CASES AND MATERIALS ON
TAXATION OF BUSINESS ENTERPRISES
Third Edition

By

Robert J. Peroni
James A. Elkins Centennial Chair in Law
The University of Texas at Austin

Steven A. Bank
Professor of Law
University of California, Los Angeles

Glenn E. Coven
Mills E. Godwin Professor of Law
College of William and Mary

AMERICAN CASEBOOK SERIES®

THOMSON
™
WEST

Mat # 40349136

American Casebook Series and West Group are trademarks
registered in the U.S. Patent and Trademark Office.

© West, a Thomson business, 1998, 2002
© 2006 Thomson/West
  610 Opperman Drive
  P.O. Box 64526
  St. Paul, MN 55164–0526
  1–800–328–9352

ISBN–13: 978–0–314–15990–8
ISBN–10: 0–314–15990–8

 *TEXT IS PRINTED ON 10% POST CONSUMER RECYCLED PAPER*

The authors dedicate this book to our friend and colleague, Richard Pugh, who is an inspiration and teacher to us all and who was one of the original authors of this book, first published by CCH.

Professor Peroni also dedicates this book to his loving and supportive parents, his late father, Emil Peroni, and his mother, Betty Peroni.

Professor Bank also dedicates this book to Julie, Reuben, and Asher.

Professor Coven also dedicates this book to his friend and wife, Joan B. Coven.

*

Preface

This book adopts the classic casebook approach to the study of C corporations, S corporations, partnerships, and limited liability companies, while at the same time incorporating an expanded number of problem sets. These materials should reasonably accommodate every instructional style; they will also provide a ready means to greater or lesser concentration on the various subject areas. In a course that covers the entire range of business taxation, some selectivity will have to be exercised. There is ample material for a three- or four-credit course on the taxation of C corporations and for a two-credit course focusing on corporate reorganizations. For the courses that focus on the taxation of "pass-through" entities, the coverage of the Subchapter S, partnership, and limited liability company areas should prove more than adequate to the need.

This third edition incorporates major developments in the law through May 17, 2006. As revised, the book is intended as a teaching tool adaptable to the newly emerging as well as more traditional law school and business school course offerings in partnership and corporate tax law.

This book adopts a number of otherwise unnoted editing practices. Most footnotes from judicial opinions have been deleted. Those that do appear retain their original numbers as reported in the opinions. Ellipses indicate the omission of portions of court opinions, revenue rulings and revenue procedures, legislative reports, and other excerpted materials.

Paragraph numbers are used to identify discrete portions of the materials. This usage makes it easier for professors who are inclined to assign only selected portions of the materials. It also facilitates cross-references.

The authors wish to thank the University of Texas School of Law, the College of William and Mary School of Law, and the UCLA School of Law for their support of this project. This book has benefitted from cross-editing by its authors of all portions of the book. It also reflects valuable suggestions from adopters of the former CCH editions and the two prior West editions to whom we are very much indebted. The authors wish to express their special appreciation to two of our co-authors on prior editions of this book, Professors Bobbi Barton and Richard Pugh, and to Professor Deborah Geier for her extensive and helpful suggestions. Comments from readers and users are warmly encouraged and welcomed.

ROBERT J. PERONI
STEVEN A. BANK
GLENN E. COVEN

*

Summary of Contents

	Page
PREFACE	v
TABLE OF CASES	xxxv
TABLE OF INTERNAL CODE SECTIONS	xli
TABLE OF TREASURY REGULATIONS	lxiii
TABLE OF TEMPORARY TREASURY REGULATIONS	lxxi
TABLE OF PROPOSED TREASURY REGULATIONS	lxxiii
TABLE OF REVENUE RULINGS	lxxv
TABLE OF REVENUE PROCEDURES	lxxvii
TABLE OF IRS NOTICES	lxxix
TABLE OF LETTER RULINGS	lxxxi

Chapter 1. Introduction — 1
A. Overview and History of the Corporate Income Tax — 1
B. Computation of C Corporation's Taxable Income — 4
C. Corporate and Shareholder Tax Rates — 6
D. Alternative Minimum Tax — 10
E. Consolidated Returns — 14
F. Introduction to Choice of Entity Considerations — 15
G. Policy Issues in Taxation of Corporations and Shareholders — 19
H. What is a Corporation? — 40
I. Identifying the Proper Taxpayer — 59
J. A Roadmap for the Trip Ahead — 61

Chapter 2. Corporate Formation — 66
A. Overview — 66
B. Requirements of Section 351(A) — 68
C. Transactions Denied Nonrecognition Under Section 351 — 88
D. Boot in Section 351 Transactions — 89
E. Basis Adjustments and Related Consequences of a Section 351 Incorporation — 93
F. Assumption of Liabilities by the Corporation — 98
G. Tax Problems Upon Incorporation of an Existing Business — 137
H. Tax Treatment of Contributions to Capital — 146
I. Tax Treatment of Corporation's Organizational Expenditures — 153

Chapter 3. Planning the Corporate Capital Structure — 155
A. Introduction — 155
B. Basic Components of Capital Structure — 155
C. Classification Issues: Stock v. Debt — 158
D. Tax Treatment of a Corporation's Investors — 177
E. Policy Considerations — 193

Page

Chapter 4. Dividend Distributions 194
A. Introduction 194
B. The Statutory Pattern for Taxing Distributions 196
C. The Taxation of Dividends 197
D. Earnings and Profits 198
E. Qualified Dividends and the 15 Percent Solution 203
F. Distributions of Property 205
G. Disguised and Constructive Dividends 209
H. Corporate Shareholders 217

Chapter 5. Redemptions of Stock 227
A. Introduction 227
B. Interest–Reducing Redemptions 228
C. Redemptions to Pay Death Taxes 263
D. Effect of Redemptions on the Distributing Company 265
E. Redemptions Through Related Corporations 266
F. Redemptions as an Acquisitive Technique 273
G. Partial Liquidations 286

Chapter 6. Stock Dividends 293
A. Introduction 293
B. History of Taxation of Stock Dividends 293
C. Nontaxable Stock Dividends 295
D. Taxable Stock Dividends 295
E. Impact of Stock Dividend on Distributing Corporation 310
F. Section 306 Stock 311
G. Summary of Distributions by Continuing Corporations 319

Chapter 7. The Corporation as a Tax Avoidance Device 321
A. Introduction 321
B. Personal Holding Company Provisions 323
C. Unreasonable Accumulations of Earnings 328

Chapter 8. Sales and Liquidations of Corporations 341
A. Introduction 341
B. Simple Corporate Liquidations 341
C. Taxable Corporate Acquisitions 358

Chapter 9. Introduction to Corporate Reorganizations 378
A. Historical Background 378
B. Types of Reorganizations 380
C. Tax Treatment of Reorganization Exchanges 386
D. Judicially Developed Prerequisites to Reorganization Qualification 389

Chapter 10. Acquisitive Reorganizations 407
A. Overview 407

Page

B. Meeting the Requirements of the Basic Acquisitive Reorganization Definitions 408
C. Triangular Reorganizations 452
D. Multi–Step Acquisitions 461
E. Acquisitions Partly Tax-Free and Partly Taxable 466
F. Treatment of Boot Paid Incident to Reorganization 475
G. Proposals for Reform of the Taxation of Acquisitions 507

Chapter 11. Single Corporation Reorganizations **517**
A. Introduction 517
B. The "E" Reorganization 518
C. The "F" Reorganization 527
D. Nondivisive "D" Reorganization 534
E. Liquidation–Reincorporation Transactions 540

Chapter 12. Corporate Divisions **554**
A. Introduction to Tax–Free Divisions Under Section 355 554
B. Requirements to Prevent Bail–Out of Corporate Earnings 557
C. Divisions Incident to "D" Reorganizations 581
D. Effects on Distributees and Distributing Corporations 582
E. Combining a Corporate Division With an Acquisition 587
F. Consequences of Failure of Corporate Division to Qualify Under Section 355 616
G. Distribution of Rights 616
H. Carryover of Corporate Attributes 620

Chapter 13. Carryover and Carryback of Tax Attributes **624**
A. Overview 624
B. Introduction to Section 381 624
C. Earnings and Profits 626
D. Net Operating Loss Carryovers 627
E. Net Operating Loss Carrybacks 664

Chapter 14. Multiple Corporations **667**
A. Introduction 667
B. Restrictions on Multiple Allowances 668
C. Reallocation of Income 669
D. Consolidated Returns 678

Chapter 15. S Corporations and Their Shareholders **685**
A. Introduction to Conduit Taxation 685
B. Creation of an S Corporation 691
C. Eligibility to Elect/Maintain Election 709
D. Reporting of Net Income From Operations 732
E. Distributions 765
F. Dispositions of Stock 772
G. Complications to Corporation From Midstream Elections 775
H. Termination of the S Election 787

Page

Chapter 16.   Introduction And Definition Of Partnerships -- **792**
A. Introduction -- 792
B. Defining a Partnership for Tax Purposes: Business Enterprise
     Classification --- 796
C. Anti–Abuse Rules: IRS Disregard of the Partnership Form ------- 824
D. Choice of Entity Considerations ----------------------------------- 829

Chapter 17.   Partnership Formation ----------------------------------- **830**
A. Introduction --- 830
B. Contributions of Capital -- 830
C. Effect of Partnership Debt on Partners' Basis --------------------- 838
D. Contribution of Services -- 843
E. Organization and Syndication Expenses -------------------------- 881

Chapter 18.   Operation of the Partnership -------------------------- **883**
A. Reporting and Taxing Partnership Income ------------------------ 883
B. Partnership Allocations --- 906
C. Family Partnerships --- 967
D. Simplified Flow–Through Regime for Electing Large Partner-
     ships --- 979

**Chapter 19.   Partner's Basis And Other Limitations On Al-
     located Losses** -- **982**
A. Introduction --- 982
B. Initial Basis --- 983
C. Adjustments to Basis -- 983
D. Timing and Priorities --- 987
E. Limitations on the Deduction of Losses -------------------------- 988

**Chapter 20.   Characterizing Transactions Between Part-
     ners and the Partnership** -------------------------------------- **1001**
A. Introduction -- 1001
B. Payments for Services and the Use of Property ------------------ 1002
C. Distinguishing Between Sales and Current Distributions -------- 1025
D. Limitations on Certain Sales --------------------------------------- 1049

Chapter 21.   Sale of a Partnership Interest ------------------------- **1052**
A. Introduction -- 1052
B. Treatment of the Seller—In General ----------------------------- 1053
C. Sales Subject to Section 751 --------------------------------------- 1059
D. Other Entity versus Aggregate Issues ---------------------------- 1071
E. Treatment of the Purchasing Partner ----------------------------- 1076
F. The Sale of an Interest: A Comprehensive Illustration ---------- 1093

Chapter 22.   Current Distributions to Partners ------------------- **1099**
A. Introduction -- 1099
B. Partner Level Consequences -------------------------------------- 1100
C. Partnership Level Consequences ---------------------------------- 1117
D. Treatment of Precontribution Gain or Loss on Certain In–Kind
     Partnership Distributions: So-Called "Mixing Bowl" Transac-
     tions --- 1129

Page

E. Distributions of Marketable Securities (Section 731(c)) ------------ 1134
F. Distributions That Alter a Partner's Interest in Ordinary Income Property -- 1140

Chapter 23. Liquidating Distributions --------------------------------- **1155**
A. Introduction --- 1155
B. The Structure of Section 736 -- 1156
C. Section 736(b) Payments -- 1157
D. Section 736(a) Payments -- 1162
E. Planning for Liquidations: Section 736(a) v. Section 736(b) ------ 1167
F. Relationship Between Sections 752 and 736 ------------------------ 1168
G. Taxing Deferred Section 736 Payments ---------------------------- 1169
H. The Comprehensive Illustration Revisited ------------------------ 1170
I. Liquidations Distinguished From Sales ---------------------------- 1174
J. Abandoning Partnership Interests -------------------------------------- 1178

Chapter 24. Partnership Terminations ------------------------------- **1191**
A. Voluntary Terminations of the Business ---------------------------- 1191
B. Statutory Terminations --- 1199
C. Partnership Mergers and Divisions ---------------------------------- 1209
D. Conversions of Partnership Interests ---------------------------------- 1224

Chapter 25. Death of a Partner --- **1231**
A. Introduction --- 1231
B. Effect on Current Year's Income ------------------------------------ 1231
C. Basis Adjustments -- 1232

INDEX -- 1243

*

Table of Contents

___

	Page
PREFACE	v
TABLE OF CASES	xxxv
TABLE OF INTERNAL CODE SECTIONS	xli
TABLE OF TREASURY REGULATIONS	lxiii
TABLE OF TEMPORARY TREASURY REGULATIONS	lxxi
TABLE OF PROPOSED TREASURY REGULATIONS	lxxiii
TABLE OF REVENUE RULINGS	lxxv
TABLE OF REVENUE PROCEDURES	lxxvii
TABLE OF IRS NOTICES	lxxix
TABLE OF LETTER RULINGS	lxxxi

Chapter 1. Introduction — 1

A. Overview and History of the Corporate Income Tax — 1

B. Computation of C Corporation's Taxable Income — 4
- 1. In General — 4
- 2. The Domestic Production Deduction — 5

C. Corporate and Shareholder Tax Rates — 6
- 1. Historic Relationship Between Top Corporate and Individual Tax Rates — 6
- 2. Corporate Tax Rates Under Current Law — 7
- 3. Tax Rates of Individual Shareholders — 8

D. Alternative Minimum Tax — 10
- 1. Description of Alternative Minimum Tax System — 10
- 2. Determination of Alternative Minimum Taxable Income — 11
- 3. Credit for Prior Year Minimum Tax Liability — 12
- 4. Eligible Credits Against Alternative Minimum Tax Liability — 13
- 5. Exemption for Small Corporations — 13

E. Consolidated Returns — 14

F. Introduction to Choice of Entity Considerations — 15

G. Policy Issues in Taxation of Corporations and Shareholders — 19
- 1. Corporate Tax Integration — 19
  - Staff of Joint Committee on Taxation Federal Income Tax Aspects of Corporate Financial Structures. — 19
  - Note — 23
- 2. The Role of Non–Statutory Principles — 25
  - Cunningham & Repetti, Textualism and Tax Shelters — 25
  - Note — 32
  - United Parcel Service of America, Inc. v. Commissioner — 32
  - Notes — 39

	Page
H. What is a Corporation?	40
1. Entity Classification	40
a. Introduction	40
Littriello v. United States	41
Notes	45
b. Check-the-Box Entity Classification Regulations	46
Problems	47
c. Trust Versus Corporation Entity Classification Issue	47
2. Recognition of the Corporate Entity	48
a. Business Purpose and Business Activity	49
Moline Properties v. Commissioner	49
Note	51
b. Sham Corporations	52
c. Corporation as Agent or Nominee	53
Commissioner v. Bollinger	53
Note	59
I. Identifying the Proper Taxpayer	59
J. A Roadmap for the Trip Ahead	61
Chapter 2. Corporate Formation	**66**
A. Overview	66
Illustration	68
B. Requirements of Section 351(A)	68
1. "Transfer" of "Property"	68
2. Exchange "Solely for Stock"	69
a. General	69
b. Securities	70
c. Qualified Preferred Stock	70
Note	72
Problem	72
3. Transferors of Property in "Control" of the Corporation	72
a. Control "Immediately After the Exchange"	73
Intermountain Lumber Co. v. Commissioner	75
Problems	78
Revenue Ruling 79–70	78
Problems	79
Notes	80
b. "Accommodation" Transfers	81
Estate of Kamborian v. Commissioner	82
Revenue Ruling 79–194	85
Note	87
Problems	88
C. Transactions Denied Nonrecognition Under Section 351	88
D. Boot in Section 351 Transactions	89
1. General Effect of Boot	89
a. At the Shareholder Level	89
b. At the Corporate Level	89
2. Allocation of Boot	90
Revenue Ruling 68–55	90
Problem	92
3. Timing of Boot Recognition	92
Problems	93

Page

E. Basis Adjustments and Related Consequences of a Section 351 Incorporation 93
   1. Basis at the Shareholder Level 93
   2. Basis at the Corporate Level 94
     a. Generally 94
     b. Built–In Loss Property 95
       Note 96
   3. Holding Period 97
     Problems 97
F. Assumption of Liabilities by the Corporation 98
   1. Nonrecognition Under Section 357(a) 98
     a. Generally 98
     b. Determination of Amount of Liabilities Assumed 99
   2. Assumption of Liability Tainted by Improper Purpose 101
     Drybrough v. Commissioner 101
   3. Liabilities in Excess of Basis: Section 357(c) 107
     Revenue Ruling 95–74 108
     Problems 112
   4. Effect of an Assumed Liability on Basis 113
     a. At the Shareholder Level 113
       Black & Decker Corp. v. United States 114
       Notes 120
     b. At the Corporate Level 121
   5. Attempts by Transferor to Avoid Section 357(c) Gain 122
     Owen v. Commissioner 122
     Note 125
     Peracchi v. Commissioner 125
     Notes 136
     Problem 137
G. Tax Problems Upon Incorporation of an Existing Business 137
   1. Assignment of Income Doctrine 138
     Hempt Bros., Inc. v. United States 138
     Notes 141
   2. Clear Reflection of Income and Tax Benefit Rules 142
     Revenue Ruling 80–198 142
     Notes 144
     Problem 145
H. Tax Treatment of Contributions to Capital 146
   Commissioner v. Fink 147
   Notes 152
   Problem 153
I. Tax Treatment of Corporation's Organizational Expenditures ... 153

Chapter 3. Planning the Corporate Capital Structure **155**
A. Introduction 155
B. Basic Components of Capital Structure 155
C. Classification Issues: Stock v. Debt 158
   1. The Criteria 158
     Scriptomatic, Inc. v. United States 159
     Notes 161
     Problem 162
   2. Statutory Characterization Rules 163

Page

C. Classification Issues: Stock v. Debt—Continued
   3. Hybrid Instruments 165
     IRS Notice 94–47 165
     Note 167
   4. Sale or Section 351 Exchange 167
     Burr Oaks Corp. v. Commissioner 167
     Problem 171
   5. Shareholders' Guarantees 171
     Plantation Patterns, Inc. v. Commissioner 171
     Notes 177
D. Tax Treatment of a Corporation's Investors 177
   1. Taxation of Positive Returns on Investments 178
     a. Stock 178
     b. Debt 180
        Revenue Ruling 72–265 182
        Note 183
   2. Tax Treatment of Losses 184
     a. Debt 184
        United States v. Generes 185
        Notes 190
     b. Shareholder Guarantees 190
     c. Stock and Section 1244 191
        Problem 192
     d. Corporate Level Consequences 192
E. Policy Considerations 193

Chapter 4. Dividend Distributions **194**
A. Introduction 194
B. The Statutory Pattern for Taxing Distributions 196
C. The Taxation of Dividends 197
   Problem 198
D. Earnings and Profits 198
   1. Definition of Earnings and Profits 199
   2. Current and Accumulated Earnings and Profits 200
   3. Allocation of Earnings and Profits Among Distributees ... 201
     Problems 202
E. Qualified Dividends and the 15 Percent Solution 203
F. Distributions of Property 205
   1. Shareholder Taxation 205
   2. Corporate Level Consequences 206
   3. Effect on Earnings and Profits 207
   4. Distribution of the Corporation's Own Obligations 208
     Problems 208
G. Disguised and Constructive Dividends 209
   Tanner v. Commissioner 210
   Problems 211
   Note 211
   Honigman v. Commissioner 212
   Notes 216
H. Corporate Shareholders 217
   1. Anti–Abuse Provisions 218

Page

H. Corporate Shareholders—Continued
   2. Earnings and Profits Revisited 220
   3. Distinguishing Dividends From Sales 220
      Litton Industries, Inc. v. Commissioner 221
      Notes 226
      Problem 226

Chapter 5. Redemptions of Stock **227**
A. Introduction 227
B. Interest–Reducing Redemptions 228
   1. Substantially Disproportionate Redemptions 228
   2. Stock Attribution 229
      Problems 232
   3. Basis Consequences 233
   4. Terminations of Interest 234
      a. "Complete" Redemption 234
         Lynch v. Commissioner 234
         Notes 240
         Hurst v. Commissioner 240
      b. Ten–Year "Look Back" 247
      c. Waivers of Attribution by Entities 248
         Problems 249
   5. Redemptions "Not Essentially Equivalent to a Dividend" ... 250
      United States v. Davis 251
      Notes 254
      Revenue Ruling 75–502 255
      Notes 256
      Cerone v. Commissioner 257
      Note 262
      Problem 262
C. Redemptions to Pay Death Taxes 263
   Problems 264
D. Effect of Redemptions on the Distributing Company 265
E. Redemptions Through Related Corporations 266
   1. Brother–Sister Sales 266
   2. Parent–Subsidiary Sales 268
   3. Interrelationship of Section 304 and Section 351 269
   4. Taxing the Reconstructed Transaction 270
   5. Corporate Shareholders 271
      Problems 272
F. Redemptions as an Acquisitive Technique 273
   1. Tax Considerations From Seller's Perspective 273
      Zenz v. Quinlivan 273
      Notes 275
      Revenue Ruling 75–447 276
      Note 278
   2. Tax Considerations From the Perspective of the Buyer and
      Other Continuing Shareholders 278
      Holsey v. Commissioner 278
      Notes 280
      Revenue Ruling 69–608 281
      Notes 284
      Problem 285

Page

G. Partial Liquidations — 286
  Imler v. Commissioner — 287
  Notes — 290
  Problems — 291

Chapter 6. Stock Dividends — **293**
A. Introduction — 293
B. History of Taxation of Stock Dividends — 293
C. Nontaxable Stock Dividends — 295
  Problems — 295
D. Taxable Stock Dividends — 295
   1. Election to Receive Property or Money in Lieu of Stock — 296
     Revenue Ruling 78–375 — 298
     Note — 300
   2. Disproportionate Distributions — 300
     Revenue Ruling 77–19 — 302
     Notes — 304
   3. Distributions on Preferred Stock — 304
     Revenue Ruling 77–37 — 305
     Note — 306
     Revenue Ruling 83–119 — 307
     Note — 309
E. Impact of Stock Dividend on Distributing Corporation — 310
  Problems — 310
F. Section 306 Stock — 311
   1. Dispositions Other Than by Redemption — 312
   2. Redemptions — 313
   3. Exceptions to Section 306 Treatment — 314
     Problems — 315
   4. To What Stock Does Section 306 Apply? — 316
     a. Non–Common Stock — 316
     b. Tax–Free Stock Distribution — 317
     c. No Earnings and Profits — 318
        Problems — 318
G. Summary of Distributions by Continuing Corporations — 319

Chapter 7. The Corporation as a Tax Avoidance Device — **321**
A. Introduction — 321
B. Personal Holding Company Provisions — 323
   1. General Definition — 324
     Problem — 325
   2. Professional Corporation as Personal Holding Company — 326
     Revenue Ruling 75–67 — 326
     Note — 327
C. Unreasonable Accumulations of Earnings — 328
   1. Evidence of Purpose to Avoid Tax — 328
     United States v. Donruss Co. — 328
     Notes — 332
   2. Unreasonable Accumulations — 332
     Ivan Allen Co. v. United States — 333

Page

C. Unreasonable Accumulations of Earnings—Continued
  Note ---- 338
  3. Reasonable Business Needs ---- 338
  4. Imposition of Tax ---- 339

Chapter 8. Sales and Liquidations of Corporations ---- **341**
A. Introduction ---- 341
B. Simple Corporate Liquidations ---- 341
  1. Nonsubsidiary Liquidations; Shareholder Consequences ---- 342
    a. Shareholder Assumption of Liabilities ---- 343
    b. Installment Sales of Stock Incident to Complete Liqui-
       dation ---- 343
  2. Nonsubsidiary Liquidations; Corporate Level Consequences 344
  3. The Special Case of Property Having No Ascertainable
     Value ---- 346
     Problems ---- 348
  4. Liquidation of Corporate Subsidiaries ---- 349
     Granite Trust Co. v. United States ---- 351
     Notes ---- 356
     Revenue Ruling 70–106 ---- 357
     Notes ---- 357
     Problems ---- 358
C. Taxable Corporate Acquisitions ---- 358
  1. A Bit of History ---- 359
  2. General Acquisitive Patterns ---- 361
  3. Taxable Asset Acquisitions ---- 361
    a. The Seller's Tax Consequences ---- 362
    b. The Buyer's Tax Consequences ---- 363
  4. Taxable Stock Acquisitions ---- 366
    a. Historical Development ---- 366
       Kimbell–Diamond Milling Co. v. Commissioner ---- 366
       Notes ---- 368
    b. Section 338 ---- 369
    c. Section 338(h)(10) ---- 372
       Notes ---- 373
  5. Choosing Among the Forms of Acquisitions ---- 373
     Problems ---- 375

Chapter 9. Introduction to Corporate Reorganizations ---- **378**
A. Historical Background ---- 378
B. Types of Reorganizations ---- 380
  1. Acquisitive Reorganizations ---- 381
  2. Single Corporation Reorganizations ---- 383
  3. Corporate Divisions ---- 384
  4. Overview of Tax Consequences of Corporate Reorganiza-
     tion ---- 384
     Problems ---- 385
C. Tax Treatment of Reorganization Exchanges ---- 386
  1. Nonrecognition of Gain or Loss ---- 386
  2. Basis in Reorganizations ---- 387
  3. Holding Period for Nonrecognition Property ---- 387

Page

C. Tax Treatment of Reorganization Exchanges—Continued
4. Tax Accounting Aspects 388
D. Judicially Developed Prerequisites to Reorganization Qualification 389
1. Business Purpose Requirement 389
Gregory v. Helvering 389
Note 391
2. Form and Substance; Step Transaction Doctrine 392
King Enterprises, Inc. v. United States 393
Note 400
3. Continuity of Shareholder Interest Requirement 400
a. Origin of the Requirement 400
Note 402
b. The Survival of the Requirement 402
Southwest Natural Gas Co. v. Commissioner 403
Note 404
4. Continuity of Business Enterprise Requirement 405

Chapter 10. Acquisitive Reorganizations **407**
A. Overview 407
B. Meeting the Requirements of the Basic Acquisitive Reorganization Definitions 408
1. An Acquisition Framework 409
2. "A" Reorganization 410
a. Statutory Merger 410
Revenue Ruling 2000–5 411
Notes 413
b. Disregarded Entity Merger 414
Problems on the "A" Reorganization 415
c. Continuity of Shareholder Interest Requirement 415
J.E. Seagram Corp. v. Commissioner 419
Notes 424
Problems 427
d. Continuity of Business Enterprise Requirement 428
Revenue Ruling 81–247 430
Note 432
Problems 433
3. "C" Reorganization 433
a. The Concept of "Substantially All of the Properties" .. 433
Revenue Ruling 57–518 434
Notes 436
b. Disposition of Unwanted Assets and the Substantially All Requirement 436
Helvering v. Elkhorn Coal Co. 437
Revenue Ruling 88–48 439
Notes 441
c. The Solely for Voting Stock Requirement; The Boot–Relaxation Rule 442
Problems on the "C" Reorganization 443
4. "B" Reorganization 444
a. The Solely for Voting Stock Requirement; No Boot in a "B" 444

Page

B. Meeting the Requirements of the Basic Acquisitive Reorganization Definitions—Continued
    Turnbow v. Commissioner 445
    Notes 447
  b. The Creeping "B" Reorganization 451
    Problems on the "B" Reorganization 451
C. Triangular Reorganizations 452
  1. Background 452
  2. Triangular "B" and "C" Reorganizations and Forward Triangular Mergers 453
    Problems 454
  3. Reverse Triangular Merger 457
    Revenue Ruling 67–448 457
    Notes 458
    Problems 460
D. Multi–Step Acquisitions 461
  Revenue Ruling 2001–46 462
  Notes 466
E. Acquisitions Partly Tax-Free and Partly Taxable 466
  1. Purchase of T Shares Followed by Tender Offer 466
  2. Preferred Stock Recapitalization Preceding Stock Purchase 468
  3. Use of Section 351 469
    a. Obtaining Tax–Free Treatment for a Minority Shareholder of T in a Cash Merger 469
    Revenue Ruling 80–284 470
    Note 473
    Revenue Ruling 84–71 473
    Notes 474
    b. The "Horizontal Double–Dummy" Transaction 474
F. Treatment of Boot Paid Incident to Reorganization 475
  1. Gain Recognition by Shareholders and Creditors 475
  2. When Does Recognized Gain Have the Effect of the Distribution of a Dividend Under Section 356(a)(2)? 477
    Commissioner v. Clark 478
    Note 486
    Problems 487
  3. Concept of Stock or Securities 490
    a. Debt Obligations as Securities 490
    Revenue Ruling 59–98 490
    Notes 492
    b. Contingent or Escrowed Stock; Flexible Conversion Ratio Preferred 494
    Revenue Procedure 84–42 495
    c. Warrants to Buy Stock 497
  4. Nonrecognition of Gain or Loss by Corporate Parties to Reorganization 499
  5. Determination of Basis 500
  6. Assumption of Liabilities 501
    a. Treatment of Assumed Liabilities as Other Than Boot 502
    b. What is an Assumed Liability? 503
    Problems 505
G. Proposals for Reform of the Taxation of Acquisitions 507

Page

Chapter 11. Single Corporation Reorganizations **517**
A. Introduction 517
B. The "E" Reorganization 518
  1. Bail–Out Potential in Recapitalizations 518
    Bazley v. Commissioner 519
    Notes 522
  2. Nonqualified Preferred Stock as Boot 523
  3. No Continuity of Shareholder Interest or Continuity of
    Business Enterprise Required 523
    Revenue Ruling 82–34 524
    Notes 525
  4. Section 306 Stock in a Recapitalization 525
    Problems 526
C. The "F" Reorganization 527
  1. Introduction 527
  2. Only One Operating Corporation May Participate 528
  3. "F" Reorganization Linked to Another Transaction 529
    Revenue Ruling 96–29 529
    Notes 531
  4. No Continuity of Shareholder Interest or Continuity of
    Business Enterprise Required 533
D. Nondivisive "D" Reorganization 534
  Warsaw Photographic Associates Inc. v. Commissioner 534
  Note 539
E. Liquidation–Reincorporation Transactions 540
  1. Potential Tax Benefits 540
  2. Application of "D" Reorganization Rules to Liquidation–
    Reincorporation Transactions 542
    Reef Corp. v. Commissioner 543
    Notes 545
  3. Application of "F" Reorganization Rules to Liquidation–
    Reincorporation Transactions 548
    Reef Corp. v. Commissioner 548
  4. Liquidation–Reincorporation Transactions in Which the
    Statutory Reorganization Provisions Do Not Apply 549
    Revenue Ruling 61–156 550
    Note 552

Chapter 12. Corporate Divisions **554**
A. Introduction to Tax–Free Divisions Under Section 355 554
B. Requirements to Prevent Bail–Out of Corporate Earnings 557
  1. Overview 557
  2. Active Trade or Business 558
    Estate of Lockwood v. Commissioner 558
    Notes 563
    Revenue Ruling 86–126 564
    Notes 566
  3. Device 568
    Rafferty v. Commissioner 568
    Note 572

Page

B. Requirements to Prevent Bail–Out of Corporate Earnings—Continued
  4. Corporate Business Purpose and Continuity of Interest 573
    Revenue Ruling 2004–23 574
    Notes 577
    Problems 579
C. Divisions Incident to "D" Reorganizations 581
D. Effects on Distributees and Distributing Corporations 582
  1. Consequences to Distributee Shareholders 582
    Revenue Ruling 93–62 583
    Note 586
  2. Consequences to Distributing Corporation 586
E. Combining a Corporate Division With an Acquisition 587
  1. Corporate Division Combined With a Taxable Acquisition ... 587
    Problems 591
  2. Corporate Division Combined With a Tax–Free Acquisition 591
    a. Case Law and Administrative Developments Before the 1997 Legislation 591
      Revenue Ruling 98–27 595
      Note 597
    b. Gain Recognition Triggered under Section 355(e) by a Section 355 Distribution Related to a Tax–Free or Taxable Acquisition 597
    c. Regulations under Section 355(e) 599
      (i) Plan and Non-plan Factors 600
        Revenue Ruling 2005–65 601
        Note 605
      (ii) Safe Harbors 606
      (iii) Agreement, Understanding, Arrangement, or Substantial Negotiations 608
      (iv) Options 608
        Problems 608
    d. Determination of "Control" in Divisions Involving Asset Transfers 610
      Problems 611
    e. Consolidated Return Changes 611
    f. Disqualified investment corporations 615
F. Consequences of Failure of Corporate Division to Qualify Under Section 355 616
G. Distribution of Rights 616
H. Carryover of Corporate Attributes 620
  Revenue Ruling 77–133 621
  Notes 622

Chapter 13. Carryover and Carryback of Tax Attributes 624
A. Overview 624
B. Introduction to Section 381 624
C. Earnings and Profits 626
  Problems 626
D. Net Operating Loss Carryovers 627
  1. Outline of Section 382 628

Page

D. Net Operating Loss Carryovers—Continued
Staff of Joint Comm. on Tax'n General Explanation of the Tax
Reform Act of 1986 629
Note 632
2. Triggering Event Under Section 382 632
3. Attribution Rules 634
4. "Stock" 635
5. Testing Period 635
6. Effect of a Section 382 Ownership Change 635
7. Value of Stock of Old Loss Corporation 636
Berry Petroleum Co. v. Commissioner 637
Note 653
8. Built–In Gains And Losses 653
9. Section 383 Restrictions on Use of Carryovers of Various
Excess Credits and Capital Losses 655
10. Section 384 Restrictions on Use of Pre–Acquisition Losses
of Acquiring Corporation Against Built–In Gains of Ac-
quired Corporation 655
11. Rules to Prevent Avoidance of Section 382 656
Problems 656
12. Limitations On Nol Carryforwards After Worthless Stock
Loss Deduction 658
13. Ongoing Significance of Section 269 658
14. Consolidated Return Regulations 659
a. Application of Sections 382 and 383 to Consolidated
Groups 659
b. Separate Return Limitation Year (SRLY) Rules 661
c. SRLY Limitation on Built–In Losses 662
E. Net Operating Loss Carrybacks 664
1. General Rules 664
2. Limitation of NOL Carrybacks Following Corporate Equi-
ty–Reducing Transaction (CERT) 664
Problem 666

Chapter 14. Multiple Corporations **667**
A. Introduction 667
B. Restrictions on Multiple Allowances 668
C. Reallocation of Income 669
1. The "Arm's Length" Standard 670
2. Transfers of Tangible Property 670
3. Transfers of Intangible Property 672
4. Effect of Inconsistent Legal Restrictions 672
Texaco, Inc. v. Commissioner 673
Notes 677
5. Common Control 678
D. Consolidated Returns 678
1. Defining the "Affiliated Group" 679
2. Consolidated Income and Loss 679
3. Intercompany Transactions 680
4. Investment Adjustments 682

Page

D. Consolidated Returns—Continued
   a. Stock Basis Adjustments ---------------------------------- 682
   b. Excess Loss Accounts -------------------------------------- 683
   c. Earnings and Profits -------------------------------------- 684
     Problems -- 684

Chapter 15.   S Corporations and Their Shareholders ---------- **685**
A. Introduction to Conduit Taxation ----------------------------- 685
  1. Historical Background to Subchapter S --------------------- 686
  2. Comparison of Partnerships, LLCs, C Corporations, and S
     Corporations --- 687
    a. S Corporations Contrasted with Partnerships and LLCs   687
    b. S Corporations Contrasted with C Corporations ----------- 688
    c. Overview of Policy Issues Raised by Subchapter S -------- 689
  3. Illustrative Example ------------------------------------- 690
B. Creation of an S Corporation --------------------------------- 691
  1. Applicability of Subchapter C Provisions on Formation ------- 691
    Wiebusch v. Commissioner --------------------------------- 691
    Notes -- 692
  2. Planning the Capital Structure --------------------------- 694
  3. Making the Election -------------------------------------- 694
    a. A Timely Filing --- 694
      Notes --- 695
      Revenue Procedure 97–48 -------------------------------- 696
      Revenue Procedure 2003–43 ------------------------------ 697
      Revenue Procedure 2004–48 ------------------------------ 701
      Note --- 702
      Problems --- 703
    b. Effective Date of Election ------------------------------ 703
    c. Who Must Consent to the Election ----------------------- 705
      Kean v. Commisioner ---------------------------------- 705
      Notes --- 708
      Problems --- 709
C. Eligibility to Elect/Maintain Election ----------------------- 709
  1. Shareholder Level Requirements -------------------------- 710
    a. 100–Shareholder Limit ---------------------------------- 710
      Revenue Ruling 94–43 ----------------------------------- 710
      Notes --- 711
    b. Nature of Authorized Shareholders, In General ---------- 712
  2. Trusts and Other (In)eligible Shareholders -------------- 713
    a. Grantor and Grantor–Like Trusts ----------------------- 713
    b. Qualified Subchapter S Trusts -------------------------- 714
      Notes --- 714
    c. Trusts in the Two-Year, Post–Death Period ------------- 715
      Problems --- 715
    d. Electing Small Business Trust (ESBT) ------------------- 717
      Notes --- 718
      Problems --- 718
    e. Nonresident Aliens: Ineligibility as Shareholders and
      Trust Beneficiaries ------------------------------------ 718

Page

C. Eligibility to Elect/Maintain Election—Continued
    f. Qualified Exempt Organizations and Select S Corporations as Eligible Shareholders _____ 719
  3. Corporate Level Eligibility Requirements _____ 719
    a. Permissible Affiliate Status _____ 720
    b. The Wholly Owned "Qualified Subchapter S Subsidiary" _____ 721
    c. One Class of Stock _____ 722
      Revenue Ruling 85–161 _____ 724
      Notes _____ 725
    d. Avoiding Corporate Limitations by Multi–Tier Structures and Partnerships _____ 726
      Letter Ruling 8819040 _____ 726
      Note _____ 728
  4. Impact of Ineligible and Quasi–Ineligible Shareholders _____ 728
    Letter Ruling 8814042 _____ 728
    Notes _____ 730

D. Reporting of Net Income From Operations _____ 732
  1. Corporate Level Computations and Determinations _____ 732
    a. Computations, In General _____ 732
    b. Nature of Passed-Through Items _____ 733
    c. Accounting Methods and Other Elections _____ 734
    d. Fringe Benefits _____ 734
    e. Distributions of Property in Kind _____ 735
      Problems _____ 735
  2. Shareholders' Reporting of Corporate Income and Expenses __ 736
    a. Date Includible _____ 736
    b. Allocation in Proportion to Stock Ownership _____ 737
      Problems _____ 737
    c. Family Owned S Corporations _____ 738
      Speca v. Commissioner _____ 738
      Notes _____ 743
  3. Impact of Operations on Shareholders' Basis _____ 744
    a. In General _____ 744
      Problems _____ 746
    b. Effect of Cancellation-of-Debt Income at the Corporate Level _____ 747
      Notes _____ 751
    c. Relevance of Loans by Shareholders _____ 752
      Bolding v. Commissioner _____ 753
      Notes _____ 759
      Revenue Ruling 75–144 _____ 761
      Note _____ 763
    d. Restoration of Basis _____ 763
  4. Other Limits on Shareholders' Reportable Losses _____ 764
    a. Worthlessness _____ 764
    b. Tax Shelter Limitations _____ 764

E. Distributions _____ 765
  1. Earnings and Profits _____ 765
  2. Corporations Lacking Earnings and Profits _____ 766
  3. Corporations Having Earnings and Profits _____ 766
    a. Accumulated Adjustments Account _____ 766

Page

E. Distributions—Continued
     b. Three–Tier Distribution Scheme 767
     c. Elective Second-Tier Distributions 768
     d. Pre–1983 S Corporations 768
        Problems 769
     e. Redemptions 769
        Revenue Ruling 95–14 769
        Problems 771
F. Dispositions of Stock 772
    1. General Consequences 772
        Problems 774
    2. Dispositions at Death 775
G. Complications to Corporation From Midstream Elections 775
    1. LIFO Inventory 776
    2. Built–In Gains 777
        Problems 778
        Letter Ruling 8849015 779
        Notes 781
    3. Passive Investment Income 783
       a. Stage One: Double Taxation 783
       b. Stage Two: Termination 784
       c. Defining Passive Investment Income 784
    4. No Carryforward or Carryback of Losses From C Corpora-
        tion Year to S Corporation Year 786
H. Termination of the S Election 787
    1. Methods of Terminating the Election 787
    2. Impact of Termination on Reporting Income 788
        Problems 789
    3. Post–Termination Transition Period 790

Chapter 16. Introduction And Definition Of Partnerships .. 792
A. Introduction 792
    1. The Statutory Framework and Its Historical Evolution 793
    2. The Basic Rules of Subchapter K 794
    3. A Simplified Illustration 795
    4. Some Useful References 796
B. Defining a Partnership for Tax Purposes: Business Enterprise
    Classification 796
    1. Partnership Versus Nonentity 797
        Revenue Ruling 75–374 797
        Revenue Ruling 77–332 798
        Madison Gas & Electric Co. v. Commissioner 801
        Revenue Procedure 2002–22 806
        Note 812
        Problem 812
    2. Electing Out of Subchapter K 813
    3. Limited Partnership Versus Corporation: Former Associa-
        tion Regulations 813
    4. The Rise of Limited Liability Companies 815
    5. "Check–The–Box" Entity Classification Regulations 817
        Notes 820
        Problems 821

Page

B. Defining a Partnership for Tax Purposes: Business Enterprise Classification—Continued
- 6. Publicly Traded Partnerships 822

C. Anti–Abuse Rules: IRS Disregard of the Partnership Form 824

D. Choice of Entity Considerations 829

Chapter 17. Partnership Formation **830**

A. Introduction 830

B. Contributions of Capital 830
- 1. Taxation of the Transfer 830
  - Revenue Ruling 99–5 832
  - *Note* 834
- 2. Tax Versus Financial Accounting: The "Capital Account" ... 836
  - *Problems* 837
- 3. Capital Contribution or Sale? 837

C. Effect of Partnership Debt on Partners' Basis 838
- 1. The General Scheme of Section 752 838
- 2. Allocation of Partnership Debt Among the Partners 839
  - a. Recourse Debt 840
  - b. Nonrecourse Debt 841
- 3. Contributions of Encumbered Property 841
  - *Problems* 843

D. Contribution of Services 843
- 1. Receipt of Capital Interest 844
- 2. Receipt of Profits Interest 847
  - *Diamond v. Commissioner* 847
  - *Notes* 851
  - Revenue Procedure 93–27 853
  - Revenue Procedure 2001–43 854
  - *Notes* 855
- 3. 2005 Proposed Regulations and the Liquidation Value Safe Harbor 857
  - IRS Notice 2005–43 857
  - *Problems* 872
- 4. Services or Properties Contributed? 873
  - *United States v. Stafford* 873
  - *Problems* 881

E. Organization and Syndication Expenses 881

Chapter 18. Operation of the Partnership **883**

A. Reporting and Taxing Partnership Income 883
- 1. Computation of Partnership Income 884
  - *United States v. Basye* 884
  - *Note* 887
- 2. Taxable Year of the Partnership 887
- 3. Classification and Determination of Partnership Income and Expenses 888
  - Revenue Ruling 68–79 889
  - *Note* 890
  - *Demirjian v. Commisioner* 891
  - *Notes* 893
- 4. Assignment of Income 895

Page

A. Reporting and Taxing Partnership Income—Continued
    Schneer v. Commissioner 896
    Notes 906
B. Partnership Allocations 906
  1. Flexible Approach Permitted by Local Law 906
  2. Economic Allocations 907
  3. Judicial Analysis 908
    Orrisch v. Commissioner 908
  4. Thrust of the Regulations 913
  5. Illustrative Examples—The Stakes 914
  6. "Substantial Economic Effect" Under the Allocation Regulations 916
    a. Economic Effect 916
      Revenue Ruling 92–97 918
      Revenue Ruling 97–38 923
    b. "Substantiality" of the Economic Effect 926
      Revenue Ruling 99–43 927
    c. Inability to Satisfy Substantial Economic Effect .. 932
      Problems 933
      Note 934
  7. Allocations Attributable to Nonrecourse Debt 935
    Problem 937
  8. Allocations With Respect to Contributed Property .. 937
    a. Section 704(c) Requirements for Allocation 937
      Problems 943
    b. Special Problems in Allocating Depreciation ... 944
      Problems 945
    c. Character of Gain or Loss 946
      Problems 946
  9. Allocation of Partnership Liabilities 947
    a. Introduction 947
    b. Effect of Partnership Recourse Liabilities 948
    c. Effect of Partnership Nonrecourse Liabilities ... 950
      Note 951
      Revenue Ruling 95–41 952
      Problems 957
  10. Retroactive Allocations 959
    a. The Varying Interest Rule 959
      Revenue Ruling 77–119 959
    b. Section 706(d) 960
    c. Shifting Interests Not Accompanied by Contributions 961
      Lipke v. Commissioner 961
      Problems 966
C. Family Partnerships 967
  1. Recognition of Transferee Partner 967
    Carriage Square, Inc. v. Commissioner 968
    Note 977
    Problems 977
  2. Apportionment of Income 978
D. Simplified Flow–Through Regime for Electing Large Partnerships 979

Page

Chapter 19. Partner's Basis And Other Limitations On Allocated Losses ----- **982**
A. Introduction ----- 982
B. Initial Basis ----- 983
C. Adjustments to Basis ----- 983
    Revenue Ruling 96–11 ----- 985
D. Timing and Priorities ----- 987
    Problems ----- 988
E. Limitations on the Deduction of Losses ----- 988
    1. Inadequate Basis ----- 988
        Sennett v. Commissioner ----- 989
        Problems ----- 992
    2. Section 465 at Risk Limitations ----- 992
    3. Passive Activity Loss Limitations ----- 993
    4. Judicial Limitations on Partnership Losses ----- 995
        Estate of Franklin v. Commissioner ----- 995
        Notes ----- 999

Chapter 20. Characterizing Transactions Between Partners and the Partnership ----- **1001**
A. Introduction ----- 1001
B. Payments for Services and the Use of Property ----- 1002
    1. The Statutory Trichotomy ----- 1002
        a. The Entity Approach ----- 1002
        b. The Aggregate Approach ----- 1003
        c. The Hybrid Approach ----- 1003
    2. The Consequences of Characterization ----- 1004
    3. Distinguishing Between Types of Payments ----- 1006
        a. Section 707(a) ----- 1006
            Pratt v. Commissioner ----- 1007
            Revenue Ruling 81–301 ----- 1012
        b. The 1984 Amendments ----- 1014
            Problems ----- 1016
        c. Section 707(c) ----- 1017
            Gaines v. Commissioner ----- 1017
            Revenue Ruling 81–300 ----- 1021
            Notes ----- 1023
            Problems ----- 1025
C. Distinguishing Between Sales and Current Distributions ----- 1025
    1. The Judicial Background ----- 1026
        Otey v. Commissioner ----- 1026
        Jupiter Corp. v. United States ----- 1033
        Note ----- 1042
    2. The 1992 Regulations ----- 1042
    3. The 2004 Proposed Regulations ----- 1045
        Problems ----- 1048
D. Limitations on Certain Sales ----- 1049
    Note ----- 1050
    Problems ----- 1050

Page

Chapter 21. Sale of a Partnership Interest 1052
A. Introduction 1052
B. Treatment of the Seller—In General 1053
   1. Effect of Partnership Liabilities 1054
     Revenue Ruling 77–402 1054
     Note 1056
   2. Effect of Current Year's Income 1058
     Problems 1058
C. Sales Subject to Section 751 1059
   1. Section 751 Property 1060
     a. Unrealized Receivables 1060
        Logan v. Commissioner 1060
        Notes 1065
     b. Inventory Items 1065
        Holbrook v. Commissioner 1066
        Notes 1068
   2. Determination of Gain or Loss on the Section 751(a) and the Section 741 Portions of the Sale 1068
     Problems 1071
D. Other Entity Versus Aggregate Issues 1071
   1. Installment Sale Reporting of Gain From the Sale of a Partnership Interest 1072
     Revenue Ruling 89–108 1072
     Notes 1074
   2. Capital Gain Look–Through Rules for Sales or Exchanges of Partnership Interests 1074
E. Treatment of the Purchasing Partner 1076
   1. Section 743(b) Basis Adjustment 1077
     Estate of Dupree v. United States 1078
     Note 1083
   2. Mandatory Basis Adjustment for Partnership With a Substantial Built–In Loss 1084
   3. Calculating and Allocating the Section 743(b) Basis Adjustment 1086
     Problems 1092
F. The Sale of an Interest: A Comprehensive Illustration 1093
   1. Determination of Gain (or Loss) on the Sale of a Partner's Interest 1094
   2. Determination of Basis to the Purchaser 1096

Chapter 22. Current Distributions to Partners 1099
A. Introduction 1099
B. Partner Level Consequences 1100
   1. Cash Distributions 1100
     Helmer v. Commissioner 1101
     Note 1103
     Problems 1104
   2. Property Distributions 1104
   3. Distributions of Stock of a Controlled Corporation to a Corporate Partner 1108

Page

B. Partner Level Consequences—Continued
    4. Elective Basis Adjustment to Distributee _____ 1110
    5. Disposition of Distributed Property_____ 1111
       Problems _____ 1112
    6. Effect of Partnership Liabilities _____ 1113
       Revenue Ruling 79–205 _____ 1114
       Problem _____ 1116
C. Partnership Level Consequences _____ 1117
    1. The Section 754 Election _____ 1118
    2. Allocating the Section 734(b) Basis Adjustment _____ 1119
    3. Effect of Operating Distributions on Partners' Capital Accounts _____ 1121
       Problem _____ 1122
    4. Tiered Partnership Distributions_____ 1123
       Revenue Ruling 92–15_____ 1123
       Note _____ 1128
D. Treatment of Precontribution Gain or Loss on Certain In–Kind Partnership Distributions: So-Called "Mixing Bowl" Transactions _____ 1129
    1. Distributions of Contributed Property to Another Partner (Section 704(c)(1)(B)) _____ 1129
    2. Distributions of Other Property to The Contributing Partner (Section 737) _____ 1131
E. Distributions of Marketable Securities (Section 731(c)) _____ 1134
   *Problems*_____ 1139
F. Distributions That Alter a Partner's Interest in Ordinary Income Property _____ 1140
    1. Current Law_____ 1140
       Problems _____ 1144
    2. Alternative Approaches for Reform of Section 751(b)_____ 1146
       IRS Notice 2006–14 _____ 1147
       Note _____ 1154

Chapter 23. Liquidating Distributions_____**1155**
A. Introduction _____ 1155
B. The Structure of Section 736 _____ 1156
C. Section 736(b) Payments _____ 1157
D. Section 736(a) Payments _____ 1162
   Revenue Ruling 75–154_____ 1164
E. Planning for Liquidations: Section 736(a) v. Section 736(b) _____ 1167
F. Relationship Between Sections 752 and 736 _____ 1168
G. Taxing Deferred Section 736 Payments _____ 1169
H. The Comprehensive Illustration Revisited_____ 1170
   *Problems*_____ 1172
I. Liquidations Distinguished From Sales_____ 1174
   *Cooney v. Commissioner*_____ 1174
   Note _____ 1178
J. Abandoning Partnership Interests _____ 1178
   *Citron v. Commissioner*_____ 1179
   Revenue Ruling 93–80 _____ 1186
   Problem _____ 1190

Page

Chapter 24.　Partnership Terminations 1191

A. Voluntary Terminations of the Business 1191
　Revenue Ruling 77–412 1192
　Note 1193
　Revenue Ruling 84–111 1193
　Notes 1198
B. Statutory Terminations 1199
　1. Generally 1199
　　a. Complete Cessation of Business in the Partnership
　　　Form—Section 708(b)(1)(A) 1200
　　　Revenue Ruling 99–6 1200
　　　Note 1203
　　b. Constructive Terminations—Section 708(b)(1)(B) 1203
　　　Notes 1206
　2. Tiered Partnerships 1206
　　Revenue Ruling 87–51 1207
　　Note 1208
　　Problems 1209
C. Partnership Mergers and Divisions 1209
　1. Mergers 1209
　2. Divisions 1214
　3. Application of Mixing Bowl Rules to Partnership Mergers 1216
　　Revenue Ruling 2004–43 1217
D. Conversions of Partnership Interests 1224
　Revenue Ruling 84–52 1225
　Revenue Ruling 95–37 1227
　Notes 1229

Chapter 25.　Death of a Partner 1231

A. Introduction 1231
B. Effect on Current Year's Income 1231
C. Basis Adjustments 1232
　1. Fair Market Value Basis 1232
　2. Carryover Basis: Income in Respect of a Decedent 1233
　　Quick Trust v. Commissioner 1234
　　Woodhall v. Commissioner 1238
　　Notes 1241
　3. Property Contributed by the Deceased Partner With a
　　Built-In Loss 1242

Index 1243

*

Table of Cases

The principal cases are in bold type. Cases cited or discussed in the text are roman type. References are to paragraphs. Cases cited in principal cases and within other quoted materials are not included.

Ach v. Commissioner, 42 T.C. 114 (Tax Ct.1964), 1130

ACM Partnership v. Commissioner, T.C. Memo. 1997–115 (U.S.Tax Ct.1997), 16085

Adams v. Commissioner, 74 T.C. 4 (U.S.Tax Ct.1980), 3125

Aetna Cas. & Sur. Co. v. United States, 568 F.2d 811 (2nd Cir.1976), 11075

American Bantam Car Co. v. Commissioner, 11 T.C. 397 (Tax Ct.1948), 2045, 2070, 9075

American Nurseryman Publishing Co. v. Commissioner, 75 T.C. 271 (U.S.Tax Ct.1980), 15080

Arkansas Best Corp. v. Commissioner, 485 U.S. 212, 108 S.Ct. 971, 99 L.Ed.2d 183 (1988), 21055

Armstrong v. Phinney, 394 F.2d 661 (5th Cir.1968), 15235, 20010

Arrowsmith v. Commissioner, 344 U.S. 6, 73 S.Ct. 71, 97 L.Ed. 6 (1952), 8015

ASA Investerings Partnership v. Commissioner, T.C. Memo. 1998–305 (U.S.Tax Ct.1998), 16085

Associated Mach. v. Commissioner, 403 F.2d 622 (9th Cir.1968), 11060, 13135

Associated Wholesale Grocers, Inc. v. United States, 927 F.2d 1517 (10th Cir. 1991), 8050

A.W. Chesterton Co., Inc. v. Chesterton, 128 F.3d 1 (1st Cir.1997), 15465

Bardahl Mfg. Corp. v. Commissioner, T.C. Memo. 1965–200 (Tax Ct.1965), 7070

Bard–Parker Co. v. Commissioner, 218 F.2d 52 (2nd Cir.1954), 11115

Bashford, Helvering v., 302 U.S. 454, 58 S.Ct. 307, 82 L.Ed. 367 (1938), 10150

Basye, United States v., 410 U.S. 441, 93 S.Ct. 1080, 35 L.Ed.2d 412 (1973), **18005,** 18040

Bateman v. Commissioner, 40 T.C. 408 (Tax Ct.1963), 10290

Bausch & Lomb Optical Co. v. Commissioner, 267 F.2d 75 (2nd Cir.1959), 10115

Bazley v. Commissioner, 331 U.S. 737, 67 S.Ct. 1489, 91 L.Ed. 1782 (1947), **11015**

Bentsen v. Phinney, 199 F.Supp. 363 (S.D.Tex.1961), 9105

Bergstrom v. United States, 37 Fed.Cl. 164 (1996), 19065

Berry Petroleum Co. v. Commissioner, 104 T.C. No. 30, 104 T.C. 584 (U.S.Tax Ct.1995), **13070**

B. Forman Co. v. Commissioner, 453 F.2d 1144 (2nd Cir.1972), 14045

Bhada v. Commissioner, 89 T.C. No. 67, 89 T.C. 959 (U.S.Tax Ct.1987), 5150

Black & Decker Corp. v. United States, 436 F.3d 431 (4th Cir.2006), **2210**

Bolding v. Commissioner, 117 F.3d 270 (5th Cir.1997), **15295**

Bollinger, Commissioner v., 485 U.S. 340, 108 S.Ct. 1173, 99 L.Ed.2d 357 (1988), **1120**

Brown Group, Inc. and Subsidiaries v. Commissioner, 104 T.C. No. 5, 104 T.C. 105 (U.S.Tax Ct.1995), 18040

Burnet v. Logan, 283 U.S. 404, 51 S.Ct. 550, 75 L.Ed. 1143 (1931), 8030

Burr Oaks Corp. v. Commissioner, 365 F.2d 24 (7th Cir.1966), **3050**

Byrne v. Commissioner, 361 F.2d 939 (7th Cir.1966), 15285

Campbell v. Commissioner, T.C. Memo. 1990–162 (U.S.Tax Ct.1990), 17075

Carlberg v. United States, 281 F.2d 507 (8th Cir.1960), 10290

Carriage Square, Inc. v. Commissioner, 69 T.C. 119 (U.S.Tax Ct.1977), **18230**

Centennial Sav. Bank FSB, United States v., 499 U.S. 573, 111 S.Ct. 1512, 113 L.Ed.2d 608 (1991), 6000

Cerone v. Commissioner, 87 T.C. No. 1, 87 T.C. 1 (U.S.Tax Ct.1986), **5105**

Chamberlin v. Commissioner, 207 F.2d 462 (6th Cir.1953), 6100

Chapman v. Commissioner, 618 F.2d 856 (1st Cir.1980), 10135

Chevron U.S.A., Inc. v. Natural Resources Defense Council, Inc., 467 U.S. 837, 104 S.Ct. 2778, 81 L.Ed.2d 694 (1984), 16075

Citron v. Commissioner, 97 T.C. No. 12, 97 T.C. 200 (U.S.Tax Ct.1991), **23070**

City Bank of Washington v. Commissioner, 38 T.C. 713 (Tax Ct.1962), 8005

Clark, Commissioner v., 489 U.S. 726, 109 S.Ct. 1455, 103 L.Ed.2d 753 (1989), **10250**

Coady v. Commissioner, 33 T.C. 771 (Tax Ct.1960), 12025

Commissioner v. _____ (see opposing party)

Cooney v. Commissioner, 65 T.C. 101 (U.S.Tax Ct.1975), **23055**

Cortland Specialty Co. v. Commissioner, 60 F.2d 937 (2nd Cir.1932), 9080

Cottage Sav. Ass'n v. Commissioner, 499 U.S. 554, 111 S.Ct. 1503, 113 L.Ed.2d 589 (1991), 3095, 6000

Court Holding Co., Commissioner v., 324 U.S. 331, 65 S.Ct. 707, 89 L.Ed. 981 (1945), 4055, 8075, 12100

Crane v. Commissioner, 331 U.S. 1, 67 S.Ct. 1047, 91 L.Ed. 1301 (1947), 8015, 21010

Crosswhite v. United States, 438 F.Supp. 368 (D.Or.1977), 4095

Culbertson, Commissioner v., 337 U.S. 733, 69 S.Ct. 1210, 93 L.Ed. 1659 (1949), 18225

Cumberland Public Service Co., United States v., 338 U.S. 451, 70 S.Ct. 280, 94 L.Ed. 251 (1950), 4055, 12100

D'Agostino, United States v., 145 F.3d 69 (2nd Cir.1998), 4087

Davant v. Commissioner, 366 F.2d 874 (5th Cir.1966), 11060

Davis, United States v., 397 U.S. 301, 90 S.Ct. 1041, 25 L.Ed.2d 323 (1970), **5085**

Demirjian v. Commissioner, 457 F.2d 1 (3rd Cir.1972), **18035**

Diamond v. Commissioner, 492 F.2d 286 (7th Cir.1974), 17075

Diamond v. Commissioner, 56 T.C. 530 (U.S.Tax Ct.1971), **17070**

Dilts v. United States, 845 F.Supp. 1505 (D.Wyo.1994), 15235

Donruss Co., United States v., 393 U.S. 297, 89 S.Ct. 501, 21 L.Ed.2d 495 (1969), **7045**

Drybrough v. Commissioner, 376 F.2d 350 (6th Cir.1967), **2185**

Dunlap and Associates, Inc. v. Commissioner, 47 T.C. 542 (Tax Ct.1967), 11055

Dupree's Estate v. United States, 391 F.2d 753 (5th Cir.1968), **21105**

Eisner v. Macomber, 252 U.S. 189, 40 S.Ct. 189, 64 L.Ed. 521 (1920), 1020, 6000

Eli Lilly and Company and Subsidiaries v. Commissioner, 84 T.C. No. 65, 84 T.C. 996 (U.S.Tax Ct.1985), 14020

Elkhorn Coal Co., Helvering v., 95 F.2d 732 (4th Cir.1937), **10100**

Elliotts, Inc. v. Commissioner, 716 F.2d 1241 (9th Cir.1983), 4095

Ellis v. Commissioner, T.C. Memo. 1989–280 (U.S.Tax Ct.1989), 15310

Estate of (see name of party)

Feingold v. Commissioner, 49 T.C. 461 (Tax Ct.1968), 15450

Fink, Commissioner v., 483 U.S. 89, 107 S.Ct. 2729, 97 L.Ed.2d 74 (1987), **2290**

Flint v. Stone Tracy Co., 220 U.S. 107, 31 S.Ct. 342, 55 L.Ed. 389 (1911), 1000

Franklin's Estate v. Commissioner, 544 F.2d 1045 (9th Cir.1976), **19060**

Frontier Chevrolet Co. v. Commissioner, 116 T.C. No. 23, 116 T.C. 289 (U.S.Tax Ct.2001), 5125

Frontier Sav. Ass'n. and Subsidiaries v. Commissioner, 87 T.C. No. 40, 87 T.C. 665 (U.S.Tax Ct.1986), 6025

Fuchs v. Commissioner, 80 T.C. 506 (U.S.Tax Ct.1983), 18040

Gaines v. Commissioner, T.C. Memo. 1982–731 (U.S.Tax Ct.1982), **20055**

General Utilities & Operating Co. v. Helvering, 296 U.S. 200, 56 S.Ct. 185, 80 L.Ed. 154 (1935), 4055, 8075

Generes, United States v., 405 U.S. 93, 92 S.Ct. 827, 31 L.Ed.2d 62 (1972), **3110**

Gitlitz v. Commissioner, 531 U.S. 206, 121 S.Ct. 701, 148 L.Ed.2d 613 (2001), 15287

Golconda Mining Corp. v. Commissioner, 58 T.C. 736 (U.S.Tax Ct.1972), 7050

Golconda Mining Corp. v. Commissioner, 58 T.C. 139 (U.S.Tax Ct.1972), 7050

Gordon, Commissioner v., 391 U.S. 83, 88 S.Ct. 1517, 20 L.Ed.2d 448 (1968), 9065

Granite Trust Co. v. United States, 238 F.2d 670 (1st Cir.1956), **8045**

Greenberg v. Commissioner, 62 T.C. 331 (U.S.Tax Ct.1974), 1110

Gregory v. Helvering, 293 U.S. 465, 55 S.Ct. 266, 79 L.Ed. 596 (1935), **9055**

Gregory, Helvering v., 69 F.2d 809 (2nd Cir.1934), 9065

Grojean v. Commissioner, 248 F.3d 572 (7th Cir.2001), 15300

Groman v. Commissioner, 302 U.S. 82, 302 U.S. 654, 58 S.Ct. 108, 82 L.Ed. 63 (1937), 10150

Haley Bros. Const. Corp. v. Commissioner, 87 T.C. No. 26, 87 T.C. 498 (U.S.Tax Ct.1986), 15170

Hamrick v. Commissioner, 43 T.C. 21 (Tax Ct.1964), 10135

Helmer v. Commissioner, T.C. Memo. 1975–160 (U.S.Tax Ct.1975), **22010**

Helvering v. _____ (see opposing party)

Hempt Bros., Inc. v. United States, 490 F.2d 1172 (3rd Cir.1974), **2260**

Hendler, United States v., 303 U.S. 564, 58 S.Ct. 655, 82 L.Ed. 1018 (1938), 2170, 10145, 10305

Hesse, Estate of v. Commissioner, 74 T.C. 1307 (U.S.Tax Ct.1980), 25005

Heverly v. Commissioner, 621 F.2d 1227 (3rd Cir.1980), 10135

Hickok v. Commissioner, 32 T.C. 80 (Tax Ct.1959), 11030

Hillsboro Nat. Bank v. Commissioner, 460 U.S. 370, 103 S.Ct. 1134, 75 L.Ed.2d 130 (1983), 2275, 21065

Holbrook v. Commissioner, T.C. Memo. 1975–294 (U.S.Tax Ct.1975), **21060**

Holsey v. Commissioner, 258 F.2d 865 (3rd Cir.1958), **5200**

Home Const. Corp. of America v. United States, 439 F.2d 1165 (5th Cir.1971), 11060

Honbarrier v. Commissioner, 115 T.C. No. 23, 115 T.C. 300 (U.S.Tax Ct.2000), 10070

Honigman v. Commissioner, 466 F.2d 69 (6th Cir.1972), **4090**

Hook v. Commissioner, 58 T.C. 267 (U.S.Tax Ct.1972), 15465

Howell v. Commissioner, 57 T.C. 546 (U.S.Tax Ct.1972), 15450

Hubert Enterprises, Inc. and Subsidiaries v. Commissioner, 125 T.C. No. 6, 125 T.C. 72 (U.S.Tax Ct.2005), 19045

Hurst v. Commissioner, 124 T.C. No. 2, 124 T.C. 16 (U.S.Tax Ct.2005), 5040, **5045**

Imler v. Commissioner, 11 T.C. 836 (Tax Ct.1948), **5230**

Intermountain Lumber Co. and Subsidiaries v. Commissioner, 65 T.C. 1025 (U.S.Tax Ct.1976), **2050**

Ivan Allen Co. v. United States, 422 U.S. 617, 95 S.Ct. 2501, 45 L.Ed.2d 435 (1975), **7060**

Jackson Inv. Co., Commissioner v., 346 F.2d 187 (9th Cir.1965), 23025

Jacobson v. Commissioner, 96 T.C. No. 21, 96 T.C. 577 (U.S.Tax Ct.1991), 20087

James Armour, Inc. v. Commissioner, 43 T.C. 295 (Tax Ct.1964), 11115

J.E. Seagram Corp. v. Commissioner, 104 T.C. No. 4, 104 T.C. 75 (U.S.Tax Ct.1995), **10045**

John A. Nelson Co. v. Helvering, 296 U.S. 374, 56 S.Ct. 273, 80 L.Ed. 281 (1935), 10040, 10055

Johnson v. Commissioner, 78 T.C. 564 (U.S.Tax Ct.1982), 11020

Jones v. United States, 531 F.2d 1343 (6th Cir.1976), 8020

Jupiter Corp. v. United States, 2 Cl.Ct. 58 (Cl.Ct.1983), **20085**

Kamborian, Estate of v. Commissioner, 469 F.2d 219 (1st Cir.1972), **2080**

Kass v. Commissioner, 60 T.C. 218 (U.S.Tax Ct.1973), 10040

Kean v. Commissioner, 469 F.2d 1183 (9th Cir.1972), **15075**

Keller v. Commissioner, 77 T.C. 1014 (U.S.Tax Ct.1981), 1130

Kenroy, Inc. v. Commissioner, T.C. Memo. 1984–232 (U.S.Tax Ct.1984), 17075

Kenyatta Corp. v. Commissioner, 86 T.C. No. 12, 86 T.C. 171 (U.S.Tax Ct.1986), 7030

Kimbell–Diamond Mill. Co. v. Commissioner, 14 T.C. 74 (Tax Ct.1950), **8110,** 9065

King Enterprises, Inc. v. United States, 189 Ct.Cl. 466, 418 F.2d 511 (Ct.Cl. 1969), 2045, 9065, **9070**

Kinsey v. Commissioner, 477 F.2d 1058 (2nd Cir.1973), 8020

Kobor v. United States, 62 A.F.T.R.2d (RIA) 5047 (C.D.Cal.1987), 17075

Krahenbuhl v. Commissioner, T.C. Memo. 1968–34 (Tax Ct.1968), 15275

Krause v. Commissioner, 57 T.C. 890 (U.S.Tax Ct.1972), 18230

Larson v. Commissioner, 66 T.C. 159 (U.S.Tax Ct.1976), 16060, 16080

Leavitt, Estate of v. Commissioner, 90 T.C. No. 16, 90 T.C. 206 (U.S.Tax Ct.1988), 15300

Lebowitz v. Commissioner, 917 F.2d 1314 (2nd Cir.1990), 19065

Ledoux v. Commissioner, 77 T.C. 293 (U.S.Tax Ct.1981), 21050

Lessinger v. Commissioner, 872 F.2d 519 (2nd Cir.1989), 2015, 2285

Le Tulle v. Scofield, 308 U.S. 415, 60 S.Ct. 313, 84 L.Ed. 355 (1940), 9080

Libson Shops, Inc. v. Koehler, 353 U.S. 382, 77 S.Ct. 990, 1 L.Ed.2d 924 (1957), 13030

Liddon v. Commissioner, 230 F.2d 304 (6th Cir.1956), 11115

Lipke v. Commissioner, 81 T.C. No. 41, 81 T.C. 689 (U.S.Tax Ct.1983), **18210**

Litton Industries, Inc. v. Commissioner, 89 T.C. No. 75, 89 T.C. 1086 (U.S.Tax Ct.1987), **4120**

Littriello v. United States, 95 A.F.T.R.2d (RIA) 2581 (W.D.Ky.2005), **1082**

Lockwood's Estate v. Commissioner, 350 F.2d 712 (8th Cir.1965), **12010**

Logan v. Commissioner, 51 T.C. 482 (Tax Ct.1968), **21045**

Long Term Capital Holdings v. United States, 330 F.Supp.2d 122 (D.Conn. 2004), 1074, 16085

Lucas v. Earl, 281 U.S. 111, 50 S.Ct. 241, 74 L.Ed. 731 (1930), 1130, 18045

Lukens v. Commissioner, 945 F.2d 92 (5th Cir.1991), 19065

Lynch v. Commissioner, 801 F.2d 1176 (9th Cir.1986), **5035**

Madison Gas and Elec. Co. v. Commissioner, 633 F.2d 512 (7th Cir.1980), **16040**

Manhattan Bldg. Co. v. Commissioner, 27 T.C. 1032 (Tax Ct.1957), 2045

Marett, United States v., 325 F.2d 28 (5th Cir.1963), 12025

Marr v. United States, 268 U.S. 536, 45 S.Ct. 575, 69 L.Ed. 1079 (1925), 9000

Mathis v. Commissioner, 19 T.C. 1123 (Tax Ct.1953), 11115

McDonald's Restaurants of Illinois, Inc. v. Commissioner, 688 F.2d 520 (7th Cir. 1982), 10040

McManus v. Commissioner, 65 T.C. 197 (U.S.Tax Ct.1975), 18040

Miller v. Commissioner, 84 F.2d 415 (6th Cir.1936), 10040

Moline Properties v. Commissioner, 319 U.S. 436, 63 S.Ct. 1132, 87 L.Ed. 1499 (1943), **1100**

Morrissey v. Commissioner, 296 U.S. 344, 56 S.Ct. 289, 80 L.Ed. 263 (1935), 1080

Morris Trust, Commissioner v., 367 F.2d 794 (4th Cir.1966), 12100

Mountain State Steel Foundries, Inc. v. Commissioner, 284 F.2d 737 (4th Cir. 1960), 7070

Mountain Water Co. of La Crescenta v. Commissioner, 35 T.C. 418 (Tax Ct.1960), 8005

Movielab, Inc. v. United States, 204 Ct.Cl. 6, 494 F.2d 693 (Ct.Cl.1974), 11060

Murphy Logging Co. v. United States, 378 F.2d 222 (9th Cir.1967), 3070

Nash v. United States, 398 U.S. 1, 90 S.Ct. 1550, 26 L.Ed.2d 1 (1970), 2275

New Jersey Mortg. & Title Co. v. Commissioner, 3 T.C. 1277 (Tax Ct.1944), 10315

Niederkrome v. Commissioner, 266 F.2d 238 (9th Cir.1958), 4095

OBH, Inc. v. United States, 397 F.Supp.2d 1148 (D.Neb.2005), 4105

Ogiony v. Commissioner, 617 F.2d 14 (2nd Cir.1980), 1105

Old Virginia Brick Co. v. C I. R., 44 T.C. 724 (Tax Ct.1965), 15140

Orrisch v. Commissioner, 55 T.C. 395 (U.S.Tax Ct.1970), **18075**

O'Sullivan Rubber Co. v. Commissioner, 120 F.2d 845 (2nd Cir.1941), 7010

Otey v. Commissioner, 70 T.C. 312 (U.S.Tax Ct.1978), **20080**

Owen v. Commissioner, 881 F.2d 832 (9th Cir.1989), **2230**

Paige v. United States, 580 F.2d 960 (9th Cir.1978), 15180

Penrod (Robert A.) v. Commissioner, 88 T.C. No. 79, 88 T.C. 1415 (U.S.Tax Ct.1987), 10040

Peracchi v. Commissioner, 143 F.3d 487 (9th Cir.1998), **2240**

Performance Systems, Inc. v. United States, 382 F.Supp. 525 (M.D.Tenn.1973), 11060

Peterson v. Commissioner, T.C. Memo. 1997–377 (U.S.Tax Ct.1997), 15320

Phellis, United States v., 257 U.S. 156, 42 S.Ct. 63, 66 L.Ed. 180 (1921), 9000

Plantation Patterns, Inc. v. Commissioner, 462 F.2d 712 (5th Cir.1972), **3065**, 15300

Pleasant Summit Land Corp. v. Commissioner, 863 F.2d 263 (3rd Cir.1988), 19065

Pollock v. Farmers' Loan & Trust Co., 157 U.S. 429, 15 S.Ct. 673, 39 L.Ed. 759 (1895), 1000

Pope & Talbot & Subsidiaries v. Commissioner, 104 T.C. No. 29, 104 T.C. 574 (U.S.Tax Ct.1995), 4055

Portage Plastics Co., Inc. v. United States, 486 F.2d 632 (7th Cir.1973), 15180

Pratt v. Commissioner, 64 T.C. 203 (U.S.Tax Ct.1975), **20035**

Pridemark, Inc. v. Commissioner, 345 F.2d 35 (4th Cir.1965), 11080

Putnam v. Commissioner, 352 U.S. 82, 77 S.Ct. 175, 1 L.Ed.2d 144 (1956), 3120

Quick's Trust v. Commissioner, 54 T.C. 1336 (U.S.Tax Ct.1970), **25020**

Rafferty v. Commissioner, 452 F.2d 767 (1st Cir.1971), **12035**

Rath v. Commissioner, 101 T.C. No. 13, 101 T.C. 196 (U.S.Tax Ct.1993), 15220

Redding v. Commissioner, 630 F.2d 1169 (7th Cir.1980), 12180

Reef Corp. v. Commissioner, 368 F.2d 125 (5th Cir.1966), 9065, 11075, **11110, 11120**

Reynolds Metals Co. v. Commissioner, 105 T.C. No. 20, 105 T.C. 304 (U.S.Tax Ct.1995), 2295

Rockefeller v. United States, 257 U.S. 176, 42 S.Ct. 68, 66 L.Ed. 186 (1921), 9000, 12000

Roebling III v. Commissioner, 143 F.2d 810 (3rd Cir.1944), 10055

Rooney v. United States, 305 F.2d 681 (9th Cir.1962), 2265

Rushing v. Commissioner, 441 F.2d 593 (5th Cir.1971), 8020

Schneer v. Commissioner, 97 T.C. No. 45, 97 T.C. 643 (U.S.Tax Ct.1991), **18050**

Scriptomatic, Inc. v. United States, 555 F.2d 364 (3rd Cir.1977), **3015**

Selfe v. United States, 778 F.2d 769 (11th Cir.1985), 15300

Sennett v. Commissioner, 752 F.2d 428 (9th Cir.1985), **19035**

Shellabarger Grain Products Co. v. Commissioner, 146 F.2d 177 (7th Cir.1944), 2305

Sleiman v. Commissioner, 187 F.3d 1352 (11th Cir.1999), 15300

Smothers v. United States, 642 F.2d 894 (5th Cir.1981), 11115

Southland Ice Co. v. Commissioner, 5 T.C. 842 (Tax Ct.1945), 10315

Southwest Consol. Corp., Helvering v., 315 U.S. 194, 62 S.Ct. 546, 86 L.Ed. 789 (1942), 10315

Southwest Natural Gas Co. v. Commissioner, 189 F.2d 332 (5th Cir.1951), **9095**

Speca v. Commissioner, 630 F.2d 554 (7th Cir.1980), **15270**

Sperl v. Commissioner, T.C. Memo. 1993–515 (U.S.Tax Ct.1993), 15280

Stafford, United States v., 727 F.2d 1043 (11th Cir.1984), **17095**

Stauffer's Estate v. Commissioner, 403 F.2d 611 (9th Cir.1968), 11060, 13135

St. Charles Inv. Co. v. Commissioner, 232 F.3d 773 (10th Cir.2000), 15453

St. John v. United States, 53 A.F.T.R.2d (RIA) 718 (C.D.Ill.1983), 17075

Stoddard v. Commissioner, 141 F.2d 76 (2nd Cir.1944), 10315

Tanner v. Commissioner, T.C. Memo. 1983–230 (U.S.Tax Ct.1983), **4080**

Texaco, Inc. v. Commissioner, 98 F.3d 825 (5th Cir.1996), **14035**

Textron, Inc. v. United States, 561 F.2d 1023 (1st Cir.1977), 13105

Towne v. Eisner, 245 U.S. 418, 38 S.Ct. 158, 62 L.Ed. 372 (1918), 6000

Tufts, Commissioner v., 461 U.S. 300, 103 S.Ct. 1826, 75 L.Ed.2d 863 (1983), 18125, 21010

Turnbow v. Commissioner, 368 U.S. 337, 82 S.Ct. 353, 7 L.Ed.2d 326 (1961), **10130**

Underwood v. Commissioner, 63 T.C. 468 (U.S.Tax Ct.1975), 15310

United Parcel Service of America, Inc. v. Commissioner, 254 F.3d 1014 (11th Cir.2001), **1073**

United States v. ———— **(see opposing party)**

Walton, United States v., 909 F.2d 915 (6th Cir.1990), 1110

Warsaw Photographic Associates, Inc. v. Commissioner, 84 T.C. No. 3, 84 T.C. 21 (U.S.Tax Ct.1985), **11090**

Western Federal Sav. and Loan Ass'n v. Commissioner, 880 F.2d 1005 (8th Cir. 1989), 6025

Whipple v. Commissioner, 373 U.S. 193, 83 S.Ct. 1168, 10 L.Ed.2d 288 (1963), 3105

Wiebusch v. Commissioner, 59 T.C. 777 (U.S.Tax Ct.1973), **15030**

Wilhelm v. United States, 257 F.Supp. 16 (D.Wyo.1966), 15235

Williams, United States v., 875 F.2d 846 (11th Cir.1989), 4087

Woodhall v. Commissioner, 454 F.2d 226 (9th Cir.1972), **25025**

Wortham Machinery Co. v. United States, 521 F.2d 160 (10th Cir.1975), 4095

Wright v. United States, 482 F.2d 600 (8th Cir.1973), 5100

Wyman Bldg. Trust v. Commissioner, 45 B.T.A. 155 (B.T.A.1941), 1090

Yoc Heating Corp. v. Commissioner, 61 T.C. 168 (U.S.Tax Ct.1973), 11080

Zenz v. Quinlivan, 213 F.2d 914 (6th Cir. 1954), **5175**

*

Table of Internal Revenue Code Sections

UNITED STATES

UNITED STATES CODE ANNOTATED

26 U.S.C.A.—Internal Revenue Code

Sec.	This Work Para.
1(b)(11)	4000
1(h)	1005
1(h)	1020
1(h)	3080
1(h)	15,385
1(h)	18,030
1(h)	18,030
1(h)	21,092
1(h)(9)	15,385
1(h)(9)	18,030
1(h)(9)	21,092
1(h)(11)	4042
1(h)(11)	6020
1(h)(11)	11,000
1(h)(11)	15,385
1(h)(11)	16,075
1(h)(11)	21,092
1(h)(11)(D)(i)	4042
11	1000
11	1015
11(a)(2)	1130
11(b)	14,005
11(b)(1)	1010
11(b)(2)	1015
29	18,250
38(c)	1040
42	18,250
47	18,250
53	1035
53	1040
55	15,215
55—59	1025
55(a)	1025
55(b)(1)(B)	1025
55(d)	14,005
55(d)(2)	1025
55(e)(1)	1045
55(e)(1)(A)	1045
55(e)(1)(B)	1045
55(e)(2)	1045
55(e)(3)	1045
55(e)(5)	1045
56(a)(1)	1025
56(a)(1)	1030
56(a)(4)	1025

UNITED STATES CODE ANNOTATED

26 U.S.C.A.—Internal Revenue Code

Sec.	This Work Para.
56(a)(6)	1025
56(a)(6)	1030
56(d)	1025
56(g)(1)	1030
56(g)(3)	1030
56(g)(4)	1030
57(a)(5)	1030
59(a)	1040
59A	14,005
61	1005
61	6000
61	17,060
61	17,075
61	17,084
61	20,020
61(a)	20,065
61(a)(12)	3135
61(a)(12)	11,020
63(a)	1005
67	18,250
67(b)	18,250
83	2025
83	3005
83	15,190
83	17,065
83	17,065
83	17,075
83	17,084
83	6000
83(a)	2010
83(a)	17,065
83(b)	2010
83(b)	15,190
83(b)	17,065
83(c)(1)	17,075
83(c)(2)	17,075
83(h)	17,065
83(h)	2010
96–30	12,115
108	3135
108	15,015
108	15,287
108	18,040
108(a)	15,287
108(a)	18,040
108(b)	15,287
108(b)	18,040
108(b)(5)	18,040
108(c)(3)	18,040

UNITED STATES CODE ANNOTATED

26 U.S.C.A.—Internal Revenue Code

Sec.	This Work Para.
108(d)(6)	18,040
108(d)(7)	15,015
108(d)(7)(A)	15,287
108(e)(6)	2295
108(e)(6)	3135
108(e)(8)	11,020
108(e)(8)	3135
111	18,020
112(g)(1)(B)	10,135
118	2295
118(a)	2285
118(a)	2295
118(b)	2295
118(e)(2)	2295
119	15,235
119	20,010
151	18,250
151(d)(3)	1010
162	17,060
162	20,020
162	20,065
162(a)(1)	2010
162(k)	5125
162(l)	20,065
162(m)	1005
163(d)	1005
163(d)	4042
163(e)	3025
163(j)	3025
163(l)	3025
165	2285
165(b)	19,000
165(d)	18,020
165(g)	3000
165(g)	3100
165(g)	3105
165(g)	3115
165(g)	13,105
165(g)	15,320
166	3115
166	15,220
166(a)	15,220
166(c)	2275
166(d)	3100
166(d)	3105
166(d)	3120
166(d)	15,220
166(d)	15,320
166(e)	3105
168	4025
168(g)(2)	4025
168(n)	4025
170(b)(2)	1005
170(b)(2)	18,250
170(e)	19,025
171	3085
172	13,135
172	15,453
172	18,020
172	18,250

UNITED STATES CODE ANNOTATED

26 U.S.C.A.—Internal Revenue Code

Sec.	This Work Para.
172(b)	15,453
172(b)(1)(A)	13,020
172(b)(1)(H)	13,020
172(h)	13,140
172(h)	13,145
172(h)(3)(B)	13,140
172(h)(3)(C)	13,140
175	18,020
175(b)	18,020
179	18,020
179(d)(6)	14,005
179(d)(8)	18,020
183	1005
195	18,000
195(b)	17,105
195(b)(1)	17,105
197	5125
197	8095
197	21,110
197	23,025
203(h)(1)(A)	10,100
212	18,250
243	1005
243	1030
243	4100
243	4105
243	4110
243	5215
243	5235
243	15,220
243(a)	5180
243(a)(1)	4100
243(a)(3)	1050
243(a)(3)	4100
243(b)	4100
243(c)	4100
246(c)	4105
246A	4042
246A	4105
246A(c)(2)(A)	4105
246A(d)(3)(A)	4105
248	2305
248(a)(2)	2305
248(b)	2305
249	3085
249	11,020
263	20,065
263(a)	2010
263(c)	18,020
265	4025
265(a)(2)	4105
267	2095
267	4025
267	4055
267	8025
267	8075
267	15,230
267(a)(1)	8025
267(a)(1)	20,105
267(a)(2)	15,230

UNITED STATES CODE ANNOTATED 26 U.S.C.A.—Internal Revenue Code		UNITED STATES CODE ANNOTATED 26 U.S.C.A.—Internal Revenue Code	
Sec.	This Work Para.	Sec.	This Work Para.
267(a)(2)	20,010	301(c)(3)	4010
267(a)(2)	20,035	301(d)	15,240
267(b)	10,240	301(d)	4050
267(b)	12,090	301(e)	4110
267(b)	12,140	302	1015
267(b)	20,010	302	1135
267(b)	20,035	302	4005
267(b)	22,066	302	5015
267(b)(2)	4055	302	5115
267(b)(3)	4055	302	5120
267(c)	20,105	302	5130
267(c)(3)	20,105	302	5135
267(c)(4)	5015	302	5145
267(d)	20,105	302	5155
267(d)	20,110	302	6050
267(d)	4055	302	6120
267(e)	15,230	302	6140
267(e)	20,010	302	6170
267(e)	20,035	302	10,245
267(e)	20,070	302	12,175
269	13,020	302	15,380
269	13,110	302(a)	5005
269	13,125	302(a)	5125
269(a)	13,110	302(a)	5225
269(a)(2)	13,110	302(b)	5005
269(b)	8125	302(b)	5135
269A	1130	302(b)	5140
269A	7020	302(b)	5170
269A(1)	1130	302(b)	6115
269A(2)	1130	302(b)	10,255
269A(a)	1130	302(b)	10,260
274	15,280	302(b)(1)	5005
279	3025	302(b)(1)	5050
301	4005	302(b)(1)	5080
301	4042	302(b)(1)	5100
301	4065	302(b)(1)	5135
301	5005	302(b)(1)	10,245
301	6020	302(b)(1)	10,255
301	6035	302(b)(1)	10,260
301	6040	302(b)(1)—(b)(3)	5005
301	6115	302(b)(2)	5005
301	11,045	302(b)(2)	5010
301	12,070	302(b)(2)	5020
301	12,100	302(b)(2)	5050
301	12,175	302(b)(2)	5080
301	15,380	302(b)(2)	5100
301	15,470	302(b)(2)	5135
301—318	6000	302(b)(2)	10,245
301—304	6000	302(b)(2)	10,255
301—385	1000	302(b)(2)	10,260
301(a)	12,180	302(b)(2)(B)	5010
301(a)	4005	302(b)(2)(C)	5010
301(a)	4010	302(b)(3)	5005
301(b)	4050	302(b)(3)	5025
301(b)	4065	302(b)(3)	5050
301(b)(1)	11,020	302(b)(3)	5060
301(b)(2)	4070	302(b)(3)	5080
301(c)	12,180	302(b)(3)	5175
301(c)	4010	302(b)(4)	5225
301(c)(2)	4010	302(b)(4)	5235

UNITED STATES CODE ANNOTATED 26 U.S.C.A.—Internal Revenue Code		UNITED STATES CODE ANNOTATED 26 U.S.C.A.—Internal Revenue Code	
Sec.	**This Work Para.**	**Sec.**	**This Work Para.**
302(b)(4)(A)	5225	304(c)(3)(B)(ii)(II)	5160
302(c)(1)	5015	305	1135
302(c)(2)	5180	305	4005
302(c)(2)(A)(i)	5030	305	4010
302(c)(2)(A)(i)	5040	305	5115
302(c)(2)(B)	5050	305	6000
302(c)(2)(B)	6120	305	6040
302(c)(2)(C)	5060	305	6050
302(d)	5005	305	6065
302(d)	5175	305	6100
302(e)	5225	305	6140
302(e)	5235	305	10,205
302(e)(1)	5225	305	10,290
302(e)(2)	5225	305—307	6000
302(e)(4)	5225	305(a)	6010
303	1135	305(a)	6015
303	4005	305(a)	6020
303	5115	305(a)	6025
303	5115	305(a)	6040
303	5120	305(a)	6080
303	5125	305(a)	6170
303	7070	305(a)	6180
303(a)(1)	5120	305(b)	6020
303(a)(2)	5120	305(b)	6040
303(b)(2)	5115	305(b)	6055
303(b)(2)(B)	5115	305(b)(1)	6020
303(b)(3)	5115	305(b)(1)	6025
303(b)(4)	5115	305(b)(1)	6035
303(c)(1)(B)(ii)	6170	305(b)(1)	6040
304	1135	305(b)(1)	6085
304	4005	305(b)(1)	6180
304	5130	305(b)(2)	6025
304	5135	305(b)(2)	6035
304	5140	305(b)(2)	6040
304	5145	305(b)(2)	6050
304	5150	305(b)(2)	6085
304	5155	305(b)(3)	6040
304	5160	305(b)(3)	6085
304	5215	305(b)(4)	6020
304	6170	305(b)(4)	6055
304	10,240	305(b)(4)	6065
304(a)	5155	305(b)(5)	6040
304(a)(1)	5135	305(c)	6020
304(a)(1)	5145	305(c)	6040
304(a)(1)	5160	305(c)	6050
304(a)(2)	10,050	305(c)	6065
304(a)(2)	5140	305(c)(2)	6020
304(a)(2)	5150	305(c)(2)	6065
304(a)(2)	5160	305(c)(3)	6020
304(b)(1)	5135	305(c)(5)	6020
304(b)(2)	5135	306	1135
304(b)(3)	5145	306	4005
304(b)(3)(B)	5145	306	4010
304(b)(3)(B)(i)	5215	306	5115
304(c)	5135	306	6000
304(c)	11,085	306	6100
304(c)	11,105	306	6110
304(c)	11,115	306	6115
304(c)(3)	11,105	306	6120
304(c)(3)(B)	11,105	306	6135

UNITED STATES CODE ANNOTATED

26 U.S.C.A.—Internal Revenue Code

Sec.	This Work Para.
306	6140
306	6145
306	6160
306	6170
306	6170
306	6170
306	6172
306	6175
306	6180
306	10,240
306	10,260
306	11,045
306	11,050
306	11,100
306(a)	6120
306(a)(1)	6110
306(a)(1)(A)	21,055
306(a)(1)(A)(ii)	4035
306(a)(1)(D)	6100
306(a)(2)	6115
306(b)	6120
306(b)(1)	6120
306(b)(1)(A)	6120
306(b)(2)	6120
306(b)(3)	6120
306(b)(4)(A)	6120
306(b)(4)(A)	6135
306(b)(4)(B)	6120
306(c)	6145
306(c)(1)(A)	6170
306(c)(1)(B)	11,045
306(c)(1)(B)	11,045
306(c)(1)(B)	11,100
306(c)(1)(C)	6120
306(c)(1)(C)	6170
306(c)(2)	6172
306(c)(3)	6170
306(c)(3)(A)	6170
307	4005
307	6000
307	6010
307	6140
311	10,295
311	12,175
311	14,065
311	2110
311	4005
311	4065
311	5125
311	8075
311(a)	15,240
311(a)	2110
311(a)	4055
311(a)	8015
311(a)(1)	6080
311(b)	14,065
311(b)	15,240
311(b)	2110
311(b)	4055
311(b)	4060

UNITED STATES CODE ANNOTATED

26 U.S.C.A.—Internal Revenue Code

Sec.	This Work Para.
311(b)	4095
311(b)	6080
311(b)(1)(A)	4065
311(b)(1)(B)	4055
311(d)	4055
312	4025
312	4110
312(a)(2)	4065
312(a)(3)	4060
312(a)(3)	4060
312(b)	4060
312(b)(1)	4060
312(b)(2)	4060
312(d)(1)	6080
312(h)(1)	12,185
312(k)	4025
312(k)	4110
312(n)	4025
312(n)	4110
312(n)(7)	5125
316	4010
316	4020
316	4030
316(a)(1)	4030
316(a)(2)	4030
317	4065
317	5150
317(a)	10,290
317(a)	12,180
317(a)	4065
317(a)	5135
317(a)	6000
317(b)	5000
318	5015
318	5060
318	5100
318	5135
318	5959
318	7010
318	10,240
318	12,172
318	14,005
318(a)	10,245
318(a)	11,045
318(a)	11,105
318(a)	11,115
318(a)	13,045
318(a)(1)	5015
318(a)(1)	5025
318(a)(2)	5015
318(a)(2)	12,090
318(a)(2)(C)	5015
318(a)(2)(C)	12,090
318(a)(2)(C)	12,115
318(a)(3)	5015
318(a)(4)	5015
318(a)(5)	5015
318(a)(5)(C)	5015
318(a)(5)(C)	5020
331	4005

UNITED STATES CODE ANNOTATED

26 U.S.C.A.—Internal Revenue Code

Sec.	This Work Para.
331	5000
331	8010
331	8015
331	8030
331	8040
331	8090
331	8135
331(a)	8010
331(a)	8020
331(a)	12,175
331(b)	8010
332	4005
332	5000
332	8040
332	8040
332	8050
332	8060
332	8065
332	8123
332	11,060
332	12,025
332	13,000
332	13,005
332	13,005
332	15,175
332	15,220
332	15,425
332(b)(1)	8060
332(b)(2)	8060
332(b)(3)	8060
334	8065
334	8135
334(a)	8010
334(a)	8015
334(b)	13,000
334(b)(1)	8040
336	4005
336	8025
336	8030
336	8040
336	8075
336	8090
336	8135
336	15,240
336(a)	8025
336(a)	12,175
336(d)	8025
336(d)	8035
336(d)	12,175
336(d)(1)	8025
336(d)(1)	8025
336(d)(1)	8075
336(d)(2)	8025
336(d)(2)	8075
336(d)(2)(B)(i)(II)	8025
336(d)(2)(B)(ii)	8025
336(d)(3)	8040
336(d)(3)	8065
337	4005
337	8040

UNITED STATES CODE ANNOTATED

26 U.S.C.A.—Internal Revenue Code

Sec.	This Work Para.
337	8040
337	8065
337	12,175
337	15,175
337(b)(1)	8040
338	8115
338	8120
338	8120
338	8123
338	8125
338	8130
338	8135
338	8135
338	10,195
338	12,090
338	13,025
338	13,080
338	13,085
338	13,140
338	15,220
338	15,425
338(a)	8120
338(a)(1)	8120
338(b)(1)(B)	8120
338(b)(2)	8120
338(b)(5)	8095
338(b)(6)(A)	8120
338(d)(3)	8120
338(e)	8120
338(f)	8120
338(g)	15,425
338(h)(10)	12,090
338(h)(10)	8123
338(h)(10)	8130
338(h)(11)	8120
346	5225
346(a)	8005
351	1135
351	2000
351	2005
351	2010
351	2020
351	2025
351	2030
351	2040
351	2045
351	2055
351	2070
351	2075
351	2130
351	2135
351	2140
351	2145
351	2150
351	2155
351	2160
351	2170
351	2175
351	2180
351	2190

UNITED STATES CODE ANNOTATED		UNITED STATES CODE ANNOTATED	
26 U.S.C.A.—Internal Revenue Code		26 U.S.C.A.—Internal Revenue Code	
	This Work		This Work
Sec.	Para.	Sec.	Para.
351	2205	351(a)	2045
351	2225	351(a)	2070
351	2265	351(a)	2075
351	2275	351(a)	2140
351	2285	351(a)	2155
351	3005	351(a)	2220
351	3045	351(a)	2255
351	3055	351(a)	2275
351	4025	351(a)	2300
351	5135	351(a)	9022
351	5145	351(a)	10,235
351	5150	351(b)	2015
351	5155	351(b)	2155
351	5160	351(b)	2170
351	5215	351(b)	10,235
351	5240	351(b)	10,295
351	6000	351(c)	12,160
351	6120	351(c)(1)	2035
351	6170	351(c)(1)	2040
351	6175	351(c)(2)	12,115
351	8025	351(d)(1)	2010
351	8035	351(d)(2)	2010
351	8135	351(d)(3)	2010
351	9035	351(e)	2100
351	9075	351(e)	17,005
351	10,000	351(e)(1)	2100
351	10,180	351(e)(1)(B)	2100
351	10,210	351(e)(2)	2100
351	10,230	351(f)	2110
351	10,235	351(g)	2025
351	10,240	351(g)	2035
351	10,275	351(g)	2040
351	10,305	351(g)	6175
351	10,315	351(g)	9030
351	11,085	351(g)	11,025
351	12,055	351(g)(1)	2025
351	12,090	351(g)(1)(A)	10,230
351	12,100	351(g)(2)	10,040
351	12,160	351(g)(2)	10,205
351	12,175	351(g)(2)	10,230
351	13,075	351(g)(2)	12,070
351	14,065	351(g)(2)	12,085
351	14,080	351(g)(2)(A)	2025
351	15,020	351(g)(2)(A)	10,240
351	15,025	351(g)(2)(B)	2025
351	15,175	351(g)(2)(B)	10,240
351	15,245	351(g)(2)(C)	2025
351	15,415	351(g)(2)(C)(i)(I)	10,205
351	16,070	351(g)(2)(C)(i)(II)	10,205
351	17,000	351(g)(2)(C)(ii)	10,230
351	17,005	351(g)(3)	2025
351	20,075	351(g)(3)(A)	10,240
351	24,020	351(g)(3)(A)	2025
351(a)	2000	351(g)(4)	2025
351(a)	2010	354	6000
351(a)	2015	354	9030
351(a)	2020	354	10,240
351(a)	2025	354	10,290
351(a)	2035	354	10,315
351(a)	2040	354	11,100

UNITED STATES CODE ANNOTATED

26 U.S.C.A.—Internal Revenue Code

Sec.	This Work Para.
354	12,065
354(a)	10,160
354(a)	10,290
354(a)(1)	10,160
354(a)(1)	10,290
354(a)(1)	11,015
354(a)(1)	11,115
354(a)(2)	10,240
354(a)(2)	10,265
354(a)(2)	10,275
354(a)(2)	10,290
354(a)(2)	11,020
354(a)(2)	11,040
354(a)(2)	9030
354(a)(2)(A)(i)	10,240
354(a)(2)(B)	10,240
354(a)(2)(B)	10,275
354(a)(2)(C)	10,240
354(a)(2)(C)	9030
354(a)(2)(C)(i)	11,025
354(a)(2)(C)(ii)	11,025
354(a)(2)(C)(ii)(II)	11,025
354(b)(1)	11,085
354(b)(1)	12,195
354(b)(1)(A)	11,115
354(b)(1)(B)	11,115
355	1135
355	5225
355	5225
355	5240
355	6000
355	9020
355	10,085
355	10,090
355	10,110
355	11,085
355	12,000
355	12,040
355	12,045
355	12,055
355	12,060
355	12,065
355	12,085
355	12,090
355	12,095
355	12,100
355	12,100
355	12,115
355	12,155
355	12,160
355	12,165
355	12,170
355	12,172
355	12,175
355	12,180
355	12,185
355	13,005
355	15,425
355(a)	12,090
355(a)(1)	12,070

UNITED STATES CODE ANNOTATED

26 U.S.C.A.—Internal Revenue Code

Sec.	This Work Para.
355(a)(1)	12,095
355(a)(1)(B)	12,005
355(a)(1)(B)	12,040
355(a)(1)(B)	12,055
355(a)(3)(A)	12,070
355(a)(3)(B)	12,070
355(a)(3)(B)	12,085
355(a)(3)(C)	12,070
355(a)(3)(D)	12,070
355(a)(4)	12,070
355(b)	12,025
355(b)(1)	12,005
355(b)(1)	12,090
355(b)(1)(A)	12,100
355(b)(2)	12,005
355(b)(2)	12,090
355(b)(2)(D)	12,005
355(b)(3)	12,025
355(b)(3)(i)	12,090
355(b)(3)(iii)	12,090
355(c)	12,085
355(c)(1)	12,090
355(c)(2)	12,085
355(c)(2)	12,090
355(c)(2)	12,115
355(c)(2)(A)	12,085
355(c)(2)(C)	12,085
355(d)	12,085
355(d)	12,090
355(d)	12,115
355(d)(2)	12,090
355(d)(3)	12,090
355(d)(3)(B)(ii)	12,090
355(d)(5)(B)	12,090
355(d)(5)(C)	12,090
355(d)(6)	12,090
355(d)(7)	12,090
355(d)(7)(B)	12,090
355(d)(8)	12,090
355(d)(8)(A)	12,090
355(d)(8)(A)	12,115
355(e)	12,085
355(e)	12,115
355(e)	12,120
355(e)	12,125
355(e)	12,160
355(e)	12,170
355(e)(1)	12,090
355(e)(1)	12,115
355(e)(2)(A)(ii)	12,120
355(e)(2)(B)	12,115
355(e)(2)(C)	12,170
355(e)(2)(D)	12,115
355(e)(3)(A)	12,115
355(e)(3)(B)	12,115
355(e)(4)	12,115
355(e)(4)(C)(ii)	12,115
355(f)	12,170
355(g)	12,172
356	5000

UNITED STATES CODE ANNOTATED		UNITED STATES CODE ANNOTATED	
26 U.S.C.A.—Internal Revenue Code		**26 U.S.C.A.—Internal Revenue Code**	
Sec.	**This Work Para.**	**Sec.**	**This Work Para.**
356	9030	357(c)	12,085
356	10,240	357(c)	15,040
356	10,290	357(c)	15,175
356	11,100	357(c)	17,050
356	12,065	357(c)(1)	2190
356	12,070	357(c)(3)	2190
356(a)	10,240	357(c)(3)	2205
356(a)	10,275	357(c)(3)	2215
356(a)	12,070	357(c)(3)	2225
356(a)(1)	10,145	357(c)(3)	2255
356(a)(1)	12,070	357(c)(3)	17,030
356(a)(2)	4035	357(c)(3)(A)	2250
356(a)(2)	6170	357(c)(3)(A)(i)	2190
356(a)(2)	9030	357(c)(3)(B)	2190
356(a)(2)	10,245	357(d)	2175
356(a)(2)	10,260	357(d)	2190
356(a)(2)	11,000	357(d)	4050
356(a)(2)	11,020	357(d)	10,315
356(a)(2)	11,045	357(d)(1)	2175
356(a)(2)	11,100	357(d)(1)	2235
356(a)(2)	11,105	357(d)(1)(A)	2235
356(b)	12,070	357(d)(1)(A)	3070
356(c)	10,240	357(d)(2)	2175
356(c)	9030	358	2105
356(d)	10,265	358	2130
356(d)	10,275	358	2135
356(d)	11,020	358	2145
356(d)	11,040	358	2175
356(d)(2)(A)	10,240	358	2190
356(d)(2)(B)	10,290	358	9035
356(d)(2)(B)	10,290	358	10,315
356(d)(2)(C)	12,070	358	15,020
356(e)	10,240	358	17,005
356(e)	11,045	358	22,090
357	2175	358(a)	2005
357	2235	358(a)	2140
357(a)	2170	358(a)	2165
357(a)	2170	358(a)	2190
357(a)	2180	358(a)	10,300
357(a)	2190	358(a)(1)	2000
357(a)	5145	358(a)(1)	2140
357(a)	10,310	358(a)(1)(A)(ii)	2170
357(a)	10,315	358(a)(2)	2140
357(a)(3)	10,315	358(c)	12,080
357(b)	2170	358(c)	12,170
357(b)	2180	358(d)	10,315
357(b)	2190	358(d)(1)	2170
357(b)	10,310	358(d)(1)	2205
357(b)	10,315	358(d)(1)	2215
357(b)	10,320	358(d)(2)	2190
357(b)	17,050	358(d)(2)	2215
357(b)	20,090	358(h)	2215
357(c)	2170	358(h)	10,315
357(c)	2175	358(h)(1)	2215
357(c)	2190	358(h)(1)	10,315
357(c)	2190	358(h)(1)(A)	2215
357(c)	2245	358(h)(2)	2215
357(c)	2250	361	9030
357(c)	10,315	361	9045
357(c)	10,325	361(a)	10,160

UNITED STATES CODE ANNOTATED

26 U.S.C.A.—Internal Revenue Code

Sec.	This Work Para.
361(a)	10,295
361(a)	10,320
361(b)(1)	10,295
361(b)(1)	12,085
361(b)(1)(A)	10,295
361(b)(1)(B)	10,295
361(b)(2)	10,295
361(b)(3)	10,295
361(b)(3)	12,085
361(c)	9030
361(c)	10,295
361(c)(1)	10,295
361(c)(1)	9030
361(c)(2)	12,085
361(c)(2)(A)	10,295
361(c)(2)(B)	10,295
361(c)(2)(B)	12,085
361(c)(2)(C)	12,085
361(c)(3)	10,295
362	2105
362	2135
362	2145
362	2150
362	2175
362	9035
362	17,005
362	24,020
362(a)	2000
362(a)	2005
362(a)	2130
362(a)	2145
362(a)	2165
362(a)	2175
362(a)	2190
362(a)	2220
362(a)	17,050
362(a)(1)	2145
362(a)(1)	15,020
362(a)(2)	2145
362(a)(2)	2285
362(a)(2)	2295
362(b)	10,160
362(b)	10,160
362(b)	10,300
362(b)	10,315
362(b)	11,100
362(b)	13,000
362(b)	9035
362(c)(1)	2295
362(c)(2)	2295
362(d)	10,315
362(d)(1)	2190
362(d)(1)	2220
362(d)(2)	2220
362(e)	2165
362(e)	8025
362(e)(1)	10,300
362(e)(1)	2150
362(e)(1)	2155
362(e)(1)(B)	2155

UNITED STATES CODE ANNOTATED

26 U.S.C.A.—Internal Revenue Code

Sec.	This Work Para.
362(e)(1)(C)	2155
362(e)(2)	2100
362(e)(2)	2150
362(e)(2)	2165
362(e)(2)	8025
362(e)(2)	8035
362(e)(2)	10,300
362(e)(2)	15,035
362(e)(2)	15,220
362(e)(2)(A)	2150
362(e)(2)(B)	2150
362(e)(2)(C)	15,035
362(e)(2)(C)	2150
362(e)(2)(C)	8035
368	1135
368	8070
368	10,000
368	15,220
368(a)(1)	9005
368(a)(1)	9030
368(a)(1)	10,240
368(a)(1)	11,100
368(a)(1)	13,005
368(a)(1)(A)	9010
368(a)(1)(A)	9090
368(a)(1)(A)	10,015
368(a)(1)(A)	10,025
368(a)(1)(A)	10,155
368(a)(1)(A)	10,160
368(a)(1)(A)	10,260
368(a)(1)(A)	10,290
368(a)(1)(A)	12,100
368(a)(1)(A)	13,090
368(a)(1)(B)	9005
368(a)(1)(B)	9010
368(a)(1)(B)	9025
368(a)(1)(B)	10,135
368(a)(1)(B)	10,140
368(a)(1)(B)	10,175
368(a)(1)(B)	12,100
368(a)(1)(C)	10,115
368(a)(1)(C)	10,120
368(a)(1)(C)	10,160
368(a)(1)(C)	10,160
368(a)(1)(C)	10,315
368(a)(1)(C)	13,090
368(a)(1)(D)	9020
368(a)(1)(D)	10,030
368(a)(1)(D)	10,100
368(a)(1)(D)	10,110
368(a)(1)(D)	12,065
368(a)(1)(D)	12,100
368(a)(1)(D)	13,090
368(a)(1)(E)	9015
368(a)(1)(E)	11,000
368(a)(1)(E)	11,015
368(a)(1)(F)	9015
368(a)(1)(F)	11,000
368(a)(2)(B)	10,115
368(a)(2)(B)	10,120

UNITED STATES CODE ANNOTATED

26 U.S.C.A.—Internal Revenue Code

Sec.	This Work Para.
368(a)(2)(B)	10,135
368(a)(2)(B)	10,135
368(a)(2)(C)	10,150
368(a)(2)(C)	10,160
368(a)(2)(C)	10,160
368(a)(2)(D)	9010
368(a)(2)(D)	10,000
368(a)(2)(D)	10,080
368(a)(2)(D)	10,150
368(a)(2)(D)	10,155
368(a)(2)(D)	10,160
368(a)(2)(D)	10,175
368(a)(2)(D)	10,260
368(a)(2)(E)	9010
368(a)(2)(E)	10,000
368(a)(2)(E)	10,080
368(a)(2)(E)	10,150
368(a)(2)(E)	10,160
368(a)(2)(E)	10,165
368(a)(2)(E)	10,175
368(a)(2)(E)	10,180
368(a)(2)(E)	10,185
368(a)(2)(G)	10,090
368(a)(2)(H)	11,105
368(a)(2)(H)	11,115
368(a)(2)(H)(i)	11,085
368(a)(2)(H)(ii)	12,160
368(b)	9030
368(b)	10,160
368(b)	10,295
368(c)	2000
368(c)	2010
368(c)	2035
368(c)	2040
368(c)	2095
368(c)	9020
368(c)	10,140
368(c)	10,150
368(c)	10,240
368(c)	11,105
368(c)	12,100
381	9045
381	12,185
381	13,005
381	13,005
381—384	13,005
381(a)	13,005
381(a)	8040
381(a)(2)	12,195
381(a)(2)(C)	13,045
381(b)	11,055
381(b)	13,135
381(b)(1)	11,055
381(b)(1)	13,005
381(b)(2)	13,005
381(b)(3)	11,055
381(b)(3)	13,135
381(c)	13,005
381(c)(2)(A)	13,010
381(c)(2)(B)	13,010

UNITED STATES CODE ANNOTATED

26 U.S.C.A.—Internal Revenue Code

Sec.	This Work Para.
381(c)(2)(C)	11,100
382	9045
382	13,020
382	13,025
382	13,040
382	13,045
382	13,055
382	13,060
382	13,065
382	13,080
382	13,085
382	13,090
382	13,095
382	13,100
382	13,105
382	13,110
382	13,115
382	13,120
382	13,125
382	13,130
382(a)	13,025
382(a)	13,110
382(b)	13,120
382(b)(1)	13,025
382(b)(2)	13,060
382(c)	13,025
382(c)(2)	13,025
382(e)(1)	13,065
382(e)(2)	13,065
382(f)	13,035
382(g)	13,040
382(g)(1)	13,040
382(g)(4)(A)	13,040
382(g)(4)(B)(ii)	13,040
382(g)(4)(D)	13,105
382(h)	13,025
382(h)	13,080
382(h)	13,130
382(h)(1)(C)	13,080
382(h)(2)(B)	13,080
382(h)(2)(B)	13,130
382(h)(3)	13,080
382(h)(3)	13,130
382(h)(3)(B)	13,130
382(h)(3)(B)(i)	13,080
382(h)(3)(B)(ii)	13,080
382(i)	13,055
382(i)(2)	13,055
382(i)(3)	13,055
382(j)	13,130
382(k)(1)	13,060
382(k)(2)	13,060
382(k)(6)	13,050
382(l)(1)	13,065
382(l)(3)(A)	13,045
382(l)(3)(A)(iv)	13,045
382(l)(3)(A)(v)	13,045
382(l)(4)	13,025
382(l)(4)(A)	13,075
382(l)(4)(D)	13,065

UNITED STATES CODE ANNOTATED

26 U.S.C.A.—Internal Revenue Code

Sec.	This Work Para.
382(*l*)(4)(E)	13,065
383	9045
383	13,110
383	13,115
383	13,120
383	13,125
383(a)	13,085
383(b)	13,085
384	9045
384	13,090
384	13,090
385	3025
422	2025
422	3005
444	15,250
444	18,015
447	1005
447(c)	1005
447(d)	1005
447(d)(2)(C)(ii)	11,025
447(e)	11,025
448	1005
448(b)(2)	1005
448(b)(3)	1005
448(d)(2)	1015
453	2025
453	2130
453	8030
453	9025
453	15,395
453	15,415
453	23,035
453(e)	8020
453(f)	8020
453(h)	8030
453(h)	8075
453(h)	8090
453(h)	8135
453(h)(1)(A)	8090
453(j)(2)	8030
453(k)	8020
453B	4070
453B(a)	8135
465	1005
465	15,325
465	15,325
465	19,000
465	19,045
465	19,050
465	19,065
465(a)(1)(B)	1005
465(a)(3)	1005
465(b)	19,045
465(b)(6)	19,045
465(c)(3)(D)	19,065
469	1005
469	15,325
469	15,325
469	15,450
469	15,453

UNITED STATES CODE ANNOTATED

26 U.S.C.A.—Internal Revenue Code

Sec.	This Work Para.
469	19,000
469	19,050
469	19,065
469(a)(2)(B)	1005
469(a)(2)(C)	1005
469(b)	15,453
469(c)(1)	19,050
469(c)(2)	19,050
469(c)(3)(A)	19,050
469(c)(7)	19,050
469(e)(2)	1005
469(g)	15,453
469(h)(2)	19,050
469(i)	19,050
469(i)(3)	19,050
469(i)(6)(C)	19,050
482	1130
482	1135
482	2275
482	7020
482	14,010
482	14,015
482	14,020
482	14,025
482	14,030
482	14,040
482	14,045
483	10,135
483	23,035
483	8030
531	7035
532	7035
532(b)	7035
532(c)	7050
533(a)	7040
533(b)	7040
535(a)	7075
535(c)	14,005
535(c)(2)	7075
537	7070
537(a)(2)	7070
541	7005
541	15,450
542(a)	7010
542(c)	7010
543(a)	7010
543(a)(1)—(a)(5)	7010
543(a)(3)	15,450
543(a)(4)	15,450
544	7010
545	7010
547	7010
565	7010
565	7075
565(c)(2)	7010
615	18,020
641	1090
641(c)	15,145
643(b)	15,130
651	1090

UNITED STATES CODE ANNOTATED

26 U.S.C.A.—Internal Revenue Code

Sec.	This Work Para.
652	1090
661	1090
662	1090
671—677	15,120
676	15,140
678	15,120
678	15,140
678(a)	15,125
691	15,395
691	25,015
691	25,030
701	1000
701	1055
701	16,010
701	16,085
701	17,105
701—761	16,000
702	1000
702	1055
702	16,010
702	17,084
702	18,000
702	20,015
702	21,107
702(a)	18,020
702(b)	18,020
702(b)	18,155
702(b)	18,250
702(c)	18,020
703	18,000
703	18,020
703(a)	15,220
703(a)	18,000
703(a)(2)	19,010
703(b)	18,000
703(b)	18,020
703(b)(1)	18,040
704	1055
704	16,005
704	16,010
704	16,065
704	17,084
704	18,000
704	18,190
704(a)	18,065
704(b)	15,255
704(b)	16,075
704(b)	17,045
704(b)	18,045
704(b)	18,065
704(b)	18,070
704(b)	18,085
704(b)	18,090
704(b)	18,095
704(b)	18,125
704(b)	18,135
704(b)	18,175
704(b)	18,245
704(b)	19,045
704(b)	21,110

UNITED STATES CODE ANNOTATED

26 U.S.C.A.—Internal Revenue Code

Sec.	This Work Para.
704(b)	21,125
704(b)	22,067
704(b)	24,040
704(b)(2)	18,080
704(c)	15,255
704(c)	15,260
704(c)	17,045
704(c)	18,045
704(c)	18,065
704(c)	18,120
704(c)	18,135
704(c)	18,135
704(c)	18,145
704(c)	18,175
704(c)	18,185
704(c)	18,245
704(c)	21,070
704(c)	21,095
704(c)	21,110
704(c)	21,115
704(c)	21,125
704(c)	22,020
704(c)	22,095
704(c)	22,095
704(c)	22,105
704(c)	22,120
704(c)	24,040
704(c)	24,070
704(c)(1)	18,135
704(c)(1)	22,090
704(c)(1)	22,095
704(c)(1)(A)	18,055
704(c)(1)(A)	18,135
704(c)(1)(A)	22,090
704(c)(1)(B)	16,085
704(c)(1)(B)	18,135
704(c)(1)(B)	20,000
704(c)(1)(B)	20,090
704(c)(1)(B)	22,000
704(c)(1)(B)	22,020
704(c)(1)(B)	22,090
704(c)(1)(B)	22,095
704(c)(1)(B)	22,100
704(c)(1)(B)	24,040
704(c)(1)(B)	24,070
704(c)(1)(B)	24,077
704(c)(1)(B)(i)	22,090
704(c)(1)(B)(ii)	22,090
704(c)(1)(B)(iii)	22,090
704(c)(1)(C)	18,135
704(c)(1)(C)	21,095
704(c)(1)(C)	21,110
704(c)(1)(C)	23,010
704(c)(1)(C)	24,070
704(c)(1)(C)	25,035
704(c)(2)	22,090
704(c)(3)	22,090
704(d)	1055
704(d)	18,165
704(d)	19,000

UNITED STATES CODE ANNOTATED

26 U.S.C.A.—Internal Revenue Code

Sec.	This Work Para.
704(d)	19,030
704(e)	18,045
704(e)	18,065
704(e)(1)	15,275
704(e)(1)	18,225
704(e)(2)	18,245
704(e)(2)	18,245
704(e)(3)	18,245
705	16,010
705	19,010
705	21,025
705	21,107
705(a)	19,020
705(a)(1)	18,040
705(a)(1)	19,020
705(a)(1)	20,110
705(a)(1)(A)	19,010
705(a)(1)(B)	19,010
705(a)(2)	17,030
705(a)(2)	19,010
705(a)(2)	20,110
705(a)(2)	22,005
705(a)(2)(A)	19,010
705(a)(2)(A)	19,010
705(a)(2)(B)	19,010
706(a)	17,065
706(a)	18,000
706(a)	18,015
706(a)	18,195
706(a)	20,015
706(a)	21,025
706(b)	15,250
706(b)	18,015
706(b)(1)(C)	18,015
706(c)	18,065
706(c)(1)	24,025
706(c)(2)(A)	21,025
706(c)(2)(A)	25,005
706(d)	15,465
706(d)	18,065
706(d)	18,205
706(d)(1)	18,205
706(d)(1)	21,025
706(d)(1)	25,005
706(d)(2)	18,205
706(d)(2)(B)	18,205
706(d)(2)(B)(iv)	18,120
707	16,005
707	17,075
707	17,085
707	20,000
707	20,000
707	20,005
707	20,045
707	20,065
707	20,090
707	20,095
707	22,000
707	22,005
707(a)	17,020

UNITED STATES CODE ANNOTATED

26 U.S.C.A.—Internal Revenue Code

Sec.	This Work Para.
707(a)	20,010
707(a)	20,015
707(a)	20,020
707(a)	20,025
707(a)	20,030
707(a)	20,045
707(a)	20,050
707(a)	20,065
707(a)	20,070
707(a)(1)	20,010
707(a)(1)	20,045
707(a)(2)	20,045
707(a)(2)	22,005
707(a)(2)	22,020
707(a)(2)	23,015
707(a)(2)(A)	20,045
707(a)(2)(A)	20,047
707(a)(2)(A)	20,090
707(a)(2)(B)	20,090
707(a)(2)(B)	20,095
707(a)(2)(B)	22,095
707(a)(2)(B)	22,095
707(a)(2)(B)	22,105
707(a)(2)(B)	23,045
707(a)(2)(B)	24,037
707(a)(2)(B)	24,045
707(a)(2)(B)	24,070
707(b)	10,240
707(b)	12,140
707(b)(1)	12,090
707(b)(1)	20,105
707(b)(1)	20,110
707(b)(1)	22,066
707(b)(2)	20,105
707(b)(3)	20,105
707(c)	20,020
707(c)	20,025
707(c)	20,045
707(c)	20,050
707(c)	20,065
707(c)	20,070
707(c)	23,015
707(c)(1)(B)	20,100
708	24,025
708	24,095
708	25,005
708(b)(1)(A)	24,025
708(b)(1)(A)	24,030
708(b)(1)(A)	24,037
708(b)(1)(B)	22,090
708(b)(1)(B)	22,095
708(b)(1)(B)	24,025
708(b)(1)(B)	24,040
708(b)(1)(B)	24,045
708(b)(1)(B)	24,050
708(b)(1)(B)	24,060
708(b)(1)(B)	24,070
708(b)(2)(A)	24,070
708(b)(2)(B)	24,075
709	17,105

UNITED STATES CODE ANNOTATED	**UNITED STATES CODE ANNOTATED**
26 U.S.C.A.—Internal Revenue Code	**26 U.S.C.A.—Internal Revenue Code**
This Work	**This Work**
Sec. — **Para.**	**Sec.** — **Para.**
709(b)(1) — 17,105	731(a)(2) — 23,010
709(b)(2) — 17,105	731(a)(2) — 23,010
709(b)(3) — 17,105	731(b) — 22,055
721 — 16,010	731(b) — 22,067
721 — 17,000	731(b) — 22,067
721 — 17,005	731(b) — 22,090
721 — 17,020	731(c) — 19,020
721 — 17,060	731(c) — 22,000
721 — 17,070	731(c) — 22,020
721 — 18,135	731(c) — 22,020
721 — 19,005	731(c) — 22,060
721 — 20,075	731(c) — 22,095
721 — 20,090	731(c) — 22,100
721 — 20,095	731(c) — 22,100
721 — 24,070	731(c) — 22,100
721(b) — 17,005	731(c) — 22,100
721(c) — 17,005	731(c) — 22,120
722 — 16,010	731(c) — 23,010
722 — 17,005	731(c) — 24,040
722 — 17,008	731(c)(1) — 20,095
722 — 17,030	731(c)(1) — 22,100
722 — 19,010	731(c)(2) — 22,105
723 — 16,010	731(c)(2) — 23,045
723 — 17,005	731(c)(2)(A) — 22,100
723 — 24,070	731(c)(2)(B)(i)—(c)(2)(B)(iv) — 22,100
724 — 18,155	731(c)(2)(B)(v) — 22,100
724 — 21,055	731(c)(2)(B)(vi) — 22,100
724 — 22,030	731(c)(2)(C) — 22,100
724(a) — 18,155	731(c)(3)(A)(i) — 22,100
724(b) — 18,155	731(c)(3)(A)(ii) — 22,100
724(c) — 18,155	731(c)(3)(A)(iii) — 22,100
731 — 15,240	731(c)(3)(B) — 22,100
731 — 16,005	731(c)(4) — 22,100
731 — 16,010	731(c)(4) — 23,010
731 — 17,020	731(c)(4)(A) — 22,100
731 — 17,050	731(c)(4)(B) — 22,100
731 — 20,015	731(c)(5) — 22,060
731 — 20,075	731(c)(5) — 22,100
731 — 20,090	731(c)(6) — 22,100
731 — 20,095	731(c)(7) — 22,100
731 — 22,012	731(d) — 22,100
731 — 22,020	732 — 15,240
731 — 22,055	732 — 22,020
731 — 23,010	732 — 22,025
731 — 23,040	732 — 22,055
731 — 23,065	732 — 22,065
731 — 24,000	732 — 22,090
731—733 — 22,040	732 — 22,100
731—733 — 22,115	732 — 23,010
731(a) — 22,005	732 — 24,000
731(a) — 22,065	732 — 24,070
731(a)(1) — 17,050	732(a) — 22,022
731(a)(1) — 19,020	732(a)(1) — 22,020
731(a)(1) — 22,005	732(a)(2) — 22,020
731(a)(1) — 22,100	732(b) — 22,055
731(a)(1) — 22,100	732(b) — 23,010
731(a)(1) — 22,100	732(b) — 24,070
731(a)(1) — 24,070	732(b) — 25,010
731(a)(1) — 25,010	732(c) — 22,020
731(a)(2) — 22,005	732(c) — 22,022

UNITED STATES CODE ANNOTATED

26 U.S.C.A.—Internal Revenue Code

Sec.	This Work Para.
732(c)	22,025
732(c)	23,010
732(c)(1)	23,040
732(c)(1)(A)(i)	22,020
732(c)(1)(A)(i)	23,010
732(c)(1)(A)(ii)	22,020
732(c)(1)(A)(ii)	23,010
732(c)(1)(B)(i)	22,020
732(c)(1)(B)(i)	23,010
732(c)(1)(B)(ii)	22,020
732(c)(1)(B)(ii)	23,010
732(c)(2)(A)	23,010
732(c)(2)(B)	23,010
732(c)(3)	22,020
732(c)(3)(A)	22,020
732(c)(3)(A)	23,010
732(c)(3)(B)	22,020
732(c)(3)(B)	23,010
732(d)	21,075
732(d)	22,025
732(d)	22,035
732(d)	24,065
732(f)	22,020
732(f)	22,022
732(f)(1)	22,022
732(f)(2)	22,022
732(f)(3)(A)	22,022
732(f)(3)(B)	22,022
732(f)(4)	22,000
732(f)(4)	22,020
732(f)(4)(A)	22,022
732(f)(4)(B)	22,022
732(f)(5)	22,022
732(f)(8)	22,022
733	19,010
733	22,100
733	23,040
733(a)(1)	22,005
733(a)(2)	22,020
734	21,100
734	21,108
734	22,060
734	22,060
734	22,065
734	22,100
734	22,120
734	23,010
734	25,010
734(b)	18,135
734(b)	22,060
734(b)	22,066
734(b)	22,075
734(b)	22,085
734(b)	22,090
734(b)	22,095
734(b)	23,010
734(b)	23,035
734(b)	25,010
734(b)(1)(A)	25,010
734(b)(1)(B)	22,065

UNITED STATES CODE ANNOTATED

26 U.S.C.A.—Internal Revenue Code

Sec.	This Work Para.
734(b)(2)	22,065
734(b)(2)(B)	22,065
734(b)(2)(B)	25,010
734(d)(1)	22,060
734(d)(2)	22,060
734(d)(2)	23,010
734(e)	23,010
735	22,030
735	23,040
735	24,000
735(a)	22,030
735(a)(2)	22,030
735(c)(2)(a)	22,030
736	16,010
736	23,000
736	23,005
736	23,015
736	23,030
736	23,035
736	23,040
736	23,050
736	24,000
736	25,000
736	25,010
736	25,015
736	25,030
736(a)	23,005
736(a)	23,010
736(a)	23,015
736(a)	23,015
736(a)	23,025
736(a)	23,030
736(a)	23,035
736(a)	23,040
736(a)	23,050
736(a)	23,060
736(a)	25,015
736(a)	25,030
736(a)(1)	23,015
736(a)(2)	23,015
736(b)	23,005
736(b)	23,010
736(b)	23,015
736(b)	23,025
736(b)	23,035
736(b)	23,040
736(b)	23,045
736(b)	23,060
736(b)	25,015
736(b)(1)	23,035
737	16,005
737	16,085
737	18,135
737	20,000
737	20,090
737	22,000
737	22,020
737	22,020
737	22,095
737	22,100

UNITED STATES CODE ANNOTATED

26 U.S.C.A.—Internal Revenue Code

Sec.	This Work Para.
737	22,120
737	24,040
737	24,070
737	24,077
737(a)	22,095
737(a)(1)	22,095
737(b)	22,095
737(b)	22,095
737(c)(1)	22,095
737(c)(2)	22,095
737(d)	22,095
737(d)(1)	22,095
737(d)(2)	22,095
741	16,010
741	17,050
741	21,005
741	21,035
741	21,055
741	21,070
741	21,075
741	21,092
741	21,108
741	23,050
741	24,070
742	19,005
742	21,095
742	21,110
742	24,070
742	25,010
743	18,135
743	24,020
743	25,010
743(a)	21,095
743(a)	21,100
743(a)	21,108
743(b)	21,100
743(b)	21,107
743(b)	21,108
743(b)	21,110
743(b)	21,130
743(b)	22,020
743(b)	22,025
743(b)	22,085
743(b)	24,040
743(b)	24,070
743(b)	25,010
743(b)	25,030
743(d)	21,100
743(d)	25,010
743(d)(1)	21,108
743(d)(1)	21,130
743(d)(1)	25,010
743(d)(2)	21,108
743(d)(2)	22,060
743(d)(2)	23,010
743(e)	21,108
743(e)(1)	21,108
743(e)(2)	21,108
743(e)(6)	21,108
743(f)	22,060

UNITED STATES CODE ANNOTATED

26 U.S.C.A.—Internal Revenue Code

Sec.	This Work Para.
743(f)	23,010
743(f)(1)	21,108
743(f)(2)	21,108
751	16,005
751	21,005
751	21,030
751	21,035
751	21,040
751	21,050
751	21,055
751	21,065
751	21,070
751	21,080
751	21,090
751	21,125
751	22,030
751	22,055
751	22,100
751	22,110
751	22,115
751	23,010
751(a)	21,005
751(a)	21,035
751(a)	21,040
751(a)	21,055
751(a)	21,065
751(a)	21,070
751(a)	21,075
751(a)	21,092
751(a)	21,125
751(a)	22,110
751(a)	24,000
751(b)	22,000
751(b)	22,020
751(b)	22,095
751(b)	22,100
751(b)	22,110
751(b)	22,115
751(b)	22,120
751(b)	22,130
751(b)	23,010
751(b)	23,015
751(b)	23,035
751(b)	23,040
751(b)	24,000
751(b)(1)(A)(ii)	22,110
751(b)(3)	21,065
751(b)(3)	22,110
751(b)(3)	23,040
751(b)(3)(A)	22,110
751(b)(3)(B)	22,110
751(c)	21,040
751(c)	21,050
751(c)	21,070
751(c)	21,110
751(c)	21,130
751(c)	22,030
751(c)	22,110
751(c)	23,015
751(c)	23,040

UNITED STATES CODE ANNOTATED

26 U.S.C.A.—Internal Revenue Code

Sec.	This Work Para.
751(c)(2)	21,050
751(d)	21,040
751(d)	21,055
751(d)	21,065
751(d)	22,110
751(d)(1)	21,055
751(d)(1)	22,110
751(d)(1) (former)	22,110
751(d)(1)(A) (former)	21,065
751(d)(2)	21,055
751(d)(2)	22,110
751(d)(3)	21,055
751(f)	21,055
752	15,290
752	16,005
752	16,065
752	16,075
752	17,025
752	17,030
752	17,035
752	18,165
752	18,170
752	18,180
752	18,190
752	19,005
752	19,045
752	21,020
752	21,070
752	21,095
752	22,005
752	22,040
752	23,030
752	23,035
752	23,080
752	24,070
752(a)	17,030
752(a)	17,050
752(a)	19,005
752(a)	22,012
752(a)	22,040
752(b)	17,030
752(b)	17,050
752(b)	18,095
752(b)	20,090
752(b)	21,010
752(b)	22,012
752(b)	22,040
752(b)	23,030
752(b)	23,065
752(b)	24,070
752(c)	20,090
752(c)	21,020
752(d)	21,010
752(d)	21,020
753	25,015
753	25,030
754	21,075
754	21,100
754	21,107
754	21,108

UNITED STATES CODE ANNOTATED

26 U.S.C.A.—Internal Revenue Code

Sec.	This Work Para.
754	21,110
754	21,115
754	22,020
754	22,025
754	22,035
754	22,060
754	22,070
754	22,075
754	22,085
754	22,090
754	22,095
754	22,110
754	23,010
754	23,025
754	23,035
754	23,040
754	23,045
754	24,040
754	24,065
754	25,010
755	21,110
755	21,130
755	22,065
755	22,065
755	24,040
755(c)	22,066
755(c)(1)	22,066
755(c)(2)	22,066
761(a)	16,025
761(a)	16,055
761(c)	18,195
761(e)	24,040
771	18,250
771—777	18,250
772	18,250
772—777	18,250
772(a)	18,250
772(c)(1)	18,250
772(c)(4)	18,250
773	21,100
773(a)(1)	18,250
773(a)(2)	18,250
773(b)(1)	18,250
773(b)(3)	18,250
774	18,250
774(a)(1)	21,100
774(c)	24,045
775	21,100
775	22,060
775	24,045
775(a)(1)(A)	18,250
775(b)(1)	18,250
775(b)(2)	18,250
775(b)(3)	18,250
775(c)	18,250
775(d)	18,250
776	18,250
851	16,080
871	16,085
881	16,085

UNITED STATES CODE ANNOTATED

26 U.S.C.A.—Internal Revenue Code

Sec.	This Work Para.
1001	10,315
1001	10,315
1001(a)	21,025
1001(c)	10,315
1011	21,095
1012	2245
1012	17,075
1012	19,005
1012	21,095
1012	21,110
1014	1055
1014	5115
1014	8090
1014	8130
1014	15,395
1014	19,005
1014	25,010
1014	25,015
1014	25,030
1014(c)	25,015
1014(f)	25,010
1015	19,005
1016(a)(1)	2285
1022	25,010
1031	4025
1031	18,140
1031	22,090
1031(a)(2)	16,055
1032	2000
1032	2005
1032	2110
1032	6080
1032	9030
1032	10,295
1032	11,020
1032	21,107
1032(a)	2010
1033	18,040
1036	6000
1041	5215
1041	15,385
1041(b)	15,385
1044	3080
1045	3080
1059	4105
1059	5135
1059	5155
1059	5235
1059(a)	4105
1059(a)(2)	5155
1059(e)	4105
1059(e)	5155
1059(e)(1)	5235
1059(e)(1)(A)(iii)(II)	5155
1060	8090
1060	8095
1060	8120
1060	21,110
1202	1020
1202	3080

UNITED STATES CODE ANNOTATED

26 U.S.C.A.—Internal Revenue Code

Sec.	This Work Para.
1202	15,090
1202	15,220
1202(a)	15,220
1202(b)	3080
1202(c)(2)(A)	3080
1202(c)(3)	3080
1202(d)(1)	3080
1202(d)(2)	3080
1202(e)(1)	3080
1202(e)(3)	3080
1202(g)	15,220
1202(k)	3080
1211	1020
1211	3100
1211	10,245
1211(a)	1005
1212(a)(1)(A)	1005
1212(a)(1)(B)	1005
1221	23,025
1223(1)	2160
1223(1)	2165
1223(1)	9040
1223(1)	12,085
1223(1)	17,005
1223(1)	17,008
1223(1)	24,070
1223(2)	17,005
1223(2)	24,070
1223(2)	2160
1223(2)	2165
1223(2)	9040
1231	2160
1231	15,225
1231	15,390
1231	17,005
1231	17,008
1231	18,020
1231	18,135
1231	18,250
1231	18,250
1231	21,050
1231	21,055
1231	21,108
1231	21,110
1231	22,030
1231	22,065
1231	23,025
1231	23,040
1231(b)	16,080
1237	15,220
1237(a)	15,220
1237(a)(2)(A)	15,245
1239	20,105
1244	3115
1244	3125
1244	3130
1244	8010
1244	15,220
1244	15,320
1245	17,015

UNITED STATES CODE ANNOTATED

26 U.S.C.A.—Internal Revenue Code

Sec.	This Work Para.
1245	18,135
1245	21,120
1245	23,025
1245	23,040
1245(a)(2)(A)	22,030
1250	18,030
1250	21,092
1251	18,135
1256	15,450
1272	23,035
1272	3085
1272—1274	11,020
1273(a)	3085
1274	3085
1274	8030
1274	10,135
1275	10,135
1361	15,075
1361	16,065
1361	1055
1361—1379	1000
1361(a)	1000
1361(a)	15,000
1361(b)	15,070
1361(b)	15,090
1361(b)	16,077
1361(b)(1)	15,145
1361(b)(1)	15,165
1361(b)(1)(A)	15,095
1361(b)(1)(B)	15,110
1361(b)(1)(C)	15,110
1361(b)(1)(C)	15,155
1361(b)(1)(D)	15,165
1361(b)(1)(D)	15,180
1361(b)(2)	15,165
1361(b)(2)(A)	15,170
1361(b)(3)	15,170
1361(b)(3)	15,175
1361(b)(3)	15,425
1361(b)(3)(A)	15,175
1361(b)(3)(B)	15,175
1361(b)(3)(C)	15,175
1361(b)(3)(D)	15,175
1361(c)(1)	15,095
1361(c)(1)	15,140
1361(c)(1)(A)(i)	15,105
1361(c)(1)(A)(ii)	15,080
1361(c)(1)(A)(ii)	15,105
1361(c)(1)(B)	15,105
1361(c)(1)(C)	15,105
1361(c)(2)	15,110
1361(c)(2)(A)	15,105
1361(c)(2)(A)(i)	15,120
1361(c)(2)(A)(i)	15,140
1361(c)(2)(A)(i)	15,155
1361(c)(2)(A)(ii)	15,135
1361(c)(2)(A)(iii)	15,135
1361(c)(2)(A)(iii)	15,140
1361(c)(2)(A)(v)	15,105
1361(c)(2)(A)(v)	15,145

UNITED STATES CODE ANNOTATED

26 U.S.C.A.—Internal Revenue Code

Sec.	This Work Para.
1361(c)(2)(A)(vi)	15,115
1361(c)(2)(B)(i)	15,140
1361(c)(2)(B)(iii)	15,140
1361(c)(2)(B)(v)	15,105
1361(c)(2)(B)(v)	15,145
1361(c)(3)	15,110
1361(c)(4)	15,180
1361(c)(5)	15,190
1361(c)(6)	15,110
1361(c)(6)	15,160
1361(c)(6)	15,170
1361(d)	15,120
1361(d)	15,140
1361(d)(1)(B)	15,125
1361(d)(1)(C)	15,325
1361(d)(2)(B)(ii)	15,130
1361(d)(3)	15,125
1361(d)(3)(B)	15,130
1361(e)	15,145
1361(e)	15,145
1361(e)(1)(A)(ii)	15,145
1361(e)(1)(C)	15,145
1361(e)(2)	15,145
1362	15,075
1362	15,450
1362	16,077
1362(a)	15,045
1362(a)(2)	15,070
1362(b)	15,045
1362(b)(1)	15,070
1362(b)(2)(B)(ii)	15,070
1362(b)(3)	15,070
1362(b)(5)	15,055
1362(c)	15,140
1362(d)	15,455
1362(d)(1)(A)	15,455
1362(d)(1)(B)	15,455
1362(d)(1)(C)	15,455
1362(d)(2)	15,455
1362(d)(3)	15,080
1362(d)(3)	15,445
1362(d)(3)	15,455
1362(d)(3)(C)(i)	15,450
1362(d)(3)(C)(iii)	15,450
1362(d)(3)(D)	15,450
1362(d)(3)(E)	15,450
1362(d)(3)(F)	15,450
1362(e)	15,460
1362(e)(2)	15,460
1362(e)(3)	15,460
1362(e)(6)(D)	15,460
1362(f)	15,065
1362(f)	15,070
1362(f)	15,080
1362(f)	15,210
1362(f)	15,445
1362(f)	15,455
1362(g)	15,460
1363	1055
1363(a)	15,215

UNITED STATES CODE ANNOTATED

26 U.S.C.A.—Internal Revenue Code

Sec.	This Work Para.
1363(b)	15,220
1363(b)	15,220
1363(b)(1)	15,225
1363(b)(2)	15,225
1363(c)	15,230
1363(d)	15,405
1363(d)	15,405
1363(d)(5)	15,405
1366	1000
1366	1055
1366	15,240
1366	15,385
1366	15,453
1366	16,065
1366(a)	15,030
1366(a)	15,215
1366(a)(1)	15,225
1366(a)(1)	15,250
1366(a)(1)	15,255
1366(a)(1)(A)	15,287
1366(b)	15,225
1366(b)	15,245
1366(d)(1)	15,030
1366(d)(1)	15,280
1366(d)(1)(B)	15,290
1366(d)(2)	15,325
1366(d)(2)(A)	15,280
1366(d)(2)(B)	15,385
1366(d)(3)	15,280
1366(d)(3)	15,325
1366(d)(3)	15,470
1366(d)(3)	15,470
1366(e)	15,275
1366(f)(2)	15,410
1366(f)(3)	15,440
1367	15,280
1367	15,350
1367(a)(1)	15,280
1367(a)(1)	15,290
1367(a)(1)	15,385
1367(a)(1)(A)	15,287
1367(a)(2)	15,280
1367(a)(2)(A)	15,280
1367(a)(2)(A)	15,340
1367(a)(2)(B)	15,280
1367(a)(2)(C)	15,280
1367(a)(2)(D)	15,280
1367(a)(2)(D)	15,405
1367(b)(2)(A)	15,290
1367(b)(2)(B)	15,315
1367(b)(3)	15,320
1367(b)(4)	15,395
1368	15,330
1368	15,335
1368	15,355
1368	15,365
1368	15,415
1368(b)	13,360
1368(b)	15,370
1368(b)(1)	15,340

UNITED STATES CODE ANNOTATED

26 U.S.C.A.—Internal Revenue Code

Sec.	This Work Para.
1368(b)(2)	15,340
1368(c)	13,350
1368(c)	15,345
1368(c)	15,355
1368(e)(1)	15,350
1368(e)(1)(B)	13,350
1368(e)(1)(B)	15,380
1368(e)(3)	13,360
1371(a)	15,025
1371(a)	15,220
1371(b)(1)	15,453
1371(b)(2)	15,453
1371(b)(3)	15,453
1371(c)(1)	15,405
1371(e)	15,470
1372	15,235
1374	1000
1374	15,410
1374	15,410
1374	15,415
1374	15,425
1374	15,440
1374(b)(1)	15,415
1374(b)(2)	15,410
1374(c)(1)	15,410
1374(d)(1)	15,410
1374(d)(2)(A)(i)	15,410
1374(d)(2)(A)(ii)	15,410
1374(d)(2)(B)	15,410
1374(d)(3)	15,410
1374(d)(4)	15,410
1374(d)(7)	15,410
1374(d)(8)	15,410
1374(d)(8)	15,425
1375	1000
1375	8090
1375	15,210
1375	15,440
1375	15,440
1375	15,445
1375	15,450
1375	15,450
1375(b)	15,440
1375(b)(1)(B)	15,450
1375(d)	15,440
1377	15,470
1377(a)	15,385
1377(a)	15,460
1377(a)(1)	15,255
1377(a)(1)	15,385
1377(a)(2)	15,385
1377(b)	15,470
1377(b)(3)(A)	15,470
1377(b)(3)(B)	15,470
1378	15,250
1378(a)	15,250
1378(b)	15,250
1441	16,085
1501	14,050
1501—1504	1050

UNITED STATES CODE ANNOTATED

26 U.S.C.A.—Internal Revenue Code

Sec.	This Work Para.
1502	14,050
1504	10,050
1504	12,170
1504	14,050
1504(a)	1050
1504(a)	4100
1504(a)	12,025
1504(a)	12,170
1504(a)	14,055
1504(a)(2)	8060
1504(a)(4)	13,140
1504(a)(4)	1050
1504(b)	10,050
1504(b)	1050
1504(b)(8)	15,170
1551	14,005
1561	14,005
1561(a)(3)	1025
1563	14,005
1563	14,045
1563(d)	14,005
1563(e)	14,005
1563(f)(5)	14,000
2053	5120
2054	5120
2056(b)(5)	15,125
2056(b)(7)	15,125
2056(b)(7)	15,140
2503(c)	15,125
6011	16,085
6031(a)	18,000

UNITED STATES CODE ANNOTATED

26 U.S.C.A.—Internal Revenue Code

Sec.	This Work Para.
6038A	16,085
6072(a)	18,000
6111	16,085
6112	16,085
6221—6255	18,000
6240—6255	18,250
6501(e)	18,020
6707A	16,085
6708	16,085
7519	15,250
7519	18,015
7701(a)(2)	16,025
7701(a)(3)	1080
7701(g)	21,070
7701(g)	2175
7701(l)	16,085
7704	1000
7704	1085
7704	16,070
7704	16,080
7704	16,080
7704(b)	16,080
7704(b)	21,005
7704(c)	16,080
7704(c)(3)	16,080
7704(d)	16,080
7704(e)	16,080
7704(f)	16,080
7704(g)	16,080
7872	15,180

Table of Treasury Regulations

TREASURY REGULATIONS

Sec.	This Work Para.
1.1(h)–1	15,385
1.1(h)–1(b)	21,092
1.1(h)–1(c)	21,092
1.1(h)–1(d)	21,092
1.1(h)–1(f), Ex. 5	21,092
1.1(h)–1(f), Exs. 1–3	21,092
1.83–3(b)	17,085
1.83–3(c)	17,075
1.83–3(d)	17,075
1.118–1	2285
1.166–9(b)	3120
1.248–1(b)(1)	2305
1.248–1(b)(2)	2305
1.248–1(b)(3)(i)	2305
1.248–1(b)(3)(ii)	2305
1.269–7	13,110
1.301–1(g)	4050
1.302–2(c)	5020
1.302–3(a)	5010
1.302–4(d)	5040
1.303–2(d)	5115
1.303–2(f)	5115
1.305–2(a)	6085
1.305–3(b)	6040
1.305–3(e), Ex. 1	6085
1.305–3(e), Ex. 2	6085
1.305–3(e), Ex. 10	6050
1.305–4(b), Ex. 1	6085
1.305–5(b)	10,205
1.305–5(b)(3)	6065
1.305–6	6085
1.306–3(d)	11,045
1.306–3(d)	11,045
1.307–1(a)	6010
1.312–3	4070
1.312–10(a)	12,185
1.312–10(b)	12,185
1.312–10(c)	12,185
1.316–2(b)	4035
1.316–2(c)	4035
1.316–2(c)	4040
1.318–1(b)(3)	5015
1.332–2(b)	8040
1.332–7	8040
1.338–3(b)(5)	8120
1.338–3(b)(5)	8125
1.338–4(b)(1)	8120
1.338–4(b)(2)(iii)	8120
1.338–4(c)(1)	8120
1.338–4(e)	8120

TREASURY REGULATIONS

Sec.	This Work Para.
1.338–5	8120
1.338–5(b)(2)(iii)	8120
1.338–6	8095
1.338–8	8120
1.338(b)–6	8120
1.338(h)(10)–1(d)	8123
1.351–1(a)(1)	2030
1.351–1(a)(1)	2045
1.351–1(a)(1)(ii)	2075
1.351–1(a)(1)(ii)	2090
1.351–1(a)(2), Ex. 3	2075
1.351–1(a)(3)	2070
1.354–1(e)	10,055
1.354–1(e)	10,290
1.355–2(b)	12,045
1.355–2(b)—(c)	12,005
1.355–2(b)(1)	12,045
1.355–2(b)(1)	12,125
1.355–2(b)(2)	12,055
1.355–2(b)(3)	12,005
1.355–2(b)(4)	12,040
1.355–2(b)(5), Ex. 3	12,055
1.355–2(b)(5), Ex. 4	12,055
1.355–2(b)(5), Ex. 8	12,125
1.355–2(c)	12,045
1.355–2(c)	12,090
1.355–2(c)(1)	12,045
1.355–2(d)	12,005
1.355–2(d)	12,030
1.355–2(d)	12,040
1.355–2(d)(2)	12,040
1.355–2(d)(2)(i)	12,040
1.355–2(d)(3)	12,040
1.355–2(d)(3)(i)	12,040
1.355–2(d)(3)(ii)	12,040
1.355–2(d)(5)	12,040
1.355–3	12,005
1.355–3	12,025
1.355–3(b)(2)(ii)	12,025
1.355–3(b)(2)(iii)	12,025
1.355–3(b)(2)(iv)	12,025
1.355–3(c), Ex. 4	12,025
1.355–3(c), Ex. 5	12,025
1.355–3(c), Ex. 6	12,015
1.355–3(c), Ex. 7	12,015
1.355–3(c), Exs. 9–11	12,025
1.355–3(c), Ex. 12	5235
1.355–3(c), Ex. 13	5235
1.355–6	12,090
1.355–6(b)(2)(iii)	12,090

TREASURY REGULATIONS

Sec.	This Work Para.
1.355–6(b)(3)(i)	12,090
1.355–6(b)(3)(ii)	12,090
1.355–6(b)(3)(iii)	12,090
1.355–6(b)(3)(iv), Ex. 1	12,090
1.355–6(d)(2)(iv)	12,090
1.355–7(b)(1)	12,120
1.355–7(b)(1)	12,125
1.355–7(b)(1)	12,135
1.355–7(b)(2)	12,120
1.355–7(b)(3)	12,125
1.355–7(b)(4)	12,125
1.355–7(c)	12,140
1.355–7(c)(1)	12,125
1.355–7(c)(2)	12,125
1.355–7(c)(3)	12,125
1.355–7(c)(4)	12,125
1.355–7(d)	12,120
1.355–7(d)	12,140
1.355–7(e)(1)	12,150
1.355–7(e)(4)	12,150
1.355–7(f)	12,150
1.355–7(h)(1)	12,145
1.355–7(h)(5)	12,140
1.355–7(h)(10)	12,140
1.356–1(d)	11,020
1.357–1(c)	2200
1.357–2	2200
1.357(b)–2(b)	2190
1.358–2	12,080
1.358–2(a)	12,090
1.358–2(a)(2)(i)	10,300
1.358–2(a)(2)(vii)	10,300
1.358–2(b)(2)	2140
1.358–6(c)(1)	10,160
1.358–6(c)(2)	10,180
1.358–6(c)(3)	10,160
1.368–1(b)	9060
1.368–1(b)	9100
1.368–1(b)	10,060
1.368–1(b)	10,070
1.368–1(b)	10,150
1.368–1(b)	11,040
1.368–1(b)	11,080
1.368–1(c)	9060
1.368–1(d)	9105
1.368–1(d)	10,060
1.368–1(d)	10,150
1.368–1(d)(3)(i)	10,070
1.368–1(e)	9100
1.368–1(e)	10,040
1.368–1(e)	10,050
1.368–1(e)(2)	10,040
1.368–1(e)(3)(i)(A)	10,050
1.368–2(b)(1)(i)—(b)(1)(iii)	10,030
1.368–2(b)(1)(ii)	10,025
1.368–2(b)(1)(ii)(B)	10,035
1.368–2(b)(2)	10,160
1.368–2(c)	10,140
1.368–2(d)(1)	10,160
1.368–2(e)	11,005
1.368–2(g)	9060
1.368–2(j)(3)(i)	10,175

TREASURY REGULATIONS

Sec.	This Work Para.
1.368–2(j)(3)(iii)	10,175
1.368–2(j)(6)	10,180
1.368–2(j)(6), Ex. 4	10,235
1.368–2(j)(6), Ex. 5	10,235
1.368–2(k)	10,160
1.368–2(k)(1)	10,160
1.368–2(k)(2)	10,160
1.381(a)–1(b)(2)	13,005
1.381(a)–1(b)(2)(ii), Exs. 2–4	13,005
1.381(a)–1(b)(3)	13,005
1.381(b)–1(a)(2)	13,005
1.381(b)–1(b)(3)	13,005
1.383–1	13,085
1.383–1(d)	13,085
1.453–11(a)(2)	8090
1.482–1(b)(1)	14,015
1.482–1(c)	14,020
1.482–1(f)	14,040
1.482–1(h)(2)	14,030
1.482–1(i)(4)	14,045
1.482–1(i)(4)—(i)(6)	14,045
1.482–2	14,015
1.482–3(a)	14,020
1.482–3(b)	14,020
1.482–3(c)	14,020
1.482–3(d)	14,020
1.482–4(f)(2)	14,025
1.482–5	14,020
1.482–6	14,020
1.537–1(b)(1)	7070
1.537–2(b)(3)	7070
1.643(b)–1	15,130
1.651(b)–3(a)	15,140
1.701–1	18,000
1.701–2	15,200
1.701–2	16,005
1.701–2	20,000
1.701–2	20,090
1.701–2	22,000
1.701–2	22,020
1.701–2	22,055
1.701–2(b)	16,085
1.701–2(c)	16,085
1.701–2(d)	16,085
1.701–2(d), Ex. 2	15,200
1.701–2(d), Ex. 9	22,055
1.701–2(d), Ex. 10	22,055
1.701–2(d), Ex. 11	22,055
1.701–2(e)	16,085
1.701–2(f)	16,085
1.701–2(i)	16,085
1.702–1(a)	18,000
1.702–1(a)(8)(i)	18,020
1.703–1(b)(1)	18,020
1.704–1(b)	18,125
1.704–1(b)(1)(i)	18,090
1.704–1(b)(1)(i)	18,110
1.704–1(b)(2)(i)	18,090
1.704–1(b)(2)(i)	18,115
1.704–1(b)(2)(ii)	18,095
1.704–1(b)(2)(ii)(a)	18,115
1.704–1(b)(2)(ii)(b)	18,115

TREASURY REGULATIONS

Sec.	This Work Para.
1.704–1(b)(2)(ii)(*b*)	18,125
1.704–1(b)(2)(ii)(*b*)	22,067
1.704–1(b)(2)(ii)(*b*)(*1*)	17,010
1.704–1(b)(2)(ii)(*b*)(*2*)	23,010
1.704–1(b)(2)(ii)(*d*)	18,095
1.704–1(b)(2)(ii)(*d*)	18,115
1.704–1(b)(2)(ii)(*d*)	18,125
1.704–1(b)(2)(ii)(*i*)	18,115
1.704–1(b)(2)(iii)(*a*)	18,105
1.704–1(b)(2)(iii)(*c*)	18,105
1.704–1(b)(2)(iii)(*c*)	18,115
1.704–1(b)(2)(iv)	18,095
1.704–1(b)(2)(iv)	22,067
1.704–1(b)(2)(iv)(*b*)	17,010
1.704–1(b)(2)(iv)(*b*)	22,067
1.704–1(b)(2)(iv)(*c*)	22,012
1.704–1(b)(2)(iv)(*d*)	17,010
1.704–1(b)(2)(iv)(*e*)	17,010
1.704–1(b)(2)(iv)(*e*)(*1*)	22,067
1.704–1(b)(2)(iv)(*e*)(*1*)	23,010
1.704–1(b)(2)(iv)(*f*)	18,120
1.704–1(b)(2)(iv)(*f*)	22,067
1.704–1(b)(2)(iv)(*f*)(*5*)(*i*)	18,115
1.704–1(b)(2)(iv)(*f*)(*5*)(*ii*)	22,067
1.704–1(b)(2)(iv)(*f*)(*5*)(*ii*)	23,010
1.704–1(b)(2)(iv)(*g*)(*1*)	18,140
1.704–1(b)(2)(iv)(*l*)	21,030
1.704–1(b)(2)(iv)(*l*)	24,040
1.704–1(b)(3)	18,115
1.704–1(b)(3)(i)	18,110
1.704–1(b)(3)(iii)	18,095
1.704–1(b)(3)(iii)	18,115
1.704–1(b)(4)(i)	18,120
1.704–1(b)(5), Ex. 5	18,105
1.704–1(b)(5), Ex. 13(v)	24,040
1.704–1(b)(5), Ex. 14	18,120
1.704–1(b)(5), Ex. 17	18,105
1.704–1(b)(5), Ex. 18	18,120
1.704–1(d)(1)	19,030
1.704–1(d)(2)	19,020
1.704–1(d)(2)	19,030
1.704–1(e)(1)(i)	18,135
1.704–1(e)(2)	18,225
1.704–1(e)(3)	18,240
1.704–2	18,125
1.704–2(b)(1)	18,125
1.704–2(e)	18,125
1.704–2(f)	18,125
1.704–2(i)(1)	18,125
1.704–3(a)(1)	18,135
1.704–3(a)(2)	18,135
1.704–3(a)(2)	24,040
1.704–3(a)(3)(i)	24,040
1.704–3(a)(6)(ii)	21,110
1.704–3(a)(7)	18,135
1.704–3(a)(7)	22,090
1.704–3(a)(8)(i)	18,140
1.704–3(a)(10)	18,135
1.704–3(b)	18,135
1.704–3(b)	18,140
1.704–3(b)	22,105
1.704–3(b)(1)	18,135

Sec.	This Work Para.
1.704–3(b)(2), Ex. 1	18,150
1.704–3(c)	18,135
1.704–3(c)	18,140
1.704–3(c)	18,145
1.704–3(c)	18,150
1.704–3(c)(1)	18,135
1.704–3(c)(2)	18,135
1.704–3(c)(3)(i)	18,135
1.704–3(c)(3)(ii)	18,135
1.704–3(c)(3)(iii)(A)	18,135
1.704–3(d)	18,135
1.704–3(d)	18,140
1.704–3(d)	18,150
1.704–3(d)	21,070
1.704–3(d)	21,110
1.704–3(d)(1)	18,135
1.704–3(d)(1)	18,145
1.704–3(d)(3)	18,135
1.704–3(d)(3)	18,145
1.704–3(d)(4)(ii)	18,135
1.704–3(e)(1)	18,135
1.704–3(e)(2)	18,135
1.704–3(e)(3)	18,135
1.704–4(a)	22,090
1.704–4(a)(2)	22,105
1.704–4(a)(4)(ii)	24,040
1.704–4(b)	22,090
1.704–4(c)(3)	22,090
1.704–4(c)(3)	24,040
1.704–4(c)(4)	22,090
1.704–4(c)(5)	22,090
1.704–4(c)(6)	22,090
1.704–4(d)(2)	22,090
1.704–4(d)(3)	22,090
1.704–4(e)(1)	22,090
1.704–4(e)(2)	22,090
1.704–4(e)(3)	22,090
1.704–4(f)(1)	16,085
1.704–4(f)(1)	22,090
1.704–4(f)(2), Ex. 1	22,090
1.704–4(f)(2), Ex. 2	22,090
1.705–1(a)(1)	19,020
1.705–2(b)(1)	21,107
1.706–1(c)(2)(ii)	21,025
1.707–1(a)	20,010
1.707–1(c)	20,020
1.707–1(c)	20,065
1.707–1(c), Ex. 2	20,065
1.707–3(a)(2)	20,090
1.707–3(b)(1)	20,090
1.707–3(b)(2)	20,090
1.707–3(b)(2)(iii)	20,090
1.707–3(c)(1)	20,090
1.707–3(d)	20,090
1.707–3(f), Ex. 4	20,090
1.707–4	20,095
1.707–4(a)	20,090
1.707–4(a)	20,095
1.707–4(b)	20,090
1.707–4(b)	20,095
1.707–5(a)	20,090
1.707–5(a)(6)	20,090

TREASURY REGULATIONS

Sec.	This Work Para.
1.707–5(a)(7)	20,090
1.707–5(b)(1)	20,090
1.708–1(b)(2)	24,040
1.708–1(b)(2)	24,050
1.708–1(b)(2)	24,060
1.708–1(b)(3)	24,025
1.708–1(b)(4)	24,040
1.708–1(b)(4), Ex. (ii)	24,040
1.708–1(b)(5)	24,040
1.708–1(c)(1)	24,070
1.708–1(c)(3)(i)	24,070
1.708–1(c)(3)(ii)	24,070
1.708–1(c)(4)	24,070
1.708–1(c)(5), Ex. 3	24,070
1.708–1(c)(5), Ex. 4	24,070
1.708–1(c)(5), Ex. 5	24,070
1.708–1(c)(6), Ex.	24,070
1.708–1(c)(6)(i)	24,070
1.708–1(c)(6)(ii)	24,070
1.708–1(d)(1)	24,075
1.708–1(d)(2)(ii)	24,075
1.708–1(d)(3)(i)	24,075
1.708–1(d)(3)(i)(A)	24,075
1.708–1(d)(3)(i)(B)	24,075
1.708–1(d)(3)(ii)(A)	24,075
1.708–1(d)(4)(i)	24,075
1.708–1(d)(5), Ex. 1	24,075
1.708–1(d)(5), Ex. 2	24,075
1.708–1(d)(5), Ex. 3	24,075
1.708–1(d)(5), Ex. 6	24,075
1.708–1(d)(6)	24,075
1.709–2(a)	17,105
1.709–2(c)	17,105
1.721–1(b)(1)	17,065
1.731–1(a)(1)(i)	22,035
1.731–1(a)(1)(ii)	19,020
1.731–1(a)(1)(ii)	22,005
1.731–1(a)(1)(ii)	22,015
1.731–1(a)(1)(ii)	22,040
1.731–1(a)(2)	23,010
1.731–1(c)(2)	22,005
1.731–1(c)(2)	22,015
1.731–2(b)(1)	22,100
1.731–2(b)(2)	22,100
1.731–2(c)(3)(i)	22,100
1.731–2(c)(3)(ii)	22,100
1.731–2(d)(1)(i)	22,100
1.731–2(d)(1)(ii)	22,100
1.731–2(d)(1)(iii)	22,100
1.731–2(d)(2)	22,100
1.731–2(e)	22,100
1.731–2(f)(1)(i)	22,100
1.731–2(f)(1)(i)	23,010
1.731–2(f)(1)(ii)	22,100
1.731–2(f)(2)	22,060
1.731–2(f)(2)	22,100
1.731–2(g)(1)(i)	22,100
1.731–2(g)(1)(ii)	22,100
1.731–2(g)(1)(iii)(B)	22,100
1.731–2(g)(2)	24,040
1.731–2(h)	22,100
1.732–1(a)	22,020

TREASURY REGULATIONS

Sec.	This Work Para.
1.732–1(a), Ex. 1	22,020
1.732–1(a), Ex. 2	22,020
1.732–1(a), Ex. 2	22,035
1.732–1(c)(1)(i)	22,020
1.732–1(c)(1)(i)	23,010
1.732–1(c)(1)(ii)	22,020
1.732–1(c)(1)(ii)	23,010
1.732–1(c)(2)(i)	22,020
1.732–1(c)(2)(i)	23,010
1.732–1(c)(2)(ii)	23,010
1.732–1(c)(3)	23,010
1.732–1(c)(3)	23,010
1.732–1(c)(4), Ex. 1	23,010
1.732–1(c)(4), Ex. 2	23,010
1.732–1(c)(4), Ex. 3	23,010
1.732–1(c)(4), Ex. 4	23,010
1.732–1(d)(1)(iii)	22,025
1.732–1(d)(4)	22,025
1.732–1(g)(2)(i)	22,020
1.732–2	22,020
1.733–1	22,020
1.736–1(a)(4)	23,015
1.736–1(a)(5)	23,035
1.736–1(a)(6)	23,030
1.736–1(a)(6)	24,000
1.736–1(b)(2)	23,005
1.736–1(b)(3)	23,005
1.736–1(b)(5)	23,035
1.736–1(b)(5)(iii)	23,035
1.737–1(a)	22,095
1.737–1(b)	22,095
1.737–1(c)	22,095
1.737–1(d)	22,095
1.737–2(a)	22,095
1.737–2(a)	24,040
1.737–2(b)(1)	22,095
1.737–2(b)(2)	22,095
1.737–2(c)	22,095
1.737–2(d)(2)	22,095
1.737–3(a)	22,095
1.737–3(b)	22,095
1.737–3(c)(1)	22,095
1.737–3(c)(4)	22,095
1.737–4(a)	16,085
1.737–4(a)	22,095
1.737–4(b), Ex. 1	22,095
1.737–4(b), Ex. 2	22,095
1.743–1(b)	21,110
1.743–1(d)(1)	21,110
1.743–1(d)(2)	21,110
1.743–1(d)(3)	21,110
1.743–1(h)(1)	24,040
1.743–1(h)(2)(i)	24,020
1.743–1(h)(2)(iii)	24,020
1.743–1(j)(1)	21,100
1.743–1(j)(1)	21,110
1.743–1(j)(2)	21,100
1.743–1(j)(3)(i)	21,110
1.743–1(j)(4)(i)	21,110
1.743–1(j)(4)(ii)	21,110
1.743–2(h)(2)(ii)	24,020
1.751–1(a)(1)	18,180

TREASURY REGULATIONS

Sec.	This Work Para.
1.751–1(a)(2)	18,180
1.751–1(a)(2)	21,035
1.751–1(a)(2)	21,070
1.751–1(d)(2)(ii)	22,110
1.751–1(g), Ex. 1	21,070
1.751–1(g), Ex. 3(c)	22,115
1.751–1(g), Ex. 4(c)	22,115
1.752–1	17,030
1.752–1(a)(1)	18,170
1.752–1(a)(1)	18,175
1.752–1(a)(2)	18,170
1.752–1(a)(4)(i)	18,170
1.752–1(f)	24,070
1.752–1(g), Ex. 1	24,070
1.752–1(i)	18,175
1.752–2	17,040
1.752–2	23,030
1.752–2(a)	18,170
1.752–2(b)(1)	18,170
1.752–2(b)(3)	18,170
1.752–2(b)(4)	17,030
1.752–2(b)(4)	18,170
1.752–2(b)(5)	18,170
1.752–2(b)(6)	18,170
1.752–2(c)(1)	18,175
1.752–2(c)(1)	18,190
1.752–2(f), Ex. 1	18,115
1.752–2(f), Ex. 2	18,115
1.752–2(f), Ex. 2	18,190
1.752–2(f), Ex. 3	18,190
1.752–2(f), Ex. 4	18,190
1.752–2(f), Ex. 5	18,190
1.752–2(h)(1)	18,170
1.752–2(h)(2)	18,170
1.752–2(i)	18,170
1.752–3(a)	18,175
1.752–3(a)(1)	18,175
1.752–3(a)(1)	23,030
1.752–3(a)(2)	18,175
1.752–3(a)(3)	18,175
1.752–3(a)(3)	18,185
1.752–3(b)(1)	18,175
1.752–4(a)	18,170
1.752–7	18,175
1.755–1(a)(1)	21,110
1.755–1(a)(2)	21,110
1.755–1(a)(3)	21,110
1.755–1(a)(4)	21,110
1.755–1(a)(5)	21,110
1.755–1(b)(1)(i)	21,110
1.755–1(b)(1)(ii)	21,110
1.755–1(b)(1)(ii), Ex. 2	21,110
1.755–1(b)(2)(i)	21,110
1.755–1(b)(2)(ii), Ex. 1	21,110
1.755–1(b)(3)(i)	21,110
1.755–1(b)(3)(ii)	21,110
1.755–1(b)(3)(ii), Ex. 1	21,110
1.755–1(b)(3)(iii)(A)	21,110
1.755–1(b)(3)(iii)(B)	21,110
1.755–1(b)(3)(iv), Ex. 1	21,110
1.755–1(b)(3)(iv), Ex. 2	21,110
1.755–1(b)(4)(i)	25,030

TREASURY REGULATIONS

Sec.	This Work Para.
1.755–1(b)(4)(ii), Ex.	25,030
1.755–1(c)(1)(i)	22,065
1.755–1(c)(1)(ii)	22,065
1.755–1(c)(2)	22,065
1.755–1(c)(3)	22,065
1.755–1(c)(4)	22,065
1.755–1(c)(6), Ex.	22,065
1.761–2(a)	16,055
1.1001–3	10,315
1.1001–3(e)(1)	10,315
1.1001–3(e)(3)(ii)	10,315
1.1060–1(c)(4)	8095
1.1221–3(f), Ex. 2	21,070
1.1223–3	21,092
1.1223–3(b)(1)	17,008
1.1223–3(b)(2)	21,005
1.1223–3(b)(2)	22,012
1.1223–3(b)(3)	22,012
1.1223–3(b)(4)	21,070
1.1223–3(b)(5)	21,005
1.1223–3(c)(1)	17,008
1.1223–3(c)(1)	21,005
1.1223–3(c)(2)(i)	21,005
1.1223–3(c)(2)(ii)	21,005
1.1223–3(d)(1)	22,012
1.1223–3(d)(2)	17,008
1.1223–3(d)(2)	22,012
1.1223–3(f), Ex. 1	17,008
1.1223–3(f), Ex. 1	21,005
1.1223–3(f), Ex. 3	21,005
1.1223–3(f), Ex. 4	17,008
1.1223–3(f), Ex. 5	21,005
1.1223–3(f), Ex. 6	21,005
1.1223–3(f), Ex. 7	22,012
1.1223–3(f), Ex. 8	22,012
1.1244(c)–2(b)(2)	3130
1.1245–1(e)(2)	18,135
1.1250–1(f)	18,135
1.1273–2(j)	3085
1.1361–1(b)(3)	15,085
1.1361–1(d), Ex. 1	15,175
1.1361–1(e)(1)	15,080
1.1361–1(e)(1)	15,085
1.1361–1(e)(1)	15,095
1.1361–1(e)(2)	15,085
1.1361–1(e)(2)	15,105
1.1361–1(g)	15,155
1.1361–1(h)(1)(i)	15,120
1.1361–1(h)(1)(ii)	15,135
1.1361–1(h)(1)(iv)	15,135
1.1361–1(j)(1)(i)	15,130
1.1361–1(j)(9)	15,130
1.1361–1(j)(10)	15,130
1.1361–1(l)(1)	15,180
1.1361–1(l)(2)(i)	15,180
1.1361–1(l)(2)(iii)(A)	15,180
1.1361–1(l)(2)(iii)(B)	15,180
1.1361–1(l)(2)(vi), Ex. 1	15,180
1.1361–1(l)(2)(vi), Ex. 2	15,180
1.1361–1(l)(2)(vi), Ex. 3	15,180
1.1361–1(l)(2)(vi), Ex. 4	15,180
1.1361–1(l)(2)(vi), Ex. 5	15,180

TREASURY REGULATIONS

Sec.	This Work Para.
1.1361–1(*l*)(2)(vi), Ex. 8	15,180
1.1361–1(*l*)(2)(vi), Ex. 9	15,180
1.1361–1(*l*)(3)	15,190
1.1361–1(*l*)(4)	15,180
1.1361–1(*l*)(4)(ii)(2)	15,180
1.1361–1(*l*)(4)(iii)	15,190
1.1361–1(*l*)(5)(i)	15,190
1.1361–1(*l*)(5)(ii)	15,190
1.1361–1(*l*)(5)(iv)	15,180
1.1361–1(*l*)(5)(iv)	15,190
1.1361–1(*l*)(5)(v)	15,180
1.1361–2(a)	15,175
1.1361–2(b)	15,175
1.1361–4	15,175
1.1361–5(b)	15,175
1.1361–5(c)	15,175
1.1362–2(c)(5)(ii)(A)(*1*)	15,450
1.1362–2(c)(5)(ii)(A)(*2*)	15,450
1.1362–2(c)(5)(ii)(A)(*3*)	15,450
1.1362–2(c)(5)(ii)(B)(*1*)	15,450
1.1362–2(c)(5)(ii)(B)(*2*)	15,450
1.1362–3(a)	15,460
1.1362–3(b)	15,460
1.1362–5(a)	15,210
1.1362–5(a)	15,460
1.1362–6(a)(2)(i)	15,080
1.1362–6(a)(2)(ii)(C)	15,055
1.1362–6(a)(2)(iii), Ex. 1	15,055
1.1362–6(a)(3)(i)	15,455
1.1362–6(a)(3)(i)	15,465
1.1362–6(b)(2)	15,080
1.1362–6(b)(3)(ii), Ex. 2	15,080
1.1363–1(a)(1)	15,215
1.1363–1(a)(2)	15,215
1.1363–1(c)	15,230
1.1363–2	15,405
1.1366–1(a)(1)	15,215
1.1366–1(a)(1)	15,250
1.1366–1(a)(2)	15,225
1.1366–1(b)	15,245
1.1366–1(b)(1)	15,225
1.1366–1(b)(2)	15,225
1.1366–1(b)(3)	15,225
1.1366–2(a)(1)	15,280
1.1366–2(a)(1)(ii)	15,290
1.1366–2(a)(2)	15,280
1.1366–2(a)(5)	15,385
1.1366–2(b)	15,280
1.1366–2(b)(2)	15,470
1.1366–3(a)	15,275
1.1366–3(b), Ex. 2	15,275
1.1366–4(b)	15,410
1.1367–1(b)	15,280
1.1367–1(c)(1)	15,280
1.1367–1(c)(2)	15,280
1.1367–1(c)(3)	15,280
1.1367–1(d)(1)	15,280
1.1367–1(f)	15,280
1.1367–1(g)	15,280
1.1367–2(b)	15,290
1.1367–2(c)	15,315
1.1367–2(d)(1)	15,315

TREASURY REGULATIONS

Sec.	This Work Para.
1.1368–1(c)	15,370
1.1368–1(d)(2)	15,365
1.1368–1(d)(2)(ii)	15,350
1.1368–1(e)(2)	15,370
1.1368–1(f)(2)(i)	13,360
1.1368–1(f)(3)	13,360
1.1368–1(g)	15,390
1.1368–2(a)(1)	15,350
1.1368–2(a)(2)	15,350
1.1368–2(a)(3)	13,350
1.1368–2(a)(3)(iii)	15,370
1.1368–2(a)(5)	13,350
1.1368–2(b)	13,350
1.1368–2(d)	13,350
1.1368–2(d)(1)	15,380
1.1368–3, Ex. 2	15,370
1.1368–3, Ex. 7	13,360
1.1368–3, Ex. 8	13,350
1.1368–3, Ex. 9	15,380
1.1374–1A(d)(1)	15,410
1.1374–1(d)	15,410
1.1374–1(e)	15,425
1.1374–2	15,410
1.1374–3	15,410
1.1374–4	15,410
1.1374–4(h)	15,415
1.1374–8	15,410
1.1374–8	15,425
1.1374–8(c)	15,425
1.1377–1(a)	15,385
1.1377–1(b)	15,385
1.1377–2	15,470
1.1502–11	14,060
1.1502–11(a)	14,060
1.1502–12	14,060
1.1502–13(a)(2)	14,065
1.1502–13(c)(1)(i)	14,065
1.1502–13(c)(7), Ex. 7	14,065
1.1502–13(c)(7)(ii), Ex. 1(f)	14,065
1.1502–15	13,130
1.1502–15(a)(1)	13,130
1.1502–15(b)(1)	13,130
1.1502–15(c)(1)	13,130
1.1502–15(c)(2)	13,130
1.1502–19(a)(2)	14,080
1.1502–19(b)(2)(ii)	14,080
1.1502–19(c)	14,080
1.1502–19(g)	12,170
1.1502–21	14,060
1.1502–21(b)	13,130
1.1502–21(c)	13,125
1.1502–21(c)(2)	13,125
1.1502–32(a)	14,075
1.1502–32(a)(3)(iii)	14,075
1.1502–32(b)(2)	14,075
1.1502–33(a)	14,085
1.1502–33(e)	14,085
1.1502–76(b)	15,070
1.1502–80(b)	10,050
1.1502–91—1.1502–93	13,115
1.1502–91(a)(1)	13,120
1.1502–91(c)(1)	13,120
1.1502–91(d)(1)	13,120

TREASURY REGULATIONS

Sec.	This Work Para.
1.1502–92(b)(1)(i)	13,120
1.1502–92(b)(1)(ii)	13,120
1.1502–93	13,120
1.1502–93(b)	13,120
1.1502–93(c)(2)	13,120
1.1502–94—1.1502–95	13,115
1.1502–94(b)	13,120
1.1502–94(b)(1)	13,120
1.1502–95(c)	13,120
1.1563–1(a)(3)	14,005
1.6011–4	16,085
301.7701–1—301.7701–4	1080
301.7701–1(a)(1)	16,050
301.7701–1(a)(1)	16,070
301.7701–1(a)(2)	16,025
301.7701–1(a)(2)	16,030
301.7701–1(a)(2)	16,040
301.7701–1(a)(2)	16,050
301.7701–1(a)(2)	16,070
301.7701–2 (former)	16,060
301.7701–2 (former)	16,065
301.7701–2(a)	16,070
301.7701–2(a)(1) (former)	16,060
301.7701–2(b)	16,070

TREASURY REGULATIONS

Sec.	This Work Para.
301.7701–2(b)	1085
301.7701–2(b)(8)	16,070
301.7701–3(a)	1085
301.7701–3(a)	16,070
301.7701–3(a)	17,065
301.7701–3(b)(1)	1085
301.7701–3(b)(1)	16,070
301.7701–3(b)(2)	16,070
301.7701–3(b)(3)	16,070
301.7701–3(c)	1085
301.7701–3(c)	16,070
301.7701–3(c)(1)(iv)	16,070
301.7701–3(c)(1)(v)(C)	15,064
301.7701–3(c)(1)(v)(C)	16,077
301.7701–3(f)	16,070
301.7701–3(g)	16,070
301.7701–3(g)(1)(i)	16,070
301.7701–3(g)(1)(i)	24,020
301.7701–3(g)(1)(ii)	16,070
301.7701–3(g)(1)(ii)	24,095
301.7701–3(g)(1)(iii)	16,070
301.7701–3(g)(1)(iv)	16,070
301.7701–4(a)	1090
301.7701–4(a)	1090

*

Table of Temporary Treasury Regulations

TEMPORARY TREASURY REGULATIONS

Sec.	This Work Para.
1.163–8T	20,090
1.382–2T(e)(1)	13,040

TEMPORARY TREASURY REGULATIONS

Sec.	This Work Para.
1.382–2T(e)(2)	13,040
15A.453–1(d)(2)(iii)	8030

*

Table of Proposed Treasury Regulations

PROPOSED TREASURY REGULATIONS

Sec.	This Work Para.
1.83–3(e)	17,065
1.83–3(e)	17,075
1.83–3(*l*)	17,065
1.83–3(*l*)	17,075
1.368–2(b)(1)	10,030
1.368–2(m)	11,075
1.368–2(m)	11,085
1.368–2(m)(3)(ii)	11,075
1.453–1(f)(3)	2130
1.453–1(f)(3)	2135
1.453–1(f)(3)(ii)	2130
1.453–1(f)(3)(iii), Ex. 2	2135
1.704–1(b)(2)(iv)(b)(1)	17,065
1.707–1(c)	17,065
1.707–3(a)	20,095
1.707–7(a)(1)	20,095
1.707–7(a)(2)(i)	20,095
1.707–7(a)(2)(ii)(A)	20,095
1.707–7(a)(2)(ii)(C)	20,095
1.707–7(a)(2)(ii)(D)	20,095
1.707–7(a)(4)	20,095
1.707–7(a)(7)	24,037
1.707–7(a)(8)	20,095

PROPOSED TREASURY REGULATIONS

Sec.	This Work Para.
1.707–7(a)(8)	24,045
1.707–7(b)(1)	20,095
1.707–7(b)(2)	20,095
1.707–7(b)(2)(ii)	20,095
1.707–7(c)	20,095
1.707–7(d)	20,095
1.707–7(e)	20,095
1.707–7(f)	20,095
1.707–7(g)	20,095
1.707–7(j)(1)	20,095
1.707–7(j)(2)	20,095
1.707–7(j)(3)	20,095
1.721–1(b)(1)	17,075
1.721–1(b)(2)	17,065
1.721–1(b)(4)(i)	17,065
1.721–1(b)(4)(ii)	17,065
1.751–1(c)(1)(ii)	21,045
1.761–1(b)	17,065
1.1041–2	5215
1.1361–1(j)(12)	15,147
1.1361–1(m)(1)(ii)(C)	15,145
1.1361–1(m)(4)(i)	15,105
1.1361–1(m)(4)(vii)	15,105
1.1361–1(m)(4)(vii)	15,145
1.1361–1(m)(5)(iii)	15,145
301.7701–3(g)	1085

*

Table of Revenue Rulings

REVENUE RULINGS

Rev.Rul.	This Work Para.
54–396	10,115
56–330	9105
56–373	12,195
56–584	5050
57–276	11,055
57–465	10,025
57–518	**10,085**
57–586	10,290
58–422	11,055
59–98	**10,270**
59–98	10,275
61–156	11,075
61–156	**11,130**
61–156	11,135
63–29	9105
64–56	2010
64–73	10,160
64–251	10,290
66–23	10,040
66–94	19,020
66–112	10,290
66–142	2190
66–365	10,135
67–275	10,135
67–448	**10,170**
67–448	10,175
67–448	10,180
67–448	10,235
67–448	11,085
68–55	**2120**
68–79	**18,025**
68–603	12,100
68–603	12,100
68–629	2245
69–357	2010
69–608	5195
69–608	**5210**
69–608	5215
70–106	**8055**
70–108	10,135
70–225	12,100
70–225	12,110
70–434	12,100
70–521	4095
72–265	**3090**
72–265	3095
72–522	10,135
73–54	10,135
73–102	10,135
73–427	10,235

REVENUE RULINGS

Rev.Rul.	This Work Para.
74–503	10,180
75–67	**7025**
75–144	**15,305**
75–144	15,310
75–154	23,015
75–154	**23,020**
75–188	15,450
75–250	7020
75–374	**16,030**
75–406	12,100
75–447	**5185**
75–447	5190
75–502	**5095**
75–502	5100
75–561	13,135
76–123	10,235
76–258	6025
77–19	**6045**
77–19	6050
77–37	**6060**
77–119	**18,200**
77–119	18,205
77–133	**12,190**
77–226	5180
77–245	5225
77–293	5050
77–332	**16,035**
77–402	**21,015**
77–412	**24,005**
77–415	11,040
77–455	6120
78–250	10,235
78–294	2070
78–371	1090
78–375	6025
78–375	**6030**
78–401	5100
79–70	**2060**
79–77	1090
79–194	**2085**
79–205	**22,045**
79–273	10,235
80–198	2265
80–198	**2270**
80–198	2275
80–284	**10,215**
80–284	10,220
81–41	5010
81–186	11,045
81–247	**10,065**

REVENUE RULINGS

Rev.Rul.	This Work Para.
81–300	**20,060**
81–301	**20,040**
81–301	20,045
82–34	**11,035**
82–34	11,040
83–119	6055
83–119	**6070**
83–119	6075
83–120	6075
84–30	10,050
84–52	**24,085**
84–52	24,095
84–71	**10,225**
84–71	10,230
84–111	**24,015**
84–111	24,020
84–111	24,070
85–32	17,105
85–161	**15,185**
85–164	2160
86–73	24,040
86–126	**12,020**
87–50	24,050
87–51	**24,055**
87–51	24,060
87–132	5115
88–48	**10,105**
88–48	10,110
88–48	10,175
88–76	16,065
88–77	17,030
88–77	18,170
89–7	18,020
89–63	6120
89–108	**21,087**
89–108	21,090
90–13	5225
90–95	8125
91–26	20,065
92–15	**22,080**
92–15	22,085
92–97	18,040
92–97	**18,100**
92–97	22,040
93–13	23,035
93–36	15,220
93–38	16,065
93–61	10,255
93–62	11,020
93–62	**12,075**
93–80	**23,075**
94–4	22,040
94–43	**15,100**

REVENUE RULINGS

Rev.Rul.	This Work Para.
94–43	15,105
94–43	15,155
95–14	**15,375**
95–14	15,390
95–37	**24,090**
95–37	24,095
95–41	18,175
95–41	**18,185**
95–55	16,065
95–55	24,095
95–74	**2195**
96–10	20,110
96–11	19,010
96–11	**19,015**
96–29	**11,070**
96–29	11,075
96–30	12,100
97–38	**18,102**
98–27	**12,105**
98–27	12,110
98–37	16,065
98–37	16,065
98–44	12,110
99–5	16,077
99–5	**17,007**
99–6	**24,035**
99–43	**18,107**
2000–5	10,015
2000–5	**10,020**
2000–5	10,025
2000–5	10,030
2001–24	10,160
2001–25	10,175
2001–26	10,185
2001–46	**10,190**
2001–46	10,195
2003–38	12,015
2003–52	12,055
2003–74	12,055
2003–75	12,055
2003–110	12,055
2004–23	12,045
2004–23	**12,050**
2004–23	12,055
2004–43	24,077
2004–43	**24,078**
2004–59	24,020
2004–78	10,240
2005–10	24,077
2005–15	24,077
2005–65	**12,130**
2005–65	12,135

Table of Revenue Procedures

REVENUE PROCEDURES

Rev.Proc.	This Work Para.
67–14	4095
77–37	10,080
77–37	10,135
77–37	10,290
77–37, § 3.07	2090
84–42	10,135
84–42	**10,285**
86–42	10,080
89–50	10,090
93–27	17,075
93–27	**17,080**
93–27	17,085
95–10	16,065
96–30	12,045
97–48	15,055
97–48	**15,060**
97–48	15,065
97–48	15,080
98–23	15,147
98–55	15,065

REVENUE PROCEDURES

Rev.Proc.	This Work Para.
2001–43	17,075
2001–43	**17,082**
2001–43	17,085
2002–22	**16,043**
2003–43	15,055
2003–43	**15,062**
2003–43	15,065
2003–43	15,080
2003–43, § 2.02	15,175
2003–43, § 2.03	15,130
2003–43, § 2.03	15,147
2003–43, § 2.03	15,147
2003–43, § 4	15,130
2003–43, § 4	15,147
2003–43, § 4	15,147
2003–43, § 4	15,175
2003–43, § 4	15,210
2004–48	15,055
2004–48	**15,063**
2004–48	15,065
2004–48	16,077

*

Table of IRS Notices

IRS NOTICES

No.	This Work Para.
94–47	**3035**
94–47	3040
94–48	16,085
95–14	16,065
95–14	16,070
97–12	15,105
97–12	15,145
97–49	15,145

IRS NOTICES

No.	This Work Para.
2005–43	17,065
2005–43	17,075
2005–43	17,083
2005–43	**17,085**
2005–91	15,105
2006–14	**22,125**

*

Table of Letter Rulings

LETTER RULINGS

Ltr.Rul.	This Work Para.
8443039	15,070
8621013	15,210
8807070	**15,050**
8814042	**15,205**
8814042	15,210
8819040	**15,195**
8821020	15,210
8839006	15,130

LETTER RULINGS

Ltr.Rul.	This Work Para.
8842024	13,350
8846013	15,210
8848065	15,445
8849015	**15,420**
8849015	15,425
9224027	15,210
9241035	15,210
9452037	15,210

*

CASES AND MATERIALS ON
TAXATION OF BUSINESS ENTERPRISES

Third Edition

*

Chapter 1

INTRODUCTION

[¶ 1000]

A. OVERVIEW AND HISTORY OF THE CORPORATE INCOME TAX

The federal income tax system, with certain exceptions, treats corporations and their shareholders as separate and distinct taxpayers. Thus, the earnings of a corporation generally are subject to two levels of federal income taxation—one at the corporate level under Section 11 on the corporation's "taxable income" and a second at the shareholder level when the corporation's net income is distributed to its shareholders or the shareholders dispose of their stock in the corporation. A corporation's net losses may be deducted only by the corporation and do not flow through to the corporation's shareholders.

By contrast, as discussed in Chapters 16 through 25 of this book, a partnership is not treated as a taxpaying entity for federal income tax purposes. § 701. Under Section 702, a partnership's net income is subject to only one level of federal income tax, imposed at the partner level. A partnership's net losses pass through and are reported on the partners' own returns. This single, partner level tax regime for partnerships also often applies to a hybrid entity known as the "limited liability company," which may elect to be treated as a partnership for federal tax purposes. The single, partner level tax regime, however, does not apply to certain publicly traded partnerships, which Section 7704 treats as corporations for federal tax purposes (see ¶ 16,080).

This distinction between corporations and partnerships did not always exist. Under the income tax in effect during most of the Civil War and Reconstruction, 13 Stat. 223, 282 (1864), stockholders were taxed on their allocable, but undistributed, share of corporate profits just as partners were taxed on their allocable, but undistributed, share of partnership profits. While certain corporations were subject to a tax on their dividends and undistributed profits, this tax was not imposed because of their corporate status, but rather because of their membership in specific industries such as transportation and banking.

Congress first enacted an entity-level tax directed against corporations generally in 1894. The 1894 Act, 28 Stat. 553, 556 (1894), imposed a tax of two percent on the incomes of both individuals and corporations. The latter was considered more of a prepayment of the individual tax than a separate corporate tax, though, because dividends were exempt from individual income tax and most corporations distributed all of their taxable income as dividends each year.[1] In any event, the tax was never enforced because of the Supreme Court's decision in Pollock v. Farmers' Loan & Trust Co., 157 U.S. 429 (1895), reh. denied, 158 U.S. 601 (1895). The Court held that the 1894 Act's income tax was a "direct tax" that was unconstitutional because it was not apportioned among the states in proportion to their populations as required by Article I, Section 9, Clause 4 of the U.S. Constitution. The Court did suggest, though, that unapportioned "excise taxes on business, privileges, employments, and vocations" might be constitutionally permissible. Id. at 637.

Amidst calls for the reintroduction of an income tax, Congress attempted to toe the line drawn in *Pollock* by enacting a corporate excise tax as part of the Payne–Aldrich Tariff Act of 1909.[2] The 1909 Act, 36 Stat. 112 (1909), imposed "a special excise tax with respect to the carrying on or doing of business by [every] corporation, joint stock company or association, or insurance company." This tax was applied at the rate of one percent of the entity's net income in excess of $5,000. The validity of this tax was challenged under the doctrine of *Pollock* in Flint v. Stone Tracy Co., 220 U.S. 107 (1911), but the Court upheld it as an excise tax "upon the doing of business with the advantages which inhere in the peculiarities of corporate or joint stock organizations of the character described." Id. at 145–46.

The modern corporate income tax did not begin to emerge until the Sixteenth Amendment was ratified. As in 1894, Congress' first post-amendment corporate income tax, 38 Stat. 166, 172 (1913), operated like a prepayment of the individual income tax rather than as a separate levy. Dividends were exempt from the base, or "normal," tax of one percent on individual income. Although they were subject to the graduated surtax of up to six percent in the case of higher incomes, the corporate tax rate was identical to the normal tax rate, allowing for essentially complete integration of the two taxes as a single system.[3]

---

1. See Bank, "Entity Theory as Myth in the Origins of the Corporate Income Tax," 43 Wm. & Mary L. Rev. 447 (2001).

2. Another rationale offered for the adoption of a corporate excise tax at this time was its ability to serve as a tool of corporate regulation. See Avi–Yonah, "Corporations, Society, and the State: A Defense of the Corporate Tax," 90 Va. L. Rev. 1193 (2004); Kornhauser, "Corporate Regulation and the Origins of the Corporate Income Tax, 66 Ind. L.J. 53 (1990).

3. Because there was an exemption of $3,000 that applied to individuals but not corporations, the integration of the two systems was not complete. Those relatively few

Corporate income was subject to a one percent rate at the corporate level and up to a six percent surtax rate at the shareholder level, just as income earned individually was subject to a one percent normal rate and up to a six percent surtax rate. During World War I, however, the corporate and normal rates began to diverge, lessening the value of the dividend exemption and reinforcing the separate status of the corporation for tax purposes. In 1936, the dividend exemption was repealed entirely, introducing the full double taxation of corporate income that has been characteristic of the modern system for most of the last century. See ¶ 1060 for discussion of proposals to reintegrate the corporate and individual income taxes.

The double taxation of corporate earnings has tended to discourage use of the corporate form by closely held businesses even where nontax considerations make the corporate form desirable. To mitigate this problem, in 1958, Congress adopted the Subchapter S provisions. Under these provisions, a closely held corporation that meets certain conditions set forth in Section 1361 may elect to be taxed under the provisions of Subchapter S (Sections 1361 through 1379). The Code refers to a corporation that makes the Subchapter S election as an "S corporation," while a corporation that does not have an S corporation election in effect for a taxable year is called a "C corporation." § 1361(a). Under the S corporation election, the corporation's net income generally passes through and is taxed to the corporation's shareholders, regardless of whether the income is distributed to those shareholders. § 1366. Similarly, under this election, the corporation's net losses generally pass through and are reported on the shareholders' own returns. § 1366. An S corporation generally bears no separate income tax at the corporate level, except in the case of certain built-in gains (i.e., gains attributable to appreciation in the corporation's assets accruing before the effective date of the Subchapter S election), and certain amounts of passive investment income. See §§ 1374, and 1375. The Subchapter S provisions are considered in detail in Chapter 15 of this book. The provisions of Subchapter C of the Code (Sections 301 through 385) are the primary focus of Chapters 1 through 13 of this book.

For additional commentary concerning the provisions of Subchapter C, see the following helpful reference materials: H. Abrams & R. Doernberg, Federal Corporate Taxation (5th ed. 2002); B. Bittker & J. Eustice, Federal Income Taxation of Corporations and Shareholders–Student Edition (7th ed. 2000); and D. Kahn & J. Lehman, Corporate Income Taxation (5th ed. 2005).

shareholders who would not otherwise be subject to tax because of the individual exemption would be indirectly burdened by the application of the corporate tax.

B. COMPUTATION OF C CORPORATION'S TAXABLE INCOME

[¶ 1005]

1. IN GENERAL

A C corporation calculates its taxable income in a manner that parallels the calculation of an individual's taxable income, but with some important variations. §§ 61 and 63(a). For example, a corporation may not claim deductions for personal exemptions or the standard deduction. The Code currently contains no rate preference for a corporation's long-term capital gain income, whereas Section 1(h) generally limits the top rate on an individual's net long-term capital gains to 15 percent.[4] A corporation cannot deduct capital losses in excess of capital gains (Section 1211(a)), and generally may carry back such excess capital losses only to each of the three years before the loss and carry forward such excess capital losses to each of the five years following the loss (Section 1212(a)(1)(A) and (B)). A corporation's charitable contribution deduction may not exceed 10 percent of its taxable income (as specially computed for this purpose). § 170(b)(2). A publicly held corporation cannot deduct compensation in excess of $1 million per year paid to its chief executive officer or to any of its other four most highly compensated officers unless the compensation relates to achieving certain performance goals. § 162(m).

Further, special limits are placed on a corporation's choice of a tax accounting method. Sections 447 and 448 generally require a corporation to use the accrual method of accounting. However, in general personal service corporations, corporations having average annual gross receipts of $5 million or less, and small farms are excepted from this rule. §§ 447(c) and (d) and 448(b)(2) and (3).

On the other hand, a corporation is entitled to some deductions that are not available to individual taxpayers. For example, one important deduction that is central to tax planning in the Subchapter C area—the dividends-received deduction in Section 243—may allow a corporation to deduct an amount equal to 70, 80, or 100 percent of the dividends it receives from other corporations (depending on its percentage of stock ownership in the corporate payor and on certain other conditions). See ¶ 4100. (Since this deduction is based upon a receipt, rather than an expenditure, it would have been less confusing to call it an exclusion.)

Further, a C corporation is entitled, with some exceptions, to claim deductions free of the at risk rules in Section 465 and the special limits on the deductibility of investment interest in Section 163(d), so-called hobby losses in Section 183, and passive activity losses in Section 469. However, certain closely held C corporations are subject to the at risk rules of Section 465. See § 465(a)(1)(B) and (a)(3). In addition, the

---

4. For gain from the sale of capital assets that are "collectibles" and that are held for more than one year, the top rate remains 28 percent. For certain depreciation recapture gain on depreciable real property, the top rate is 25 percent.

Section 469 passive activity loss limits apply to certain personal service corporations and, in modified form, to certain closely held C corporations (other than personal service corporations). See § 469(a)(2)(B) and (C), and (e)(2).

Finally, a separate array of other statutory measures, relating to both income and deductions, cover dealings between corporations and their shareholders. These statutory measures are discussed throughout the remainder of Chapters 1 through 15 of this book.

[¶ 1007]

2. THE DOMESTIC PRODUCTION DEDUCTION

For many years, Congress sought to stimulate exports through a variety of income tax subsidies. However, the WTO ruled that those provisions constituted an export subsidy that was prohibited by WTO agreements. Accordingly, in 2004 that approach was replaced by a special deduction that was made available to a broad range of manufacturers and other producers without regard to whether their products are exported. Unlike most deductions, the deduction extended by Section 199 is not attributable to an expenditure. Rather, the deduction is equal to a percentage of the taxpayer's net income from "qualified production activities." The general effect of the provision, therefore, is to exempt a portion of the favored income from tax. After a phase-in period that began in 2005 and continues to 2010, the percentage of qualified income that will be exempt from tax will be nine percent. Since business income is generally taxed at approximately 35 percent, that nine percent deduction was intended to provide tax relief roughly equivalent to a three percent reduction in the tax rate. The deduction is available to all taxpayers, incorporated or not, and thus includes partnerships and individuals. The deduction may not exceed 50 percent of the wages paid by the taxpayer during the year.

The principal source of qualified production activities income will be income attributable to the sale or lease of personal property, software, or sound recordings manufactured or produced by the taxpayer "in whole or in significant part" in the United States. However, the favored income also includes income attributable to (a) the sale or lease of motion pictures if over 50 percent of the compensation paid in producing the film is attributable to services performed in the United States, (b) the sale of electricity, natural gas, or potable water produced in the United States and (c) construction preformed in the United States.

Because the deduction is intended to assist U. S. manufacturing, income derived from the provision of services or retailing is not eligible for the deduction. As a result, the provision requires some difficult line drawing. For example, the legislative history suggests that making sausages at a meat packing place would qualify but making sausages by the chef at a restaurant would not. Similarly, it is not always clear which firm is the manufacturer entitled to the deduction. For example, when one firm contracts with another for the processing of inventory, the deduction may belong to the "principal" rather than to the physical manufacturer. See IRS Notice 2005–14, 2005–7 I.R.B. 498; Seago, "Who Is Worthy of the Producers' Deduction for Production Under Contract?," 38 Tax Notes 721 (2005).

The qualified production activities income taken into account for this purpose cannot exceed the taxpayer's taxable income for the year. Somewhat oddly for a provision designed to assist the struggling U. S. manufacturing sector, this limitation means that if a taxpayer incurs a loss for the year, either attributable to current losses or net operating loss carryovers from other years, the taxpayer is not entitled to any deduction and thus obtains no benefit from this provision. That restriction creates an incentive for taxpayers to devise ways to shift the benefit of the deduction to other taxpayers with which they contract.

To compute the amount of its deduction, the taxpayer must first allocate its gross receipts between its qualified and non-qualified activities. For an integrated manufacturer/retailer, that will require allocating the proceeds of the final sale of an item between the value created by manufacturing and the value added by the distribution activities. The taxpayer must then allocate its expenses, which would include general overhead expenses, between the qualified and non-qualified activities in order to compute the net qualified production activities income.

C. CORPORATE AND SHAREHOLDER TAX RATES

[¶ 1010]

1. HISTORIC RELATIONSHIP BETWEEN TOP CORPORATE AND INDIVIDUAL TAX RATES

Historically, the top corporate tax rate was lower (and, at many times, substantially lower) than the top individual tax rate. For example, upon enactment of the Internal Revenue Code of 1954, the top corporate rate was 48 percent and the top individual rate was 91 percent. In 1981, before the rate cuts made by the Economic Recovery Act of 1981, the top corporate rate was 46 percent and the top individual rate was 70 percent. In 1986, before the rate cuts made by the Tax Reform Act of 1986, the top corporate rate was 46 percent and the top individual rate was 50 percent. As discussed in Chapter 7, this gap between the top corporate and individual tax rates led to efforts by individual taxpayers to shift income from themselves to their corporations in order to have the income taxed at the lower corporate rates. These efforts, in turn, led to the enactment of Code provisions designed to discourage such income shifting, including the provisions relating to personal holding companies,

¶ 7005, unreasonable accumulations of corporate earnings and profits, ¶ 7035, collapsible corporations (now repealed), and commonly controlled multiple corporations, ¶ 14,005.

The 1986 Act, however, reduced the top individual rate to 28 percent and the top corporate rate to 34 percent, thus inverting the historic relationship between the top corporate and individual tax rates. Although Congress in 1990 raised the top individual rate to 31 percent, it left the top corporate rate at 34 percent. For the period from 1987 to 1992, this inversion in the relationship of the top corporate and individual tax rates led to greater use of the partnership and S corporation forms by new businesses, an increase in the number of Subchapter S elections by qualifying existing C corporations, and the disincorporation of some existing businesses that had been operating in the C corporation form. The 1993 Act restored the historic relationship between the top corporate and individual tax rates by raising the top nominal individual rate to 39.6 percent and the top nominal corporate rate to 35 percent.[5] This change, however, did not lead to a return to the use of the C corporation form of doing business, because the double tax on a C corporation's earnings still served as a disincentive. The 2001 and 2003 Acts left corporate tax rates unchanged but enacted a gradual reduction in individual rates. In 2006, the maximum individual rate of 35 percent was the same as the maximum corporate tax rate, thus further discouraging the use of C corporations.

[¶ 1015]

2. CORPORATE TAX RATES UNDER CURRENT LAW

Under Section 11, the taxable income of a corporation is subject to tax at the following rates:

Taxable Income	Rates
Up to $50,000	15 percent
$50,001 to $75,000	25 percent
$75,001 to $10,000,000	34 percent
Over $10,000,000	35 percent

The rates below 34 percent are phased out for a corporation with taxable income in excess of $100,000 in any taxable year[6] and the 34

---

5. Certain individuals who are subject to various floors on, and phaseouts of, itemized deductions and the phaseout of personal exemptions in Section 151(d)(3) may face an effective top marginal rate greater than the top nominal individual marginal rate. Moreover, certain corporations face an effective top marginal rate greater than 35 percent because of provisions in Section 11(b)(1) that phase out the corporate rates below 35 percent.

6. Section 11(b)(1) increases the amount of tax fixed under the above graduated rate table by the lesser of (a) five percent of that excess or (b) $11,750. Thus, a corporation with taxable income of between $335,000 and $10,000,000 is taxed at a flat rate of 34 percent, and a corporation with taxable income of between $100,000 and $335,000 has

percent rate is phased out for a corporation with taxable income in excess of $15,000,000.[7] The current statute contains no rate preference for a corporation's net long-term capital gains; thus, such gains are taxed at the regular rates in Section 11.[8]

Since the first $50,000 of a corporation's taxable income is taxed at only 15 percent and the next $25,000 of taxable income at a rate of only 25 percent, a strong incentive exists for individuals subject to the higher individual marginal tax rates on income to shift relatively small amounts of taxable income to corporations. While C corporations can be used in this manner to reduce the income tax burden on some small businesses, it is no longer desirable for an individual engaged in rendering personal services to set up a corporation to perform those services and collect the income. Section 11(b)(2) provides that the taxable income of a "qualified personal service corporation" is to be taxed at a flat rate of 35 percent. A qualified personal service corporation is a corporation of which (i) substantially all of the activities involve performing services in the fields of health, law, engineering, architecture, accounting, actuarial science, performing arts, and consulting and (ii) substantially all of the stock is held by employees or retired employees or by their estates or beneficiaries of their estates. §§ 11(b)(2) and 448(d)(2).

[¶ 1020]

3. TAX RATES OF INDIVIDUAL SHAREHOLDERS

Under the doctrine of Eisner v. Macomber, 252 U.S. 189 (1920), corporate earnings are not taxable to the shareholders until that wealth is realized either through a distribution or a sale of the stock in the corporation. Until 2003, the typical individual investor faced two widely different rates of tax upon the withdrawal of funds from a corporation depending upon which of those paths were chosen. Earnings distributed as a dividend were subject to tax at ordinary income tax rates. However, since the stock was a capital asset, its sale would produce a capital gain or loss. Throughout most of the history of the income tax, capital gains were taxed at a rate roughly one-half of the rate applicable to ordinary income. In that environment corporate tax planners attempted to find ways for an individual shareholder to enjoy the value of corporate earnings at the lower capital gains tax rates through either a sale or

---

an effective top *marginal* tax rate of 39 percent (34 percent plus the supplementary tax of five percentage points).

7. Section 11(b)(1) increases the amount of tax fixed under the above graduated rate table by the lesser of (a) three percent of that excess or (b) $100,000. Thus, a corporation with taxable income of $18,333,334 or more is taxed at a flat rate of 35 percent, and a corporation with taxable income of between $15,000,000 and $18,333,334 has

an effective top *marginal* tax rate of 38 percent (35 percent plus the supplementary tax of three percentage points).

8. Section 1201(a) provides an alternative rate of 35 percent on a corporation's net capital gain. However, that provision has no effect unless Congress raises the top rate in Section 11 above 35 percent (determined without regard to the phaseout provisions in Section 11(b)(1)).

exchange of the shareholder's stock or a distribution from the corporation that is treated, for tax purposes, as a sale or exchange of the shareholder's stock. Thus, for example, if a corporate distribution could be structured as a redemption that qualified for exchange treatment under Section 302, the shareholder's gain on the redemption would be taxed at the lower capital gains rates, rather than the higher rates applicable to ordinary dividend income.

In 2003, however, Congress provided that most dividends received by non-corporate shareholders would be taxed at the rates applicable to a long-term capital gain rather than the rates applicable to ordinary income. § 1(h). Moreover, that rate of tax on either sales of stock or dividends was reduced to a maximum of 15 percent. For taxpayers whose ordinary income is taxed at a rate below 25 percent, the rate is only 5 percent and is scheduled to be reduced to zero beginning in 2008. The 2003 provisions, however, are presently scheduled to expire at the end of the 2010 tax year.[9] Those 2003 capital gains rates compare quite favorably to the rate of tax imposed on ordinary income which in 2006 reached a maximum of 35 percent.

In that changed environment, for many individual taxpayers the realization of corporate earnings at capital gains rates has lost much of its importance. On a sale, the taxpayer might be entitled to a tax-free return of tax basis, a benefit that is not available for dividends, but the amount taxed is taxed at the same rate. Nevertheless, for corporate taxpayers and for some individual taxpayers, the distinction between dividends and gains on the sale of stock remains crucial. All of this is examined in detail in Chapter 4.

Regardless of the rate of tax imposed on dividend income, the distinction between ordinary income and capital gains remains important, particularly in connection with the claiming of capital losses. Under Section 1211, capital losses may be offset, in the case of corporations, only against capital gains and, in the case of individuals, only against capital gains and up to $3,000 of ordinary income. Thus, a taxpayer with significant capital losses will want income to be characterized as capital gain so that a current deduction may be claimed for the capital losses. Moreover, a short-term capital gain remains taxable at ordinary income tax rates. Accordingly, and somewhat oddly, the gain on the sale of stock held for less than one year, i.e., a short-term capital gain, may be taxed far more heavily than a dividend.

---

9. Moreover, in 1993 Congress added Section 1202 to the Code to allow noncorporate taxpayers who hold qualified small business stock for more than five years to exclude 50 percent of any gain realized on the sale or exchange of the stock if certain conditions are met, thus reducing the *effec-* *tive* top tax rate on a qualifying long-term capital gain to 14 percent (i.e., 50 percent of the 28 percent top tax rate that applies to long-term capital gain from the sale of small business stock since such gain does not qualify for the lower rates discussed above). See ¶ 3080.

D. ALTERNATIVE MINIMUM TAX

[¶ 1025]

1. DESCRIPTION OF ALTERNATIVE MINIMUM TAX SYSTEM

As a response to the fact that many taxpayers with high economic incomes paid little or no federal income tax, Congress enacted in 1969 a "minimum tax on tax preferences," under which a tax of 10 percent was imposed on a corporate or individual taxpayer's items of tax preference. The tax evolved into a 15 percent "add-on minimum tax," which was added to a corporation's regular tax liability. Relatively few taxpayers were affected in a material way by this levy.

The Tax Reform Act of 1986, however, contained an alternative minimum tax, which made sweeping changes in the earlier versions of the minimum tax and which has a far greater impact than its predecessors. The alternative minimum tax is set forth in Sections 55 through 59. The tax rate was raised from 15 to 20 percent for corporations and the items treated as tax preference items were substantially expanded with a view to preventing corporations from avoiding significant tax through use of exclusions, deductions, and credits that are taken into account in computing their regular tax liability. As a result, many major U.S. corporations have to pay substantial alternative minimum tax even though they are substantially or completely exempt from the regular corporate tax.

Like the alternative tax for individuals, the corporate alternative tax has never been popular with taxpayers and calls for its repeal recur frequently. Most recently, in 2005 the final report of the President's Advisory Panel on Federal Tax Reform included provisions recommending the repeal of both the individual and corporate alternative minimum taxes. Thus far, however, those recommendations remain unheeded.

The alternative minimum tax creates a tax system largely independent of the regular corporate tax system. Three basic steps are involved in calculating the alternative minimum tax:

1.   The corporate taxpayer calculates its corporate income tax in the normal way, using all available exclusions and deductions and using the normal corporate tax rates.

2.   Then a "tentative minimum tax" is computed as follows:

(a) The corporation recomputes its taxable income by adding to it the tax preference items described in Section 57 and by making the adjustments called for in Sections 56 and 58. § 55(b)(2). The result is alternative minimum taxable income, which is intended to produce a tax base that is closer to the taxpayer's true economic income than is taxable income determined in the usual way.

¶ 1025

(b) Alternative minimum taxable income is then reduced by an exemption amount of $40,000. § 55(d)(2). This amount, however, is reduced (but not below zero) by 25 percent of the amount by which alternative minimum taxable income exceeds $150,000, and the exemption disappears when alternative minimum taxable income reaches or exceeds $310,000. (A controlled group of corporations is entitled to only one exemption amount. § 1561(a)(3).)

(c) The flat rate of 20 percent for corporations is then applied to alternative minimum taxable income reduced by the exemption amount (if any) and the corporation's alternative minimum tax foreign tax credit (if any) is then subtracted from this amount, producing a tentative minimum tax. § 55(b)(1)(B).

3. If the tentative minimum tax exceeds the regular income tax, the excess must be paid in addition to the regular tax. § 55(a).

The most striking difference between the alternative minimum tax and the add-on minimum tax that was in place before the 1986 changes is that under prior law, add-on items of tax preference for a given taxable year did not have collateral effects on tax liability in subsequent years. By contrast, the present alternative minimum tax is a distinct alternative system for computing tax liability, under which tax preferences of one year may affect the computation of tax liability in subsequent years. For example, in some cases, alternative minimum taxable income uses slower depreciation rates than may be used in computing "regular" taxable income (Section 56(a)(1)), and in computing gain on the disposition of the assets for alternative minimum tax purposes the adjusted basis is determined with reference to alternative minimum tax depreciation. § 56(a)(6). Also, the net operating loss for alternative minimum tax purposes is computed with reference to alternative minimum taxable income, and the alternative minimum tax net operating loss deduction is carried back and/or forward to offset up to 90 percent of alternative minimum taxable income in other years. § 56(a)(4) and (d). Thus, under the alternative minimum tax, corporations potentially affected are required to maintain two separate sets of books for tax purposes—the regular tax set and the alternative minimum tax set.

[¶ 1030]

2. DETERMINATION OF ALTERNATIVE MINIMUM TAXABLE INCOME

Alternative minimum taxable income is determined by adding items of tax preference and making a variety of other adjustments to taxable income. Some of these adjustments that serve to highlight the sweep of the alternative minimum tax system are summarized below:

1. ***Adjusted current earnings (ACE) adjustment***. For many corporations, this adjustment will be the most significant and it produces

an alternative tax liability for many corporations that owe little regular corporate tax. Corporations are required to include in their alternative minimum taxable income 75 percent of the excess (if any) of the corporation's adjusted current earnings over alternative minimum taxable income computed without this adjustment. § 56(g)(1). "Adjusted current earnings" for this purpose means alternative minimum taxable income as *further* adjusted to reflect certain items that otherwise are excludible from income or deductible for alternative minimum taxable income purposes. The general effect of these adjustments is to approximate the computation of earnings and profits (a concept that is used in determining whether a corporation's distributions to its shareholders are taxable "dividends" for federal income tax purposes, as will be discussed in Chapter 4). See § 56(g)(3) and (4). This current earnings adjustment is aimed primarily at large corporations that report large earnings to their shareholders but pay little or no federal tax because their earnings consist largely of such items as tax-exempt state and local governmental bond interest, dividends exempt from tax under Section 243, and similar items of economic, but not taxable, income.

2. *Accelerated depreciation*. A corporation computes depreciation for alternative minimum tax purposes under special rules that may provide smaller depreciation deductions in the early years of the asset's useful life than does the accelerated cost recovery system. § 56(a)(1). As noted above, the adjusted basis for computing alternative minimum tax gain on the disposition of depreciable assets is determined with reference to alternative minimum tax depreciation. § 56(a)(6).

3. *Tax-exempt interest*. Corporations must include in alternative minimum taxable income interest on certain otherwise tax exempt "private activity" state and local governmental bonds (generally, those bonds the proceeds of which are used in private businesses), reduced by the amount of deductions not allowed for regular income tax purposes that would be allowed if interest on the bonds were includible in gross income. § 57(a)(5).

[¶ 1035]

3. CREDIT FOR PRIOR YEAR MINIMUM TAX LIABILITY

As illustrated in the preceding section, a portion of the alternative minimum tax liability is attributable to timing differences between the alternative tax and the regular tax and a portion is attributable to items that are permanently excluded from the regular tax. To prevent income from being taxed twice, once when it is taken into account under the alternative minimum tax calculation and again when it is taken into account under the regular income tax calculation, corporations are permitted to credit any alternative minimum tax liability paid in previous taxable years that is attributable to timing differences against regular tax liability for any later year (to the extent that such regular tax liability exceeds the corporation's tentative minimum tax liability for the year and after reduction of regular tax liability for certain other tax credits). § 53.

[¶ 1040]

4. ELIGIBLE CREDITS AGAINST ALTERNATIVE MINIMUM TAX LIABILITY

Only a few credits (other than the Section 53 credit described above) may be used by a corporation to reduce its alternative minimum tax liability. One such credit is the general business credit, which may be used for alternative minimum tax purposes to the limited extent provided in Section 38(c). In addition, a corporation may reduce its alternative minimum tax liability by applying the alternative minimum tax foreign tax credit. § 59(a).

[¶ 1045]

5. EXEMPTION FOR SMALL CORPORATIONS

Congress came to believe that the alternative minimum tax inhibits capital formation and business enterprise and is inordinately complex, particularly for small businesses. H.R. Rep. No. 148, 105th Cong., 1st Sess. 351–52 (1997). Accordingly, under a provision enacted as part of the Taxpayer Relief Act of 1997, a corporation that satisfies certain gross receipts tests is treated as a "small corporation" that is exempt from the alternative minimum tax during the period that it remains a small corporation. § 55(e)(1). A corporation initially qualifies as a small corporation if it had average gross receipts of $5,000,000 or less for the three-year period that ended with its first taxable year beginning after 1996. § 55(e)(1)(A). A corporation that initially qualifies as a small corporation will continue to be exempt from the alternative minimum tax for so long as its average gross receipts for the previous three years are $7,500,000 or less. § 55(e)(1)(B).

If a corporation loses its small corporation status because it fails to satisfy the $7,500,000 gross receipts test, the corporation will then become liable for the alternative minimum tax. The determination of the corporation's alternative minimum tax liability, however, is modified so that certain preferences and adjustments are based only on transactions and investments that were entered into after the corporation lost its status as a small corporation. § 55(e)(2) and (e)(3). Moreover, the amount of the corporation's Section 53 alternative minimum tax credit is subject to a special limit. § 55(e)(5).

[¶ 1050]

E. CONSOLIDATED RETURNS

Pursuant to Sections 1501 through 1504 the members of an affiliated group of corporations are permitted to file a single consolidated federal income tax return (rather than separate returns for all members) if all members of the group consent. As discussed in more detail in Chapter 14, there are several tax advantages that may be obtained from using consolidated returns. First, operating losses of one member of the affiliated group generally may be offset against the income of another member of the affiliated group. Second, capital losses of one member of the affiliated group may be offset against the capital gains of another member of the affiliated group. Third, gains or income on intercompany transactions between members of the affiliated group are deferred and, thus, not subject to current income tax. Of course, a potential disadvantage of filing a consolidated return is that losses on such intercompany transactions are also deferred. Fourth, deductions or credits that contain limits based on a taxpayer's gross or taxable income are generally applied on the basis of the consolidated income of the group members. Finally, intercompany dividends paid by one group member to another group member are eliminated from consolidated income and, thus, are not taxable. Note, however, that whether or not consolidated returns are filed, it is possible to avoid tax on intercompany dividend distributions received by one member of an affiliated group from another member by virtue of a 100 percent dividends-received deduction under Section 243(a)(3). See ¶ 4100.

An "affiliated group" is defined as one or more chains of "includible corporations," which are all corporations (with certain exceptions spelled out in Section 1504(b)), connected through stock ownership with an includible corporation common parent, provided that: (1) the common parent directly owns stock possessing at least 80 percent of the total voting power of at least one of the other includible corporations and having a value equal to at least 80 percent of the total value of the stock of that corporation, and (2) stock meeting the 80 percent tests in each includible corporation (other than the common parent) is owned directly by one or more of the other includible corporations. § 1504(a). For purposes of the 80 percent tests, "stock" does not include certain nonvoting and nonconvertible preferred stock. § 1504(a)(4).

The right to offset losses of one corporation against income of another included in a consolidated return sometimes encourages an affiliated group that is profitable overall to acquire a corporation or an affiliated group that has accumulated losses. There are important restrictions on the use of losses of an acquired corporation (or affiliated group) to offset and thereby eliminate taxes on the income of an acquiring corporation or group. These restrictions are discussed at ¶¶ 13,110 through 13,125.

[¶ 1055]

F. INTRODUCTION TO CHOICE OF ENTITY CONSIDERATIONS

In planning for the formation of any business enterprise, one inevitable question is whether the business should be incorporated or conducted through a partnership or other unincorporated business form. That important decision will depend on a wide range of legal and financial considerations, tax and nontax, with often contradictory implications. The following discussion is intended to be introductory in nature and discusses only some of the tax and nontax factors that influence the choice of entity determination.

Nontax factors. Raising capital from outside investors is usually facilitated by use of a corporation rather than a partnership or other unincorporated business form. This is because certain types of outside investors, such as financial institutions, are subject to legal restrictions on their ability to invest in unincorporated enterprises. Also, some venture capitalists and public shareholders simply are hesitant to invest in an entity other than a corporation.

In addition, business lawyers often place considerable weight on the relative certainty of the corporate governance rules provided by state law, a factor that favors the corporate form for conducting a business enterprise. For example, a minority shareholder in a corporation can readily be given the right to veto certain actions sought by the majority but it is more difficult to achieve a comparable result in a partnership because of the broad authority of a general partner to bind the partnership vis-à-vis a third party. Nevertheless, a carefully drafted partnership agreement can normally resolve most of the governance issues of concern to the parties.

If the participants want limited liability for their business venture, that factor may favor the corporate form for conducting the business. However, the venture could be conducted through a hybrid form of business entity, the "limited liability company" (LLC), an entity which has the corporate attribute of limited liability for all equity owners but which can be operated in a manner similar to a partnership. (Prior to the widespread use of the LLC, a modified form of limited liability was achieved by structuring the enterprise as a limited partnership with a corporation as the sole general partner.) Importantly, the owners of an LLC normally may elect to cause it to be taxed either as a corporation or as a partnership. The LLC has an important advantage over a limited partnership in that all members of an LLC enjoy limited liability and still may participate in the management of the entity, whereas limited partners generally may not participate in the management of the partnership without losing their limited liability shield. On the other hand, in any closely held business enterprise, actually attaining limited liability may be problematic. Creditors of a closely held corporations often require the corporation's shareholders to guarantee loans made to the corporation, and courts may pierce the corporate veil to reach the shareholders' assets to discharge a judgment in tort litigation against an undercapitalized, closely held corporation.

Estate planning lawyers may also voice a preference for the corporate form for a number of reasons. For example, gifts or bequests of shares of a corporation may readily be effected to family members, charities, and others. Gifts of interests in a general or limited partnership, on the other hand, may present complications or even insuperable obstacles.

Finally, it is often much cheaper to form a corporation than a partnership. Today the preparation of a corporate charter and bylaws is often a matter of filling in blanks on a form that resides on a lawyer's computer while partnership agreements and the operating agreements of LLCs are more commonly tailor-made and thus far more time-consuming to prepare.

Tax factors. Frequently, of course, the controlling factor in the choice of an entity is the desire to minimize the overall income tax burdens on the owners of the business enterprise. A business enterprise conducted through a partnership or an LLC treated as a partnership for tax purposes is subject to only one level of tax, at the partner level. § 701. Further, the federal tax law allows the partners or LLC members considerable flexibility in making special allocations of the income and deductions of the partnership's or LLC's business enterprise among themselves if they so desire. See § 704. An S corporation also generally is subject to only one level of tax, at the shareholder level (Sections 1363 and 1366), but only corporations meeting certain requirements may make the Subchapter S election and there is a limit on the number and types of shareholders that may hold stock in an S corporation. However, these restrictions have been liberalized continuously. See § 1361. Further, an S corporation generally must allocate its income and deductions in accordance with the shareholders' stock ownership and thus does not have the flexibility accorded partnerships to make special allocations of income and deductions. See § 1366.

By contrast, a C corporation (or an LLC that is taxed as a corporation) generally is subject to two levels of tax on its earnings, one at the corporate level and a second at the shareholder level when the net earnings are distributed to the shareholders or the shareholders sell their corporate stock. The significance of that double tax is primarily a function of the relationship among the different rates of tax applicable to different types of income: the individual rates on business income, dividends or capital gains and the corporate tax rate.[10] In recent years, Congress has altered these relationships repeatedly, sometimes dramatically. That volatility in tax rates has greatly complicated tax planning in general and the proper choice of entity in particular.

Since the maximum tax rates applicable to the business income of an individual at present are roughly identical to the maximum tax rates applicable to the income of a corporation, any additional tax imposed on the realization of corporate profits by shareholders (as upon a dividend or sale of stock) will cause the overall tax burden on corporate income to exceed the burden imposed on the income of partnerships. For example, at present partnership income is taxed at a single maximum rate of 35 percent. Corporate income is also taxed at 35 percent but is in addition subject to a 15 percent tax upon distribution to individual shareholders. The combined effect of a corporate tax rate of 35 percent and an individual rate of 15 percent produces an overall rate of tax of nearly 45 percent. Given this rate relationship, in most instances the income tax burden on the shareholders of a C corporation will be greater than the income tax burden on the partners of a partnership or members of an LLC that has elected to be taxed as a partnership.

In many instances, however, the relative disadvantage of the C corporation form can be offset by rules or techniques that reduce either the corporate level or the shareholder level tax, or both. For example, the corporate level tax may be avoided to the extent that the corporation can transfer funds out of corporate solution to its shareholders in a manner that is deductible rather than as nondeductible dividends. Thus, payments characterized as salaries for services rendered by the shareholders to the corporation, as rent for property owned by the shareholders and leased by the corporation, or as interest on loans made to the corporation by the shareholders all avoid the corporate level tax.

Second, the income of small corporations is not taxed at the maximum rate. In fact, since the first $75,000 of corporate income is taxed at rates of 15 and 25 percent, that amount of corporate income may be taxed at a rate that is lower than the tax that would be paid on that income if it were derived directly by an individual. Accordingly, the C corporate form may produce a smaller tax on businesses that generate relatively low levels of taxable income.

Until 2003, the burden of the shareholder level tax could be reduced if the corporation avoided distributing dividends, accumulated its earnings, and allowed the shareholder to benefit from those earnings at a later date through sales of stock (perhaps including sales back to the

---

10. Double taxation does not necessarily mean heavy taxation. The aggregate burden of the taxes imposed at both the corporate and shareholder levels can be, and during some periods were, lower than the burden imposed upon partnership income derived by individual partners.

issuing corporation). However, because dividends and gain on the sale of stock are now taxed at the same rate, that strategy will only have a material effect if the shareholder has a high tax basis for the stock being sold so that a significant portion of the proceeds of sale will not be subject to tax. In general, that means that the burden of the shareholder level tax can be reduced only if the corporate stock is held until death and benefits from a step-up in tax basis under Section 1014.

In sum, except for these few special cases, C corporations are taxed more heavily than is unincorporated business or S corporations. However, under current law that additional burden is relatively small and can be reduced. As a result, the additional tax burden may not outweigh the importance of non-tax factors that favor incorporation.

If the business venture is expected to experience tax losses (i.e., allowable deductions in excess of gross income) in its early years, the participants in the venture may want to deduct those losses immediately on their own returns. That factor strongly favors use of the partnership, LLC, or S corporation forms for conducting the business venture because the losses of such an entity flow through to its partners, members, or shareholders and may be deducted on their own returns (subject to certain limits). See §§ 702 and 1366. By contrast, the net losses of a C corporation may be deducted only by the corporation and do not flow through to its shareholders. However, those losses can be carried forward and deducted by the corporation in future years.

Moreover, if the entity's operations are to be financed substantially with funds borrowed by the entity, that factor favors use of a partnership or an LLC treated as a partnership for tax purposes because the partners or members will obtain a basis increase in their partnership or LLC interests to reflect their share of liabilities incurred by the entity. This basis increase will support the deduction by such partners or members of losses flowing through from the entity. See § 704(d). By contrast, the shareholders of an S corporation generally cannot include their share of the corporation's liabilities in their adjusted basis for the corporation's stock.

In helping one's clients to resolve the choice of entity question, the tax adviser must consider each of the three distinct patterns of taxation applicable to partnerships and LLCs electing to be taxed as partnerships (in Subchapter K), S corporations (in Subchapter S), and C corporations (in Subchapter C). As you progress through Chapters 2 through 14 of this book which focus on the taxation of C corporations and their shareholders, it will be useful to compare the nontax attributes of each of the forms of conducting a business enterprise as well as to compare the federal income tax consequences produced by Subchapter C with the consequences that would have been produced by the other two regimes of business taxation.

¶ 1055

G. POLICY ISSUES IN TAXATION OF CORPORATIONS AND SHAREHOLDERS

[¶ 1060]

1. CORPORATE TAX INTEGRATION

A number of policy issues arise out of the fact that corporations and their shareholders are separate taxable entities. The issue given most attention has been the double tax imposed first on income at the corporate level and again at the shareholder level either on the distribution of dividends or on gains from the disposition of stock. As explained in the following excerpt, critics of the dual tax regime argue that this regime creates inequities and inefficiencies that could be solved by so-called integration of corporate and shareholder taxes, which would eliminate (or, at least, mitigate) the double taxation of corporate earnings.

[¶ 1065]

STAFF OF JOINT COMMITTEE ON TAXATION FEDERAL INCOME TAX ASPECTS OF CORPORATE FINANCIAL STRUCTURES.

101st Cong., 1st Sess., 84–88 (Jan. 18, 1989).

Advocates of integration contend that the relationship of the separate corporate and individual income taxes tends to create certain distortions in economic decisions that should be alleviated by providing some form of relief from the two-tier tax. Such advocates generally contend that the tax system should seek to provide (1) neutrality between corporate and noncorporate investment, (2) neutrality between debt and equity financing at the corporate level, and (3) neutrality between retention and distribution of corporate earnings.

Corporate vs. noncorporate investment.—The two-tier tax may discourage some from deciding to carry on business in corporate form in situations where nontax considerations indicate that corporate operations would be preferable. (The S corporation rules were developed to address this concern.) The extent to which this may occur depends in large part upon where the corporate tax ultimately falls: whether it is passed on to consumers, employees, or others, or borne by the owners of the corporation's stock.

Debt vs. equity finance.—The two-tier tax in its present form tends to encourage financing corporate investment with debt rather than new equity, because deductible interest payments on corporate debt reduce corporate taxes while nondeductible dividends do not.

¶ 1065

Accordingly, there may be an incentive for corporations to finance investment in excess of retained earnings with new debt rather than equity. To the extent that there is a bias in favor of debt financing, the risk of bankruptcy is increased for corporations, particularly those in cyclical industries.

Some investors, however, may prefer equity to debt. The corporate dividends received deduction provides an incentive for a corporation to invest in stock rather than debt of another corporation. In addition, an issuing corporation with tax losses, or an inability to utilize fully interest deductions for other reasons, may issue preferred stock with characteristics very similar to debt—effectively passing through some of the benefit of its losses to corporate shareholders. * * *

Retention vs. distribution of corporate income.—A further issue is whether the two-tier tax distorts decisions to retain or to distribute corporate earnings. Where shareholders are better able than the corporation to put capital to its most productive use, a tax-based disincentive to distribute earnings creates economic inefficiency.

The two-tier tax on dividend distributions can make it more desirable for a corporation to use retained earnings rather than new equity for its investments. Shareholders can find such earnings retention attractive (subject to the accumulated earnings tax and personal holding company rules) where the shareholder expects to defer tax on capital gains for a substantial period, or intends to hold stock until death (so that appreciation can be passed to his heirs free of individual income tax).

There also may be an incentive under present law to retain earnings if the corporation's effective tax rate on reinvestment is lower than the shareholder tax rate on distributed earnings. By contrast, where the shareholder's tax rate is significantly lower than the corporation's effective tax rate—for example, if the shareholder is a tax-exempt entity or is a corporation entitled to a dividends received deduction—there may be a tax incentive to distribute earnings.

* * *

A RATIONALE FOR INTEGRATION

* * * Billion dollar mergers, acquisitions, and leveraged buyouts are perhaps the most visible transactions facilitating the flow of equity out of corporate solution; however, equity contraction also may be accomplished by redemption, debt-for-equity swaps (including unbundled stock units), and extraordinary distributions. Many commentators have concluded that the unintegrated two-tier income tax encourages these transactions.

To the extent that corporate restructurings are influenced by tax rather than efficiency considerations, the unintegrated income tax may

¶ 1065

be causing a waste of resources. Rising corporate debt levels also may increase the risk of corporate insolvency and the associated costs of bankruptcy. Some economists have suggested that Congress amend the Code to provide partial or full integration of the income tax. * * *

Others argue that relief from the two-tier tax would require substantial tax increases to ensure revenue neutrality. Thus, the economic benefits of integration (if any) would need to be weighed against the economic costs of revenue balancing taxes.

A further consideration in the decision to provide relief from double taxation is the uncertainty about the extent to which the two-tier tax in fact distorts corporate financial decisions. While income taxes generally are considered to provide a disincentive to savings and investment, there is little agreement concerning the effect of the two-tier tax on economic activity. One source of the uncertainty is the widely varying circumstances of corporations and their shareholders, such as differing effective tax rates, need for external funds to finance investment, and ability to pass on corporate taxes to consumers or workers. This uncertainty raises the possibility that measures to relieve double taxation may not have the intended results.

2. *Forms of integration*

There are two broad categories of integration: (1) complete integration, and (2) dividend relief. Complete integration eliminates double taxation of both dividends and retained corporate earnings. S corporations are taxed under a regime of complete integration since earnings of an S corporation, whether retained or distributed, are treated as income of the shareholders for tax purposes.

Dividend relief, unlike complete integration, reduces the double taxation on distributed earnings, with no change in the taxation of retained earnings. Dividend relief may be accomplished by reducing tax at either the corporate or shareholder level. At the corporate level, the tax burden on distributed earnings can be alleviated by means of a dividends-paid deduction or a lower corporate income tax on distributed versus retained income (i.e., a split-rate corporate income tax). At the shareholder level, the tax burden on dividends may be reduced by exemption or by crediting shareholders with tax paid by the corporate distributee (i.e., the imputation method).

COMPLETE INTEGRATION

Relief from the two-tier tax can be achieved by eliminating the corporate tax and including undistributed, as well as distributed, earnings in shareholders' gross income. Under this approach, a corporation's undistributed earnings would be deemed to have been distributed to and reinvested by the shareholders each year. Tax could be collected at the corporate level (in effect using the corporation as a withholding agent for

¶ **1065**

shareholders), or tax could be collected solely at the shareholder level without withholding. Shareholders would be subject to income tax on their allocated earnings and would adjust basis in their shares accordingly.

In one form of this mechanism, all corporations would be treated in a manner similar to either partnerships or S corporations; this treatment would include the passing through of credits and losses as well as the character (ordinary or capital gain) and source (domestic or foreign) of income. Other versions would provide for the pass through of net income but not losses in excess of income, as is the case with real estate investment trusts.

The burden on both distributed and retained corporate earnings also could be relieved, in part, by reducing the corporate income tax rate. Reducing the corporate tax rate to zero, however, would turn corporations into the equivalent of nondeductible individual retirement accounts, since retained earnings and reinvestment income would accumulate tax free within the corporation.

DIVIDEND RELIEF AT THE CORPORATE LEVEL

The double taxation of dividends could be alleviated at the corporate level by allowing a deduction for dividends paid to shareholders. A portion of the double tax on dividends could be eliminated by means of a partial dividends paid deduction, which reduces the corporate tax on distributed as compared to retained corporate income. In 1985, the [Reagan] Administration proposed a deduction of 10 percent of the dividends paid from earnings of a domestic corporation that have borne the regular corporate tax. A similar proposal was included in the House-passed version of the 1986 Act.

DIVIDEND RELIEF AT THE SHAREHOLDER LEVEL

One method for relieving the tax burden on dividends at the shareholder level would be to exclude a portion of dividends from gross income. This alternative has been criticized as reducing the progressivity of the income tax, since the tax benefit of exemption is greatest for shareholders in the highest tax bracket. Shareholders might be required to reduce stock basis, to the extent of tax exempt dividends, to prevent deduction of capital losses associated with untaxed dividends.

An alternative to a shareholder exemption is to give shareholders an income tax credit to reflect all or a portion of the corporate-level tax paid with respect to dividends. The amount of the credit could be adjusted based on the degree to which partial relief from the two-tier tax is desired. Under such a system, shareholders who receive dividends would be required to "gross up" the dividend by the amount of the credit for corporate taxes paid, and include the grossed-up amount in income, while using the credit as an offset to their tax liability. The gross-up and

¶ 1065

credit mechanism is analogous to the credit for taxes withheld on wages under present law.

Gross-up and credit systems, also known as "imputation" systems, are used by several foreign countries including West Germany, France, Canada, and the United Kingdom. A number of these countries grant the shareholder credit only to the extent that the corporation actually has paid tax on dividends (this is accomplished by a corporate minimum tax on distributions). West Germany has a "hybrid" system, with a reduced income tax rate on distributed income at the corporate level, and a gross-up and credit at the shareholder level.

[¶ 1067]

Note

Treasury and ALI corporate integration studies. In January 1992, the Treasury Department issued its corporate integration study, which defines four integration prototypes and describes how each prototype would work:

(1) ***Dividend exclusion prototype***. Under this approach to integration, a corporation would continue to pay tax at the entity level, but shareholders would exclude dividends from income (because they have already been taxed at the corporate level). This approach would require little structural change in the Internal Revenue Code.

(2) ***Shareholder allocation prototype***. Under this approach to integration, all corporate income would be allocated to shareholders and taxed in a manner similar to partnership income under current law.

(3) ***Comprehensive business income tax prototype***. Under this approach to integration, shareholders and bondholders would exclude dividends and interest received from a corporation from income, but neither type of payment would be deductible by the corporation. The Treasury Department indicated that this prototype better achieves tax neutrality because corporate debt and equity receive the same treatment. Further, the Treasury Department concluded that this prototype would be "self-financing" and would permit the corporate rate to be lowered to the then-maximum individual rate of 31 percent on a revenue-neutral basis (even if shareholders' capital gains on corporate stock were fully exempt from tax). However, this prototype would represent a much more comprehensive change from current law and hence would require a longer transition period and a more extensive revision of the current statute to become fully effective.

(4) ***Imputation credit prototype***. Under this approach, the corporate income tax would serve as a withholding tax. Dividends

paid to shareholders would carry a credit for the corporate tax paid on the amount distributed, which would be fully refundable to the shareholders. As an alternative, the corporation would be allowed a deduction for dividends paid to shareholders.

See U.S. Treas. Dep't, Report on Integration of the Individual and Corporate Tax Systems; Taxing Business Income Once (Jan. 6, 1992).

The Treasury Department did not make any legislative proposal in this study but did seem to indicate its preference for the comprehensive business income tax prototype in relation to all of the others and the dividend exclusion prototype to the imputation credit prototype. Because of administrative and complexity concerns, the Treasury Department indicated in this study that it could not recommend the shareholder allocation prototype.

In December 1992, the Treasury Department issued a second, follow-up report to its earlier January 6, 1992, study on corporate integration and recommended enactment of a system similar to the dividend exclusion prototype of corporate integration. Under the proposed dividend exclusion system, a corporation would compute its taxable income and pay tax at the corporate level as under current law. Any distribution out of the corporation's taxable income that remained after paying tax and after making certain adjustments to taxable income (called adjusted taxable income under the proposed system) would be treated as a dividend and would be excludible by the shareholders when received. Distributions in excess of adjusted taxable income would be treated as a nontaxable return of capital to the extent of the shareholder's adjusted basis in the stock and as capital gain to the extent that the distributions were in excess of the shareholder's adjusted basis in the stock. Under this proposal, the integration benefits would not be extended to foreign shareholders by statute but could be extended to such shareholders by treaty.

By contrast, a study by the American Law Institute, issued in 1993, recommended adoption of the shareholder credit method of integration, which would convert the separate corporate income tax into a withholding tax with respect to dividends. Under this approach, a withholding tax would be imposed on dividend distributions, and payments of corporate tax would be fully creditable against the withholding tax. The shareholders would receive a refundable tax credit for the dividend withholding tax. Certain corporate tax preferences (such as tax-exempt bond interest) would be passed through to the shareholders and thus result in no withholding tax upon distribution. Finally, to minimize the differential treatment of debt and equity, a withholding tax would be imposed on corporate payments of interest. That tax, in turn, would be fully creditable by and refundable to the recipients of the interest payments. See Federal Income Tax Project: Integration of the Individual and Corporate Income Taxes (A.L.I. 1993).

¶ 1067

Although these relatively sophisticated approaches to integration have not to date attracted support in the United States, Congress has moved to reduce the burden of the double tax. While rejecting the Administration's proposal in 2003 to eliminate the taxation of dividends, Congress did reduce the rate of tax on dividends to a maximum of 15 percent. That reduction, which is roughly equivalent to exempting half of all dividends received from tax, can be seen as a step in the direction of corporate tax integration.

[¶ 1070]

2.   THE ROLE OF NON–STATUTORY PRINCIPLES

The proper approach to interpreting the rules embodied in the Internal Revenue Code has been the subject of an on-going debate since the inception of the income tax. A literal application of those rules furthers the desirable goals of certainly and predictability and at times may appear more fair. One the other hand, an overly literal interpretation can produce unreasonable results and facilitates taxpayer manipulation of the tax rules. Recently this debate has taken on greater importance as the following passage suggests.

[¶ 1071]

CUNNINGHAM & REPETTI, TEXTUALISM AND TAX SHELTERS*

24 Virginia Tax Review 1 (2004).

I.   INTRODUCTION

During the last decade, a substantial debate has developed over the approaches courts use to interpret statutes. Some have argued that the search for a statute's meaning and purpose should focus on the text itself and should not include consulting legislative history. In contrast, others have argued that it is difficult to determine the meaning of a statute without consulting legislative history to determine the legislature's purpose for enacting the statute.

The debate about the appropriate method for interpreting statutes underlies a crisis in the administration of tax law. The recent proliferation of tax shelters has, at least in part, been facilitated by the ascendancy of textualism. Our conversations with practitioners indicate that tax advisors have become more aggressive in structuring transactions that comply with the form of the tax statutes even though the transactions may be highly questionable in light of the legislation's history or underlying purpose. The result has been a cottage industry where investment banks and accounting firms market tax shelters that triumph in form, but not substance, at the expense of the fisc. Because most tax shelters are hidden,[5] it is difficult to ascertain their revenue impact. It is estimated that tax shelters reduced tax revenues by approximately $10 to $24 billion in 1999.

In addition, practitioners and government officials worry that the use of shelters is eroding confidence in the tax system. * * *

* * *

II. THE ROLE OF LEGISLATIVE INTENT AND LEGISLATIVE HISTORY IN INTERPRETING STATUTES

Scholars have identified four methods of statutory interpretation that courts have used: intentionalism, purposivism, textualism, and the practical reason (or dynamic) method. The first three of these methods have been termed "foundational" because each identifies the primary source for interpreting a statute. In this part, we describe the four types of statutory interpretation. We explain that courts in the United States have traditionally used the intentionalist and purposivist methods of interpretation. We conclude that textualism is inappropriate for interpreting statutes in general and is particularly inappropriate for interpreting tax statutes.

In vogue through the 1920s, intentionalism seeks to determine what the legislature intended the statute to mean by examining committee reports and floor statements by sponsors. This method of interpretation reflects a view that in interpreting a statute, a court acts as the agent of Congress. Under this view, it is appropriate to consult legislative history, even where the statutory language is clear, to insure that the interpretation does not conflict with the legislature's intent.

The purposivist, in contrast, does not inquire what the legislature intended the statute to mean, but rather asks what the statute's purpose was as the time of enactment in order to interpret the statute in a manner consistent with that purpose. The intentionalist and purposivist methods are quite similar. Indeed, purposivism has been described as the fall-back from the concept of legislative intent. The major theoretical difference between the two is that while the intentionalists try to determine what the legislature's intent actually was at the time of enactment, the purposivists try to determine what the statute would have meant at the time of enactment when read by a reasonably

---

5. Most tax shelters are organized as partnerships that are not subject to tax, but instead flow-through their income and losses to partners. In 2002, the Service audited only 0.39% of the tax returns for flow-through entities such as partnerships. Staff of Joint Comm. on Taxation, 108th Cong., Report Relating to the Internal Revenue Service as Required by the IRS Reform and Restructuring Act of 1998, at 37 (Joint Comm. Print 2003).

¶ 1071

intelligent and informed reader. To identify this purpose, the purposivist will also examine legislative history.

The textualist, in contrast, eschews all legislative history, considering it highly suspect. Instead, the textualist looks to the statute's language and other sources to identify the text's meaning. Justice Scalia has stated that the textualist should seek " 'objectified' intent—the intent that a reasonable person would gather from the text of the law, placed alongside the remainder of the corpus juris." He has elaborated on this search for objectified intent in a judicial opinion:

> The meaning of terms on the statute books ought to be determined, not on the basis of which meaning can be shown to have been understood by a larger handful of the Members of Congress; but rather on the basis of which meaning is (1) most in accord with context and ordinary usage, and thus most likely to have been understood by the whole Congress which voted on the words of the statute (not to mention the citizens subject to it), and (2) most compatible with the surrounding body of law into which the provision must be integrated—a compatibility which, by a benign fiction, we assume Congress always has in mind.[34]

Under the textualist method, an interpreter is not limited to examining the text of the statute, itself, and related statutes, but may also consult various textual authorities existing at the time of enactment, such as dictionaries, case law, and possibly treatises. In addition, the interpreter should apply "statutory clear statement rules," strong canons of statutory interpretation setting forth policy presumptions that may only be overcome by statutory text clearly to the contrary. As mentioned above, the one text not consulted is legislative history, except to determine the background context of the legislation where such background may be independently verified.

The fourth method of statutory interpretation is the practical reasoning or dynamic interpretation. This method, developed by William N. Eskridge and Philip P. Frickey, holds that all three foundational methods are not only flawed but also do not reflect what the courts actually do. The practical reasoning method does not reject the foundational methods per se, but rather "refuses to privilege intention, purpose or text as the sole touchstone of interpretation." An interpreter under this model will look

> at a broad range of evidence—text, historical evidence, and the text's evolution—and thus form a preliminary view of the statute. The interpreter then develops that preliminary view by testing various possible interpretations against the multiple criteria of fidelity to the text, historical accuracy, and conformity to circumstances and val-

---

34. Green v. Bock Laundry Mach. Co., 490 U.S. 504, 528 (1989) (Scalia, J., concurring).

ues. Each criterion is relevant, yet none necessarily trumps the others.[41]

What is most important for present purposes is the last aspect of this analysis, the conformity to contemporary circumstances and values. In his book on dynamic interpretation, Professor Eskridge states "the interpreter asks 'not only what the statute means abstractly, or even on the basis of legislative history, but also what it ought to mean in terms of the needs and goals of our present day society.' " He further states, "[s]ometimes the circumstances will be materially different from those contemplated by the statutory drafters, and in that event any application of the statute will be dynamic in a strong sense, going against the drafters' expectations, which have been negated because important assumptions have been undone."

No matter what method of statutory interpretation courts employ, the starting point is always the same: the text. Nevertheless, for over one hundred years the courts have been willing to look at the legislative history of a statute to clarify ambiguities, and to avoid applying the law in ways that produce unintended results. Frequently, the courts will use legislative history to limit the scope of a statute's application in situations that literally fall within the statute's language.

* * *

Legislative history has played an important role in the development of the tax law. Over the past several decades, the Supreme Court has examined tax provisions first by analyzing the language and then by placing those words in the context of the Code and the provision's legislative history. The Court has stated that "the words of statutes— including revenue acts—should be interpreted where possible in their ordinary, everyday senses."[52] But it has tempered this statement by observing:

> We have noted that "[t]he true meaning of a single section of a statute in a setting as complex as that of the revenue acts, however precise its language, cannot be ascertained if it be considered apart from related sections, or if the mind be isolated from the history of the income tax legislation of which it is an integral part."[53]

* * *

III. Textualism Legitimizes Tax Shelters

The ascendancy of textualism has had its greatest impact by facilitating the promotion and sale of "abusive" tax shelters. An "abusive"

---

41. William N. Eskridge, Jr. & Philip P. Frickey, Statutory Interpretation as Practical Reasoning, 42 Stan. L. Rev. 321, 352 (1990).

52. Malat v. Riddell, 383 U.S. 569, 571 (1966) (quoting Crane v. Commissioner, 331 U.S. 1, 6 (1947)).

53. Commissioner v. Engle, 464 U.S. 206, 223 (1984) (quoting Helvering v. Morgan's, Inc., 293 U.S. 121, 126 (1934)).

tax transaction, from the perspective of the Treasury, is a transaction which is designed to technically comply with the letter of the law, but which produces tax savings that are inappropriate to the underlying purposes of the statutory scheme and inconsistent with the economic reality of the transaction.[99] It is in the nature of abusive transactions that the statute in question is inadequate to address the abuse. Thus, the courts, using the intentionalist and purposivist approaches, have crafted additional doctrines that permit the reviewing agency or court to go beyond the literal wording of the statute in order to effectuate its purpose. The use of textualism, however, challenges the legitimacy of these doctrines and supports literal interpretations that are the keystone of tax shelters.

In Part III, we will first briefly describe the doctrines that the courts developed to combat abusive tax transactions using the purposivist and intentionalist methods of interpretation. We will then discuss the manner in which tax advisors have utilized the textualist approach to avoid the judicial doctrines in structuring and rendering legal opinions about tax shelters. The most important of the doctrines, business purpose and economic substance, could not have been developed under textualism and therefore are vulnerable to attack.

A. Judicially–Crafted Doctrines

1. The Business Purpose Doctrine

Using the purposivist and intentionalist methods of statutory interpretation, the courts have developed two broad doctrines to curb abusive transactions: the business purpose doctrine and substance-over-form doctrine. The business purpose doctrine provides that a tax statute will not be applied to a transaction unless the transaction serves some business purpose, other than tax avoidance. Although the courts created the business purpose doctrine based on legislative history that accompanied the adoption of the corporate reorganization tax provisions, they readily applied the doctrine in other tax contexts, including partnerships. In 1949, Judge Learned Hand explained the scope of the doctrine in circumstances other than reorganizations: "The doctrine . . . means that in construing . . . a tax statute which describe[s] commercial or industrial transactions we are to understand [it] to refer to transactions entered upon for commercial or industrial purposes and not to include transactions entered upon for no other motive but to escape taxation."[104]

Where the tax benefit claimed does not relate to a commercial transaction, the business purpose doctrine cannot be applied easily.

---

99. Treas. Reg. § 1.701–2 (as amended in 1995); see also Alan Gunn, The Use and Misuse of Antiabuse Regulations: Lessons from the Partnership Antiabuse Regulations, 54 SMU L. Rev. 159, 164 (2001) (defining abusive transactions).

104. Commissioner v. Transp. Trading & Terminal Corp., 176 F.2d 570, 572 (2d Cir. 1949), cert. denied, 338 U.S. 955 (1950).

¶ 1071

Consequently, the courts have modified application of the doctrine in these settings. * * *

* * *

It is likely that these doctrines would never have been developed by textualists. No statutory language authorized the business purpose doctrine or its subsequent expansion in *Goldstein* [364 F.2d 734 (2d Cir. 1966), cert. denied, 385 U.S. 1005 (1967)]. Rather, the doctrines resulted from the application of the intentionalist and purposivist methods of statutory interpretation by the Court of Appeals in *Gregory*.[109]

2. The Substance–Over–Form Doctrine

The substance-over-form doctrine also originated in the context of corporate taxation.[110] In contrast to the business purpose doctrine, the substance-over-form doctrine is rather amorphous because it applies differently in different contexts and is sometimes known by different names. In general, under this doctrine, courts seek to tax a transaction pursuant to its economic effect, rather than its form. For example, the "step transaction" doctrine disregards steps in a transaction that lack independent economic significance.[111] Similarly, under the "sham transaction" doctrine, where a transaction involves a circular flow of cash or property such that each party does not change its legal or economic position, the transaction will be disregarded.[112] It is likely that a textualist would have developed the step-transaction and sham-transaction doctrines because they seek to characterize facts, not to interpret statutes.

This is not true, however, for the most important variation of the substance-over-form doctrine, the "economic substance" doctrine. Under this doctrine, the courts will deny tax benefits if the purported pre-tax economic profit is insubstantial in relation to the value of the expected tax benefits from the transaction. The economic substance doctrine is a supplement to the business purpose doctrine. The Court of Appeals for the Fourth Circuit has stated that both a business purpose and economic substance must be lacking before it will disregard a transaction.[114] In other words, the presence of either a business purpose or profit motive will suffice to respect the transaction. Consistent with this suggestion,

---

109. See Helvering v. Gregory, 69 F.2d 809, 811 (2d Cir. 1934), aff'd, 293 U.S. 465 (1935).

110. See Commissioner v. Court Holding Co., 324 U.S. 331, 334 (1945).

111. See, e.g., True v. United States, 190 F.3d 1165, 1174–76 (10th Cir. 1999); Associated Wholesale Grocers, Inc. v. United States, 927 F.2d 1517, 1521–22 (10th Cir. 1991).

112. See, e.g., Higgins v. Smith, 308 U.S. 473, 477–78 (1940); Griffiths v. Helver-ing, 308 U.S. 355, 356–58 (1939); Rev. Rul. 78–397, 1978–2 C.B. 150.

114. Rice's Toyota World, Inc. v. Commissioner, 752 F.2d 89, 91–92 (4th Cir. 1985) (stating that the court will disregard a transaction if it finds "that the taxpayer was motivated by no business purposes other than obtaining tax benefits ... *and* that the transaction has no economic substance because no reasonable possibility of a profit exists") (emphasis added).

¶ 1071

most courts apply the economic substance doctrine only after concluding that the transaction does not serve a nontax business purpose other than generating a profit.* * *

In evaluating the profit motive, some courts will compare the magnitude of the profit potential to the tax benefits. Sheldon v. Commissioner[118] is a good example of this approach. There, the court found that no business purpose was present and concluded that the possibility of only an "incidental" profit for a preplanned transaction could not justify the tax benefits.[119] The Tax Court and the Courts of Appeal for the Third, Sixth, and Tenth Circuits have similarly employed this balancing test. Other courts, however, have not engaged in such an explicit balancing test.[122]

The courts would not have developed the economic substance doctrine if they had been using the textualist method of statutory interpretation. The economic substance doctrine, like the business purpose doctrine, is the result of a purposivist or intentionalist method of interpretation. It imposes an additional requirement that is not explicitly expressed in the statutory language. It is based on the judiciary's view that a transaction must have some purpose other than tax avoidance before it may benefit from the provisions of the tax statute.

B. Textualism and Purposive Activity

Despite the potentially wide application of these doctrines, tax advisors have frequently diminished their significance in structuring abusive transactions.[123] Textualism is a major contributor to the problem

---

118. 94 T.C. 738 (1990).

119. Id. at 767–69; see also Kenneth W. Gideon, Mrs. Gregory's Grandchildren: Judicial Restriction of Tax Shelters, 5 Va. Tax Rev. 825, 835–39 (1986) (discussing early cases that address this issue).

122. See, e.g., IES Indus., Inc. v. United States, 253 F.3d 350, 351–56 (8th Cir. 2001). In IES, the Eighth Circuit allowed the taxpayer to claim a capital loss and a foreign tax credit in the following transaction. The taxpayer, IES, purchased foreign stock with the right to receive a dividend that would be subject to a 15% foreign withholding tax. The purchase price for the stock was market value plus 85% of the expected gross dividend. IES sold the stock shortly thereafter for the price it had paid, less the dividend, since it retained the right to receive the dividend. The subsequent receipt of the dividend by IES, less the 15% withholding, allowed IES to fully recover its investment. When the dust had settled, IES had incurred no pre-tax economic gain or loss, but was able to claim a foreign tax credit for the amount withheld on the divi-dend and a capital loss from the stock sale. The Service sought to disallow the foreign tax credit and capital loss, arguing that the transaction was a sham since there was no economic benefit. The Court of Appeals concluded that the transaction was not a sham because an economic profit existed. The court reasoned that the profit was 100% of the gross dividend amount, less the 85% amount attributable to the dividend that the taxpayer paid on acquiring the stock. Although IES never received the 15% of the dividend that was withheld, the court treated such amount as profit because it provided a benefit to the taxpayer; it satisfied IES's tax liability. The court made no attempt to balance this "profit" with the tax benefits the taxpayer obtained from the transaction. See also Compaq Computer Corp. v. Commissioner, 277 F.3d 778, 779–88 (5th Cir. 2001) (engaging in the same analysis for an identical transaction).

123. The advisors' willingness to do so can be attributed to a number of factors, some of which are not related to textualism. First, the audit lottery heavily favors tax-for two reasons. First, textualism undermines the legitimacy of the business purpose and economic substance doctrines, since it is likely that a textualist would never have formulated the doctrines. The textualist would not have consulted the legislative history that the Second Circuit examined in *Gregory* to determine that Congress intended the reorganization provisions to apply to bona fide business transactions. Moreover, a textualist would not have reshaped the business purpose requirement into a general requirement of purposive activity without express statutory support.

Second, textualism limits the sources that a court may consult in interpreting a statute. The elimination of legislative history as a tool to determine a statute's purpose makes it less likely that the court will find authority to limit application of the statute's literal text.

[¶ 1072]

Note

The authors attach considerable importance to the application of judicially crafted doctrines to taxpayers' transactions in the effort to retard, if not prevent, the abuse of statutory rules, as would most commentators. However, ultimately it is a generalist federal judge that must decide whether the highly complex transaction under scrutiny, which appears to conform to the statutory requirements, can be recast under a subjective judicial standard. The following case illustrates the perils faced by the IRS in seeking to prevent tax avoidance behavior through reliance on judicial doctrines. If such broad doctrines cannot be relied upon to prevent taxpayer abuse, what can be relied upon?

[¶ 1073]

UNITED PARCEL SERVICE OF AMERICA, INC. v. COMMISSIONER

United States Court of Appeals, Eleventh Circuit, 2001.
254 F.3d 1014.

COX, CIRCUIT JUDGE:

The tax court held United Parcel Service of America, Inc. (UPS) liable for additional taxes and penalties for the tax year 1984. UPS appeals, and we reverse and remand.

payers investing in tax shelters organized as partnerships because there is a low audit rate for partnerships. Many practitioners we spoke to in Boston and New York have never had a tax shelter partnership client audited by the Service other than family limited partnerships used in estate planning. In 2002, the Service only audited 0.39% of the tax returns for flow-through entities such as partnerships. Staff of Joint Comm. on Taxation, 108th Cong., Report of the Joint Committee on Taxation Relating to the Internal Revenue Service as Re-

quired by the IRS Reform and Restructuring Act of 1998, at 37 (Comm. Print 2003). Consequently, most abusive transactions are not even identified as such, much less litigated. Second, because of the complexity of the abusive transactions, it is likely that, even if audited, the examining Service agents will lack the sophistication to identify the abuse. Practitioners have frequently told us of the complexity of tax shelter structures where several layers of partnerships and other entities are used to obfuscate the transaction.

I. Background

UPS, whose main business is shipping packages, had a practice in the early 1980s of reimbursing customers for lost or damaged parcels up to $100 in declared value.[1] Above that level, UPS would assume liability up to the parcel's declared value if the customer paid 25¢ per additional $100 in declared value, the "excess-value charge." If a parcel were lost or damaged, UPS would process and pay the resulting claim. UPS turned a large profit on excess-value charges because it never came close to paying as much in claims as it collected in charges, in part because of efforts it made to safeguard and track excess-value shipments. This profit was taxed; UPS declared its revenue from excess-value charges as income on its 1983 return, and it deducted as expenses the claims paid on damaged or lost excess-value parcels.

UPS's insurance broker suggested that UPS could avoid paying taxes on the lucrative excess-value business if it restructured the program as insurance provided by an overseas affiliate. UPS implemented this plan in 1983 by first forming and capitalizing a Bermuda subsidiary, Overseas Partners, Ltd. (OPL), almost all of whose shares were distributed as a taxable dividend to UPS shareholders (most of whom were employees; UPS stock was not publicly traded). UPS then purchased an insurance policy, for the benefit of UPS customers, from National Union Fire Insurance Company. By this policy, National Union assumed the risk of damage to or loss of excess-value shipments. The premiums for the policy were the excess-value charges that UPS collected. UPS, not National Union, was responsible for administering claims brought under the policy. National Union in turn entered a reinsurance treaty with OPL. Under the treaty, OPL assumed risk commensurate with National Union's, in exchange for premiums that equal the excess-value payments National Union got from UPS, less commissions, fees, and excise taxes.

Under this plan, UPS thus continued to collect 25¢ per $100 of excess value from its customers, process and pay claims, and take special measures to safeguard valuable packages. But UPS now remitted monthly the excess-value payments, less claims paid, to National Union as premiums on the policy. National Union then collected its commission, excise taxes, and fees from the charges before sending the rest on to OPL as payments under the reinsurance contract. UPS reported neither revenue from excess-value charges nor claim expenses on its 1984 return, although it did deduct the fees and commissions that National Union charged.

---

1. These facts synopsize the high points of the tax court's long opinion, which is published at 78 T.C.M. (CCH) 262.

¶ **1073**

The IRS determined a deficiency in the amount of the excess-value charges collected in 1984, concluding that the excess-value payment remitted ultimately to OPL had to be treated as gross income to UPS. UPS petitioned for a redetermination. Following a hearing, the tax court agreed with the IRS.

It is not perfectly clear on what judicial doctrine the holding rests. The court started its analysis by expounding on the assignment-of-income doctrine, a source rule that ensures that income is attributed to the person who earned it regardless of efforts to deflect it elsewhere. *See United States v. Basye,* 410 U.S. 441, 450 * * * (1973). The court did not, however, discuss at all the touchstone of an ineffective assignment of income, which would be UPS's control over the excess-value charges once UPS had turned them over as premiums to National Union. *See Comm'r v. Sunnen,* 333 U.S. 591, 604 * * * (1948). The court's analysis proceeded rather under the substantive-sham or economic-substance doctrines, the assignment-of-income doctrine's kissing cousins. *See United States v. Krall,* 835 F.2d 711, 714 (8th Cir.1987) (treating the assignment-of-income doctrine as a subtheory of the sham-transaction doctrine). The conclusion was that UPS's redesign of its excess-value business warranted no respect. Three core reasons support this result, according to the court: the plan had no defensible business purpose, as the business realities were identical before and after; the premiums paid for the National Union policy were well above industry norms; and contemporary memoranda and documents show that UPS's sole motivation was tax avoidance. The revenue from the excess-value program was thus properly deemed to be income to UPS rather than to OPL or National Union. The court also imposed penalties.

UPS now appeals, attacking the tax court's economic-substance analysis and its imposition of penalties. The refrain of UPS's lead argument is that the excess-value plan had economic substance, and thus was not a sham, because it comprised genuine exchanges of reciprocal obligations among real, independent entities. The IRS answers with a before-and-after analysis, pointing out that whatever the reality and enforceability of the contracts that composed the excess-value plan, UPS's postplan practice equated to its preplan, in that it collected excess-value charges, administered claims, and generated substantial profits. The issue presented to this court, therefore, is whether the excess-value plan had the kind of economic substance that removes it from "shamhood," even if the business continued as it had before. The question of the effect of a transaction on tax liability, to the extent it does not concern the accuracy of the tax court's fact-finding, is subject to de novo review. *Kirchman v. Comm'r,* 862 F.2d 1486, 1490 (11th Cir.1989); *see Karr v. Comm'r,* 924 F.2d 1018, 1023 (11th Cir.1991). We agree with UPS that this was not a sham transaction, and we therefore do not reach UPS's challenges to the tax penalties.

¶ 1073

II.   DISCUSSION

I.R.C. §§ 11, 61, and 63 together provide the Code's foundation by identifying income as the basis of taxation. Even apart from the narrower assignment-of-income doctrine—which we do not address here—these sections come with the gloss, analogous to that on other Code sections, that economic substance determines what is income to a taxpayer and what is not. *See Caruth Corp. v. United States,* 865 F.2d 644, 650 (5th Cir.1989) (addressing, but rejecting on the case's facts, the argument that the donation of an income source to charity was a sham, and that the income should be reattributed to the donor); *United States v. Buttorff,* 761 F.2d 1056, 1061 (5th Cir.1985) (conveying income to a trust controlled by the income's earner has no tax consequence because the assignment is insubstantial); *Zmuda v. Comm'r,* 731 F.2d 1417, 1421 (9th Cir.1984) (similar). This economic-substance doctrine, also called the sham-transaction doctrine, provides that a transaction ceases to merit tax respect when it has no "economic effects other than the creation of tax benefits." *Kirchman,* 862 F.2d at 1492.[2] Even if the transaction has economic effects, it must be disregarded if it has no business purpose and its motive is tax avoidance. *See Karr,* 924 F.2d at 1023 (noting that subjective intent is not irrelevant, despite *Kirchman*'s statement of the doctrine); *Neely v. United States,* 775 F.2d 1092, 1094 (9th Cir.1985); *see also Frank Lyon Co. v. United States,* 435 U.S. 561, 583–84 * * * (1978) (one reason requiring treatment of transaction as genuine was that it was "compelled or encouraged by business or regulatory realities"); *Gregory v. Helvering,* 293 U.S. 465, 469 * * * (1935) (reorganization disregarded in part because it had "no business or corporate purpose").

The kind of "economic effects" required to entitle a transaction to respect in taxation include the creation of genuine obligations enforceable by an unrelated party. *See Frank Lyon Co.,* 435 U.S. at 582–83 * * * (refusing to deem a sale-leaseback a sham in part because the lessor had accepted a real, enforceable debt to an unrelated bank as part of the deal). The restructuring of UPS's excess-value business generated just such obligations. There was a real insurance policy between UPS and National Union that gave National Union the right to receive the excess-value charges that UPS collected. And even if the odds of losing money on the policy were slim, National Union had assumed liability for the losses of UPS's excess-value shippers, again a genuine obligation. A history of not losing money on a policy is no guarantee of such a future. Insurance companies indeed do not make a habit of issuing policies whose premiums do not exceed the claims anticipated, but that fact does

---

2. *Kirchman,* which is binding in this circuit, differs in this respect from the oft-used statement of the doctrine derived from *Rice's Toyota World, Inc. v. Comm'r,* 752 F.2d 89, 91–92 (4th Cir.1985). *Rice's Toyota World,* unlike *Kirchman,* requires a tax-avoidance purpose as well as a lack of substance; *Kirchman* explicitly refuses to examine subjective intent if the transaction lacks economic effects.

not imply that insurance companies do not bear risk. Nor did the reinsurance treaty with OPL, while certainly reducing the odds of loss, completely foreclose the risk of loss because reinsurance treaties, like all agreements, are susceptible to default.

The tax court dismissed these obligations because National Union, given the reinsurance treaty, was no more than a "front" in what was a transfer of revenue from UPS to OPL. As we have said, that conclusion ignores the real risk that National Union assumed. But even if we overlook the reality of the risk and treat National Union as a conduit for transmission of the excess-value payments from UPS to OPL, there remains the fact that OPL is an independently taxable entity that is not under UPS's control. UPS really did lose the stream of income it had earlier reaped from excess-value charges. UPS genuinely could not apply that money to any use other than paying a premium to National Union; the money could not be used for other purposes, such as capital improvement, salaries, dividends, or investment. These circumstances distinguish UPS's case from the paradigmatic sham transfers of income, in which the taxpayer retains the benefits of the income it has ostensibly forgone. *See, e.g., Zmuda v. Comm'r,* 731 F.2d at 1417 (income "laundered" through a series of trusts into notes that were delivered to the taxpayer as "gifts"). Here that benefit ended up with OPL. There were, therefore, real economic effects from this transaction on all of its parties.

The conclusion that UPS's excess-value plan had real economic effects means, under this circuit's rule in *Kirchman,* that it is not per se a sham. But it could still be one if tax avoidance displaced any business purpose. The tax court saw no business purpose here because the excess-value business continued to operate after its reconfiguration much as before. This lack of change in how the business operated at the retail level, according to the court, betrayed the restructuring as pointless.

It may be true that there was little change over time in how the excess-value program appeared to customers. But the tax court's narrow notion of "business purpose"—which is admittedly implied by the phrase's plain language—stretches the economic-substance doctrine farther than it has been stretched. A "business purpose" does not mean a reason for a transaction that is free of tax considerations. Rather, a transaction has a "business purpose," when we are talking about a going concern like UPS, as long as it figures in a bona fide, profit-seeking business. *See ACM P'ship v. Comm'r,* 157 F.3d 231, 251 (3d Cir.1998). This concept of "business purpose" is a necessary corollary to the venerable axiom that tax-planning is permissible. *See Gregory v. Helvering,* 293 U.S. 465, 469 * * * (1935) ("The legal right of a taxpayer to decrease the amount of what otherwise would be his taxes, or altogether avoid them, by means which the law permits, cannot be doubted."). The Code treats lots of categories of economically similar behavior differently. For instance, two ways to infuse capital into a corporation, borrowing and sale of equity, have different tax consequences; interest is usually

¶ 1073

deductible and distributions to equityholders are not. There may be no tax-independent reason for a taxpayer to choose between these different ways of financing the business, but it does not mean that the taxpayer lacks a "business purpose." To conclude otherwise would prohibit tax-planning.

The caselaw, too, bears out this broader notion of "business purpose." Many of the cases where no business purpose appears are about individual income tax returns, when the individual meant to evade taxes on income probably destined for personal consumption; obviously, it is difficult in such a case to articulate any *business* purpose to the transaction. *See, e.g., Gregory,* 293 U.S. at 469 * * * (purported corporate reorganization was disguised dividend distribution to shareholder); *Knetsch v. United States,* 364 U.S. 361, 362–65 * * * (1960) (faux personal loans intended to generate interest deductions); *Neely v. United States,* 775 F.2d 1092, 1094 (9th Cir.1985) (one of many cases in which the taxpayers formed a trust, controlled by them, and diverted personal earnings to it). Other no-business-purpose cases concern tax-shelter transactions or investments by a business or investor that would not have occurred, *in any form,* but for tax-avoidance reasons. *See, e.g., ACM P'ship,* 157 F.3d at 233–43 (sophisticated investment partnership formed and manipulated solely to generate a capital loss to shelter some of Colgate–Palmolive's capital gains); *Kirchman,* 862 F.2d at 1488–89 (option straddles entered to produce deductions with little risk of real loss); *Karr,* 924 F.2d at 1021 (façade of energy enterprise developed solely to produce deductible losses for investors); *Rice's Toyota World, Inc. v. Comm'r,* 752 F.2d 89, 91 (4th Cir.1985) (sale-leaseback of a computer by a car dealership, solely to generate depreciation deductions). By contrast, the few cases that accept a transaction as genuine involve a bona fide business that—perhaps even by design—generates tax benefits. *See, e.g., Frank Lyon,* 435 U.S. at 582–84 * * * (sale-leaseback was part of genuine financing transaction, heavily influenced by banking regulation, to permit debtor bank to outdo its competitor in impressive office space); *Jacobson v. Comm'r,* 915 F.2d 832, 837–39 (2d Cir.1990) (one of many cases finding that a bona fide profit motive provided a business purpose for a losing investment because the investment was not an obvious loser ex ante).

The transaction under challenge here simply altered the form of an existing, bona fide business, and this case therefore falls in with those that find an adequate business purpose to neutralize any tax-avoidance motive. True, UPS's restructuring was more sophisticated and complex than the usual tax-influenced form-of-business election or a choice of debt over equity financing. But its sophistication does not change the fact that there was a real business that served the genuine need for customers to enjoy loss coverage and for UPS to lower its liability exposure.

¶ 1073

We therefore conclude that UPS's restructuring of its excess-value business had both real economic effects and a business purpose, and it therefore under our precedent had sufficient economic substance to merit respect in taxation. It follows that the tax court improperly imposed penalties and enhanced interest on UPS for engaging in a sham transaction. The tax court did not, however, reach the IRS's alternative arguments in support of its determination of deficiency, the reallocation provisions of I.R.C. §§ 482 and 845(a). The holding here does not dispose of those arguments, and we therefore must remand for the tax court to address them in the first instance.

III. Conclusion

For the foregoing reasons, we reverse the judgment against UPS and remand the action to the tax court for it to address in the first instance the IRS's contentions under §§ 482 and 845(a).

REVERSED AND REMANDED.

RYSKAMP, DISTRICT JUDGE, dissenting:

I respectfully dissent. Although I agree with the majority's recitation of the facts as well as its interpretation of the applicable legal standard, I find that its reversal of the tax court is contrary to the great weight of the evidence that was before the lower court. The majority, as well as the tax court below, correctly finds that the question before the Court is whether UPS's insurance arrangements with NUF and OPL are valid under the sham-transaction doctrine. Under the sham-transaction doctrine, UPS's transaction ceases to merit tax respect when it has no "economic effects other than the creation of tax benefits," *Kirchman v. Comm'r*, 862 F.2d 1486, 1492 (11th Cir.1989), or has no business purpose and its sole motive is tax avoidance. *See Karr v. Comm'r*, 924 F.2d 1018, 1023 (11th Cir.1991). Thus the question before the Court is not strictly whether UPS had a tax avoidance motive when it formulated the scheme in question, but rather whether there was some legitimate, substantive business reason for the transaction as well. There clearly was not.

As the tax court articulated in great detail in its well-reasoned 114–page opinion, the evidence in this case overwhelmingly demonstrates that UPS's reinsurance arrangement with NUF and OPL had no economic significance or business purpose outside of UPS's desire to avoid federal income tax, and was therefore a sham transaction. First, the tax court based its decision upon evidence that the scheme in question was subjectively motivated by tax avoidance. For example, the evidence showed that tax avoidance was the initial and sole reason for the scheme in question, that UPS held off on the plan for some time to analyze tax legislation on the floor of the United States House of Representatives, and that a letter sent to AIG Insurance from UPS detailing the scheme claimed that AIG would serve in merely a "fronting" capacity and would

¶ 1073

bear little or no actual risk. The evidence thus showed that this scheme was hatched with only tax avoidance in mind.

Second, the tax court based its decision on overwhelming evidence that UPS's scheme had no real economic or business purpose outside of tax avoidance. For example, the evidence showed that NUF's exposure to loss under the plan (except in the very unlikely event of *extreme* catastrophe) was infinitesimal, and that UPS nevertheless continued to fully bear the administrative costs of the EVC program. NUF was only liable for losses not covered by another insurance policy held by UPS, yet UPS still collected the EVC's and deposited the money into UPS bank accounts, still processed EVC claims, and continued to pay all EVC claims out of UPS bank accounts (while collecting the accrued interest for itself). All NUF really did in the scheme was collect over $1 million in fees and expenses before passing the EVC income on to OPL, which was of course wholly owned by UPS shareholders. In essence, NUF received an enormous fee from UPS in exchange for nothing.

Moreover, the tax court systematically rejected every explanation of the scheme put forth by UPS. UPS claimed that the scheme was meant to avoid violation of state insurance laws, yet the evidence showed no real concern for such laws and that in fact UPS was well aware that federal preemption of these state laws likely made its old EVC plan legal. UPS claimed that it intended OPL to become a full-line insurer someday, yet the evidence showed that it was nevertheless unnecessary to specifically use *EVC income* for such a capital investment. UPS claimed that elimination of the EVC income allowed it to increase its rates, yet one of its own board members testified that this explanation was untrue. I also note that UPS's claim that OPL was a legitimate insurance company fails in light of the fact that OPL was charging a substantially inflated rate for EVCs. Evidence in the tax court showed that in an arms-length transaction with a legitimate insurance company, EVC rates would have been approximately half those charged by UPS (and in turn passed on to OPL), providing further evidence that the transaction was a sham. In sum, UPS failed to show any legitimate business reason for giving up nearly $100 million in EVC income in 1984.

For these reasons, I would affirm the holding of the tax court and find that UPS's arrangement with NUF and OPL was a sham transaction subject to federal tax liability.

[¶ 1074]

Notes

1. In the latter part of the Twentieth Century, established financial institutions, including major accounting firms, aggressively marketed "products" designed to reduce income taxes to a range of corporate clients that included well known publicly owned corporations. The legitimacy of these products varied widely, from the maybe OK to the maybe

criminal. When the scheme did not involve fraud and did bear some relationship to the business of the taxpayer, as in *UPS*, the IRS has had a difficult time in recasting the transaction under the accepted judicial doctrines. However, when the court could be persuaded that the scheme bore no relationship to the taxpayer's business and made little sense aside from the desire to avoid taxes, the IRS has had greater success. See, e.g., Long Term Capital Holdings v. United States, 330 F. Supp.2d 122 (D. Conn. 2004).

2. While the scope of such judicial doctrines as business purpose, economic substance, and step-transaction is unavoidably fuzzy, as the foregoing materials disclose, it is entirely clear that a transaction is not entitled to its sought after tax benefits merely because it complies with the literal requirements of the Code. Anticipating when a transaction can be successfully attacked under one or another judicial doctrine is one of the most challenging features of a tax practice. As you progress through the following pages, pay close attention to the factors that will cause a court to recast a transaction under one of these doctrines.

[¶ 1075]

H. WHAT IS A CORPORATION?

Subchapter C of the Code applies only to a business entity treated as a "corporation" for federal income tax purposes. The different dimensions of the question of what activities do or do not meet that definition are examined here.

1. ENTITY CLASSIFICATION

[¶ 1080]

a. *Introduction*

Section 7701(a)(3) of the Code defines the term "corporation" to include "associations, joint stock companies and insurance companies." The question of what should be treated as an "association" taxable as a corporation has led to considerable controversy over the years. For many years the controlling authority on that issue was the decision in Morrissey v. Commissioner, 296 U.S. 344 (1935), in which the Supreme Court held that a trust created to develop certain real estate was taxable as a corporation for federal income tax purposes. In that decision, the Supreme Court established that whether an entity was an association was to be determined, not by formalities, but by a facts and circumstances inquiry into whether the entity more nearly resembled a classic corporation than an unincorporated entity. To make that determination, the Court required an evaluation of six factors, a test that was subsequently embodied in regulations and is described in the following case. See former Reg. §§ 301.7701–1 through 301.7701–4.

¶ 1074

The most significant classification issue under these regulations concerned whether certain entities formed as limited partnerships or limited liability companies under state law, often as the vehicle for a tax shelter, would be treated as corporations for federal tax purposes. As discussed in Chapters 16 through 25 of this book, since a partnership's net losses flow through to its partners and may be deducted on those partners' own tax returns (subject to certain limits) but corporate losses are trapped at the corporate level and do not flow through to its shareholders, the tax stakes riding on this classification issue were often significant.

Over the years, the development under state laws of new forms of business entities, especially the LLC, undercut the traditional nontax distinctions between corporations and other types of business entities. As a result, taxpayers and their advisers often were able to structure the business enterprise to achieve partnership classification for tax purposes for entities that in all meaningful respects resembled a corporation. Accordingly, the Treasury Department concluded that the traditional entity classification regulations were increasingly formalistic and inefficient and should be discarded. In their place, the Treasury adopted in 1996 a simplified system of elective entity classification (often called the "check-the-box" system) for many types of business entities. The following case is the first in which the validity of the Treasury's approach has been challenged.

[¶ 1082]

LITTRIELLO v. UNITED STATES

United States District Court,W.D. Kentucky, 2005.
2005–1 U.S.T.C. (CCH) ¶ 50,385, 95 A.F.T.R.2d (RIA) 2005–2581.

MEMORANDUM OPINION

HEYBURN, CHIEF JUDGE:

Kentuckiana Healthcare, LLC (the "Company"), a limited liability company formed under the laws of Kentucky, operated a nursing home in Scottsburg, Indiana, under the trade name Scott County Healthcare Center. It failed to pay withholding and FICA taxes for some of the tax periods ending between 12/2000 and 3/2002. Frank Littriello ("Littriello"), the plaintiff in this case, was the sole member of the Company during the tax periods in question. The IRS notified Littriello of its intent to levy his property to enforce previously filed notices of federal tax liens for the Company's unpaid withholding and FICA taxes. Littriello requested a due process hearing with the IRS Appeals office in Louisville, Kentucky.

The Appeals Office determined that Littriello was individually liable for the Company's unpaid withholding and FICA taxes. It held that under Treas. Reg. § 301.7701–3(b)(1)(iii), a single member limited liability company that did not elect to be treated as a corporation is considered as a disregarded entity for federal tax purposes. As such, its activities are treated in the same manner as a sole proprietorship, division or branch of the owner under Treas. Reg. § 301.7701–3(a). Through this federal action Littriello seeks judicial review and redetermination of that decision.

The real dispute here concerns the validity of the so-called "check-the-box" regulations for corporations and partnerships. Treas. Reg. § 301.7701–1 through 3. Littriello contends that the check-the-box regulations constitute an invalid exercise of the Treasury's authority to issue interpretive regulations under Internal Revenue Code ("IRC") § 7805(a) and are, thus, unenforceable. If the regulations are invalid, then the Company alone is liable for the taxes at issue. The Commissioner argues that the regulations are valid and that as applied here Littriello is individually liable for the Company's tax obligation. Both sides have moved for summary judgment.

I.

The IRS and the Treasury Department proposed the check-the-box regulations in 1996 to simplify entity classification for tax purposes, believing that the prior regulations had become unnecessarily cumbersome, complex and risky for affected entities. The current regulations function in a relatively straightforward fashion. The Internal Revenue Code treats business entities differently depending upon whether the business entity is classified as a corporation or a partnership. IRC § 7701(a)(3) defines the term "corporation" to include associations, joint-stock companies, and insurance companies. IRC § 7701(a)(2) defines the term "partnership" to include any syndicate, group, pool, joint venture, or other unincorporated organization, through or by means of which any business, financial operation, or venture is carried on, and which is not, within the meaning of this title, a trust or estate or a corporation. The regulations provide that for the purposes of IRC § 7701(a)(3) any unincorporated business entity that is not a publically traded partnership covered by IRC § 7704 may elect whether or not to be classified as an association. Thus, an unincorporated business entity like the Company can generally elect whether or not to be subject to the corporate tax. A default treatment applies under a variety of circumstances where a business entity chooses not to be considered a corporation. If an unincorporated business entity with more than one member elects not to be treated as an association, it will be treated for federal tax purposes as a partnership. If an unincorporated business entity with only one member elects not to be treated as an association, it will be treated for federal tax purposes as a disregarded entity and taxed as a sole proprietorship. Treas. Reg. § 301.7701–3(a).

¶ 1082

II.

The Court now considers the validity of the check-the-box regulations. *Chevron, U.S.A., Inc. v. Natural Resources Defense Council, Inc.,* 467 U.S. 837 * * * (1989), governs the analysis for reviewing agency regulations. The Supreme Court established a two-part analysis:

> When a court reviews an agency's construction of the statute which it administers, it is confronted with two questions. First, always, is the question whether Congress has directly spoken to the precise question at issue. If the intent of Congress is clear, that is the end of the matter; for the court, as well as the agency, must give effect to the unambiguously expressed intent of Congress. If, however, the court determines Congress has not directly addressed the precise question at issue, the court does not simply impose its own construction on the statute, as would be necessary in the absence of an administrative interpretation. Rather, if the statute is silent or ambiguous with respect to the specific issue, the question for the court is whether the agency's answer is based on a permissible construction of the statute.

Id. at 842–43 (footnotes omitted). The Sixth Circuit has employed *Chevron* when assessing the validity of interpretive Treasury regulations. *Hospital Corporation of America & Subsidiaries v. Commissioner,* 348 F.3d 136, 140 (6th Cir.2003); *Ohio Periodical Distributors, Inc. v. Commissioner,* 105 F.3d 322, 324–326 (6th Cir.1997).

A.

Under step one of the *Chevron* analysis the Court looks to whether the intent of Congress is clear on the precise issue of business classification for federal tax purposes. The IRC defines "partnership" and "corporation" as being mutually exclusive. A business entity for tax purposes is defined either as a partnership or as a corporation. Littriello contends that the check-the-box regulations violate this manifest intent because two identical business entities may elect different classifications. The Commissioner responds that the term "association" in the statutory definition of a corporation is ambiguous.

Read together IRC § 7701(a)(2) and § 7701(a)(3) do not seem to make a clear distinction between an "association" which is treated for tax purposes as a corporation and a "group pool or joint venture" which is treated for tax purposes as a partnership. The definition of the "corporation" in the IRC dates from the Revenue Act of 1918 and the definition of the term "partnership" was added in 1932. Since then, Kentucky has endorsed the limited liability company as a popular business form. Business entities formed under state law most often seek to combine the limited liability of a corporation with the tax benefits of a partnership exacerbating the ambiguity in the definitions section of the statute. A business entity registered in Kentucky as a limited liability

¶ 1082

company does not fall squarely in either the partnership or corporation category as defined in the IRC. This is undoubtedly true in most other states as well. Indeed, the ambiguity is part of the reason for providing unincorporated business entities with a choice of treatment. Therefore, the Court concludes that the Commissioner's argument that the statute is ambiguous on this point is more persuasive than Littriello who seeks to impose clarity where the Court finds none.

B.

Step two of the *Chevron* analysis requires the Court to decide "whether the agency's answer is based on a permissible construction of the statute." *Id.* at 843. The Treasury promulgated the check-the-box regulations pursuant to its general authority to issue "needful rules and regulations for the enforcement of [the IRC]." IRC § 7701(a). The regulations at issue interpret the definitions sections of the IRC. The classification of a business entity affects how the IRS assesses tax liability.

Littriello argues that the plain meaning of the Internal Revenue Code forecloses the possibility of an elective regime because "taxation as intended by Congress is based on the realistic nature of the business entity." *Pls.' Mot. for Summ. J.* p 8. Littriello's primary evidence in support of this contention appears to be the previous Treasury regulations, effective prior to January 1, 1997. Former Treas. Reg. § 301.7701–2(1960). These regulations, commonly referred to as the Kintner regulations, looked to six corporate characteristics to determine the tax status of a business entity. The Kintner regulations enumerated the factors used by the Supreme Court in *Morrissey v. Commissioner,* 296 U.S. 344, 56 S.Ct. 289, 80 L.Ed. 263 (1935) to define the characteristics of a pure corporation: (1) associates; (2) an objective to carry on a business and divide the gains there from; (3) continuity of life; (4) centralization of management; (5) liability for corporate debts limited to property; and (6) free transferability of interests. Most every business entity has associates and an objective to carry out a business and profit. Before the check-the-box regulations, any business entity the IRS found to meet three of the remaining four corporate characteristics was classified as a association and taxed as a corporation. Business entities that contained only two of the remaining four where classified and taxed as a partnership. Former Treas. Reg. § 301.7701–2(a)(1).

Littriello is correct that under the former regulations the Company might have been classified differently. Of course, under the current regulations, the Company could have elected to be classified differently. Moreover, Congressional intent does not attach to the previous regulations. Indeed, Congress appears only to have spoken on this issue through the existing statutes. The check-the-box regulations are only a more formal version of the informally elective regime under the Kintner regulations. A business entity could pick at will which two corporate characteristics to avoid in order to qualify as a partnership under the Kintner regulations. The importance of the change is that under the current regulations a business entity may elect to be taxed as a corporation without specific reference to its corporate characteristics.

While some reasonable arguments support Littriello's position, the Court ultimately finds them unpersuasive. Under the circumstances, the check-the-box regulations seem to be a reasonable response to the changes in the state law industry of business formation. The rise of the limited liability corporation presents a malleable corporate form incompatible with the definitions of the IRC. The newer regulations allow similar flexibility to the Kintner regulations, with more certainty of results and consequences. Considering the difficulty in defining for federal tax purposes the precise character of various state sanctioned business entities, the regulations also seem to provide a flexible permissible construction of the statute.

C.

Littriello advances a number of arguments that the Court finds not sufficiently persuasive to change its basic analysis. Littriello says that the check-the-box regulations violate the basic principle of treating like entities alike under the IRC. It is fundamentally wrong, according to Littriello, that two business entities identical in every relevant respect would be classified and thereby taxed differently solely because of a box checked on a form. A single member LLC with all six of the pure corporation characteristics could elect not to be treated as a corporation for federal tax purposes. Conversely a single member LLC with no traditionally corporate characteristics could nevertheless elect to be classified and taxed as a corporation perhaps with the goal of limiting the assets available to that organization's tax liability. This elective function is of course the very point of the check-the-box regulations. In today's business environment, not all corporations are alike and not all partnerships share the same characteristics. In response to an ambiguous statutory definition coupled with a variety of legally created business forms, the Treasury decided that entities may choose their form for tax purposes within the limits of the IRC. Business entities get the good and the bad with their choice. This new criterion added with the check-the-box regulations appears eminently reasonable.

* * *

The Court will grant Defendant's motion for summary judgment on the issue of the validity of the check-the-box regulations. The Court will enter an order consistent with this Memorandum Opinion.

[¶ 1083]

Notes

1. There are two distinct aspects to any evaluation of the check-the-box regulations. The first is whether it is sound income tax policy for

important Code definitions to be elective. The second is whether the Treasury Department has the authority to issue regulations creating such an election. On the second question, the regulations are plainly inconsistent with the decision of the Supreme Court in *Morrissey*. Why is the Treasury not bound by that decision?

2. The check-the-box regulations have proven to be very popular with tax practitioners. Under the regulations, one can be quite confident of the tax classification of a business entity even though that classification is completely inconsistent with the classification of the entity under other bodies of law. For example, a business corporation might wish to separately incorporate the assets of a risky aspect of the business to obtain limited liability under state law but would nevertheless need to have all of the business assets treated as owned by a single corporation for federal income tax purposes. If the corporation creates a subsidiary that is an LLC, those inconsistent objectives can be accomplished.

[¶ 1085]

b. *Check-the-Box Entity Classification Regulations*

While the implications of check-the-box for entities formed under foreign law continue to evolve, for domestic entities this reform has proven quite successful in simplifying the administration of the entity classification rules and in eliminating disputes between taxpayers and the IRS. Under the regulations, some entities are automatically classified as corporations for federal tax purposes (the "per se" entities) and are not eligible to elect a different classification. Reg. § 301.7701–2(b). These entities include organizations incorporated under a state or federal general corporation law and certain similar foreign organizations. In addition, publicly traded partnerships are treated as corporations under Section 7704 and may not elect partnership classification.

A business entity that is not required to be treated as a corporation is an "eligible entity" and may elect its classification for federal tax purposes. Reg. § 301.7701–3(a). Eligible entities at least include general and limited partnerships, limited liability companies, and limited liability partnerships. The regulations are unclear on the question of exactly what constitutes an "entity" that can elect classification. Thus, it is not entirely clear whether a sole proprietorship or branch of a corporation can elect to be treated as a separate corporation although the IRS apparently is of the view that those business activities do not constitute entities.

Eligible entities with two or more members may elect to be treated as either an association taxable as a corporation or as a partnership for federal tax purposes. Eligible entities with only one owner may elect to be treated as either an association taxable as a corporation or disregarded as an entity separate from its owner for federal tax purposes. If the sole owner of a "disregarded" entity is an individual, the entity will be

¶ 1083

treated as a sole proprietorship and its items of income and expense included on a Schedule C attached to the tax return of the individual. If the sole owner is a corporation, then the disregarded entity will be treated as a branch of that corporation.

To provide most eligible entities with the classification they most likely would want without requiring them to file an election, the regulations contain default rules. Under these default rules, in the absence of an election, a domestic eligible entity is treated as a partnership if it has two or more members, and is disregarded if it has only one owner. Reg. § 301.7701–3(b)(1).

If an eligible entity chooses not to be classified under the default rules or wants to change its entity classification, it must file an entity classification election on Form 8832. Reg. § 301.7701–3(c). A change in the classification of an entity will have tax consequences. For example, if an entity that has elected corporation status changes its classification to a partnership, the change in status will be treated as a liquidation of the corporation subject to the rules discussed in Chapter 8. See Reg. § 301.7701–3(g).

These check-the-box, entity classification regulations are discussed in more detail at ¶ 16,070.

[¶ 1087]

Problems

1.   If an LLC can be disregarded and treated as a sole proprietorship or a corporate branch, why cannot a sole proprietorship or branch be regarded and treated as a corporation? Would that be sensible from a tax policy perspective? How would one demonstrate what assets were owned by the "corporation"?

2.   Three of your friends have started a computer repair business. They formed an LLC and each of them became a member of the organization. Although they did remember to obtain a taxpayer identification number, they did not make any other filings with the IRS. How will they be classified for tax purposes? Will that be in accord with their desires?

[¶ 1090]

c.   Trust Versus Corporation Entity Classification Issue

The Supreme Court's *Morrissey* decision itself involved a different classification issue than the one discussed above—the issue of whether a trust would be treated as a corporation for tax purposes. This classification issue arises because, in effect, a trust is only a quasi-taxpaying entity for federal income tax purposes. Thus, although Section 641 treats a trust as a separate taxpayer, the net income of a trust may bear only one level of tax, at the beneficiary level, if the trust distributes, or is required to distribute, its income for the year. This result occurs because a trust (unlike a corporation) may qualify for a distribution deduction, thus eliminating the entity level tax to the extent of the deduction. §§ 651, 652, 661, and 662.

In determining whether an arrangement will be treated as a trust or a business entity for tax purposes, Reg. § 301.7701–4(a) provides that "an arrangement will be treated as a trust * * * if it can be shown that the purpose of the arrangement is to vest in trustees responsibility for the protection and conservation of property for beneficiaries who cannot share in the discharge of this responsibility and, therefore, are not associates in a joint enterprise for the conduct of business for profit." Thus, if the trustee's activities are confined to protecting or conserving the trust property, the trust will not be classified as a business entity for tax purposes. See, e.g., Rev. Rul. 79–77, 1979–1 C.B. 448 (entity classified as a trust where trustee restricted to dealing with a single piece of trust property leased on a net lease basis and hence was not carrying on a business); Wyman Building Trust v. Commissioner, 45 B.T.A. 155 (1941) (acq.) (similar facts). By contrast, if the trustee is empowered to do more than merely protect and conserve trust property and engages in business activity, the trust will be classified as a business entity for federal tax purposes and may elect to be treated as an association taxable as a corporation or as a partnership. See, e.g., Rev. Rul. 78–371, 1978–2 C.B. 344 (trust classified as a corporation where trustees managed a number of contiguous parcels of real estate owned by the trust and had broad powers to purchase and sell contiguous parcels of real estate, to accept contributions of contiguous real estate by the beneficiaries or members of their families, to raze or erect any building or other structure and make whatever improvements they deemed appropriate on the trust's real estate, to borrow money, and to mortgage and lease the trust property).

[¶ 1095]

2. RECOGNITION OF THE CORPORATE ENTITY

Plainly, a corporate charter is not essential to the classification of an entity as a corporation for tax purposes. On the other hand, operating under a formal corporate charter does not always assure that the corporate entity will be respected as a separate taxable entity for tax purposes. The following cases provide illustrations of circumstances in which the issue of recognition of the corporation has arisen.

a. *Business Purpose and Business Activity*

[¶ 1100]

MOLINE PROPERTIES v. COMMISSIONER

Supreme Court of the United States, 1943.
319 U.S. 436.

MR. JUSTICE REED delivered the opinion of the Court.

Petitioner seeks to have the gain on sales of its real property treated as the gain of its sole stockholder and its corporate existence ignored as merely fictitious.

* * *

Petitioner was organized by Uly O. Thompson in 1928 to be used as a security device in connection with certain Florida realty owned by him. The mortgagee of the property suggested the arrangement, under which Mr. Thompson conveyed the property to petitioner, which assumed the outstanding mortgages on the property, receiving in return all but the qualifying shares of stock, which he in turn transferred to a voting trustee appointed by the creditor. The stock was to be held as security for an additional loan to Mr. Thompson to be used to pay back taxes on the property. Thompson owned other real property, title to which he held individually. In 1933 the loan which occasioned the creation of petitioner was repaid and the mortgages were refinanced with a different mortgagee; control of petitioner reverted to Mr. Thompson. The new mortgage debt was paid in 1936 by means of a sale of a portion of the property held by petitioner. The remaining holdings of the petitioner were sold in three parcels, one each in 1934, 1935 and 1936, the proceeds being received by Mr. Thompson and deposited in his bank account.

Until 1933 the business done by the corporation consisted of the assumption of a certain obligation of Thompson to the original creditor, the defense of certain condemnation proceedings and the institution of a suit to remove restrictions imposed on the property by a prior deed. The expenses of this suit were paid by Thompson. In 1934 a portion of the property was leased for use as a parking lot for a rental of $1,000. Petitioner has transacted no business since the sale of its last holdings in 1936 but has not been dissolved. It kept no books and maintained no bank account during its existence and owned no other assets than as described. The sales made in 1934 and 1935 were reported in petitioner's income tax returns, a small loss being reported for the earlier year and a gain of over $5,000 being reported for 1935. Subsequently, on advice of his auditor, Thompson filed a claim for refund on petitioner's behalf for 1935 and sought to report the 1935 gain as his individual return. He reported the gain on the 1936 sale.

¶ 1100

The question is whether the gain realized on the 1935 and 1936 sales shall be treated as income taxable to petitioner, as the Government urges, or as Thompson's income. The Board of Tax Appeals held for petitioner on the ground that because of its limited purpose, the corporation "was a mere figmentary agent which should be disregarded in the assessment of taxes." * * * The Circuit Court of Appeals reversed on the ground that the corporate entity, chosen by Thompson for reasons sufficient to him, must now be recognized in the taxation of the income of the corporation. * * *

The doctrine of corporate entity fills a useful purpose in business life. Whether the purpose be to gain an advantage under the law of the state of incorporation or to avoid or to comply with the demands of creditors or to serve the creator's personal or undisclosed convenience, so long as that purpose is the equivalent of business activity or is followed by the carrying on of business by the corporation, the corporation remains a separate taxable entity. * * * In *Burnet v. Commonwealth Improvement Co.*, 287 U.S. 415, this Court appraised the relation between a corporation and its sole stockholder and held taxable to the corporation a profit on a sale to its stockholder. This was because the taxpayer had adopted the corporate form for purposes of his own. The choice of the advantages of incorporation to do business, it was held, required the acceptance of the tax disadvantages.

To this rule there are recognized exceptions. * * * In general, in matters relating to the revenue, the corporate form may be disregarded where it is a sham or unreal. In such situations the form is a bald and mischievous fiction. *Higgins v. Smith*, 308 U.S. 473, 477–78; *Gregory v. Helvering*, 293 U.S. 465.

The petitioner corporation was created by Thompson for his advantage and had a special function from its inception. At that time it was clearly not Thompson's *alter ego* and his exercise of control over it was negligible. It was then as much a separate entity as if its stock had been transferred outright to third persons. The argument is made by petitioner that the force of the rule requiring its separate treatment is avoided by the fact that Thompson was coerced into creating petitioner and was completely subservient to the creditors. But this merely serves to emphasize petitioner's separate existence. * * * Business necessity, i.e., pressure from creditors, made petitioner's creation advantageous to Thompson.

When petitioner discharged its mortgages held by the initial creditor and Thompson came into control in 1933, it was not dissolved, but continued its existence, ready again to serve his business interests. It again mortgaged its property, discharged that new mortgage, sold portions of its property in 1934 and 1935 and filed income tax returns showing these transactions. In 1934 petitioner engaged in an unambiguous business venture of its own—it leased a part of its property as a parking lot, receiving a substantial rental. The facts, it seems to us, compel the conclusion that the taxpayer had a tax identity distinct from its stockholder.

Petitioner advances what we think is basically the same argument of identity in a different form. It urges that it is a mere agent for its sole stockholder and "therefore the same tax consequences follow as in the case of any corporate agent or fiduciary." There was no actual contract of agency, nor the usual incidents of an agency relationship. Surely the mere fact of the existence of a corporation with one or several stockholders, regardless of the corporation's business activities, does not make the corporation the agent of its stockholders. Therefore the question of agency or not depends upon the same legal issues as does the question of identity previously discussed. * * *

* * *

[¶ 1105]

Note

In Ogiony v. Commissioner, 617 F.2d 14 (2d Cir.), cert. denied, 449 U.S. 900 (1980), taxpayers (members of a partnership) planned to construct rental apartments. To avoid the usury laws in obtaining financing, it was necessary to transfer title to corporations to obtain mortgage loans. Loan proceeds were paid over to the partnership and the partnership received all income and paid all expenses. Net losses incurred by the partnership were allocated to the partners. Upon challenge by the Commissioner, the Second Circuit held that the loss deductions claimed by the partners were not allowable on the ground that the income and expenses of the apartment operations were attributable to the corporations as owners of the property. The court stated (617 F.2d at 16):

> The Tax Court below held that neither Garden Corporation nor Losson Corporation could be disregarded for federal tax purposes. Noting that the instant case is virtually indistinguishable from *Strong v. Commissioner*, 66 T.C. 12, aff'd on the opinion below, 553 F.2d 94 (2d Cir.1977), Judge Hall ruled that the individual partners were not entitled to deduct their distributive shares of the net operating losses incurred with respect to the apartment complexes. We agree and reaffirm the holding of the Tax Court in *Strong* that "income from property must be taxed to the corporate owner, and will not be attributed to the shareholders, unless the corporation is a *purely passive dummy* or is used for a tax-avoidance purpose." 60 T.C. at 22. Neither exception to the rule in *Strong* exist here. *Strong v. Comm'r supra*, at 22–25; see *Moline Properties, Inc. v. Commissioner*, 319 U.S. 436 * * * (1943).

¶ 1105

Consider in connection with the Supreme Court's decision in Commissioner v. Bollinger, at ¶ 1120, under what circumstances the agency doctrine may be invoked in this context.

[¶ 1110]

b. *Sham Corporations*

While the doctrine requiring the recognition of the separate entity of corporations is quite strong in federal tax law, as the Court noted in *Moline Properties* in extreme cases a corporation will be wholly disregarded. The following passage from United States v. Walton, 909 F.2d 915, 928 (6th Cir.1990), illustrates the typical context in which such a determination is made:

> In determining whether the separate corporate identity should be disregarded, each case is *sui generis* and must be decided in accordance with its own underlying facts * * *. The courts have employed a number of criteria in determining whether a corporation is an alter ego justifying piercing the corporate veil. Such criteria include: (1) the absence of normal corporate formalities * * *; (2) commingling of personal and corporate funds * * *; (3) siphoning of corporate funds by a dominant stockholder * * *; and (4) the fact that the corporation is merely a facade for the personal operations of the dominant stockholder * * *.

> Each one of these factors justifies disregarding the corporate form in this case. [The Academy, the corporate defendant,] clearly failed to observe corporate formalities. The bookkeeping records of the corporation were woefully inadequate, as illustrated by the fact that there was virtually no documentation at all of the corporation's activities during 1977. Walton has admitted to extensive commingling of personal and corporate assets. The admission is supported by numerous facts on the record. As noted above, Walton made personal use of assets nominally owned by the Academy including the Strathcona house, the Grumman aircraft, and several luxury cars. Walton also admitted on the record that he had used corporate funds to pay personal obligations, and that certain sales recorded on the Academy's books were in fact for his personal account.

> From these facts it is clear that Walton, who at all times had exclusive control over [the Academy], used the assets of the corporation as if they were his own and attempted to hide his own holdings under the veil of the corporate form. These circumstances justified the district court in piercing the veil and holding Walton and the Academy jointly and severally liable for the full amount of taxes and penalties owed by each.

In Greenberg v. Commissioner, 62 T.C. 331 (1974), aff'd per curiam, 526 F.2d 588 (4th Cir.1975), cert. denied, 423 U.S. 1052 (1976), the taxpayer was a real estate developer. With two other business associates, he created five separate corporations referred to as the "Colt" corporations to develop, construct, and sell single-family homes. Of the group, only Colt Development, Inc., had any employees and that corporation had arranged for all the engineering and project development costs, which were allocated among the several Colt corporations. The other Colt corporations took title to the lots, paid the construction costs of the houses and, when the project was completed, liquidated. The taxpayer reported the distribution as the proceeds of a corporate liquidation entitled to capital gains taxation. Largely because the taxpayer was unable to establish any business purpose for the separate corporations, the court agreed with the Commissioner that the four corporations lacked substance and that the entire distribution should be regarded as attributable to the single viable corporation, Colt Development. Since that corporation remained in existence, the distributions were treated as ordinary dividends.

[¶ 1115]

c.　*Corporation as Agent or Nominee*

In *Moline Properties* the shareholder sought to have items of income taxed to himself, rather than to the corporation, on the ground that the corporation was acting as "a mere agent for its sole stockholder." While the court rejected that argument on the facts, it held open the possibility that such an agency arrangement could be established. Such a technique would have been useful to the partnership in *Ogiony* in seeking to deduct losses on property technically owned by the corporation. The following case is the Supreme Court's most recent decision on the issue of when this agency theory may properly be invoked.

[¶ 1120]

COMMISSIONER v. BOLLINGER

Supreme Court of the United States, 1988.
485 U.S. 340.

JUSTICE SCALIA delivered the opinion of the Court.

Petitioner the Commissioner of Internal Revenue challenges a decision by the United States Court of Appeals for the Sixth Circuit holding that a corporation which held record title to real property as agent for the corporation's shareholders was not the owner of the property for purposes of federal income taxation. * * * We granted certiorari * * * to resolve a conflict in the Courts of Appeals over the tax treatment of corporations purporting to be agents for their shareholders. * * *

I

Respondent Jesse C. Bollinger, Jr., developed, either individually or in partnership with some or all of the other respondents, eight apartment complexes in Lexington, Kentucky. (For convenience we will refer to all the ventures as "partnerships.") Bollinger initiated development of the first apartment complex, Creekside North Apartments, in 1968. The Massachusetts Mutual Life Insurance Company agreed to provide permanent financing by lending $1,075,000 to "the corporate nominee of Jesse C. Bollinger, Jr." at an annual interest rate of eight percent, secured by a mortgage on the property and a personal guaranty from Bollinger. The loan commitment was structured in this fashion because Kentucky's usury law at the time limited the annual interest rate for noncorporate borrowers to seven percent. * * * Lenders willing to provide money only at higher rates required the nominal debtor and record title holder of mortgaged property to be a corporate nominee of the true owner and borrower. On October 14, 1968, Bollinger incorporated Creekside, Inc., under the laws of Kentucky; he was the only stockholder. The next day, Bollinger and Creekside, Inc., entered into a written agreement which provided that the corporation would hold title to the apartment complex as Bollinger's agent for the sole purpose of securing financing, and would convey, assign, or encumber the property and disburse the proceeds thereof only as directed by Bollinger; that Creekside, Inc., had no obligation to maintain the property or assume any liability by reason of the execution of promissory notes or otherwise; and that Bollinger would indemnify and hold the corporation harmless from any liability it might sustain as his agent and nominee.

Having secured the commitment for permanent financing, Bollinger, acting through Creekside, Inc., borrowed the construction funds for the apartment complex from Citizens Fidelity Bank and Trust Company. Creekside, Inc., executed all necessary loan documents including the promissory note and mortgage, and transferred all loan proceeds to Bollinger's individual construction account. Bollinger acted as general contractor for the construction, hired the necessary employees, and paid the expenses out of the construction account. When construction was completed, Bollinger obtained, again through Creekside, Inc., permanent financing from Massachusetts Mutual Life in accordance with the earlier loan commitment. These loan proceeds were used to pay off the Citizens Fidelity construction loan. Bollinger hired a resident manager to rent the apartments, execute leases with tenants, collect and deposit the rents, and maintain operating records. The manager deposited all rental receipts into, and paid all operating expenses from, an operating account, which was first opened in the name of Creekside, Inc., but was later changed to "Creekside Apartments, a partnership." The operation of Creekside North apartments generated losses for the taxable years 1969, 1971, 1972, 1973, and 1974, and ordinary income for the years 1970, 1975, 1976, and 1977. Throughout, the income and losses were reported by Bollinger on his individual income tax returns.

Following a substantially identical pattern, seven other apartment complexes were developed by respondents through seven separate partnerships. For each venture, a partnership executed a nominee agreement with Creekside, Inc., to obtain financing. (For one of the ventures, a different Kentucky corporation, Cloisters, Inc., in which Bollinger had a 50 percent interest, acted as the borrower and titleholder. For convenience, we will refer to both Creekside and Cloisters as "the corporation.") The corporation transferred the construction loan proceeds to the partnership's construction account, and the partnership hired a construction supervisor who oversaw construction. Upon completion of construction, each partnership actively managed its apartment complex, depositing all rental receipts into, and paying all expenses from, a separate partnership account for each apartment complex. The corporation had no assets, liabilities, employees, or bank accounts. In every case, the lenders regarded the partnership as the owner of the apartments and were aware that the corporation was acting as agent of the partnership in holding record title. The partnerships reported the income and losses generated by the apartment complexes on their partnership tax returns, and respondents reported their distributive share of the partnership income and losses on their individual tax returns.

The Commissioner of Internal Revenue disallowed the losses reported by respondents, on the ground that the standards set out in *National Carbide Corp. v. Commissioner*, 336 U.S. 422 (1949), were not met. The Commissioner contended that *National Carbide* required a corporation to have an arm's-length relationship with its shareholders before it could be recognized as their agent. Although not all respondents were shareholders of the corporation, the Commissioner took the position that the funds the partnerships disbursed to pay expenses should be deemed contributions to the corporation's capital, thereby making all respondents constructive stockholders. Since, in the Commissioner's view, the corporation rather than its shareholders owned the real estate, any losses sustained by the ventures were attributable to the corporation and not respondents. Respondents sought a redetermination in the United States Tax Court. The Tax Court held that the corporation was the agent of the partnerships and should be disregarded for tax purposes. * * * On appeal, the United States Court of Appeals for the Sixth Circuit affirmed. * * * We granted the Commissioner's petition for certiorari.

II

For federal income tax purposes, gain or loss from the sale or use of property is attributable to the owner of the property. See *Helvering v. Horst*, 311 U.S. 112, 116–117 (1940); *Blair v. Commissioner*, 300 U.S. 5, 12 (1937); see also *Commissioner v. Sunnen*, 333 U.S. 591, 604 (1948). The problem we face here is that two different taxpayers can plausibly be regarded as the owner. Neither the Internal Revenue Code nor the regulations promulgated by the Secretary of the Treasury provide significant guidance as to which should be selected. It is common ground between the parties, however, that if a corporation holds title to property as agent for a partnership, then for tax purposes the partnership and not the corporation is the owner. Given agreement on that premise, one would suppose that there would be agreement upon the conclusion as well. For each of respondents' apartment complexes, an agency agreement expressly provided that the corporation would "hold such property as nominee and agent for" the partnership, * * * and that the partnership would have sole control of and responsibility for the apartment complex. The partnership in each instance was identified as the principal and owner of the property during financing, construction, and operation. The lenders, contractors, managers, employees, and tenants—all who had contact with the development—knew that the corporation was merely the agent of the partnership, if they knew of the existence of the corporation at all. In each instance the relationship between the corporation and the partnership was, in both form and substance, an agency with the partnership as principal.

The Commissioner contends, however, that the normal indicia of agency cannot suffice for tax purposes when, as here, the alleged principals are the controlling shareholders of the alleged agent corporation. That, it asserts, would undermine the principle of *Moline Properties v. Commissioner*, 319 U.S. 436 (1943), which held that a corporation is a separate taxable entity even if it has only one shareholder who exercises total control over its affairs. Obviously, *Moline's* separate-entity principle would be significantly compromised if shareholders of closely held corporations could, by clothing the corporation with some attributes of agency with respect to particular assets, leave themselves free at the end of the tax year to make a claim—perhaps even a good-faith claim—of either agent or owner status, depending upon which choice turns out to minimize their tax liability. The Commissioner does not have the resources to audit and litigate the many cases in which agency status could be thought debatable. Hence, the Commissioner argues, in this shareholder context he can reasonably demand that the taxpayer meet a prophylactically clear test of agency.

We agree with the principle, but the question remains whether the test the Commissioner proposes is appropriate. The parties have debated at length the significance of our opinion in *National Carbide Corp. v. Commissioner, supra.* In that case, the three corporations that were wholly owned subsidiaries of another corporation agreed to operate their production plants as "agents" for the parent, transferring to it all profits except for a nominal sum. The subsidiaries reported as gross income only this sum, but the Commissioner concluded that they should be taxed on the entirety of the profits because they were not really agents. We agreed, reasoning first, that the mere fact of the parent's control over the subsidiaries did not establish the existence of an agency, since such control is typical of all shareholder-corporation relationships, *id.*, at 429–434; and second, that the agreements to pay the parent all profits above

¶ 1120

a nominal amount were not determinative since income must be taxed to those who actually earn it without regard to anticipatory assignment, *id.*, at 435–436. We acknowledged, however, that there was such a thing as "a true corporate agent ... of [an] owner-principal," *id.*, at 437, and proceeded to set forth four indicia and two requirements of such status, the sum of which has become known in the lore of federal income tax law as the "six *National Carbide* factors":

> "[1] Whether the corporation operates in the name and for the account of the principal, [2] binds the principal by its actions, [3] transmits money received to the principal, and [4] whether receipt of income is attributable to the services of employees of the principal and to assets belonging to the principal are some of the relevant considerations in determining whether a true agency exists. [5] If the corporation is a true agent, its relations with its principal must not be dependent upon the fact that it is owned by the principal, if such is the case. [6] Its business purpose must be the carrying on of the normal duties of an agent." * * *

We readily discerned that these factors led to a conclusion of nonagency in *National Carbide* itself. There each subsidiary had represented to its customers that it (not the parent) was the company manufacturing and selling its products; each had sought to shield the parent from service of legal process; and the operations had used thousands of the subsidiaries' employees and nearly $20 million worth of property and equipment listed as assets on the subsidiaries' books. *Id.*, at 425, 434, 438, and n.21.

The Commissioner contends that the last two *National Carbide* factors are not satisfied in the present case. To take the last first: The Commissioner argues that here the corporation's business purpose with respect to the property at issue was not "the carrying on of the normal duties of an agent," since it was acting not as the agent but rather as the owner of the property for purposes of Kentucky's usury laws. We do not agree. It assuredly was not acting as the owner in fact, since respondents represented themselves as the principals to all parties concerned with the loans. Indeed, it was the lenders themselves who required the use of a corporate nominee. Nor does it make any sense to adopt a contrary-to-fact legal presumption that the corporation was the principal, imposing a federal tax sanction for the apparent evasion of Kentucky's usury law. To begin with, the Commissioner has not established that these transactions were an evasion. Respondents assert without contradiction that use of agency arrangements in order to permit higher interest was common practice, and it is by no means clear that the practice violated the spirit of the Kentucky law, much less its letter. It might well be thought that the borrower does not generally require usury protection in a transaction sophisticated enough to employ a corporate agent—assuredly not the normal *modus operandi* of the loan shark. That the [Kentucky] statute positively envisioned corporate nominees is suggested by a provision

¶ 1120

which forbids charging the higher corporate interest rates "to a corporation, the principal asset of which shall be the ownership of a one (1) or two (2) family dwelling," * * *—which would seem to prevent use of the nominee device for ordinary home-mortgage loans. In any event, even if the transaction did run afoul of the usury law, Kentucky, like most States, regards only the lender as the usurer, and the borrower as the victim. * * * Since the Kentucky statute imposed no penalties upon the borrower for allowing himself to be victimized, nor treated him as *in pari delicto*, but to the contrary enabled him to pay back the principal without any interest, and to sue for double the amount of interest already paid (plus attorney's fees), * * * the United States would hardly be vindicating Kentucky law by depriving the usury victim of tax advantages he would otherwise enjoy. In sum, we see no basis in either fact or policy for holding that the corporation was the principal because of the nature of its participation in the loans.

Of more general importance is the Commissioner's contention that the arrangements here violate the fifth *National Carbide* factor—that the corporate agent's "relations with its principal must not be dependent upon the fact that it is owned by the principal." The Commissioner asserts that this cannot be satisfied unless the corporate agent and its shareholder principal have an "arm's-length relationship" that includes the payment of a fee for agency services. The meaning of *National Carbide's* fifth factor is, at the risk of understatement, not entirely clear. Ultimately, the relations between a corporate agent and its owner-principal are *always* dependent upon the fact of ownership, in that the owner can cause the relations to be altered or terminated at any time. Plainly that is not what was meant, since on that interpretation all subsidiary-parent agencies would be invalid for tax purposes, a position which the *National Carbide* opinion specifically disavowed. We think the fifth *National Carbide* factor—so much more abstract than the others— was no more and no less than a generalized statement of the concern, expressed earlier in our own discussion, that the separate-entity doctrine of *Moline* not be subverted.

In any case, we decline to parse the text of *National Carbide* as though that were itself the governing statute. As noted earlier, it is uncontested that the law attributes tax consequences of property held by a genuine agent to the principal; and we agree that it is reasonable for the Commissioner to demand unequivocal evidence of genuineness in the corporation-shareholder context, in order to prevent evasion of *Moline*. We see no basis, however, for holding that unequivocal evidence can only consist of the rigid requirements (arm's-length dealing plus agency fee) that the Commissioner suggests. Neither of those is demanded by the law of agency, which permits agents to be unpaid family members, friends, or associates. See Restatement (Second) of Agency §§ 16, 21, 22 (1958). It seems to us that the genuineness of the agency relationship is adequately assured, and tax-avoiding manipulation adequately avoided,

¶ 1120

when the fact that the corporation is acting as agent for its shareholders with respect to a particular asset is set forth in a written agreement at the time the asset is acquired, the corporation functions as agent and not principal with respect to the asset for all purposes, and the corporation is held out as the agent and not principal in all dealings with third parties relating to the asset. Since these requirements were met here, the judgment of the Court of Appeals is [affirmed].

* * *

[¶ 1125]

Note

Is the test of agency status articulated by the Court adequate to prevent what the Court referred to as the subversion of the separate entity doctrine of the *Moline* case? How hard would it be to pass the Court's test?

[¶ 1130]

I. IDENTIFYING THE PROPER TAXPAYER

Simply because a corporation is recognized as a separately taxable entity does not mean that the corporation, rather than one or more of its shareholders, must be taxed on a receipt formally derived by the corporation. Under general principles of income taxation derived from such cases as Lucas v. Earl, 281 U.S. 111 (1930), the IRS has the authority to require the reporting of items of income by the taxpayer who economically generated the item rather than by the taxpayer who received the payment of the income. Accordingly, even though the IRS may not be able to ignore a corporate entity, it may nevertheless be able to tax the income of the corporation directly to the shareholders of the corporation under assignment of income principles.

In the taxation of business income, the general authority of the IRS is strengthened by the specific mandate of Section 482. That provision specifically authorizes the IRS to reallocate items of income and expense among two or more businesses under common control to the extent necessary clearly to reflect the income of each business. While Section 482 more commonly is applied to transactions among subsidiaries of a single parent corporation, and is examined in that context in Chapter 14, it may also require the reallocation of an item of income from a corporation to an individual who is its controlling shareholder.

For example, one recurring type of case has involved an individual taxpayer who for many years operated a profitable and unincorporated business based upon the personal services of the taxpayer (one case involved a well known entertainer). Presumably because corporations were subject to a lower rate of tax than was the individual (or a particular corporation had a net operating loss carryover), the individual taxpayer transferred the business to a new or existing corporation, all of the stock of which was owned by the taxpayer (or the taxpayer's children). The taxpayer then became the principal employee of the corporation and continued the business in much the same manner as in the past. However, since the individual was only paid a nominal salary, substantially all of the profits of the business would be taxed to the corporation at its lower rate.

In the early cases of this type, the corporation made little contribution to the production of income and the individual taxpayer was severely undercompensated. On those facts the IRS was reasonably successful in invoking assignment of income principles or Section 482 to tax the individual on all or most of the income from the business and thus deny the tax benefits of incorporation. See, e.g., Ach v. Commissioner, 42 T.C. 114 (1964), aff'd, 358 F.2d 342 (6th Cir.), cert. denied, 385 U.S. 899 (1966). However, in later cases, the contribution by the corporation to the production of the income through other employees or independent contractors was emphasized and the compensation paid to the shareholder-employee was less inadequate. On those facts, the courts have a great deal more trouble concluding that the income generated by the business should be taxed to the employee rather than to the corporate employer (all of the stock of which happened to be owned by the employee or the employee's relatives).

In Keller v. Commissioner, 77 T.C. 1014 (1981), aff'd, 723 F.2d 58 (10th Cir.1983), for example, a doctor who was a partner in a medical partnership and a shareholder-employee in a related corporation formed his own personal services corporation which contracted to provide his services to the existing entities. The purpose of the arrangement appears to have been to create deferred compensation arrangements (in which the other employees could not participate) to shelter Dr. Keller's salary from current tax. Because the value of the overall compensation package was not greatly reduced by the arrangement, the court declined to apply Section 482 notwithstanding the lack of any real business purpose for his corporation. Decisions like *Keller* demonstrated that the then existing tax provisions, such as Section 482, were inadequate to prevent the inappropriate use of the corporate form to reduce tax liability.

Since the corporate entity cannot easily be disregarded and the assignment of income doctrine cannot always be invoked, the IRS turned to its third line of attack. In a series of statutory amendments, Congress sought to specifically identify the tax avoidance behavior it regarded as improper and to withdraw any tax benefits from the use of a corporation for those purposes. An early effort to deter the shifting of investment income and certain personal service income to a corporation was embodied in the personal holding company rules and is examined in Chapter 7. Those provisions, however, could generally be avoided through careful planning. A second attempt is contained in Section 269A.

¶ 1130

On its face, Section 269A appears to add little to the existing command of Section 482; the new section merely authorizes a reallocation of income or loss between a corporation and its owner-employee to prevent tax avoidance or to clearly reflect income—as does Section 482. Indeed, the application of Section 269A is limited by the two requirements in Section 269A(a). Paragraph (1) imposes the factual limitation that substantially all of the services provided by the corporation be provided to a single taxpayer, and paragraph (2) imposes the subjective requirement that the corporation be formed or availed of for the principal purpose of avoiding tax or obtaining a tax benefit. Nevertheless, the legislative history to Section 269A indicates that the purpose of the section was to overrule the decision in *Keller* and to instruct the courts to more actively restrict the use of the corporate form solely for the purpose of obtaining tax benefits. H.R. Conf. Rep. No. 760, 97th Cong., 2d Sess. 633–34 (1982).

It was Congress' final line of attack on the use of a corporation to reduce tax on the earned income of its owners, however, that proved to be its most successful. In an additional series of statutory amendments, Congress simply eliminated the tax benefits of incorporation for businesses like Dr. Keller's. Most significantly, as discussed at ¶ 1015, Section 11(a)(2) now provides that personal service corporations may not benefit from the lower graduated tax rates otherwise available to corporations and that all of their income is taxed at the maximum 35 percent rate. In addition, a general revision of the rules governing deferred compensation arrangements conformed the benefits available to the owners-employees of closely held corporate businesses to the level of benefits available to the owners of an unincorporated business. These revisions, along with Section 269A, have made it vastly more difficult for individual taxpayers to reduce their tax liabilities by causing a corporation lacking in substance to report items of income otherwise reportable by the individual.

[¶ 1135]

J. A ROADMAP FOR THE TRIP AHEAD

The taxation of business entities is undeniably a complicated subject. The following chapters, however, break that subject down into easily digestible pieces. It will help in mastering those chapters to see how all of the pieces of this grand puzzle fit together and that is the purpose of these pages. We have already examined the question of what entities formed under state or federal law are to be treated for federal income tax purposes as a corporation subject to the rules of subchapter C. The remaining rules governing the taxation of C corporations are almost entirely devoted to prescribing the consequences of the transfer of property between corporations and their shareholders (which may, of course, be corporations themselves). In this book, those rules are addressed in a sequence that follows the life cycle of the corporation.

While the incorporation of a previously unincorporated business as a technical matter would be a realization event that would trigger taxation of the unrealized appreciation in the properties transferred to the corporation, Congress long ago concluded that it would not be appropriate to impose a tax at that time. To defer the taxation of that gain, Section 351 provides for nonrecognition of gain or loss upon the transfer of property to a corporation in exchange for the corporation's stock. That favorable rule is not limited to transfers incident to the creation of a corporation; it can also defer taxation on transfers to existing corporations. However, not all transfers of property to a corporation are entitled to nonrecognition. Deferral of tax seems appropriate when the ownership of a business continues largely unchanged notwithstanding its change in form from unincorporated to incorporated but does not seem appropriate when property is merely being sold. Section 351 defines when the ownership of property transferred to a corporation has been sufficiently continued to be entitled to nonrecognition and is examined in Chapter 2.

As a corporate law matter the economic ownership and control of a corporation is represented in the equity and debt securities that the corporation issues. In allocating those interests, corporations have available a wide range of securities, such as common or preferred stock, debt in various forms, and options or convertible securities. Each type of security may have different income tax consequences to both the corporation and the security holder. As a result, the design of the capital structure of a corporation can become a complex matter of balancing competing tax and non-tax considerations. Chapter 3 covers the basic rules governing the tax consequences of differing equity and debt securities.

The typical distribution of the profits derived by a corporation to its shareholders constitutes a dividend, the taxation of which is considered in Chapter 4. By contrast, the sale of stock in the corporation by a shareholder is treated like any other sale of property. Between those polar extremes lies the sale of stock in a corporation back to the corporation itself, a redemption. That transaction can have an economic consequence similar to a sale of the stock to another shareholder, but it can also have an economic consequence that is nearly identical to a dividend. However, dividends and sales may be taxed quite differently. The Code's solution here is to tax redemptions as either dividends or as sales depending upon the consequences of the redemption. Sections 302 and 303, considered in Chapter 5, draw this very important line. The line between a dividend and a sale becomes even harder to draw when one or more shareholders own not one but several corporations. If the stock of one of such corporations is sold to another, causing the first corporation to become a subsidiary of the second, is that transaction really a sale of

¶ 1135

the first corporation or is it a disguised dividend by the second? That difficult issue is addressed by Section 304.

The liquidation of a corporation and the distribution of all of its assets to its shareholders in extinguishment of their stock interests is so much like a sale of stock that it is almost always treated as a sale and accorded capital gains taxation. In practice, however, the liquidation of a corporation is usually just one step in the sale of the business of one corporation to another. Either one corporation has sold its assets to a second and thereafter dissolved and distributed the proceeds of sale to its shareholders or the second corporation has purchased the stock of the first corporation from the shareholders of the first corporation and then dissolved that corporation in order to combine the assets of the two corporations. Chapter 8, therefore, considers the taxation of the liquidation of a corporation in the context of these different forms of taxable corporate acquisitions.

A corporation may distribute a dividend, not of cash but of additional shares of its stock. Sometimes such a stock dividend may look like a mere subdivision of the existing stock interest and not a taxable event but sometimes it may look like the shareholder has received something that he or she did not have before and which therefore should be subject to tax. Here again, the solution adopted by the Code is to treat stock dividends as either taxable or tax free depending upon the effect of the distribution. That means another line must be drawn and Sections 305 and 306, discussed in Chapter 6, undertake that task.

Incorporating a business in order to reduce income taxes is perfectly legitimate. However, over the years taxpayers have discovered methods of using corporations to reduce taxes in ways that Congress did not regard as legitimate. Particularly when corporate tax rates are materially lower than individual rates, shareholders might cause their corporations to retain earnings that were not needed in the business, or might shift income into corporations, in order to avoid the higher individual tax rates. Chapter 7 discusses some of the approaches Congress has taken to discourage use of such schemes including the personal holding company and accumulated earnings tax rules.

When the businesses of two, previously separate, corporations are combined, the transaction can resemble a sale of one business to the other which should be subject to tax. However, and particularly when the former owners of the two businesses end up owning the stock in the surviving corporation, the transaction may look like a mere change in the form of the ownership of the businesses and thus not an appropriate occasion for the imposition of tax. To allow such business combinations to go forward with a minimum of income tax obstacles, Congress created, and the courts refined, the concept of a reorganization. If a merger or other business combination falls within the very exact definition of a reorganization contained in Section 368, then the transaction will be free

¶ 1135

of tax, in whole or in part, at both the corporate and shareholder levels. The concept of a reorganization is one of the most highly developed under the income tax laws—which makes the study of this area both fascinating and complex. Chapter 9 provides a basic overview of the tax treatment of reorganizations, including a description of the nature of those transactions and the historical development of the judicial and statutory requirements for nonrecognition. Chapters 10 and 11 present a more detailed examination of acquisitive reorganizations and the restructuring of a single corporation, respectively. The tax accounting aspects of reorganizations, including the important question of the extent to which the carried over tax losses of an acquired corporation may be used by the acquiring corporation, are addressed in Chapter 13.

Chapter 12 explores the reverse of a merger: the division of a preexisting corporation into two or more successor corporations. In appropriate cases, the conversion of one corporation into two commonly owned corporations will be a tax free, nonrecognition transaction like a merger. However, because the division of a corporation can closely resemble an ordinary dividend, Section 355 imposes a series of restrictions on the availability of nonrecognition treatment for divisions.

Big business, and sometimes little business, is often conducted, not through a single corporation but through a family of commonly owned corporations. That fact of corporate life has required the development of rules governing transactions among these related companies. To prevent the arbitrary shifting of income from one corporation to another, the regulations under Section 482 have crafted extremely elaborate rules governing the price at which property and services may be transferred between related corporations. In addition, the Code allows a common parent corporation and all of its domestic subsidiaries to file a single consolidated income tax return. Chapter 14 provides just a glimpse of both of those sets of rules.

While in general corporations are subject to two levels of tax and partnerships are subject to just a single level of tax, in one situation corporations are only subject to one level of taxation. If a corporation elects to be taxed under the provisions of Subchapter S, the income of the corporation is taxed directly to its shareholders and one level of tax is achieved, somewhat like the taxation of partnerships. However, S corporations are taxed very differently from partnerships; the S corporation rules are quite rigid and not especially favorable to taxpayers. Moreover, only a tightly defined set of corporations can make this election. The rules governing this curious hybrid are discussed in Chapter 15.

While we tend to think of partnerships as more primitive and simpler than corporations, somewhat perversely, the tax rules governing partnerships are markedly more complex than the rules governing corporations. There are several reasons, some good, some bad, for this

¶ 1135

unhappy situation. One is that the rules of Subchapter K must deal, not only with transactions between partnerships and their partners, but also with the allocation and reporting of income by the partners. Second, Congress has always been a bit unsure about how much significance should be attached to the existence of the partnership entity. As a result, in some transactions the entity is given effect (as would be a corporation) while in others it is not (as if the partners were merely tenants in common) and in many others, the partners may elect (within limits) either entity or nonentity treatment. That makes for a lot of complexity. Chapters 16 through 25 approach these problems in small, manageable steps but keep the aspirin handy. As in the taxation of corporations, these chapters are arranged in a life cycle sequence.

¶ 1135

Chapter 2

CORPORATE FORMATION

[¶ 2000]

A. OVERVIEW

When a corporation is organized, the corporation generally obtains assets by issuing stock in exchange for a transfer of cash or other property. Ordinarily, these transactions do not result in the recognition of taxable gain or loss by either the shareholder-transferors of property or the transferee corporation. This may seem surprising in view of the apparent accession to wealth by the corporate recipient and the obvious realization event by those who relinquished their properties in exchange for stock of the transferee. Section 351 and related sections account for this nonrecognition treatment. For the shareholder-transferor, Section 351(a) provides that no gain or loss shall be recognized if one or more persons transfer "property" to a corporation "solely in exchange for stock" of the corporation and the transferor or transferors hold 80 percent "control" of the transferee corporation immediately after the exchange within the meaning of Section 368(c). For the transferee corporation, Section 1032 provides that no gain or loss is recognized upon the receipt of property in exchange for its stock, regardless of whether the requirements of Section 351 are met.

Tax on the gain realized but not recognized by the transferor-shareholder is not forgiven, but is deferred, and the mechanism used to achieve this result is the rules for determining basis. Under Section 358(a)(1), the transferor's basis in the stock received from the corporation in the Section 351 exchange is generally the same as the transferor's former basis in the property transferred to the corporation (sometimes called a "substituted basis") and, under Section 362(a), the transferee corporation's basis in the property received from the transferor is generally the same as the transferor's former adjusted basis in the property (sometimes called a "carryover basis"). These rules for "substituted" or "carryover" basis ensure that gain not recognized when property is exchanged for stock in a qualifying Section 351 exchange will be recognized if and when the transferor-shareholder sells the stock received in the exchange or the corporation sells the property. When both the transferor-shareholder sells the stock and the corporation sells the property, however, the basis rules result in double taxation. There are different rules for the transfer of loss properties, but that will be covered later in the Chapter.

Sometimes, in addition to receiving stock of the new corporation, the shareholders-transferors receive other property "to boot," such as cash, debt, or any other non-stock property. This "boot" property is taxed currently. It does not, however, disqualify the incorporation transaction from nonrecognition treatment altogether. Rather, the taxation of boot property is an exception to the general rule of nonrecognition of gain with respect to Section 351 exchanges in the organization of a corporation. The basis rules are adjusted to ensure that any non-cash boot property is not taxed again upon a subsequent disposition of the corporate stock.

The nonrecognition of gain regime applicable to transfers of property to controlled corporations carries out two recurrent congressional policies.[1] The first is that a change in form but not in substance should not trigger the imposition of tax, especially when there is a continuity of interest in the transferred properties. It follows that tax should not be imposed when shareholders shift ownership of properties from themselves individually or from a partnership in which they are partners to their controlled corporation because what occurs is a mere change in form of ownership; the transferor-shareholders have simply exchanged their direct ownership of the transferred property for indirect ownership interests in the property through their equity interests in the transferee corporation. A second congressional policy pertains to economic efficiency: the notion that the imposition of tax could deter the implementation of sound business purposes for shifting from an unincorporated enterprise to an incorporated enterprise. Both policies also explain the nonrecognition treatment authorized for other corporate restructurings discussed in Chapters 8 and 9, such as corporate reorganizations and liquidations of controlled subsidiaries into their parent corporations.

---

1. Early on in the history of the income tax, incorporation transactions were apparently considered taxable. In 1918, the Senate Finance Committee proposed nonrecognition treatment, but the proposal was struck from the Revenue Act of 1918 by the Conference Committee. One commentator has suggested that this resistance was due to Congress' concern about distinguishing incorporations from barter transactions in which merchants contributed their goods for corporate stock. See Jensen, "Of Form and Substance: Tax–Free Incorporations and Other Transactions Under Section 351," 11 Va. Tax Rev. 349, 382 (1991). Soon after the 1918 Act passed, though, the Secretary of the Treasury recommended extending nonrecognition treatment to incorporation transactions and Congress enacted the forerunner to Section 351 in 1921. Revenue Act of 1921, § 202(c)(3), 42 Stat. 227, 230.

¶ 2000

[¶ 2005]

Illustration

Antoine and Bernadette organized the A & B Corporation with an initial capital of $200,000. Each received 1,000 shares of common stock with a par value of $100. Antoine paid cash of $100,000 for his shares. Bernadette transferred an unencumbered small building worth $100,000, with an adjusted basis of $60,000, which she had purchased five years earlier. Both Antoine and Bernadette are U.S. taxpayers.

This is a classic Section 351 incorporation exchange in that Antoine and Bernadette have collectively transferred "property" to a corporation "solely in exchange for stock" in that corporation and they "control" the A & B Corporation immediately after the exchange by virtue of their ownership of 100 percent of the outstanding stock. As a consequence, Bernadette will not recognize the $40,000 gain realized on the contribution of her building pursuant to Section 351 and A & B Corporation will not recognize any gain on the distribution of its stock in exchange for property pursuant to Section 1032. To preserve the gain for recognition upon a future taxable transaction, Bernadette will hold her stock in A & B corporation with a substituted basis of $60,000 under Section 358(a). The A & B Corporation holds the property contributed by Bernadette with a carryover basis under Section 362(a), thus preserving gain at the corporate level as well. Antoine holds his stock with a basis equal to the $100,000 he exchanged, which reflects the fact that the property he contributed was cash and therefore did not have any built-in gain.

B. REQUIREMENTS OF SECTION 351(A)

[¶ 2010]

1. "TRANSFER" OF "PROPERTY"

Section 351(a) nonrecognition treatment applies only to "transfers" of "property." The term "property" as used in that subsection is a broad term; apart from the exceptions discussed below, it encompasses most things of value, whether real or personal, or tangible or intangible, that might be transferred to a corporation in exchange for its stock. Intellectual properties and properties created by personal efforts fall within the term. See, e.g., Rev. Rul. 64–56, 1964–1 (pt. 1) C.B. 133 (goodwill, patents, and secret processes). The term property also includes U.S. or foreign currency. Rev. Rul. 69–357, 1969–1 C.B. 101.

Although "property" is defined broadly for purposes of Section 351, there are several codified exceptions. First, a contribution of past or future services is expressly excluded from the term "property." § 351(d)(1). Thus, an individual who receives stock in exchange for services must include in income the excess of the fair market value of that stock over its cost (if any) in the tax year when the stock becomes transferable or not subject to a substantial risk of forfeiture. § 83(a).[2] Such income is ordinary compensation income.

A contribution of services might qualify as property if the services are embodied in property. Thus, for example, the transfer of certain intellectual property, such as patents and knowhow, involve an element of services provided by the transferor to enable the transferee to make effective use of the transferred property. The provision of services in this case may be considered part of a property transfer rather than being a transfer distinct from the property itself. In Rev. Rul. 64–56, 1964–1 (pt. 1) C.B. 133, 134, services are assimilated to proprietary knowhow transferred in a Section 351 exchange if the services are ancillary and subsidiary to the proprietary knowhow. Thus, services involved in assisting the transferee in incorporating transferred knowhow in its manufacturing operations would be treated as ancillary and subsidiary to the knowhow, and therefore the stock received would be eligible for nonrecognition treatment, while continuing services after the start-up phase of the transferee's manufacturing would not and stock received would be taxable. Id.[3]

Second, debt obligations owed by the corporate transferee to the transferor, but "not evidenced by a security," as well as any interest on the transferee's debts which accrued as income in the hands of the transferor, cannot qualify as "property" entitled to nonrecognition treatment. § 351(d)(2) and (3). If the latter rule were otherwise, that former creditor-turned-shareholder might avoid reporting as ordinary income amounts already earned as interest, but then converted by the transfer into stock of the debtor.

2. EXCHANGE "SOLELY FOR STOCK"

[¶ 2015]

a. General

The second requirement for nonrecognition treatment is that the transferor of property to a controlled corporation receive solely stock in exchange—i.e., an equity interest in the corporation that preserves the

---

2. Even if the stock is not transferrable and subject to forfeiture, the individual may elect to include that excess in income in the tax year in which the stock is received. § 83(b). The issuance of stock for services is tax-free to the corporation under Section 1032(a). If the stock represents compensation, the corporation may treat the fair market value of the stock as a deduction under Section 162(a)(1) or as a capital expenditure under Section 263(a), depending on the circumstances. If the stock is deductible compensation, the corporation may not take a deduction until the recipient includes the compensation in income. § 83(h).

3. Note that if the individual rendering services that are not ancillary to a transfer of intellectual property also concurrently transfers a more than insubstantial amount of property to the corporation in exchange for stock, that transferor's total stockholdings (regardless of whether received for property or for services) can be counted in measuring whether the control requirement of Section 351(a) and 368(c) is met. See ¶ 2075.

transferor's ongoing, albeit indirect, ownership in the transferred property. § 351(a). Although the literal wording of Section 351(a) confers nonrecognition treatment only upon a transfer "solely in exchange for stock," Section 351(b) makes clear that partial nonrecognition can be achieved notwithstanding a transferor's receipt of boot in addition to stock.

Despite the requirement that the transferor receive stock, a shareholder who owns 100 percent of a corporation may, on transferring additional property to that entity, be deemed to have engaged in a Section 351 exchange even without receiving additional stock in exchange. Lessinger v. Commissioner, 872 F.2d 519 (2d Cir.1989). The Second Circuit in *Lessinger* unsurprisingly concluded that issuance of stock in this situation "would be a meaningless gesture." 872 F.2d at 522. In substance the result would be the same whether or not the wholly owned corporation issued additional shares to its sole shareholder; only the number of shares held would differ. See also *Peracchi v. Commissioner*, at ¶ 2240.

[¶ 2020]

b. Securities

Prior to 1989, there was some uncertainty as to whether a purported sale of property to a corporation in exchange for "debt" could be recharacterized as a transfer in exchange for a disguised "equity" interest; an affirmative answer meant that Section 351(a) and related basis provisions could apply. Section 351(a) formerly extended nonrecognition treatment beyond stock to "securities" (i.e., relatively long-term debt obligations), suggesting that debt might be qualified property. However, in 1989 the reference to "securities" in Section 351(a) was repealed. Thus, it is now clear that debt securities are boot requiring the recognition of gain, although the inclusion of the boot gain may often be reported on the installment sale method of Section 453.[4] See ¶ 2130.

[¶ 2025]

c. Qualified Preferred Stock

While debt is clearly excluded from the definition of "stock," up until 1997 all stock interests, common and preferred and voting and nonvoting, continued to qualify as "stock" for purposes of Section 351. In 1997, however, Congress enacted Section 351(g), which restricted the definition of stock for purposes of 351(a). Section 351(g)(1) specifies that certain preferred stock, called "nonqualified preferred stock," must be treated as boot. There was concern that preferred stock was being used

---

4. Vestiges of the pre–1989 law remain in the multiple (and now incorrect) references in the Section 351 regulations to non- recognition property in the form of stock or (and) securities.

to disguise what is in substance the distribution of debt instruments, which would normally be considered boot in a Section 351 transaction. For purposes of Section 351(g), preferred stock is defined as stock with limited preferences, such as rights to fixed dividend payments and to payment of its par value on redemption or liquidation, and which does not significantly participate in the growth of the corporation (e.g., through a conversion privilege). § 351(g)(3)(A). In 2004, this definition was tightened to provide that "[s]tock shall not be treated as participating in corporate growth to any significant extent unless there is a real and meaningful likelihood of the shareholder actually participating in the earnings and growth of the corporation." Id. Congress further clarified the definition in 2005 by adding that the mere possibility that dividends will be paid beyond the limits set in the preference terms, such as through certain contingent participation rights, will be disregarded for purposes of determining whether the stock is limited and preferred as to dividends. Id.

Preferred stock status, however, does not by itself cause the preferred to be characterized as "nonqualified preferred" and hence excluded from the definition of stock. Rather, under Sections 351(g)(2)(A) and 351(g)(3) preferred stock will be classified as nonqualified preferred only if it has certain characteristics that are normally associated with a debt rather than an equity interest. More specifically, preferred stock will be "nonqualified preferred stock" if (i) the holder of such stock has the right to require the issuer or a related person to redeem or purchase the stock; (ii) the issuer or a related person is required to redeem or purchase such stock; (iii) the issuer or the related person has the right to redeem or purchase the stock and, as of the issue date, it is more likely than not that such right will be exercised; or (iv) the dividend rate on such stock varies in whole or in part (directly or indirectly) with reference to interest rates, commodity prices, or other similar indices. § 351(g)(2)(A). In the first three examples, the preferred stock will be treated as nonqualified only if the obligation cited may be exercised within the 20–year period beginning on the date the obligation is issued and the obligation is not subject to a contingency that, as of the issue date, would appear to make the likelihood of redemption or purchase remote. § 351(g)(2)(B). In the case of stock that is not publicly-traded, exceptions are provided for rights that may only be exercised upon the death, disability, or mental incapacity of the holder, or, in the case of compensation-related rights, the separation of the holder from the issuer's employment. § 351(g)(2)(C). See ¶ 10,240, where the exceptions to this definition and the definition of related person are further discussed.

While nonqualified preferred stock is not "stock" for purposes of Section 351, the legislative history indicates that it still may be considered "stock" for other purposes unless and until Treasury issues regulations to the contrary under Section 351(g)(4).[5] This is further discussed in connection with tax-free reorganizations in Chapter 10.

[¶ 2030]

Note

It is clear from the regulations that neither stock warrants nor other stock rights constitute "stock" for purposes of Section 351. Reg. § 1.351–1(a)(1). However, this does not mean that receipt of stock warrants and stock rights necessarily gives rise to immediate income recognition. Other rules aside from Section 351 may delay recognition until some later date, such as upon sale in the case of incentive stock options under Section 422 or upon exercise in the case of options subject to a substantial risk of forfeiture under Section 83.

[¶ 2035]

Problem

Consider the illustration at the beginning of this Chapter (¶ 2005). Antoine and Bernadette organized the A & B Corporation with an initial capital of $200,000. Each received 1,000 shares of common stock with a par value of $100. Antoine paid cash of $100,000 for his shares. Bernadette transferred an unencumbered small building worth $100,000, with an adjusted basis of $60,000, which she had purchased five years earlier. Both Antoine and Bernadette are U.S. taxpayers.

a. What if instead of receiving $100,000 in stock, Bernadette receives from the A & B Corporation 1,000 shares of stock worth $90,000 and $10,000 in corporate bonds issued by the A & B Corporation?

b. How would the result change, if at all, if Bernadette received from the A & B Corporation in lieu of the $10,000 in bonds, eight percent preferred stock with a par value and fair market value of $10,000 issued by the A & B Corporation, which the corporation was obligated to redeem (i.e., repurchase) at par in ten years. See § 351(g). Is this result appropriate?

[¶ 2040]

3. TRANSFERORS OF PROPERTY IN "CONTROL" OF THE CORPORATION

The third requirement imposed as a condition to treatment of an exchange as tax-free under Section 351(a) is that the person or persons transferring property to the corporation in exchange for stock must as a group be in "control" of the corporation "immediately after the exchange." Thus, under circumstances to be examined below, prompt

---

5. Staff of Joint Comm. on Tax'n, 105th Cong., 1st Sess., General Explanation of   Tax Legislation Enacted in 1997, at 210, 213 (1997).

relinquishment of control by the transferor(s) may prevent qualification under Section 351(a) and result in recognition of gain or loss.[6]

Although the definition of "control" differs in various contexts under Subchapter C, Section 351(a) specifically invokes for its purposes the definition contained in Section 368(c). The latter defines "control" to mean ownership of at least 80 percent of the total combined voting power of the corporation and at least 80 percent of the total number of shares of each class, taken separately, of nonvoting stock. These tests serve to reinforce the characterization of the transfer as effecting a change in form, not substance, from direct ownership by the transferor-shareholder(s) to indirect ownership through control of the transferee-corporation.

In the event that "nonqualified preferred stock" is issued to a transferor in exchange for property, the impact on the "control" requirement is as yet unsettled. The legislative history in the Conference Committee Report accompanying the enactment of Section 351(g) indicates an intent that such stock should be treated as stock for purposes of determining control "unless and until regulations provide otherwise."[7]

[¶ 2045]

a. Control "Immediately After the Exchange"

The regulations do not construe the requirement of Section 351(a) that the persons who transfer property to the corporation in exchange for its stock must be in control of the corporation immediately after the exchange literally, and for good reason. A literal interpretation of "immediately after the exchange" would require incorporators to act in virtual unison. Instead, the regulations provide that the phrase "does not necessarily require simultaneous exchanges by two or more persons, but comprehends a situation where the rights of the parties have been

---

6. The one codified exception, which is significant in connection with corporate restructurings discussed in later chapters, is Section 351(c)(1). This section provides that in determining whether the control requirement of Section 351(a) is met, the fact that a corporation distributes to its shareholders the stock it received in exchange for property is not to be taken into account.

7. H.R. Conf. Rep. No. 220, 105th Cong., 1st Sess. 545 (1997). Ironically, the example presented in the Report to demonstrate the latter point fails as an illustration because its outcome would have been the same whether or not the nonqualified preferred stock counted as stock. In the example, T–1 contributes appreciated property for all of the corporation's common stock while T–2 receives all of the nonquali-fied preferred stock in exchange for cash. The Report concludes that a nontaxable event occurs for T–1 by virtue of counting the preferred stock as stock—an outcome that would have been precisely the same on these facts had the preferred stock not counted as stock.

By contrast, if the facts had described T–2 as furnishing services rather than property, then indeed the tax results to T–1 would have depended on whether the nonqualified preferred stock counted as a class of qualifying preferred stock for purposes of the control requirement. For if that stock did so count, then the control necessary for nontaxable Section 351 treatment would be lacking because transferors of property would not have had the requisite 80 percent of each class of stock.

previously defined and the execution of the agreement proceeds with an expedition consistent with orderly procedure." Reg. § 1.351–1(a)(1).

An important interpretive issue under Section 351 and its statutory predecessors has been how long and under what circumstances the transferor's controlling stock must be retained and whether either a plan or a binding obligation to dispose of enough shares to bring the transferor's stockholdings below the requisite 80 percent floor would preclude meeting the statutory requirement as to control immediately after the exchange. In the context of Section 351(a), will a momentary controlling ownership after the transfer suffice? Or, under what circumstances (if any) should a planned disposition of stock needed to meet the control test by the original transferors of property constitute an integral part of the incorporation transaction that will disqualify the transaction for purposes of Section 351? These questions are the subject of the materials that follow.

Determining whether two steps separated in time (i.e., in this case the exchange of property for stock and the disposition of stock needed to meet the control test) will be treated as integral parts of the same transaction involves an application of what has come to be called the "step transaction doctrine." When this doctrine is applied, two separate steps are treated as parts of a single transaction. There are a number of formulations of the circumstances under which the step transaction doctrine will be applied. The formulations as applied to a particular set of circumstances may overlap and produce the same or different results. The issue of what formulation should be used sometimes arises in the context of Section 351, as the following materials illustrate. Under the so-called "binding commitment" test, which is the primary test courts have used in the Section 351 context, the step transaction doctrine is applied with the result that the requisite control is absent "immediately after the exchange" only when the transferor-shareholders are under an obligation at the time that they receive their shares to sell or otherwise transfer enough of them to bring the transferor-shareholders below the requisite 80–percent threshold. Another formulation that is more frequently invoked in the context of corporate reorganizations, discussed at ¶ 9065, is often called the "interdependence" test. Application of this test turns on whether the steps taken were so interdependent that the legal relations created by one transaction would have been fruitless without a completion of the series. See, e.g., American Bantam Car Co. v. Commissioner, 11 T.C. 397 (1948), aff'd per curiam, 177 F.2d 513 (3d Cir.1949), cert. denied, 339 U.S. 920 (1950); Manhattan Bldg. Co. v. Commissioner, 27 T.C. 1032, 1042 (1957) (acq.). Yet another formulation is frequently labeled the "end result" test. Under this test, separate steps will be integrated only if they were taken in furtherance and for the purpose of reaching the end result. E.g., King Enterprises, Inc. v. United States, 418 F.2d 511, 516 (Ct.Cl.1969). As the case and rulings

¶ 2045

below illustrate, whether the Section 351(a) control test is met may turn on how the step transaction doctrine is formulated.

Note that in the following case, which deals with the circumstances under which the step transaction doctrine will be applied in the context of Section 351(a), it is the taxpayer who seeks to avoid compliance with the requirements of Section 351.

[¶ 2050]

INTERMOUNTAIN LUMBER CO. v. COMMISSIONER

United States Tax Court, 1976.
65 T.C. 1025.

[Shook owned and operated a sawmill as an individual proprietor. Wilson was a customer for whom Shook processed logs into rough lumber for a fee. In addition, Shook and Wilson, as equal shareholders, operated a separate finishing plant for processing rough lumber. In March 1964, Shook's sawmill was damaged by fire. To replace it with a larger one required more capital than Shook alone could provide. Wilson agreed to assist in obtaining financing for the new mill on the condition that Shook sell to him an equal interest in a newly organized corporation, S & W Sawmill, Inc. (S & W), which was to take over Shook's damaged sawmill and rebuild it. An agreement by Shook to sell 182 shares (50 percent) of S & W stock to Wilson was entered into concurrently with the conveyance by Shook of his sawmill to S & W in exchange for 364 shares of S & W stock. Pursuant to the agreement with Wilson, Shook promptly placed 182 shares in escrow for Wilson and granted Wilson an irrevocable proxy to vote them.]

WILES, JUDGE:

* * *

* * * The only issue for decision is whether a certain corporate formation was nontaxable under section 351(a). This depends solely upon whether the primary incorporator had "control" of the requisite percentage of stock immediately after the exchange within the meaning of section 368(c).

* * *

In this case, respondent is in the unusual posture of arguing that a transfer to a corporation in return for stock was nontaxable under section 351, and Intermountain is in the equally unusual posture of arguing that the transfer was taxable because section 351 was inapplicable. The explanation is simply that Intermountain purchased all stock of the corporation, S & W, from its [the latter's] incorporators, and that Intermountain and S & W have filed consolidated income tax returns for [the] years in issue. Accordingly, if section 351 was applicable to the

¶ 2050

incorporators when S & W was formed, S & W and Intermountain must depreciate the assets of S & W on their consolidated returns on the incorporators' basis. Sec. 362(a). If section 351 was inapplicable, and the transfer of assets to S & W was accordingly to be treated as a sale, S & W and Intermountain could base depreciation on those returns on the fair market value of those assets at the time of incorporation, which was higher than the incorporators' cost and which would accordingly provide larger depreciation deductions. Secs. 167(g), 1011, and 1012.

Petitioner thus maintains that the transfer to S & W of all of S & W's property at the time of incorporation by the primary incorporator, one Dee Shook, was a taxable sale. It asserts that section 351 was inapplicable because an agreement for sale required Shook, as part of the incorporation transaction, to sell almost half of the S & W shares outstanding to one Milo Wilson over a period of time, thereby depriving Shook of the requisite percentage of stock necessary for "control" of S & W immediately after the exchange.

Respondent, on the other hand, maintains that the agreement between Shook and Wilson did not deprive Shook of ownership of the shares immediately after the exchange, as the stock purchase agreement merely gave Wilson an option to purchase the shares. Shook accordingly was in "control" of the corporation and the exchange was thus nontaxable under section 351.

* * *

Since Wilson was not a transferor of property and therefore cannot be counted for control under section 351, * * * we must determine if Shook alone owned the requisite percentage of shares for control. This determination depends upon whether, under all facts and circumstances surrounding the agreement for sale of 182 shares between Shook and Wilson, ownership of those shares was in Shook or Wilson.

A determination of "ownership," as that term is used in section 368(c) and for purposes of control under section 351, depends upon the obligations and freedom of action of the transferee with respect to the stock when he acquired it from the corporation. Such traditional ownership attributes as legal title, voting rights, and possession of stock certificates are not conclusive. If the transferee, as part of the transaction by which the shares were acquired, has irrevocably foregone or relinquished at that time the legal right to determine whether to keep the shares, ownership in such shares is lacking for purposes of section 351. By contrast, if there are no restrictions upon freedom of action at the time he acquired the shares, it is immaterial how soon thereafter the transferee elects to dispose of his stock or whether such disposition is in accord with a preconceived plan not amounting to a binding obligation. * * *

¶ 2050

After considering the entire record, we have concluded that Shook and Wilson intended to consummate a sale of the S & W stock, that they never doubted that the sale would be completed, that the sale was an integral part of the incorporation transaction, and that they considered themselves to be coowners of S & W upon execution of the stock purchase agreement in 1964. These conclusions are supported by minutes of the first stockholders meeting on July 7, 1964, at which Shook characterized the agreement for sale as a "sale"; minutes of a special meeting on July 15, 1964, at which Shook stated Wilson was to "purchase" half of Shook's stock; the "Agreement for Sale and Purchase of Stock" itself, dated July 15, 1964, which is drawn as an installment sale and which provides for payment of interest on unpaid principal; Wilson's deduction of interest expenses in connection with the agreement for sale, which would be inconsistent with an option; the S & W loan agreement, in which Shook and Wilson held themselves out as the "principal stockholders" of S & W and in which S & W covenanted to equally insure Shook and Wilson for $100,000; the March 1965 stock purchase agreement with S & W, which indicated that Shook and Wilson "*are* to remain *equal*" (emphasis added) shareholders in S & W; the letter of May 1967 from Shook and Wilson to Intermountain, which indicated that Wilson owed Shook the principal balance due on the shares as an unpaid obligation; and all surrounding facts and circumstances leading to corporate formation and execution of the above documents. Inconsistent and self-serving testimony of Shook and Wilson regarding their intent and understanding of the documents in evidence is unpersuasive in view of the record as a whole to alter interpretation of the transaction as a sale of stock by Shook to Wilson.

We accordingly cannot accept respondent's contention that the substance varied from the form of this transaction, which was, of course, labeled a "sale." The parties executed an "option" agreement on the same day that the "agreement for sale" was executed, and we have no doubt that they could and indeed did correctly distinguish between a sale and an option.

* * *

We thus believe that Shook, as part of the same transaction by which the shares were acquired (indeed, the agreement for sale was executed before the sawmill was deeded to S & W), had relinquished when he acquired those shares the legal right to determine whether to keep them. Shook was under an obligation, upon receipt of the shares, to transfer the stock as he received Wilson's principal payments. * * * We note also that the agreement for sale gave Wilson the right to prepay principal and receive all 182 shares at any time in advance. Shook therefore did not own, within the meaning of section 368(c), the requisite percentage of stock immediately after the exchange to control the corporation as required for nontaxable treatment under section 351.

¶ **2050**

We note also that the basic premise of Section 351 is to avoid recognition of gain or loss resulting from transfer of property to a corporation which works a change of form only. See Bittker & Eustice, Federal Income Taxation of Corporations and Shareholders, par. 3.01, p. 3–4 (3d ed. 1971). Accordingly, if the transferor sells his stock as part of the same transaction, the transaction is taxable because there has been more than a mere change in form. * * * In this case, the transferor agreed to sell and did sell 50 percent of the stock to be received, placed the certificates in the possession of an escrow agent, and granted a binding proxy to the purchaser to vote the stock being sold. Far more than a mere change in form was effected.

We accordingly hold for petitioner. * * *

[¶ 2055]

Problems

1. Why did the taxpayer (petitioner) in *Intermountain Lumber* argue against the applicability of Section 351?

2. Would the result have been different if Shook's sale of stock to Wilson had been pursuant to a plan but not a binding obligation?

3. Suppose that Shook insisted on a tax-free incorporation, yet needed capital from Wilson to finance the rebuilding of the sawmill. What planning might have achieved Shook's goal? Consider the following materials.

[¶ 2060]

REVENUE RULING 79–70

1979–1 C.B. 144.

Issue

Is the control requirement of Section 351(a) * * *, which provides for nonrecognition of gain or loss on transfers of property to a controlled corporation, satisfied where part of the stock of the controlled corporation received by a transferor in exchange for property is sold to another person who transferred property to the corporation in exchange for securities?

Facts

Corporation X transferred property to a newly organized corporation, Newco, in exchange for all of Newco's stock (a single class of voting common stock). Pursuant to a prearranged binding agreement between X and corporation Y, X sold 40 percent of its Newco stock for its fair market value to Y, and Y purchased securities for cash from Newco. Newco would not have been formed if Y had not agreed to purchase securities for cash from Newco and part of the Newco stock from X.

LAW AND ANALYSIS

* * *

Since the sale of Newco stock by X to Y was an integral part of the incorporation and pursuant to a binding agreement entered into prior to the exchange, the control requirement of section 351(a) is determined after the sale. See *Hazeltine Corp. v. Commissioner*, 89 F.2d 513 (3d Cir.1937), *Intermountain Lumber Co. v. Commissioner*, 65 T.C. 1025 (1976), and Rev. Rul. 70–522, 1970–2 C.B. 81, all of which hold that the control requirement of section 351(a) is not satisfied where, pursuant to a binding agreement entered into prior to the transfer of property to the corporation, a transferor loses control of a corporation by a sale of stock received in the transfer to a third party, who does not transfer property to the corporation in the transaction. After the sale was completed in the instant case, 60 percent of the Newco stock was owned by X and 40 percent of the stock was owned by Y. However, since Y was not a "transferor" of property to Newco with respect to Newco stock, Y's ownership of the Newco stock purchased from X cannot be counted in determining whether the control requirement of section 351(a) was met. The fact that Y transferred cash to Newco in exchange for securities as part of the transaction does not make Y a transferor for purposes of the control requirement of section 351(a). See Rev. Rul. 73–472, 1973–2 C.B. 114, and Rev. Rul. 73–473, 1973–2 C.B. 115, which hold that a person who receives only securities from a corporation in exchange for property, and who is not a shareholder prior to the exchange, is not a "transferor" for purposes of satisfying the section 351 control requirement.

HOLDING

Since X only owned 60 percent of the Newco stock "immediately after the exchange" within the meaning of section 351(a) * * *, the 80 percent control requirement of section 351(a) was not satisfied. Gain or loss to X will be determined and recognized under section 1001.

[¶ 2065]

Problems

1. Would a taxable event for X likewise have occurred if the facts were the same as in Rev. Rul. 79–70, except that Y received nonqualified preferred stock rather than securities in exchange for Y's transfer of cash to the corporation?

2. Suppose, instead, that, in exchange for property transferred to the corporation by X, all the stock of the corporation, consisting of 50 percent common and 50 percent of voting nonqualified preferred stock, was issued initially to X. X, in turn, pursuant to a pre-existing binding obligation, sold all the nonqualified preferred to Z, who had not transferred anything to the corporation. Would X's transfer to the corporation be taxable?

3. Anastasia (A) incorporated her sole proprietorship and received all of the common stock of the corporation in exchange for the net assets transferred to the corporation. Assume that the net assets have a fair market value of $150,000 and a basis of $50,000. What are A's tax consequences on the following facts?

a. Immediately following the incorporation, A discharged a $45,000 debt that she owed by transferring 30 percent of the stock to Boris, who was A's pre-existing creditor and who insisted on this payment as a condition to permitting the incorporation.

b. Compare the tax results if A contributed her property to the corporation and Boris contributed his claim against A to the corporation, with the parties receiving 70 and 30 percent, respectively, of the common stock.

[¶ 2070]

Notes

1. Reg. § 1.351–1(a)(3) provides that if a person acquires corporate stock from an underwriter in a qualified underwriting transaction, that person is treated as transferring cash directly to the corporation in exchange for its stock and the ownership of the underwriter is disregarded. A qualified underwriting includes a case in which the underwriter acts as an agent of the corporate issuer (e.g., the underwriter agrees to use its best efforts to find buyers of the stock but does not itself purchase the shares for resale). It also includes the more common case in which the underwriter buys the issuer's stock (in a firm commitment underwriting) and resells it to investors, provided that the underwriter's ownership is transitory. What is the significance of treating the investors in these two situations as transferring cash directly to the corporation? Why in the second case is it required that the underwriter's ownership be transitory? Cf. Rev. Rul. 78–294, 1978–2 C.B. 141.

2. Under the cases and rulings examined above, it appears that the Section 351(a) control test will not be met if, pursuant to a binding obligation, the transferor(s) of property in exchange for stock dispose of enough stock of the transferee corporation to bring their ownership below the 80–percent threshold. Until the promulgation of regulations in late 1998, there was a continuity of shareholder interest requirement that applied in the context of tax-free acquisitive reorganizations under which former shareholders of the acquired corporation were required to retain the shares they received in the acquiring corporation for a reasonable period of time or until a change of circumstances made disposition of the acquiring corporation's shares necessary. As discussed further in Chapter 10, Treasury abandoned this temporal aspect of the continuity of shareholder interest requirement in the 1998 regulations. In a tax-free acquisitive reorganization, the former shareholders of the acquired corporation are now free to dispose of their acquiring corpora-

tion's shares to a third party immediately after the reorganization and may be under a binding obligation at the time of the acquisition to do so. This development invites the inquiry why in a Section 351 exchange, if the transferors of property own 80 percent of the stock of the transferee corporation immediately after the exchange, they should be precluded from disposing of any or all of the transferee corporation's shares pursuant to a binding obligation or otherwise.

3.   Suppose the issue is not, as in *Intermountain Lumber*, whether a transferor-shareholder has disposed of enough stock after the incorporation pursuant to a binding commitment to cease to have control of the transferee corporation but whether one or more transfers of property in exchange for stock of a corporation, separated in time, should be treated as part of a single incorporation for purposes of the control test. Consider, for example, American Bantam Car Co. v. Commissioner, 11 T.C. 397 (1948), aff'd per curiam, 177 F.2d 513 (3d Cir.1949), cert. denied, 339 U.S. 920 (1950). In *American Bantam Car*, the taxpayer corporation was organized as a new corporation to take over the assets of a bankrupt corporation in exchange for common stock. As part of the plan, the new corporation offered shares of preferred stock to the public through an underwritten offering. The underwriter negotiated to receive common stock owned by the organizers of the corporation if a certain amount of preferred stock was sold. The agreement was reached orally on the date of incorporation, but was not reduced to writing until five days later. Pursuant to the agreement, the organizers of the corporation deposited common stock in escrow to be distributed to the underwriters in the event they reached their sales goals. The underwriters reached those goals and received the common stock approximately sixteen months after the incorporation date. Under both the mutual interdependence test and, notwithstanding the oral nature of the agreement, the binding commitment test, the court held that the subsequent transfer of stock to the underwriters should not be integrated with the original transaction. Thus, it was a valid Section 351 incorporation. If the transfers to the underwriters had been integrated with the original incorporation transaction, it would have failed the "control" test. The underwriters could not be considered part of the control group because they acquired their stock for services rather than property.

[¶ 2075]

b.   "Accommodation" Transfers

In determining whether the control requirement is met, as a general rule all stock of the corporation owned by persons who transfer property to the corporation "concurrently" (within the meaning of the authorities discussed in the previous section) will be taken into account. Stock belonging to someone who contributed services or property for stock earlier than, not concurrently with, the other transferors, is not counted toward meeting the 80–percent control test. If, however, that person joins the others in currently transferring property to the corporation, all of that person's stock (including the portion issued for services or for an earlier property contribution) usually counts in determining whether the current transferors of property have the requisite control of the corporation. Reg. § 1.351–1(a)(1)(ii) and (2), Ex. 3.

The regulations, however, disallow so-called "accommodation transfers" from having any impact for purposes of testing for control under Section 351. Reg. § 1.351–1(a)(1)(ii). Instead, they specify that a transfer of property for stock is to be disregarded if (i) its value is relatively small compared to the value of the stock already owned (or to be received for services) by that same transferor and (ii) the primary purpose of this particular transfer is to qualify the transfers by other persons for Section 351 nonrecognition treatment. In other words, when the conditions of this regulation apply, the consequence of disregarding the accommodation transfer is that none of the stock belonging to that transferor counts in determining whether co-transferors of property as a group own sufficient stock immediately after the exchange to satisfy the "control" test of Section 351(a). The following case upholds the validity of this regulation.

[¶ 2080]

ESTATE OF KAMBORIAN v. COMMISSIONER

United States Court of Appeals, First Circuit, 1972.
469 F.2d 219.

[The taxpayers were four individuals who owned approximately 76 percent of the stock of X Corporation, and two of them, as trustees under a trust for the benefit of the wife of another, held 50,000 additional shares, or slightly in excess of 13 percent. Taxpayers individually owned all of the stock of Y Corporation. For bona fide business reasons X acquired the Y stock in exchange for 22,871 X shares worth about $275,000. The exchange was effected pursuant to a formal agreement which included, with the wife's consent, the purchase by the trust of 418 shares of X for about $5,000 in cash. This resulted in increasing the taxpayers' combined holdings in X to 77.3 percent; the trust's interest in X was reduced to just under 13 percent, notwithstanding its purchase of additional X shares. However, the combined holdings of taxpayers and the trust remained in excess of 80 percent. The taxpayers took the position before the Tax Court that the transaction, accordingly, qualified as a tax-free exchange under Section 351(a). The Commissioner disagreed, claiming that the "control" group was limited to the taxpayers as the former owners of the Y stock, exclusive of the trust. In refusing to include the trust's purchase, the Commissioner relied, in part, upon Reg. § 1.351–1(a)(1)(ii). Specifically, the Commissioner determined that the

418 shares of X purchased by the trust for approximately $5,000 were "of relatively small value" in relation to the 50,000 X shares worth about $600,000 previously owned by the trust and that the primary purpose for the trust's transfer was to qualify the exchange of the holders of Y shares for nonrecognition treatment under Section 351(a). The taxpayers argued first that the regulation was invalid. The Tax Court sustained the regulation stating that "[f]ar from being unreasonable or inconsistent with the statute, the regulation promotes its purpose by helping to ensure substantial compliance with the control requirement." 56 T.C. 847, 864. Second, the taxpayers argued that even if the regulation was valid, the primary purpose of the transfer by the trust was not to qualify the exchanges by the other taxpayers. A trustee testified that the trust had participated in the transaction to minimize dilution of the trust's interest in X corporation and because it was a "good investment." The Tax Court noted that the trust's investment left it with only a .08 percent greater interest in X than if the trust had not purchased the additional X shares, and that while the trustee may have taken the dilution factor and the quality of the investment into account, the purchase was made primarily to qualify the exchanges of the other X shareholders under Section 351.]

ALDRICH, SENIOR CIRCUIT JUDGE:

* * *

The Tax Court ruled in favor of the Commissioner, * * * and taxpayers seek review. Basically, they make a frontal attack on the regulation, urging us to hold it invalid as going beyond what they claim is a plain and positive statute.[2]

Taxpayers' brief contains a wistful aside that there is involved a large tax and only a small discrepancy. We are not moved, legally or emotionally, by this fact. But in order to avoid any overfall therefrom, we will imagine another case that would have to be decided against the government if taxpayers are correct and all arranged transactions, regardless of their purpose or their connection with one another, are to be viewed as a single exchange. Let us suppose that P owns 10% and S 90% of the stock of W, and P owns all of the stock of Z. If P transfers his Z stock to W for further W shares, ending up with a 30% interest, it is obviously not a tax-free exchange. But if P induces S to buy, contemporaneously, one share of W stock for cash, the present petitioners would say that P and S are to be considered jointly as exchanging property, and since together they owned over 80% of the transferee corporation, P may claim the statutory exception.

2. Alternatively, taxpayers argue that even if the regulation is valid, the Tax Court erred in applying it to their transaction. This claim is patently erroneous. After a review of the record it is clear that the Tax Court's findings were not only reasonably supported, but manifestly correct.

¶ 2080

Our analysis does not lead to such a result. By the term "property [that] is transferred," the statute contemplates a single transaction, even though, as it goes on to recognize, there may be a number of transferors or participants. What is a transaction must be determined in the light of the statutory purpose, lest taxpayers be allowed to frustrate that purpose by manipulation of clearly taxable exchanges. * * * We stated that purpose long ago in speaking of the predecessor of section 351, which contains no presently material variance.

> "It is the purpose of Section 112(b) (5) to save the taxpayer from an immediate recognition of a gain, or to intermit the claim of a loss, in certain transactions where gain or loss may have accrued in a constitutional sense, but where in a popular and economic sense there has been a mere change in the form of ownership and the taxpayer has not really 'cashed in' on the theoretical gain, or closed out a losing venture."

Portland Oil Co. v. Commissioner, 1 Cir., 1940, 109 F.2d 479, 488, cert. denied 310 U.S. 650.

Thus in our hypothetical, considering P alone, there was not a "mere change in the form of ownership." Before the transaction P "owned" Z corporation, since he owned 100% of its stock. After the transaction his ownership of Z was reduced to 30% because he held only a 30% interest in W, the transferee corporation. In keeping with "economic sense" a taxpayer may be allowed a certain amount of slack. This has been ruled to be 20%; and had P ended with an 80% interest in W, and thus of Z, his ownership of the latter would not be thought to be materially changed. 1954 Int.Rev.Code § 368(c). But where P does not own that 80% it can be permissible to consider transfers by other owners only if those transfers were, in economic terms, sufficiently related to P's to make all of the transfers part of a single transaction.

It is possible that a valid association may exist even when different types of property are transferred to the transferee corporation by different transferors. Thus in Halliburton v. Commissioner, 9 Cir., 1935, 78 F.2d 265, funds contributed by other parties were found to be as necessary to the overall purpose of the transaction as was the exchange by the litigating taxpayers. In our P and S case, however, there is no economic connection, and hence no basis for regarding the two transfers as parts of one transaction, and hence of considering P and S as a unit in terms of control. If a taxpayer were able, so simply, to effect a concatenation and say that the statute applied to him, the statute would be meaningless.

The instant case presents no better claim of a connection in an economic sense. The four shareholders of Y decided it would be advantageous to merge Y with X. Finding themselves short of the requirements for tax-free treatment, they persuaded a shareholder of X, who was a complete stranger to Y, to make a token purchase of X shares. Other than the fact that the trust's participation was incorporated into the acquisition agreement, there was no relation between the exchange of Y shares and this very minor purchase. The trust transferred no Y shares. The cash it contributed to X—$5,000 for 418 shares of a corporation with nearly 400,000 shares outstanding—could have had no significant impact on X's ability to conduct its business. The trustees' desire to help the Y stockholders avoid taxes, warrantably found by the Tax Court to have been the primary motive for the trust's purchase,[3] cannot be used to make a single transaction out of otherwise unrelated transfers.

Without going into every ramification of the Regulation, in this case it appropriately and fairly fits our interpretation of the statute. Taxpayers' criticisms of the Tax Court's opinion in this regard are not readily persuasive. However, if, in some fashion, taxpayers could remove the Regulation from consideration or application altogether, it would avail them nothing.

* * *

[¶ 2085]

REVENUE RULING 79-194

1979–1 C.B. 145.

Issue

Is the control requirement of section 351(a) * * *, which provides for nonrecognition of gain or loss on transfers of property to a controlled corporation, satisfied where part of the stock of the controlled corporation received by a transferor in exchange for property is sold to other persons who also transferred property to the corporation in exchange for stock?

Facts

Situation (1)

Corporation Z and a group of investors, pursuant to a binding agreement between them, transferred property to a newly organized corporation, Newco, in exchange for all of Newco's stock (a single class of voting common stock). Z and the investors received 80 percent and 20 percent, respectively, of Newco's stock. Pursuant to the agreement Z sold an amount of its Newco stock for its fair market value to the investors to bring its ownership down to 49 percent. Newco would not have been formed if the investors had not agreed to transfer property to

---

3. The court's use of "primary motive" was to coincide with the language of the Regulation. On the basis of its findings it seems apparent that it was the sole motive. The only effect we can see from the point of view of the trust was to reduce its income.

it and their agreement to do so was conditioned on the sale by Z to them of part of Z's Newco stock.

Situation (2)

X, a domestic corporation, operates a branch in a foreign country. The foreign country enacted a nationalization law that required that the business that X's branch was engaged in be incorporated in the foreign country and that its citizens be the majority owners of such corporation. A governmental agency in the foreign country directed X to transfer all of the assets of its branch to a newly formed foreign country corporation that is, or will be, at least 51 percent owned by its citizens. Accordingly, X and a group of investors, who were citizens of the foreign country, pursuant to a binding agreement between them, transferred property to Newco, a corporation newly organized in the foreign country, in exchange for all of Newco's stock (a single class of voting common stock). X and the investors received 99 percent and one percent, respectively, of Newco's stock. Pursuant to the agreement, X sold an amount of its Newco stock for its fair market value to the investors to bring its ownership down to 49 percent; the investors would pay X in a series of yearly installments. Newco would not have been formed if the investors had not agreed to transfer property to it and their agreement to do so was conditioned on the sale by X to them of part of X's Newco stock. Further, the investors transferred property to Newco in order to become co-transferors with X, and they purchased X's Newco stock in lieu of the assets of X's branch because of the foreign governmental agency's directive. * * * The fair market value of each asset transferred is in excess of its basis.

Law and Analysis

* * *

Since the sales of Newco stock by Z to the investors, and of Newco stock by X to the investors, were integral parts of the incorporations and pursuant to binding agreements entered into prior to the exchanges, the control requirement of section 351(a) * * * is determined after the respective sales. See *Hazeltine Corp. v. Commissioner,* 89 F.2d 513 (3d Cir.1937), *Intermountain Lumber Co. v. Commissioner,* 65 T.C. 1025 (1976) and Rev. Rul. 70–522, 1970–2 C.B. 81.

In Situation (1), after the sales were completed, 49 percent of the Newco stock was owned by Z and 51 percent of the stock was owned by the investors. Therefore, the persons transferring property to Newco in exchange for Newco stock owned 100 percent of the Newco stock "immediately after the exchange" within the meaning of section 351(a). The fact that there was a shift in ownership of stock among the transferors after their exchanges with Newco does not affect the application of section 351(a). See example (1) under section 1.351–1(b) of the

* * * Regulations in which transfers of property to a new corporation qualify under section 351 even though a shift in the ownership of stock among the transferors is considered to have occurred subsequent to the transfers.

In Situation (2), after the sales were completed, 49 percent of the Newco stock was owned by X and 51 percent of the Newco stock was owned by the investors. Because the amount of stock issued directly to the investors for property is of relatively small value in comparison to the value of all the stock received by them in the transaction, the stock received by the investors is not taken into account in considering whether the transaction qualifies under section 351(a) * * *. Compare section 1.351–1(a)(1)(ii) of the regulations. Thus, for purposes of determining control under section 351, the investors were not transferors. Therefore, since the person (X) transferring property to Newco in exchange for Newco stock owned only 49 percent of the Newco stock "immediately after the exchange", the control requirement of section 351(a) is not satisfied. The fact that there was a shift in ownership of 49 percent of the Newco stock from a transferor (X) to a non-transferor (the investors) after their exchanges with Newco affects the application of section 351(a).

Compare Rev. Rul. 79–70 [at ¶ 2060], which holds that the control requirement of section 351(a) is not satisfied where part of the stock of the controlled corporation is sold to another person who transferred property to the corporation in exchange for securities.

HOLDING

Situation (1)

The control requirement of section 351(a) * * * is satisfied. No gain or loss is recognized to Z or the investors under section 351(a) on the transfer of property to Newco. Gain or loss to Z upon the sale of the Newco stock will be determined and recognized under section 1001.

Situation (2)

The control requirement of section 351(a) * * * is not satisfied. Gain is recognized to X on the transfer of property to Newco pursuant to section 1001. Gain or loss, if any, to X upon the sale of the Newco stock to the investors will be determined and recognized under section 1001.

[¶ 2090]

Note

In Rev. Proc. 77–37, § 3.07, 1977–2 C.B. 568, 570, the IRS stated that the property transferred will not be considered of relatively small value for purposes of Reg. § 1.351–1(a)(1)(ii) "if the fair market value of the property transferred is equal to, or in excess of, 10 percent of the fair market value of the stock * * * already owned (or to be received for services)'' by the transferor. Does this interpretation of the "relatively small value" language in Reg. § 1.351–1(a)(1)(ii) reasonably effectuate the intended anti-abuse purpose of the regulation?

[¶ 2095]

Problems

1.   Assume that 20 years ago Tracy (T) organized T Corporation, a family owned for-profit recreational and wildlife facility, with a capital contribution of $200,000. The capital of the corporation consisted solely of common stock of 20,000 shares, $10 par value. Through the years, T made gifts of stock to family members. At this time, T, his wife, and their three adult children own 4,000 shares apiece (20 percent interests) worth $300 per share. The family business has continued to prosper and it is necessary to expand its grounds. T owns adjacent land which is suitable for an extension of the facility. T purchased the land 10 years ago at a cost of $10,000; the tract now has a fair market value of $150,000. T consults with you as to the tax consequences of the following alternative proposals:

a.   T will transfer the property to the corporation in exchange for 500 shares of common stock that have a fair market value of $150,000.

b.   Alternatively, at the same time as the transfer described in Problem 1.a., each of the other family members will purchase an additional 10 shares of common stock at their full value of $300 per share.

2.   Assume the same facts as in Problem 1, except that T had acquired the land 10 years ago at a cost of $100,000 (its then value) and now sells the property to the corporation at its current fair market value of $60,000. See § 267. How does the determination of "ownership" in Section 267 differ from that of Section 368(c), and why?

[¶ 2100]

C.   TRANSACTIONS DENIED NONRECOGNITION UNDER SECTION 351

Section 351(e) contains two statutory exceptions to nonrecognition treatment. The first is Section 351(e)(1) which treats transfers to a controlled corporation as taxable where the recipient is an "investment company"—defined in the regulations as a corporation with an 80–percent concentration of holdings in passive assets—because such transfers would effect a diversification of the transferor's investments. Disallowance of nontaxable investment swaps was the congressional target. Originally, passive assets in the form of stock and debt securities were the sole objects of attention, but the statute has since been significantly

¶ 2090

expanded to cover other diverse assets of a passive nature, many of which are listed in Section 351(e)(1)(B). The second exception is Section 351(e)(2) which precludes nonrecognition treatment for transfers of properties by bankrupt corporate debtors. Prior to the enactment of Section 362(e)(2), transfers in such cases could have produced potential losses for the transferee because the bases of the properties of such debtors were likely to be higher than their fair market values. See ¶ 2145.

D. BOOT IN SECTION 351 TRANSACTIONS

1. GENERAL EFFECT OF BOOT

[¶ 2105]

a. At the Shareholder Level

The nonrecognition of gain does not apply to the extent that a transferor receives in the exchange, in addition to nonrecognition stock, any nonqualifying "boot," such as cash and certain other property. Instead, as with other nonrecognition provisions in the Code, realized gain (but not loss) must be currently recognized to the extent that the gain is "cashed out" through the receipt of boot. § 351(b).

Assume, for example, that a transferor contributes property with a basis of $75 and a fair market value of $100 to a corporation in exchange for $100 worth of property from the corporation, consisting of common stock worth $90 plus $10 cash. The transferor must currently recognize $10 of the $25 realized gain as a result of receiving the $10 of boot property. By contrast, realized losses remain unrecognized, regardless of the receipt of boot (i.e., receipt of property other than nonrecognition stock of the transferee corporation). Id.

As discussed below, the receipt of boot, which results in recognition of gain under Section 351(b), in turn, affects the adjusted basis of the stock and other property received from the corporation by the transferor as well as the adjusted basis to the corporation for the transferred property. §§ 358 and 362. See ¶¶ 2140–2155.

[¶ 2110]

b. At the Corporate Level

Under Section 351(f), Section 311 governs whether the corporation has recognized gain or loss on the transfer of boot to the transferor-shareholder(s). A corporation recognizes gain on the transfer of appreciated boot unless it is a debt obligation of the corporation or is nonqualified preferred stock. §§ 311(b) and 1032. A corporation does not recognize loss on a transfer of depreciated boot property. § 311(a).

¶ 2110

[¶ 2115]

2. ALLOCATION OF BOOT

The application of the rules relating to the boot becomes more complex if the transferor who receives the boot transfers more than one item of property to the corporation. In such a case, an allocation must be made among the various properties (whether their values are more or less than their tax bases) transferred in order to calculate the amount and character of the gain recognized by the transferor on each property and the respective new basis of each in the hands of the transferee-corporation. Further, boot property which is in the form of the corporation's own debt obligation (and perhaps nonqualified preferred stock as well), raises a question of whether the transferor can report the gain from that boot under the Section 453 installment sale method. The materials that follow explore these issues.

[¶ 2120]

REVENUE RULING 68–55

1968–1 C.B. 140.

Advice has been requested as to the correct method of determining the amount and character of the gain to be recognized by Corporation X under section 351(b) * * * under the circumstances described below.

Corporation Y was organized by X and A, an individual who owned no stock in X. A transferred $20x$ dollars to Y in exchange for stock of Y having a fair market value of $20x$ dollars and X transferred to Y three separate assets and received in exchange stock of Y having a fair market value of $100x$ dollars plus cash of $10x$ dollars.

In accordance with the facts set forth in the table below if X had sold at fair market value each of the three assets it transferred to Y, the result would have been as follows:

	Asset I	Asset II	Asset III
Character of asset	Capital asset held more than [18] months.	Capital asset held not more than [18] months.	Section 1245 property.
Fair market value	$22x	$33x	$55x
Adjusted basis	40x	20x	25x
Gain (loss)	($18x)	$13x	$30x
Character of gain or loss	Long-term capital loss.	Short-term capital gain.	Ordinary income.

* * *

The first question presented is how to determine the amount of gain to be recognized under section 351(b) * * *. The general rule is that each asset transferred must be considered to have been separately exchanged. See the authorities cited in Revenue Ruling 67–192, C.B. 1967–2, 140, and in Revenue Ruling 68–23, [1968–1 C.B. 144], which hold that there is no netting of gains and losses for purposes of applying sections 367 and 356(c) * * *. Thus, for purposes of making computations under Section 351(b), it is not proper to total the bases of the various assets transferred and to subtract this total from the fair market value of the total consideration received in the exchange. Moreover, any treatment other than an asset-by-asset approach would have the effect of allowing losses that are specifically disallowed by section 351(b)(2) * * *.

The second question presented is how, for purposes of making computations under section 351(b) * * *, to allocate the cash and stock received to the amount realized as to each asset transferred in the exchange. The asset-by-asset approach for computing the amount of gain realized in the exchange requires that for this purpose the fair market value of each category of consideration received must be separately allocated to the transferred assets in proportion to the relative fair market values of the transferred assets. See section 1.1245–4(c)(1) of the * * * Regulations which, for the same reasons, requires that for purposes of computing the amount of gain to which section 1245 * * * applies each category of consideration received must be allocated to the properties transferred in proportion to their relative fair market values.

Accordingly, the amount and character of the gain recognized in the exchange should be computed as follows:

	Total	Asset I	Asset II	Asset III
Fair market value of asset transferred . . .	$110x	$22x	$33x	$55x
Percent of total fair market value	--------	20%	30%	50%
Fair market value of Y stock received in exchange.	$100x	$20x	$30x	$50x
Cash received in exchange	10x	2x	3x	5x
Amount realized	$110x	$22x	$33x	$55x
Adjusted basis	--------	40x	20x	25x
Gain (loss) realized	--------	($18x)	$13x	$30x

Under section 351(b)(2) * * * the loss of 18x dollars realized on the exchange of Asset Number I is not recognized. Such loss may not be used to offset the gains realized on the exchanges of the other assets. Under section 351(b)(1) * * *, the gain of 13x dollars realized on the exchange of Asset Number II will be recognized as short-term capital gain in the amount of 3x dollars, the amount of cash received. Under sections 351(b)(1) and 1245(b)(3) * * *, the gain of 3x dollars realized on the exchange of Asset Number III will be recognized as ordinary income in the amount of 5x dollars, the amount of cash received.

¶ 2120

[¶ 2125]

Problem

Sole shareholder A transfers two assets to X Corporation in exchange for all of its 120 shares of stock, worth $120,000, plus $40,000 of cash. Asset 1, a nondepreciable capital asset, has a fair market value of $40,000 and an adjusted basis of $50,000. Asset 2, which is primarily held for sale to customers in the ordinary course of business and is therefore excepted from the capital asset definition in Section 1221, has a fair market value of $120,000 and an adjusted basis of $50,000.

How is the boot allocated? How much gain or loss is recognized? What are the bases of Asset 1 and Asset 2 in the hands of X Corporation? What is the basis for the shares of stock received by A?

[¶ 2130]

3. TIMING OF BOOT RECOGNITION

In general, a transferor who receives boot in connection with a Section 351 exchange must currently recognize the realized gain up to the fair market value of the boot. If, however, the boot consists of the corporation's own debt obligation, it may be possible to report the gain on the sale only as the debt representing the boot is collected.

Proposed regulations allow a transferor of property in a Section 351 exchange to use installment sale reporting upon receipt of the corporation's debt, provided that the transaction otherwise qualifies for installment sale reporting. See Prop. Reg. § 1.453–1(f)(3).[8] Under these rules, an increase in the transferor's basis under Section 358 attributable to the realized gain occurs at the time of the Section 351 exchange, even though the transferor will recognize the gain only over time as payments on the corporation's installment debt obligation are received. Prop. Reg. § 1.453–1(f)(3)(ii). By contrast, under these proposed regulations, the transferee corporation's increase in basis under Section 362(a) attributable to the transferor's recognized gain occurs only as the transferor actually recognizes the gain under Section 453. Id. This proposed delay in the transferee's basis increase is at variance with the immediate cost basis allowed for property purchased with debt.

The legislative history of Section 351(g) indicates that the Treasury Secretary has regulatory authority to apply installment sale-type rules to preferred stock classified as non-qualified under Section 351(g). See Staff

---

8. These proposed regulations were written before Congress, in 1989, amended Section 351 to treat all debt obligations received in a Section 351 exchange as boot. The legislative history of that amendment supports the conclusion that gain on receipt of a debt obligation constituting boot may be reported under the installment sale method (unless one of the exceptions to installment sale reporting in Section 453 applies). See H.R. Rep. No. 247, 101st Cong., 1st Sess. 1226–27 (1989); S. Prt. 101–56, 101st Cong., 1st Sess. 58 (1989); H.R. Conf. Rep. No. 239, 101st Cong., 1st Sess. 556 (1989).

of the Joint Committee on Tax'n, 105th Cong., 1st Sess., General Explanation of Tax Legislation Enacted in 1997, at 212 (1997). To date, though, no such regulations have been issued. In the absence of a regulation permitting installment sales-type treatment, nonqualified preferred stock would not appear to be sufficiently analogous to debt to qualify for the installment sale method.

[¶ 2135]

Problems

1. Tanya (T) owns unimproved land with a basis of $100,000 and a fair market value of $300,000. In an exchange to which Section 351 applies, T transfers the land to a newly formed corporation in exchange for stock of the corporation (worth $200,000) and a $100,000 installment obligation (bearing adequate interest). The installment obligation is payable in a single payment three years from the date of the exchange. Determine the federal income tax consequences to T and the corporation on account of this transfer, including T's adjusted basis in the corporation's stock under Section 358 and the corporation's adjusted basis in the land under Section 362. See Prop. Reg. § 1.453–1(f)(3).

2. How would your answer in Problem 1 change if T's adjusted basis in the land were $250,000? See Prop. Reg. § 1.453–1(f)(3)(iii), Ex. 2.

E. BASIS ADJUSTMENTS AND RELATED CONSEQUENCES OF A SECTION 351 INCORPORATION

[¶ 2140]

1. BASIS AT THE SHAREHOLDER LEVEL

Shareholders typically hold the stock they receive in a Section 351 exchange with the same basis as they held the property contributed in the exchange. Thus, for example, were a taxpayer in an exchange covered by Section 351(a) to transfer property with a basis of $75 and fair market value of $100 to a corporation in exchange for the transferee corporation's common stock likewise worth $100, the $25 of gain realized by the transferor-shareholder on the exchange would not be recognized currently but recognition would be deferred and reflected in a substituted basis of $75 assigned to the stock (worth $100) received in the exchange. § 358(a)(1). As discussed below at ¶ 2150, under certain circumstances the corporation and the shareholder may elect to have the shareholder hold the property with a fair market basis when the transferred property has a built-in loss.

When taxable boot is introduced into the transaction, the aggregate basis must be adjusted to ensure that the gain is not recognized again upon sale of the stock. Thus, assume that the taxpayer in the previous example received stock of the corporation with a fair market value of $90, plus other non-cash property with a value of $10. If the transaction otherwise qualified under Section 351(a), the presence of boot ($10 value on a transfer of property with a realized gain of $25) results in recognition of gain, but not in excess of the value ($10) of the boot received. Recognition of the transferor's $15 of additional realized gain would be deferred and reflected in the $85 basis for the properties received in the exchange (i.e., transferor's former $75 basis in the property transferred, increased by the transferor's $10 of recognized gain). § 358(a)(1). The basis is allocated $10 to the boot property and then the remaining $75 in basis is allocated to the stock received in the exchange. § 358(a)(2).

If more than one class of stock is received in exchange for an item of property, basis as determined under Section 358(a) is allocated to the classes in proportion to their respective fair market values. Reg. § 1.358–2(b)(2).

2. BASIS AT THE CORPORATE LEVEL

[¶ 2145]

a. Generally

When appreciated properties (i.e., the fair market value at the time of transfer exceeds the basis in the transferor's hands) or properties with a basis equal to fair market value are acquired by the corporate transferee incident to nontaxable Section 351 transfers, the preexisting bases for the properties are retained for the properties in the hands of the transferee corporation, producing a "carryover basis" for each of those properties from the shareholders to the corporate transferee. § 362(a)(1). Thus, in the basic example of the preceding section, upon a nontaxable Section 351 transfer by the shareholders of property with an adjusted basis of $75 and value of $100 in exchange for common stock worth $100, the corporation would take over the property with a carryover basis of $75 under Section 362(a), thereby preserving the gain in the property for possible future recognition. Or, as in the second example, if the corporation instead had transferred other property with a fair market value of $10 as well as common stock worth $90 for the property worth $100, the basis for the property in the hands of the corporation would increase to $85 under Section 362(a) (the carryover basis of $75 increased by the shareholder's $10 of recognized gain). A carryover basis likewise results under Section 362 for property acquired by the corporation in the form of a shareholder contribution to capital. § 362(a)(2).

This general carryover basis rule has the effect of duplicating gains and losses. Because of Section 358, the shareholder will hold the common stock it receives with a basis that preserves the gain or loss not recognized in the transaction. Thus, in the basic example without boot, the shareholder would hold the stock with a $25 built-in gain. In the second example with $10 worth of gain recognized currently because of the boot, the shareholder would hold the stock with a $15 built-in gain. At the same time, because of Section 362(a), the corporation would hold the property it received in the two exchanges with a $25 and $15 built-in gain, respectively. The result is to duplicate the gain on a sale by the corporation of the property and by the shareholder of the stock. This may make it undesirable to satisfy the requirements for Section 351 in the case of an incorporation involving gain property. Conversely, a transferor may prefer to qualify under Section 351 in an incorporation involving loss property. What is the policy justification, if any, for the duplication of gains and losses in a Section 351 transaction?

[¶ 2150]

b.   Built–In Loss Property

Although the potential for loss duplication was a longstanding feature of the carryover basis rules, Congress recently became concerned about its potential for abuse. One of the revelations from a 2004 Joint Committee on Taxation Report was that corporations were taking advantage of the carryover basis rules in Section 362 to shelter phantom income. Through Section 351 transfers, high-basis, low-value assets were being transferred to corporations so the built-in losses could be realized twice, at both the corporate and shareholder levels.[9] Section 362(e)(2), enacted as part of the American Jobs Creation Act of 2004, is designed to prevent loss duplication transactions using Section 351.

Section 362(e)(2) provides that either the corporate-transferee must hold the property at a fair market value basis or, if the parties jointly elect, the corporate transferee can hold the property with a carryover basis and the shareholder-transferor will then hold its stock with a fair market value basis. This election ensures that the loss could be realized at either the shareholder or the corporate level, but not at both levels, on a subsequent hypothetical transfer of the stock or the property.

Thus, for example, if a domestic taxable shareholder transferred property with a fair market value of $75 and a basis of $100 to a corporation for stock valued at $75 in a Section 351 exchange, the corporation would hold the property with a basis of $75 unless the parties jointly elected to have the shareholder's basis in the stock lowered to the fair market value of the property transferred ($75). In that case, the corporation would be able to hold the property with a $100 basis and take advantage of depreciation deductions or realize the loss on

---

9. See S. Rep. No. 192, 108th Cong., 1st Sess. 125 (2003) (discussing the 2004 Act) ("The Joint Committee on Taxation staff's investigative report of the Enron Corporation and other information reveal that taxpayers are engaging in various tax motivated transactions to duplicate a single economic loss and, subsequently deduct such loss more than once.") Id.

a subsequent sale. § 362(e)(2). If, however, the shareholder-transferor was a non-U.S. taxpayer or a tax-exempt entity, then the election would not be available. The corporate-transferee would have to hold the property with a basis of the $75 fair market value. § 362(e)(1)

The determination of whether there is a net built-in loss is not made on a property-by-property basis under Section 362(e)(2). The aggregate adjusted bases of the transferred properties are compared with the aggregate fair market value of those properties. § 362(e)(2)(A). If the former exceeds the latter, the aggregate adjusted bases of the property must be reduced to match the aggregate fair market values. § 362(e)(2)(A). This reduction in basis is then allocated among the transferred properties in proportion to their respective built-in losses immediately prior to the transaction. § 362(e)(2)(B). This prevents the basis of any property from being stepped-up to fair market value.

For example, assume a transferor contributes three properties in a transaction that qualifies under Section 351: (1) Property A with a fair market value of $500 and a basis of $200, (2) Property B, with a fair market value of $200 and a basis of $500, and (3) Property C, with a fair market value of $100 and a basis of $400. The aggregate fair market value of the transferred properties is $800 and the aggregate bases of the transferred properties is $1100. Thus, the net built-in loss is $300. In the absence of an election to reduce the shareholder's basis in his or her stock under Section 362(e)(2)(C), there would be a $300 reduction in the corporation's basis that would be allocated among the three properties in proportion to their respective built-in losses. Thus, the bases of Properties B and C would each be reduced by $150 to $350 and $250, respectively.

[¶ 2155]

Note

1. Why did Congress legislate to prevent loss duplication, but fail to take any action to prevent gain duplication? This omission is particularly incongruous when considered in light of the movement to reduce the double taxation of dividends discussed in Chapter 4.

2. As part of the same legislation designed to prevent loss duplication, Congress enacted Section 362(e)(1) to prevent loss importation. Section 362(e)(1) provides that if a "transaction" otherwise qualifying under Section 351(a) or (b) would result in an "importation of a net built-in loss," then the basis of the transferred properties in the hands of the corporate transferee becomes the fair market value of the properties at the time of the transfer rather than the carryover basis. The term "importation" refers to a situation where there would have been no U.S. income tax consequences to the seller if the property had been sold in a transaction not covered by Section 351, but there will be U.S. income tax consequences if the property is sold by the corporate-transferee in a hypothetical subsequent disposition. § 362(e)(1)(B). This forecloses

transactions where a foreign or tax-exempt transferor transfers built-in loss property to a U.S. corporation in a Section 351 exchange so that the corporation can realize the loss for U.S. tax purposes on the sale of the property.

As with the loss duplication rules, in a Section 351 transfer involving the importation of multiple properties this determination of whether there is a built-in loss is not done property-by-property. The aggregate fair market value of the transferred properties is compared with the aggregate bases of the properties. If the aggregate bases exceed the aggregate fair market value, it is considered a "net built-in loss." § 362(e)(1)(C). Unlike with the loss duplication rules, the basis of each of the transferred properties is adjusted to fair market value. Thus, the basis adjustment is not in one direction. For properties with a built-in gain, it would require a step up in basis to fair market value, while properties with a built-in loss would require a step down in basis to fair market value. In the case of a Section 351 transfer involving multiple transferors, each transferor is examined separately on the basis of the aggregate fair market values and aggregate bases of the properties that they transferred.[10]

[¶ 2160]

3. HOLDING PERIOD

The transferor-shareholder's holding period for stock received in a Section 351 transaction includes (or is "tacked" on to) the holding period of the property transferred in exchange for such stock, provided that the property is a capital asset or Section 1231 property. § 1223(1). If more than one property is transferred, the respective holding periods will attach to shares having value equal to each property. Thus, different shares may have different holding periods and bases. The transferor-shareholder may not allocate specific shares received for specific properties. Holding periods and basis are allocated across the shares received in proportion to their values whether they represent one or multiple classes. See Rev. Rul. 85–164, 1985–2 C.B. 117.

With both gain and loss assets, the corporation's holding period for each asset acquired in a Section 351 exchange includes (has tacked on to it) the transferor's holding period for the asset. § 1223(2).

[¶ 2165]

Problems

Carolyn and Dennis organized the C & D corporation, a Delaware corporation, with an initial capital of $200,000. Each received 1,000

---

10. See H.R. Conf. Rep. No. 755, 108th Cong., 2d Sess. 635 (2004) ("Thus, for example, if in a tax-free incorporation, some properties are received by a corporation from U.S. persons subject to tax, and some properties are received from foreign persons not subject to U.S. tax, this provision applies to limit the adjusted basis of each property received from the foreign persons to the fair market value of the property.").

shares of common stock with a par value of $100. Carolyn transferred Asset X, with a fair market value of $100,000 and a basis in her hands of $150,000. She has held Asset X for five years. Dennis transferred Assets Y and Z. Asset Y had a fair market value of $75,000 and a basis of $100,000. Asset Z had a fair market value of $25,000 and a basis of $10,000. Dennis has held both Assets Y and Z for six months.

1. Discuss the relevant tax consequences to the two incorporators and to the C & D corporation, i.e., (i) would any of the parties recognize gain or loss on this exchange; (ii) what basis and holding period does the C & D Corporation have for each asset (see Sections 362(a) and (e) and 1223(2)); and, (iii) what is the basis of the stock in the hands of the incorporators and their initial holding periods for their stock (see Sections 358(a), 362(e)(2), and 1223(1))?

2. If Asset Z had a fair market value of $100,000 rather than $25,000, how would the tax results to all parties referred to in Problem 1 be affected?

F. ASSUMPTION OF LIABILITIES BY THE CORPORATION

1. NONRECOGNITION UNDER SECTION 357(a)

[¶ 2170]

a. *Generally*

In the absence of the special rule set forth in Section 357(a), a transferor who is relieved from a liability in a Section 351 exchange, for example, by transferring property subject to indebtedness to a transferee corporation would be considered to receive the equivalent of a cash benefit and hence "boot" under Section 351(b). United States v. Hendler, 303 U.S. 564, reh. denied, 304 U.S. 588 (1938). However, Section 357(a) provides for a contrary result. If the transferee corporation assumes a liability of the transferor-shareholder in a Section 351 exchange, the assumption is not generally treated as boot. Section 357(a) thus serves a very important function by facilitating the tax-free incorporation of an existing business notwithstanding the presence, as is commonly the case, of accounts payable, other debts, or assets encumbered by liabilities associated with the business. The tax on gain, if any, attributable to liabilities shifted by a transferor to the corporation is not forgiven, but its imposition is deferred through a correlative reduction in the transferor's basis in the stock received. § 358(a)(1)(A)(ii) and (d)(1).

However, as discussed below, there are two important exceptions to the nonrecognition of gain rule of Section 357(a). Under Section 357(b) all transferred liabilities will be treated as boot if the transfer of any of them had a tax avoidance purpose or lacked a business purpose. Under Section 357(c), the transferor must in any event recognize gain to the extent that the total liabilities assumed by the transferee corporation exceed the total bases of the properties transferred to it in the Section 351 exchange.

[¶ 2175]

b. **Determination of Amount of Liabilities Assumed**

Under prior law, any liability of the transferor assumed by the transferee corporation and any liability to which property transferred to the corporation was subject were considered to be transferred liabilities for purposes of the Sections 351, 357, 358, and 362 and the reorganization provisions. This broad definition caused problems because of certain ambiguities regarding (1) whether a liability was assumed by the transferee because the property was taken "subject to" a liability, even if the transferor or someone else remained liable and (2) whether the transferee assumed the entire liability when it acquired only one of the two or more properties securing (or cross-collateralizing) a single liability.

In the mid-to-late 1990s, corporations began to exploit these ambiguities in tax shelter transactions. The problem arose when the transferor was a corporation not subject to tax on gain recognized under Section 357(c) (e.g., a foreign corporation or a U.S. corporation with a net operating loss). If, for example, such a corporation had two assets, each with a basis of $25,000 and a fair market value of $50,000, which secured a liability of $100,000, the corporation might transfer each asset to a separate controlled corporation in a Section 351 exchange and argue that each subsidiary acquired the property transferred to it subject to the entire $100,000 liability. The tax-exempt transferor corporation would have a recognized gain of $75,000 under Section 357(c) on each transfer, resulting in total recognized gain of $150,000, none of which would be subject to U.S. tax, but under Section 362(a), the basis of each of the assets would be stepped up to $100,000. In effect, the single liability of $100,000 would be double-counted in determining the basis of the encumbered properties in the hands of the transferee corporations. See S. Rep. No. 2, 106th Cong., 1st Sess. 75 (1999).

In order to deal with this potential for abuse, Section 357(d), enacted in 1999, for the first time provided a definition of liabilities assumed for purposes of Sections 357, 358 and 362 and the tax-free reorganization provisions. Section 357(d) narrowed the scope of the prior law in two respects. First, this legislation substantially narrowed the pre–1999 Act law in which a recourse liability was subject to Section 357 even if the parties agreed that the transferor would pay the debt. Thus, under Section 357(d)(1) liabilities assumed include:

> (i) a recourse liability (or portion thereof) if, based on the facts and circumstances, the transferee has agreed to, and is expected to, satisfy the liability (or portion) whether or not the transferor has been relieved of it, and

¶ 2175

(ii) any nonrecourse liability to which property transferred to the corporation is subject, but the amount of such a nonrecourse liability may be reduced to prevent potential abuse of Sections 357(c) and 358.

Second, this legislation reduced the amount of a nonrecourse liability deemed to be assumed by the transferee corporation to prevent potential abuse of Sections 357(c) and 358 by a transfer to two or more corporations of two or more properties securing (or cross-collateralizing) a single liability. While the scheme might have been successfully attacked by the IRS in litigation, Congress eliminated the potential abuse by enacting Section 357(d)(2), under which the Section 357(c) gain is calculated by allocating the nonrecourse liability among the properties securing it in proportion to their respective fair market values.

Specifically, Section 357(d)(2) provides that any nonrecourse liability treated as assumed by a transferee corporation is reduced by the smaller of (i) the amount of the liability that an owner of other assets not transferred to the corporation that are also subject to the liability has agreed with the transferee to, and is expected to, satisfy or (ii) the fair market value of the other assets. § 357(d)(2).

The Senate Report on the 1999 legislation change explains the change as follows:

Under the provision, the distinction between the assumption of a liability and the acquisition of an asset subject to a liability generally is eliminated. First, except as provided in Treasury regulations, a recourse liability (or any portion thereof) is treated as having been assumed if, as determined on the basis of all facts and circumstances, the transferee has agreed to, and is expected to satisfy the liability or portion thereof (whether or not the transferor has been relieved of liability). Thus, where more than one person agrees to satisfy a liability or portion thereof, only one would be expected to satisfy such liability or portion thereof. Second, except as provided in Treasury regulations, a nonrecourse liability (or any portion thereof) is treated as having been assumed by the transferee of any asset that is subject to the liability. However, this amount is reduced in cases where an owner of other assets subject to the same nonrecourse liability agrees with the transferee to, and is expected to, satisfy the liability (up to the fair market value of the other assets, determined without regard to section 7701(g)).

In determining whether any person has agreed to and is expected to satisfy a liability, all facts and circumstances are to be considered. In any case where the transferee does agree to satisfy a liability, the transferee also will be expected to satisfy the liability in the absence of facts indicating the contrary.

In determining any increase to the basis of property transferred to the transferee as a result of gain recognized because of the assumption of liabilities under section 357, in no event will the increase cause the basis to exceed the fair market value of the property (determined without regard to sec. 7701(g)).

If gain is recognized to the transferor as the result of an assumption by a corporation of a nonrecourse liability that also is secured by any assets not transferred to the corporation, and if no person is subject to Federal income tax on such gain, then for purposes of determining the basis of assets transferred, the amount of gain treated as recognized as the result of such assumption of liability shall be determined as if the liability assumed by the transferee equaled such transferee's ratable portion of the liability, based on the relative fair market values (determined without regard to sec. 7701(g) of all assets subject to such nonrecourse liability). In no event will the gain cause the resulting basis to exceed the fair market value of the property (determined without regard to sec. 7701(g)).

S. Rep. No. 2, 106th Cong., 1st Sess. 75–76 (1999).

[¶ 2180]

2. ASSUMPTION OF LIABILITY TAINTED BY IMPROPER PURPOSE

One of the important exceptions to the nonrecognition of gain treatment of assumed liabilities under Section 357(a) is set forth in Section 357(b). The latter subsection requires the corporate assumption of *all* transferred liabilities from a transferor-shareholder to be treated as boot in a Section 351 exchange if the transferor-shareholder's principal purpose for shifting *any* of the liabilities to the corporation was to avoid federal income taxes or was not a bona fide business purpose. A classic illustration is a case in which the transferor places a mortgage on real property very shortly before transferring the encumbered property (but not the cash received in the mortgage) to the corporation in an attempt to obtain a tax-free cashing out of gain inherent in the encumbered property.

[¶ 2185]

DRYBROUGH v. COMMISSIONER

United States Court of Appeals, Sixth Circuit, 1967.
376 F.2d 350.

[In 1953, the taxpayer borrowed $700,000 secured by a mortgage upon four parcels of real estate. Part of these funds was used to liquidate prior real estate loans. In addition, the taxpayer applied $200,000 to the purchase of tax-exempt securities in his wife's name. As of June 1, 1957, a balance of $600,000 was due on the 1953 loan. On that date, the taxpayer transferred the four properties which secured the 1953 loan to four separate corporations in exchange for all the stock issued by each corporation. Each corporation assumed a portion of the total indebtedness of $600,000. On June 28, 1957, the taxpayer and his son transferred another parcel of real estate, described as "620 South Fifth Street" property, to a fifth corporation, subject to a mortgage indebtedness of $149,000. The stock of this corporation was issued to the taxpayer and his son in proportion to their respective interests. The son's interest in the transferred real estate had been acquired by gift from his father. The mortgage loan on this property had been obtained by the taxpayer in March 1957, and the proceeds used to purchase tax-exempt securities. The taxpayer, in reliance upon Section 357(c)(1), reported gain for the year 1957 in the amount by which the mortgage indebtedness assumed by the several corporations exceeded his basis for each of the properties transferred.]

O'SULLIVAN, CIRCUIT JUDGE:

* * *

* * * The Commissioner, however, assessed a deficiency, claiming that Section 357(b) * * * controlled, on his assertion that Drybrough had failed to prove that his principal purpose in arranging these transactions was not that of tax avoidance and was not for a bona fide business purpose and, therefore, the assumption of the liabilities should be treated as money received on the exchange. A deficiency of $170,306.89 was assessed for the year 1957.

The Commissioner also disallowed Drybrough's deduction of the interest paid on $200,000.00 of the $700,000.00 borrowed in 1953, on the claim that this sum was used to purchase tax exempt securities. Section 265(a)(2) IRC 1954 forbids such deduction. A deficiency arising from the disallowance of these interest deductions was accordingly assessed.

The Tax Court sustained the Commissioner's determinations in the above respects. We reverse the Tax Court's holding that the assumption of a total of $600,000.00 of the 1953 borrowing by the four corporations organized on June 1, 1957, was taxable in full. We affirm its holding as to the assumption of the $149,000 mortgage by 620 South Fifth Street, Inc. (the 1957 borrowing); and we affirm the disallowance of the interest paid on $200,000 of the 1957 mortgage of $700,000.

* * *

Until the Supreme Court's 1938 decision in United States v. Hendler, 303 U.S. 564 * * * (1938), taxpayers and the Treasury Department had assumed that no taxable event occurred when a taxpayer transferred encumbered assets to a controlled corporation which assumed the obligations of the encumbrance. Such an assumption was not considered as "other property or money" as those terms were used in Code sections precedent to §§ 351 IRC 1954 and 112(b)(5) IRC 1939, the sections

¶ 2185

which provided for the familiar "tax free exchanges" identified under the term "Transfer to Corporation Controlled by Transferor." The simplest form of such a tax free exchange was the changing of a business enterprise from a proprietorship to the corporate form. Even though the assets transferred had acquired a market value in excess of their cost, or [basis], and consequently the stock shares received by the transferor were worth the enhanced value of the transferred assets, still no taxable gain was then [recognized]. Such gain, however, did not escape taxation because upon subsequent sale or other transfer, the stock shares carried the same basis as the original assets that had been transferred. The *Hendler* decision, however, held that the amount of such an assumed obligation was equivalent to "other property or money" and required that the gain be immediately recognized by the transferor. Continued application of this rule forebode serious consequences to the federal treasury as well as to taxpayers, and Congress was quick to provide amelioration by enactment of the predecessor to § 357. * * * Section 112(k)[now Section 357(a)] was adopted as the needed remedy, providing that in an otherwise tax-free exchange if "as part of the consideration another party (the transferee) to the exchange assumes a liability of the taxpayer (the transferor) or acquires from the taxpayer property subject to a liability, such assumption or acquisition shall not be considered as 'other property or money' received by the taxpayer * * * ".

To guard against abuse of the privilege granted, Congress attached an exception which now as part of § 357 provides in subsection (b) * * * that if in making the exchange, the principal purpose of the taxpayer with respect to the assumption or acquisition was a purpose to avoid federal income tax "*on the exchange,*" or if not such purpose, was not a bona fide business purpose, then the assumption or acquisition should in the total amount thereof be considered "as money received by the taxpayer on the exchange." This section also provides that in determining the principal purpose of the taxpayer there should be taken "into consideration the nature of the liability and the circumstances in the light of which the arrangement for the assumption or acquisition was made." Notwithstanding this broad contextual area to be considered, we emphasize that the purpose to avoid income tax is precisely narrowed to a purpose "*with respect to the assumption*" and to a purpose to avoid income tax "*on the exchange.*"

We read this language as excluding from identification as a purpose to avoid tax *on the exchange*, the original and unrelated motivation for borrowing the money which created the assumed obligation. In this case, Drybrough in 1953 borrowed $700,000; substantially one-half of this sum was used to pay off existing mortgage indebtedness and expenses connected with the borrowing, and the other half was deposited in Drybrough's bank account. Of this latter amount, Drybrough used $203,602 to pay accrued interest and principal on a note allegedly owing to his wife * * *. We may accept the Tax Court's unclear assertion that the

¶ 2185

note to Drybrough's wife was a sham, and that of the money allegedly paid thereon, $200,000 had been in truth borrowed and used to purchase tax exempt securities. We cannot find or infer, however, that the purposes thus served revealed as a matter of fact or law a purpose to avoid income tax "on the exchange" made *four years later* when in 1957 Drybrough's business as an investor in real estate was converted from a proprietorship to corporate enterprises. Assuming an intent by Drybrough to save or avoid income tax by the 1953 purchase of tax exempt securities, such purpose cannot be said to be a part of "the principal purpose of the taxpayer (Drybrough) with respect to the assumption" of the balance of the 1953 loan by the corporations which came into existence in 1957.

It is clear that the Tax Court was of the view that under the facts of this case a purpose to avoid income tax "on the exchange" could be found by inquiry into the reasons for, and the use of the proceeds of, the 1953 borrowing. Its opinion extensively details facts relevant to this subject and then observes:

> "Drybrough urges that the focal point of our inquiry should be his purpose with respect to the assumption on the exchange and contends that Congress was concerned with the 'taxpayer's specific purpose in having a liability assumed and not with taxpayer's reason for entering into the tax free exchange.' [We do not necessarily subscribe fully to this broad assertion by Drybrough]. In view of the introductory language of section 357(b), i.e., 'taking into consideration the nature of the liability and the circumstances in the light of which the arrangement for the assumption * * * was made,' we cannot read this section in the restrictive manner urged by Drybrough. *We believe that it is relevant to the 1957 assumption of Drybrough's liabilities by the newly formed corporations to consider the nature of the liability assumed.*" 42 T.C. at 1043. (Emphasis supplied.)

Under the statute's language, it was proper to consider "the nature of the liability assumed" but under the facts of this case we do not consider that the use that Drybrough made of the 1953 borrowing was of controlling importance here. * * *

* * *

With reference to the inquiry into the use made by Drybrough of the proceeds of the 1953 borrowing, the language of the Ninth Circuit in Easson v. C.I.R., 294 F.2d 653, 659 (C.A.9, 1961) is pertinent:

> "The test suggested by the Commissioner looks to the origin of the encumbrance and to the use of the proceeds derived from it. Section 112(k) [predecessor to § 357], however, says nothing about the origin of the encumbrance. It says only that if a corporation acquires from the taxpayer property subject to *a* liability such * * * acquisi-

tion shall not be considered as boot, unless the taxpayer's principal purpose regarding the acquisition is tax avoidance or not a bona fide business purpose. *Nor is there anything in the section which deals with the reasons for the encumbrance, or the manner in which the proceeds are used.*" (Emphasis supplied.)

There was evidence also that part of the motivation for incorporating was to allow the long term retirement of Drybrough's debt out of the corporate earnings; such earnings, when applied to the 1953 loan, would likely be taxed at a lower rate than they would be in Drybrough's own tax bracket. Drybrough's expectation, however, that income tax would be saved by the lower rate that would apply to the corporate earnings as contrasted with his own income tax exposure was not, in our view, a purpose to avoid "Federal income tax *on the exchange.*" We read such to be the holding of the Tax Court's own decision in W. H. B. Simpson v. Commissioner, 43 T.C. 900 (1965) announced some months after the decision before us. In *Simpson*, the Tax Court said,

> "We do not believe it (§ 357(b)) was intended to require recognition of gain on bona fide transactions designed to rearrange one's business affairs in such a manner as to minimize *taxes in the future*, consistent with existing provisions of the law." (Emphasis supplied.) 43 T.C. at 916.

and further observed therein,

> " * * * We do not believe the fact alone that the income which will be used to pay off the liabilities to which the securities were subjected will be taxed at a lower rate falls within the tax-avoidance purpose contemplated in section 357(b)." 43 T.C. at 917.

In *Simpson*, supra, the Tax Court held the exchange there made to be tax free and in seeking to distinguish *Simpson* from its earlier decision of the *Drybrough* case which we now review, said:

> "Unlike in the Drybrough case, and in W.H. Weaver, 32 T.C. 411 (1959), affirmed sub nom, Bryan v. Commissioner, 281 F.2d 238 (C.A.4, 1960), petitioner did not incur the liabilities to which the transferred securities were subject *immediately prior to the transfer and solely in anticipation thereof.*" 43 T.C. at 917. (Emphasis supplied.)

But in the case before us the 1953 mortgage liability of Drybrough had not been incurred "immediately prior to the transfer" and was not incurred "solely in anticipation" of the forming of the corporations in 1957.

While the Tax Court did not with desirable clarity give separate treatment to the tax avoidance purpose as distinguished from the need of Drybrough to prove also that his 1957 incorporations had "a bona fide business purpose," we read its decision as a finding that Drybrough did not have "a bona fide business purpose" for the 1957 incorporations.

¶ 2185

This was error. Drybrough testified that included in his motivation for not paying off the $600,000 mortgage before incorporating was his desire to keep as liquid as possible to be able to make further investments; to put the involved real estate investments in a more manageable condition for estate planning; and generally to obtain the advantages that attend operating in the corporate form. The Tax Court's suggestion that Drybrough by liquidating other assets could have obtained sufficient cash to pay off the $600,000 so that the corporate assets would be debt free is not impressive. Such conduct would be unwise and certainly not good practice. For many years Drybrough was engaged in the business of buying and holding downtown Louisville real estate, and operating those holdings in various enterprises such as parking lots. The conversion of these businesses into corporate form was clearly to serve a bona fide business purpose. What was done here was substantially the "garden variety" of tax free exchange—the shift of a proprietorship to a wholly owned corporation which assumed the debts of the proprietorship.

We are aware that we are not at liberty to set aside findings of fact made by the Tax Court unless we can say that such findings of fact are clearly erroneous. Commissioner of Internal Revenue v. Duberstein, 363 U.S. 278 * * * (1960). If we are, or would be, required to view as findings of fact the critical finding that Drybrough had failed to meet his burden of proving that his principal purpose in having his four corporations assume the existing 1953 indebtedness was not "to avoid Federal income tax on the exchange," and that Drybrough also failed to show that what he did was for a bona fide business purpose, we would, and do, hold such findings clearly erroneous. We are of the view, however, that the Tax Court's use of impermissible tests in assessing Drybrough's purposes amounted to an error of law subject to our review, and we reverse its determination that the assumption in question is controlled by § 357(b) * * *.

* * *

We sustain the Tax Court's holding that the assumption by 620 South Fifth Street, Inc., on June 28, 1957, of the $150,000 mortgage which had been placed on the assets transferred to that corporation on March 15, 1957, had not been proven by Drybrough to be otherwise than for a principal purpose "to avoid income tax on the exchange." In late 1956 Drybrough had, with reference to the 620 South Fifth Street property, written to National Life "620 South Fifth and the Mexican Village property are both clear and I am eager to mortgage them to the limit before combining these two properties in a corporation." This was a clear expression that the creation of the debt was directly in anticipation of, and connected in purpose with, having the corporation assume the debt, thus releasing to Drybrough $150,000 of the value of this asset without a present realization of taxable gain on the exchange. The borrowed money was used to purchase tax-exempt securities; it was not

¶ 2185

used to carry on the purposes of the business enterprise of 620 South Fifth Street, Inc., nor in furtherance of Drybrough's general real estate investments, justifying also a finding that the assumption could not be accommodated under the "bona fide business purpose" requirement of § 357(b)(1)(B). We think it was a fair inference too that Drybrough's conduct was equivalent to a pro tanto liquidation of the involved asset, and that his purpose "with respect to the assumption" disclosed a plan to avoid realization of gain on this liquidation by selling the mortgaged asset to his controlled corporation. It was permissible for the Tax Court to find in this transaction "a purpose to avoid Federal income tax on the exchange," § 357(b)(1)(A).

We find no fault with the legal standard employed to reach the above conclusions; and cannot hold as clearly erroneous the factual findings involved.

* * *

[¶ 2190]

3. LIABILITIES IN EXCESS OF BASIS: SECTION 357(c)

Whereas Section 357(a) provides as a general rule that a corporation's assumption of the transferor's debts in a Section 351 exchange is not to be treated as boot, this is subject not only to the exception in Section 357(b), discussed immediately above, but also to a second exception contained in Section 357(c). This latter subsection requires the transferor to recognize gain to the extent that the total liabilities assumed by the corporation exceed the total basis of the properties transferred in the exchange. As in the case of Section 357(a) and (b), liabilities assumed include recourse and nonrecourse liabilities to the extent specified in Section 357(d), discussed at ¶ 2175. The rule of Section 357(c) prevents the possibility of a negative basis for the stock received by the transferor. The recognition of gain under Section 357(c) occurs notwithstanding a valid business purpose for the corporation's assumption of the debt. However, in the event that both subsections (b) and (c) apply, the former takes precedence and requires the entire amount of assumed liabilities to be treated as boot, not merely the excess of the liabilities over the bases of the transferred properties.

Section 357(c) is applied to each transferor separately. Rev. Rul. 66–142, 1966–1 C.B. 66. Section 357(c) gain, which is treated as recognized gain, not boot, is allocated among all of the properties (including loss properties) transferred by that transferor in proportion to their respective fair market values and is characterized as long-or short-term capital gain or ordinary income, depending on the nature and holding period of each property transferred. Reg. § 1.357(b)–2(b). Section 357(c) gain is taken into account for basis purposes in the same way as recognized boot gain for purposes of Sections 358(a) and 362(a), but Section 362(d)(1), as amended in 1999, prevents any increase in the basis of transferred property above its fair market value as a result of the assumption of liabilities by the transferee corporation.

Absent special statutory relief, Section 357(c)(1) could produce harsh results for a cash method transferor who incorporates a sole proprietorship or partnership. Although operations may have been profitable, with the value of the assets exceeding the amount of the liabilities, those assets may consist largely of unrealized accounts receivable having a zero basis, which is exceeded by the amount of debts arising from day-to-day operations (e.g., for rent, salaries, and trade accounts payable). The resulting tax problem that could thus be presented under Section 357(c) because liabilities assumed by the corporate transferee exceed the basis of the assets transferred to the corporation is peculiar to cash method taxpayers. Accrual method taxpayers, by contrast, obtain a basis for receivables upon taking them into income, even though that income may be sheltered from tax by deductions allowed for accrued but unpaid obligations arising from operations. The relief provided by Section 357(c)(3) attempts to achieve parity for cash method taxpayers.

Under Section 357(c)(3), a liability that, when paid, would give rise to a deduction or creation of or an increase in the basis of property is excluded for purposes of Section 357(c) in determining the amount of the liabilities assumed. § 357(c)(3)(A)(i) and (B). As a corollary, Section 358(d)(2) provides that such a liability also does not reduce the transferor's Section 358 substituted basis in the stock received on the exchange.

Liabilities that would neither give rise to a deduction nor an increase in the basis of property when paid are, as usual, taken into account by Section 357(c) in determining whether liabilities exceed the basis of assets transferred. To ignore such liabilities would allow the transferor an undue benefit. For example, even for a cash method taxpayer, the obligation arising from the purchase of property with debt is reflected in the basis of that asset, and therefore should not be ignored in measuring the excess of liabilities over basis.

[¶ 2195]

REVENUE RULING 95–74

1995–2 C.B. 36.

Issues

(1) Are the liabilities assumed by S in the § 351 exchange described below liabilities for purposes of §§ 357(c)(1) and 358(d)?

(2) Once assumed by S, how will the liabilities in the § 351 exchange described below be treated?

¶ 2190

FACTS

Corporation *P* is an accrual basis, calendar-year corporation engaged in various ongoing businesses, one of which includes the operation of a manufacturing plant (the Manufacturing Business). The plant is located on land purchased by *P* many years before. The land was not contaminated by any hazardous waste when *P* purchased it. However, as a result of plant operations, certain environmental liabilities, such as potential soil and groundwater remediation, are now associated with the land.

In Year 1, for bona fide business purposes, *P* engages in an exchange to which § 351 * * * applies by transferring substantially all of the assets associated with the Manufacturing Business, including the manufacturing plant and the land on which the plant is located, to a newly formed corporation, *S*, in exchange for all of the stock of *S* and for *S*'s assumption of the liabilities associated with the Manufacturing Business, including the environmental liabilities associated with the land. *P* has no plan or intention to dispose of (or have *S* issue) any *S* stock. *S* is an accrual basis, calendar-year taxpayer.

P did not undertake any environmental remediation efforts in connection with the land transferred to *S* before the transfer and did not deduct or capitalize any amount with respect to the contingent environmental liabilities associated with the transferred land.

In Year 3, *S* undertakes soil and groundwater remediation efforts relating to the land transferred in the § 351 exchange and incurs costs (within the meaning of the economic performance rules of § 461(h)) as a result of those remediation efforts. Of the total amount of costs incurred, a portion would have constituted ordinary and necessary business expenses that are deductible under § 162 and the remaining portion would have constituted capital expenditures under § 263 if there had not been a § 351 exchange and the costs for remediation efforts had been incurred by *P*. *See* Rev. Rul. 94–38, 1994–1 C.B. 35 (discussing the treatment of certain environmental remediation costs).

LAW AND ANALYSIS

Issue 1: * * *.

* * *

A number of cases concerning cash basis taxpayers were litigated in the 1970s with respect to the definition of "liabilities" for purposes of § 357(c)(1), with sometimes conflicting analyses and results. * * * In response to this litigation, Congress enacted § 357(c)(3) to address the concern that the inclusion in the § 357(c)(1) determination of certain deductible liabilities resulted in "unforeseen and unintended tax difficulties for certain cash basis taxpayers who incorporate a going business." S. Rep. No. 1263, 95th Cong., 2d Sess. 184–85 (1978) * * *.

¶ 2195

Congress concluded that including in the § 357(c)(1) determination liabilities that have not yet been taken into account by the transferor results in an overstatement of liabilities of, and potential inappropriate gain recognition to, the transferor because the transferor has not received the corresponding deduction or other corresponding tax benefit. *Id.* To prevent this result, Congress enacted § 357(c)(3)(A) to exclude certain deductible liabilities from the scope of § 357(c), as long as the liabilities had not resulted in the creation of, or an increase in, the basis of any property (as provided in § 357(c)(3)(B)). P.L. 95–600 (Revenue Act of 1978), sec. 365 * * *; *see also* S. Rep. No. 1263, 95th Cong., 2d Sess. 185 (1978) * * *.

While § 357(c)(3) explicitly addresses liabilities that give rise to deductible items, the same principle applies to liabilities that give rise to capital expenditures as well. Including in the § 357(c)(1) determination those liabilities that have not yet given rise to capital expenditures (and thus have not yet created or increased basis) with respect to the property of the transferor prior to the transfer also would result in an overstatement of liabilities. Thus, such liabilities also appropriately are excluded in determining liabilities for purposes of § 357(c)(1). *Cf.* Rev. Rul. 95–45, 1995–1 C.B. 4 (short sale obligation that creates basis treated as a liability for purposes of §§ 357 and 358); Rev. Rul. 88–77, 1988–2 C.B. 129 (accrued but unpaid expenses and accounts payable are not liabilities of a cash basis partnership for purposes of computing the adjusted basis of a partner's interest for purposes of § 752).

In this case, the contingent environmental liabilities assumed by *S* had not yet been taken into account by *P* prior to the transfer (and therefore had neither given rise to deductions for *P* nor resulted in the creation of, or increase in, basis in any property of *P*). As a result, the contingent environmental liabilities are not included in determining whether the amount of the liabilities assumed by *S* exceeds the adjusted basis of the property transferred by *P* pursuant to § 357(c)(1).

Due to the parallel constructions and interrelated function and mechanics of §§ 357 and 358, liabilities that are not included in the determination under § 357(c)(1) also are not included in the § 358 determination of the transferor's basis in the stock received in the § 351 exchange. See *Focht v. Commissioner*, 68 T.C. 223 (1977); S. Rep. No. 1263, 95th Cong., 2d Sess. 183–85 (1978) * * *. Therefore, the contingent environmental liabilities assumed by *S* are not treated as money received by *P* under § 358 for purposes of determining *P*'s basis in the stock of *S* received in the exchange.

Issue 2: In *Holdcroft Transp. Co. v. Commissioner*, 153 F.2d 323 (8th Cir.1946), the Court of Appeals for the Eighth Circuit held that, after a transfer pursuant to the predecessor to § 351, the payments by a transferee corporation were not deductible even though the transferor partnership would have been entitled to deductions for the payments had the partnership actually made the payments. The court stated generally that the expense of settling claims or liabilities of a predecessor entity did not arise as an operating expense or loss of the business of the transferee but was a part of the cost of acquiring the predecessor's property, and the fact that the claims were contingent and unliquidated at the time of the acquisition was not of controlling consequence.

In Rev. Rul. 80–198, [at ¶ 2270] * * *, an individual transferred all of the assets and liabilities of a sole proprietorship, which included accounts payable and accounts receivable, to a new corporation in exchange for all of its stock. The revenue ruling holds, subject to certain limitations, that the transfer qualifies as an exchange within the meaning of § 351(a) and that the transferee corporation will report in its income the accounts receivable as collected and will be allowed deductions under § 162 for the payments it makes to satisfy the accounts payable. In reaching these holdings, the revenue ruling makes reference to the specific congressional intent of § 351(a) to facilitate the incorporation of an ongoing business by making the incorporation tax free. The ruling states that this intent would be equally frustrated if either the transferor were taxed on the transfer of the accounts receivable or the transferee were not allowed a deduction for payment of the accounts payable. See also Rev. Rul. 83–155, 1983–2 C.B. 38 (guaranteed payments to a retired partner made pursuant to a partnership agreement by a corporation to which the partnership had transferred all of its assets and liabilities in a § 351 exchange were deductible by the corporation as ordinary and necessary business expenses under § 162(a)).

The present case is analogous to the situation in Rev. Rul. 80–198. For business reasons, P transferred in a § 351 exchange substantially all of the assets and liabilities associated with the Manufacturing Business to S, in exchange for all of its stock, and P intends to remain in control of S. The costs S incurs to remediate the land would have been deductible in part and capitalized in part had P continued the Manufacturing Business and incurred those costs to remediate the land. The congressional intent to facilitate necessary business readjustments would be frustrated by not according to S the ability to deduct or capitalize the expenses of the ongoing business.

Therefore, on these facts, the Internal Revenue Service will not follow the decision in *Holdcroft Transp. Co. v. Commissioner,* 153 F.2d 323 (8th Cir.1946). Accordingly, the contingent environmental liabilities assumed from P are deductible as business expenses under § 162 or are capitalized under § 263, as appropriate, by S under S's method of accounting (determined as if S has owned the land for the period and in the same manner as it was owned by P).

HOLDINGS

(1) The liabilities assumed by S in the § 351 exchange described above are not liabilities for purposes of § 357(c)(1) and § 358(d) because

the liabilities had not yet been taken into account by P prior to the transfer (and therefore had neither given rise to deductions for P nor resulted in the creation of, or increase in, basis in any property of P).

(2) The liabilities assumed by S in the § 351 exchange described above are deductible by S as business expenses under § 162 or are capital expenditures under § 263, as appropriate, under S's method of accounting (determined as if S has owned the land for the period and in the same manner as it was owned by P).

LIMITATIONS

The holdings described above are subject to § 482 and other applicable sections of the Code and principles of law, including the limitations discussed in Rev. Rul. 80–198, 1980–2 C.B. 113 (limiting the scope of the revenue ruling to transactions that do not have a tax avoidance purpose).
* * *

[¶ 2200]

Problems

1. Assume that Antoine and Bernadette organized the A & B Corporation with an initial capital of $200,000. Each received 1,000 shares of common stock with a par value of $100 per share. Antoine paid cash of $100,000 for his shares. Bernadette received her shares in exchange for a transfer by her to the corporation of a building with a basis of $60,000 and a fair market value of $125,000, subject to a mortgage debt of $25,000, which had been incurred five years before to finance improvements to the property. (The original principal amount of the debt was $25,000, none of which had been repaid). What are the tax consequences of this transfer to Bernadette and the A & B Corporation?

2. Developer Tompkins (T) owned, among his other assets, a parcel of improved real estate which had an adjusted cost basis of $100,000 and a fair market value of $500,000. On January 2, T borrowed $250,000 on a nonrecourse loan secured by a first mortgage on the property. These funds were used by T in another business venture. On January 10, T transferred the property subject to the mortgage of $250,000 to a newly organized corporation in exchange for all the stock of the corporation.

a. How much taxable gain does T recognize upon the transfer of the property to the corporation? What is T's basis for his stock?

b. Would your answers differ if the borrowed funds were not put immediately into another business venture, but were instead invested in tax-exempt bonds?

3. Marla (M) converted her proprietorship into a wholly owned corporation by transferring all her assets and liabilities in exchange for all the issued stock of the corporation. The assets had an aggregate basis of $55,600. The liabilities totalled $25,000. M regularly reported income

on the accrual method. The opening balance sheet disclosed the following:

M Corporation

Assets	Basis	Fair Market Value	Liabilities	
Cash	$ 3,000	$ 3,000	Accounts Payable	$ 5,000
Accounts receivable	20,000	20,000	Mortgage payable	20,000
Inventory	27,000	27,000		
Land	2,000	5,000	Equity	
Building	–0–	35,000	Common stock	75,000
Machinery	3,600	10,000		
	$55,600	$100,000		$100,000

What would be the tax consequences of the incorporation in each of the following circumstances?

a.   Assume that the land and building were transferred subject to the mortgage in the amount of $20,000. Reg. § 1.357–2.

b.   Assume in addition that the accounts payable included an obligation of $2,000 for a gold watch which M had purchased for her husband three days before the incorporation. Reg. § 1.357–1(c). What if it had been purchased three years before?

4.   EFFECT OF AN ASSUMED LIABILITY ON BASIS

[¶ 2205]

a.   *At the Shareholder Level*

The rules for determining the basis of stock received by a transferor of property in a Section 351 exchange must be adjusted for liabilities assumed by the transferee corporation. Under Section 358(a), the transferor's basis in nonrecognition property received is the basis of the property transferred decreased by

(1) the fair market value of any boot property (except money) received and

(2) the amount of money received, and

increased by the amount of gain recognized to the transferor. Under Section 358(d)(1), an assumed liability, other than a liability excluded under Section 357(c)(3), is treated as money received for purposes of Section 358(a).

Prior to 2000, the exception in Sections 358(d)(1) and 357(c)(3) to the above basis rule for contingent liabilities, when combined with Rev. Rul. 95–74, opened up the potential for abuse. The case below describes one such potentially abusive scheme.

¶ 2205

[¶ 2210]

BLACK & DECKER CORP. v. UNITED STATES

United States Court of Appeals, Fourth Circuit, 2006.
436 F.3d 431.

MICHAEL, CIRCUIT JUDGE:

A corporate taxpayer paid $561 million to a controlled subsidiary in exchange for 10,000 shares of the subsidiary's stock and the subsidiary's assumption of a $560 million contingent liability of the taxpayer. The taxpayer then sold the shares for $1 million, claimed a $560 million capital loss on its federal income tax return, and sought a refund based on that loss. The Internal Revenue Service declined to pay because it concluded that the capital loss stemmed from an illegal tax shelter. After the taxpayer sued, the district court denied the IRS's summary judgment motion and granted the taxpayer's summary judgment motion. The IRS appeals. We conclude that neither the IRS nor the taxpayer is entitled to summary judgment under the controlling tax statutes. Under the sham transaction doctrine, however, the validity of the claimed loss turns on unresolved issues of material fact. Accordingly, we affirm the denial of the IRS's motion, reverse the grant of the taxpayer's motion, and remand for further proceedings.

I.

A.

The Black & Decker Corporation (BDC), its wholly-owned subsidiary Black & Decker Inc. (BDI), and their direct and indirect subsidiaries constitute a major manufacturer of power tools and home improvement products. (The subsidiaries involved are Emhart Industries, Inc., Price Pfister, Inc., and Kwikset Corp., all of which are domestic corporations controlled by BDC. BDC is also owner of Black & Decker Canada, Inc. (the "Canadian subsidiary), which does not file a tax return in the United States. We will refer to BDC and its domestic direct and indirect subsidiaries as, collectively, "Taxpayer."). Taxpayer provides medical and dental insurance benefits to its current and retired employees, who number in the thousands. The aggregated future health benefits claims constitute a contingent liability because their precise cost is not known in the present. Thus, Taxpayer can estimate but cannot predict with certainty how many of its employees or retirees will be diagnosed with particular illnesses in future years.

In 1998 Taxpayer realized nearly $303 million in capital gains income from the sale of three businesses. Taxpayer sought to offset that income against a large loss to prevent the imposition of a substantial federal income tax obligation. To this end Taxpayer executed a transaction that gave rise to what it intended to be a significant capital loss.

The Deloitte & Touche accounting firm had designed the transaction and advised some 30 corporate clients, including Taxpayer, on its implementation as a tax strategy. The transaction involved a subsidiary called Black & Decker Healthcare Management Inc. (BDHMI). Taxpayer owned all of BDHMI's common stock. BDHMI's preferred shareholders included an affiliate of William M. Mercer, Inc. (Taxpayer's benefits consultant and a subsidiary of Marsh & McLennan Companies, Inc.) and Taxpayer's Canadian subsidiary. The participation of outside investors permitted BDHMI to file a federal income tax return separate from Taxpayer's.

The transaction consisted of two phases. Phase One was an exchange on November 25, 1998, between Taxpayer and its Canadian subsidiary on the one hand and BDHMI on the other. Taxpayer and the Canadian subsidiary paid BDHMI approximately $561 million in cash with funds Taxpayer had borrowed from its banks for 30 days. In return BDHMI (1) gave Taxpayer and the Canadian subsidiary 10,000 shares of BDHMI's series C preferred stock and (2) assumed liability for the future health benefits claims against Taxpayer and the Canadian subsidiary from 1999 to 2007, which had an estimated net present value of $560 million. According to the exchange agreement the companies executed, BDHMI's assumption of liability "[did] not constitute either a legal defeasance of the Benefits Liabilities by [Taxpayer] or a novation and consequently, [Taxpayer] . . . continued to be primarily liable for the payment and performance of the Benefits Liabilities." J.A. 217. Thus, Taxpayer remained liable on the underlying obligations transferred to BDHMI.

The companies executed Phase Two on December 29, 1998. Taxpayer and the Canadian subsidiary sold the 10,000 BDHMI shares at a price of $1 million to an unrelated third-party trust benefitting a former BDC executive. Also that day, BDHMI promised to lend BDI approximately $564 million, most of which was to be repaid in monthly installments according to the terms of three lending agreements. BDI's installment payments on the loans were "designed to provide [BDHMI] with sufficient funds to pay" the benefits liabilities as they came due. J.A. 127. Although BDHMI continued to hold the benefits liabilities, Taxpayer reported all of the income from the businesses and employees that gave rise to those liabilities.

As one of BDHMI's outside investors put it, "The rationale behind the establishment of the subsidiary [BDHMI] is that a loss equal to the reserve for the liabilities can be recognized upfront for tax purposes and the [special purpose vehicle, BDHMI] may be able to deduct the amount of the claims a second time as they are actually incurred." J.A. 3235. Formally, the investors in BDHMI stood to earn a positive return on their investment in the event that Taxpayer's actual health care liabilities fell short of the expected cost of those liabilities, so that Taxpayer's repayment on the loan would exceed BDHMI's payments on the medical claims, creating net income for BDHMI. But as a practical matter

¶ 2210

Taxpayer expected BDHMI to generate net operating losses because the health expenses were likely to consistently exceed BDHMI's interest income from the loan to Taxpayer. Or, in the words of Taxpayer's in-house accountants, "BDHMI will generate net operating losses since the interest income on the note receivable is not likely to exceed annual claims paid which are recognized for tax purposes when paid." J.A. 148.

B.

In its 1998 tax return Taxpayer characterized Phase One as the purchase of the BDHMI shares for $561 million and Phase Two as the sale of those shares for $1 million, generating a $560 million capital loss. Taxpayer claimed that its basis in the BDHMI stock was equal to the cash payment without reduction by the benefits liabilities BDHMI assumed in Phase One. The large capital loss offset the capital gains from Taxpayer's divestitures earlier in the year. Further, the large loss had both retrospective and prospective tax-reducing effects under the Internal Revenue Code of 1986, * * * allowing Taxpayer to file for refunds on its returns for the 1995 through 2000 tax years. The refunds sought totaled approximately $57 million.

Because the IRS did not pay the refunds for more than six months, Taxpayer commenced a civil action in the U.S. District Court for the District of Maryland. 26 U.S.C. §§ 7422; 6532(a)(1). The IRS filed a counterclaim for tax, interest, and penalties of approximately $215 million. The IRS construed the tax laws as requiring Taxpayer to state its basis in the shares sold as $1 million, not $560 million. Taxpayer took the opposite view. Moving for summary judgment, the IRS argued that under IRC § 357(c)(3)(A) Taxpayer, the transferor, had to reduce its stock basis by the amount of the contingent liability assumed by BDHMI, the transferee. The district court denied the motion. Taxpayer then moved for summary judgment, arguing that the transfer of the benefits liabilities was not a sham transaction that could be disregarded for tax purposes. The district court granted the motion, * * * The district court stated that because BDHMI was constituted for a valid business purpose, BDHMI and all of its transactions were "objectively reasonable" and thus could not be disregarded for tax purposes. * * * This appeal by the IRS followed.

II.

The IRS first contends that it was entitled to summary judgment because, on the undisputed facts, the statutes governing the transaction required the basis reduction. Preliminarily, we note that if Taxpayer were to engage in the contingent liability transfer today, it would be required to reduce its basis by the amount of the transferred liabilities under IRC § 358(h), which Congress enacted as part of the Community Renewal Tax Relief Act of 2000. * * * That statute does not control here because it does not apply retroactively. In addition, in 2001 the IRS

¶ 2210

issued Notice 2001–17 on contingent liability tax shelters, which put corporations on notice that the IRS would challenge transactions of the type at issue here. These legal and enforcement policy developments took place after Taxpayer engaged in the contingent liability transaction. Consequently, the question before us is whether the law at the time Taxpayer executed this transaction required Taxpayer to reduce its basis in the stock by the amount of the benefits liabilities transferred. In answering this question, we first briefly survey the pertinent statutes. Then we turn to the parties' specific statutory arguments on whether summary judgment should have been granted in the IRS's favor.

A.

On appeal the parties agree that the transaction is to be analyzed under IRC § 351. Section 351(a) provides that no gain or loss shall be recognized—that is, the transaction is tax-free—if property (here, the cash from Taxpayer) is transferred to a corporation (BDHMI) by "one or more persons" (here, members of a consolidated group, Taxpayer) solely in exchange for voting stock in BDHMI, and immediately after the exchange the transferor is in control of the transferee. *See* * * * § 351(a). Taxpayer did not, however, transfer property to BDHMI "solely" in exchange for BDHMI stock because BDHMI also assumed the contingent liability. So the transfer does not fit within the exact terms of § 351(a).

Taxpayer would nevertheless continue to enjoy the tax-free benefit of § 351(a) if Taxpayer could successfully invoke § 357(a). Under § 357(a) transactions are treated as § 351(a) tax-free transactions if they would satisfy § 351(a) were it not for the fact that the transferee, in consideration for the transferor's property, not only gave its stock but *also* assumed the transferor's liability. In such cases, § 357(a) prevents the transferee's assumption of liability from being treated as taxable money or property received by the transferor. This tax-free benefit is not available, however, when the exceptions of §§ 357(b) and (c) apply. *See* * * * § 357(a). * * *

Separate from the concept of gain or loss recognition is the concept of basis computation. The income tax consequences of selling property hinge on the taxpayer's basis in that property. Except as otherwise provided, "the basis of property shall be the cost of such property." * * * § 1012. (Usually, basis is "the original cost of property used in computing capital gains or losses for income tax purposes." *Lessinger v. Comm'r,* 872 F.2d 519, 525 n.3 (2d Cir. 1989) (quoting *Webster's Third New International Dictionary* 182 (1963)). In general, when a taxpayer sells an asset for more than its basis, he records a capital gain; when he sells the asset for less than its basis, he records a capital loss.) In the § 351 transaction at issue here, Taxpayer's basis in the BDHMI stock is determined under § 358. *See* * * * § 351(h)(2). Under § 358(a)(1) a § 351 transferor's basis in the stock received from the transferee is the same as the basis of the property the transferor surrendered, reduced by the amount of any "money received." 26 U.S.C. § 358(a)(1). Section 358(d)(1) further provides that, in § 358 analysis, an assumption of liability by the transferee shall be treated as "money received" by the transferor. A transferor reduces its basis in the stock received from the transferee by the amount of any liability the transferee assumed in exchange. But the statute also provides that § 358(d)(1) does *not* apply if the liability assumed is one that would be excluded under § 357(c)(3). * * * § 358(d)(2). Section 357(c)(3), in turn, excludes "liability the payment of which ... would give rise to a deduction." * * * § 357(c)(3)(A).

B.

To prevail on summary judgment the IRS must demonstrate that as a matter of law Taxpayer was not entitled to the § 357(c)(3) exception. This demonstration turns on statutory meaning. "It is well established that when the statute's language is plain, the sole function of the courts—at least where the disposition required by the text is not absurd—is to enforce it according to its terms." *Lamie v. United States Trustee,* 540 U.S. 526 * * * (2004) (punctuation omitted); *see Coleman v. Cmty. Trust Bank (In re Coleman),* 426 F.3d 719, 724–25 (4th Cir. 2005). When the language of the statute is unclear, we "may consult its legislative history as a guide to congressional intent." *Yi v. Fed. Bureau of Prisons,* 412 F.3d 526, 533 (4th Cir. 2005). The fact that a tax statute is at issue here does not render inapplicable these general principles of statutory interpretation.

The benefits liabilities Taxpayer transferred to BDHMI fall within the plain terms of the § 357(c)(3) exception if, in the event that the claims are paid, a person would be able to deduct the amounts paid from that person's taxable income. The statute does not specify, however, whether the person taking the deduction would be the liability's transferee (BDHMI) or the transferor (Taxpayer). Because the statute does not clearly identify the person who would take the hypothetical deduction the statute envisions, it is appropriate to examine the legislative history so far as is necessary to identify that person.

Section 357(c) was first enacted in 1978 and rewritten into its present form two years later by the next Congress. The Senate Report that presaged the 1980 revision explained:

> In general, liabilities the payment of which would give rise to a deduction include trade accounts payable and other liabilities (e.g., interest and taxes) which relate to the transferred trade or business. However, such liabilities may be excluded under this provision only to the extent payment thereof by the transferor would have given rise to a deduction.

¶ 2210

S. Rep. No. 96–498, at 62 (1979) * * *. The second sentence quoted resolves the uncertainty in § 357(c)(3)'s "would give rise to a deduction" phrase by clarifying that Congress had in mind the deductibility by the transferor. A liability falls within the § 357(c)(3) exception so long as, if the transfer had not taken place and the transferor had paid the liability, the transferor could have taken a deduction. To see why this condition is satisfied here, let us suppose that the health care claims had remained with Taxpayer. In that case, when Taxpayer incurred medical expenses as its employees and retirees received health care, Taxpayer could have deducted those expenses from income.

The IRS presses two arguments for why Taxpayer cannot claim the § 357(c)(3) exception. The first argument relies on legislative history. The IRS focuses on sentences such as the first of the two from the Senate Report quoted. It contends that Congress crafted the exception to protect a parent corporation from a tax double whammy when transferring both assets *and* associated liabilities to a subsidiary in exchange for stock. From this perspective, Congress wanted to prevent such parent corporations from being twice penalized by (1) deprivation of the right to deduct the transferred liabilities as they accrued and (2) mandatory reduction of the stock basis by the amount of the liabilities transferred. Since Taxpayer only transferred the health claims but not the assets generating those claims, the IRS argues that Congress did not intend for Taxpayer to benefit from § 357(c)(3). Further, the IRS reads the quoted phrase "would have given rise to a deduction," S. Rep. No. 96–498, at 62, to mean a deduction unavailable to the transferor once the liability has been transferred.

The legislative history argument does not persuade us. The prototypical transaction Congress had in mind in drafting § 357(c)(3) may well have been one in which a corporation exchanged liabilities as part of a transfer of an entire trade or business to a controlled subsidiary, but nothing in the section's plain language embraces such a limitation. As a result we find no ambiguity in the statute that requires us to parse the congressional record and discern what *type* of business transactions Congress originally envisioned in enacting the section. The Senate Report's use of the phrase "would have given rise" also does not go as far as the IRS would have us take it. On the contrary, we agree with one commentator's observation that this language "does not imply ... that Congress silently contemplated a case in which liabilities are transferred but the deduction is retained by the transferor and [then] concluded that § 357(c)(3) should not apply." Ethan Yale, *Reexamining Black & Decker's Contingent Liability Tax Shelter*, 108 Tax Notes 223, 234 (July 11, 2005).

The IRS's second argument is based on sound administration of the tax laws, because the Taxpayer should not be allowed to take the "functional equivalent of a double deduction." Appellant's Br. at 59. Although Taxpayer has not claimed the employee health expenses as a

¶ **2210**

deduction (BDHMI, not a party to this suit, claims them instead), the IRS argues that Taxpayer has the legal right to seek these deductions as health care costs accrue. In the IRS's view, the $560 million loss that Taxpayer reported effectively accelerates deductions for uncertain future health care costs through the year 2007. Such acceleration would contravene the prohibition against claiming a deduction in a given tax year for an estimate of liabilities that have not become fixed by the end of that year. Here, receipt of medical care and filing of proper claims forms would fix the annual health care liability. *United States v. Gen. Dynamics Corp.*, 481 U.S. 239, 242–45 * * *.

Again, we are not convinced that the language of § 357(c)(3) is so unclear as to permit us to rely on this policy argument and adopt the IRS's reading. In addition, because BDHMI files a tax return separate from Taxpayer's and has been taking the deductions for the health care expenses as the expenses are incurred, the "double deduction" argument would only work if we were to treat BDHMI and Taxpayer as a single entity. We see no justification on the present record for disregarding the distinct corporate taxpayer identities of BDHMI and Taxpayer. Rather, we agree with Taxpayer: "BDHMI pays the claims; BDHMI takes the deductions—not Taxpayer." Appellee's Br. at 27.

We conclude that the contingent liability Taxpayer transferred to BDHMI falls within the § 357(c)(3) exception for "liability the payment of which ... would give rise to a deduction." Therefore, under § 358(d)(2)'s exception to the general rule of § 358(d)(1), the liability need not be treated as "money received" by Taxpayer for basis reduction purposes. For this reason the district court's denial of the IRS's summary judgment motion was correct.

* * *

[The court affirmed the grant of summary judgment in the Taxpayer's favor on the IRS argument that the transaction violated Section 357(b), but reversed and remanded for consideration as to whether the transaction violated the sham transaction doctrine.]

AFFIRMED IN PART, REVERSED IN PART, AND REMANDED.

[¶ 2215]

Notes

1. To shut down contingent liability tax shelters like the one described in *Black & Decker*, Congress enacted Section 358(h). Under this provision, when the basis of the nonrecognition property received by the shareholder-transferor in the transaction would exceed its fair market value under the normal basis rules, the basis must be reduced by the amount of any liability assumed that was not otherwise reduced under Section 358(d)(1). § 358(h)(1). In other words, notwithstanding the exception in Section 358(d)(2) for liabilities excluded under Section

357(c)(3), the basis must be reduced by any liability assumed unless the exception described in Note 2 below applies. Thus, for example, if a corporation transfers a single asset with an adjusted basis and fair market value of $200 to its wholly owned corporation and the transferee corporation assumes $80 of liabilities (the payment of which would have given rise to a deduction or an increase in the basis of property if paid by the transferor), the value of the stock received by the transferor is $120. The basis of the stock will be reduced from $200 (which it would be in the absence of Section 358(h)(1)) to $120 under Section 358(h)(1). The effect of Section 358(h) is to make explicit what the IRS argued in *Black & Decker* was implicit in Section 357(c)(3), which is to prevent double deductions by preserving the loss for the subsidiary, but denying a second loss to the parent corporation.

    2.   Under Section 358(h), the basis reduction requirement does not apply where the trade or business with which the liability is associated is transferred to the corporation as part of the exchange or where substantially all of the assets with which the liability is associated are transferred to the person assuming the liability as part of the exchange. § 358(h)(2). This exception obviates the need to value assets in such cases. As the statutory language implies, the exception is not intended to apply to a situation involving the selective transfer of assets that may bear some relationship to the liability; rather the assets must represent the full scope of the trade or business (or substantially all of the assets) transferred. Moreover, the Section 358(h)(1) basis reduction applies only if, as is usually the case, the liability is assumed by a person other than the transferor. § 358(h)(1)(A).

[¶ 2220]

b. *At the Corporate Level*

    The basis of property received by a transferee corporation in a Section 351(a) exchange is generally the basis of the property to the transferor increased by any gain recognized to the transferor. § 362(a). However, the gain recognized to the transferor as the result of the assumption by the transferee of a liability of the transferor cannot increase the basis of the property in the hands of the transferee corporation to more than the fair market value of the property. § 362(d)(1). Moreover, for reasons discussed above, at ¶ 2175, if gain is recognized to the transferor as a result of the assumption of a nonrecourse liability by a transferee which is also secured by assets not transferred to the transferee and no one is subject to tax on that gain (e.g., because the transferor is a tax-exempt entity or is a foreign corporation), then in determining the transferee's basis in the property, the amount of gain recognized by the transferor as a result of assumption of the liability is determined as if the liability assumed by the transferee equaled the transferee's ratable share of such liability based on the ratio of the value of the property transferred to the transferee to the value of all the property securing the liability. § 362(d)(2).

[¶ 2225]

5. ATTEMPTS BY TRANSFEROR TO AVOID SECTION 357(c) GAIN

When the liabilities assumed by a corporation incident to a Section 351 transfer cannot be disregarded under the authority of Section 357(c)(3), might recognition of gain be avoided by the transferor either (i) continuing to remain personally liable for the debts or (ii) contributing a promissory note equal to the excess of the liabilities assumed over the basis of the properties transferred? Such planning efforts were at the heart of the following cases. Should either or both have succeeded?

[¶ 2230]

OWEN v. COMMISSIONER

United States Court of Appeals, Ninth Circuit, 1989.
881 F.2d 832, cert. denied, 493 U.S. 1070 (1990).

THOMPSON, CIRCUIT JUDGE:

William and Gretchen Owen appeal the tax court's decision * * * forcing them to recognize a taxable gain on a 1981 transfer of equipment. * * * We affirm.

I

FACTS

Over the years, William Owen participated in several business ventures with Stephen McEachron. In 1977, they formed a general partnership called McO Investment ("McO"), in which they were equal partners. In 1980, Owen and McEachron entered the seismic drilling business. They borrowed money to buy drilling equipment, secured the loan by the equipment, gave their personal guaranties to the lender, and placed title to the equipment in McO. They then leased most of the equipment to Western Exploration, Inc. ("Western"), a corporation in which they had equal ownership interests. Western conducted the seismic drilling operations.

* * *

By 1981, the petroleum industry had suffered economic reversals, and Owen and McEachron decided to sell. Their tax attorney advised them the best way to do that was to get the assets of the business into one corporate entity. So, in 1981, all of McO's assets were transferred to Western. At that time, the indebtedness secured by the assets exceeded the assets' adjusted basis.

¶ 2220

* * * The Commissioner * * * assessed a capital gain tax against the Owens on their 1981 return based upon McO's transfer of the equipment to Western. The capital gain tax was calculated with reference to the amount by which the indebtedness secured by the equipment exceeded the equipment's adjusted basis on the date of the transfer. The Commissioner's position, relative to this appeal, was upheld by the tax court. The Owens appeal.

* * *

III

THE 1981 TRANSFER

The tax court held that section 357(c) requires the Owens to recognize a gain on the 1981 transfer of equipment from McO to Western. The court calculated the gain by subtracting the adjusted basis of the equipment from the total liabilities secured by the equipment on the date of the transfer. The Owens argue that the tax court should have excluded liabilities secured by the property which they had personally guaranteed and for which they remained liable following the transfer. We disagree.

Under I.R.C. § 357(c), the Owens' continuing personal liability for the loans secured by the transferred equipment is irrelevant. "So long as the transferred property remains liable on the debt, then, such debt can be a section 357(c) liability even if the petitioner retained personal, unrelieved liability on it." *Smith v. Commissioner*, 84 T.C. 889, 909 (1985); *see also Beaver v. Commissioner*, 41 T.C.M. (CCH) 52, 54 (1980); *Rosen v. Commissioner*, 62 T.C. 11, 19 (1974), *aff'd without published opinion*, 515 F.2d 507 (3d Cir.1975).

First, the Owens ask us to reject the authority of *Smith*, *Rosen* and *Beaver*, and to hold that I.R.C. § 357(c) only applies where a taxpayer realizes an economic benefit from the transfer. We decline the Owens' invitation because section 357(c)'s plain language makes no special provision for transfers not resulting in an economic benefit to the transferor. *Cf. Commissioner v. Asphalt Products Co.*, 482 U.S. 117, 120–21 * * * (1987) (per curiam) (courts must give effect to the plain language of the internal revenue code); *Commissioner v. Tufts*, 461 U.S. 300, 307 * * * (1983) (taxpayer may realize a taxable gain under I.R.C. § 1001 even without receiving a net economic benefit from the transferee).

Second, the Owens claim that our decision *Jackson v. Commissioner*, 708 F.2d 1402 (9th Cir.1983) (per curiam), supports their assertion that section 357(c) only applies to transactions resulting in a gain cognizable under I.R.C. § 1001. *Jackson* offers no support for this argument. Indeed, in *Jackson*, we assumed that sections 351 and 357(c) were applicable despite our holding that section 1001's requirements for "a taxable transfer were not met." *Jackson*, 708 F.2d at 1404–05.

Third, the Owens assert that *Jackson* held that section 357(c)'s provisions do not apply to liabilities which are guaranteed by the transferor. We disagree. *Jackson* held that a partner did not have a section 357(c) gain when he transferred his partnership interest to his wholly owned corporation even though his share of the joint venture's liabilities exceeded his adjusted basis in the partnership interest. *Id.* at 1404–05; *id.* at 1406 (Duniway, J., concurring and dissenting). In *Jackson*, the taxpayer remained liable on the partnership loans after the transfer of the partnership interest. The Owens claim that *Jackson* stands for the proposition that a taxpayer's continued liability for loans secured by the transferred property prevents the Commissioner from treating the loans as section 357(c) liabilities. The Owens suggest that *Jackson* rejected, *sub silentio*, the holdings of *Rosen* and *Beaver*. We conclude that *Jackson* is distinguishable.

Jackson involved the transfer of an interest in an ongoing partnership, and the interest was not encumbered by any liabilities. Thus, the property, *i.e.*, the partnership interest, transferred was not "subject to" a liability which could trigger a section 357(c) gain. The case presently before us involves the transfer of equipment which the tax court found to be subject to substantial liabilities in excess of the equipment's adjusted basis. In such a case, section 357(c) applies.[4]

Furthermore, *Jackson* was decided without the benefit of the Supreme Court's opinion in *Commissioner v. Tufts*, 461 U.S. 300, 307 * * * (1983). *Tufts* and *Jackson* were published at approximately the same time. Relying in part on dicta from *Crane v. Commissioner*, 331 U.S. 1 * * * (1947), *Jackson* concluded that section 1001, and the tax system as a whole, require that the transferor receive "economically significant consideration." *Jackson*, 708 F.2d at 1404. *Tufts* clarified the scope of *Crane* and rejected *Crane*'s "limited theory of economic benefit." *Tufts*, 461 U.S. at 307. *Tufts* undercuts the authority supporting the *Jackson* decision.

Fourth, the Owens contend that section 357(c)'s categories of (1) assumed liabilities and (2) liabilities to which the transferred property is subject are mutually exclusive. They assert that the latter category only applies to nonrecourse, unassumable liabilities. We disagree. The tax court decisions in *Smith*, *Rosen* and *Beaver* applied section 357(c) to recourse liabilities secured by the transferred property. *Smith*, 84 T.C. at 909; *Rosen*, 62 T.C. at 19; *Beaver*, 41 T.C.M. (CCH) at 54; *see also* Treas.Reg. § 1.357–2 (1988) (section 357(c) gain will occur "whether or

---

4. In *Jackson*, we did not consider whether any property of the partnership was used to secure the loans. *Cf. Smith*, 84 T.C. at 910 (partnership interests "were in substance" subject to the section 357 (c) liabilities which were secured by the partnership's real property).

not the liability is assumed by the transferee"). We hold that section 357(c) applies to recourse liabilities to which the transferred property is subject even if the transferor remains subject to the liabilities following the transfer.

* * *

AFFIRMED.

[¶ 2235]

Note

As a result of enactment of Section 357(d)(1)(A) in 1999, discussed at ¶ 2175, the transferor of a recourse debt need only have the transferee corporation agree that it will not pay the debt to exclude the debt from the operation of Section 357. Thus, *Owen* might be decided differently under Section 357(d)(1) if the facts established that the corporation had not agreed to and was not expected to satisfy the transferred liability.

[¶ 2240]

PERACCHI v. COMMISSIONER

United States Court of Appeals, Ninth Circuit, 1998.
143 F.3d 487.

KOZINSKI, CIRCUIT JUDGE:

We must unscramble a Rubik's Cube of corporate tax law to determine the basis of a note contributed by a taxpayer to his wholly-owned corporation.

THE TRANSACTION

The taxpayer, Donald Peracchi, needed to contribute additional capital to his closely-held corporation (NAC) to comply with Nevada's minimum premium-to-asset ratio for insurance companies. Peracchi contributed two parcels of real estate. The parcels were encumbered with liabilities which together exceeded Peracchi's total basis in the properties by more than half a million dollars. As we discuss in detail below, under section 357(c), contributing property with liabilities in excess of basis can trigger immediate recognition of gain in the amount of the excess. In an effort to avoid this, Peracchi also executed a promissory note, promising to pay NAC $1,060,000 over a term of ten years at 11% interest. Peracchi maintains that the note has a basis equal to its face amount, thereby making his total basis in the property contributed greater than the total liabilities. If this is so, he will have extracted himself from the quicksand of section 357(c) and owe no immediate tax on the transfer of property to NAC. The IRS, though, maintains that (1) the note is not genuine indebtedness and should be treated as an unenforceable gift; and (2)

¶ 2240

even if the note is genuine, it does not increase Peracchi's basis in the property contributed.

The parties are not splitting hairs: Peracchi claims the basis of the note is $1,060,000, its face value, while the IRS argues that the note has a basis of zero. If Peracchi is right, he pays no immediate tax on the half a million dollars by which the debts on the land he contributed exceed his basis in the land; if the IRS is right, the note becomes irrelevant for tax purposes and Peracchi must recognize an immediate gain on the half million. The fact that the IRS and Peracchi are so far apart suggests they are looking at the transaction through different colored lenses. To figure out whether Peracchi's lens is rose-tinted or clear, it is useful to take a guided tour of sections 351 and 357 and the tax law principles undergirding them.

Into the Lobster Pot: Section 351[2]

The Code tries to make organizing a corporation pain-free from a tax point of view. A capital contribution is, in tax lingo, a "nonrecognition" event: A shareholder can generally contribute capital without recognizing gain on the exchange. It's merely a change in the form of ownership, like moving a billfold from one pocket to another. See I.R.C. § 351. So long as the shareholders contributing the property remain in control of the corporation after the exchange, section 351 applies: It doesn't matter if the capital contribution occurs at the creation of the corporation or if—as here—the company is already up and running. The baseline is that Peracchi may contribute property to NAC without recognizing gain on the exchange.

Gain Deferral: Section 358(a)

Peracchi contributed capital to NAC in the form of real property and a promissory note. Corporations may be funded with any kind of asset, such as equipment, real estate, intellectual property, contracts, leaseholds, securities or letters of credit. The tax consequences can get a little complicated because a shareholder's basis in the property contributed often differs from its fair market value. The general rule is that an asset's basis is equal to its "cost." See I.R.C. § 1012. But when a shareholder like Peracchi contributes property to a corporation in a nonrecognition transaction, a cost basis does not preserve the unrecognized gain. Rather than take a basis equal to the fair market value of the property exchanged, the shareholder must substitute the basis of that property for what would otherwise be the cost basis of the stock. This preserves the gain for recognition at a later day: The gain is built into

---

2. "Decisions to embrace the corporate form of organization should be carefully considered, since a corporation is like a lobster pot: easy to enter, difficult to live in, and painful to get out of." Boris I. Bittker & James S. Eustice, Federal Income Taxation of Corporations and Shareholders ¶ 2.01[3] (6th ed. 1997).

the shareholder's new basis in the stock, and he will recognize income when he disposes of the stock.

The fact that gain is deferred rather than extinguished doesn't diminish the importance of questions relating to basis and the timing of recognition. In tax, as in comedy, timing matters. Most taxpayers would much prefer to pay tax on contributed property years later—when they sell their stock—rather than when they contribute the property. Thus what Peracchi is seeking here is gain deferral: He wants the gain to be recognized only when he disposes of some or all of his stock.

CONTINUITY OF INVESTMENT: BOOT AND SECTION 351(B)

Continuity of investment is the cornerstone of nonrecognition under section 351. Nonrecognition assumes that a capital contribution amounts to nothing more than a nominal change in the form of ownership; in substance the shareholder's investment in the property continues. But a capital contribution can sometimes allow a shareholder to partially terminate his investment in an asset or group of assets. For example, when a shareholder receives cash or other property in addition to stock, receipt of that property reflects a partial termination of investment in the business. The shareholder may invest that money in a wholly unrelated business, or spend it just like any other form of personal income. To the extent a section 351 transaction resembles an ordinary sale, the nonrecognition rationale falls apart.

Thus the central exception to nonrecognition for section 351 transactions comes into play when the taxpayer receives "boot"—money or property other than stock in the corporation—in exchange for the property contributed. See I.R.C. § 351(b). Boot is recognized as taxable income because it represents a partial cashing out. It's as if the taxpayer contributed part of the property to the corporation in exchange for stock, and sold part of the property for cash. Only the part exchanged for stock represents a continuation of investment; the part sold for cash is properly recognized as yielding income, just as if the taxpayer had sold the property to a third party.

Peracchi did not receive boot in return for the property he contributed. But that doesn't end the inquiry: We must consider whether Peracchi has cashed out in some other way which would warrant treating part of the transaction as taxable boot.

ASSUMPTION OF LIABILITIES: SECTION 357(A)

The property Peracchi contributed to NAC was encumbered by liabilities. Contribution of leveraged property makes things trickier from a tax perspective. When a shareholder contributes property encumbered by debt, the corporation usually assumes the debt. And the Code normally treats discharging a liability the same as receiving money: The taxpayer improves his economic position by the same amount either way.

¶ 2240

See I.R.C. § 61(a)(12). NAC's assumption of the liabilities attached to Peracchi's property therefore could theoretically be viewed as the receipt of money, which would be taxable boot. *See United States v. Hendler*, 303 U.S. 564 * * * (1938).

The Code takes a different tack. Requiring shareholders like Peracchi to recognize gain any time a corporation assumes a liability in connection with a capital contribution would greatly diminish the nonrecognition benefit section 351 is meant to confer. Section 357(a) thus takes a lenient view of the assumption of liability: A shareholder engaging in a section 351 transaction does not have to treat the assumption of liability as boot, even if the corporation assumes his obligation to pay. See I.R.C. § 357(a).

This nonrecognition does not mean that the potential gain disappears. Once again, the basis provisions kick in to reflect the transfer of gain from the shareholder to the corporation: The shareholder's substitute basis in the stock received is decreased by the amount of the liability assumed by the corporation. See I.R.C. § 358(d), (a). The adjustment preserves the gain for recognition when the shareholder sells his stock in the company, since his taxable gain will be the difference between the (new lower) basis and the sale price of the stock.

SASQUATCH AND THE NEGATIVE BASIS PROBLEM: SECTION 357(C)

Highly leveraged property presents a peculiar problem in the section 351 context. Suppose a shareholder organizes a corporation and contributes as its only asset a building with a basis of $50, a fair market value of $100, and mortgage debt of $90. Section 351 says that the shareholder does not recognize any gain on the transaction. Under section 358, the shareholder takes a substitute basis of $50 in the stock, then adjusts it downward under section 357 by $90 to reflect the assumption of liability. This leaves him with a basis of minus $40. A negative basis properly preserves the gain built into the property: If the shareholder turns around and sells the stock the next day for $10 (the difference between the fair market value and the debt), he would face $50 in gain, the same amount as if he sold the property without first encasing it in a corporate shell.[8]

But skeptics say that negative basis, like Bigfoot, doesn't exist. Compare *Easson v. Commissioner*, 33 T.C. 963, 970 * * * (1960) (there's no such thing as a negative basis) with Easson v. Commissioner, 294 F.2d 653, 657–58 (9th Cir.1961) (yes, Virginia, there is a negative basis). Basis normally operates as a cost recovery system: Depreciation deductions reduce basis, and when basis hits zero, the property cannot be depreciated farther. At a more basic level, it seems incongruous to

---

8. If the taxpayer sells the property outright, his amount realized includes the full amount of the mortgage debt, see *Crane v. Commissioner*, 331 U.S. 1, 14 * * * (1947), and the result is as follows: Amount realized ($10 cash + $90 debt)—$50 basis = $50 gain.

¶ 2240

attribute a negative value to a figure that normally represents one's investment in an asset. Some commentators nevertheless argue that when basis operates merely to measure potential gain (as it does here), allowing negative basis may be perfectly appropriate and consistent with the tax policy underlying nonrecognition transactions. * * * Whatever the merits of this debate, it seems that section 357(c) was enacted to eliminate the possibility of negative basis. * * *

Section 357(c) prevents negative basis by forcing a shareholder to recognize gain to the extent liabilities exceed basis. Thus, if a shareholder contributes a building with a basis of $50 and liabilities of $90, he does not receive stock with a basis of minus $40. Instead, he takes a basis of zero and must recognize a $40 gain.

Peracchi sought to contribute two parcels of real property to NAC in a section 351 transaction. Standing alone the contribution would have run afoul of section 357(c): The property he wanted to contribute had liabilities in excess of basis, and Peracchi would have had to recognize gain to the extent of the excess, or $566,807:[10]

	Liabilities	*Basis*
Property #1	1,386,655	349,774
Property #2	161,558	631,632
	1,548,213	981,406
Liabilities	1,548,213	
Basis	981,406	
Excess (357(c))		566,807

THE GRIFT: BOOSTING BASIS WITH A PROMISSORY NOTE

Peracchi tried to dig himself out of this tax hole by contributing a personal note with a face amount of $1,060,000 along with the real property. Peracchi maintains that the note has a basis in his hands equal to its face value. If he's right, we must add the basis of the note to the basis of the real property. Taken together, the aggregate basis in the property contributed would exceed the aggregate liabilities:

	Liabilities	*Basis*
Property #1	1,386,655	349,774
Property #2	161,558	631,632
Note	0	1,060,000
	1,548,213	2,041,406

Under Peracchi's theory, then, the aggregate liabilities no longer exceed the aggregate basis, and section 357(c) no longer triggers any

---

10. Peracchi remained personally liable on the debts encumbering the property transferred to NAC. NAC took the property subject to the debts, however, which is enough to trigger gain under the plain language of section 357(c). See *Owen v. Commissioner*, 881 F.2d 832, 835–36 (9th Cir. 1989).

¶ 2240

gain. The government argues, however, that the note has a zero basis. If so, the note would not affect the tax consequences of the transaction, and Peracchi's $566,807 in gain would be taxable immediately.

ARE PROMISES TRULY FREE?

Which brings us (phew!) to the issue before us: Does Peracchi's note have a basis in Peracchi's hands for purposes of section 357(c)?[12] The language of the Code gives us little to work with. The logical place to start is with the definition of basis. Section 1012 provides that "[t]he basis of property shall be the cost of such property. . . . " But "cost" is nowhere defined. What does it cost Peracchi to write the note and contribute it to his corporation? The IRS argues tersely that the "tax-payers in the instant case incurred no cost in issuing their own note to NAC, so their basis in the note was zero." * * * *See Alderman v. Commissioner*, 55 T.C. 662, 665 (1971); Rev. Rul. 68–629, 1968–2 C.B. 154, 155.[13] Building on this premise, the IRS makes Peracchi out to be a grifter: He holds an unenforceable promise to pay himself money, since the corporation will not collect on it unless he says so.

It's true that all Peracchi did was make out a promise to pay on a piece of paper, mark it in the corporate minutes and enter it on the corporate books. It is also true that nothing will cause the corporation to enforce the note against Peracchi so long as Peracchi remains in control. But the IRS ignores the possibility that NAC may go bankrupt, an event that would suddenly make the note highly significant. Peracchi and NAC are separated by the corporate form, and this gossamer curtain makes a difference in the shell game of C Corp organization and reorganization. Contributing the note puts a million dollar nut within the corporate shell, exposing Peracchi to the cruel nutcracker of corporate creditors in the event NAC goes bankrupt. And it does so to the tune of $1,060,000, the full face amount of the note. Without the note, no matter how deeply the corporation went into debt, creditors could not reach Peracchi's personal assets. With the note on the books, however, creditors can

---

12. Peracchi owned all the voting stock of NAC both before and after the exchange, so the control requirement of section 351 is satisfied. Peracchi received no boot (such as cash or securities) which would qualify as "money or other property" and trigger recognition under 351(b) alone. Peracchi did not receive any stock in return for the property contributed, so it could be argued that the exchange was not "solely in exchange for stock" as required by section 351. Courts have consistently recognized, however, that issuing stock in this situation would be a meaningless gesture: Because Peracchi is the sole shareholder of NAC, issuing additional stock would not affect his economic position relative to other shareholders. *See, e.g., Jackson v. Commissioner*, 708 F.2d 1402, 1405 (9th Cir.1983).

13. We would face a different case had the Treasury promulgated a regulation interpreting section 357(c). A revenue ruling is entitled to some deference as the stated litigating position of the agency which enforces the tax code, but not nearly as much as a regulation. Ruling 68–629 offers no rationale, let alone a reasonable one, for its holding that it costs a taxpayer nothing to write a promissory note, and thus deserves little weight.

¶ 2240

reach into Peracchi's pocket by enforcing the note as an unliquidated asset of the corporation.

The key to solving this puzzle, then, is to ask whether bankruptcy is significant enough a contingency to confer substantial economic effect on this transaction. If the risk of bankruptcy is important enough to be recognized, Peracchi should get basis in the note: He will have increased his exposure to the risks of the business—and thus his economic investment in NAC—by $1,060,000. If bankruptcy is so remote that there is no realistic possibility it will ever occur, we can ignore the potential economic effect of the note as speculative and treat it as merely an unenforceable promise to contribute capital in the future.

When the question is posed this way, the answer is clear. Peracchi's obligation on the note was not conditioned on NAC's remaining solvent. It represents a new and substantial increase in Peracchi's investment in the corporation.[14] The Code seems to recognize that economic exposure of the shareholder is the ultimate measuring rod of a shareholder's investment. Cf. I.R.C. § 465 (at-risk rules for partnership investments). Peracchi therefore is entitled to a step-up in basis to the extent he will be subjected to economic loss if the underlying investment turns unprofitable. Cf. *HGA Cinema Trust v. Commissioner*, 950 F.2d 1357, 1363 (7th Cir.1991) (examining effect of bankruptcy to determine whether long-term note contributed by partner could be included in basis). See also Treas. Reg. § 1.704–1(b)(2)(ii)(c)(1) (recognizing economic effect of promissory note contributed by partner for purposes of partner's obligation to restore deficit capital account).

The economics of the transaction also support Peracchi's view of the matter. The transaction here does not differ substantively from others that would certainly give Peracchi a boost in basis. For example, Peracchi could have borrowed $1 million from a bank and contributed the cash to NAC along with the properties. Because cash has a basis equal to face value, Peracchi would not have faced any section 357(c) gain. NAC could then have purchased the note from the bank for $1 million which, assuming the bank's original assessment of Peracchi's creditworthiness was accurate, would be the fair market value of the note. In the end the corporation would hold a million dollar note from Peracchi—just like it does now—and Peracchi would face no section 357(c) gain.[15] The only

14. We confine our holding to a case such as this where the note is contributed to an operating business which is subject to a non-trivial risk of bankruptcy or receivership. NAC is not, for example, a shell corporation or a passive investment company; Peracchi got into this mess in the first place because NAC was in financial trouble and needed more assets to meet Nevada's minimum premium-to-asset ratio for insurance companies.

15. In a similar vein, Peracchi could have first swapped promissory notes with a third party. Assuming the bona fides of each note, Peracchi would take a cost basis in the third party note equal to the face value of the note he gave up. Peracchi could then contribute the third party note to NAC, and (thanks to the added basis) avoid any section 357(c) gain. NAC could then close the circle by giving the third party note back to the third party in exchange for

¶ 2240

economic difference between the transaction just described and the transaction Peracchi actually engaged in is the additional costs that would accompany getting a loan from the bank. Peracchi incurs a "cost" of $1 million when he promises to pay the note to the bank; the cost is not diminished here by the fact that the transferor controls the initial transferee. The experts seem to agree: "Section 357(c) can be avoided by a transfer of enough cash to eliminate any excess of liabilities over basis; and since a note given by a solvent obligor in purchasing property is routinely treated as the equivalent of cash in determining the basis of the property, it seems reasonable to give it the same treatment in determining the basis of the property transferred in a § 351 exchange." Bittker & Eustice ¶ 3.06[4][b].

We are aware of the mischief that can result when taxpayers are permitted to calculate basis in excess of their true economic investment. See *Commissioner v. Tufts*, 461 U.S. 300 * * * (1983). For two reasons, however, we do not believe our holding will have such pernicious effects. First, and most significantly, by increasing the taxpayer's personal exposure, the contribution of a valid, unconditional promissory note has substantial economic effects which reflect his true economic investment in the enterprise. The main problem with attributing basis to nonrecourse debt financing is that the tax benefits enjoyed as a result of increased basis do not reflect the true economic risk. Here Peracchi will have to pay the full amount of the note with after-tax dollars if NAC's economic situation heads south. Second, the tax treatment of nonrecourse debt primarily creates problems in the partnership context, where the entity's loss deductions (resulting from depreciation based on basis inflated above and beyond the taxpayer's true economic investment) can be passed through to the taxpayer. It is the pass-through of losses that makes artificial increases in equity interests of particular concern. See, e.g., *Levy v. Commissioner*, 732 F.2d 1435, 1437 (9th Cir.1984). We don't have to tread quite so lightly in the C Corp context, since a C Corp doesn't funnel losses to the shareholder.[16]

Peracchi's note, leaving Peracchi and NAC in exactly the same position they occupy now.

The IRS might attack these maneuvers as step transactions, but that would beg the question: Does the contribution of a shareholder's note to his wholly-owned corporation have any real economic effect, or is it just so much window dressing? If the debt has real economic effect, it shouldn't matter how the shareholder structures the transaction.

The only substantive difference between the avoidance techniques just discussed— swapping notes or borrowing from a third

party—and the case here is the valuation role implicitly performed by the third party. A bank would not give Peracchi the face value of the note unless his credit warranted it, while we have no assurance that NAC wouldn't do so. We readily acknowledge that our assumptions fall apart if the shareholder isn't creditworthy. Here, the government has stipulated that Peracchi's net worth far exceeds the value of the note, so creditworthiness is not at issue. But we limit our holding to cases where the note is in fact worth approximately its face value.

16. Our holding therefore does not extend to the partnership or S Corp context.

We find further support for Peracchi's view by looking at the alternative: What would happen if the note had a zero basis? The IRS points out that the basis of the note in the hands of the corporation is the same as it was in the hands of the taxpayer. Accordingly, if the note has a zero basis for Peracchi, so too for NAC. *See* I.R.C. § 362(a).[17] But what happens if NAC—perhaps facing the threat of an involuntary petition for bankruptcy—turns around and sells Peracchi's note to a third party for its fair market value? According to the IRS's theory, NAC would take a carryover basis of zero in the note and would have to recognize $1,060,000 in phantom gain on the subsequent exchange, even though the note did not appreciate in value one bit. That can't be the right result.

Accordingly, we hold that Peracchi has a basis of $1,060,000 in the note he wrote to NAC. The aggregate basis exceeds the liabilities of the properties transferred to NAC under section 351, and Peracchi need not recognize any section 357(c) gain.

Genuine Indebtedness or Sham?

The Tax Court never reached the issue of Peracchi's basis in the note. Instead, it ruled for the Commissioner on the ground that the note is not genuine indebtedness. The court emphasized two facts which it believed supported the view that the note is a sham: (1) NAC's decision whether to collect on the note is wholly controlled by Peracchi and (2) Peracchi missed the first two years of payments, yet NAC did not accelerate the debt. These facts certainly do suggest that Peracchi paid imperfect attention to his obligations under the note, as frequently happens when debtor and creditor are under common control. But we believe the proper way to approach the genuine indebtedness question is to look at the face of the note and consider whether Peracchi's legal obligation is illusory. And it is not. First, the note's bona fides are adequate: The IRS has stipulated that Peracchi is creditworthy and likely to have the funds to pay the note; the note bears a market rate of interest commensurate with his creditworthiness; the note has a fixed term. Second, the IRS does not argue that the value of the note is

---

17. But see *Lessinger v. Commissioner*, 872 F.2d 519 (2d Cir.1989). In *Lessinger*, the Second Circuit analyzed a similar transaction. It agreed with the IRS's (faulty) premise that the note had a zero basis in the taxpayer's hands. But then, brushing aside the language of section 362(a), the court concluded that the note had a basis in the *corporation's* hands equal to its face value. The court held that this was enough to dispel any section 357(c) gain to the taxpayer, proving that two wrongs sometimes do add up to a right.

We agree with the IRS that *Lessinger's* approach is untenable. Section 357(c) con-

templates measuring basis of the property contributed in the hands of the taxpayer, not the corporation. Section 357 appears in the midst of the Code sections dealing with the effect of capital contributions on the shareholder; sections 361 et seq., on the other hand, deal with the effect on a corporation, and section 362 defines the basis of property contributed in the hands of the corporation. Because we hold that the note has a face value basis to the shareholder for purposes of section 357(c), however, we reach the same result as *Lessinger*.

¶ 2240

anything other than its face value; nothing in the record suggests NAC couldn't borrow against the note to raise cash. Lastly, the note is fully transferable and enforceable by third parties, such as hostile creditors. On the basis of these facts we hold that the note is an ordinary, negotiable, recourse obligation which must be treated as genuine debt for tax purposes. * * *

The IRS argues that the note is nevertheless a sham because it was executed simply to avoid tax. Tax avoidance is a valid concern in this context; section 357(a) does provide the opportunity for a bailout transaction of sorts. For example, a taxpayer with an unencumbered building he wants to sell could take out a nonrecourse mortgage, pocket the proceeds, and contribute the property to a newly organized corporation. Although the gain would be preserved for later recognition, the taxpayer would have partially cashed out his economic investment in the property: By taking out a nonrecourse mortgage, the economic risk of loss would be transferred to the lender. Section 357(b) addresses this sort of bailout by requiring the recognition of gain if the transaction lacks a business purpose.

Peracchi's capital contribution is not a bailout. Peracchi contributed the buildings to NAC because the company needed additional capital, and the contribution of the note was part of that transaction. The IRS, in fact, stipulated that the contribution had a business purpose. Bailout potential exists regardless of whether the taxpayer contributes a note along with the property; section 357(b), not 357(c), is the sword the Service must use to attack bailout transactions.

Is the Note a Gift?

The IRS also offers a more refined version of the sham transaction argument: The note was really a gift to NAC because Peracchi did not receive any consideration from the exchange. The IRS admits that the tax deferral resulting from avoiding section 357(c) gain is a benefit to Peracchi. It argues, nonetheless, that this is not enough to make the bargain enforceable because it works no detriment to NAC. This argument would classify all contributions of capital as gifts. A corporation never gives up anything explicitly when it accepts a capital contribution. Instead, the corporation implicitly promises to put the money to good use, and its directors and officers undertake the fiduciary duty to generate the highest possible return on the investment. The contribution of the note was no more a gift than the contribution of $1 million in cash to the corporation would have been; it does not reflect the "detached and disinterested generosity" which characterizes a gift for purposes of federal income taxation. *See Commissioner v. Duberstein*, 363 U.S. 278, 285 * * * (1960).

The Aftermath

We take a final look at the result to make sure we have not placed our stamp of approval on some sort of exotic tax shelter. We hold that

¶ 2240

Peracchi is entitled to a step up in basis for the face value of the note, just as if he contributed cash to the corporation. See I.R.C. § 358. If Peracchi does in fact keep his promise and pay off the note with after tax dollars, the tax result is perfectly appropriate: NAC receives cash, and the increase in basis Peracchi took for the original contribution is justified. Peracchi has less potential gain, but he paid for it in real dollars.

But what if, as the IRS fears, NAC never does enforce the note? If NAC goes bankrupt, the note will be an asset of the estate enforceable for the benefit of creditors, and Peracchi will eventually be forced to pay in after tax dollars. Peracchi will undoubtedly have worked the deferral mechanism of section 351 to his advantage, but this is not inappropriate where the taxpayer is on the hook in both form and substance for enough cash to offset the excess of liabilities over basis. By increasing his personal exposure to the creditors of NAC, Peracchi has increased his economic investment in the corporation, and a corresponding increase in basis is wholly justified.[20]

CONCLUSION

We hold that Peracchi has a basis of $1,060,000 in the note, its face value. As such, the aggregate liabilities of the property contributed to NAC do not exceed its basis, and Peracchi does not recognize any section 357(c) gain. The decision of the Tax Court is REVERSED. The case is remanded for entry of judgment in favor of Peracchi.

FERNANDEZ, CIRCUIT JUDGE, DISSENTING:

Is there something that a taxpayer, who has borrowed hundreds of thousands of dollars more than his basis in his property, can do to avoid taxation when he transfers the property? Yes, says Peracchi, because by using a very clever argument he can avoid the strictures of * * * § 357(c). He need only make a promise to pay by giving a "good," though unsecured, promissory note to his corporation when he transfers the property to it. That is true even though the property remains subject to the encumbrances. How can that be? Well, by preparing a promissory note the taxpayer simply creates basis without cost to himself. But see * * * § 1012; Rev. Rul. 68–629, 1968–2 C.B. 154; *Alderman v. Commissioner*, 55 T.C. 662, 665 (1971). Thus he can extract a large part of the value of the property, pocket the funds, use them, divest himself of the property, and pay the tax another day, if ever at all.

---

20. What happens if NAC does not go bankrupt, but merely writes off the note instead? Peracchi would then face discharge of indebtedness income to the tune of $1,060,000. This would put Peracchi in a worse position than when he started, since discharge of indebtedness is normally treated as ordinary income. Peracchi, having increased his basis in the stock of the corporation by $1,060,000 would receive a capital loss (or less capital gain) to that extent. But the shift in character of the income will normally work to the disadvantage of a taxpayer in Peracchi's situation.

But as with all magical solutions, the taxpayer must know the proper incantations and make the correct movements. He cannot just transfer the property to the corporation and promise, or be obligated, to pay off the encumbrances. That would not change the fact that the property was still subject to those encumbrances. According to Peracchi, the thaumaturgy that will save him from taxes proceeds in two simple steps. He must first prepare a ritualistic writing—an unsecured promissory note in an amount equal to or more than the excess of the encumbrances over the basis. He must then give that writing to his corporation. That is all.[1] But is not that just a "promise to pay," which "does not represent the paying out or reduction of assets?" *Don E. Williams Co. v. Commissioner*, 429 U.S. 569, 583 * * * (1977). Never mind, he says. He has nonetheless increased the total basis of the property transferred and avoided the tax. I understand the temptation to embrace that argument, but I see no real support for it in the law.

Peracchi says a lot about economic realities. I see nothing real about that maneuver. I see, rather, a bit of sortilege that would have made Merlin envious. The taxpayer has created something—basis—out of nothing.

Thus, I respectfully dissent.

[¶ 2245]

Notes

1. Both *Owen* and *Peracchi* illustrate a trap for the unwary: the risk that incorporation of an insolvent business will trigger recognition of gain. In both cases, the IRS asserted an income tax deficiency against the transferor even though that transferor suffered an economic loss with respect to the properties transferred to the corporation. Can finding taxable income in such circumstances be justified on policy grounds?

2. Section 1012 provides, in a relevant part, that "the basis of property shall be the cost of such property," and in Rev. Rul. 68–629, 1968–2C.B. 154, the IRS ruled that gain is recognized under Section 357(c) when the transferor issues and transfers to the corporation a promissory note for the excess of liabilities over the adjusted basis of assets of a sole proprietorship transferred to a corporation. Because, in the view of the IRS, the transferor does not incur any cost in issuing the promissory note, the transferor has a basis in the note of zero under Section 1012. Is the Ninth Circuit's rejection of this analysis persuasive? Can the result in *Peracchi* be squared with the Ninth Circuit's earlier decision in *Owen*? Is it solely the risk of the transferee's bankruptcy that confers a face value basis on the note? If so, how great must that risk be?

---

1. What is even better, he need not even make payments on the note until after the IRS catches up with him. I, by the way, am dubious about the proposition that the Tax Court clearly erred when it held that the note was not even a genuine indebtedness.

[¶ 2250]

Problem

Lulu (L), a sole proprietor, was engaged in a wholesale distribution business. Her business had regularly reported its income on the accrual method. As a result, accounts receivable and accounts payable (owed to suppliers and others who provided supplies or services to the business) were already reflected in taxable income.

On January 1, she transferred this business, including uncollected receivables and unpaid liabilities, to her wholly owned corporation in exchange for all the stock of the corporation. The balance sheet of the corporation immediately after the transfer was as follows:

L Corporation

Assets	Basis	Per Books	Liabilities	Per Books
Cash...............	$ 5,000	$ 5,000	Accounts payable ...	$ 30,000
Accounts receivable	80,000	80,000	Bank loans	90,000
Equipment	15,000	15,000		
			Capital stock	(20,000)
	$100,000	$100,000		$100,000

    a. To what extent would Section 357(c) require L to recognize gain upon the incorporation?

    b. What if the accounts payable represented expenses that, because contested, could be deducted only when paid? Recall § 357(c)(3)(A).

    c. Would your answer to Problem a. change if, alternatively, L issued her promissory note to L Corporation in the amount of $20,000?

    d. Would your answer to Problem a. change if Lulu agreed to remain personally liable for the debts transferred to L Corporation?

[¶ 2255]

G. TAX PROBLEMS UPON INCORPORATION OF AN EXISTING BUSINESS

A number of tax issues arise upon the incorporation of an existing proprietorship or partnership, particularly one that has been reporting income on the cash method. Several of these were discussed above. One involves the excess of liabilities of a cash method taxpayer in the form of accounts payable over bases of assets, including accounts receivable, the subject of Section 357(c)(3). A second is the possible nondeductibility of business expenses incurred (but unpaid) by a cash method taxpayer, and later paid by the transferee corporation—a payor that could not claim the items as its own business expenses. A third is the conflict between nonrecognition treatment under Section 351(a) and the recognition of income dictated by other principles such as the assignment of income doctrine and the tax benefit rule. The following materials further explore these issues.

1. ASSIGNMENT OF INCOME DOCTRINE

[¶ 2260]

HEMPT BROS., INC. v. UNITED STATES

United States Court of Appeals, Third Circuit, 1974.
490 F.2d 1172.

[A cash method partnership engaged in the business of quarrying and selling stone, sand, gravel, ready-mix concrete, and related products transferred its assets to a newly organized corporation in a Section 351 transaction. Among the assets transferred were accounts receivable in excess of $662,820. In a subsequent audit of the corporate operations, the IRS concluded that the business should be placed upon an accrual basis, and issued a notice of deficiency accordingly. The taxpayer corporation paid the amounts noticed, then filed claims for refund, and brought suit claiming as one of its major propositions that it did not have taxable income upon the collection of the transferred accounts receivable.]

ALDISERT, CIRCUIT JUDGE:

In this appeal by a corporate taxpayer from a grant of summary judgment in favor of the government in a claim for refund, we are called upon to decide the proper treatment of accounts receivable * * * transferred from a cash basis partnership to a corporation organized to continue the business under * * * § 351(a). * * *

* * *

I.

Taxpayer argues here, as it did in the district court, that because the term "property" as used in Section 351 does not embrace accounts receivable, the Commissioner lacked statutory authority to apply principles associated with Section 351. The district court properly rejected the legal interpretation urged by the taxpayer.

* * *

The taxpayer * * * makes a strenuous argument that "[t]he government is seeking to tax the wrong person." It contends that the assignment of income doctrine as developed by the Supreme Court applies to a Section 351 transfer of accounts receivable so that the transferor, not the transferee-corporation, bears the corresponding tax liability. It argues that the assignment of income doctrine dictates that where the right to receive income is transferred to another person in a transaction not giving rise to tax at the time of transfer, the transferor is taxed on the income when it is collected by the transferee; that the only requirement for its application is a transfer of a right to receive ordinary income; and that since the transferred accounts receivable are a present right to future income, the sole requirement for the application of the doctrine is squarely met. In essence, this is a contention that the nonrecognition provision of Section 351 is in conflict with the assignment of income doctrine and that Section 351 should be subordinated thereto. Taxpayer relies on the seminal case of Lucas v. Earl, 281 U.S. 111 * * * (1930), and its progeny for support of its proposition that the application of the doctrine is mandated whenever one transfers a right to receive ordinary income.

On its part, the government concedes that a taxpayer may sell for value a claim to income otherwise his own and he will be taxable upon the proceeds of the sale. Such was the case in Commissioner v. P. G. Lake, Inc., 356 U.S. 260 * * * (1958), in which the taxpayer-corporation assigned its oil payment right to its president in consideration for his cancellation of a $600,000 loan. Viewing the oil payment right as a right to receive future income, the Court applied the reasoning of the assignment of income doctrine, normally applicable to a gratuitous assignment, and held that the consideration received by the taxpayer-corporation was taxable as ordinary income since it essentially was a substitute for that which would otherwise be received at a future time as ordinary income.

Turning to the facts of this case, we note that here there was the transfer of accounts receivable from the partnership to the corporation pursuant to Section 351. We view these accounts receivable as a present right to receive future income. In consideration of the transfer of this right, the members of the partnership received stock—a valid consideration. The consideration, therefore, was essentially a substitute for that which would otherwise be received at a future time as ordinary income to the cash basis partnership. Consequently, the holding in *Lake* would normally apply, and income would ordinarily be realized, and thereby taxable, by the cash basis partnership-transferor at the time of receipt of the stock.

But the terms and purpose of Section 351 have to be reckoned with. By its explicit terms Section 351 expresses the Congressional intent that transfers of property for stock or securities will not result in recognition. It therefore becomes apparent that this case vividly illustrates how Section 351 sometimes comes into conflict with another provision of the Internal Revenue Code or a judicial doctrine, and requires a determination of which of two conflicting doctrines will control.

As we must, when we try to reconcile conflicting doctrines in the revenue law, we endeavor to ascertain a controlling Congressional man-

¶ **2260**

date. Section 351 has been described as a deliberate attempt by Congress to facilitate the incorporation of ongoing businesses and to eliminate any technical constructions which are economically unsound.[7]

Appellant-taxpayer seems to recognize this and argues that application of the Lake rationale when accounts receivable are transferred would not create any undue hardship to an incorporating taxpayer. "All a taxpayer [transferor] need do is withhold the earned income items and collect them, transferring the net proceeds to the Corporation. Indeed . . . the transferor should retain both accounts receivable and accounts payable to avoid income recognition at the time of transfer and to have sufficient funds with which to pay accounts payable. Where the taxpayer [transferor] is on the cash method of accounting [as here], the deduction of the accounts payable would be applied against the income generated by the accounts receivable." (Appellant's Brief at 32.)

While we cannot fault the general principle "that income be taxed to him who earns it," to adopt taxpayer's argument would be to hamper the incorporation of ongoing businesses; additionally it would impose technical constructions which are economically and practically unsound. None of the cases cited by taxpayer, including *Lake* itself, persuades us otherwise. In *Lake* the Court was required to decide whether the proceeds from the assignment of the oil payment right were taxable as ordinary income or as long term capital gains. Observing that the provision for long term capital gains treatment "has always been narrowly construed so as to protect the revenue against artful devices," 356 U.S. at 265, * * * the Court predicated its holding upon an emphatic distinction between a conversion of a capital investment—"income-producing property"—and an assignment of income *per se*. "The substance of what was assigned was the right to receive future income. The substance of what was received was the present value of income which the recipient would otherwise obtain in the future." *Ibid.*, at 266 * * *. A Section 351 issue was not presented in *Lake*. Therefore the case does not control in weighing the conflict between the general rule of assign-

---

7. "One of the purposes of this section [Section 202(c)(3) of the Revenue Act of 1921] was to permit changes in form [of business] involving no change in substance to be made without undue restriction from the tax laws." Note, Section 351 of the Internal Revenue Code and "Mid–Stream" Incorporations, 38 U.Cin.L.Rev. 96 (1969). *See*, S.Rep.No.275, 67th Cong., 1st Sess. 11 (1921). This intention is also reflected in the report of the House of Representatives accompanying § 351 of the Internal Revenue Code of 1954. H.R.Rep.No.1337, 83rd Cong., 2d Sess. 34 (1954).

The House Ways and Means Committee recommended that nonrecognition treatment be granted for incorporation, reorganization and certain other types of exchanges to "permit business to go forward with the readjustments required by existing conditions" and to prevent "taxpayers from taking colorable losses in wash sales and other fictitious exchanges." *See* H.R.Rep. 350, 67th Cong., 1st Sess. 10 (1921). The Senate Finance Committee added that such treatment would eliminate "many technical constructions which are economically unsound." See S.Rep.275, 67th Cong., 1st Sess. 12 (1921). * * *

ment of income and the Congressional purpose of nonrecognition upon the incorporation of an ongoing business.

We are persuaded that, on balance, the teachings of *Lake* must give way in this case to the broad Congressional interest in facilitating the incorporation of ongoing businesses. As desirable as it is to afford symmetry in revenue law, we do not intend to promulgate a hard and fast rule. We believe that the problems posed by the clash of conflicting internal revenue doctrines are more properly determined by the circumstances of each case. Here we are influenced by the fact that the subject of the assignment was accounts receivable for partnership's goods and services sold in the regular course of business, that the change of business form from partnership to corporation had a basic business purpose and was not designed for the purpose of deliberate tax avoidance, and by the conviction that the totality of circumstances here presented fit the mold of the Congressional intent to give nonrecognition to a transfer of a total business from a non-corporate to a corporate form.

But this too must be said. Even though Section 351(a) immunizes the transferor from immediate tax consequences, Section 358 retains for the transferors a potential income tax liability to be realized and recognized upon a subsequent sale or exchange of the stock certificates received. As to the transferee-corporation, the tax basis of the receivables will be governed by Section 362.

* * *

[¶ 2265]

Notes

1. The problem presented in *Hempt Bros.* is particularly acute in the incorporation of a seasonal business, such as farming, in which income is reported on the cash method. In such a case, there is a potential for distortion of income if the business is incorporated midstream after substantial expenses have been incurred and prior to the realization of income from the annual crop. See, e.g, Rooney v. United States, 305 F.2d 681 (9th Cir.1962), discussed in Rev. Rul. 80–198, at ¶ 2270.

2. Is the *Hempt Bros.* court's flexible, facts and circumstances approach sound (i.e., in applying the assignment of income doctrine, or not, to override nonrecognition under Section 351 depending upon ad hoc determinations of whether the facts at issue fit within the congressional intent underlying Section 351)? Under what circumstances would the assignment of income doctrine trump the nonrecognition rules of Section 351?

¶ 2265

2. CLEAR REFLECTION OF INCOME AND TAX BENEFIT RULES

[¶ 2270]

REVENUE RULING 80-198

1980-2 C.B. 113.

ISSUE

Under the circumstances described below, do the nonrecognition of gain or loss provisions of section 351 * * * apply to a transfer of the operating assets of an ongoing sole proprietorship (including unrealized accounts receivable) to a corporation in exchange solely for the common stock of a corporation and the assumption by the corporation of the proprietorship liabilities?

FACTS

Individual *A* conducted a medical practice as a sole proprietorship, the income of which was reported on the cash receipts and disbursements method of accounting. *A* transferred to a newly organized corporation all of the operating assets of the sole proprietorship in exchange for all of the stock of the corporation, plus the assumption by the corporation of all of the liabilities of the sole proprietorship. The purpose of the incorporation was to provide a form of business organization that would be more conducive to the planned expansion of the medical services to be made available by the business enterprise.

The assets transferred were tangible assets having a fair market value of $40,000 and an adjusted basis of $30,000 and unrealized trade accounts receivable having a face amount of $20,000 and an adjusted basis of zero. The liabilities assumed by the corporation consisted of trade accounts payable in the face amount of $10,000. The liabilities assumed by the corporation also included a mortgage liability, related to the tangible property transferred, of $10,000. *A* had neither accumulated the accounts receivable nor prepaid any of the liabilities of the sole proprietorship in a manner inconsistent with normal business practices in anticipation of the incorporation. If *A* had paid the trade accounts payable liabilities, the amounts paid would have been deductible by *A* as ordinary and necessary business expenses under section 162 * * *. The new corporation continued to utilize the cash receipts and disbursements method of accounting.

LAW AND ANALYSIS

The applicable section of the Code is section 351(a) * * *.

* * *

¶ 2270

The facts of the instant case are similar to those in *Hempt Bros.* [at ¶ 2260] in that there was a valid business purpose for the transfer of the accounts receivable along with all of the assets and liabilities of *A*'s proprietorship to a corporate transferee that would continue the business of the transferor. Further, *A* had neither accumulated the accounts receivable nor prepaid any of the account payable liabilities of the sole proprietorship in anticipation of the incorporation, which is an indication that, under the facts and circumstances of the case, the transaction was not designed for tax avoidance.

Holding

The transfer by *A* of the operating assets of the sole proprietorship (including unrealized accounts receivable) to the corporation in exchange solely for the common stock of the corporation and the assumption by the corporation of the proprietorship liabilities (including accounts payable) is an exchange within the meaning of section 351(a) * * *. Therefore, no gain or loss is recognized to *A* with respect to the property transferred, including the accounts receivable. For transfers occurring on or after November 6, 1978 (the effective date of the Revenue Act of 1978 * * * with respect to sections 357(c)(3) and 358(d)(2) * * *) the assumption of the trade accounts payable that would give rise to a deduction if *A* had paid them is not, pursuant to section 357(c)(3), considered as an assumption of a liability for purposes of sections 357(c)(1) and 358(d). * * * The corporation, under the cash receipts and disbursements method of accounting, will report in its income the account receivables as collected, and will be allowed deductions under section 162 for the payments it makes to satisfy the assumed trade accounts payable when such payments are made.

A's basis in the stock received in the exchange of property for stock under section 358(a)(1) * * * is $20,000 which is calculated by decreasing *A*'s $30,000 basis in the assets transferred by the $10,000 mortgage liability under sections 358(a)(1)(A)(ii) and 358(d)(1). No adjustment to such basis is made under section 358(a)(1)(A)(ii) because of the assumption by the corporation of the $10,000 in accounts payable inasmuch as the general rule of section 358(d)(1), which requires the basis in the stock received to be decreased by the liabilities assumed, does not apply by reason of section 358(d)(2), which provides that section 358(d)(1) does not apply to the amount of any liabilities defined in section 357(c)(3) such as accounts payable that would have been deductible by *A* as ordinary and necessary business expenses under section 162 in the taxable year paid if *A* had paid these liabilities prior to the exchange. * * *

Limitations

Section 351 * * * does not apply to a transfer of accounts receivable which constitute an assignment of an income right in a case such as

¶ 2270

Brown v. Commissioner, 40 B.T.A. 565 (1939), *aff'd* 115 F.2d 337 (2d Cir.1940). In *Brown*, an attorney transferred to a corporation, in which he was the sole owner, a one-half interest in a claim for legal services performed by the attorney and his law partner. In exchange, the attorney received additional stock of the corporation. The claim represented the corporation's only asset. Subsequent to the receipt by the corporation of the proceeds of the claim, the attorney gave all of the stock of the corporation to his wife. The United States Court of Appeals for the Second Circuit found that the transfer of the claim for the fee to the corporation had no purpose other than to avoid taxes and held that in such a case the intervention of the corporation would not prevent the attorney from being liable for the tax on the income which resulted from services under the assignment of income rule of *Lucas v. Earl*, 281 U.S. 111 (1930). Accordingly, in a case of a transfer to a controlled corporation of an account receivable in respect of services rendered where there is a tax avoidance purpose for the transaction (which might be evidenced by the corporation not conducting an ongoing business), the Internal Revenue Service will continue to apply assignment of income principles and require that the transferor of such a receivable include it in income when received by the transferee corporation.

Likewise, it may be appropriate in certain situations to allocate income, deductions, credits, or allowances to the transferor or transferee under Section 482 * * * when the timing of the incorporation improperly separates income from related expenses. See *Rooney v. United States*, 305 F.2d 681 (9th Cir.1962), where a farming operation was incorporated in a transaction described in section 351(a) after the expenses of the crop had been incurred but before the crop had been sold and income realized. The transferor's tax return contained all of the expenses but none of the farming income to which the expenses related. The United States Court of Appeals for the Ninth Circuit held that the expenses could be allocated under Section 482 to the corporation, to be matched with the income to which the expenses related. Similar adjustments may be appropriate where some assets, liabilities, or both, are retained by the transferor and such retention results in the income of the transferor, transferee, or both, not being clearly reflected.

[¶ 2275]

Notes

1. As indicated in Rev. Rul. 80–198, several theories might be invoked to require recognition of gain notwithstanding literal compliance with Section 351(a). Besides the assignment of income doctrine, the ruling in its final paragraph discusses the possible recognition of gain in order to achieve a proper matching of income and deductions. Unlike the assignment of income doctrine, which Rev. Rul. 80–198 and *Hempt* would apply only in an instance of a tax motivated transfer, the clear

reflection of income doctrine under Section 482 could apply to prevent distortions of taxable income even when tax avoidance was not involved.

2.   The tax benefit rule might also override Section 351. Suppose, for example, that a taxpayer transfers to a corporation some materials and supplies having short lives, their cost having been deducted by the transferor at acquisition on the premise that they would be consumed in less than a year. Would the tax benefit rule give rise to recapture of income on the theory that the current transfer to the corporation was fundamentally inconsistent with the prior full deduction of the costs of the materials and supplies? See Hillsboro Nat'l Bank v. Commissioner and United States v. Bliss Dairy, Inc., 460 U.S. 370 (1983). In *Bliss Dairy*, the Court did so hold, requiring income recognition by a corporation upon its distribution in liquidation of cattle feed, the cost of which had previously been deducted at acquisition, and notwithstanding that Section 336 as it then read, if applied literally, would have precluded recognition.

3.   In Nash v. United States, 398 U.S. 1 (1970), a taxpayer incorporated an accrual method partnership under Section 351. Among the assets transferred to the new corporation were the accounts receivable of the partnership which the taxpayer had previously taken into income and against which the taxpayer had previously claimed deductions, under former Section 166(c), based upon estimated uncollectible bad debts. The IRS argued for income in the amount of the prior bad debt deductions reflected in the partnership's bad debt reserve. The Supreme Court, however, held otherwise because the fair market value of the receivables transferred to the corporation was equal to their face amount less the bad debt reserve. Thus, the Court found that the reserve was still an accurate estimate of the debts that would ultimately prove uncollectible and, hence, that the earlier deduction of the bad debt was consistent with the later transfer of the receivables to the corporation. Implicitly, the outcome could be different if the prior bad debt deductions appear excessive by the date at which accounts receivables are transferred to a corporation under Section 351.

[¶ 2280]

Problem

Titian (T), a sole proprietor, was engaged in a service business as a painting contractor and had regularly reported his income on the cash method. On January 1, T transferred his business, including uncollected receivables and unpaid liabilities, to his wholly owned corporation in exchange for all the stock of the corporation. The balance sheet of the corporation immediately following the transfer was as follows:

T Corporation

Assets	Basis	Per Books	Liabilities	Per Books
Cash	$ 1,000	$ 1,000	Accounts payable	$ 40,000
Accounts receivable	–0–	89,000	Bank loans	10,000
Prepaid rent and insurance	1,000	1,000		
Equipment (Cost $14,000, less depreciation $5,000)	9,000	9,000	Capital stock (5,000 shares, $10 par)	50,000
	$11,000	$100,000		$100,000

T had consistently followed the practice of deferring the deduction of prepaid rent and insurance premiums.

a.   To what extent would the collection of the accounts receivable by the corporation constitute taxable income to the corporation, to T, or to both?

b.   To what extent could the corporation properly deduct the expenses that had accrued while T was operating as a sole proprietor?

c.   If T had consistently followed the practice of deducting his short-term prepayments at the date when paid, would he have income to recognize on his transfer to the corporation of the remaining unexpired rental term and insurance premiums?

[¶ 2285]

H.   TAX TREATMENT OF CONTRIBUTIONS TO CAPITAL

If a sole shareholder transfers cash or other property to a corporation and does not receive consideration in exchange, the transfer in substance is a capital contribution and will be characterized as a Section 351 exchange even though no additional stock certificates are issued in return for the transferred property. See *Peracchi v. Commissioner*, at ¶ 2240; *Lessinger v. Commissioner*, 872 F.2d 519 (2d Cir.1989). The same should hold true if all the shareholders make pro rata transfers of property to the corporation.

By contrast, if some shareholders transfer property to the corporation and others do not, the resulting disproportionate transfers are more difficult to characterize. If they constitute "contributions to capital," they are not immediate taxable events to either the contributing shareholder or the recipient corporation. Apart from the exception discussed in Note 5 at ¶ 2295 for capital contributions of the corporation's own debt obligations, Section 118(a) generally allows the transferee corporation to exclude shareholders' capital contributions from its gross income. Under Section 362(a)(2), the corporation's basis in the contributed property is the same as the contributing shareholder's basis in such

¶ 2280

property (a carryover basis). At the shareholder level, the regulations generally treat a capital contribution as "an additional price paid for" the contributing shareholder's stock and not as a deductible loss or expense. Reg. § 1.118–1. This means that the contributor is allowed to increase the basis of that shareholder's stock by the amount of cash or the adjusted basis of the property contributed to the corporation. § 1016(a)(1). However, under certain circumstances (as when, for example, the remaining shareholders are members of the contributor's family), the contributor's capital contribution may be viewed as a gift to those other shareholders whose interests in the corporation increased in value as a result of the disproportionate capital contribution.

These nonrecognition results for capital contributions may appear unduly harsh to a shareholder who has made a transfer that reduced that shareholder's net worth. For example, suppose that a shareholder owns less than all the stock of a financially troubled corporation. In order to make the corporation more attractive to outside investors, the shareholder voluntarily either transfers assets to the corporation or surrenders some of her shares to the corporation without receiving consideration in exchange, thereby reducing her proportionate interest in the corporation. Can the shareholder deduct the basis of either the transferred assets or the surrendered shares as an ordinary loss under Section 165? The Supreme Court provides at least a partial answer to this question in the case below.

[¶ 2290]

COMMISSIONER v. FINK

Supreme Court of the United States, 1987.
483 U.S. 89.

JUSTICE POWELL delivered the opinion of the Court.

The question in this case is whether a dominant shareholder who voluntarily surrenders a portion of his shares to the corporation, but retains control, may immediately deduct from taxable income his basis in the surrendered shares.

I

Respondents Peter and Karla Fink were the principal shareholders of Travco Corporation, a Michigan manufacturer of motor homes. Travco had one class of common stock outstanding and no preferred stock. Mr. Fink owned 52.2 percent, and Mrs. Fink 20.3 percent, of the outstanding shares. Travco urgently needed new capital as a result of financial difficulties it encountered in the mid–1970's. The Finks voluntarily surrendered some of their shares to Travco in an effort to "increase the attractiveness of the corporation to outside investors." * * * Mr. Fink surrendered 116,146 shares in December 1976; Mrs. Fink surrendered

80,000 shares in January 1977. As a result, the Finks' combined percentage ownership of Travco was reduced from 72.5 percent to 68.5 percent. The Finks received no consideration for the surrendered shares, and no other shareholder surrendered any stock. The effort to attract new investors was unsuccessful, and the corporation eventually was liquidated.

On their 1976 and 1977 joint federal income tax returns, the Finks claimed ordinary loss deductions totaling $389,040, the full amount of their adjusted basis in the surrendered shares. The Commissioner of Internal Revenue disallowed the deductions. He concluded that the stock surrendered was a contribution to the corporation's capital. Accordingly, the Commissioner determined that the surrender resulted in no immediate tax consequences, and that the Finks' basis in the surrendered shares should be added to the basis of their remaining shares of Travco stock.

In an unpublished opinion, the Tax Court sustained the Commissioner's determination for the reasons stated in *Frantz v. Commissioner*, 83 T.C. 162, 174–182 (1984), aff'd, 784 F.2d 119 (C.A.2 1986) * * *. In *Frantz* the Tax Court held that a stockholder's non pro rata surrender of shares to the corporation does not produce an immediate loss. The court reasoned that "[t]his conclusion ... necessarily follows from a recognition of the purpose of the transfer, that is, to bolster the financial position of [the corporation] and, hence, to protect and make more valuable [the stockholder's] retained shares." 83 T.C., at 181. Because the purpose of the shareholder's surrender is "to decrease or avoid a loss on his overall investment," the Tax Court in *Frantz* was "unable to conclude that [he] sustained a loss at the time of the transaction." *Ibid.* "Whether [the shareholder] would sustain a loss, and if so, the amount thereof, could only be determined when he subsequently disposed of the stock that the surrender was intended to protect and make more valuable." *Ibid.* The Tax Court recognized that it had sustained the taxpayer's position in a series of prior cases. *Id.*, at 174–175. But it concluded that these decisions were incorrect, in part because they "encourage[d] a conversion of eventual capital losses into immediate ordinary losses." *Id.*, at 182.

In this case, a divided panel of the Court of Appeals for the Sixth Circuit reversed the Tax Court. 789 F.2d 427 (1986). The court concluded that the proper tax treatment of this type of stock surrender turns on the choice between "unitary" and "fragmented" views of stock ownership. Under the "fragmented view," "each share of stock is considered a separate investment," and gain or loss is computed separately on the sale or other disposition of each share. *Id.*, at 429. According to the "unitary view," "the 'stockholder's entire investment is viewed as a single indivisible property unit,' "*ibid.* (citation omitted), and a sale or disposition of some of the stockholder's shares only produces "an ascertainable gain or loss when the stockholder has disposed of his remaining shares." *Id.*, at 432. The court observed that both it and the Tax Court generally had adhered to the fragmented view, and concluded that "the facts of the instant case [do not] present sufficient justification for abandoning" it. *Id.*, at 431. It therefore held that the Finks were entitled to deduct their basis in the surrendered shares immediately as an ordinary loss, except to the extent that the surrender had increased the value of their remaining shares. The Court of Appeals remanded the case to the Tax Court for a determination of the increase, if any, in the value of the Finks' remaining shares that was attributable to the surrender.

Judge Joiner dissented. Because the taxpayers' "sole motivation in disposing of certain shares is to benefit the other shares they hold[,] . . . [v]iewing the surrender of each share as the termination of an individual investment ignores the very reason for the surrender." *Id.*, at 435. He concluded: "Particularly in cases such as this, where the diminution in the shareholder's corporate control and equity interest is so minute as to be illusory, the stock surrender should be regarded as a contribution to capital." *Ibid.*

We granted certiorari to resolve a conflict among the circuits, * * * and now reverse.

II

A

It is settled that a shareholder's voluntary contribution to the capital of the corporation has no immediate tax consequences. * * * § 263; [Reg. §] 1.263(a)–2(f) (1986). Instead, the shareholder is entitled to increase the basis of his shares by the amount of his basis in the property transferred to the corporation. See * * * § 1016(a)(1). When the shareholder later disposes of his shares, his contribution is reflected as a smaller taxable gain or a larger deductible loss. This rule applies not only to transfers of cash or tangible property, but also to a shareholder's forgiveness of a debt owed to him by the corporation. [Reg. §] 1.61–12(a) (1986). Such transfers are treated as contributions to capital even if the other shareholders make proportionately smaller contributions, or no contribution at all. * * * The rules governing contributions to capital reflect the general principle that a shareholder may not claim an immediate loss for outlays made to benefit the corporation. * * * We must decide whether this principle also applies to a controlling share-holder's non pro rata surrender of a portion of his shares.[6]

B

The Finks contend that they sustained an immediate loss upon surrendering some of their shares to the corporation. By parting with

6. The Finks concede that a pro rata stock surrender, which by definition does not change the percentage ownership of any shareholder, is not a taxable event. Cf., *Eisner v. Macomber*, 252 U.S. 189 (1920) (pro rata stock dividend does not produce taxable income).

the shares, they gave up an ownership interest entitling them to future dividends, future capital appreciation, assets in the event of liquidation, and voting rights.[7] Therefore, the Finks contend, they are entitled to an immediate deduction. See * * * §§ 165(a) and (c)(2). In addition, the Finks argue that any non pro rata stock transaction "give[s] rise to immediate tax results." * * * For example, a non pro rata stock dividend produces income because it increases the recipient's proportionate ownership of the corporation. * * * By analogy, the Finks argue that a non pro rata surrender of shares should be recognized as an immediate loss because it reduces the surrendering shareholder's proportionate ownership.

Finally, the Finks contend that their stock surrenders were not contributions to the corporation's capital. They note that a typical contribution to capital, unlike a non pro rata stock surrender, has no effect on the contributing shareholder's proportionate interest in the corporation. Moreover, the Finks argue, a contribution of cash or other property increases the net worth of the corporation. For example, a shareholder's forgiveness of a debt owed to him by the corporation decreases the corporation's liabilities. In contrast, when a shareholder surrenders shares of the corporation's own stock, the corporation's net worth is unchanged. This is because the corporation cannot itself exercise the right to vote, receive dividends, or receive a share of assets in the event of liquidation. * * *

III

A shareholder who surrenders a portion of his shares to the corporation has parted with an asset, but that alone does not entitle him to an immediate deduction. Indeed, if the shareholder owns less than 100 percent of the corporation's shares, any non pro rata contribution to the corporation's capital will reduce the net worth of the contributing shareholder.[10] A shareholder who surrenders stock thus is similar to one who forgives or surrenders a debt owed to him by the corporation; the latter gives up interest, principal, and also potential voting power in the event of insolvency or bankruptcy. But, as stated above, such forgiveness of corporate debt is treated as a contribution to capital rather than a

---

7. As a practical matter, however, the Finks did not give up a great deal. Their percentage interest in the corporation declined by only four percent. Because the Finks retained a majority interest, this reduction in their voting power was inconsequential. Moreover, Travco, like many corporations in financial difficulties, was not paying dividends.

10. For example, assume that a shareholder holding an 80 percent interest in a corporation with a total liquidation value of $100,000 makes a non pro rata contribution to the corporation's capital of $20,000 in cash. Assume further that the shareholder has no other assets. Prior to the contribution, the shareholder's net worth was $100,000 ($20,000 plus 80 percent of $100,000). If the corporation were immediately liquidated following the contribution, the shareholder would receive only $96,000 (80 percent of $120,000). Of course such a non pro rata contribution is rare in practice. Typically a shareholder will simply purchase additional shares.

current deduction. * * *. The Finks' voluntary surrender of shares, like a shareholder's voluntary forgiveness of debt owed by the corporation, closely resembles an investment or contribution to capital. See B. Bittker & J. Eustice, Federal Income Taxation of Corporations and Shareholders § 3.14, p. 3–59 (4th ed. 1979) ("If the contribution is voluntary, it does not produce gain or loss to the shareholder.") We find the similarity convincing in this case.

* * *

The Finks concede that the purpose of their stock surrender was to protect or increase the value of their investment in the corporation. * * * They hoped to encourage new investors to provide needed capital and in the long run recover the value of the surrendered shares through increased dividends or appreciation in the value of their remaining shares. If the surrender had achieved its purpose, the Finks would not have suffered an economic loss. * * *

Finally, treating stock surrenders as ordinary losses might encourage shareholders in failing corporations to convert potential capital losses to ordinary losses by voluntarily surrendering their shares before the corporation fails. In this way shareholders might avoid the consequences of * * * § 165(g)(1), which provides for capital-loss treatment of stock that becomes worthless. Similarly, shareholders may be encouraged to transfer corporate stock rather than other property to the corporation in order to realize a current loss.

We therefore hold that a dominant shareholder who voluntarily surrenders a portion of his shares to the corporation, but retains control, does not sustain an immediate loss deductible from taxable income. Rather, the surrendering shareholder must reallocate his basis in the surrendered shares to the shares he retains.[15] The shareholder's loss, if any, will be recognized when he disposes of his remaining shares. A reallocation of basis is consistent with the general principle that "[p]ayments made by a stockholder of a corporation for the purpose of protecting his interest therein must be regarded as [an] additional cost of his stock," and so cannot be deducted immediately. *Eskimo Pie Corp.*

---

15. The Finks remained the controlling shareholders after their surrender. We therefore have no occasion to decide in this case whether a surrender that causes the shareholder to lose control of the corporation is immediately deductible. In related contexts, the Code distinguishes between minimal reductions in a shareholder's ownership percentage and loss of corporate control. See § 302(b)(2) (providing "exchange" rather than divided treatment for a "substantially disproportionate redemption of stock" that brings the shareholder's ownership percentage below 50 percent); § 302(b)(3) (providing similar treatment when the redemption terminates the share-

holder's interest in the corporation). [See ¶¶ 5005–5025.]

In this case we use the term "control" to mean ownership of more than half of a corporation's voting shares. We recognize, of course, that in larger corporations—especially those whose shares are listed on a national exchange—a person or entity may exercise control in fact while owning less than a majority of the voting shares. See Securities Exchange Act of 1934, § 13(d) * * * (requiring persons to report acquisition of more than 5 percent of a registered equity security).

v. Commissioner, 4 T.C. at 676 (1945) * * *. We conclude only that a controlling shareholder's voluntary surrender of shares, like contributions of other forms of property to the corporation, is not an appropriate occasion for the recognition of gain or loss.

IV

For the reasons we have stated, the judgment of the Court of Appeals for the Sixth Circuit is reversed.

* * *

[Concurring and dissenting opinions have been omitted.]

[¶ 2295]

Notes

1. Note that the Supreme Court in footnote 15 of the *Fink* decision expressly left open whether the result in *Fink* would have been different if the majority shareholder's surrender of the stock to the corporation had caused the shareholder to lose control of the corporation. Why might loss of control change the result in *Fink*?

2. Compare the result in *Fink* with Reynolds Metals Co. v. Commissioner, 105 T.C. 304 (1995), aff'd, 114 F.3d 1177 (4th Cir.1997). In that case, a parent corporation was denied a current capital loss deduction and was treated instead as making a capital contribution to its subsidiary, upon surrendering shares of stock in that subsidiary to the latter's creditors. In exchange for the surrendered stock, the parent corporation received from the creditors debentures of a lesser value than the subsidiary had earlier issued and which the parent had guaranteed it would reacquire at the election of the creditors.

3. Contributions to the capital of a corporation by persons other than shareholders are subject to rules somewhat different from those applicable to shareholders' contributions to capital. Contributions from both groups generally may be excluded from the corporation's gross income under Section 118(a). However, under Section 362(c)(1), the corporation's basis in noncash property contributed by a nonshareholder is zero. (Compare the more favorable carryover basis rule that applies under Section 362(a)(2) to property contributed by a shareholder.) Further, in the case of a nonshareholder's cash contribution to capital, Section 362(c)(2) requires the corporation to reduce the adjusted basis of property it acquires within 12 months after the cash contribution by the amount of the contribution. Why are nonshareholder contributions to capital subject to less favorable rules than shareholder contributions to capital?

4. Note that Section 118(b) provides that a corporation may not exclude from gross income as a capital contribution "any contribution in aid of construction or any other contribution by a customer or potential

customer." Thus, for example, a utility company may not exclude from gross income a contribution made to assist it to extend service to a particular site. Why does Congress not allow a corporation to exclude such contributions from gross income? What is the transferee corporation's adjusted basis in property acquired by it as a contribution falling within Section 118(b)?

5. Nor is a corporation entitled to exclude from gross income a capital contribution to it by a shareholder of the corporation's own debt. Such a contribution obviously results in cancellation of the corporation's debt. In such a case, Section 118(e)(2) displaces the general nonrecognition rule of Section 118 by deferring instead to the regime of Section 108(e)(6). Under Section 108(e)(6), the corporation is treated as having satisfied the debt with cash equal to the shareholder's basis in the contributed debt.

[¶ 2300]

Problem

Anita and Byron are unrelated individuals. Anita owns 60 shares of the common stock of Xanadu Corporation with a total fair market value of $12,000 and a basis of $6,000; Byron owns the remaining 40 shares with a total fair market value of $8,000 and a basis of $2,000. Anita contributes to the capital of the corporation property with a fair market value of $6,000 and a basis to Anita of $3,000. Byron contributes property with a fair market value of $4,000 and a basis of $1,000. The corporation issues no stock in exchange for the contributed property.

a. What are the tax consequences to Anita, Byron, and the Xanadu Corporation? Does Section 351(a) apply?

b. What are the consequences if Byron makes the described contribution, but Anita does not?

c. What if Byron contributes 20 shares of his Xanadu stock worth $4,000 to the corporation and Anita makes no contribution?

[¶ 2305]

I. TAX TREATMENT OF CORPORATION'S ORGANIZATIONAL EXPENDITURES

In the absence of any special Code provision, a corporation's organizational expenditures would be treated as capital expenditures because they create an asset (the corporate organization and charter) that generally does not have a limited useful life (i.e., the usual corporation charter provides for a perpetual life). Thus, such expenditures normally would not be deductible by the corporation except as a loss in the year that the corporation dissolves and abandons its corporate franchise. See, e.g., H.R. Rep. No. 1337, 83d Cong., 2d Sess. 31 (1954); Shellabarger Grain Products Co. v. Commissioner, 146 F.2d 177 (7th Cir.1944).

However, Section 248 allows a corporation to elect to currently deduct a limited amount of certain "organizational expenditures." The corporation may deduct as much as $5,000 of its actual organizational expenditures, but such amount is reduced by the amount the organizational expenditures exceed $50,000. Thus, if the organizational expenditures reach $55,000, no current deduction is available. The remaining expenses are deductible ratably over a 15–year period, beginning on the date the corporation begins business. § 248(a)(2). Prior to 2004, no current deduction was permitted, but expenses were deductible over a five-year period. The change in 2004 brings the deductibility of organizational expenses other than the first $5,000 in line with the time period available for amortization of intangibles under Section 197. If a corporation does not elect to amortize its organizational expenditures under Section 248, the corporation may not deduct such expenditures except, presumably, as a loss in the year in which it liquidates.

For purposes of Section 248, an "organizational expenditure" is any expenditure that is (i) incident to the creation of the corporation; (ii) chargeable to the capital account; and (iii) of a character that, if expended incident to the creation of a corporation having a limited life, would be amortizable over such life. § 248(b) and Reg. § 1.248–1(b)(1). The regulations list the following items as examples of expenditures that meet the definition of "organizational expenditure" and qualify for the Section 248 election: legal and accounting services incident to the organization of the corporation, expenses of organizational meetings of directors or shareholders, and state incorporation fees. Reg. § 1.248–1(b)(2).

By contrast, the regulations provide that the Section 248 election does not apply to the costs of issuing or selling shares of stock or other securities (such as underwriting commissions, professional fees, and printing costs). Reg. § 1.248–1(b)(3)(i). Nor does the Section 248 election apply to expenditures connected with the transfer of assets to a corporation. Reg. § 1.248–1(b)(3)(ii). Why not? As discussed in Chapter 17, a similar dichotomy exists between amortizable organizational expenditures and nondeductible syndication fees of a partnership or limited liability company.

¶ 2305

Chapter 3

PLANNING THE CORPORATE CAPITAL STRUCTURE

[¶ 3000]

A. INTRODUCTION

As a part of the formation of any corporation, its capital structure must be designed in a manner that properly allocates the various interests in the corporation among investors. Those fundamental interests are: the interest in current income, the interest in accumulated income and capital and the interest in control. Under modern corporate law, the organizers of a corporation have almost infinite flexibility in the design of the capital structure to accomplish the desired allocation with great precision, a reality that can either simplify or complicate the task. In recent years, that flexibility has resulted in an endless stream of innovative, if not bizarre, financial products. This Chapter, however, focuses upon the basics of corporate finance that are of importance to even the smallest of corporations.

On a semantic note, the Code is inconsistent in the meaning it attaches to the word "securities." In Section 165(g) it is defined as including both equity securities (stock) and debt securities (bonds, etc.). However, in Subchapter C the phrase "stock and securities" often appears and in that context the word means only debt securities. In this book we try to avoid using the unmodified word securities but when we do, we use it to mean both debt and equity.

[¶ 3005]

B. BASIC COMPONENTS OF CAPITAL STRUCTURE

A corporation's capital structure consists of the securities issued by the corporation in exchange for the cash or other property or services contributed, or to be contributed, to it. The classic components of a capital structure include stock, which is understood to represent the ownership, or equity, interest in the corporation, and debt, which reflects a creditor interest, although, as shall be seen, the line between those two forms of securities can become very fine.

Common stock. Every corporation must have outstanding at least one class of common stock, although under most state laws a different label (such as "Class A Stock") can be used. Common stock represents the residual interest in the corporation. Thus, the common stockholders are entitled to all of the corporate profits and increase in value, and all of the rights to vote for directors and on other matters, assigned to shareholders that have not been granted to others under the corporate charter. On the other hand, common stock is the most junior security in that common stockholders are entitled to their residual rights only after the required allocations are made to other, more senior, security holders. A corporation may issue more than one class of common stock, assigning somewhat different rights, usually different voting rights, to the different classes.

Preferred stock. Not uncommonly corporations issue one or more classes of a more senior security called preferred stock. Notwithstanding its traditional label, the key characteristic of preferred stock is not its preference but the fact that the rights of the holders of preferred stock in either current income or accumulated capital, or both, are limited. Thus, each share of preferred stock typically bears a stated liquidation preference, say $1,000, which will be the full amount to be paid on the normal retirement of the stock and therefore will also be the amount paid to the corporation upon the acquisition of the stock. The interest of preferred stock in current income is typically limited to a percentage of this liquidation preference, say 7 percent. While most states allow preferred stockholders to be given a right to vote, typically preferred stock is nonvoting. As can be seen, a $1,000 nonvoting 7% preferred stock is not very different from a loan. Nevertheless, for tax purposes preferred stock has generally been treated as "stock"—along with common stock. There is, however, a slight trend in recent tax legislation towards treating some forms of preferred stock more like debt and you should watch for instances of that.

Debt. Extensions of credit to a corporation can assume an extremely broad range of forms. Debt can represent a long-term investment in the corporation not unlike preferred stock or it may reflect the very short-term loan created by purchasing goods or services on credit, like the monthly telephone bill. Loans to the corporation from banks and other investors will have widely varying attributes, such as whether they are secured by a mortgage on corporate properties, but those terms generally only control the relative interests of different classes of creditors. Absent a very clear agreement to the contrary (which would be unusual), all debt is senior to all stock so that interest on the debt must be paid before

¶ **3005**

dividends can be paid and debt is repaid first on the dissolution of the corporation. Various labels are attached to debt instruments, such as bond or debenture, but those labels have no income tax significance. Lenders (other than trade creditors) to small corporations quite commonly insist that one or more shareholders of the corporation guarantee repayment of their loan in the event the corporation is unable to do so.

Options. A corporation may sell a right to purchase stock of the corporation at a future time for a fixed price. Such an arrangement allows the purchaser to participate in the future appreciation in the value of the corporate stock for little, if any, current investment. Stock options are commonly used as a form of compensation and the tax consequences of such options are prescribed by such Code sections as 83 and 422, which are not considered here. The treatment of options sold to investors is governed by general tax principles.

Hybrid securities. It is not unusual for a single security to contain attributes of different types of securities. Perhaps the most common form of hybrid security, but by no means the only form, is the convertible security, which combines an option with another form of investment. The terms of a debt instrument, for example, may allow the holder to exchange the instrument for a fixed number of shares of stock in the corporation. Hybrid securities can present difficult problems of classification, some of which are considered below.

In deciding what form of investment to make in a corporation, an investor's choice is not merely between one form of security or another. Nothing prohibits an investor from acquiring two or more different types of securities in a corporation and that strategy will often be the most beneficial. Thus, an investor trying to balance the tax efficiency and relative security of debt against the appreciation potential in stock will most likely be trying to decide what proportion of his or her investment should be for common stock and what proportion for debt.

Choosing the right balance between debt and equity financing from the perspective of either the corporation or an individual investor is a daunting task. A multitude of tax and nontax aspects of the respective securities, often pointing in conflicting directions, must inform that decision. Nevertheless, on balance there is normally a significant bias in favor of the use of debt rather than equity. Corporate profits distributed on stock are subject to the double tax imposed upon corporations in this country. Lowering the shareholder level tax to 15 percent reduced, but did not eliminate, this double tax. On the other hand, earnings distributed on debt avoid the double tax. In particular, because payments of interest generally are deductible, corporate earnings distributed as interest are not subject to the corporate income tax. That single difference between debt and stock is sufficiently important to most corporations to account for the preference for debt. In addition, however, debt may provide the investor greater security of repayment should the business

¶ **3005**

fail and normally provides a more stable and reliable annual return than do dividends on stock.

On the other hand, in other respects, both tax and non-tax factors favor stock. On incorporation, for example, stock, but not debt, can often be received free of tax. Moreover, having too much debt in the capital structure can impair the corporation's credit standing and the need to meet large interest obligations can create a destructive cash flow drain on the business. And, as discussed below, having too much debt in the capital structure can result in the loss of the interest deduction.

Preferred stock is normally used when it is desirable for an investment to be represented by stock, rather than debt (perhaps so that the security can be obtained free of tax in a Section 351 exchange), but the investors wish to allocate their capital investment differently from the allocation of voting control. For example, institutional investors may be issued nonvoting preferred stock while the employee-shareholders are issued voting common stock. Similarly, it may be useful to exchange the common stock of a retiring employee-shareholder for preferred stock, having a fixed income but reduced vote, thereby shifting the ownership of the common stock to the next generation. However, the use of preferred stock is not always wise. For example, a corporation with outstanding preferred stock is barred from electing S corporation status. As you explore corporate taxation, especially the taxation of stock dividends, try to identify other reasons for small corporations to issue—or not issue—preferred stock.

[¶ 3010]

C. CLASSIFICATION ISSUES: STOCK v. DEBT

1. THE CRITERIA

Whether an instrument obtained by an investor in exchange for a contribution to a corporation is to be treated as stock or as debt for income tax purposes is a matter to be resolved by the income tax rules themselves and not by the label affixed to the instrument by the parties or by state law. Given the nature of the differences in tax attributes between debt and equity, this characterization issue is of great importance both to taxpayers and to the proper administration of the tax laws. Yet the tax law rules in this area remain unsatisfactorily vague and uncertain, as indicated by the still apt summary in the following excerpt from a pamphlet prepared by the Staff of the Joint Committee on Taxation, 101st Cong., lst Sess., Federal Income Tax Aspects of Corporate Financial Structures, at 35–36 (Jan. 18, 1989):

> The characterization of an investment in a corporation as debt or equity for Federal income tax purposes is generally determined by the economic substance of the investor's interest in the corporation.

The form of the instrument representing the investment and the taxpayer's characterization of the interest as debt or equity is not necessarily controlling. However, taxpayers have considerable latitude in structuring the terms of an instrument so that an interest in a corporation will be considered to be debt or equity, as so desired.

There is presently no definition in the Code or the regulations which can be used to determine whether an interest in a corporation constitutes debt or equity for tax purposes. Such a determination must be made under principles developed in case law. Courts have approached the issue of distinguishing debt and equity by trying to determine whether the particular investment at issue in each case more closely resembles a pure debt interest or a pure equity interest. It is generally understood that a pure debt instrument is ordinarily represented by a written, unconditional promise to pay a principal sum certain, on demand or before a fixed maturity date not unreasonably far in the future, with interest payable in all events and not later than maturity. Conversely, a pure equity interest is generally understood as an investment which places the funds contributed by the investor at the risk of the enterprise, provides for a share of any future profits, and carries with it rights to control or manage the enterprise.

The determination of whether an interest constitutes debt or equity is generally made by analyzing and weighing the relevant facts and circumstances of each case. * * *

[¶ 3015]

SCRIPTOMATIC, INC. v. UNITED STATES

United States Court of Appeals, Third Circuit, 1977.
555 F.2d 364.

VAN DUSEN, CIRCUIT JUDGE:

The question in this case is whether payments made on two series of obligations (denominated "debentures") of Scriptomatic, Inc. (plaintiff) were deductible as interest under * * * § 163, or were, in reality, disguised dividends and therefore not deductible by the corporation. On June 24, 1975, the district court entered judgment for plaintiff notwithstanding a December 1973 jury verdict answering special questions in favor of defendant, * * * from which the government appeals. The judgment n.o.v. having been properly entered, we affirm the district court order.

I.

In *Fin Hay Realty Co. v. United States*, 398 F.2d 694 (3d Cir.1968), this Court enumerated sixteen criteria which, as we stated there, have been isolated by the courts and commentators as factors which have been used in evaluating "the nature of an instrument which is in form a debt." 398 F.2d at 696. However, those criteria were never intended to obtain talismanic significance. The essence of *Fin Hay* is contained in the following quotation from it:

"[N]either any single criterion nor any series of criteria can provide a conclusive answer in the kaleidoscopic circumstances which individual cases present.

* * *

"The various factors which have been identified in the cases are only aids in answering the *ultimate question whether the investment, analyzed in terms of its economic reality, constitutes risk capital entirely subject to the fortunes of the corporate venture or represents a strict debtor-creditor relationship*. Since there is often an element of risk in a loan, just as there is an element of risk in an equity interest, the conflicting elements do not end at a clear line in all cases.

"In a corporation which has numerous shareholders with varying interests, the *arm's-length* relationship between the corporation and a shareholder who supplies funds to it inevitably results in a transaction whose form mirrors its substance. Where the corporation is closely held, however, and the same persons occupy both sides of the bargaining table, form does not necessarily correspond to the intrinsic *economic nature of the transaction*, for the parties may mold it at their will with no countervailing pull. This is particularly so where a shareholder can have the funds he advances to a corporation treated as corporate obligations instead of contributions to capital without affecting his proportionate equity interest. Labels, which are perhaps the best expression of the subjective intention of parties to a transaction, thus lose their meaningfulness.

"To seek economic reality in objective terms of course disregards the personal interest which a shareholder may have in the welfare of the corporation in which he is a dominant force. But an objective standard is one imposed by the very fact of his dominant position and is much fairer than one which would presumptively construe all such transactions against the shareholder's interest. Under an objective test of economic reality it is useful to compare the form which a similar transaction would have taken had it been between the corporation and an outside lender, and if the shareholder's advance is far more speculative than what an outsider would make, it is obviously a loan in name only." [Footnote omitted. Emphasis added.]

398 F.2d At 697.

Under *Fin Hay*, then, the ultimate issue is measurement of the transaction by objective tests of economic reality, and the touchstone of

¶ 3015

economic reality is whether the transaction would have taken the same form had it been between the corporation and an outside lender—whether, in sum, "the shareholder's advance is far more speculative than what an outsider would make." The analysis suggested by this approach to the debt-equity question may be expressed in terms of two lines of inquiry: assuming that the obligation is debt in form, (1) did the form result from an arm's-length relationship, and/or (2) would an outside investor have advanced funds on terms similar to those agreed to by the shareholder.

If question one is answered in the affirmative (the form did result from arm's-length dealings), the obligation is debt. If question two is answered in the affirmative (an outsider would have advanced funds on terms similar to those agreed to by the shareholder), the obligation is debt—despite the fact that the negotiations leading to its issuance were not at arm's length. As is apparent, if there is proof or agreement that an outsider would have purchased an instrument on the terms available to a shareholder, the question as to whether the form of the obligation resulted from arm's-length negotiation is irrelevant to resolution of the debt-equity issue. The crucial issue is the economic reality of the marketplace: what the market would accept as debt is debt.

It is only within this framework that the many factors listed in *Fin Hay* and in other court decisions in this area have any meaning or function. One or more of those factors may be relevant to the threshold question of whether the instrument is debt in form. One or more of those criteria may, in the same sense, be helpful in evaluating whether there was an arm's-length relationship. Certain of those elements may also bear on the fundamental inquiry, whether an obligation is commercially valuable as an obligation and, therefore, debt in "economic reality." However, the criteria which will be relevant to each of those three areas of inquiry will vary from case to case, as will the weight which should be accorded each criterion. For this reason, two court decisions in this area will rarely present comparable situations and it will be unusual for any particular case to have controlling effect in any other case on the basis of the particular factors applied or the weight accorded a specific criterion. The weight of precedent in the realm of debt-equity determinations flows from the framework of analysis on the basis of factors such as those enumerated in *Fin Hay*.

* * *

[¶ 3020]

Notes

1. Had the government prevailed in *Scriptomatic*, what would have been the tax outcome?

2. If the answer to the second question posed by the court is in the negative, what effect does that have? The instrument may not automati-

cally be treated as debt but does it follow that the instrument should be treated as stock? Might it not also be said that an outsider would not have advanced funds to the corporation in exchange for stock on the terms agreed to by the shareholder?

Put differently, should the test be whether this instrument meets an arm's length standard for debt or whether this instrument more nearly resembles debt or equity? From the taxpayer's perspective, which test is more favorable?

3.   The sixteen criteria enumerated in *Fin Hay* were: (1) The intent of the parties; (2) the identity between creditors and shareholders; (3) the extent of participation in management by the holder of the instrument; (4) the ability of the corporation to obtain funds from outside sources; (5) the "thinness" of the capital structure in relation to debt; (6) the risk involved; (7) the formal indicia of the arrangement; (8) the relative position of the obligee as to other creditors regarding the payment of interest and principal; (9) the voting power of the holder of the instrument; (10) the provision of a fixed rate of interest; (11) a contingency on the obligation to repay; (12) the source of the interest payments; (13) the presence or absence of a fixed maturity date; (14) a provision for redemption by the corporation; (15) a provision for redemption at the option of the holder; and (16) the timing of the advance with reference to the organization of the corporation.

4.   The "thinness" of a corporation's capital structure refers to the ratio of debt to equity. A high ratio, indicating far more has been invested for debt than for equity, reveals a "thin" corporation—one lacking in equity contributions. The lack of an "equity cushion" increases the riskiness of the debt investment and that is a factor in recharacterizing the security as stock. Because the computation of the debt-equity ratio of a corporation can be mechanical and has the appearance of being more objective than other criteria, it is often used in statutory rules that disallow interest deductions, as described in the following section. Appearances, however, can be misleading. There is no consensus in the caselaw concerning how the ratio is to be computed. Should the debt side of the ratio include just shareholder held debt or also non-shareholder debt? If non-shareholder debt is included, should that be just long-term debt or also include trade creditors? On the equity side, it might be supposed that contributions should be taken into account at market value, rather than tax basis, and that retained earnings be included along with paid-in capital but that may not always be the case. Obviously, how these questions are answered in a particular case can have a dramatic effect on the computation of the ratio.

[¶ 3023]

Problem

Assume that four unrelated individuals have brought together business assets and employees and have arranged financing for a new venture involving the collection and disposal of industrial waste which they hope to take public after a few good years of operations. The four will form a corporation to which they will contribute property worth $3 million in exchange for all of the common stock of the corporation. A bank has agreed to loan the venture $4 million which will be secured by some of the properties and all of the accounts receivable of the venture.

An insurance company has agreed to invest $14 million in the corporation which will be used to acquire additional properties and to provide working capital. The insurance company is willing to take back long-term debt convertible into common stock bearing an interest rate of 7 percent or preferred stock bearing a dividend rate of 8 percent or a combination of both.

The bank has insisted that no payments of principal may be made to the insurance companies until its loan has been retired but there may be some flexibility in that position. The bank is also requiring an opinion of counsel to the effect that all payments of interest will be deductible for federal income tax purposes.

You represent the four promoters of this venture and it is your opinion that the bank requests. How will you insist that the investment by the insurance companies be structured? Can any of the investment by the four promoters be for debt? Bear in mind that the more that is paid in taxes by the venture, the less likely it is that the venture will succeed.

[¶ 3025]

2. STATUTORY CHARACTERIZATION RULES

Because of the complexity of applying a facts and circumstances test that employs as many factors as were listed in *Fin Hay* and the resulting uncertainty of tax result, Congress has on several occasions sought to provide guidance in this heavily litigated area. The most general assistance has to date proved to be the least successful. Section 385, enacted in 1969, authorized the Commissioner to promulgate regulations that would govern the determination of whether an interest in a corporation was to be treated as stock or as debt. The section sets forth five factors that the drafters of the regulations might take into account in the inquiry. After some 11 years, the Treasury Department issued proposed regulations in March 1980 that became "final" on December 29 of that year and had an original effective date of May 1981. However, in response to a flood of criticism of these regulations, the Treasury twice postponed the effective date of the final regulations. On December 30, 1981, the Treasury issued new proposed regulations, but these regulations never became effective. Finally, in July 1983, the Treasury announced that both versions of the Section 385 regulations were being withdrawn. The Treasury has not issued any additional regulations under Section 385 to date. The difficulty of reducing this complex area to workable regulatory rules appears insurmountable.

One aspect of this failed regulatory project is worth some reflection. Under the judicial approach to characterization as represented by *Scriptomatic*, the result is all or nothing. Either the entire block of securities held by the particular taxpayer is stock or it is debt. By contrast, the regulations took a bifurcation approach under which the investment in the corporation was allocated between stock and debt. To achieve this allocation, a value for the debt portion of the instrument issued by the corporation was derived by taking account of all of the features of the instrument, including the interest rate paid. The derived amount was then treated as debt and the balance of the investment was treated as for stock. While appearing a reasonable compromise, bifurcation had one odd consequence. Most debt-equity cases arise from attempts by the IRS to disallow interest deductions. Under bifurcation, however, it was not the interest deduction that was reduced; it was the principal amount of the purported indebtedness. Perhaps it is not surprising that the Treasury Department lost interest in the Section 385 regulations.

In narrower contexts, Congress has itself enacted mandatory rules that limit or disallow the deduction of interest on debt issued by corporations. These rules do not always explicitly bifurcate these instruments or characterize the payments for which deductions are disallowed as dividends. However, the objective of each of these sets of rules is to identify investments in corporations that, either because of their riskiness or for other reasons, more nearly resemble equity than debt. For example, Section 279 disallows interest deductions on "junk bonds" issued in the process of acquiring the stock or assets of another corporation. To fall within this section, the bonds must be subordinated to other debt, convertible into stock of the issuing corporation, and produce a ratio of debt to equity of more than 2:1. In addition, the section only applies to disallow the annual deduction of junk bond interest in excess of $5 million. Because these definitions are so easily skirted, Section 279 has never had much effect. A somewhat similar provision in Section 163(j) is intended to disallow the deduction of very large interest payments by the U. S. subsidiaries of foreign corporations on payments to their foreign parents when those foreign corporations are not taxable on the interest received from U. S. sources. Section 163(*l*) takes a different approach. It disallows any deduction for interest that is payable in stock of the issuer or a related corporation or is measured by the value of such stock.

Section 163(e) is of interest because it does expressly bifurcate certain instruments. This provision applies to debt instruments that are issued at a very large discount which, in turn, would reflect an unreasonably high interest rate. In that event, the excessive discount is treated as a dividend and not as interest to the recipient and a deduction for the excessive amount is disallowed to the payor.

¶ 3025

[¶ 3030]

3. HYBRID INSTRUMENTS

As the first question posed by the court in *Scriptomatic* illustrates, traditionally the debt-equity dispute has only involved purported debt held by stockholders. If the debt is held by persons who are not stockholders or related to stockholders, then the loan by definition meets an arms' length standard and will be considered debt. However, the issue also arises in a different context.

Efforts to capture the "best of all possible worlds" when tailoring a corporation's financial instruments have produced a variety of financial vehicles best characterized as "hybrids." These instruments contain complex mixtures of the classic features of debt and equity that are designed to combine security of principal with participation in profits. In general, the classification of hybrid instruments employs the same facts and circumstances inquiry that applies to the analysis of shareholder held debt.

[¶ 3035]

IRS NOTICE 94–47

1994–1 C.B. 357.

In a number of recent transactions, instruments have been issued that are designed to be treated as debt for federal income tax purposes but as equity for regulatory, rating agency, or financial accounting purposes. These instruments typically contain a combination of debt and equity characteristics.

Upon examination, the Service will scrutinize instruments of this type to determine if their purported status as debt for federal income tax purposes is appropriate. Of particular interest to the Service are instruments that contain a variety of equity features, including an unreasonably long maturity or an ability to repay the instrument's principal with the issuer's stock. Analysis of these instruments must take into account the cumulative effect of these features and other equity features.

General Debt/Equity Analysis

The characterization of an instrument for federal income tax purposes depends on the terms of the instrument and all surrounding facts and circumstances. Among the factors that may be considered in making this determination are: (a) whether there is an unconditional promise on the part of the issuer to pay a sum certain on demand or at a fixed maturity date that is in the reasonably foreseeable future; (b) whether holders of the instruments possess the right to enforce the payment of principal and interest; (c) whether the rights of the holders of the instruments are subordinate to rights of general creditors; (d) whether the instruments give the holders the right to participate in the management of the issuer; (e) whether the issuer is thinly capitalized; (f) whether there is identity between holders of the instruments and stockholders of the issuer; (g) the label placed upon the instruments by the parties; and (h) whether the instruments are intended to be treated as debt or equity for non-tax purposes, including regulatory, rating agency, or financial accounting purposes. No particular factor is conclusive in making the determination of whether an instrument constitutes debt or equity. The weight given to any factor depends upon all the facts and circumstances and the overall effect of an instrument's debt and equity features must be taken into account.

PAYABLE IN STOCK

The Service is aware of recent offerings in which taxpayers may be relying on Rev. Rul. 85–119, 1985–2 C.B. 60. In that ruling, a bank holding company issued instruments (the Notes) that permitted the principal amount to be repaid with the company's stock at maturity. The Service held that the Notes constituted debt based on all the facts and circumstances, including the fact that, in substance, a holder of the Notes had the right to obtain repayment either in cash or in stock.

The holding in Rev. Rul. 85–119 is limited to the facts of that ruling. Instruments that are similar to the Notes but that, on balance, are more equity-like are unlikely to qualify as debt for federal income tax purposes. For example, an instrument does not qualify as debt if it has terms substantially identical to the Notes except for a provision that requires the holder to accept payment of principal solely in stock of the issuer (or, in certain circumstances, a related party). Similarly, an instrument does not qualify as debt if it has terms substantially identical to the Notes except that (a) the right to elect cash is structured to ensure that the holder would choose the stock, or (b) the instrument is nominally payable in cash but does not, in substance, give the holder the right to receive cash because, for example, the instrument is secured by the stock and is nonrecourse to the issuer.

UNREASONABLY LONG MATURITIES

The Service also is aware of recent offerings of instruments that combine long maturities with substantial equity characteristics. Some taxpayers are treating these instruments as debt for federal income tax purposes, apparently based on authorities such as *Monon Railroad v. Commissioner*, 55 T.C. 345 (1970), *acq.*, 1973–2 C.B. 3, which involved an instrument with a 50-year term.

The Service cautions taxpayers that, even in the case of an instrument having a term of less than 50 years, *Monon Railroad* generally does not provide support for treating an instrument as debt for federal income tax purposes if the instrument contains significant equity characteristics not present in that case. The reasonableness of an instrument's

¶ 3035

term (including that of any relending obligation or similar arrangement) is determined based on all the facts and circumstances, including the issuer's ability to satisfy the instrument. A maturity that is reasonable in one set of circumstances may be unreasonable in another if sufficient equity characteristics are present.

[¶ 3040]

Note

In keeping with tradition, Notice 94–47 above recites a series of factors frequently relied upon by authorities in deciding how to characterize a purported debt instrument; it also endorses the appropriateness of a facts and circumstances inquiry. However, the Notice appears to attach special importance to two particular factors. Why should those factors be given extra importance in the debt-equity analysis?

[¶ 3045]

4. SALE OR SECTION 351 EXCHANGE

While, as noted above, the debt-equity issue most commonly arises in disputes over the deductibility of interest on shareholder held debt, this issue also emerges in quite different contexts. As discussed in Chapter 2, when property is transferred to a corporation upon its formation, whether the shareholder is entitled to nonrecognition treatment, or the corporation is entitled to a fair market value basis in the contributed properties, depends in part upon the character of the instrument received by the transferor. Only the receipt of stock by the transferor is entitled to the nonrecognition benefit of Section 351. When property has been transferred to a corporation by a shareholder or a person related to a shareholder in exchange for a purported debt instrument, the IRS may seek to recharacterize the debt as stock and further assert that the stock was obtained in a Section 351 exchange. In disputes such as this, the courts tend to frame this issue as whether the property has been transferred to the corporation in a sale or in a Section 351 exchange. That issue, however, is largely resolved through the application of the traditional debt-equity analysis to the security issued in exchange for the property as the following case illustrates.

[¶ 3050]

BURR OAKS CORP. v. COMMISSIONER

United States Court of Appeals, Seventh Circuit, 1966.
365 F.2d 24.

KNOCH, CIRCUIT JUDGE:

The petitioners, Burr Oaks Corporation, A. Aaron Elkind and Rosella Elkind, Harold A. Watkins and Fannie G. Watkins, Maurice Ritz and

¶ **3050**

Esther Leah Ritz, instituted these proceedings in the Tax Court to contest deficiencies in income taxes determined against them. Mrs. Elkind, Mrs. Watkins and Mrs. Ritz are in these cases only because joint income tax returns were filed. * * * The Tax Court held that the transfer of certain land by the petitioners A. Aaron Elkind, Harold A. Watkins and Maurice Ritz (hereinafter called "the individual appellants") to the corporate appellant represented a contribution to capital and not a sale. Accordingly, the Tax Court determined a deficiency * * *.

* * *

The three individual appellants acquired a tract of undeveloped land in 1957 for $100,000, which the appellants state to be less than the then market value.

After discarding plans to develop a regional shopping center or an industrial park, the individual appellants decided to subdivide the land, improve it and sell lots. The Burr Oaks Corporation was formed. The individual appellants transferred the land to it, and, in return, each received a two-year 6% promissory note in the principal amount of $110,000. The sum of $30,000 still due on the original purchase was entered on the corporation's books as "Mortgage Payable." Another account "Land Contract Payable" in the amount of $330,000 represented the three notes.

At the trial in the Tax Court, the appellants' expert witness testified that the property transferred to the corporation was worth at least $360,000. The Tax Court, however, found more convincing the testimony of the Commissioner's expert witness * * *. On the basis of all the evidence adduced, the Tax Court found a fair market value of not more than $165,000 at the time of the transfer.

* * *

The Tax Court decided that the three promissory notes did not represent a true indebtedness. In 1959, these three notes, in the amount of $110,000 each, were surrendered by payment of $23,000 in cash on each note, and a new one-year promissory note dated November 1, 1959, in the amount of $87,000 at 6% was given in exchange for each of these three notes. Later the same year, the corporation paid $8,000 to each of three noteholders and issued new promissory notes in the amount of $79,000. On December 29, 1959, the corporation purported to pay these notes, although at the close of business that day it had a bank balance of only $5,398.88. Immediately after such purported payment, the three individual appellant-noteholders each lent the corporation $79,000 in return for three new one-year promissory notes dated December 31, 1959, in the amount of $79,000 each. The Tax Court construes this transaction as a mere extension of the maturity date. * * * Additional payments were made to each of the three individual appellants as follows:

¶ 3050

8/31/60	$ 8,000
1/31/61	15,000
12/31/61	10,000

Leaving a balance of $46,000 due each at the time of the trial. None of the earnings of the corporation were [sic] distributed to any of the shareholders of record.

Although the appellants all treated the transfer of the land in November, 1957, as a sale, the three individual appellants reported no gain until 1959 when the corporation "paid" the promissory notes issued at the transfer. In their returns for 1959, the three reported long-term capital gains of $85,729.06. The Commissioner determined that this was ordinary income. The Commissioner increased the corporation's taxable income for 1958 through 1960 on the ground that the corporation claimed too high a basis or cost for the land it sold during that period.

The Tax Court considered the "notes" to be preferred stock because the three holders occupied a preferred position compared to the common stockholders, the 6% interest constituting a prior charge on the earnings of the corporation.

The three individual appellants contend that they transferred the Burr Oaks property, a capital asset * * * to the corporation in return for promissory notes, valid indebtednesses incurred by the corporation, resulting in gain properly reportable in 1959 when the notes were paid in full. * * *

The corporation asserts that it bought the Burr Oaks property at a cost of $360,000 and that that should be its correct basis.

The Tax Court disregarded the form of the transaction and determined the substance of it to be not a sale but an equity contribution. Substance, rather than form, is the controlling factor in determining proper tax treatment. * * *

The Tax Court found the transfer lacking the essential characteristics of a sale, but, on the contrary, possessed of the elements normally found in equity contribution. See Emanuel N. Kolkey, 1956, 27 T.C. 37, affirmed, Kolkey v. Commissioner * * *, 7 Cir., 1958, 254 F.2d 51. In that case, certain criteria were established:

Was the capital and credit structure of the new corporation realistic? What was the business purpose, if any, of organizing the new corporation? Were the noteholders the actual promoters and entrepreneurs of the new adventure? Did the noteholders bear the principal risks of loss attendant upon the adventure? Were payments of "principal and interest" on the notes subordinated to dividends and to the claims of creditors? Did the noteholders have substantial control over the business operations; and, if so, was such control reserved to them, as an integral part of the plan under which

¶ 3050

the notes were issued? Was the "price" of the properties, for which the notes were issued, disproportionate to the fair market value of such properties? Did the noteholders, when default of the notes occurred, attempt to enforce the obligations?

In this case, the corporation was organized with a paid-in capital of only $4500, but shortly thereafter reflected liability of $360,000 on its books. Although it was anticipated that the City of Madison, Wisconsin, would pay the major costs of improvement of the tract to be subdivided, the corporation would have to incur development costs estimated at $100,000 or more. Within two months, the corporation borrowed $15,000 from individual appellant Aaron Elkind and on February 28, 1958, borrowed another $10,000 from him. Although the taxpayers assert that a number of lots were ready for sale and that heavy capitalization was therefore unnecessary, the sales were not so quickly made as to eliminate the need to borrow. The land was the corporation's only asset.

When the payment to the transferors is dependent on the success of an untried undercapitalized business with uncertain prospects, a strong inference arises that the transfer is an equity contribution.

* * *

* * * The three individual appellants challenge the finding that they controlled the corporation as their "notes" gave them no voting rights. Actually, the three individual appellants and their wives and brothers all transferred some property (land or money) to the corporation. All received equity interests of some kind, although not at exactly the same time, in the same transaction. Camp Wolters Enterprises v. Commissioner * * *, 5 Cir., 1956, 230 F.2d 555, 559, affirming 22 T.C. 737, 1954, cert. den. 352 U.S. 826 * * *. The Tax Court also observes that the Income Tax Regulations, § 1.351–1(a)(1) provide that the phrase "immediately after the exchange" does not necessarily require simultaneous exchanges by two or more persons, but also includes a situation where the rights of the parties have been previously defined and the execution of the agreement proceeds expeditiously consistent with orderly procedure.

The Tax Court thus fixed the corporation's basis for its property at $100,000, a carry-over basis from the transferors, pursuant to § 362(a)(1).

The Tax Court found the payments to the three individual appellants were governed by § 302(d) and that to the extent of the corporation's earnings and profits, these should be treated as dividends.

After close scrutiny of the entire record, we conclude that the decisions of the Tax Court are correct and must be affirmed.

* * *

¶ 3050

[¶ 3055]

Problem

Cases like *Burr Oaks* arise when taxpayers seek to avoid Section 351, normally to obtain a step-up in the basis of the property contributed to the corporation. As a result of changes in Section 351 over the years, achieving that result is not as difficult today as it once was. The use of nonqualified preferred stock which is treated as boot in a Section 351 exchange would seem to be one easy path to that result. Accordingly, only poorly advised taxpayers should lose a step-up in the basis of contributed property as a result of a debt-equity challenge. How would you structure an incorporation to assure the corporation a fair market value basis for its properties?

[¶ 3060]

5.   SHAREHOLDERS' GUARANTEES

In *Burr Oaks* the shareholders, or members of their family, transferred property to the corporation in exchange for purported debt, which the court then recharacterized as stock. An alternative approach to a comparable end result would be for the corporation to borrow from a bank or other unrelated lender and pay the borrowed funds over to the shareholder in exchange for the properties transferred to it. The corporation would be left in the same position except that it is indebted to the bank rather than the shareholder. The shareholder is somewhat better off in that the shareholder has cash in hand today rather than upon the maturity of the debt instrument. Unfortunately for tax purposes, to induce a bank to lend large sums to a new and often under-capitalized company, the shareholder usually must guarantee repayment of the bank's loan to the corporation. That factor has led the IRS to question whether the shareholder might be the real borrower in the transaction.

[¶ 3065]

PLANTATION PATTERNS, INC. v. COMMISSIONER

United States Court of Appeals, Fifth Circuit, 1972.
462 F.2d 712.

SIMPSON, CIRCUIT JUDGE:

[John S. Jemison, Jr. and Jemison Investment Company, of which he was the president and controlling shareholder, formed a new corporation, New Plantation, to purchase all of the stock of Old Plantation from unrelated individuals. All of the stock of New Plantation was issued to Mrs. Marie Jemison in exchange for a contribution of $5,000. Although Mr. Jemison was active in the management of New Plantation, Mrs. Jemison was not. New Plantation then obtained a loan from Bradford and Company in the amount of $150,000 in exchange for 6½% debentures which were subordinated to all other debt of New Plantation and which were not guaranteed. This loan was made to New Plantation "as an inducement to Mr. Jemison to place Mr. Bradford's son with New Plantation."

The payments for the stock of Old Plantation (exclusive of the amount paid for a portion of the business which was immediately resold to two of the selling shareholders) consisted of a down payment in cash of $100,000 and 5½% notes in the principal amount of $609,878.33. These notes, which were to be retired at the rate of $50,000 annually, were guaranteed by Mr. Jemison and by the Jemison Investment Company. Except for $100,000 of the notes, they were subordinated to all other debt of New Plantation except the notes to Bradford and Company. New Plantation paid principal and interest on each of these notes as it became due out of its earnings.

In a notice of deficiency to New Plantation, the Commissioner disallowed the deduction for interest on the 5½% notes.]

The Tax Court held that all steps taken by Mr. Jemison and the shareholders of Old Plantation were parts of a single transaction for the purchase by New Plantation of the wrought iron furniture business of Old Plantation, and, applying the relevant factors with respect to debt-equity situations to the facts here, one of which was found to be thin capitalization, that the guaranteed debt must be treated as an indirect contribution to New Plantation's capital by Mr. Jemison. Therefore, it held that New Plantation was not entitled to deductions claimed under Code Section 163 for interest on the 5½% serial notes in its taxable years ended September 30, 1963 to September 30, 1966 and that the Jemisons were taxable in 1963 under Code Sections 301 and 316 with the principal and interest payments on these guaranteed notes in that year.[7] Their deficiency was fixed at $28,403.91.

II.   THE ISSUES ON APPEAL

The issues presented for our consideration are these:

1.   Whether $100,000 of guaranteed 5½% serial debentures issued by New Plantation to the sellers of Old Plantation are to be treated as debt for income tax purposes where the notes were not subordinated and were paid when due by New Plantation without recourse to other financing?

2.   Whether $509,878.33 of guaranteed 5½% notes issued by New Plantation to the sellers of Old Plantation are to be treated as debt for income tax purposes where the notes were subordinated to general

---

7.   The Tax Court allowed the Jemisons a deduction for interest paid the sellers by New Plantation.

creditors but were senior to $150,000 of other debentures which the Tax Court did treat as debt for income tax purposes?

3. Whether Jemison Investment Company, a co-guarantor, rather than John S. Jemison, Jr., a co-guarantor, should be deemed to have made the contribution to the equity capital of New Plantation in the event that any of the $609,878.33 principal amount of 5½% notes is deemed to represent a contribution to the equity capital of New Plantation?

III. THE RELEVANT LAW

The criteria for adjudicating debt-equity cases were set forth most clearly by Judge Jones for this Court in 1963 in Montclair, Inc. v. C. I. R., 5 Cir., 1963, 318 F.2d 38. At page 40 of Volume 318 F.2d the factors which bear most strongly on the determination of the label to be applied to the transaction are enunciated:

> "(1) The names given to the certificates evidencing the indebtedness; (2) the presence or absence of a maturity date; (3) the source of the payments; (4) the right to enforce the payment of principal and interest; (5) participation in management; (6) a status equal to or inferior to that of regular corporate creditors; (7) the intent of the parties; (8) 'thin' or adequate capitalization; (9) identity of interest between creditor and stockholder; (10) payment of interest only out of 'dividend' money; (11) the ability of the corporation to obtain loans from outside lending institutions."

Since *Montclair, Inc.* consideration of debt-equity cases has frequently demanded the attention of this Court. * * * In applying these factors, each case must be decided on its own facts, and no one standard is controlling. * * * The tests are not "talismans of magical power", and the most that can be said is that they are a source of helpful guidance. * * * Thus we decide debt-equity issues by a case by case analysis, applying the *Montclair* rubrics as best we can to the facts at hand.

IV. TREATMENT OF THE $100,000 UNSUBORDINATED 5½% DEBENTURES AND THE $509,878.33 PARTIALLY SUBORDINATED 5½% NOTES

* * *

* * * Taxpayers contend that it is anomalous and inconsistent for the Tax Court to characterize the $509,878.33 partially subordinated debentures as equity while at the same time characterizing inferior fully subordinated debentures held by Bradford and Company as debt, arguing that if the fully subordinated 6½% notes held by Bradford and Company are equity, surely the $509,878.33 debentures are entitled to the same treatment.

* * *

Without receding from their strong stand that the 5½% debentures constitute debt, the taxpayers alternatively argue that if the court should hold that such notes do not constitute debt, the same equity treatment should be given to the 6½% subordinated debentures held by Bradford and Company. Stated otherwise, they argue that if the 5½% *partially* subordinated debentures are to be regarded as equity, then the 6½% totally subordinated debentures should logically be deemed to constitute preferred stock in New Plantation. Taxpayers point out that long-term debt held by non-stockholders has been held to be an equity interest in the nature of preferred stock. Foresun, Inc. v. Commissioner of Internal Revenue, 6 Cir. 1965, 348 F.2d 1006, affirming 41 T.C. 706 (1964). Taxpayers claim that they were denied the right to further trial on this point in the Tax Court, and they contend that at the very least this Court should remand the case to the Tax Court to permit development of further evidence as to the treatment to be given the $150,000 in Bradford and Company notes. If these notes are regarded as equity, taxpayers argue that the debt-equity ratio of New Plantation would be approximately 4 to 1 ($609,878.33 to $155,000), and not the plus 125 to 1 ratio which the government asserts is the proper debt-equity ratio ($759,878.33 to $5,000). This would effectively demolish the Tax Court finding of thin capitalization.

The Commissioner answers these contentions with the familiar tax law precept: substance and not form determines proper tax treatment for a transaction, urging that the substance of this transaction is that a corporation was sold for a price more than $600,000 in excess of its net worth, with payment promised by a new corporation without significant capital or other assets, whose only solidarity was the guarantee of the individual taxpayer, Mr. Jemison. The Commissioner continues that the guarantee was in reality a contribution of capital and that in substance the payments on the notes were dividends on the Jemison capital investment taxable to them as income.

* * *

Resolving these two conflicting views of this amorphous transaction is no easy task, but we are not persuaded that the taxpayers have successfully demonstrated the incorrectness of the position taken by the Tax Court. Certainly we recognize that this transaction was initially cast to have all of the outward appearances of a debt transaction, complete with instruments styled "debentures" which had fixed maturity dates. But these surface considerations do not end our examination. Closer scrutiny establishes that the other factors which would give the transaction the aura of debt are noticeable by their absence.

Of critical importance in determining whether financial input is debt or equity is whether or not the money is expended for capital assets. In the instant case the substantial portion of the $609,878.33 was directed to the purchase of capital assets and to finance initial operations. In

¶ 3065

contrast, only $5,000.00 was set up as equity to finance launching of the corporate venture.

Other equity factors exist. While the sellers were ostensibly to look to the corporation for payment of the debt, it is apparent from the meager capital position of the company that Mr. Jemison's guarantee was regarded as the real undergirding for the deal. Our conclusion is reinforced by noting that the sellers apparently considered financially acceptable the agreement to subordinate the great majority of the 5½% debentures to almost all other corporate indebtedness so long as the debentures were guaranteed by Mr. Jemison. Mr. Jemison's guarantee was, of course, an obligation primary in nature.

Further, while Mrs. Jemison was the stockholder of record, and Mr. Jemison on the surface was only a guarantor, surrounding circumstances clearly demonstrate that Mr. Jemison completely controlled the shares held by Mrs. Jemison. Mrs. Jemison seldom attended the meetings of the corporation, and took little active interest in it. In contrast, Mr. Jemison was intimately and continuously involved in the operations of New Plantation. Regarding Mr. Jemison as the "constructive" owner of the stock, we have an identity of interest between the stockholder and the guarantor—a factor which points strongly toward equity treatment.

The record cannot support a determination by us that the Tax Court's finding that New Plantation was thinly capitalized is "clearly erroneous". The balance sheet of the corporation showed that its quick assets (cash and accounts receivables) of $317,000 could not cover its current liabilities of approximately $490,000. This ratio is one of the acid test indicators used by businessmen to determine the health of a business. After the dissolution of Old Plantation the new corporation had tangible assets, at fair market value, of approximately $1,064,000 securing debts of approximately $1,078,000. We regard this as thin capitalization, as did the Tax Court.

The guarantee enabled Mr. Jemison to put a minimum amount of cash into New Plantation immediately, and to avoid any further cash investment in the corporation unless and until it should fall on hard times. At the same time he exercised total control over its management. Adding together the personal guarantee of Mr. Jemison to the guarantee of Jemison Investment Company, which was wholly owned by him and Mr. Jemison's control of New Plantation, we think that the result is that Mr. Jemison's guarantee simply amounted to a covert way of putting his money "at the risk of the business". Stated differently, the guarantee enabled Mr. Jemison to create borrowing power for the corporation which normally would have existed only through the presence of more adequate capitalization of New Plantation.

We do not regard as significant the fact that ultimately things progressed smoothly for New Plantation and that its debts were paid without additional financing. The question is not whether, looking back

¶ 3065

in time, the transaction was ultimately successful or not, but rather whether at its inception there was a reasonable expectation that the business would succeed on its own. The transaction must be judged on the conditions that existed when the deal was consummated, and not on conditions as they developed with the passage of time. * * * When New Plantation was incorporated its prospects of business success were questionable indeed without the Jemison guarantees.

We hold also that the Tax Court was correct in refusing to give value to the intangible financial skills of Mr. Jemison for purposes of computing the corporation's debt-equity ratio. * * * In our view courts should be wary in giving weight to such intangible assets as those attributed to Mr. Jemison. Certainly business acumen or financial wizardry of stockholders or corporate management could not properly be valued and placed on the corporate balance sheet under generally accepted principles of accounting, although they might afford window dressing in a footnote. * * * [W]e conclude that intangible assets such as those claimed for Mr. Jemison have no place in assessing debt-equity ratio unless it can be shown by convincing evidence that the intangible asset has a direct and primary relationship to the well-being of the corporation. Additionally it seems clear to us that the assets sought to be valued must be something more than management skills and normal business contacts. These are expected of management in the direction of any corporation.

* * *

Our holding does not require that we find the notes held by Bradford and Company to be equity interests. While the Bradford and Company notes were subordinated, subordination is far from the sole criterion for determining whether an interest is debt or equity. It is not controlling. Aside from this single factor this record is productive of nothing to indicate that this was not a bona fide loan made by Bradford with the primary motive of inducing New Plantation to employ young Bradford. We agree with the Tax Court that this was a legitimate loan.

V. SHOULD THE EQUITY CONTRIBUTION BE DEEMED TO HAVE BEEN MADE BY JEMISON INVESTMENT COMPANY RATHER THAN BY MR. JEMISON?

The Tax Court found that the equity contribution was to be attributed to Mr. Jemison and not to Jemison Investment Company. Although acknowledging that Jemison Investment Company received a fee of $15,000.00 for its guarantee on the notes, the Tax Court reasoned that inasmuch as Mr. Jemison controlled both Jemison Investment and New Plantation, the fee for the guarantee was either a matter of internal accounting or for cosmetic effect, and not an indication that the sellers of Old Plantation realistically looked to Jemison Investment Company for any security. It is uncontested that practically all of Mr. Jemison's assets consisted of stock in Jemison Investment Company. It owned the house he lived in and the automobile he drove, but he owned it in its entirety. Furthermore, the Tax Court found that the sellers of Old Plantation only investigated the credit of Mr. Jemison, and that the Messrs. Jernigans as sellers looked at all times to Mr. Jemison's guarantee as the real insurance for the notes.

Although the appellants cast some doubt on the Tax Court's finding that the sellers did not investigate the financial statements of the Jemison Investment Company, in no other respect have they demonstrated error in the Tax Court's conclusion that through all of the haze of corporate red tape, the real financial keystone supporting the entire deal, the person to whom the sellers ultimately looked for their protection in the event of the failure of New Plantation was Mr. John S. Jemison, Jr.

VI.   Conclusion

Error is not demonstrated on this record. None of the Tax Court's Findings and Conclusions based upon stipulated facts are shown to be "clearly erroneous". The decision of the Tax Court as to all matters raised by this appeal is

Affirmed.

[¶ 3070]

Notes

1.   Note carefully the court's holding. Were the 5½% notes held by non-shareholders recharacterized as stock? If not, why exactly was the debt-equity analysis even relevant, much less dispositive?

2.   In *Plantation Patterns* the debt to equity ratio was extreme and that factor influenced the court. On less extreme facts, the Commissioner has had less success in attacking the character of shareholder guaranteed loans. See, e.g., Murphy Logging Co. v. United States, 378 F.2d 222 (9th Cir.1967).

3.   If Jemison is regarded as borrowing an amount equal to the purchase price for the stock of Old Plantation and contributing that amount to the capital of New Plantation, should not New Plantation be regarded as having assumed Jemison's liability? How would that assumption be treated under Section 357(d)(1)(A) (which was enacted long after the decision in *Plantation Patterns*)?

[¶ 3075]

D.   TAX TREATMENT OF A CORPORATION'S INVESTORS

In designing the capital structure of a corporation, the income tax consequences of the various securities to their holders will be one of the more important considerations. Since investors tend to be optimists, their primary focus normally is on the taxation of the anticipated profit from the investment. Their customary objective is to convert the corporate earnings into cash in the hands of the investor at the lowest overall tax cost. Tax advisors, however, need to be more pessimistic. While seeking to reduce the tax burden on profitable ventures, the advisor must keep one eye on maximizing the tax benefit obtained on withdrawing from unsuccessful ventures. The following materials address both sides of the coin.

[¶ 3080]

1. TAXATION OF POSITIVE RETURNS ON INVESTMENTS

a. *Stock*

Under current law, shareholders are subject to a maximum rate of tax of 15 percent upon the realization of their share of corporate earnings—whether realized as a dividend or as gain on the sale of stock held for one year or longer. Gain on stock held for a shorter term is taxed as ordinary income at rates ranging up to 35 percent. That 15 percent rate of tax compares quite favorably, of course, to the taxation of other types of ordinary income, including interest. Nevertheless, returns on stock, at least those paid to individuals, are the most heavily taxed method of transmitting wealth from the corporation to the investors. When that 15 percent rate is combined with the corporate income tax, the overall rate of tax on corporate profits is almost always greater than the tax imposed on profits distributed in other ways or on the profits of an unincorporated enterprise. Accordingly, from the perspective of withdrawing funds from a continuing corporation, stock is the least attractive security.

The 15 percent rate of tax on dividends has created one exception to that generalization. If the taxable income of the corporation is below $100,000, the combination of the corporate and shareholder level rates of tax on dividends may be lower than the combination of the individual rate of tax on salary and the social security taxes on salary which now exceed 15 percent. As a result, at some point it may become preferable for a corporation to stop paying deductible salary to a shareholder-employee and start paying dividends.

On a sale of stock, as on any sale of property, the seller is entitled to offset the cost or other tax basis of the property sold against the proceeds of sale in the computation of the taxable gain. That basis is thus recovered free of tax. Since no such basis recovery is allowable on the receipt of a dividend, the proceeds of a sale will generally be subject to less tax than would a dividend. Moreover, if the corporation can qualify under one of the provisions designed to encourage investment in small business, that rate can be reduced further.

¶ 3075

Section 1202. Section 1202 provides an opportunity for noncorporate investors, including owners of pass-through entities, to exclude up to 50 percent of the capital gains from dispositions of "qualified small business stock" held for more than five years. When initially enacted, this 50 percent exclusion meant that gains eligible for Section 1202 treatment qualified for an effective maximum tax rate of no more than one-half the investor's usual long-term capital gain tax rate. No longer, however, does the tax break under Section 1202 reduce by a full one-half the preferential capital gain rates that would otherwise apply in its absence. This is because Section 1(h) excepts the preferentially treated Section 1202 gains from the most favorable capital gain rates now available—which can be as low as 5 percent. Consequently, under the Section 1202 relief, the effective maximum tax rate on eligible qualified gains will continue to equal one-half of 28 percent. Obviously, today the tax benefit under Section 1202 is not as significant as it was in the past.

Section 1202 imposes a number of restrictions, all integral to the statutory purpose of stimulating an infusion of new equity/risk capital into small start-up ventures in fields not excluded by the statute. To implement this goal, eligible stock is confined to that issued after August 10, 1993, by certain corporations of a limited size[1] that are engaged in actively conducting a qualified trade or business (e.g., a business generally not heavily invested in real estate or securities and not operating in designated lines of activity, such as the performance of certain services).[2] To ensure that the benefits extend only to newly attracted capital, the provision contains anti-churning rules[3] and restricts its benefits to stock issued initially in exchange for cash or property or as compensation. Thus, stock issued in exchange for other stock does not generally qualify. However, tax free rollovers of qualified stock incident to Section 351 or reorganization exchanges will not cause a forfeiture of benefits for the substituted stock. To ensure that the potential exclusion applies only to gains developed from and engendered by investments in a qualified small business, "built-in gains" on property contributed to a qualified corporation do not qualify for favorable treatment; rather, basis for purposes of determining qualified gain is the fair market value at date of contribution of property contributed to a qualified small business.

Not all gains from stock in a qualified small business are eligible for Section 1202 treatment. Eligible stock includes only that held for more than five years. Furthermore, the maximum gain that can qualify for Section 1202 treatment is the greater of (i) $10 million total cumulative

---

1. The aggregate gross assets of the corporation cannot exceed $50 million at any time between August 10, 1993, and the date the stock is issued. § 1202(d)(1) and (2).

2. At least 80 percent of the corporate assets must be used in businesses other than (i) professional services such as law and medicine, (ii) banking and finance, (iii) farming, (iv) production or extraction of minerals for which percentage depletion is available, and (v) hotels, motels and restaurants. § 1202(c)(2)(A) and (e)(1) and (3).

3. These rules disqualify stock issued relatively shortly before or after the corporation's retirement of other stock. § 1202(c)(3).

¶ 3080

gain per issuer ($5 million per spouse in the case of married individuals filing separately) or (ii) 10 times the taxpayer's adjusted basis in the qualified stock disposed of by the taxpayer during the year. § 1202(b). In addition, Section 1202(k) authorizes regulations to prevent taxpayers' avoidance of the purpose of the statute by, for example, dividing corporate activity into multiple entities so as to circumvent the statutory monetary ceilings.

Sections 1044 and 1045. A companion provision enacted with Section 1202, but of more modest reach, is Section 1044. This provision authorizes taxpayers by election to defer realized gains from dispositions of publicly traded securities if the proceeds are promptly (within 60 days) reinvested in a specialized small business investment company. Section 1044 can operate independently from or as a supplement to Section 1202. Annual ceilings cap the amount excludable on a qualifying rollover. For individuals, these are the lesser of (i) $50,000 ($25,000 if married and filing a separate return) or (ii) $500,000 ($250,000 if married and filing a separate return) reduced by any gain previously excludible under Section 1044. For C corporations, the limits are increased to the lesser of (i) $250,000 annually or (ii) $1 million cumulatively.

The corporations and partnerships that qualify for status as "specialized small business investment companies" are those licensed by the Small Business Administration under Section 301(d) of the Small Business Investment Act of 1958, (i.e., investment companies that finance small businesses owned by disadvantaged taxpayers). The "publicly traded" securities that qualify for tax-free rollover treatment are securities that are traded on an established exchange and presumably include debt as well as equity interests.

Section 1045 authorizes an additional and analogous election to roll over the gains arising from dispositions of stock described in Section 1202 and held for more than six months. As with Section 1044, in order to avoid recognizing the realized gain, Section 1045 requires a reinvestment within 60 days of the disposition into other "qualified small business stock" described in Section 1202.

[¶ 3085]

b. Debt

Interest, the current return to the holder of a debt security, is not eligible for the 15 percent tax rate and thus remains taxable to the investor at ordinary income tax rates. While, from the perspective of the investor, interest is thus taxed more heavily than are dividends, the overall tax burden on amounts paid by a corporation as interest is far less than the tax burden on amounts distributed as dividends because the payment of interest is normally deductible by the payor. That deduction eliminates the corporate level tax on the earnings distributed as interest and thus effectively removes those earnings from the double tax system. Accordingly, debt is generally regarded as superior to stock as a vehicle for removing cash from corporate solution.

Amounts distributed by a corporation in retirement of a debt instrument normally are not deductible by the payor and thus corporate earnings used for that purpose do not avoid the corporate level tax. However, in most instances, a debt holder will have a tax basis for the debt approximately equal to the amounts paid in retirement of the security. As a result, the repayment normally will be free of tax to the investor. Since the transfer of cash from the corporation to the investor in retirement of a debt instrument is generally subject to only a single level of tax, it also will be taxed more lightly than the sale or redemption of stock.

Original issue discount. If a debt instrument is issued in exchange for an amount that is materially less than the amount that will be paid to the investor upon the retirement of the debt, that difference is referred to as "discount." When that discount arises at the time the debt instrument is originally sold to the investor, it is referred to as "original issue discount" or OID. OID, which arises because the debt does not bear an adequate stated interest, is treated as interest for virtually all purposes under the Code. § 1272. OID is equal to the excess of the redemption price of the instrument at maturity over the issue price although OID in an amount less than 1/4 of 1 percent per year is ignored. § 1273(a). The amount of OID attributable to each day that the instrument is to be outstanding is calculated using semiannual compounding of interest. That daily amount must then be taken into income by the holder of the instrument, and deducted by the issuer, on a daily basis notwithstanding that the amount of the discount will not in fact be paid prior to the maturity of the instrument. The tax basis of an instrument is increased annually by the OID included in income. Because taxpayers are understandably unwilling to report income that they will not receive currently, most instruments containing significant OID are held by tax-exempt entities such as pension trusts.

The identification of the issue price for a debt instrument is slightly complicated when the instrument is issued in exchange for property. In principle, the issue price should be the market value of the property given in exchange. However, to avoid difficult valuation issues, the Code treats the issue price of such a security as the computed value of the debt security on the date it is issued, on the assumption that the value of the security should be equal to the value of the property exchanged for the security. § 1274. The value of the security is computed by discounting the amount of all payments due under the instrument to present value using a discount rate equal to the "applicable Federal rate," which the Treasury Department determines and publishes monthly.

If a debt instrument having a principal amount of $2 million or less is issued in exchange for property and the seller-lender uses the cash method of accounting, the parties may jointly elect to avoid the OID rules. In the event of such an election, both the borrower and the lender will report the interest on the instrument under the cash method.

If a debt instrument is issued as one component of an investment unit that is sold for a single price, the selling price must be allocated between the debt instrument and the stock or option included in the unit on the basis of the value of each component. The amount allocated to the debt instrument constitutes the issue price for the debt security. Interestingly, no such allocation is required when a convertible debt instrument is sold. Although convertible debt is equivalent to an investment unit consisting of a debt security and an option, the regulations treat the entire amount paid for the security as the issue price of the debt instrument. Reg. § 1.1273–2(j). The principal effect of this rule is to disallow any deduction for this element of discount to the issuer.

Bond premium. When the stated interest on a debt instrument is higher than a market rate of interest, the bond will be sold at a premium, rather than a discount. To the issuer, the premium received is an offset to the interest that must be paid and thus must be taken into income to offset the interest deduction. To the purchaser of the bond, premium is effectively a return of a portion of the interest received. The purchaser is allowed to allocate that premium over all interest payments to be received using the same principles applicable to OID and to take an annual deduction for the allocated amounts. § 171.

Redemption premium. When the terms of a debt security allow the issuer to redeem the security prior to maturity, the issuer may be required to pay an amount in excess of the normal redemption price upon such an early retirement. Such a call premium protects the investor against the loss of the benefit of his or her bargain. Normally, such a premium is deductible by the issuer and income to the investor. However, if the security is convertible, the issuer is prohibited from deducting the portion of the premium attributable to the conversion feature. § 249. Rather, the deduction is limited to the amount of a normal call premium on non-convertible debt.

Conversion. The terms of a debt instrument sometimes provide that the instrument may be exchanged for a fixed number of shares of stock in the issuer. The following ruling addresses the income tax consequences of that exchange.

[¶ 3090]

REVENUE RULING 72–265

1972–1 C.B. 222.

Advice has been requested concerning the Federal income tax consequences to the owner of a corporate debenture of his exercise of the right, provided for in the debenture, to surrender it and to receive in exchange common stock of the corporation.

A purchased on the open market in 1967 for 500x dollars a debenture of Y corporation with a principal amount of 500x dollars. The terms of the offering of this issue of debentures in 1965 had included a provision that, at any time before January 1, 1970, the holder of any debenture could surrender all or part (in multiples of 100x dollars of principal amount) of his holdings of this issue of debentures and would receive 20 shares of Y common stock for each 100x dollars of principal amount of the debentures surrendered. In 1969 A exercised the right to surrender the debenture and received therefor 100 shares of Y common stock with a total fair market value of 1000x dollars.

Section 1001(a) * * * provides that the gain from the sale or other disposition of property shall be the excess of the amount realized therefrom over the adjusted basis for determining gain, and the loss shall be the excess of the adjusted basis for determining loss over the amount realized.

The conclusion that no gain or loss is realized upon the conversion of a corporate debenture into stock of the obligor corporation was initially stated in Article 1563 of Treasury Regulations 45 (1920 edition) under the Revenue Act of 1918. This rule remains applicable except where provisions of the Code specifically require that gain be recognized. See Revenue Ruling 72–264, [1972–1 C.B. 131]. No gain is therefore realized by A upon his exercise of the right to surrender the debenture for common stock. Similarly, the unadjusted basis of the 100 shares of Y common stock is 500x dollars, the cost of the debenture. The conversion of a debenture into stock of a different corporation, however, is a taxable event. See Revenue Ruling 69–135, C.B.1969–1, 198.

[¶ 3095]

Note

The conclusion that no gain is realized on the conversion of a debt instrument is difficult to square with more modern authorities such as Cottage Savings Assn. v. Commissioner, 499 U.S. 554 (1991). A better basis for the result reached in Rev. Rul. 72–265 might be that the gain, while realized, would not be recognized. The difficulty with that theory, however, is that nonrecognition is for Congress to grant, not the courts or the Treasury Department, and Congress has not done so. The conversion might be viewed as an open transaction with the tax consequences to await the final disposition of the investment. But, the normal justification for open transaction reporting, the inability to value the amount realized, seems to be missing. Whatever the theoretical weakness, the result in Rev. Rul. 72–265 is firmly established.

[¶ 3100]

2. TAX TREATMENT OF LOSSES

Normally an investment in a corporation, whether in the form of stock or debt, will be a capital asset in the hands of the investor. As a result, if the investment is sold at a loss, the loss will be a capital loss and subject to the rather strict limitations on the ability to deduct capital losses in Section 1211. Even when the investment becomes worthless, the loss remains a capital loss. See §§ 165(g) and 166(d). There are, however, some important exceptions to this unhappy generalization. Unfortunately, the opportunities for ordinary losses are quite different for stock and debt. Accordingly, the ability to claim a loss on an investment is another factor to be taken into account in planning the capital structure of a corporation.

[¶ 3105]

a. Debt

A loss incurred by an individual on a loan to a corporation will be deductible as an ordinary loss, rather than subject to the capital loss limitations, if the loan is not evidenced by an investment grade security (see Sections 166(e) and 165(g)) and the loan can avoid classification as a "nonbusiness" debt under Section 166(d). In general that means that the debt must be created or acquired in connection with a trade or business of the lending taxpayer or that the loss must be incurred in the taxpayer's trade or business.

In Whipple v. Commissioner, 373 U.S. 193 (1963), the taxpayer had organized several corporations engaged in various business activities and devoted substantially all of his time to these business activities. After a loan to one such corporation had become worthless, the taxpayer sought a bad debt deduction which the Court denied, observing that:

> Devoting one's time and energies to the affairs of a corporation is not of itself, and without more, a trade or business of the person so engaged. Though such activities may produce income, profit or gain in the form of dividends or enhancement in the value of an investment, this return is distinctive to the process of investing and is generated by the successful operation of the corporation's business as distinguished from the trade or business of the taxpayer himself. When the only return is that of an investor, the taxpayer has not satisfied his burden of demonstrating that he is engaged in a trade or business since investing is not a trade or business and the return to the taxpayer, though substantially the product of his services, legally arises not from his own trade or business but from that of the corporation. Even if the taxpayer demonstrates an independent trade or business of his own, care must be taken to distinguish bad debt losses arising from his own business and those

¶ 3100

actually arising from activities peculiar to an investor concerned with, and participating in, the conduct of the corporate business.

373 U.S. At 202.

Since the taxpayer was not himself engaged in the business of forming corporations for the purpose of selling them to customers nor in the business of loaning money to corporations, the worthlessness of the loans constituted nonbusiness bad debts. After *Whipple*, few promoters could avoid capital loss treatment for their loans. On the other hand, an individual's employment does constitute a trade or business and that rule opened one small window for ordinary loss treatment.

[¶ 3110]

UNITED STATES v. GENERES

Supreme Court of the United States, 1972.
405 U.S. 93.

MR. JUSTICE BLACKMUN delivered the opinion of the Court.

A debt a closely held corporation owed to an indemnifying share-holder-employee became worthless in 1962. The issue in this federal income tax refund suit is whether, for the shareholder-employee, that worthless obligation was a business or a nonbusiness bad debt within the meaning and reach of §§ 166(a) and (d) * * *, and of the implementing Regs. § 1.166–5.

The issue's resolution is important for the taxpayer. If the obligation was a business debt, he may use it to offset ordinary income and for carryback purposes under § 172 of the Code * * *. On the other hand, if the obligation is a nonbusiness debt, it is to be treated as a short-term capital loss subject to the restrictions imposed on such losses by § 166(d)(1)(B) and §§ 1211 and 1212, and its use for carryback purposes is restricted by § 172(d)(4). The debt is one or the other in its entirety, for the Code does not provide for its allocation in part to business and in part to nonbusiness.

In determining whether a bad debt is a business or a nonbusiness obligation, the Regulations focus on the relation the loss bears to the taxpayer's business. If, at the time of worthlessness, that relation is a "proximate" one, the debt qualifies as a business bad debt and the aforementioned desirable tax consequences then ensue.

The present case turns on the proper measure of the required proximate relation. Does this necessitate a "dominant" business motivation on the part of the taxpayer or is a "significant" motivation sufficient?

* * *

¶ 3110

I

The taxpayer as a young man in 1909 began work in the construction business. His son-in-law, William F. Kelly, later engaged independently in similar work. During World War II the two men formed a partnership * * *. In 1954 Kelly–Generes Construction Co., Inc., was organized as the corporate successor to the partnership. It engaged in the heavy-construction business, primarily on public works projects.

The taxpayer and Kelly each owned 44% of the corporation's outstanding capital stock. The taxpayer's original investment in his shares was $38,900. The remaining 12% of the stock was owned by a son of the taxpayer and by another son-in-law. Mr. Generes was president of the corporation and received from it an annual salary of $12,000. Mr. Kelly was executive vice-president and received an annual salary of $15,000.

* * *

Taxpayer Generes from time to time advanced personal funds to the corporation to enable it to complete construction jobs. He also guaranteed loans made to the corporation by banks for the purchase of construction machinery and other equipment. In addition, his presence with respect to the bid and performance bonds is of particular significance. Most of these were obtained from Maryland Casualty Co. That underwriter required the taxpayer and Kelly to sign an indemnity agreement for each bond it issued for the corporation. In 1958, however, in order to eliminate the need for individual indemnity contracts, taxpayer and Kelly signed a blanket agreement with Maryland whereby they agreed to indemnify it, up to a designated amount, for any loss it suffered as surety for the corporation. Maryland then increased its line of surety credit to $2,000,000. The corporation had over $14,000,000 gross business for the period 1954 through 1962.

In 1962 the corporation seriously underbid two projects and defaulted in its performance of the project contracts. It proved necessary for Maryland to complete the work. Maryland then sought indemnity from Generes and Kelly. The taxpayer indemnified Maryland to the extent of $162,104.57. In the same year he also loaned $158,814.49 to the corporation to assist it in its financial difficulties. The corporation subsequently went into receivership and the taxpayer was unable to obtain reimbursement from it.

In his federal income tax return for 1962 the taxpayer took his loss on his direct loans to the corporation as a nonbusiness bad debt. He claimed the indemnification loss as a business bad debt and deducted it against ordinary income. Later he filed claims for refund for 1959–1961, asserting net operating loss carrybacks under § 172 to those years for the portion, unused in 1962, of the claimed business bad debt deduction.

In due course the claims were made the subject of the jury trial refund suit in the United States District Court for the Eastern District

¶ 3110

of Louisiana. At the trial Mr. Generes testified that his sole motive in signing the indemnity agreement was to protect his $12,000–a-year employment with the corporation. The jury, by special interrogatory, was asked to determine whether taxpayer's signing of the indemnity agreement with Maryland "was proximately related to his trade or business of being an employee" of the corporation. The District Court charged the jury, over the Government's objection, that *significant* motivation satisfies the Regulations' requirement of proximate relationship.[6] The court refused the Government's request for an instruction that the applicable standard was that of *dominant* rather than significant motivation.[7]

After twice returning to the court for clarification of the instruction given, the jury found that the taxpayer's signing of the indemnity agreement was proximately related to his trade or business of being an employee of the corporation. Judgment on this verdict was then entered for the taxpayer.

The Fifth Circuit majority approved the significant-motivation standard so specified * * *.

II

A. The fact responsible for the litigation is the taxpayer's dual status relative to the corporation. Generes was both a shareholder and an employee. These interests are not the same, and their differences occasion different tax consequences. In tax jargon, Generes' status as a shareholder was a nonbusiness interest. * * * On the other hand, Generes' status as an employee was a business interest. * * *

Thus, for tax purposes it becomes important and, indeed, necessary to determine the character of the debt that went bad and became uncollectible. Did the debt center on the taxpayer's business interest in the corporation or on his nonbusiness interest? If it was the former, the taxpayer deserves to prevail here. * * *

B. Although arising in somewhat different contexts, two tax cases decided by the Court in recent years merit initial mention. In each of these cases a major shareholder paid out money to or on behalf of his

---

6. "A debt is proximately related to the taxpayer's trade or business when its creation was significantly motivated by the taxpayer's trade or business, and it is not rendered a non-business debt merely because there was a non-qualifying motivation as well, even though the non-qualifying motivation was the primary one."

7. "You must, in short, determine whether Mr. Generes' dominant motivation in signing the indemnity agreement was to protect his salary and status as an employee or was to protect his investment in the Kelly–Generes Construction Co.

"Mr. Generes is entitled to prevail in this case only if he convinces you that the dominant motivating factor for his signing the indemnity agreement was to insure the receiving of his salary from the company. It is insufficient if the protection or insurance of his salary was only a significant secondary motivation for his signing the indemnity agreement. It must have been his dominant or most important reason for signing the indemnity agreement."

¶ **3110**

corporation and then was unable to obtain reimbursement from it. In each he claimed a deduction assertable against ordinary income. In each he was unsuccessful in this quest:

1. In Putnam v. Commissioner, 352 U.S. 82 (1956), the taxpayer was a practicing lawyer who had guaranteed obligations of a labor newspaper corporation in which he owned stock. He claimed his loss as fully deductible * * *. The Court rejected this approach and held that the loss was a nonbusiness bad debt subject to short-term capital loss treatment * * *.

2. In Whipple v. Commissioner, 373 U.S. 193 (1963), the taxpayer had provided organizational, promotional, and managerial services to a corporation in which he owned approximately an 80% stock interest. He claimed that this constituted a trade or business and, hence, that debts owing him by the corporation were business bad debts when they became worthless in 1953. The Court also rejected that contention and held that Whipple's investing was not a trade or business, that is, that "[d]evoting one's time and energies to the affairs of a corporation is not of itself, and without more, a trade or business of the person so engaged." 373 U.S., at 202. The rationale was that a contrary conclusion would be inconsistent with the principle that a corporation has a personality separate from its shareholders and that its business is not necessarily their business. * * * The Court also carefully noted the distinction between the business and the nonbusiness bad debt for one who is both an employee and a shareholder.[8]

* * *

III

We conclude that in determining whether a bad debt has a "proximate" relation to the taxpayer's trade or business, as the Regulations specify, and thus qualifies as a business bad debt, the proper measure is that of dominant motivation, and that only significant motivation is not sufficient. We reach this conclusion for a number of reasons:

A. The Code itself carefully distinguishes between business and nonbusiness items. * * * It does this despite the fact that the latter are just as adverse in financial consequence to the taxpayer as are the former. But this distinction has been a policy of the income tax structure ever since the Revenue Act of 1916, § 5(a), 39 Stat. 759, provided differently for trade or business losses than it did for losses sustained in another transaction entered into for profit. * * *

The point, however, is that the tax statutes have made the distinction, that the Congress therefore intended it to be a meaningful one, and

---

8. "Even if the taxpayer demonstrates an independent trade or business of his own, care must be taken to distinguish bad debt losses arising from his own business and those actually arising from activities peculiar to an investor concerned with, and participating in, the conduct of the corporate business." 373 U.S., at 202.

that the distinction is not to be obliterated or blunted by an interpretation that tends to equate the business bad debt with the nonbusiness bad debt. We think that emphasis upon the significant rather than upon the dominant would have a tendency to do just that.

B. Application of the significant-motivation standard would also tend to undermine and circumscribe the Court's holding in Whipple and the emphasis there that a shareholder's mere activity in a corporation's affairs is not a trade or business. As Chief Judge Lumbard pointed out in his separate and disagreeing concurrence in Weddle, supra, 325 F.2d at 852–853, both motives—that of protecting the investment and that of protecting the salary—are inevitably involved, and an inquiry whether employee status provides a significant motivation will always produce an affirmative answer and result in a judgment for the taxpayer.

C. The dominant-motivation standard has the attribute of workability. It provides a guideline of certainty for the trier of fact. * * *

* * *

IV

The conclusion we have reached means that the District Court's instructions, based on a standard of significant rather than dominant motivation, are erroneous and that, at least, a new trial is required. We have examined the record, however, and find nothing that would support a jury verdict in this taxpayer's favor had the dominant-motivation standard been embodied in the instructions. Judgment n.o.v. for the United States, therefore, must be ordered. * * *

As Judge Simpson pointed out in his dissent, 427 F.2d at 284–285, the only real evidence offered by the taxpayer bearing upon motivation was his own testimony that he signed the indemnity agreement "to protect my job," that "I figured in three years' time I would get my money out," and that "I never once gave it [his investment in the corporation] a thought."

The statements obviously are self-serving. In addition, standing alone, they do not bear the light of analysis. What the taxpayer was purporting to say was that his $12,000 annual salary was his sole motivation, and that his $38,900 original investment, the actual value of which prior to the misfortunes of 1962 we do not know, plus his loans to the corporation, plus his personal interest in the integrity of the corporation as a source of living for his son-in-law and as an investment for his son and his other son-in-law, were of no consequence whatever in his thinking. The comparison is strained all the more by the fact that the salary is pre-tax and the investment is taxpaid. With his total annual income about $40,000, Mr. Generes may well have reached a federal income tax bracket of 40% or more for a joint return in 1958–1962. §§ 1 and 2 of the 1954 Code * * *. The $12,000 salary thus would produce for him only about $7,000 net after federal tax and before any state income tax. This is the figure, and not $12,000, that has any possible significance for motivation purposes, and it is less than 1/5 of the original stock investment.

We conclude on these facts that the taxpayer's explanation falls of its own weight, and that reasonable minds could not ascribe, on this record, a dominant motivation directed to the preservation of the taxpayer's salary as president of Kelly–Generes Construction Co., Inc.

The judgment is reversed and the case is remanded with direction that judgment be entered for the United States.

* * *

[Concurring and dissenting opinions omitted.]

[¶ 3115]

Notes

1. What factual showing might have prompted the Supreme Court to affirm the jury verdict in the taxpayer's favor?

2. Assume that the facts had established that the taxpayer's losses were business bad debts. On those same facts, would he also have been entitled to ordinary (business) loss treatment had he provided the funds to the corporation in the form of a stock investment rather than incident to a loan or indemnification agreement? Compare Section 165(g) as to worthless stock with Section 166 on business bad debts. Is a taxpayer therefore better advised from a tax perspective to make advances to a risky venture in the form of loans rather than capital contributions? Consider Section 1244, discussed at ¶ 3125, before answering. Also recall that the issuing corporation does not face taxable income from nonrepayment of equity investments, unlike its potential cancellation of indebtedness income resulting from nonrepayment of debt.

[¶ 3120]

b. *Shareholder Guarantees*

If an individual who has guaranteed repayment of a loan to a corporation is called upon by the lender to discharge the corporation's obligation, normally the guarantor steps into the shoes of the creditor and acquires the creditor's right of repayment against the corporate borrower. Accordingly, if the guarantor is not repaid by the corporation and sustains a loss in the transaction, the loss remains a bad debt loss. Thus, as in the case of direct loans, capital loss treatment can be avoided only if the guarantee grew out of a trade or business of the guarantor rather than out of an investment activity of the guarantor. Putnam v. Commissioner, 352 U.S. 82 (1956). Regardless of the original rationale for this rule, the regulations take the position that all losses arising out of a guarantee or indemnity are subject to the limitations of Section 166(d). Reg. § 1.166–9(b). Thus, a payment by a shareholder-guarantor to a creditor to be released from the guarantee normally will only give rise to a short-term capital loss.

[¶ 3125]

c. Stock and Section 1244

As the preceding materials demonstrate, obtaining ordinary loss treatment for an uncollectible loan to a corporation is difficult for the average investor. Moreover, because success depends upon the state of highly variable factors, the organizers of a corporation can rarely be confident of achieving a favorable result years later when the loss is incurred. While in general losses on equity investments also produce capital losses, in one situation an ordinary loss on stock can be obtained. And, because that loss is attributed to an explicit statutory preference, the availability of the loss is relatively assured. Accordingly, within the limits imposed by Section 1244, an investment in stock can produce a far better result than an investment in debt should the corporate business fail.

Under Section 1244, a shareholder is allowed for any taxable year an ordinary loss deduction not to exceed $100,000 in the case of a joint return ($50,000 in the case of a single taxpayer or a married taxpayer filing a separate return) with respect to a loss incurred upon the disposition or worthlessness of stock of a "small business corporation." Section 1244 stock may be either common or preferred stock and need not be voting stock. Only individuals and partnerships can claim an ordinary loss under Section 1244. To qualify for this benefit, the stock must have been initially issued to the individual or partnership claiming the loss. That means, for example, that if stock is originally issued to an investment partnership and the partnership later dissolves and distributes the stock to the individual partners, the stock is no longer eligible for Section 1244 treatment!

The courts have been alert to prevent the avoidance of these restrictions. For example, in Adams v. Commissioner, 74 T.C. 4 (1980), the corporation redeemed substantially all of its stock from its original shareholder and a few months later sold a similar number of shares to a new investor who later incurred a loss. The court held that the stock was not eligible for Section 1244 treatment because the transaction was a mere substitution for preexisting capital and did not result in the infusion of new capital into the corporation.

Ordinary loss treatment cannot be claimed if, during the five taxable years preceding the loss, the issuing corporation derived more than 50 percent of its gross receipts from passive investment activities. Moreover, at the time the stock was issued, the corporation may not have received throughout its existence, in the aggregate, more than $1,000,000 in exchange for its stock or as a contribution to its capital.

With most positive returns to stock taxed at 15 percent, has Section 1244 become too generous?

[¶ 3130]

Problem

These several limitations on the availability of Section 1244 can require close attention by the organizers of a corporation. Consider, for example, how the organization of a corporation should proceed if half of the investors are to be corporations and $3 million is to be raised through sales of stock but only $1 million will be raised in the initial stock offering. Unfortunately, while stock issued to corporate investors cannot be Section 1244 stock, the amounts received upon the sale of that stock do reduce the $1 million ceiling. Under the regulations, in the year in which the corporation exceeds the $1 million limitation, the corporation may designate which shares are Section 1244 stock and which shares are not. Reg. § 1.1244(c)–2(b)(2). What use could be made of that regulation here?

[¶ 3135]

d. Corporate Level Consequences

As described in Chapter 5, when a corporation redeems its own stock, the corporation does not have income—even if the amount paid for the stock is less than the amount originally received on the sale of the stock. However, if the corporation retires indebtedness for an amount less than the issue price for the debt, the corporate debtor normally will have ordinary income in the nature of cancellation of indebtedness (COD) income to the extent of the difference. §§ 61(a)(12) and 108. There are, however, numerous exceptions to this rule, two of which are presently worth noting.

If a shareholder-lender contributes the indebtedness to the issuer corporation as a contribution to its capital, the corporation is treated as discharging the debt for an amount equal to the shareholder's tax basis in the debt. § 108(e)(6). Such a transaction might occur, for example, if a controlling shareholder wished to improve the appearance of the corporate balance sheet. This rule usually allows the corporation to escape any COD income upon the extinguishment of shareholder held debt. Second, if a corporation issues its stock to a creditor in exchange for its indebtedness, the corporation is treated as discharging the debt for an amount equal to the value of the stock issued to the creditor. § 108(e)(8).

[¶ 3140]

E. POLICY CONSIDERATIONS

The increased divergence of debt instruments from the traditional model of obligations bearing fixed due dates and fixed payments of interest and principal places great strains on the ability of the tax system to sort out the appropriate tax consequences of each transaction. The tax law itself bears heavy responsibility for encouraging these developments by its generally disparate treatment of equity and debt, particularly in Subchapter C.

Elimination of the dual tax on corporate earnings by permitting deductions for dividends or other forms of "integration" would certainly reduce the reliance on debt financing, as would further restrictions on the corporate interest deduction itself. For elaboration of the policy considerations and proposed solutions, see generally the discussion of corporate integration proposals by the Treasury Department and the American Law Institute in Chapter 1.

Chapter 4

DIVIDEND DISTRIBUTIONS

[¶ 4000]

A. INTRODUCTION

As described in Chapter 1, the classical system for taxing corporate profits as traditionally used in the United States imposes two levels of tax, a corporate level tax and a shareholder level tax. The following chapters explore the second, shareholder level tax, including the techniques used by taxpayers to minimize that second tax, and the congressional responses to those efforts.

Unlike the corporate level tax, the shareholder level tax is not imposed at the time profits are earned by the corporation but rather is deferred until those profits are realized by the shareholder. That realization can occur in a variety of ways. Profits may simply be distributed to the shareholder as a dividend, or may be paid out in exchange for stock in the corporation itself (a transaction referred to as a redemption), or may be realized upon a sale of stock to a third party. The actual burden of the shareholder level tax can vary quite widely depending upon which method for obtaining the corporate profits is used. Adding to the complexity, the income tax treatment of a corporation in its capacity as a shareholder in another corporation is often the reverse of the treatment of individuals and other non-corporate shareholders.

The traditional approach to the taxation of distributions of profits to individual shareholders, now partially abandoned, has been built on the following principles.

(a) The distribution of profits by the corporation is not deductible. That principle, which is necessary to preserve the first or corporate level tax, differs sharply from the treatment of interest and thus encourages the use of debt in corporate capital structures and results in the debt-equity controversies examined in Chapter 3.

(b) Shareholders are taxable on the distribution of those profits in the form of dividends at ordinary income tax rates. When combined with the corporate level tax, this principle created a substantial tax burden on currently distributed profits.

(c) Gain on the sale of stock by an investor, including sales of stock back to the issuing corporation, are capital gains. Traditionally the rate of tax imposed on such capital gains has been substantially lower than the rate of tax imposed on ordinary income.

This traditional regime contains substantial biases. Because of the double tax, shareholders have an incentive to avoid any realization of profits and instead generally prefer to obtain cash from the corporation in other ways that are deductible at the corporate level, such as interest or salary, or that are not taxable at the shareholder level, such as a loan. Secondly, when profits must be distributed, shareholders have a substantial tax incentive to avoid making current distributions of dividends and instead prefer to realize those profits through transactions that can be characterized as sales entitled to capital gains rates of taxation. Accordingly, in times when the taxation of corporations is subject to this regime, the provisions of the Code that draw the line between ordinary income dividends and capital gain sales are extremely important to individual taxpayers and their advisors.

In 2003, Congress significantly altered this traditional regime. Pursuant to Section 1(h)(11), most dividends received by individuals became subject to the same rate of tax that applied to long-term capital gains. That change dramatically reduced the incentive for individual shareholders to design distributions of corporate profits to be treated as sales of stock rather than simply as a dividend. Secondly, the rate of tax applicable to dividends and long-term capital gains was reduced to 15 percent. That change somewhat reduced the burden of the double tax and thus the incentive to avoid distributions of corporate earnings to shareholders. Under this new regime, the rules of the Code governing the taxation of distributions to individual shareholders are far less important than they were under the traditional regime to taxpayers and their advisors—and to students of taxation.

On the other hand, this 2003 revision in the taxation of distributions did not alter the manner of taxing corporate shareholders. For such shareholders, capital gains are taxed at the same rate as ordinary income while dividends received by corporate shareholders are taxed very lightly or not at all. Accordingly, for corporate shareholders and their advisors, the line between dividends and sales continues to be a matter of considerable importance.

While for individual shareholders the distribution provisions of the Code have become less important, they have not become unimportant. The distinction must still be mastered by tax advisors for at least all of the following reasons.

(a) Even with a 15 percent tax rate on shareholders, corporate profits remain more heavily taxed overall than are other forms of income and thus some incentive remains to avoid any realization of corporate earnings through either dividends or sales of stock.

(b) While dividends are treated as capital gains for the purpose of applying the 15 percent tax, they are not treated as capital gains for any other purpose and thus are treated differently from capital gains under a variety of important Code provisions. For example, while the amount of taxable capital gains may be offset by capital losses, dividends cannot be so offset.

(c) In a sale, taxpayers are entitled to offset their tax basis in the property sold against the proceeds of sale and recover that amount free of tax. Dividends, by contrast, are not entitled to any such recovery of basis. As a result, the receipt of a dividend will often require the payment of a greater tax than would the receipt of the proceeds from a sale of stock. The higher the shareholder's basis for the stock, the more important this difference in treatment becomes.

(d) On the other hand, short-term capital gains are not subject to the 15 percent rate. Rather, such gains remain taxed as ordinary income at rates that range up to 35 percent. Thus, gains on the sale of stock held for less than one year are taxed quite differently from dividends.

(e) Most importantly, if tax history teaches anything, it is that nothing is permanent. The regime of 2003 could disappear as quickly as it arrived and the rules governing the distinction between dividends and capital gains could regain their former importance to individual shareholders. (Indeed, it is presently scheduled to expire for tax years starting after 2010!)

With all of that in mind, we turn to the study of the taxation of corporate distributions.

[¶ 4005]

B. THE STATUTORY PATTERN FOR TAXING DISTRIBUTIONS

Shareholders may realize their share of corporate earnings in different ways. Those opportunities might be viewed as a continuum of transactions ranging from a current distribution of earnings to a sale or exchange of the corporate stock. While any of these transactions can place cash in the hands of the shareholders, dividends are taxed very differently from sales. The statutory provisions governing the taxation of different types of distributions can be viewed as an attempt to draw a line across this continuum between distributions taxed as dividends and distributions taxed as sales.

¶ 4000

The termination of an investment through the complete liquidation of the corporation can present the closest analogy to a sale of stock. Generally, therefore, shareholders receiving liquidating distributions are taxed under Section 331 as they would be on a sale of their stock. The consequences of the liquidation to the distributing corporation are governed by Section 336. If the shareholder is a corporation that owns 80 percent or more of the stock of the liquidating corporation, Sections 332 and 337 prescribe a special rule extending nonrecognition of gain or loss. Those and related Code provisions are considered in Chapter 8.

If the distribution is in form a redemption of the stock of the shareholder, i.e., a sale of the stock back to the issuing corporation, distinguishing between transactions entitled to taxation as a sale and transactions that must be treated as a dividend becomes more difficult. Sections 302, 303, and 304 provide rules for determining how to make that distinction and are considered in Chapter 5. Section 311 governs the tax consequences to the corporation of a distribution of property either in redemption of its stock or as an ordinary dividend.

The distribution by a corporation of its own stock presents special income tax problems. In that event, the threshold issue may be whether the distribution should be taxable at all. Those problems are addressed by Sections 305, 306, and 307 and are considered in Chapter 6.

Corporations may be created or used to reduce income taxes and, in general, that is entirely proper. However, Congress has concluded that some uses of corporations to reduce taxes are not proper and has enacted a number of rules designed to discourage the accumulation of profits at the corporate level in an attempt to defer unduly the shareholder level tax. Chapter 7 examines some of those rules.

If the taxation of a corporate distribution is not governed by one of these specific tax regimes, it is subject to tax as an ordinary current distribution under Section 301(a). Although most distributions are in fact governed by Section 301, that section by its terms ("Except as otherwise provided") is a residual provision that only applies when a more specific provision does not. Section 301 and sections related to it are considered in this Chapter.

[¶ 4010]

C. THE TAXATION OF DIVIDENDS

Tracing the taxation of ordinary distributions requires examining a surprising number of Code sections. Section 301(a) applies only to a distribution of property "as defined in section 317(a)." Because that Section excludes stock of the distributing corporation from the definition of property, it serves to reserve the taxation of stock dividends to Sections 305 and 306.

¶ 4010

The taxation of distributions of property is prescribed by Section 301(c), which, in paragraph (1), somewhat mysteriously subjects the "portion of the distribution which is a dividend" to tax. The odd language is used because, as a matter of the technical tax terminology used in Section 316, the word "dividend" refers only to a distribution "out of" earnings and profits (E & P). A distribution in excess of E & P is technically not a dividend in the tax sense of that word although in everyday conversation, such technicalities are not observed. In any event, distributions in excess of E & P are treated first as nontaxable returns of capital to the extent of the basis for the stock on which the dividend is distributed and thereafter as gain from the sale of that stock. § 301(c)(2) and (3). Plainly, the computation of E & P is critical to an understanding of the taxation of distributions.

At the corporate level, the distribution of a dividend in cash is unremarkable; the transaction does not have any income tax consequences, apart from causing a reduction in the distributing corporation's E & P. The more complicated consequences of the distribution of other forms of property are addressed at ¶¶ 4045 through 4060.

[¶ 4015]

Problem

To explore the taxation of distributions first on a conceptual level, assume that an individual invested $10,000 in a newly formed corporation, thereby becoming its sole shareholder. Over the years the corporation made money and lost money and now has come out exactly even. After not making any distributions since it was formed, the corporation now distributes $500 to its sole shareholder.

    a.   Should the distribution be taxable to the shareholder?

    b.   Would it matter if the corporation had unrealized appreciation in its assets of $2,000?

    c.   Would it matter if the corporation had no net taxable income because it had claimed accelerated depreciation but would show a profit of $2,000 if it had claimed only economic depreciation?

[¶ 4020]

D.   EARNINGS AND PROFITS

It would not be unreasonable to treat any distribution on stock as a fully taxable dividend just as other investment returns are treated as fully taxable interest or rents. Indeed, that approach might be more consistent with the treatment of the corporation as a legal entity separate from its shareholders. The tax law did not develop along those lines, however. Rather, tax law follows the corporate law in treating a dividend as a division of profits that implies the existence of corporate

¶ 4010

level profits. Absent corporate earnings, therefore, there cannot be a dividend for income tax purposes.

The use of a profitability limitation on the definition of a dividend makes it necessary to define the corporate profits that will support dividend treatment. The simplest approach, of course, would have been to use accumulated taxable income as the measure of profitability. However, as we know, taxable income is frequently far smaller than economic income because of the myriad of preferential allowances that taxpayers are entitled to claim for tax purposes. Those allowances reduce corporate taxable income and thus the corporate tax. If they were also allowed to reduce the amount of corporate distributions that are taxable to shareholders, then the preferences would reduce the shareholder level tax as well as the corporate level tax.

To limit the extent to which corporate preferences may "pass through" to the shareholders and produce a second exclusion from income, Section 316 uses a measure of profitability other than accumulated taxable income. Corporations are required to maintain a separate accounting of their "earnings and profits" (E & P), and that separate account is the measure of profitability that governs the taxation of distributions. That account, of course, does not represent an actual pool of funds available for distribution but rather is merely a bookkeeping entry that reflects the historic profitability of the corporation.

[¶ 4025]

1. DEFINITION OF EARNINGS AND PROFITS

Surprisingly, perhaps, the Code does not contain a comprehensive definition of earnings and profits. Rather, to compute E & P one generally must begin with taxable income and make the series of specific adjustments that are required by Section 312, the regulations, and case law. In general, those adjustments are designed to bring the computation of E & P more in line with the corporation's real economic income. As a result, E & P more accurately reflects the real profitability and dividend-paying capacity of a corporation than would taxable income.

Historically, relatively little attention was paid to the definition of E & P. The reason for this benign neglect was that most corporations had E & P well in excess of amounts distributed to shareholders and thus all distributions unquestionably would be covered by E & P. The precise level of the E & P account really did not matter. Today, however, the alternative minimum tax has given that definition a new importance by in effect including 75 percent of E & P in alternative minimum taxable income. See Chapter 1.

In computing E & P, the fundamental accounting or timing rules of the Code, including the realization requirement and nonrecognition of gain provisions, are generally respected. Thus, gain not recognized under such provisions as Sections 1031 and 351 does not increase E & P. However, when those timing rules seem unduly preferential, Section 312(n) may prohibit their use. Thus, for example, neither the installment method of reporting gain from sales nor the completed contract method of accounting for long-term contracts may be used.

In contrast to the deferral of income, items of income that are wholly exempt from tax are generally included in E & P because they do increase the corporation's capacity to make distributions. Thus, both tax-exempt municipal bond interest and the deductible portion of an inter-corporate dividend must be added to E & P. Of course, the proceeds of a loan are not added to E & P since a borrowing does not reflect a gain. Because the domestic production deduction granted by Section 199 is like the dividends-received deduction in that it does not reflect a disbursement, presumably E & P will not be reduced by the amount of the deduction.

Similarly, disbursements for which no tax benefit is allowable may reduce E & P. Thus, the payment of federal income taxes reduces E & P as do losses and payments that are not deductible under such sections as 265 and 267. And, of course, when a distribution is treated as out of E & P and thus taxable as a dividend, to that extent the E & P account must be reduced.

On the other hand, when the tax law is overly generous, the allowance for E & P purposes may be trimmed back. Importantly, under Section 312(k), E & P cannot be reduced by accelerated methods of depreciation or cost recovery allowances under Section 168. Rather, only straight-line depreciation using the longer lives specified in Section 168(g)(2) may be used. Also, under subsection (n), the tax deductions for certain capital expenditures, such as intangible drilling costs, are converted to amortization allowances deductible over 60 months.

The E & P accounts may be reduced below zero by losses to produce an account deficit. Distributions, however, do not reduce the account below zero.

[¶ 4030]

2. CURRENT AND ACCUMULATED EARNINGS AND PROFITS

Under Section 316, the E & P account is actually two accounts, one reflecting the cumulative experience from February 28, 1913, to the date of the distribution (accumulated E & P) and one reflecting the earnings for the entire current year of the distribution (current E & P). The interplay between these two accounts is somewhat tricky.

Distributions are first tested for dividend treatment against the current account. If current E & P exists, the distribution will be treated as a dividend to that extent, even if there is a deficit in the accumulated E & P account that is greater than the positive balance in the current account. For example, assume that on balance the corporation over its history has incurred a net loss and thus has a deficit in its accumulated

E & P account of $100,000. This year, however, is one of the profitable ones; the corporation has current E & P of $30,000. If the corporation makes a distribution to shareholders of $25,000, the entire amount will be treated as a dividend out of E & P. One of the happy consequences of the use of a current E & P account is that, because corporations distributing dividends usually have current earnings, it is generally unnecessary to demonstrate the size of the accumulated account by analyzing all adjustments to the account since 1913.

Under Section 316(a)(2), current E & P must be computed as of the end of the taxable year, without reduction for distributions during the year. Thus, the current E & P balance cannot be known with precision when a distribution is made. In our example, if a distribution of $25,000 occurs in July, the computation of current E & P must nevertheless wait until December 31. If by then losses were incurred and the current E & P balance turned out to be only $10,000, only that amount would be treated as a dividend, and the balance would become a tax-free return of capital or a capital gain. On the other hand, if the distribution were deferred until January 5 of the following year, the current E & P account would have been folded into the accumulated account as of the beginning of that following year and would have disappeared. If the current account stood at a positive $30,000 at the year's end, the accumulated account would start at negative $70,000 for the second year. The consequences of the January 5 distribution would not be known until the end of the second year when current E & P for that year can be computed!

The reverse is also true. If the corporation has a deficit in current earnings (or the distribution exceeds the positive balance in the current account), the distribution is then tested against the accumulated account. The computation of the accumulated account includes the experience of the current year but only to the date of the distribution. That is, in sharp contrast to the year-end computation of current E & P, accumulated earnings must be allocated between the pre-and post-distribution period. Accordingly, the portion of the current deficit in E & P attributable to the part of the year preceding the distribution reduces accumulated E & P and thus the amount of the distribution treated as a dividend.

While of little significance today, it is noteworthy that Section 316(a)(1) bars the retroactive effect of the income tax laws. Accumulated E & P includes only income derived on or after March 1, 1913, the effective date of the current income tax system.

[¶ 4035]

3. ALLOCATION OF EARNINGS AND PROFITS AMONG DIS-TRIBUTEES

Current E & P is allocated ratably to all distributions during the year in proportion to the amount of the distributions but without regard to the chronological order of the distributions within the year. Reg. § 1.316–2(b). By contrast, accumulated E & P is allocated to distributions in chronological order. The regulations helpfully illustrate the interaction at Reg. § 1.316–2(c).

The E & P account is a corporate account and is not personal to any shareholder. Thus, the fact that a corporation has not generated any earnings during the period of time in which a specific shareholder has held stock in the corporation is not relevant to the taxation of distributions to that shareholder. If the corporation has E & P, the distribution will be taxable as a dividend notwithstanding that the earnings occurred prior to the shareholder's acquisition of stock in the corporation.

E & P is allocated in proportion to distributions, not stockholdings. As a result, a shareholder may receive a disproportionate distribution of E & P. For example, assume that a corporation with three equal shareholders has current E & P of $20,000 (but no accumulated E & P). One of the shareholders causes the corporation to pay a personal expense in the amount of $15,000 and that payment is successfully characterized by the IRS as a constructive dividend. The entire $15,000 will be treated as out of current E & P and taxable to that shareholder. That result should be contrasted to the proration rule contained in Sections 306(a)(1)(A)(ii) and 356(a)(2), discussed in Chapters 6 and 10, respectively.

[¶ 4040]

Problems

1. Universal Corporation was organized in year 1 and uses the calendar year as its accounting period. Its sole shareholder, Jones, acquired her stock for $50,000 in cash. Assume that Universal began year 3 with an accumulated deficit in E & P of $30,000 although its assets had appreciated in value. On September 1 of year 3, it borrowed funds from a bank and distributed $80,000 to Jones. How is the September distribution taxed under the following alternative assumptions?

a. By September 1 of year 3, Universal had $40,000 of current E & P.

b. For all of year 3 Universal had $40,000 of current E & P.

c. For all of year 3 Universal had $10,000 of current E & P.

d. Under the assumption contained in Problem 1.c., what would be the effect of the distribution on the E & P accounts of the corporation?

e. Universal had $40,000 of E & P in year 3 but the distribution to Jones was postponed to January 10 of year 4. In year 4, Universal's current E & P netted to zero.

¶ 4035

f. Under the assumption contained in Problem 1.b., would it alter the answer if the distribution of any dividend were illegal under state law?

2. Assume, instead, that Universal had accumulated E & P of $30,000 at the beginning of year 3 and incurred a deficit in current E & P for that year of $20,000.

a. How would a distribution of $20,000 on June 30 of year 3 be taxed to Jones?

b. Would it matter if the entire deficit were incurred prior to June 30 and for the balance of the year Universal broke even?

c. Assume that in June, but prior to the distribution, Smith contributed $60,000 to Universal for stock and became an equal shareholder with Jones. If, on June 30, Universal distributes $10,000 to each of the shareholders, how will they be taxed?

3. Continental Corporation has accumulated E & P of $10,000 and current E & P of $28,000. During the year it distributed $30,000 to its sole shareholder on March 1 and $10,000 on September 1. How are the two distributions taxed? See Reg. § 1.316–2(c).

4. Would the answer in Problem 3 change if all of the stock in Continental were sold to a new investor on July 1 and that new investor received the September distribution?

5. Assume that during a corporation's first year of operation it derived taxable income of $100,000 as to which it paid a federal income tax of $30,000. During the year the corporation sold property for deferred payments that it reported under the installment method. As a result of that accounting method, the corporation deferred tax on a gain of $50,000. The corporation made a distribution to its shareholders totaling $10,000 during December. What is the accumulated E & P account for the corporation as it starts its second year?

[¶ 4042]

E. QUALIFIED DIVIDENDS AND THE 15 PERCENT SOLUTION

Taxing corporate profits at both the corporate and shareholder levels has often been criticized as creating an excessive tax burden. Many commentators have argued that the tax system could be made more efficient and less distorting of investment decisions if the United States adopted a form of integration such as that used by most European countries. In 2003 a limited step was taken in that direction. In time, that step may prove to have been the first step towards the adoption of a scheme of full integration that completely eliminates the double taxation of corporate profits.

Under Section 1(h)(11), "qualified" dividends are to be subject to tax at the same rate as long term capital gains. That rate, as described more fully in Chapter 1, is a maximum of 15 percent but can be as low as 5 percent (or even zero after 2007). As a result, under current law, dividends are taxed at a rate that is less than one-half the rate applicable to most other items of ordinary income. Many of the more dramatic tax reductions in recent years have been enacted on a temporary basis and the 15 percent rate is no exception; it is scheduled to expire for tax years starting after 2010. Whether that will occur remains to be seen.

Nearly all dividends from domestic corporations are eligible for this reduced rate of taxation. The principal exceptions are for dividends, the payment of which generated an income tax deduction to the payor corporation, and distributions from mutual funds to the extent not attributable to qualified dividends received by the fund. On the other hand, dividends from foreign corporations are eligible for the reduced rate only if the corporation is (a) incorporated in a possession, (b) is incorporated in a country with which the United States has an income tax treaty that provides for the exchange of tax information with the United States and is eligible for the benefits of that treaty, or (c) the stock with respect to which the dividend is paid is traded on a U. S. stock exchange. To qualify for this reduced rate on a dividend from any corporation, the shareholder must hold the stock for at least 60 days although that period may, in whole or in part, follow the payment of the dividend.

Subject to these narrow exceptions, the reduced rate is apparently available for any distribution that is treated as a dividend under Section 301. Accordingly, the reduced rate should be available for disguised or constructive dividends considered at ¶ 4075. Presumably that means that if the IRS disallows a deduction at the corporate level for the payment of salary or rent or another payment to a shareholder because the payment is properly characterized as a dividend, the recipient shareholder would become taxable on the payment at the 15 percent rate rather than the higher ordinary income rate. That may justify a refund of tax to the shareholder if the statute of limitations has not run on the relevant tax year.

This generally taxpayer favorable provision was not without its twists. Much stock held for investment is held in margin accounts with brokers. Without specific notice to the customer, that stock may be lent by the broker to another customer for use in a short sale. If a dividend is paid on stock which has been the subject of a short sale, a payment in lieu of the dividend is made to the investor by the broker. That payment is not eligible for the 15 percent rate.

Like any preferential rate of tax, Section 1(h)(11) raises a host of policy issues that will have to be worked out over the years. For example, if a taxpayer is required to repay a dividend, should the amount of the deduction for the repayment be limited? One obvious issue was addressed in Section 1(h)(11)(D)(i). Under Section 163(d), the amount of the deduction for investment interest is limited to the amount of a taxpayer's investment income which normally would include dividends. However, it would be improper to allow a deduction for interest against income taxed at full ordinary income rates if the dividends generated by the investment of the loan proceeds are taxed only at the 15 percent rate. Accordingly, clause (i) provides that dividend income taken into account under Section 163 for the purpose of increasing the deduction for interest is not eligible for the 15 percent rate. That treatment should be compared to the similar result produced by Section 246A, described at ¶ 4105.

[¶ 4045]

F. DISTRIBUTIONS OF PROPERTY

Historically, distributions of appreciated property could result in significant tax avoidance at the corporate and, sometimes, shareholder levels. Through a series of amendments to the Code during the 1980s, Congress largely conformed the taxation of property distributions to the taxation of cash distributions. However, some additional complexities in the tax treatment remain.

[¶ 4050]

1. SHAREHOLDER TAXATION

Distributions of property are taxed to the shareholder very much like distributions of cash. Under Section 301(b), the amount of the distribution is the fair market value of the property distributed, reduced by the amount of any liability assumed by the shareholder. Like a distribution of cash, that net amount distributed will be taxed as a dividend to the extent of the corporation's E & P. Correspondingly, the tax basis of distributed property to the distributee will be the fair market value of the property on the date of distribution. § 301(d).

On the receipt of a dividend of encumbered property, or of liabilities along with assets, the recipient calculates the amount of the distribution and its basis in much the same way as does a purchaser of encumbered property. However, for the purpose of determining whether, and to what extent, a liability has been assumed by a shareholder, the rules of Section 357(d), described in Chapter 2, are applicable. Reg. § 1.301–1(g). To illustrate, if property is worth $5,000 but encumbered by a $2,000 debt, a purchaser will pay a net price of $3,000 and receive a cost basis of $5,000 for the encumbered property. (Recall that the repayment of the debt will not affect basis.) A dividend distributee of such property will treat the $3,000 net value as the amount received and will likewise obtain a basis in the property of its full fair market value of $5,000.

[¶ 4055]

2. CORPORATE LEVEL CONSEQUENCES

Prior to 1986, the distribution of property, even highly appreciated property, generally did not have any income tax consequences to the distributing corporation. Under the so-called *General Utilities* doctrine, a unilateral distribution of property with respect to stock was not treated as a recognition event at the corporate level. See General Utilities and Operating Co. v. Helvering, 296 U.S. 200 (1935). As might be expected, that rule had a dramatic effect on tax planning for corporations. If appreciated corporate property were sold and the proceeds distributed to shareholders, two levels of tax would be incurred. However, if the property were first distributed to shareholders and then sold by them, only the shareholder level tax would be imposed.

Over several decades, the IRS sought to minimize the consequences of the *General Utilities* doctrine while accepting its basic premise. Thus, for example, when officers of the corporation assisted in the purported shareholder level sale of distributed property, the IRS might argue that the sale had occurred for tax purposes at the corporate level and seek to impose the corporate level tax. Compare Commissioner v. Court Holding Co., 324 U.S. 331 (1945), with United States v. Cumberland Pub. Serv. Co., 338 U.S. 451 (1950). Ultimately, however, the incentive for tax motivated transactions created by the doctrine became intolerable. Finally, in the Tax Reform Act of 1986, the *General Utilities* doctrine and all of its accompanying baggage were discarded by Congress and replaced by the far more sensible rule that now appears in Section 311(b). Today, the distribution of appreciated property by a corporation is treated as a recognition event *to the corporation*, as well as to the shareholder. As a result, the same corporate level tax will be imposed whether the property is sold by the corporation or distributed to the shareholders.

The meaning of the literal language of Section 311(b) was considered by the Tax Court in Pope & Talbot, Inc. v. Commissioner, 104 T.C. 574 (1995), aff'd, 162 F.3d 1236 (9th Cir.1999). The corporate taxpayer had contributed extensive landholdings to a partnership and thereafter distributed interests in the partnership to each of its shareholders as a dividend, resulting in the creation of a publicly held partnership. The taxpayer argued that for the purposes of Section 311(b)(1)(B), the fair market value of the distributed property should equal the aggregate amount for which the partnership interests traded immediately following the distribution, an amount said to be $40,325,775. That, it was argued, reflected the gain that would be realized "if such property were sold to the distributee." The IRS contended that the correct value was the amount for which the land could have been sold by the corporate taxpayer as a single parcel, an amount said to be $115,610,385. Observing that "the purpose underlying section 311(d) was to tax the appreciation in value that had occurred while the distributing corporation held the property and to prevent a corporation from avoiding tax on the inherent gain by distributing such property to its shareholders," (104 T.C. at 579), the court agreed with the IRS.

Logically, perhaps, the taxation of gain following the repeal of the *General Utilities* doctrine should have been matched by the allowance of a loss to a corporation that distributed property having a tax basis in excess of the value of the property. However, Congress' traditional reluctance to allow losses when property is transferred to a related taxpayer, such as a shareholder, resulted in a different rule. Under Section 311(a), a corporation cannot claim a loss as a result of the nonliquidating distribution of property. That disallowed loss is not preserved through an adjustment to the basis of other corporate property and thus is permanently lost.

To obtain a tax benefit from loss property at the corporate level, the property must be sold, not distributed to shareholders. However, a sale of the loss property to those shareholders may not produce a better result. Under Section 267, losses on sales of property between related parties, including a corporation and a controlling shareholder, may be disallowed. See § 267(b)(2) and (3). Note, however, that the transferee may obtain some future benefit from the disallowed loss. See § 267(d).

[¶ 4060]

3. EFFECT ON EARNINGS AND PROFITS

To the extent that a distribution of cash or property is treated as "out of" E & P, the account balance must be reduced. However, the effect of a property distribution on E & P is slightly more complex than the effect of a cash distribution. If appreciated property is distributed, the distribution results in gain to the corporation under Section 311(b), and E & P must be increased by that gain. § 312(b)(1). In addition, Section 312(a)(3) and (b)(2) together require that the current E & P account balance be reduced by the fair market value of the distributed property (although not below zero). The net effect of these rules is to reduce E & P by the adjusted basis of the distributed property. (Of course, if an income tax is payable as a result of the distribution, the payment of that tax will also reduce E & P.) Recognizing that the rules governing the computation of E & P differ from the rules governing the computation of taxable income, Section 312(b) clarifies that, for these purposes, the adjusted basis of property is its basis determined under the rules for computing E & P.

When the basis of the property equals or exceeds its value, a consistent result is reached directly by Section 312(a)(3): E & P is reduced by the adjusted basis of the distributed property. That reduction

¶ 4060

applies, of course, notwithstanding that for the purposes of computing the taxable income of the corporation, the loss was not allowable. E & P is properly reduced by nondeductible losses.

[¶ 4065]

4. DISTRIBUTION OF THE CORPORATION'S OWN OBLIGATIONS

The distribution by a corporation of its own stock is not governed by Section 301 because Section 317(a) excludes stock from the definition of property. Significantly, however, Section 317 does not exclude from the scope of Section 301 a debt instrument issued by the distributing corporation. Thus, the distribution of a corporation's own debt obligation is taxed to the shareholder just as any other distribution of property would be taxed. The amount distributed for the purposes of Section 301(b) is the value of the obligation and that amount will be taxed as a dividend, assuming the availability of adequate E & P.

At the level of the distributing corporation, however, special rules are required. It is generally understood that a corporation does not have a basis in its own securities. Thus, the distribution of a debt obligation could result in gain to the corporation under the current version of Section 311. That result, however, is barred by the parenthetical expression in Section 311(b)(1)(A). Notwithstanding the absence of gain, the corporation's E & P is reduced by the principal amount of the obligation (or the issue price of an obligation with original issue discount). § 312(a)(2). Of course, when the obligation is retired, E & P is not reduced a second time.

[¶ 4070]

Problems

1.   R & B Distributors, Inc. has accumulated E & P of $200,000 but no E & P for the current year aside from any that may be generated by the following transactions. Bellas, the sole shareholder, has a basis of $100,000 in his shares. Assume that Bellas receives a distribution of vacant land that Distributors has held as an investment. The land had a cost basis to Distributors of $50,000 and a value of $300,000 on the date of distribution. (Ignore the effect on E & P of the payment of the income tax on this transaction.)

a.   What are the income tax consequences of the distribution to Distributors?

b.   What is the effect of the distribution on Distributors' E & P?

c.   What are the income tax consequences of the distribution to Bellas?

d.   What is the tax basis of the land in Bellas' hands?

¶ 4060

2.   Assume instead that the value of the land is only $30,000. What now would be the consequences to Distributor and Bellas of a distribution in kind?

3.   How would the answer to Problem 2 change if Distributors sold the land to an unrelated purchaser for $30,000 and distributed the proceeds to Bellas?

4.   How would the answer to Problem 2 change if the land were sold to Bellas for $30,000 and the proceeds thereafter distributed to him?

5.   Many years ago the Moonbeam Corporation acquired 300 acres of land at a cost of $30,000 which it held as an investment. Moonbeam had accumulated E & P of $100,000 at the beginning of year 1 but will have no E & P in the current year aside from earnings that may be generated by the following transactions. Moonbeam sold the land during year 1 for $120,000. The buyer paid $20,000 down and gave an installment promissory note for the balance of $100,000, payable in equal installments of $20,000 per year over the next five years with interest at the prevailing market rate. Assume that on a gain of $15,000, Moonbeam would pay an income tax of $5,000.

During year 1, the corporation distributed cash of $150,000 to Adam, the sole shareholder of Moonbeam. During year 2 the corporation distributed the installment note, which had a fair market value of $100,000 on the date of distribution.

Ignoring the payment of interest, what are the tax consequences of the distributions in years 1 and 2 to the corporation and to Adam? See § 453B. The most likely treatment of the income tax payments is that they reduce E & P for the year in which the gain being taxed is reported.

6.   The Quest Products Corporation has no accumulated E & P and has current E & P of $15,000 aside from earnings that may be generated by the following transaction. It distributes to Solomon, its sole shareholder, a building worth $50,000 which has an adjusted basis of $25,000. The building is mortgaged in the amount of $20,000 and Solomon assumes the mortgage. What are the tax consequences to the corporation and its shareholder? See § 301(b)(2) and Reg. § 1.312–3.

[¶ 4075]

G.   DISGUISED AND CONSTRUCTIVE DIVIDENDS

Because the distribution of profits in the form of dividends is subject to tax at both the corporate and shareholder levels, the owners of closely held corporations have a substantial incentive to attempt to withdraw funds from their corporations in a manner that will reduce tax at the corporate level or avoid tax at the shareholder level. That incentive has

¶ 4075

led to numerous controversies with the IRS which the following cases explore.

[¶ 4080]

TANNER v. COMMISSIONER

United States Tax Court, 1983.
T.C. Memo. 1983–230.

WILES, JUDGE: Respondent determined deficiencies in petitioners' 1977 and 1978 Federal income taxes in the amounts of $522 and $517, respectively. After concessions, the issues for decision are whether petitioners received constructive dividends from their personal use of automobiles owned by their closely held corporation and, if so, the amount of such dividends.

* * *

At all relevant times, petitioners were minority shareholders in Ray Tanner Motors, Inc. (hereinafter Tanner Motors or the corporation), an Arizona corporation with a principal office in Phoenix, Arizona. The officers of Tanner Motors include: Ray Tanner, Sr., President; petitioner, Ray Tanner, Jr., Vice President; and George Wylie, Vice President. During the years in issue, it was the policy of Tanner Motors to provide each officer with the use of new Volvo automobiles under a personal car purchase plan for which documents of title and license registrations were held in the name of the corporation. Between 1977 and 1978, petitioners obtained three automobiles exclusively for personal use under this plan. Petitioners used each automobile for approximately one year before obtaining a new model each spring. Petitioners did not own any other vehicles during the years in issue and they did not reimburse Tanner Motors for the personal use of these automobiles.

The cost to the corporation of providing these vehicles to petitioners was approximately $500 per year which included maintenance expenses, licensing and registration fees, and insurance premiums on each vehicle. Petitioners paid all gasoline costs. Each of the cars was covered by the manufacturer's warranty during the periods that petitioners used them, and repair costs charged to the corporation were paid by the manufacturer. After each car was driven approximately 6,000 miles, it was sold at a profit through the corporation's used car sales department. All such profit was included in the income of Tanner Motors.

In the notice of deficiency, respondent determined that the fair market value of petitioners' personal use of Volvo automobiles owned by Tanner Motors constituted constructive dividends in the amounts of $1,440 in each of 1977 and 1978. Accordingly, their taxable income was increased by $1,440 in both 1977 and 1978, resulting in deficiencies in their Federal income taxes of $522 and $517, respectively.

OPINION

The issue for decision is whether petitioners received constructive dividends from their personal use of corporate automobiles and, if so, the amount of such dividends.

It is well settled that corporate expenditures, or the making available of corporate-owned property to stockholders for their personal benefit, may constitute constructive dividends taxable to those stockholders. * * * Under sections 301 and 316, a dividend is any corporate distribution to its shareholders out of earnings and profits. That the formalities of a dividend are lacking or that the distribution is not recorded on the corporation books is of no consequence. * * * The amount of a constructive dividend generally is equal to the fair market value of the benefits conferred. * * *

The record in the instant case establishes that petitioners enjoyed, for their personal benefit, the free use of Volvo automobiles owned by Tanner Motors. Petitioners have failed to prove that Tanner Motors did not have earnings and profits for the years in issue in amounts at least equal to the fair market value of the use of the Volvo automobiles. See sections 301(c) and 316(a). Moreover, petitioners have failed to present any evidence that the fair market value of their personal use of the Volvo automobiles was less than that determined by respondent. Consequently, we uphold respondent's determination that petitioners' use of the Volvo automobiles owned by Tanner Motors constituted constructive dividends for 1977 and 1978 in the amount of $1,440 per year. * * *

* * *

[¶ 4085]

Problems

1. Why was the value of the use of the Volvos treated as a constructive dividend rather than as compensation? What difference would it have made to the Tanners in 1978 if the amounts had been treated as compensation? To Tanner Motors?

2. What different would it have made to the Tanners today if the amounts has been treated as compensation?

3. What difference would it have made to the Tanners if Tanner Motors had not had E & P at least equal to the value of the use of the cars?

[¶ 4087]

Note

In one recurring scenario, shareholders in a closely held corporation who have diverted corporate funds to their personal use but have failed to report the receipt as income find themselves prosecuted for criminal tax evasion. A question that has arisen in that context is whether the taxpayers may defend themselves on the ground that the corporation did not have any E & P. In United States v. Williams, 875 F.2d 846 (11th Cir.1989), the Eleventh Circuit had held that in such a case the government was not required to characterize the income that the taxpayer was accused of failing to report. Since the taxpayer could be prosecuted for concealing generic income, the absence of E & P was immaterial. In United States v. D'Agostino, 145 F.3d 69 (2d Cir.1998), however, the Second Circuit declined to follow the earlier case, holding that "[i]n this Circuit, corporate funds lawfully diverted by a shareholder constitute taxable income only to the extent that the corporation had earnings and profits during the tax year in which the diversion occurred." 145 F.3d at 72. On the other hand, the court noted that "the 'no earnings and profits, no income' rule would not necessarily apply in a case of *unlawful* diversion, such as embezzlement, theft, a violation of corporate law, or an attempt to defraud third party creditors." 145 F.3d at 73.

What distinction is the court in *D'Agostino* drawing? Is that distinction viable in the context of the taxation of corporations and their shareholders?

If withdrawals are subject to tax notwithstanding the absence of E & P, should they be taxed at full ordinary income tax rates or at 15 percent?

[¶ 4090]

HONIGMAN v. COMMISSIONER

United States Court of Appeals, Sixth Circuit, 1972.
466 F.2d 69.

PHILLIPS, CHIEF JUDGE:

* * *

The principal controversy involves the tax consequences of the sale of corporate property below market value to a minority shareholder. * * *

I.

* * * The National Building Corporation was incorporated under the laws of Michigan in 1946 to engage in the ownership and operation of commercial real estate. Its principal stockholders were the Honigman family (35%), the Silberstein family (35%) and the Galperin family (20)%. A member of each family held a position as a director and officer of National.

In early 1963 steps were undertaken to effect a complete liquidation of National. A preliminary agreement to sell its principal asset, the First National Building in Detroit, was entered into in February 1963. At that time, National's only unsuccessful investment was the Pantlind Hotel in downtown Grand Rapids, Michigan, which it had acquired in 1951. Taxpayers were aware that the Pantlind should be sold prior to adoption of the liquidation plan in order to permit the corporation to recognize the loss on this sale * * *. During this time, unsuccessful efforts were made to sell the hotel at offering prices ranging from $200,000 to $250,000 over its $590,000 mortgage. At an informal meeting of the directors in April, Jason Honigman proposed that the property be sold for a "nominal" price of $50,000 over mortgage. The hotel had not been offered previously at this price, nor was such an offer ever made to outsiders. Ben Silberstein initially indicated an interest in the transaction, but subsequently declined the purchase. Honigman later decided to buy the property at the "nominal" price.

The Pantlind Hotel Corporation was organized under Michigan law to purchase the hotel for some $661,000, representing assumption of the mortgage and a $21,000 tax liability, and $50,000 cash. Mrs. Edith Honigman, wife of Jason Honigman, was the sole stockholder. Title was transferred on May 27, 1963. Two days later a further adjustment of about $38,000 was paid to National. At the time of the sale, National's adjusted basis in the Pantlind was approximately $1,486,000.

In August 1963 National adopted a qualified liquidation plan. All assets were sold within one year and the proceeds distributed pro rata to the shareholders.

The Honigmans reported no income from the May transaction on their 1963 joint income tax return. National deducted the difference between the sale price and the basis of the Pantlind as a business loss on its corporate tax return. The Commissioner determined a deficiency against the Honigmans individually, asserting that they had received a taxable dividend from the Pantlind sale equal to the excess of the fair market value over the purchase price. The fair market value was asserted by the Commissioner to have been $1,300,000. A further deficiency was asserted against the Honigmans as transferees of National, the Commissioner disallowing National's claimed loss deduction on the ground that the constructive dividend to the Honigmans was not recognizable as a loss by the corporation. Similar transferee liability was asserted against the Silbersteins and Galperins.

These deficiencies were contested in a consolidated Tax Court proceeding. The Tax Court found that the fair market value of the Pantlind at the time of sale was $830,000. The court held the transaction to have been a dividend to the Honigmans to the extent of the difference between the market value and sale price and a sale to the extent of the difference between adjusted basis and market value. The former was held to be includible as income to the Honigmans and not deductible by National. The latter was held to be deductible by National.

¶ 4090

A threshold question is whether the Tax Court's finding as to the fair market value was clearly erroneous. * * *

The finding of the Tax Court as to fair market value is further supported by an alternative rough valuation approach. Taxpayers' expert witness testified that hotels were selling at between six and eight times annual earnings at the time of the sale. This expert's own projected earnings of $116,500 yields a value between $699,000 and $932,000. The Tax Court figure of $135,000 yields a value between $810,000 and $1,080,000. On the record before us, we decline to set aside the Tax Court's finding of fair market value in the amount of $830,000.

The principal legal argument on behalf of the taxpayers is that the excess of fair market value over purchase price of an asset purchased from a corporation by a stockholder is a necessary but not sufficient condition for the declaration of a constructive dividend to the extent of the excess. It is urged that there also must be an intent to distribute a dividend and that such intent is negated by a showing that the sale was made in good faith for a valid business purpose to a noncontrolling stockholder.

We do not accept this argument. A dividend, includible in the recipient's gross income under § 301(c) and not recognizable as a loss by the corporation under § 311(a), is defined in § 316 * * *. * * * As stated by the Supreme Court:

> "[I]t is clear that when a corporation sells corporate property to stockholders or their assignees at less than its fair market value, thus diminishing the net worth of the corporation, it is engaging in a 'distribution of property' as that term is used in § 316. Such a sale thus results in a dividend to shareholders unless some specific exception or qualification applies." Commissioner of Internal Revenue v. Gordon, 391 U.S. 83, 89–90 * * * (1968) (Footnote omitted.)

> "If a distribution meets the requirements of the statutory definition of a dividend, then it is regarded as such notwithstanding the fact that it was intended to be a payment of some other kind. * * * It is not necessary that the dividend be formally declared, or that the payment be termed a dividend, or that the payment be made to all the shareholders. * * * For example, distributions have been regarded as dividends where a corporation makes a loan to a shareholder and later cancels the indebtedness, or sells property to a shareholder for a purchase price far below its fair market value, or pays compensation to an officer-shareholder in an amount in excess of the value of his services. In cases such as these and others involving the same problem, courts have had little difficulty in holding the distribution, or that part of it in excess of the *quid pro quo*, to be a dividend, notwithstanding the fact that neither the shareholder no[r] the corporation 'intended' that a dividend be paid. It is not the intent of the parties that governs the characterization

of the distribution, but rather the economic and consequent legal effect of their actions." * * *

* * *

II.

We turn next to the cross appeal of the Commissioner. The Tax Court held that the sale of the Pantlind Hotel by National to the Honigmans was partly a constructive dividend and partly a sale. To reiterate the details of this transaction, the hotel had an adjusted basis to National of $1,468,168.51. The Honigmans purchased the hotel for $661,280.21. The Tax Court found that its fair market value was $830,000. It held that the transfer of the hotel to the Honigmans was to be treated for tax purposes as in part a dividend to the Honigmans in an amount equal to the difference between the purchase price and the hotel's fair market value (i.e., a constructive dividend of $168,719.79); and in part a sale to the extent of the excess of basis over fair market value. The Tax Court thus fragmented the transaction into part dividend, part sale. It further held that only the sale portion constituted a taxable event with respect to National. National was allowed a recognizable loss on this transaction to the extent of the difference between the fair market value of the hotel and its adjusted basis. Under the holding, National was allowed to allocate 100 per cent of the hotel's basis to the sale portion of the transaction.

The Commissioner asserts that this part of the decision of the Tax Court is in direct contravention of the congressional purpose and nonrecognition mandate contained in § 311(a) * * *. * * * We agree with the Commissioner.

The portion of the hotel transaction which the Tax Court held to be a constructive dividend distribution to the Honigmans represented a distribution to shareholders with respect to National's stock under § 301. The non-recognition of loss provision contained in § 311 would prohibit any recognition of loss on this part of the transaction. Yet, by allowing National a loss on the transaction measured by the difference between the hotel's adjusted basis and its fair market value, the Tax Court has permitted National to receive the benefit of a loss on that portion of the transaction held to be a distribution with respect to National's stock. We agree with the Commissioner that in order to give effect to the requirement of § 311, the basis of the hotel must be fragmented proportionately between the sales aspect and the distribution aspect of the transaction. The sale portion should be given recognition only to the extent that the basis allowable to the sale exceeds the consideration paid. Since the Honigmans paid $661,280 for the hotel property which had a fair market value of $830,000, they have purchased in their capacity as buyers a fractional interest represented by $661,280/$830,000. The loss resulting to National from the sale portion of the transaction thus should be computed by allocating a like per cent of the adjusted basis ($1,174,534) to the sale portion, which would result in a recognized loss to National of the difference between the consideration paid and the proportionate share of the basis allocated to the consideration paid.

In the present case, using approximate figures for the purchase price ($660,000), market value ($830,000) and adjusted basis ($1,470,000), approximately 66/83 of the property was sold and 17/83 was distributed as a dividend.

Therefore, we reverse as to that part of the decision of the Tax Court covered by the cross-appeal of the Commissioner. We remand for recomputation of the loss properly recognizable by National and the resulting amount of transferee liability for each of the taxpayers.

* * *

[¶ 4095]

Notes

1. With the repeal of the *General Utilities* doctrine, the allocation of basis undertaken by the court will be of no consequence if property, which is the subject of a bargain sale to shareholders, has a value in excess of its basis. With respect to the distribution of property containing a built-in loss, however, the law today is the same as it was when *Honigman* was decided.

2. Rev. Rul. 70–521, 1970–2 C.B. 72, holds that the distribution by a corporation to its shareholders of an option to acquire corporate property at a price below its fair market value constitutes a dividend to the extent of the value of the right on the date of distribution, which value would approximate the spread between the exercise price and the value of the property. Thus, for example, if a corporation distributed an option to purchase property worth $1,000 for $600, the shareholder would be treated as receiving a dividend in the amount of $400. If the option were exercised at a time when the property was worth $1,100, under the ruling the gain to the corporation would be limited to the excess of the $600 exercise price over the *entire* basis for the property to the corporation.

Rev. Rul. 70–521, however, was issued long before the repeal of the *General Utilities* doctrine. What should be the consequences under Section 311(b) today upon the distribution of the option and its subsequent exercise?

3. In addition to the situations considered above, the presence of a disguised dividend is commonly asserted in the following contexts:

¶ 4090

a. Payment by the corporation of a debt owed by a shareholder to a personal creditor. Wortham Machinery Co. v. United States, 521 F.2d 160 (10th Cir.1975).

b. Sale of property by a shareholder to the corporation at an excessive price. Crosswhite v. United States, 438 F.Supp. 368 (D.C.Ore. 1977).

c. Corporate loans to a shareholder where there is no intention that the loan will be repaid. Niederkrome v. Commissioner, 266 F.2d 238 (9th Cir.1958), cert. denied, 359 U.S. 945 (1959).

d. Corporate payments of salary found to be excessive to a shareholder or member of a shareholder's family. See, e.g., the seemingly interminable saga of Elliotts, Inc. v. Commissioner, 716 F.2d 1241 (9th Cir.1983), on remand, T.C. Memo. 1984–516, aff'd, 782 F.2d 1051 (9th Cir.1986).

4. On occasion some, but not all, shareholders in a corporation will temporarily waive their right to dividends. Corporate insiders, for example, may be required by state securities laws to execute such a waiver in connection with an offering of stock. Or, the controlling stockholders may be trying to put the corporation on a sounder financial basis. The IRS will not assert that a portion of the dividend actually distributed to the non-waiving shareholders should be treated as if it were constructively distributed to the waiving shareholders as long as there is a business purpose for the waiver and relatives of the waiving shareholders do not receive more than 20 percent of the amount of the actual distribution. Rev. Proc. 67–14, 1967–1 C.B. 591.

[¶ 4100]

H. CORPORATE SHAREHOLDERS

If the foregoing rules were applied without modification when the shareholder receiving the dividend is also a corporation, corporate profits would be subject to multiple tiers of taxation before coming to rest in the hands of the ultimate individual owners of the business. That Congress has elected not to do. On the other hand, completely exempting dividends received by corporate shareholders from tax has not seemed entirely appropriate, either. Under that approach, individuals might hold their stock investments through closely held corporations. If these "personal holding companies" collected and reinvested, but did not distribute, dividends, the second tier, shareholder level tax could be deferred indefinitely.

Congress has compromised these concerns in Section 243. While the relief from tax extended by that section is termed the "dividends-received deduction," the effect of the section is to exclude from the income of a corporate shareholder all or a major portion of a dividend

¶ 4100

received from a domestic corporate payor. If the corporate shareholder (by itself or together with other related corporations) owns at least 80 percent of the voting power and value of the stock of the payor corporation, the dividend generally will be fully deductible, i.e., wholly exempt from tax. §§ 243(a)(3) and (b) and 1504(a). If the corporate shareholder owns 20 percent or more of the stock of the payor corporation but less than 80 percent, the shareholder may deduct 80 percent of the dividend (reducing the effective tax rate to 7 percent). § 243(c). Finally, if a lesser interest is held, a mere "portfolio" investment, the corporate shareholder is entitled to deduct 70 percent of the amount of the dividend from income. § 243(a)(1). If the otherwise applicable corporate tax rate would be 35 percent, the 70 percent deduction reduces the effective rate of tax on intercorporate dividends to 10.5 percent. Does that adequately offset the deferral potential of a personal holding company?

While Section 243 may be amply justified by the need to avoid excessively high rates of tax on income passing through multiple tiers of corporations, the section nonetheless has some perverse effects. In particular, it means that corporations prefer to derive income in the form of dividends. In sharp contrast to individual shareholders who, as we have seen, tend to avoid dividends, corporations are taxed more lightly on dividends than on other forms of income, including gains from the sale of stock. The following sections explore some of the ramifications of Section 243.

[¶ 4105]

1. ANTI–ABUSE PROVISIONS

Section 243 creates a category of exempt, or partially exempt, income. As do other forms of tax-favored income, the section thus creates the potential for manipulative transactions that would improperly enlarge upon the relief intended by Congress. That potential has led to the enactment of several provisions designed to limit the abuse of the tax exemption.

Stock may, of course, be purchased with borrowed money. If a corporate shareholder were allowed to deduct the interest paid on money borrowed to purchase stock, the taxpayer could pair a nontaxable receipt with a deductible expenditure. In connection with tax-exempt bonds, just such a scheme is barred by Section 265(a)(2). In the context of the dividends-received deduction, Section 246A produces a similar result. Instead of reducing the interest deduction, however, Section 246A increases the proportion of the intercorporate dividend that is subject to tax by the percentage of the purchase price for the stock attributable to borrowed funds.

For example, assume that a corporate taxpayer purchased stock for $1,000, using $400 of its own funds and $600 of the proceeds of a loan. The "average indebtedness percentage" would be 60 percent. Thus, the

¶ 4100

percentage of any dividend on that stock that the taxpayer could exclude from income would be reduced from 70 to 70 times the equity percentage of 40 (100 percent less 60 percent) or 28 percent. Thus, of a dividend of $100, $72 would be subject to tax. Significantly, however, Section 246A generally does not apply to dividends from subsidiaries if 50 percent or more of the subsidiary's stock is owned by the taxpayer. See § 246A(c)(2)(A).

For Section 246A to apply, the necessary connection must be established between the borrowing and the stock purchase and under Section 246A(d)(3)(A) that connection is that the borrowing must be "directly attributable" to the stock investment. One court has held that this language requires a direct tracing of the proceeds of the borrowing into the stock purchase and does not permit the use of accounting conventions such as prorata allocations or last in–first out assumptions. OBH, Inc. v. United States, 397 F.Supp.2d 1148 (D.Neb. 2005). Given the complexity of the cash flows in a large corporation, that ruling would sharply limit the application of Section 246A.

Section 1059 applies to similar potential mismatching of exempt income and allowable loss. That section applies when a corporate shareholder receives an unusually large dividend, referred to as an "extraordinary dividend," on stock that it has held for less than two years. Following such a dividend, the value of the payor's stock normally would fall by an amount approximating the amount of the extraordinary dividend. A sale of the stock might then produce a loss that could be offset against fully taxable gains. In net effect, the transaction might be an economic wash. However, it would produce a loss that was fully deductible and an equal amount of income that was only lightly taxed or not taxed at all. To prevent that result, Section 1059 requires that the basis of the stock in the payor corporation be reduced by the amount of the extraordinary dividend that was not subject to tax because of the dividends-received deduction. In addition, however, if the untaxed portion of the dividend exceeds that basis, the excess is taxed as gain from the sale of the stock in the year of the dividend.

The general effect of Section 1059 is to treat an "extraordinary dividend" as a return of capital rather than as tax-free income. The original consequence of that characterization was to prevent an abuse of the dividends-received deduction by eliminating an artificial loss. In Section 1059(e), however, Congress has extended the concept of that section to address a very different problem. Some Code sections convert what would otherwise be a capital gain into an ordinary dividend in order to increase the tax cost of a transaction. However, because of the dividends-received deduction, that recharacterization would have an effect upon a corporate shareholder that was exactly the opposite of the tax increase that Congress intended. In certain of those situations, Congress has provided that the reconstructed dividend will be treated as an extraordinary dividend subject to Section 1059(a) without regard to the length of time the stock has been held by the corporate shareholder. As a result, for a corporate shareholder, the transaction remains taxed as a sale and is not treated as a tax-free dividend. This aspect of Section 1059 is discussed more fully in Chapter 5.

In a further anti-abuse provision, Section 246(c) attacks the practice of purchasing stock only for the purpose of obtaining the dividends-received deduction. The deduction is entirely barred unless the stock upon which the dividend is paid is held for more than 45 days.

[¶ 4110]

2. EARNINGS AND PROFITS REVISITED

In discussing the computation of E & P, we noted that several preferential allowances used in the computation of taxable income cannot be used in the computation of E & P. The effect of that rule is to increase E & P and thereby prevent the pass-through of preference items to shareholders. When the shareholder is a corporation, however, that scheme does not work very well. In that context, increasing E & P (and thus the amount of the distribution that is treated as a dividend) increases the amount deducted (i.e., effectively excluded) from the income of the corporate shareholder under Section 243! As a result, the amount of the nontaxable receipt by the corporate shareholder could exceed the amount taxed to the payor corporation. Because the purpose of the dividends-received deduction is to prevent subjecting corporate earnings to a second corporate tax, logically the amount treated as a dividend eligible for the deduction should not exceed the taxable income of the payor corporation. In this context, therefore, for E & P to exceed taxable income appears to produce the wrong result.

To address this consequence of Section 243, Section 301(e) eliminates for corporate shareholders some of the increases in E & P required by Section 312 for individual shareholders. Section 301(e) applies whenever a dividend is received by a corporate shareholder that owns 20 percent or more of the stock of the payor corporation, measured by vote or value. For the purpose of determining the amount of any dividend received by such a shareholder, the E & P of the payor corporation is computed without regard to subsection (k) and most of subsection (n) of Section 312. This rule reduces the amount of E & P and thus the amount of the distribution that is eligible for the dividends-received deduction.

[¶ 4115]

3. DISTINGUISHING DIVIDENDS FROM SALES

Individual shareholders, who generally are taxed more heavily on dividends than on long-term gains from the sale of a capital asset, rarely have any incentive to convert a capital gain into a dividend. Indeed, the focus of the next Chapter on redemptions is the conversion of dividends into capital gains. One of the perverse effects of the dividends-received deduction, however, is that corporate shareholders, who have no capital gain preference under current law and thus may be taxed at rates up to 35 percent on their capital gains, often have a great deal of incentive to convert capital gains into dividends. While that topic is the subject of Chapter 5, the issue can arise in other contexts as the following case illustrates.

[¶ 4120]

LITTON INDUSTRIES, INC. v. COMMISSIONER

United States Tax Court, 1987.
89 T.C. 1086.

CLAPP, JUDGE: Respondent determined a deficiency in petitioner's Federal corporate income tax for the year ended July 29, 1973, in the amount of $11,583,054. After concessions, the issue for decision is whether Litton Industries received a $30 million dividend from Stouffer Corp., its wholly owned subsidiary, or whether that sum represented proceeds from the sale of Stouffer stock to Nestle Corp.

* * *

Litton Industries, Inc. (petitioner), and its subsidiaries manufactured and sold, inter alia, business systems and equipment, defense and marine systems, industrial systems and equipment, and microwave cooking equipment. It maintained its principal office in Beverly Hills, California, at the time it filed its petition in this case.

On October 4, 1967, petitioner acquired all the outstanding stock of Stouffer Corp. (Stouffer), a corporation whose common stock was listed and traded on the New York stock exchange. Stouffer manufactured and sold frozen prepared food, and operated hotels and food management services and restaurants. * * *

In early 1972, Charles B. Thornton (Thornton), the chairman of Litton's board of directors; Joseph Imirie, president of Stouffer; and James Biggar, an executive of Stouffer, discussed project "T.I.B.," i.e., the sale of Stouffer. In July 1972, Litton's board of directors discussed the mechanics and problems of selling Stouffer. As of August 1, 1972, Stouffer's accumulated earnings and profits exceeded $30 million. On August 23, 1972, Stouffer declared a $30 million dividend which it paid to Litton in the form of a $30 million negotiable promissory note, and at that time, Thornton believed that Litton would have no difficulty in receiving an adequate offer for Stouffer. Two weeks later, on September 7, 1972, petitioner announced publicly its interest in disposing of Stouffer. Subsequent to said announcement, Litton received inquiries from a number of interested sources, including TWA, Green Giant, investment banking houses, and business brokers about the possible purchase of all or part of the Stouffer business.

Beginning in mid-September 1972, Litton and several underwriters discussed the feasibility of a public offering of Stouffer Stock. * * * During November 1972, petitioner, Stouffer, and Hornblower and Weeks prepared a partial public offering of Stouffer stock. * * * In mid-December 1972, Litton decided that a complete public offering was preferable and abandoned the idea of a partial public offering. The S–1 Registration Statement, which Stouffer filed with the Securities and Exchange Commission, stated that $30 million of the proceeds would be used to pay the promissory note which Litton received as a dividend.

On March 1, 1973, Nestle Alimentana S.A. Corp. (Nestle), a Swiss corporation, offered to buy all of Stouffer's stock for $105 million. On March 5, 1973, Nestle paid Litton $74,962,518 in cash for all the outstanding stock of Stouffer and $30 million in cash for the promissory note. Because Litton sold Stouffer to Nestle, the underwriters stopped work on the scheduled public offering.

OPINION

The issue for decision is whether the $30 million dividend declared by Stouffer on August 23, 1972, and paid to its parent, Litton, by means of a negotiable promissory note was truly a dividend for tax purposes or whether it should be considered part of the proceeds received by Litton from the sale of all of Stouffer's stock on March 1, 1973. If, as petitioner contends, the $30 million constitutes a dividend, petitioner may deduct 85 percent of that amount as a dividend-received credit pursuant to section 243(a), as that section read during the year at issue. However, if the $30 million represents part of the selling price of the Stouffer stock, as contended by respondent, the entire amount will be added to the proceeds of the sale and taxed to Litton as additional capital gain. Respondent's approach, of course produces the larger amount of tax dollars.

The instant case is substantially governed by *Waterman Steamship Corp. v. Commissioner*, 50 T.C. 650 (1968), revd. 430 F.2d 1185 (5th Cir.1970), cert. denied 401 U.S. 939 (1971). * * * For the reasons set forth below, we conclude that the $30 million distribution constituted a dividend which should be recognized as such for tax purposes. We believe that the facts in the instant case lead even more strongly than did the facts in *Waterman Steamship* to the conclusion that the $30 million was a dividend. Accordingly, we hold that the Stouffer distribution to Litton was a dividend within the meaning of section 243(a).

In many respects, the facts of this case and those of *Waterman Steamship* are parallel. The principal difference, and the one which we find to be most significant, is the timing of the dividend action. In *Waterman Steamship*, the taxpayer corporation received an offer to purchase the stock of two of its wholly owned subsidiary corporations, Pan–Atlantic and Gulf Florida, for $3,500,000 cash. The board of directors of Waterman Steamship rejected that offer but countered with an offer to sell the two subsidiaries for $700,000 after the subsidiaries declared and arranged for payments of dividends to Waterman Steamship amounting in the aggregate to $2,800,000. Negotiations between the parties ensued, and the agreements which resulted therefrom included, in specific detail, provisions for the declaration of a dividend by Pan–Atlantic to Waterman Steamship prior to the signing of the sales agreement and the closing of that transaction. Furthermore, the agreements called for the purchaser to loan or otherwise advance funds to Pan–Atlantic promptly in order to pay off the promissory note by which the dividend had been paid. Once the agreement was reached, the entire transaction was carried out by a series of meetings commencing at 12 noon on January 21, 1955, and ending at 1:30 p.m. the same day. At the first meeting, the board of directors of Pan–Atlantic met and declared a dividend in the form of a promissory note in the amount of $2,799,820. The dividend was paid by execution and delivery of the promissory note. At 12:30 p.m., the board of directors of the purchaser's nominee corporation (Securities) met and authorized the purchase and financing of Pan–Atlantic and Gulf Florida. At 1 p.m., the directors of Waterman authorized the sale of all outstanding stock of Pan–Atlantic and Gulf Florida to Securities. Immediately following that meeting, the sales agreement was executed by the parties. The agreement provided that the purchaser guaranteed prompt payment of the liabilities of Pan–Atlantic and Gulf Florida including payment of any notes given by either corporation as a dividend.

Finally, at 1:30 p.m., the new board of directors of Pan–Atlantic authorized the borrowing of sufficient funds from the purchaser personally and from his nominee corporation to pay off the promissory note to Waterman Steamship, which was done forthwith. As the Fifth Circuit pointed out, "By the end of the day and within a ninety minute period, the financial cycle had been completed. Waterman had $3,500,000, hopefully tax-free, all of which came from Securities and McLean, the buyers of the stock." 430 F.2d at 1190. This Court concluded that the distribution from Pan–Atlantic to Waterman was a dividend. The Fifth Circuit reversed, concluding that the dividend and sale were one transaction. 430 F.2d at 1192.

The timing in the instant case was markedly different. The dividend was declared by Stouffer on August 23, 1972, at which time the promissory note in payment of the dividend was issued to Litton. There had been some general preliminary discussions about the sale of Stouffer, and it was expected that Stouffer would be a very marketable company which would sell quickly. However, at the time the dividend was declared, no formal action had been taken to initiate the sale of Stouffer. It was not until 2 weeks later that Litton publicly announced that Stouffer was for sale. There ensued over the next 6 months many discussions with various corporations, investment banking houses, business brokers, and underwriters regarding Litton's disposition of Stouffer through sale of all or part of the business to a particular buyer, or through full or partial public offerings of the Stouffer stock. All of this culminated on March 1, 1973, over 6 months after the dividend was declared, with the purchase by Nestle of all of Stouffer's stock. Nestle also purchased the outstanding promissory note for $30 million in cash.

In the instant case, the declaration of the dividend and the sale of the stock were substantially separated in time in contrast to *Waterman Steamship* where the different transactions occurred essentially simultaneously. In *Waterman Steamship*, it seems quite clear that no dividend would have been declared if all of the remaining steps in the transaction had not been lined up in order on the closing table and did not in fact take place. Here, however, Stouffer declared the dividend, issued the promissory note, and definitely committed itself to the dividend before even making a public announcement that Stouffer was for sale. Respondent argues that the only way petitioner could ever receive the dividend was by raising revenue through a sale of Stouffer. Therefore, respondent asserts the two events (the declaration of the dividend and then the sale of the company) were inextricably tied together and should be treated as one transaction for tax purposes. In our view, respondent ignores the fact that Stouffer could have raised sufficient revenue for the dividend from other avenues, such as a partial public offering or borrowing. Admittedly, there had been discussions at Litton about the sale of Stouffer which was considered to be a very salable company. However, there are many slips between the cup and the lip, and it does not take much of a stretch of the imagination to picture a variety of circumstances under which Stouffer might have been taken off the market and no sale consummated. Under these circumstances, it is unlikely that respondent would have considered the dividend to be a nullity. On the contrary, it would seem quite clear that petitioner would be charged with a dividend on which it would have to pay a substantial tax. Petitioner committed itself to the dividend and, thereby, accepted the consequences regardless of the outcome of the proposed sale of Stouffer stock. * * *

* * * The parties have stipulated that Stouffer had earnings and profits exceeding $30 million at the time the dividend was declared. This Court has recognized that a dividend may be paid by a note. * * * Based on these criteria, the $30 million distribution by Stouffer would clearly constitute a dividend if the sale of Stouffer had not occurred. We are not persuaded that the subsequent sale of Stouffer to Nestle changes that result merely because it was more advantageous to Litton from a tax perspective.

It is well established that a taxpayer is entitled to structure his affairs and transactions in order to minimize his taxes. This proposition does not give a taxpayer carte blanche to set up a transaction in any

¶ 4120

form which will avoid tax consequences, regardless of whether the transaction has substance. *Gregory v. Helvering*, 293 U.S. 465 (1935). A variety of factors present here preclude a finding of sham or subterfuge. Although the record in this case clearly shows that Litton intended at the time the dividend was declared to sell Stouffer, no formal action had been taken and no announcement had been made. There was no definite purchaser waiting in the wings with the terms and conditions of sale already agreed upon. At that time, Litton had not even decided upon the form of sale of Stouffer. Nothing in the record here suggests that there was any prearranged sale agreement, formal or informal, at the time the dividend was declared.

Petitioner further supports its argument that the transaction was not a sham by pointing out Litton's legitimate business purposes in declaring the dividend. Although the code and case law do not require a dividend to have a business purpose, it is a factor to be considered in determining whether the overall transaction was a sham. *T.S.N. Liquidating Corp. v. United States*, 624 F.2d 1328 (5th Cir.1980). Petitioner argues that the distribution allowed Litton to maximize the gross after-tax amount it could receive from its investment in Stouffer. From the viewpoint of a private purchaser of Stouffer, it is difficult to see how the declaration of a dividend would improve the value of the stock since creating a liability in the form of a promissory note for $30 million would reduce the value of Stouffer by approximately that amount. However, since Litton was considering disposing of all or part of Stouffer through a public or private offering, the payment of a dividend by a promissory note prior to any sale had two advantages. First, Litton hoped to avoid materially diminishing the market value of the Stouffer stock. At that time, one of the factors considered in valuing a stock, and in determining the market value of a stock was the "multiple of earnings" criterion. Payment of the dividend by issuance of a promissory note would not substantially alter Stouffer's earnings. Since many investors were relatively unsophisticated, Litton may have been quite right that it could increase its investment in Stouffer by at least some portion of the $30 million dividend. Second, by declaring a dividend and paying it by a promissory note prior to an anticipated public offering, Litton could avoid sharing the earnings with future additional shareholders while not diminishing to the full extent of the pro rata dividend, the amount received for the stock. Whether Litton could have come out ahead after Stouffer paid the promissory note is at this point merely speculation about a public offering which never occurred. The point, however, is that Litton hoped to achieve some business purpose, and not just tax benefits, in structuring the transaction as it did.

Under these facts, where the dividend was declared 6 months prior to the sale of Stouffer, where the sale was not prearranged, and since Stouffer had earnings and profits exceeding $30 million at the time the dividend was declared, we cannot conclude that the distribution was

¶ 4120

merely a device designed to give the appearance of a dividend to a part of the sales proceeds. In this case, the form and substance of the transaction coincide; it was not a transaction entered into solely for tax reasons, and it should be recognized as structured by petitioner.

On this record, we hold that for Federal tax purposes Stouffer declared a dividend to petitioner on August 23, 1972, and, subsequently, petitioner sold all of its stock in Stouffer to Nestle for $75 million.

* * *

[¶ 4125]

Notes

1. Why did Litton cause Stouffer to declare a dividend of $30 million in the form of a promissory note? If the answer is: "to avoid a tax of over $11 million," does that matter?

2. How significant was the intervention of Nestle? If Stouffer had gone forward with a public offering of its stock and had used $30 million of the proceeds to pay off the promissory note, would that have weakened Litton's tax position?

3. Cases like *Litton Industries* arise because gain from an intercorporate dividend is taxed differently from gain on the sale of stock in a subsidiary. Why should that be? If it is appropriate to exempt a dividend from Stouffer to Litton from tax to avoid multiple levels of taxation on corporate earnings, why would it not be similarly appropriate to exempt Litton's gain on the sale of the Stouffer stock from tax?

[¶ 4130]

Problem

Investors, Inc. owns 50 of the 1,000 outstanding shares of stock in Operating, Inc. Operating owns vacant land that it purchased many years ago for $10,000 which is now worth $100,000. If Operating distributes the land to Investors as an ordinary dividend:

a. What will be the income tax consequences of the distribution to Operating?

b. What will be the effect of the distribution on Operating's E & P account?

c. Assuming ample current E & P, what will be the income tax consequences of the distribution to Investors?

d. What will be the tax basis of the land in the hands of Investors?

Chapter 5

REDEMPTIONS OF STOCK

[¶ 5000]

A. INTRODUCTION

In the language of Section 317(b), a redemption is a transaction in which "the corporation acquires its stock from a shareholder in exchange for property." From the shareholder's perspective, the sale of stock back to the corporation that issued it looks somewhat like a sale but somewhat like the receipt of an ordinary dividend. The tax rules governing redemptions mostly refine the line between these two characterizations.

Retirement of stock by redemption occurs in a number of different contexts. The occasion may be the liquidation, recapitalization, or other reorganization of a corporation; the corporation's trading on the market in its own stock; a death or retirement that prompts a shareholder to withdraw from ownership; or simply the accommodation of a desire for funds by one or a select group of shareholders. The taxation of redemptions in different contexts is governed by different Code provisions. Redemptions in complete liquidation are governed by Section 331 or 332, while redemptions incident to reorganizations are governed by Section 356. This Chapter concerns redemptions by continuing corporations that are not incident to organic alterations of the corporation.

As was most of Subchapter C, the rules examined in this Chapter were drafted envisioning individual shareholders in a corporation. From that perspective, the rules generally sought to prevent the conversion of dividend income into a capital gain. However, in most cases, these same rules also apply to corporate shareholders in corporations and their objectives tend to be the reverse of those of the individual shareholders for whom the rules were drafted. Indeed, today these rules are of greater importance to corporate shareholders than they are to individual shareholders.

B. INTEREST–REDUCING REDEMPTIONS

Section 302(a) provides that a distribution in redemption of stock will be treated as a payment in exchange for the stock if the tests of one of the four paragraphs of Section 302(b) are met. Of those tests, the first three apply to interest-reducing redemptions and are considered here; paragraph (4) applies to partial liquidations and is taken up separately. If exchange treatment is obtained, the shareholder is treated as having sold stock to the corporation and thus generally is entitled to the relatively favorable tax consequences that the Code extends to sales. Thus, the shareholder will normally be entitled to capital gains taxation and, in measuring gain, to offset the stock basis against the proceeds of the sale. On the other hand, if the redemption fails all four tests of Section 302(b), under Section 302(d) sales treatment will be denied and the distribution will be taxed under Section 301 as an ordinary dividend to the extent of the redeeming corporation's E & P.

Section 302(b) contains alternative tests for exchange treatment; only one test need be met in order to avoid taxation as a dividend. While each test is somewhat different from the others, there is a common theme that unifies paragraphs (1), (2), and (3). The fundamental difference between a dividend, on the one hand, and a sale to an unrelated purchaser, on the other, is that the former does not alter the shareholder's proportionate interest in the corporate entity while a sale reduces or eliminates that interest. A redemption can do either; a large redemption from a small shareholder will materially reduce the shareholder's continuing interest, while a small redemption from a large shareholder may not. The rules of paragraphs (1) through (3) specify when a redemption has produced a reduction in the shareholder's interest that is sufficient to make it appropriate to tax the redemption as a sale rather than as a dividend.

1. SUBSTANTIALLY DISPROPORTIONATE REDEMPTIONS

The core of the interest-reduction principle is embodied in the safe harbor rule contained in Section 302(b)(2). Under that section, the redemption will be "substantially disproportionate" and entitled to exchange treatment if three mechanical tests are met.

First, and most importantly, the redemption must result in a greater than 20 percent reduction in the shareholder's voting stock interest. That is, after the redemption, the percentage of the voting stock held by the shareholder must be less than 80 percent of the percentage of voting stock held before the redemption. Second, the redemption must also result in a greater than 20 percent reduction in the shareholder's interest in common stock, whether voting or nonvoting. Third, after the redemption the shareholder must own less than 50 percent of the total voting power of all classes of the corporation's stock, including voting preferred.

To illustrate, assume Kate owns 20 of 100 shares of voting common stock in a corporation. If 5 shares are redeemed, after the redemption she will own 15/95 or 15.8 percent of the outstanding stock (note the reduction in the total amount of stock outstanding). Multiplying her original ownership percentage of 20 percent times 80 percent equals 16 percent. Since Kate's holdings after the redemption of 15.8 percent are less than that, her redemption is substantially disproportionate, and she is entitled to exchange treatment and capital gains taxation.

When a shareholder owns more than one class of stock in the redeeming corporation, the computation of the two greater-than–20–percent reductions must be made on an aggregate basis. For the purposes of the common stock reduction test, the Code expressly provides that the aggregation be based upon the fair market value of the shares of stock. § 302(b)(2)(C)(last sentence). However, the Code does not explain how voting stock is to be aggregated. If common shares have one vote per share but preferred shares have two votes per share, should the shares be aggregated on the basis of market value (like common stock) or on the basis of voting power (like the 50 percent test in Section 302(b)(2)(B)) or on the basis of number of shares of stock (as the language of Section 302(b)(2)(C) seems to suggest)? Which would make the most sense?

When the several tests of Section 302(b)(2) are met, all common stock and all voting preferred stock redeemed in the transaction will be entitled to exchange treatment. Notwithstanding the required reduction in common stockholdings, in Rev. Rul. 81–41, 1981–1 C.B. 121, the IRS rather generously ruled that a redemption of voting preferred stock alone could be treated as substantially disproportionate when the shareholder did not own any common stock.

Since the retirement of nonvoting preferred stock is irrelevant to the computation under Section 302(b)(2), it might be feared that the redemption of such stock could never be brought within the scope of a substantially disproportionate redemption. The regulations, however, provide that, if a redemption of other stock is treated as an exchange under Section 302(b)(2), then a simultaneous redemption of nonvoting preferred stock will also be treated as an exchange—apparently without regard to the proportion of the nonvoting preferred stock redeemed. Reg. § 1.302–3(a).

[¶ 5015]

2. STOCK ATTRIBUTION

While the redemption of five of Kate's 20 shares of voting common stock is entitled to exchange treatment, the redemption of those same shares would be treated as a dividend if Kate owned all 100 outstanding shares before the redemption. What should be the result, however, if the other 80 shares were not owned by Kate directly but were owned by her husband or by a second corporation in which she owned all of the stock?

For the purpose of testing distributions for substantial disproportion, Section 302(c)(1) generally requires that the stock attribution rules of Section 318 be applied in the computation of stock ownership. Under those rules, shareholders are treated as owning stock that is actually owned by individuals or entities that are closely related to the shareholder. For example, if the other 80 shares were owned by Kate's husband, under Section 318 Kate would be treated as "constructively" owning those shares. Thus, counting her actual and constructive ownership, she would be treated as owning 100/100 of the stock before the redemption and 95/95 of the stock after the redemption. Since her ownership, after the application of the stock attribution rules, would not have diminished at all, the redemption would be treated as a dividend.

In the context of Section 302, stock attribution attempts to prevent the manipulation of the definition of a substantially disproportionate redemption. Absent this rule, Kate could divide her stockholding among several relatives or controlled entities. A redemption of the shares held by any one of those shareholders might then qualify for exchange treatment even though the aggregate holdings of the group declined by only a trivial amount or not at all.

Two cautionary points concerning attribution must be made. First, the rules of Section 318 are highly mechanical. They only apply if the Code says they apply, and stock is attributed to a shareholder only from the individuals or entities specified in Section 318. Second, Section 318 is only one of several stock attribution rules contained in the Code and each is slightly different from the others. For example, under Section 318, stock is not attributed between brothers and sisters while under Section 267(c)(4), it is.

One form of constructive ownership results from "family attribution" of ownership among a statutorily designated range of relatives. The notion underlying this rule is that persons within the defined familial relationships are likely to possess an identity of economic interests that justifies the attribution of ownership from one to another. Accordingly, Section 318(a)(1) requires attribution of stock ownership to a taxpayer from a spouse, from a parent, and from a child or grandchild.

A second form of attribution of ownership occurs between entities and certain of their beneficial owners. Entity to owner attribution under Section 318(a)(2) requires that stock owned by a partnership, estate, trust, or another corporation be imputed *from* that entity to its beneficial owners, its partners, beneficiaries, or shareholders, in proportion to their ownership in the entity. Importantly, however, stock owned by a corporation is only attributed to a shareholder who owns a 50 percent or

¶ 5015

greater interest in the corporation—after the application of the stock attribution rules. § 318(a)(2)(C) and Reg. § 1.318–1(b)(3). For example, assume that Jake owns 40 percent of the stock in Top Company and his wife owns 20 percent. Top Company in turn owns 80 of the 100 outstanding shares of stock in Bottom Company. Because, after the application of the stock attribution rules, Jake is treated as owning 60 percent of Top Company, he would also be treated as owning 48 percent (.60 x .80) of Bottom Company.

Under Section 318(a)(3), owner to entity attribution requires the stockholdings of the owners of partnerships, estates, trusts, or corporations to be attributed in full to their entities. The same 50 percent threshold applies, however, to attribution from shareholders. For example, if Jake also owned 35 of the 100 outstanding shares of stock in X Company, Top Company would be treated as owning all 35 of those shares.

One significant complication in the application of the attribution rules is reattribution. Under Section 318(a)(5), the constructive ownership interests that result from attribution may themselves be reattributed to another. For example, under the entity to owner attribution rule of Section 318(a)(2)(C), stock that a corporation owns in a second corporation will be imputed *from* the corporation to its 50 percent shareholder. In turn, such imputed interests may be reattributed through those owners (i) further upward to a shareholder of the shareholder, (ii) downward to another entity in which the 50 percent shareholder has an interest, or (iii) to a relative covered by the family attribution rules. However, double family attribution is not allowed; otherwise the statutory definition of the family could be expanded ad infinitum. Further, the ownership interests of a shareholder, partner, or beneficiary in other entities that are imputed to an entity under Section 318(a)(3) cannot be reattributed through that entity to another owner of the same entity. Owner to owner attribution, that is, is not allowed. § 318(a)(5)(C).

Finally, stock is attributed to any person who holds an option to acquire that stock. Under that rule, stock that the holder could acquire by the exercise of an option, warrant, convertible debenture, or similar right is attributed to the holder. There is relatively little authority on what constitutes an option for the purposes of this rule. It does appear that when the right to exercise an option is subject to contingencies not within the control of the option holder, the option generally will not support attribution. However, attribution is made even though the option can only be exercised at a future time. Because the range of options covered by Section 318(a)(4) is so broad, taxpayers seeking attribution (perhaps a corporate shareholder wishing to have a redemption treated as a dividend) have been able to design relatively worthless options that fulfilled their objectives. Should a right to acquire stock that has a current value of $100 per share for $250 per share during a 30–day period 10 years in the future be treated as a basis for attribution today?

¶ 5015

[¶ 5020]

Problems

1. A, B, and C, who are unrelated, each own 33 of the 99 outstanding shares of voting common stock in First National Corporation. If the Corporation redeems 9 shares from A, will the redemption qualify for exchange treatment under Section 302(b)(2)?

2. If, instead, First National simultaneously redeems 10 shares from each of A and B, will either or both redemptions qualify under Section 302(b)(2)? Would it matter if A were redeemed in one year and B in the next?

3. L owns 70 and S owns 30 of the 100 outstanding shares of the single class of stock in Retail Corporation. How many shares must be redeemed from L for his holding to be reduced to below 80 percent of his present holding (assuming no shares of S are redeemed and that L and S are unrelated)? Would that redemption qualify under Section 302(b)(2)? How many shares must be redeemed from L to meet the tests of Section 302(b)(2)?

4. Wholesale Corporation has outstanding 1,000 shares of voting common stock and 1,000 shares of nonvoting common stock. Shares of each class of stock have the same value. Ralph owns 100 shares of each class. If Wholesale redeems 30 of his voting shares, will the transaction qualify under Section 302(b)(2)?

5. Maria and Tom each own 100 shares of stock in their family owned corporation. The shares have a value of $75 per share. Maria, who has held her shares since the corporation was formed has a basis of only $1 per share. Tom, however, recently inherited his stock and has a basis of $75 per share. The corporation plans to redeem half of the stock held by Maria and Tom.

   a. To what extent does it matter to either of them whether Section 302 will treat the redemption as a dividend?

   b. What if Maria has capital loss carryover of $50,000 from last year?

   c. What if Maria was actually a corporation, Maria, Inc.?

6. Janis is a 50–percent shareholder in a thriving record company; her brother Elvis owns the balance of the outstanding stock. If some of Janis' stock is redeemed, will she nevertheless be treated by Section 318 as the owner of 100 percent of the corporate stock by virtue of (i) the attribution of her brother's shares to her or (ii) the attribution of her brother's shares to the corporation and the reattribution of those shares to Janis (see Section 318(a)(5)(C)) or (iii) the attribution of her brother's shares to their father and the reattribution from him to Janis?

7. Taxpayer owns one of the 100 outstanding shares of the single class of stock in Sub Corporation, and she would like to have that share

redeemed. Parent Corporation owns 40 shares in Sub, and the balance is owned by unrelated persons. Of the 100 shares of stock outstanding in Parent Corporation, Taxpayer owns 30, her Brother owns 10, and Trust owns 60. Taxpayer's Mother has a one-third interest in Trust; the other interests are held by her brothers and sisters. Will the redemption qualify under Section 302(b)(2)?

[¶ 5022]

3. BASIS CONSEQUENCES

When a redemption of stock is recharacterized under Section 302 as a dividend and the corporation has adequate E & P, the entire amount of the distribution will become subject to tax. That means the shareholder does not obtain any tax benefit from whatever tax basis existed in the stock redeemed. Exactly what happens to that "disappearing" basis remains slightly murky.

The regulations currently provide that following such a redemption, a "proper adjustment" will be made to the basis of the "remaining" stock. Reg. § 1.302–2(c). When the shareholder continues to own other stock in the redeeming corporation, that rule plainly requires that the basis of the stock redeemed be added to the basis of the stock retained. However, what should happen if the shareholder does not continue to own any stock in the redeeming corporation and the redemption was treated as a dividend because stock owned by others was attributed to the shareholder? The regulations hint at the answer to that question only by providing an example involving a husband and wife. The example concludes that, when all of the stock owned by the husband is redeemed, the basis of the stock is added to the remaining stock in the corporation held by the wife.

Taxpayers have generally assumed that the rule to be derived from this example was that, when the redeemed shareholder did not continue to own any stock in the corporation, the basis in redeemed stock shifted to the individuals or entities whose stock was attributed to the shareholder and caused the transaction to be taxed as a dividend. When that expansive reading of the regulations began to be abused in tax-motivated transactions involving unrelated corporations (see IRS Notice 2001–45, 2001–2 C.B. 129), the Treasury issued a proposed regulation that would end the shifting of basis following a redemption in all circumstances. Under those regulations, the redeemed shareholder would have been entitled to a loss in the amount of the basis of the stock redeemed. However, the loss could not be taken at the time of the redemption. Rather, the loss was to be deferred under a complex set of rules that in general permitted the loss to be claimed at the time that stock was no longer attributed to the shareholder in amounts that would cause the redemption to be treated as a dividend. Apparently, the Treasury opposed allowing a loss at the time of the redemption because the redemption was being taxed as a dividend and no loss would be allowed on an actual dividend. The proposed regulation drew considerable criticism and finally was withdrawn. What approach to basis should be taken in a future revision of this proposal?

[¶ 5025]

4. TERMINATIONS OF INTEREST

At first encounter one might be puzzled as to what is added by the extension in Section 302(b)(3) of sale treatment to the complete termination of a shareholder's interest. After all, even a lesser reduction in holdings, a substantially disproportionate reduction, will achieve sale treatment for the shareholder.

What Section 302(b)(3) adds is that a shareholder, whose actual ownership interest in the corporation is completely redeemed, can waive constructive ownership under Section 318(a)(1). (Notice that the reference to paragraph (1) results in the potential waiver of family attribution only, not entity attribution.) The complete termination of interest rule of Section 302(b)(3) probably is best understood, not as a technically required element of the definition of a dividend but rather as a policy-executing provision. Paragraph (3) greatly facilitates the transfer of the ownership of family-owned corporations from one generation to the next. To attain the benefits of that rule, however, a shareholder must meet several requirements that are absent from the substantially disproportionate redemption test.

[¶ 5030]

a. *"Complete" Redemption*

To be entitled to waive family attribution, the redemption must result in a complete termination of the redeemed shareholder's interest within the meaning of Section 302(c)(2)(A)(i). The meaning of the requirement that the distributee retain "no interest in the corporation" understandably has been controversial, as the following case illustrates.

[¶ 5035]

LYNCH v. COMMISSIONER

United States Court of Appeals, Ninth Circuit, 1986.
801 F.2d 1176.

HALL, CIRCUIT JUDGE:

The Commissioner of the Internal Revenue Service (Commissioner) petitions for review of a Tax Court decision holding that a corporate redemption of a taxpayer's stock was a sale or exchange subject to capital gains treatment. The Commissioner argues that the taxpayer held a prohibited interest in the corporation after the redemption and therefore the transaction should be characterized as a dividend distribution taxable as ordinary income. We agree with the Commissioner and reverse the Tax Court.

I

Taxpayers, William and Mima Lynch, formed the W.M. Lynch Co. on April 1, 1960. The corporation issued all of its outstanding stock to William Lynch (taxpayer). The taxpayer specialized in leasing cast-in-place concrete pipe machines. He owned the machines individually but leased them to the corporation which in turn subleased the equipment to independent contractors.

On December 17, 1975 the taxpayer sold 50 shares of the corporation's stock to his son, Gilbert Lynch (Gilbert), for $17,170. Gilbert paid for the stock with a $16,000 check given to him by the taxpayer and $1,170 from his own savings. The taxpayer and his wife also resigned as directors and officers of the corporation on the same day.

On December 31, 1975 the corporation redeemed all 2300 shares of the taxpayer's stock. In exchange for his stock, the taxpayer received $17,900 of property and a promissory note for $771,920. Gilbert, as the sole remaining shareholder, pledged his 50 shares as a guarantee for the note. In the event that the corporation defaulted on any of the note payments, the taxpayer would have the right to vote or sell Gilbert's 50 shares.

In the years immediately preceding the redemption, Gilbert had assumed greater managerial responsibility in the corporation. He wished, however, to retain the taxpayer's technical expertise with cast-in-place concrete pipe machines. On the date of the redemption, the taxpayer also entered into a consulting agreement with the corporation. The consulting agreement provided the taxpayer with payments of $500 per month for five years, plus reimbursement for business related travel, entertainment, and automobile expenses. * * * The corporation never withheld payroll taxes from payments made to the taxpayer.

After the redemption, the taxpayer shared his former office with Gilbert. The taxpayer came to the office daily for approximately one year; thereafter his appearances dwindled to about once or twice per week. * * *

In addition to the consulting agreement, the taxpayer had other ties to the corporation. He remained covered by the corporation's group medical insurance policy until 1980. When his coverage ended, the taxpayer had received the benefit of $4,487.54 in premiums paid by the corporation. * * *

II

We must decide whether the redemption of the taxpayer's stock in this case is taxable as a dividend distribution * * *.

¶ 5035

* * * In order to determine whether there is a complete redemption for purposes of section 302(b)(3), the family attribution rules of section 318(a) must be applied unless the requirements of section 302(c)(2) are satisfied. Here, if the family attribution rules apply, the taxpayer will be deemed to own constructively the 50 shares held by Gilbert (100% of the corporation's stock) and the transaction would not qualify as a complete redemption within the meaning of section 302(b)(3).

* * *

The Commissioner argues that in every case the performance of post-redemption services is a prohibited interest under section 302(c)(2)(A)(i), regardless of whether the taxpayer is an officer, director, employee, or independent contractor.

The Tax Court rejected the Commissioner's argument, finding that the services rendered by the taxpayer did not amount to a prohibited interest in the corporation. In reaching this conclusion, the Tax Court relied on a test derived from *Lewis v. Commissioner*, 47 T.C. 129, 136 (1966) (Simpson, J., concurring):

> Immediately after the enactment of the 1954 Code, it was recognized that section 302(c)(2)(A)(i) did not prohibit office holding per se, but was concerned with a retained financial stake in the corporation, such as a profit-sharing plan, or in the creation of an ostensible sale that really changed nothing so far as corporate management was concerned. Thus, in determining whether a prohibited interest has been retained under section 302(c)(2)(A)(i), we must look to whether the former stockholder has either retained a financial stake in the corporation or continued to control the corporation and benefit by its operations. In particular, where the interest retained is not that of an officer, director, or employee, we must examine the facts and circumstances to determine whether a prohibited interest has been retained under section 302(c)(2)(A)(i).

Lynch v. Commissioner, 83 T.C. 597, 605 (1984) (citations omitted).

After citing the "control or financial stake" standard, the Tax Court engaged in a two-step analysis. First, the court concluded that the taxpayer was an independent contractor rather than an employee because the corporation had no right under the consulting agreement to control his actions.[5] *Id.* at 606. Second, the court undertook a "facts and circumstances" analysis to determine whether the taxpayer had a financial stake in the corporation or managerial control after the redemption. Because the consulting agreement was not linked to the future profitability of the corporation, the court found that the taxpayer had no

---

5. Finding that the taxpayer was not an employee obviated the need to decide whether the parenthetical language in section 302(c)(2)(A)(i) prohibited employment relationships per se. *See Seda v. Commis-* *sioner*, 82 T.C. 484, 488 (1984) (court stated that "section 302(c)(2)(A)(i) may not prohibit the retention of all employment relationships").

financial stake. *Id*. at 606–07. The court also found no evidence that the taxpayer exerted control over the corporation. *Id*. at 607. Thus, the Tax Court determined that the taxpayer held no interest prohibited by section 302(c)(2)(A)(i).

III

* * *

We reject the Tax Court's interpretation of section 302(c)(2)(A)(i). An individualized determination of whether a taxpayer has retained a financial stake or continued to control the corporation after the redemption is inconsistent with Congress' desire to bring a measure of certainty to the tax consequences of a corporate redemption. We hold that a taxpayer who provides post-redemption services, either as an employee or an independent contractor, holds a prohibited interest in the corporation because he is not a creditor.

The legislative history of section 302 states that Congress intended to provide "definite standards in order to provide certainty in specific instances." S. Rep. No. 1622, 83d Cong. 2d Sess. 233 * * *. "In lieu of a factual inquiry in every case, [section 302] is intended to prescribe specific conditions from which the taxpayer may ascertain whether a given redemption" will qualify as a sale or be treated as a dividend distribution. H.R. Rep. No. 1337, 83d Cong. 2d Sess. 35 * * *. The facts and circumstances approach created by the Tax Court undermines the ability of taxpayers to execute a redemption and know the tax consequences with certainty.

* * * The Tax Court's refusal to recognize that section 302(c)(2)(A)(i) prohibits *all* noncreditor interests in the corporation creates the same uncertainty as the "dividend equivalence" test.

The problem with the Tax Court's approach is apparent when this case is compared with *Seda v. Commissioner*, 82 T.C. 484 (1984). In *Seda*, a former shareholder, at his son's insistence, continued working for the corporation for two years after the redemption. He received a salary of $1,000 per month. The Tax Court refused to hold that section 302(c)(2)(A)(i) prohibits the retention of employment relations per se, despite the unequivocal language in the statute.[6] *Id*. at 488. Instead, the court applied the facts and circumstances approach to determine whether the former shareholder retained a financial stake or continued to control the corporation. The Tax Court found that the monthly payments of $1,000 constituted a financial stake in the corporation. *Id*. This result is at odds with the holding in *Lynch* that payments of $500 per month do not constitute a financial stake in the corporation. *Compare Lynch*, 83 T.C. at 606–07 *with Seda*, 82 T.C. at 488. The court also found

---

6. Eight of the seventeen Tax Court judges who reviewed *Seda* concurred in the result but would have classified all officer, director, or employee relationships as prohibited interests under section 302(c)(2)(A)(i).

in *Seda* no evidence that the former shareholder had ceased to manage the corporation. 82 T.C. at 488. Again, this finding is contrary to the holding in *Lynch* that the taxpayer exercised no control over the corporation after the redemption, even though he worked daily for a year and shared his old office with his son. *Compare Lynch*, 83 T.C. at 607 *with Seda*, 82 T.C. 488. *Seda* and *Lynch* thus vividly demonstrate the perils of making an ad hoc determination of "control" or "financial stake."

A recent Tax Court opinion further illustrates the imprecision of the facts and circumstances approach. * * *

Although the Tax Court reached the correct result in *Cerone*, its approach undermines the definite contours of the safe harbor Congress intended to create with sections 302(b)(3) and 302(c)(2)(A)(i). Whether a taxpayer has a financial stake according to the Tax Court seems to depend on two factors, length of employment and the amount of salary. Length of employment after the redemption is irrelevant because Congress wanted taxpayers to know whether they were entitled to capital gains treatment on the date their shares were redeemed. * * * As for the amount of annual salary, the Tax Court's present benchmark appears to be the $12,000 figure in *Seda*. Salary at or above this level will be deemed to be a financial stake in the enterprise, though the $6,000 annual payments in this case were held not to be a financial stake. There is no support in the legislative history of section 302 for the idea that Congress meant only to prohibit service contracts of a certain worth, and taxpayers should not be left to speculate as to what income level will give rise to a financial stake.

In this case, the taxpayer points to the fact that the taxpayers in *Seda* and *Cerone* were employees, while he was an independent contractor. On appeal, the Commissioner concedes the taxpayer's independent contractor status. We fail to see, however, any meaningful way to distinguish *Seda* and *Cerone* from *Lynch* by differentiating between employees and independent contractors. All of the taxpayers performed services for their corporations following the redemption. To hold that only the employee taxpayers held a prohibited interest would elevate form over substance. The parenthetical language in section 302(c)(2)(A)(i) merely provides a subset of prohibited interests from the universe of such interests, and in no way limits us from finding that an independent contractor retains a prohibited interest. Furthermore, the Tax Court has in effect come to ignore the parenthetical language. If employment relationships are not prohibited interests per se, then the taxpayer's status as an employee or independent contractor is irrelevant. What really matters under the Tax Court's approach is how the taxpayer fares under a facts and circumstances review of whether he has a financial stake in the corporation or managerial control.[7] Tax planners

---

7. The Tax Court's focus on managerial control or a financial stake originated with

Judge Simpson's concurrence in *Lewis*, 47 T.C. at 136–38. His interpretation of section

are left to guess where along the continuum of monthly payments from $500 to $1000 capital gains treatment ends and ordinary income tax begins.

* * *

* * * We believe that any attempt to define prohibited interests based on the level of control leads to the same difficulties inherent in making a case-by-case determination of what constitutes a financial stake.[8]

IV

Our decision today comports with the plain language of section 302 and its legislative history. * * * Taxpayers who wish to receive capital gains treatment upon the redemption of their shares must completely sever all noncreditor interests in the corporation.[9] We hold that the taxpayer, as an independent contractor, held such a noncreditor interest, and so cannot find shelter in the safe harbor of section 302(c)(2)(A)(i). Accordingly, the family attribution rules of section 318 apply and the taxpayer fails to qualify for a complete redemption under section 302(b)(3). The payments from the corporation in redemption of the taxpayer's shares must be characterized as a dividend distribution taxable as ordinary income under section 301.

REVERSED.

302(c)(2)(A) is supported by Bittker, *Stock Redemptions and Partial Liquidations Under the Internal Revenue Code of 1954*, 9 Stan. L. Rev. 13, 33 n.72 (1956). Professor Bittker argues that Congress' goal was to ensure that taxpayers who transferred only ostensible control or maintained a financial stake in the corporation did not receive the benefit of capital gains treatment. He is no doubt correct. However, the means selected by Congress to achieve this goal do not allow for an individualized determination of control and financial stakes. Instead, section 302(c)(2)(A)(i) operates mechanically: the taxpayer must sever all but a creditor's interest to avoid the family attribution rules and thereby receive capital gains treatment. Nowhere in the legislative history of section 302(c) does Congress intimate that courts may use a flexible facts and circumstances test to determine the existence of managerial control or a financial stake.

8. Determining the existence of control is particularly difficult in the context of a family-held corporation. The exercise of control often will not be obvious because a parent may influence a child, and hence corporate decisionmaking, in myriad ways. Our rule that the provision of services is a prohibited interest eliminates the need to make a speculative inquiry into whether the parent still controls the corporation after the redemption. Of course, no rule could or should prohibit post-redemption parent-child communication concerning the management of the corporation.

9. Our definition of a prohibited interest still leaves an open question as to the permissible scope of a creditor's interest under section 302(c)(2)(A)(i). *See, e.g.,* Treas. Reg. § 1.302–4(d) (a creditor's claim must not be subordinate to the claims of general creditors or in any other sense proprietary, i.e., principal payments or interest rates must not be contingent on the earnings of the corporation).

The taxpayer argues that some creditor relationships might result in an "opportunity to influence" as great or greater than any officer, director, or employee relationship. He cites Rev. Ruling 77–467, 1977–2 C.B. 92 which concluded that a taxpayer who leased real property to a corporation, after the corporation redeemed his shares, held a creditor's interest under section 302(c)(2)(A)(i). While the taxpayer here may be correct in his assessment of a creditor's "opportunity to influence" a corporation, he overlooks the fact that Congress specifically allowed the right to retain such an interest.

[¶ 5040]

Notes

1.   Does the decision in *Lynch* achieve appropriate results from a tax policy point of view? By the time that the first generation shareholders wish to end their financial involvement in the corporation, the second generation may not have acquired all the technical information or know-how required to operate the business. Can a redemption under these circumstances achieve exchange treatment under *Lynch*? For example, would an agreement by the retiring shareholders to provide services to the corporation without charge satisfy the court?

2.   Section 302(c)(2)(A)(i) specifically authorizes the retention of an interest as a creditor. However, Reg. § 1.302–4(d) suggests that if stock is redeemed for a note but the note contains too many equity characteristics, such as an interest rate that is geared to earnings, the former shareholder would be regarded as having an interest other than as a creditor. Could that, appropriately, be the result if the note were nevertheless regarded as debt rather than stock under the Section 385 debt-equity analysis?

3.   If the redeemed shareholder cannot retain any employment relationship with the corporation, can the shareholder's spouse? The following case addresses that issue and others. In reading *Hurst*, compare the general approach of the court with the approach taken in *Lynch*.

[¶ 5045]

HURST v. COMMISSIONER

United States Tax Court, 2005.
124 T. C. 16.

HOLMES, JUDGE: Richard Hurst founded and owned Hurst Mechanical, Inc. (HMI), a thriving small business in Michigan that repairs and maintains heating, ventilating, and air conditioning (HVAC) systems. He bought, with his wife Mary Ann, a much smaller HVAC company called RHI; and together they also own the building where HMI has its headquarters.

When the Hursts decided to retire in 1997, they sold RHI to HMI, sold HMI to a trio of new owners who included their son, and remained HMI's landlord. Mary Ann Hurst stayed on as an HMI employee at a modest salary and with such fringe benefits as health insurance and a company car.

The Hursts believe that they arranged these transactions to enable them to pay tax on their profit from the sale of HMI and RHI at capital gains rates over a period of fifteen years. The Commissioner disagrees.

¶ 5035

FINDINGS OF FACT

* * *

In April 1979, the Hursts opened their own HVAC business, working out of their basement and garage. Mr. Hurst handled the technical and sales operations while Mrs. Hurst did the bookkeeping and accounting. The business began as a proprietorship, but in November of that year they incorporated it under Michigan law, with Mr. Hurst as sole shareholder of the new corporation, named Hurst Mechanical, Inc. (HMI). In 1989, HMI elected to be taxed under subchapter S of the Code, and that election has never changed. The firm grew quickly, and after five years it had about 15 employees; by 1997, it had 45 employees and over $4 million in annual revenue.

After leaving the Hursts' home, HMI moved to * * * Belmont, Michigan, in a building on Safety Drive. The Hursts bought this building in their own names and leased it to HMI. In early 1994, the Hursts bought another HVAC business, Refrigerator Man, Inc., which they renamed R.H., Inc. (RHI). Each of the Hursts owned half of RHI's stock.

[In 1996, in anticipation of their retirement, the Hursts agreed to sell the business to three key employees, one of whom was their son, Todd Hurst.]

* * *

Everything came together on July 1, 1997: HMI bought 90 percent of its 1000 outstanding shares from Mr. Hurst for a $2 million note. Richard Hurst sold the remaining 100 shares in HMI to Todd Hurst (51 shares), Dixon (35 shares), and Tuori (14 shares). The new owners each paid $2500 a share, also secured by promissory notes. HMI bought RHI from the Hursts for a $250,000 note. (All these notes, from both HMI and the new owner, had an interest rate of eight percent and were payable in 60 quarterly installments.) HMI also signed a new 15–year lease for the Safety Drive property, with a rent of $8,500 a month, adjusted for inflation. The lease gave HMI an option to buy the building from the Hursts, and this became a point of some contention—described below—after the sale. And, finally, HMI also signed a ten-year employment contract with Mrs. Hurst, giving her a small salary and fringe benefits that included employee health insurance.

If done right, the deal would have beneficial tax and nontax effects for the Hursts. From a tax perspective, a stock sale would give rise to long-term capital gain, taxed at lower rates than dividends.[3] And by

---

3. This was an important consideration to the Hursts—although HMI was an S corporation at the time of these transactions, and thus subject only to a single tier of tax, secs. 1363, 1366, it had been a C corporation until 1989 and still had $383,000 in accumulated earnings from those years that had not been distributed to Mr. Hurst. Without careful planning, these earnings might end up taxed as dividends under section 1368(c).

taking a 15–year note, rather than a lump sum, they could qualify for installment treatment under section 453, probably letting them enjoy a lower effective tax rate.

There were also nontax reasons for structuring the deal this way. HMI's regular bank had no interest in financing the deal, and the parties thought that a commercial lender would have wanted a security interest in the corporations' assets. By taking a security interest only in the stock, the Hursts were allowing the buyers more flexibility should they need to encumber corporate assets to finance the business.

But this meant that they themselves were financing the sale. And spreading the payments over time meant that they were faced with a lack of diversification in their assets and a larger risk of default. To reduce these risks, the parties agreed to a complicated series of cross-default and cross-collateralization provisions, the net result of which was that a default on any one of the promissory notes or the Safety Drive lease or Mrs. Hurst's employment contract would constitute a default on them all. Since the promissory notes were secured by the HMI and RHI stock which the Hursts had sold, a default on any of the obligations would have allowed Mr. Hurst to step in and seize the HMI stock to satisfy any unpaid debt.

As it turned out, these protective measures were never used, and the prospect of their use seemed increasingly remote. Under the management of Todd Hurst, Dixon, and Tuori, HMI boomed. The company's revenue increased from approximately $4 million annually at the time of the sale to over $12 million by 2003. Not once after the sale did any of the new owners miss a payment on their notes or the lease.

The Hursts reported the dispositions of both the HMI and RHI stock on their 1997 tax return as installment sales of long-term capital assets. The Commissioner disagreed, and recharacterized these dispositions as producing over $400,000 in dividends and over $1.8 million in immediately recognized capital gains. In the resulting notice of deficiency for the Hursts' 1997 tax year, he determined that this (and a few much smaller adjustments) led to a total deficiency of $538,114, and imposed an accuracy-related penalty under section 6662 of $107,622.80. The Hursts were Michigan residents when they filed their petition, and trial was held in Detroit.

OPINION

* * *

Given the stakes involved, the Hursts and their advisers tried to steer this deal toward the comparatively well-lit safe harbor of section 302(b)(3)—the "termination redemption." Reaching their destination depended on redeeming the HMI stock in a way that met the rules defining complete termination of ownership. And one might think that a termination redemption would be easy to spot, because whether a taxpayer did or didn't sell all his stock looks like a simple question to answer. Congress, however, was concerned that taxpayers would manipulate the rules to get the tax benefits of a sale without actually cutting their connection to the management of the redeeming corporation. The problem seemed especially acute in the case of family-owned businesses, because such businesses often don't have strict lines between the roles of owner, employee, consultant, and director.

The Code addresses this problem by incorporating rules attributing stock ownership of one person to another (set out in section 318) in the analysis of transactions governed by section 302. Section 318(a)(1)(A)(ii), which treats stock owned by a child as owned by his parents, became a particular obstacle to the Hursts' navigation of these rules because their son Todd was to be one of HMI's new owners. This meant that the note that Mr. Hurst received from HMI in exchange for 90 percent of his HMI stock might be treated as a section 301 distribution, because he would be treated as if he still owned Todd's HMI stock—making his "termination redemption" less than "complete".

But this would be too harsh a result when there really is a complete termination both of ownership and control. Thus, Congress provided that if the selling family member elects to keep no interest in the corporation other than as a creditor for at least ten years, the Commissioner will ignore the section 318 attribution rules. Sec. 302(c)(2); sec. 1.302–4, Income Tax Regs.

By far the greatest part of the tax at issue in this case turns on whether Richard Hurst proved that the sale of his HMI stock was a termination redemption, specifically whether he kept an interest "other than an interest as a creditor" in HMI. * * *

A. Complete Termination of Interest in HMI

The Hursts' argument is simple—they say that Richard (who had owned all the HMI stock) walked completely away from the company, and has no interest in it other than making sure that the new owners keep current on their notes and rent. The Commissioner's argument is more complicated. While acknowledging that each relationship between the Hursts and their old company—creditor under the notes, landlord under the lease, employment of a non-owning family member—passes muster, he argues that the total number of related obligations resulting from the transaction gave the Hursts a prohibited interest in the corporation by giving Richard Hurst a financial stake in the company's continued success.

In analyzing whether this holistic view is to prevail, we look at the different types of ongoing economic benefits that the Hursts were to receive from HMI: (a) The debt obligations in the form of promissory notes issued to the Hursts by HMI and the new owners, (b) their lease of the Safety Drive building to HMI; and (c) the employment contract between HMI and Mrs. Hurst.

1. *Promissory Notes*

There were several notes trading hands at the deal's closing. One was the $250,000 note issued by HMI to the Hursts for their RHI stock. The second was the $2 million, 15–year note, payable in quarterly installments, issued to Mr. Hurst by HMI in redemption of 90 percent (900 of 1000) of his HMI shares. Mr. Hurst also received three 15–year notes payable in quarterly installments for the remaining 100 HMI shares that he sold to Todd Hurst, Dixon, and Tuori. All these notes called for periodic payments of principal and interest on a fixed schedule. Neither the amount nor the timing of payments was tied to the financial performance of HMI. Although the notes were subordinate to HMI's obligation to its bank, they were not subordinate to general creditors, nor was the amount or certainty of the payments under them dependent on HMI's earnings. See *Dunn v. Commissioner,* 615 F.2d 578, 582–583 (2d Cir.1980), affg. 70 T.C. 715, 726–727 (1978); *Estate of Lennard v. Commissioner,* 61 T.C. 554, 563 & n. 7 (1974). All of these contractual arrangements had cross-default clauses and were secured by the buyers' stock. This meant that should *any* of the notes go into default, Mr. Hurst would have the right to seize the stock and sell it. The parties agree that the probable outcome of such a sale would be that Mr. Hurst would once again be in control of HMI.

Respondent questions the cross-default clauses of the various contractual obligations, and interprets them as an effective retention of control by Mr. Hurst. But in *Lynch v. Commissioner,* 83 T.C. 597 (1984), revd. on other grounds 801 F.2d 1176 (9th Cir.1986), we held that a security interest in redeemed stock does not constitute a prohibited interest under section 302. We noted that "The holding of such a security interest is common in sales agreements, and * * * not inconsistent with the interest of a creditor." *Id.* at 610; see also *Hoffman v. Commissioner,* 47 T.C. 218, 232 (1966), affd. 391 F.2d 930 (5th Cir.1968). Furthermore, at trial, the Hursts offered credible evidence from their professional advisers that these transactions, including the grant of a security interest to Mr. Hurst, were consistent with common practice for seller-financed deals.

2. *The Lease*

HMI also leased its headquarters on Safety Drive from the Hursts. As with the notes, the lease called for a fixed rent in no way conditioned upon the financial performance of HMI. Attorney Ron David, who was intimately familiar with the transaction, testified convincingly that there was no relationship between the obligations of the parties and the financial performance of HMI. The transactional documents admitted into evidence do not indicate otherwise. There is simply no evidence that the payment terms in the lease between the Hursts and HMI vary from those that would be reasonable if negotiated between unrelated parties. And the Hursts point out that the IRS itself has ruled that an arm's-length lease allowing a redeeming corporation to use property owned by a former owner does not preclude characterization as a redemption. Rev. Rul. 77–467, 1977–2 C.B. 92.

The Commissioner nevertheless points to the lease to bolster his claim that Mr. Hurst kept too much control, noting that in 2003 he was able to persuade the buyers to surrender HMI's option to buy the property. Exercising this option would have let HMI end its rent expense at a time of low mortgage interest rates, perhaps improving its cash-flow—and so might well have been in the new owners' interest. But the Hursts paid a price when the new owners gave it up. Not only did the deal cancel the option, but it also cut the interest rate on the various promissory notes owed to the Hursts from eight to six percent. So we think the Commissioner is wrong in implicitly asserting that the buyers should have engaged in every behavior possible that would be adverse to the elder Hursts' interest, and focus on whether the elder Hursts kept "a financial stake in the corporation or continued to control the corporation and benefit by its operations." *Lynch,* 83 T.C. at 604. Ample and entirely credible testimony showed that the discussions about HMI's potential purchase of the Safety Drive location were adversarial: The Hursts as landlords wanted to keep the rent flowing, and the new owners wanted to reduce HMI's cash outlays. Though the Hursts kept their rents, the new owners did not give up the option gratuitously—making this a negotiation rather than a collusion.

3. *Employment of Mrs. Hurst*

At the same time that HMI redeemed Mr. Hurst's stock and signed the lease, it also agreed to a ten-year employment contract with Mrs. Hurst. Under its terms, she was to receive a salary that rapidly declined to $1000/month and some fringe benefits—including health insurance, use of an HMI-owned pickup truck, and free tax preparation.

In deciding whether this was a prohibited interest, the first thing to note is that Mrs. Hurst did not own any HMI stock. Thus, she is not a "distributee" unable to have an "interest in the corporation (including an interest as officer, director, or employee), other than an interest as a creditor." Sec. 302(c)(2)(A)(i). The Commissioner is thus forced to argue that her employment was a "prohibited interest" for Mr. Hurst. And he does, contending that through her employment Mr. Hurst kept an ongoing influence in HMI's corporate affairs. He also argues that an employee unrelated to the former owner of the business would not continue to be paid were she to work Mrs. Hurst's admittedly minimal schedule. And he asserts that her employment was a mere ruse to provide Mr. Hurst with his company car and health benefits, bolstering this argument with proof that the truck used by Mrs. Hurst was the same one that her husband had been using when he ran HMI.

None of this, though, changes the fact that her compensation and fringe benefits were fixed, and again—like the notes and lease—not subordinated to HMI's general creditors, and not subject to any fluctuation related to HMI's financial performance. Her duties, moreover, were various administrative and clerical tasks—some of the same chores she had been doing at HMI on a regular basis for many years. And there was no evidence whatsoever that Mr. Hurst used his wife in any way as a surrogate for continuing to manage (or even advise) HMI's new owners. Cf. *Lynch,* 801 F.2d at 1179 (former shareholder himself providing post-redemption services).

It is, however, undisputed that her employment contract had much the same cross-default provisions that were part of the lease and stock transfer agreements. The Commissioner questions whether, in the ordinary course of business, there was reason to intertwine substantial corporate obligations with the employment contract of only one of 45 employees. He points to this special provision as proof that the parties to this redemption contemplated a continuing involvement greater than that of a mere creditor.

In relying so heavily on the cross-default provisions of the Hursts' various agreements, though, the Commissioner ignores the proof at trial that there was a legitimate creditor's interest in the Hursts' demanding them. They were, after all, parting with a substantial asset (the corporations), in return for what was in essence an IOU from some business associates. Their ability to enjoy retirement in financial security was fully contingent upon their receiving payment on the notes, lease, and employment contract. As William Gedris, one of the Hursts' advisers, credibly testified, it would not have been logical for Mr. Hurst to relinquish shares in a corporation while receiving neither payment nor security.

The value of that security, however, depended upon the financial health of the company. Repossessing worthless shares as security on defaulted notes would have done little to ensure the Hursts' retirement. The cross-default provisions were their canary in the coal mine. If at any point the company failed to meet any financial obligation to the Hursts, Mr. Hurst would have the option to retrieve his shares immediately, thus protecting the value of his security interest instead of worrying about whether this was the beginning of a downward spiral. This is perfectly consistent with a creditor's interest, and there was credible trial testimony that multiple default triggers are common in commercial lending.

We find that the cross-default provisions protected the Hursts' financial interest as creditors of HMI, for a debt on which they had received practically no downpayment, and the collection of which (though not "dependent upon the earnings of the corporation" as that phrase is used in section 1.302–4(d), Income Tax Regs.) was realistically contingent upon HMI's continued financial health. The buyers likewise

¶ 5045

had a motivation to structure the transaction as they did—their inability to obtain traditional financing without unduly burdening HMI's potential for normal business operations. Even one of the IRS witnesses showed this understanding of Mr. Hurst's relationship to the new owners after the redemption—the revenue agent who conducted the audit accurately testified that Mr. Hurst was "going to be the banker and wanted his interests protected."

The number of legal connections between Mr. Hurst and the buyers that continued after the deal was signed did not change their character as permissible security interests. Even looked at all together, they were in no way contingent upon the financial performance of the company except in the obvious sense that all creditors have in their debtors' solvency.

Moreover, despite the Commissioner's qualms, we find as a matter of fact that Mr. Hurst has not participated in any manner in any corporate activity since the redemptions occurred—not even a Christmas party or summer picnic. His only dealing with HMI after the sale was when, as noted above, he dickered with the buyers over their purchase option on the Safety Drive property. These facts do not show a continuing proprietary stake or control of corporate management.

* * *

[¶ 5050]

b.   Ten–Year "Look Back"

The termination of interest rule is obviously susceptible to abuse. Consider, for example, a taxpayer desiring to withdraw funds from a wholly owned corporation but unable to qualify the transaction under Section 302(b)(1) or (2). The taxpayer might make a gift of a large block of stock to a spouse or child and shortly thereafter cause the corporation to redeem either all of the stock now held by the donee or all of the stock retained by the taxpayer, in each case hoping to qualify the redemption under Section 302(b)(3). If the transaction is merely a scheme to withdraw funds from the corporation at capital gains rates but without materially altering the continuing ownership of the corporation, the redemption should not be treated as a complete termination of interest. On the other hand, Section 302(b)(3) is designed to facilitate the transfer of the stock interest of a retiring shareholder to the next generation. If the transaction is a step in such a plan, it should be entitled to be treated as a complete termination.

Section 302(c)(2)(B) attempts to draw that line. In general, if stock has been divided among related taxpayers (within the meaning of Section 318) during the 10–year period preceding the redemption, by either sale or gift, the redemption of any of that stock from either the transferor or the transferee is not eligible for complete termination treatment. However, if tax avoidance was not one of the principal purposes of the earlier stock transfer, then the limitation does not apply and the redemption regains eligibility for complete termination treatment. In administering this provision, the IRS has stated:

> The structure and legislative history of section 302 * * * make it clear that the purpose of section 302(c)(2)(B) is not to prevent the reduction of capital gains through gifts of appreciated stock prior to the redemption of the remaining stock of the transferor, but to prevent the withdrawal of earnings at capital gains rates by a shareholder of a family controlled corporation who seeks continued control and/or economic interest in the corporation through the stock given to a related person or the stock he retains. * * *

> Tax avoidance within the meaning of section 302(c)(2)(B) * * * would occur, for example, if a taxpayer transfers stock of a corporation to a spouse in contemplation of the redemption of the remaining stock of the corporation and terminates all direct interest in the corporation in compliance with section 302(c)(2)(A), but with the intention of retaining effective control of the corporation indirectly through the stock held by the spouse. Another example, which would generally constitute tax avoidance within the meaning of this provision, is the transfer by a taxpayer of part of the stock of a corporation to a spouse in contemplation of the subsequent redemption of the transferred stock from the spouse. * * *

Rev. Rul. 77–293, 1977–2 C.B. 91.

As a result, when the initial transfer of stock has been for a business reason, including a bona fide shift in ownership, the IRS has been quite willing to treat a later redemption of stock as eligible for complete termination treatment. Taxpayer successes in avoiding Section 302(c)(2)(B) usually occur when a retiring shareholder gives or sells some stock to children and causes the remaining stock to be redeemed. However, redemptions from donees have also secured complete termination treatment when the stock was given to the donee child in the hope that the child would assume control of the business but the plan unraveled, the child departed, and the stock was redeemed. See Rev. Rul. 56–584, 1956–2 C.B. 179.

[¶ 5060]

c. Waivers of Attribution by Entities

What happens if the first generation waits too long to have their stock redeemed under Section 302(b)(3) and dies before the transaction can occur? Can the heirs or the estate avoid dividend treatment if the holdings acquired from the decedent are redeemed? The answer to that question remains terribly important under current law. Since the stock will have received a step-up in tax basis to its value, if the redemption

¶ 5050

can avoid dividend treatment it will not be subject to any tax at all. Unfortunately the answer is a bit tricky and depends in large part upon whether the heirs already own stock in the corporation.

Assume Father and Child owns all of the stock in a corporation; Mother does not own any. We know that if Father's stock is redeemed, it will be a complete termination allowing the waiver of attribution from Child and thus securing treatment as a sale. Assume that Father dies, leaving his entire estate to Mother. If the estate causes the stock to be redeemed, stock held by its beneficiaries will be attributed to it. While Mother, the only beneficiary, does not own any stock directly, Child does and under the general rule of Section 318, stock can be attributed under the family attribution rule (from Child to Mother) and then reattributed under the attribution to entities rule (from Mother to the estate). However, under Section 302(c)(2)(C), an entity, such as the estate, can waive *family* attribution in connection with a complete termination of its actual holdings. Thus, the *estate* can waive attribution of the stock held by Child to Mother and thereby avoid dividend treatment. Note that for an entity to be able to waive family attribution, both the entity and all persons holding stock that might be attributed to the entity must meet all of the requirements that Father would have had to meet to obtain complete termination treatment.

If the stock were distributed to Mother and redeemed by her, complete termination treatment would be somewhat less assured. Mother, who just acquired her stock from the estate, would thereby fall under the 10–year look back rule and that could prevent her from waiving family attribution from Child. However, if there were no indication that Mother intended to control the corporation through her child, the transfer of stock to her should not be regarded as occurring for a tax-avoidance purpose.

On the other hand, if Child were also a beneficiary of the estate, the holdings of Child would be attributed to the estate under the attribution to entities rule and that attribution cannot be waived. Under these circumstances, the estate could not obtain complete termination treatment and its redemption would likely be taxed as a dividend as long as the Child remained a beneficiary of the estate. Note that it would not improve the situation for the stock to be distributed to Child for Child would also be unable to obtain complete termination treatment.

[¶ 5075]

Problems

1. Father and Son each owned 50 percent of the stock of Chemical Corporation, and each was active in its business. However, Father has now retired and all of his stock has been redeemed by the corporation. How would the redemption be taxed under each of the following circumstances?

a. Father agreed in writing to provide technical assistance to the corporation for a period of three years without charge, but no request for assistance was ever made.

b. Father and Son did not enter into any formal agreement concerning technical assistance. On three occasions in the year following the redemption Son called upon Father for assistance and reimbursed Father's travel expenses in the total amount of $4,500.

c. Father's stock was redeemed in exchange for a note in the principal amount of $500,000, which amount equalled 50 percent of the net worth of the corporation. The note carried a market rate of interest, and principal was payable in five equal annual installments but no installment was to exceed 75 percent of the net profits for the year.

d. After five years, Son dies and Father inherits all of his stock.

e. Father purchased his stock from Son five years before the redemption because he thought it would be a good investment.

f. Son acquired his stock by gift from Father five years before the redemption of Father's stock.

2. Father and Mother each owned 50 percent of the stock in Family, Inc. Upon Father's death, his stock passed to his estate of which Mother and Child are equal beneficiaries. The executor of Father's estate has the discretion to distribute the stock to either Mother or Child. All of the parties now wish to have just Father's stock redeemed if dividend treatment can be avoided. How should the executor proceed?

a. Can the stock simply be redeemed from the estate?

b. If the stock is distributed to Child, can it shortly thereafter be redeemed without dividend treatment?

c. The estate can distribute other assets to Mother in complete satisfaction of her inheritance in which event Mother would no longer be a beneficiary of the estate. If that occurred, could the estate thereafter cause the stock to be redeemed?

[¶ 5080]

5. REDEMPTIONS "NOT ESSENTIALLY EQUIVALENT TO A DIVIDEND"

Redemptions that fail to qualify as substantially disproportionate under Section 302(b)(2) or as terminations of interest under Section 302(b)(3) may still qualify for exchange treatment under Section 302(b)(1). The following case remains the leading interpretation of this provision.

¶ 5075

[¶ 5085]

UNITED STATES v. DAVIS

Supreme Court of the United States, 1970.
397 U.S. 301.

MR. JUSTICE MARSHALL delivered the opinion of the Court.

In 1945, taxpayer and E.B. Bradley organized a corporation. In exchange for property transferred to the new company, Bradley received 500 shares of common stock, and taxpayer and his wife similarly each received 250 such shares. Shortly thereafter, taxpayer made an additional contribution to the corporation, purchasing 1,000 shares of preferred stock at a par value of $25 per share.

The purpose of this latter transaction was to increase the company's working capital and thereby to qualify for a loan previously negotiated through the Reconstruction Finance Corporation. It was understood that the corporation would redeem the preferred stock when the RFC loan had been repaid. Although in the interim taxpayer bought Bradley's 500 shares and divided them between his son and daughter, the total capitalization of the company remained the same until 1963. That year, after the loan was fully repaid and in accordance with the original understanding, the company redeemed taxpayer's preferred stock.

* * *

The Court of Appeals held that the $25,000 received by taxpayer was "not essentially equivalent to a dividend" within the meaning of that phrase in § 302(b)(1) of the Code because the redemption was the final step in a course of action that had a legitimate business (as opposed to a tax avoidance) purpose. That holding represents only one of a variety of treatments accorded similar transactions under § 302(b)(1) in the circuit courts of appeals. We granted certiorari, * * * in order to resolve this recurring tax question involving stock redemptions by closely held corporations. We reverse.

I.

* * * The basic question in this case is whether the $25,000 distribution by the corporation to taxpayer falls under that section—more specifically, whether its legitimate business motivation qualifies the distribution under § 302(b)(1) of the Code. Preliminarily, however, we must consider the relationship between § 302(b)(1) and the rules regarding the attribution of stock ownership found in § 318(a) * * *.

* * *

Taxpayer * * * argues that the attribution rules do not apply in considering whether a distribution is essentially equivalent to a dividend under § 302(b)(1). * * * However, the plain language of the statute

¶ 5085

compels rejection of the argument. In subsection (c) of § 302, the attribution rules are made specifically applicable "in determining the ownership of stock for purposes of this section." Applying this language, both courts below held that § 318(a) applies to all of § 302, including § 302(b)(1)—a view in accord with the decisions of the other courts of appeals, a longstanding treasury regulation, and the opinion of the leading commentators.

* * *

Indeed, it was necessary that the attribution rules apply to § 302(b)(1) unless they were to be effectively eliminated from consideration with regard to § 302(b)(2) and (3) also. For if a transaction failed to qualify under one of those sections solely because of the attribution rules, it would according to taxpayer's argument nonetheless qualify under § 302(b)(1). We cannot agree that Congress intended so to nullify its explicit directive. We conclude, therefore, that the attribution rules of § 318(a) do apply; and, for the purposes of deciding whether a distribution is "not essentially equivalent to a dividend" under § 302(b)(1), taxpayer must be deemed the owner of all 1,000 shares of the company's common stock.

II.

After application of the stock ownership attribution rules, this case viewed most simply involves a sole stockholder who causes part of his shares to be redeemed by the corporation. We conclude that such a redemption is always "essentially equivalent to a dividend" within the meaning of that phrase in § 302(b)(1) and therefore do not reach the Government's alternative argument that in any event the distribution should not on the facts of this case qualify for capital gains treatment.

* * *

In explaining the reason for adding the "essentially equivalent" test, the Senate Committee stated that the House provisions "appeared unnecessarily restrictive, particularly, in the case of redemptions of preferred stock which might be called by the corporation without the shareholder having any control over when the redemption may take place." S. Rep. No. 1622, 83d Cong., 2d Sess., 44 * * *. This explanation gives no indication that the purpose behind the redemption should affect the result. Rather, in its more detailed technical evaluation of § 302(b)(1), the Senate Committee reported as follows:

> The test intended to be incorporated in the interpretation of paragraph (1) is in general that currently employed under section 115(g)(1) of the 1939 Code. Your committee further intends that in applying this test for the future that the inquiry will be devoted solely to the question of whether or not the transaction by its nature may properly be characterized as a sale of stock by the redeeming

shareholder to the corporation. For this purpose the presence or absence of earnings and profits of the corporation is not material. Example: X, the sole shareholder of a corporation having no earnings or profits causes the corporation to redeem half of its stock. Paragraph (1) does not apply to such redemption notwithstanding the absence of earnings and profits.

S. Rep. No. 1622, *supra*, at 234 * * *.

The intended scope of § 302(b)(1) as revealed by this legislative history is certainly not free from doubt. However, we agree with the Government that by making the sole inquiry relevant for the future the narrow one whether the redemption could be characterized as a sale, Congress was apparently rejecting past court decisions that had also considered factors indicating the presence or absence of a tax-avoidance motive. At least that is the implication of the example given. Congress clearly mandated that pro rata distributions be treated under the general rules laid down in §§ 301 and 316 rather than under § 302, and nothing suggests that there should be a different result if there were a "business purpose" for the redemption. Indeed just the opposite inference must be drawn since there would not likely be a tax-avoidance purpose in a situation where there were no earnings or profits. We conclude that the Court of Appeals was therefore wrong in looking for a business purpose and considering it in deciding whether the redemption was equivalent to a dividend. Rather, we agree with the Court of Appeals for the Second Circuit that "the business purpose of a transaction is irrelevant in determining dividend equivalence" under § 302(b)(1). Hasbrook v. United States, 343 F.2d 811, 814 (1965).

Taxpayer strongly argues that to treat the redemption involved here as essentially equivalent to a dividend is to elevate form over substance. Thus, taxpayer argues, had he not bought Bradley's shares or had he made a subordinated loan to the company instead of buying preferred stock, he could have gotten back his $25,000 with favorable tax treatment. However, the difference between form and substance in the tax law is largely problematical, and taxpayer's complaints have little to do with whether a business purpose is relevant under § 302(b)(1). It was clearly proper for Congress to treat distributions generally as taxable dividends when made out of earnings and profits and then to prevent avoidance of that result without regard to motivation where the distribution is in exchange for redeemed stock.

We conclude that that is what Congress did when enacting § 302(b)(1). If a corporation distributes property as a simple dividend, the effect is to transfer the property from the company to its shareholders without a change in the relative economic interests or rights of the stockholders. Where a redemption has that same effect, it cannot be said to have satisfied the "not essentially equivalent to a dividend" requirement of § 302(b)(1). Rather, to qualify for preferred treatment under

¶ 5085

that section, a redemption must result in a meaningful reduction of the shareholder's proportionate interest in the corporation. Clearly, taxpayer here, who (after application of the attribution rules) was the sole shareholder of the corporation both before and after the redemption, did not qualify under this test. The decision of the Court of Appeals must therefore be reversed and the case remanded to the District Court for dismissal of the complaint.

* * *

MR. JUSTICE DOUGLAS, with whom MR. JUSTICE BRENNAN concurs, dissenting.

I agree with the District Court, 274 F.Supp. 466, and with the Court of Appeals, 408 F.2d 1139, that respondent's contribution of working capital in the amount of $25,000 in exchange for 1,000 shares of preferred stock with a par value of $25 was made in order for the corporation to obtain a loan from the RFC and that the preferred stock was to be redeemed when the loan was repaid. For the reasons stated by the two lower courts, this redemption was not "essentially equivalent to a dividend," for the bona fide business purpose of the redemption belies the payment of a dividend. As stated by the Court of Appeals:

> Although closely-held corporations call for close scrutiny under the tax law, we will not, under the facts and circumstances of this case, allow mechanical attribution rules to transform a legitimate corporate transaction into a tax avoidance scheme.

408 F.2d, at 1143–1144.

When the Court holds it was a dividend, it effectively cancels § 302(b)(1) from the Code. This result is not a matter of conjecture, for the Court says that in case of closely held or one-man corporations a redemption of stock is "always" equivalent to a dividend. I would leave such revision to the Congress.

[¶ 5090]

Notes

1. In rejecting the contention that a distribution is "not essentially equivalent to a dividend" if made for sound business reasons of the corporation rather than to benefit the distributee-shareholder, what content did the Court give to the phrase "not essentially equivalent to a dividend"?

2. Would the taxpayer have been better off lending money to the corporation and subordinating his interest to that of outside creditors? Did the Court adequately answer the taxpayer's argument that his investment resembled a loan and should be taxed in the same manner?

3. How many shares must be redeemed in order to satisfy the Court's "meaningful reduction" test? See the following materials.

¶ 5085

[¶ 5095]

REVENUE RULING 75–502

1975–2 C.B. 111.

Advice has been requested whether, under the circumstances described below, a redemption of common stock will qualify as an exchange under section 302(a) * * *.

X corporation had outstanding one class of stock consisting of 1,750 shares of common stock. An estate owned 250 shares of the common stock and individual A, the sole beneficiary of the estate, owned 750 shares of the common stock. Individual B, who was not related to individual A within the meaning of section 318(a)(1) * * *, owned the remaining 750 shares of X common stock. Through the application of the attribution rules of section 318(a)(3)(A), the estate owned A's common stock. Thus, prior to the redemption described below, the estate owned, actually and constructively, approximately 57 percent of the total voting rights of the outstanding common stock of X.

X redeemed for cash all of the common stock held by the estate. After the redemption, the common stock held by A represented 50 percent of the total voting rights of the then outstanding stock of X. Such stock continued to be owned by the estate through the application of section 318(a)(3)(A). Thus, the redemption reduced the estate's voting rights in X from 57 percent to 50 percent.

* * *

In the instant case the redemption of the estate's common stock did not qualify as a substantially disproportionate redemption under section 302(b)(2) * * * because the estate owned 50 percent of the voting rights of X after the redemption. Moreover, the estate's constructive ownership of the X stock also prevented the redemption from qualifying as a complete termination of interest under section 302(b)(3). The question, therefore, is whether the redemption was not essentially equivalent to a dividend within the meaning of section 302(b)(1).

* * *

In *United States v. Davis*, 397 U.S. 301 (1970), * * * the Supreme Court of the United States held that a redemption must result in a meaningful reduction of the shareholder's proportionate interest in the corporation in order to qualify as not essentially equivalent to a dividend within the meaning of section 302(b)(1) * * * and that the business purpose of the redemption is irrelevant to this determination. The Supreme Court further held that section 318(a) applies for the purpose of determining whether a distribution is "not essentially equivalent to a dividend" under section 302(b)(1).

¶ **5095**

The Supreme Court in *Davis* did not indicate what constitutes an "interest" and what constitutes a "meaningful reduction" in situations different from the factual pattern contained in *Davis* wherein the shareholder owned 100 percent of the redeeming corporation before and after the transaction. The Court of Appeals for the Second Circuit has defined the rights inherent in a shareholder's interest. In *Himmel v. Commissioner*, 338 F.2d 815 (2d Cir.1964), the court defined a shareholder's interest to include: (1) the right to vote and thereby exercise control; (2) the right to participate in current earnings and accumulated surplus; and (3) the right to share in net assets on liquidation. A redemption which reduces these rights may result in a meaningful reduction in a shareholder's proportionate interest in a corporation within the meaning of *Davis* and, thus, qualify such redemption as not essentially equivalent to a dividend under section 302(b)(1) * * *. Therefore, *A*'s interest in *X* before and after the redemption must be examined in determining whether the redemption resulted in a meaningful reduction of *A*'s interest under the facts and circumstances of the instant case.

In applying the above principles to the instant case, it is significant that the redemption reduced the estate's voting rights in *X* from 57 percent to 50 percent and also correspondingly reduced the estate's right to participate in current earnings and accumulated surplus and the estate's right to share in net assets on liquidation. Moreover, the reduction of the estate's voting rights from 57 percent to 50 percent produced a situation in which the other 50 percent of the voting rights of *X* were held by a single unrelated shareholder. Thus, under the facts and circumstances of the instant case, the redemption constituted a meaningful reduction of the estate's interest in *X* within the meaning of *Davis*.

Accordingly, the redemption was not essentially equivalent to a dividend within the meaning of section 302(b)(1) * * * and, therefore, qualified as an exchange under section 302(a).

If in the instant case, the stock of *X* held by the estate was reduced by less than 7 percent the redemption would not qualify under section 302(b)(1) because the estate would continue to have dominant voting rights in *X* by virtue of its ownership of more than 50 percent of the *X* stock.

[¶ 5100]

Notes

1. While the redemption in *Davis* did not receive exchange treatment, it certainly was appropriate to test the redemption under Section 302(b)(1) because the redemption of only preferred stock could not qualify under Section 302(b)(2). It is less clear that redemptions of voting common stock that fail the test of Section 302(b)(2) should be given a second chance under Section 302(b)(1). Rev. Rul. 75–502 is

typical in not only applying the test of Section 302(b)(1) to a voting common stock redemption but in doing so rather liberally.

2.   Would you anticipate a different outcome in the ruling if the estate's interest dropped as it did from 57 percent to 50 percent, and the remaining shares were scattered among several unrelated shareholders? In Rev. Rul. 78–401, 1978–2 C.B. 127, it was held that reduction of a shareholder's interest from 90 percent to 60 percent was *not* a "meaningful reduction" inasmuch as he continued to retain day-to-day control of corporate affairs. The remaining 40 percent was held by an unrelated taxpayer. Compare Wright v. United States, 482 F.2d 600 (8th Cir.1973), in which a drop in the taxpayer's voting interests from 85 percent to 61.7 percent was held to be meaningful in view of the significance of a two-thirds vote under state law (for amending articles of incorporation and approving a merger or consolidation or liquidation). The court went on to observe that the taxpayer's "23.3 per cent less of a right to dividends and to assets upon liquidation * * * in itself is of considerable significance."

3.   Under the tripartite test derived from *Himmel*, "meaningfulness" is determined by reference both to economic interests and voting power interests. In granting exchange treatment to relatively small redemptions that result in a loss of control over the corporation, the IRS has placed a surprising degree of importance on the latter.

4.   After *Davis*, it was clear that a meaningful reduction was to be determined after the application of the stock attribution rules. However, those rules could not apply to Section 302(b)(1) in the same way that they apply to Section 302(b)(2). Under the safe harbor test in Section 302(b)(2), exchange treatment is determined by a mathematical computation. Under Section 302(b)(1), even after the attribution rules are applied, the question remains whether the redemption is essentially equivalent to a dividend. That difference has allowed taxpayers to argue that, under Section 302(b)(1), the rules of Section 318 should be applied more flexibly, as the following case illustrates.

[¶ 5105]

CERONE v. COMMISSIONER

United States Tax Court, 1986.
87 T.C. 1.

PARKER, JUDGE: * * *.

* * *

Petitioner Michael N. Cerone (petitioner or "Mike") and his son (Michael L. Cerone—the son or "Mick") owned and operated the Stockade Cafe (the corporate taxpayer herein), each owning 50 percent of the stock of the corporation. The father and son had a volatile relationship and frequently disagreed over management decisions. Over the years their disagreements became more serious, and finally they decided one of them should buy the other's interest in the business. Petitioner did not think he could run the business alone, so it was decided that the corporation would redeem all of his stock. After the redemption, petitioner worked at the Stockade Cafe for several years, but he did not exercise any control over the corporation. This case involves the tax treatment of the payments or distributions petitioner received for his stock. Specifically, the issue is whether the distributions are dividends under section 301(a) taxable as ordinary income or payments in exchange for stock under section 302(a) taxable as capital gain. The family attribution rules of section 318 play a prominent role in this determination.

* * * According to section 302(c)(1), "Except as provided in paragraph (2) of this subsection, section 318(a) shall apply in determining the ownership of stock for purposes of this section." Under section 318(a), certain individuals and entities are treated as owning stock actually owned by certain related individuals and entities. * * * Unless petitioner can bring himself within some exception to this family attribution rule, he would own 100 percent of the stock of the Stockade Cafe both before and after the redemption. * * *

Petitioner's first argument is that the family attribution rules of section 318(a)(1) should be ignored in determining whether the corporation's redemption of his stock satisfies the requirements of either section 302(b)(1) or section 302(b)(3). Without the attribution rules, petitioner says, the redemption satisfies both of those sections. Petitioner's position is that the hostility between him and his son negates or nullifies the family attribution rules of section 318(a)(1). Secondly, petitioner argues that even if the attribution rules apply, the redemption so reduced his economic interests or rights in and control over the corporation that the distribution was not essentially equivalent to a dividend within the meaning of section 302(b)(1).

Conversely, respondent argues that section 318(a)(1) clearly applies in determining whether the redemption satisfies the requirements of either section 302(b)(1) or section 302(b)(3). Respondent contends that under section 318(a)(1)(A)(ii) petitioner is treated as owning all of his son's stock in the corporation. Thus, both before and after the redemption, petitioner actually and/or constructively owned 100 percent of the corporation's stock. This, respondent continues, precludes the redemption from being not essentially equivalent to a dividend within the meaning of section 302(b)(1). Respondent also argues that petitioner's constructive ownership of his son's stock prevents the redemption from satisfying the complete termination of interest requirement of section 302(b)(3). Respondent maintains that there is only one other way the redemption could qualify under section 302(b)(3), that is, if petitioner satisfied the requirements of section 302(c)(2). In such a case, the

¶ 5105

attribution rules of section 318(a)(1) would not apply, and, the corporation's redemption of all of the stock petitioner actually owned would be a complete redemption within the meaning of section 302(b)(3). Petitioner cannot satisfy the requirements of section 302(c)(2), respondent insists, because petitioner retained an interest in the corporation as an employee in violation of section 302(c)(2)(A)(i).

I. FAMILY HOSTILITY AND THE ATTRIBUTION RULES

Petitioner vigorously argues that the hostility between him and his son should negate or nullify the family attribution rules of section 318(a)(1) in determining whether the corporation's redemption of his stock qualifies for sale or exchange treatment under section 302(b)(1) or section 302(b)(3). Petitioner stresses that the disagreements between him and his son, the corporation's two equal shareholders, increased in frequency and intensity as the years went by. Petitioner also emphasizes that he and his son began negotiating the redemption only after the Omaha vice squad raided the corporation's premises searching for evidence of petitioner's gambling activities and a representative of the Nebraska Liquor Control Commission warned the son that petitioner might cause the corporation to lose its liquor license. Petitioner points to the numerous heated arguments he had with his son throughout the approximately one-year period during which they negotiated the redemption agreement. He notes that those arguments continued even after the redemption agreement was signed. He further notes that the redemption was not consummated until approximately two months after the signing of the agreement.

Respondent's primary position[28] is that the discord between petitioner and his son does not affect petitioner's constructive ownership of his son's 100–percent interest in the corporation after the redemption. For the reasons stated below, we agree that there is no family hostility exception in this case to the section 318 family attribution rules.

In making his family hostility argument, petitioner acknowledges, as he must, the importance of the Supreme Court's decision in *United States v. Davis*, 397 U.S. 301 (1970). In *Davis*, the Supreme Court held

---

28. Respondent questions whether petitioner and his son exaggerate the hostility that existed between them before the redemption. The Court is inclined to think that they do. Respondent points to their long working relationship. They had worked together for some 12 years before the redemption and continued to work together for at least five years after the redemption. Respondent also notes that petitioner did not want to run the corporation's business without his son's help. Clearly, the relationship between Mike and Mick was always volatile and because of Mike's gambling activity had become more so the year before the redemption. The father and son continued to work together during the redemption negotiations, although they were not speaking to each other at times. Thus, we have no doubt that there were arguments and some degree of hostility between petitioner and his son prior to the redemption. Whether this hostility was such as to bring into operation any "family hostility" exception to the attribution rules, we need not decide in this case. For purposes of this case, we assume the existence of the requisite degree of family hostility whatever that may be.

that: (1) the constructive ownership rules of section 318 apply to dividend equivalency determinations under section 302(b)(1); (2) redemptions of stock held by a sole shareholder, including a "constructive" sole shareholder, are always essentially equivalent to a dividend under section 302(b)(1); (3) business purpose is irrelevant in determining dividend equivalency under section 302(b)(1); and (4) in order to avoid dividend equivalency, the redemption must result in a "meaningful reduction" in the shareholder's proportionate interest in the corporation. * * *

Petitioner correctly observes that the facts in Davis did not involve family discord. Thus, the Supreme Court was not required to decide what effect, if any, family hostility has on the application of the attribution rules in the context of section 302. Petitioner cites *Haft Trust v. Commissioner*, 510 F.2d 43 (1st Cir.1975), vacating and remanding 61 T.C. 398 (1973) and 62 T.C. 145 (1974) (supplemental opinion), as authority for the proposition that family hostility may negate or nullify the attribution rules of section 318 in determining whether a redemption satisfies the requirements of section 302(b)(1) or section 302(b)(3). In *Haft Trust*, the taxpayer-trusts argued that the attribution rules of section 318(a)(1) should not apply when hostility exists among the members of a family. *Haft Trust v. Commissioner*, supra, 61 T.C. at 403. We rejected that argument * * *.

* * *

On appeal, the First Circuit analyzed the law differently. The First Circuit construed Davis as not requiring that the dividend equivalency inquiry end after taking into account the attribution rules. It pointed out that section 1.302–2(b), Income Tax Regs., only requires that constructive stock ownership caused by section 318 be one of the facts considered in determining dividend equivalency. The First Circuit interpreted *Davis'* meaningful reduction requirement as permitting, if not mandating, an examination of the facts and circumstances to determine the effect of the transaction going beyond a mere mechanical application of the attribution rules. *Haft Trust v. Commissioner*, supra, 510 F.2d at 47, 48. The First Circuit believed that, by retaining the section 302(b)(1) dividend equivalency test as an alternative to the more objective tests of section 302(b)(2) and section 302(b)(3), Congress showed itself willing to tolerate some administrative and judicial inconvenience brought about by inquiries into "the uncertain shifting quagmires of family relationships" for the sake of taxpayer equity. *Haft Trust v. Commissioner*, supra, 510 F.2d at 48. * * *

* * *

In *Metzger Trust* [*v. Commissioner*, 76 T.C. 42 (1981) (Court reviewed), affd. 693 F.2d 459 (5th Cir.1982), cert. denied 463 U.S. 1207 (1983)], the taxpayer-trust relied upon the First Circuit's opinion in *Haft*

¶ 5105

Trust v. Commissioner, supra, for the proposition that family hostility is a factor to be considered in mitigation of the attribution rules of section 318 in determining dividend equivalency under section 302(b)(1). We again analyzed the legislative history of section 318, and concluded that the end product of the legislative process, the statute itself, makes application of the attribution rules mandatory. *Metzger Trust v. Commissioner,* 76 T.C. at 56–58. We stated as follows:

> * * * Some commentators have suggested that it would be better to ignore the attributions rules where family discord is present. But courts should not attempt to rewrite statutes because they feel that the scheme Congress created could be improved upon. *United States v. Calamaro,* 354 U.S. 351, 357 (1957).

> * * *

> Although section 318 assumes * * * a "unity of action and of interest within the family which is frequently lacking," a Court should not make an exception to a statutory rule on the basis of that Court's determination that Congress established the rule on the basis of a faulty set of assumptions. * * *

Although we rejected the taxpayer-trust's argument that family discord could preclude application of the attribution rules, we nonetheless noted that family discord does have a role, albeit a limited one, in testing for dividend equivalency under section 302(b)(1). We reasoned that under *United States v. Davis, supra,* the proper analysis is as follows: First, the attribution rules are plainly and straightforwardly applied. Second, a determination is made whether there has been a reduction in the stockholder's proportionate interest in the corporation. If not, the inquiry ends because, if there is no change in the stockholder's interest, dividend equivalency results. If there has been a reduction, then all the facts and circumstances must be examined to see if the reduction was meaningful under *United States v. Davis, supra.* It is at this point, *and only then,* that family hostility becomes an appropriate factor for consideration. *Metzger Trust v. Commissioner,* 76 T.C. at 61.

> * * *

II. Section 302(b)(1)—Dividend Equivalency Test

* * * [W]e reach the following conclusions: Under the attribution rules of section 318(a)(1)(A)(ii), petitioner owned 100 percent of the corporation's outstanding stock both before and after the redemption. Before the redemption, petitioner directly owned 50 shares. He also constructively owned, under section 318(a)(1)(A)(ii), the 50 shares actually owned by his son. After the corporation redeemed the 50 shares petitioner actually owned, he still constructively owned his son's 50 shares, which then constituted all of the corporation's outstanding stock.

Because petitioner is treated as owning 100 percent of the corporation's stock both before and after the redemption, the redemption did not cause any reduction in petitioner's proportionate interest in the corporation. Therefore, the redemption was essentially equivalent to a dividend within the meaning of section 302(b)(1). * * *

III. SECTION 302(b)(3)—COMPLETE REDEMPTION TEST

[The Tax Court concluded that the redemption could not qualify as a complete termination of interest because "petitioner's employment relationship with the corporation after the redemption was a prohibited interest within the meaning of section 302(c)(2)(A)(i)."]

IV. CONCLUSION

The corporation's redemption of petitioner's stock failed to satisfy the requirements of either section 302(b)(1) or section 302(b)(3). Thus, the redemption must be treated as a distribution of property to which section 301 applies. See sec. 302(d). Under sections 301 and 316, a distribution of property is treated as ordinary income to the extent it is made out of the corporation's earnings and profits. Secs. 301(a), 301(c)(1), and 316(a). Petitioners do not suggest that the corporation's payments to petitioner were not made out of its earnings and profits. Consequently, all such payments are ordinary income to the individual petitioners * * *.

* * *

[¶ 5110]

Note

Although the Court in *Cerone* left the door open to a family hostility argument, the opening is scarcely a crack. In most family owned corporations in which the argument might be important, 100 percent of the stock of the corporation will be attributed to the taxpayer both before and after the redemption—as in *Cerone*.

[¶ 5112]

Problem

Assume that the Cerones had each owned 40 percent of the Stockade Café and the remaining 20 percent had been owned by Lucky Baritone, an unrelated taxpayer. If the other facts were unchanged and all of the taxpayer's stock had been redeemed, should the taxpayer be entitled to treat the redemption as a sale?

[¶ 5115]

C. REDEMPTIONS TO PAY DEATH TAXES

In designing our wealth transfer tax system, one of Congress' concerns has been the individual whose wealth consists primarily of an ownership interest in a closely held farm or small business. Because it may be difficult to convert such an interest to cash, the payment of the estate tax could be unusually burdensome and might result in an economically inefficient contraction of the business or even its dismemberment. Several provisions of the income tax are designed to mitigate these effects of the estate tax; the one of present interest is Section 303.

If the various requirements of that section are met, the redemption of a specified amount of stock in the closely held corporation by the deceased shareholder's estate or heirs will automatically be treated as an exchange, and not as a dividend, notwithstanding that none of the tests for exchange treatment under Section 302 is met. This dispensation has substantial value. Since the stock being redeemed will have received a step-up in tax basis to its date of death value under Section 1014, the redemption will produce little, if any, income tax liability.

Because Section 303 is intended to be a relief provision for illiquid estates, its benefits are available only if at least 35 percent of the value of the decedent's gross estate (less most deductions other than charitable bequests) consists of stock in the corporation whose stock is being redeemed. § 303(b)(2). While the focus of Section 303 may be on closely held businesses, the decedent's stock ownership may meet the 35 percent of gross estate test even though the decedent only held a trivial proportion of the outstanding stock of the corporation—and thus the corporation was not very closely held at all.

While Section 303 is generally beneficial to taxpayers, the 35–percent limitation can be inconsistent with normal lifetime estate planning desires. One typical estate plan would be to make lifetime gifts of stock for the purpose of reducing the size of the estate. If that plan is pursued too aggressively, qualification under Section 303 could be lost. On the other hand, the likelihood of qualifying under this section may be increased by lifetime gifts of other property.

If the decedent's business interests are spread over several sister corporations rather than concentrated in a single corporation (which might have a number of subsidiaries), the 35–percent test might not be met with respect to the stock of any one corporation. To avoid the necessity of "mergers in contemplation of death," Section 303(b)(2)(B) treats the stock of all corporations in which the decedent owns 20–percent or more of the value of the outstanding stock as stock in a single corporation. Moreover, if the decedent and the decedent's spouse owned stock jointly, the entire value of the holding may be counted towards the

20 percent test. Notice that if the taxpayer relies on the 20–percent rule, the decedent and his or her spouse must actually own a substantial (20 percent!) interest in the business entities *and* the value of those entities must equal a substantial (35 percent) fraction of the estate.

The amount of stock that is eligible for Section 303 exchange treatment normally is equal to the total amount of state and federal estate or inheritance taxes plus the amount of funeral and administrative expenses of the estate. However, the benefits of Section 303 are not limited to the persons who pay those expenses but rather may be claimed by any person who economically bears the burden of those expenses. See § 303(b)(3) and Reg. § 1.303–2(f). If the redemption is delayed for more than four years following the decedent's death, the amount of the qualifying redemption is reduced by Section 303(b)(4).

The Treasury has been quite generous in applying Section 303. In Rev. Rul. 87–132, 1987–2 C.B. 82, the estate was an equal shareholder in a corporation with an unrelated party. To allow a redemption without reducing the estate's control, the corporation distributed a nonvoting preferred stock dividend. Immediately thereafter, the estate redeemed two-thirds of the preferred stock issued to it. The IRS held that the redemption qualified under Section 303 notwithstanding (a) the obvious possible application of the step transaction doctrine, (b) that the immediate conversion of the stock dividend to cash could have caused the stock dividend to become taxable under Section 305 (see Chapter 6), and (c) that, if the stock dividend was not taxable under Section 305, the preferred stock was Section 306 stock (see Reg. § 1.303–2(d)(last sentence)). The policy in favor of the preservation of small businesses is strong indeed.

[¶ 5120]

Problems

1. Maude died leaving an estate having a value (net of amounts deductible under Sections 2053 and 2054) of $1 million. Most of her assets consisted of stock in three corporations that together had conducted the family business, as follows:

	percentage owned	value included in estate
A Corporation	25	$200,000
B Corporation	35	100,000
C Corporation	15	400,000

a. Can Maude's executor redeem stock in any of these corporations and qualify the transaction under Section 303?

b. Whether Section 303 applies or not, how likely would it be that the executor could obtain exchange treatment under Section 302 for a redemption of any amount of stock?

2. Harold died owning all of the stock in Partytime Balloons, Inc. and the value of that stock exceeded the 35–percent requirement of

Section 303. The amount of the taxes and expenses qualifying under Section 303(a)(1) and (2) equalled $100,000, all of which was paid by the executor of Harold's estate. Under Harold's will, an amount of property equal to $500,000 is to be transferred to his surviving wife and the balance of his estate is to be transferred to their one surviving child. Prior to distributing the estate, the executor caused Partytime Balloons to redeem stock worth $60,000. The executor thereafter distributed the assets of the estate, including stock in Partytime Balloons, to both the wife and child. Shortly thereafter, the corporation redeemed an additional $30,000 of its stock from each of the wife and the child. To what extent do these redemptions qualify under Section 303?

[¶ 5125]

D. EFFECT OF REDEMPTIONS ON THE DISTRIBUTING COMPANY

The income tax consequences of a redemption to the distributing corporation are identical to the consequences of a simple dividend. Section 311, which governs both transactions, does not distinguish among nonliquidating distributions. Thus, gain will be recognized on the distribution of appreciated property but no loss will be allowed.

The effect of a redemption treated as an exchange under Section 302(a) on E & P, however, differs from that occasioned by a dividend. Section 312(n)(7) provides that, in a Section 302(a) or 303 distribution, E & P must be reduced by the pro rata portion of the E & P attributable to the stock redeemed. Thus, in the simple case of a corporation with only one class of stock outstanding, a redemption will cause a percentage reduction in E & P equal to the percentage of the outstanding stock that has been redeemed. Since no amount of the distribution will be taxed to the shareholder as a dividend, one might question why a redemption should produce any reduction in E & P. Congress presumably concluded that a redemption is similar to a liquidation, albeit of only a portion of the outstanding interests, and in a liquidation, E & P completely disappears.

The amount paid by a corporation to redeem its stock is, of course, not deductible and Section 162(k) extends that result to any expense incurred in connection with the redemption. That disallowance originally was intended to discourage so-called greenmail payments to corporate raiders but applies to the expenses of any redemption. Section 162(k) evidently does not apply to payments made to a former shareholder-employee pursuant to a covenant not to compete with the corporation entered into at the time the employee retired and submitted the stock for redemption. The IRS, however, has argued that Section 197, described at ¶ 8095, does apply and thus that any payments made on the covenant must be amortized over 15 years regardless of the terms of the covenant. See Frontier Chevrolet Co. v. Commissioner, 116 T.C. 289 (2001).

E. REDEMPTIONS THROUGH RELATED CORPORATIONS

Although, as we now know, the redemption of a few shares out of a larger holding is likely to be treated as a dividend, the sale of those same shares to another shareholder would produce a capital gain. While controlling shareholders might wish to avoid dividends, the sale of common stock in a family owned corporation to an outsider is not an attractive option. That line of reasoning has led many taxpayers to consider selling stock in one corporation to a second corporation owned by themselves or by members of their family. Such a transaction, it might be hoped, would produce the tax consequences of a sale but would not actually result in a dilution of the ownership interest in the corporation being sold. Unfortunately for those who would avoid dividend treatment, Section 304 addresses precisely such a transaction.

As we will see, conceptually Section 304 is an extension of the notion of a redemption that is taxed as a dividend. Like Section 302, the importance of Section 304 to *individual* shareholders is greatly diminished in an environment in which capital gains and dividends are taxed at the same rate. The importance of Section 304 to corporate shareholders remains rather complex as described in ¶ 5155.

1. BROTHER–SISTER SALES

The application of Section 304 requires a two-step analysis in which the first step is to determine whether the stock sale falls within the scope of either of the two transactions described by the section. Section 304(a)(1) will apply when one or more persons in control of a corporation (the "issuing" corporation) transfer stock in that corporation to a second corporation (the "acquiring" corporation) that they also control in exchange for cash or other property. Control for this purpose is defined in Section 304(c) to mean the ownership of 50 percent or more of the stock of the corporation, measured by either voting power or value. As under Section 302, the stock deemed owned includes stock attributable to the taxpayer under Section 318, although for this purpose the corporate-shareholder attribution rule is somewhat broadened.

If such a sale occurs, the second step must be taken: the transaction is reconstructed under the very precise rules of Section 304. Section 304(a)(1) requires that the sale of stock in the issuing corporation to the acquiring corporation be treated as a sale of stock in the acquiring corporation to the acquiring corporation—in other words, as a redemption. That alone does not adversely affect the shareholder/sellers; redemptions can be entitled to capital gains taxation, too. However, Section 304(b)(1) goes on to provide that the redemption is to be tested for dividend equivalence under the rules of Section 302(b). Moreover, Section 302(b) is to be applied by reference to the change in proportionate ownership of the stock of the issuing corporation, i.e., the one whose stock was sold (not of the acquiring corporation, i.e., the one whose stock is treated as having been redeemed). Finally, if sale treatment is barred by Section 302, the amount of the distribution that is treated as a dividend is determined by reference to the E & P of both corporations. § 304(b)(2).

Without a doubt, the blending of the treatment of the issuing and the acquiring corporation is very confusing, but the final result effectively prevents avoiding dividend treatment through sales of stock of one corporation to a related corporation. An example might help. Assume that Bob owns all 100 outstanding shares in I Corporation and 60 of the 100 outstanding shares in A Corporation. Since any attempted redemption of his stock in I Corporation would result in dividend treatment, Bob sells 30 shares to A Corporation for $30,000.

The conditions for the application of Section 304 are present. Bob is in control of both corporations, and he transferred stock in one corporation to the other in exchange for property. Therefore, the transaction is viewed for tax purposes as a redemption of the stock of A Corporation. Whether that redemption will be taxable as a dividend is determined by reference to Bob's change in interest in I Corporation. Prior to the redemption he owned 100 percent of I Corporation. After the redemption he owns 70 shares directly and 18 shares (60/100 x 30) by attribution from A Corporation. Since his interest in I Corporation is 88/100 and that is greater than 80 percent of his prior interest, Bob fails the safe harbor rule of Section 302(b)(2). (He would also fail the 50–percent requirement of the safe harbor.) Unless Bob can pass the general test of Section 302(b)(1), which is most unlikely, the amount he received from A Corporation on the purported sale of his I Corporation stock will be taxed as a dividend to the extent of the E & P, first of A Corporation and then of I Corporation.

If the distribution is taxed as a dividend, Section 304(a)(1) carries the reconstruction a step further (perhaps a step too far) to explain how the stock of the issuing corporation is converted into stock of the acquiring corporation. Bob is treated as if he transferred the I Corporation stock to A Corporation in a Section 351 exchange (even though the requirements of that section have not been met) for A Corporation stock which A Corporation thereafter redeems. The net effect of this step on individual shareholders is merely to shift the basis that Bob had in the I Corporation stock to his A Corporation stock. For corporate shareholders, however, this step has dire consequences for it permits the applica-

¶ 5135

tion of Section 1059, as noted below. A second consequence of this step is to give the acquiring corporation a carryover basis for the stock of the issuing corporation that it acquires.

Because of the stock attribution rules, the true scope of Section 304 is far broader than this example suggests. For example, the result would be unchanged if (1) Bob owned only 40 shares in I Corporation and the rest were owned by his parents and (2) he owned no stock in A Corporation at all but 60 percent of the A Corporation stock was owned by his children.

Section 304 would also apply if, after the application of the stock attribution rules, Bob was treated as owning 51 shares of each corporation before he sold 30 shares of I Corporation to A Corporation. In that event, however, Bob's reconstructed transaction would pass the test of Section 302(b)(2) because his interest in I Corporation would decline from 51 shares to 36.3 shares (21 + (.51 x 30)), 71 percent of his prior holding. The Code is not very clear about just how Section 304 is to apply when the reconstructed transaction is not taxed as a dividend but the result now seems settled. Because the second sentence of Section 304(a) does not apply when no dividend is created, A corporation is treated as having purchased the I corporation stock from Bob. Thus, A corporation would have a cost basis in that stock of $30,000. Bob would be taxed on the $30,000 proceeds of the sale, less his basis in the 30 shares of I corporation stock that he sold to A corporation, at capital gains rates. Apparently Bob would be treated as selling his A corporation stock rather than his I corporation stock but that point seems of no practical importance. In any event, Bob's final basis in his A corporation stock would be the same after the transaction as it was before the transaction.

Section 304 only applies if stock in one corporation is transferred to another in exchange for "property" within the meaning of Section 317(a). As a result, if stock is transferred to an acquiring corporation in exchange for stock in that corporation, Section 304 does not apply. On the other hand, if the shareholders receive both stock and property, such as cash or a debt obligation of the acquiring corporation, Section 304 may apply to the receipt of the property.

[¶ 5140]

2. PARENT–SUBSIDIARY SALES

The same result that Bob tried to achieve with his brother-sister corporations could be attempted with a parent-subsidiary arrangement. For example, assume that Bobbie owns 75 of the 100 outstanding shares in Parent Corporation and the Parent has a wholly owned subsidiary. If Bobbie sells five of her shares to Parent, the receipt would be taxed as a dividend. If instead she sells those shares to the subsidiary, she has engaged in an apparent sale that does not materially diminish her interest in the corporations. However, she has also run afoul of the second type of transaction covered by Section 304. Section 304(a)(2) applies to the sale of stock of one (the issuing) corporation to a second (the acquiring) corporation if the issuing corporation controls the acquiring corporation. In that event, the sale is reconstructed as a redemption of the stock of the issuing corporation, that is, of Parent Corporation.

It is noteworthy that Section 304(a)(2) applies regardless of the amount of stock that the selling shareholder owns in the issuing corporation. Thus, the section would apply to Bobbie even if, after the attribution rules, she owned only six shares. However, as the fraction of the stock of the issuing corporation owned by the shareholder decreases, the more likely it becomes that the redemption will pass at least one of the tests of Section 302(b).

[¶ 5145]

3. INTERRELATIONSHIP OF SECTION 304 AND SECTION 351

A transaction that falls within the scope of Section 304(a)(1) might also constitute a Section 351 transaction. That might occur, for example, if all of the shareholders of a corporation transferred their stock in the corporation to a second corporation in exchange for stock and boot, provided that after the exchange, the transferor shareholders owned 80 percent, rather than merely 50 percent, of the second corporation. Section 304 would not apply to the receipt of stock in the second corporation, since that is not "property," but might apply to the receipt of the boot. After a period of uncertainty, Section 304(b)(3) now makes clear that, if a Section 351 transaction also falls within the scope of Section 304, then with only minor exceptions the taxation of any boot received will be determined under the rules of Section 304 rather than the rules of Section 351.

Aside from Section 304, the receipt of the boot would be subject to tax under the principles of Section 351. However, under those principles, the boot would be taxed as the proceeds of a sale. Thus, the amount taxed would be limited to the gain on the exchange and the tax would generally be at capital gains rates. By contrast, to the extent that Section 304 applies, the boot would be subject to tax as a dividend. In fact, the application of Section 304 in the context of a Section 351 transaction should be viewed as a rule taxing boot in a Section 351 transaction as a dividend if it is equivalent to a dividend under the tests of Sections 304 and 302.

When Section 304(b)(3) was enacted, the application of Section 304 rather than Section 351 increased the tax cost of withdrawing funds from a corporation in connection with what was essentially a reincorporation. Today, however, given that dividends and long-term capital gains are subject to the same 15 percent tax rate, this provision has little, if

¶ 5145

any, significance to individual shareholders and can only benefit corporate shareholders.

You may recall that the assumption of a liability by the corporation in a Section 351 exchange is generally not taxable by virtue of Section 357(a). Nevertheless, the value of that assumption would constitute a distribution of property which might be subject to tax under Section 304. That result is frequently prevented by Section 304(b)(3)(B), which provides that the assumption by the acquiring corporation of a liability incurred to acquire the stock being transferred will not be treated as a distribution of property and thus will not be subject to tax. The unstated implication of that provision is that the assumption of other kinds of liabilities in a Section 351 exchange might be taxable.

[¶ 5150]

4. TAXING THE RECONSTRUCTED TRANSACTION

Section 304 requires the reconstruction of a transaction and the imposition of tax in accordance with the revised form. In that respect, the section can be viewed as a statutory version of the familiar substance over form doctrine. One of the difficulties in applying that doctrine is determining the tax consequences of the reconstructed transaction. That problem is well illustrated by the facts of Bhada v. Commissioner, 89 T.C. 959 (1987), aff'd, 892 F.2d 39 (6th Cir.1989) and sub nom. Caamano v. Commissioner, 879 F.2d 156 (5th Cir.1989).

Petitioners were shareholders in a Delaware corporation (McDermott) which owned all of the stock of a foreign corporation (International). To reduce U.S. taxes on International, it was decided to "invert" the corporate structure and make International the parent of McDermott. That was accomplished by having the petitioners and other shareholders transfer their stock in McDermott to International in exchange for cash and stock of International. When the dust settled, the individual shareholders controlled International and International controlled McDermott. McDermott, however, retained all of the outstanding nonvoting preferred stock of International. Because that class of stock was held by a non-transferor (McDermott) to International, the transfer to International did not constitute a Section 351 transaction.

The parties agreed that Section 304(a)(2) applied to the receipt of the cash. The issue was whether the section applied to the receipt of the International stock. Section 304 applies only to the receipt of "property" and Section 317 excludes from the definition of property "stock in the corporation making the distribution." The petitioners therefore argued that Section 304 did not apply to the International stock issued to them by International.

The IRS argued that Section 304(a)(2) reconstructed the transaction as a distribution of stock of International, not by International, but by

McDermott in redemption of its own stock. Thus, the exclusion in Section 317 did not apply, the International stock was property for these purposes, and Section 304 did apply. The Tax Court ultimately agreed with the petitioners. Section 317 applied to the actual exchange with International, not the reconstructed exchange with McDermott. Thus, the exclusion applied, the International stock was not "property," and Section 304 did not apply. Is that what you normally would expect in the application of the step transaction doctrine?

[¶ 5155]

5. CORPORATE SHAREHOLDERS

The effect of Section 304 on individual shareholders is normally adverse; it converts what otherwise would be a sale into a more heavily taxed dividend. However, Section 304 also applies to corporate shareholders and, as we know, corporations are more heavily taxed on the sale of stock in a subsidiary than they are on the receipt of a dividend. Accordingly, if Section 304 applied to a transfer of stock by a corporate shareholder in the same manner as it applies to individual shareholders, the effect of the section normally would be favorable. Indeed, in the past, corporations with multiple subsidiaries were able to rely on Section 304 to eliminate income taxation on the transfer of the stock of a subsidiary among the members of the corporate group. However, any dividend to a corporate shareholder created by Section 304 is treated as an extraordinary dividend for the purposes of Section 1059. § 1059(e)(1)(A)(iii)(II). As a result, instead of having the proceeds of the sale of stock treated as a tax-free dividend, the proceeds are applied in reduction of the tax basis of the corporate shareholder's stock in the acquiring corporation. However, under the flush language following clause (II), only the basis of the stock treated under Section 304(a) as being redeemed is reduced, not the basis of any other stock in the subsidiary that might be owned by the shareholder. Thus, the proceeds of the hypothetical redemption in excess of the basis of the stock redeemed will be taxed immediately as a capital gain under Section 1059(a)(2).

To illustrate, assume that Top Corp. owns all of the stock of A Corp. and B Corp. Top's basis in the A stock is $100 and its basis in B stock is $10,000. Top sells all of its A stock to B Corp. for $5,000. Under Section 304(a), the transaction is treated as if Top had contributed the A stock to B in a Section 351 transaction in exchange for B stock which B immediately redeemed. That redemption is treated as a $5,000 dividend under Section 302 but as an extraordinary dividend under Section 1059(e). Thus, the $100 basis in the B stock that was hypothetically issued and redeemed is reduced to zero and the balance of the proceeds of $4,900 is taxed as a capital gain.

As a final result, the actual sale by Top is converted into a redemption which is converted into a dividend which is converted into a sale! It might be observed that the result here is identical to the result that would have been reached if Congress had merely said that Section 304 did not apply to corporate shareholders. Would that have been a better solution? In fact, why should Congress ever allow a rule designed to prevent individuals from avoiding dividend treatment to be used by corporations to obtain dividend treatment?

[¶ 5160]

Problems

1. Ted owns 60 of the 100 outstanding shares of Target Corporation stock; the balance is owned by unrelated individuals. Ted's basis in the 60 shares is $6,000. He also owns 90 of the 100 outstanding shares of Acquiring Corporation. The E & P of Target is $50,000; the E & P of Acquiring is $4,000. Assume that Ted sells 30 shares of his Target stock to Acquiring for their fair market value of $20,000.

   a.   How is this sale taxed under Section 304?

   b.   What effect will the transaction have on Ted's remaining basis for the Target stock and his basis in the Acquiring stock?

   c.   What is the effect of the transaction on the E & P accounts of both corporations?

2. Assume instead that Ted only owns 55 of the 100 shares in Acquiring Corporation. Now how would the sale be taxed?

3. Assume instead that Ted does not directly own any stock in Acquiring Corporation but his daughter owns 90 shares of Acquiring stock. Does that change the result? Under this assumption, where should the basis for the transferred Target stock go?

4. A, B, C, and D each owns 25 percent of Manufacturing Co. and of Sales Co. A sells one half of her stock in Manufacturing Co. to Sales Co.

   a.   Assuming that the four shareholders are unrelated to each other, does Section 304 apply to the sale?

   b.   Assuming that B and C are A's children, does Section 304 apply to the sale?

5. Individual Y owns 10 percent of the stock in P corporation and 100 percent of the stock in S corporation. Y sells three percent of the P stock to S.

   a.   Does Section 304(a)(1) apply to the sale?

   b.   Does Section 304(a)(2) apply to the sale? In applying the stock attribution rules for the purposes of this question, note carefully the unusual rule contained in Section 304(c)(3)(B)(ii)(II)!

6. Reba owned all of the stock of Elder Corporation. Upon the formation of Newer Corporation, she transferred all of her Elder stock to

¶ 5155

Newer in exchange for 85 of the 100 outstanding shares of Newer common stock plus a debt obligation of Newer in the principal amount of $10,000. Elder Corporation has E & P of $200,000. What will be the tax consequences to Reba of the formation of Newer Corporation under Sections 351 and 304?

[¶ 5165]

F. REDEMPTIONS AS AN ACQUISITIVE TECHNIQUE

Aside from income tax considerations, one wishing to acquire all or part of the stock in a corporation might purchase the stock from an existing shareholder. In turn, the purchaser might recover the expenditure by obtaining distributions from the acquired corporation. The tax cost of that approach, however, would be high. Moving cash from the corporation to the purchaser would be taxable, probably as an ordinary dividend. In addition, the payment of that cash to the selling shareholder would incur a second tax to the extent of the gain on the sale. By contrast, if the ownership of the corporation can be shifted by redeeming the stock of the selling shareholder, one layer of tax may be avoided. Such transactions, often referred to as "bootstrap" acquisitions because the corporation seems to be purchasing itself, are valuable acquisitive techniques. However, tax pitfalls exist for both the seller and the purchaser.

[¶ 5170]

1. TAX CONSIDERATIONS FROM SELLER'S PERSPECTIVE

For the seller, a simple sale of shares to the purchaser virtually guarantees capital gains treatment. But, what tax would result if a few shares were sold and the balance redeemed by the corporation? Would the redemption qualify under any paragraph of Section 302(b)? Should it make any difference whether the redemption precedes or follows the sale of shares to the purchaser? The following case remains the leading authority on those questions.

[¶ 5175]

ZENZ v. QUINLIVAN
United States Court of Appeals, Sixth Circuit, 1954.
213 F.2d 914.

GOURLEY, DISTRICT JUDGE:

* * *

Appellant is the widow of the person who was the motivating spirit behind the closed corporation which engaged in the business of excavating and laying of sewers. Through death of her husband she became the owner of all shares of stock issued by the corporation. She operated the business until remarriage, when her second husband assumed the management. As a result of a marital rift, separation, and final divorce, taxpayer sought to dispose of her company to a competitor who was anxious to eliminate competition.

* * * [The] buyer purchased part of taxpayer's stock for cash. Three weeks later, after corporate reorganization and corporate action, the corporation redeemed the balance of taxpayer's stock, purchasing the same as treasury stock which absorbed substantially all of the accumulated earnings and surplus of the corporation.

Taxpayer, in her tax return, invoked Section 115(c) [current law § 302(b)(3)] * * * as constituting a cancellation or redemption by a corporation of all the stock of a particular shareholder, and therefore was not subject to being treated as a distribution of a taxable dividend.

The District Court sustained the deficiency assessment of the Commissioner that the amount received from accumulated earnings and profits was ordinary income since the stock redeemed by the corporation was "at such time and in such manner as to make the redemption thereof essentially equivalent to the distribution of a taxable dividend" under Section 115(g) [current law § 302(d)] * * *.

The District Court's findings were premised upon the view that taxpayer employed a circuitous approach in an attempt to avoid the tax consequences which would have attended to the outright distribution of the surplus to the taxpayer by the declaration of a taxable dividend.

* * *

We cannot concur with the legal proposition enunciated by the District Court that a corporate distribution can be essentially equivalent to a taxable dividend even though that distribution extinguishes the shareholder's interest in the corporation. To the contrary, we are satisfied that where the taxpayer effects a redemption which completely extinguishes the taxpayer's interest in the corporation, and does not retain any beneficial interest whatever, that such transaction is not the equivalent of the distribution of a taxable dividend as to him.

* * *

The use of corporate earnings or profits to purchase and make payment for all the shares of a taxpayer's holdings in a corporation is not controlling, and the question as to whether the distribution in connection with the cancellation or the redemption of said stock is essentially equivalent to the distribution of a taxable dividend under the Internal Revenue Code and Treasury Regulation must depend upon the circumstances of each case.

* * *

¶ 5175

In view of the fact that the application of Section 115(g) [current law § 302(d)] * * * contemplates that the shareholder receiving the distribution will remain in the corporation, the circumstances of this proceeding militate against treating taxpayer's sale as a distribution of a taxable dividend.

* * *

We conclude that under the facts and circumstances of the present case the District Court was in error, and the taxpayer is not liable as a distributee of a taxable dividend under Section 115(g) [current law § 302(d)] * * *.

The decision and judgment of the District Court is reversed and the case remanded with instructions to enter judgment in accordance with this opinion.

[¶ 5180]

Notes

1. The payment of cash by the corporation in a bootstrap acquisition depends on the existence of substantial liquid assets or substantial unneeded assets that may be sold to provide needed funds. It is obviously undesirable to sell major operating assets in order to fund payments to the seller. A common variation where dispensable assets are not present is to use future profits of the business itself by paying for the retired stock with a corporate note. The obligation may either be fixed or contingent upon profits, but in either case it is anticipated that the profits generated by the business will provide the funds with which the obligation will be satisfied. In such a case, there is an obvious risk that the obligation will be recharacterized as stock, and the payments on the obligation as dividends, under the debt-equity analysis considered in Chapter 3. There is also a more subtle danger that the seller/redeemed shareholder will be treated as having a continuing interest in the corporation that would violate the requirements of Section 302(c)(2) for a complete termination of interest.

2. If the selling shareholder is a corporation, it may well be in the taxpayer's interest to argue that the redemption was essentially equivalent to a dividend, which would give rise to an intercorporate dividends-received deduction, rather than a sale. See § 243(a). But cf. Rev. Rul. 77–226, 1977–2 C.B. 90 (applying the *Zenz* case to the taxpayer's disadvantage).

3. While *Zenz* involved integrating sales and redemptions in connection with a complete termination of interest, the following ruling extends the principle of that case to a substantially disproportionate redemption.

¶ 5180

[¶ 5185]

REVENUE RULING 75–447

1975–2 C.B. 113.

Advice has been requested as to the Federal income tax consequences, in the situations described below, of the redemption by a corporation of part of its stock.

Situation 1

Corporation *X* had outstanding 100 shares of voting common stock of which *A* and *B* each owned 50 shares. In order to bring *C* into the business with an equal stock interest, and pursuant to an integrated plan, *A* and *B* caused *X* to issue, at fair market value, 25 new shares of voting common stock to *C*. Immediately thereafter, as part of the same plan, *A* and *B* caused *X* to redeem 25 shares of *X* voting common stock from each of them. Neither *A*, *B*, nor *C* owned any stock of *X* indirectly under section 318 * * *.

Situation 2

Corporation *X* had outstanding 100 shares of voting common stock of which *A* and *B* each owned 50 shares. In order to bring *C* into the business with an equal stock interest, and pursuant to an integrated plan, *A* and *B* each sold 15 shares of *X* voting common stock to *C* at fair market value and then caused *X* to redeem five shares from both *A* and *B*. Neither *A*, *B*, nor *C* owned any stock of *X* indirectly under section 318 * * *.

Section 302(b)(2) * * * states that section 302(a), which provides for treating a redemption of stock as a distribution in part or full payment in exchange for the stock, will apply if the distribution is substantially disproportionate with respect to the shareholder. * * *

In *Zenz v. Quinlivan*, 213 F.2d 914 (6th Cir.1954), a sole shareholder of a corporation, desiring to dispose of her entire interest therein, sold part of her stock to a competitor and shortly thereafter sold the remainder of her stock to the corporation for an amount of cash and property approximately equal to its earned surplus. The Government contended that the redemption was a dividend on the grounds that the result was the same as if the steps had been reversed, that is, as if the stock had been redeemed first and the sale of stock to the competitor had followed. The United States Court of Appeals rejected the Government's contention and held that the purchase of the stock by the corporation (when coupled with the sale of stock to the competitor) was not a dividend to the selling shareholder and that the proceeds should be treated as payment for the stock surrendered under the provisions of the Internal Revenue Code of 1939.

¶ 5185

Rev. Rul. 55–745, 1955–2 C.B. 223, states that in situations similar to that in *Zenz*, the amount received by the shareholder from the corporation will be treated as received in payment for the stock surrendered under section 302(a) * * * since the transaction when viewed as a whole results in the shareholder terminating his interest in the corporation within the meaning of section 302(b)(3).

In determining whether the "substantially disproportionate" provisions of section 302(b)(2) * * * have been satisfied in *Situation 1* and in *Situation 2*, it is proper to rely upon the holding in *Zenz* that the sequence in which the events (that is, the redemption and sale) occur is irrelevant as long as both events are clearly part of an overall plan. Therefore, in situations where the redemption is accompanied by an issuance of new stock (as in *Situation 1*), or a sale of stock (as in *Situation 2*), and both steps (the sale, or issuance, of stock, as the case may be, and the redemption) are clearly part of an integrated plan to reduce a shareholder's interest, effect will be given only to the overall result for purposes of section 302(b)(2) and the sequence in which the events occur will be disregarded.

Since the *Zenz* holding requires that effect be given only to the overall result and proscribes the fragmenting of the whole transaction into its component parts, the computation of the voting stock of the corporation owned by the shareholder *immediately before* the redemption for purposes of section 302(b)(2)(C)(ii) * * * should be made before any part of the transaction occurs. Likewise, the computation of the voting stock of the corporation owned by the shareholder *immediately after* the redemption for purposes of section 302(b)(2)(C)(i) should be made after the whole transaction is consummated. Making the immediately before and the immediately after computations in this manner properly reflects the extent to which the shareholder involved in each situation actually reduces his stock holdings as a result of the whole transaction.

Therefore, for purposes of the computations required by section 302(b)(2)(C) * * *, A and B, in *Situation 1*, will each be viewed as having owned 50 percent (50/100 shares) of X before the transaction and 33 1/3 percent (25/75 shares) immediately thereafter. In *Situation 2*, A and B will each be viewed as having owned 50 percent (50/100 shares) of X before the transaction and 33 1/3 percent (30/90 shares) immediately thereafter. Furthermore, in each situation, the result would be the same if the redemption had preceded the issuance, or sale, of stock.

Accordingly, in both *Situations 1* and 2, the requirements of section 302(b)(2) of the Code are satisfied. Therefore, the amounts distributed to A and B in both situations are distributions in full payment in exchange for the stock redeemed pursuant to section 302(a).

¶ 5185

Note

Does Rev. Rul. 75–447 take matters too far? What would have been the result in *Situation 1* if *A* and *B* each had had only one share redeemed? Their interest would have declined from 50/100 to 49/123 or 79.7 percent of their prior interest! Should C's investment insulate the old shareholders from dividend treatment?

2. TAX CONSIDERATIONS FROM THE PERSPECTIVE OF THE BUYER AND OTHER CONTINUING SHAREHOLDERS

As a general proposition, the use of corporate funds for the benefit of a shareholder should result in dividend treatment to that shareholder. When a transfer of the ownership of an interest in a corporation is accomplished through the use of corporate funds to redeem stock, should that general rule result in a dividend to the shareholders whose proportionate interest in the corporation is increased? That question is of great importance to the thousands of shareholders who have entered into shareholder agreements requiring that on the death or retirement of a shareholder, the remaining shareholders must buy that shareholder's stock.

When the continuing shareholder has initially entered into a binding obligation to acquire the stock of the retiring shareholder and the corporation thereafter discharges that obligation, the IRS has long held that the continuing shareholder is indeed in receipt of a taxable constructive dividend. See, e.g., Rev. Rul. 69–608, at ¶ 5210, Situations 1 and 2. While that rule is well established, so are the broad limitations on the scope of that rule. To understand where that line is drawn, one needs to understand the basis for the general rule. There are two possible approaches to sustaining the position of the IRS. In the following case, the IRS initially asserted the traditional argument that the mere assumption of the shareholder's obligation should result in a constructive dividend.

HOLSEY v. COMMISSIONER

United States Court of Appeals, Third Circuit, 1958.
258 F.2d 865.

[The taxpayer owned 50 percent of the outstanding stock of an Oldsmobile dealership, J.R. Holsey Sales Company (Holsey Company). The remaining shares were owned by Greenville Auto Sales Company, a Chevrolet dealership in which the taxpayer's father had a 76–percent ownership interest and the taxpayer was a vice president and director. On June 28, 1946, the Greenville Company gave the taxpayer an option to purchase its 50–percent interest in the Holsey Company at a purchase price of $80,000, although the evidence suggested that the corporation was worth over $300,000. The option was in favor of the taxpayer individually and could only be assigned to another company in which he held an interest of at least 50 percent. On January 19, 1951, the taxpayer assigned his option to the Holsey Company which immediately exercised it, paying Greenville Company the $80,000 purchase price. As a result the taxpayer became the owner of all the outstanding shares of the Holsey Company. The Commissioner determined that the effect of the transaction was that the taxpayer received a constructive dividend in the amount of $80,000 and the Commissioner's determination was sustained by the Tax Court, from which the taxpayer then appealed.]

MARIS, CIRCUIT JUDGE:

* * * Here the distribution was made to the Greenville Company, not to the taxpayer. This the Government, of course, concedes but urges that it was made for the benefit of the taxpayer. It is true that it has been held that a distribution by a corporation in redemption of stock which the taxpayer stockholder has a contractual obligation to purchase is essentially the equivalent of a dividend to him since it operates to discharge his obligation. *Wall v. United States*, 4 Cir., 1947, 164 F.2d 462 * * *. But where, as here, the taxpayer was never under any legal obligation to purchase the stock held by the other stockholder, the Greenville Company, having merely an option to purchase which he did not exercise but instead assigned to the Holsey Company, the distribution did not discharge any obligation of his and did not benefit him in any direct sense.

It is, of course, true that the taxpayer was benefited indirectly by the distribution. The value of his own stock was increased, since the redemption was for less than book value, and he became sole stockholder. But these benefits operated only to increase the value of the taxpayer's stock holdings; they could not give rise to taxable income within the meaning of the Sixteenth Amendment until the corporation makes a distribution to the taxpayer or his stock is sold. *Eisner v. Macomber*, 1920, 252 U.S. 189 * * *.

* * *

The question whether payments made by a corporation in the acquisition and redemption of its stock are essentially equivalent to the distribution of a taxable dividend has been often before the courts and certain criteria have been enunciated. The most significant of these is said to be whether the distribution leaves the proportionate interests of the stockholders unchanged as occurs when a true dividend is paid. *Ferro v. Commissioner of Internal Revenue*, 3 Cir., 1957, 242 F.2d 838, 841. The application of that criterion to the facts of this case compels the conclusion that in the absence of a direct pecuniary benefit to the taxpayer the Tax Court erred in holding the distribution in question taxable to him. For in this case prior to the distribution the taxpayer and the Greenville Company each had a 50% interest in the Holsey Company whereas after it was over the taxpayer had 100% of the outstanding stock and the Greenville Company none.

The Government urges the lack of a corporate purpose for the distribution and the taxpayer seeks to establish one. But we do not consider this point for, as we have recently held, "It is the effect of the redemption, rather than the purpose which actuated it, which controls the determination of dividend equivalence." *Kessner v. Commissioner of Internal Revenue*, 3 Cir., 1957, 248 F.2d 943, 944. Nor need we discuss the present position of the Government that the transaction must be treated as a sham and the purchase of the stock as having been made by the taxpayer through his alter ego, the Holsey Company. For the Tax Court made no such finding, doubtless in view of the fact that at the time the taxpayer owned only 50% of the stock and was in a minority on the board of directors. On the contrary that court based its decision on the benefit which the distribution by the corporation to the Greenville Company conferred upon the taxpayer, which it thought gave rise to taxable income in his hands.

For the reasons stated we think that the Tax Court erred in its decision. The decision will accordingly be reversed and the cause remanded for further proceedings not inconsistent with this opinion.

[¶ 5205]

Notes

1. Sensing, perhaps, the fatal weakness in their economic benefit argument, on appeal the government sought to invoke a form of step transaction analysis but the Court, without considering the argument in great depth, rejected it as well. What facts should cause a court to conclude that the real transaction to be taxed was a transfer of shares from one shareholder to another followed by a transfer of those shares to the corporation by way of a redemption that (normally) would be taxable as a dividend?

2. The following ruling discloses where the IRS believes the line between assumptions of shareholder obligations that result in constructive dividends and assumptions that do not result in constructive dividends should be drawn. As you examine the ruling, consider the extent to which the IRS continues to rely on an economic benefit theory rather than a step transaction theory.

3. The *Holsey* case was complicated by the fact that the taxpayer held an option to purchase the stock of the Greenville Company at a bargain price. In that event, the taxpayer would indeed have derived an economic benefit from the transaction. Do you agree with the court's

conclusion that taxing that income was barred by the decision in *Eisner v. Macomber*? Not taxing the taxpayer may nevertheless be correct because the source of the benefit was the Greenville Company (and thus the taxpayer's father) rather than the Holsey Company. Should the father have been taxed on a dividend?

[¶ 5210]

REVENUE RULING 69–608

1969–2 C.B. 42.

Advice has been requested as to the treatment for Federal income tax purposes of the redemption by a corporation of a retiring shareholder's stock where the remaining shareholder of the corporation has entered into a contract to purchase such stock.

Where the stock of a corporation is held by a small group of people, it is often considered necessary to the continuity of the corporation to have the individuals enter into agreements among themselves to provide for the disposition of the stock of the corporation in the event of the resignation, death, or incapacity of one of them. Such agreements are generally reciprocal among the shareholders and usually provide that on the resignation, death, or incapacity of one of the principal shareholders, the remaining shareholders will purchase his stock. Frequently such agreements are assigned to the corporation by the remaining shareholder and the corporation actually redeems its stock from the retiring shareholder.

Where a corporation redeems stock from a retiring shareholder, the fact that the corporation in purchasing the shares satisfies the continuing shareholder's executory contractual obligation to purchase the redeemed shares does not result in a distribution to the continuing shareholder provided that the continuing shareholder is not subject to an existing primary and unconditional obligation to perform the contract and that the corporation pays no more than fair market value for the stock redeemed.

On the other hand, if the continuing shareholder, at the time of the assignment to the corporation of his contract to purchase the retiring shareholder's stock, is subject to an unconditional obligation to purchase the retiring shareholder's stock, the satisfaction by the corporation of his obligation results in a constructive distribution to him. The constructive distribution is taxable as a distribution under section 301 * * *.

If the continuing shareholder assigns his stock purchase contract to the redeeming corporation prior to the time when he incurs a primary and unconditional obligation to pay for the shares of stock, no distribution to him will result. If, on the other hand, the assignment takes place after the time when the continuing shareholder is so obligated, a

¶ **5210**

distribution to him will result. While a pre-existing obligation to perform in the future is a necessary element in establishing a distribution in this type of case, it is not until the obligor's duty to perform becomes unconditional that it can be said a primary and unconditional obligation arises.

The application of the above principles may be illustrated by the situations described below.

SITUATION 1

A and B are unrelated individuals who own all of the outstanding stock of corporation X. A and B enter into an agreement that provides in the event B leaves the employ of X, he will sell his X stock to A at a price fixed by the agreement. The agreement provides that within a specified number of days of B's offer to sell, A will purchase at the price fixed by the agreement all of the X stock owned by B. B terminates his employment and tenders the X stock to A. Instead of purchasing the stock himself in accordance with the terms of the agreement, A causes X to assume the contract and to redeem its stock held by B. In this case, A had a primary and unconditional obligation to perform his contract with B at the time the contract was assigned to X. Therefore, the redemption by X of its stock held by B will result in a constructive distribution to A. See William J. and Georgia K. Sullivan v. United States of America, 244 F.Supp. 605 (1965), affirmed, 363 F.2d 724 (1966), certiorari denied, 387 U.S. 905 (1967), rehearing denied, 388 U.S. 924 (1967).

SITUATION 2

A and B are unrelated individuals who own all of the outstanding stock of corporation X. An agreement between them provides unconditionally that within ninety days of the death of either A or B, the survivor will purchase the decedent's stock of X from his estate. Following the death of B, A causes X to assume the contract and redeem the stock from B's estate.

The assignment of the contract to X followed by the redemption by X of the stock owned by B's estate will result in a constructive distribution to A because immediately on the death of B, A had a primary and unconditional obligation to perform the contract.

* * *

SITUATION 4

A and B owned all of the outstanding stock of X corporation. A and B entered into a contract under which, if B desired to sell his X stock, A agreed to purchase the stock or to cause such stock to be purchased. If B chose to sell his X stock to any person other than A, he could do so at any time. In accordance with the terms of the contract, A caused X to redeem all of B's stock in X.

¶ 5210

At the time of the redemption, *B* was free to sell his stock to *A* or to any other person, and *A* had no unconditional obligation to purchase the stock and no fixed liability to pay for the stock. Accordingly, the redemption by *X* did not result in a constructive distribution to *A*. * * *

SITUATION 5

A and *B* owned all of the outstanding stock of *X* corporation. An agreement between *A* and *B* provided that upon the death of either, *X* will redeem all of the *X* stock owned by the decedent at the time of his death. In the event that *X* does not redeem the shares from the estate, the agreement provided that the surviving shareholder would purchase the unredeemed shares from the decedent's estate. *B* died and, in accordance with the agreement, *X* redeemed all of the shares owned by his estate.

In this case *A* was only secondarily liable under the agreement between *A* and *B*. Since *A* was not primarily obligated to purchase the *X* stock from the estate of *B*, he received no constructive distribution when *X* redeemed the stock.

SITUATION 6

B owned all of the outstanding stock of *X* corporation. *A* and *B* entered into an agreement under which *A* was to purchase all of the *X* stock from *B*. *A* did not contemplate purchasing the *X* stock in his own name. Therefore, the contract between *A* and *B* specifically provided that it could be assigned by *A* to a corporation and that, if the corporation agreed to be bound by the terms, *A* would be released from the contract.

A organized *Y* corporation and assigned the stock purchase contract to it. *Y* borrowed funds and purchased all of the *X* stock from *B* pursuant to the agreement. Subsequently *Y* was merged into *X* and *X* assumed the liabilities that *Y* incurred in connection with the purchase of the *X* stock and subsequently satisfied these liabilities.

The purchase by *Y* of the stock of *X* did not result in a constructive distribution to *A*. Since *A* did not contemplate purchasing the *X* stock in his own name, he provided in the contract that it could be assigned to a corporation prior to the closing date. *A* chose this latter alternative and assigned the contract to *Y*. *A* was not personally subject to an unconditional obligation to purchase the *X* stock from *B*. * * *

SITUATION 7

A and *B* owned all of the outstanding stock of *X* corporation. An agreement between the shareholders provided that upon the death of either, the survivor would purchase the decedent's shares from his estate at a price provided in the agreement. Subsequently, the agreement was rescinded and a new agreement entered into which provided that upon

¶ 5210

the death of either *A* or *B*, *X* would redeem all of the decedent's shares of *X* stock from his estate.

The cancellation of the original contract between the parties in favor of the new contract did not result in a constructive distribution to either *A* or *B*. At the time *X* agreed to purchase the stock pursuant to the terms of the new agreement, neither *A* nor *B* had an unconditional obligation to purchase shares of *X* stock. The subsequent redemption of the stock from the estate of either pursuant to the terms of the new agreement will not constitute a constructive distribution to the surviving shareholder.

[¶ 5215]

Notes

1. What exactly is the substantive difference between *Situations 1* and *2* and *Situations 6* and *7*? Does the benefit to the shareholders differ?

2. The simplest form of bootstrap acquisition involves a redemption by the corporation, the ownership of which is being transferred. However, if the seller insists on a shareholder level sale of stock and refuses to enter into a redemption, a similar result can be achieved if the buyer forms a new corporation to make the purchase. See *Situation 6*. The transfer of funds from the target corporation to the newly formed acquiring corporation will be free of tax under the intercorporate dividends-received deduction in Section 243.

Extending the point further, after an individual purchases stock in exchange for the purchaser's note, the stock might be transferred to a newly formed corporation which would assume the purchaser's liability on the note. As before, funds can now be withdrawn from the target corporation to pay off the note to the seller without tax. The transfer of stock to the new corporation would be free of tax if the transaction qualified under Section 351. While Section 304 could result in dividend treatment to the purchaser/transferor, Section 304 does not apply to the assumption of a purchase money obligation. § 304(b)(3)(B)(i).

3. One occasion on which a shareholder's interest in a corporation is retired is following the divorce of the principal owners of a family business. Depending upon how the transaction is structured, the redemption can be treated as (a) a redemption by the withdrawing spouse entitled to sales treatment under Situation 4 or as (b) a transfer of the stock from the withdrawing spouse to the remaining spouse followed by a redemption treated as a dividend under Situation 2. Under the Situation 2 scenario, the transfer of the stock between spouses would not be subject to tax under Section 1041. Even though under current law the tax imposed on the transaction would be roughly the same regardless of the characterization, the treatment would matter a great deal to the parties: under Situation 4, the withdrawing spouse is taxed; under

Situation 2, the remaining spouse is taxed. In a fairly unusual provision, the regulations to Section 1041 provide that whether under Rev. Rul. 69–608, Situation 4 or Situation 2 would otherwise apply, the parties may agree that either the withdrawing spouse will be taxed on the redemption or the remaining spouse will be taxed on a constructive dividend. Reg. § 1.1041–2(c). Is such an election sound income tax policy?

[¶ 5220]

Problem

You are called in to advise shareholders Alice and Betty, who were the original incorporators of a corporation engaged in management and investment counseling. Their corporation, Superior Investment (SI), Inc., had been moderately successful and, at Alice's suggestion, it agreed to bring in new talent in the form of Sly, who had recently graduated from a prestigious business school. To assure the proper incentive for Sly, Alice and Betty each transferred 20 shares of common stock to him, leaving them with 80 shares apiece.

Suppose that Sly's ideas subsequently appeared reckless and imprac-tical and Alice and Betty are unwilling to put any of them on trial. Sly's pride is wounded and he demands to be bought out at a price of $125 a share so that he can invest in a business of his own. The following plans are proposed, and the clients ask you to comment on the comparative tax consequences of each plan to all of the parties (i.e., Alice and Betty, Sly, and SI, Inc.) to help Alice and Betty decide how to proceed and at what price. (Initially, of course, you will have to address the ethical issues presented by your representing all four parties.)

Plan 1: Alice and Betty will contract to buy Sly's stock and borrow the necessary $5,000 to effect the purchase. They intend later to pay off the loan with proceeds to be provided by SI, Inc., either through a cash dividend or by SI, Inc.'s redemption of their newly purchased shares or, perhaps, by SI, Inc.'s direct payment of their $5,000 debt.

Plan 2: SI, Inc. instead will purchase the shares from Sly for $5,000 pursuant to an arrangement negotiated directly between Sly and the corporation.

Plan 3: Alternatively, if Alice and Betty do enter into the contract contemplated by Plan 1, they might assign their rights under the contract to SI, Inc. which would then acquire the stock from Sly.

Plan 4: Alice and Betty will create a new corporation, Newco, to which they will transfer their shares in SI, Inc. in exchange for Newco stock. Thereafter, Newco will purchase Sly's stock. Newco will derive funds with which to discharge its liability to Sly by receiving an intercor-porate dividend from SI, Inc.

Plan 5: Alice and Betty will purchase the shares from Sly, financing the purchase by a loan from a bank. Thereafter, Alice and Betty will transfer the newly acquired shares, along with their obligations to pay Sly for the shares, to a newly created corporation, Newco, in exchange for all of Newco's stock.

[¶ 5225]

G. PARTIAL LIQUIDATIONS

The interest-reducing redemptions just considered condition exchange treatment upon the substantial reduction in the shareholder's continuing interest in the corporation. A distribution in complete liquidation, however, is entitled to exchange treatment notwithstanding that the distribution is entirely pro rata. Given those principles, how should a distribution be taxed that, on the one hand, is a pro rata distribution from a continuing corporation but, on the other hand, represents the proceeds of the liquidation of a material portion of the corporate business? From the shareholder's perspective, such a distribution would indeed resemble a dividend. However, from the corporate perspective, the distribution would not seem to be the equivalent of a dividend because it more nearly resembles a distribution in liquidation. That, at least, is the position now embodied in Section 302(b)(4); a distribution to a noncorporate distributee in partial liquidation of the distributing corporation (as defined in Section 302(e)) is treated as an exchange rather than as a dividend and thus will be taxed in the same manner as other Section 302(a) redemptions. Under Section 302(e)(4) the fact that a distribution is pro rata to shareholdings cannot even be considered in determining whether the transaction constitutes a partial liquidation

Under prior law, qualification as a partial liquidation was particularly valuable because it was the only way that a pro rata distribution from a continuing corporation could achieve taxation at capital gains rates of tax. Today, however, given the uniform 15–percent tax, qualification is less important; it allows shareholders to offset the tax basis for their stock against the proceeds of the partial liquidation and it may allow them to deduct capital losses.

Section 302(b)(4)(A) appears to require an actual redemption of stock in order to obtain partial liquidation treatment. However, the IRS has ruled that, at least where the distribution is pro rata, an actual surrender of stock is not required because it would be a meaningless step. Rev.Rul. 90–13, 1990–1 CB 65. Indeed, even if some shares are surrendered, the IRS has ruled that for the purpose of determining gain, the shareholders will be deemed to have surrendered the same proportion of their stock as the proportion of the corporate assets distributed in partial liquidation. Rev.Rul. 77–245, 1977–2 CB 105.

¶ 5220

The scope of the exchange treatment available under Section 302(e) is, of course, a function of the description of the transactions that will be treated as partial liquidations and thus eligible for this favorable treatment. The core of the definition is contained in the so-called safe harbor rule of Section 302(e)(2). Under that provision, a distribution in partial liquidation includes the distribution of the proceeds attributable to the termination of an active business that had been conducted by the redeeming corporation for at least five years, or the distribution of the assets of such a business, provided that following the distribution the corporation continues to conduct another active business which it has also conducted for five years.

There is an obvious relationship between the distribution of the assets of an entire division of a single corporation, which is governed by Section 302(e), and the distribution of the stock of a subsidiary, which is governed by Section 355. In both contexts, the avoidance of dividend treatment turns, in part, upon the divestiture of all of the assets of an actively conducted business rather than a portion of a business or mere investment assets. The definition of what is meant by an actively conducted business thus becomes critical. For this definition, the regulations relating to Section 302(e) (which are still issued under Section 346, the statutory predecessor to Section 302(e)) achieve a commendable degree of consistency by incorporating the definition contained in the regulations under Section 355. See Chapter 12.

A distribution that does not meet the safe harbor rule of Section 302(e)(2) may nevertheless be treated as a partial liquidation if it meets the broader, residual test of Section 302(e)(1). Under that provision, any distribution may obtain the favorable partial liquidation treatment if it is not "essentially equivalent to a dividend (determined at the corporate level rather than at the shareholder level)." What transactions that do not amount to the termination of a discrete business activity should be entitled to partial liquidation treatment? Not surprisingly, the scope of this rule has generated controversy. In the 1954 revision of the partial liquidation rule, the Senate Finance Committee stated it was "intended that a genuine contraction of the business as under present law will result in a partial liquidation." S. Rep. No. 1622, 83d Cong., 2d Sess. 262 (1954). In this connection the Congress was relying upon the decision in *Imler*, which follows.

[¶ 5230]

IMLER v. COMMISSIONER

United States Tax Court, 1948.
11 T.C. 836.

The Commissioner determined a deficiency of $2,410.27 in the petitioner's income and victory tax for the year 1943. The sole question is, Was the retirement of certain shares of its stock by Imler Supply Company in 1942 accomplished at such time and in such manner as to make the distribution and cancellation and redemption essentially equivalent to a taxable dividend? The question arises on the following facts:

* * *

Previous to December 1, 1941, the company was engaged in the business of retinning and soldering metals and in the rental of excess space in buildings owned by the company. The company owned five buildings, consisting of a 7–story brick building and 4 smaller buildings. The main building was equipped with a large freight elevator capable of carrying automobiles. The company rented space in its buildings to the Allegheny County Milk Exchange at a fixed rental of $650 per month, the exchange being entitled to whatever space it required for its operations. Prior to December 1, 1941, the Exchange used all of the sixth floor of the main building and one-half of the seventh floor. The rental allocable to this space was from $100 to $125 per floor. The portion of the seventh floor that was not used in the actual operation by the Exchange was rented for storing various items of freight, including automobiles.

On December 1, 1941, a fire destroyed the two upper floors of the main building. This building was covered by insurance and in April 1942, the company recovered $28,603 as insurance proceeds on account of the fire.

After the insurance proceeds were received, the company obtained an estimate as to the cost of rebuilding the two top floors of the main building, which had been destroyed by the fire. It was estimated that the cost would run from $40,000 to $50,000. * * * The company decided to remove the 2 top floors of the main building which had been burned out and to place a roof over the fifth floor. It was estimated that the cost of this operation would be $15,340. The Company thereupon removed the remains of the two top floors and placed a roof over the building at the fifth floor, making a 5–story out of what had been a 7–story building.

* * * [A]t a meeting of the directors of the Company held April 6, 1942, a resolution was adopted in which the following appeared:

> Mr. Imler stated to the Meeting that the loss occasioned by the fire on December 1, 1941 had been settled with the insurance companies for the sum of $28,603.00; that it had been deemed advisable to tear down the walls of the sixth and seventh floors of the seven-story building damaged by fire and not rebuild that portion of the building, so that we now have instead of a seven-story building a five story building. He further stated that after the payment of repairs and damages caused by the fire that we would have about $15,000.00 more cash than was needed to operate the Company. He stated that in his opinion he thought it advisable that

the stockholders of the Company sell to the Company and the Company buy from the stockholders 300 shares of the Capital Stock of the Company at $50.00 a share totaling $15,000.00.

* * *

The cash working capital of the company for some years prior to December 1, 1941, ranged from $7,500 to $9,000. The cash balance of the company, exclusive of the estimated fire proceeds left after reconstruction of the building, was $9,628.76. At that time approximately $4,500 had been expended on the damaged building and it was estimated that the total cost of repairing and reroofing the building would amount to $15,340. This estimated cost proved to be excessive in the amount of $175.81.

Except for the remaining proceeds of fire insurance, the company could not have paid a dividend in the amount of $15,000 on April 6, 1942, without borrowing money.

After the building was repaired and reduced in size, Imler Supply Company discontinued its retinning and soldering activities and has never resumed the same. This cessation of activity was primarily due to the fact that the corporation lacked space for storage of articles required in its retinning and soldering operations, together with the fact that war conditions and scarcity of materials made such operations unprofitable.

* * *

VAN FOSSAN, JUDGE: The issue here raised presents a question of fact depending on the circumstances of the particular case. * * * No sole or universally applicable test can be laid down. * * * The statutory provision is couched in broad terms—"at such time and in such manner." Though decided cases are not controlling, they are helpful as indicating what elements have been considered important, viz., the presence or absence of a real business purpose, the motives of the corporation at the time of the distribution, the size of the corporate surplus, the past dividend policy, and the presence of any special circumstance relating to the distribution.

In our findings of fact we have indicated our conclusions of fact that the acquisition and cancellation by Imler Supply Company of certain shares of its capital stock in 1942 were not made at such time and in such manner as to be essentially equivalent to a distribution of a taxable dividend * * *; or, as stated otherwise, that the transaction constituted a partial liquidation under section 115(c) [1986 Code § 302(b)(4)].

The principal building owned by the company had been damaged by fire in 1941. When the company undertook to repair the building it was found that because of war conditions, the shortage of building materials, and high costs, it was advisable to abandon 2 damaged floors and reduce the 7–story building to one of 5 stories. The consequence was that the

¶ 5230

company found its facilities inadequate to carry on the retinning and soldering operations formerly engaged in. Moreover, these operations had proven unprofitable in recent experience because of war conditions and shortage of necessary materials. For these reasons the company discontinued the retinning and soldering operations. This reduction in operations likewise reduced the amount of capital necessary for carrying on the business activities of the company. This was a bona fide contraction of business operations and consequent reduction in capital used. The company thus had a real and legitimate purpose for reducing its outstanding capital stock.

The motives of the corporation were all related to the above business purpose and were, therefore, legitimate and properly conceived. If the excess of insurance proceeds be set to one side, the surplus of the company had remained almost constant for 10 years. The company had followed a conservative dividend policy throughout its history and had not paid a dividend since 1934. The original issuance of the stock had occurred many years before and there was no connection between the issuance and the redemption of the same. There was no special circumstance or condition relating to the distribution excepting the fact that the company had in its hands the excess insurance proceeds which formed the basis of the distribution. We are convinced that, except for the fire and the excess insurance proceeds, there would have been no distribution.

* * *

[¶ 5235]

Notes

1. The facts in *Imler* show that, prior to the fire, the taxpayer had been in two businesses: retinning and soldering metals and rental of excess space in the building. Would the facts have fit the safe harbor of Section 302(e)?

2. Should the rental of excess space be treated as the active conduct of a trade or business? See Reg. § 1.355–3(c), Exs. 12 and 13.

3. What facts were critical to the court's decision that the distribution was not a disguised dividend? For example, would the court have reached the same result if there were no war shortages, or if there had not been a fire? Did the history of a conservative dividend policy hurt or help the taxpayer's case?

4. Corporate distributees are excluded from the reach of Section 302(b)(4). Thus, the receipt of a distribution in partial liquidation by a corporate shareholder is always treated as a dividend. Because of the dividends-received deduction, this treatment could be more favorable than if the corporate shareholder were entitled to partial liquidation treatment. That, however, was not what Congress intended. To prevent

that benefit, partial liquidating distributions are treated as extraordinary dividends under Section 1059. See § 1059(e)(1). As a result, the corporate shareholder's tax basis in the stock in the distributing corporation must be reduced by an amount equal to the portion of the dividend that is not taxable under Section 243 and any amount received in excess of that basis is taxed as a capital gain. Oddly, that treatment may still be more favorable than the treatment of individual shareholders.

[¶ 5240]

Problems

Assume that your client, X Corporation, has a net worth of $300,000, including $100,000 in retained E & P from the established business which it has conducted over the past fifteen years. X Corporation's two shareholders, who are individuals, would like to withdraw cash from the corporation but are unwilling to be taxed on dividend income.

a. Would you advise your client that a distribution to the two individual shareholders of one-third of the corporation's assets ($100,000) would represent a bona fide contraction that would qualify as a redemption in partial liquidation?

b. If X Corporation instead used the $100,000 to purchase an active business which it then distributed in kind to its shareholders, would such a distribution shortly after the purchase qualify as a partial liquidation?

c. If, solely in order to preclude dividend consequences, X Corporation retained and actively conducted the newly acquired business for five years and a day, would its distribution of the assets of that business, or of the proceeds from sale of those assets, give rise to exchange treatment by the recipient shareholders?

d. Suppose that X Corporation, on acquiring the new business more than five years ago, had placed that business in a new subsidiary corporation. Now could it distribute the stock of that subsidiary corporation as a partial liquidation? Apparently not. The consequences of the distribution of stock in a subsidiary are governed instead by Section 355. That section permits shareholders to receive stock of a controlled subsidiary or subsidiaries free of tax, but only if such distribution complies with the very rigorous requirements of Section 355. Not too surprisingly, those tests for nonrecognition treatment are stricter than the tests for partial liquidation treatment. See Chapter 12.

e. If X Corporation actively conducted the newly acquired business for a period shorter than five years, might its distribution of that business or of the proceeds from sale of its assets count as a partial liquidation nonetheless? What facts might be relevant to your answer?

f. Suppose that the shareholders transferred to an existing X Corporation, in a transfer complying with the terms of Section 351, a business acquired by them four years ago and operated during that period in partnership form. If X Corporation two years later distributed the proceeds of the sale of the assets of the contributed business, would this distribution meet the statutory safe harbor test? Why should it?

¶ 5240

Chapter 6

STOCK DIVIDENDS

[¶ 6000]

A. INTRODUCTION

The materials in this Chapter turn from a corporation's distribution of cash or property, either as a dividend or in redemption of a shareholder's stock, to distributions made as dividends but comprised of the corporation's own stock. Section 317(a) provides that, for purposes of "this part" (referring to Sections 301 through 318), the term "property" does not include the distributing corporation's own stock or rights to acquire such stock. As a result, the taxation of the distribution of such stock or rights is not governed by the Code sections studied in the preceding Chapters, Sections 301 through 304. Rather, it is governed by Sections 305, 306, and 307.

Not all distributions of a corporation's own stock are the subject of this chapter. Sections 305 through 307 govern a corporation's distribution of its own stock "with respect to its stock," that is, distributions to a shareholder in his or her capacity as shareholder. They do not control the tax consequences of other transfers of stock, such as (i) a transfer of stock to an employee as compensation (see Section 83), (ii) a distribution of stock in exchange for contributed property (see Section 351, discussed in Chapter 2), (iii) a stock swap pursuant to a Section 1036 exchange, or (iv) a distribution incident to a corporate reorganization or division (see Sections 354 and 355, discussed in Chapters 9 through 12). It is a "stock dividend" that is the focus of this chapter.

B. HISTORY OF TAXATION OF STOCK DIVIDENDS

Over the years, the taxation of stock dividends has generated considerable litigation and has been altered by Congress repeatedly. In Towne v. Eisner, 245 U.S. 418 (1918), the Supreme Court held that a dividend of common stock distributed with respect to outstanding common stock was not income within the meaning of the predecessor of Section 61. This case was followed by Eisner v. Macomber, 252 U.S. 189 (1920), where the Court held that a provision of the Revenue Act of 1916 that specifically imposed a tax on stock dividends was unconstitutional as it applied to a dividend of common on common. The Court held that the distributees did not "realize" income upon such a distribution because nothing had been severed from the corporation and delivered to the shareholders; the transaction altered the form but not the substance of the taxpayer's stockholdings.

Congress responded to *Eisner v. Macomber* by excluding all stock dividends in the Revenue Act of 1921. The situation remained thus for 15 years. During this period, however, it became clear that stock dividends having the effect of increasing the proportionate interests of shareholders were not within the rationale of *Eisner v. Macomber* and were properly taxable but, by virtue of the 1921 Act, were escaping tax.

In 1936, Congress again revised its treatment of stock dividends. This time the statute provided that a stock dividend "shall not be treated as a dividend to the extent that it does not constitute income to the shareholder within the meaning of the Sixteenth Amendment to the Constitution." Revenue Act of 1936, § 115(f)(1), 49 Stat. 1688 (1936). The Act also provided that a stock dividend would be taxable as a dividend if the shareholder could elect to receive either property or stock. Id. at § 115(f)(2). However, this test left a significant middle ground where the "proportionate interest" test was difficult to apply because of uncertainty as to the constitutional bounds.

Section 305 of the 1954 Code once again amended the statutory tests of taxable stock dividends in order to simplify this area and to establish some degree of certainty. It provided that a stock dividend was not to be included in gross income, except (i) where any of the shareholders could elect to receive either stock or property and (ii) where the stock dividend was in discharge of preference dividends for the taxable year of the corporation in which the distribution was made or for the preceding taxable year. Although this accomplished the purposes of simplification and certainty, the new version removed many current distributions from exposure to tax and encouraged some corporations to arrange their capital structures in a manner giving shareholders, indirectly, an option to receive current property distributions or to increase their proportionate equity interests in the corporation.

The tax avoidance design of these corporate capital structures led to the eventual recasting of Section 305 in the form in which it presently appears. No longer does there seem to be any serious constitutional question as to whether stock dividends can be subjected to tax. Today the realization principle has at the very least receded as a constitutional limit on the taxability of unrealized gains if it has not disappeared altogether. See Cottage Savings Ass'n v. Commissioner, 499 U.S. 554 (1991), and United States v. Centennial Savings Bank FSB, 499 U.S. 573 (1991).

[¶ 6010]

C. NONTAXABLE STOCK DIVIDENDS

Under the general rule of Section 305(a), the receipt of stock (or rights to acquire stock) distributed with respect to stock is not subject to income taxation. While the exceptions to Section 305(a) will demand more of your attention than will this general rule, the fact remains that most distributions of additional shares of stock to existing shareholders are not subject to federal income taxation. Thus, the typical stock split or stock dividend of common stock on the same class of common stock is exempt from income taxation.

When a shareholder receives a nontaxable distribution of stock, the basis consequences of the distribution are governed by Section 307. Since the conceptual premise for not taxing the distribution is that it more nearly resembles a subdivision of property than a realization of gain, the rule prescribed by the regulations under that section should not come as a surprise. A shareholder's tax basis in the stock with respect to which the distribution was made must be allocated between the previously held shares and the newly issued shares on the basis of their relative fair market values on the date of distribution. See Reg. § 1.307–1(a).

[¶ 6015]

Problems

1. Is it more accurate to view the general rule of Section 305(a) as an exclusion from income or a deferral of income?

2. Rich has a tax basis of $30,000 in the 1,000 shares of common stock that he owns in a corporation. Prior to this transaction, the shares had an aggregate value of $100,000. Rich has now received a tax-free distribution of 500 shares of nonconvertible preferred stock on his common shares. The aggregate value of the preferred stock is $20,000. What is Rich's tax basis in the common stock and in the preferred stock after the distribution? Do not overlook the fact that the distribution of the preferred stock will affect the value of the common stock!

[¶ 6020]

D. TAXABLE STOCK DIVIDENDS

Subsections (b) and (c) of Section 305 contain very broad exceptions to the favorable general rule of subsection (a). If a stock distribution is described in one of these exceptions, then it is treated as a distribution of property taxable under Section 301. That, of course, normally means ordinary dividend treatment and today means that the distribution is usually taxed at the 15 percent rate. While the exceptions from tax-free treatment cover a broad range of transactions, they basically implement just two policies for the taxation of stock distributions. Subsection (b)(1) reflects expanded notions of constructive receipt; a stock distribution will be taxable if the recipient could have elected to receive cash instead. The other subsections implement the view that a stock distribution that increases the shareholder's proportionate interest in the corporation ought to be subject to tax. Paragraphs (2), (3), and (5), as embellished by subsection (c), tax the receipt of a stock distribution by some shareholders if, in one form or another, other shareholders received cash or property. Paragraph (4) treats all distributions on preferred stock as taxable increases in the distributee's proportionate interest.

Because Section 305(b) cross refers to Section 301, if a stock distribution is taxable, it will be taxed at the 15 percent rate if it is a qualified dividend under Section 1(h)(11) received by an individual.

[¶ 6025]

1. ELECTION TO RECEIVE PROPERTY OR MONEY IN LIEU OF STOCK

Under Section 305(b)(1) it is clear that, if a resolution of the board of directors specifically authorizes shareholders to elect between the receipt of payment of a dividend in stock or in cash, a shareholder electing to receive solely stock will nonetheless be subject to tax on the value of the stock received. Under what other situations would Section 305(b)(1) apply to tax a shareholder who receives only stock as a dividend? One example is the issuance of a stock dividend with a concurrent authorization for shareholders, at their option, immediately to have the distributed stock redeemed for cash. See Rev. Rul. 76–258, 1976–2 C.B. 95.

The matter becomes somewhat more complicated, however, if the corporation retains a right to refuse to cash in the shares. For example, in Frontier Savings Ass'n v. Commissioner, 87 T.C. 665 (1986), aff'd sub nom. Colonial Savings Ass'n v. Commissioner, 854 F.2d 1001 (7th Cir.1988), the Tax Court's rejection of dividend treatment was upheld on appeal even though the corporation granted the shareholders an opportunity to have their stock dividends redeemed and did in fact redeem all such stock presented for redemption. In the words of the Tax Court:

> Respondent concedes that the [issuing corporation] did not completely abdicate its discretionary authority to redeem its stock but respondent argues that that authority was exercised so consis-

¶ 6020

tently in favor of redemption that [the shareholders], as a practical matter, had the option or election to have excess shares redeemed at any time. * * *

* * *

We recognize that the issuance * * * of stock dividends instead of or in addition to cash dividends was motivated in part by tax considerations. We cannot conclude, however, on the facts before us that the stock dividends were a mere subterfuge for cash distributions * * *, or that the [issuing company] had relinquished its discretionary authority to decline to grant stock redemption requests.

87 T.C. at 677–78.

Three judges concurred in the result by an opinion that stated:

If a discretionary act of the board of directors of a shareholder corporation to redeem stock dividends becomes a routine matter, it might, in my opinion, develop into an "option" that arises after the distribution or a distribution pursuant to a "plan." * * * In such a situation, it seems the redemptions might be periodic rather than isolated. The broad rules of section 305 could invoke different consideration under other circumstances.

87 T.C. at 679.

An additional factor militated against treating the shareholders as having an "option" to redeem: the shareholders were member banks controlled by the Federal Home Loan Bank Board, the regulations of which prevented some of the shareholder banks from having their shares redeemed. The cases since *Frontier Savings* have uniformly rejected the government's argument that a shareholder-bank makes a de facto election governed by Section 305(b)(1) by failing to tender shares of stock for redemption. See, e.g., Western Federal Savings & Loan Ass'n v. Commissioner, 880 F.2d 1005 (8th Cir.1989).

In *Frontier Savings,* the taxpayer did not redeem any of the shares distributed to it and thus sought to benefit from the deferral of tax that Section 305(a) extends. Do you suppose that the banks that did redeem all of the distributed shares were benefitted or harmed by the decision in this case?

Another example of a situation that may invite tax under Section 305(b)(1) is an automatic dividend reinvestment plan. As indicated by Rev. Rul. 78–375, which follows, such a plan may be taxable under Section 301, under Section 305(b)(1), under Section 305(b)(2), or under all three provisions.

¶ **6025**

[¶ 6030]

REVENUE RULING 78–375

1978–2 C.B. 130.

Advice has been requested as to the treatment for federal income tax purposes of a "dividend reinvestment plan" where the shareholder may not only elect to receive stock of greater fair market value than the cash dividend such shareholder might have received instead, but also the shareholder may, through the plan, purchase additional stock from the corporation at a discount price which is less than the fair market value of the stock.

X is a corporation engaged in commercial banking whose shares of common stock are widely held and are regularly traded in the over-the-counter market. In order to raise additional equity capital for corporate expansion and to provide holders of X's common stock with a simple and convenient way of investing their cash dividends and optional payments in additional shares of X common stock without payment of any broker-age commission, X established an automatic dividend reinvestment plan. An independent agent will administer the plan and will receive the stock from X in the manner described below on behalf of a participating shareholder.

The plan provides the following:

(1) Shareholders can elect to have all their cash dividends (less a quarterly service charge of 3x dollars that is paid to an independent agent of the shareholder) otherwise payable on common stock registered in the name of the shareholder automatically reinvested in shares of X common stock. * * * The shareholders who elect to participate in the plan acquire X stock at a price equal to 95 percent of the fair market value of such stock on the dividend payment date. The shareholder's option to receive a dividend in additional common stock in lieu of a cash dividend is not transferable apart from a transfer of the common shares themselves.

(2) A shareholder who participates in the dividend reinvestment aspect of the plan as described in paragraph (1) above, in addition, has the option to invest additional amounts to purchase shares of X common stock at a price equal to 95 percent of the fair market value of such stock on the dividend payment date. * * * The shareholder's right to invest additional amounts under the plan is not transferable apart from a transfer of the common shares themselves.

There is no requirement to participate in the plan and shareholders who do not participate receive their cash dividend payments in full. Certain shareholders have chosen not to participate; therefore, they receive their regular quarterly cash dividend. While the plan continues in effect, a participant's dividends will continue to be invested without further notice to X.

* * *

A participant may withdraw from the plan at any time, upon written request. Upon withdrawal, certificates for whole shares credited to the participant's account under the plan will be issued and a cash payment based upon the market value of the participant's fractional share interest will be paid by X, through the participant's agent, to the participant. * * *

* * *

Section 1.305–3(b)(2) of the regulations provides that in order for a distribution of stock to be considered as one of a series of distributions, it is not necessary that such distribution be pursuant to a plan to distribute cash or property to some shareholders and to increase the proportionate interests of other shareholders. It is sufficient if there is an actual or deemed distribution of stock and, as a result of such distribution, some shareholders receive cash or property and other shareholders increase their proportionate interests. This is so whether the stock distributions and the cash distributions are steps in an overall plan or are independent and unrelated. In addition, section 1.305–3(b)(3) states that there is no requirement that both elements of section 305(b)(2) * * * (receipt of cash or property by some shareholders and an increase in proportionate interests of other shareholders) occur in the form of a distribution or series of distributions as long as the result of a distribution of stock is that some shareholders' proportionate interests increase and other shareholders in fact receive cash or property.

* * *

Rev. Rul. 76–53, 1976–1 C.B. 87, concerns a situation where a widely held corporation that regularly distributes its earnings and profits adopted a plan permitting the shareholders to choose to have all of the cash dividends, otherwise payable on common shares owned by the shareholder, automatically invested to purchase additional shares of the corporation's stock. The shareholders who elect to participate under this plan acquire the company's stock at a price equal to 95 percent of the fair market value of such stock on the dividend payment date. That Revenue Ruling concludes that the distributions made by the corporation while the plan is in effect are properly treated as payable either in stock or in cash at the election of the shareholder within the meaning of section 305(b)(1) * * *, and, therefore, such participating shareholders will be treated as having received a distribution to which section 301 applies by reason of section 305(b)(1).

Rev. Rul. 77–149, 1977–1 C.B. 82, concerns a situation where a corporation established a dividend reinvestment plan administered by a

¶ **6030**

local bank, acting as agent for the shareholders. At a shareholder's direction the shareholder's cash dividends would be received by the participating shareholders' agent, the bank, who would then purchase the corporation's stock on the open market at 100 percent of fair market value. That Revenue Ruling held that section 301 applies directly to the cash dividends without reference to section 305(b)(1) because the distribution is payable by the corporation only in cash, and the shareholders of the corporation do not have the election of receiving their dividend distribution from the corporation in either stock or cash.

In the present case, the distributions made by X while the plan is in effect are properly treated as payable either in X's stock or in cash at the election of X's common shareholders within the meaning of section 305(b)(1) * * *. The acquisition of stock through the dividend reinvestment aspect of the plan is identical to the situation in Rev. Rul. 76–53. Further, the present case and Rev. Rul. 76–53 are distinguishable from Rev. Rul. 77–149 because the distribution described in Rev. Rul. 77–149 was payable by the corporation only in cash, and the shareholder, through the agent, purchased the corporation's stock on the open market.

The optional investment aspect of the present case results in an increase in the proportionate interests of the shareholders making the purchase at a 5 percent discount, and this event increases their proportionate interests in the assets or earnings and profits of X within the meaning of section 305(b)(2)(B) * * *. Furthermore, the fact that X shareholders who do not participate in the plan receive cash dividends constitutes a receipt of property by those shareholders within the meaning of section 305(b)(2)(A).

* * *

[¶ 6035]

Note

What difference does it make, if any, whether the shareholder was taxable on the distribution under the terms of Section 301, Section 305(b)(1), or Section 305(b)(2)?

[¶ 6040]

2. DISPROPORTIONATE DISTRIBUTIONS

The second general theme of the exclusions from Section 305(a) is that an increase in a taxpayer's percentage interest in corporate equity resulting from a stock distribution is subject to tax. Under Section 305(b)(2), (3), and (5), a taxable increase in interest occurs if a number of related distributions have the effect of distributing cash or property to one group of shareholders while another group obtains an increased proportionate interest in the corporation. Section 305(b)(2) sets forth this general rule and requires that the receipt of the increased interest, as well as the receipt of the cash or property, be subject to tax. It may be that the second requirement of Section 305(b)(2), that one group of shareholders receive cash or property, is unnecessary to the purposes of the section; the increased interest of those who receive stock is sufficient to justify tax. Perhaps for that reason, the regulations under this provision broadly associate any cash or property distributions with a stock distribution to create the premise for the application of Section 305(b)(2). See Reg. § 1.305–3(b).

The classic transaction covered by Section 305(b)(2) is the distribution of stock to one group of shareholders and the distribution of cash to the others. The coverage of this disproportionate distribution rule thus substantially overlaps the constructive receipt rule of Section 305(b)(1). Section 305(b)(2), however, is broader than (b)(1); it applies even in the absence of an election. The scope of Section 305(b)(2) is also far broader than this classic transaction as the ruling below illustrates.

Section 305(b)(3) expands the disproportionate distribution concept by treating preferred stock as property for this purpose. Thus, if one group of common shareholders receives an increased interest in the common stock while another group receives preferred stock, a taxable distribution results. In this case, both the distribution of the common stock and the distribution of the preferred stock will be taxable under Section 301 by virtue of Section 305(b)(3). While preferred stock is generally treated the same as common stock under the Code (whether that makes sense or not), in this context Congress perceived an important distinction. Much like a bond, preferred stock reflects a fixed dollar interest in the corporate issuer. Thus, even though some common shareholders receive common stock and others receive preferred stock having the same present value, the transaction would nevertheless give the first group of shareholders an increased proportionate interest in the residual equity of the corporation. For the purposes of Section 305, therefore, preferred stock more nearly resembles property than it resembles common stock.

Section 305(b)(5) describes a more subtle variant of this same problem. A distribution of preferred stock convertible into common stock will have the effect of some shareholders receiving an increased interest in common stock while others receive preferred stock if some shareholders convert the stock and others do not. When the nature of the conversion feature indicates that a partial conversion is likely, then the receipt of the convertible preferred will be taxed to all shareholders.

Section 305(c) expands upon all of these rules by making clear that a broad range of transactions that may have the effect of increasing a shareholder's proportionate interest in a corporation but which would not normally be considered a distribution will nevertheless be treated as a distribution for the purposes of Section 305(b).

[¶ 6045]

REVENUE RULING 77–19

1977–1 C.B. 83.

Advice has been requested whether under the circumstances described below, past redemptions and a current redemption by a corporation constitute a periodic redemption plan the effect of which is to increase the proportionate interests of certain shareholders within the meaning of section 305(b)(2) and (c) * * *.

Corporation X is a publicly held corporation with 450,000 shares of common stock outstanding. Its stock has been traded over-the-counter, but no active market for X stock currently exists.

Although no formal plan or resolution has been adopted calling for X to redeem shares of its stock, X, over the previous 36 months, has redeemed 20,000 shares of its common stock in 20 separate transactions. The redeeming shareholders have consisted principally of retiring employees of X or the estates of deceased shareholders. Eighteen of these transactions were distributions in redemption of stock within the meaning of section 302(a) * * *. The remaining two were distributions to which section 301 applied.

The management of X has now determined that it would be beneficial to eliminate shareholders who do not own a significant amount of X stock.

Accordingly, pursuant to a merger under section 368(a)(1)(A) * * *, X corporation was merged with and into Y corporation, a corporation newly formed by X for the purpose of effecting the merger. In the merger, Y issued shares of its common stock and cash to the exchanging shareholders of X corporation. The exchange ratio called for the exchange of one share of Y's common stock for 200 shares of X's common stock. Shareholders with less than 200 shares of X common stock received 20x dollars in cash for each share of X stock surrendered. In the transaction, Y issued 2,000 shares of its common stock to former X shareholders; and, numerous shareholders of X who owned in the aggregate 50,000 shares of X common stock received only cash. As a result, corporation Y has 81 percent fewer shareholders than X. As provided in Rev. Rul. 74–515, 1974–2 C.B. 118, those X shareholders who received only cash in exchange for their X stock are treated as having their X stock redeemed under section 302.

* * *

Section 1.305–3(b)(3) of the regulations provides, in part, that a distribution of property incident to an isolated redemption of stock (for example, pursuant to a tender offer) will not cause section 305(b)(2) to apply even though the redemption distribution is treated as a distribution of property to which section 301, 871(a)(1)(A), 881(a)(1), or 356(a)(2) applies.

Section 1.305–3(b)(4) of the regulations provides, in part, that where the receipt of cash or property occurs more than 36 months following a distribution or series of distributions of stock, or where a distribution or series of distributions of stock is made more than 36 months following the receipt of cash or property, such distribution or distributions will be presumed not to result in the receipt of the cash or property by some shareholders and an increase in the proportionate interest of other shareholders, unless the receipt of cash or property and the distribution or series of distributions of stock are made pursuant to a plan.

Example (10) of section 1.305–3(e) of the regulations involves a situation where corporation *P* has 1,000 shares of stock outstanding. *T* owns 700 shares of the *P* stock and *G* owns 300 shares of the *P* stock. In a single and isolated redemption to which section 301 * * * applies, the corporation redeems 150 shares of *T*'s stock. Since this is an isolated redemption and is not part of a periodic redemption plan, *G* is not treated as having received a deemed distribution under section 305(c) to which section 305(b)(2) and 301 apply even though *G* has an increased proportionate interest in the assets and earnings and profits of the corporation. Sections 305(c) and 305(b)(2) * * * are intended to apply to corporate stock redemptions that are in pursuance of a plan to periodically redeem the interest of some of a corporation's shareholders. See *S. Rep. No. 522*, 91st Cong., 1st Sess. (1969), 1969–3 C.B. 423, 521, which provides, in part, as follows:

> A periodic redemption plan may exist, for example, where a corporation agrees to redeem a small percentage of each common shareholders stock annually at the election of the shareholder. The shareholders whose stock is redeemed receive cash, and the shareholders whose stock is not redeemed receive an automatic increase in their proportionate interests. However, the committee does not intend that this regulatory authority is to be used to bring isolated redemptions of stock under the disproportionate distribution rule (of sec. 305(b)(2)).

In the instant case, all of the redemptions that occurred in the past 36 months were principally from retiring employees of *X* or the estates of deceased shareholders. Also, the redemptions completely terminated the direct ownership of the redeemed shareholders. The circumstances surrounding the prior redemptions indicate there was no direct relation between the prior redemptions and the redemptions that were effected pursuant to the merger agreement. Furthermore, the magnitude of the latter is of such a nature that it should be considered as an isolated redemption. The redemptions were not distributions to which section 305(b)(2) * * * applies by reason of application of section 1.305–3(b)(3) of the regulations even though the redemption had the effect of transac-

¶ 6045

tions described in that section since one group of shareholders increased their proportionate interest in the assets and earnings and profits of the corporation while other shareholders may have received cash in a transaction to which section 301 applied. * * *

This is consistent with the conclusion reached in example (10) of section 1.305–3(e) of the regulations where isolated redemptions do not cause section 305(b)(2) * * * to apply even though there are increased proportionate interests in the assets and earnings and profits of the corporation by some shareholders and receipts of property by other shareholders.

Accordingly, in the instant case the redemptions are not deemed, under section 305(c) * * *, to result in distributions to which sections 305(b)(2) and 301 apply.

[¶ 6050]

Notes

1. Notice that the shareholders whose shares were in fact redeemed were taxed under Section 302. It was the others who did not participate in a redemption whose interests increased and therefore for whom the issue of taxability under Section 305(b)(2) arose.

2. All non-pro rata redemptions result in one or more shareholders receiving cash or property while others receive an increased proportionate interest in the corporation and thus literally might appear to fall within the scope of Section 305(b)(2) and (c). Were that to be the case, all redemptions would result in the taxation of the non-redeeming shareholders under Section 305! While Congress clearly did not intend that result, the proper scope of Section 305 is not as clear. One limitation is suggested by Section 305(c), which authorizes treating redemptions taxed as dividends, not all redemptions, as property distributions. But, as Rev. Rul. 77–19 illustrates, that limitation still allows an overly broad application of Section 305. Drawing on the legislative history to Section 305, the regulations have created a second limitation in the "isolated transaction" rule.

3. How do you decide whether a redemption is "isolated" and thus does not create constructive dividends to the non-redeemed shareholders? Rev. Rul. 77–19 suggests that the concept is broader than the single transaction described in Reg. § 1.305–3(e), Ex. 10, but there is little further guidance.

[¶ 6055]

3. DISTRIBUTIONS ON PREFERRED STOCK

Preferred stock by definition represents a limited interest in corporate equity. As a result, any distribution of stock, whether common or preferred, on preferred stock results in an increased proportionate

¶ 6045

interest in corporate equity to the recipient. Under Section 305(b)(4), that increased interest is taxable without the need to show that any other group of shareholders received cash or property. The original focus of paragraph (4) was on the distribution of stock in lieu of accrued but unpaid cash dividends on preferred stock. However, the IRS has more creatively expanded the scope of this provision than it has the remainder of Section 305(b) as Rev. Rul. 83–119 below illustrates.

In some circumstances a distribution on preferred stock, viewed together with other transactions, does not result in an increased interest but rather in avoiding a decreased interest. In that event, the distribution will not be taxable, as the following ruling indicates.

[¶ 6060]

REVENUE RULING 77–37
1977–1 C.B. 85.

Advice has been requested whether an increase in the conversion ratio of convertible preferred stock to reflect a distribution of stock to the common shareholders under section 355 * * * is a distribution to which section 301 applies because of the application of section 305(b) and (c).

X corporation has outstanding both common stock and convertible preferred stock. The preferred stock is convertible into the common stock at a fixed ratio. Pursuant to a consent decree entered into with an agency of the United States Government, X distributed all the stock in its wholly owned subsidiary, Y, to its common shareholders in a nontaxable spin-off under section 355 * * *. No other property was distributed to the shareholders. Since the distribution of the Y stock diluted the conversion value of the preferred stock by decreasing the value of the X common stock, X increased the conversion ratio of the preferred stock to the extent necessary to fully protect the preferred shareholders' investments from such dilution.

* * *

Section 305(c) * * * provides, in part, that the Secretary of the Treasury shall prescribe regulations under which a change in conversion ratio shall be treated as a distribution for purposes of section 305 with respect to any shareholder whose proportionate interest in the earnings and profits or assets of the corporation is increased by such change.

Section 1.305–7(b) of the * * * Regulations provides, in part, that for purposes of applying section 305(c) * * * in conjunction with section 305(b), a change in the conversion ratio of convertible preferred stock made pursuant to a bona fide, reasonable, adjustment formula that has the effect of preventing dilution of the interest of the holders of such stock will not be considered to result in a deemed distribution of stock.

The regulation adds that an adjustment in the conversion ratio to compensate for cash or property distributions to other shareholders that are taxable under section 301, 356(a)(2), 871(a)(1)(A), 881(a)(1), 852(b), or 857(b) will not be considered as made pursuant to a bona fide adjustment formula.

The increase in the conversion ratio of the convertible preferred stock in the instant case was made to the extent necessary to fully protect the preferred shareholders' investments from dilution caused by a nontaxable spin-off of the Y stock under section 355 * * *.

For this reason, and since sections 301, 356(a)(2), 871(a)(1)(A), 881(a)(1), 852(b), and 857(b) * * * are not applicable to the spin-off, the increase in conversion ratio is made pursuant to a bona fide, reasonable, adjustment formula that has the effect of preventing dilution of the interest of the convertible preferred shareholders.

Accordingly, the increase in the conversion ratio of the preferred stock will not be treated as a deemed distribution of stock to which section 301 applies because of the application of section 305(b) and (c).

[¶ 6065]

Note

There is an obvious parallel between the issuance of a debt instrument at a discount from its face amount and the sale of preferred stock for an amount less than the amount to be paid upon its retirement. That parallel is strongest when the issuing corporation is required to redeem the preferred stock at a predetermined time (such as the death of the holder of the stock) and for a predetermined amount. Acknowledging that similarity, the expansion of Section 305(b)(4) contained in the second sentence of subsection 305(c) now requires that the redemption premium on preferred stock be taxed in the same manner as original issue discount on debt. That means that the difference between the issue price and the redemption price for the preferred stock is treated as a distribution of additional shares of preferred stock in annual increments over the period during which the preferred stock is outstanding. The amount of each taxable distribution is determined under the same economic accrual principles that determine the annual amount of original issue discount and is subject to the same de minimis exception.

When the preferred stock is not subject to a mandatory redemption but rather may be redeemed at the option of the issuer, or "called," the analogy is less clear. A premium paid for the premature retirement of the preferred stock for the benefit of the issuer has elements of gain as well as potential elements of ordinary investment return. Under these circumstances, Section 305(c)(2) and the regulations treat a redemption premium as a periodic distribution taxable under Section 305 only if (a) the call is more likely than not to occur and (b) the premium is not merely a penalty for the premature redemption. Reg. § 1.305–5(b)(3).

¶ 6060

The following ruling illustrates the reach of Section 305(b)(4) and its significance for closely held corporations. It was issued prior to the enactment of the rules just described and at a time in which the regulations applied rules similar to the more vague rules now applicable to callable preferred to all redemption premiums. How would the result in the ruling be changed by the current regulations?

[¶ 6070]

REVENUE RULING 83–119

1983–2 C.B. 57.

ISSUE

In a recapitalization where a corporation issues preferred stock that must be redeemed on the holder's death at the price in excess of one hundred and ten percent of the issue price, is the amount of the excess redemption premium treated, by reason of section 305(c) * * *, as a distribution with respect to preferred stock within the meaning of section 305(b)(4)? If so, when is this distribution deemed to be received?

FACTS

A domestic corporation, X, had outstanding 100 shares of common stock. A owned 80 shares of the X common stock and B, A's child, owned the other 20 shares. A was actively engaged in X's business as its president, and B was a key employee. A retired from the business and resigned as a director, officer, and employee of X with no intention to take part in the future activities of X. Pursuant to a plan of recapitalization for the purpose of transferring control and ownership of the common stock to B in conjunction with A's retirement, a single class of nonvoting, dividend paying preferred stock (as defined in section 1.305–5(a) of the * * * Regulations) was authorized. There are no redemption provisions with regard to the preferred stock, except that on the death of a shareholder of the preferred stock, X is required to redeem the preferred stock from the shareholder's estate or beneficiaries at its par value of 1,000x dollars per share. On January 1, 1981, A had a life expectancy of 24 years determined by using the actuarial tables provided in section 1.72–9 of the regulations. On January 1, 1981, A exchanged 80 shares of common stock for 80 shares of preferred stock. Following this exchange, A held all of the preferred stock, and B held all of the common stock that X then had outstanding.

On the date of the exchange the X common stock surrendered had a fair market value of 1,000x dollars per share, and the X preferred stock had a par value of 1,000x dollars per share. The one-for-one exchange ratio resulted because the par value of the preferred stock was presumed to represent its fair market value. However, the fair market value of the preferred stock was only 600x dollars per share. See Rev. Rul. 83–120,

¶ 6070

* * * for factors taken into account in valuing common and preferred stock. Thus, *A* surrendered *X* common stock with a fair market value of 80,000*x* dollars (80 x 1,000*x* dollars) in exchange for *X* preferred stock with a fair market value of 48,000*x* dollars (80 x 600*x* dollars).

The exchange of all of *A*'s *X* common stock for *X* preferred stock is a recapitalization within the meaning of section 368(a)(1)(E) * * *. Under section 354, no gain or loss will be recognized to *A* with regard to the receipt of the preferred stock to the extent of its 48,000*x* dollars fair market value. However, the 32,000*x* dollars excess in the fair market value of the *X* common stock surrendered by *A* as compared to the fair market value of the preferred stock *A* received will be treated as having been used to make a gift, pay compensation, satisfy obligations of any kind, or for whatever purposes the facts indicate. Section 356(f) * * * and Rev. Rul. 74–269, 1974–1 C.B. 87.

Law and Analysis

* * *

One element which is necessary to taxability under sections 305(b) and (c) is that there must be a distribution. Regarding this requirement, section 305(b) deals with actual distributions, and section 305(c) deems certain transactions which are not actual distributions to be distributions for section 305 purposes. Certain recapitalizations, even if isolated, are treated as distributions under regulations section 1.305–7(c). That is, an actual exchange of stock, even though clearly isolated, can be treated as a distribution if the exchange is pursuant to a larger plan to periodically increase a shareholder's proportionate interest. * * *

Although an exchange of stock in an isolated recapitalization would not in itself result in section 305(b) and (c) applicability, the terms of the preferred stock used in the exchange may result in this applicability. The difference between issue price and redemption price (section 1.305–7(a) of the regulations) and the fact that the stock cannot be called for redemption for a specific period of time (section 1.305–5(b) of the regulations) are the factors which combine to produce a deemed distribution. The imposition of tax results from the deemed distribution of additional preferred stock over the period the stock cannot be called or presented for redemption.

* * *

In the present situation, *X* common stock was exchanged by *A* for *X* preferred stock. Since the exchange was not part of a plan to periodically increase a shareholder's proportionate interest, the recapitalization itself did not result in a deemed distribution. However, the preferred stock will be redeemed by *X* on the death of a shareholder at a price of 1,000*x* dollars per share. Since the preferred stock had a fair market value of

¶ 6070

600x dollars per share on the date of issuance, the preferred stock has a redemption premium of 400x dollars per share. There is no evidence that a call premium in excess of 60x dollars was reasonable. Because (1) the X stock is closely held, (2) no public offerings are planned, (3) the X stock is held by members of a family group within the meaning of section 318(a), and (4) the stock is not readily marketable, it is presumed that, at the time of the exchange, the shareholders intended that A would not transfer the preferred stock, and, therefore, redemption would occur upon A's death. Although the exact duration of A's life is not yet known, A's life is "a specified period of time" within the meaning of section 1.305–5(b)(1) of the regulations. Because A has a life expectancy of 24 years, the 400x dollar redemption premium on the X preferred stock has substantially the same effect as a 400x dollar redemption premium payable at the end of a fixed term of 24 years.

HOLDING

The recapitalization in which X issues X preferred stock that must be redeemed on the shareholder's death at a price (1,000x dollars) which exceeds the issue price (600x dollars) results in the recipient, A, being deemed to receive a distribution of additional stock with respect to preferred stock, within the meaning of section 305(b)(4) * * *, by reason of section 305(c), in the amount of 340x dollars (400x dollars less a deemed reasonable redemption premium of 60x dollars) on each share of preferred stock. This amount will be constructively received ratably (14.16x dollars per share per year) over A's life expectancy of 24 years, and will be treated as a distribution to which section 301 applies. If A should die earlier, any part of the 340x dollars per share not yet constructively received by A would be deemed received at the time of A's death.

[¶ 6075]

Note

In Rev. Rul. 83–120, 1983–2 C.B. 170, which was referred to in Rev. Rul. 83–119, the IRS set forth its views on valuing preferred stock. One critical factor in such a valuation is the dividend rate which, the IRS asserted, should be geared to the rate payable on publicly traded preferred stock. That base rate must then be increased to reflect the greater risk of an investment in the taxpayer's stock relative to publicly traded preferred stock. As a result of these rules, to avoid the Section 305 problem described in Rev. Rul. 83–119, taxpayers would be required to pay a substantial dividend on the preferred stock—a result taxpayers often seek to avoid.

[¶ 6080]

E. IMPACT OF STOCK DIVIDEND ON DISTRIBUTING CORPORATION

Under the general rule of Section 311(a)(1), a corporation that makes a distribution of its own stock with respect to its stock will not recognize any gain or loss. This result is not altered by Section 311(b) as it is for distributions of other appreciated property. Even where the corporation purchases its stock on the market for an amount less than its value at the time of the later distribution of the stock to shareholders, the distribution of this appreciated asset will not trigger income to the corporation. Upon analysis, this result is not surprising. Were the rule otherwise, the corporation would simply retire the stock it bought on the market and instead distribute newly issued stock which would be protected from a reportable gain to the corporation by Section 1032.

Although the corporation recognizes neither gain nor loss on distributing its own stock, its E & P might decline as a result of the distribution. This would be so if the stock distribution produced dividend income to the distributee. In that case, E & P is reduced in the same manner as if cash had been distributed and reported as dividend income by the distributees. Of course, if the distribution is exempt from tax under Section 305(a), no reduction in E & P occurs. See § 312(d)(1) and (3).

[¶ 6085]

Problems

Assume that each of the following corporations was newly organized three years ago and has sufficient E & P to cover all distributions.

1. X Corporation, with only common stock outstanding, declared a dividend permitting each shareholder to elect to receive either $5 cash per share or one additional share of common stock for each twenty shares currently owned. The stock of the corporation has a fair market value of $100 per share. All shareholders elected to take stock.

a. Is the distribution a taxable distribution? § 305(b)(1) and Reg. § 1.305–2(a).

b. What are the consequences to the distributing corporation?

2. Y Corporation has two classes of common stock: Class A and Class B. Each share of stock is entitled to share equally in the assets and earnings of the corporation. The corporation distributed a $5 per share dividend to the Class A common shareholders and one additional share of Class B common for each 20 shares of Class B held by a Class B shareholder. The Class B common has a fair market value of $100 per

share. The Class A and Class B shares are not held by the same group of shareholders.

a.   Is the distribution of the stock dividend on Class B common a taxable distribution? § 305(b)(2) and Reg. § 1.305–3(e), Ex. 1.

b.   Would the result be different if the Class A stock were preferred stock? Reg. § 1.305–3(e), Ex. 2.

3.   Z Corporation has Class A common and Class B common as its only outstanding stock. The different classes of stock are held by different groups of shareholders. The corporation distributes a stock dividend of one share of Class A common for each Class A share outstanding, and one share of a new class of five percent preferred stock, redemption value $10 per share, for each share of Class B stock outstanding. Are either of these distributions taxable dividends? § 305(b)(3) and Reg. § 1.305–4(b), Ex. 1.

4.   X Corporation has only two classes of stock outstanding, one common and one nonconvertible preferred. A dividend of one share of common stock is declared with respect to each share of common and each share of preferred.

a.   What is the result to the holders of the preferred? The holders of the common?

b.   Suppose that the preferred is convertible into two shares of common. A dividend of one share of common is declared on each share of common. No dividend is declared on the preferred, but the conversion ratio of the preferred is doubled. What results to the holders of the common and the convertible preferred?

c.   Suppose that the conversion ratio of the preferred is doubled but the distribution on the common was of cash, not stock. What results to the holders of the common and the convertible preferred?

5.   Y Corporation has only one class of common stock outstanding. A dividend of convertible preferred is distributed. What results to the holders? Reg. § 1.305–6.

6.   What result if instead Y Corporation had distributed a dividend consisting of common stock in Y–2, a subsidiary of Y Corporation?

[¶ 6100]

F.   SECTION 306 STOCK

When a shareholder sells non-voting preferred stock for its fair market value, the shareholder gives up nothing of importance in the corporation. The stock simply represents a finite economic interest which has been converted to cash and thus has the same effect as the distribution of a dividend. In the past, taxpayers sought to exploit this financial reality in the following manner. Instead of distributing a dividend, the corporation would distribute a class of preferred stock in a manner that was free of tax under Section 305. The stock would then be sold to a financial intermediary, such as an insurance company, and the transaction reported as a sale taxable at capital gains rates. Sometime later, the stock would be redeemed by the corporation at little or no gain. If the final redemption were sufficiently separated from the issuance of the stock to avoid challenge under the step transaction doctrine, the net effect of the transaction to the shareholder was identical to the distribution of a dividend except that it was taxed at the more favorable rate. See Chamberlin v. Commissioner, 207 F.2d 462 (6th Cir. 1953), cert. denied, 347 U.S. 918 (1954).

To prevent this socalled "preferred stock bailout," Congress enacted Section 306. That section was based upon the premise that some dividends of preferred stock served legitimate business purposes and thus should not be penalized. Accordingly, the section did not impose a tax on the distribution of the preferred stock, as did section 305, but rather adopted a socalled "wait and see" approach. It is only upon the disposition of "Section 306 stock" in a manner that suggests it is being used to avoid dividends that a tax is imposed. In general, at least on a sale other than a redemption, Section 306 first identifies the amount that would have been taxed as a dividend if the distribution of the preferred stock had been taxable. That portion of the proceeds of sale are then treated as ordinary income rather than as capital gain.

Under Section 306(a)(1)(D), however, that element of ordinary income is treated as a dividend for the purposes of Section 1. Since under current law dividends generally are taxed at the same rate as capital gains, that means Section 306 has little remaining significance. Nevertheless, the section has not been repealed and it does have some significance to shareholders who run afoul of its provisions. As we glance over the section, however, you will have to look carefully to find a continuing role for Section 306 under current law.

One of the oddities of Section 306 is that it treats sales quite differently from redemptions.

[¶ 6110]

1. DISPOSITIONS OTHER THAN BY REDEMPTION

Upon a sale or other taxable disposition of Section 306 stock (other than by a redemption), Section 306(a)(1) treats the entire proceeds of sale, not merely the gain, as dividend equivalent ordinary income, but only to the extent that the initial distribution of the preferred stock would have been taxed as a dividend if cash had been distributed in lieu of the preferred stock. In general, that qualification means that dividend equivalent treatment upon a sale of Section 306 stock is limited to the stock's ratable share of the corporation's E & P *at the time the preferred stock was distributed.* If the proceeds of sale exceed this amount, they are treated first as a tax-free return of the basis of the stock sold and thereafter as gain from the sale of the stock and thus eligible for capital gains treatment.

Because, under Section 306, this dividend equivalent element is taxed first and without regard to the tax basis of the preferred stock, Section 306 can result in a greater tax than would a sale not subject to Section 306. For example, assume the preferred stock has a value of $100 and a tax basis of $35 and that its ratable share of E & P at the time it was issued was $80. On a sale of non-Section 306 stock there would be a gain of only $65 and that is all that could be taxed. However, under Section 306 there would be dividend equivalent income of $80 and that larger amount would be taxed. On the other hand, if the ratable share of E & P had been only $60, whether or not Section 306 applied, there would be income of $65 taxed at the 15 percent rate (for Section 306 stock there would be dividend equivalent income of $60 and a capital gain of $5). Thus, the consequences of the sale of the Section 306 stock nearly would be identical to the sale of non-Section 306 stock.

While the Section 306 ordinary income is treated as a dividend for the purposes of the rate schedule, it apparently is not treated as a dividend for other purposes. Thus, for example, the amount of ordinary income generated on a sale does not reduce the corporation's E & P account. In addition, the consequences of a charitable contribution of Section 306 stock may be very different from the consequences of a gift of other stock.

[¶ 6115]

2. REDEMPTIONS

If Section 306 stock is redeemed by the issuing corporation, the proceeds are treated as a distribution taxable under Section 301. That characterization means, among other things, that the proceeds will be treated as a dividend to the full extent of the E & P of the corporation *at the time of the redemption.* Also, if the amount of the distribution exceeds E & P, the excess will be free of tax to the extent of the full basis of all of the shareholder's stock in the corporation, not just the basis of the stock redeemed.

The only significance of applying Section 306 to a redemption is that Section 306(a)(2) does not permit the redemption to avoid dividend treatment by complying with the tests of Section 302(b); rather, the taxpayer is sent directly to Section 301. However, Section 306 contains its own set of exceptions to dividend treatment that roughly parallel Section 302(b).

¶ 6115

3. EXCEPTIONS TO SECTION 306 TREATMENT

Not every disposition of Section 306 stock results in dividend equivalent treatment. The point of the wait-and-see approach is that dividend equivalent taxation is only to be imposed if the shareholder in fact uses the preferred stock in an attempt to avoid dividend treatment upon the extraction of corporate earnings. Section 306(b) lists the circumstances under which the disposition of the preferred stock will not be regarded as creating the potential for such a bailout of E & P.

Under Section 306(b)(1) and (2), if the disposition of the preferred stock is part of a transaction that terminates the shareholder's entire interest in the corporation, Section 306(a) will not apply. The principles considered in connection with Section 302 in Chapter 5 plainly indicate that such a disposition is not the equivalent of a dividend. However, when the disposition is by sale rather than redemption or liquidating distribution, the definition of a complete termination of interest for the purposes of Section 306 is unusually strict. The taxpayer may neither waive family attribution nor transfer the stock to any person whose ownership would be attributed back to the taxpayer. § 306(b)(1)(A).

The IRS, however, has softened that relatively harsh limitation. If a shareholder transfers all of his or her holdings to a related taxpayer under circumstances that, if Section 302 applied, would not be treated as a tax avoidance transaction for the purposes of Section 302(c)(2)(B), while Section 306(b)(1) cannot apply, the exception contained in Section 306(b)(4)(B) will. Thus Section 306 treatment can generally be avoided when shareholders transfer ownership of a corporation to the next generation. See Rev. Rul. 77–455, 1977–2 C.B. 93. Note that for the (4)(B) exception to apply, apparently the taxpayer must first or simultaneously dispose of all of the common stock with respect to which the preferred stock was issued.

Under Section 306(b)(3), Section 306 does not apply when stock is disposed of in a nonrecognition transaction. In such an event, however, the Section 306 "taint" follows the stock into the hands of the transferee. § 306(c)(1)(C). Thus, if Section 306 stock is the subject of a gift or a Section 351 exchange (having no taxable boot), the transferor will not be subject to tax, but the stock in the hands of the donee or transferee corporation will continue to be Section 306 stock. On the other hand, stock acquired from a decedent will not be Section 306 stock. Death purges the taint of Section 306 because the transferee does not obtain a carryover basis.

In the years following the adoption of Section 306, it was generally understood that the section was primarily addressed to closely held corporations and that it would be applied to publicly held corporations in only the more abusive circumstances. Accordingly, unless preferred stock was issued pursuant to a plan to redeem the stock within a short period of time, the IRS would rule under Section 306(b)(4)(A) that the issuance of the preferred stock by a publicly held corporation was not for a tax avoidance purpose. In Rev. Rul. 89–63, 1989–1 C.B. 90, however, the IRS reversed that 35–year history and held that preferred stock of a widely held corporation was no longer automatically entitled to exemption from Section 306 treatment. What practical effect would you expect that change of position to have?

[¶ 6140]

Problems

1. Atlantic Corp. has outstanding 1,000 shares of common stock, which are owned in equal shares by five shareholders, A, B, C, D, and E, each of whom has a tax basis of $300 per share. On December 31 of year 1, when the corporation had a net worth of $1,500,000 and E & P (current and accumulated) totaling $200,000, it distributed a dividend of one share of nonvoting, nonconvertible preferred stock on each share of common. The preferred stock had a liquidation preference and fair market value of $500 per share.

    a. Would the receipt of the preferred stock be subject to tax?

    b. Would the preferred stock be Section 306 stock?

    c. What would be the tax basis of the preferred stock in the hands of the shareholders?

2. In year 3, when Atlantic Corp. had total E & P of $400,000, the following occurred:

    a. A caused the corporation to redeem 100 shares of her preferred stock for their then value of $450 per share, but she retained the balance of her holdings.

    b. B sold 100 shares of his preferred stock to X, an unrelated individual, for $450 per share.

    c. C died and his executor caused the corporation to redeem just C's preferred stock for $500 per share.

    d. D sold all of his common and preferred stock to a trust for the benefit of his minor children for $450 per share.

    e. E gave all of her preferred stock to a public charity.

Compute the taxable income to each shareholder produced by these transactions under Sections 302, 305, 306, and 307.

3. Assume that the value of the preferred stock declined to $250 per share and that B sold his 100 shares at that price. What would result? Would the transaction affect B's basis in his remaining shares?

4. Assume instead that Atlantic Corp. sustained heavy losses and in year 3 its E & P account had been reduced to zero. Now what

¶ 6140

consequence if B sells 100 shares of preferred stock for $250 per share to an unrelated purchaser? What result if the stock is redeemed at that price?

5. Kim is the sole shareholder in Pacific Corp. At a time when the corporation has E & P of $1 million, it distributed as a stock dividend 100 shares of preferred stock having an aggregate value of $200,000. Two years later, when the value of the preferred has risen to $250,000, Kim gave all of the preferred stock to her 14 year old child. In the following year, the child disposed of the preferred stock for $250,000.

     a.   What consequences to Kim and the child in the year of the gift?

     b.   What consequences to the child if the stock is sold to an unrelated purchaser?

     c.   If the stock is redeemed?

[¶ 6145]

4.   TO WHAT STOCK DOES SECTION 306 APPLY?

In order to achieve the conversion of ordinary dividend income into a capital gain that resulted in *Chamberlin*, two factors must be present. The stock cannot represent a residual interest in corporate equity and the receipt of the stock cannot have been taxable. Both requirements are reflected in the definition of Section 306 stock contained in Section 306(c).

[¶ 6150]

a.   Non–Common Stock

The tax free distribution of common stock on common stock, followed by the sale of the distributed stock, is not different from the mere sale of the underlying common stock. While the selling shareholder may obtain capital gains treatment of the sale, that benefit is an established feature of the corporate tax system. What distinguishes the *Chamberlin* transaction is that preferred stock can be distributed and sold without giving up any continuing proportional interest in the corporation and thus can serve as the functional equivalent of a cash dividend. Section 306 is rather narrowly targeted at that transaction. For that reason, Section 306 stock is defined as stock "other than common stock."

The key characteristic of stock that is "other than common stock" is that it lacks an unlimited interest in the residual value of the corporation. Thus, for example, if the class of stock is redeemable at the option of the corporation, the IRS is likely to conclude that it lacks a sufficient residual interest and thus may constitute Section 306 stock. What the stock is labeled or whether it possesses voting rights seems irrelevant. It should be stressed that the essence of "preferred" stock in general and

¶ 6140

Section 306 stock in particular is not so much that it possess a preferred economic interest but rather that its economic interest is limited.

[¶ 6170]

b. Tax–Free Stock Distribution

Because a bailout potential will only exist if stock can be placed in the hands of shareholders free of tax, the basic definition of Section 306 stock encompasses a stock dividend distributed free of tax under Section 305(a). § 306(c)(1)(A). However, preferred stock can also be distributed to shareholders free of tax in transactions more complex than a simple stock dividend. In particular, preferred stock can be distributed to shareholders in connection with a merger or other form of tax-free reorganization. To address that potential, Section 303(c)(1)(B)(ii) extends the definition of Section 306 stock to preferred stock received in a tax-free reorganization if the effect of the transaction is the same as the receipt of a stock dividend.

If the Code stood alone, it would be quite difficult to decide, even on a conceptual level, when the receipt of preferred stock in the acquiring corporation in a statutory merger would have the effect of a stock dividend. The regulations, however, helpfully specify that the receipt of preferred stock will be treated as having such an effect if cash distributed in lieu of the preferred stock would have been taxed as a dividend rather than gain on a sale under the rules governing the taxation of cash received in reorganizations. See § 356(a)(2) and Chapter 10.

Tax under Section 306 normally is not triggered by the disposition of Section 306 stock in a nonrecognition transaction. However, to prevent the avoidance of ordinary income treatment, the Section 306 taint carries over to any stock, the tax basis of which is determined by reference to the Section 306 stock. § 306(c)(1)(C). Thus, for example, when Section 306 stock is the subject of a gift, the stock in the hands of the donee remains Section 306 stock. This rule can produce some surprising results when Section 306 stock is transferred to a corporation in a Section 351 transaction. In that event, the transferred stock in the hands of the corporation of course becomes Section 306 stock. However, the stock in the new corporation issued in exchange for the old Section 306 stock also becomes Section 306 stock (thus doubling the potential Section 306 tax) and that is true even if the stock issued by the new corporation is solely common stock. In this situation, even classic common stock can become Section 306 stock!

In general, preferred stock obtained in exchange for the transfer of property to a corporation should not be Section 306 stock; such an exchange does not amount to a bailing out of E & P. However, a Section 351 exchange can be used as a substitute for a tax-free stock dividend or reorganization. For example, the shareholders of existing Corporation A, which has only common stock outstanding, might transfer all of their stock to newly formed Corporation B in exchange for both common and preferred stock in Corporation B. To address that possibility, Section 306(c)(3) provides that preferred stock received in such a Section 351 exchange will be Section 306 stock if cash received in lieu of the preferred stock would have been treated as a dividend to any extent. You may recall that cash received in a Section 351 exchange may be treated as a dividend if the transaction falls within the scope of Section 304. Accordingly, if the controlling shareholders of one corporation transfer their stock to a second corporation in a Section 351 exchange for both common and preferred stock, the preferred stock will be Section 306 stock if cash issued in lieu of the preferred stock would have been taxed as a dividend under Sections 304 and 302. As discussed below, preferred stock issued by a newly formed corporation generally avoids Section 306 treatment because the corporation lacks any E & P. However, for this purpose the E & P of the old corporation is taken into account. § 306(c)(3)(A).

Presumably nonqualified preferred stock received in a Section 351 exchange and taxed as boot should not be Section 306 stock because it cannot be used as a substitute for a dividend. Nevertheless, it is not expressly excluded from the definition. Instead, the legislative history accompanying the 1997 adoption of the nonqualified preferred stock rules stated that the treatment of the new category of preferred stock under various Code sections, including Section 306, could be addressed by regulation but that in the interim, nonqualified preferred stock would continue to be treated as stock. H. R. Rep. No. 220, 105th Cong., 1st Sess. 544 (1997). Does that help?

[¶ 6172]

c. *No Earnings and Profits*

One final feature of the definition of Section 306 stock is that, under Section 306(c)(2), stock cannot be treated as Section 306 stock if the corporation has no E & P in the year in which the stock was issued. That provision places considerable importance on corporate tax planning. Preferred stock issued on the formation of a corporation may escape Section 306 while preferred stock issued thereafter may be Section 306 stock. This limitation on Section 306 treatment can be largely technical, however. If the corporation has even a single dollar of E & P, the stock may be Section 306 stock. However, the extent to which such Section 306 stock will produce dividend equivalent income depends upon whether the stock is sold or redeemed.

[¶ 6175]

Problems

1. Martha owned 60 of 100 outstanding shares of stock in Shipping Company which has accumulated E & P of $500,000. Martha transferred

¶ 6170

all of her stock in Shipping to Transport Corp. upon its incorporation in exchange for 100 shares of Transport Common Stock and 100 shares of Transport Preferred Stock, constituting all of the outstanding stock of Transport. By the end of the year, Transport Corp. has no E & P.

    a. Would the Transport Preferred Stock be Section 306 stock?

    b. If the stock is Section 306 stock and Martha retains the stock until her death, will the Section 306 characterization of the stock have any adverse income tax consequences?

    c. If the Transport Preferred Stock was "nonqualified preferred stock" within the meaning of Section 351(g), could the stock nevertheless be Section 306 stock?

    2. If the Transport Preferred Stock is Section 306 stock, what would be the consequence if Martha transfers that stock to a second newly formed corporation in a Section 351 exchange for solely common stock of the new corporation and then sells all of the stock of that new corporation?

    3. Assume that Donald owns 90 percent of the single class of stock in a corporation and his son Pluto owns the remaining 10 percent. In a tax-free recapitalization, Donald exchanges all of his common stock for newly authorized preferred stock of equal value. Is the preferred stock Section 306 stock?

[¶ 6180]

G.   SUMMARY OF DISTRIBUTIONS BY CONTINUING CORPORATIONS

    To consolidate your understanding of the tax rules governing corporate distributions encountered in these chapters, try your hand at working through the following problems.

    1. Final Exams, Inc. has E & P of $100,000. Its six shareholders each own 50 shares of the single outstanding class of common stock. Each block of 50 shares has a tax basis of $5,000 and a value of $30,000. Final Exams has distributed land which it held as an investment and which had a tax basis of $10,000 and a value of $30,000.

    a. What sections of the Code *might* apply to the distribution? What facts would determine whether a particular section applied?

    b. Compare the different patterns of taxation that would apply to the distribution, looking at both the corporation and its shareholders, depending upon whether the distribution is:

    (1) pro rata to all shareholders,

    (2) to just two of the six shareholders in exchange for a portion of their stock,

¶ 6180

(3) to just two shareholders but all six of them are members of the same family, or

(4) pro rata to all but the land was a profitable cabbage farm instead of an investment.

c. What if the property distributed was not land but was all of the stock of a subsidiary corporation which owned the land? What would that change?

2. Assume that Final Exams, Inc. distributes a dividend of voting preferred stock pro rata to its six common stockholders. Three years later four of the shareholders sell the preferred stock for cash to a corporation.

a. What sections of the Code *might* apply to the distribution and/or to the later sale? What facts would determine whether a particular section applied?

b. Assuming that the sale is to an unrelated corporation, compare the different patterns of taxation that would apply, looking at both the corporation and its shareholders, depending upon whether the Code sections governing the distribution are:

(1) Section 305(a) but not Section 306,

(2) Section 305(a) and Section 306, or

(3) Section 305(b)(1).

c. Assume instead that Section 305(a) applies to the distribution (and Section 306 may or may not) but the preferred stock is sold back to Final Exams itself.

d. Assume instead that the preferred stock is sold to Patsy, Inc., all of the stock of which is owned by the four shareholders of Final Exams who are selling their stock.

¶ 6180

Chapter 7

THE CORPORATION AS A TAX AVOIDANCE DEVICE

[¶ 7000]

A. INTRODUCTION

From the very beginning of the income tax, Congress has been concerned that individuals would find ways to use corporations to reduce their individual income tax liability. One concern was that individuals would transfer to corporations income producing activities that had no reason to be conducted in corporate form other than the reduction of tax liability. During the early years of the income tax in which the marginal rates facing individuals were materially higher than the rates facing corporations, there was good reason for that concern. In 1934, for example, the maximum individual rate was 63 percent but the maximum corporate rate was only 13.75 percent. Those concerns led Congress to enact provisions, such as the personal holding company rules adopted in that year, that were designed to eliminate any tax benefit from shifting certain categories of income to corporations.

Over the years, however, the relationship between the individual and corporate rates have changed dramatically and that has altered the ability to use corporations to avoid individual income taxes. In 2006, for example, the maximum individual and corporate rates were the same—both stood at 35 percent. In that tax environment, the opportunities to reduce income taxes by shifting income to C corporations has become very limited.

One small opportunity was described in Chapter 1. On low levels of income not attributable to personal services, the tax paid by a corporation will often be lower than the tax paid by an individual on the same amount of income. To exploit that aspect of the progressive rate structure applicable to corporations, an incorporated manufacturing or retailing business can divide its income between the corporation and its individual shareholders by making deductible payments of salary (or interest or rent). If the earnings left in the corporation are relatively small, under $100,000 or so, a tax savings may be obtained. However, much of those savings will be lost when the earnings are distributed and subjected to the shareholder level tax unless the distribution can be deferred until the stock in the corporation receives a step-up in tax basis as a result of the death of the shareholder.

A second opportunity is presented by the intercorporate dividends-received deduction described in Chapter 4. On a portfolio investment in the stock of another corporation, corporations are only subject to tax on 30 percent of any dividends received, producing a rate of tax of 10.5 percent. By contrast, under current law, the rate of tax imposed on dividends received by individuals is 15 percent. On the other hand, gains on the sale of stock are taxed to corporations at the full 35 percent rate while the capital gains derived by individuals are taxed at only 15 percent. Given these rate relationships, it is possible for the investment income of a corporation that does not engage in much selling of its holdings to be taxed at a lower rate than if those investment returns were derived by an individual. Again, however, that savings will be offset by the shareholder level tax when the earnings are distributed.

All in all, under current law, the opportunities to save income taxes by shifting income into a C corporations are very limited. Accordingly, the provisions of the tax law designed to deny taxpayers these tax savings opportunities are of far less importance than in the past. Nevertheless, as we have seen before, Congress is very slow to repeal provisions once they are in place. The personal holding company provisions remain a part of the tax law, largely as a trap for the unwary.

A second congressional concern, dating from the very adoption of the income tax, was that corporations would fail to distribute to shareholders earnings from businesses legitimately incorporated in order to avoid the shareholder level tax. When such a strategy by shareholders would be rational is worth understanding.

Contrary to what one might suppose, there is no tax benefit from merely deferring the distribution of funds from a corporation. To be clear about it, compare two strategies. In the first, the earnings of a corporation are immediately distributed to the shareholders and subjected to the shareholder level tax. Those funds are then invested and reinvested by the shareholder for a period of time. In the second, the earnings are retained by the corporation and invested and reinvested by the corporation for the same period of time. At the end of the period, the accumulation is distributed to the shareholders and subjected to the shareholder level tax. Which strategy will put more money in the hands of the shareholders? Notwithstanding the deferral of the shareholder level tax under the second strategy, the answer is, assuming the same rate of tax applies to all income (and assuming that the shareholders and the corporation can earn the same rate of return), they come out the same. Under either strategy, the shareholders end up with exactly the same amount of money! The mere accumulation of funds in a corporation is not a tax avoidance strategy.

On the other hand, if all rates of tax are not equal, an accumulation strategy could be beneficial. During most of the history of the income tax, the tax rates imposed on the income of corporations were significantly lower than the rates of tax imposed on the income of individuals. Moreover, the rate of tax imposed upon a shareholder attributable to a deferred distribution from a corporation would often be the lower capital gains tax imposed on a sale or redemption while the rate of tax imposed on a current distribution was the higher ordinary income tax rate. Given that rate relationship, shareholders who accumulated funds at the corporate level and later withdrew them through sales or redemptions would come out far ahead of shareholders who received current distributions. Accordingly, in that tax environment, Congress had good reason to be concerned that corporations would accumulate their earnings in order to avoid the shareholder level tax. Congress addressed that concern with provisions such as the accumulated earnings tax.

Under the rates of tax prevailing in 2006, however, not only are the individual and corporate tax rates the same but the rates of tax imposed on current dividends and deferred redemptions are the same. In that tax environment, the accumulation strategy does not avoid taxes. Accordingly, there is not the same reason for Congress to be concerned about corporations accumulating their earnings. (Of course, there might be important non-tax reasons for not wanting corporations to accumulate their earnings excessively.) Indeed, as long as the 15 percent rate of tax on dividends is scheduled to expire in 2010, there may be an incentive to pay out current dividends and avoid accumulations to take advantage of the low rate of tax. Again, however, the provisions enacted during a quite different time remain in the Code and practitioners must be aware of their potential impact.

[¶ 7005]

B. PERSONAL HOLDING COMPANY PROVISIONS

Section 541 imposes a penalty tax upon the undistributed income of a personal holding company. As a tax upon the so-called incorporated pocketbook, the personal holding company provisions are designed principally to bar the use of the corporate form as a vehicle for receiving and accumulating investment income on behalf of its controlling shareholders. The provisions also penalize the shifting to a separate corporate entity of income produced by personal services rendered by a talented controlling shareholder. As mentioned above, the incentive to use personal holding companies has diminished. However, the personal holding company provisions are also still important, in part because of the risk that taxpayers may inadvertently fall within their scope.

[¶ 7010]

1. GENERAL DEFINITION

Under Section 542(a), a corporation must meet two basic requirements to fall within the personal holding company provisions: an income requirement and a stock ownership requirement. Under the income requirement, at least 60 percent of the corporation's adjusted ordinary gross income must be personal holding company income as defined in Section 543(a). The definition primarily includes classic passive income such as dividends, interest, rents, patent royalties, mineral royalties, and copyright royalties. Significantly, however, it does not include capital gains. Personal holding company income also includes amounts received under personal service contracts performed by a designated individual shareholder who at some time during the taxable year owned 25 percent or more of the outstanding stock of the corporation. There are various exceptions to the general definition for certain rents, interest, and royalties, and for active business computer software royalties. See § 543(a)(1) through (5).

The stock ownership requirement is met if at any time during the last half of the taxable year more than 50 percent in value of the corporation's outstanding stock is owned by not more than five individuals. For purposes of determining stock ownership, stock attribution rules similar (but not identical) to the rules of Section 318 are applied. § 544. Certain types of corporations are excluded from the personal holding company provisions, including banks, savings and loan associations, life insurance companies, and certain lending and finance companies. § 542(c).

A corporation that is not a personal holding company in one year may become one in a later year with little warning. For example, a corporation may redeem shares upon the death or retirement of a shareholder, or one shareholder may sell shares to others, with the result that more than 50 percent in value of the total shares may be owned by not more than five individuals. Similarly, the mix of the corporation's gross income may change from year to year. The corporation's receipt of an increased portion of its gross income in the form of interest or other passive income from investments may cause the corporation to meet the 60 percent income threshold and thereby become a personal holding company. See O'Sullivan Rubber Co. v. Commissioner, 120 F.2d 845 (2d Cir.1941).

Under prior law, if a corporation was a personal holding company, a flat tax at the highest individual rate (in 2002, that would have been 38.6 percent) was imposed upon the undistributed personal holding company income of the corporation—in addition to the normal corporate income tax. However, since the intended effect of the personal holding company tax is to impose the same tax as if all of the earnings of the corporation were distributed as a dividend, when the general rate of tax on dividends was reduced to 15 percent, the personal holding company tax was conformed. Accordingly, the current rate of the personal holding company tax is 15 percent.

In what may be one of the Code's most confusing definitions, "undistributed personal holding company income" is *not* limited to the personal holding company income used in defining a personal holding company. Rather, the taxable undistributed personal holding company income comprises the entire taxable income of the corporation, subject to certain adjustments that resemble the adjustments made in computing E & P. Thus, the corporation may deduct federal income taxes and the amount of any dividends paid but cannot claim the intercorporate dividends-received deduction. In addition, however, capital gains are excluded from the definition of undistributed personal holding company income. § 545.

Although the personal holding company tax is similar to the tax that would be imposed if the corporation distributed a dividend and the shareholder reinvested the same amount, the personal holding company tax is harsher because it does not result in an increase in the tax basis of the shareholder's stock. That result can be avoided by the consent dividend procedure established by Section 565. If the shareholder consents, the shareholder is taxed as if a dividend in the agreed upon amount had been paid, that amount may then be deducted by the corporation in computing its undistributed personal holding company income, and the basis of the shareholder's stock is increased by a like amount. See § 565(c)(2). Relief from the penalty tax can also be obtained through a deficiency dividend, which can be distributed following a determination that the corporation is subject to the penalty tax. See § 547.

[¶ 7015]

Problem

Tom is the sole shareholder of Holding Co., Inc. No dividends of any kind have been paid or consented to for the current year. The income and expenses of the corporation for the year are as follows:

	Income	Expenses
Cash dividends	$50,000	—
Commercial building:		
Rental income	100,000	—
Depreciation	—	$30,000
Repairs	—	20,000
Taxes and interest	—	20,000
Long-term capital gains from sale of stock	$ 10,000	—
	$160,000	$70,000

¶ 7015

Does the personal holding company tax apply?

[¶ 7020]

2. PROFESSIONAL CORPORATION AS PERSONAL HOLDING COMPANY

At one stage in the development of efforts to limit the abuse of the corporate form, Congress expanded the scope of the personal holding company provisions to include certain types of personal service corporations. Today, more sophisticated provisions, such as Sections 269A and 482, attack that problem, but the personal holding company rules remain to ensnare the unwary. Initially, there was some uncertainty as to whether professional corporations might be vulnerable under the personal holding company provisions. This concern was alleviated with the issuance of the following ruling. See also Rev. Rul. 75–250, 1975–1 C.B. 172 (accountant).

[¶ 7025]

REVENUE RULING 75–67

1975–1 C.B. 169.

Advice has been requested whether, under the circumstances described below, a corporation will be considered to have received personal holding company income within the meaning of section 543(a)(7) * * *.

B, a doctor specializing in a certain area of medical services, owns 80 percent of the outstanding stock of L, a domestic professional service corporation. B is the only officer of L who is active in the production of income for L, and he is the only medical doctor presently employed by L. B performs medical services under an employment contract with L. L furnishes office quarters and equipment, and employs a receptionist to assist B. P, a patient, solicited the services of and was treated by B.

Section 543(a)(7) * * * provides, in part, that the term personal holding company income includes amounts received under a contract whereby a corporation is to furnish personal services if some person other than the corporation has the right to designate, by name or description, the individual who is to perform the services, or if the individual who is to perform the services is designated, by name or description, in the contract.

In dealing with a professional service corporation providing medical services, an individual will customarily solicit and expect to receive the services of a particular physician, and he will usually be treated by the physician sought.

¶ 7015

A physician-patient relationship arises from such a general agreement of treatment. Either party may terminate the relationship at will, although the physician must give the patient reasonable notice of his withdrawal and may not abandon the patient until a replacement, if necessary, can be obtained. *C. Morris & A. Moritz, Doctor and Patient and the Law* 135 (5th ed. 1971). Moreover, if a physician who has entered into a general agreement of treatment is unable to treat the patient when his services are needed, he may provide a qualified and competent substitute physician to render the services. *C. Morris & A. Moritz, supra*, at 138, 374–75.

Thus, when an individual solicits, and expects, the services of a particular physician and that physician accepts the individual as a patient and treats him, the relationship of physician-patient established in this manner does not constitute a designation of the individual who is to perform the services under a contract for personal services within the meaning of section 543(a)(7) * * *.

If, however, the physician or the professional service corporation contracts with the patient that the physician personally will perform particular services for the patient, and he has no right to substitute another physician to perform such services, there is a designation of that physician as the individual to perform services under a contract for personal services within the meaning of section 543(a)(7) * * *.

The designation of a physician as an individual to perform services can be accomplished by either an oral or written contract. * * *

Moreover, if *L* agreed to perform the type of services that are so unique as to preclude substitution of another physician to perform such services, there is also a designation.

Accordingly, since in the instant case there is no indication that *L* has contracted that *B* will personally perform the services or that the services are so unique as to preclude substitution, it is held that income earned by *L* from providing medical service contracts will not be considered income from personal service contracts within the meaning of section 543(a)(7) * * *.

[¶ 7030]

Note

In Kenyatta Corp. v. Commissioner, 86 T.C. 171 (1986), aff'd, 812 F.2d 577 (9th Cir. 1987), the court examined the income of a corporation, over 50 percent of the stock of which was owned by Bill Russell, a former professional basketball player. The corporation had employed Russell to provide a variety of services such as lecturing and appearing as host on ABC Sports. The court found that in each of the corporation's agreements to provide services, the contracts specified that Russell himself was to provide the services and that therefore the income from the services was personal holding company income.

[¶ 7035]

C. UNREASONABLE ACCUMULATIONS OF EARNINGS

Historically, the gap between the top individual rates and the top corporate rate created a significant incentive to accumulate earnings within a corporation rather than distribute them. To discourage this activity, Section 531 imposes an additional tax on the "accumulated taxable income" of a corporation. Pursuant to Section 532, the tax applies to "every corporation * * * formed or availed of for the *purpose* of avoiding the income tax with respect to its shareholders or the shareholders of any other corporation, by permitting earnings and profits to accumulate instead of being divided or distributed." (Emphasis added.) It does not apply, however, to personal holding companies or to corporations exempt from tax. § 532(b). This penalty tax has its roots in the Revenue Act of 1913, the first tax act enacted after ratification of the Sixteenth Amendment. Consistent with the personal holding company tax, the rate of the accumulated earnings tax is presently 15 percent.

[¶ 7040]

1. EVIDENCE OF PURPOSE TO AVOID TAX

Section 533(a) provides that accumulation of earnings and profits "beyond the reasonable needs of the business shall be determinative of the purpose to avoid the income tax with respect to shareholders, unless the corporation by the preponderance of the evidence shall prove to the contrary." If a corporation is a mere holding or investment company, that fact is prima facie evidence of the tax avoidance purpose. § 533(b). In the following case, the Supreme Court further diminished the role of purpose in the application of the tax.

[¶ 7045]

UNITED STATES v. DONRUSS CO.

Supreme Court of the United States, 1969.
393 U.S. 297.

MR. JUSTICE MARSHALL delivered the opinion of the Court.

This case involves the application of §§ 531–537 * * *, which impose a surtax on corporations "formed or availed of for the purpose of avoiding the income tax with respect to ... [their] shareholders ... by permitting earnings and profits to accumulate instead of being divided or distributed."

¶ 7030

Respondent is a corporation engaged in the manufacture and sale of bubble gum and candy and in the operation of a farm. Since 1954, all of respondent's outstanding stock has been owned by Don B. Wiener. In each of the tax years from 1955 to 1961, respondent operated profitably, increasing its undistributed earnings from $1,021,288.58 to $1,679,315.37. The company did not make loans to Wiener or provide him with benefits other than a salary, nor did it make investments unrelated to its business, but no dividends were declared during the entire period.

Wiener gave several reasons for respondent's accumulation policy; among them were capital and inventory requirements, increasing costs, and the risks inherent in the particular business and in the general economy. Wiener also expressed a general desire to expand and a more specific desire to invest in respondent's major distributor, the Tom Huston Peanut Company. There were no definite plans during the tax years in question, but in 1964 respondent purchased 10,000 shares in Tom Huston at a cost of $380,000.

The Commissioner of Internal Revenue assessed accumulated earnings taxes against respondent for the years 1960 and 1961. Respondent paid the tax and brought this refund suit. At the conclusion of the trial, the Government specifically requested that the jury be instructed that:

"[I]t is not necessary that avoidance of shareholder's tax be the sole purpose for the unreasonable accumulation of earnings; it is sufficient if it is one of the purposes for the company's accumulation policy."

The instruction was refused and the court instructed the jury in the terms of the statute that tax avoidance had to be "the purpose" of the accumulations. The jury, in response to interrogatories, found that respondent had accumulated earnings beyond the reasonable needs of its business, but that it had not retained its earnings for the purpose of avoiding income tax on Wiener. Judgment was entered for respondent and the Government appealed.

The Court of Appeals reversed and remanded for a new trial, holding that "the jury might well have been led to believe that tax avoidance must be the sole purpose behind an accumulation in order to impose the accumulated earnings tax." *Donruss Co. v. United States*, 384 F. 2d 292, (C.A. 6th Cir. 1967). The Court of Appeals rejected the Government's proposed instruction and held that the tax applied only if tax avoidance was the "dominant, controlling, or impelling motive" for the accumulation. *Ibid.* We granted the Government's petition for certiorari to resolve a conflict among the circuits over the degree of "purpose" necessary for the application of the accumulated earnings tax, and because of the importance of that question in the administration of the tax. * * *

I.

* * *

The dispute before us is a narrow one. The Government contends that in order to rebut the presumption contained in § 533(a), the taxpayer must establish by the preponderance of the evidence that tax avoidance with respect to shareholders was not "one of the purposes" for the accumulation of earnings beyond the reasonable needs of the business. Respondent argues that it may rebut that presumption by demonstrating that tax avoidance was not the "dominant, controlling, or impelling" reason for the accumulation. Neither party questions the trial court's instructions on the issue of whether the accumulation was beyond the reasonable needs of the business, and respondent does not challenge the jury's finding that its accumulation was indeed unreasonable. We intimate no opinion about the standards governing reasonableness of corporate accumulations.

We conclude from an examination of the language, the purpose, and the legislative history of the statute that the Government's construction is the correct one. Accordingly, we reverse the judgment of the court below and remand the case for a new trial on the issue of whether avoidance of shareholder tax was one of the purposes of respondent's accumulations.

II.

Both parties argue that the language of the statute supports their conclusion. Respondent argues that Congress could have used the article "a" in §§ 532 and 533 if it had intended to adopt the Government's test. Instead, argues respondent, Congress used the article "the" in the operative part of the statute, thus indicating that tax avoidance must at least be the dominant motive for the accumulation. The Government argues that respondent's construction gives an unduly narrow effect to the word "the." Instead, contends the Government, this Court should focus on the entire phrase "availed of for the purpose." Any language of limitation should logically modify "availed of" rather than "purpose" and no such language is present. * * *

We find both parties' arguments inconclusive. The phrase "availed of for the purpose" is inherently vague, and there is no indication in the legislative history that Congress intended to attach any particular significance to the use of the article "the." * * * Since the language of the statute does not provide an answer to the question before us, we have examined in detail the relevant legislative history. That history leads us to conclude that the test proposed by the Government is consistent with the intent of Congress and is necessary to effectuate the purpose of the accumulated earnings tax.

¶ 7045

III.

The accumulated earnings tax is one congressional attempt to deter use of a corporate entity to avoid personal income taxes. The purpose of the tax "is to compel the company to distribute any profits not needed for the conduct of its business so that, when so distributed, individual stockholders will become liable" for taxes on the dividends received * * *. * * *

* * *

* * * [T]he legislative history of the accumulated earnings tax demonstrates a continuing concern with the use of the corporate form to avoid income tax on a corporation's shareholders. Numerous methods were employed to prevent this practice, all of which proved unsatisfactory in one way or another. Two conclusions can be drawn from Congress' efforts. First, Congress recognized the tremendous difficulty of ascertaining the purpose for corporate accumulations. Second, it saw that accumulation was often necessary for legitimate and reasonable business purposes. It appears clear to us that the congressional response to these facts has been to emphasize unreasonable accumulation as the most significant factor in the incidence of the tax. The reasonableness of an accumulation, while subject to honest difference of opinion, is a much more objective inquiry, and is susceptible of more effective scrutiny, than are the vagaries of corporate motive.

Respondent would have us adopt a test that requires that tax avoidance purpose need be dominant, impelling, or controlling. It seems to us that such a test would exacerbate the problems that Congress was trying to avoid. Rarely is there one motive, or even one dominant motive, for corporate decisions. Numerous factors contribute to the action ultimately decided upon. Respondent's test would allow taxpayers to escape the tax when it is proved that at least one other motive was equal to tax avoidance. We doubt that such a determination can be made with any accuracy, and it is certainly one which will depend almost exclusively on the interested testimony of corporate management. Respondent's test would thus go a long way toward destroying the presumption that Congress created to meet this very problem. * * *

* * *

Finally, we cannot subscribe to respondent's suggestion that our holding would make purpose totally irrelevant. It still serves to isolate those cases in which tax avoidance motives did not contribute to the decision to accumulate. Obviously in such a case imposition of the tax would be futile. In addition, "purpose" means more than mere knowledge, undoubtedly present in nearly every case. It is still open to the taxpayer to show that even though knowledge of the tax consequences was present, that knowledge did not contribute to the decision to accumulate earnings.

¶ 7045

Reversed and remanded.

[Concurring and dissenting opinions omitted.]

[¶ 7050]

Notes

1.   The practical effect of the decision in *Donruss* was virtually to eliminate the purpose defense to the accumulated earnings tax in the normal case. Was that an appropriate result, bearing in mind that the defense is only important to a taxpayer who has "unreasonably" accumulated earnings? One consequence of the decision was to significantly increase the potency of the penalty in the hands of the IRS.

2.   One context in which the statutory purpose continues to play a role is the publicly held corporation. In practice, the accumulated earnings tax has been applied only to closely held corporations. In the 1954 revisions of the Code, a provision in the House bill which would have exempted publicly held corporations was deleted in the Senate, and the Senate Finance Committee Report indicated that the tax was "theoretically applicable" to publicly held corporations, although, as a "practical matter" it had been applied only "where 50 percent or more of the stock of a corporation is held by a limited group." S. Rep. No. 1622, 83d Cong., 2d Sess. 69 (1954). The Tax Court sustained the application of the tax to a publicly held corporation but was reversed by the Ninth Circuit. Golconda Mining Corp. v. Commissioner, 58 T.C. 139 and 58 T.C. 736 (1972), rev'd, 507 F.2d 594 (9th Cir.1974). In the Tax Reform Act of 1984, Congress resolved the theoretical issue by adding Section 532(c), which provides that the application of the accumulated earnings tax to a corporation is determined without regard to the number of shareholders of the corporation. The amendment, however, has had little practical importance.

[¶ 7055]

2.   UNREASONABLE ACCUMULATIONS

The statutory provisions suggest that, to establish liability for the tax, the entire historical earnings of the corporation must be compared to the entire cumulative needs of the business for cash. In a practice that has evolved over the past three decades, such a burdensome analysis is not undertaken. Rather, the liquid asset balances of the corporate taxpayer are compared to the needs of the business for current assets. The penalized behavior, therefore, has become the accumulation by a corporation of relatively liquid investment assets. That judicial rewriting of the accumulated earnings tax received final approval in the following case.

¶ 7045

[¶ 7060]

IVAN ALLEN CO. v. UNITED STATES

Supreme Court of the United States, 1975.
422 U.S. 617.

MR. JUSTICE BLACKMUN delivered the opinion of the Court.

Sections 531–537 * * * subject most corporations to an "accumulated earnings tax." * * *

The issue here is whether, in determining the application of § 533(a), listed and readily marketable securities owned by the corporation and purchased out of its earnings and profits, are to be taken into account at their cost to the corporation or at their net liquidation value, that is, fair market value less the expenses of, and taxes resulting from, their conversion into cash.

* * *

The petitioner, Ivan Allen Company (the taxpayer), is a Georgia corporation incorporated in 1902 and actively engaged in the business of selling office furniture, equipment, and supplies in the metropolitan Atlanta area. * * *

* * *

Throughout fiscal 1965 and 1966, the taxpayer owned various listed and unlisted marketable securities. Prominent among these were listed shares of common stock and listed convertible debentures of Xerox Corporation that, in prior years, had been purchased out of earnings and profits. Specifically, on June 30, 1965, the corporation owned 11,140 shares of Xerox common, with a cost of $116,701 and a then fair market value of $1,573,525, and $30,600 Xerox convertible debentures, with a cost to it of $30,625 and a then fair market value of $48,424. On June 30, 1966, the corporation owned 10,090 shares of Xerox common, with a cost of $102,479 and a then fair market value of $2,479,617, and the same $30,600 convertible debentures, with their cost of $30,625 and a then fair market value of $69,768. * * *

According to its returns as filed, the taxpayer's undistributed earnings as of June 30, 1965, and June 30, 1966, were $2,200,184.77 and $2,360,146.52, respectively. * * * The taxpayer points out that the marketable portfolio assets represented an investment, as measured by cost, of less than 7% of its undistributed earnings and of less than 5% of its total assets. * * *

It is also apparent, however, that the Xerox debentures and common shares had proved to be an extraordinarily profitable investment, although, of course, because these securities continued to be retained, the gains thereon were unrealized for federal income tax purposes. The

¶ 7060

debentures had increased in fair market value more than 50% over cost by the end of June 1965, and more than 100% over cost one year later; the common shares had increased in fair market value more than 13 times their cost by June 30, 1965, and more than 24 times their cost by June 30, 1966.

Throughout fiscal 1965 and 1966 the taxpayer's two major shareholders, Ivan Allen, Sr., and Ivan Allen, Jr., respectively owned 31.20% and 45.46% of the taxpayer's outstanding voting stock. * * *

Following an examination of the taxpayer's federal income tax returns for fiscal 1965 and 1966, the Commissioner of Internal Revenue determined that the taxpayer had permitted its earnings and profits for each of those years to accumulate beyond the reasonable and reasonably anticipated needs of its business, and that one of the purposes of the accumulation for each year was to avoid income tax with respect to its shareholders. Based upon this determination, the Commissioner assessed against the corporation accumulated earnings taxes of $77,383.98 and $73,131.87 for 1965 and 1966, respectively.

* * *

It is agreed that the taxpayer had reasonable business needs for operating capital amounting to $1,198,309 and $1,455,222 at the close of fiscal 1965 and fiscal 1966, respectively. * * * It is stipulated, in particular, that if the taxpayer's marketable securities are to be taken into account at *cost*, its net liquid assets (current assets less current liabilities), at the end of each of those taxable years, and fully available for use in its business, were then exactly equal to its reasonable business needs for operating capital, that is, the above-stated figures of $1,198,309 and $1,455,222. It would follow, accordingly, that the earnings and profits of the two taxable years had *not* been permitted to accumulate beyond the taxpayer's reasonable and reasonably anticipated business needs, within the meaning of § 533(a), * * * and no accumulated earnings taxes were incurred. It is still further stipulated, however, that if the taxpayer's marketable securities are to be taken into account at *fair market value* (less the cost of converting them into cash), as to the ends of those fiscal years, the taxpayer's net liquid assets would then be $2,235,029 and $3,152,009, respectively. * * * From this it would follow that the earnings and profits of the two taxable years *had* been permitted to accumulate beyond the taxpayer's reasonable and reasonably anticipated business needs. Then, if those accumulations had been for "the purpose of avoiding the income tax with respect to its shareholders," under § 532(a), accumulated earnings taxes would be incurred.

The issue, therefore, is clear and precise: whether, for purposes of applying § 533(a), the taxpayer's readily marketable securities should be taken into account at cost, as the taxpayer contends, or at net liquidation value, as the Government contends.

The District Court held that the taxpayer's readily marketable securities were to be taken into account at cost. Accordingly, it entered judgment for the petitioner-taxpayer. 349 F. Supp. 1075 (1972). * * *

The United States Court of Appeals for the Fifth Circuit reversed. 493 F.2d 426 (1974). * * * The case was remanded, as the parties had agreed, * * * "for the additional factual determination of whether one purpose for the accumulation was to avoid income tax on behalf of the shareholders." 493 F.2d, at 428.

* * *

Under our system of income taxation, corporate earnings are subject to tax at two levels. First, there is the tax imposed upon the income of the corporation. Second, when the corporation, by way of a dividend, distributes its earnings to its shareholders, the distribution is subject to the tax imposed upon the income of the shareholders. Because of the disparity between the corporate tax rates and the higher gradations of the rates on individuals, a corporation may be utilized to reduce significantly its shareholders' overall tax liability by accumulating earnings beyond the reasonable needs of the business. Without some method to force the distribution of unneeded corporate earnings, a controlling shareholder would be able to postpone the full impact of income taxes on his share of the corporation's earnings in excess of its needs. * * *

In order to foreclose this possibility of using the corporation as a means of avoiding the income tax on dividends to the shareholders, every Revenue Act since the adoption of the Sixteenth Amendment in 1913 has imposed a tax upon unnecessary accumulations of corporate earnings effected for the purpose of insulating shareholders.

* * *

It is to be noted that the focus and impositions of the accumulated earnings tax are upon "accumulated taxable income," § 531. This is defined in § 535(a) to mean the corporation's "taxable income," as adjusted. The adjustments consist of the various items described in § 535(b), including federal income tax, the deduction for dividends paid, defined in § 561, and the accumulated earnings credit defined in § 535(c). The adjustments prescribed by §§ 535(a) and (b) are designed generally to assure that a corporation's "accumulated taxable income" reflects more accurately than "taxable income" the amount actually available to the corporation for business purposes. This explains the deductions for dividends paid and for federal income taxes; neither of these enters into the computation of taxable income. Obviously, dividends paid and federal income taxes deplete corporate resources and must be recognized if the corporation's economic condition is to be properly perceived. Conversely, § 535(b)(3) disallows, for example, the deduction, available to a corporation for income tax purposes under

¶ 7060

§ 243, on account of dividends received; dividends received are freely available for use in the corporation's business.

The purport of the accumulated earnings tax structure established by §§ 531–537, therefore, is to determine the corporation's true economic condition before its liability for tax upon "accumulated taxable income" is determined. The tax, although a penalty and therefore to be strictly construed, Commissioner v. Acker, 361 U.S. 87, 91 * * * (1959), is directed at economic reality.

It is important to emphasize that we are concerned here with a tax on "accumulated taxable income," § 531, and that the tax attaches only when a corporation has permitted "earnings and profits to accumulate instead of being divided or distributed," § 532(a). What is essential is that there be "income" and "earnings and profits." This at once eliminates, from the measure of the tax itself, any unrealized appreciation in the value of the taxpayer's portfolio securities over cost, for any such unrealized appreciation does not enter into the computation of the corporation's "income" and "earnings and profits."

The corporation's readily marketable portfolio securities and their unrealized appreciation, nonetheless, are of profound importance in making the entirely discrete determination whether the corporation has permitted what, concededly, are earnings and profits to accumulate beyond its reasonable business needs. If the securities, as here, are readily available as liquid assets, then the recognized earnings and profits that have been accumulated may well have been unnecessarily accumulated, so far as the reasonable needs of the business are concerned. On the other hand, if those portfolio securities are not liquid and are not readily available for the needs of the business, the accumulation of earnings and profits may be viewed in a different light. Upon this analysis, not only is such accumulation as has taken place important, but the liquidity otherwise available to the corporation is highly significant. In any event—and we repeat—the tax is directed at the accumulated taxable income and at earnings and profits. The tax itself is not directed at the unrealized appreciation of the liquid assets in the securities portfolio. The latter becomes important only in measuring reasonableness of accumulation of the earnings and profits that otherwise independently exist. What we look at, then, in order to determine its reasonableness or unreasonableness, in the light of the needs of the business, is any failure on the part of the corporation to distribute the earnings and profits it has.

* * * What is required, then, is a comparison of accumulated earnings and profits with "the reasonable needs of the business." Business *needs* are critical. And need, plainly, to use mathematical terminology, is a function of a corporation's liquidity, that is, the amount of idle current assets at its disposal. The question, therefore, is not how much capital of all sorts, but how much in the way of quick or liquid

¶ 7060

assets, it is reasonable to keep on hand for the business. * * * *Smoot Sand & Gravel Corp. v. Commissioner*, 274 F.2d 495, 501 (C.A.4), cert. denied, 362 U.S. 976 * * * (1960) (liquid assets provide "a strong indication" of the purpose of the accumulation) * * *.

The taxpayer itself recognizes, and accepts, the liquidity concept as a basic factor, for it "has agreed that the full amount of its realized earnings invested in its liquid assets—their cost—should be taken into account in determining the applicability of Section 533(a)." * * * It concedes that if this were not so, "the tax could be avoided by any form of investment of earnings and profits." * * * But the taxpayer would stop at the point of cost and, when it does so, is compelled to compare earnings and profits—not the amount of readily available liquid assets, net—with reasonable business needs.

We disagree with the taxpayer and conclude that cost is not the stopping point; that the application of the accumulated earnings tax, in a given case, may well depend on whether the corporation has available readily marketable portfolio securities; and that the proper measure of those securities, for purposes of the tax, is their net realizable value. Cost of the marketable securities on the assets side of the corporation's balance sheet would appear to be largely an irrelevant gauge of the taxpayer's true financial condition. Certainly, a lender would not evaluate a potential borrower's marketable securities at cost. Realistic financial condition is the focus of the lender's inquiry. It also must be the focus of the Commissioner's inquiry in determining the applicability of the accumulated earnings tax.[11]

This taxpayer's securities, being liquid and readily marketable, clearly were available for the business needs of the corporation, and their fair market value, net, was such that, according to the stipulation, the taxpayer's undistributed earnings and profits for the two fiscal years in question were permitted to accumulate beyond the reasonable and reasonably anticipated needs of the business.

* * *

The arguments advanced by the taxpayer do not persuade us:

1. The taxpayer, of course, quite correctly insists that unrealized appreciation of portfolio securities does not enter into the determination of "earnings and profits," within the meaning of § 533(a). As noted above, we agree. The Government does not contend otherwise. It does not follow, however, that unrealized appreciation is never to be taken into account for purposes of the accumulated earnings tax.

11. We see little force in any observation that our emphasis on liquid assets means that a corporate taxpayer may avoid the accumulated earnings tax by merely investing in nonliquid assets. If such a step, in a given case, amounted to willful evasion of the accumulated earnings tax, it would be subject to criminal penalties. See, *e.g.*, § 7201 * * *.

¶ 7060

As has been pointed out, the tax is imposed only upon accumulated taxable income, and this is defined to mean taxable income as adjusted by factors that have been described. The question is not whether unrealized appreciation enters into the determination of earnings and profits, which it does not, but whether the accumulated taxable income, in the determination of which earnings and profits have entered, justifiably may be retained rather than distributed as dividends. The tax focuses, therefore, on current income and its retention or distribution. If the corporation has freely available liquid assets in excess of its reasonable business needs, then accumulation of taxable income may be unreasonable and the tax may attach. Utilizable availability of the portfolio assets is measured realistically only at net realizable value. The fact that this value is not included in earnings and profits does not foreclose its being considered in determining whether the corporation is subject to the accumulated earnings tax.

* * *

Affirmed.

[Dissenting opinion omitted.]

[¶ 7065]

Note

While the court in *Ivan Allen* focused on liquid assets as the measure of an unreasonable accumulation, it would seem that any asset that is not required for the conduct of one of the corporate businesses should be treated as a part of the accumulation of earnings. For example, if a corporate taxpayer invested the earnings from its New Jersey sheet metal fabrication business in vacant land in Montana, that investment strategy should not defeat the application of the accumulated earnings tax. However, what would happen if the taxpayer asserted that it had entered the real estate development business in Montana?

[¶ 7070]

3. REASONABLE BUSINESS NEEDS

The accumulation of liquid assets by a corporation will not be penalized if the accumulation can be justified by the needs of the business for cash. See § 537. In measuring the needs of the business for cash, courts tend to disregard the ability of the business to borrow and to allow an accumulation sufficient to finance the entire business operation out of retained earnings.

In *Ivan Allen* the parties apparently stipulated that the reasonable needs of the business included over $1 million for operating or working capital. Working capital is the cash needed to operate a business, from the purchase of raw materials and labor through the sale of inventory and the collection of payment. For many businesses, the need for working capital is the principal justification for the accumulation of liquid assets. The amount of working capital required by a business can be computed for the purposes of the accumulated earnings tax under a formula developed in Bardahl Manufacturing Corp. v. Commissioner, T.C. Memo. 1965–200, and subsequently refined, which is based upon a simplified computation of the operating cycle of the business and is derived from the financial statements of the corporation.

One customary need of the business for cash is an anticipated expansion of the business or an anticipated need to repair or refurbish existing facilities. The regulations to Section 537, however, caution that there must be a demonstrated need for the expansion or renovation, that the corporation's plans must be "specific, definite, and feasible," and that the plans be executed within a reasonable period of time. Regs. § 1.537–1(b)(1).

In general, the courts have not been willing to equate the needs of the shareholders with the needs of the business. Thus, accumulations of liquid assets cannot be justified by the anticipated need to redeem the stock of a shareholder. In some cases, however, it has been argued successfully that the continued investment by a shareholder is harmful to the business and that the redemption of that particular shareholder's stock, therefore, is a need of the business. See Mountain State Steel Foundries, Inc. v. Commissioner, 284 F.2d 737 (4th Cir.1960).

In two specific circumstances, Section 537 authorizes accumulations for the purpose of redeeming stock but the scope of both rules is quite narrow. Section 537(a)(2), for example, permits an accumulation to fund a Section 303 redemption but only in the year of a decedent's death or later years. Thus, an accumulation in advance of the decedent's death is not protected from penalty.

Suppose that, instead of accumulating earnings in advance in order to fund a redemption, a corporation borrows the amount necessary to redeem the interest of a major shareholder and then accumulates earnings in order to discharge the indebtedness. In this connection, see Reg. § 1.537–2(b)(3), which permits the accumulation of funds "for the retirement of bona fide indebtedness created in connection with the trade or business." If an accumulation in advance of the redemption would not be considered a need of the business, could an indebtedness incurred to fund the redemption nevertheless be "created in connection with the trade or business"? Some cases, such as *Mountain State*, seem to find that an accumulation to retire debt incurred in a redemption easier to justify than one that takes place before a redemption. Is there a reasonable basis for this distinction?

[¶ 7075]

4. IMPOSITION OF TAX

If the net liquid assets of the corporation exceed the reasonable needs of the business for current assets, there will be an unreasonable accumulation within the meaning of the accumulated earnings tax as interpreted in the foregoing opinions. However, that accumulation is not directly subject to the 15 percent penalty tax. Rather, as described by the Court in *Ivan Allen*, the tax is imposed on accumulated taxable income—an amount closely related to undistributed personal holding company income. However, Section 535(a) allows the reduction of accumulated taxable income by an "accumulated earnings credit" for the reasonable needs of the business. As a result, the amount subject to tax should never be greater than the excess of liquid assets over the needs of the business for cash. On the other hand, if that excess is greater than the accumulated taxable income for the year, only the lesser amount is subject to tax. In addition, an operating business is entitled to a minimum credit of $250,000 ($150,000 in the case of certain personal service corporations) before it can become subject to the accumulated earnings tax. § 535(c)(2).

As in the case of a personal holding company, the amount otherwise subject to tax is reduced by dividends paid during the year, including consent dividends under Section 565.

¶ 7075

Chapter 8

SALES AND LIQUIDATIONS
OF CORPORATIONS

[¶ 8000]

A. INTRODUCTION

The complete liquidation of a corporation can involve the dismemberment of a business and the distribution of the proceeds of any sales of individual business assets. Such a transaction, however, should be rare because the dismemberment would destroy the intangible value of the business as a going concern. A corporation also might be liquidated because the shareholders desire to conduct the business in unincorporated form. As we will see, however, that transaction would not be common because of the high tax cost of moving from incorporated to unincorporated form. Rather, the most likely reason for liquidating a corporation is that its business has been sold intact to a new corporate owner and the proceeds of the sale are being distributed to the old owners. For that reason, we will examine corporate liquidations in the context of corporate acquisitions. In general, however, the basic tax rules applicable to both corporations and their shareholders are the same regardless of the reason for the liquidation. Thus, we will examine those basic rules first.

[¶ 8005]

B. SIMPLE CORPORATE LIQUIDATIONS

A liquidation for income tax purposes is not exactly the same as the state law dissolution of the corporation although, of course, the concepts are similar. An income tax liquidation occurs when the corporation ceases to conduct business and distributes substantially all of its assets in retirement of all of its outstanding stock. To produce the income tax consequences of a liquidation, it is not necessary that the corporation be dissolved under state law.

341   ¶ 8005

Under several of the Code sections encountered in this chapter, however, a pattern of taxation is available only for transactions occurring after the adoption of a "plan of liquidation." Normally, the date of the adoption of such a plan by a corporation's shareholders is unambiguous. On occasion, however, taxpayers begin liquidations before the formal adoption of a plan with potentially disastrous consequences. For example, under Section 346(a), each distribution in a series may be taxed as a liquidating distribution if it is pursuant to a plan of liquidation while distributions in the absence of a plan would be redemptions or dividends. In analogous circumstances courts have saved careless taxpayers by finding an "informal" adoption of a plan in the actions of officers. See Mountain Water Co. of La Crescenta v. Commissioner, 35 T.C. 418 (1960).

In other circumstances, careful taxpayers have sought to improve upon the tax consequences of a liquidation by timing some transactions to occur just before the formal adoption of a plan of liquidation and others to occur just after. In those circumstances, the courts generally respect the formal adoption of the plan and thus permit taxpayers to "straddle" the plan of liquidation. See City Bank of Washington v. Commissioner, 38 T.C. 713 (1962). While such transactions were common under the pre–1986 rules governing liquidations, they are far less common today.

Sharply different tax rules apply to both corporations and shareholders depending upon whether the corporation being liquidated is at least 80 percent owned by another corporation. We turn first to the rules governing nonsubsidiary liquidations.

[¶ 8010]

1. NONSUBSIDIARY LIQUIDATIONS; SHAREHOLDER CONSEQUENCES

Throughout its existence, a corporation will have accumulated its earnings, perhaps in a calculated effort to avoid distributing dividends to its shareholders. The complete liquidation of that corporation finally requires the distribution of both the realized and unrealized corporate earnings and represents the last opportunity the taxing authorities will have to impose the second tier, shareholder level tax at the income tax rates applicable to dividends. Nevertheless, the liquidation of a corporation is expressly not treated as a final dividend to the extent of the corporate E & P. § 331(b). Rather, under Section 331(a), the liquidating distributions are taxed in the same manner as if they were received on a sale of the stock. That means that the shareholder generally will be entitled to capital gains taxation on the difference between the sum of the amount of cash and the value of any property distributed and the tax basis for the stock. Consistent with that treatment, the basis to the shareholder of any property distributed will be the value of the property.

¶ 8005

§ 334(a). Of course, under the tax rate relationships that exist in 2006, the difference between the taxation of dividends and capital gains has been narrowed substantially.

As described in the preceding chapters, Section 331's capital gains treatment can be overridden by other, more specific rules. On the loss side, for example, Section 1244 may create ordinary loss treatment for individual shareholders.

[¶ 8015]

a. Shareholder Assumption of Liabilities

In computing a shareholder's gain upon receiving a liquidating distribution, the amount of any corporate liability assumed by the shareholder will reduce the fair market value of the property received and thus the amount subject to tax under Section 331. Thus, for example, on a distribution in a complete liquidation of property having a gross value of $10,000, but subject to a liability of $3,000, to a shareholder having a basis of $1,000 for her stock, the shareholder would have an amount realized of $7,000 and a gain of $6,000.

While Section 334(a) might seem to imply the contrary, the basis of the property to the shareholder should equal the fair market value of the property ignoring the liability, or $10,000 in our example. In effect, the shareholder is given a basis credit for the liability under the assumption that she will later pay off the liability. As a result, the later payment of the assumed liabilities generally should not have any tax consequences, which is consistent with the treatment of debt generally under the tax laws. See Crane v. Commissioner, 331 U.S. 1 (1947), and its progeny.

If the shareholder ultimately is required to pay more to discharge the liability than was taken into account in the measurement of gain, some tax benefit from the excess payment would be required. For example, if the amount of the liability assumed were contingent, such as a pending tort claim against the corporation, the payment needed to discharge the liability might be more than was predicted at the time of liquidation. Thus, in our example a contingent liability might have been valued at $3,000 but ultimately discharged for a payment of $4,000. Upon her payment of the $4,000 the shareholder must be given a tax benefit for the additional $1,000. Unfortunately for the shareholder, that tax benefit is probably limited to a capital loss under Arrowsmith v. Commissioner, 344 U.S. 6 (1952), if the prior receipt of the proceeds of liquidation were taxable at capital gains rates.

[¶ 8020]

b. Installment Sales of Stock Incident to Complete Liquidation

Normally under Section 331(a), the distributee shareholders must recognize the full amount of their gain at the time of liquidation.

However, in the past some shareholders have succeeded in deferring their gain through an installment sale of their stock in advance of the liquidation. Several cases upheld the efficacy of such planning. See, e.g., Rushing v. Commissioner, 441 F.2d 593 (5th Cir.1971).

Today an the installment sale must overcome several hurdles to succeed in deferring the gain. First, under Section 453(e) and (f), if, as is common, the buyer is the shareholder's child or other related person, the buyer's subsequent disposition of the stock within two years of the installment sale (including a surrender of the stock in exchange for a liquidating distribution) will cause an acceleration of the deferred gain unless a lack of tax avoidance motive is proven. Second, the sale must be of stock not traded on an established market. See § 453(k).

Third, an otherwise qualifying sale of stock must be sufficiently timely to forestall application of the assignment of income doctrine. Otherwise the liquidation proceeds will be treated as earned by, and therefore taxable to, the selling shareholder. The same constraint applies to gifts of stock in connection with a planned liquidation of a corporation. In Kinsey v. Commissioner, 477 F.2d 1058 (2d Cir.1973), for example, a shareholder made a gift to a university of 56 percent of the shares in a corporation after a plan of liquidation had been approved by a two-thirds shareholder vote but before the date set for the liquidation distribution. Even though a majority interest had been transferred, the liquidation distribution was, as a practical matter, assured, since neither the university nor any other shareholders could be expected to vote to rescind the plan, particularly in view of the adverse tax consequences which might ensue. For this reason, the court held that the transfer of the shares was an anticipatory assignment of the liquidation proceeds and thus the proceeds were includible in the donor's gross income. Although the taxpayer in *Kinsey* clearly had control of the corporation, the same result has been reached where a taxpayer owned only 10 percent of the outstanding shares. Jones v. United States, 531 F.2d 1343 (6th Cir.1976).

[¶ 8025]

2. NONSUBSIDIARY LIQUIDATIONS; CORPORATE LEVEL CONSEQUENCES

In general, the corporate level consequences of distributions in liquidation are identical to other distributions with respect to stock. That means that a distribution of cash will not have any income tax consequences. Moreover, the effect of the distribution on the E & P account of the corporation is of no significance since the account will be extinguished by the liquidation. And, as occurs on nonliquidating distributions, the distribution of appreciated property requires the corporation to recognize gain as if the property were sold to the distributee for its value. § 336(a).

¶ 8020

The distribution of loss property, however, is treated quite different-ly in a liquidating distribution. Unlike the rule of Section 311(a) govern-ing nonliquidating distributions, Section 336(a) generally allows the liquidating corporation to recognize loss on the distribution of property having a tax basis in excess of its value. That favorable rule, however, is subject to the broad and complex limitations of Section 336(d), which may limit the amount of loss that may be claimed or disallow the loss entirely.

To put Section 336(d) at least somewhat in context, recall that under Section 267(a)(1) losses are disallowed on all *sales* between related persons, which include a corporation and a more than 50 percent shareholder, determined after the application of stock attribution rules. Thus, on sales of corporate property to a majority shareholder in anticipation of a corporate liquidation, the loss would be disallowed. While Section 267 applies to sales in anticipation of a liquidation, it does not apply to the liquidating distributions themselves. Rather, Section 336(d) applies.

Under Section 336(d)(1), corporate level losses on the *distribution* of property in liquidation may be disallowed if the property is distributed to the related persons covered by Section 267, including controlling share-holders. Section 336, however, is not automatically applicable as is Section 267; the disallowance produced by Section 336(d)(1) applies only in two circumstances. First, losses are disallowed on the portion of the property distributed to related persons if the distribution is not pro rata as to all shareholders. Second, losses are disallowed if they are attribut-able to property distributed to a related person that was contributed to the corporation within the last five years in a Section 351 transaction or a contribution to capital. This so-called anti-stuffing rule was designed to prevent the contribution of property containing a built-in loss to a corporation in a carryover basis transaction in anticipation of a liqui-dation. While the contribution would not be subject to tax, absent Section 336(d)(1), the distribution might produce recognized losses at both the corporate (on the sale or distribution of the property) and shareholder (on the receipt of the distribution of the proceeds) levels. However, if Section 336(d)(1) applies, any post-contribution loss is disal-lowed along with any pre-contribution loss.

If the liquidating corporation has acquired property in a Section 351 transaction or as a contribution to capital and the loss is not disallowed under Section 336(d)(1), generally because the property was transferred to an unrelated person, the amount of loss that may be claimed on the disposition of the property may be limited by Section 336(d)(2). If Section 336(d)(2) applies, only loss economically accruing after the transfer of the property to the corporation may be deducted; pre-contribution, or built-in, loss is disallowed by reducing the basis of the contributed property by the amount of the built-in loss at the time of the contribution. The scope of (d)(2) is broader than the scope of (d)(1). It applies even if the property was acquired more than five years ago and it applies to transfers to any person, whether or not related. Significantly, Section 336(d)(2) applies to all forms of dispositions, sales as well as distributions.

This broad scope to Section 336(d)(2) is restricted by the further provision that the limitation on loss applies only if a principal purpose of the acquisition of the property by the corporation was to create a loss for the corporation in the subsequent liquidation. § 336(d)(2)(B)(i)(II). Because that purpose might be difficult to prove, the section further provides that property acquired by the corporation during the two years preceding the adoption of the plan of liquidation will be treated as acquired for the prohibited purpose except as provided by regulation. § 336(d)(2)(B)(ii). Because that blanket rule appeared too harsh, the Conference Report admonishes that the regulations should provide that presumed prohibited purpose will be ignored if the property transferred to the corporation bore a substantial relationship to the corporation's business. H.R. Conf. Rep. 841, 99th Cong. 2d Sess. at II–201 (1986).

Section 336(d), however, was enacted before Congress adopted Section 362(e)(2). Under that provision, if the *aggregate* tax basis of property contributed by a specific transferor in a Section 351 exchange exceeds the *aggregate* fair market value of that property, the aggregate basis to the transferee corporation must be reduced to equal that aggregate value (unless the parties elect to reduce the basis of the transferor's stock instead). See ¶ 2150. Given that newer and more draconian rule, the continued need for Section 336(d) is unclear because the tax avoidance transaction that Section 336(d) addressed can no longer occur. Indeed, if Section 336(d) applied to eliminate a loss at the corporate level after the parties had elected under Section 362(e) to eliminate the loss at the shareholder level, the effect of Section 336(d) would be excessively harsh. Nevertheless, Section 336(d) remains in the Code and can have a material impact in the liquidation of a corporation. Because Section 362(e) operates on the aggregate built-in loss, after its operation specific items of property may continue to have a precontribution built-in loss. See ¶ 2150. Since Section 336(d)(2) apparently applies to specific items of property, it would disallow that remaining built-in loss. And, of course, since Section 336(d)(1) disallows both pre-and post-contribution losses, it continues to have a role in the taxation of liquidating distributions.

[¶ 8030]

3. THE SPECIAL CASE OF PROPERTY HAVING NO ASCERTAINABLE VALUE

The otherwise logical scheme of Sections 331 and 336 is difficult to apply when the liquidating corporation distributes property in kind that is so difficult to value that it may be said to have no ascertainable fair market value. That issue is presented by such properties as contract rights to payments that are contingent upon factors entirely out of the control of the taxpayer, such as royalties based upon productivity (e.g., of a mine) or use (e.g., of a patent) or the right to commissions on the renewal of insurance contracts generated in the course of the corporate business. Frequently, however, such contract rights arise from the sale of the corporate business itself in anticipation of the liquidation and call for future payments determined by the profitability of the business sold.

Under the doctrine of Burnet v. Logan, 283 U.S. 404 (1931), an actual sale or exchange of property for rights to payment having no ascertainable value may be held "open" for tax purposes. In that event, rather than valuing the rights received and taxing the seller on that value in the year of sale or exchange, tax is imposed as payments are made pursuant to the contract. Under Section 336, a distribution of property is to be taxed to the corporation as if the property had been sold. However, following a liquidating distribution, the corporate taxpayer will cease to exist and it therefore seems impossible to apply the *Burnet v. Logan* doctrine to the liquidating corporation. Yet, it is not entirely clear what does happen under Section 336. Must the corporation make its best effort to value the rights and pay tax on that value in the year of liquidation or, since the value of the rights is by hypothesis "unascertainable," is no amount taxable? In the more likely event that some value must be taxed, in many instances the assigned value will be substantially less than the amount ultimately paid to the holders of the rights. In these cases, the liquidation will result in the elimination of the corporate level tax on a significant amount of income or gain. That result seems especially troublesome when the contract rights were created by the sale of the corporate business in contemplation of the liquidation.

The taxation of the shareholder recipient of the impossible-to-value property is similarly unclear, but the stakes are not quite so great. Payments on the liquidation of a corporation may constitute an installment sale under Section 453. However, aside from the limited exception provided by Section 453(h), the receipt of third-party contract rights from the liquidating corporation are not eligible for installment reporting; they constitute "payments" that are to be taxed in the year that the contract rights are distributed. That much seems clear. However, if the payments (in the form of contract rights) received in an installment sale do not have an ascertainable value, how are they to be taxed?

The unresolved issue is whether taxation of the contract rights can be deferred under *Burnet v. Logan* until payments are made pursuant to the contracts or whether Section 453 itself requires that all "payments" be valued and taxed in the year of liquidation. If that issue is resolved in favor of the deferral of tax, as seems probable, the timing of any recovery of basis must be determined. Normally under *Burnet v. Logan* open transaction reporting, the taxpayer's entire basis in the property exchanged may be recovered before any gain must be reported. However,

¶ 8030

Section 453(j)(2) appears to bar that result in the context of an installment sale. All of this is further confused, if that is possible, by the ability to elect out of installment reporting. But see Temp. Reg. § 15A.453–1(d)(2)(iii)(open transaction reporting available only in rare and extraordinary cases).

These are timing issues, however. No income should escape tax to the shareholder as might occur at the corporate level; the areas of doubt involve whether the reporting of income may be deferred and whether the recovery of basis may be accelerated. The resolutions of these issues, however, might also affect the characterization of the shareholders' gain on the liquidation. At one time, open transaction reporting meant that the full amount of all payments received was treated as attributable to the liquidation and thus was taxable as a capital gain. Today, however, if the receipt of the contract rights constitutes a payment under a contract for the sale of property, Section 483 (or the similar Section 1274) would impute an interest charge on the deferred payment and thus convert a portion of the gain on the liquidation to ordinary income, whether *Burnet v. Logan* applied or not. Presumably Section 483 (or Section 1274) ought to apply to the receipt of payments on the liquidation of a corporation. That issue, however, has not been authoritatively resolved.

[¶ 8035]

Problems

1.   Terminator Corp. owns cash of $250 and an asset with a tax basis of $50 and a fair market value of $750 and has no liabilities. Cher, the sole shareholder in the corporation, invested $100 for all of its stock many years ago. Assume that the corporate tax rate is 30 percent and the individual capital gains rate is a flat 20 percent. What will be the tax consequences to Terminator and to Cher, and what will be the after tax proceeds to Cher, if:

a.   Terminator sells its asset for $750, pays its tax liability and liquidates?

b.   Terminator distributes its assets in kind, less the amount needed to pay its tax liability, and Cher retains the assets. What will be Cher's basis in the asset?

c.   What result if instead Cher sells the stock of Terminator? For what could the stock be sold? $790?

2.   How would your answer to Problem 1.b. change if the asset were subject to a liability of $300 that Cher assumed when the property was distributed?

3.   Upon the formation of Double–Whammy, Inc., Sonny contributed the following three items of property in a transaction qualifying under Section 351:

	Fair Market Value	**Basis**
Asset A	$100	$ 500
Asset B	200	400
Asset C	400	100
	$700	$1000

Assume that 18 months later, Double–Whammy is liquidated. During that 18 months, the value and basis of the contributed properties did not change except that the value of Asset B declined by 150 to 50. What would be the results under Sections 362(e)(2) and 336(d) if

a. Double–Whammy sells all three assets to an unrelated purchaser and distributes the after-tax proceeds in liquidation?

b. Double–Whammy distributes the assets in kind to Sonny?

c. Assume that following the Section 351 exchange, the parties elected under Section 362(e)(2)(C) to reduce the basis of Sonny's stock to $700 rather than reducing the basis of the assets in the hands of the corporation. Now what consequences if Double–Whammy sells the assets to an unrelated purchaser and distributes the proceeds?

[¶ 8040]

4. LIQUIDATION OF CORPORATE SUBSIDIARIES

Speaking generally, the liquidation rules just described treat the transfer of the corporate assets as a sale of those assets to the shareholders. That treatment does not seem sensible when the shareholder is a sole corporate parent of the liquidating corporation. The transfer of the business of the subsidiary to the parent more nearly resembles the kind of alteration in the form of doing business that is normally extended nonrecognition treatment than it resembles a sale. For that reason, the different rules of Sections 332 and 337 apply to the liquidation of a corporation when 80 percent or more of its stock is owned by a parent corporation. Under those rules, the taxation of the liquidation of a subsidiary has more in common with the tax-free reorganization provisions described in Chapters 9 and 10 than it does with nonsubsidiary liquidations.

Under the pattern of taxation created by Sections 332 and 337, in general neither the liquidating subsidiary nor the distributee parent corporation is subject to tax on any gain. Rather, under Section 334(b)(1), the bases of the subsidiary's assets carry over to the parent corporation, thus preserving the unrealized appreciation (or other income, such as depreciation recapture) that would otherwise have been taxable to the subsidiary. In addition, the other tax attributes of the subsidiary, including its E & P account, survive the liquidation and carry over to the parent corporation. § 381(a).

¶ 8040

On the other hand, the parent's tax basis in the subsidiary's stock disappears along with that stock, and the parent's investment gain or loss permanently escapes tax consequences. Since the corporate level tax is preserved in the carryover basis for the subsidiary assets, the elimination of tax on the gain in the subsidiary's stock serves the same purpose as the intercorporate dividends-received deduction—the avoidance of multiple tiers of taxation. Somewhat inconsistently, if the repayments on a debt instrument of the subsidiary held by the parent exceed the tax basis of that debt, the resulting gain is recognized. Reg. § 1.332–7.

Under prior law, the nonrecognition rule applicable to the subsidiary now contained in Section 337 only applied to distributions with respect to stock and not to retirements of debt. Thus, when much of a parent's investment in the liquidating subsidiary was in the form of debt, complex tax planning was required to ensure that property lacking appreciation was used to discharge that debt in order to avoid a taxable gain to the subsidiary. That marshalling of assets is no longer required. Under Sections 337(b)(1) and 334(b)(1), the transfer of property to the parent corporation in retirement of a debt obligation incident to a Section 332 liquidation is treated in the same manner as a transfer in retirement of stock—as a nonrecognition/carryover basis transaction. However, Section 332 apparently applies only if some distribution is made with respect to stock and thus might not apply to distributions in retirement of the debt obligations of an insolvent subsidiary. Reg. § 1.332–2(b). Accordingly, and somewhat oddly, an insolvent subsidiary would recognize gain or loss on the distribution of property in complete liquidation.

Since the special rules of Sections 332 and 337 apply to 80 percent owned subsidiaries, a subsidiary being liquidated under those rules may also have minority shareholders. The taxation of those shareholders is not governed by Section 332 but rather remains controlled by Section 331. Thus, the gain or loss recognized by the minority shareholders will be fully subject to tax. Similarly, in the event that property is distributed to the minority shareholders, Section 336, and not Section 337, will apply to the liquidating corporation. Thus, the subsidiary will be subject to tax on any appreciation in property distributed to the minority shareholders. However, under the special rule of Section 336(d)(3), no loss can be recognized.

In general, Sections 332 and 337 are favorable and taxpayers would seek their application, but the blessing is mixed. If the parent has a loss in the stock of the subsidiary or the subsidiary has a loss in its assets, it might prefer the tax consequences of Sections 331 and 336. Or, inheriting the E & P account of the subsidiary might not be desirable. These preferences might lead to tax planning in advance of a contemplated liquidation with a view towards altering its consequences. However, in creating two distinct patterns for taxing liquidations, Congress may not have intended to allow taxpayers to elect the treatment they desired.

¶ 8040

Nevertheless, whenever an arbitrary definition, such as 80 percent ownership, leads to different tax consequences, the potential for manipulation arises. The following is one of the earliest cases to explore that pervasive issue.

[¶ 8045]

GRANITE TRUST CO. v. UNITED STATES

United States Court of Appeals, First Circuit, 1956.
238 F.2d 670.

MAGRUDER, CHIEF JUDGE:

* * *

In 1928 the Building Corporation was organized by Granite Trust Company for the purpose of acquiring land and constructing an office building thereon to be occupied by the bank. The land and building cost over $1,000,000 and were financed through the purchase by the taxpayer bank of all the stock of the Building Corporation. * * *

Beginning at least as early as 1936, the amount at which the stock of the Building Corporation was carried upon the taxpayer's books was subjected to continuous criticism by various banking authorities. As a result, the taxpayer wrote down the value of the stock on its books, but nevertheless the examining authorities continued to press for further annual reductions.

At some time prior to October, 1943, the taxpayer's management commenced the formulation of a plan to bring this issue to a close by the expedient of having Granite Trust Company purchase the real estate from the Building Corporation for $550,000, a fair current appraisal, after which the subsidiary Building Corporation was to be liquidated. The practical problem in the execution of this plan resulted from the fact that the distribution in the liquidation of the subsidiary corporation was expected to amount to something between $65 and $66 per share upon the shares of common stock in the Building Corporation for which the taxpayer had paid $100 per share. In thus contributing to the simplification of the corporate structure of the taxpayer as a holding company, an end deemed desirable by the Congress, Granite Trust Company naturally wanted to be assured that its prospective loss to be realized upon the liquidation of its subsidiary would lawfully be "recognized" at once so as to be available as a tax deduction.

In order that this forthcoming loss upon its investment might not be denied recognition by § 112(b)(6) of the Internal Revenue Code of 1939 [§ 332 of the 1954 and the 1986 Codes], the taxpayer, on advice of counsel, proceeded to divest itself of some of its shares of common stock in the Building Corporation by means of several purported sales and of a gift, the facts concerning which are as follows:

* * * On December 6, 1943, the taxpayer sold to, or went through the form of selling to, Howard D. Johnson Company 1,025 shares of common stock of the Building Corporation, that being 20.5 per cent of the outstanding voting stock. Howard D. Johnson Company paid $65.50 per share * * *.

At a meeting of the Building Corporation stockholders held on December 10, 1943, the taxpayer submitted a written offer to purchase the real estate for $550,000. The stockholders voted to accept this offer, and at the same meeting the following vote was taken:

> "That if and when this Corporation shall receive $550,000, adjusted as provided in the vote with regard to the sale of the Corporation's real estate, this Corporation shall be completely liquidated, * * * provided, however, that such liquidation and distribution shall be made and shall be entirely completed prior to December 30, 1943."

* * *

Thereafter, on December 13, 1943, the taxpayer sold, or went through the form of selling, ten shares each of the common stock in the Building Corporation to Howard D. Johnson individually and to one Ralph E. Richmond, for a price of $65.50 per share. On the same day the taxpayer donated to the Greater Boston United War Fund two shares of the common stock of the Building Corporation. Johnson and Richmond duly paid by check for the shares they bought, and the taxpayer delivered to them and to the United War Fund certificates sufficient to cover the shares sold or donated, which certificates were held by Johnson, Richmond, and the United War Fund until surrendered by them on December 17 in the course of the final liquidation of the Building Corporation.

At no time after the making of the above sales and gift did the taxpayer acquire any additional common stock in the Building Corporation.

On December 15, 1943, the real estate was conveyed to the taxpayer by the Building Corporation, and the taxpayer paid the Building Corporation the price of $550,000, appropriately adjusted for local taxes, rentals and insurance. The real estate was thereby brought on to the taxpayer's books at a cost equivalent to current fair market value, thus satisfying the banking authorities.

* * *

On December 30, 1943, a final meeting of the Building Corporation stockholders was held, there being represented at the meeting the taxpayer, Howard D. Johnson Company, Howard D. Johnson, Ralph E. Richmond, and Greater Boston United War Fund. Dissolution was voted,

¶ 8045

with authority to the corporation's directors and officers to take all steps necessary or advisable to that end.

The taxpayer concedes that it would not have made the sales described above had it not been for § 112(b)(6) of the Internal Revenue Code of 1939 [now § 332]. * * *

The precise issue before us is whether or not to give effect for tax purposes to the aforesaid sales and gift by the taxpayer. * * *

Although there is no dispute that the transactions in form at least purport to be sales and a gift, the Commissioner nevertheless maintains that we should not accord them that significance. The Commissioner's argument is in two parts: The first proposition derives from the basic finding of the district court that the taxpayer effected the liquidation "in such manner as to achieve a tax reduction" and that this was "without legal or moral justification." The Commissioner attempts to bolster this argument by his traditional corporation reorganization analysis to the effect that, so long as the "end-result" of the transactions involved complies with the "criteria of the statute," intermediary steps (in this case the sales and gift) should be ignored as if they were nonexistent. His reasoning is that, if the final outcome is complete liquidation of a subsidiary corporation which at the outset was wholly owned by the taxpayer, the entire procedure comes within the intendment of the statute and "[c]ircuitous steps to avoid Section 112(b)(6)" occurring prior to the ultimate liquidation should be disregarded.

The Commissioner's second proposition is that there were in fact no valid sales or gift of stock made by the taxpayer. This argument rests on the taxpayer's admission that the transfers were motivated solely by tax considerations and were made in a friendly atmosphere to friendly people who knew of the decision to liquidate the corporation before the end of the year. As the Commissioner points out, the liquidation took place shortly after the transfers, and the transferees then received back the money they had paid in, plus a small profit. Therefore, the Commissioner argues, relying heavily on Gregory v. Helvering, 1935, 293 U.S. 465, that "the stock transfers in question had no independent purpose or meaning—either for the transferor or the transferees—but constituted merely a transitory and circuitous routing of legal title for the purpose of avoiding taxes, within the meaning of Helvering v. Gregory, supra. It was not expected or intended by any of the parties that the transferees should become true stockholders. Legal title passed; but beneficial ownership surely never passed. The transferees who paid money for their stock knew that the subsidiary would be liquidated in a few days and that they would get their money back—as in fact they did, with additional amounts to pay them for their cooperation in serving as conduits of title." The gift of stock to the United War Fund is dismissed as "nothing more than a gift of the cash."

* * *

Our conclusion is that the Commissioner's arguments must be rejected, and that the taxpayer should be permitted to "recognize" the loss on its investment, which it undoubtedly realized upon the liquidation of the Building Corporation.

* * *

Turning then to the basic contentions of the Commissioner, not much need be said with reference to the proposition that the tax motive for the sales and gift rendered the transactions "immoral" and thus vitiated them. Again and again the courts have pointed out that a "purpose to minimize or avoid taxation is not an illicit motive."

* * *

As for the Commissioner's "end-result" argument, the very terms of § 112(b)(6) [now § 332] make it evident that it is not an "end-result" provision, but rather one which prescribes specific conditions for the nonrecognition of realized gains or losses, conditions which, if not strictly met, make the section inapplicable. In fact, the Commissioner's own regulations * * * emphasize the rigid requirements of the section and make no allowance for the type of "step transaction" theory advanced in this case.

* * *

The more specific and more important bit of legislative history is found in the Report of the Senate Finance Committee at the time that § 112(b)(6) was reenacted, with amendments, as § 332 of the Internal Revenue Code of 1954. At this time, when Congress was engaged in a comprehensive reexamination of the Internal Revenue Code, the well-known case of Commissioner of Internal Revenue v. Day & Zimmermann, Inc., 3 Cir., 1945, 151 F.2d 517, had been decided in favor of the taxpayer, and it reasonably could be supposed that Congress, had it disapproved of the decision in that case, would have overturned its conclusion by making over § 112(b)(6) into an "end-result" provision. In the Day & Zimmermann case, the taxpayer, admittedly in order to avoid the nonrecognition provisions of § 112(b)(6), had sold at public auction a sufficient number of shares of a wholly owned subsidiary corporation to reduce its holdings below 80 per cent. These shares were bought, after general bidding, by the treasurer of the taxpayer, who, after receiving cash dividends in the subsequent liquidation of the companies, reported his gain and paid income tax thereon. The Third Circuit held that § 112(b)(6) did not apply to the liquidation, emphasizing that the treasurer had paid a fair price for the shares, had used his own money, had not been directed by anyone to bid, and that there had been no showing of any understanding existing between him and the corporation by which the latter was to retain any sort of interest in the securities or in the proceeds therefrom. * * *

¶ 8045

Commissioner of Internal Revenue v. Day & Zimmermann, Inc., is not to be distinguished, as the Commissioner suggests, on the ground that the sale of stock was at public auction, without specific negotiation between the treasurer and the taxpayer. The significant thing in the case is its ultimate rationale that the purported sales of stock to the treasurer were in fact sales, notwithstanding the tax motive which prompted the corporation to enter into the transaction; from which it would seem to be irrelevant how the transfer was arranged, or whether or not it occurred at a public auction or exchange, so long as the beneficial as well as legal title was intended to pass and did pass.

[Relying on the Senate Finance Committee Report, the court concluded that Congress had not intended to alter the conclusion reached in *Day & Zimmermann*.]

* * *

We come then to the Commissioner's second major contention, resting on Helvering v. Gregory, supra, that the sales of stock by the corporation should be ignored on the ground that they were not bona fide, and that the taxpayer therefore retained "beneficial ownership". The Commissioner characterizes the transfers as artificial, unessential, transitory phases of a completed tax avoidance scheme which should be disregarded.

In answer to this contention, it is first necessary to determine precisely what the Gregory case held. Judge Learned Hand, in Chisholm v. Commissioner, 2 Cir., 1935, 79 F. 2d 14, 15 * * * analyzed the case as follows:

> *"The question always is whether the transaction under scrutiny is in fact what it appears to be in form*; a marriage may be a joke; a contract may be intended only to deceive others; an agreement may have a collateral defeasance. In such cases the transaction as a whole is different from its appearance. * * * In Gregory v. Helvering, supra, 293 U.S. 465 * * * the incorporators adopted the usual form for creating business corporations; but their intent, or purpose, was merely to draught the papers, in fact not to create corporations as the court understood that word. That was the purpose which defeated their exemption, not the accompanying purpose to escape taxation; that purpose was legally neutral. Had they really meant to conduct a business by means of the two reorganized companies, they would have escaped whatever other aim they might have had, whether to avoid taxes, or to regenerate the world." [Italics added.]

In the present case the question is whether or not there actually were sales. Why the parties may wish to enter into a sale is one thing, but that is irrelevant under the Gregory case so long as the consummated agreement was no different from what it purported to be.

¶ 8045

Even the Commissioner concedes that "[l]egal title" passed to the several transferees on December 13, 1943, but he asserts that "beneficial ownership" never passed. We find no basis on which to vitiate the purported sales, for the record is absolutely devoid of any evidence indicating an understanding by the parties to the transfers that any interest in the stock transferred was to be retained by the taxpayer. If Johnson or Richmond had gone bankrupt, or the assets of both had been attached by creditors, on the day after the sales to them, we do not see how the conclusion could be escaped that their Building Corporation stock would have been included in their respective assets; and if Johnson or Richmond had died, surely the holdings of stock of each would have passed to his executors or administrators, or legatees.

In addition to what we have said, there are persuasive reasons of a general nature which lend weight to the taxpayer's position. To strike down these sales on the alleged defect that they took place between friends and for tax motives would only tend to promote duplicity and result in extensive litigation as taxpayers led courts into hairsplitting investigations to decide when a sale was not a sale. It is no answer to argue that, under Helvering v. Gregory, there is an inescapable judicial duty to examine into the actuality of purported corporate reorganizations, for that was a special sort of transaction, whose bona fides could readily be ascertained by inquiring whether the ephemeral new corporation was in fact transacting business, or whether there was in fact a continuance of the proprietary interests under an altered corporate form. * * *

What we have said so far is related chiefly to the validity of the sales. When we turn to the gift on December 13, 1943, to the United War Fund, the taxpayer is on even firmer ground. * * * Charitable contributions of low-cost securities are an everyday type of transfer motivated by tax purposes. The gift to the United War Fund, being valid, transferred two shares from the taxpayer after the adoption of the plan of liquidation, and alone sufficed to put the liquidation beyond the reach of the nonrecognition provisions of § 112(b)(6).

In short, though the facts in this case show a tax avoidance, they also show legal transactions not fictitious or so lacking in substance as to be anything different from what they purported to be, and we believe they must be given effect in the administration of § 112(b)(6) as well as for all other purposes.

* * *

[¶ 8050]

Notes

1. Was the court correct to reject the argument of the IRS that the facts of *Day & Zimmermann* were distinguishable? Not all courts would

be as slow as was the court in *Granite Trust* to apply the step transaction doctrine to prevent the avoidance of nonrecognition under Section 332. See Associated Wholesale Grocers, Inc. v. United States, 927 F.2d 1517 (10th Cir.1991) (sale of assets and repurchase by parent treated as Section 332 liquidation).

2. The other side of the *Granite Trust* coin is the last minute attempt to come within Section 332. Is the following ruling consistent with that case?

[¶ 8055]

REVENUE RULING 70–106

1970–1 C.B. 70.

Minority shareholders owned twenty-five percent of the capital stock of corporation X. The remaining seventy-five percent of the capital stock of X was owned by Corporation Y. Y desired to liquidate X in a transaction to which section 332 * * * would apply in order that Y would recognize no gain on the transaction. The minority shareholders agreed to have their stock of X redeemed. Following the distribution to the minority shareholders, Y owned all the stock of X. Y then adopted a formal plan of complete liquidation of X and all of the remaining assets of X were distributed to Y.

Held, all of the shareholders of X received a distribution in liquidation under the provisions of section 331 * * *, and the gain is recognized to Y and gain or loss is recognized to the minority shareholders under section 331 * * *. The liquidation fails to meet the eighty percent stock ownership requirements of section 332(b)(1) * * * since the plan of liquidation was adopted at the time Y reached the agreement with the minority shareholders and at such time, Y owned seventy-five percent of the stock of X.

[¶ 8060]

Notes

1. Was is appropriate to conclude that a plan of liquidation was constructively adopted as of a date when taxpayer Y would not have agreed to such a plan?

2. Section 332(b)(1) imposes two requirements for obtaining non-recognition of gain: a "control" requirement and a timing requirement. The parent must own stock in the subsidiary "meeting the requirements of section 1504(a)(2)." This control requirement is the familiar 80 percent stock ownership, except that Section 332 excludes nonvoting stock limited and preferred as to dividends. See § 1504(a)(2). The requisite control must exist at all times from the date of adoption of the plan of liquidation until the receipt of the liquidating distribution.

The timing requirement involves two alternatives: (i) the liquidation must be completed within the taxable year or (ii) it must be completed within three years from the close of the taxable year of the subsidiary in which the first in a series of liquidating distributions occurs. § 332(b)(2) and (3). The effective difference in the time requirements is in the additional administrative formalities that attend the longer time period. In particular, if the longer period is used, the plan of liquidation must specifically provide for completion within the specified time.

[¶ 8065]

Problems

1. S Corporation owns assets having a net fair market value of $100,000 and a tax basis of $30,000. P Corporation owns all of the stock of S Corporation and has a basis in that stock of $10,000. Assume that S Corporation is liquidated in a manner that complies with the requirements of Section 332.

a. What gain or loss, if any, will be recognized by P Corporation under Section 332?

b. What will be P Corporation's aggregate basis in the assets it acquires from S Corporation under Section 334?

c. What gain or loss, if any, will be recognized by S Corporation upon its liquidation under Sections 336(d)(3) and 337?

2. How, if at all, would your answer change if a loan in the amount of $20,000 from P Corporation to S Corporation were outstanding at the time of liquidation?

3. How would your answer change if P Corporation's basis in the S Corporation stock were $60,000?

[¶ 8070]

C. TAXABLE CORPORATE ACQUISITIONS

Traditionally, the various transactions through which one corporation transfers the ownership of some or all of its business assets to another corporation have been classified under two broad headings: (i) tax-free acquisitive reorganizations and (ii) taxable acquisitions. That classification of this interesting but complex area may not be the most helpful. Because the corporate and shareholder level taxes are imposed independently of each other, acquisitions may be taxable at one level but tax-free at the other. Moreover, in some situations, so-called taxable acquisitions may not actually result in a tax, while reorganizations may. A more modern approach to classification focuses upon what is generally the most significant consequence of the transaction: whether, at the corporate level, assets are transferred in a taxable/cost basis or a nonrecognition/carryover basis transaction. Nevertheless, there is some benefit for our purposes in dealing with acquisitions that constitute reorganizations within the meaning of Section 368 separately from acquisitions that do not so qualify. This portion of the book focuses on acquisitions that are not reorganizations.

[¶ 8075]

1. A BIT OF HISTORY

More than in most other areas of the tax law, the rules governing corporate acquisitions can only be fully understood in the light of the long and convoluted evolution of those rules. By contrast to the study of reorganizations, tax history thankfully has become markedly less important in the study of taxable acquisitions. Nevertheless, even here a brief historical summary may prove helpful.

In the first decades of the income tax, notions of income and gain were far more limited than they are today. In particular, the unilateral transfer of property was not regarded as producing an amount realized to the transferor and thus did not result in a taxable gain or loss. Thus, making a gift to a child or charity did not result in taxable gain to the donor. Similarly, the distribution of property to shareholders did not result in taxable gain or loss to the distributing corporation. In the corporate sphere, that principle was confirmed by the Supreme Court in the case of General Utilities and Operating Co. v. Helvering, 296 U.S. 200 (1935), and came to be known as the *General Utilities* doctrine. In that case the taxpayer had declared and paid a dividend consisting of shares of stock in a subsidiary which the taxpayer had purchased long ago for $2,000 but which were now worth over $1 million. The Supreme Court held that the taxpayer did not realize any taxable gain because the distribution of the dividend was not a "sale."

Corporate planners blended the *General Utilities* doctrine with other rules governing corporate acquisitions to produce dramatically favorable tax results. A corporate dealer in, say, beans might normally sell a boxcar of beans, which had appreciated in value, to its distributor, understanding that the gain would be taxed at ordinary rates. If the after-tax proceeds of the sale were distributed to the shareholders as a dividend, a second ordinary income tax would be imposed on those shareholders. Instead of following that normal course of action, the bean dealer might liquidate, distributing all of its assets to its shareholders. That distribution would be taxed to the shareholders at capital gains rates and they would obtain a fair market value basis in the distributed beans. However, under *General Utilities*, no tax would be imposed on the distributing corporation. The shareholders could then, of course, sell the beans to the distributor who also would obtain a cost basis in the product. At a minimum, the net tax consequences of the transaction would include the avoidance of the corporate tax on the appreciation in the bean inventory. In addition, the transaction might convert an ordinary dividend to the shareholders into a liquidating distribution taxable at capital gains rates.

In the context of a corporate acquisition, the combination of the cost basis to an acquiring corporation with the failure to tax the target corporation on a distribution of its assets meant that the corporate assets, the beans in our illustration, obtained a tax-free step-up in basis and that the corporate level tax on the target corporation's gain was permanently forgiven. Surprisingly, perhaps, the *General Utilities* result was accepted and even extended by Congress. Under the 1954 Code, through a statutory extension of the principle of that case, all sales (as well as distributions) of assets incident to a complete liquidation were made exempt from the corporate level tax.

While scholarly opinion on the merits of the *General Utilities* doctrine itself varied, there could be no question but that the combination of that doctrine with the step-up in basis to the acquiring corporation was improper. That impropriety provided a substantial tax incentive to corporate acquisitions. By liquidating a corporation and transferring its business to a new corporate owner, the corporate level tax on highly appreciated assets, including intangible assets, could be avoided. It was the revenue loss from the unseemly spectacle of a high volume of tax motivated acquisitions, rather than its theoretical deficiencies, that eventually resulted in the repeal of the *General Utilities* doctrine. After a period of chipping away at the doctrine, it was entirely eliminated in the Tax Reform Act of 1986. Sections 336 and 311 were amended to impose a tax at the corporate level on distributions to shareholders and the provisions exempting sales of property incident to liquidations from tax were repealed.

During the *General Utilities* era, the tax consequences of a sale of property by the corporation followed by a distribution of the proceeds (two potential levels of tax) might differ substantially from the consequences of a distribution of property to shareholders followed by a sale by them (one level of tax). That difference spawned a subset of step transaction cases, beginning with Commissioner v. Court Holding Co., 324 U.S. 331 (1945), that are of continuing significance. In *Court Holding* the corporate taxpayer had been seeking to sell its principal asset. In the midst of negotiations with a buyer, the corporation distributed the asset to its shareholders who then completed the sale on the terms that had been arranged by the corporate officers. The issue was whether the sale by the shareholders should be treated as a sale by the corporation (and a distribution of the proceeds) since the shareholders had seemed to serve as little more than a conduit for the corporate assets. In *Court Holding* Supreme Court treated the transaction as a taxable sale by the corporation although later cases suggested that minimal attention to corporate formalities could produce a different result.

¶ 8075

After the repeal of the *General Utilities* doctrine, the *"Court Holding* problem" is not nearly as significant as it once was. On occasion, however, it still matters whether a sale occurs at the corporate or shareholder level. For example, on the disposition of property at a loss in connection with a liquidation, the loss disallowance rules of Sections 267 and 336(d)(1) and (2) vary in their application depending on whether the corporation sells or distributes the property. Similarly, the installment reporting option provided by Section 453(h) for certain liquidating distributions, discussed below, is only available for property sold at the corporate level. Today, however, taxpayers will normally prefer the tax consequences of corporate level sales to those of distributions followed by shareholder level sales. Given that, how today might a dispute such as was involved in *Court Holding* arise?

[¶ 8080]

2. GENERAL ACQUISITIVE PATTERNS

As a factual matter, an acquisition would normally proceed along one of two general paths:

(i) *Stock Acquisitions*. The shareholders of the target corporation may sell their stock to new owners. If those new owners are individuals, the target corporation will become a sister corporation of any other corporations owned by the acquiring shareholders. More commonly, the new owner will be an acquiring corporation, in which event the target corporation will become a subsidiary of the acquiring corporation.

(ii) *Asset Acquisitions*. Alternatively, the target corporation may sell its assets to the acquiring corporation or one of its subsidiaries. Following the sale of its business assets, the target corporation may retain and invest the proceeds, perhaps in a new business venture, or it may liquidate and distribute the proceeds to its shareholders.

From the nontax perspective, these and other more complex acquisitive techniques are merely different mechanical steps to an identical result. Ideally, when that is the case, the income tax consequences of the different acquisitive mechanics should also be identical. In the complex world of corporate acquisitions, however, that is not at all true. To the contrary, form remains as important as substance to the final income tax burden of the acquisition, as we are about to see.

[¶ 8085]

3. TAXABLE ASSET ACQUISITIONS

With the few and relatively minor exceptions that are noted in the following paragraphs, the Code does not contain special rules governing the income tax consequences of asset acquisitions that do not constitute reorganizations. As a result, the sale of assets and liquidation of the

¶ 8085

target corporation generally have the same tax consequences as do sales and liquidations not in the context of an acquisition.

[¶ 8090]

a.   *The Seller's Tax Consequences*

The sale of corporate assets by a target corporation, whether individually or in bulk to a single acquiring corporation, is a fully taxable transaction to the target corporation. Moreover, the distribution of some or all of the assets to shareholders instead will not alter that tax burden. Under the present version of Section 336, an identical corporate level tax will be imposed.

To the extent that the sale of certain assets, such as capital assets, produces capital gains against which capital losses may be offset, target corporations would have some incentive to manipulate the allocation of the purchase price for the assets. Similarly, the acquiring corporation will have an incentive to allocate the purchase price to the most rapidly depreciable assets. The flexibility available to both target and acquiring corporations has been sharply curtailed by Section 1060, described below.

If the target corporation is liquidated and its assets distributed to its shareholders, a second, shareholder level tax will be imposed under Section 331 on the full value of the distribution, less the shareholders' bases in their stock, whether the distribution consists of the business assets in kind or the proceeds of the sale of those assets. Thus, a taxable asset acquisition followed by a liquidation of the target corporation will result in the imposition of two full levels of taxation. There is nothing unfair about the imposition of two levels of tax; our system for taxing corporations contemplates the imposition of two levels of taxation on corporate profits. Nevertheless, the nearly simultaneous imposition of two taxes will surely strike the shareholders of the target as harsh, if not unfair. As a result, it is common to attempt to structure an acquisition to produce only a single level of tax.

Avoiding the shareholder level tax following an asset acquisition, however, is not easy. The target corporation could stay in existence and acquire a new business, although the shareholders are rarely interested in that option. Moreover, the target corporation with its existing tax history, including its E & P account, might not be a good vehicle for acquiring another business in any event. Allowing the target corporation to remain in existence and invest the proceeds of the sale of the business assets in a passive activity subjects the investment return to double taxation and may run afoul of the penalty taxes, such as the accumulated earnings tax, considered in Chapter 7. The corporation might be eligible to elect S corporation status, which would eliminate both the double tax and the potential imposition of the penalty taxes, but Congress has discouraged just this use of the S corporation with a special penalty tax on investment income. § 1375. Of course, if a major block of the stock in the target corporation will soon benefit from a step-up in basis attributable to the death of a shareholder under Section 1014, the cost of keeping the corporation in existence may well be worth paying.

If liquidation (and incurring the second-tier tax) is the best among unsavory alternatives, there is one small window through which that tax burden can be softened. If the target corporation sells all or a portion of its assets for one or more deferred payments and then distributes the right to the deferred payments to its shareholders in complete liquidation, under Section 453(h), the shareholders are treated as if they sold their stock to the purchaser of the corporate assets. See Reg. § 1.453–11(a)(2). As a result, the shareholders report their gain attributable to the deferred payments under the installment method unless they elect out of installment reporting. Moreover, the nature of the assets of the corporation is irrelevant. The shareholders are entitled to report their gain on the hypothetical stock sale under the installment method even though the corporation could not have reported its gain in some or all of its assets under that method because the assets were excluded from eligibility for installment reporting.

If Section 453(h) applies, the shareholders will not be taxed on the receipt of the obligations of the purchaser of the target assets. Rather, the tax will be deferred until payments are received by the shareholders on the distributed obligations. Under Section 453(h)(1)(A), this installment reporting benefit is only available if certain formalities are observed. The corporation must first adopt a plan of complete liquidation and must in fact liquidate within one year following that adoption. If that occurs, installment reporting of deferred payment obligations is allowed but only for obligations received on the sale of assets after the plan of liquidation is adopted.

Because under current law a taxable asset acquisition generally incurs two full levels of tax, the seller faces a powerful income tax disincentive to engaging in this form of acquisition. One exception to this obstacle arises if tax attributes of either the target corporation or its shareholders would reduce or eliminate one of the levels of tax. The most common circumstance in which that occurs is when the target corporation has a sufficiently large net operating loss carryforward to absorb a major portion of the gain on the sale of its assets. Absent such a loss carryover, therefore, tax considerations normally will cause the seller to prefer a stock acquisition.

[¶ 8095]

b. The Buyer's Tax Consequences

In any acquisition, the principal tax concern of the buyer is likely to be the availability of income tax benefits from the payment of the purchase price. If there are no tax consequences to a payment by the buyer for the target assets, the after tax burden of the payment of $1 will remain $1. However, if a buyer that generally is subject to a 35 percent income tax rate can immediately deduct a payment, the after-tax burden of the payment is reduced to 65 cents. While few acquisition costs may be currently deductible, many acquired assets will be subject to depreciation or amortization. The amount paid for depreciable assets will produce a tax benefit that is spread over the period of depreciation. However, the faster the allowable depreciation, the greater the tax benefit, and the lower the net after-tax cost of the acquisition. Accordingly, the tax planning for the acquiring corporation in an acquisition involves efforts to allocate the purchase price to the most rapidly depreciable assets. However, two Code provisions largely control the buyer's allocation.

During periods in which taxable corporate acquisitions are popular, it is not uncommon for purchasers to pay considerably more for a business than the apparent value of the identifiable assets. For many years, taxpayers and the IRS disputed whether that premium should be prorated over all the acquired assets, including rapidly depreciable assets, or largely allocated to what prior to the enactment of Section 197 was nondepreciable goodwill. Section 1060 has resolved that disagreement for any "applicable asset acquisition" against the purchaser of a profitable business. The reach of Section 1060 is even broader than the acquisitions addressed here; the section applies to any taxable acquisition of assets constituting a trade or business. Thus, the section may apply to the acquisition of less than all of the assets of a corporation or to the acquisition of a business conducted by a partnership or sole proprietor.

Section 1060 is actually little more than a curious cross-reference to the regulations under Section 338(b)(5). Those regulations, however, which appear at Reg. § 1.338–6, divide all of the assets of the corporation into seven classes. The most significant assets assigned to those classes are: (I) cash on hand, (II) marketable securities, (III) accounts receivable, (IV) inventory, (V) all assets not assigned to another class, which would include virtually all of the tangible assets of the business, (VI) most section 197 assets, and (VII) goodwill and going concern value. The purchase price must be allocated first to the Class I assets in proportion to their fair market value to the full extent of that value. The remaining consideration is then allocated in a like matter to each of the higher classes in turn until it has been fully allocated. Any portion of the purchase price in excess of the value of the assets in the first six classes, including the entire premium paid for the business, must thus be allocated to intangibles assets in the nature of goodwill.

The use of this so-called residual or subtraction method of allocation is, of course, designed to prevent acquiring corporations from making purchase price allocations in a manner that would produce tax bases in inventory or depreciable assets that exceed the value of those assets.

¶ 8095

However, this approach can also be beneficial to taxpayers. If the assets of a business are purchased at a discount, rather than a premium, basis is allocated to the depreciable assets or inventory up to the amount of their value and the discount is be applied entirely to goodwill.

The allocation required by Section 1060 applies to the seller as well as the buyer. Thus, the basis step-up claimed by the acquiring corporation for categories of assets must be consistent with the gain reported by the target corporation. If the parties agree among themselves on the allocation of the consideration over classes of assets, the agreement is binding on the parties unless it would be invalid under state law. The regulations note, however, that the agreed upon allocation is not at all binding on the IRS. Reg. § 1.1060–1(c)(4).

A second former area of dispute involving the purchasers of businesses was the scope of the concept of nondepreciable goodwill. Prior to 1993, goodwill could not be amortized for tax purposes although intangibles closely related to goodwill could be amortized if their value and useful life could be established. Not surprisingly, purchasers devoted substantial effort to identifying, sometimes with substantial creativity, intangible assets having a limited life that could be separated from goodwill, thus generating deductible amortization. The array of assets identified by taxpayers included customer lists, vending machine locations, and patients' charts. In addition, when a major shareholder of the target corporation was also active in its business, a significant portion of the purchase price might be allocated to a covenant by the shareholder not to compete with the transferred business for a specified period of time. Amounts paid for such a covenant could be amortized over the relatively brief life of the agreement.

Under Section 197, the incentive to identify amortizable intangibles and to allocate the purchase price to such intangibles generally has been eliminated. Under this provision, taxpayers are permitted to amortize over a 15–year life the cost of any purchased "section 197 intangible" which is held for use in a trade or business. For taxpayers, the good news is that purchased goodwill is a Section 197 intangible and thus may be amortized for tax purposes. The bad news is that all of the other intangibles that taxpayers had so laboriously carved out of goodwill are also Section 197 intangibles and are thus subject to the same 15–year amortization. As a result, little purpose is served by the effort to separate discrete intangibles from goodwill.

The scope of Section 197 goes far beyond resolving the endless debate over goodwill. Section 197 intangibles include so-called customer-based and supplier-based intangibles, such as customer lists or shelf space in retail outlets, and also include government permits, patents, trademarks, franchises, and, notably, covenants not to compete (regardless of their duration). All such purchased intangibles must be amortized over 15 years regardless of their provable useful life.

¶ 8095

[¶ 8100]

4. TAXABLE STOCK ACQUISITIONS

From the perspective of the seller, a stock acquisition generally seems the most attractive. A single tax, usually at the favorable capital gains rate, is imposed on the gain from the sale of stock and the seller is relieved of the necessity for liquidating the corporation to receive the cash proceeds of the sale.

The benefit to the seller of avoiding the corporate level tax by a stock sale, however, is balanced by the imposition of a comparable detriment on the buyer. While the buyer will obtain a basis for the purchased stock equal to the full purchase price, that tax basis does not yield any immediate tax benefits. The depreciable assets of the business remain in the target corporation, and the basis of those assets has not been altered by the mere change in ownership of the corporate stock. Just as the imposition of two levels of tax on an asset acquisition is not "unfair," the failure to step up the basis of the target's assets following a stock acquisition is not unfair; since the corporate level gain is not subject to tax in a stock acquisition, the basis of the corporate level assets should not be altered. Nevertheless, the buyer is not obtaining a tax benefit for its purchase price payments, and it is easy to understand why buyers would view those results as harsh, if not unfair.

[¶ 8105]

a. *Historical Development*

Under prior law, acquiring corporations found an escape from this harshness in the following case. While the rule of *Kimbell-Diamond* no longer applies to the determination of asset basis following taxable stock acquisitions, the more general step transaction analysis contained in the case remains an important part of corporate taxation.

[¶ 8110]

KIMBELL–DIAMOND MILLING CO. v. COMMISSIONER

United States Tax Court, 1950.
14 T.C. 74, aff'd per curiam, 187 F.2d 718 (5th Cir.), cert. denied, 342 U.S. 827 (1951).

OPINION

BLACK, JUDGE: * * *.

* * *

The facts have been stipulated and are adopted as our findings of fact. They may be summarized as follows:

Petitioner is a Texas corporation engaged primarily in the business of milling, processing, and selling grain products, and has its principal office in Fort Worth, Texas. * * *

On or about August 13, 1942, petitioner sustained a fire casualty at its Wolfe City, Texas plant which resulted in the destruction of its mill property at that location. * * * This property was covered by insurance, and on or about November 14, 1942, petitioner collected insurance in the amount of $124,551.10 ($118,200.16 as a reimbursement for the loss sustained by the fire and $6,350.94 as a premium refund). * * *

[Pursuant to authorization by the Board of Directors, Kimbell–Diamond, on December 26, 1942, purchased 100 percent of the stock of Whaley Mill and Elevator Company, a Texas Corporation, at a cost of $210,000. Kimbell–Diamond immediately proceeded with the dissolution and distribution of the assets of Whaley. On December 31, 1942, the Secretary of State certified that Whaley had been dissolved on that date. Immediately prior to the dissolution, the adjusted tax basis to Whaley of its assets aggregated $328,736.59.]

* * *

* * * [W]e must now determine the question of petitioner's basis in Whaley's assets on the merits. Petitioner argues that the acquisition of Whaley's assets and the subsequent liquidation of Whaley brings petitioner within the provisions of section 112(b)(6) [1954 Code § 332] and, therefore, by reason of section 113(a)(15) [1954 Code § 334(b)(1)], petitioner's basis in these assets is the same basis in Whaley's hands. In so contending, petitioner asks that we treat the acquisition of Whaley's stock and the subsequent liquidation of Whaley as separate transactions. It is well settled that the incidence of taxation depends upon the substance of a transaction. *Commissioner v. Court Holding Co.*, 324 U.S. 331. It is inescapable from petitioner's minutes set out above and from the "Agreement and Program of Complete Liquidation" entered into between petitioner and Whaley, that the only intention petitioner ever had was to acquire Whaley's assets.

We think that this proceeding is governed by the principles of *Commissioner v. Ashland Oil & Refining Co.*, 99 Fed. (2d) 588, certiorari denied 306 U.S. 661. In that case the stock was retained for almost a year before liquidation. Ruling on the question of whether the stock or the assets of the corporation were purchased, the court stated:

> The question remains, however, whether if the entire transaction, whatever its form, was essentially in intent, purpose and result, a purchase by Swiss of property, its several steps may be treated separately and each be given an effect for tax purposes as though each constituted a distinct transaction. * * * And without regard to whether the result is imposition or relief from taxation, the courts have recognized that where the essential nature of a

transaction is the acquisition of property, it will be viewed as a whole, and closely related steps will not be separated either at the instance of the taxpayer or the taxing authority. * * *

We hold that the purchase of Whaley's stock and its subsequent liquidation must be considered as one transaction, namely, the purchase of Whaley's assets which was petitioner's sole intention. This was not a reorganization within section 112(b)(6), and petitioner's basis in these assets, both depreciable and nondepreciable, is, therefore, its cost * * *. Since petitioner does not controvert respondent's allocation of cost to the individual assets acquired from Whaley, both depreciable and nondepreciable, respondent's allocation is sustained.

* * *

[¶ 8115]

Notes

1. While *Kimbell-Diamond* represented a victory for the IRS, which was seeking to step down the basis of the acquired assets, taxpayers soon learned how to use the decision to their advantage. If a target corporation were liquidated promptly following a stock acquisition, the acquiring corporation would be treated as if it had purchased assets rather than stock and thus would obtain a tax basis in the assets of the target corporation equal in the aggregate to the amount paid for the stock. That result left the acquiring corporation in the same favorable tax position that it would have occupied following an actual asset acquisition. Since, under the *General Utilities* doctrine, the liquidation of the target corporation did not produce a corporate level tax, the overall effect of the taxpayer invocation of the *Kimbell-Diamond* rule was to create a tax-free step-up in the bases of the assets of the target corporation.

2. As a policy matter, the result in *Kimbell-Diamond* was entirely satisfactory because it created a consistency in the tax treatment of acquiring corporations between asset and stock acquisitions. Accordingly, the effect of the case on asset basis was soon codified and the somewhat uncertain case law application of the step transaction doctrine replaced with a statutory safe harbor: if the target corporation was liquidated within two years following the purchase of 80 percent of its stock, then the basis of the assets would become the amount paid for the target stock. Of course, nothing compelled the liquidation of the target corporation. Thus, acquiring corporations could retain the carried over basis in the target assets if they preferred by simply not liquidating the target corporation. In complex acquisitions, the requirement of an actual liquidation permitted acquiring corporations to obtain a cost basis for some assets and a carryover basis for others.

To illustrate the last point, assume that P (purchasing) Corporation wished to acquire two existing (target) corporations (A Corporation and B Corporation) that were being operated as wholly owned subsidiaries of another corporation. A Corporation held low basis ($4,000,000), high value ($10,000,000) assets. B Corporation held high basis ($10,000,000), low value ($4,000,000) assets. P Corporation could purchase the assets directly from the respective corporations at an aggregate price of $14,000,000. The assets of each business could then be transferred to separate wholly owned subsidiaries of P Corporation, but the aggregate basis of the assets of the two enterprises would be the cost of $14,000,000. Under the former Code provisions, the better strategy for P Corporation would be as follows: P Corporation would create Subsidiary Corporation with a capital contribution of $10,000,000. Subsidiary Corporation would purchase all the stock of A Corporation at a cost of $10,000,000, and then liquidate A Corporation. The assets acquired on the liquidation would take a basis of $10,000,000, and, under *General Utilities*, A Corporation would recognize no gain on its liquidation. To complete its objective, P Corporation would also acquire all the stock of B Corporation at a cost of $4,000,000. But B Corporation would *not* be liquidated; instead, it would be held as a wholly owned subsidiary, and its assets would retain their basis of $10,000,000. By this alternative procedure, P Corporation would have made the same investment of $14,000,000 in acquiring the two businesses, but the aggregate basis of the assets acquired would be $20,000,000 rather than $14,000,000.

In the most recent refinement of the *Kimbell-Diamond* rule, this "transactional" election to adjust basis or not was replaced by an explicit election extended by Section 338. While that modernization of the rule was welcome, Congress attached to Section 338 a number of complex provisions that were less welcome. In a masterstroke of irony, however, shortly after the adoption of Section 338, Congress repealed the *General Utilities* doctrine. As a result, the use of Section 338 following an acquisition declined precipitously.

[¶ 8120]

b. Section 338

In broad outline, Section 338 permits the acquiring corporation following a stock purchase to elect to be treated as if it purchased assets. As a result, the target corporation acquires a fair market value basis for its assets but it must also pay the corporate level tax on the appreciation in those assets. In its articulation of the consequences of this deemed sale, the regulations go as far as they possibly can to reproduce the income tax consequences of an actual sale of assets to, and purchase from, an unrelated corporation.

This elective treatment is available if there has been a "qualified stock purchase." § 338(d)(3). To meet that requirement, the acquiring corporation must obtain 80–percent control of the target corporation through a purchase of its stock within a 12 month acquisition period. In computing the 80–percent requirement, redemptions of the target stock during the acquisition period from unrelated shareholders are given effect. Reg. § 1.338–3(b)(5). The consequences of Section 338 are then geared to the amount paid for this "recently purchased stock" which is defined in Section 338(b)(6)(A) as target stock held by the acquiring corporation on the acquisition date and purchased by it during the 12–month acquisition period. If the Section 338 election is made following a qualified stock purchase, then the target corporation (the "old" target) is treated as if it sold all of its assets to a newly formed corporation (the "new" target) in a fully taxable transaction for their fair market value. § 338(a). In general, the old target is deemed to cease to exist on the acquisition date and all of its tax attributes disappear, although it may apply any loss carryovers against the gain recognized on the deemed sale. All of this, of course, is a tax fiction; no new corporation is actually formed and no assets are actually sold.

While Section 338(a)(1) suggests that the selling price for measuring gain to the old target is based upon the value of its assets as determined by an appraisal, in fact the regulations require that the assets be treated as having been sold for an amount based upon the amount realized on the sale of the "recently purchased target stock" as determined under general income tax rules. That amount is then grossed-up to reflect the value attributable to any other outstanding stock. Reg. § 1.338–4(b)(1) and (c)(1). See also § 338(h)(11).

Even the total amount paid for the target stock will not reflect the amount that would be paid for the assets if the corporation has liabilities. In an actual asset purchase, the assumption of those liabilities by the purchaser would, under general tax principles, constitute an additional amount paid for the assets and would increase the amount realized on the sale. Accordingly, the grossed-up basis for the stock must be further increased under Section 338(b)(2) by the amount of the liabilities of the target corporation. One of those liabilities may be the obligation to pay an income tax as a result of the Section 338 election itself. Reg. § 1.338–4(e). The resulting "aggregate deemed sale price" or ADSP should represent the full market value of Target Corp.

To illustrate the computation of the ADSP, assume that Target Corp. holds the assets of an active business and is indebted to banks in the amount of $6,000. Acquiring Corp. purchases 80 of the 100 outstanding shares of Target stock for $100 per share, or $8,000. In addition, Acquiring Corp. owns five shares of Target that it purchased several years ago for $40 per share, or $200. To compute the ADSP, the amount realized on the sale of the recently purchased stock of $8,000 must be grossed-up to reflect the entire value of the corporation by dividing that amount by the percentage of outstanding stock that the recently purchased stock represents, or 80 percent. To that result ($8,000 ÷ .80 =

¶ 8120

$10,000) must be added the liabilities of $6,000 producing an ADSP of $16,000. (Generally, any tax liability resulting from the deemed sale would also be added to the ADSP.)

Normally the most important effect of the constructive sale is to give the new target a step-up in tax basis for its assets to an amount that approximates the fair market value of those assets. Under the regulations the "adjusted grossed-up basis" or AGUB for the assets of the new target corporation is computed under a formula that resembles (but is not identical to) the computation of ADSP. Reg. § 1.338–5. AGUB consists of (a) the basis to the acquiring corporation for its recently purchased stock, (b) grossed-up to reflect the value of stock *not* owned by the acquiring corporation, (c) increased by the basis of target stock owned by the acquiring corporation but not recently purchased (referred to by Section 338(b)(1)(B) as "nonrecently purchased stock"), and (d) the liabilities of the new target.

To illustrate, in the example used above, Acquiring Corp. obtained a basis of $8,000 in the recently purchased target shares. To reflect stock owned by others, that basis must be grossed-up by dividing it by the percentage that the recently purchased stock is of all stock other than the nonrecently purchased stock, or 80/95. To the result ($8,000 ÷ 80/95 = $9,500) must be added the basis of the nonrecently purchased stock of $200 and the liabilities of $6,000 (or more, if the tax liability is taken into account), producing a AGUB of $15,700. That amount must then be allocated over the Target Corp. assets under the same rules of Reg. § 1.338(b)–6 that are applicable under Section 1060 to an actual asset acquisition.

Aside from the fact the AGUB is not grossed-up to reflect the value of the nonrecently purchased stock, in many acquisitions, ADSP and AGUB will be the same. However, in some instances, the general income tax rules governing the computation of amount realized will differ from the rules governing the computation of basis. In particular, the discounted value of a contingent obligation must normally be included in the amount realized by the seller in the year of sale but may not be reflected in the basis obtained by the buyer until a later point in time. In that event, as in an actual sale, ADSP will differ from AGUB. In addition, the regulations acknowledge that events occurring after the constructive sale may affect the basis of the assets in the hands of the new target or the amount realized by the old target under general principles of tax law. Some of those adjustments, particularly those occurring after the end of the year in which the sale occurs, may affect one computation but not the other. For example, the cancellation of a liability of the target to an unrelated party might cause a reduction in the basis of the target assets but would not affect the amount realized on the earlier sale so the AGUB would be reduced but the ADSP would not. Compare Reg. § 1.338–4(b)(2)(iii) with Reg. § 1.338–5(b)(2)(iii).

¶ 8120

Section 338 treatment is elective and reflects the congressional determination that, following the acquisition of a corporation through a taxable stock purchase, at the corporate level either nonrecognition/carryover basis or taxable/cost basis treatment is acceptable. However, when Section 338 was enacted Congress also concluded that to allow taxpayers to elect Section 338 treatment on an asset-by-asset basis, or even on a corporation-by-corporation basis, would be unduly generous. As a result, the so-called consistency requirements of Section 338(e) and (f) were adopted to execute the further congressional policy that corporate acquisitions that are partly cost basis and partly carryover basis are not acceptable.

The repeal of the *General Utilities* doctrine, however, sharply eroded the significance of the consistency rules. Since after 1986 a cost basis could not be obtained without the payment of a corporate level tax, many commentators began to question whether a rigorous set of consistency rules were worth their cost. Ultimately the Treasury accepted that analysis and in final regulations gave the consistency requirements a far narrower scope than that suggested by the statutory provisions.

If the consistency rule does apply, the acquiring corporation is required to take a carryover basis in the acquired target assets unless an express Section 338 election is made for the target. Under Reg. § 1.338–8, the focus of the asset consistency rules of subsection (e) is limited to sophisticated attempts to avoid the tax that should result from the repeal of the *General Utilities* doctrine. The rules do not apply simply because an asset has been purchased from a target corporation for which the Section 338 election has not been made. In addition, the stock consistency rule of subsection (f) has been virtually eliminated. In most situations, therefore, an acquiring corporation is permitted to make the Section 338 election for one or more related target corporations but not for others.

[¶ 8123]

c. *Section 338(h)(10)*

The desirability of the Section 338 election in the environment of today changes dramatically if the principal shareholder of the target corporation is itself a corporation. In that event, the tax on the sale of the stock in the target corporation is actually a corporate level tax imposed on the old parent of the target. If the acquiring corporation then makes the Section 338 election, multiple layers of corporation tax would be imposed on a single economic gain—an inappropriate result. To avoid that result, when the target is an 80 percent or more owned subsidiary, Section 338(h)(10) allows the old parent and the acquiring corporation to make a joint election to treat the stock sale as an asset sale followed by a liquidation of the target corporation into its old parent, normally qualifying under Section 332 for tax-free treatment. In that event, the old target will be taxable on the deemed asset sale, but the old parent corporation will not be taxed on the actual stock sale. Reg. § 1.338(h)(10)–1(d).

The making of a Section 338(h)(10) election avoids any additional tax on the sale of the target stock. In contrast to a regular Section 338 election, the resulting taxable gain on the deemed asset sale is substituted for the gain on the stock sale instead of added to it. Nevertheless, the acquiring corporation will obtain a cost basis for the target assets. Accordingly, if the selling shareholder is a corporate parent and an (h)(10) election can be made, the making of this election will often be advisable. You might observe that, in eliminating the tax on the stock sale, the policy of (h)(10) is consistent with the policy of the intercorporate dividends-received deduction.

[¶ 8125]

Notes

1. What would happen today on the facts of *Kimbell-Diamond*? In Rev. Rul. 90–95, 1990–2 C.B. 67, the IRS ruled that Section 338 is now the exclusive method for obtaining a cost basis in the assets of the target corporation following a stock purchase and that the *Kimbell-Diamond* rule no longer produces such a result. If that is so, but no Section 338 election were made, would a taxpayer today be able to get away with the benefit that the IRS successfully attacked in the original *Kimbell-Diamond* case? Almost—for the point seems to have been overlooked in drafting Section 338. However, Section 269(b) was enacted to prevent that embarrassment.

2. Can the acquisition of the requisite 80–percent interest for purposes of Section 338 be obtained through a combination of stock purchase and redemption of minority shareholders? As noted at ¶ 8120, to qualify the acquisition of target corporation under Section 338, it is necessary that the purchasing corporation acquire 80 percent or more of the target stock by purchase within a 12–month period. Assume that during a 12–month period the acquiring corporation purchases 52 percent of target stock while the target simultaneously redeems 36 percent of its stock from other shareholders. At the conclusion of these transactions, the purchasing corporation will hold an interest of 81.25 percent in target. Would this acquisition of control meet the requirements of Section 338? Apparently so. See Reg. § 1.338–3(b)(5).

[¶ 8130]

5. CHOOSING AMONG THE FORMS OF ACQUISITIONS

In the field of corporate acquisitions there are a wide variety of paths to essentially the same result. In this Chapter we have seen several approaches and even more are described in the following chapters on reorganizations. That necessarily raises the question of which form produces the superior tax result. As you might expect, the optimum form for an acquisition varies with the circumstances of the parties but some important generalizations are possible.

Usually the more important income tax results are those occurring at the corporate level. The gain potentially realized at the shareholder level is normally smaller than the appreciation in the corporate assets and it is widely distributed. Much of the shareholder level gain may have been recently excused by a step-up in basis under Section 1014. The rate of tax imposed on the shareholder level gain, especially today, may be much lower than the rate of tax imposed on the corporate level gain.

At the corporate level the choice is between an acquisition that is taxable to the target and produces a cost basis to the acquiring corporation and an acquisition that results in nonrecognition to the target and produces a carryover basis to the acquiring corporation. The benefit from a cost basis acquisition is that the basis to the acquiring corporation for depreciation or other tax benefits is increased by the difference between the target corporation's basis for those assets and the amount paid for the assets by the acquiring corporation. In other words, the basis step-up will reflect the amount of gain recognized by the target corporation. However, the gain to the target will be immediately taxable while the tax benefit from the step-up in basis will be deferred over the period of cost recovery through depreciation or other allowance. Put differently, the present value of the tax payable on the sale of the target's assets will exceed the present value of the future tax deductions thereby created for the acquiring corporation. As a result, usually the parties will minimize their combined tax liabilities by adopting a carryover basis acquisition. That means we should expect to see far more stock purchases (which avoid tax at the corporate level) than asset purchases.

Of course, this generalization does not always hold. If something reduces or eliminates the tax to the target, a cost basis acquisition might be more favorable than a carryover basis acquisition. The most common something that reduces that tax are operating loss carryovers. Thus, if the target has substantial NOLs, the optimum form of acquisition may be a taxable acquisition.

As we have just discovered, a taxable stock acquisition may become either a cost basis or a carryover basis acquisition at the corporate level. Indeed, the decision to make or not make the Section 338 election is basically the decision between a cost or carryover basis and the merits of the election must be analyzed in the same manner as the choice between different forms of acquisitions. That is, unless something offsets the tax generated by the Section 338 election, the tax benefits from making the election will be less than the tax burdens thereby created. As a result, Section 338 elections, aside from the Section 338(h)(10) election, are not commonly made.

¶ 8130

If a carryover basis is selected at the corporate level, the parties still must choose between a taxable or tax-free acquisition at the shareholder level. (A tax-free acquisition would generally be accomplished with one of the forms of reorganizations discussed in the following Chapters.) While the shareholders of the target corporation would normally prefer non-recognition, the acquiring corporation would prefer a taxable purchase for a number of reasons. A taxable acquisition generally means the consideration for the target stock is paid in the form of debt rather than stock and we learned in Chapter 3 that corporations tend to prefer to issue debt rather than equity.

In addition, in a taxable acquisition, the acquiring corporation obtains a cost basis for the acquiring stock. Traditionally, that basis has not been regarded as important as the tax imposed on the selling shareholders because no tax benefit could be obtained from the basis until the acquired stock was resold. However, the reduction in the tax rate imposed upon the capital gains of individuals has somewhat altered the equation. The stepped-up basis for the acquired stock can be offset against the proceeds of any future sale of that stock which otherwise would be taxed at the 35–percent corporate tax rate while the present gain to the target shareholders is only taxed at 15 percent or less. As a result, there has been some increase in the use of forms of acquisition that are taxable at the shareholder level rather than tax-free reorganizations.

[¶ 8135]

Problems

1. Which of the following transactions would be treated as a qualified stock purchase under Section 338? What policies underlie these results?

a. The X Corporation constructed an apartment building at a cost of $100,000. It transferred the building to the Y Corporation in a Section 351 transaction, taking back all of the stock of Y. At the date of transfer, the apartment building had a fair market value of $500,000.

b. The X Corporation purchased 20 percent of the stock of the Y Corporation in 1994, 10 percent in 1995, and the remaining 70 percent in the current year.

c. The X Corporation purchased 10 percent of the stock of the Y Corporation in 1982 and the remaining 90 percent in February of the current year.

d. The X Corporation purchased 75 percent of the stock of Y Corporation in February of the current year, and in June the target corporation redeemed from unrelated parties half of its remaining stock in a taxable redemption.

¶ 8135

2. Target Corporation, the stock of which is held by several individuals, holds assets having a fair market value of $5.0 million and an aggregate tax basis of $2.8 million. The appreciation in the assets is largely attributable to the value of various patents and other intellectual properties. Target Corporation has been profitable for several years.

a. If the business of Target is to be acquired for cash by Acquiring Corporation, would you suggest that the acquisition be of the Target stock or of the Target assets followed by the liquidation of Target? What difference would it make to either party?

b. If the acquisition is to be of stock, should the Section 338 election be made? Why or why not?

c. If the acquisition is to be of stock, would it be more or less advantageous to the Target shareholders if they received Acquiring stock in the transaction free of tax instead of cash (as in a Section 351 exchange or a reorganization)? To Acquiring Corporation?

3. Roscoe Stone owns 90 percent of the stock of Tone-with-Stone, Inc. (Tone), a failing health club which Stone and his 10–percent co-shareholder, Fountain–Of–Youth, Incorporated (FOY) organized 10 years ago with an initial cash investment of $180,000 from Stone and $20,000 from FOY. Increasing competition from the larger chains has threatened the future of Tone and the shareholders have decided to dispose of the business. The following balance sheet reflects Tone's financial condition.

Assets	Fair Market Value	Basis	*Liabilities and Equity*	
Current Assets			*Current Liabilities*	
Cash	$ 295,000	$ 295,000	Accounts Payable	$ 75,000
Receivables (net) ...	75,000	75,000	*Long-term liabilities*	
			Mortgage (land and	
Inventories	275,000	200,000	buildings)	200,000
			Total liabilities	$ 275,000
			Stockholder's Equity	
			Common stock	100,000
			Additional paid-in capi-	
Plant			tal..................	100,000
			Accum. earnings	525,000
Land	260,000	30,000		
Buildings	550,000	200,000	Total equity	725,000
Machinery	45,000	200,000		
Total Assets	$1,500,000	$1,000,000	Total Liab. & Equity	$1,000,000

a. Assume that Tone sells its assets to a single corporate purchaser who takes all the assets except cash, assumes all liabilities, and agrees to pay the $930,000 balance of the purchase price in 10 equal annual installments bearing a market rate of interest and beginning one year from the date of sale. Assume further that immediately following the sale, Tone liquidates, pays its federal income tax liability (at a flat rate of

¶ 8135

34 percent), and distributes its remaining cash and the purchaser's installment obligations. What will be the tax consequences to Tone and its shareholders? See §§ 331, 334, 336, 453(h) and 453B(a).

b. In what respects would the tax consequences to Tone or its shareholders be different if the assets were sold to various purchasers in several different transactions and Tone were thereafter liquidated?

c. In what respects would the tax consequences to Tone or its shareholders be different if Tone were first liquidated, distributing all of its assets pro rata to its shareholders, and the shareholders thereafter sold the assets?

d. Assume that after the deal for the sale of assets was made, the parties agreed that, instead, the shareholders of Tone would sell all of their stock to the corporate purchaser. What effect would that change in plans have on the tax consequences to the shareholders? In view of the parties' prior agreement, what should be the purchase price for the stock?

e. Assume that FOY declines to sell its stock, so Stone sells all of his stock in Tone for $949,500 (90 percent of the net value of the assets after allowing for a potential corporate level tax liability of $170,000) to the corporate purchaser who thereafter makes the Section 338 election. What gain to "old" Tone? What tax basis to "new" Tone?

Chapter 9

INTRODUCTION TO CORPORATE REORGANIZATIONS

[¶ 9000]

A. HISTORICAL BACKGROUND

Mergers, consolidations, and other transactions generally described as "reorganizations" of existing businesses posed special difficulties when the income tax was in its infancy. At the time, several fundamental questions with special significance for the tax treatment of reorganizations had yet to be resolved. On the one hand, it was not clear that capital gains of any sort were taxable. If capital gains were not taxable, then exchanges of stock and securities pursuant to reorganizations would not be as well. On the other hand, realization was not yet a precondition to taxation. Before *Eisner v. Macomber* was decided in 1920, the government had taken the position that stock dividends were taxable. If stock dividends were taxable, it appeared that the receipt of acquiring company stock in a merger or reorganization might be as well. Given this state of flux, it is not surprising that the Treasury Department's early pronouncements on the tax treatment of reorganizations flip-flopped between treating them as taxable and exempting them altogether.[1]

The uncertainty regarding the tax treatment of mergers and other similar transactions might have continued indefinitely if not for the onset of World War I and the dramatic increase in individual income rates. The top marginal rate on the combined normal tax and surtax, which was seven percent in 1915, more than doubled to thirteen percent in 1916 before skyrocketing to fifty-four percent in 1917 and seventy-seven percent in 1918. Coupled with the rise of participation in the equity markets and the increase in merger and acquisition activity, the stakes for stockholders involved in such transactions rose considerably. Congress responded by enacting the first tax-free reorganization provi-

---

1. See Bank, "Mergers, Taxes, and Historical Realism," 75 Tul. L. Rev. 1 (2000).

sion, which provided that "no gain or loss shall be deemed to occur" from the receipt of stock or securities in a "reorganization, merger, or consolidation" and "the new stock or securities received shall be treated as taking the place of the stock, securities, or property exchanged." Revenue Act of 1918, ch. 18, § 202(b), 40 Stat. 1057, 1060 (1919).

Nonrecognition treatment was part of a compromise designed to ensure that the gain on the receipt of stocks and securities in a reorganization transaction would be deferred, but not relieved from tax altogether. While reorganization transactions were technically "realization events," they appeared to differ from transactions where the taxpayer cashed out his investment. Unlike sales, stockholders in reorganization transactions maintained a continuing investment in the underlying business assets, which remained in corporate solution. Thus, by carrying over the tax basis in the stock or securities exchanged, which was implicit in the statute and made explicit in the Treasury regulations and later the statute itself, gain was deferred until a taxpayer did cash out his or her investment in a subsequent sale of the stock or securities. Of course, as Congress subsequently made clear, if a stockholder actually received cash or other property in addition to stock or securities in the exchange then it would constitute an actual realization with respect to the non-stock property (or "boot") and that portion of the exchange would be taxed currently.

In the ensuing years, the statute underwent a cycle of expansion, judicial gap-filling, and retrenchment. In the early 1920s, when seemingly minor readjustments of corporate form were being held taxable in the courts,[2] there were concerns that the law's "grave uncertain[ties]" were "blocking desirable business readjustments."[3] In response, Congress made "reorganization" the centerpiece of the provision and broadly defined it to include a "merger or consolidation (including the acquisition by one corporation of at least a majority of the voting stock and at least a majority of the total number of shares of all other classes of stock of another corporation, or of substantially all the properties of another corporation), recapitalization, or mere change in identity, form, or place of organization of a corporation (however effected)." Revenue Act of 1921, ch. 136, 42 Stat. 227. A further revision to the statute in 1924 added spin-off transactions and formally extended nonrecognition treatment to corporations as well. Revenue Act of 1924, ch. 234, § 203(h)(1),

---

2. See United States v. Phellis, 257 U.S. 156 (1921) (reincorporation from New Jersey to Delaware); Rockefeller v. United States, 257 U.S. 176 (1921) (division of a single business through a spin-off); Marr v. United States, 268 U.S. 536 (1925). While each of these cases involved transactions occurring prior to the institution of nonrecognition treatment in 1918, observers were worried that they would not have been covered by the statute in any event.

3. H.R. Rep. No. 350, 67th Cong., 1st Sess. at 10 (1921); An Act to Reduce and Equalize Taxation, to Amend and Simplify the Revenue Act of 1918, and for Other Purposes: Hearings on H.R. 8245 Before the Sen. Comm. On Fin., 67th Cong. 29 (1921) (statement of T.S. Adams, advisor to the Treasury Department).

¶ 9000

43 Stat. 253, 257. The resulting expansive definition left several open questions, however, such as the nature of the consideration for the transactions described in the parenthetical clause. When abusive transactions resulted, courts attempted to fills the gaps in the statute with the judicial doctrines discussed starting at ¶ 9050. At the same time, the concern that the reorganization provisions were being used as a tool of tax avoidance led to a period of statutory retrenchment. In 1933, a House Ways and Means subcommittee recommended repeal of the reorganization provisions. Congress rejected that as going too far, but did severely restrict the reorganization definition, adopting many of the requirements that form the backbone of the current Section 368. The intent was to make the reorganization provisions more useful to business while ensuring that economically similar transactions were taxed the same.

As a result of the continuing influence of this cyclical pattern, the tax-free reorganization provisions have evolved in a seemingly arbitrary and unnecessarily detailed fashion. The number of transactions eligible for nonrecognition treatment has increased as Congress tries to keep pace with the changing nature of modern mergers and acquisitions. So as to prevent abuse, however, these categories of reorganizations are tightly confined by a number of formalistic requirements. While these bright-line rules appear to at least provide certainty, they are also still subject to the sometimes unpredictable judicial doctrines. Perhaps the best way to unpack all of this detail is to keep in mind the historical evolution of the statute and its focus on distinguishing taxable sales from necessary readjustments of continuing interests in a business enterprise.

[¶ 9005]

B. TYPES OF REORGANIZATIONS

As the history of this area suggests, the term "reorganization" has evolved into a term of art for tax purposes. The term applies to three different kinds of transactions—first, to certain transactions in which two or more corporations are combined (acquisitive reorganizations); second, to readjustments of single corporations, such as changes in capital structure or place of incorporation (single corporation reorganizations), and, third, to certain transactions in which the investment of shareholders in one corporation is divided between two or more corporations (corporate divisions). In many respects, the tax concept of reorganization is very different from its meaning in the commercial and corporate law areas, although there is a tax provision for bankruptcy reorganizations not covered in this book that overlaps these three categories. § 368(a)(1)(G). In the ensuing chapters, the requirements for qualifying these transactions as reorganizations under the Code will be explored. Chapter 10 focuses on acquisitive reorganizations, Chapter

¶ 9000

11 on single corporation reorganizations, Chapter 12 on corporate divisions, and Chapter 13 on the carryover of tax attributes, such as net operating losses, in tax-free liquidations and reorganizations. In this section, we will provide a brief overview of the nature of each category of transactions and the statutory provisions that cover them. Section 368(a)(1) is the starting point in any description of the corporate reorganization provisions. It defines several basic types of corporate reorganizations and a number of variations in some of the basic types.

[¶ 9010]

1. ACQUISITIVE REORGANIZATIONS

In an acquisitive reorganization, one corporation (Acquirer) acquires the assets or stock of another corporation (Target) in exchange for Acquirer stock. This can take several forms. In a merger, the Target transfers all of its assets and liabilities to the the Acquirer and ceases to exist. The old Target shareholders become shareholders in Acquirer, the surviving corporation, although the merger agreement may specify that the merger consideration will consist of both cash and Acquirer stock. Mergers considered "statutory," which typically means conducted pursuant to the requirements of a state or federal corporate law merger statute as opposed to de facto mergers that are declared as such by a court, are called "A" reorganizations because they are governed by the requirements in Section 368(a)(1)(A). One of the benefits of the merger transaction is that the assets and liabilities of Target transfer to Acquirer by operation of state law, which means that the parties may not need to obtain the consent of creditors to transfer each individual asset or to record and pay fees or taxes on the transfer of such assets. A disadvantage, however, is that at least in the case of a publicly held corporation the Acquirer shareholders would have to vote to approve the merger and dissenters would have the right to have their shares redeemed at appraised value. This, along with the cost of complying with SEC proxy statement requirements, makes the direct merger unattractive in the public company context.

A consolidation is also governed by Section 368(a)(1)(A) and therefore considered an "A" reorganization. In a consolidation, both corporations merge into a new corporation (the "Resulting Corporation"). The stock in each of the old corporations converts to stock in the Resulting Corporation. While this has some of the same advantages of a merger, it also means that the franchises and tax attributes of both merging corporations go out of existence. For this reason, consolidations are a much less common form of acquisitive reorganization.

A recent variant on the "A" reorganization is what is called the "disregarded entity merger." In this transaction, a single-member limited liability company is the acquiring corporation for state law purposes, but because, as discussed in Chapter 16, it is disregarded as an entity separate from its owner for federal income tax purposes, it is treated as a direct merger of the Target into the acquiring corporation's owner. This type of "A" reorganization has only become available in recent years because of the spread of state-law limited liability company statutes and changes in Treasury regulations reflecting this development. The primary advantage of a disregarded entity merger is that the Target assets and liabilities are held in a separate entity for state law liability purposes, but are held by the acquiring corporation's owner for federal income tax purposes. It also avoids the problem of dissenters because the owner's shareholders are not members of the limited liability company.

A second type of acquisitive reorganization is a "stock-for-assets" transaction, which is called a "C" reorganization because it is governed by Section 368(a)(1)(C). This transaction resembles the statutory merger, but is not effected pursuant to statutory authority. It traces its origins to the parenthetical clause of the 1921 provision, which permitted certain merger-like transactions, such as the acquisition of "substantially all the properties of another corporation," to qualify for nonrecognition treatment. See ¶ 9000. At one point, the principal benefit of this was to allow parties in states without merger statutes to participate in tax-free reorganizations. Now that all states have such statutes, though, one of the benefits of a stock-for-assets reorganization is that it permits the acquisition of a Target's business without the acquisition of its liabilities, as occurs in a merger. The "C" reorganization is almost never used to acquire the assets of a large complex Target, though, in part because cumbersome and expensive individual transfers of the Target's assets and liabilities would usually be required.

A third type of acquisitive reorganization is a "stock-for-stock" transaction, which is called a "B" reorganization because it is governed by Section 368(a)(1)(B). In a stock-for-stock reorganization, Acquirer receives Target stock directly from the former Target shareholders in exchange for Acquirer stock. This may permit Acquirer to side step Target management, as might occur in a tender offer situation. While it also traces its origins to the 1921 parenthetical clause, it is less like the merger because both parties to the reorganization survive. This is also one of the benefits of the transaction, since it ensures that not only the Target liabilities remain separate from Acquirer assets, but that Target retains its separate identity and tax attributes. However, a disadvantage is that the Acquirer would almost never obtain all of the shares of the Target if it is publicly held. To force out the Target's minority shareholders, a subsequent merger of the Target and a new subsidiary of Acquirer may be required, resulting in additional transactional costs.

Finally, in more recent times, several variants on the standard acquisitive reorganization transactions have emerged, called "triangular reorganizations." These are transactions in which a third party is involved, typically a controlled subsidiary created specifically for this purpose. In the earliest triangular reorganizations, the Acquirer used

¶ 9010

stock of its parent corporation (Parent) to engage in a stock-for-assets or stock-for-stock reorganization, which is called a "triangular C" or a "triangular B" reorganization, respectively. This enabled a controlled subsidiary to hold the assets or stock rather than the Parent itself. More recently, the triangular reorganization has been used in connection with a statutory merger. In one version, Target merges with a controlled subsidiary of Parent in exchange for Parent stock, rather than stock of the controlled subsidiary. The merger is a state-law merger that would qualify as an "A" reorganization if it had been directly with the Parent. The benefit of conducting the merger at the subsidiary level, though, is to avoid subjecting the Parent to any Target liabilities. Because of the involvement of a subsidiary and the direction of the transaction, this is called a "forward subsidiary merger" and is governed by Section 368(a)(2)(D). When the parties wish for the Target corporation rather than the controlled subsidiary to survive, the flow of assets change direction and the controlled subsidiary merges into the Target, with the latter surviving. The former Target shareholder's stock is then exchanged for Parent stock in this second form of triangular reorganization, called a "reverse subsidiary merger" and governed by Section 368(a)(2)(E).

[¶ 9015]

2. SINGLE CORPORATION REORGANIZATIONS

The most common form of single corporation reorganization is a recapitalization of a single pre-existing corporation, which is called an "E" reorganization because it is governed by Section 368(a)(1)(E). A recapitalization may involve replacement of one series of outstanding bonds with another series or the exchange by a corporation's bondholders of their bonds for common or preferred stock of that corporation. Exchanges of common stock for another type of common stock or for preferred stock or a combination of common and preferred stock or an exchange of preferred stock for another type of preferred stock or preferred stock for common stock, all may constitute recapitalizations.

Another form of single corporation reorganization technically does involve a second corporation, but falls into this category because only one business is involved. This is the "reincorporation merger," which is called an "F" reorganization because it is governed by Section 368(a)(1)(F). In a reincorporation merger, a corporation seeks to change its place of corporation from one state to another. Often, the reincorporation is into Delaware in preparation for an initial public offering since Delaware's corporate laws and governance system is considered more predictable by the investment community. If, for example, it is desired to convert a corporation organized in Colorado into a Delaware corporation, the Colorado corporation may be merged into a new corporation organized under Delaware law. The shareholders will surrender their Colorado corporation shares in exchange for shares of the new Delaware corporation. While this appears to also qualify as an "A" reorganization, the "F" reorganization allows the surviving Delaware corporation to succeed to the tax attributes of the former Colorado corporation.

[¶ 9020]

3. CORPORATE DIVISIONS

Like a single corporation reorganization, a division begins with a single corporation. It differs, though, in that the division ends with two or more corporations, each conducting a separate business formerly operated in the original corporation. Divisions typically take one of three forms: (1) a spin-off, which involves the distribution of the stock of a subsidiary pro rata to the parent corporation's shareholders; (2) a split-off, in which some of the parent corporation shareholders surrender their parent stock in exchange for the stock in the subsidiary; and (3) a split-up, in which the parent corporation distributes stock in two or more corporate subsidiaries in complete liquidation. Originally, corporate divisions were governed by the reorganization rules even though the spin-off did not involve an exchange of stock while the split-off and split-up did. Eventually, all three types of transactions were moved out of the reorganization section and are now governed by their own rules in Section 355. Currently, while corporate divisions are often preceded by a contribution of part of a corporation's assets to a newly-created subsidiary, which is called a "D" reorganization because it is governed by Section 368(a)(1)(D), divisions are not considered reorganizations at all.

[¶ 9022]

4. OVERVIEW OF TAX CONSEQUENCES OF CORPORATE RE-ORGANIZATION

As will be more fully examined below, in a tax-free reorganization, the tax on unrecognized gain is not forgiven but is deferred through the preservation or carryover of tax basis of stock or assets exchanged. Recognition of realized loss is also deferred through the same mechanisms. For example, in a tax-free acquisitive reorganization, the former basis of the shareholders of the acquired corporation in its stock becomes, sometimes with adjustments, their basis in the stock they receive in the acquiring corporation. The basis to the acquiring corporation of any assets acquired is the former basis of those assets in the acquired corporation's hands. The unrecognized gain or loss represented by the difference between the value and the basis of the stock exchanged or assets transferred is taxed only if and when the stock or assets are subsequently disposed of in a taxable transaction. The nonrecognition and basis provisions applicable to reorganizations function very much like their counterparts in the context of Section 351(a) exchanges discussed in Chapter 2 and the liquidation of an 80–percent owned corporate subsidiary into its corporate parent discussed in Chapter 8.

[¶ 9025]

Problems

1.   Mr. and Mrs. Johnson own 75,000 shares of the common stock of Galaxy Corporation (Galaxy), which they established 35 years ago to engage in the business of providing market research services and of which they remain Chairman and President, respectively. The remaining 25,000 shares of the Galaxy common stock are owned by other Galaxy employees. The Galaxy shares are not publicly traded. The business has been and remains highly profitable. The Johnsons are now in their early seventies and are considering an offer by Cosmos Marketing Corporation (Cosmos), a prestigious and successful publicly held advertising and marketing services corporation, to acquire all of Galaxy's common stock, which is worth $500 per share. Cosmos has offered to acquire all of the Galaxy shares either for Cosmos voting common stock or for debt obligations issued by Cosmos with a term to maturity of ten years. Cosmos pays annual dividends on its common shares equal to about two percent of their fair market value. These shares are traded on the New York Stock Exchange. If the consideration takes the form of Cosmos shares, the shareholders of Galaxy would emerge from the transaction owning about one percent of the outstanding Cosmos common stock. If the consideration takes the form of Cosmos debt obligations, those obligations would bear an interest rate of eight percent. Cosmos enjoys a AA credit rating. There would be no market for these obligations. If Cosmos stock is used, the transaction would qualify as a tax-free reorganization under Section 368(a)(1)(B). If Cosmos debt obligations are used, the acquisition would be taxable, but the transaction would qualify for installment sale treatment under Section 453.

The Johnsons' basis in their Galaxy shares is $50 per share. They would like to retire, and the prospect of selling Galaxy to a prominent and well capitalized public corporation is attractive to them and most of the other Galaxy shareholder-employees. From the Johnsons' perspective, what are the basic pros and cons of the alternative offers?

2.   From the perspective of Cosmos, what are the pros and cons of the alternative offers? Assume that the aggregate adjusted tax bases of the tangible and intangible assets of Galaxy are $20 million while their fair market value is $70 million; Galaxy has liabilities of $20 million.

C. TAX TREATMENT OF REORGANIZATION EXCHANGES

[¶ 9030]

1. NONRECOGNITION OF GAIN OR LOSS

Qualifying a transaction under one of the definitions of Section 368(a)(1) and the judicially developed prerequisites, discussed at ¶ 9050, does not assure to all participants tax-free treatment. Qualification of the transaction as a reorganization earns each taxpayer involved only the right to submit the particular reorganization exchange to the rules of Section 354, 356, or 361. These are the operative sections that actually determine the extent to which gain or loss is to be recognized. A shareholder or securityholder who participates in a reorganization looks to Section 354 or 356. Under Section 354, certain exchanges of stock or securities may be effected without tax. Thus, for example, under Section 354, in a qualifying statutory merger, common stock of the acquired corporation may be exchanged for common stock of the acquiring corporation without the recognition of gain or loss.

If a reorganization exchange partially fails to qualify for nonrecognition treatment under Section 354 because, in addition to qualifying stock or securities, other property (such as cash) is received by the exchanging shareholder or securityholder, then under Section 356 gain realized by that person will be recognized and taxed to the extent of the value of that other property, usually called "boot." The major limitation on the right of an exchanging shareholder or securityholder to receive stock or securities without recognition of gain is Section 354(a)(2), which limits debt securities that may be so received to those having a principal amount no greater than that of debt securities surrendered. Thus, if stock is exchanged for debt securities, realized gain equal to the value of the securities is recognized. In addition, if a shareholder receives nonqualified preferred stock, as defined in Section 351(g), in exchange for common or other preferred stock, the value of the nonqualified preferred is treated as boot. §§ 354(a)(2)(C) and 356(c). As discussed at ¶ 10,245, gain recognized as a result of the presence of boot is taxed as a gain from the exchange of property or as a dividend, depending on the circumstances. § 356(a)(2).

In a qualifying reorganization, the transferor (often an acquired) corporation qualifies as a "party to the reorganization" pursuant to Section 368(b) and is subject to Section 361, which provides for nonrecognition of gain or loss if that corporation exchanges property solely for stock or securities in another corporation that is a party to the reorganization. Even if boot is received by the transferor, gain will not be recognized if the boot is distributed to the transferor's shareholder(s).

¶ 9030

§ 361(c)(1). However, under Section 361(c), gain may be recognized on the distribution of boot consisting of certain appreciated property. The acquiring corporation is not subject to tax when it acquires assets or stock of the acquired corporation in exchange for acquiring corporation stock. § 1032.

[¶ 9035]

2. BASIS IN REORGANIZATIONS

Like Section 351, the reorganization sections are commonly said to result in tax deferral with respect to transfers of appreciated property rather than tax forgiveness. This view is somewhat unrealistic, however, because the deferral, in many cases, proves to be indefinite, if not permanent. The mechanism adopted to secure deferral is embodied in the basis provisions of Sections 358 and 362. Section 358 governs the basis of the exchanging shareholder or securityholder. In the simplest case, it provides that nonrecognition property, such as stock, received in the reorganization by an exchanging shareholder of the acquired corporation takes a substituted basis equal to the basis of the stock surrendered. A shareholder owning 100 shares of the common stock of X Corporation, the acquired corporation, with a basis of $10 per share and a value of $100 per share exchanges that stock in a "B" reorganization solely for 1,000 voting common shares of Y Corporation, the acquiring corporation, worth $10 each. Under Section 358, the shareholder's realized gain of $9,000 is not recognized but the $1,000 basis in the shares surrendered attaches to, and becomes the shareholder's substituted basis for, the Y Corporation stock worth $10,000. Thus, recognition of the shareholder's $9,000 gain is deferred unless and until the shareholder disposes of the Y shares in a taxable transaction. This basic principle is subject to adjustments specified in Section 358 in more complicated situations involving the receipt of boot and the assumption of liabilities.

When a corporation acquires the assets of another corporation in a reorganization—as in an "A" merger or a "C"—the basis of those assets in the hands of the acquiring corporation is determined under Section 362(b). The principle is that of a carryover basis. The basis of the assets in the hands of the acquired corporation is carried over to the acquiring corporation. The same rule applies under Section 362(b) if the acquiring corporation acquires the stock of the acquired corporation in a "B" reorganization. The basis of the acquiring corporation in the acquired shares is the basis that the acquired corporation's shareholder(s) had in those shares immediately before the acquisition, increased by the gain recognized by the transferor.

[¶ 9040]

3. HOLDING PERIOD FOR NONRECOGNITION PROPERTY

The holding period for stock or securities that are received in a reorganization and that qualify as nonrecognition property includes the holding period of stock or securities surrendered in exchange for them, provided that the stock or securities surrendered were held as capital assets. § 1223(1). That is, the holding period of the stock or securities (held as capital assets) surrendered is tacked on to the holding period of the nonrecognition stock or securities received.

The holding period for property received by the transferee corporation in a reorganization also includes the transferor's holding period in the property. § 1223(2).

[¶ 9045]

4. TAX ACCOUNTING ASPECTS

In the case of a stock for stock acquisitive "B" reorganization, there is no change in the corporate tax accounting attributes, the taxable year, or carryovers of net operating or capital losses of the target corporation because its corporate existence remains intact. The same is true of the "E" and "F" reorganizations because they actually involve (the "E") or are deemed to involve (the "F") only a single corporation.

In an acquisitive reorganization involving a transfer of assets governed by Section 361 from one corporation to another with differing shareholders, the taxable year of the acquired corporation terminates on date of the transfer, and the tax attributes of the acquired corporation carryover to the acquiring corporation to the extent prescribed in Section 381. This regime is applicable to all reorganizations except the "B," "E," and "F" reorganizations. Thus, such items as basis of assets, E & P, most accounting methods, inventories, depreciation methods, and net operating and capital losses are carried over to the acquiring corporation.

However, in the case of acquisitive reorganizations and purchases of corporate stock, if there is a sufficiently substantial change in the stock ownership of a corporation with losses, the post-acquisition use of the corporation's net operating loss and capital loss carryovers, built-in losses, and certain other tax attributes is subject to special restrictions contained in Sections 382, 383, and 384, which are discussed in Chapter 13. Moreover, net operating losses incurred by an acquiring corporation after a reorganization cannot be carried back against pre-reorganization income of the acquired corporation except in the case of the "B," "E," and "F" reorganizations.

[¶ 9050]

D. JUDICIALLY DEVELOPED PRE-REQUISITES TO REORGANIZA-TION QUALIFICATION

As originally enacted in 1921 and revised in 1924, the reorganization provisions remained sufficiently general in phraseology to afford the taxpayer extensive and highly inviting opportunities to avoid tax by specially tailoring a considerable variety of transactions in order to meet the statutory requirements for a qualifying tax-free reorganization. In view of the tempting advantages to be gained and the relative ease with which the statutory tests could be met, it was only a matter of time before the courts were presented with taxpayer efforts to claim tax-free reorganization benefits for transactions that had been cast in the statutory molds but that failed to comply with the presuppositions on which the justification for nonrecognition of gain rested.

In response to these efforts, the courts played a dynamic role in construing and elaborating upon the statutory structure. Many of the landmark judicial doctrines of this period have remained essential features of reorganization topography and have cast their shadows in many other corners of the tax scene. While most of these doctrines are in some form or another codified in the Treasury regulations discussed in the next Chapter, the cases themselves remain the touchstone of judicial analysis and therefore constitute prerequisites to reorganization treatment.

1. BUSINESS PURPOSE REQUIREMENT

[¶ 9055]

GREGORY v. HELVERING

Supreme Court of the United States, 1935.
293 U.S. 465.

MR. JUSTICE SUTHERLAND delivered the opinion of the Court.

Petitioner in 1928 was the owner of all the stock of United Mortgage Corporation. That corporation held among its assets 1,000 shares of the Monitor Securities Corporation. For the sole purpose of procuring a transfer of these shares to herself in order to sell them for her individual profit, and, at the same time, diminish the amount of income tax which would result from a direct transfer by way of dividend, she sought to bring about a "reorganization" under § 112(g) of the Revenue Act of 1928, set forth later in this opinion. To that end, she caused the Averill Corporation to be organized under the laws of Delaware on September 18, 1928. Three days later, the United Mortgage Corporation transferred

¶ 9055

to the Averill Corporation the 1,000 shares of Monitor stock, for which all the shares of the Averill Corporation were issued to the petitioner. On September 24, the Averill Corporation was dissolved, and liquidated by distributing all its assets, namely, the Monitor shares, to the petitioner. No other business was ever transacted, or intended to be transacted, by that company. Petitioner immediately sold the Monitor shares for $133,333.33. She returned for taxation as capital net gain the sum of $76,007.88, based upon an apportioned cost of $57,325.45. Further details are unnecessary. It is not disputed that if the interposition of the so-called reorganization was ineffective, petitioner became liable for a much larger tax as a result of the transaction.

The Commissioner of Internal Revenue, being of opinion that the reorganization attempted was without substance and must be disregarded, held that petitioner was liable for a tax as though the United corporation had paid her a dividend consisting of the amount realized from the sale of the Monitor shares. In a proceeding before the Board of Tax Appeals, that body rejected the commissioner's view and upheld that of petitioner. * * * Upon a review of the latter decision, the circuit court of appeals sustained the commissioner and reversed the board, holding that there had been no "reorganization" within the meaning of the statute. * * * Petitioner applied to this court for a writ of certiorari, which the government, considering the question one of importance, did not oppose. We granted the writ.

Section 112 of the Revenue Act of 1928 deals with the subject of gain or loss resulting from the sale or exchange of property. Such gain or loss is to be recognized in computing the tax, except as provided in that section. The provisions of the section, so far as they are pertinent to the question here presented, follow:

"Sec. 112. (g) *Distribution of stock on reorganization.*—If there is distributed, in pursuance of a plan of reorganization, to a shareholder in a corporation a party to the reorganization, stock or securities in such corporation or in another corporation a party to the reorganization, without the surrender by such shareholder of stock or securities in such a corporation, no gain to the distributee from the receipt of such stock or securities shall be recognized. . . .

"(i) *Definition of reorganization.*—As used in this section . . .

"(1) The term 'reorganization' means . . . (B) a transfer by a corporation of all or a part of its assets to another corporation if immediately after the transfer the transferor or its stockholders or both are in control of the corporation to which the assets are transferred, . . ."

It is earnestly contended on behalf of the taxpayer that since every element required by the foregoing subdivision (B) is to be found in what was done, a statutory reorganization was effected; and that the motive of the taxpayer thereby to escape payment of a tax will not alter the result

¶ 9055

or make unlawful what the statute allows. It is quite true that if a reorganization in reality was effected within the meaning of subdivision (B), the ulterior purpose mentioned will be disregarded. The legal right of a taxpayer to decrease the amount of what otherwise would be his taxes, or altogether avoid them, by means which the law permits, cannot be doubted. * * * But the question for determination is whether what was done, apart from the tax motive, was the thing which the statute intended. The reasoning of the court below in justification of a negative answer leaves little to be said.

When subdivision (B) speaks of a transfer of assets by one corporation to another, it means a transfer made "in pursuance of a plan or reorganization" [§ 112(g)] of corporate business; and not a transfer of assets by one corporation to another in pursuance of a plan having no relation to the business of either, as plainly is the case here. Putting aside, then, the question of motive in respect of taxation altogether, and fixing the character of the proceeding by what actually occurred, what do we find? Simply an operation having no business or corporate purpose— a mere device which put on the form of a corporate reorganization as a disguise for concealing its real character, and the sole object and accomplishment of which was the consummation of a preconceived plan, not to reorganize a business or any part of a business, but to transfer a parcel of corporate shares to the petitioner. No doubt, a new and valid corporation was created. But that corporation was nothing more than a contrivance to the end last described. It was brought into existence for no other purpose; it performed, as it was intended from the beginning it should perform, no other function. When that limited function had been exercised, it immediately was put to death.

In these circumstances, the facts speak for themselves and are susceptible of but one interpretation. The whole undertaking, though conducted according to the terms of subdivision (B), was in fact an elaborate and devious form of conveyance masquerading as a corporate reorganization, and nothing else. The rule which excludes from consideration the motive of tax avoidance is not pertinent to the situation, because the transaction upon its face lies outside the plain intent of the statute. To hold otherwise would be to exalt artifice above reality and to deprive the statutory provision in question of all serious purpose.

Judgment affirmed.

[¶ 9060]

Note

The business purpose requirement, in a variety of different formulations, is now codified in a number places in the Treasury regulations. See Reg. §§ 1.368–1(b) ("the purpose of the reorganization provisions of the Code is to except from the general rule certain specifically described transactions * * * as are required by business exigencies") and (c) ("A scheme * * * the object and accomplishment of which is the consummation of a preconceived plan having no business or corporate purpose, is not a plan of reorganization") and 1.368–2(g) ("the readjustments involved in the exchanges or distributions effected in the consummation [of a plan of reorganization] must be undertaken for reasons germane to the continuance of the business of a corporation a party to the reorganization.").

[¶ 9065]

2. FORM AND SUBSTANCE; STEP TRANSACTION DOCTRINE

In *Gregory v. Helvering*, the Supreme Court, in holding that Mrs. Gregory's corporate manipulations failed to qualify as a tax-free reorganization, characterized the transaction as "a mere device which put on the form of a corporate reorganization as a disguise for concealing its true character," and indicated that to hold the transaction tax-free would "be to exalt artifice above reality." As a consequence, the *Gregory* case is often cited not only as the source of the business purpose doctrine but also of the broad doctrine that, in characterizing a transaction for tax purposes, it is the "reality" or "substance" of what occurred in fact that controls, rather than the form adopted. The principle that substance controls over form plays a role in every tax controversy when a question of fact is presented as to whether the actual facts establish that the transaction (or status) concerned meets the statutory requirements for prescribed tax treatment. Commonly, the issue boils down to whether the transaction (or status) involved "is what it purports to be." In some cases, the IRS or a court may determine that an alleged transaction should be disregarded for tax purposes because it was not in fact carried out. More often the problem involves determining whether a particular transaction (or status) has in reality, when all of the relevant circumstances are examined, the particular character that produces the tax advantage sought by the taxpayer. It should be emphasized that, although the existence of enforceable legal rights and duties created by the formal arrangements between the parties is relevant in determining the proper characterization of the transaction or status for tax purposes, it is not controlling.

In evaluating the risk presented in a particular situation that the IRS may seek to disregard the formal arrangements adopted, one is inclined to start with Judge Learned Hand's celebrated comment in Helvering v. Gregory, 69 F.2d 809, 810 (2d Cir.1934):

> [A] transaction, otherwise within an exception of the tax law, does not lose its immunity because it is actuated by a desire to avoid or, if one choose, to evade, taxation. Anyone may so arrange his affairs that his taxes shall be as low as possible; he is not bound to choose that pattern which will best pay the Treasury; there is not even a patriotic duty to increase one's taxes.

¶ 9060

In many aspects of reorganizations, it is clear that form will control, at least when the Code envisages and permits the adoption of more than one formal route to the same economic end. Thus, the same practical results can often be achieved in an acquisition situation, whether an "A," "B," or "C" reorganization is employed, but the form adopted will usually be respected and will determine the tax results. Indeed, it is generally incumbent on a taxpayer seeking tax-free reorganization treatment to cast the transaction in a form that will fall squarely within one of the reorganization definitions. The difficult problem is to judge whether a particular reorganization or some transaction involved in it may be vulnerable because the form does not comport with economic reality.

The reorganizations area is replete with examples of the IRS and the courts looking through form to substance. A notable illustration is the so-called step transaction doctrine, previously encountered in connection with transfers of property to a corporation under Section 351, at ¶ 2045, pursuant to which a series of separate transactions will, under certain circumstances, be treated as a single integrated transaction for tax purposes. As discussed in the following case, the step transaction doctrine has been given a variety of different formulations in applying the tax-free reorganization provisions. Some stress objective criteria. For example, steps will be integrated only if, when the first step is taken, the taxpayer is under a binding commitment to take the subsequent step. Commissioner v. Gordon, 391 U.S. 83 (1968) (the "binding commitment" test), or only if the steps are so interdependent that the legal relations created by one transaction would have been fruitless without completion of the other transaction (the "interdependence" test). Reef Corp. v. Commissioner, 368 F.2d 125 (5th Cir.1966), cert. denied, 386 U.S. 1018 (1967). Another looks to more subjective criteria, notably the taxpayer's "intent" or "plan." Kimbell–Diamond Milling Co. v. Commissioner, 14 T.C. 74. (1950), aff'd per curiam, 187 F.2d 718 (5th Cir.1951), cert. den., 342 U.S. 827 (1951). For example, steps will be integrated only if they were taken in furtherance of and for the purpose of reaching the end result. King Enterprises, Inc. v. United States, 418 F.2d 511, 516 (Ct.Cl.1969) (the "end result" test). In the following case note the court's evaluation of the "binding commitment" formulation in the reorganization context.

[¶ 9070]

KING ENTERPRISES, INC. v. UNITED STATES

United States Court of Claims, 1969.
418 F.2d 511.

PER CURIAM:

* * * Since the court agrees with the [trial] commissioner's opinion, findings and recommended conclusion of law, as hereinafter set forth, it

hereby adopts the same as the basis for its judgment in this case without oral argument. * * *

* * *

* * * BERNHARDT, COMMISSIONER:

This is an action to recover Federal income taxes paid by petitioner for the fiscal year ended June 30, 1960. The issues involve the proper characterization for tax purposes of the transaction in question, and the tax treatment of the resulting gain. The facts detailed in the accompanying report, condensed here, sustain the conclusion that the petitioner is entitled to recover.

Petitioner, King Enterprises, Inc., is a Tennessee corporation presently engaged in the business, *inter alia*, of holding and managing various investments. Prior to October 30, 1961, petitioner's business, then styled Fleetwood Coffee Company, was the sale of roasted coffee. It was one of 11 shareholders in Tenco, Inc., a corporation organized in 1951 to supply its shareholders with a reliable source of instant coffee for them to market under their own brand names. Tenco was financially successful over the years, and by 1959 had become the second largest producer of soluble coffee in the United States. Despite its financial success there was stockholder discontent.

Minute Maid Corporation had become by 1958 one of the nation's principal producers of frozen concentrated citrus juices. Because of financial reverses in 1957 Minute Maid decided to acquire other businesses in order to stabilize its income. Between January and July 29, 1959, Minute Maid submitted and the Tenco directors rejected three separate proposals for acquisition of Tenco stock. A fourth proposal was approved by the respective boards on August 25, 1959, and on September 3, 1959, petitioner and other Tenco shareholders signed an agreement with Minute Maid entitled "Purchase and Sale Agreement."

Pursuant to the Agreement providing for the sale of their Tenco stock to Minute Maid, the Tenco shareholders received a total consideration consisting of $3,000,000 in cash, $2,550,000 in promissory notes, and 311,996 shares of Minute Maid stock valued at $5,771,926. Petitioner's share of the total consideration consisted of $281,564.25 in cash, $239,329.40 in promissory notes, and 29,282 shares of Minute Maid stock valued at $541,717. The Minute Maid stock received by Tenco stockholders represented 15.62 percent of the total outstanding Minute Maid shares, and constituted in excess of 50 percent of the total consideration received.

On December 10, 1959, the Minute Maid directors approved the November 24th recommendation of its general counsel to merge the company's four subsidiaries, including Tenco, into the parent company, and authorized that the merger be submitted to its stockholders for approval at a meeting scheduled for February 1960. Minute Maid's

¶ 9070

annual report to stockholders announced the merger plan about December 3, 1959. On January 5, 1960, Minute Maid requested a ruling from the Commissioner of Internal Revenue whether in the event of the proposed Tenco merger the basis of Tenco assets in Minute Maid's hands would be determined under section 334(b)(2) [now Section 338(b)] of the Internal Revenue Code of 1954. This was approved by the Commissioner by ruling of February 25, 1960 that "Under the provisions of section 334(b)(2) [now Section 338(b)] that basis of the property received by Minute Maid upon the complete liquidation of Tenco will be determined by reference to the adjusted basis of the Tenco stock in the hands of Minute Maid." On April 30 and May 2, 1960, in accordance with the applicable state laws, Tenco and certain other subsidiaries were merged into Minute Maid.

On its income tax return for the fiscal year ended June 30, 1960, petitioner reported the cash and notes received as dividend income, subject to the 85 percent intercorporate dividends received deduction. The value of the Minute Maid stock received by petitioner was not reported, it being petitioner's position that such stock was received in connection with a nontaxable corporate reorganization. The District Director of Internal Revenue assessed a deficiency on the ground that the gain portion of the total consideration received (cash, notes, and Minute Maid stock) constituted taxable capital gain from the sale of a capital asset. Petitioner paid the deficiency, then sued here.

Petitioner contends that the transfer by the Tenco stockholders of their Tenco stock to Minute Maid in exchange for Minute Maid stock, cash and notes, followed by the merger of Tenco into Minute Maid, were steps in a unified transaction qualifying as a reorganization under section 368(a)(1)(A) * * *. Consequently, petitioner continues, the Minute Maid stock was received by it pursuant to the plan of reorganization and is nontaxable as such, while the cash and notes received constitute a dividend distribution to which the 85 percent intercorporate dividends received deduction is applicable. The Government asserts that the transfer of Tenco stock to Minute Maid was an independent sales transaction; therefore, the entire gain realized by petitioner on the payment to it of cash, notes and Minute Maid stock is taxable as gain from the sale of a capital asset.

I

THE REORGANIZATION ISSUE

The threshold issue is whether the transfer of Tenco stock to Minute Maid is to be treated for tax purposes as an independent transaction of sale, or as a transitory step in a transaction qualifying as a corporate reorganization. Significant tax consequences turn on which characterization is determined to be proper.

¶ 9070

The general rule is that when property is sold or otherwise disposed of, any gain realized must also be recognized, absent an appropriate nonrecognition provision in the Internal Revenue Code. One such non-recognition provision, section 354(a)(1), provides in pertinent part:

> No gain or loss shall be recognized if stock or securities in a corporation a party to a reorganization are, in pursuance of the plan of reorganization, exchanged solely for stock or securities in such corporation or in another corporation a party to the reorganization.

By its terms, this exception to the general rule of taxation depends for its operation on the existence of a corporate reorganization. The term "reorganization", moreover, is a word of art in tax law and is specifically defined in section 368(a)(1) as comprising six [now seven] types of transactions, exclusively.

* * *

The premise of the corporate reorganization provisions is that certain transactions constitute corporate readjustments and are not the proper occasion for the incidence of taxation. Congressional policy is to free from tax consequences those corporate reorganizations involving a continuity of business enterprise under modified corporate form and a continuity of interest on the part of the owners before and after, where there is no basic change in relationships and not a sufficient "cashing in" of proprietary interests to justify contemporaneous taxation.

It is not disputed that there was a Type A reorganization in April 1960 when Tenco and Minute Maid were merged in accordance with state law. Nor does the Government dispute that Minute Maid continued the business of Tenco following the merger, or that the former Tenco shareholders had a continuity of interest in the enterprise by virtue of their ownership of stock in Minute Maid received in the exchange. The disagreement centers on whether the initial exchange of stock was a step in a unified transaction pursuant to a "plan of reorganization".

The underlying theory of the petitioner's claim is that the tax consequences of business transactions are properly determined by their substance and not by the form in which they are cast. Thus petitioner views the substance of the transaction under review to be an acquisition by Minute Maid of Tenco's assets in exchange for transferring Minute Maid stock, cash and notes to Tenco's stockholders. * * * The value of the Minute Maid stock received, which exceeded 50 percent of the total consideration, constituted a sufficient continuity of interest to support a Type A reorganization. Petitioner concludes, therefore, that the net result of the entire transaction is a reorganization, not to be altered by splitting the entire transaction into its component transitory steps. * * * Petitioner's conclusion is justified in fact and in law.

The problem of deciding whether to accord the separate steps of a complex transaction independent significance, or to treat them as related

¶ 9070

steps in a unified transaction, is a recurring problem in the field of tax law. The principle that even extended business transactions have determinate limits for tax purposes is based on a strong preference for "closed transactions" upon which to impose tax consequences. This preference is tempered, however, with respect for the integrity of an entire transaction. Accordingly, the essence of the step transaction doctrine is that an "integrated transaction must not be broken into independent steps or, conversely, that the separate steps must be taken together in attaching tax consequences". Bittker and Eustice, Federal Income Taxation of Corporations and Shareholders, p. 18 (1966) * * *. The mere recitation of the doctrine, however, does not clarify the necessary relationship between the steps requisite to characterization as an integrated transaction.

Analysis of the reported cases and the diverse business transactions they encompass reveals that there is no universal test applicable to step transaction situations * * *. It has been persuasively suggested that "the aphorisms about 'closely related steps' and 'integrated transactions' may have different meanings in different contexts, and that there may be not one rule, but several, depending on the substantive provision of the Code to which they are being applied". Mintz and Plumb, Step Transactions, pp. 247, 252–253 (1954).

In their attempt to define the criteria upon which application of step transaction principles depend, the courts have enunciated two basic tests. The "interdependence test" requires an inquiry as to "whether on a reasonable interpretation of objective facts the steps were so interdependent that the legal relations created by one transaction would have been fruitless without a completion of the series". Paul and Zimet, Step Transactions, Selected Studies in Federal Taxation (2d Series, 1938), pp. 200, 254. * * * The "end result" test, on the other hand, establishes a standard whereby:

> * * * purportedly separate transactions will be amalgamated into a single transaction when it appears that they were really component parts of a single transaction intended from the outset to be taken for the purpose of reaching the ultimate result.

Despite the real differences between the tests, each is faithful to the central purpose of the step transaction doctrine; that is, to assure that tax consequences turn on the substance of a transaction rather than on its form.

In support of its position that the step transaction doctrine is inapplicable to the facts of this case the Government correctly points out that there was no binding commitment for the merger of Tenco to follow the acquisition of its stock. Defendant erroneously concludes, however, that the absence of such a commitment here renders the step transaction doctrine inapplicable. The binding commitment requirement, relied upon by the Government, was enunciated by the Supreme Court in Commissioner v. Gordon, [391 U.S. 83] at 96, * * * wherein the Court said "if one transaction is to be characterized as a 'first step' there must be a binding commitment to take the later steps". Analysis of the statement in its proper context, however, dispels its application to the case before us. * * *

* * *

The opinion in *Gordon* contains not the slightest indication that the Supreme Court intended the binding commitment requirement to be the touchstone of the step transaction doctrine in tax law. Nor is there any indication that the Court intended to overrule any prior decisions applying the step transaction doctrine to other types of transactions where there were no binding commitments. On the contrary, the opinion addressed a narrow situation (a D reorganization) involving a specific statutory requirement (divestiture of control), and limited the potential for dilution and circumvention of that requirement by prohibiting the indefinite extension of divestiture distributions. Its interpretation should be so limited. Clearly, the step transaction doctrine would be a dead letter if restricted to situations where the parties were *bound* to take certain steps.

The doctrine derives vitality, rather, from its application where the form of a transaction *does not require* a particular further step be taken; but, once taken, the substance of the transaction reveals that the ultimate result was intended from the outset. * * * In the majority of cases, it is the Government that relies on the step transaction doctrine for tax characterization. General application of the binding commitment requirement would effectively insure taxpayers of virtual exemption from the doctrine merely by refraining from such commitments. * * *

In the alternative, the Government asserts that the step transaction doctrine has no application to this case because the merger of Tenco into Minute Maid was not the intended end result from the outset. Although the appropriate standard is invoked, defendant's assertion is inconsistent with the inferences to be drawn from the record.

The operative facts emerging from the record in this case suggest that Minute Maid, desirous of diversifying its operations in order to stabilize its income, was presented with the opportunity to acquire the entire stock of Tenco for a bargain "price". Tenco's record of financial success and its asking price for Tenco stock of seven or eight times its earnings (while other companies were asking 20 times their earnings), without more, constituted an attractive investment. After the stock acquisition, moreover, Minute Maid was at liberty to operate Tenco as a wholly owned subsidiary, if it so desired. There is no persuasive evidence, however, that Minute Maid's appetite was limited to these goals, though worthy, when there was more in sight. On the contrary, the record reveals that, prior to the acquisition of Tenco stock, the officers of Minute Maid considered merging its existing subsidiaries into the parent in order to eliminate some of the general ledgers and extra taxes, and to bring about other savings. In fact, the merger of subsidiaries as a money-saving device was Mr. Speeler's (Minute Maid's vice president and general counsel) pet idea, which he discussed with Minute Maid's President Fox before the initial agreement with Tenco.

Shortly after the stock acquisition, Minute Maid instituted steps to consummate the merger of Tenco into Minute Maid. The proposed merger was motivated by a desire to avoid additional income tax on inter-corporate dividends, to eliminate duplicate costs in the approximate amount of $50,000, and to obtain a stepped-up basis for stock in foreign corporations and other assets owned by Tenco. The potential step-up in basis for the foreign stock was estimated at $750,000 and the step-up for Tenco's other assets, although unable to be precisely ascertained, was considerable and probably sufficient as a justification for the merger independent of the other assigned reasons.

Minute Maid applied for on January 5, 1960, and received on February 25, 1960, a ruling by the Internal Revenue Service that Minute Maid's basis in property received upon the complete liquidation of Tenco would be determined under section 334(b)(2) [now Section 338(b)] by reference to the adjusted basis of Tenco stock in Minute Maid's hands. Subsequently, on April 30 and May 2, 1960, in accordance with applicable state laws, Tenco and certain other subsidiaries were merged into Minute Maid.

No express intention on the part of Minute Maid to effect a merger of Tenco surfaces in the record until after the initial agreement to exchange stock. It strains credulity, however, to believe other than that the plan to merge was something more than inchoate, if something less than announced, at the time of such exchange. One gains the impression that the record of intentions is edited, so in reconstruction we must lean heavily on the logic of tell-tale facts and lightly on chameleon words. It is difficult to believe that sophisticated businessmen arranging a multimillion dollar transaction fraught with tax potentials were so innocent of knowledge of the tax consequences as the testimony purports. Perhaps testimony from private tax authorities serving the parties would have yielded more explicit knowledge of the questions asked and the advice given, but a trial record is rarely perfect in retrospect and a decision must be reached on an objective appraisal of the facts, including the inferences to be squeezed from them.

The operative facts in this case clearly justify the inference that the merger of Tenco into Minute Maid was the intended result of the transaction in question from the outset, the initial exchange of stock constituting a mere transitory step. Accordingly, it is concluded that the initial exchange and subsequent merger were steps in a unified transac-

¶ 9070

tion qualifying as a Type A reorganization, and that petitioner received its Minute Maid stock pursuant to the plan of reorganization shown by the facts and circumstances above to have existed.

* * *

[¶ 9075]

Note

As *King Enterprises* suggests, step transaction issues arise frequently in the reorganization area. Why does the court conclude that the step transaction doctrine would become a dead letter in the reorganization context if two steps could be integrated only if, when the first step is taken, the parties are committed to take the second? See also the discussion of liquidation-reincorporation transactions at ¶¶ 11,100 et seq. Under Section 351, the binding commitment formulation is generally applied to determine whether an original transferor of property meets the requirement that it have control immediately after the exchange if, after the exchange, it sells enough stock in the transferee to bring it below the control threshold. *Intermountain Lumber Co. v. Commissioner*, at ¶ 2050. When the issue is whether two transfers of property for stock, separated in time, should be treated as a single transfer in applying the control test, the "interdependence" test has been invoked. American Bantam Car Co. v. Commissioner, 11 T.C. 397 (1948), aff'd, 177 F.2d 513 (3d Cir.1949), cert. denied, 339 U.S. 920 (1950).

[¶ 9080]

3. CONTINUITY OF SHAREHOLDER INTEREST REQUIRE-MENT

a. *Origin of the Requirement*

Early on, the difficulty with the reorganization provisions was that they failed to provide a clear line distinguishing a "reorganization," involving the continuation of the transferor's proprietary interest, from a "sale," which essentially terminated that interest. One of the first cases to grapple with this problem was Cortland Specialty Co. v. Commissioner, 60 F.2d 937 (2d Cir.1932). In the *Cortland Specialty Co.* case, substantially all of the properties of X Corporation were transferred to Y Corporation in exchange for cash and Y serial promissory notes, of which the longest maturity was 14 months. Although the transaction fell within the literal terms of the reorganization definition as it was then drafted, the court held that the transaction failed to qualify because there was no "continuance of interest on the part of the transferor in the properties transferred." 60 F.2d at 940.

¶ 9070

Subsequently, the Supreme Court considered whether the result would be different if the consideration received by shareholders of the acquired corporation consisted exclusively of relatively long-term debt instruments. In Le Tulle v. Scofield, 308 U.S. 415 (1940), substantially all of the assets of the Irrigation Company were transferred to the Water Company for $50,000 in cash and $750,000 in bonds issued by the Water Company payable serially over 11 years. In holding that the transaction did not qualify as a reorganization, notwithstanding compliance with the definitional requirements, the Court stated:

> * * * [T]he judgment must be affirmed on the ground that no tax-free reorganization was effected within the meaning of the statute.

> Section 112(i) provides, so far as material:

> "(1) The term reorganization means (A) a merger or consolidation (including the acquisition by one corporation of at least a majority of the voting stock and at least a majority of the total number of shares of all other classes of stock of another corporation, or substantially all the properties of another corporation)...."

> As the court below properly stated, the section is not to be read literally, as denominating the transfer of all the assets of one company for what amounts to a cash consideration given by the other a reorganization. We have held that where the consideration consists of cash and short term notes the transfer does not amount to a reorganization within the true meaning of the statute, but is a sale upon which gain or loss must be reckoned. We have said that the statute was not satisfied unless the transferor retained a substantial stake in the enterprise and such a stake was thought to be retained where a large proportion of the consideration was in common stock of the transferee, or where the transferor took cash and the entire issue of preferred stock of the transferee corporation.
> * * *

> * * *

> We are of opinion that the term of the obligations is not material. Where the consideration is wholly in the transferee's bonds, or part cash and part such bonds, we think it cannot be said that the transferor retains any proprietary interest in the enterprise. On the contrary, he becomes a creditor of the transferee; and we do not think that the fact referred to by the Circuit Court of Appeals, that the bonds were secured solely by the assets transferred and that, upon default, the bondholder would retake only the property sold, changes his status from that of a creditor to one having a proprietary stake, within the purview of the statute.

¶ **9080**

We conclude that the Circuit Court of Appeals was in error in holding that, as respects any of the property transferred to the Water Company, the transaction was other than a sale or exchange upon which gain or loss must be reckoned in accordance with the provisions of the revenue act dealing with the recognition of gain or loss upon a sale or exchange.

* * *

308 U.S. at 419.

[¶ 9085]

Note

In the *Cortland Specialty Co.* and *Le Tulle* cases, the timing of gain recognition was at stake—either immediate recognition based on the value of the debt obligations if the transaction was not a reorganization or recognition deferred until collection of the obligations at maturity if it was. The stakes were potentially much higher in *Le Tulle*, in which the obligations were payable over 11 years than in *Cortland Specialty Co.*, in which the maximum maturity was 14 months. Today, under some circumstances, installment method reporting under Section 453 would produce deferred recognition even in the absence of a qualifying reorganization.

[¶ 9090]

b. The Survival of the Requirement

The continuity of interest requirement was in part necessitated by Congress' failure in the early Revenue Acts to specify the consideration necessary for one of the parenthetical clause transactions to qualify as a "merger or consolidation." In 1934, however, Congress modified the merger category of reorganization in the predecessor to Section 368(a)(1)(A) to require a "statutory" merger or consolidation. To some contemporary observers, this meant that the judicial doctrine of continuity of interest was no longer applicable. The assumption was that the state law requirements for mergers would be sufficient to distinguish mergers from sales. Under this line of thought, as long as the transaction constituted a "merger" for purposes of the state law merger statute, it would qualify as a reorganization. Treasury disputed this interpretation, but for a long time the issue was unresolved. The following case was one of several to finally address the post–1934 Act relevance of the continuity of interest requirement.

[¶ 9095]

SOUTHWEST NATURAL GAS CO. v. COMMISSIONER

United States Court of Appeals, Fifth Circuit, 1951.
189 F.2d 332.

RUSSELL, CIRCUIT JUDGE:

The correctness of asserted deficiencies for corporate income tax for the year 1941 and of declared value excess profits tax and excess profits tax for 1942 due by Southwest Natural Gas Company depends upon whether a merger of Peoples Gas & Fuel Corporation with the taxpayer, effected in accordance with the laws of Delaware, was a sale, as asserted by the Commissioner, or a "reorganization" within the terms of Section 112(g) of the Internal Revenue Code of 1939,[4] as contended by the taxpayer. The parties so stipulated the issue in the Tax Court. That Court upheld the Commissioner's determination. Southwest Natural Gas Company has petitioned this Court for review.

The facts found by the Tax Court (which, as facts, are not challenged) and the grounds for its judgment in law thereon are fully set forth in its published opinion. In substance that Court held that literal compliance with the provisions of a state law authorizing a merger would not in itself effect a "reorganization" within the terms applicable under Internal Revenue Statutes; that the test of continuity of interest was nevertheless applicable; and that the transaction in question did not meet this test. * * *

Consideration of the underlying purposes of the terms and provisions of Section 112 of the Internal Revenue Code in its entirety and of this Section (g)(1)(A) as involved here, in particular, as being enacted "to free from the imposition of an income tax purely 'paper profits or losses' wherein there is no realization of gain or loss in the business sense but merely the recasting of the same interests in a different form, the tax being postponed to a future date when a more tangible gain or loss is realized," Commissioner of Internal Revenue v. Gilmore's Estate, 3 Cir., 130 F.2d 791, 794, and thus applicable to transactions which affect only the "readjustment of continuing interest in property under modified corporate forms," clearly discloses, we think, that the accomplishment of a statutory merger does not *ipso facto* constitute a "reorganization" within the terms of the statute here involved. * * * The authorities are clearly to the effect that the terms expressed in the statute are not to be given merely a literal interpretation but are to be considered and applied in accordance with the purpose of Section 112. Thus the benefits of the reorganization provision have been withheld "in situations which might

---

4. Section 112(g) provided: "As used in this section * * * (1) the term 'reorganiza- tion' means (A) a statutory merger or con- solidation."

¶ 9095

have satisfied the provision of the section treated as inert language, because they were not reorganizations of the kind with which § 112, in its purpose and particulars concerns itself." * * *

It is thus clear that the test of "continuity of interest" announced and applied by these cited authorities, supra, must be met before a statutory merger may properly be held a reorganization within the terms of Section 112(g)(1)(A), supra. Each case must in its final analysis be controlled by its own peculiar facts. While no precise formula has been expressed for determining whether there has been retention of the requisite interest, it seems clear that the requirement of continuity of interest consistent with the statutory intent is not fulfilled in the absence of a showing: (1) that the transferor corporation or its shareholders retained a substantial proprietary stake in the enterprise represented by a material interest in the affairs of the transferee corporation, and, (2) that such retained interest represents a substantial part of the value of the property transferred.

Among other facts, the Tax Court found that under the merger all of Peoples' assets were acquired by the petitioner in exchange for specified amounts of stock, bonds, cash and the assumption of debts. There was a total of 18,875 shares common stock of Peoples' entitled to participate under the agreement of merger. The stockholders were offered Option A and Option B. The holders of 7,690 of such shares exercised Option B of that agreement and received $30.00 in cash for each share, or a total of $230,700.00. In respect to the stock now involved, the stockholders who exercised Option A, the holders of 59.2 per cent of the common stock received in exchange 16.4 per cent of petitioner's outstanding common stock plus $340,350.00 principal amount of six per cent mortgage bonds (of the market value of 90 per cent of principal), which had been assumed by petitioner in a prior merger, and $17,779.59 cash. The 16.4 per cent of the common stock referred to was represented by 111,850 shares having a market value of $5,592.50, or five cents per share, and represented the continuing proprietary interest of the participating stockholders in the enterprise. This was less than one per cent of the consideration paid by the taxpayers.

We think it clear that these and other facts found by the Tax Court find substantial support in the evidence, and the conclusion of the Tax Court that they failed to evidence sufficient continuity of interest to bring the transaction within the requirements of the applicable statute is correct.

The decision of the Tax Court is Affirmed.

[Dissenting opinion has been omitted.]

[¶ 9100]

Note

Eventually, the continuity of interest requirement was codified in the Treasury regulations. See Reg. §§ 1.368–1(b) (permitting reorganizations "which effect only a readjustment of continuing interest in property under modified corporate forms.") and –1(e). As will be more fully described in Chapter 10, this requirement contains three components: (1) a qualitative component, requiring stock rather than debt consideration (see *Cortland Specialty* and *Le Tulle,* at ¶ 9080), (2) a quantitative component, requiring that a substantial part of the consideration (at least 38%) consist of Acquirer stock (see the discussion of *Nelson v. Helvering,* at ¶ 10,040), and (3) a temporal component. The temporal aspect of the continuity of shareholder interest prerequisite for nonrecognition treatment was reflected in the requirement that the shareholders of the acquired corporation hold the continuity stock for an appropriate period after the acquisitive reorganization. At least with respect to sales to parties not associated with the Acquirer, this requirement has been eliminated under Reg. § 1.368–1(e), issued in January 1998, and is discussed at ¶ 10,040.

[¶ 9105]

4. CONTINUITY OF BUSINESS ENTERPRISE REQUIREMENT

While the continuity of interest requirement addressed the question of shareholder level continuity of stock ownership, it did not address whether the Acquirer must continue to own or operate the former Target business. Theoretically, the Acquirer could sell all of the assets of the Target after the transaction, which would equate to a sale of Acquirer stock for cash by Target shareholders. In such a transaction, Target shareholders would have effectively cashed out their appreciated investment in the Target assets tax-free. Moreover, the continuity of interest in a surviving corporation that neither owns the former Target assets nor uses them in a business appeared to be meaningless because the underlying investment had changed so significantly. According to the court in *Cortland Specialty,* at ¶ 9080, this was contrary to the intentions of the framers of the reorganization provisions. Therefore, in addition to specifying that a reorganization requires continuity of shareholder stock ownership, the court made clear that "[r]eorganization presupposes continuance of business under modified corporate form." 60 F.2d at 940. While this continuity of business enterprise requirement appeared to be very closely related to the continuity of interest requirement, it evolved into a separate requirement of its own.

At one point, the Service took the position that continuity of business enterprise meant that the Acquirer must actually continue to operate the Target's business after the reorganization. See Rev. Rul. 56–330, 1956–2 C.B. 204. This position, however, failed several times in court. In one such case, Bentsen v. Phinney, 199 F. Supp. 363 (S.D. Tex. 1961), the assets of three land development corporations were transferred to a newly created life insurance corporation in exchange for its stock and the land development corporations dissolved after the transaction. The life insurance corporation continued to own the former land development corporation's assets, but used them in the insurance business. The court rejected the government's argument that there was no continuity of business enterprise because the corporation engaged in a different line of business. According to the court, "[t]o qualify as a 'reorganization' under the applicable statutes, the new corporation does not have to engage in an identical or similar type of business. All that is required is that there must be continuity of business activity." Id. at 367. As a result of losses such as this one, the Service revoked its prior position. Rev. Rul. 63–29, 1963–1 C.B. 77. See Reg. § 1.368–1(d). For further discussion of the modern continuity of business enterprise requirement, see ¶ 10,060.

¶ 9105

Chapter 10

ACQUISITIVE REORGANIZATIONS

[¶ 10,000]

A. OVERVIEW

Most of the tax-free reorganizations one encounters in the business world involve the acquisition of the assets or stock of one corporation by another. As discussed in Chapter 9, the basic tax motivation for the use of a tax-free reorganization rather than a taxable purchase of the stock or assets of the target corporation is to avoid the one or two levels of tax that are imposed on gain realized by the target corporation and/or its shareholders in one of the taxable transactions discussed in Chapter 8.

The three basic types of reorganization used for the acquisition of one corporation by another are the "A" (statutory merger), the "B" (stock-for-stock), and the "C" (assets-for-stock). Each of these can be carried out in what is called "triangular" fashion when stock of a corporation in control of the acquiring corporation is the sole or the predominant consideration paid to the shareholders of the target corporation. In the case of the statutory merger, the triangular transaction can take either of two forms, the forward triangular merger under Section 368(a)(2)(D), in which the target corporation is merged into a subsidiary of the acquiring corporation (identified as the issuing corporation in the regulations under Section 368), and the reverse triangular merger under Section 368(a)(2)(E), in which a subsidiary of the acquiring (issuing) corporation is merged into the target corporation. Moreover, as discussed below at ¶ 10,210, in some cases Section 351 can play a pivotal role in connection with a corporate acquisition that is partially but not wholly tax-free.

In many cases when the target and acquiring corporation are both closely held, any of the reorganization forms could potentially be used as the vehicle for the acquisition. The choice may turn on business considerations, such as the amount of the consideration that will constitute boot, whether the equity portion of the consideration will consist of voting or nonvoting stock, and whether the target corporation has special attributes that make it desirable to keep it in existence. When the target or the acquiring corporation is publicly held, tax-free acquisitions are often effected by a forward triangular merger to avoid dissenters while permitting the widest latitude in structuring consideration. Alternatively, if it is desirable to keep the target corporation in existence to preserve certain attributes or a special status it may enjoy, the acquisition will often be implemented by a reverse triangular merger.

In the materials that follow, we start with the most basic form of reorganization—the statutory merger or "A" reorganization. All of the other types of acquisitive reorganizations are subject to requirements designed to ensure that the transactions resemble the prototypical statutory merger. We next proceed to the stock-for-assets acquisition, or "C" reorganization, both because it is considered a de facto form of merger and because it involves two basic requirements also found in other reorganization definitions. These are the requirements that the acquiring corporation obtain "substantially all of the properties" of the target and that it use solely voting stock for consideration. The discussion of the stock-for-stock acquisition, or "B" reorganization, follows and revolves principally around its stricter form of the solely for voting stock requirement. Finally, we conclude the examination of acquisitive reorganizations with the triangular reorganizations. While in many respects the triangular reorganizations are expansions of the three basic types of reorganization and therefore could be separated and considered in association with their respective "A," "B," or "C" counterparts, their growth in importance and their unique requirements makes them worthy of independent study.

[¶ 10,005]

B. MEETING THE REQUIREMENTS OF THE BASIC ACQUISITIVE REORGANIZATION DEFINITIONS

It has long been a fundamental principle of taxation that economic substance usually prevails over the form adopted for a transaction in determining the appropriate tax consequences under the Code when the form adopted by the taxpayer does not reflect the underlying realities. This principle has frequently been asserted by the IRS and supported by the courts. However, in the reorganization context, the form adopted for a transaction is often of pivotal importance. If the transaction does not meet the formal requirements of a reorganization definition, it usually cannot qualify for tax-free treatment. Moreover, it is the taxpayer who normally bears the burden of ensuring that the formal requirements of the reorganization definition are met if the transaction is to be tax free. It is important to recognize, though, that essentially the same economic

¶ 10,000

results can often be achieved in a transaction that qualifies as a tax-free reorganization as would be achieved in a transaction that because of essentially formal differences would not so qualify. Thus, by making formal changes in the structure of the acquisition transaction, the transaction may be brought within the definition of a tax-free reorganization even though without those formal changes the economic results (aside from the recognition and taxation of realized gain or loss) would be substantially the same. However, the adoption of formal arrangements that meet the statutory requirements for a reorganization is not necessarily the end of the inquiry. The judicially developed prerequisites, discussed at ¶¶ 9050 et seq., must also be met. Of these the most pervasive is that the form chosen must comport with the economic substance of the transaction. See *Gregory v. Helvering*, at ¶ 9055. If they do not, as Mrs. Gregory learned to her chagrin, the IRS and the courts are not bound to respect the form adopted by the taxpayer.

The challenge for the tax planner is to determine whether an acquisition transaction can be structured in a way that will enable the transaction to qualify as a tax-free reorganization. Needless to say, the qualification or not of the transaction as a tax-free reorganization is often of great importance to the shareholders of the target who have a much lower basis in their target shares than the present value of those shares. The risk borne by the tax planner and his client in this context can be eliminated if, time permitting, an advance ruling that the transaction will qualify as a reorganization can be obtained from the IRS. The IRS will frequently issue a ruling if the transaction involves issues that have not been definitively resolved by controlling authority. If uncertainty as to the applicable law or time does not permit obtaining a ruling or the IRS declines to rule favorably, the planner must decide whether to give the client a favorable opinion, and the client must decide whether to go forward with the transaction on the strength of this opinion.

[¶ 10,010]

1. AN ACQUISITION FRAMEWORK

In order to focus on the formal definitional requirements of the acquisitive reorganization definitions and the relationship between the formal requirements and the economic realities of the transaction, we consider whether the basic types of acquisitive reorganization can be used to implement an acquisition involving the following facts. The threshold issue for the planner is whether the transaction can be cast in the form of a qualifying reorganization without distorting the parties' business objectives and without creating a formal facade unsupported by economic reality.

The balance sheet of Target Corporation (Target) is as follows:

¶ 10,010

Assets		Liabilities	
Cash	$ 80,000	Bank Debt	$100,000
Inventory	$320,000	Common Stock	$275,000
Real Estate	$ 75,000	Earned Surplus	$100,000
	$475,000		$475,000

Acquirer Corporation (Acquirer) intends to acquire Target. In negotiations between Acquirer and Target's shareholders the fair market value of the equity in Target is agreed to be $500,000. Target has outstanding 50,000 common shares with an agreed fair market value of $10 each. Acquirer desires to use up to 450,000 shares of its own voting common stock as consideration for the acquisition of Target. The controlling shareholders of Acquirer feel that the issuance of more than 450,000 shares would jeopardize their control of Acquirer. Acquirer's common stock is presently trading on the American Exchange at $1 per share, which is agreed by the parties to be its fair market value. Acquirer proposes to add $50,000 to its 450,000 shares of common stock to make up the total consideration of $500,000. Target's shareholders have a basis of 10 cents per Target share. They are willing to enter into the transaction only if their recognized gain will be limited to the cash they receive.

In connection with the materials and problems that follow, consider under what circumstances the proposed acquisition can be effected as an "A," "C," or "B" reorganization.

[¶ 10,015]

2. "A" REORGANIZATION

a. *Statutory Merger*

To fit literally within Section 368(a)(1)(A), a transaction need only comply with the terms for a merger or consolidation under a "statute." Traditionally, this has meant the corporation law of the applicable state (or of the United States, a territory, or the District of Columbia). Many state merger provisions, though, are very broad. Transactions which in substance are tantamount to a sale of corporate assets can frequently be designed to qualify as state law mergers. Rev. Rul. 2000–5, discussed below, was at least in part prompted by a new form of state merger statute enacted in 1989 by the legislature of Texas to permit "divisive" mergers in which more than one corporation emerges from the transaction.

[¶ 10,020]

REVENUE RULING 2000–5

2000–1 C.B. 436.

ISSUES

Whether a transaction in which (1) a target corporation "merges" under state law with and into an acquiring corporation and the target corporation does not go out of existence, or (2) a target corporation "merges" under state law with and into two or more acquiring corporations and the target corporation goes out of existence, qualifies as a reorganization under § 368(a)(1)(A) of the Internal Revenue Code?

FACTS

Situation (1). A target corporation transfers some of its assets and liabilities to an acquiring corporation, retains the remainder of its assets and liabilities, and remains in existence following the transaction. The target corporation's shareholders receive stock in the acquiring corporation in exchange for part of their target corporation stock and they retain their remaining target corporation stock. The transaction qualifies as a merger under state X corporate law.

Situation (2). A target corporation transfers some of its assets and liabilities to each of two acquiring corporations. The target corporation liquidates and the target corporation's shareholders receive stock in each of the two acquiring corporations in exchange for their target corporation stock. The transaction qualifies as a merger under state X corporate law.

DISCUSSION

The purpose of the reorganization provisions of the Code is to provide tax-free treatment to certain exchanges incident to readjustments of corporate structures made in one of the specified ways described in the Code. Section 1.368–1(b) of the Income Tax Regulations. In 1921, Congress defined a reorganization as including "... a merger or consolidation (including the acquisition by one corporation ... of substantially all the properties of another corporation)." In 1934, Congress separated this rule into two distinct provisions. In the predecessor of current § 368(a)(1)(C), an "acquisition by one corporation ... of substantially all the properties of another corporation" continued to be a reorganization where payment was effectuated with the acquiror's voting stock. In the predecessor of current § 368(a)(1)(A), the terms "merger or consolidation" were qualified by requiring that they be "statutory" mergers and consolidations. The word "statutory" was added to the definition of a reorganization so that the definition "will conform more closely to the general requirements of [state] corporation law." See H. R. Rep. No. 704, 73d Cong., 2 d Sess. 14 (1934).

Historically, corporate law merger statutes have operated to ensure that "[a] merger ordinarily is an absorption by one corporation of the properties and franchises of another whose stock it has acquired. The merged corporation ceases to exist, and the merging corporation alone survives." Cortland Specialty Co. v. Commissioner, 60 F.2d 937, 939 (2d Cir.1932), cert. denied, 288 U.S. 599 (1933); * * *. Thus, unlike § 368(a)(1)(C), in which Congress included a "substantially all the properties" requirement, it was not necessary for Congress to explicitly include a similar requirement in § 368(a)(1)(A) because corporate law merger statutes contemplated an acquisition of the target corporation's assets by the surviving corporation by operation of law.

Compliance with a corporate law merger statute does not by itself qualify a transaction as a reorganization. See, e.g., Southwest Natural Gas Co. v. Commissioner, 189 F.2d 332 (5th Cir.1951), cert. denied, 342 U.S. 860 (1951) (holding that a state law merger was not a reorganization under § 368(a)(1)(A)); * * *. In addition to satisfying the requirements of business purpose, continuity of business enterprise and continuity of interest, in order to qualify as a reorganization under § 368(a)(1)(A), a transaction effectuated under a corporate law merger statute must have the result that one corporation acquires the assets of the target corporation by operation of the corporate law merger statute and the target corporation ceases to exist. The transactions described in Situations (1) and (2) do not have the result that one corporation acquires the assets of the target corporation by operation of the corporate law merger statute and the target corporation ceases to exist. Therefore, these transactions do not qualify as reorganizations under § 368(a)(1)(A).

In contrast with the operation of corporate law merger statutes, a divisive transaction is one in which a corporation's assets are divided among two or more corporations. Section 355 provides tax-free treatment for certain divisive transactions, but only if a number of specific requirements are satisfied. Congress intended that § 355 be the sole means under which divisive transactions will be afforded tax-free status and, thus, specifically required the liquidation of the acquired corporation in reorganizations under both §§ 368(a)(1)(C) and 368(a)(1)(D) in order to prevent these reorganizations from being used in divisive transactions that did not satisfy § 355. See S. Rep. No. 1622, 83d Cong., 2d Sess. 274 (1954); S. Rep. No. 169, 98th Cong., 2d Sess. 204 (1984). No specific liquidation requirement was necessary for statutory mergers because corporate law merger statutes contemplated that only one corporation survived a merger. The transaction described in Situation (1) is divisive because, after the transaction, the target corporation's assets and liabilities are held by both the target corporation and acquiring corporation and the target corporation's shareholders hold stock in both

¶ 10,020

the target corporation and acquiring corporation. The transaction described in Situation (2) is divisive because, after the transaction, the target corporation's assets and liabilities are held by each of the two acquiring corporations and the target corporation's shareholders hold stock in each of the two acquiring corporations.

HOLDING

The transactions described in Situations (1) and (2) do not qualify as reorganizations under § 368(a)(1)(A). However, the transactions described in Situations (1) and (2) possibly may qualify for tax-free treatment under other provisions of the Code.

[¶ 10,025]

Notes

1. As the ruling indicates, permitting such a transaction to qualify as an "A" reorganization would subvert the carefully articulated requirements that must be met if a corporate division is to qualify as tax-free under Section 355. See Chapter 15.

2. Arguably, the statutory merger requirement was an anachronism for more than just the potential for atypical state law merger provisions such as those described in Rev. Rul. 2000–5. It was inconsistent with the de-linking of the Code from state law reflected in the check-the-box regulations. Moreover, the statutory merger requirement introduced unjustifiable differences in tax consequences based on differences in applicable state corporate laws. This suggested that the statutory merger requirement should be eliminated in favor of a uniform federal standard. See Bank, "Federalizing the Tax–Free Merger: Toward an End to the Anachronistic Reliance on State Corporation Laws," 77 N.C.L. Rev. 1307 (1999).

3. In May of 2000, Treasury issued proposed regulations that adopted what amounts to a federal definition of "merger" for purposes of the "A" reorganization. Final regulations were approved in January of 2003. Under Reg. § 1.368–2(b)(1)(ii), a statutory merger or consolidation is a transaction in which all of the assets and liabilities of Target become assets and liabilities of Acquirer and Target "ceases its separate legal existence for all purposes." This incorporated the definition set forth in Rev. Rul. 2000–5.

4. Despite the introduction of a federal definition of "merger," participants to merger transactions continued to comply with the requirement in Section 368(a)(1)(A) that transactions also be "statutory," or, according to regulations in existence prior to 2006, "effected pursuant to the laws of the United States or a State or the District of Columbia." This comported with Treasury's long-standing view that "foreign mergers," or mergers effected under the laws of a non-U.S. jurisdiction, could not qualify as "A" reorganizations even if one of the

¶ 10,025

parties was a U.S. corporation or some of the shareholders were U.S. taxpayers. See Rev. Rul. 57–465, 1957–2 C.B. 250. Because of the growth of foreign mergers and the absence of any domestic law requirement in Section 368(a)(1)(A), this interpretation came under attack. Thus, effective January 23, 2006, Treasury adopted final regulations requiring only that a merger be completed "pursuant to the statutes necessary to effect the merger or consolidation." Reg. § 1.368–2(b)(1)(ii). This permits foreign mergers to qualify as "A" reorganizations.

[¶ 10,030]

b. *Disregarded Entity Merger*

As discussed in Chapter 1, the check-the-box regulations provided for "disregarded entities," or entities that are disregarded as separate from their owners for tax purposes. One of the most common forms of disregarded entities to emerge from the adoption of check-the-box in 1997 is the single member limited liability company (LLC). An LLC that is wholly owned by a corporation is treated as a division of its owner for tax purposes. Thus, theoretically a merger between a corporation and the single member LLC of another corporation pursuant to state law will be treated as a direct statutory merger for purposes of Section 368(a)(1)(A). This would have the advantage of permitting public corporations to avoid some of the more stringent requirements of the other types of reorganizations while maintaining the limited liability advantages of effecting the merger at a level below the parent corporation.

One potential obstacle to the disregarded entity merger was the requirement in the regulations that the transaction be effected pursuant to the "corporation laws" of the United States, a State, or the District of Columbia. While not all states permitted LLCs to merge with corporations, those that did often did so pursuant to the state LLC statute rather than the corporation law statute. In May 2000, however, as part of the proposed regulations issued to adopt the merger definition, Treasury formally abandoned the requirement that the statutory merger be effected pursuant to a corporation law statute.

Notwithstanding this broadening of the "A" reorganization regulations to encompass non-corporate mergers such as those involving LLCs, Treasury's original proposed regulations would not have permitted mergers between corporations and disregarded entities to qualify as "A" reorganizations. Treasury and the IRS changed their position and issued in November 2001 a revised Prop. Reg. § 1.368–2(b)(1), which permitted a merger of a corporation into another corporation's single member LLC to qualify as an "A" reorganization. A merger in the opposite direction, however, where the single-member LLC merged into another corporation, was still not permitted. The rationale was that because the owner of the single member LLC survived in the latter transaction, it resembled either a sale or the divisive transaction that Treasury had denied

"A" reorganization treatment to in Rev. Rul. 2000–5. Final regulations issued in January 2006 adopted the revised proposed regulations' split treatment of disregarded entity mergers. Reg. §§ 1.368–2(b)(1)(i)-(iii).

[¶ 10,035]

Problems on the "A" Reorganization

Method One: Acquirer acquires all of the assets and liabilities of Target in exchange for Acquirer stock and Target liquidates, thus ceasing its existence. In California, where the transaction took place and the parties are incorporated, a court declares that the acquisition satisfies the predicates for a de facto merger pursuant to applicable case law. Assume that, except for the filing requirement, the requirements for a de facto merger under California case law are identical to the requirements pursuant to state statute.

Can this qualify as an "A" reorganization? What if the transaction was effected pursuant to a merger statute in Bermuda, but Target continued to exist for the purpose of participating in a lawsuit relating to events that occurred prior to the merger? See Reg. § 1.368–2(b)(1)(ii)(B).

Method Two: Pursuant to state statute, Target merges into the single member LLC of a publicly traded corporation (Owner) in exchange for stock of the Owner.

Can this qualify as an "A" reorganization? What if the state statute authorizing the transaction was the state LLC statute rather than the state corporation law?

Method Three: Pursuant to state statute, the single member LLC of a publicly-traded corporation (Owner) merges into Target and stock in Target converts to stock in Owner as a result of the transaction.

Can this qualify as an "A" reorganization?

Method Four: Pursuant to state statute, Target merges into Acquirer, which is the surviving corporation, and Target ceases to exist. Each Target shareholder receives in exchange for each Target share, nine shares of Acquirer and $1 cash.

Can this qualify as an "A" reorganization? Are there any restrictions in the statutory definition of the "A" reorganization on the nature of the consideration that may be used? See the discussion of the continuity of shareholder interest requirement in the next section.

[¶ 10,040]

c. Continuity of Shareholder Interest Requirement

As we discussed in Chapter 9, one of the judicial doctrines that developed early on in the history of the tax-free reorganization provisions was the requirement that target corporation shareholders, taken as a whole, maintain a continuing interest in the underlying target assets by receiving shares of stock in the acquiring corporation. See ¶ 9080. Originally, this judicial doctrine was necessary with respect to all types of reorganizations because the early Revenue Acts failed to specify the requisite consideration for a transaction to qualify as a tax-free reorganization. As we will see, while the continuity of interest requirement still applies to all reorganizations, it is now most relevant in the case of the "A" reorganization.

The continuity of shareholder interest requirement has historically been regarded as having three distinct elements: a qualitative, a quantitative, and a temporal aspect.

Qualitative: The qualitative element is the requirement that some of the consideration received by one or more of the shareholders of an acquired corporation consist of voting or nonvoting stock of the acquiring corporation (or, in a triangular acquisitive reorganization, of a corporation in control of it). Only the receipt of stock will enable the shareholders of the acquired corporation to emerge from the transaction with the requisite proprietary or equity interest in the acquiring corporation (or its parent) exchanged for their equity interest in the acquired corporation. See the *Cortland Specialty Co.* and *Le Tulle* cases at ¶ 9080.

Under the qualitative aspect of the continuity of interest requirement, debt instruments cannot constitute a proprietary interest. This can produce artificial results that belie economic reality. For example, nonparticipating, nonconvertible, and nonvoting preferred stock, which is nonqualified preferred stock under Section 351(g)(2), may satisfy the qualitative element while long-term income debentures (on which interest is payable only out of income of the debtor) may not. Similarly, a merger of a small, closely held corporation into a large, publicly traded corporation may be treated as a tax-free reorganization even if, after the merger, the former sole shareholder of the closely held corporation owns only a quarter of one percent of the outstanding stock of the publicly traded corporation.

Quantitative: The quantitative aspect of the continuity of interest test requires that a substantial part of the consideration paid by the acquiring corporation consist of its stock or stock of a corporation in control of it. See the *Southwest Natural Gas Co.* case at ¶ 9095. The question is what percentage of the stock is sufficient to be considered "substantial." Until 2005, the IRS required for ruling purposes that the consideration paid include stock worth at least 50 percent of the value of the acquired corporation's stock. See Rev. Proc. 77–37, 1977–2 C.B. 568. However, the Supreme Court has held that the continuity test was met when 38 percent of the consideration was nonvoting, callable preferred stock and 62 percent was cash. John A. Nelson Co. v. Helvering, 296 U.S. 374 (1935). Additionally, at least one court held that a mere 25 percent stock would suffice, Miller v. Commissioner, 84 F.2d 415 (6th Cir.1936), although the Tax Court denied continuity in a case in which the

¶ 10,040

consideration was only 16 percent stock. Kass v. Commissioner, 60 T.C. 218 (1973), aff'd without opinion, 491 F.2d 749 (3d Cir.1974). Given this precedent, for years the conventional wisdom among practitioners appeared to be that 40 percent stock would be sufficient for purposes of rendering a tax opinion on a transaction, although it was understood that 50 percent stock was safer. In its commentary on the new continuity of interest regulations that became effective on September 15, 2005, the IRS reversed its historic position and announced that it would apply the 40–percent standard for purposes of testing continuity of interest. Reg. § 1.368–1(e); T.D. 9225, 2005–2 C.B. 739.

Prior to 2005, the quantitative requirement also posed a potential obstacle even in the case of transactions that appeared to meet the minimum requirement for continuity. This was because the IRS measured continuity as of the effective date of the transaction. Absent a last-minute renegotiation of the amount of the stock consideration, publicly traded stock subject to the vagaries of the market valuation could fall below the 40–percent minimum by the time the transaction became effective. The new continuity of interest regulations, however, reduced this obstacle. Under these regulations, the consideration is valued on the last business day before the first date the contract becomes binding, assuming the consideration is fixed rather than contingent. Reg. § 1.368–1(e)(2). The consideration is generally considered fixed if the contract stipulates the specific consideration or the percentage of each type of consideration. This would appear to rule out tender offers, but the regulations provide that a contract that provides shareholders an option of cash or stock may still qualify as fixed consideration if the contract specifies the minimum and maximum amount, or percentage, of each type of consideration.

There is no requirement that all of the shareholders of the acquired corporation emerge from the reorganization with a continuing proprietary interest in the acquiring corporation (or its parent). Indeed, in many cases involving an "A" reorganization, shareholders of the acquired corporation who vote against the transaction have a right to have their shares redeemed for cash at their appraised value. Moreover, when the acquired corporation is closely held, it is not uncommon for its shareholders to agree among themselves that some will receive all stock in the acquiring corporation, while others will receive cash or other consideration. It is enough that the acquired corporation's shareholders in the aggregate emerge from the transaction with the requisite continuing equity interest in the acquiring corporation.

Temporal: Until early 1998, there was a temporal aspect of the continuity of shareholder interest test. Shareholders of the acquired corporation were required to hold the requisite quantity of stock of the acquiring corporation (or its parent) for a reasonable period of time after the reorganization or to demonstrate that any disposition of the continuity stock after the reorganization was not pursuant to a plan in effect at the time of the reorganization. In Rev. Rul. 66–23, 1966–1 C.B. 67, the IRS stated its position as follows:

> It is the position of the Internal Revenue Service that the continuity of interest requirement of a reorganization can be satisfied where the shareholder of the transferor corporation receives stock of the transferee corporation without any preconceived plan or arrangement for disposing of any of the stock and with unrestricted rights of ownership for a period of time sufficient to warrant the conclusion that such ownership is definite and substantial, notwithstanding that at the time of the reorganization the shareholder is required by a court decree to dispose of the stock before the end of such period. Ordinarily, the Service will treat 5 years of unrestricted rights of ownership as a sufficient period for the purpose of satisfying the continuity of interest requirements of a reorganization.

A holding for a period of less than five years might have been acceptable if the decision to sell the continuity stock was dictated by a post-reorganization change in circumstances, such as an unanticipated urgent personal need for funds. Penrod v. Commissioner, 88 T.C. 1415 (1987).

In this temporal aspect, the continuity of shareholder interest test was also applicable to "B" and "C" reorganizations. Thus, even though the shareholders of the acquired corporation received solely voting stock of the acquiring corporation for their shares or the assets of the acquired corporation so that the transaction met the literal definition of a "B" or "C" reorganization, failure to meet the temporal aspect of the continuity requirement could have resulted in disqualification of the transaction as a tax-free reorganization. The temporal aspect of the continuity of interest test was applied by the court of appeals in McDonald's Restaurants of Illinois v. Commissioner, 688 F.2d 520 (7th Cir.1982). The court held that the merger of a number of corporations operating McDonald's franchises owned by a group of investors in exchange for McDonald's Corporation (McDonald's) stock was taxable, resulting in a stepped-up basis in the acquired assets to McDonald's. The court found that the continuity of interest test was not met because the group of investors had sold their McDonald's shares six months after receiving them from McDonald's pursuant to a plan and under demand registration rights that satisfied "the spirit, if not the letter, of the 'binding commitment' test." 688 F.2d at 525.

An analogous aspect of the temporal dimension of the continuity of shareholder interest test was whether sales of the stock of a corporation to third parties by its "historic" shareholders prior to acquisition of the corporation by an acquiring corporation could jeopardize compliance with the continuity of interest requirement. This issue played a pivotal role in the following case and provides a backdrop to the elimination in 1998 of the temporal aspect of the continuity of shareholder interest and

¶ 10,040

of the relevance of the holdings of "historic" shareholders of the acquired corporation.

[¶ 10,045]

J.E. SEAGRAM CORP. v. COMMISSIONER

United States Tax Court, 1995.
104 T.C. 75.

NIMS, JUDGE: * * *.

[The petitioner, J.E. Seagram Corp. (JES), commenced a cash tender offer for a large portion of the publicly traded stock of Conoco. Conoco thereafter entered into an agreement with DuPont Holdings, Inc. (DuPont Tenderer or DT), a subsidiary of E.I. DuPont de Nemours and Co. (DuPont), pursuant to which DT commenced a competing tender offer of cash or publicly traded DuPont stock for all the stock of Conoco. The Conoco–DT agreement called for Conoco to be merged into DT if DT acquired more than 50 percent of Conoco's stock. When withdrawal rights of tendering shareholders of Conoco under the DT tender offer expired, DT had been tendered more than 50 percent of Conoco's stock while petitioner had acquired about 32 percent. Because DT had acquired control of Conoco, petitioner tendered its Conoco stock in exchange for DuPont stock. Thereafter, Conoco merged into DT and petitioner claimed that its realized loss on the exchange of its Conoco stock for DuPont stock should be recognized on the theory that the merger did not qualify as a reorganization.]

* * *

The ultimate issue for decision is whether, for tax purposes, petitioner had a recognized loss upon the exchange of its Conoco stock for DuPont stock. Whether such a loss is to be recognized depends upon the effect to be given section 354(a)(1) under the above facts. * * *

Thus, if DuPont Tenderor, and Conoco were parties to a reorganization, and if the statutory merger of Conoco into DuPont Tenderor was in pursuance of a plan of reorganization, then no loss is to be recognized by petitioner upon the exchange of its Conoco stock for DuPont stock.

[Petitioner challenged the validity of the putative reorganization on a number of grounds, including an alleged failure to meet the continuity of shareholder interest requirement. The court had the following to say on this issue.]

* * *

We first address the question of whether Conoco's merger into DuPont was pursuant to a plan of reorganization, as contemplated by section 354(a)(1). Simply stated, petitioner claims that DuPont's tender offer and the subsequent merger squeezing out the remaining Conoco shareholders were separate and independent transactions. Consequently, petitioner argues that the exchange of Conoco stock for DuPont pursuant to DuPont's tender offer rather than pursuant to the merger could not have been in pursuance of a plan of reorganization, as section 354 requires.

* * *

Petitioner insists that the DuPont tender offer was a legally binding contract that closed prior to the merger and irrespective of whether the subsequent merger would even have been consummated. Petitioner argues that the tender offer was "plainly not a 'step' engaged in by DuPont for tax planning reasons. Rather the tender offer was the essential transaction by which DuPont obtained control of Conoco."

* * *

In *Commissioner v. Gordon*, [391 U.S. 83, 96 (1968)] * * * the Supreme Court held that * * * "if one transaction is to be characterized as a 'first step' there must be a binding commitment to take the later steps." This requirement has been met. While DuPont's acquisition of control of Conoco by means of the tender offer unquestionably had economic significance, "independent" or not, and unquestionably was not a "meaningless step," DuPont and DuPont Tenderor were under a binding and irrevocable commitment to complete the culminating merger—the second step—upon the successful completion of the DuPont tender offer—the first step.

* * *

Petitioner also argues that even if the DuPont tender offer and merger were to be treated as an integrated transaction, the merger does not qualify as a reorganization because it fails the "continuity of interest" requirement.

* * *

On the date of the Conoco/DuPont Agreement, July 6, 1981, there were approximately 85,991,896 Conoco shares outstanding. Petitioner is essentially arguing that because it acquired approximately 32 percent of these shares for cash pursuant to its own tender offer, and DuPont acquired approximately 46 percent of these shares for cash pursuant to its tender offer, the combined 78 percent of Conoco shares acquired for cash after the date of the Agreement destroyed the continuity of interest requisite for a valid reorganization. We think petitioner's argument, and the logic that supports it, miss the mark.

Pursuant to its two-step tender offer/merger plan of reorganization, DuPont acquired approximately 54 percent of the "initial" 85,992,896 shares of Conoco in exchange for DuPont stock, which included petitioner's recently acquired Conoco shares that it tendered pursuant to Du-

Pont's tender offer. If the 54 percent had been acquired by DuPont from Conoco shareholders in a "one-step" merger-type acquisition, there would be little argument that continuity of interest had been satisfied. Sec. 368(a)(1)(A).

* * *

The parties stipulated that petitioner and DuPont, through their wholly owned subsidiaries, were acting independently of one another and pursuant to competing tender offers. Furthermore, there is of course nothing in the record to suggest any prearranged understanding between petitioner and DuPont that petitioner would tender the Conoco stock purchased for cash if petitioner by means of its own tender offer failed to achieve control of Conoco. Consequently, it cannot be argued that petitioner, although not a party to the reorganization, was somehow acting in concert with DuPont, which was a party to the reorganization. If such had been the case, the reorganization would fail because petitioner's cash purchases of Conoco stock could be attributed to DuPont, thereby destroying continuity.

* * *

Petitioner cites *Yoc Heating Corp. v. Commissioner*, 61 T.C. 168, 177 (1973) for the proposition that continuity requires looking at shareholders "immediately prior to the inception of the series of transactions" in an integrated transaction. Again, we look at the facts: R, the acquiring corporation, purchased for cash over 85 percent of the stock of O, and then caused O to transfer its assets, subject to liabilities, to R's wholly owned subsidiary, N. N issued one share of its stock to R in exchange for every three shares of O held by R plus cash to be paid to the minority shareholders of O.

The Commissioner argued in *Yoc Heating* that the taxpayer's series of transactions constituted a reorganization within the meaning of section 368(a)(1)(F) or, alternatively, section 368(a)(1)(D). We held, however, that the acquisition by N of O's assets constituted a purchase under the "integrated transaction" (step transaction) doctrine, rather than a reorganization under either section proposed by the Commissioner. *Id.* at 117–178. Thus *Yoc Heating's* comparison of stock ownership immediately prior and immediately after the series of transactions is perfectly appropriate to the facts of that case, where the acquiring corporation acquired control of the target for cash and then effected the corporate combination, because the shareholders of O before the acquisition by R lacked the requisite continuing interest in the affairs of O after the acquisition.

Petitioner also attempts to apply cases involving prearranged post-acquisition sales of acquiring corporation stock by shareholders of the acquired corporation. Petitioner points out that these cases hold that a sale that was not pursuant to the plan of reorganization was fatal to continuity of interest where the sale "[established an] intent to divest * * * [the old stockholders] of their proprietary interest." *Heintz v. Commissioner*, 25 T.C. 132, 143 (1955). Petitioner also cites *McDonald's Restaurants of Illinois, Inc. v. Commissioner*, 688 F.2d 520 (7th Cir. 1982), revg. 76 T.C. 972 (1981), which involved a similar fact pattern and reached a result parallel with that in *Heintz*.

By citing *Heintz* and *McDonald's Restaurants of Illinois*, petitioner is attempting to draw an analogy between the post-reorganization sales of these cases and the sales by Conoco shareholders to petitioner during the course of the reorganization transactions in this case. We quote petitioner's memorandum:

> The Commissioner clearly would agree that there would be insufficient continuity if the public shareholders who exchanged Conoco shares for DuPont shares sold their shares of DuPont to Seagram the day after the merger. It is both inequitable and illogical to count dispositions to third parties the day after an alleged reorganization as in *Heintz* and *McDonald's*, against continuity, but not to similarly count actual dispositions made in the allegedly integrated reorganization period immediately prior to the merger.

We do not believe petitioner's analogy is appropriate, because in a case such as the one before us we must look not to the identity of the target's shareholders, but rather to what the shares represented when the reorganization was completed. In this case, a majority of the old shares of Conoco were converted to shares of DuPont in the reorganization, so that in the sense, at least, that a majority of the consideration was the acquiring corporation's stock, the test of continuity was met. In this aspect of the case step transaction and continuity questions would have arisen only had there been some preexisting intention or arrangement for the disposal of the newly acquired DuPont shares, but there were none.

Respondent points out, correctly we believe, that the concept of continuity of interest advocated by petitioner would go far toward eliminating the possibility of a tax-free reorganization of any corporation whose stock is actively traded. Because it would be impossible to track the large volume of third party transactions in the target's stock, all completed transactions would be suspect. Sales of target stock for cash after the date of the announcement of an acquisition can neither be predicted nor controlled by publicly held parties to a reorganization. A requirement that the identity of the acquired corporation's shareholders be tracked to assume a sufficient number of "historic" shareholders to satisfy some arbitrary minimal percentage receiving the acquiring corporation's stock would be completely unrealistic.

Such a mandate to look only to historic shareholder identity to determine continuity was rejected by the Supreme Court in *Helvering v. Alabama Asphaltic Limestone Co.*, 315 U.S. 179 (1942). In *Alabama*

¶ 10,045

Asphaltic, unsecured noteholders of an insolvent corporation commenced a bankruptcy proceeding against the corporation. The noteholders bought the corporate assets from the trustee and transferred them to a newly formed corporation in exchange for its stock. In discussing these facts, the Supreme Court stated:

> When the equity owners are excluded and the older creditors become the stockholders of the new corporation, it conforms to realities to date their equity ownership from the time when they invoked the processes of the law to enforce their rights of full priority. *At that time they stepped into the shoes of the old stockholders.* The sale "did nothing but recognize officially what had before been true in fact." * * *

* * *

In reaching this conclusion, the Supreme Court upheld the finding of a valid "A" reorganization by this Court. *Alabama Asphaltic Limestone Co. v. Commissioner*, 41 B.T.A. 324, 336 (1940), affd. 119 F.2d 819 (5th Cir.1941), 315 U.S. 179 (1942).

In the "integrated" transaction before us petitioner, not DuPont, "stepped into the shoes" of 32 percent of the Conoco shareholders when petitioner acquired their stock for cash via the JES competing tender offer, held the 32 percent transitorily, and immediately tendered it in exchange for DuPont stock. For present purposes, there is no material distinction between petitioner's tender of the Conoco stock and a direct tender by the "old" Conoco shareholders themselves. Thus, the requirement of continuity of interest has been met.

Petitioner extended its tender offer even after DuPont had been tendered a "significant majority" of the outstanding shares of Conoco and withdrawal rights had closed. At that time petitioner announced that it was accepting the shares tendered to it and "was seeking additional shares to increase its investment in Conoco." And as we recited earlier, petitioner, in connection with its tender of its just-acquired Conoco stock issued a press release quoting Edgar M. Bronfman, Seagram's chairman and CEO, as saying that Seagram's was pleased at the prospect of becoming "a large stockholder of the *combined DuPont and Conoco*." (Emphasis added.) We also noted that petitioner did not report a loss on the exchange of its Conoco stock for DuPont stock for financial accounting purposes. Instead, petitioner ascribed its carrying cost for its Conoco stock to the DuPont stock. None of these acts is consistent with the recognized loss petitioner claimed on its tax return.

For reasons stated in this opinion, we hold that a loss cannot be recognized by petitioner on its exchange of Conoco stock for DuPont

stock, made pursuant to the DuPont–Conoco plan of reorganization.
* * *

* * *

[¶ 10,050]

Notes

1. The relevance of sales by the shareholders of the acquired corporation to third parties either before or after an acquisitive reorganization and the need to identify historic shareholders of the acquired corporation were effectively eliminated by Reg. § 1.368–1(e), which became effective on January 28, 1998. The commentary accompanying the regulation states, in part, T.D. 8760, 1999–2 C.B. 701, as follows:

> The purpose of the continuity of interest [COI] requirement is to prevent transactions that resemble sales from qualifying for nonrecognition of gain or loss available to corporate reorganizations. The final regulations provide that the COI requirement is satisfied if in substance a substantial part of the value of the proprietary interest in the target corporation (T) is preserved in the reorganization. A proprietary interest in T is preserved if, in a potential reorganization, it is exchanged for a proprietary interest in the issuing corporation (P), it is exchanged by the acquiring corporation for a direct interest in the T enterprise, or it otherwise continues as a proprietary interest in T. The issuing corporation means the acquiring corporation (as the term is used in section 368(a)), except that, in determining whether a reorganization qualifies as a triangular reorganization (as defined in § 1.358–6(b)(2)), the issuing corporation means the corporation in control of the acquiring corporation. However, a proprietary interest in T is not preserved if, in connection with the potential reorganization, it is acquired by P for consideration other than P stock, or P stock furnished in exchange for a proprietary interest in T in the potential reorganization is redeemed. All facts and circumstances must be considered in determining whether, in substance, a proprietary interest in T is preserved.

Rationale for the COI Regulations

> The proposed and final regulations permit former T shareholders to sell P stock received in a potential reorganization to third parties without causing the reorganization to fail to satisfy the COI requirement. Some commentators have questioned whether the regulations are consistent with existing authorities. The COI requirement was applied first to reorganization provisions that did not specify that P exchange a proprietary interest in P for a proprietary interest in T. Supreme Court cases imposed the COI requirement to further Congressional intent that tax-free status be accorded only to

transactions where P exchanges a substantial proprietary interest in P for a proprietary interest in T held by the T shareholders rather than to transactions resembling sales. See LeTulle v. Scofield, 308 U.S. 415 (1940); Helvering v. Minnesota Tea Co., 296 U.S. 378 (1935); Pinellas Ice & Cold Storage Co. v. Commissioner, 287 U.S. 462 (1933). See also Cortland Specialty Co. v. Commissioner, 60 F.2d 937 (2d Cir.1932), cert. denied, 288 U.S. 599 (1933).

None of the Supreme Court cases establishing the COI requirement addressed the issue of whether sales by former T shareholders of P stock received in exchange for T stock in the potential reorganization cause the COI requirement to fail to be satisfied. Since then, however, some courts have premised decisions on the assumption that sales of P stock received in exchange for T stock in the potential reorganization may cause the COI requirement to fail to be satisfied. McDonald's Restaurants of Illinois, Inc. v. Commissioner, 688 F.2d 520 (7th Cir.1982); Penrod v. Commissioner, 88 T.C. 1415 (1987); Heintz v. Commissioner, 25 T.C. 132 (1955), nonacq., 1958–2 C.B. 9 * * *. The apparent focus of these cases is on whether the T shareholders intended on the date of the potential reorganization to sell their P stock and the degree, if any, to which P facilitates the sale. Based on an intensive inquiry into nearly identical facts, some of these cases held that as a result of the subsequent sale the potential reorganization did not satisfy the COI requirement; others held that satisfaction of the COI requirement was not adversely affected by the subsequent sale. The IRS and Treasury Department have concluded that the law as reflected in these cases does not further the principles of reorganization treatment and is difficult for both taxpayers and the IRS to apply consistently.

Therefore, consistent with Congressional intent and the Supreme Court precedent which distinguishes between sales and reorganizations, the final regulations focus the COI requirement generally on exchanges between the T shareholders and P. Under this approach, sales of P stock by former T shareholders generally are disregarded.

The final regulations will greatly enhance administrability in this area by both taxpayers and the government. The regulations will prevent "whipsaw" of the government, such as where the former T shareholders treat the transaction as a tax-free reorganization, and P later disavows reorganization treatment to step up its basis in the T assets based on the position that sales of P stock by the former T shareholders did not satisfy the COI requirement. See, e.g., McDonald's Restaurants, supra. In addition, this approach will prevent unilateral sales of P stock by former majority T shareholders from adversely affecting the section 354 nonrecognition treatment expected by former minority T shareholders.

¶ 10,050

Dispositions of T Stock

The proposed COI regulations do not specifically address the effect upon COI of dispositions of T stock prior to a potential reorganization, but ask for comments on that issue. The IRS and Treasury Department believe that issues concerning the COI requirement raised by dispositions of T stock before a potential reorganization correspond to those raised by subsequent dispositions of P stock furnished in exchange for T stock in the potential reorganization. As requested by commentators, the final regulations apply the rationale of the proposed COI regulations to transactions occurring both prior to and after a potential reorganization. Cf. J.E. Seagram Corp. v. Commissioner, 104 T.C. 75 (1995) (sales of T stock prior to a potential reorganization do not affect COI if not part of the plan of reorganization). The final regulations provide that, for COI purposes, a mere disposition of T stock prior to a potential reorganization to persons not related to P is disregarded and a mere disposition of P stock received in a potential reorganization to persons not related to P is disregarded. * * *

In soliciting comments on the effect upon COI of dispositions of T stock prior to a potential reorganization, the preamble to the proposed COI regulations specifically requests comments on King Enterprises, Inc. v. United States, 418 F.2d 511 (Ct.Cl.1969) (COI requirement satisfied where, pursuant to a plan, P acquires the T stock for 51 percent P stock and 49 percent debt and cash, and T merges upstream into P), and Yoc Heating Corp. v. Commissioner, 61 T.C. 168 (1973) (COI requirement not satisfied where, pursuant to a plan, P acquires 85 percent of the T stock for cash and notes, and T merges into P's newly formed subsidiary with minority shareholders receiving cash). Consistent with these cases, where the step transaction doctrine applies to link T stock purchases with later acquisitions of T, the final regulations provide that a proprietary interest in T is not preserved if, in connection with the potential reorganization, it is acquired by P for consideration other than P stock. Whether a stock acquisition is made in connection with a potential reorganization will be determined based on the facts and circumstances of each case. See generally § 1.368–1(a). * * *

2. As a result of the 1998 regulations, the COI requirement is met if a substantial part of the value of the proprietary interest in the acquired (or target) corporation (T) is preserved in the reorganization. In most cases, the shareholders' proprietary interest in T is preserved when their T shares are exchanged for a proprietary interest in the "issuing" corporation (P). The issuing corporation is either the acquiring corporation or, in the case of a triangular reorganization, a corporation in control of the acquiring corporation.

¶ 10,050

As long as the shareholders of T immediately before the acquisition receive stock of P (i.e., the acquiring corporation or corporation in control of it), the transaction will meet the COI test even if the T shareholders bought their T shares from third parties immediately before and in contemplation of the reorganization (as arbitrageurs frequently do) and even if the T shareholders sell to third parties the P shares they receive from P immediately after the reorganization pursuant to a pre-existing binding commitment. Thus, while the qualitative and quantitative aspects of the COI test are retained, the temporal aspects (including the focus on historic shareholders of T) of the COI are "history" in connection with corporate reorganizations except for "D" reorganizations and Section 355 transactions.

The COI test will not be met in connection with a potential reorganization, however, to the extent that P or a related person acquires T stock with consideration other than P stock or if P or a related person redeems P stock exchanged for T stock.

There are two categories of related persons for purposes of the COI test. The first category includes corporations that are members of the same affiliated group under Section 1504, without regard to the exceptions in Section 1504(b). Reg. § 1.368–1(e)(3)(i)(A). The second category includes two corporations if a purchase of the stock of one by the other would be treated as a distribution in redemption of the stock of the first under Section 304(a)(2) (determined without regard to Reg. § 1.1502–80(b)). See ¶ 5130.[1]

[¶ 10,055]

Problems

X Corporation proposes to acquire Y Corporation by statutory merger. X Corporation has outstanding 200,000 shares of no par common stock which are widely dispersed among approximately 500 shareholders. Y Corporation is closely held and has outstanding 2,000 shares of no par common stock. Y Corporation also has outstanding $800,000 of 20–year, eight-percent debentures owned by the Security Insurance Company. The fair market value of the outstanding X stock is approximately $30 per share and of the Y stock is approximately $300 per share.

1. Can the acquisition be effected as a tax-free statutory merger of Y into X if the consideration received by all of the Y shareholders consists of any one of the following alternative packages in exchange for each 100 shares of Y stock:

a. 10,000 warrants, each having a fair market value of $1 and each giving the holder the right for five years to purchase one share of X stock

---

1. Under an exception to the related person rule, the requisite proprietary interest in T is preserved to the extent that those persons who were direct or indirect owners of T prior to the potential reorganization maintain a direct or indirect proprietary interest in P. See, e.g., Rev. Rul. 84–30, 1984–1 C.B. 114.

for $32, plus 20 18–year, nine-percent $1,000 debentures issued by X, each debenture having a fair market value of $1,000. See Reg. § 1.354–1(e);

b. 300 shares of $100 nonvoting preferred stock (which is not nonqualified preferred stock) issued by X with a cumulative preferred dividend of seven percent. See John A. Nelson Co. v. Helvering, 296 U.S. 374 (1935); or

c. 100 shares of newly issued X common stock plus 27 20–year, 9–percent $1,000 debentures issued by X. See Roebling III v. Commissioner, 143 F.2d 810 (3d Cir.), cert. denied, 323 U.S. 773 (1944)?

2. Will the continuity of shareholder interest requirement be met if half of the shareholders of Y Corporation are paid exclusively with X Corporation debentures, while the remaining shareholders receive exclusively X Corporation stock?

3. In Problem 1, to what extent are the tax consequences to the shareholders of Y affected by whether there is a qualifying continuity of shareholder interest?

4. Does the fact that holders of debentures of Y Corporation exchange them for debentures issued by X Corporation have any bearing on whether the continuity of shareholder interest requirement is met? Could recognition of gain on the exchange of Y debentures for X debentures depend upon which of the packages described in Problem 1 is selected?

[¶ 10,060]

d. *Continuity of Business Enterprise Requirement*

Reg. § 1.368–1(b) provides that a prerequisite to a reorganization under the Code is "a continuity of the business enterprise" of the acquired corporation. As discussed in Chapter 9, the government's interpretation of this requirement has varied over the years. Its thinking is now reflected in Reg. § 1.368–1(d), issued in 1998, which states, in part, as follows:

(1) *General rule.* Continuity of business enterprise (COBE) requires that the issuing corporation (P) * * * either continue the target corporation's (T's) historic business or use a significant portion of T's historic business assets in a business. The application of this general rule to certain transactions, such as mergers of holding companies, will depend on all facts and circumstances. The policy underlying this general rule, which is to ensure that reorganizations are limited to readjustments of continuing interests in property under modified corporate form, provides the guidance necessary to make these facts and circumstances determinations.

While continuity of business enterprise is determined at the corporate level and continuity of interest is determined at the shareholder level, both are based on the underlying assumption that a tax-free reorganization effects only a readjustment of continuing interests under modified corporate form.

The commentary that introduced Reg. § 1.368–1(d) offered the following observations on the underlying rationale of the continuity of business enterprise test, T.D. 8760, 1998–1 C.B. 4, 6:

> The COBE requirement is fundamental to the notion that tax-free reorganizations merely readjust continuing interests in property. In § 1.368–1(d), as effective prior to these final regulations, COBE generally required the acquiring corporation to either continue a significant historic T business or use a significant portion of T's historic business assets in a business. However, a valid reorganization may qualify as tax-free even if the acquiring corporation does not directly carry on the historic T business or use the historic T assets in a business. See section 368(a)(2)(C). See also Rev. Rul. 68–261 (1968–1 C.B. 147); Rev. Rul. 81–247 (1981–1 C.B. 87).

> Consistent with the view that the acquiring corporation need not directly conduct the T business or use the T assets, the final regulations provide rules under which, in an otherwise qualifying corporate reorganization, the assets and the businesses of the members of a qualified group of corporations are treated as assets and businesses of the issuing corporation. Accordingly, in the final regulations, COBE requires that the issuing corporation either continue T's historic business or use a significant portion of T's historic business assets in a business.

> A qualified group is one or more chains of corporations connected through stock ownership with the issuing corporation, but only if the issuing corporation owns directly stock meeting the requirements of section 368(c) in at least one of the corporations, and stock meeting the requirements of section 368(c) in each of the corporations is owned directly by one of the other corporations.

> The judicial continuity of interest doctrine historically included a concept commonly known as remote continuity of interest. Commonly viewed as arising out of Groman v. Commissioner, 302 U.S. 82 (1937), and Helvering v. Bashford, 302 U.S. 454 (1938), remote continuity of interest focuses on the link between the T shareholders and the former T business assets following the reorganization. In § 1.368–1(d), as effective prior to these final regulations, COBE focuses on the continuation of T's business, or the use of T's business assets, by the acquiring corporation. Section 1.368–1(d), as revised herein, expands this concept by treating the issuing corporation as conducting a T business or owning T business assets if these activities are conducted by a member of the qualified group or, in

¶ 10,060

certain cases, by a partnership that has a member of the qualified group as a partner.

[¶ 10,065]

REVENUE RULING 81–247

1981–2 C.B. 87.

ISSUE

Will the application of the continuity of business enterprise rules of section 1.368–1(d) of the * * * Regulations to *Situations 1, 2,* and *3,* prevent the transactions between X and Y in each of the situations from qualifying as tax free reorganizations under sections 368(a)(1)(A) and (a)(2)(C) * * *?

FACTS

Situation 1:

In a transaction meant to qualify as a tax free reorganization under sections 368(a)(1)(A) and (a)(2)(C) * * *, corporation X, a holding company, acquired, under the applicable merger laws of State M, a significant portion of the historic business assets of corporation Y, a manufacturing business. Immediately thereafter, X transferred all assets received from Y to corporation Z, its wholly-owned subsidiary engaged in a manufacturing business. Z then used the assets in its manufacturing business.

Situation 2:

The facts are the same as in *Situation 1* except that X was also engaged in a manufacturing business, and X transferred less than a significant portion of Y's assets to Z and retained less than a significant part of Y's assets. Both X and Z used their respective parts of Y's assets (which together totaled more than a significant portion of the historic business assets of Y) in their separate manufacturing businesses.

Situation 3:

The facts are the same as in *Situation 1*, except that X transferred a part of the assets received from Y to each of three wholly owned manufacturing subsidiaries. The separate parts of the assets transferred to the three wholly owned subsidiaries each represented less than a significant portion of the historic business assets X received from Y. However, the total of all of the assets X transferred to the three subsidiaries represented all the assets X received from Y which, as stated above, was a significant portion of Y's historic business assets.

In none of the situations described above did X, Z or any of X's other subsidiaries, continue an historic trade or business of Y.

¶ 10,060

LAW AND ANALYSIS

Section 1.368–1(b) of the regulations provides, in part, that requisite to a reorganization is the continuity of the business enterprise under the modified corporate form.

Section 1.368–1(d) of the regulations provides the general rule that continuity of business enterprise requires that the transferee (acquiring corporation) in a corporate reorganization either (i) continue the transferor's (acquired corporation) historic business, or (ii) use a significant portion of the acquired corporation's historic business assets in a business.

The second sentence of section 1.368–1(d)(2) states that the application of this general rule to certain transactions, such as mergers of holding companies, will depend on all facts and circumstances. That section goes on to state that the policy underlying this general rule, which is to ensure that reorganizations are limited to readjustments of continuing interests in property under modified corporate form, provides the guidance necessary to make these facts and circumstances determinations.

Section 368(a)(1)(A) * * * provides that the term "reorganization" includes a statutory merger or consolidation. Section 1.368–2(b) of the regulations provides that the words "statutory merger or consolidation" refer to a merger or consolidation made under the corporation laws of the United States, a state, or territory, or the District of Columbia. Section 368(a)(2)(C) provides, in part, that a transaction otherwise qualifying under paragraph (1)(A) of section 368(a) will not be disqualified because part or all of the assets that were acquired in the transaction are transferred by the corporation to another corporation it controls.

In Rev. Rul. 68–261, 1968–1 C.B. 147, a parent corporation acquired all the assets of a target corporation. The target had conducted its business through six divisions. Immediately after the merger of the parent and the target corporation, the parent transferred the assets of each of the six divisions of the target to six wholly owned subsidiaries of the parent. The revenue ruling concludes that the transaction is a reorganization within the meaning of sections 368(a)(1)(A) and 368(a)(2)(C) * * *.

In Rev. Rul. 64–73, 1964–1 (Part I) C.B. 142, a parent corporation acquired the assets of a target corporation in a reorganization under sections 368(a)(1)(C) and 368(a)(2)(C) * * *. Some of the target assets were transferred to the parent and some of the assets were transferred to a second tier subsidiary of the parent, wholly owned by a wholly owned subsidiary of the parent. The revenue ruling states that neither the assets transferred to the subsidiary nor to the parent constituted separately substantially all of the target assets, but together constituted

¶ 10,065

all of the target's assets. The revenue ruling concludes that the transaction qualifies as a reorganization as defined in section 368(a)(1)(C).

Both Rev. Rul. 68–261 and Rev. Rul. 64–73 are consistent with the legislative intent of section 368(a)(2)(C) * * *, which permits transactions to continue to qualify as reorganizations within the meaning of section 368(a)(1)(A) and 368(a)(1)(C) whether any of the assets received by the acquiring corporation are transferred to corporations it controls.

HOLDING

The application of the continuity of business enterprise rules of section 1.368–1(d) of the regulations to *Situations 1, 2,* and *3* will not prevent the transactions between *X* and *Y,* in each of the situations, from qualifying as tax free reorganizations under sections 368(a)(1)(A) and (a)(2)(C) * * *, because the significant portion of *Y*'s historical business assets received by *X* remained with *X* or corporations directly controlled by *X.* Therefore, in *Situations 1, 2,* and *3* the mergers of *Y* into *X,* followed by the specific transfers described in each situation, are statutory mergers within the meaning of sections 368(a)(1)(A) and 368(a)(2)(C).

The above holdings regarding *Situations 1, 2,* and *3* would also apply in situations that meet the qualifications of an asset acquisition under section 368(a)(1)(C) and (a)(2)(C) or a stock acquisition within the meaning of section 368(a)(1)(B) and (a)(2)(C) * * *.

[¶ 10,070]

Note

The Tax Court in Honbarrier v. Commissioner, 115 T.C. 300 (2000), held that a merger failed to qualify as a tax free "A" reorganization because the continuity of business enterprise was not met. Reg. § 1.368–1(b). Colonial Motor Freight Line, Inc. (Colonial), all of the stock of which was owned by petitioner, Archie Honbarrier, was a trucking company operating under grants of authority from the ICC and the State of North Carolina. In 1988, as a result of financial losses, Colonial ceased business operations. By August 1992, Colonial had sold all of its operating assets except its ICC authority and invested the proceeds almost exclusively in about $7 million worth of tax-exempt bonds and a municipal bond fund. Some of these bonds and the fund were converted to approximately $2.5 million of cash immediately before the merger. Central Transport, Inc. (Central) was a highly successful trucking company engaged in the transport of liquid and dry chemicals under authorities from the ICC, various states, and Canada. Central held working capital in the form of short-term liquid assets, such as certificates of deposit. It did not invest in tax-exempt securities. All of Central's stock was owned by Mr. and Mrs. Honbarrier and their children. On December 31, 1993, Colonial was merged into Central, and Mr. Honbarrier received shares of Central in exchange for his Colonial shares. The court found that Colonial had abandoned its trucking business well before the merger and, at the time of the merger, Colonial's historic business was acquiring and holding tax-exempt bonds worth about $4.5 million. Three days after the merger these tax-exempt bonds were distributed to Mr. Honbarrier. The court held that the continuity of business enterprise requirement of Reg. § 1.368–1(d)(3)(i) was not met because Central did not use in its business a significant portion of Colonial's historic business assets. Consequently, the merger was taxable and Mr. Honbarrier had a recognized gain of about $7 million.

[¶ 10,075]

Problems

1.   As part of a plan, T Corporation sells all of the assets of its hardware business on June 1 for cash, then on September 1 merges into P Corporation with the T shareholders receiving P shares. Is the COBE requirement met?

2.   If the facts are the same as in Problem 1, except that all of the stock of T Corporation is acquired solely for stock of P Corporation, is the COBE requirement met?

3.   Assume that the facts are the same as in Problem 1, except that T Corporation reinvests the proceeds of the sale of its hardware business in a portfolio of stock and securities, which it manages until November 1, when T Corporation merges into P Corporation, a regulated investment company. Is the COBE requirement met?

4.   T Corporation is engaged in the retail paint business and the wholesale paint business each of which produces about 50 percent of T's revenue. On February 1, T Corporation merges into P Corporation. P Corporation immediately sells the retail paint business for cash and operates only the wholesale paint business. Is the COBE requirement met?

5.   T Corporation manufactures tennis rackets. P Corporation owns all of the stock of SB1, SB1 owns all of the stock of SB2 and SB2 owns all of the stock of SB3. T merges into SB1 and the T shareholders receive P shares in return for their T stock. As part of the plan and for bona fide business reasons, SB1 transfers all of the T assets to SB2 and SB2 transfers all of these assets to SB3, which is engaged already in the manufacture of tennis balls. Is the COBE requirement met?

3.   "C" REORGANIZATION

[¶ 10,080]

a.   The Concept of "Substantially All of the Properties"

The "C" reorganization definition requires the acquisition of "substantially all of the properties" of the transferor corporation by the

¶ 10,080

transferee corporation. And, as we will see in subsequent sections in this Chapter, with the word "assets" substituted for "properties," this is also a requirement of transactions qualifying as "D" reorganizations in which the transferor corporation distributes stock of the controlled corporation in liquidation under Section 354. Similarly, in forward and reverse triangular mergers under Section 368(a)(2)(D) and (E) there is a requirement that the surviving subsidiary acquire (or retain) substantially all of the properties of the acquired corporation.

Rev. Proc. 77–37, 1977–2 C.B. 568, states that the IRS will rule favorably on a "substantially all" question where "there is a transfer * * * of assets representing at least 90 percent of the fair market value of the net assets and at least 70 percent of the fair market value of the gross assets held by the corporation immediately prior to the transfer." All payments by the transferor corporation to its shareholders who dissent, amounts used to pay reorganization expenses, and all redemptions and distributions (except for regular, normal distributions) which were made by the corporation immediately preceding the transfer and which are part of the plan of reorganization will be considered as assets held by the corporation immediately prior to the transfer. Rev. Proc. 86–42, 1986–2 C.B. 722. These revenue procedures only state the ruling policy of the IRS and are not an attempt to determine the outer limits of "substantially all." Indeed, those limits cannot be described by a simple mechanical formula; the kind of assets that are not transferred and the use made of the nontransferred assets are of primary importance. The retention of a large amount of cash or accounts receivable may be approved, particularly if used to satisfy creditors, whereas retention of a similar amount of operating assets would disqualify the transaction.

[¶ 10,085]

REVENUE RULING 57–518

1957–2 C.B. 253.

The M and N corporations were engaged in the fabrication and sale of various items of steel products. For sound and legitimate business reasons, N corporation acquired most of M corporation's business and operating assets. Under a plan of reorganization, M corporation transferred to N corporation (1) all of its fixed assets (plant and equipment) at net book values, (2) 97 percent of all its inventories at book values, and (3) insurance policies and other properties pertaining to the business. In exchange therefor, N corporation issued shares of its voting common stock to M corporation.

The properties retained by M corporation include cash, accounts receivable, notes, and three percent of its total inventory. The fair market value of the assets retained by M was roughly equivalent to the amount of its liabilities. M corporation proceeded to liquidate its retained properties as expeditiously as possible and applied the proceeds to its outstanding debts. The property remaining after the discharge of all its liabilities was turned over to *N* corporation, and *M* corporation was liquidated.

Section 368 * * *, in defining corporate reorganizations, provides in part:

(a) REORGANIZATION.—

(1) IN GENERAL.—* * * the term "reorganization" means—

* * *

(C) The acquisition by one corporation, in exchange solely for all or a part of its voting stock (or in exchange solely for all or a part of the voting stock of a corporation which is in control of the acquiring corporation), of substantially all of the properties of another corporation, * * *.

The specific question presented is what constitutes "substantially all of the properties" as defined in the above section of the Code. The answer will depend upon the facts and circumstances in each case rather than upon any particular percentage. Among the elements of importance that are to be considered in arriving at the conclusion are the nature of the properties retained by the transferor, the purpose of the retention, and the amount thereof. In *Milton Smith, et al. v. Commissioner*, 34 B.T.A. 702 * * * withdrawing nonacquiescence, C.B. XV–2, 46 (1936), a corporation transferred 71 percent of its gross assets. It retained assets having a value of $52,000, the major portion of which was in cash and accounts receivable. It was stated that the assets were retained in order to liquidate liabilities of approximately $46,000. Thus, after discharging its liabilities, the outside figure of assets remaining with the petitioner would have been $6,000, which the court stated was not an excessive margin to allow for the collection of receivables with which to meet its liabilities. No assets were retained for the purpose of engaging in any business or for distribution to stockholders. In those circumstances, the court held that there had been a transfer of "substantially all of the assets" of the corporation. The court very definitely indicated that a different conclusion would probably have been reached if the amount retained was clearly in excess of a reasonable amount necessary to liquidate liabilities. Furthermore, the court intimated that transfer of all of the net assets of a corporation would not qualify if the percentage of gross assets transferred was too low. Thus, it stated that, if a corporation having gross assets of $1,000,000 and liabilities of $900,000 transferred only the net assets of $100,000, the result would probably not come within the intent of Congress in its use of the words "substantially all."

[In] the instant case, of the assets not transferred to the corporation, no portion was retained by *M* corporation for its own continued use inasmuch as the plan of reorganization contemplated *M*'s liquidation.

¶ 10,085

Furthermore, the assets retained were for the purpose of meeting liabilities, and these assets, at fair market values, approximately equaled the amount of such liabilities. Thus, the facts in this case meet the requirements established in the case of *Milton Smith, supra.*

* * *

[¶ 10,090]

Notes

1. Why should there be a "substantially all" requirement? Should retention of assets not needed in the business (such as excess cash) ever prevent satisfaction of the requirement? What limits are appropriate with respect to the amount and type of assets retained to discharge liabilities? Rather than requiring the transfer of substantially all the properties of a corporate entity, should the definition simply require the transfer of substantially all the properties of a single active business? This would allow a corporation having several active businesses to qualify by transfer of what might be well under 50 percent of its total assets. This would also permit the transferor to split its businesses tax-free between two corporations. These results would not appear to be appropriate because Section 355, discussed in Chapter 12, provides a special set of requirements that must be met if a division of corporate businesses between two or more corporations is to qualify as tax-free. Thus, the substantially all requirement of the "C" reorganization (and of the forward and reverse triangular mergers and the nondivisive "D" reorganization) helps preserve the integrity of the Section 355 requirements for tax-free corporate divisions.

2. Section 368(a)(2)(G) requires that the acquired corporation in a "C" reorganization be liquidated unless a waiver is granted by the IRS. The sole purpose for which such a waiver will be granted is preservation of the corporate charter of the acquired corporation for sale to an unrelated party for whom it may have value (e.g., because the corporation held a bank charter). Rev. Proc. 89–50, 1989–2 C.B. 631. This liquidation requirement has effectively eliminated some of the significance of the substantially all requirement in the context of the "C" reorganization because the corporation from which the assets are acquired can no longer be the repository of operating assets not transferred to the acquiring corporation.

[¶ 10,095]

b. Disposition of Unwanted Assets and the Substantially All Requirement

The "substantially all" requirement still has a potentially important role to play when the acquired corporation has significant assets that the acquiring corporation does not want to acquire. As noted at ¶ 10,080,

¶ 10,085

redemptions or other dispositions of assets by the acquired corporation before the acquisition of its assets in a "C" reorganization and as part of the same plan of reorganization are taken into account in determining whether substantially all of the properties of the acquired corporation have been acquired by the acquiring corporation. The same is generally true of the other reorganizations that have a substantially all requirement. The risk posed to a "C" reorganization by certain dispositions by the acquired corporation of assets not wanted by the acquiring corporation has its roots in the following decision.

[¶ 10,100]

HELVERING v. ELKHORN COAL CO.

United States Court of Appeals, Fourth Circuit, 1937.
95 F.2d 732, cert. denied, 305 U.S. 605 (1938).

[The Elkhorn Coal & Coke Company (Elkhorn or old company) transferred certain unwanted mining properties to a newly created corporation (new corporation) on December 18. The new corporation's shares were immediately distributed to the shareholders of Elkhorn in a spin-off transaction that qualified for nonrecognition of gain under Section 203(h)(1)(A), the statutory predecessor of Sections 355 and 368(a)(1)(D). Then, as part of the same plan, on December 31, Elkhorn transferred its remaining mining assets to Mill Creek Coal & Coke Company (Mill Creek) for voting stock and assumption of liabilities in what purported to be a "C" reorganization.]

* * *

The Board [of Tax Appeals] was of opinion that all of these transactions were carried through pursuant to prearranged plan, saying: "We do not doubt that before a single step was taken a plan had been formulated for regrouping the corporate assets"; and "The stipulated facts justify the inference that one of the motives which the stockholders of Elkhorn had in organizing the new corporation and causing the three corporations to adopt the several steps or plans of reorganization which were adopted and carried out, was to make the transfer of the mining properties from Elkhorn to Mill Creek without resulting tax liability to Elkhorn or to themselves." The Board thought, however, with five members dissenting, that because the transfers from the old company to the new were genuine and were separate and distinct from the transfer to the Mill Creek Company, the latter must be treated as a transfer of substantially all of the properties of the corporation within the meaning of the reorganization statute, summing up its conclusions as follows: "In our opinion, the facts show affirmatively that the transfer to Mill Creek was completely separate and distinct from the earlier transfer by Elkhorn to the new corporation. The transfer made on December 18 was complete within itself, regardless of what Elkhorn planned to do later, or

¶ 10,100

did subsequently do. It was not a sham or a device intended to obscure the character of the transaction of December 31. The stipulated facts do not suggest other than a bona fide business move. The transfer made on December 31, was also complete within itself, and was made for reasons germane to the business of both corporations. This transfer falls within the terms of clause (A) of section 203(h)(1), whether or not Elkhorn was dissolved.''

While we are bound by the Board's findings of evidentiary facts, we are not bound by the foregoing conclusion set forth in the opinion and embodying a mixed question of law and fact. As said by the Supreme Court in the recent case of Helvering v. Tex–Penn Oil Co., 300 U.S. 481, * * *: "The ultimate finding is a conclusion of law or at least a determination of a mixed question of law and fact. It is to be distinguished from the findings of primary, evidentiary, or circumstantial facts. It is subject to judicial review and, on such review, the court may substitute its judgment for that of the Board.''

A careful consideration of the evidentiary facts discloses no purpose which could have been served by the creation of the new company and the transfer of the assets to it, except to strip the old company of all of its properties which were not to be transferred to the Mill Creek Company, in anticipation of that transfer. The creation of the new company and its acquisition of the assets of the old was not a corporate reorganization, therefore, within the meaning of the statute or within any fair meaning of the term "reorganization." It did not involve any real transfer of assets by the business enterprise or any rearranging of corporate structure, but at most a mere shifting of charters, having no apparent purpose except the avoidance of taxes on the transfer to the Mill Creek Company which was in contemplation. To use in part the language of the Supreme Court in Gregory v. Helvering, 293 U.S. 465, 469, * * * it was "simply an operation having no business or corporate purpose—a mere device which put on the form of a corporate reorganization as a disguise for concealing its real character, and the sole object and accomplishment of which was the consummation of a preconceived plan, not to reorganize a business or any part of a business," but to give to the intended transfer to the Mill Creek Company the appearance of a transfer of all the corporate assets so as to bring it within the nonrecognition provision of section 203(h)(1)(A).

* * *

It is suggested in the opinion of the Board that the case before us is analogous to that which would have been presented if the old company, prior to the transfer to Mill Creek, had distributed to its stockholders all of the assets except those destined for such transfer; but the distinction is obvious. In the case supposed, the business enterprise would have definitely divested itself of the property distributed. Here it did not divest itself of the property at all, but merely made certain changes in

¶ 10,100

the legal papers under which it enjoyed corporate existence. No rule is better settled than that in tax matters we must look to substance and not to form; and no one who looks to substance can see in the mere change of charters, which is all that we have here, any reason for permitting a transfer of a part of the corporate assets to escape the taxation to which it is subject under the statute.

Congress has seen fit to grant nonrecognition of profit in sale or exchange of assets only under certain conditions, one of which is that one corporation shall transfer "substantially all" of its properties for stock in another. If nonrecognition of profit can be secured by the plan adopted in this case, the exemption is broadened to cover all transfers of assets for stock, whether "substantially all" or not, if only the transferor will go to the slight trouble and expense of getting a new charter for his corporation and making the transfer of assets to the new corporation thus created in such way as to leave in the old only the assets to be transferred at the time the transfer is to be made. We do not think the statutory exemption may be thus broadened by such an artifice.

Having reached this conclusion, it is unnecessary to decide whether the unity of the plan under which the transfer was made brings it, without a unifying contract, within the principles laid down in Starr v. Commissioner (C.C.A. 4th) 82 F.(2d) 964, 968, wherein we said: "Where transfers are made pursuant to such a plan of reorganization, they are ordinarily parts of one transaction and should be so treated in application of the well-settled principle that, in applying income tax laws, the substance, and not the form, of the transaction shall control. * * * This is demanded also by the principle, equally well settled, that a single transaction may not be broken up into various elements to avoid a tax. * * * "

For the reasons stated, the decision of the Board will be reversed, and the cause will be remanded to it for further proceedings in accordance with this opinion.

Reversed.

[Dissenting opinion has been omitted.]

[¶ 10,105]

REVENUE RULING 88–48

1988–1 C.B. 117.

* * *

X and Y were unrelated corporations that for many years were engaged in the hardware business. X operated two significant lines of business, a retail hardware business and a wholesale plumbing supply business. Y desired to acquire and continue to operate X's hardware business but did not desire to acquire the other business. Accordingly, pursuant to an overall plan, the following steps were taken. First, in a taxable transaction, X sold its entire interest in the plumbing supply business (constituting 50 percent of its total historic business assets) to purchasers unrelated to either X or Y or their shareholders. Second, X transferred all of its assets, including the cash proceeds from the sale, to Y solely for Y voting stock and the assumption of X's liabilities. Finally, in pursuance of the plan of reorganization, X distributed the Y stock (the sole asset X then held) to the X shareholders in complete liquidation.

Except for the issue relating to the "substantially all" requirement, the transfer of assets from X to Y constituted a corporate reorganization within the meaning of section 368(a)(1)(C) * * *.

LAW AND ANALYSIS

Section 368(a)(1)(C) * * * defines a corporate reorganization to include the acquisition by one corporation, in exchange solely for all or part of its voting stock, of substantially all the properties of another corporation.

Section 368(a)(1)(C) * * * is intended to accommodate transactions that are, in effect, mergers, but which fail to meet the statutory requirements that would bring them within section 368(a)(1)(A). *See* S. Rep. No. 558, 73d Cong., 2d Sess. 16, 17 (1939) * * *.

Congress intended that transactions that are divisive in nature not qualify under section 368(a)(1)(C) * * *, but, instead, be subject to the tests under section 368(a)(1)(D). *See* S. Rep. No. 1622, 83d Cong., 2d Sess. 274 (1954). The enactment of section 368(a)(2)(G) indicates the continuing interest in furthering this underlying objective of preventing divisive "C" reorganizations.

Rev. Rul. 57–518, 1957–2 C.B. 253, concerns whether, in a "C" reorganization, assets may be retained to pay liabilities. The ruling states that what constitutes "substantially all" for purposes of section 368(a)(1)(C) * * * depends on the facts and circumstances in each case. Rev. Rul. 57–518 exemplifies the Service's longstanding position that where some assets are transferred to the acquiring corporation and other assets retained, then the transaction may be divisive and so fail to meet the "substantially all" requirement of section 368(a)(1)(C). *See also* Rev. Rul. 78–47, 1978–1 C.B. 113.

In the present situation, 50 percent of the X assets acquired by Y consisted of cash from the sale of one of X's significant historic businesses. Although Y acquired substantially all the assets X held at the time of transfer, the prior sale prevented Y from acquiring substantially all of X's historic business assets. The transaction here at issue, however, was not divisive. The sale proceeds were not retained by the transferor corporation or its shareholders, but were transferred to the acquiring corporation. Moreover, the prior sale of the historic business assets was to unrelated purchasers, and the X shareholders retained no interest, direct or indirect, in these assets. Under these circumstances, the "substantially all" requirement of section 368(a)(1)(C) was met because all of the assets of X were transferred to Y.

HOLDING

The transfer of all of its assets by X to Y met the "substantially all" requirement of section 368(a)(1)(C) * * *, even though immediately prior to the transfer X sold 50 percent of its historic business assets to unrelated parties for cash and transferred that cash to Y instead of the historic assets.

[¶ 10,110]

Notes

1. Because the basic purpose of the substantially all test is to prevent tax-free divisive asset transfers that fail to meet the special requirements imposed on such transfers by Sections 355 and 368(a)(1)(D), the court's conclusion in *Elkhorn* seems eminently reasonable. Why does the IRS conclude that the transaction in Rev. Rul. 88–48, at ¶ 10,105, is not divisive?

2. The *Elkhorn* decision, at least as decided by the Board of Tax Appeals, involves an early analysis of what came to be called the step transaction doctrine, under which interrelated steps may be treated as a single integrated transaction for purposes of the reorganization provisions. See ¶ ¶ 9065 through 9075. The Board of Tax Appeals rejected the application of the doctrine. The court of appeals, having held the spin-off to be an artifice, apparently concluded that it did not have to reach the question of whether the step transaction doctrine was applicable.

3. The outer limits of the *Elkhorn* decision remain somewhat uncertain. For example, suppose the unwanted assets are sold to an unrelated party and the proceeds are distributed to the shareholders of the *acquired* corporation before the acquisition of the wanted assets in a putative "C" reorganization. Alternatively, suppose the acquired corporation distributes the unwanted assets to its shareholders in a taxable distribution in redemption of some of their stock before a putative "C" reorganization. In these cases the transaction does not involve a tax-free division of corporate assets between two corporations, and arguably *Elkhorn* should not be controlling. Do the *Elkhorn* case and Rev. Rul. 88–48, at ¶ 10,105, provide guidance with respect to these transactions?

Moreover, there is no substantially all test applicable to a straight (i.e., non-triangular) "A" reorganization or to a "B" reorganization. Thus, a disposition of an unwanted business by a corporation can precede a qualifying tax-free non-triangular merger of that corporation with another corporation. It can also precede a qualifying "B" reorganization. However, if the pre-acquisition disposition takes the form of a tax-free spin-off under Section 355 of a controlled subsidiary after a transfer to it of the unwanted business, special rules apply. See the discussion at ¶¶ 12,100 et seq.

[¶ 10,115]

c.   The Solely for Voting Stock Requirement; The Boot–Relaxation Rule

Although Section 368(a)(1)(C) defines the "C" reorganization as the acquisition of substantially all of the properties of the acquired corporation solely in exchange for voting stock of the acquiring corporation (or a corporation in control of it), it goes on to provide that the solely for voting stock test will be met even if liabilities of the acquired corporation are shifted to the acquiring corporation. As discussed in Chapter 2, in the absence of a special statutory provision to the contrary, the assumption of liabilities could be characterized as the transfer of money to the target to pay off its debt and therefore treated as something other than stock.

A significant revision of the "C" reorganization definition is contained in Section 368(a)(2)(B), which is frequently referred to as the boot-relaxation rule. This rule permits up to 20 percent of the fair market value of all of the property of the acquired corporation to be acquired for money or other property (i.e., for boot). Thus, 20 percent of the consideration paid may take the form of boot. While this appears to be good news, the bad news is that if any boot is included in the consideration package along with voting stock of the acquiring corporation (or its parent), all liabilities of the acquired corporation shifted to the acquiring corporation are treated as boot.

In most cases, the boot-relaxation rule is without practical effect. Because most corporations have liabilities that exceed 20 percent of the value of their assets, if any consideration other than voting stock and assumed liabilities of the acquired corporation is involved, liabilities will be considered boot, the boot-relaxation test will not be met, and the acquisition will not qualify as a "C" reorganization.

Prior to 2000, the acquisition of assets of a corporation in which the acquirer was already a 20 percent or more owner of the stock posed potential problems under the boot-relaxation rule. This became known as the "*Bausch & Lomb* problem" after the court's decision in Bausch & Lomb Optical Co. v. Commissioner, 267 F.2d 75 (2d Cir.), cert. denied, 361 U.S. 835 (1959). In this case, Bausch & Lomb owned 79.9 percent of Riggs and acquired all of the assets of Riggs in exchange for Bausch & Lomb stock. Riggs then liquidated and the Bausch & Lomb stock was distributed to the former Riggs' stockholders, including back to Bausch & Lomb. The court held that the transaction did not qualify as a "C" reorganization because 79.9 percent of the Riggs assets was acquired, not in exchange for voting stock of Bausch & Lomb, but as a liquidating distribution in exchange for the 79.9 percent of Riggs stock previously owned by Bausch & Lomb. Since 79.9 percent of the assets was acquired in exchange for Riggs shares, the transaction could not qualify as an acquisition of substantially all of the Riggs properties in exchange for Bausch & Lomb voting stock. *Bausch & Lomb* sustained the position of the IRS previously articulated in Rev. Rul. 54–396, 1954–2 C.B. 147. Based on a substantially identical fact situation the ruling stated, in part:

> * * * Under the circumstances presented, the M corporation, already the owner of 79 percent of N corporation stock, acquired only the remaining 21 percent of the assets of N through the exchange of stock. The remaining 79 percent of the assets were acquired by M as a liquidating dividend in exchange for the stock of N which had been acquired by cash purchase in prior years.

The court in *Bausch & Lomb* emphasized that the transaction failed to meet the formal requirements of the definition of "C" reorganization:

> * * * [T]he Congress has defined in Section 112(g)(1)(C) [predecessor of Section 368(a)(1)(C)] how a reorganization thereunder may be effected, and the only question for us to decide * * * is whether the necessary requirements have been truly fulfilled. It is for the Congress and not for us to say whether some other alleged equivalent set of facts should receive the same tax free status.

> * * *

> Of course, the fact that Bausch & Lomb "could have" merged with Riggs and hence qualified the transaction as a reorganization under Section 112(g)(1)(A) [predecessor of Section 368(a)(1)(A)] is beside the point. For reasons of its own it chose not to do so. This is clearly not an "A" reorganization.

267 F.2d at 77.

In 2000, Reg. § 1.368–2(d)(4)(i) was amended to reverse the result in *Bausch & Lomb*. This regulation provides that prior ownership of more than 20 percent of the stock of Target does not generally prevent qualification of a transaction described in *Bausch & Lomb* from qualifying as a "C" reorganization. From a policy point of view this change was long overdue, particularly since it reflected the reality that had the *Bausch & Lomb* transaction been differently structured, it would have been tax-free.

[¶ 10,120]

Problems on the "C" Reorganization

Method One: Acquirer acquires all of the assets of Target (and assumes the $100,000 bank debt) for 450,000 shares of Acquirer voting common stock and $50,000 cash.

Target liquidates, distributing the 450,000 shares of Acquirer common stock and the $50,000 cash to its shareholders.

Can this qualify as a "C" reorganization under Section 368(a)(1)(C) and (a)(2)(B)?

Has Acquirer acquired the properties of Target "solely for * * * its voting stock" within the meaning of Section 368(a)(1)(C)? Under Section 368(a)(1)(C) must Acquirer's assumption of the $100,000 bank debt be regarded as consideration in addition to the Acquirer voting stock? Has Acquirer acquired 80 percent of the fair market value of Target's property "solely for voting stock" under the boot-relaxation rule of Section 368(a)(2)(B)?

Method Two: Target uses its $80,000 of cash to pay off $80,000 of its bank loan. Following this, Acquirer acquires all the remaining assets of Target in exchange for 450,000 shares of its common stock and $50,000 in cash and assumes the remaining $20,000 bank debt.

Target liquidates, distributing to its shareholders the 450,000 Acquirer shares and the $50,000 cash.

Can this qualify as a "C" reorganization? Did Acquirer acquire "substantially all of the properties" of Target? Did Acquirer satisfy the "solely for * * * voting stock" requirement of Section 368(a)(2)(B)(iii)? Does meeting the latter test turn on whether the repayment of $80,000 of the bank loan was pursuant to, or independent of, the acquisition plan?

Method Three: Target transfers all of its property to Acquirer except for $50,000 in cash, which it retains. Acquirer gives Target in exchange 450,000 shares of its common stock and assumes the $100,000 bank debt.

Following this, Target liquidates, distributing to its shareholders the 450,000 shares of Acquirer common stock and the $50,000 cash.

Can this qualify as a "C" reorganization? Did Acquirer acquire "substantially all of the properties" of Target? Did Acquirer satisfy the "solely for voting stock" requirement of Section 368(a)(1)(C)?

4. "B" REORGANIZATION

[¶ 10,125]

a. The Solely for Voting Stock Requirement; No Boot in a "B"

The solely for voting stock requirement of the "B" reorganization definition is not tempered by any statutory exception like the boot-relaxation rule in the "C" reorganization. See ¶ 10,115. The question was bound to arise whether "solely" was intended by Congress to be as inflexible as the statutory terminology would seem.

¶ 10,120

[¶ 10,130]

TURNBOW v. COMMISSIONER

Supreme Court of the United States, 1961.
368 U.S. 337.

MR. JUSTICE WHITTAKER delivered the opinion of the Court.

* * *

The facts are simple and undisputed. Petitioner owned all of the 5,000 shares of outstanding stock of International Dairy Supply Company ("International"), a Nevada corporation. In 1952, petitioner transferred all of the International stock to Foremost Dairies, Inc. ("Foremost"), a New York corporation, in exchange for 82,375 shares (a minor percentage) of Foremost's common (voting) stock of the fair market value of $15 per share or $1,235,625 *plus cash* in the amount of $3,000,000. Petitioner's basis in the International stock was $50,000, and his expenses in connection with the transfer were $21,933.06. Petitioner therefore received for his International stock property and money of a value exceeding his basis and expenses by $4,163,691.94.

In his income tax return for 1952, petitioner treated his gain as recognizable only to the extent of the cash he received. The Commissioner concluded that the whole of the gain was recognizable and accordingly proposed a deficiency. * * *

Because of the arbitrary and technical character, and of the somewhat "hodgepodge" form, of the statutes involved, the interpretation problem presented is highly complicated; and although both parties rely upon the "plain words" of these statutes, they arrive at diametrically opposed conclusions. That plausible arguments can be and have been made in support of each conclusion must be admitted; and, as might be expected, they have hardly lightened our inescapable burden of decision.

* * * By definition, contained in § 112(g)(1)(B) [1939 Code predecessor of Section 368(a)(1)(B), which is materially different], the term "reorganization" means "the acquisition by one corporation, in exchange *solely* for all or a part of its voting stock, of at least 80 per centum of the ... stock of another corporation." (Emphasis added.) This type of reorganization is commonly called a "(B) reorganization."

There is no dispute between the parties about the fact that the transaction involved was not a "reorganization," as defined in § 112(g)(1)(B), because "the acquisition by" Foremost was not "in exchange *solely* for ... its voting stock," but was partly for such stock and partly for cash. *Helvering v. Southwest Consolidated Corp.*, 315 U.S. 194. Nor is there any dispute that the transaction was not actually within the terms of § 112(b)(3) [predecessor of Section 354(a)(1)] because the exchange was not of "stock ... in ... a party to a reorganization," "in pursuance of [a] plan of reorganization," nor "for stock . . . in another corporation [which was] a party to the reorganization."

But petitioner contends that § 112(c)(1) [predecessor of Section 356(a)(1)] authorizes the indulging of assumptions, contrary to the actual facts, hypothetically to supply the missing elements that are necessary to make the exchange a "reorganization," as defined in § 112(g)(1)(B) and as used in § 112(b)(3), and the case turns on whether that is so. Section 112(c)(1) provides:

> "Gains from exchanges not solely in kind. (1) If an exchange would be within the provisions of subsection (b)(1), (2), (3), or (5), or within the provisions of subsection (1), of this section if it were not for the fact that the property received in exchange consists not only of property permitted by such paragraph or by subsection (1) to be received without the recognition of gain, but also of other property or money, then the gain, if any, to the recipient shall be recognized, but in an amount not in excess of the sum of such money and the fair market value of such other property."

Centering upon this section, petitioner argues that "if it were not for the fact that the property [he] received in [the] exchange" consisted not only of voting stock—"property permitted [by § 112(b)(3)] to be received [if in a corporation which is a party to a reorganization] without the recognition of gain"—but also of cash, the exchange *would have been* a "reorganization," as defined in § 112(g)(1)(B), because, in that case, "the acquisition by" Foremost would have been "in exchange *solely* for . . . its voting stock"; and the exchange also *would have been* within the terms of § 112(b)(3) because, in that case, the exchange would have been of "stock . . . in . . . a party to a reorganization," "in pursuance of [a] plan of reorganization," and "for stock . . . in another corporation [which was] a party to the reorganization." Petitioner then argues that inasmuch as his transaction *would have been* a "reorganization," as defined in § 112(g)(1)(B) and used in § 112(b)(3), and hence "would [have been] within the provisions of subsection (b) . . . (3)," "if it were not for the fact that the property [he] received" consisted "not only of" voting stock "but also of . . . money," § 112(c)(1) authorizes the *assumption*, as respects the Foremost stock he received, that the exchange *was* a "reorganization," as defined in § 112(g)(1)(B) and used in § 112(b)(3), and hence precludes recognition of his gain "in excess of the . . . money" he received.

But we cannot agree that § 112(c)(1) authorizes the assumption, contrary to the actual facts, of a "reorganization," as defined in § 112(g)(1)(B) and used in § 112(b)(3). To indulge such an assumption would actually be to permit the negation of Congress' carefully composed definition and use of "reorganization" in those subsections, and to permit nonrecognition of gains on what are, in reality, only sales, the full gain from which is immediately recognized and taxed under the general rule of § 112(a). To the contrary, we think that an actual "reorganization," as defined in § 112(g)(1) and used in § 112(b)(3) must exist before § 112(c)(1) can apply thereto. We are also agreed that § 112(c)(1) can apply only if the exchange actually consists *both* of "property permitted by [subsection (b)(1), (2), (3), or (5), or subsection (1) of § 112] ... to be received without the recognition of gain" *and* "other property or money." And we think it is clear that the "property permitted by [§ 112(b)(3)] ... to be received without the recognition of gain" is "stock or securities in ... a party to a reorganization" "in pursuance of [a] plan of reorganization," and "for stock ... in such corporation or in another corporation [which is] a party to the reorganization." Since, as is admitted, none of the property involved in this exchange actually met that description, none of it was "property permitted by [§ 112(b)(3)] ... to be received without the recognition of gain," and therefore § 112(c)(1) does not apply to postpone recognition of petitioner's gain from the Foremost stock.

This, of course, is not to say that § 112(c)(1) is without purpose or function. It is to say only that it does not apply unless some part, at least, of the property exchanged *actually* meets the particular description contained in the applicable section or subsection of the Code. But, inasmuch as § 112(g)(1)(B) defines "reorganization" to mean "the acquisition by one corporation, in exchange solely for all or a part of its voting stock, of at least 80 per centum of the ... stock of another corporation," an exchange of stock *and* cash—approximately 30 per centum in stock and 70 per centum in cash—for "at least 80 per centum of the ... stock of another corporation" cannot be a "reorganization," as defined in § 112(g)(1)(B), nor hence of "stock ... in ... a party to a reorganization" as required by § 112(b)(3), and thus § 112(c)(1) cannot be applicable to petitioner's transaction. That holding determines this case and is all we decide.

Affirmed.

* * *

[¶ 10,135]

Notes

1. Compare the "B" reorganization definition contained in Section 112(g)(1)(B) with the lengthier Section 368(a)(1)(B) of the 1986 Code. Notice particularly the difference in language bearing on control. Whereas Section 112(g)(1)(B) required the acquisition of 80 percent of the stock of the acquired corporation in the transaction, Section 368(a)(1)(B) requires only that the acquiring corporation be in control immediately after the acquisition. This change allowed "creeping control" to meet the control test. See ¶ 10,140.

¶ 10,135

2. In Heverly v. Commissioner, 621 F.2d 1227 (3d Cir.1980), cert. dismissed, 451 U.S. 1012 (1981), the issue was whether the acquisition by the International Telephone and Telegraph Corporation (ITT) of stock of the Hartford Fire Insurance Company constituted a "B" reorganization. In November 1968, ITT purchased six percent of the Hartford stock for cash and between November 1968 and January 1969 purchased another two percent for cash. For purposes of the proceeding, which was a motion for summary judgment, it was assumed that these purchases were made "for the purpose of furthering ITT's efforts to acquire Hartford."

In May 1970, ITT made an exchange offer to all Hartford shareholders, offering to exchange ITT voting stock for stock of Hartford. Pursuant to this offer it acquired from independent parties more than 80 percent of Hartford's then outstanding stock. Following the transaction, ITT owned more than 95 percent of all Hartford stock. The court in *Heverly* stated:

> The major issue presented by these consolidated appeals from the United States Tax Court and the United States District Court for the District of Delaware is whether the use of consideration other than voting stock is allowable in a tax deferred stock for stock reorganization as defined in § 368(a)(1)(B) * * *. In the vernacular, the question is whether "boot" may be used in a clause B corporate reorganization. Both courts below agreed with the taxpayers that other consideration is allowable so long as "control" of the target corporation is obtained "solely for ... voting stock," and thus allowed them to defer recognition of their gain under § 354(a)(1) * * *. We hold that, in a stock for stock transaction in which control is achieved, the acquiring corporation may exchange no consideration other than voting stock to effect a tax deferred clause B reorganization. * * *

621 F.2d at 1228.

One of taxpayer's arguments was that not allowing boot in a "B" reorganization would result in a peculiar mismatch in the reorganization provisions because of Section 368(a)(2)(B), which allows boot in a "C" reorganization. As to this the court noted:

> The provision allowing cash or other property in a clause C transaction was added in 1954. * * * Contrary to what taxpayers argue, this provision, § 368(a)(2)(B), does not allow substantially more flexibility in clause C transactions than in clause B transactions. If cash or other property is given, the liabilities assumed by the acquiring corporation must be included in the total twenty percent allowable nonstock consideration, whereas the assumption of liabilities need not be counted against the solely for voting stock requirement if no nonstock consideration is exchanged. Thus, since provision must be made for creditors, and since rarely will the transferor

corporation have less than twenty percent of its asset value encumbered by liabilities, the apparent permissibility of cash or other property under clause C is almost inevitably illusory. We believe Congress was fully aware of, and probably intended, this limitation on nonstock consideration under clause C. * * *

621 F.2d at 124. The First Circuit also concluded that there can be no boot in a "B" reorganization in the case of another Hartford Fire shareholder-taxpayer involved in the same ITT–Hartford acquisition. Chapman v. Commissioner, 618 F.2d 856 (1st Cir.1980), cert. dismissed, 451 U.S. 1012 (1981).

The finding of disqualifying boot in the ITT acquisition of Hartford assumed for purposes of the motion for summary judgment that the 1968 and 1969 cash transactions (or at least one of them) had to be considered together with the 1970 stock-for-stock transaction. The Third Circuit remanded this question for consideration by the trial courts. Whether two steps should, for tax purposes, be considered as separate or as part of a single transaction under the step transaction doctrine is considered at ¶ 9065.

3. The solely for voting stock requirement is common to the "B" and the "C" reorganizations. As noted in ¶ 10,115, the boot-relaxation rule of Section 368(a)(2)(B) permits some boot in a "C," but because, if there is any consideration other than voting stock and assumed liabilities, the liabilities are also treated as boot, and because most businesses have substantial liabilities, any boot will usually disqualify a putative "C" reorganization.

4. The solely for voting stock requirement relates only to the consideration paid by the acquiring corporation to the shareholders of the acquired corporation for the stock of the acquired corporation. Therefore, a stock-for-stock acquisition will not be disqualified as a "B" reorganization if the acquiring corporation pays off or assumes liabilities of the acquired corporation, lends funds to the acquired corporation, or pays cash to shareholders of the acquired corporation as consideration for something other than their shares in the acquired corporation. The acquiring corporation may also make capital contributions to, or may purchase stock directly from, the acquired corporation without disqualifying the transaction as a "B" reorganization, provided that none of the cash is distributed to, or used for the benefit of, the acquired corporation's shareholders. Rev. Rul. 72–522, 1972–2 C.B. 215. Moreover, prior to and as a part of a "B" reorganization, the acquired corporation may redeem its own shares so long as the cash does not come from the acquiring corporation.

5. One significant relaxation of the rule that there can be no boot in a "B" reorganization (and the similar rule that applies as a practical matter to most "C" reorganizations) is that the acquiring corporation may pay cash to the acquired corporation's shareholders in lieu of

issuing fractional shares, so long as the cash represents merely a mechanical rounding off of the fractions in the exchange and is not separately bargained for consideration. Rev. Rul. 66–365, 1966–2 C.B. 116. This de minimis exception is adopted to eliminate the administrative inconvenience to the acquiring corporation of having to deal with fractional shares.

6. A problem that has involved considerable uncertainty over the years is whether assumption and payment by the acquiring corporation of certain liabilities of the acquired corporation related to the reorganization constitute boot. The IRS has ruled that the acquiring corporation may assume and pay expenses of the acquired corporation and its shareholders that are "solely and directly related to" a "B" or "C" reorganization, such as underwriting and SEC registration costs, legal and accounting fees, finder's fees, administrative costs, appraisal fees, transfer taxes, and transfer agents' fees. The acquiring corporation may not, however, transfer cash to the acquired corporation or its shareholders so that they can pay these expenses, and the acquiring corporation may not pay other expenses of those shareholders, such as legal, accounting, and investment advisory fees. Rev. Rul. 73–54, 1973–1 C.B. 187. Except for the rare case in which the boot-relaxation rule under Section 368(a)(2)(B) applies, in a "C" reorganization the acquiring corporation may not assume the acquired corporation's liability to redeem the shares of dissenters because the liability runs to its shareholders with respect to their stock. Rev. Rul. 73–102, 1973–1 C.B. 186.

7. Payment by the acquiring corporation of its own expenses in registering its stock is not boot even though registration facilitates the disposition by the acquired corporation's shareholders of the shares of the acquiring corporation they receive. The theory is that the registration promotes the orderly marketing of the acquiring corporation's shares. Rev. Rul. 67–275, 1967–2 C.B. 142.

8. If the shareholders of the acquired corporation receive, in addition to acquiring corporation voting stock, an option to purchase additional shares of this stock or a right exercisable within five years (see ¶ 10,040) to require the acquiring corporation to redeem the shares (i.e., a "put"), the option or put would probably constitute disqualifying boot. See Rev. Rul. 70–108, 1970–1 C.B. 78. If, however, voting stock of the acquiring corporation received by shareholders of the acquired corporation is convertible without further payment into another class of stock (e.g., voting preferred convertible into common), the conversion feature is treated as an attribute of the convertible stock rather than as boot.

If the shareholders of the acquired corporation are granted a contingent right to receive additional voting shares of the acquiring corporation without making any additional payment (for example, as a bonus if the post-acquisition earnings of the acquired corporation exceed a specified level), the contingent right is not considered boot. James Hamrick v.

Commissioner, 43 T.C. 21 (1964) (acq.). Similarly, shares of the acquiring corporation held in escrow to be released to the acquired corporation's shareholders upon the occurrence of certain events (e.g., if the acquired corporation meets certain post-acquisition goals) will not constitute boot. The IRS has issued guidelines indicating the circumstances under which it will issue favorable rulings in situations involving contingent or escrowed stock. Rev. Proc. 77–37, 1977–2 C.B. 568, as amplified by Rev. Proc. 84–42, 1984–1 C.B. 521. In the case of contingent stock arrangements, if adequate interest on delayed issuances of stock is not stated, the imputed interest or original discount rules apply. See §§ 483, 1274, and 1275.

[¶ 10,140]

b.   *The Creeping "B" Reorganization*

Section 368(a)(1)(B) does not require the acquiring corporation to acquire 80 percent of the outstanding stock in the acquisition under consideration; the acquiring corporation must simply be in "control" (as defined in Section 368(c)) immediately after the acquisition. Assume Acquirer had acquired 500 of the 1,000 outstanding shares of Target in a separate transaction five years ago. Even if it had acquired those shares solely for cash in a taxable transaction, Acquirer could now comply with Section 368(a)(1)(B) by acquiring only 300 additional Target shares solely for its voting stock because, following that acquisition, it would be in control of Target. Indeed, if Acquirer had purchased 800 shares of Target five years ago, it could now engage in a "B" reorganization by the acquisition of only one Target share. (However, the reorganization would obviously have limited effect: nonrecognition of gain and carryover of basis would apply only to the Target shareholder disposing of the single share.) The process of acquiring 80 percent of the stock of a corporation in two or more separate transactions is often said to involve acquisition of "creeping control" and the tax-free acquisition of Target stock as a creeping "B" reorganization. But note that the earlier acquisition or acquisitions, if not solely for voting stock, must be independent of the current acquisition. If Acquirer, as part of the same transaction, acquired 100 shares of Target for cash and 700 for Acquirer voting stock, there would be no "B" reorganization because the "solely for voting stock" requirement would not be met. See Reg. § 1.368–2(c).

[¶ 10,145]

Problems on the "B" Reorganization

Method One: Acquirer acquires all of the outstanding shares of Target from the Target shareholders. In exchange for each share of Target stock, Acquirer gives nine shares of Acquirer stock and $1 cash.

Can this qualify as a "B" reorganization? Would the exchanges by the Target shareholders qualify under Section 356(a)(1)? Would Section

354 have applied to the exchange if only Acquirer stock had been received?

Method Two: Acquirer purchases 5,000 shares of Target stock from shareholder Smith for $50,000. Smith owns no other Target shares.

As part of the same transaction, Acquirer acquires the other 45,000 Target shares from the other Target shareholders for 450,000 shares of Acquirer stock.

Can the transaction constitute a "B" reorganization?

Method Three: Target redeems 5,000 shares of Target stock from shareholder Smith for $50,000. Smith owns no other Target shares and is not related to any other Target shareholder.

As part of the same transaction, Acquirer acquires the other 45,000 Target shares from the other Target shareholders for 450,000 shares of Acquirer stock.

Can the transaction constitute a "B" reorganization?

Method Four: Target shareholders, collectively, borrow $50,000 on the security of their Target corporation stock. Following this borrowing, Acquirer acquires all the Target stock, subject to the $50,000 liability, from the Target shareholders for 450,000 shares. Can this qualify as a "B" reorganization? See United States v. Hendler, 303 U.S. 564 (1938), discussed at ¶ 10,305. Suppose the Target shareholders had borrowed the $50,000 on their Target stock five years earlier, before they had thought of selling out to Acquirer?

C. TRIANGULAR REORGANIZATIONS

[¶ 10,150]

1. BACKGROUND

Triangular acquisitive reorganizations, so-called because they involve a third corporation in addition to the acquired and acquiring corporations, may take a number of forms. For example, the acquiring corporation may acquire the assets or stock of the acquired corporation in exchange for shares of a corporation in control of the acquiring corporation or the acquiring corporation may acquire the assets or stock of the acquired corporation in exchange for the acquiring corporation's stock and then the acquired assets or stock may be dropped down to a subsidiary of the acquiring corporation.

Both of these transactions encountered early roadblocks in the form of Supreme Court decisions which adopted what came to be known as the "remote continuity of interest doctrine." In 1937, the Supreme Court in Groman v. Commissioner, 302 U.S. 82 (1937), decided that the continuity of shareholder interest test was not met when transferors of stock of the acquired corporation received stock of the acquiring corpora-

¶ 10,145

tion's parent corporation rather than of the acquiring corporation itself. An equity interest in the parent of the acquiring corporation was too remote from the acquired property. The same result was reached in Helvering v. Bashford, 302 U.S. 454 (1938), in which the acquired properties were transferred to the parent corporation itself and were then transferred by it to a wholly owned subsidiary.

Over the years Congress has greatly limited the remote continuity of interest doctrine by specifically authorizing a broad range of triangular acquisitive transactions. An "A" reorganization may be cast as a forward triangular merger under Section 368(a)(2)(D) or as a reverse triangular merger under Section 368(a)(2)(E). Parenthetical phrases in the definitions of the "B" and "C" reorganizations permit use of stock of a parent corporation in control (as defined in Section 368(c)) of the corporation acquiring stock or assets of the acquired corporation, and under Section 368(a)(2)(C), assets or stock acquired by an acquiring corporation may be dropped down to an 80–percent owned subsidiary without disqualifying the transaction as an "A," "B," or "C" reorganization. Under Section 368(b), all of the corporations participating in a qualifying triangular reorganization are treated as parties to the reorganization.

Changes made in 1998 to Reg. § 1.368–1(b) and (d) curtail even further the remote continuity doctrine for purposes of the continuity of shareholder interest requirement, discussed at ¶ 10,040, and the continuity of business enterprise requirement, discussed at ¶ 10,060. These regulations permit transfers or successive transfers of acquired assets or stock under Section 368(a)(2)(C) to members of a "qualified group" of corporations or to partnerships under specified circumstances without disqualifying the acquisition transaction as an "A," "B," "C," or "G" reorganization. (Section 368(a)(2)(C) does not apply by its terms to acquisitive "D" or to "F" reorganizations.)

"Qualified group" is defined as one or more chains of corporations connected through stock ownership meeting the 80–percent test of Section 368(c). For purposes of the continuity of business enterprise test, a corporate transferor partner will be treated as conducting the business of a partnership to which assets have been transferred if such partner has an active and substantial management function in the partnership business or the partner's interest in the partnership is significant.

[¶ 10,155]

2. TRIANGULAR "B" AND "C" REORGANIZATIONS AND FORWARD TRIANGULAR MERGERS

The earlier arrivals to the triangular scene included the triangular "B" and "C" reorganizations and the forward triangular merger. The adjective "triangular" derives from the fact that the corporate vehicle actually used to implement the acquisition is a controlled subsidiary of the acquiring corporation the shares of which are received by the former shareholders of the acquired corporation in exchange for their acquired corporation shares.

In the case of triangular "B" and "C" reorganizations, the transactions must still meet the stricter requirements for consideration specified in those types of reorganizations. By contrast, under Section 368(a)(2)(D), a merger of an acquired corporation into a subsidiary controlled by an acquiring corporation, called a forward triangular or forward subsidiary merger, may qualify as a statutory merger under Section 368(a)(1)(A). Stock of the acquiring parent corporation is received by the former shareholders of the acquired corporation in exchange for their acquired corporation stock.

To qualify for the looser consideration permitted for an "A" reorganization, the forward triangular merger must meet several requirements, not all of which are applied in a normal statutory merger. Under Section 368(a)(2)(D), a forward triangular merger will qualify as a statutory merger if (i) substantially all of the properties of the acquired corporation are acquired by a subsidiary in exchange for stock of a corporation in control of it, (ii) the transaction would have qualified as a statutory merger if the merger had been into the controlling corporation, and (iii) no stock of the acquiring subsidiary is used.

Consider the scope of these triangular forms of reorganization in connection with the following Problems.

[¶ 10,160]

Problems

1. Parent, Inc., owns all of the outstanding stock of Subsidiary Corporation. It wants Subsidiary to obtain all the assets of Target Corporation, an unrelated corporation. The Target shareholders will not approve any transaction unless it is completely tax-free. They are willing to exchange their Target stock for an appropriate number of shares of either Parent or Subsidiary or both. Parent, however, is not willing to issue any Subsidiary shares in the transaction since, for ease of management, it wants to continue to own all of Subsidiary's stock. The transaction must therefore be done with Parent stock. Thus, Target shareholders exchange their Target shares for Parent shares.

Consider the following plan: Parent transfers an appropriate number of shares of its voting stock to Subsidiary. Subsidiary thereupon acquires all of the Target assets and liabilities in exchange for the Parent stock. Target then liquidates, distributing the Parent stock to its shareholders.

a. Does the transaction qualify as a reorganization within the meaning of Section 368(a)(1)(C)? Did Target exchange its properties "solely for stock * * * in another corporation a party to the reorganization" within the meaning of Section 361(a)? Did the Target shareholders, on the liquidation of Target, exchange their Target shares "solely for stock * * * in another corporation a party to the reorganization" within the meaning of Section 354(a)(1)? See § 368(b). What is Subsidiary's basis in the former assets of Target? See § 362(b). What is the basis of Parent in the stock of Subsidiary after the reorganization? See Reg. § 1.358–6(c)(1).

b.   Suppose in the above transaction Subsidiary acquired all the properties of Target and gave as consideration half Parent stock and half its own stock. Would this constitute a reorganization pursuant to Section 368(a)(1)(C)? See Reg. § 1.368–2(d)(1). Suppose 80 percent of the consideration given by Subsidiary consisted of its own stock and 20 percent of Parent stock. Would this constitute a reorganization pursuant to Section 368(a)(1)(C)? Would the answer depend on whether the Target properties were transferred free of liabilities? Is Reg. § 1.368–2(d)(1) supported by the language of the Code? Is it appropriate as a matter of policy?

c.   Suppose Parent acquired all the assets of Target in exchange for stock of Subsidiary. Would the transaction qualify as a "C" reorganization?

d.   Suppose Parent owns all the stock of Subsidiary and Subsidiary owns all the stock of Grand–Sub. Could an acquisition of all the properties of Target qualify as a "C" reorganization if Subsidiary acquired the properties solely for voting stock of Parent and then transferred them to Grand–Sub? Could it qualify if Grand–Sub acquired the properties directly, using solely voting stock of Parent? Could it qualify if Parent acquired the properties using solely its own voting stock and then transferred the properties through Subsidiary to Grand–Sub? See Rev. Rul. 64–73, 1964–1 C.B. 142, which analyzed the transaction as an acquisition by Parent that qualified under Section 368(a)(2)(C).

2.   Suppose Parent transfers an appropriate number of shares of its voting stock to Subsidiary. Subsidiary thereupon acquires 90 percent of the shares of Target in exchange for the Parent stock. Does the transaction qualify as a "B" reorganization? What is Parent's basis in the shares of Subsidiary after the reorganization? See Reg. § 1.358–6(c)(3). What is Subsidiary's basis in the shares of Target? See § 362(b). Would the transaction qualify as a "B" reorganization if Subsidiary transferred the shares acquired by it to Grand–Sub?

3.   Suppose after the transfer of Parent shares to Subsidiary, Target merged into Subsidiary and the Target shareholders exchanged their Target shares for the shares of Parent held by Subsidiary. Assume that the transaction qualifies as a merger under applicable state law. Does it constitute a reorganization under Section 368(a)(1)(A)? Do the exchanges by the Target shareholders of their Target shares for Parent shares qualify under Section 354(a)? See Section 368(a)(2)(D), which provides that merging Target into Subsidiary in exchange for shares of

Parent qualifies as a forward triangular merger if the statutory requirements are met. These requirements include:

(i) Subsidiary (the acquiring corporation) must acquire "substantially all of the properties" of Target. See the discussion of the similar requirements of the "C" reorganization at ¶ 10,080.

(ii) No stock of Subsidiary may be used.

(iii) The transaction would have qualified as a statutory merger under Section 368(a)(1)(A) if Target had been merged into Parent.

The third requirement taken literally would seem to disqualify the forward triangular merger if for some reason under applicable state or federal law, Target could not have been merged into Parent. The regulations indicate, however, that this requirement simply confirms that the judicially developed business purpose, continuity of shareholder interest, and continuity of business enterprise requirements must be fulfilled. These requirements, which would have to be met if Target were merged into Parent, must also be met if the forward triangular merger is to qualify as a tax-free reorganization under Section 368(a)(2)(D). Reg. § 1.368–2(b)(2).

What is the basis of Parent in the stock of Subsidiary after the reorganization? See Reg. § 1.358–6(c)(1).

Note that pursuant to Section 368(a)(2)(C), Parent could acquire the assets of Target in a direct statutory merger and immediately transfer all or part of the assets to Subsidiary. Under the corporate law of many states this would require a vote of Parent's shareholders to approve the merger, and dissenters would normally have a right to have their Parent shares redeemed by Parent at their appraised value. This factor often makes use of a forward triangular merger or a reverse triangular merger attractive; in a triangular merger only Parent (Subsidiary's sole shareholder) need approve the merger on the acquiring corporation side.

4. Suppose Parent transfers the stock of its acquiring subsidiary (S) to another controlled subsidiary (S1) of Parent as part of a plan of reorganization, following the merger of Target into S. Will it qualify as a forward triangular merger even though, under the step transaction doctrine, S1, a second-tier subsidiary, could be recast as the acquirer of Target assets, which would eliminate Parent's control? See Rev. Rul. 2001–24, 2001–1 C.B. 182. Under this type of circumstance, the IRS elected not to apply the step transaction doctrine because if S had merged into Target, under Reg. § 1.368(2)(k)(2), the transaction would have qualified as a reverse triangular merger under Section 368(a)(2)(E) even if the stock (or assets) of the surviving corporation (Target) were transferred to a subsidiary or sub-subsidiary controlled by the transferor, and the legislative history of Section 368(a)(2)(E) suggests that forward and reverse triangular mergers should be treated similarly. See S. Rep. No. 1533, 91st Cong., 2d Sess. 2 (1970). In 2004, Treasury issued

¶ 10,160

proposed regulations that would codify the principle announced in Rev. Rul. 2001–24 by expanding Reg. § 1.368–2(k)(1), which already permitted transfers to controlled subsidiaries in "A," "B,", "C," and "G" reorganizations, to other reorganizations. See Prop. Reg. § 1.368–2(k) (2004).

[¶ 10,165]

3. REVERSE TRIANGULAR MERGER

The difficulty with the forward triangular merger is that the Target has to merge out of existence. Sometimes, because of certain franchises or tax benefits held by the Target, the parties desire the Target to continue in existence as a legal entity while still utilizing the convenience of the triangular form. Prior to enacting Section 368(a)(2)(E) in 1971, Treasury issued the following ruling to address such a circumstance.

[¶ 10,170]

REVENUE RULING 67–448

1967–2 C.B. 144.

Advice has been requested whether the transaction described below qualifies as a reorganization within the meaning of section 368(a)(1)(B) * * *.

Corporation P and Corporation Y, incorporated in the same state, are publicly owned corporations. Corporation P wanted to acquire the business of Corporation Y but could do so with an effective result only if the corporate entity of Y were continued intact due to the necessity of preserving its status as a regulated public utility. P also desired to eliminate the possibility of minority shareholders in the event less than all of the shareholders of Y agreed to the transaction. Since an outright acquisition of stock pursuant to a reorganization as defined in section 368(a)(1)(B) * * * would not achieve this result, the plan of reorganization was consummated as follows:

(a) P transferred shares of its voting stock to its newly formed subsidiary, S, in exchange for shares of S stock.

(b) S (whose only asset consisted of a block of the voting stock of P) merged into Y in a transaction which qualified as a statutory merger under the applicable state law.

(c) Pursuant to the plan of reorganization and by operation of state law, the S stock owned by P was converted into Y stock. At the same time the Y stock held by its shareholders was exchanged for the P stock received by Y on the merger of S into Y. The end result of these actions was that P acquired from the shareholders of Y in exchange for its own voting stock more than 95 percent of the stock of Y.

(d) Y shareholders owning less than five percent of the stock of Y dissented to the merger and had the right to receive the appraised value of their shares paid solely from the assets of Y. No funds, or other property, have been or will be provided by P for this purpose.

Thus, upon the consummation of the plan of reorganization Y became a wholly owned subsidiary of P.

At the time of the transaction P had no plan or intention to liquidate Y or to merge it into any other corporation.

The transaction described above does not constitute a reorganization within the meaning of either section 368(a)(1)(A) or section 368(a)(1)(C) * * * because no assets of Y were transferred to nor acquired by another corporation in the transaction but rather all assets (except for amounts paid to dissenting shareholders) were retained in the same corporate entity.

Section 368(a)(1)(B) * * * provides in part that the term "reorganization" means the acquisition by one corporation, in exchange solely for all or a part of its voting stock, of stock of another corporation if, immediately after the acquisition, the acquiring corporation has control of such other corporation (whether or not such acquiring corporation had control immediately before the acquisition).

It is evident that the shortest route to the end result described above would have been achieved by a transfer of P voting stock directly to the shareholders of Y in exchange for their stock. This result is not negated because the transaction was cast in the form of a series of interrelated steps. The transitory existence of the new subsidiary, S, will be disregarded. The effect of all the steps taken in the series is that Y became a wholly owned subsidiary of P, and P transferred solely its voting stock to the former shareholders of Y.

Accordingly, the transaction will be treated as an acquisition by P, in exchange solely for part of its voting stock, of stock of Y in an amount constituting control (as defined in section 368(c) * * *) of Y, which qualifies as a reorganization within the meaning of section 368(a)(1)(B) * * *.

[¶ 10,175]

Notes

1. What practical or business advantages might this reverse merger "B" reorganization under Rev. Rul. 67–448 have over a straight "B" reorganization? Over a forward triangular "A" reorganization under Section 368(a)(2)(D)?

2. One of the problems with classifying the transaction in Rev. Rul. 67–448 as a "B" reorganization is that it subjects parties to the zero boot tolerance rule of Section 368(a)(1)(B). A few years later, however Congress created the reverse triangular merger under Section 368(a)(2)(E), which accomplishes the same result without being classified as a "B" reorganization. Like the forward triangular merger, however, the transaction must satisfy several requirements in addition to the judicial doctrines applied to the "A" reorganization. These include that—

(i) the surviving corporation (the acquired corporation) hold substantially all of its properties and of the properties of the merged corporation (other than stock of the controlling corporation) (again, "substantially all" has the same meaning as in the case of the "C" reorganization, see ¶ 10,080), and

(ii) the shareholders of the surviving (acquired) corporation must exchange acquired corporation stock constituting "control," as defined in Section 368(c), for voting stock of the acquiring corporation.

As a result of the second requirement, the reverse triangular merger is not available if the acquiring corporation has already acquired over 20 percent of the stock of the acquired corporation in an independent transaction. However, assuming that the acquiring corporation owns no stock in the acquired corporation, the Section 368(a)(2)(E) merger permits acquisition of up to 20 percent of the stock of the acquired corporation for boot in the acquisition transaction and in that regard is more flexible than the reverse merger "B" reorganization under Rev. Rul. 67–448 in which no boot could be used. Note also that Target can pay off dissenters with cash or other property and their shares are not counted in determining whether "control" has been acquired for acquiring corporation voting stock. Reg. § 1.368–2(j)(3)(i). This disposition of cash or property, however, is taken into account in applying the "substantially all" test. Reg. § 1.368–2(j)(3)(iii).

3. One commentator suggests that Section 368(a)(2)(E) was passed to accommodate the transaction of a particular taxpayer that could not comply with the requirements of Rev. Rul. 67–448:

The Committee Reports recommending passage of the new provision afford little insight into either the problems impelling the legislation or the anticipated consequences of its enactment.

Reputedly, pursuant to the pressure of a prominent corporation which found itself in tax difficulties, Congress chose to create the new "E" type reorganization. The author understands that after the initial legislation was drafted to help this company, it was sent over to the Treasury Department because Treasury complained that the draft opened up too many loopholes. Congress told Treasury it was free to write as many restrictions as it wished into Subsection E provided that the company in question was relieved of its tax difficulties. Consequently, it is not surprising that the legislative history did not shed too much light on the background of the unusual statutory requirements of the section.

Stutsman, "Triangular Mergers," 50 Taxes 820, 825–26 (1972).

That history could explain the convoluted, makeshift nature of the section. Certainly there is little explanation in the legislative history. The House Ways and Means Committee report stated simply that the Committee "sees no reason why a merger in one direction should be taxable when a merger in the other direction [under Section 368(a)(2)(D)], in identical circumstances, is tax-free. Moreover, it sees no reason why in cases of this type the acquisition needs to be made solely for stock." H.R. Rep. No. 1778, 91st Cong., 2d Sess. 2 (1970).

Despite its narrow purpose, the reverse triangular merger has been widely used. One of its principal advantages is that, like the reverse merger treated as a "B" reorganization in Rev. Rul. 67–448, the reverse triangular merger keeps the acquired corporation intact; its assets are not transferred and its attributes are not altered. This may be important if the acquired corporation enjoys a special status, such as that of a regulated public utility, or holds assets that would be difficult or impossible to transfer or that could be transferred only with the consent of another party. Such assets might include franchises, leases, licenses, and interests in joint ventures.

4. Does the target corporation (Target) "hold" substantially all of its properties and the properties of the merged corporation, under Section 368(a)(2)(E), if Target sells for cash a substantial portion of its assets after the merger and retains the cash proceeds? Rev. Rul. 2001–25, 2001–1 C.B. 1291, holds that a transaction that otherwise qualifies as a reverse triangular merger under Section 368(a)(2)(E) will not be disqualified if, as part of the plan of reorganization, the Target sells 50 percent of its assets for cash to an unrelated corporation after the reverse merger and retains the cash proceeds. This result is consistent with Rev. Rul. 88–48, 1988–1 C.B. 117, which holds that the "substantially all" test of the "C" reorganization is met if before the acquisition the Target sells a substantial part of its assets for cash and transfers the cash proceeds and its remaining assets to the acquiring corporation.

[¶ 10,180]

Problems

Consider the following Section 368(a)(2)(E) transaction. Parent, pursuant to Section 351, forms Subsidiary, transferring to Subsidiary voting stock of Parent in exchange for all of Subsidiary's stock. Subsidiary merges into Target. All Target shareholders exchange their Target shares for the Parent voting stock held by Subsidiary. Parent exchanges its Subsidiary shares for Target shares.

¶ 10,175

1. What is the basis of Parent Stock in Subsidiary's hands? See Rev. Rul. 74–503, 1974–2 C.B. 117, holding that whether Parent stock is treasury stock or newly issued stock, its basis in subsidiary's hands is zero.

2. Does Subsidiary have gain recognized on the disposition of Parent stock? What provision applies? Suppose for some reason (e.g., failure to meet the substantially all test or failure to acquire "control" of Target stock) the transaction fails to qualify under Section 368(a)(2)(E). Will Subsidiary have gain recognized? Is there any way to avoid this?

3. What is the basis of Parent in the stock of Target? See Reg. § 1.358–6(c)(2).

4. What are the advantages of a reverse triangular merger under Section 368(a)(2)(E) over a reverse merger characterized as a "B" reorganization under Rev. Rul. 67–448?

5. Can a reverse triangular merger that fails to qualify under Section 368(a)(2)(E) qualify as a "B" reorganization? Suppose Acquirer owns 21 percent of Target stock before the acquisition? See Reg. § 1.368–2(j)(6), Exs. 4 and 5. Suppose Target disposes of substantial unwanted assets before but in contemplation of the acquisition? What are the advantages of Rev. Rul. 67–448 over Section 368(a)(2)(E)?

D. MULTI–STEP ACQUISITIONS

[¶ 10,185]

It is often said that in the case of mergers and acquisitions, tax drives the structure of the transaction. While this is true in most cases, there are times when considerations such as regulatory restrictions, securities laws, stock exchange rules, loan covenants, and other non-tax elements require a multi-step transaction. For example, parties may desire to acquire sufficient control as a first step in order to effect the larger transaction without requiring the consents of the dissenting shareholders. In multi-step transactions, the parties typically seek to have the step transaction doctrine (discussed at ¶¶ 9065–9075) applied to qualify the transaction as a reorganization, notwithstanding the fact that some or all of the individual steps would not so qualify.

In recent years, the IRS has treated such multi-step transactions flexibly so as to allow the parties to comply with the requirements of the reorganization provisions. For example, in Rev. Rul. 2001–26, 2001–1 C.B. 1297, the IRS concluded that a reverse triangular merger may be preceded by a tender offer by the acquiring corporation for stock of the target corporation. Under the facts of that ruling, the first step was a tender offer by the Parent corporation for 51 percent of the stock of the Target solely for Parent voting stock. Then, as a second step, Parent formed a wholly owned subsidiary, Corporation S, which merged into

Target in a reverse statutory merger. Each of the Target shareholders holding the remaining 49 percent of the Target stock received a combination of consideration consisting of two-thirds voting stock and one-third cash. The ruling assumes that under the step transaction doctrine, the two steps are treated as parts of an integrated acquisition by Parent of all of the Target stock, and holds that the integrated transaction qualifies as a reverse triangular merger under Section 368(a)(2)(E). The result is the same if the tender offer is initiated by S and it acquires 51 percent of the Target stock for Parent stock provided by Parent prior to the merger of S into Target.

While Rev. Rul. 2001-26 assumed that the step transaction doctrine would apply to permit integration of the two steps, the following ruling provides potential guidance for the application of that principle in a multi-step acquisition.

[¶ 10,190]

REVENUE RULING 2001–46

2001–2 C.B. 321.

* * *

Issue

Under the facts described below, what is the proper tax treatment if, pursuant to an integrated plan, a newly formed wholly owned subsidiary of an acquiring corporation merges into a target corporation, followed by the merger of the target corporation into the acquiring corporation?

Facts

Situation (1)

Corporation X owns all the stock of Corporation Y, a newly formed wholly owned subsidiary. Pursuant to an integrated plan, X acquires all of the stock of Corporation T, an unrelated corporation, in a statutory merger of Y into T (the "Acquisition Merger"), with T surviving. In the Acquisition Merger, the T shareholders exchange their T stock for consideration, 70 percent of which is X voting stock and 30 percent of which is cash. Following the Acquisition Merger and as part of the plan, T merges into X in a statutory merger (the "Upstream Merger"). Assume that, absent some prohibition against the application of the step transaction doctrine, the step transaction doctrine would apply to treat the Acquisition Merger and the Upstream Merger as a single integrated acquisition by X of all the assets of T. Also assume that the single integrated transaction would satisfy the nonstatutory requirements of a reorganization under § 368(a) of the Internal Revenue Code.

¶ 10,185

Situation (2)

The facts are the same as in Situation (1) except that in the Acquisition Merger the T shareholders receive solely X voting stock in exchange for their T stock, so that the Acquisition Merger, if viewed independently of the Upstream Merger, would qualify as a reorganization under § 368(a)(1)(A) by reason of § 368(a)(2)(E).

Law

Section 338(a) provides that if a corporation makes a qualified stock purchase and makes an election under that section, then the target corporation (i) shall be treated as having sold all of its assets at the close of the acquisition date at fair market value and (ii) shall be treated as a new corporation which purchased all of its assets as of the beginning of the day after the acquisition date. Section 338(d)(3) defines a qualified stock purchase as any transaction or series of transactions in which stock (meeting the requirements of § 1504(a)(2)) of one corporation is acquired by another corporation by purchase during a 12–month acquisition period. Section 338(h)(3) defines a purchase generally as any acquisition of stock, but excludes acquisitions of stock in exchanges to which § 351, § 354, § 355, or § 356 applies.

Rev. Rul. 90–95 (1990–2 C.B. 67) (Situation 2), holds that the merger of a newly formed wholly owned domestic subsidiary into a target corporation with the target corporation shareholders receiving solely cash in exchange for their stock, immediately followed by the merger of the target corporation into the domestic parent of the merged subsidiary, will be treated as a qualified stock purchase of the target corporation followed by a § 332 liquidation of the target corporation. As a result, the parent's basis in the target corporation's assets will be the same as the basis of the assets in the target corporation's hands. The ruling explains that even though "the step-transaction doctrine is properly applied to disregard the existence of the [merged subsidiary]," so that the first step is treated as a stock purchase, the acquisition of the target corporation's stock is accorded independent significance from the subsequent liquidation of the target corporation and, therefore, is treated as a qualified stock purchase regardless of whether a § 338 election is made.

Section 1.338–3(d) of the Income Tax Regulations incorporates the approach of Rev. Rul. 90–95 into the regulations by requiring the purchasing corporation (or a member of its affiliated group) to treat certain asset transfers following a qualified stock purchase (where no § 338 election is made) independently of the qualified stock purchase. In the example in § 1.338–3(d)(5), the purchase for cash of 85 percent of the stock of a target corporation, followed by the merger of the target corporation into a wholly owned subsidiary of the purchasing corporation, is treated (other than by certain minority shareholders) as a

¶ 10,190

qualified stock purchase of the stock of the target corporation followed by a § 368 reorganization of the target corporation into the subsidiary. As a result, the subsidiary's basis in the target corporation's assets is the same as the basis of the assets in the target corporation's hands.

Section 368(a)(1)(A) defines the term "reorganization" as a statutory merger or consolidation. Section 368(a)(2)(E) provides that a transaction otherwise qualifying under § 368(a)(1)(A) shall not be disqualified by reason of the fact that stock of a corporation (controlling corporation), which before the merger was in control of the merged corporation, is used in the transaction if (i) after the transaction, the corporation surviving the merger holds substantially all of its properties and the properties of the merged corporation, and (ii) in the transaction, former shareholders of the surviving corporation exchange, for an amount of voting stock of the controlling corporation, an amount of stock in the surviving corporation which constitutes control of such corporation.

In Rev. Rul. 67–274 (1967–2 C.B. 141), Corporation Y acquires all of the stock of Corporation X in exchange for some of the voting stock of Y and, thereafter, X completely liquidates into Y. The ruling holds that because the two steps are parts of a plan of reorganization, they cannot be considered independently of each other. Thus, the steps do not qualify as a reorganization under § 368(a)(1)(B) followed by a liquidation under § 332, but instead qualify as an acquisition of X's assets in a reorganization under § 368(a)(1)(C).

Analysis

Situation (1)

Because of the amount of cash consideration paid to the T shareholders, the Acquisition Merger could not qualify as a reorganization under § 368(a)(1)(A) and § 368(a)(2)(E). If the Acquisition Merger and the Upstream Merger in Situation (1) were treated as separate from each other, as were the steps in Situation (2) of Rev. Rul. 90–95, the Acquisition Merger would be treated as a stock acquisition that is a qualified stock purchase, because the stock is not acquired in a § 354 or § 356 exchange. The Upstream Merger would qualify as a liquidation under § 332.

However, if the approach reflected in Rev. Rul. 67–274 were applied to Situation (1), the transaction would be treated as an integrated acquisition of T's assets by X in a single statutory merger (without a preliminary stock acquisition). Accordingly, unless the policies underlying § 338 dictate otherwise, the integrated asset acquisition in Situation (1) is properly treated as a statutory merger of T into X that qualifies as a reorganization under § 368(a)(1)(A). See King Enterprises, Inc. v. United States, 418 F.2d 511 (Ct.Cl.1969) (in a case that predated § 338, the court applied the step transaction doctrine to treat the acquisition of the stock of a target corporation followed by the merger of the target corporation into the acquiring corporation as a reorganization under § 368(a)(1)(A)); J.E. Seagram Corp. v. Commissioner, 104 T.C. 75 (1995) (same). Therefore, it is necessary to determine whether the approach reflected in Rev. Rul. 90–95 applies where the step transaction doctrine would otherwise apply to treat the transaction as an asset acquisition that qualifies as a reorganization under § 368(a).

Rev. Rul. 90–95 and § 1.338–3(d) reject the approach reflected in Rev. Rul. 67–274 where the application of that approach would treat the purchase of a target corporation's stock without a § 338 election followed by the liquidation or merger of the target corporation as the purchase of the target corporation's assets resulting in a cost basis in the assets under § 1012. The rejection of step integration in Rev. Rul. 90–95 and § 1.338–3(d) is based on Congressional intent that § 338 "replace any nonstatutory treatment of a stock purchase as an asset purchase under the Kimbell–Diamond doctrine." H.R. Rep. No. 760, 97th Cong., 2d Sess. 536 (1982), 1982–2 C.B. 600, 632. (In Kimbell–Diamond Milling Co. v. Commissioner, 14 T.C. 74, aff'd per curiam, 187 F.2d 718 (1951), cert. denied, 342 U.S. 827 (1951), the court held that the purchase of the stock of a target corporation for the purpose of obtaining its assets through a prompt liquidation should be treated by the purchaser as a purchase of the target corporation's assets with the purchaser receiving a cost basis in the assets.) Rev. Rul. 90–95 and § 1.338–3(d) treat the acquisition of the stock of the target corporation as a qualified stock purchase followed by a separate carryover basis transaction in order to preclude any nonstatutory treatment of the steps as an integrated asset purchase.

The policy underlying § 338 is not violated by treating Situation (1) as a single statutory merger of T into X because such treatment results in a transaction that qualifies as a reorganization under § 368(a)(1)(A) in which X acquires the assets of T with a carryover basis under § 362, and does not result in a cost basis for those assets under § 1012. Thus, in Situation (1), the step transaction doctrine applies to treat the Acquisition Merger and the Upstream Merger not as a stock acquisition that is a qualified stock purchase followed by a § 332 liquidation, but instead as an acquisition of T's assets through a single statutory merger of T into X that qualifies as a reorganization under § 368(a)(1)(A). Accordingly, a § 338 election may not be made in such a situation.

Situation (2)

Situation (2) differs from Situation (1) only in that the Acquisition Merger, if viewed independently of the Upstream Merger, would qualify as a reorganization under § 368(a)(1)(A) by reason of § 368(a)(2)(E). This difference does not change the result from that in Situation (1). The transaction is treated as a single statutory merger of T into X that qualifies as a reorganization under § 368(a)(1)(A) without regard to § 368(a)(2)(E).

¶ 10,190

HOLDING

Under the facts presented, if, pursuant to an integrated plan, a newly formed wholly owned subsidiary of an acquiring corporation merges into a target corporation, followed by the merger of the target corporation into the acquiring corporation, the transaction is treated as a single statutory merger of the target corporation into the acquiring corporation that qualifies as a reorganization under § 368(a)(1)(A).

* * *

EFFECT ON OTHER DOCUMENTS

Rev. Rul. 67–274 is amplified and Rev. Rul. 90–95 is distinguished.

[¶ 10,195]

Notes

1.   In Situations 1 and 2, how, if at all, was the tax treatment of the shareholders of Corporation T affected by application of the step transaction doctrine?

2.   The ruling suggests that one reason to integrate the transactions is that it would not violate the "policy underlying § 338." What is the policy underlying Section 338? Does it apply the same in taxable transactions as it does in tax-free transactions?

3.   For a critical view of Rev. Rul. 2001–46 and its reliance on *King Enterprises*'s use of the step transaction doctrine, see Kwall & Maynard, "Dethroning King Enterprises," 58 Tax Law. 1 (2004).

E.   ACQUISITIONS PARTLY TAX-FREE AND PARTLY TAXABLE

[¶ 10,200]

1.   PURCHASE OF T SHARES FOLLOWED BY TENDER OFFER

A number of techniques have been developed to combine the benefits of an acquisition that is tax-free for some holders of the acquired corporation shares (sometimes an identifiable group that owns a substantial block of highly appreciated stock) with the benefits of a cash purchase for others. Not infrequently, the acquiring corporation will commence its efforts to acquire a publicly owned target corporation (T) by buying some of T's shares for cash on a stock exchange or in the over-the-counter market. After having acquired a position in the T stock, the management of the acquiring corporation will approach T's management with an acquisition proposal, often involving a triangular merger, in which the shareholders of T would receive acquiring corporation stock, cash, or debt securities, or some combination thereof. With the support of T's management or, in some cases, over its opposition, the acquiring corporation may initiate a tender offer directed to T shareholders, in which the acquiring corporation offers to acquire their T shares. If the tender offer is supported by T's management, the offer may involve consideration in the form of cash, stock, and/or debt securities. If the tender offer is opposed by T's management, the offered consideration is likely to be in cash because cash permits the acquisition to proceed much more quickly than would use of stock or debt securities, which would usually have to be registered with the SEC and certain state securities agencies. The second step in the acquisition of T may be considerably easier to accomplish if the acquiring corporation can offer the option of a tax-free acquisition to holders of large blocks of highly appreciated T corporation stock who may exercise effective control over T.

If the total consideration received by the shareholders of T in a forward triangular merger transaction includes enough stock of the parent (P) of the acquiring corporation to meet the continuity of shareholder interest test, discussed at ¶ 10,040, the merger of T into P's wholly owned subsidiary (S) will be tax-free to the T shareholders receiving P stock. In applying the continuity of shareholder interest test, any cash paid to purchase T shares in the initial purchase will usually have to be taken into account as part of the merger transaction under the step transaction doctrine, discussed at ¶ 9065. It is also possible to offer T shareholders an election to receive P stock or cash (or debt securities) in the triangular merger. In order to ensure that the continuity of shareholder interest test is met, however, a limit would be imposed on the amount of cash or debt obligations that would be paid to T shareholders in the aggregate. This limit would ensure that a substantial percentage (at least 40 percent) of the total consideration would consist of P stock. See ¶ 10,040. If some or all of those shareholders elected to receive an aggregate amount of cash or debt obligations in excess of the limit, the cash or debt obligations up to the limit would be prorated among the shareholders so electing, and the rest of the consideration received by them would consist of P stock. The transaction is, of course, tax-free to T shareholders who receive only P stock and is a recognition event with respect to gains for those who receive only cash or debt obligations. For T shareholders who, by choice or as a result of proration, receive a combination of P stock and cash or debt obligations, the amount of cash and the fair market value of the obligations are boot and are, to the extent of the gain realized, taxable as capital gain or as qualified dividend income (and therefore at the same rate as capital gains, but without basis offset), depending on the circumstances; no loss would be recognized. Capital gain treatment will generally be available only to a T shareholder for whom the receipt of cash or debt obligations results in a meaningful reduction in his or her proportionate equity interest in relation to the equity interest in P he or she would have received if all of the consideration had been P stock. See ¶ 10,255.

¶ 10,200

[¶ 10,205]

2. PREFERRED STOCK RECAPITALIZATION PRECEDING STOCK PURCHASE

Even though the great majority of the Target (T) shareholders may prefer to sell their T shares for cash, in some rather special circumstances it may be possible to achieve tax-free treatment for one or more T shareholders but not for the holders of a majority of the T shares. This possibility may be important to certain T shareholders who have a low basis in their T shares, but who do not have in the aggregate a large enough holding in T to meet the continuity of shareholder interest test, if, in a forward triangular merger of T into S, they were to receive P stock while the majority shareholders of T received cash.

One technique that might be feasible in these circumstances would be to have a cash purchase of T stock follow a recapitalization of T in which the T shareholders, who do not want to have a taxable gain, exchange their old T stock for a new class of nonvoting preferred stock of T. Such a recapitalization is one type of reorganization in which no continuity of shareholder interest is required, ¶ 11,030, and the exchange of T common stock for T preferred stock would not be a taxable event, provided that the preferred is not nonqualified preferred stock, as defined in Section 351(g)(2). See ¶ 10,240. If it is nonqualified preferred, it is taxable boot. Thus, while the terms of the preferred stock might include measures designed to protect the holder as a minority shareholder, those terms could not include debt-like features that would result in classification of the preferred as nonqualified preferred stock, such as giving the holder a right to put the preferred stock to T for a fixed price after five years or requiring T redeem the preferred after five years.

If T is publicly held, corporate and securities law considerations will often require that all of the shareholders of T be offered the preferred stock, and therefore this technique may not work unless the preferred stock can be structured in a way (e.g., with a low dividend) that makes it attractive only to those T shareholders holding T stock with a low basis who attach paramount importance to avoiding a taxable gain. However, the preferred may not be attractive even to such shareholders if they cannot be assured that they, or their estates, can sell the preferred or have it redeemed. If the preferred carries a low dividend and the holder cannot be given a right to put the stock to T or have T redeem it, the preferred stock recapitalization may not be viable. Even though a holder's right to put the preferred to T or T's obligation to redeem would generally result in classification of the preferred as nonqualified preferred stock, Section 351(g)(2)(C)(i)(I) contains an exception if the holder's put or T's obligation to redeem may be exercised only on the death, disability, or mental incompetency of the holder. However, this exception is available only if neither the T stock surrendered nor the preferred stock received in exchange is in a corporation any class of the stock of which is readily tradable. Hence, this exception is not available if any stock of T or of the acquiring corporation is readily tradable. Thus, as a practical matter, it is only when both corporations are closely held that this exception will apply.

Another exception applies if the holder's put or the issuer's obligation to redeem is transferred in connection with the performance of services for the issuer (or a related person) and is exercisable only upon the holder's separation from service. § 351(g)(2)(C)(i)(II). This exception applies even if the stock of T and the stock of the acquiring corporation are readily tradable.

Thus, the bottom line appears to be that, as a practical matter, a preferred stock recapitalization for minority shareholders of T seeking to avoid recognition of gain, coupled with a purchase of T shares owned by other shareholders, can achieve the desired results only if the shares of neither T nor the acquiring corporation are readily tradable or if the preferred stock of the acquiring corporation is issued in connection with the performance of services for that corporation.

Under certain circumstances the use of the preferred stock recapitalization involves risk that the IRS may treat the preferred as involving a taxable distribution under Section 305. See ¶ 6070. Moreover, the regulations require a redemption premium on certain preferred stock to be treated as distributed to shareholders on an economic accrual basis. See Reg. § 1.305–5(b).

3. USE OF SECTION 351

[¶ 10,210]

a. Obtaining Tax–Free Treatment for a Minority Shareholder of T in a Cash Merger

Another technique that has been used to provide tax-free treatment to some shareholders who hold low basis T shares while the holders of most of the T shares sell for cash involves use of Section 351. This scheme involves offering the T shareholders a choice of receiving, in exchange for their T stock, either cash or a low-dividend preferred stock in S, a subsidiary of T. Although if T is publicly held, legal considerations may require offering a choice between the low-dividend preferred and cash to all T shareholders, the low-dividend preferred stock would presumably be attractive only to T shareholders who have highly appreciated stock and who are desirous of avoiding a large capital gains tax (e.g., elderly T shareholders who will obtain a stepped-up basis at death under current law). The T shareholders seeking nonrecognition of gain treatment transfer their T shares to S in a putative Section 351 exchange for the low-dividend preferred stock of S. P transfers the cash needed to purchase the remaining T stock to S in exchange for all of its common stock. S then organizes, and transfers the cash to, a wholly owned new sub-subsidiary which merges into T, with the remaining T shareholders receiving cash (received from P by S and transferred to its new sub-subsidiary) for their T stock. This approach was adopted in the 1978 acquisition by Unilever of National Starch and Chemical Corporation. The chief executive officer (and major shareholder) of National Starch had a very low basis in his stock and was opposed to bearing the tax that would have been imposed on a sale of his shares. To avoid this result, this individual was willing to accept a low-dividend preferred stock in S in exchange for his National Starch stock in what purported to be a Section 351 exchange. The S preferred stock, while offered to all of National Starch's shareholders in exchange for their common stock, was chosen by relatively few. The IRS originally issued a private ruling determining that the failure to meet the continuity of shareholder interest test for an acquisitive reorganization did not preclude the applicability of Section 351(a) to prevent recognition of gain on the transfers of T common stock in exchange for preferred stock of S even though these transfers were an integral part of an acquisition transaction. Letter Ruling 7839060 (1978).

[¶ 10,215]

REVENUE RULING 80–284

1980–2 C.B. 117.

* * *

T, a manufacturing corporation, had outstanding $1,000x$ shares of capital stock. The fair market value of *T* was $100,000x$ dollars, and the fair market value of each share of its outstanding stock was $100x$ dollars. *T*'s president and chairman of the board, *A*, owned $140x$ shares of its capital stock (14 percent). The remaining $860x$ shares of *T*'s capital stock (86 percent) were publicly held. *P*, a large publicly traded corporation unrelated to *T*, wished to purchase the stock of *T* and thereafter to have *T*'s business continued by a wholly owned subsidiary. While the other shareholders of *T* were willing to accept cash for their *T* stock, *A*, who was of an advanced age and who had a very low basis in his $140x$ shares, was unwilling to sell the *T* stock for cash because the sale would result in recognition of taxable gain.

In order to accommodate *A*'s wish to avoid recognition of gain, *P* and *A* agreed in January, 1980, to organize a new corporation, *S*, for the purpose of acquiring and holding all of the stock of *T*. Several months later, pursuant to the agreement, *P* transferred $86,000x$ dollars in cash together with other property to *S* solely in exchange for all of *S*'s common stock, and *A* transferred his $140x$ shares of *T* stock to *S* solely in exchange for all of *S*'s preferred stock. It was intended that this transaction would be a tax-free exchange under section 351(a) * * *. Thereafter, and as part of the overall plan *S*, organized a new corporation, D, by transferring the 86,000x dollars in cash to D solely in exchange for all of D's stock. D was then merged into T under applicable state law, and pursuant thereto each share of T stock, except those shares transferred by A to S, was surrendered in exchange for 100x dollars in cash. The T stock acquired by D for cash was canceled and, pursuant to state law, each share of D stock was converted into stock of T. Although S could theoretically have acquired the remaining 86 percent of the T stock directly from the T shareholders for cash, the acquisition was made pursuant to the state merger laws because this method was more expeditious and convenient. T remains in existence as an operating company, and S remains in existence as a holding company.

LAW AND ANALYSIS

Section 351(a) * * * provides that no gain or loss is recognized if persons who control a corporation transfer property to the corporation solely in exchange for stock or securities. Section 351(a) is an exception to the general rule that gain or loss must be recognized on any sale or exchange of property. See [Reg. §] 1.1002–1(b) * * *, which states that exceptions to the general rule (including section 351(a)) "are strictly construed and do not extend either beyond the words or the underlying assumptions and purposes of the exception. Nonrecognition is accorded by the Code only if the exchange is one which satisfies both (1) the specific description in the Code of an excepted exchange, and (2) the underlying purpose for which such exchange is excepted from the general rule."

Thus, while A's exchange of common stock for preferred stock may satisfy all of the literal requirements of section 351 of the Code, it does not follow that Congress meant to cover such an exchange, even though "the facts answer the dictionary definition of each term used in the statute." See *Helvering v. Gregory*, 69 F.2d 809, 810 (2d Cir. 1934) (Hand, J.), *aff'd*, 293 U.S. 465 (1935) * * *.

Section 351(a) * * * is intended to apply to "certain transactions where gain or loss may have accrued in a constitutional sense, but where in a popular and economic sense there has been a mere change in the form of ownership and the taxpayer has not really 'cashed in' on the theoretical gain, or closed out a losing venture." *Portland Oil Co. v. Commissioner*, 109 F.2d 479, 488 (1st Cir.1940), *cert. denied*, 310 U.S. 650 (1940). * * * On the other hand, section 351(a) is not intended to apply to transactions that sufficiently resemble a sale so that gain is recognized in a popular and economic sense. Thus, the issue presented is whether, in terms of economic substance, there has been a mere exchange in the form of investment or a cashing in of that investment.

A's exchange of common stock for preferred stock is an integral part of a larger transaction. In the larger transaction, P, acting through its subsidiary S, acquires all the stock of an unrelated third corporation T.

¶ 10,215

Thus, viewed from the perspective of all the parties, the larger transaction fits a pattern common to acquisitive reorganizations. * * *

A well-established continuity of interest test applies to acquisitive reorganizations. See section 1.368–1(b) of the Regulations and Rev. Rul. 66–224, 1966–2 C.B. 114. The object of the continuity of interest test is to identify acquisitive transactions that sufficiently resemble a sale so gain is recognized in the ordinary business sense. * * *

Under the continuity of interest test, a substantial portion of the consideration paid must consist of stock in the acquiring corporation. * * * If an acquisitive transaction fails the continuity of interest test, then the transaction as a whole sufficiently resembles a sale so all the parties recognize gain in the ordinary business sense.

The larger acquisitive transaction in which S obtains the stock of T fails the continuity of interest test. It follows that the transaction as a whole sufficiently resembles a sale so all the parties (including A) recognize gain in the ordinary business sense. Because section 351 * * * is not intended to apply where gain is recognized in the ordinary business sense, A's exchange is not within the "underlying assumptions and purposes" of section 351. See section 1.1002–1(b) of the regulations.

No other conclusion would be consistent with the history and purpose of continuity of interest. In a series of decided cases, the courts have denied nonrecognition treatment to acquisitive transactions that lacked continuity of interest. * * * The defect in each case was entirely one of substance; the transaction at issue satisfied all of the technical requirements for nonrecognition under the statutory provisions that were directly relevant. A defect of this kind cannot be remedied by means that are essentially formal. In particular it cannot be remedied merely by rearranging the form of an acquisitive transaction so that the technical requirements of section 351 * * * are satisfied, but without altering the substance of the transaction.

In this ruling, the facts reveal an acquisitive transaction which does not meet the continuity of interest test and thus is equivalent to a sale. Accordingly, although the technical requirements of section 351(a) * * * are satisfied, the transaction is beyond the underlying assumptions and purposes of section 351(a). Therefore, its substance as a sale remains the same, and the transaction will be treated as a taxable exchange. Compare Rev. Rul. 80–285, [1980–2 C.B. 119] this page, this Bulletin, which reaches the same result when assets, instead of stock, are acquired under similar circumstances.

HOLDING

A's exchange of capital stock in T for preferred stock in S does not qualify for nonrecognition treatment under section 351(a) * * *, and gain is therefore recognized on the exchange.

¶ 10,215

[¶ 10,220]

Note

If the transaction described in Rev. Rul. 80–284 had been implemented and the position adopted by the IRS had been sustained by the courts, how would the tax consequences of the transaction have differed?

[¶ 10,225]

REVENUE RULING 84–71

1984–1 C.B. 106.

The Internal Revenue Service has reconsidered Rev. Rul. 80–284, 1980–2 C.B. 117 * * *, in which transfers that satisfied the technical requirements of section 351(a) * * * were nevertheless held to constitute taxable exchanges because they were part of larger acquisitive transactions that did not meet the continuity of interest test generally applicable to acquisitive reorganizations.

In Rev. Rul. 80–284, fourteen percent of *T* corporation's stock was held by *A*, president and chairman of the board, and eighty-six percent by the public. *P*, an unrelated, publicly held corporation wished to purchase the stock of *T*. All the *T* stockholders except *A* were willing to sell the *T* stock for cash. *A* wished to avoid recognition of gain.

In order to accommodate these wishes, the following transactions were carried out as part of an overall plan. First, *P* and *A* formed a new corporation, *S*. *P* transferred cash and other property to *S* in exchange solely for all of *S*'s common stock; *A* transferred *T* stock to *S* solely in exchange for all of *S*'s preferred stock. These transfers were intended to be tax-free under section 351 of the Code. Second, *S* organized a new corporation, *D*, and transferred to *D* the cash it had received from *P* in exchange for all the *D* common stock. Third, *D* was merged into *T* under state law. As a result of the merger, each share of *T* stock, except those shares held by *S*, were surrendered for cash equal to the stock's fair market value and each share of *D* stock was converted into *T* stock.

Rev. Rul. 80–284 concluded that if a purported section 351 exchange is an integral part of a larger transaction that fits a pattern common to acquisitive reorganizations, and if the continuity of shareholder interest requirement of section 1.368–1(b) of the * * * Regulations is not satisfied with respect to the larger transaction, then the transaction as a whole resembles a sale and the exchange cannot qualify under section 351 because that section is not intended to apply to sales. * * *

Upon reconsideration, the Service has concluded that the fact that "larger acquisitive transactions," such as those described in Rev. Rul. 80–284 * * *, fail to meet the requirements for tax-free treatment under the reorganization provisions * * * does not preclude the applicability of section 351(a) to transfers that may be described as part of such larger

¶ 10,225

transactions, but also, either alone or in conjunction with other transfers, meet the requirements of section 351(a).

* * *

Rev. Rul. 80–284 * * * [is] revoked.

[¶ 10,230]

Notes

1. What explains the IRS's change of heart? Should the IRS have given up on this issue without litigating it?

2. Note that the acquisitive scheme using Section 351, blessed in Rev. Rul. 84–71, will not avoid gain recognition if the preferred stock received by a T shareholder in exchange for T stock is nonqualified preferred stock as defined in Section 351(g)(2) because such preferred is now treated as boot in a Section 351 exchange. § 351(g)(1)(A). After reviewing the material on nonqualified preferred stock discussed at ¶ 10,240, consider how much the treatment of nonqualified preferred limits the use of Section 351 to effect an acquisition of a publicly held corporation that is tax-free to a minority of the target corporation shareholders while it is taxable to the majority. Note that if the issuer's obligation to redeem preferred stock (at its or the holder's option) is triggered at the death or disability of the holder, the stock will not be nonqualified preferred stock unless the preferred stock or stock for which it is exchanged is readily tradable. § 351(g)(2)(C)(ii). Is the utility of Section 351 effectively limited to acquisitions in which the stock of neither T nor the acquiring corporation is readily tradable or in which the preferred stock is issued in connection with the performance of services for the issuer? See the discussion at ¶ 10,205.

[¶ 10,235]

b. The "Horizontal Double–Dummy" Transaction

Two corporations, T1 and T2, which are both organized under Delaware law and which both want to combine tax-free but retain their separate identities, may use Section 351 to effect the transaction in a way that would not qualify as a tax-free reorganization. Assume that the shares of T1 and T2 are traded on the New York Stock Exchange, each wants to retain its name, assets, and status after the combination, and neither wants to have to transfer its assets (which include various contracts, joint ventures, and franchises). T1's shareholders are to receive common stock worth $500 million and T2's shareholders are to receive common stock worth $400 million and 15–year debentures worth $200 million. The objective is to have neither the shareholders of T1 or T2 recognize gain with respect to stock received in the transaction.

¶ 10,225

The horizontal double-dummy Section 351 transaction involves formation of a new corporation (e.g., under Delaware law) (Newco), which establishes two wholly owned subsidiaries, S1 and S2, under Delaware law solely for the purpose of effectuating the transaction. In accordance with an integrated plan, S1 is merged into T1, the T1 shareholders receive shares of Newco worth $500 million, T1 stays in existence with its assets, status, and tax attributes unaffected, and T1 becomes a wholly owned subsidiary of Newco.

The transaction, taken by itself, would qualify as a reverse triangular merger or as a reverse merger B-type reorganization, but, when treated as an integral part of the entire transaction, the S1–T1 merger becomes part of a Section 351(a) exchange. S2 is merged into T2, T2's shareholders exchange their T2 shares for Newco shares worth $400 million and Newco 15–year debentures worth $200 million. T2 becomes a wholly owned subsidiary of Newco. The merger of S2 into T2, taken by itself, would not qualify as a reverse triangular merger because more than 20 percent of the T2 shares would be exchanged for boot (the Newco debentures). However, when treated as an integral part of the entire transaction, and, if the existence of S2 is disregarded, the S2–T2 merger is part of a Section 351 exchange. Section 351 is applicable because the mergers are parts of a single plan, and the former T1 and T2 shareholders are in control of Newco immediately after the exchange. See Rev. Rul. 76–123, 1976–1 C.B. 94. The transaction is tax-free to the former T1 shareholders, and the former T2 shareholders are taxable only to the extent of the lesser of the fair market value of the Newco debentures received or the gain realized. § 351(b). Their recognized gain will normally be taxed as capital gain. Treatment of the transactions as parts of a Section 351 exchange is dependent on disregarding the transitory existence of S1 and S2, which is supported by a number of rulings. See, e.g., Rev. Rul. 79–273, 1979–2 C.B. 125; Rev. Rul 78–250, 1978–1 C.B. 83; Rev. Rul. 73–427, 1973–2C.B. 301; Rev. Rul 67–448, at ¶ 10,170; cf. Reg. § 1.368–2(j)(6), Exs. 4 and 5. If Newco, T1, and T2 file a consolidated return, Newco's interest payments on the debentures will be deductible by the consolidated group, and dividends paid by T1 and T2 to Newco will be exempt from tax on receipt by Newco.

F. TREATMENT OF BOOT PAID INCIDENT TO REORGANIZATION

[¶ 10,240]

1. GAIN RECOGNITION BY SHAREHOLDERS AND CREDITORS

If the transaction qualifies as a reorganization because it meets both the literal terms of one of the Section 368(a)(1) definitions and the relevant judicially developed tests examined at ¶¶ 9050 et seq., gain or loss realized by the shareholders and creditors involved in the transaction will go unrecognized to the extent prescribed in Sections 354 and 356.

A shareholder who, pursuant to a plan of reorganization, exchanges stock for other stock generally enjoys nonrecognition of any gain realized. If, however, the shareholder exchanges some stock for boot, gain realized by the exchanging shareholder is recognized to the extent of the fair market value of the boot under Section 356(a). Boot includes, for example, cash and the value of the principal amount of any securities received in exchange for the stock surrendered. § 354(a)(2). Loss is not recognized even if boot is involved. § 356(c).

If a creditor holding debt securities (who may also be a shareholder) exchanges those securities for other debt securities pursuant to a plan of reorganization, the creditor will enjoy nonrecognition of any gain realized to the extent that the principal amount of securities received does not exceed the principal amount of the securities surrendered. §§ 354(a)(2)(A)(i) and 356(d)(2)(A). This is true even if the remaining term on the securities might otherwise be deemed too short to constitute securities under applicable case law. See Rev. Rul. 2004–78, 2004–2 C.B. 108 (allowing the exchange of securities with only two years remaining on the term). To the extent that there is an excess, the fair market value of the excess constitutes boot and is potentially taxable. § 356(d)(2)(B). Any stock or other property received in exchange for accrued interest is also boot. § 354(a)(2)(B).

As discussed in Chapter 2, the Taxpayer Relief Act of 1997 created a new class of boot called "nonqualified preferred stock." Although preferred stock is generally nonrecognition property, preferred stock with certain debt-like characteristics is labeled nonqualified preferred stock and is treated as boot. §§ 354(a)(2)(C) and 356(e). The preferred stock subject to this treatment includes stock that is limited and preferred as to dividends and that does not participate significantly (e.g., through a conversion privilege) in corporate growth. § 351(g)(3)(A). Stock is not treated as participating in corporate growth unless there is a real and meaningful likelihood that dividends beyond any preference limit will actually be paid. Such preferred stock is treated as boot if (1) the holder has the right to require the issuer or a related person (within the meaning of Sections 267(b) and 707(b)) to redeem or purchase the stock, (2) the issuer or a related person is required to redeem or purchase the stock, (3) the issuer (or related person) has the right to redeem or purchase the stock and, as of the issue date, it is more likely than not that such right will be exercised, or (4) the dividend rate on the stock varies in whole or in part (directly or indirectly) with reference to interest rates, commodity prices, or other similar indices. § 351(g)(2)(A). For this purpose, the rules of (1), (2), and (3) apply if the right or obligation may be exercised within 20 years of the date the instrument is issued and such right or obligation is not subject to a contingency which, as of the issue date, makes remote the likelihood of redemption or purchase. § 351(g)(2)(B). In addition, if neither the stock surrendered nor the stock received in the exchange is stock of a corporation (or of a related corporation) any class of stock of which is publicly traded, a right or obligation is disregarded if it may be exercised only upon the death, disability, or mental incompetency of the holder. Also, a right or obligation is disregarded in the case of stock transferred in connection with the performance of services if it may be exercised only upon the holder's separation from service.

The Treasury has regulatory authority to (1) apply installment sale-type rules to nonqualified preferred stock in appropriate cases and (2) prescribe treatment of nonqualified preferred stock under other provisions of the Code (e.g., Sections 304, 306, 318, and 368(c)). Until regulations are issued, nonqualified preferred stock will continue to be treated as stock under other provisions of the Code.

The rationale for treating the nonqualified preferred stock as boot is presumably that its features make it sufficiently similar to debt obligations to warrant boot treatment when received in a Section 351 exchange or a reorganization in exchange for stock. Consistent with this rationale the following exchanges are excluded from this gain recognition rule: (1) exchanges of nonqualified preferred stock for nonqualified preferred stock of the same or lesser value; (2) an exchange of nonqualified preferred stock for common stock; (3) certain exchanges of debt securities for nonqualified preferred stock of the same or lesser value; and (4) exchanges of stock in certain recapitalizations of family owned corporations, see ¶ 11,025.

[¶ 10,245]

2. WHEN DOES RECOGNIZED GAIN HAVE THE EFFECT OF THE DISTRIBUTION OF A DIVIDEND UNDER SECTION 356(a)(2)?

For years there was controversy over how to determine whether, under Section 356(a)(2), dividend treatment was appropriate for gain recognized by a shareholder in a reorganization because that shareholder exchanged shares of the acquired corporation for a combination of nonrecognition property (e.g., voting common stock of the acquiring corporation) and boot. Section 356(a)(2) provides relatively little guidance in stating that, if the exchange of shares for boot has the effect of a dividend, it will be treated as the distribution of a dividend (determined with the application of Section 318(a)) to the extent of each exchanging shareholder's ratable share of accumulated E & P. This issue was particularly important prior to 2003, when dividends and redemptions were taxed at significantly different rates. Given that qualified dividend income is taxed at the same preferential tax rates as long-term capital gains, though, it makes little difference under current law how the boot is characterized (except for purposes of the capital loss limitation in Section 1211). See Chapter 4 for a discussion of the narrowing of the differences between dividend and redemption treatment under current law, which is scheduled to expire in 2010.

At the time, there was broad agreement that if, as a result of receiving some boot along with nonrecognition property, a shareholder had recognized a gain, that shareholder could appropriately be treated as if shares had been redeemed for the boot. This analysis, in turn, led the courts to apply by analogy the rules of Section 302 and the constructive ownership rules of Section 318(a) for determining when a redemption will qualify for exchange rather than dividend treatment. The boot would not be treated as having the effect of a dividend if the hypothetical redemption met the substantially disproportionate test of Section 302(b)(2) or the not essentially equivalent to a dividend test of Section 302(b)(1), which, according to the Supreme Court in the *Davis* case, at ¶ 5085, required a meaningful reduction in the shareholder's interest.

An issue that sharply divided the courts in the context of acquisitive reorganizations involving boot, however, was whether the hypothetical redemption should be regarded as having occurred before the reorganization, so that it was a redemption by the acquired corporation, or as having occurred as a part of the reorganization, so that it should be treated as a redemption by the acquiring corporation. The split was reflected in the *Wright* and *Shimberg* cases discussed by the Supreme Court in the *Clark* case, below, and this issue appears to have been laid to rest by the Court. What appears to be the Court's alternative holding, however, opens new vistas for controversy.

[¶ 10,250]

COMMISSIONER v. CLARK

Supreme Court of the United States, 1989.
489 U.S. 726.

JUSTICE STEVENS delivered the opinion of the Court.

* * *

The relevant facts are easily summarized. For approximately 15 years prior to April 1979, the taxpayer was the sole shareholder and president of Basin Surveys, Inc. (Basin), a company in which he had invested approximately $85,000. The corporation operated a successful business providing various technical services to the petroleum industry. In 1978, N.L. Industries, Inc. (NL), a publicly owned corporation engaged in the manufacture and supply of petroleum equipment and services, initiated negotiations with the taxpayer regarding the possible acquisition of Basin. On April 3, 1979, after months of negotiations, the taxpayer and NL entered into a contract.

The agreement provided for a "triangular merger," whereby Basin was merged into a wholly owned subsidiary of NL. In exchange for transferring all of the outstanding shares in Basin to NL's subsidiary, the taxpayer elected to receive 300,000 shares of NL common stock and cash boot of $3,250,000, passing up an alternative offer of 425,000 shares of NL common stock. The 300,000 shares of NL issued to the taxpayer amounted to approximately 0.92% of the outstanding common shares of NL. If the taxpayer had instead accepted the pure stock-for-stock offer, he would have held approximately 1.3% of the outstanding common shares. The Commissioner and the taxpayer agree that the merger at issue qualifies as a reorganization under §§ 368(a)(1)(A) and (a)(2)(D).

Respondents filed a joint federal income tax return for 1979. As required by § 356(a)(1), they reported the cash boot as taxable gain. In calculating the tax owed, respondents characterized the payment as long-term capital gain. The Commissioner on audit disagreed with this characterization. In his view, the payment had "the effect of the distribution of a dividend" and was thus taxable as ordinary income up to $2,319,611, the amount of Basin's accumulated earnings and profits at the time of the merger. The Commissioner assessed a deficiency of $972,504.74.

Respondents petitioned for review in the Tax Court, which, in a reviewed decision, held in their favor, 86 T.C. 138 (1986). The court started from the premise that the question whether the boot payment had "the effect of the distribution of a dividend" turns on the choice between "two judicially articulated tests." *Id.*, at 140. Under the test advocated by the Commissioner and given voice in *Shimberg v. United States*, 577 F.2d 283 (C.A.5 1978), cert. denied, 439 U.S. 1115 (1979), the boot payment is treated as though it were made in a hypothetical redemption by the acquired corporation (Basin) immediately *prior* to the reorganization. Under this test, the cash payment received by the taxpayer indisputably would have been treated as a dividend. The second test, urged by the taxpayer and finding support in *Wright v. United States*, 482 F.2d 600 (C.A.8 1973), proposes an alternative hypothetical redemption. Rather than concentrating on the taxpayer's pre-reorganization interest in the acquired corporation, this test requires that one imagine a pure stock-for-stock exchange, followed immediately by a *post-*reorganization redemption of a portion of the taxpayer's shares in the acquiring corporation (NL) in return for a payment in an amount equal to the boot. Under § 302 of the Code, which defines when a redemption of stock should be treated as a distribution of dividend, NL's redemption of 125,000 shares of its stock from the taxpayer in exchange for the $3,250,000 boot payment would have been treated as capital gain.[6]

---

6. * * * As the Tax Court explained, receipt of the cash boot reduced the taxpayer's potential holdings in NL from 1.3% to 0.92%. 86 T.C., at 153. The taxpayer's hold- ings were thus approximately 71% of what they would have been absent the payment. *Ibid.* This fact, combined with the fact that the taxpayer held less than 50% of the

The Tax Court rejected the pre-reorganization test favored by the Commissioner because it considered it improper "to view the cash payment as an isolated event totally separate from the reorganization." 86 T.C., at 151. Indeed, it suggested that this test requires that courts make the "determination of dividend equivalency fantasizing that the reorganization does not exist." *Id.*, at 150 (footnote omitted). The court then acknowledged that a similar criticism could be made of the taxpayer's contention that the cash payment should be viewed as a post-reorganization redemption. It concluded, however, that since it was perfectly clear that the cash payment would not have taken place without the reorganization, it was better to treat the boot "as the equivalent of a redemption *in the course of implementing the reorganization,*" than "as having occurred *prior to and separate from the reorganization.*" *Id.*, at 152 (emphasis in original).[7]

The Court of Appeals for the Fourth Circuit affirmed, 828 F.2d 221 (1987). Like the Tax Court, it concluded that although "[s]ection 302 does not explicitly apply in the reorganization context," *id.*, at 223, and although § 302 differs from § 356 in important respects, *id.*, at 224, it nonetheless provides "the appropriate test for determining whether boot is ordinary income or a capital gain," *id.*, at 223. Thus, as explicated in § 302(b)(2), if the taxpayer relinquished more than 20% of his corporate control and retained less than 50% of the voting shares after the distribution, the boot would be treated as capital gain. However, as the Court of Appeals recognized, "[b]ecause § 302 was designed to deal with a stock redemption by a single corporation, rather than a reorganization involving two companies, the section does not indicate which corporation [the taxpayer] lost interest in." *Id.*, at 224. Thus, like the Tax Court, the Court of Appeals was left to consider whether the hypothetical redemption should be treated as a pre-reorganization distribution coming from the acquired corporation or as a post-reorganization distribution coming from the acquiring corporation. It concluded:

> "Based on the language and legislative history of § 356, the change-in-ownership principle of § 302, and the need to review the reorganization as an integrated transaction, we conclude that the boot should be characterized as a post-reorganization stock redemption by N.L. that affected [the taxpayer's] interest in the new corporation. Because this redemption reduced [the taxpayer's] N.L. holdings by more than 20%, the boot should be taxed as a capital gain." *Id.*, at 224–225.

voting stock of NL after the hypothetical redemption, would have qualified the "distribution" as "substantially disproportionate" under § 302(b)(2).

7. The Tax Court stressed that to adopt the pre-reorganization view "would in ef-

fect resurrect the now discredited 'automatic dividend rule' . . . , at least with respect to pro rata distributions made to an acquired corporation's shareholders pursuant to a plan of reorganization." * * *

This decision by the Court of Appeals for the Fourth Circuit is in conflict with the decision of the Fifth Circuit in *Shimberg v. United States*, 577 F.2d 283 (1978), in two important respects. In *Shimberg*, the court concluded that it was inappropriate to apply stock redemption principles in reorganization cases "on a wholesale basis." *Id.*, at 287; see also *ibid*, n. 13. In addition, the court adopted the pre-reorganization test, holding that "§ 356(a)(2) requires a determination of whether the distribution would have been taxed as a dividend if made prior to the reorganization or if no reorganization had occurred." *Id.*, at 288.

To resolve this conflict on a question of importance to the administration of the federal tax laws, we granted certiorari. 485 U.S. 933 (1988).

II

We agree with the Tax Court and the Court of Appeals for the Fourth Circuit that the question under § 356(a)(2) of whether an "exchange ... has the effect of the distribution of a dividend" should be answered by examining the effect of the exchange as a whole. We think the language and history of the statute, as well as a common-sense understanding of the economic substance of the transaction at issue, support this approach.

The language of § 356(a) strongly supports our understanding that the transaction should be treated as an integrated whole. Section 356(a)(2) asks whether "*an exchange* is described in paragraph (1)" that "has the effect of the distribution of a dividend." (Emphasis supplied.) The statute does not provide that boot shall be treated as a dividend if its payment has the effect of the distribution of a dividend. Rather, the inquiry turns on whether the "exchange" has that effect. Moreover, paragraph (1), in turn, looks to whether "the property received in *the exchange* consists not only of property permitted by section 354 or 355 to be received without the recognition of gain but also of other property or money." (Emphasis supplied.) Again, the statute plainly refers to one integrated transaction and, again, makes clear that we are to look to the character of the exchange as a whole and not simply its component parts. Finally, it is significant that § 356 expressly limits the extent to which boot may be taxed to the amount of gain realized in the reorganization. This limitation suggests that Congress intended that boot not be treated in isolation from the overall reorganization. * * *

Our reading of the statute as requiring that the transaction be treated as a unified whole is reinforced by the well-established "step-transaction" doctrine, a doctrine that the Government has applied in related contexts * * *. Under this doctrine, interrelated yet formally distinct steps in an integrated transaction may not be considered independently of the overall transaction. By thus "linking together all interdependent steps with legal or business significance, rather than taking them in isolation," federal tax liability may be based "on a realistic view of the entire transaction." 1 B. Bittker, Federal Taxation of Income, Estates and Gifts, ¶ 4.3.5, p. 4–52 (1981).

Viewing the exchange in this case as an integrated whole, we are unable to accept the Commissioner's pre-reorganization analogy. The analogy severs the payment of boot from the context of the reorganization. Indeed, only by straining to abstract the payment of boot from the context of the overall exchange, and thus imagining that Basin made a distribution to the taxpayer independently of NL's planned acquisition, can we reach the rather counterintuitive conclusion urged by the Commissioner—that the taxpayer suffered no meaningful reduction in his ownership interest as a result of the cash payment. We conclude that such a limited view of the transaction is plainly inconsistent with the statute's direction that we look to the effect of the entire exchange.

The pre-reorganization analogy is further flawed in that it adopts an overly expansive reading of § 356(a)(2). As the Court of Appeals recognized, adoption of the pre-reorganization approach would "result in ordinary income treatment in most reorganizations because corporate boot is usually distributed pro rata to the shareholders of the target corporation." 828 F.2d, at 227 * * *. Such a reading of the statute would not simply constitute a return to the widely criticized "automatic dividend rule" (at least as to cases involving a pro rata payment to the shareholders of the acquired corporation), see n. [7], *supra*, but also would be contrary to our standard approach to construing such provisions. The requirement of § 356(a)(2) that boot be treated as dividend in some circumstances is an exception from the general rule authorizing capital gains treatment for boot. In construing provisions such as § 356, in which a general statement of policy is qualified by an exception, we usually read the exception narrowly in order to preserve the primary operation of the provision. * * * Given that Congress has enacted a general rule that treats boot as capital gain, we should not eviscerate that legislative judgment through an expansive reading of a somewhat ambiguous exception.

The post-reorganization approach adopted by the Tax Court and the Court of Appeals is, in our view, preferable to the Commissioner's approach. Most significantly, this approach does a far better job of treating the payment of boot as a component of the overall exchange. Unlike the pre-reorganization view, this approach acknowledges that there would have been no cash payment absent the exchange and also that, by accepting the cash payment, the taxpayer experienced a meaningful reduction in his potential ownership interest.

Once the post-reorganization approach is adopted, the result in this case is pellucidly clear. Section 302(a) of the Code provides that if a redemption fits within any one of the four categories set out in § 302(b), the redemption "shall be treated as a distribution in part or full payment in exchange for the stock," and thus not regarded as a dividend. As the Tax Court and the Court of Appeals correctly determined, the hypothetical post-reorganization redemption by NL of a portion of the taxpayer's shares satisfies at least one of the subsections of § 302(b).[8] In particular, the safe harbor provisions of subsection (b)(2) provide that redemptions in which the taxpayer relinquishes more than 20% of his or her share of the corporation's voting stock and retains less than 50% of the voting of stock after the redemption, shall not be treated as distributions of a dividend. See n. 6, *supra*. Here, we treat the transaction as though NL redeemed 125,000 shares of its common stock (*i.e.*, the number of shares of NL common stock foregone in favor of the boot) in return for a cash payment to the taxpayer of $3,250,000 (*i.e.*, the amount of the boot). As a result of this redemption, the taxpayer's interest in NL was reduced from 1.3% of the outstanding common stock to 0.9%. See 86 T.C., at 153. Thus, the taxpayer relinquished approximately 29% of his interest in NL and retained less than a 1% voting interest in the corporation after the transaction, easily satisfying the "substantially disproportionate" standards of § 302(b)(2). We accordingly conclude that the boot payment did not have the effect of a dividend and that the payment was properly treated as capital gain.

III

The Commissioner objects to this "recasting [of] the merger transaction into a form different from that entered into by the parties," Brief for the Petitioner 11, and argues that the Court of Appeals' formal adherence to the principles embodied in § 302 forced the court to stretch to "find a redemption to which to apply them, since the merger transaction entered into by the parties did not involve a redemption," *id.*, at 28. There are a number of sufficient responses to this argument. We think it first worth emphasizing that the Commissioner overstates the extent to which the redemption is imagined. As the Court of Appeals for the Fifth Circuit noted in *Shimberg*, "[t]he theory behind tax-free corporate reorganizations is that the transaction is merely 'a continuance of the proprietary interests in the continuing enterprise under modified corporate form.' "*Lewis v. Commissioner of Internal Revenue*, 176 F.2d 646, 648 (C.A.1 1949); Treas. Reg. § 1.368–1(b). * * * 577 F.2d, at 288. As a result, the boot-for-stock transaction can be viewed as a partial repurchase of stock by the continuing corporate enterprise—*i.e.*, as a redemption. It is of course true that both the pre-reorganization and post-reorganization analogies are somewhat artificial in that they imagine that the redemption occurred outside the confines of the actual reorgani-

---

8. Because the mechanical requirements of subsection (b)(2) are met, we need not decide whether the hypothetical redemption might also qualify for capital gains treatment under the general "not essentially equivalent to a dividend" language of subsection (b)(1). Subsections (b)(3) and (b)(4), which deal with redemptions of all of the shareholder's stock and with partial liquidations, respectively, are not at issue in this case.

zation. However, if forced to choose between the two analogies, the post-reorganization view is the less artificial. Although both analogies "recast the merger transaction," the post-reorganization view recognizes that a reorganization has taken place, while the pre-reorganization approach recasts the transaction to the exclusion of the overall exchange.

Moreover, we doubt that abandoning the pre-and post-reorganization analogies and the principles of § 302 in favor of a less artificial understanding of the transaction would lead to a result different from that reached by the Court of Appeals. Although the statute is admittedly ambiguous and the legislative history sparse, we are persuaded—even without relying on § 302—that Congress did not intend to except reorganizations such as that at issue here from the general rule allowing capital gains treatment for cash boot. * * * § 356(a)(1). The legislative history of § 356(a)(2), although perhaps generally "not illuminating," *Estate of Bedford*, 325 U.S., at 290, suggests that Congress was primarily concerned with preventing corporations from "siphon[ing] off" accumulated earnings and profits at a capital gains rate through the ruse of a reorganization. See Golub, 58 Taxes, at 905. This purpose is not served by denying capital gains treatment in a case such as this in which the taxpayer entered into an arm's length transaction with a corporation in which he had no prior interest, exchanging his stock in the acquired corporation for less than a one percent interest in the acquiring corporation and a substantial cash boot.

Section 356(a)(2) finds its genesis in § 203(d)(2) of the Revenue Act of 1924. See 43 Stat. 257. Although modified slightly over the years, the provisions are in relevant substance identical. The accompanying House Report asserts that § 203(d)(2) was designed to "preven[t] evasion." H.R. Rep. No. 179, 68th Cong., 1st Sess. 15 (1924). Without further explication, both the House and Senate Reports simply rely on an example to explain, in the words of both Reports, "[t]he necessity for this provision." *Ibid*; S. Rep. No. 398, 68th Cong., 1st Sess., 16 (1924). Significantly, the example describes a situation in which there was no change in the stockholders' relative ownership interests, but merely the creation of a wholly owned subsidiary as a mechanism for making a cash distribution to the shareholders:

> "Corporation A has capital stock of $100,000, and earnings and profits accumulated since March 1, 1913, of $50,000. If it distributes the $50,000 as a dividend to its stockholders, the amount distributed will be taxed at the full surtax rates.
>
> On the other hand, Corporation A may organize Corporation B, to which it transfers all its assets, the consideration for the transfer being the issuance by B of all its stock and $50,000 in cash to the stockholders of Corporation A in exchange for their stock in Corporation A. Under the existing law, the $50,000 distributed with the stock of Corporation B would be taxed, not as a dividend, but as a

capital gain, subject only to the 12 1/2 per cent rate. The effect of such a distribution is obviously the same as if the corporation had declared out as a dividend its $50,000 earnings and profits. If dividends are to be subject to the full surtax rates, then such a amount so distributed should also be subject to the surtax rates and not to the 12½ per cent rate on capital gain." *Ibid*, at 16; H.R. Rep. No. 179, at 15.

The "effect" of the transaction in this example is to transfer accumulated earnings and profits to the shareholders without altering their respective ownership interests in the continuing enterprise.

Of course, this example should not be understood as exhaustive of the proper applications of § 356(a)(2). It is nonetheless noteworthy that neither the example, nor any other legislative source, evinces a congressional intent to tax boot accompanying a transaction that involves a bona fide exchange between unrelated parties in the context of a reorganization as though the payment was in fact a dividend. To the contrary, the purpose of avoiding tax evasion suggests that Congress did not intend to impose an ordinary income tax in such cases. Moreover, the legislative history of § 302 supports this reading of § 356(a)(2) as well. In explaining the "essentially equivalent to a dividend" language of § 302(b)(1)—language that is certainly similar to the "has the effect ... of a dividend" language of § 356(a)(2)—the Senate Finance Committee made clear that the relevant inquiry is "whether or not the transaction by its nature may properly be characterized as a sale of stock...." S. Rep. No. 1622, 83d Cong., 2d Sess., 234 (1954); cf. *United States v. Davis*, 397 U.S., at 311.

Examining the instant transaction in light of the purpose of § 356(a)(2), the boot-for-stock exchange in this case "may properly be characterized as a sale of stock." Significantly, unlike traditional single corporation redemptions and unlike reorganizations involving commonly owned corporations, there is little risk that the reorganization at issue was used as a ruse to distribute dividend. Rather, the transaction appears in all respects relevant to the narrow issue before us to have been comparable to an arm's-length sale by the taxpayer to NL. This conclusion, moreover, is supported by the findings of the Tax Court. The court found that "[t]here is not the slightest evidence that the cash payment was a concealed distribution from BASIN." 86 T.C., at 155. As the Tax Court further noted, Basin lacked the funds to make such a distribution:

> "Indeed, it is hard to conceive that such a possibility could even have been considered, for a distribution of that amount was not only far in excess of the accumulated earnings and profits ($2,319,611), but also of the total assets of BASIN ($2,758,069). In fact, only if one takes into account unrealized appreciation in the value of BASIN's assets, including good will and/or going concern value, can one

possibly arrive at $3,250,000. Such a distribution could only be considered as the equivalent of a complete liquidation of BA-SIN...." Ibid.

In this context, even without relying on § 302 and the post-reorganization analogy, we conclude that the boot is better characterized as a part of the proceeds of a sale of stock than as a proxy for a dividend. As such, the payment qualifies for capital gains treatment.

The judgment of the Court of Appeals is accordingly

Affirmed.

[Dissenting opinion has been omitted.]

[¶ 10,255]

Note

In an apparent alternative holding, the Court reasoned that Congress's intention was that the relevant inquiry be whether or not the transaction "may properly be characterized as a sale of stock." Even without relying on the application by analogy of the Section 302(b) rules, the Court concluded that, in the light of the entire integrated transaction, "the boot is better characterized as a part of the proceeds of the sale of stock than as a proxy for a dividend." What are the parameters of this analysis? In the event that the boot distribution failed to meet one of the Section 302(b) tests, under what circumstances might the Court nonetheless, under its alternative holding, allow capital gain treatment? The only specific situations that the Court reserved for dividend consequences are the two referred to in the opinion. It is unclear whether in still other cases the particular facts would have any bearing on the availability of capital gain treatment.

In the *Clark* case, the taxpayer received a stock interest in the acquired company that was only 71 percent of what he would have received had only stock been given as consideration for the acquisition, a difference that easily met the reduction in interest required to qualify for the threefold test of Section 302(b)(2) as substantially disproportionate. Had the amount of cash received been smaller, and the taxpayer's stock interest in the acquiring company correlatively larger, the boot might have failed the Section 302(b)(2) tests but might have qualified as "not essentially equivalent to a dividend" under Section 302(b)(1) because the taxpayer emerged from the acquisition with a relatively insignificant stock interest in the acquiring company.

Under the *Clark* decision, the shareholders of the acquired corporation may have the opportunity, if the negotiations with the acquiring corporation permit, to bargain for a large enough percentage of the total consideration in the form of boot in lieu of acquiring corporation stock to ensure that the boot distribution will meet the substantially disproportionate test of Section 302(b)(2).

In Rev. Rul. 93–61, 1993–2 C.B. 118, the IRS reacted to the *Clark* decision as follows:

> In an acquisitive reorganization, the determination of whether boot is treated as a dividend distribution under section 356(a)(2) of the Code is made by comparing the interest the shareholder actually received in the acquiring corporation in the reorganization exchange with the interest the shareholder would have received in the acquiring corporation if solely stock had been received.

Has the IRS implicitly rejected the Supreme Court's alternative holding?

[¶ 10,260]

Problems

1. Target Corporation was merged into a new wholly owned subsidiary of Acquirer Corporation, pursuant to applicable state law, in a manner that qualified as a forward triangular merger under Sections 368(a)(1)(A) and 368(a)(2)(D).

Before the merger, Target Corporation had outstanding 1,000 shares of common stock with a fair market value of $200 per share. It also had outstanding 100 15–year, seven-percent debentures, each with a principal amount of $1,000 and a fair market value of $1,100. Acquirer Corporation had outstanding 100,000 shares of voting common stock with a fair market value of $50 per share.

The plan of reorganization provides that each share of Target common stock is to be exchanged for:

> (i) three shares of Acquirer voting common stock, worth $50 per share;

> (ii) one Acquirer 15–year, eight-percent debenture, with a principal amount of $20 and a fair market value of $20;

> (iii) one share of the common stock of the General Match Corporation worth $20. General Match is an unrelated corporation; Acquirer simply owned as a portfolio investment 1,000 shares of General Match common stock which it had purchased a year before for $5 per share; and

> (iv) $10 cash.

If the transaction had been an all stock and no boot transaction, each share of Target common would have been exchanged for four shares of Acquirer voting common stock, and the total number of Acquirer shares outstanding after the acquisition would have been 104,000 shares.

The plan of reorganization provides that each Target debenture is to be exchanged for 55 Acquirer 15–year, eight-percent debentures, each with a fair market value of $20 and a principal amount of $20.

The merger is consummated on December 31. Both Acquirer and Target are on a calendar year. Target had current E & P for the year of the merger of $50,000 but prior to the year of the merger had an accumulated deficit in E & P of $35,000.

Compute the gain (loss) realized and the gain (loss) recognized for the following Target shareholders:

A, an individual owning 100 shares of Target which she purchased two years ago for $100 per share.

B, an individual owning 100 shares of Target which he purchased one year ago for $180 per share.

C, an individual owning 100 shares of Target which she purchased three years ago for $250 per share.

Will any recognized gain of A, B, or C be treated as a dividend or as gain from the exchange of stock?

An individual, D, owning no Target common stock, exchanges his five Target debentures for 275 15–year, eight-percent Acquirer debentures pursuant to the plan of reorganization. D had purchased his Target debentures two years ago (during a depressed bond market) for $900 each.

How much gain is realized by D? Recognized? Treated as a dividend?

2. Assume that, as in *Clark,* an acquisition is effected through a forward triangular merger and that all of the Target stock is owned by a single individual. Apply the Section 302(b) tests under the Court's integrated transaction analysis and its apparent alternative holding to determine how the boot will be taxed under each of the following variations in factual assumptions:

a. Target Smaller than Acquirer

Before the merger, Target had equity with a fair market value (FMV) of $200,000 and had 1,000 shares of voting common outstanding with a value of $200 per share.

Before the merger, Acquirer had equity with a FMV of $800,000 and had 4,000 shares of voting common outstanding with a value of $200 per share.

The combined equity of Acquirer and Target after a "no boot" or all voting stock merger would be $1 million, represented by 5,000 shares of voting common with a value of $200 per share.

In a no boot or all voting stock merger, Target's shareholders would have received 1,000 shares of stock of Acquirer with a FMV of $200,000, which would have represented 20 percent of Acquirer's outstanding shares (1,000/5,000).

Instead, Target's shareholders agreed to take 700 shares of Acquirer worth $200 per share, or a total of $140,000, and $60,000 of boot.

¶ 10,260

Consequently, in the actual merger, Target's shareholders received 700 of a total of 4,700 shares of Acquirer outstanding, or 14.9 percent.

b.   Target Larger than Acquirer

Before the merger, Target's situation is as stated above.

Before the merger, Acquirer had equity with a FMV of $100,000 and had 500 shares of voting common outstanding with a value of $200 per share.

The combined equity of Acquirer and Target after a no boot or all voting stock merger would have a FMV of $300,000, represented by 1,500 shares worth $200 per share.

In a no boot merger, Target's shareholders would have received 1,000 shares of stock of Acquirer with a total FMV of $200,000 and would have owned 66⅔ percent of the outstanding Acquirer shares (1,000/1,500).

Instead, Target's shareholders agreed to take 700 shares of Acquirer shares worth $200 per share, or a total of $140,000, plus $60,000 of boot. Consequently, in the actual merger, Target's shareholders received 700 of Acquirer's 1,200 shares or 58⅓ percent of Acquirer's outstanding shares.

c.   Target Equal in Size to Acquirer

Before the merger, Target's situation is as stated above.

Before the merger, Acquirer had equity with a FMV of $200,000 and had 1,000 shares of voting common outstanding with a value of $200 per share.

The combined equity of Acquirer and Target after a no boot or all voting stock merger would have a FMV of $400,000 represented by 2,000 shares worth $200 per share.

In a no boot merger, Target's shareholders would have received 1,000 shares of stock of Acquirer with a total FMV of $200,000 and would have owned 50 percent of the outstanding Acquirer shares (1,000/2,000).

Instead, Target's shareholders agreed to take 700 shares of Acquirer stock worth $200 per share, or a total of $140,000, plus $60,000 of boot. Consequently, in the actual merger, Target's shareholders received 700 of Acquirer's 1,700 shares or 41.1 percent of Acquirer's outstanding shares.

3.   If, under Section 356(a)(2) and *Clark,* the receipt of boot by the shareholders of the acquired corporation results in dividend treatment, how does that treatment differ from dividend treatment under Section 302(d)?

4.   How much more boot in lieu of Acquirer stock would be required in Problems 1.b. and 1.c., above, to ensure that the constructive redemp-

tion would meet the substantially disproportionate test of Section 302(b)(2)?

5.   Would the not essentially equivalent to a dividend test of Section 302(b)(1) be met in Problems 1.a., 1.b., and 1.c., above?

6.   How does the *Clark* case affect the likelihood that preferred stock issued incident to an acquisitive or a single corporation reorganization will be classified as Section 306 stock?

3. CONCEPT OF STOCK OR SECURITIES

[¶ 10,265]

a. *Debt Obligations as Securities*

When a holder of debt obligations issued by a corporation that is a party to a reorganization surrenders those obligations in exchange for other debt obligations issued by that corporation (in an "E" recapitalization) or by another corporation (in an acquisitive reorganization) that is a party to the reorganization, nonrecognition of gain and loss is accorded only if both the obligations surrendered and the obligations received in exchange qualify as "securities." Thus, if securities are surrendered in a reorganization in exchange for debt obligations that are not securities, the exchange is taxable. Similarly, if the debt holder surrenders debt obligations in exchange for stock, nonrecognition will apply only if the debt obligations surrendered are "securities." When "securities" are involved, nonrecognition of gain or loss applies to the extent prescribed in Sections 354(a)(2) and 356(d).

Any other exchanges of debt obligations for other debt obligations or for stock will be outside the reorganization provisions and any gain or loss realized will be recognized. For example, a surrender of short-term debt obligations that do not qualify as securities in exchange for securities will be taxable, as will a surrender of short-term debt obligations for stock and a surrender of securities for debt obligations that are not securities.

[¶ 10,270]

REVENUE RULING 59–98
1959–1 C.B. 76.

Advice has been requested whether the exchange of bonds and accrued interest thereon for stock of the corporation which issued such bonds is a recapitalization under the terms of section 368(a)(1)(E) * * * and whether such bonds constitute "securities" within the meaning of section 354(a)(1) * * *.

In 1957, the corporation here involved, which had been in serious financial difficulties for several years, exchanged newly issued common stock for all its outstanding first mortgage bonds and the accrued unpaid interest thereon, so that after the exchange the former bondholders owned 40 percent of the common stock outstanding. The bonds surrendered had been issued in 1946 and had originally been payable in from three to 10 years, the average time to maturity at issuance being six and one-half years. The corporation had not deducted any of the unpaid interest, either in its computation of income or in its computation of earnings and profits. Before the bonds were surrendered none of the bondholders owned any of the common stock. The exchange of stock for bonds was arranged in order to bring the corporation out of the financial difficulties which had made it unable to pay the principal and interest of the bonds when due. The fair market value of the stock issued for each bond was substantially less than the principal amount of the bond. All of the bonds were purchased at issuance by various individuals as investments.

Section 354(a)(1) * * * states, in part, that no gain or loss shall be recognized if *securities* in a corporation a party to a reorganization are, in pursuance of a plan of reorganization, exchanged solely for stock in such corporation. Section 368(a)(1)(E) states that a "reorganization" includes a *recapitalization*.

The meaning of the word "securities" is not defined in the Internal Revenue Code of 1939 and is similarly not defined in the Internal Revenue Code of 1954. However, in *Camp Wolters Enterprises, Inc. v. Commissioner*, 22 T.C. 737, affirmed, 230 Fed. (2d) 555, the Tax Court of the United States discussed the meaning of the term as it appeared in section 112(b)(5) of the 1939 Code, saying, in part, as follows:

> * * * The test as to whether notes are securities is not a mechanical determination of the time period of the note. Though time is an important factor, the controlling consideration is an over-all evaluation of the nature of the debt, degree of participation and continuing interest in the business, the extent of proprietary interest compared with the similarity of the note to a cash payment, the purpose of the advances, etc.

In view of the foregoing, since in the instant case the bonds were secured by a mortgage on the corporate property, since they had an average life of six and one-half years when issued, and since they were purchased for investment purposes by persons other than the stockholders, it is held that these bonds constitute securities for purposes of subchapter C, chapter 1, of the Code. Thus the change in the capital structure of the corporation constitutes a recapitalization and, therefore, a reorganization as defined in section 368(a)(1)(E) * * *. Accordingly, under section 354(a) * * *, no gain or loss is recognized to the bondholders from the exchange of the mortgage bonds, together with the unpaid accrued interest thereon, for capital stock of the corporation.

¶ 10,270

[¶ 10,275]

Notes

1.   Section 354(a)(2)(B) now requires that any gain realized on the exchange of accrued interest for stock, securities, or other property, be recognized.

2.   The Tax Court in *Camp Wolters Enterprises, Inc. v. Commissioner*, cited in Rev. Rul. 59–98, held that nonnegotiable, unsecured installment notes coming due five to nine years after issuance (but containing rights of prepayment which were, in fact, exercised within two years) were securities. In formulating the test quoted by Rev. Rul. 59–98, the court reviewed the authorities as follows:

> * * * The line is drawn somewhere between long-term bonds and short-term notes. Short-term notes are not "securities." *Pinellas Ice & Cold Storage Co. v. Commissioner*, 287 U.S. 462 (3½-month notes); * * * *Neville Coke & Chemical Co.*, 3 T.C. 113, affirmed 148 F.2d 599 (3–, 4–, and 5–year notes); *Pacific Public Service Co.*, 4 T.C. 742 (demand notes); *Wellington Fund, Inc.*, 4 T.C. 185 (12–month notes). On the other hand, long-term bonds have been held to be "securities." *Helvering v. Watts*, 296 U.S. 387 (mortgage bonds); *Daniel H. Burnham*, 33 B.T.A. 147, affirmed 86 F.2d 776 (10–year unsecured notes); *Commissioner v. Freund*, 98 F.2d 201, affirming B.T.A. Memorandum Opinion (6–year bonds); *Globe-News Publishing Co.*, 3 T.C. 1199 (25–year scrip).

> * * *

In *Wellington Fund, Inc.*, supra, we said at p. 189:

> The question of the meaning of the term "securities," as used in various revenue statutes, has been considered by the courts in a number of cases. The rule appears to be settled that where such an act does not define the term, it denotes an obligation of a character giving the creditor some assured participation in the business of the debtor, or, in other words, an investment in the business, and that the term does not include evidences of indebtedness for short term loans representing temporary advances for current corporate needs.
> * * *

> In our recent decision in *Neville Coke & Chemical Co.*, 3 T.C. 113, we held that a creditor holding three, four, and five-year notes of a corporation, evidencing advances made to meet current liabilities, was not, because of that fact, a holder of securities of the corporation, since such notes could not be considered investments in the business and thus did not constitute securities * * *.

> * * *

22 T.C. at 751.

3. In Rev. Rul. 59–98, assuming that the bondholders had purchased the bonds at their principal or face amount when they were originally issued by the corporation, was the loss they realized on the exchange recognized?

4. To the extent that securities are exchanged in a reorganization for other securities, gain is recognized (i) to the extent of the fair market value of any excess of the principal amount of the securities received over the principal amount of the securities surrendered and (ii) to the extent of any accrued interest on the securities surrendered. §§ 356(d) and 354(a)(2)(B). As noted above, if either the debt obligations surrendered or those received do not constitute securities, gain or loss realized will be recognized. Thus, in addition to the issue raised in Rev. Rul. 59–98, the question of whether a debt obligation is a security may arise with respect to the obligations received in a reorganization exchange. In a reorganization, if securities are surrendered in exchange for other securities of equal or lesser principal amount, recognition of gain or loss will be deferred until the securities received are paid off or disposed of; if they are exchanged for obligations that are not securities, gain or loss will be recognized in full immediately.

5. If, in a qualifying reorganization, stock in one corporation is exchanged by a shareholder for stock and debt obligations issued by another corporation, both corporations being parties to the reorganization, the fair market value of the debt instruments is taxable as boot whether they constitute securities or not. If the obligations are securities, their receipt is governed by Sections 354(a)(2) and 356(a) and (d). If they are not securities, it is governed by Section 356(a).

6. In "Securities—Continuity of Interest," 58 Harv. L. Rev. 705 (1945), Dean Griswold argued that the term "securities" should be construed, for purposes of the reorganization sections, to include all corporate debt obligations. He referred to the narrower construction it has received as a "situation in which a literalism, faithful not to the statute itself, but to an unnecessary construction of the statute, has been allowed to go far towards preventing the statute from being applied to cases which seem to be clearly within its intended scope."

Do you agree? What purpose is served by a narrow construction of the term "securities"? Is it sound policy to permit nonrecognition of gain when relatively long-term debt obligations (securities) are exchanged in a reorganization for similar obligations of an equal or lesser principal amount and not do the same when short-term debt obligations are exchanged? Does the fact that a holder of securities has a longer term stake in the corporation than the holder of short-term obligations justify the difference in treatment?

7. The issue whether debt obligations do or do not constitute "securities" is controlling only with respect to nonrecognition of gain or loss under Sections 354(a)(2) and 356(a) and (d). In other contexts, a

¶ 10,275

distinction is drawn between debt obligations and equity interests, and the distinction between a "security" and another debt obligation is immaterial. For example, when the continuity of shareholder interest test is being applied, the controlling distinction is generally between debt and equity. As noted above, if the consideration received by the shareholders of the acquired corporation in an acquisitive reorganization consists predominantly of debt obligations issued by the acquiring corporation, the transaction will not meet the continuity of shareholder interest test and the transaction will not qualify as a reorganization. See ¶ 10,040. This will be true whether or not the debt obligations received qualify as "securities."

8. Note that in a Section 351 exchange, securities issued by the transferee corporation are always treated as boot. If, however, they are exchanged for securities in the same corporation, the transaction will be treated as a recapitalization, and the reorganization rules apply. See ¶ 11,005.

9. A separate issue is whether, when debt obligations are surrendered (for example, in a "C" reorganization) in exchange for other debt obligations, there has been an "exchange" of differing obligations or simply an assumption by the acquiring corporation of the liability represented by the surrendered obligations. If debt obligations of a corporation are surrendered for essentially similar obligations, the transaction will normally be treated as simply an assumption of the debt concerned. See ¶ 10,315.

[¶ 10,280]

b. *Contingent or Escrowed Stock; Flexible Conversion Ratio Preferred*

An acquisitive reorganization may involve what are in effect acquisition price adjustments following the closing. For example, a post-closing audit may disclose that the acquiring corporation received less than it bargained for, or, more specifically, less than the target represented it would receive. One method for dealing with this issue is to place some acquiring corporation stock in escrow to be returned to it if the target's assets transferred prove to be of less value than represented by the target or its shareholders. The target shareholders may have the right to vote and to receive dividends on the escrowed shares or the escrow agent may receive these dividends and pay them to the target shareholders if the shares are released by the escrow agent to them. If a downward price adjustment is called for, an appropriate number of shares is returned by the escrow agent to the acquiring corporation and the rest released to the target shareholders.

A post-closing adjustment in the number of acquiring corporation shares to be included in the purchase price may also be required because the parties agree that the number of shares should be increased if the target exceeds a specified level of profitability after the closing or if the stock of the acquiring corporation decreases in value after the closing. These adjustments may be funded by an escrow arrangement or they may be implemented by a contingent stock arrangement. Under the latter scheme the acquiring corporation is obligated to issue additional shares to target shareholders if the target's post-closing business generates profits in excess of a specified amount (an "earn-out" arrangement) or if the value of the acquiring corporation stock falls by a specified amount (a "contingent stock" arrangement).

An earn-out or contingent stock arrangement can, alternatively, be embodied in a flexible conversion ratio on preferred stock which forms part or all of the consideration package. The preferred is convertible into common stock at a specified ratio. This basic conversion ratio is subject to adjustment upward (i.e., the preferred is convertible into a larger number of common shares) or downward (i.e., into a smaller number) to reflect the earn-out or contingent stock arrangement.

[¶ 10,285]

REVENUE PROCEDURE 84–42

1984–1 C.B. 521.

* * *

Sec. 2. Procedure

.01 Section 3.03 of Rev. Proc. 77–37 is amplified to read as follows:

In transactions under sections 368(a)(1)(A), 368(a)(1)(B), 368(a)(1)(C), 368(a)(1)(D), 368(a)(1)(E), and 351 * * *, it is not necessary that all the stock which is to be issued in exchange for the requisite stock or property, be issued immediately provided (1) that all the stock will be issued within 5 years from the date of transfer of assets or stock for reorganizations under sections 368(a)(1)(A), 368(a)(1)(C), 368(a)(1)(D), and 368(a)(1)(E), or within 5 years from the date of the initial distribution in the case of transactions under sections 368(a)(1)(B) and 351; (2) there is a valid business reason for not issuing all the stock immediately, such as difficulty in determining the value of one or both of the corporations involved in the transaction; (3) the maximum number of shares which may be issued in the exchange is stated; (4) at least 50 percent of the maximum number of shares of each class of stock which may be issued is issued in the initial distribution; (5) the agreement evidencing the right to receive stock in the future prohibits assignment (except by operation of law) or if the agreement does not prohibit assignment, the right must not be evidenced by negotiable certificates of any kind and must not be readily marketable; (6) such right can give rise to the receipt only of additional stock of the corporation making the underlying distribution; (7) such stock issuance will not be triggered by

¶ 10,285

an event the occurrence or nonoccurrence of which is within the control of shareholders; (8) such stock issuance will not be triggered by the payment of additional tax or reduction in tax paid as a result of a Service audit of the shareholders or the corporation either (a) with respect to the reorganization or section 351 transaction in which the contingent stock will be issued, or (b) when the reorganization or section 351 transaction in which the contingent stock will be issued involves persons related within the meaning of section 267(c)(4) * * *; and (9) the mechanism for the calculation of the additional stock to be issued is objective and readily ascertainable. Stock issued as compensation, royalties or any other consideration other than in exchange for stock or assets will not be considered to have been received in the exchange. Until the final distribution of the total number of shares of stock to be issued in the exchange is made, the interim basis of the stock of the issuing corporation received in the exchange by the shareholders (not including that portion of each share representing interest) will be determined, pursuant to section 358(a), as though the maximum number of shares to be issued (not including that portion of each share representing interest) has been received by the shareholders.

In connection with item 3.03(8) above, the Service reserves the right to refuse to rule if, based on all the facts and circumstances of a case, it is determined that the principal purpose of the triggering mechanism is the reduction in federal income taxes (see section 3.02(1) of Rev. Proc. 84–22, 1984–13 I.R.B. 18).

.02 Section 3.06 of Rev. Proc. 77–37 is amplified to read as follows:

In transactions under section 368(a)(1)(A), 368(a)(1)(B), 368(a)(1)(C), 368(a)(1)(D), 368(a)(1)(E), and 351 * * *, a portion of the stock issued in exchange for the requisite stock or property may be placed in escrow by the exchanging shareholders, or may be made subject to a condition pursuant to the agreement, or plan of reorganization or of the transaction, for possible return to the issuing corporation under specified conditions provided (1) there is a valid business reason for establishing the arrangement; (2) the stock subject to such arrangement appears as issued and outstanding on the balance sheet of the issuing corporation and such stock is legally outstanding under applicable state law; (3) all dividends paid on such stock will be distributed currently to the exchanging shareholders; (4) all voting rights of such stock (if any) are exercisable by or on behalf of the shareholders or their authorized agent; (5) no shares of such stock are subject to restrictions requiring their return to the issuing corporation because of death, failure to continue employment, or similar restrictions; (6) all such stock is released from the arrangement within 5 years from the date of consummation of the transaction (except where there is a bona fide dispute as to whom the stock should be released); (7) at least 50 percent of the number of shares of each class of stock issued initially to the shareholders (exclusive of shares of stock to be issued at a later date as described in .01 above) is not subject to the arrangement; (8) the return of stock will not be triggered by an event the occurrence or nonoccurrence of which is within the control of shareholders; (9) the return of stock will not be triggered by the payment of additional tax or reduction in tax paid as a result of a Service audit of the shareholders or the corporation either (a) with respect to the reorganization or section 351 transaction in which the escrowed stock will be issued, or (b) when the reorganization or section 351 transaction in which the escrowed stock will be issued involves persons related within the meaning of section 267(c)(4) * * *; and (10) the mechanism for the calculation of the number of shares of stock to be returned is objective and readily ascertainable.

In connection with item 3.06(9) above, the Service reserves the right to refuse to rule if, based on all the facts, and circumstances of a case, it is determined that the principal purpose of the triggering mechanism is the reduction in federal income taxes * * *.

* * *

[¶ 10,290]

c. *Warrants to Buy Stock*

In Bateman v. Commissioner, 40 T.C. 408 (1963) (nonacq.), the Tax Court considered whether stock warrants qualified as stock within the meaning of Section 354(a). In a statutory merger which qualified as a reorganization under Section 368(a)(1)(A) the taxpayer exchanged stock of the acquired corporation for stock and stock warrants of the acquiring corporation. The warrants were assignable and had a life of ten years. Each warrant entitled its holder to buy one share of common stock of the acquiring corporation at a price of $10 per share during the first five years and at a price of $15 per share during the second five years. At the time of receipt the warrants were worth almost $3 each. The court said (40 T.C. at 414):

* * *

In *Helvering v. Southwest Corp.*, 315 U.S. 194 (1942) warrants to purchase voting stock were held not to be voting stock. In *E.P. Raymond*, 37 B.T.A. 423 (1938), we held stock purchase warrants to be securities and in so doing apparently accepted as a fact that these securities were not stock. The Court of Claims in *Goodhue v. United States*, 17 F.Supp. 86 (1936), held stock rights not to constitute stock but to represent a contractual right to purchase stock. In *Carlberg v. United States*, [281 F.2d 507 (8th Cir.1960)], in holding certain certificates of contingent interest to represent stock, the Court considered the rights connected with such certificates to differ from the "contractual" rights of the warrants involved in *Helvering v. Southwest Corp.*, *supra*. One of the major differences which the

¶ 10,290

taxpayer had urged and the Court apparently approved was that the warrants in the *Southwest* case gave no rights in the stock to the holder until a payment for the stock was made, whereas in the *Carlberg* case the holder of certificates of contingent interests needed to take no positive action or provide any additional consideration to become entitled to the reserved stock. * * * Also in the *Carlberg* case the holder of the certificates of contingent interest was entitled to the accumulated dividends on the stock when and if the contingency was removed and the stock certificates issued to her. * * * In the instant case a payment was required before the warrant holder would be entitled to receive stock and the warrants did not entitle the holder to any dividends or other rights of stockholders until exercised with the required payments to receive the stock. The provisions of the warrants here involved are not distinguishable in any material respect from those involved in *Helvering v. Southwest Corp., supra.* We, therefore, hold that the stock purchase warrants did not constitute stock. If they were securities, section 354(a)(1) is made inapplicable to this exchange by the provisions of section 354(a)(2)(B) and the fair market value of the warrants is recognized as gain to the extent provided in section 356 just as it would be if the warrants were not securities but were "other property."

Neither party takes the position that these warrants were not property at all. Both apparently recognize that the warrants are "property."

* * *

In a ruling apparently based on the same facts as Carlberg v. United States, 281 F.2d 507 (8th Cir.1960), the IRS reached a conclusion contrary to the Eighth Circuit. The ruling dealt with negotiable certificates issued to shareholders of an acquired corporation in a statutory merger that represented contingent interests in shares of the common stock of the acquiring (surviving) corporation to be issued in certain eventualities along with cash representing the value of dividends that would have been paid on the contingent shares in the meantime. The IRS ruled that since the certificates represented transferable interests that contained a dividend income element, they constituted something more than a right only to receive additional stock and must be characterized as "other property." Rev. Rul. 57–586, 1957–2 C.B. 249; cf. Rev. Rul. 64–251, 1964–2 C.B. 338. But the IRS has ruled that a nonassignable contract right to receive only additional voting stock contingent on future earnings did not violate the "solely for voting stock" requirement of a "B" reorganization. Rev. Rul. 66–112, 1966–1 C.B. 68; see also Rev. Proc. 77–37, 1977–2 C.B. 568.

In the *Bateman* case, is the court's conclusion correct that, if the warrants are "securities," the tax result is the same as if they are "other property"? Is the court merely suggesting that under Section 356 the fair market value of the warrants would be taxed as "boot"? Under the provisions of Section 356(d)(2)(B), if securities are received on an exchange but none are surrendered it appears that the amount of gain recognized cannot be greater than the "entire principal amount of the securities received." In *Bateman* that amount would be zero using the normal definition of principal amount, i.e., the amount due upon maturity of an obligation. If this is true, then it will certainly make a difference under *Bateman* whether the warrants are securities or other property.

Reg. § 1.354–1(e) formerly stated that stock rights or warrants were not included in the term "stock or securities". Effective March 9, 1998, it was amended to provide that for purposes of Section 354 the term "securities" includes rights issued by a corporate party to a reorganization to acquire its stock. It also provides that for purposes of Sections 354 and 356(d)(2)(B) a right to acquire stock has no principal amount. In the reorganization context, a right to acquire stock has the same meaning as it does under Sections 305 and 317(a). Reg. § 1.354–1(e). In the light of the changes in Reg. § 1.354–1(e), consider the following exchange: Taxpayer surrenders $100,000 worth of common stock and a long-term bond with both a principal amount and a fair market value of $1,000; taxpayer receives $70,000 worth of stock and $31,000 worth of warrants such as those in *Bateman*. On such an exchange would Section 354(a)(1) apply, unlimited by any provision of Section 354(a)(2)?

[¶ 10,295]

4. NONRECOGNITION OF GAIN OR LOSS BY CORPORATE PARTIES TO REORGANIZATION

Section 361(a) applies to the corporate transferor of property in a reorganization. It provides that, as a general rule, no gain or loss will be recognized by a corporate transferor on any exchange of property for stock or securities pursuant to the plan of reorganization. The transferor and the corporation whose stock or securities are received must each be a "party to the reorganization" as that term is defined in Section 368(b).

Section 361(b) provides for the recognition of gain realized by the corporate transferor if the transferor receives boot along with the nonrecognition property. However, under Section 361(b)(1)(A), gain is not recognized by the transferor if all of the boot is distributed in pursuance of the plan of reorganization. The rationale for this treatment is that the transferor corporation is simply a "conduit" for passing the boot to its shareholders, even though particular shareholders may have a loss on the transaction with the result that, insofar as appreciated boot distributed to them is concerned, the gain will not be recognized either at the corporate or at the shareholder level. If some or all of the boot is retained by the transferor, any gain realized must be recognized up to the value of the boot retained. § 361(b)(1)(B). For purposes of Section 361(b)(1), a transfer of boot to creditors in connection with the reorganization is treated as a distribution pursuant to the plan of reorganization. § 361(b)(3). If a loss is realized by the corporate transferor, the loss is not recognized whether or not boot is received. § 361(b)(2).

Because in a direct and a forward triangular "A" reorganization the acquired corporation disappears by operation of law and in a "C" the acquired corporation must be liquidated (unless a special waiver is granted), no gain will be recognized to the transferor with respect to boot received in the acquisition; the boot is necessarily distributed.

Section 361(c) deals with the tax consequences of distributions by the transferor corporation to its shareholders (or creditors) in pursuance of the plan of reorganization which parallel those mandated by Section 311. Although Section 361(c)(1) provides generally for nonrecognition of gain (and loss) on the distribution by a corporation of property to its shareholders in pursuance of a plan of reorganization, Section 361(c)(2)(A) requires recognition of gain (but not loss) on the distribution of property to shareholders (or creditors) other than "qualified property." Qualified property is defined in Section 361(c)(2)(B) to include stock, stock rights, or debt obligations of the corporations that are parties to the reorganization. It therefore includes essentially all of the consideration received from the acquiring corporation in the form of equity or debt. In addition, a corporation recognizes no gain (or loss) on the transfer of qualified property to the corporation's creditors in payment of its debt obligations in connection with the reorganization. § 361(c)(3). Section 361(c)(2)(A) is most likely to apply to require recognition of gain with respect to gain inherent in property owned by the acquired corporation before the acquisition of its assets that is not transferred by the acquired corporation to the acquiring corporation but is distributed instead to the shareholders (or creditors) of the acquired corporation.

The acquiring corporation in an acquisitive reorganization is not covered by Section 361 and must rely on Section 1032 to avoid recognition of gain when it exchanges its stock for assets or stock of the transferor. Suppose as part of the consideration the acquiring corporation transfers vacant land with a fair market value of $800,000 and a basis of $400,000? What is the result? What Code provision governs?

[¶ 10,300]

5. DETERMINATION OF BASIS

As noted above, two separate sets of provisions govern the determination of basis in reorganizations. Section 358(a) deals with determination of the basis a participating shareholder or securityholder will have in nonrecognition property received in a reorganization. It provides that the basis in stock or securities surrendered will be substituted (with prescribed adjustments) for the basis in nonrecognition property received.

¶ 10,295

Section 362(b) governs the basis of property acquired by a corporation in a reorganization. It provides for a carryover of the basis of the transferor to the acquiring corporation (with prescribed adjustments). Under both Sections 358(a) and 362(b), basis must be increased by gain recognized to the transferor.

The carryover basis rule of Section 362(b) is simple to apply when assets of the target corporation are acquired. The target can advise the acquiring corporation as to the former basis of the acquired assets in its hands which carries over to the acquiring corporation. It is more difficult when stock of a publicly owned target is acquired for voting stock of the acquiring corporation in a "B" reorganization. Technically, the basis of the target shares in the hands of its shareholders carries over under Section 362(b) to become the basis of those shares in the hands of the acquiring corporation. It is often not feasible, however, to determine the basis of target shares in the hands of each of its shareholders. Formerly, the IRS permitted the acquiring corporation to determine its basis in the target's shares using an averaging method in which the acquiring corporation would obtain a sample of the target shareholders' basis and use an appropriate statistical method for determining its overall basis in the target's shares. In 2006, Treasury issued final regulations adopting a tracing method in which the basis of each share of stock received is the same as the basis of the allocable share of stock surrendered. Reg. § 1.358–2(a)(2)(i). To the extent that the terms of the exchange fail to specify which shares of acquiring corporation stock are received in exchange for a particular share of target stock, the regulations provide that a pro rata portion of the shares of stock of each class received is treated as received in exchange for the target stock surrendered, based on the fair market values of the surrendered stock. Reg. § 1.358–2(a)(2)(vii).

As discussed in Chapter 2, Congress changed the basis rules in 2004 for incorporation transactions by enacting Section 362(e)(2), which prevents loss duplication. See ¶ 2150. While this rule does not apply in the case of reorganization transactions, Section 362(e)(1) does apply in the context of loss importations in tax-free reorganizations. These occur when property that has not been taxed in the U.S. system, such as property owned by a foreign corporation or a tax-exempt organization, are acquired by a U.S. corporation in a tax-free reorganization. Under Section 362(e)(1), such property would be held by the U.S. corporation at fair market value basis. See ¶ 2155.

[¶ 10,305]

6. ASSUMPTION OF LIABILITIES

As discussed in Chapter 2, the Supreme Court held that the assumption by the acquiring corporation of a debt of the acquired corporation in a statutory merger constituted boot in United States v. Hendler, 303

U.S. 564 (1938). See ¶ 2170. The decision caused considerable consternation and uncertainty in the tax world. Especially disturbing to the IRS was the question of whether bases of assets acquired in tax-free reorganizations or Section 351 exchanges that had occurred in prior years had to be stepped up to the assets' fair market values at the time of the original exchange. This step-up would have been required to reflect gain recognized because the assumption of liabilities constituted boot, even though tax was generally not paid on the gain because it was widely believed before *Hendler* that such assumptions of liability did not constitute boot. As a result of the step-up in basis, taxpayer depreciation deductions would be increased for all years for which the statute of limitations had not run without correlative recognition of gain on the original transfer on which the statute had run. Large tax revenue losses were at stake.

[¶ 10,310]

a. *Treatment of Assumed Liabilities as Other Than Boot*

Not surprisingly, soon after the *Hendler* decision, Congress reversed the holding retroactively by enacting the predecessors of subsections 357(a) and (b). H.R. Rep. No. 855, 76th Cong., 1st Sess. 18 (1939), stated:

> It has long been the policy in our income tax law to give due consideration to the exigencies of business in connection with corporate reorganizations by postponing, in certain specifically described instances, the recognition of gain realized in such transactions. In general, if gain is realized in such a transaction, non-recognition of the entire gain is allowed only where, under the specifically defined circumstances, the taxpayer transfers property and receives in exchange therefor stock or securities in a corporation which is a party to the reorganization. If, in addition to such stock or securities, other property or money is received, gain is recognized to the extent of such other property or money.

> The recent Supreme Court case of *United States v. Hendler* (303 U.S. 564 (1938)) has been broadly interpreted to require that, if a taxpayer's liabilities are assumed by another party in what is otherwise a tax-free reorganization, gain is recognized to the extent of the assumption. In typical transactions changing the form or entity of a business it is not customary to liquidate the liabilities of the business and such liabilities are almost invariably assumed by the corporation which continues the business. Your committee therefore believes that such a broad interpretation as is indicated above will largely nullify the provisions of existing law which postpone the recognition of gain in such cases. To enable bona fide transactions of this type to be carried on without the recognition of gain, the committee has recommended section 213 of the bill [the predecessor of § 357(a)].

b. What is an Assumed Liability?

As a result of legislation enacted in 1999, we now have a definition of what is meant by a liability assumed by a transferee in an exchange under Section 351 and for purposes of the reorganization provisions, including provisions relating to the exchanging shareholder's basis in nonrecognition property received (Section 358(d) and (h)), the corporate transferee's basis in property received (Section 362(b) and (d)), and the definition of a "C" reorganization. Under Section 357(d), liabilities assumed include the amount of (i) a recourse liability (or portion thereof) if, based on the facts and circumstances, the transferee has agreed to, and is expected to, satisfy the liability (or portion) whether or not the transferor has been relieved of it and (ii) any nonrecourse liability to which property transferred to the corporation is subject. A nonrecourse liability transferred to a corporate transferee may be reduced, however, if necessary to prevent potential abuse of Sections 357(c) and 358. See ¶ 2175.

Under another 1999 Act change, the basis of stock received in a reorganization exchange cannot (with certain exceptions) be reduced to reflect an assumed liability (including a liability covered by Section 357(a)(3)) to less than the stock's fair market value. § 358(h)(1). See ¶ 2215.

The 1999 statutory changes do not, however, resolve all issues relating to the treatment of liabilities. The issue whether a particular aspect of a reorganization transaction involves "an assumption of a liability" for purposes of the reorganization provisions can arise in a number of contexts. For example, if, in a statutory merger, the old debt obligations of the acquired corporation are exchanged for new debt obligations of the acquiring corporation, is there an "exchange" (a realization event under Section 1001) for purposes of Section 354 or merely an assumption? To what extent is the answer of significance for an "A" reorganization? For a "C"? Is the exchange versus assumption issue affected by whether the debt obligations constitute "securities"?

Surrender of debt obligations of the acquired corporation in exchange for identical obligations of the acquiring corporation would be treated as an assumption rather than an exchange. Issuance of new bonds with slightly different terms has been held to be an assumption. See e.g., New Jersey Mortgage & Title Co. v. Commissioner, 3 T.C. 1277 (1944) (acq.). But issuance of a secured mortgage bond for an unsecured note did not qualify as an assumption. Stoddard, Jr. v. Commissioner, 141 F.2d 76 (2d Cir.1944).

Reg. § 1.1001–3 provides rules for determining whether a modification of the terms of a debt instrument (including an exchange of a new instrument for an existing debt instrument) results in an exchange for purposes of Section 1001(c). There is a Section 1001 exchange under the regulation if there is "a significant modification" of the original instrument surrendered. This test is met if the original instrument is surrendered in a reorganization in exchange for a modified instrument that differs materially either in kind or in extent from the surrendered instrument. The regulation sets forth standards for determining whether a modification is significant and includes examples. Generally, a modification is significant "only if based on all facts and circumstances, the legal rights or obligations that are altered and the degree to which they are altered are economically significant." Reg. § 1.1001–3(e)(1). For example, a difference between the yield of a debt instrument surrendered in a reorganization and the yield of a debt instrument received in exchange therefor will be a significant modification if it is more than the greater of 1/4 of one percent or five percent of the annual yield of the surrendered instrument. Reg. § 1.001–3(e)(3)(ii).

The assumption issue may arise in the context of an acquisitive reorganization in which it is required that the consideration consist solely of voting stock. For example, if the acquiring corporation assumes an obligation of the acquired corporation that arises in connection with a "C" reorganization, the question may arise whether such an assumption is an "assumption of a liability" of the acquired corporation for purposes of Section 357(a) and the definition of a "C" reorganization or is consideration that violates the solely for voting stock requirement.

Helvering v. Southwest Consol. Corp., 315 U.S. 194 (1942), involved a corporation in financial difficulty which, pursuant to a plan approved by a Delaware court, reformed itself into a new corporation. As a part of the plan, the old corporation borrowed $106,680 from a bank and used it to pay off certain of its bonds (at substantially less than their face amount). Also as part of the plan the new corporation acquired the assets of the old corporation and assumed the $106,680 bank debt. The Court held that the assumption of the bank debt did not qualify under the predecessor to Section 368(a)(1)(C) as "the assumption by the acquiring corporation of a liability of the other." As a result the transaction did not fulfill the "solely for voting stock" requirement of a "C" reorganization. The Court reasoned:

> In the first place, security holders of the old company owning $440,000 face amount of obligations were paid off in cash. That cash was raised, during the reorganization, on a loan from a bank. Since that loan was assumed by respondent, it is argued that the requirement of [solely for voting stock] was satisfied. But, in substance, the transaction was precisely the same as if respondent had paid cash plus voting stock for the properties. We search the legislative history of the 1939 amendment in vain for any indication that it was designed to do more than to alter the rule of the Hendler case. That case dealt with a situation where an indebtedness which antedated the transaction in question was assumed by the transferee. There

¶ 10,315

the debt assumed clearly was a "liability of the other" corporation. The situation here is quite different * * *. Though the liability assumed had its origin in obligations of the transferor, its nature and amount were determined and fixed in the reorganization. It therefore cannot be labelled as an obligation of the "other" or predecessor corporation. * * *

315 U.S. at 199.

Does the *Southwest Consol. Corp.* reasoning apply to all liabilities incurred by the transferor corporation during the course of the reorganization? If other liabilities amounting to 20 percent or more of the value of its assets are to be assumed by the acquiring corporation, must transferor corporations in a "C" reorganization reserve enough cash to pay their own lawyers and accounting fees? Despite the above language from *Southwest Consol. Corp.*, the IRS has ruled that the acquiring corporation may pay such expenses and certain others that arise in connection with the reorganization without violating the solely for voting stock requirement. See ¶ 10,135.

Does Section 357(b) provide an adequate check against tax avoidance through the incurring of borrowings to generate cash shortly before the acquisition? Does the reservation of cash by the acquired corporation for payment of its own liabilities pose a similar threat? Does the "substantially all of the properties" requirement (¶ 10,080) provide a sufficient check? See Southland Ice Co. v. Commissioner, 5 T.C. 842 (1945) (acq).

[¶ 10,320]

Problems

Household, Inc., a manufacturer of prefabricated houses, has one class of stock outstanding which is worth one dollar per share. It acquires three small corporations in "C" reorganizations. They are Chair, Inc., Table, Inc., and the Glassware Corporation.

a. **Chair has assets as follows**:

	Adjusted Basis	Fair Market Value
Inventory	$60,000	$ 50,000
Land	10,000	100,000
Cash	50,000	50,000

Household acquires Chair's assets for 200,000 shares of its voting common stock worth $1 per share.

Assume, pursuant to the plan of reorganization, Chair liquidates and distributes 100,000 Household shares each to Jones and Smith, its two 50–percent shareholders. Jones has a total adjusted basis of $200,000 for the Chair shares he surrenders in the liquidation; Smith has an adjusted basis of only $50,000 for her Chair shares. What basis

¶ **10,320**

will Smith and Jones have for their Household shares? Is this result reasonable? What is the basis of the Chair assets in Household's hands?

b. Table has a bank debt of $12,000 and has assets as follows:

	Adjusted Basis	Fair Market Value
Land	$10,000	$70,000
Inventory	40,000	40,000

Household acquires all the assets of Table, subject to the $12,000 bank debt, in exchange for 90,000 Household shares, $6,000 in cash, and 200 shares of XYZ Corporation. XYZ is an unrelated corporation, the stock of which has a fair market value of $10 per share. Household's adjusted basis for the XYZ stock is $5 per share.

Table is liquidated pursuant to the plan of reorganization. It distributes 45,000 Household shares, $3,000 in cash, and 100 XYZ shares to Black in exchange for her 1,000 Table shares which have a total basis of $20,000. It makes a like distribution to White in exchange for his 1,000 Table shares which have a total basis of $50,000.

What are the tax consequences to Household, to Table, and to Black and White of the transfer of the XYZ shares by Household to Table and their subsequent distribution in liquidation by Table to Black and White?

What are the tax consequences to Table of the assumption of its liability by Household?

What is the basis of the Household shares and the XYZ shares in the hands of Black? Of White? Is this reasonable? What is the basis of the Table assets in the hands of Household?

c. Glassware has assets as follows:

	Adjusted Basis	Fair Market Value
Land	$10,000	$100,000
Inventory	35,000	35,000

Glassware has a bank debt of $100,000. Household acquires all the assets of Glassware, subject to the $100,000 debt, for 35,000 shares of Household stock. Glassware liquidates, distributing the 35,000 shares of Household stock to its sole shareholder, Blue, who has a basis for her Glassware stock of $30,000.

Is any gain recognized to Glassware? If so, how much? Suppose Section 357(b) applied? If no gain is recognized to Glassware, has Glassware received a windfall?

Would Glassware have any recognized gain if its transaction with Household constituted a "D" reorganization—that is, if following the exchange of its assets for Household stock Glassware was in "control" of

¶ 10,320

Household and if immediately thereafter Glassware completely liquidated? Would Section 361(a) protect Glassware from recognition of gain?
See § 357(c).

[¶ 10,325]

G. PROPOSALS FOR REFORM OF THE TAXATION OF ACQUISITIONS

The existing rules relating to acquisitive reorganizations that have
been considered in the preceding materials are freighted with irrational
distinctions and inconsistencies and almost numbing complexity. It is
hardly surprising therefore that they have generated a chorus of criticism and a number of proposals for reform.

The first major effort to review the acquisitive reorganization area
was reflected in the proposals contained in the Federal Income Tax
Project: Subchapter C: Proposals on Corporate Acquisitions and Dispositions (A.L.I. 1982). The basic thrust of these proposals was to acknowledge that the existing system enabled sophisticated tax planners to elect
an appropriately tailored transaction and thereby to determine to what
extent (i) tax-free, carryover basis treatment or (ii) taxable, fair market
value basis treatment (and in certain cases some of each) would apply.
The objective usually was, of course, to minimize the tax burden since
there are few substantive economic differences between various types of
transactions. The A.L.I. proposals embraced the elective feature of the
existing system by suggesting that taxpayers be given the right to dictate
the result by simply making an explicit election. This would avoid the
possibility that certain procedural requirements of one transaction or
another, such as board approval for an asset acquisition, would not
impede parties from achieving their desired tax results. Rather than
linking the tax treatment to corporate procedure that is itself elective,
the A.L.I. proposed to make it independently elective. The A.L.I. proposals contemplated a set of default rules to be applied in the absence of an
election, such as making any stock acquisition a carryover-basis transaction and any asset acquisition a cost-basis transaction.

Next to weigh in was the Staff of the Senate Finance Committee.
This Committee issued in 1983 a report entitled The Reform and
Simplification of the Income Taxation of Corporations, S. Prt. No. 95,
98th Cong., 1st Sess. 27 (1983), which concluded that "[t]he statutory
scheme prescribing nonrecognition treatment for those acquisitions defined as reorganizations is extremely complex and many of the differences between the types of transactions defy rationalization." This
report, at p. 5, recommended the following four fundamental changes to
the then-existing rules, also opting to give the parties the right to elect
between tax-free and taxable treatment at the corporate, but not at the
shareholder, level:

¶ 10,325

* * * First, in corporate acquisitions the parties would be able to choose, at the corporate level, between recognition and nonrecognition transactions. This express flexibility does not substantially liberalize present law. Not only is nonrecognition treatment available (so long as continuity of interest is maintained) under the reorganization rules, but corporate nonrecognition is always available if the purchaser acquires stock, rather than assets. Accordingly, the complex definitional rules for acquisitive reorganizations would be repealed. Second, transferees from corporations would be entitled to claim a cost basis only if the corporate transferor recognized gain. Thus, the general nonrecognition rules of the *General Utilities* case and its codification, which the Congress has repeatedly limited over the past 20 years, would be repealed. [This proposal was essentially implemented in the Tax Reform Act of 1986.] Third, shareholders would be permitted to receive stock tax-free in an acquisition without regard to the characterization of the transaction at the corporate level, or the terms of the exchange with other shareholders. Fourth, the complex collapsible corporation rules of section 341 would be repealed in their entirety. Those rules would no longer be necessary because the unrealized gain, ultimately, would always be taxed to the corporation.

A primary argument for an elective regime is that the present system is, in effect, elective for the taxpayer with a sophisticated tax lawyer. At p. 84, the report reasons:

* * * By making corporate nonrecognition treatment expressly elective, the law will reduce the premium placed on sophisticated tax planning. The technical requirements for qualifying a transaction as a tax-free reorganization under present law are sufficiently complex that small businesses that cannot afford to hire sophisticated tax counsel may inadvertently fail to meet them. The proposals would eliminate many of these pitfalls. As a result, like taxpayers will be more often treated alike. Additionally, the transaction costs incident to legitimate transactions will be reduced.

Then, in 1985, the Staff of the Senate Finance Committee prepared a report to accompany The Subchapter C Revision Act of 1985, which was not enacted. This report summarized the proposals contained in the bill, which also opted for elective treatment, as follows (S. Prt. No. 47, 99th Cong., 1st Sess. 50–53 (1985)):

A. *Definition of qualified acquisition (new section 364 of the Code)*

In general, the bill consolidates, simplifies, and makes uniform the rules classifying corporate mergers and acquisitions, whether treated under current law as a "reorganization", a liquidating sale * * *, or a section 338 stock acquisition.

New section 364 defines "qualified acquisition" as meaning any "qualified stock acquisition" or any "qualified asset acquisition." A qualified stock acquisition is defined as any transaction or series of transactions during the 12–month acquisition period in which one corporation acquires stock representing control of another corporation. A qualified asset acquisition means (1) any statutory merger or consolidation, or (2) any other transaction in which one corporation acquires at least 70 percent of the gross fair market value and at least 90 percent of the net fair market value of the assets of another corporation held immediately before the acquisition, and the transferor corporation distributes, within 12 months of the acquisition date, all of its assets (other than assets retained to meet claims) to its shareholders or creditors.

For these purposes, the definition of "control" is conformed to that contained in section 1504(a)(2) of the Code.

Where an acquiring corporation makes a qualified stock acquisition of a target corporation and the target corporation owns stock in a subsidiary, a special rule would treat the acquiring corporation as having also acquired the stock of the subsidiary, for purposes of determining whether the acquiring corporation has made a qualified stock acquisition of the subsidiary.

A special rule is also provided where an acquisition might qualify as both a qualified asset acquisition and a qualified stock acquisition. For example, where an acquiring corporation acquires all of the assets of a target corporation, and certain of those assets consist of all of the stock of a subsidiary, the transaction is treated as a qualified stock acquisition of the subsidiary and a qualified asset acquisition of all of the other assets of the target corporation.

The common-law doctrines of continuity of interest, continuity of business enterprise, and business purpose would have no applicability in determining whether a transaction qualifies as a qualified acquisition.

The bill repeals section 368. Acquisitive reorganizations ("A" "B" and "C" reorganizations and subsidiary mergers) under current law would be replaced by the rules for qualified acquisitions. The "D" reorganization rules would be replaced by special rules (described below) relating to qualified acquisitions between related parties. Transactions qualifying under current law as an "E" reorganization (a recapitalization) and an "F" reorganization (a mere change in identity, form, or place of organization of one corporation) are conformed to the definition of qualified acquisitions. Finally, the "G" reorganization rules (bankruptcy reorganizations), developed largely in response to continuity of interest problems in those types of transactions, are no longer needed and therefore are repealed.

B. *Elective tax treatment of qualified acquisitions (new section 365 of the Code)*

The corporate level tax consequences of a qualified acquisition are explicitly made elective. Under new section 365, all qualified acquisitions are treated as "carryover basis acquisitions" unless an election to be treated as a "cost basis acquisition" is made.

In general, elections may be made on a corporation-by-corporation basis. Thus, for example, if an acquiring corporation makes a qualified stock acquisition of both a target corporation and a target subsidiary, a cost basis election may be made for the target corporation but, if desired, no such election need be made for the target subsidiary.

Within a single corporation, the same election must generally apply for all of the assets of the corporation. A consistency rule would provide that assets that are acquired which were held by a single corporation during the consistency period must be treated consistently, either as all cost basis or all carryover basis.

* * *

C. *Corporate level tax consequences of qualified acquisitions (sections 361, 362 and 381 of the Code)*

The corporate level tax consequences of a qualified acquisition result directly from the election made at the corporate level. For example, in the case of a carryover basis acquisition, no gain or loss is recognized by the target corporation and the acquiring corporation obtains a carryover basis in any assets acquired. Attributes carry over under section 381.

In the case of a cost basis acquisition, the target corporation recognizes gain or loss and the acquiring corporation obtains a basis in any assets acquired determined under section 1012. Attributes do not carry over. Where the cost basis acquisition is a qualified stock acquisition, the target corporation is deemed to have sold all of its assets for fair market value at the close of the acquisition date in a transaction in which gain or loss is recognized, and then is treated as a new corporation which purchased all of such assets as of the beginning of the day after the acquisition date.

* * *

Under the bill, section * * * 338 of current law [is] repealed.

D. *Shareholder level tax consequences of qualified acquisitions (sections 354, 356, and 358 of the Code)*

In general, shareholder level tax consequences of a qualified acquisition are determined independent of the corporate level tax consequences and independent of the election made at the corporate level. Thus, even if a transaction is treated as a cost basis acquisition at the corporate level, it may be wholly or partly taxfree at the shareholder level. In addition, shareholder level consequences are generally determined shareholder-by-shareholder, and the consequences to one shareholder do not affect the tax treatment of other shareholders or investors of the target corporation.

As a general rule, nonrecognition treatment is provided to shareholders or security holders of the target corporation upon receipt of "qualifying consideration," i.e., stock or securities of the acquiring corporation and, where the acquiring corporation is a member of an affiliated group, of the common parent of such group and any other member of such group specified in regulations. The nonrecognition rule applies to the receipt of securities only to the extent the issue price of any securities received does not exceed the adjusted basis of any securities surrendered.

* * *

Receipt of "nonqualifying consideration" (*i.e.*, any consideration other than qualifying consideration) generally results in recognition of gain to the shareholder or security holder. Such gain is treated as gain from the sale or exchange of property unless the receipt of nonqualifying consideration has the effect of a distribution of a dividend. The determination of dividend effect is made by treating the shareholder as having received only qualifying consideration in the exchange, and then as being redeemed of all or a portion of such qualifying consideration (to the extent of the nonqualifying consideration received). For these purposes, earnings and profits of both the target and acquiring corporations are generally taken into account.

* * *

In general, shareholders or security holders obtain a substitute basis in any [qualifying] consideration received, and a fair market value basis in any nonqualifying consideration received. Controlling corporate shareholders of the target corporation generally obtain a basis in any qualifying consideration received equal to the lesser of substitute basis or fair market value basis.

An obvious concomitant of an elective regime for taxing acquisitions is that, within broad parameters, taxpayers are free to select a tax free or a taxable mode of acquisition, whichever produces the more favorable tax results. This freedom of choice necessarily implies a tax subsidy to certain acquisitions and a correlative loss of tax revenue as compared with the results that would obtain under a uniform mandatory system of taxing acquisitions.

Consider the following excerpts from Coven, "Taxing Corporate Acquisitions: A Proposal for Mandatory Uniform Rules," 44 Tax L. Rev. 145, 203, 162–63, 166–67, 173, 184–85, 190–91 (1989):[2]

¶ **10,325**

The question of how a corporate acquisition ought to be subject to tax does not have a technically perfect answer. The fundamental structure of the taxing system contains inherent contradictions which preclude deriving an answer that can be defended through the elaboration of principles upon which all students of taxation would agree. As a result, rationalizing this area of the taxing system requires identifying the pattern of taxation that will result in the least economic distortion and will be most compatible with the other broad features of the legal system. The suggestion here is that those requirements are best achieved through a mandatory carryover basis system.

* * *

Historically, a number of different features in the pattern of taxing corporations might have produced a low marginal rate of tax on target corporations in cost basis acquisitions. In the current tax environment, however, the most common explanation for a low rate of tax upon a target corporation will be the existence of net operating losses in the target or the consolidated group of which it is a member. If the gain produced by a cost basis acquisition can be absorbed in whole or in part by loss carryforwards available to the target, its overall tax burden may be reduced to an amount less than the tax benefit obtained by the acquiring corporation from the resulting basis adjustment. Cost basis acquisitions are economically rational, therefore, only when the resulting tax is absorbed by operating losses.

* * *

The tax burdens produced by cost and carryover basis treatments * * * are not equally acceptable. To the contrary, in an elective system for taxing acquisitions, the cost basis election results in an improper reduction of the corporate income tax. A cost basis election becomes advantageous only when it creates a value for operating losses as a result of an acquisition that is greater than the value of those losses to the continuing business of the target. That value constitutes a tax subsidy of acquisitive transactions that violates sound congressional income tax policy.

A carryover basis pattern of taxing an acquisition should produce a tax burden on the transferred business in the hands of the acquiring corporation that replicates the burden that would have been imposed upon the target corporation in the absence of the acquisition. No income tax is accelerated and the tax attributes of the target corporation survive. Under prior law, that equation was frequently disturbed by the ability of acquiring corporations to use operating losses at a faster rate than could the target corporation from which they were inherited. Since the operating loss thereby became more valuable to the acquiring corporation than it was to the target, the loss itself provided an incentive to the acquisition.

In a recent revision of § 382, Congress addressed the distortion of normal market forces created by the favorable treatment of operating losses in the hands of acquiring corporations. The revised section was designed expressly to limit the value of transferred operating losses to the value the loss had in the hands of the target corporation. That equivalence is sought by not allowing the acquiring corporation in any year to use an amount of target losses in excess of an amount equal to a reasonable rate of return on the value of the target assets. Since that limitation approximates the maximum amount of income that the target itself might generate with its own assets, the operating losses cannot be used by the acquiring corporation at a faster rate than they could be used by the target, and thus, the losses will not have a greater value to the acquiring corporation than they did to the target. Under current law, therefore, the treatment of transferred losses under a carryover basis system in the hands of the acquiring corporation also replicates the treatment of those losses in the hands of the target.

* * * [C]ost basis treatment will only be elected when it results in a greater after-tax economic benefit to the parties to the acquisition than would carryover basis treatment. Since the tax burden of a carryover basis pattern of taxing an acquisition reproduces the tax burden that would have been imposed upon the target corporation in the absence of an acquisition, it necessarily follows that electing taxable, cost basis treatment produces a reduction in the corporate income tax relative to that level of taxation.

To ensure that business combinations are pursued for reasons that have economic justification, the taxing system ought not to provide a tax incentive to corporation acquisitions. Under current law, that principle of tax neutrality between continuing and acquired businesses is not a mere abstract ideal; rather, it has become a firmly established congressional policy. The repeal of the *General Utilities* doctrine, the revision of § 382, and other related legislation all reflect the entirely proper ascension of that policy of neutrality.

In an elective system for taxing corporation acquisitions, the cost basis election plainly violates that congressional policy. That pattern of taxation enhances the value of tax attributes in the course of an acquisition relative to the value those attributes otherwise would possess had the acquisition not occurred. The value so created constitutes a tax subsidy for those acquisitions for which a cost basis election produces a favorable result. Accordingly, the existence of the cost basis alternative improperly reduces the burden of the corporate income tax and serves as an incentive to acquisitive corporate behavior.

* * *

The rejection of elective treatment of corporate acquisitions requires the adoption of a mandatory scheme of taxation. In principle, the optimum mandatory pattern might be either a single pattern of taxation applicable to all acquisitions, either a fully taxable cost basis, or a nonrecognition carryover basis pattern, or a pattern in which cost and carryover basis consequences were assigned to transactions that are clearly distinguishable on the basis of substantial nontax factors.

The most important criterion for selecting a pattern for taxing corporate acquisitions is that the resulting tax burden be logically and fairly related to the other broad features of the taxing system. A corporate acquisition is merely one form of economic behavior subject to the provisions of the tax laws, and the treatment of that form of activity ought not be disproportionate to other applications of the taxing system. In the context of a corporate acquisition, the development of a rational pattern of taxation requires reconciling the inherent inconsistencies between the taxation of stock and asset acquisitions created by the separate entity, double tax system. Further, the resulting system must successfully distinguish between transactions that are essentially dispositive, and thus taxable, and those that are essentially a nontaxable continuation of a business activity.

The decision to impose a mandatory pattern of taxation on all acquisitions, however, implies constraints beyond fairness and rationality. In sharp contrast to the transactional and express elections permitted under current law, a mandatory system requires a clear and defensible definition of the set of transactions that are to be subject to the mandatory system. Absent such a definition, the system will remain elective. * * *

* * *

Concededly, the proposed definitional line, under current law or in the future, can never achieve crystal clarity; taxpayers desiring to alter the consequences of their transaction would not be deprived of all possible avenues of manipulation. However, because of the accumulated experience under § 355 and similar provisions, the existing tax law does contain a developed and discernible line between the transfer of a bundle of assets that constitute a business and the transfer of something less. That line could be used to create a workable definition of a corporate acquisition. Moreover, upon reviewing the continuum of corporate transactions from the sale of a single asset to the sale of a single share of stock, only one discontin-

¶ 10,325

uity that could serve as the basis for an enforceable definition of a corporate acquisition emerges. A distinction based upon the transfer of an entire business activity is the definitional line that is, at the very least, the most defensible in practice of all possible lines.

* * *

Under current law, carryover basis treatment for asset acquisitions is available only in a reorganization where the consideration received by the shareholders of the target must consist of stock in the acquiring corporation. However, and somewhat inconsistently, carryover basis treatment is always available following a stock acquisition, regardless of the nature of the consideration. The proposal here is, in general effect, to extend to asset transfers that comprise an entire business the carryover basis treatment that presently extends to stock acquisitions. That parallel treatment is entirely consistent with sound income tax policy. To the extent that stock and asset transfers produce essentially identical economic results, differences in tax treatment are improper. Accordingly, it is entirely appropriate to define carryover basis acquisitions without reference to the nature of the consideration paid by the acquiring corporation. In this respect, the proposal here is similar to the proposals of the American Law Institute pursuant to which the corporate level consequences of an acquisition would not depend upon the nature of the consideration received by the target shareholders.

* * *

Any mandatory pattern for taxing corporate acquisitions would result in enormous simplification of the taxing system. Under present law, acquisitions must be distinguished from nonacquisitive stock purchases on one side and from nonacquisitive asset transfers on the other. Moreover, reorganization-type carryover basis acquisitions must be distinguished from all other forms of acquisitions. Under any mandatory pattern, most of those arbitrary and scarcely enforceable lines would be abandoned.

Firstly, the entire complicated set of rules defining and taxing reorganizations would be entirely repealed. If a cost basis pattern were adopted, the reorganization provisions would be inconsistent with the pattern selected and would have to be eliminated. Conversely, if the carryover basis pattern suggested here were selected, the reorganization rules would be entirely subsumed with the scope of the new definition of an acquisition and would be unnecessary.

That measure of simplification, however, would only be achieved if a mandatory pattern actually were adopted. While the practical possibility of enacting a rigorous carryover basis pattern of taxation is far from clear, the likelihood that a mandatory cost basis pattern

¶ 10,325

of taxation would be adopted is virtually nonexistent. There are simply too many forms of corporate transactions, such as simple reincorporations, that present a highly appealing case for nonrecognition carryover basis treatment for the reorganization provisions to be wholly repealed. Absent that repeal, both cost and carryover basis acquisitions would continue to exist and there would not be a mandatory pattern of taxation. Rather, the existing line between cost and carryover basis acquisitions, at best, would merely have been somewhat rationalized. Accordingly, the only real possibility for substantially simplifying the taxation of corporate acquisitions is the adoption of a mandatory carryover basis pattern of taxation.

Secondly, under any mandatory system, at least for the purposes of the corporate level tax, only a single definitional line need be drawn. Under the proposal made here, there would be no occasion to define a corporate acquisition by reference to stock acquisitions for the purposes of universally applicable Code provisions, for stock transfers, regardless of their nature, would not have corporate level consequences. Rather, the only definition needed would be of the transfer of a sufficient bundle of assets to constitute a separate trade or business. The drawing of such a single definitional line would greatly simplify the taxing system. Since stock transfers are inherently carryover basis transactions and assets transfers are inherently cost basis transactions, the task of drawing one or more lines across the continuum of transactions is unavoidable. However, the fewer the lines that are drawn, the less complex and less arbitrary will be the statutory pattern. Distinguishing between asset transfers involving an entire business activity and those that do not provide a single definitional line between cost and carryover basis acquisitions and thus would contribute the maximum possible degree of simplification. Even were it assumed that the use of that definition to define an acquisition would increase the pressure on that definition, that cost would be more than offset by the simplification resulting from the use of a single definitional line.

Chapter 11

SINGLE CORPORATION REORGANIZATIONS

[¶ 11,000]

A. INTRODUCTION

Although most reorganizations, including particularly the acquisitive reorganizations discussed in Chapter 10, involve two or more corporations, there are three types of reorganizations that involve, either in form or in substance, a single corporation. These include the "E," "F," and the nondivisive "D" reorganizations.

Most of the normal rules with respect to nonrecognition of gain or loss, taxation of boot, and basis adjustments that apply in multiple corporation reorganizations also apply in the single corporation reorganizations. However, because of certain characteristics of these reorganizations, some special rules apply. For example, as discussed below, the continuity of shareholder interest and the continuity of business enterprise requirements of the acquisitive reorganizations do not apply to a recapitalization under § 368(a)(1)(E) or to a "mere change in identify, form, or place of organization" under § 368(a)(1)(F). Moreover, in an "F" reorganization, unlike the acquisitive reorganizations, the taxable year of the transferor corporation does not end on the date of the transfer, and a post-reorganization loss realized by the transferee corporation can often be carried back against the pre-reorganization income of the transferor corporation.

Historically, two principal sets of problems arose in connection with single corporation reorganizations. The first was the use of an "E" recapitalization or an "F" reorganization as the vehicle for effecting a distribution (a "bail-out") of E & P that would be taxed to individual shareholders as long-term capital gain rather than as dividend income. With the advent of qualified dividend income and the resulting narrowing of the differences between the tax treatment of capital gains and dividends, the bailout issue has declined in significance. The second involved a taxpayer adopting the form of a complete liquidation of a controlled corporation with accumulated earnings which was intended to result in the treatment of the liquidating distribution of those earnings as long-term capital gain notwithstanding the reincorporation of the operating business assets (but not the bulk of the liquid assets) in a new corporation. The latter scenario, which has many variations, all with bail-out implications, is usually referred to as the liquidation-reincorporation transaction. To combat the bail-out potential in the liquidation-reincorporation context, the IRS often attempted to have the transaction characterized for tax purposes as a reorganization in order to have recognized boot gain treated as an ordinary income dividend under Section 356(a)(2). The demise of the *General Utilities* doctrine, resulting in recognition of gain to a corporation that distributes appreciated property, sharply limited the circumstances in which a liquidation-reincorporation offered potential advantages. The advent of the concept of qualified dividend income in Section 1(h)(11), which taxes dividends at the same rate as net capital gains, reduced such circumstances even further. Nevertheless, as discussed in Chapter 4, the differences between exchange treatment and qualified dividend income have not disappeared completely and they may reappear if the change in dividend treatment is not made permanent. Thus, it is worth considering both types of bailout transactions in some detail.

[¶ 11,005]

B. THE "E" REORGANIZATION

The "E" reorganization involves a rearranging or "reshuffling" of the capital structure of a single existing corporation through the exchange of one class of stock or securities for another. For example, voting common stock may be exchanged for a combination of voting and nonvoting common stock; common stock may be exchanged for a combination of common and preferred stock; preferred stock may be exchanged for common stock or preferred stock with different terms; common or preferred stock may be exchanged for debt securities or a combination of stock and debt securities; and debt securities may be exchanged for other debt securities or for stock. See Reg. § 1.368–2(e).

[¶ 11,010]

1. BAIL–OUT POTENTIAL IN RECAPITALIZATIONS

There is no definition in the Code or regulations of the "E" reorganization. The lack of definitional restraints might be thought to open the door to casting transactions in the form of recapitalizations with a view to bailing out corporate earnings as long-term capital gain exchanges rather than as qualified dividend income with no basis offset.

The following case curtailed the potential for abuse through this strata-
gem even before a statutory bar was enacted.

[¶ 11,015]

BAZLEY v. COMMISSIONER

Supreme Court of the United States, 1947.
331 U.S. 737.

MR. JUSTICE FRANKFURTER delivered the opinion of the Court.

The proper construction of provisions of the Internal Revenue Code
relating to corporate reorganizations is involved in both these cases.
Their importance to the Treasury as well as to corporate enterprise led
us to grant certiorari * * *. While there are differences in detail to
which we shall refer, the two cases may be disposed of in one opinion.

In the *Bazley* case, * * * the Commissioner of Internal Revenue
assessed an income tax deficiency against the taxpayer for the year 1939.
Its validity depends on the legal significance of the recapitalization in
that year of a family corporation in which the taxpayer and his wife
owned all but one of the Company's one thousand shares. These had a
par value of $100. Under the plan of reorganization the taxpayer, his
wife, and the holder of the additional share were to turn in their old
shares and receive in exchange for each old share five new shares of no
par value, but of a stated value of $60, and new debenture bonds, having
a total face value of $400,000, payable in ten years but callable at any
time. Accordingly, the taxpayer received 3,990 shares of the new stock
for the 798 shares of his old holding and debentures in the amount of
$319,200. At the time of these transactions the earned surplus of the
corporation was $855,783.82.

The Commissioner charged to the taxpayer as income the full value
of the debentures. The Tax Court affirmed the Commissioner's determination, against the taxpayer's contention that as a "recapitalization" the
transaction was a tax-free "reorganization" and that the debentures
were "securities in a corporation a party to a reorganization," "exchanged solely for stock or securities in such corporation" "in pursuance
of a plan of reorganization," and as such no gain is recognized for
income tax purposes. * * * §§ 112(g)(1)(E) and 112(b)(3) [predecessors
of §§ 368(a)(1)(E) and 354 (a)(1) of the current Code]. The Tax Court
found that the recapitalization had "no legitimate corporate business
purpose" and was therefore not a "reorganization" within the statute.
The distribution of debentures, it concluded, was a disguised dividend,
taxable as earned income * * *. * * * The Circuit Court of Appeals for
the Third Circuit, sitting *en banc*, affirmed, two judges dissenting. * * *

Unless a transaction is a reorganization contemplated by § 112(g),
any exchange of "stock or securities" in connection with such transac-

tion, cannot be "in pursuance of the plan of reorganization" under § 112(b)(3). While § 112(g) informs us that "reorganization" means, among other things, "a recapitalization," it does not inform us what "recapitalization" means. "Recapitalization" in connection with the income tax has been part of the revenue laws since 1921. * * * Congress has never defined it and the Treasury Regulations shed only limited light. * * * One thing is certain. Congress did not incorporate some technical concept, whether that of accountants or of other specialists, into § 112(g), assuming that there is agreement among specialists as to the meaning of recapitalization. And so, recapitalization as used in § 112(g) must draw its meaning from its function in that section. It is one of the forms of reorganization which obtains the privileges afforded by § 112(g). Therefore, "recapitalization" must be construed with reference to the presuppositions and purpose of § 112(g). It was not the purpose of the reorganization provision to exempt from payment of a tax what as a practical matter is realized gain. Normally, a distribution by a corporation, whatever form it takes, is a definite and rather unambiguous event. It furnishes the proper occasion for the determination and taxation of gain. But there are circumstances where a formal distribution, directly or through exchange of securities, represents merely a new form of the previous participation in an enterprise, involving no change of substance in the rights and relations of the interested parties one to another or to the corporate assets. As to these, Congress has said that they are not to be deemed significant occasions for determining taxable gain.

These considerations underlie § 112(g) and they should dominate the scope to be given to the various sections, all of which converge toward a common purpose. Application of the language of such a revenue provision is not an exercise in framing abstract definitions. In a series of cases this Court has withheld the benefits of the reorganization provision in situations which might have satisfied provisions of the section treated as inert language, because they were not reorganizations of the kind with which § 112, in its purpose and particulars, concerns itself. * * *

Congress has not attempted a definition of what is recapitalization and we shall follow its example. The search for relevant meaning is often satisfied not by a futile attempt at abstract definition but by pricking a line through concrete applications. Meaning frequently is built up by assured recognition of what does not come within a concept the content of which is in controversy. Since a recapitalization within the scope of § 112 is an aspect of reorganization, nothing can be a recapitalization for this purpose unless it partakes of those characteristics of a reorganization which underlie the purpose of Congress in postponing the tax liability.

No doubt there was a recapitalization of the Bazley corporation in the sense that the symbols that represented its capital were changed, so

¶ 11,015

that the fiscal basis of its operations would appear very differently on its books. But the form of a transaction as reflected by correct corporate accounting opens questions as to the proper application of a taxing statute; it does not close them. Corporate accounting may represent that correspondence between change in the form of capital structure and essential identity in fact which is of the essence of a transaction relieved from taxation as a reorganization. What is controlling is that a new arrangement intrinsically partake of the elements of reorganization which underlie the congressional exemption and not merely give the appearance of it to accomplish a distribution of earnings. In the case of a corporation which has undistributed earnings, the creation of new corporate obligations which are transferred to stockholders in relation to their former holdings, so as to produce, for all practical purposes, the same result as a distribution of cash earnings of equivalent value, cannot obtain tax immunity because cast in the form of a recapitalization-reorganization. The governing legal rule can hardly be stated more narrowly. To attempt to do so would only challenge astuteness in evading it. And so it is hard to escape the conclusion that whether in a particular case a paper recapitalization is no more than an admissible attempt to avoid the consequences of an outright distribution of earnings turns on details of corporate affairs, judgment on which must be left to the Tax Court. * * *

What have we here? No doubt, if the Bazley corporation had issued the debentures to Bazley and his wife without any recapitalization, it would have made a taxable distribution. Instead, these debentures were issued as part of a family arrangement, the only additional ingredient being an unrelated modification of the capital account. The debentures were found to be worth at least their principal amount, and they were virtually cash because they were callable at the will of the corporation which in this case was the will of the taxpayer. One does not have to pursue the motives behind actions, even in the more ascertainable forms of purpose, to find, as did the Tax Court, that the whole arrangement took this form instead of an outright distribution of cash or debentures, because the latter would undoubtedly have been taxable income whereas what was done could, with a show of reason, claim the shelter of the immunity of a recapitalization-reorganization.

The Commissioner, the Tax Court and the Circuit Court of Appeals agree that nothing was accomplished that would not have been accomplished by an outright debenture dividend. And since we find no misconception of law on the part of the Tax Court and the Circuit Court of Appeals, whatever may have been their choice of phrasing, their application of the law to the facts of this case must stand. A "reorganization" which is merely a vehicle, however elaborate or elegant, for conveying earnings from accumulations to the stockholders is not a reorganization under § 112. This disposes of the case as a matter of law, since the facts as found by the Tax Court bring them within it. * * *

* * *

[Dissenting opinion has been omitted.]

[¶ 11,020]

Notes

1.   Under Sections 354(a)(2) and 356(d), to the extent that a shareholder exchanges stock for debt securities, the value of debt securities is treated as boot and the value of any excess in the principal amount of debt securities received over the principal amount of debt securities surrendered is also treated as boot. The *Bazley* case was decided before enactment of the predecessors of these provisions when a recapitalization involving an exchange of common stock for a combination of new common stock and debt securities fell literally within the definition of a reorganization and there were no statutory provisions requiring treatment of the debt securities as boot.

2.   If "securities" are exchanged for other "securities" of lesser or equal principal amount, no gain is recognized even if the fair market value of the securities received exceeds that of the securities surrendered. For a discussion of when debt obligations will constitute securities, see ¶ 10,265. If the principal amount of securities received exceeds the principal amount of securities surrendered, the fair market value of the excess is treated as boot. § 356(d). In determining "principal amount," the OID rules of Sections 1272 through 1274 apply.

3.   Whether boot distributions will be taxed as having the effect of a dividend under Section 356(a)(2) is determined by applying the rules of Section 302. Johnson v. Commissioner, 78 T.C. 564 (1982); cf. Rev. Rul. 93–62, 1993–2 C.B. 118. The amount of taxable boot is normally limited by gain realized by, and the ratable share of accumulated earnings of, the exchanging shareholder. § 356(a)(2). However, under *Bazley* the full value of securities received could be taxed as a dividend to the extent of the corporation's E & P. See Reg. § 1.356–1(d) and § 301(b)(1).

4.   If a corporation exchanges new securities for outstanding securities with a higher principal amount, Section 61(a)(12) may require the corporation to recognize cancellation of indebtedness income, subject to the exceptions and rules of Section 108. If the newly issued securities have a higher principal amount than the retired securities, the corporation may generally deduct the retirement premium as a cost of borrowing. Cf. § 249. If a corporation exchanges newly issued common or preferred stock for outstanding securities, the exchange is tax-free to the exchanging securityholders; however the corporation, if solvent, will have cancellation of indebtedness income if the principal and accrued interest on the securities retired exceed the fair market value of the

newly issued stock. § 108(e)(8). The latter value is insulated from tax under Section 1032.

2. NONQUALIFIED PREFERRED STOCK AS BOOT

The bail-out potential discussed in ¶¶ 11,010 through 11,020 also exists when certain types of preferred stock having debt-like characteristics are issued by a corporation in exchange for common stock or other preferred stock in an "E" recapitalization. Accordingly, legislation enacted in 1997 treats such preferred stock, called "nonqualified preferred stock" and defined in Section 351(g), as boot when exchanged for stock that is not itself nonqualified preferred stock. § 354(a)(2)(C)(i). See ¶ 10,240.

An exception to the gain recognition rule applies to the receipt of nonqualified preferred stock in exchange for common stock or other preferred if the exchange is part of an "E" reorganization of a family corporation meeting certain requirements. § 354(a)(2)(C)(ii). A family corporation is defined in Section 447(d)(2)(C)(i) as any corporation of which at least 50 percent of the total voting power and value of its nonvoting stock is owned by members of the same family, as defined in Section 447(e), for the eight-year period beginning five years before the recapitalization. § 354(a)(2)(C)(ii)(II).

3. NO CONTINUITY OF SHAREHOLDER INTEREST OR CONTINUITY OF BUSINESS ENTERPRISE REQUIRED

It has long been established that the continuity of shareholder interest requirement that applies to acquisitive reorganizations is not applicable to an "E" recapitalization. In Hickok v. Commissioner, 32 T.C. 80 (1959), the holders of common stock in the Hickok company exchanged their common stock for the corporation's 20 year, six percent subordinated debentures. The government argued that the plan of recapitalization could not qualify as a tax-free reorganization because the requisite continuity of shareholder interest was lacking; the exchanging shareholders emerged with only creditors' interests. After reviewing the continuity of shareholder interest cases, the court rejected the government's argument, stating:

> The foregoing cases are authority that the "continuity of interest" doctrine, which was developed by the courts to serve a necessary purpose in the merger and consolidation types of reorganizations need not be a necessary ingredient in the cases where a recapitalization occurs. It is quite apparent that the considerations which make such a doctrine necessary in the merger and consolidation cases are simply not present in a recapitalization. A recapitalization of a

single corporation often contemplates some change in interest, such as from stockholder to bondholder, and in a sense such a change might always be called an interruption of continuity. We have seen that the term "recapitalization" has a broad meaning. * * * It cannot be that the term "recapitalization" in the statute includes a requirement of the continuance of the old interest in proprietary form when recapitalization plans so often contemplate converting such interest to a non-proprietary form. We think that the "continuity of interest" doctrine has no application to a recapitalization such as took place in the instant case.

32 T.C. at 89.

[¶ 11,035]

REVENUE RULING 82–34

1982–1 C.B. 59.

* * *

Section 368(a)(1)(E) * * * provides that a "recapitalization" is a reorganization. A recapitalization has been defined as a "reshuffling of a capital structure within the framework of an existing corporation." *Helvering v. Southwest Consolidated Corp.*, 315 U.S. 194 (1942) * * *.

When a shareholder receives stock in a reorganization described in section 368(a)(1) and either before or after the transaction, the principal business assets of the transferor are sold or disposed of, a question arises whether the continuity of business enterprise requirement for a reorganization is satisfied. See sections 1.1002–1(c), 1.368–1(b) and 1.368–1(d) of the * * * Regulations.

The purpose of the reorganization provisions is to except from the general rule of recognizing gain or loss certain specifically described exchanges incident to corporate readjustments which effect only a readjustment of continuing interests in property under modified corporate forms. Section 1.368–1(b) of the regulations states that a continuity of the business enterprise under the modified corporate form is required in a reorganization.

Specifically, section 1.368–1(d) of the regulations provides, in general, that the transferee in a corporate reorganization must either (i) continue the transferor's historic business or (ii) use a significant portion of the transferor's historic business assets in a business.

The "continuity of business enterprise" requirement is closely related to "continuity of shareholder interest" requirement in section 1.368–1(b) of the regulations in that both are concerned with determining whether a transaction involves an otherwise taxable transfer of stock or assets of one corporation to another corporation, as distinguished from a tax-free reorganization, which assumes only a readjustment of continuing interests under modified corporate form. The consideration of whether a transaction involves an otherwise taxable transfer of stock or assets of one corporation to another corporation is not present in a recapitalization because a recapitalization involves only a single corporation. Therefore, Rev. Rul. 77–415, 1977–2 C.B. 311, consistent with several court decisions, concludes that continuity of shareholder interest is not a requirement for a recapitalization to qualify as a reorganization under section 368(a)(1)(E) * * *. Similarly, continuity of business enterprise is not a requirement for a recapitalization to qualify as a reorganization under section 368(a)(1)(E).

[¶ 11,040]

Notes

1. In view of the fact that, to the extent that a recapitalization calls for an exchange of stock for bonds, the bonds would constitute boot under Sections 354(a)(2) and 356(d), does the position adopted in *Hickok* have any bearing on the tax consequences of the rearrangement of the capital structure of a single corporation? Suppose that shareholders who previously owned 90 percent of the stock of the corporation exchange their stock for debt securities, while the remaining shareholders exchange their stock for new stock and debt securities. Assuming the corporation has ample E & P and the latter shareholders had a basis for their old stock that exceeded its value, could qualification of the transaction as an "E" reorganization affect the tax results? Would the answer be different if the latter shareholders exchanged their stock for new common stock?

2. All of the corporation's shareholders and securityholders need not participate in a recapitalization; it is enough if only one shareholder exchanges stock or securities for other stock or securities.

3. In 2005, to codify its position in Rev. Ruls. 82–34 and 77–415, Treasury amended Reg. § 1.368–1(b) to provide that a continuity of business enterprise and a continuity of interest are not required for a transaction to qualify as an "E" reorganization.

[¶ 11,045]

4. SECTION 306 STOCK IN A RECAPITALIZATION

If, in a reorganization, shareholders exchange some of their common stock for new preferred stock that is not nonqualified preferred stock at a time when the corporation has E & P, the preferred will constitute Section 306 stock if "the effect of the transaction was substantially the same as the receipt of a stock dividend." § 306(c)(1)(B). If cash had been received in lieu of the preferred stock and if the cash would have been taxed as a dividend, the preferred will be classified as Section 306 stock. Reg. § 1.306–3(d). For example, if X Corporation, which has only common stock outstanding, is merged in an "A" reorganization into Y Corporation and if the former X Corporation shareholders receive four shares of Y Corporation common stock and one share of Y Corporation preferred stock for each share of X Corporation common stock, the Y Corporation preferred stock will be considered to be Section 306 stock if, had cash been distributed in lieu of the preferred stock, the cash would have been taxed as a dividend under Section 356(a)(2). See ¶ 10,245. If Section 306 stock is exchanged for preferred stock which is not substantially different from the Section 306 stock surrendered, the new preferred stock will also be Section 306 stock. If the Section 306 stock is exchanged for common stock, the common stock will not be Section 306 stock. § 306(c)(1)(B); Reg. § 1.306–3(d). The constructive ownership rules of Section 318(a) do not apply in determining whether preferred stock received in a recapitalization is Section 306 stock. Rev. Rul. 81–186, 1981–2 C.B. 85.

If in an "E" reorganization boot is received in exchange for Section 306 stock, the value of the boot is treated as a Section 301 distribution. § 356(e).

[¶ 11,050]

Problems

1. A owns 50 percent of the outstanding common stock worth $100,000 of X Corporation, which has current E & P of $300,000. His son owns the remaining common stock. A exchanges all of his common for preferred stock (that is not nonqualified preferred stock) in a recapitalization. The son retains his 50 percent of the common. Is the preferred stock Section 306 stock?

2. A, the sole shareholder of Y Corporation, which has E & P of $250,000, exchanges 1,000 outstanding 18 year, seven percent debentures with a principal (face) amount of $10,000 each for 1,000 20 year, six percent debentures with a principal (face) amount of $1,100 each. Is the transaction an "E" reorganization? What are the tax consequences to A?

3. S, an individual, owns 50 percent of the common stock of Z Corporation, which has E & P of $400,000. S exchanges 1,000 shares of noncumulative $100 par value eight percent nonvoting preferred stock, issued by Z worth $100,000, which is not nonqualified preferred stock, for 500 new shares of noncumulative $100 par value five percent nonvoting preferred stock worth $50,000 that must be redeemed by the corporation within 10 years at $101 per share and 100 shares of additional common stock worth $50,000. Is the transaction an "E" reorganization? What are the tax consequences to S?

¶ 11,045

C. THE "F" REORGANIZATION

[¶ 11,055]

1. INTRODUCTION

In 1940, Randolph Paul thought the "F" reorganization had "perished from lack of use." But in 1957 and 1958 two revenue rulings put some life into it: Rev. Rul. 57–276, 1957–1 C.B. 126, and Rev. Rul. 58–422, 1958–2 C.B. 145. Both concerned changing a corporation's state of incorporation by the use of a statutory merger. That is, the owners of the old corporation caused a new corporation to be formed in a different state and then caused the old corporation to be merged into the new one. While these transactions fell within the definitions of both the "A" and "F" reorganizations, they were treated as "F" reorganizations. The reincorporation of a corporation in a different state is today the most common use of and "F" reorganization. Certain "D" and "C" reorganizations can also qualify as "F" reorganizations, in which case they are also treated as "F" reorganizations. Because the "F" reorganization is merely a "change in identity, form or place of incorporation, however effected," of a single corporation, the taxable year of the corporation does not terminate, the tax attributes of the corporation are retained, and post-reorganization net operating losses and capital losses are carried forward and back as they would be in the case of a single corporation. See § 381(b).

If a transaction qualifies as an "A," "C," or "D" reorganization, when will it make a difference whether it also qualifies as an "F"? In general, whether a transaction qualifies as an "A," "C," "D," or "F" reorganization, there is a carryover of attributes under Section 381(b). With respect to a number of issues, however, it can make a difference. Two are specifically referred to in Section 381(b):

> *Closing of taxable year*. If the old corporation and the new corporation both are on calendar years and the transaction occurs on June 30, and if the transaction is an "F" reorganization, the new corporation is regarded as a continuation of the old corporation and only one tax return for the calendar year is due. If the transaction is not an "F" reorganization, the taxable year of the old corporation terminates June 30 and separate returns for the two halves of the calendar year are due. Section 381(b)(1) provides that, except in the case of an "F" reorganization, the taxable year of the transferor ends on the date of transfer. See Dunlap and Associates, Inc. v. Commissioner, 47 T.C. 542 (1967).

> *Carryback of net operating loss*. If the new corporation realizes net operating losses or capital losses subsequent to June 30, the question arises whether losses can be carried back against pre-

reorganization income. Section 381(b)(3) deprives the new corporation of the right to carry back a net operating loss or a capital loss for a taxable year after the reorganization to a taxable year of the old corporation unless the transaction qualifies as an "F" reorganization. If it is an "F," the new corporation is deemed simply a continuation of the old corporation and the carryback is appropriate.

The role of the "F" reorganization in efforts by the IRS to limit taxpayer abuses in the liquidation-reincorporation area is discussed at ¶ 11,120.

[¶ 11,060]

2. ONLY ONE OPERATING CORPORATION MAY PARTICIPATE

In Estate of Stauffer v. Commissioner, 403 F.2d 611 (9th Cir.1968), Associated Machine v. Commissioner, 403 F.2d 622 (9th Cir.1968), and Davant v. Commissioner, 366 F.2d 874 (5th Cir.1966), cert. denied, 386 U.S. 1022 (1967), the Ninth and Fifth Circuits held that a transaction resulting in a combination of two or more operating corporations qualifies as an "F" reorganization. Both courts rejected the contention of the IRS that the "F" reorganization was limited to the reincorporation, or other mere change in the form, identity or place of incorporation, of a single operating corporation.

In Home Construction Corp. of America v. United States, 439 F.2d 1165 (5th Cir.1971), the Fifth Circuit followed its own decision in *Davant* and the decisions of the Ninth Circuit and held that the consolidation of 123 brother-sister operating corporations into a single corporation constituted an "F" reorganization (there being identity of stock ownership among the participating companies and a continuation of the businesses of the consolidated companies) so that post-consolidation losses sustained by the surviving corporation could be carried back to pre-consolidation taxable years of 83 of the constituent companies. The decisions in Movielab, Inc. v. United States, 494 F.2d 693 (Ct.Cl.1974) and Performance Systems, Inc. v. United States, 382 F.Supp. 525 (M.D.Tenn.1973), aff'd per curiam, 501 F.2d 1338 (6th Cir.1974), represented yet another judicial extension of the "F" reorganization. In those cases, the courts held that the merger of a wholly owned operating subsidiary into its parent company, also an operating company, constituted an "F" reorganization (as well as a Section 332 liquidation), so that post-liquidation losses realized by the parent could be carried back to a pre-liquidation year of the liquidated subsidiary.

What the IRS could not achieve in the courts was eventually accomplished by the Congress. Legislation enacted in 1982 restricted the "F" reorganization to a change in identity, form, or place of organization of "one corporation," which means, according to the Conference Committee Report, "a single operating corporation." H.R. Conf. Rep. No. 760, 97th Cong., 2d Sess. 541 (1982).

¶ 11,055

[¶ 11,065]

3. "F" REORGANIZATION LINKED TO ANOTHER TRANSACTION

It is not uncommon for a reincorporation of a corporation in a state with more favorable corporate laws to be related to another transaction such as a redemption, a public offering, or an acquisitive reorganization. Two such situations were considered in the following ruling.

[¶ 11,070]

REVENUE RULING 96–29

1996–1 C.B. 50.

ISSUE

Do the transactions described below qualify as reorganizations under § 368(a)(1)(F)?

FACTS

Situation 1. Q is a manufacturing corporation all of the common stock of which is owned by twelve individuals. One class of nonvoting preferred stock, representing 40 percent of the aggregate value of Q, is held by a variety of corporate and noncorporate shareholders. Q is incorporated in state M. Pursuant to a plan to raise immediate additional capital and to enhance its ability to raise capital in the future by issuing additional stock, Q proposes to make a public offering of newly issued stock and to cause its stock to become publicly traded. Q entered into an underwriting agreement providing for the public offering and a change in its state of incorporation. The change in the state of incorporation was undertaken, in part, to enable the corporation to avail itself of the advantages that the corporate laws of state N afford to public companies and their officers and directors. In the absence of the public offering, Q would not have changed its state of incorporation. Pursuant to the underwriting agreement, Q changed its place of incorporation by merging with and into R, a newly organized corporation incorporated in state N. The shares of Q stock were converted into the right to receive an identical number of shares of R stock. Immediately thereafter, R sold additional shares of its stock to the public and redeemed all of the outstanding shares of nonvoting preferred stock. The number of new shares sold was equal to 60 percent of all the outstanding R stock following the sale and redemption.

Situation 2. W, a state M corporation, is a manufacturing corporation all of the stock of which is owned by two individuals. W conducted its business through several wholly owned subsidiaries. The management of W determined that it would be in the best interest of W to acquire the business of Z, an unrelated corporation, and combine it with the business of *Y*, one of its subsidiaries, and to change the state of incorporation of *W*. In order to accomplish these objectives, and pursuant to an overall plan, *W* entered into a plan and agreement of merger with *Y* and *Z*. In accordance with the agreement, *Z* merged with and into *Y* pursuant to the law of state *M*, with the former *Z* shareholders receiving shares of newly issued *W* preferred stock in exchange for their shares of *Z* stock. Immediately following the acquisition of *Z*, *W* changed its place of organization by merging with and into *N*, a newly organized corporation incorporated in state *R*. Upon *W*'s change of place of organization, the holders of *W* common and preferred stock surrendered their *W* stock in exchange for identical *N* common and preferred stock, respectively.

Law and Analysis

Section 368(a)(1)(F) provides that a reorganization includes a mere change in identity, form, or place of organization of one corporation, however effected. This provision was amended by the Tax Equity and Fiscal Responsibility Act of 1982 * * * in order to limit its application to one corporation. Certain limitations contained in § 381(b), including those precluding the corporation acquiring property in a reorganization from carrying back a net operating loss or a net capital loss for a taxable year ending after the date of transfer to a taxable year of the transferor, do not apply to reorganizations described in § 368(a)(1)(F) "in recognition of the intended scope of such reorganizations as embracing only formal changes in a single operating corporation." H.R. Rep. No. 760, 97th Cong., 2d Sess. 540, 541 (1982). Although a change in the place of organization usually must be effected through the merger of one corporation into another, such a transaction qualifies as a reorganization under § 368(a)(1)(F) because it involves only one operating corporation. The 1982 amendment of § 368(a)(1)(F) thus overruled several cases in which a merger of two or more operating corporations could be treated as a reorganization under § 368(a)(1)(F). * * *

A transaction does not qualify as a reorganization under § 368(a)(1)(F) unless there is no change in existing shareholders or in the assets of the corporation. However, a transaction will not fail to qualify as a reorganization under § 368(a)(1)(F) if dissenters owning fewer than 1 percent of the outstanding shares of the corporation fail to participate in the transaction. Rev. Rul. 66–284, 1966–2 C.B. 115.

The rules applicable to corporate reorganizations as well as other provisions recognize the unique characteristics of reorganizations qualifying under § 368(a)(1)(F). In contrast to other types of reorganizations, which can involve two or more operating corporations, a reorganization of a corporation under § 368(a)(1)(F) is treated for most purposes of the Code as if there had been no change in the corporation and, thus, as if the reorganized corporation is the same entity as the corporation that was in existence prior to the reorganization. See § 381(b); § 1.381(b)–1(a)(2) * * *.

In Rev. Rul. 69–516, 1969–2 C.B. 56, the IRS treated as two separate transactions a reorganization under § 368(a)(1)(F) and a reorganization under § 368(a)(1)(C) undertaken as part of the same plan. Specifically, a corporation changed its place of organization by merging into a corporation formed under the laws of another state and immediately thereafter, it transferred substantially all of its assets in exchange for stock of an unrelated corporation. The ruling holds that the change in place of organization qualified as a reorganization under § 368(a)(1)(F).

Accordingly, in *Situation 1*, the reincorporation by Q in state N qualifies as a reorganization under § 368(a)(1)(F) even though it was a step in the transaction in which Q was issuing common stock in a public offering and redeeming stock having a value of 40 percent of the aggregate value of its outstanding stock prior to the offering.

In *Situation 2*, the reincorporation by W in state N qualifies as a reorganization under § 368(a)(1)(F) even though it was a step in the transaction in which W acquired the business of Z.

HOLDING

On the facts set forth in this ruling, in each of *Situations 1* and *2*, the reincorporation transaction qualifies as a reorganization under § 368(a)(1)(F), notwithstanding the other transactions effected pursuant to the same plan.

* * *

[¶ 11,075]

Notes

1. The above ruling states that generally a transaction will qualify as an "F" reorganization only if there is "no change in existing shareholders or in the assets of the corporation" although redemption of shares of dissenters owning less than one percent of the outstanding stock will be tolerated. How then in *Situation 1* could redemption of the preferred representing 40 percent of the total value of the corporation and sale of stock to new shareholders representing 60 percent of the total value of the corporation be reconciled with the conclusion that the reincorporation was a qualifying "F" reorganization? The ruling is short on reasoning. One possibility might be to treat the redemption and the public offering as transactions functionally unrelated to the reincorporation. See Reef Corp. v. Commissioner, 368 F.2d 125 (5th Cir.1966), at ¶ 11,120, holding that a simultaneous stock redemption and an "F" reorganization were "functionally unrelated." If this is the correct analysis, how could the IRS conclude that the reincorporation was "a

step in the transaction" in which the corporation was selling common stock and redeeming its preferred?

2. Treasury appears to be continuing the trend it started in Rev. Rul. 96–29 to broaden the scope of the "F" reorganization. Under Prop. Reg. § 1.368–2(m), issued in 2004, "a change that has no effect other than that of a redemption of less than all the shares of the corporation," is exempted from the general requirement that there be no change in ownership. Furthermore, the proposed regulations explicitly provide that "[r]elated events that precede or follow the transaction or series of transactions that constitutes a mere change will not cause that transaction or series of transactions to fail to qualify as a reorganization under section 368(a)(1)(F)." Prop. Reg. § 1.368–2(m)(3)(ii).

3. Assume that X Corporation owns 60 percent of the stock of Oldco, which it transfers to Newco in exchange for all of its common stock. Oldco is then merged into Newco in a tax-free statutory merger and the minority shareholders of Oldco receive X Corporation shares with the result that Newco becomes a wholly owned subsidiary of X Corporation. After this reorganization, Newco operates at a loss for several years. Can this loss be carried back to offset the pre-reorganization income of X Corporation? In the Aetna Casualty and Surety Co. v. United States, 568 F.2d 811 (2d Cir.1976), which involved a more complex but essentially similar transaction, the court held that the transactions involved a redemption of the minority shareholders and an "F" reorganization, stating:

> * * * Clearly a corporation which merely redeems its minority shareholders' stock has not undergone a reorganization at all under § 368(a)(1) and is entitled to carry back its losses under § 172. We see no reason why the result should be different simply because the redemption occurs in the course of merging one corporation into a different shell. *Casco Products Corp. v. Commissioner, supra,* 49 T.C. at 36; *Reef Corp. v. Commissioner, supra,* 368 F.2d at 134–38. If the redemption, reorganization and carryback provisions were not intended to preclude carrybacks where there has been a simple redemption, we do not believe those provisions should be construed to preclude the carryback here involved.

> Accepting arguendo the government's contention that Aetna Life had independent business reasons for freezing out the minority shareholders during the course of the merger of Old Aetna into New Aetna, we do not believe that a redemption which occurs in the course of what otherwise would be a § 368(a)(1)(F) reorganization should strip the reorganization of its subsection (F) character. Even assuming that the merger could not be separated from the redemption, as apparently it was possible for the court to do in *Reef Corp. v. Commissioner, supra,* 368 F.2d at 134, we agree with the reasoning of the Fifth Circuit that a "redemption is not a characteristic of a

reorganization...." *Id.* at 136. This view also is implicit in the Tax Court's reasoning in *Casco Products Corp. v. Commissioner, supra.*

* * * Since New Aetna was merely a corporate shell with no business of its own, none of the accounting problems which motivated § 381(b)(3) is present here. Indeed, since New Aetna had no pre-reorganization tax history of its own, application here of the carry-back prohibition contained in § 381(b)(3) would prevent New Aetna from obtaining *any* carryback of its current losses, even though § 381(b)(3) does not prevent acquiring corporations in other types of reorganizations from carrying back losses to their *own* pre-reorganization tax years. We do not believe that the mere fact that a redemption has occurred should lead to so Draconian a result, particularly since § 172 manifests a legislative policy in favor of carrybacks which ordinarily would not be affected by a simple redemption.

568 F.2d at 821.

4. The treatment of a redemption as functionally unrelated to an "F" reorganization is discussed at ¶ 11,120.

[¶ 11,080]

4. NO CONTINUITY OF SHAREHOLDER INTEREST OR CONTINUITY OF BUSINESS ENTERPRISE REQUIRED

As discussed in ¶ 11,030, both the IRS and the courts have long taken the position that the continuity of shareholder interest and business enterprise requirements do not apply to the "E" reorganization. This was not the case, however, with "F" reorganizations. In several cases, courts held that the "F" reorganization was limited to transactions in which the business enterprise continued without interruption after the transaction and in which the shareholders maintained a continuing interest in the surviving corporation. See Pridemark, Inc. v. Commissioner, 345 F.2d 35 (4th Cir. 1965); Yoc Heating Corp. v. Commissioner, 61 T.C. 168 (1973).

In 2005, Treasury clarified its position by adopting final regulations permitting transactions to qualify as "F" reorganizations without complying with the continuity of business enterprise or shareholder interest requirements. Treas. Reg. § 1.368–1(b). According to the explanation of the proposed regulations issued in 2004, "[b]ecause F reorganizations involve only the slightest change in a corporation and do not resemble sales, the IRS and the Treasury Department have concluded that applying the continuity of interest and continuity of business enterprise requirements to transactions that would otherwise qualify as F reorganizations is not necessary to protect the policies underlying the reorganization provisions."

[¶ 11,085]

D. NONDIVISIVE "D" REORGANIZATION

The paradigm transactions included in the definition of the "D" reorganizations are (i) a transfer of all of the assets of a corporation to a single new or existing corporation that is controlled by the transferor and/or its shareholders and (ii) a transfer of a part of the assets of a corporation to one or more such transferee corporations. In either case, stock and securities of the transferee corporation(s) must be distributed by the transferor. The first transaction involves essentially a reincorporation into a controlled corporation. It could also qualify as an "F" reorganization if the stock ownership of the transferor and the transferee corporations does not change other than through a redemption of less than all of the outstanding shares. See Prop. Reg. § 1.368–2(m). The second transaction is a divisive restructuring and it will qualify as a "D" reorganization only if it meets the requirements of Section 355 discussed in Chapter 12.

The nondivisive "D" reorganization definition requires that substantially all of the assets of the transferor be transferred to the commonly controlled transferee. This requirement is the same as the "substantially all" requirement found in the "C" reorganization and the forward and reverse triangular mergers. In addition, if the transaction is to qualify as a "D" reorganization, all stock or securities of the transferee and all other properties of the transferor must be distributed in liquidation. § 354(b)(1). But for the distribution requirement, this transaction would often be governed by Section 351.

Moreover, a transaction will qualify as a nondivisive "D" reorganization only if the distributing corporation and/or the distributee shareholder(s) control the distributed corporation immediately after the distribution. Under Section 368(a)(2)(H)(i), the control test for this purpose is the test of Section 304(c), which defines control as ownership of stock processing at least 50 percent of the total combined voting power of all classes of voting stock or 50 percent of the total value of all shares.

[¶ 11,090]

WARSAW PHOTOGRAPHIC ASSOCIATES INC. v. COMMISSIONER

United States Tax Court, 1985.
84 T.C. 21.

CHABOT, JUDGE: * * *.

[Warsaw Studios, Inc. (Studios) carried on a photography business in New York City. Warsaw & Co., Inc. (Warsaw) owned all of the preferred stock and 7,549 shares of the common stock of Studios. Ten employees of Studios owned about 2,000 shares of the Studios' common stock. Studios had incurred losses for a number of years, due in part to an unfavorable lease on its business premises at 34th and Madison Avenue. The ten employees believed the business could be run profitably if the burdensome lease were eliminated and they developed a plan under which a new corporation, Warsaw Photographic Associates, Inc. (petitioner), was formed. Studios transferred its operating assets (but not the lease) to the petitioner for $21,000. The ten employees surrendered their stock in Studios. Petitioner issued 100 shares of its common stock to each of them but none to Studios or to Warsaw. One of the issues considered was the petitioner's argument that the transaction was a "D" reorganization entitling petitioner to calculate depreciation on the operating assets received from Studios using a carryover basis and to use net operating losses generated by Studios.]

OPINION

* * *

In order to qualify as a nondivisive D reorganization (and thus, permit petitioner to (1) use Studios' bases for calculating depreciation and (2) * * * deduct Studios' net operating losses), the transaction in the instant case must satisfy a series of statutory requirements and also a series of judicial requirements.

Respondent contends that the transfer from Studios to petitioner does not qualify as a nondivisive D reorganization because it does not satisfy certain of the statutory and judicial requirements. Instead, respondent contends, the transfer of assets from Studios to petitioner is a sale. Respondent maintains that the transaction does not satisfy the statutory requirement that stock of the transferee corporation (i.e., petitioner) be issued and distributed in the purported reorganization. Respondent also maintains that the transaction does not satisfy the judicial requirement of continuity of interest. Specifically, respondent asserts that the continuity of interest requirement is not satisfied because either (1) "the preferred shareholder (Warsaw & Co., Inc.) had the proprietary interest in (Studios)' and did not continue an interest in petitioner, or (2) the minority shareholders who did continue an interest "had too small a proprietary interest in (Studios)."

Petitioner contends that the transaction between Studios and petitioner qualifies as a nondivisive D reorganization because it satisfies all the statutory and judicial requirements. In particular, petitioner contends that the 100 shares were given as consideration for Studios' assets and that the 100 shares were worth at least $42,727, far more than the $21,000 of cash and other property transferred by petitioner to Studios. Petitioner further contends that the fact that the 100 shares were issued directly to the 10 shareholders, rather than first to Studios and then distributed from Studios to the 10 shareholders, does not mean that petitioner's stock was not distributed within the meaning of section 354(b)(1)(B). Petitioner also asserts that the continuity of interest requirement is satisfied. In making this assertion, petitioner further contends that the proper test for applying the continuity of interest test is whether the stock of the transferee corporation (petitioner) represents a substantial part of the consideration given in the transaction and not whether a certain percentage of historic shareholders of the transferor continue as shareholders of the transferee.

We agree with respondent that the transaction is not a D reorganization because of the failure to satisfy the statutory requirement that petitioner's stock be transferred to Studios and distributed in a transaction which qualifies under sec. 354.

In order for a transaction to be a D reorganization, the transaction must be one "which qualifies under section 354 * * *.' (Sec. 368(a)(1)(D)) * * *. In order for petitioner to succeed to Studios' net operating losses under a D reorganization, Studios must have received stock of petitioner and Studios must have distributed the stock it thus received (secs. 354(a)(1) and 354(b)(1)(B)). The July 2, 1973, agreement between petitioner and Studios provides * * * that, as part of the consideration flowing from petitioner to Studios, "The Buyer is hereby issuing 10 shares of Common Stock, $.05 par value, of the Buyer to each of the shareholders of the Seller other than Warsaw & Co., Inc. who are the only shareholders of the Buyer." There was not literally a transfer of petitioner's stock from petitioner to Studios and a distribution of this stock by Studios to Studios' shareholders. Accordingly, we conclude that the statute's formal requirements have not been met in this regard.

It is true that "we have repeatedly held that, when the stock ownership of transferor and transferee is identical, the actual distribution would be a mere formality and the statute (section 368(a)(1)(D)) may be satisfied without it. * * *." * * * However, in the instant case, the stock ownerships of petitioner and Studios were not identical. Warsaw & Co., Inc., which owned about 80 percent of Studios' common stock and all of Studios' preferred stock, was not a shareholder in petitioner. The 10 shareholders, each holding 10 percent of petitioner's shares, had differing holdings in Studios. These holdings ranged from Zad's 375 shares down to Sinn's 92 shares. Indeed, apart from Shawn and Neil (each holding 250 shares); none of the 10 shareholders held the same number of Studios' shares as any of the others among the 10 shareholders * * * even though all were equal shareholders in petitioner.

Thus, the instant case does not qualify for the one exception that the courts have created regarding the stock transfer and distribution rule. Compliance with this rule is essential for the net operating loss carryover benefit sought by petitioner (secs. 381(a)(2) and 354(b)(1)(B)) and the carryover basis benefit sought by petitioner (secs. 362(b), 368(a)(1)(D), and 354(b)(1)(B)). Accordingly, we conclude that petitioner is entitled to use neither of the tax benefits it seeks to carry over from Studios.

On brief, petitioner makes the following contention regarding the stock transfer and distribution requirement:

> Code section 354(b)(1)(B) requires that all properties of the transfer-or corporation must be distributed in pursuance of the plan of reorganization. This provision is satisfied whenever, pursuant to the plan of reorganization, the shareholders of the transferor receive shares of the transferee sufficient to satisfy the control require-ments of Code section 368(a)(1)(D). A direct issuance of shares of the transferee corporation to shareholders of the transferor corpora-tion will suffice. An actual exchange of the transferor corporation's assets for shares of the transferee corporation, followed by a distri-bution of those shares to the transferor corporation's shareholders is not required. * * * Where as in the case at bar the acquiring corporation issues stock directly to the shareholders of the transfer-or corporation in consideration of the assets received from the transferor corporation, the transfer is treated as if the shares were first issued to the transferor corporation and then distributed in redemption of the outstanding shares of the transferor corporation.

We believe petitioner's reliance on the cases it cites is misplaced.

* * *

All of these authorities on which petitioner relies are distinguishable from the instant case in that the transferors and transferees in those instances had identical ownership, while in the instant case the owner-ship interests in petitioner and Studios differed widely. Further, in each of these cases in which a court has held that the requirement of an actual stock transfer and distribution may be ignored, it was respondent who urged on the court that the realities of the situation belied the form chosen by the taxpayer. In those situations where the courts have departed from the literal language of the statute, it was to counter a perceived abuse by the taxpayer, these courts having concluded that the taxpayer should not be permitted to shape the form of the transaction so as to secure an unwarranted benefit. * * * We have not found, and petitioner has not cited us to, any case in this area in which the court has acceded to a taxpayer's urging that the taxpayer be permitted to obtain a D reorganization tax benefit even though the form of the transaction which the taxpayer shaped did not meet the literal require-ments of the statute.

Petitioner contends that the "transaction in form and in substance qualified as a reorganization described in Code section 368(a)(1)(D)." Petitioner states that the transaction, and Studios' subsequent assignment for benefit of creditors, were designed as a convenient way to shed a burdensome obligation (i.e., the 34th Street lease). Petitioner concludes as follows:

> Had (Studios) followed a formal redemption/Chapter XI format, the reorganized corporation unquestionably could have carried over and utilized its pre-Chapter XI reorganization net operating losses. A different result should not obtain where the parties, on the advice of their respective counsel, achieved the same substantive results utilizing a (D) reorganization format.

We have already concluded that the transaction failed to satisfy one of the formal statutory requirements of section 368(a)(1)(D). As to the substance, we note that the parties to continue the transaction chose to create a new corporation rather than the old one; we are not persuaded that they should have the tax benefits they seek merely because they could have achieved the same business purposes by a different route that would have continued the old corporation and thereby provided these benefits.

When we examine the substance of what was done, we conclude that it points toward "sale" at least as much as toward "reorganization." Ten people put up an aggregate of $100,000 to acquire and bankroll a going business. The business had suffered substantial losses. The 10 shareholders trimmed the work force and avoided the burdens of an unfavorable lease, and apparently succeeded in reviving the business. The 10 shareholders had owned about 20 percent of the old corporation's common stock and none of its preferred. If they had purchased the remaining common stock or a controlling interest, then (as petitioner notes on brief) the corporation's tax characteristics would not be affected by the substance of the change in ownership and control. Apparently for a legitimate business reason (escaping from the burdens of the 34th Street lease), the 10 shareholders specifically turned down an opportunity to buy the old corporation, thus turning down the simple route toward retention of the old corporation's tax attributes.

If the 10 shareholders (or petitioner, their new corporation) had merely purchased Studios' assets, then the transaction would be a sale, the normal tax rules would apply (i.e., petitioner would not be entitled to use Studios' tax attributes) even though petitioner carried on the business that Studios had carried on and did so with essentially the same work force at the "same old stand."

What, in these circumstances, is the matter of substance that distinguishes the transaction from a sale? Petitioner contends that the issuance of the 100 shares is an element of substance that (1) enables the transaction to satisfy the statutory requirement of stock distribution, (2) enables the transaction to satisfy the judicial requirement that its stock be a substantial part of the consideration given by it, and (3) as an alternative, enables petitioner to substantially increase its basis in the assets received from Studios. In connection with the latter two points, petitioner contends that the 100 shares were worth $349,000.

After examining the transaction with care in light of petitioner's contentions, we note the following:

Firstly, the 100 shares effected no change, not even a subtle one, in the positions of the 10 shareholders. Each of the 10 shareholders merely had one extra piece of paper. * * * None involved in the transaction— not petitioner, Studios, the 10 shareholders, Warsaw & Co., Inc., or J. J. Warsaw—were any richer or any poorer on account of the issuance of the 100 shares, than they would have been if no shares were issued or if 1,000,000 shares were issued.

Secondly, care was taken to be sure that the 100 shares were not held by Studios at any time. This element is of some significance because Studios made a general assignment for the benefit of creditors only 3 weeks after the transaction in dispute, and the assignee was not able to find assets to make any payments to the creditors.

Thirdly, although the 100 shares were supposed to be issued to the 10 shareholders in their capacities as Studios' shareholders, they were issued * * * in proportion to the 10 shareholders' ownership of petitioner and not in proportion to the 10 shareholders' ownership of Studios.

Fourthly, petitioner contends that the 100 shares were worth a total of $349,000, while at the same time the initial 1,000 shares were worth a total of $100,000. The contentions, as to identical shares issued virtually simultaneously, are manifestly inconsistent. We are not given any hint as to why the 100 shares would be worth $3,490 each while the 1,000 shares were worth $100 each.

On answering brief, petitioner tells us that "Taxation is a practical art; labels will not replace or substitute for judgment as to the roles played by the parties and whether or not those roles were acted out in such a way as to effect a reorganization described by the Internal Revenue Code". We agree. We conclude that, as a practical matter, the appearance of the 100 shares in the transaction provides only a smell of reorganization. We will not speculate as to why the July 2, 1973, agreement provided for the issuance of the 100 shares in such a manner that their issuance satisfies neither the form nor the substance of section 368(a)(1)(D). We conclude that the 100 shares did not constitute any part of petitioner's consideration for the assets, tangible or intangible, that petitioner received from Studios. * * *

[¶ 11,095]

Note

The court emphasizes the taxpayer's burden to adopt formalities that comply with the literal language of the Code. It holds that only the IRS and the courts may depart from the literal language to find that the realities belie the form chosen by the taxpayer. Is this sound as a generalization in the reorganization context? Well-advised taxpayers seeking reorganization treatment will normally take pains to comply with the literal requirements of the reorganization requirements. But are there examples—albeit rare ones—of taxpayers successfully arguing that the realities support treating a transaction as a reorganization even though the form adopted does not fit within the literal language of the statute? See, e.g., Rev. Rul. 67–448, at ¶ 10,170.

E. LIQUIDATION–REINCORPORATION TRANSACTIONS

[¶ 11,100]

1. POTENTIAL TAX BENEFITS

Before the Tax Reform Act of 1986, there were powerful tax incentives for individual shareholders of a closely held corporation with substantial accumulated earnings to engage in a liquidation-reincorporation transaction. The basic features of the transaction are a liquidation of the old corporation and a continuation of the business in a new corporation to which the essential operating assets (but only a minimum of liquid assets needed as working capital) are transferred. When the reincorporation follows the liquidation, the distributee shareholders transfer the operating assets received in liquidation to a new corporation in exchange for its stock, and the new corporation continues the business. The shareholders' direct or indirect ownership interests in the new corporation will frequently approximate their interests in the old. The bulk of the liquid assets of the old corporation is retained by the shareholders. If the form of the transaction is respected for tax purposes, the shareholders, who are entitled to long-term capital gain treatment on the liquidating distribution from the old corporation, will have bailed out accumulated earnings of the old corporation at the cost of the tax on long-term capital gains, whereas if the earnings had been distributed as a dividend, they would have been taxed as ordinary income. In addition, elimination of the earnings of the old corporation obviates future accumulated earnings tax risk.

There are a number of other ways in which the liquidation-reincorporation transaction can be accomplished in addition to the transaction in which the reincorporation follows the liquidation of the old corporation. The reincorporation might precede the liquidation. Thus, X corporation (having large E & P) could transfer its operating assets to newly formed Y corporation, the originally issued stock of which is owned by the same shareholders and in the same proportions as X corporation, solely in exchange for newly issued Y stock. Thereafter, X would distribute its nonoperating assets and its stock in Y to the X shareholders in complete liquidation.

¶ 11,095

Needless to say, the reincorporation device was seldom, if ever, intentionally employed in forms as stark as these. New shareholders would be added in the new corporation; some shareholders of the old corporation would not acquire stock in the new corporation or would acquire a larger or smaller equity participation in the new corporation than was held in the old. A substantial interval of time might pass between the liquidation and the reincorporation. The business of the new corporation might differ in significant respects from the business of the old.

Two features of the 1986 Act, however, dramatically eroded the tax advantages of the liquidation-reincorporation device. First, the preferential rate of tax on long-term capital gain was eliminated. Second, the repeal of the *General Utilities* doctrine requires the liquidating corporation to recognize gain on the appreciation inherent in its assets when they are distributed in liquidation. This immediate tax, which was not imposed under *General Utilities* (except with respect to limited items), is usually a heavy price to pay for a stepped-up basis in the operating assets because the step-up in basis can often be recovered only over time through depreciation or amortization deductions and, in the case of other assets, such as undeveloped land, can be recovered only when and if the assets are sold.

Although a preferential tax on long-term capital gains has been restored for individuals, the 2003 changes to the tax treatment of dividends has significantly narrowed the gap between dividends and liquidating distributions. It has not, however, eliminated it entirely. Because a corporation can offset capital losses only against capital gains and an individual can offset capital losses only against such gains and a limited amount of ordinary income, but not against qualified dividend income, a taxpayer having current capital losses or capital loss carryovers or who anticipates future capital losses will have an incentive to bail-out corporate earnings through a liquidation qualifying as a capital gain transaction rather than as a dividend. Moreover, a shareholder is entitled to recover the stock basis before recognizing gain in a liquidation transaction but with respect to a dividend no basis can be recovered until all E & P of the corporation have been distributed. Finally, there may be taxpayers who wish to realize and have recognized in a taxable liquidation the loss in the value of the stock or assets of a corporation that has not been successful.

However, except in special cases, the tax to the old corporation on liquidation will be a disadvantage that will often outweigh the capital gain taxation advantage to the shareholders. These special cases in which the liquidation-reincorporation device has continuing allure typically arise when liquidation would not involve a substantial tax to the liquidating corporation. They would include situations in which the old corporation had little gain inherent in its assets, the old corporation had assets with built-in losses that would offset the built-in gain on other assets, or the old corporation had net operating loss or capital loss carryforwards that could offset the gain that would otherwise be recognized on liquidation.

Traditionally, the primary assaults of the IRS on liquidation-reincorporation transactions have been based on the reorganization provisions. If the IRS can successfully contend that the transaction falls within the definition of one of the Section 368(a)(1) reorganizations, there is the possibility of taxing some, and possibly all, of the cash and property distributed to, and retained by, the continuing shareholders as a dividend under Section 356(a)(2). Under Section 381(c)(2)(C), the new corporation would succeed to the E & P of the old. Under Section 306(c)(1)(B), preferred stock issued by the new corporation would probably bear the Section 306 taint. No losses realized by the shareholders would be recognized under Sections 354 and 356. Pursuant to Section 362(b), the basis of the old corporation's assets would carry over to the new.

[¶ 11,105]

2. APPLICATION OF "D" REORGANIZATION RULES TO LIQUIDATION–REINCORPORATION TRANSACTIONS

The "D" reorganization has long been an important part of the arsenal of weapons the IRS has employed in dealing with the liquidation-reincorporation device for bailing out corporate earnings at the cost of the preferential tax rate on long-term capital gains. If the transaction fell within the "D" definition, the cash and other liquid assets distributed to the shareholders of the old corporation would usually be treated as boot having the effect of the distribution of a dividend under Section 356(a)(2) and be taxed as qualified dividend income.

The Tax Reform Act of 1984 amended the definition of "control" for purposes of the nondivisive "D" reorganization in two important respects with the objective of making it possible to treat a broader range of liquidation-reincorporation transactions as nondivisive "D" reorganizations. First, "control" was redefined to track the control definition of Section 304(c)—ownership of stock possessing at least 50 percent (rather than 80 percent as under prior law) of the total combined voting power of all classes of voting stock or at least 50 percent of the total value of all other shares. § 368(a)(2)(H). Second, the constructive ownership of stock rules contained in Section 318(a) (with some modifications contained in 304(c)(3)(B)) were made applicable to the determination of control. § 304(c)(3).

The General Explanation of the 1984 Act prepared by the Staff of the Joint Committee on Taxation commented as follows on the changes:

> The Congress believed that the D reorganization control requirement should more closely conform to the control requirement

under section 304. In addition, the Congress believed that the absence of explicit attribution rules to determine ownership of stock for purposes of the D reorganization control requirement may have enabled taxpayers to bail out earnings and profits at capital gains rates by having their corporation transfer assets to a corporation controlled by related persons rather than to a corporation controlled by them. Generally, because attribution rules are applicable for purposes of section 304, such a bail out would not be possible if the transaction were structured as a transfer of stock rather than of assets.

* * *

It was not intended that recharacterization as a D reorganization under this provision be the exclusive means for the Service to challenge liquidation-reincorporation and similar transactions. Thus, it was not intended that this provision supersede or otherwise replace the various doctrines that have been developed by the Service and the courts to deal with such transactions. See, e.g., Rev. Rul. 61–156, 1961–2 C.B. 62; *Telephone Answering Service Co. v. Commissioner*, 63 T.C. 423 (1974), aff'd, 546 F.2d 423 (4th Cir. 1976), *cert. denied*, 431 U.S. 914 (1977); and *J.E. Smothers v. U.S.*, 642 F.2d 894 (5th Cir.1981).

Staff of Joint Comm. on Tax'n, 98th Cong., 2d Sess., General Explanation of the Revenue Provisions of the Deficit Reduction Act of 1984, at 194 (1985).

The *Reef Corp.* case below was decided under the pre-existing definition of control set forth in Section 368(c) and before the repeal of the *General Utilities* doctrine. Note the analysis underlying the court's conclusion that all the elements of a nondivisive "D" reorganization definition were present.

[¶ 11,110]

REEF CORP. v. COMMISSIONER

United States Court of Appeals, Fifth Circuit, 1966.
368 F.2d 125.

BELL, CIRCUIT JUDGE:

[Reef Fields Gasoline Corp. (Reef Fields) was a Texas corporation organized to operate a casinghead gas plant. About 52 percent of its stock was owned by the Butler group, which operated the business, and the remaining 48 percent by the Favrot group, which was not involved in business operations. A convoluted plan was adopted to buy out the Favrot group and to transfer the operating assets to a new Delaware corporation (new Reef) wholly owned by the Butler group. Part of the plan involved sale of the stock of new Reef to a straw man, Strong, who briefly owned all of the stock of new Reef and Reef Fields and who arranged to have Reef Fields sell its operating assets to new Reef before Reef Fields liquidated. At the end of the day, the Butler group controlled new Reef, which owned the operating assets, and the Favrot group's stock had been exchanged for cash and notes of new Reef. The issue was whether new Reef was entitled to a stepped-up basis on the ground that new Reef had purchased the operating assets.]

* * *

We affirm the holding of the Tax Court insofar as it disregarded the role of Strong without further discussion. He was a mere conduit in a preconceived and prearranged unified plan to redeem the stock of the Favrot group in Reef Fields. * * *

* * *

II.

This brings us to the contention of petitioner that the Tax Court erred on the depreciation question in holding that the transaction resulted in a corporate reorganization under § 368(a)(1)(D). * * *

Petitioner here contends that the old asset basis for purposes of depreciation should give way to a stepped-up basis computed on the cost of the assets to new Reef. Section 362(b) * * * requires that petitioner's basis in the assets, if this was a reorganization, shall be the same as their basis in the hands of Reef Fields. The Tax Court was of the view that the transaction between Reef Fields, Strong, and new Reef meets the definition of a reorganization set out in § 368(a)(1)(D).

The statute first requires a transfer by Reef Fields of all or a part of its assets to new Reef. This condition was met. The statute requires that immediately after the transfer one or more of the shareholders in Reef Fields, who were shareholders immediately before the transfer, be in control of new Reef. The Butler group was in control of new Reef. However, unless Strong is to be ignored, they were not shareholders immediately before the transfer of the assets because their stock had been conveyed to Strong in part and to new Reef in part. We conclude, as did the Tax Court, that Strong is to be disregarded for the purposes of this statute. * * *

But this is not the end of the matter. The statute also provides that pursuant to the plan of reorganization, and there was definitely a plan here, the stock or securities of the corporation to which the assets are transferred (new Reef) be distributed in a transaction which qualifies under § 354, 355, or 356 * * *. Only § 354 is pertinent here. * * *

Section 354(a)(1) requires the exchange of stock or securities in Reef Fields for stock or securities in new Reef. Disregarding Strong, here the

¶ 11,110

Butler group exchanged some of their Reef Fields stock for all of the new Reef stock and the balance of their Reef Fields stock for new Reef securities (notes). Thus the Butler group has complied with this requirement. The Favrot group also complied by transferring their stock for new Reef notes via Strong.

We must also find compliance with § 354(b)(1)(A) and (B). Subsection (A) requires that new Reef must have acquired substantially all of the assets of Reef Fields and the Tax Court found this to be the fact. Petitioner urges that $1,217,000 in cash was distributed to the Favrot group and therefore "substantially all of the assets" of Reef Fields were not transferred to new Reef. However, eliminating this cash, approximately eighty per cent of the assets of Reef Fields were transferred to new Reef and this is a sufficient basis for the finding by the Tax Court.

Subsection (B) requires that the stock, securities or other properties received by Reef Fields must have been distributed pursuant to the plan of reorganization. This requirement was also met. The notes of new Reef were received by Reef Fields and distributed by Reef Fields to its shareholders via Strong. Here again we disregard Strong's participation for tax purposes. The statute cannot be avoided by such a strawman procedure. We read subsection (B) as requiring that whatever is received by Reef Fields, stock, securities and property, be distributed. Only securities were received and they were indeed distributed.

These statutory tests make redundant two general requirements which must be present if the reorganization statutes are to be applied. There must be continuity of interest between Reef Fields and new Reef, * * * and also a continuity of business enterprise between the two. * * * The continuity of interest was present here through the Butler group, and the continuity of business enterprise was present since new Reef carried on the same business as Reef Fields. * * *

This was clearly a corporate reorganization within the meaning of § 368(a)(1)(D) and, accordingly, pursuant to § 362(b), new Reef's basis in the corporate assets is the same as it was in the hands of Reef Fields. The Tax Court was correct in so holding.

* * *

[The court went on to hold (with one dissent) that the transaction also was an "F" reorganization. The discussion is set forth at ¶ 11,120]

[¶ 11,115]

Notes

1.   In order to treat the transaction as a "D" reorganization it was necessary for the IRS to demonstrate that "substantially all of the assets" of the old corporation were transferred to the new. The courts proved to be quite receptive in the liquidation-reincorporation context to finding this requirement met if substantially all of the *operating* assets

of the reincorporated business were transferred to the new corporation even though large amounts of nonoperating assets were not.

Indeed, there is a rather striking contrast between the view of the courts in the liquidation-reincorporation context of the "substantially all of the assets" requirement of Section 354(b)(1)(A) and the interpretation of "substantially all of the properties" of the acquired corporation for purposes of the "C" reorganization discussed at ¶ 10,080. In Smothers v. United States, 642 F.2d 894 (5th Cir.1981), the "substantially all" requirement was found to be met when all of the operating assets, which constituted only 15 percent of the total assets, were transferred. The court stated:

> Properly interpreted, therefore, the assets looked to when making the "substantially all assets" determination should be all the assets, and only the assets, necessary to operate the corporate business—whether or not those assets would appear on a corporate balance sheet constructed according to generally accepted accounting principles. Two errors in particular should be avoided. Inclusion of assets unnecessary to the operation of the business in the "substantially all assets" assessment would open the way for the shareholders of any enterprise to turn dividends into capital gain at will. For example, if we assume that "substantially all" means greater than 90%, then a corporation need only cease declaring dividends and accumulate surplus liquid assets until their value exceeds 10% of the total value of all corporate assets. The shareholders could then transfer the assets actively used in the business to a second corporation owned by them and liquidate the old corporation. Such a liquidating distribution would be a dividend in any meaningful sense, but an interpretation of "substantially all assets" that took surplus assets into account would permit the shareholders to treat it as capital gain. Indeed, such an interpretation would perversely treat a merely nominal distribution of retained earnings as a dividend, but would permit substantial distributions to be made at capital gain rates. Courts therefore have invariably ignored all surplus assets and have focused on the operating assets of the business—the tangible assets actively used in the business—when making the "substantially all assets" assessment.

> Second, exclusion of assets not shown on a balance sheet constructed according to generally accepted accounting principles from the "substantially all assets" assessment would offer an unjustified windfall to the owners of service businesses conducted in corporate form. The most important assets of such a business may be its reputation and the availability of skilled management and trained employees, none of which show up on a standard balance sheet. Other courts have correctly recognized that in appropriate cases those intangible assets alone may constitute substantially all of the corporate assets. * * *

¶ 11,115

642 F.2d at 900.

2. The exchange and distribution requirements of Section 354(a)(1) and (b)(1)(B) were discussed as follows in James Armour, Inc. v. Commissioner, 43 T.C. 295, 307 (1964), which involved a reincorporation in which the stock ownership in the old (Armour, Inc.) and new (Excavating) corporations was identical:

> The petitioners contend, however, that the various transactions here do not constitute a reorganization within the meaning of section 368(a)(1)(D), since there has not been met the statutory requirement that stock or securities of the corporation to which the assets are transferred be distributed in a transaction which qualifies under section 354, 355 or 356 of the Code. They point out that there was no stock of Excavating actually transferred to either Armour, Inc., or the individual petitioners. However, the petitioners already owned all the stock of Excavating and it was not necessary that further stock be issued in order that they might retain their same proprietary interest in the assets received by Excavating. The issuance of further stock would have been a meaningless gesture, and we cannot conclude that the statute requires such a vain act. We conclude, therefore, that there was in substance an exchange of stock of Armour, Inc., for stock of Excavating, which meets the requirements of sections 354 and 356 * * *.

Suppose new shareholders acquire 15 percent of the stock of the new corporation while the pre-existing shareholders own 85 percent. Can a constructive issuance, exchange, and distribution of new corporation stock be found? If not, would the door be opened to controlling shareholders of any corporation with large accumulated earnings to bail out those earnings through a liquidation-reincorporation with no risk of dividend treatment simply by bringing in a small minority interest in the transferee corporation and electing not to have the transferee issue stock in exchange for the liquidated corporation's assets?

3. With respect to the requirement of Section 354(a)(1) and (b)(1)(B) that the required exchanges and distribution be in pursuance of a plan of reorganization, the courts have generally had little difficulty in holding that the series of related steps carried out by the two corporations and their shareholders in common constitutes sufficient evidence of the requisite plan. In addition to the *Reef* case, at ¶ 11,110, see, e.g., Liddon v. Commissioner, 230 F.2d 304 (6th Cir.1956); Bard–Parker Co. v. Commissioner, 218 F.2d 52, 57 n.3 (2d Cir.1954). Although the taxpayer may succeed in proving that there was in fact no plan of reorganization, e.g., Mathis v. Commissioner, 19 T.C. 1123 (1953) (acq.), as a practical matter, once the question is reduced to an evidentiary one, the IRS enjoys a strong position: The very tax benefits to be realized by the taxpayers from a successful liquidation-reincorporation encourage

¶ 11,115

the inference that the transactions were part of an integrated plan to achieve those benefits.

4. Can the controlling shareholders of the liquidated corporation insulate a liquidation-reincorporation from reorganization treatment by interposing a corporation in which they own 100 percent of the stock between themselves and the new corporation which continues the business? The possibility of avoiding "D" reorganization treatment of a liquidation-reincorporation by interposing a corporation was ended by the 1984 amendments. These provide that, in determining whether the Section 304(c) 50 percent control test of the definition of the nondivisive "D" reorganization is met, the Section 318(a) attribution rules used in relation to Section 304 are applicable. § 368(a)(2)(H). See ¶ 11,105.

3. APPLICATION OF "F" REORGANIZATION RULES TO LIQUIDATION–REINCORPORATION TRANSACTIONS

[¶ 11,120]

REEF CORP. v. COMMISSIONER

United States Court of Appeals, Fifth Circuit, 1966.
368 F.2d 125.

BELL, CIRCUIT JUDGE:

[The facts are summarized at ¶ 11,110. After holding that the transaction fell within the definition of a "D" reorganization, the majority went on to hold the transaction was an "F" reorganization.]

* * *

The reasoning which supports the conclusion of Judges Rives and Fulton that this is a § 368(a)(1)(F) reorganization follows.

* * *

The intricate and confusing facts of this case have been carefully explained. Distilled to their pure substance, two distinct and unrelated events transpired. First, the holders of 48% of the stock in Reef Fields had their stockholdings completely redeemed. Second, new Reef was formed and the assets of Reef Fields were transferred to new Reef. The business enterprise continued without interruption during both the redemption and the change in corporate vehicles.

Much confusion flows from the fact that the corporate reorganization took place simultaneously with the stock redemption. But taking the Code as a standard, these two elements were functionally unrelated. Reef Fields could have completely redeemed the stock of 48% of its shareholders without changing the state of its incorporation. A complete redemption is not a characteristic of a reorganization. Congress clearly indicated this when it defined reorganization in section 368. Section 368(a)(1)(A)

¶ 11,115

speaks of a "merger or consolidation" which looks to the joining of two or more corporations. Sections 368(a)(1)(B) and (C) look to one corporation acquiring the assets of another or control of another corporation solely for its voting stock. Section 368(a)(1)(D) looks to the consolidation of two or more corporations or the division of two or more going businesses into separate corporations. Only sections 368(a)(1)(E) and (F) look to adjustments within a corporation. But none of these provisions focuses on a complete redemption as a characteristic of a reorganization. Congress did not have redemption of stock as a primary purpose of any of the forms of a reorganization. That subject came under consideration when it undertook to enact specific legislation on complete and partial redemptions, section 302.

The boot provision, section 356, is adequate to cover a complete redemption when it occurs incident to a reorganization whose primary purpose conforms to the intent of section 354 or 355. But section 356 was principally designed to cover dividends incident to a reorganization. When the primary characteristics of the reorganization conform to those described by 368(a)(1)(F), we should parse the occurrences into their functional elements. The reorganizational characteristics present in the instant case do not conform to those generally intended to be covered by section 354 and therefore we should not be blinded by the 356 boot provision. To effectuate the intention of Congress manifested in the Code, we must separate this transaction into its two distinctly separate functional parts. The test of whether events should be viewed separately or together as part of a single plan is not temporal but is functional. * * * Applying this test to the instant case, it is clear that the redemption and the change of corporate vehicles must be viewed as separate and distinct occurrences. * * *

* * *

* * * We do not have a shift in the ownership of the proprietary interest in the sense that the assets have been sold to entirely new stockholders. At best we have a complete redemption covered by section 302 which, like all redemptions, means the remaining stockholders have increased their proprietary interest.

For the foregoing reasons, we hold that * * * this is a § 368(a)(1)(F) reorganization.

* * *

[Dissenting opinion has been omitted.]

[¶ 11,125]

4. LIQUIDATION–REINCORPORATION TRANSACTIONS IN WHICH THE STATUTORY REORGANIZATION PROVISIONS DO NOT APPLY

In cases in which the shareholders of the old corporation fail to "control" the new corporation to which the operating assets have been transferred, the IRS has had to recharacterize the transaction as a "device" for the bailout of earnings and profits through the liquidation/reincorporation transaction.

[¶ 11,130]

REVENUE RULING 61–156

1961–2 C.B. 62.

Advice has been requested whether the transaction described below should be treated, for Federal income tax purposes, as a sale of corporate assets to a newly organized corporation followed by the liquidation of the "selling" corporation under sections 337 and 331 of the Internal Revenue Code of 1954 [which prior to repeal of the *General Utilities* principle treated the sale as tax free to the corporation and the liquidation taxable only to its shareholders], or whether the transaction should be treated as a reorganization within the meaning of section 368 * * *.

Within a 12–month period following the adoption of a plan of complete liquidation, a corporation sold substantially all of its assets to a new corporation formed by the management of the selling corporation. The "purchasing" corporation paid 18,000x dollars for the assets as follows:

(a) 2,025x dollars in shares of its stock equal to 45 percent of all the shares to be issued,

(b) 4,975x dollars in long-term notes, and

(c) 11,000x dollars in cash obtained through a first mortgage borrowing on the assets acquired.

Immediately thereafter, the new corporation sold shares of its stock, equal to 55 percent of all the shares to be issued, to the public through underwriters.

The "selling" corporation was then completely liquidated, paying off its funded and unfunded liabilities and distributing the balance of its assets, including the 45 percent stock interest in the purchasing corporation, the long-term notes, and cash to its shareholders. As a result of the transaction, the business enterprise continued without interruption in the corporate form with a substantial continuing stock interest on the part of those persons who were shareholders in the selling corporation.

Section 1.331–1(c) of the * * * Regulations provides as follows:

A liquidation which is followed by a transfer to another corporation of all or part of the assets of the liquidating corporation, or which is preceded by such a transfer may, however, have the effect of the distribution of a dividend or of a transaction in which no loss is recognized and gain is recognized only to the extent of "other property." See sections 301 and 356.

¶ 11,125

In this case, if the issuance of stock to the new investors is disregarded, there is clearly a mere recapitalization and reincorporation coupled with a withdrawal of funds. The withdrawal would be treated either under section 356(a) * * * "money or other property" received in connection with a reorganization exchange of stock for stock, or under section 301 * * * as an unrelated distribution to the shareholders.

The issuance of stock to new investors can be disregarded as being a separate transaction, since even without it the dominant purpose—to withdraw corporate earnings while continuing the equity interest in substantial part in a business enterprise conducted in corporate form— was fully achieved. The issuance of stock to new investors was not needed to implement the dominant purpose and, therefore, the rest of the transaction was not fruitless without it and so dependent on it.

The transaction was shaped so as to make it essentially "a device whereby it has been attempted to withdraw corporate earnings at capital gains rates by distributing all the assets of a corporation in complete liquidation and promptly reincorporating" them. See Conference Report No. 2543, 83d Cong., to accompany H.R. 8300 (Internal Revenue Code of 1954), page 41.

It was not intended by Congress that such a device should obtain the benefits of section 337 [a provision since repealed along with *General Utilities* that sheltered the liquidating corporation from tax on appreciated assets sold] and avoid dividend taxation. In substance there was no reality to the "sale" of corporate assets or to the "liquidation" of the selling corporation, since each was only a formal step in a reorganization of the existing corporation. The entire transaction was consummated pursuant to a plan of reorganization which readjusted interests in property continuing in a modified corporate form. Sections 1.368–1(b) and 1.368–2(g) of the regulations.

The newly formed "purchasing" corporation was utilized to effect, in substance, a recapitalization and a change in identity, form or place of organization of the "selling" corporation and, at the same time, to withdraw accumulated earnings from the corporate enterprise for the benefit of the shareholders, while they nevertheless continued a substantial equity interest in the enterprise.

The fact that the shareholders of the "selling" corporation own only 45 percent of the stock of the "purchasing" corporation because of the public stock offering does not dispose of the reorganization question. A surrender of voting control, or ownership of less than 50 percent of the stock of a newly-formed corporation, does not in itself mark a discontinuity of interest. * * * It is necessary only that the shareholders continue to have a definite and substantial equity interest in the assets of the acquiring corporation.

In view of the foregoing, it is held that the transaction here described constitutes a reorganization within the meaning of sections

¶ 11,130

368(a)(1)(E) and (F) * * *. No gain or loss is recognized to the "selling" corporation on the exchange of property, as provided by section 361 * * *. The basis of the assets in the hands of the "purchasing" corporation will be the same as in the hands of the "selling" corporation, as provided in section 362(b) * * *. No gain or loss is recognized under section 354 * * * on the exchange of the stock of the "selling" corporation for stock of the "purchasing" corporation pursuant to the plan of reorganization.

With regard to the stockholders' withdrawal of money and other property from the corporate solution, it is necessary to determine whether such withdrawal is to be treated as "boot" received as part of the consideration for their stock in the "selling" corporation in accordance with section 356(a) * * * or as a separate dividend distribution taxable in accordance with the provisions of section 301 * * *. See sections 1.301–1(*l*) and 1.331–1(c) of the regulations and *J. Robert Bazley v. Commissioner*, 331 U.S. 737 (1947).

Under section 356(a)(1) * * *, gain would be recognized to the shareholders of the "selling" corporation upon the surrender of their shares of stock in exchange for stock of the "purchasing" corporation, its long-term notes, cash, and other assets, but in an amount not in excess of the sum of cash and the fair market value of the long-term notes and other assets received. Under section 356(a)(2) * * *, such gain would be taxable as a dividend to each shareholder to the extent of his ratable share of the undistributed earnings and profits of the corporation accumulated after February 28, 1913; the remainder, if any, would be treated as gain from the exchange of property. Under section 301 the distribution would be taxable as a dividend to the same extent as a dividend formally declared in the same amount.

In this case, viewing the issuance of stock of the "purchasing" corporation to new investors as a transaction separate from the reorganization, it is concluded that the distribution to stockholders of the "selling" corporation of the cash, long-term notes, and other assets should be treated as a distribution under section 301 * * *.

* * *

[¶ 11,135]

Note

Is the "functionally unrelated" doctrine applied by the Fifth Circuit in *Reef*, see ¶ 11,120, essentially similar to the approach adopted by the IRS in Rev. Rul. 61–156 with respect to the sale of 55 percent of the stock in the new corporation to the public? What is the relationship of these approaches to the step transaction doctrine discussed at ¶¶ 9065 et seq.?

To what extent is treating a redemption of shareholders of the old corporation and sale to outsiders of the stock in the new corporation as separate from the rest of the transaction likely to enable the IRS to meet the liquidation-reincorporation challenge in cases in which the shareholders of the old corporation emerge with less than 50 percent of the stock of the new?

Chapter 12

CORPORATE DIVISIONS

[¶ 12,000]

A. INTRODUCTION TO TAX–FREE DIVISIONS UNDER SECTION 355

Unlike the "A," "B," and "C" reorganizations, which involve acquisition transactions, a tax-free corporate division is a transaction in which the investment of the shareholders in a single corporation is divided between two or more corporations. The division is often effected through a distribution by the corporation to its shareholders of the stock of a controlled corporation. Alternatively, an existing corporation may transfer all of its assets to two or more controlled corporations and then distribute in a complete liquidation the shares of the controlled corporations.

Corporate divisions under Section 355 may take any of the following three transactional forms:

Spin-off: The most common form of corporate division is the spin-off, which is a distribution by one corporation to its shareholders pro rata of the stock of a controlled subsidiary corporation. The spin-off is used to divide between two corporations two separate businesses previously conducted by the distributing corporation or to divide a single business into two separate businesses. In either case, after the spin-off, one business is conducted by the distributing corporation and the other by the controlled corporation the shares of which are distributed. The controlled corporation may either be an existing subsidiary that is already conducting the business to be spun off or that business may be transferred to a newly organized subsidiary. In either case, the shares of the controlled subsidiary are distributed to the shareholders of the distributing corporation in proportion to their percentages of the stock of the distributing corporation. Thus, the distributed controlled subsidiary and the distributing corporation become brother-sister corporations owned immediately after the distribution by the same shareholders in the same proportions.

Split-off: A split-off is similar to the spin-off, except that one or more of the shareholders of the distributing parent corporation surrender some or all of their stock in the parent in exchange for the controlled subsidiary's stock and the distribution need not be pro rata. If the exchange is pro rata among the shareholders of the distributing corporation, the split-off is essentially equivalent to a spin-off. If not, the split-off results in changes in the shareholders' proportionate ownership in the two corporations. For example, a split-off could be used to divide two businesses between two shareholders of the distributing corporation. If A and B each owns 50 percent of the stock of X Corporation, which conducts two businesses, one of the businesses can be transferred to a new wholly owned subsidiary, Y Corporation. The shares of Y Corporation can then be distributed to A in exchange for all of A's shares in X Corporation. After the split-off, A will own 100 percent of the shares of Y Corporation and B will own 100 percent of the shares of X Corporation. A split-off may also be used to divide a single business between shareholders A and B.

Split-up: A split-up involves a distribution by a parent corporation in complete liquidation of its stock in two or more controlled subsidiaries. The split-up involves either a pro rata or non-pro rata distribution to the shareholders of the distributing corporation in liquidation. If non-pro rata, the split-up distribution can, like the split-off, be the vehicle for splitting the ownership of two businesses (or a single business) between two shareholders or groups of shareholders of the distributing parent corporation. X Corporation may transfer one business to a newly organized wholly owned subsidiary, Y Corporation, and another business to a newly organized wholly owned subsidiary, Z Corporation. X Corporation then liquidates and distributes the shares of Y Corporation to one of its shareholders or to a group of its shareholders and the shares of Z Corporation to another shareholder or group.

There are a variety of legitimate business reasons to effect a division of a corporation. Thus, for example, it may be the device adopted to comply with an antitrust decree or the requirements of local law to separate a regulated from a non-regulated business; to insulate a speculative from a non-speculative business; to resolve a controversy or deadlock between shareholders; or, subject to important constraints discussed at ¶¶ 12,090 et seq., to prepare for the disposition of one of the resultant corporations.

To understand the tax treatment of corporate divisions, it is useful to review a bit of history. Prior to 1924, both split-offs and split-ups were covered by the tax-free reorganization provisions because they involved exchanges. Spin-offs, by contrast, were taxed like ordinary dividends since they involved only distributions. An early case—Rockefeller v.

¶ 12,000

United States, 257 U.S. 176 (1921)—helped to illustrate the inequity and inefficiency of this disparate treatment. In that case, several oil companies in which John D. Rockefeller was a stockholder were engaged in multiple lines of business that were subject to conflicting regulatory jurisdiction: (1) oil production and sales, which were regulated by the Federal Trade Commission, and (2) oil distribution through pipe lines owned by the companies that crossed state lines, which was governed by the Interstate Commerce Commission under a 1914 Supreme Court ruling. To avoid this regulatory conflict, as well as to avoid the imposition of a gross receipts tax imposed by the state of Ohio on transportation companies that also included receipts from oil production businesses, the companies sought to transfer the transportation businesses to wholly owned corporations and distribute the stock in them to their stockholders. The Court held that the distributions were taxable dividends. Although the underlying transactions in *Rockefeller* arose prior to the enactment of the tax-free reorganization provisions in 1918, and therefore would have been taxable in any event, dissatisfaction with the outcome helped to get spin-offs added as a tax-free reorganization in the Revenue Act of 1924. The only restriction was the requirement that the stockholders in a spin-off acquire "control" in the distribution, or at least 80 percent of the voting stock and 80 percent of all other shares of outstanding stock.

The legitimate business rationale for the spin-off in Rockefeller stood in stark contrast to the spin-off effected in 1934 in the *Gregory* case, discussed in Chapter 9. See ¶ 9055. In that case, the Supreme Court ultimately found no business purpose for the distribution of the subsidiary other than as a device to effect the "bail-out" of the earnings and profits of United Mortgage Corporation—in the form of the highly appreciated shares of stock in Monitor Securities Corporation—at capital gains rates rather than the ordinary income rates normally applicable to a dividend. The decision of the Tax Court upholding the transaction, however, caused such an uproar that even before the Supreme Court had a chance to hear the case, and only days after the Second Circuit had reversed it, Congress legislatively overturned it by removing spin-offs from the tax-free reorganization definition in the Revenue Act of 1934. Thus, from 1934 through 1951, spin-offs were once again taxable while split-offs and split-ups were tax-free.

In 1951, practitioners finally prevailed upon Congress to reunify the tax treatment of corporate divisions. It did so, however, by enacting a special provision—Section 355—with several requirements unique to divisions that were designed to guard against the bail-out of corporate earnings at capital gains rates. These requirements were further developed in the 1954 Code and are discussed in detail in this chapter.

While the elimination of the rate differential between dividends and exchanges in 2003 has lessened the need to attempt to bail out corporate earnings, and therefore perhaps the need for Section 355's extensive requirements, the repeal of the General Utilities doctrine in 1986 has left spin-offs as one of the few avenues for corporations to distribute appreciated property without recognizing an entity-level tax.

B. REQUIREMENTS TO PREVENT BAIL–OUT OF CORPORATE EARNINGS

[¶ 12,005]

1. OVERVIEW

If a corporation with accumulated E & P could segregate liquid, nonoperating assets in a subsidiary corporation and distribute the stock of this subsidiary pro rata to its shareholders without taxable gain, these shareholders would be in a position to realize upon the accumulated E & P represented by these liquid assets as a capital gain, either by selling the stock of, or by liquidating, the distributed subsidiary. In order to prevent such abuses, Congress by statute and the Treasury Department by regulations have adopted the following battery of safeguards:

(1) The requirement that, immediately after the distribution, both the distributing and the controlled corporations be engaged in the active conduct of a trade or business that has been conducted for at least five years and that has not been acquired in a taxable transaction within that period. § 355(b)(1) and (2) and Reg. § 1.355–3. In addition, control of a corporation conducting such a business may not have been acquired (directly or through one or more corporations) by the distributing corporation or any distributee corporation (including members of an affiliated group of which it is a member) within that five-year period in a taxable transaction. § 355(b)(2)(D).

(2) The requirement that the transaction not be used principally as a device for the distribution of the E & P of the distributing corporation or the controlled corporation or both. § 355(a)(1)(B) and Reg. § 1.355–2(d).

(3) The requirements that the transaction be carried out for a corporate (as distinguished from a shareholder) business purpose and that there be continuity of shareholder interest on the part of the historic shareholders of the distributing corporation in both the distributing corporation and the controlled corporation. Reg. §§ 1.355–2(b)-(c).

In the light of the materials that follow, consider the purposes for the foregoing requirements, how well those purposes have been served, and whether changes are needed.

¶ 12,005

2. ACTIVE TRADE OR BUSINESS

[¶ 12,010]

ESTATE OF LOCKWOOD v. COMMISSIONER

United States Court of Appeals, Eighth Circuit, 1965.
350 F.2d 712.

VOGEL, CIRCUIT JUDGE:

The single question involved in this review of an unreported decision of the Tax Court * * * is whether the "spin-off" of part of the business conducted by the Lockwood Grader Corporation of Gering, Nebraska, (hereinafter Lockwood) through the organization of a new corporation, Lockwood Graders of Maine, Inc. (hereinafter Maine, Inc.) was tax-free to petitioners, recipients of the stock of Maine, Inc., under * * * § 355 * * *. The government contended that the spin-off was not tax-free since the requirements of § 355(b)(2)(B) relating to the conducting of an active business for five years prior to the date of distribution had not been met. The government apparently conceded and the Tax Court found that the petitioner had met all other requirements to qualify under § 355 for tax-free treatment. The Tax Court upheld the government's contention and petitioners appeal.

The now deceased Thorval J. Lockwood, whose interests herein are represented by his duly qualified executor, National Bank of Commerce Trust and Savings Association, and his wife Margaret were the sole stockholders of Lockwood and had been so since its incorporation under Nebraska law in 1946. Lockwood's predecessor, Lockwood Graders, was a partnership formed in 1935 for the purpose of producing and selling a portable potato sorting machine invented by the decedent. * * * The equipment was sold in "all of the potato growing areas of the United States" but primarily in the biggest growing areas such as North Dakota, Idaho and Colorado.

From 1946 to 1951, inclusive, Lockwood operated its business of manufacturing and selling wash lines, potato machinery, parts and supplies to potato shippers in the potato growing areas. Though Lockwood continued to have its principal place of business at Gering, Nebraska, branches were opened, as the business expanded, in Grand Forks, North Dakota; Antigo, Wisconsin; Monte Vista, Colorado; and Rupert, Idaho. These branches performed both manufacturing and sales functions. In 1952, under a reorganization plan, these branches were separately incorporated to promote greater efficiency and to properly provide for expansion. Assets of Lockwood were exchanged for all of the stock of each new corporation and the stock so exchanged was passed without consideration to Thorval and Margaret as sole stockholders of Lockwood. The reorganization plan, among other things, was specifically designed to make use of the tax-free provisions of what is now § 355.

¶ 12,010

In the early 1950's Lockwood and the other controlled corporations changed the nature of their business somewhat by selling to individual farmers as well as to potato suppliers. Lockwood had previously dealt primarily in grading equipment but at this time it began to manufacture and sell field equipment such as harvesting pieces, bin holders and vine beaters as well.

Beginning as early as 1947 Lockwood began to make some sporadic and relatively inconsequential sales in the northeastern part of the United States. From 1949 to 1955 the primary sales of products and parts in that part of the country were made to Gould & Smith, Inc., a retailer of farming and industrial equipment, of Presque Isle, Maine * * *. Such sales were found to be of a relatively small volume by the Tax Court. On November 15, 1954, Lockwood established a branch office in Presque Isle, Maine, from which to handle Lockwood products. On March 1, 1956, pursuant to the 1951 plan for reorganization * * *, the Maine branch office was incorporated under the laws of Maine with its principal place of business at Presque Isle, Maine. Maine, Inc., was a wholly owned subsidiary of Lockwood. On incorporating, Lockwood transferred to Maine, Inc., $23,500 in assets consisting of petty cash totaling $150.00, accounts receivable totaling $4,686.67, automobiles and trucks worth $1,100, shop equipment worth $295.00, office furniture and fixtures worth $81.60, and inventory worth $17,186.73. In return for these assets Maine, Inc., issued all of its stock, 235 shares at $100.00 par value, to Lockwood. On March 31, 1956, Lockwood distributed 162 of these shares of Maine, Inc., to Thorval and 73 of them to Margaret. This distribution gave rise to the controversy here involved.

The Tax Court held this distribution to be outside of § 355. According to the Tax Court there was:

> " * * * the absence of evidence that the *Maine business* was actively conducted during the months between March 31, 1951, and August 1953—a span of time totaling over 40 per cent of the requisite five-year period [required by § 355(b)(2)(B).]" (Emphasis supplied.)

The Tax Court found that the Maine business was not actively and continuously conducted until August 1953, at which time a Lockwood salesman traveled to Maine and personally solicited orders from farmers and businessmen other than Gould & Smith. We do not disagree with the factual finding of the Tax Court as to the active conduct of Lockwood's business in Maine prior to the incorporation of Maine, Inc. However, the Tax Court, for reasons set out below, erred in looking only at the business performed by Lockwood in Maine to determine if the five-year active business requirement had been met prior to the incorporation of Maine, Inc. Nothing in the language of § 355 suggests that prior business activity is only to be measured by looking at the business performed in a geographical area where the controlled corporation is eventually formed. In this case, when the entire Lockwood market is

¶ 12,010

viewed, it can be seen that Lockwood was engaged in active business as required by § 355 for the five years prior to the incorporation of Maine, Inc. Since its incorporation Maine, Inc., has carried on the same kind of manufacturing and selling business previously and concurrently performed by Lockwood. Thus all § 355 prerequisites are met and the Tax Court erred in determining this was not a tax-free transfer.

* * *

* * * After much controversy it has been determined that tax-free treatment will not be denied to a transaction under § 355 merely because it represents an attempt to divide a single trade or business. See United States v. Marett, 1963, 325 F.2d 28 (5th Cir.1963); Coady v. Commissioner, 33 T.C. 771, affirmed per curiam, 289 F.2d 490 (6th Cir.1961). The Commissioner has acceded to the holdings of Marett and Coady in Rev. Rule 64–147, 1964–1, Cum. Bull. 136, even though the Commissioner had previously insisted * * * that two or more existing businesses had to be actively operated the five years prior to distribution. * * *

Respondent in the instant case, although claiming to accept the single business interpretation, points to the language of § 355(b)(1) and argues, as did the government in Coady, that the word *"and"* in that section means that, in determining whether or not the active business requirement was met, one has to look at both the business done by the distributing corporation (Lockwood) *and* the business done as such by the controlled corporation (Maine, Inc.) and its predecessors in Maine. Contrary to the government's position, once it has been ascertained that two or more trades or businesses are not required for § 355 to apply, the crucial question becomes whether or not the two corporations existing after distribution are doing the same type of work and using the same type of assets previously done and used by the prior *single* existing business. § 355(b)(1) has no relevance to respondent's point once it has been determined that only a single business is required.

Here the five years of prior activity we are concerned with involve the prior overall activity of Lockwood. Previous to 1956 Lockwood had carried on *in toto* what Maine, Inc., would later carry on in part in the northeast. We are not concerned with the prior activity of Lockwood in the northeast only, for Congress has never intimated that such a geographical test should be applied and we are not about to apply such a test now. A perusal of the House and Senate Reports indicates conclusively that at no time did the House or the Senate contemplate any kind of geographic test in applying the five-year active business requirement. The facts clearly show that Lockwood, in fact, was actively conducting the trade or business involved five years prior to the distribution period.

One case, Patricia W. Burke v. Commissioner, 42 T.C. 1021 (1964), did discuss the past business of a controlled corporation as performed in a limited geographical area in finding the prerequisites of § 355 had been met. That case did not, however, hold that there was in fact a geographical test. * * *. * * * [T]he test, restated, is not whether active business had been carried out in the geographic area later served by the controlled corporation but, simply, whether the distributing corporation, for five years prior to distribution, had been actively conducting the type of business now performed by the controlled corporation without reference to the geographic area. In the instant case the facts are abundantly clear that Lockwood had been actively engaged in the type of business later carried on by Maine, Inc., if one refers to a national rather than just the northeastern market.

It was mentioned earlier in this opinion that beginning in 1950 Lockwood began to sell field equipment as well as grading equipment. The respondent apparently does not contend, nor do we find, that Lockwood so changed its business as to be engaged in a new business that had been active for only two years prior to the incorporation of Maine, Inc. Lockwood meets the requirements of an existing five-year active business as set out by the Conference Committee in Conference Report No. 2543 * * *:

> "It is the understanding of the managers on the part of the House, in agreeing to the active business requirements of section 355 and of section 346 (defining partial liquidations), that a trade or business which has been actively conducted throughout the 5–year period described in such sections will meet the requirements of such sections, even though such trade or business underwent change during such 5–year period, for example, *by the addition of new*, or the dropping of old, *products*, changes in production capacity, and the like, provided the changes are not of such a character as to constitute the acquisition of a new or different business." (Emphasis supplied.)

* * *

The respondent contends:

> "If the taxpayers' argument prevails, then any corporation with a five-year history could distribute any of its assets regardless of when they were acquired and regardless of what kind of business they are in after the division, as long as the distributing corporation is in an active business. In other words, taxpayer argues that the five-year history rule requires that only the business of the distributing corporation have a five-year history. For instance, suppose a large manufacturing corporation with a ten-year life acquired some data processing machines in order to better control its inventory and work-in-process flow. If taxpayers' argument is correct, a year later this corporation could transfer all the data processing equipment to a new corporation in exchange for its stock, spin off the stock and claim a tax-free distribution under Section 355 since the manufacturing corporation had more than a five-year life and the data

processing business, once an integral part of the original business, was being actively conducted after the spin-off. Moreover, the same logic would allow the spin-off of real estate owned by the manufacturing corporation and used in its business.''

The fears of the government are unfounded. The example of the manufacturing company is more closely akin to the Bonsall case [317 F.2d 61 (2d Cir.1963)], * * * and is factually distinguishable from the instant case. Here Lockwood had not just recently acquired that part or segment of its business that was spun off. Rather, what was spun off was a part of the business Lockwood had always performed in the past and which it has continued to perform since the distribution. If Lockwood had, just before distribution, acquired or opened up a new or entirely different aspect of its business unrelated to prior activities and had spun this off to the controlled corporation, a different result might ensue. In Bonsall the distributing company, a dealer in floor covering materials, attempted to assert a tax-free spin-off occurred when a rental business of *de minimis* proportions was transferred to a subsidiary with the stock of the subsidiary being distributed to the distributor's shareholders. The Second Circuit held at page 64 of 317 F.2d:

> "There is ample support for the factual determination that Albany Linoleum [the distributing company therein] was not actively conducting a real-estate rental business. * * * the portion of its income realized from real estate rentals was minute. * * * No activity appeared beyond a few casual conversations with prospective tenants. Moreover, most of the floor-space of the two buildings combined was occupied by the floor-covering business. Only a very small part was available for rental, and an even smaller part actually leased. The continuing rental to Armstrong Cork Co. which provided most of the rental income appeared to be an accommodation to a large supplier of the floor-covering business and thus an adjunct to it, rather than indicative of an independent business, for the Tax Court found that the premises were let at less than fair rental value over the five-year period. Finally, no separate records of rental income and expenses were kept. Absence of such records is at least probative of the fact that the managers of Albany Linoleum did not regard it as engaged in an independent rental business. The Tax Court was plainly justified in concluding that the small amount of rental activity was merely an incidental part of the sole business of the corporation—wholesale floor-coverings. * * * * "

Thus it is clear that in respondent's example and in Bonsall the business sought to be spun off was not actively engaged in for five years prior to distribution, which is not the situation in the instant case. Here, what was spun off was merely an integral part of what had been Lockwood's primary and only business from its inception.

¶ 12,010

Further, it should be remembered that even if the five-year active business requirement is met, there is further protection in § 355 against spin-offs being used for mere tax avoidance, which would be contrary to Congressional intent. § 355(a)(1)(B) will only allow a tax-free spin-off transaction where " * * * the transaction was not used principally as a device for the distribution of the earnings and profits of the distributing corporation or the controlled corporation or both * * *." Under this section, the government and the courts have great latitude in preventing the abuses which the respondent fears will happen by finding for petitioners in this case. * * * Herein the respondent does not contend that the purpose of the spin-off was designed primarily for tax avoidance. No earnings and profits were in fact distributed to Thorval and Margaret. The Tax Court stated that:

> * * * we do not view the distribution as running afoul of the congressional purpose behind section 355, * * *.

This being so, and since petitioners otherwise complied with § 355, the decision of the Tax Court will be reversed. The transaction herein involved cannot be treated as a taxable distribution of dividends.

[¶ 12,015]

Notes

1. The regulations adopt the position of the court in *Estate of Lockwood* that a business conducted in two geographical locations can constitute two separate businesses. Reg. § 1.355–3(c), Exs. 6 and 7.

2. *Estate of Lockwood* dealt with a geographic expansion of an existing business, but a business can expand in other ways. For instance, rather than opening a location in another state, a business can start a "location" on the internet by creating a website. In Rev. Rul. 2003–38, 2003–1 C.B. 811, a retail shoe store business that had been in business for ten years sought to spin off the internet website it had created to sell shoes. Although the internet website business had only been in operation for two years prior to the distribution, the IRS found that the website was an expansion of the retail shoe store business because they both sold shoes and the internet website relied upon the goodwill and knowhow of the retail shoe store business. Similarly, a business can expand its product line. In Rev. Rul. 2003–18, 2003–1 C.B. 467, a dealer in one brand of automobiles acquired a franchise in another brand of automobiles and less than five years later sought to spin off the original brand of automobiles. The IRS permitted it under the active trade or business doctrine, noting that the product, business activities, and operation of the new dealership were similar to that of the existing dealership and thus this constituted an expansion of an existing business rather than an acquisition of a new business.

[¶ 12,020]

REVENUE RULING 86-126

1986–2 C.B. 58.

ISSUE

Whether a corporation is considered to be engaged in the active conduct of a trade or business within the meaning of section 355(b) * * * and section 1.355–1(c) of the * * * Regulations under the following circumstances.

FACTS

A and *B* are the only officers and shareholders of *P* corporation. Each has held 50 percent of *P*'s outstanding common stock for more than 5 years. *A* and *B* are both farmers who are engaged in the business of farming their own individual tracts of farmland not owned by *P*. *P* has for more than 5 years held title to large tracts of farmland elsewhere in the same state. Each tract of land held by *P* is leased for one year at a time to a tenant farmer who has agreed with *P* to share one-half of all income and expenses of the farm. Each party to the lease is responsible for securing the financing necessary to pay that party's share of expenses. In the case of each tract leased, the planting, raising, and harvesting of corn and soybeans (the only crops grown on these farms) are done by the tenant farmer. The tenant farmer also supplies the farm equipment used in these activities. The tenant farmer repairs and maintains the equipment, and also maintains the irrigation system, fences, and other fixtures located on the property. After consulting with *A* and *B*, the tenant farmer purchases all herbicides, insecticides, and fertilizers used on the property. Also after consulting with *A* and *B*, the tenant farmer contracts to sell the crops at a future date, or sells them when harvested. Each tenant farmer is responsible for accounting to *A* and *B* for *P*'s share of the proceeds.

A and *B* each devote a substantial part of their time to the operation of their own respective farms which are unconnected with the farmland owned by *P*. After completing work on their own properties, *A* and *B*, in their capacity as officers of *P*, occasionally inspect the crops and improvements located on each leased tract. If any corrective steps must be taken, *A* or *B* points out the problem to the tenant farmer, who makes the necessary corrections in the way the tenant farmer sees fit. *A* and *B* also decide each year what portion of each tract will be leased, in the light of soil conservation needs, market conditions, and federal price support and acreage reserve programs. They review each tenant farmer's accounting of operations and sales.

For valid business reasons, *P* will transfer to a newly-formed subsidiary corporation, *S*, one-half of all the property held by *P*, and then will distribute all the S stock to B in exchange for all B's stock in P. After the distribution, P and S will continue to conduct operations in the same manner with tenant farmers as P had prior to the distribution.

Except for the question here at issue regarding the active conduct of a trade or business, the transfer will meet all the requirements of sections 368(a)(1)(D) and 355 * * * and the regulations thereunder.

LAW AND ANALYSIS

* * *

Section 355(b) * * * requires that both the distributing and controlled corporations be engaged, immediately after the distribution, in the active conduct of a trade or business that has been actively conducted throughout the 5–year period ending on the date of distribution.

To meet the requirements of section 355(b) * * *, each corporation must, as stated in *Rafferty v. Commissioner*, 452 F.2d 767, 772 (1st Cir.1971), *cert. denied*, 408 U.S. 922 (1972), "engage in entrepreneurial endeavors of such a nature and to such an extent as to qualitatively distinguish its operations from mere investments. Moreover, there should be objective indicia of such corporate operations." Such objective indicia are found in active and substantial managerial and operational activities of the corporation. In addition, this business activity has to be the activity of the corporation itself (through its officers and employees) and not the activity of independent contractors. * * *

In Rev. Rul. 73–234, it was held that a corporation engaged in farming with tenant farmers was engaged in the active conduct of a trade or business within the meaning of section 355(b) * * *. However, in that revenue ruling, Y corporation, through its employees, A and B, was engaged in hiring seasonal workers, purchasing and supplying equipment, maintaining equipment, arranging financing, planning all rotation and planting and harvesting of crops, purchasing livestock, planning livestock breeding, selling all crops and livestock, and accounting to the tenant farmers for their shares of the proceeds. This activity of Y, carried on through its own employees and constituting active and substantial managerial and operational activity, contrasts with the activity carried on by the employees of P in the present situation. Here, P either did not engage in the above activities at all, or engaged in them only on a limited basis. At best, P could be considered to engage in some managerial and operational activity but not enough to "qualitatively distinguish its operations from mere investments." Thus, Rev. Rul. 73–234 is distinguishable from the present situation.

HOLDING

Because of the absence of active and substantial operational and managerial activities, the active business requirement of section 355(b) * * * is not met and P's distribution of the S stock is not governed by section 355. *B* will recognize gain on the receipt of the *S* stock in exchange for *P* stock, and *P* will be subject to the provisions of section 311. See Rev. Rul. 74–516, 1974–2 C.B. 121.

In addition, because there is no distribution of stock or securities to *B* under section 354, 355, or 356 * * *, the transfer of property from *P* to *S* does not meet the requirements of section 368(a)(1)(D). However, this transfer does meet the requirements of section 351(a). The fact that *P* distributed the *S* stock to *B* does not violate the control requirement of Section 351(c).

[¶ 12,025]

Notes

1. As part of the 1989 revisions, the regulations under Section 355(b) (which requires that the distributing and controlled corporations be engaged in active businesses after the distribution) were revised and expanded. See Reg. § 1.355–3.

The regulations deal in some detail with the requirement that the distributed controlled corporation(s) and the distributing corporation (unless its only assets are stock and securities of controlled corporations) be engaged in the active conduct of a trade or business immediately after the distribution. The corporation concerned must carry on activities that include every operation that forms part of, or a step in, the process of earning income, including ordinarily the collection of income and payment of expenses. Reg. § 1.355–3(b)(2)(ii). Generally the corporation must perform active and substantial management and operational functions itself, not by retaining independent contractors. Reg. § 1.355–3(b)(2)(iii). It is specifically provided that the active conduct of a trade or business does not include:

(1) The holding for investment purposes of stock, securities, land, or other property, or

(2) The ownership and operation (including leasing) of real or personal property used in a trade or business, unless the owner performs significant services with respect to the operation and management of the property.

Reg. § 1.355–3(b)(2)(iv).

2. A substantial number of examples are provided in the regulations. One of these reflects acceptance of the decision in Coady v. Commissioner, 33 T.C. 771 (1960), aff'd per curiam, 289 F.2d 490 (6th Cir.1961), permitting the division by split-off of a single business between two equal shareholders to resolve their deadlock. Reg. § 1.355–3(c), Ex. 4. In United States v. Marett, 325 F.2d 28 (5th Cir.1963), the motivation was a similarly valid business purpose, i.e., the satisfaction of a major customer and retention of his account. The single business activity of packaging foods was split into two operating corporations. The

distributing corporation retained two factories and continued to produce solely as a supplier of the major customer. The remaining factory was transferred to a new corporation which continued to package goods for the remainder of the original customers and any new customers. All of the stock of this new subsidiary was distributed to the distributing corporation's shareholders in a spin-off. This division of a single business was held to comply with the active business tests, and the regulations accept this result. See Reg. § 1.355–3(c), Ex. 5.

3.   While *Lockwood*, *Coady*, and *Marett* each involved the division of a single business between different locations or assets, a thornier problem is present when a single business is divided along functional lines. For example, if the research and development division of a manufacturing corporation is spun-off, there may be a concern as to whether the R & D operation may constitute an active trade or business in its own right or whether it merely supports the manufacturing business. Prior to 1989, the IRS challenged such a division on active trade or business grounds. In the regulations issued since then, this challenge was dropped regardless of whether the R & D business contracts solely with the manufacturing business or with other businesses as well after the spin-off. Reg. § 1.355–3(c), Exs. 9–11. The regulations caution, however, that a distribution of such a supporting business may still be subject to taxation on device grounds.

4.   Under legislation enacted in 2006, the active trade or business requirement is judged by reference to the "relevant affiliated group," as determined under the consolidated return rules. §§ 355(b)(3); 1504(a). Previously, an affiliated group would have had to restructure prior to the spin-off if the distributing corporation was a holding company and less than half of the value of its gross assets consisted of stock in subsidiaries that were engaged in the active conduct of a trade or business for the five-year period preceding the distribution. One method of effecting such a reorganization would have been for the distributing corporation to cause one of its actively engaged subsidiaries to liquidate under Section 332 so that the distributing corporation could directly qualify under the active trade or business requirement and thereby eliminate the taint of its non-actively engaged or recently acquired subsidiaries. Another would be for the distributing corporation to contribute the stock of its non-actively engaged or recently acquired subsidiaries to one of its actively engaged subsidiaries so that all of its direct subsidiaries would meet the active trade or business test. To eliminate the need for such inefficient pre-distribution tailoring by holding companies, Section 355(b)(3) now provides that if at least one member of an affiliated group is actively engaged in the conduct of a trade or business, each member of such group will be treated as meeting the active trade or business test. This provision applies to transactions effected on or before December 31, 2010.

¶ 12,025

[¶ 12,030]

3. DEVICE

After suffering losses like the *Lockwood* case, the IRS eventually switched its method of attacking bail-outs from the more mechanical active trade or business test to the requirement that the transaction not be used principally as a *device* for the distribution of the earnings and profits of the distributing or the controlled corporation. This requirement is more difficult to define, as evidenced by the case below and the extensive regulations that follow. See Reg. §§ 1.355–2(d).

[¶ 12,035]

RAFFERTY v. COMMISSIONER

United States Court of Appeals, First Circuit, 1971.
452 F.2d 767, cert. denied, 408 U.S. 922 (1972).

McENTEE, CIRCUIT JUDGE:

Taxpayers, Joseph V. Rafferty and wife, appeal from a decision of the Tax Court, 55 T.C. 490, which held that a distribution to them of all the outstanding stock of a real estate holding corporation did not meet the requirements of § 355 * * * and therefore was taxable as a dividend. * * *

* * * The taxpayers own all the outstanding shares of Rafferty Brown Steel Co., Inc. (hereinafter RBS), a Massachusetts corporation engaged in the processing and distribution of cold rolled sheet and strip steel in Longmeadow, Massachusetts. In May 1960, at the suggestion of his accountant, Rafferty organized Teragram Realty Co., Inc., also a Massachusetts corporation. In June of that year RBS transferred its Longmeadow real estate to Teragram in exchange for all of the latter's outstanding stock. Thereupon Teragram leased back this real estate to RBS for 10 years at an annual rent of $42,000. In 1962 the taxpayers also organized Rafferty Brown Steel Co., Inc., of Connecticut (RBS Conn.), which corporation acquired the assets of Hawkridge Brothers, a general steel products warehouse in Waterbury, Connecticut. Since its inception the taxpayers have owned all of the outstanding stock in RBS Conn. From 1962 to 1965 Hawkridge leased its real estate in Waterbury to RBS Conn. In 1965 Teragram purchased some unimproved real estate in Waterbury and built a plant there. In the same year it leased this plant to RBS Conn. for a term of fourteen years. Teragram has continued to own and lease the Waterbury real estate to RBS Conn. and the Longmeadow realty to RBS, which companies have continued up to the present time to operate their businesses at these locations.

During the period from 1960 through 1965 Teragram derived all of its income from rent paid by RBS and RBS Conn. Its earned surplus increased from $4,119.05 as of March 31, 1961, to $46,743.35 as of

March 31, 1965. The earned surplus of RBS increased from $331,117.97 as of June 30, 1959, to $535,395.77 as of June 30, 1965. In August 1965, RBS distributed its Teragram stock to the taxpayers. Other than this distribution, neither RBS nor Teragram has paid any dividends.

Joseph V. Rafferty has been the guiding force behind all three corporations, RBS, RBS Conn., and Teragram. He is the president and treasurer of Teragram which, while it has no office or employees, keeps separate books and records and filed separate tax returns for the years in question.

On various occasions Rafferty consulted his accountant about estate planning, particularly about the orderly disposition of RBS. While he anticipated that his sons would join him at RBS, he wanted to exclude his daughters (and/or his future sons-in-law) from the active management of the steel business. He wished, however, to provide them with property which would produce a steady income. The accountant recommended the formation of Teragram, the distribution of its stock, and the eventual use of this stock as future gifts to the Rafferty daughters. The taxpayers acted on this advice and also on the accountant's opinion that the distribution of Teragram stock would meet the requirements of § 355.

In their 1965 return the taxpayers treated the distribution of Teragram stock as a nontaxable transaction under § 355. The Commissioner viewed it, however, as a taxable dividend and assessed a deficiency. He claimed (a) that the distribution was used primarily as a device for the distribution of the earnings and profits of RBS or Teragram or both, and (b) that Teragram did not meet the active business requirements of § 355.

We turn first, to the Tax Court's finding that there was no device because there was an adequate business purpose for the separation and distribution of Teragram stock. In examining this finding we are guided by the rule that the taxpayer has the burden of proving that the transaction was not used principally as a device. * * * Initially, we are disturbed by the somewhat uncritical nature of the Tax Court's finding of a business purpose. Viewing the transaction from the standpoint of RBS, RBS Conn., or Teragram, no immediate business reason existed for the distribution of Teragram's stock to the taxpayers. Over the years the businesses had been profitable, as witnessed by the substantial increase of the earned surplus of every component, yet none had paid dividends. The primary purpose for the distribution found by the Tax Court was to facilitate Rafferty's desire to make bequests to his children in accordance with an estate plan. This was a personal motive. Taxpayers seek to put it in terms relevant to the corporation by speaking of avoidance of possible interference with the operation of the steel business by future sons-in-law, pointing to Coady v. Commissioner of Internal Revenue, 33 T.C. 771 (1960), aff'd per curiam, 289 F.2d 490 (6th Cir.1961).

¶ 12,035

In *Coady*, however, the separation was in response to a seemingly irreconcilable falling-out between the owners of a business. This falling-out had already occurred and, manifestly, the separation was designed to save the business from a substantial, present problem. * * * In the case at bar there was, at best, only an envisaged possibility of future debilitating nepotism. If avoidance of this danger could be thought a viable business purpose at all, it was so remote and so completely under the taxpayers' control that if, in other respects the transaction was a "device," that purpose could not satisfy the taxpayers' burden of proving that it was not being used "principally as a device" within the meaning of the statute.

Our question, therefore, must be whether taxpayers' desire to put their stockholdings into such form as would facilitate their estate planning, viewed in the circumstances of the case, was a sufficient personal business purpose to prevent the transaction at bar from being a device for the distribution of earnings and profits. While we remain of the view, which we first expressed in Lewis v. Commissioner of Internal Revenue, 176 F.2d 646 (1st Cir.1949), that a purpose of a shareholder, qua shareholder, may in some cases save a transaction from condemnation as a device, we do not agree with the putative suggestion in Estate of Parshelsky v. Commissioner of Internal Revenue, 303 F.2d 14, 19 (2d Cir.1962), that any investment purpose of the shareholders is sufficient. Indeed, in *Lewis*, although we depreciated the distinction between shareholder and corporate purpose, we were careful to limit that observation to the facts of that case, and to caution that the business purpose formula "must not become a substitute for independent analysis." 176 F.2d at 650. For that reason we based our decision on the Tax Court's finding that the transaction was "undertaken for reasons germane to the continuance of the corporate business." *Id*. at 647.

This is not to say that a taxpayer's personal motives cannot be considered, but only that a distribution which has considerable potential for use as a device for distributing earnings and profits should not qualify for tax-free treatment on the basis of personal motives unless those motives are germane to the continuance of the corporate business. * * * We prefer this approach over reliance upon formulations such as "business purpose," and "active business." * * * The facts of the instant case illustrate the reason for considering substance. Dividends are normally taxable to shareholders upon receipt. Had the taxpayers received cash dividends and made investments to provide for their female descendants, an income tax would, of course, have resulted. Accordingly, once the stock was distributed, if it could potentially be converted into cash without thereby impairing taxpayers' equity interest in RBS, the transaction could easily be used to avoid taxes. The business purpose here alleged, which could be fully satisfied by a bail-out of dividends, is not sufficient to prove that the transaction was not being principally so used.

¶ 12,035

Given such a purpose, the only question remaining is whether the substance of the transaction is such as to leave the taxpayer in a position to distribute the earnings and profits of the corporation away from, or out of the business. The first factor to be considered is how easily the taxpayer would be able, were he so to choose, to liquidate or sell the spun-off corporation. Even if both corporations are actively engaged in their respective trades, if one of them is a business based principally on highly liquid investment-type, passive assets, the potential for a bail-out is real. The question here is whether the property transferred to the newly organized corporation had a readily realizable value, so that the distributee-shareholders could, if they ever wished, "obtain such cash or property or the cash equivalent thereof, either by selling the distributed stock or liquidating the corporation, thereby converting what would otherwise be dividends taxable as ordinary income into capital gain. . . ." Wilson v. Commissioner, * * * 42 T.C. at 923. In this connection we note that the Tax Court found that a sale of Teragram's real estate properties could be "easily arranged." 55 T.C. at 353. Indeed, taxpayers themselves stressed the fact that the buildings were capable of multiple use.

There must, however, be a further question. If the taxpayers could not effect a bail-out without thereby impairing their control over the on-going business, the fact that a bail-out is theoretically possible should not be enough to demonstrate a device because the likelihood of it ever being so used is slight. "[A] bail-out ordinarily means that earnings and profits have been drawn off without impairing the shareholder's residual equity interest in the corporation's earning power, growth potential, or voting control." B. Bittker & J. Eustice, Federal Income Taxation of Corporations and Shareholders (3d ed. 1971) § 13.06. If sale would adversely affect the shareholders of the on-going company, the assets cannot be said to be sufficiently separated from the corporate solution and the gain sufficiently crystallized as to be taxable. * * * In this case, there was no evidence that the land and buildings at which RBS carried on its steel operations were so distinctive that the sale of Teragram stock would impair the continued operation of RBS, or that the sale of those buildings would in any other way impair Rafferty's control and other equity interests in RBS.

In the absence of any direct benefit to the business of the original company, and on a showing that the spin-off put salable assets in the hands of the taxpayers, the continued retention of which was not needed to continue the business enterprise, or to accomplish taxpayers' purposes, we find no sufficient factor to overcome the Commissioner's determination that the distribution was principally a device to distribute earnings and profits.

* * *

It is our view that in order to be an active trade or business under § 355 a corporation must engage in entrepreneurial endeavors of such a nature and to such an extent as to qualitatively distinguish its operations from mere investments. Moreover, there should be objective indicia of such corporate operations. Prior to 1965 Teragram's sole venture was the leasing back to its parent of its only asset for a fixed return, an activity, in economic terms, almost indistinguishable from an investment in securities. Standing by itself this activity is the type of "passive investment" which Congress intended to exclude from § 355 treatment. Furthermore, there are hardly any indicia of corporate operations. Prior to 1965 Teragram paid neither salaries nor rent. It did not employ independent contractors, and its only activity appears to have been collecting rent, paying taxes, and keeping separate books. Prior to 1965 it failed to meet either set of criteria for an active trade or business. We need not reach the more difficult question of whether its activities in 1965 constituted an active trade or business.

Affirmed.

[¶ 12,040]

Note

In 1989, the regulations under Section 355(a)(1)(B) (requiring that the transaction not be used principally as a device for the distribution of E & P) were revised to specify "device" and "nondevice" factors to be taken into account in determining whether a transaction was used principally as such a device. Reg. § 1.355–2(d). The device requirement reflects the recognition that a tax-free Section 355 distribution of a controlled corporation by the distributing corporation may facilitate avoidance of dividend taxation through a subsequent sale of stock of one corporation coupled with retention of stock of another. Reg. § 1.355–2(d)(1).

The regulations state that there must be a corporate business purpose for the distribution even if it can be demonstrated that the distribution is not a prohibited "device," thereby rejecting the view that the potential abuses addressed by the business purpose requirement were adequately discouraged by the "device" test. The regulations, however, acknowledge that the existence of a corporate business purpose is a nondevice factor. Reg. § 1.355–2(b)(4).

Reg. § 1.355–2(d)(1) states, in part:

Generally, the determination of whether a transaction was used principally as a device will be made from all of the facts and circumstances, including, but not limited to, the presence of the device factors specified in paragraph (d)(2) of this section ("evidence of device"), and the presence of the nondevice factors specified in paragraph (d)(3) of this section ("evidence of nondevice").

After describing the device and nondevice factors in some detail, the regulations go on to identify distributions that will ordinarily be considered not to have been used principally as a device. These include (i) distributions when neither the distributing nor the controlled corporation has current or accumulated E & P that could result in dividend treatment and (ii) distributions that, in the absence of Section 355, would be redemptions treated as exchanges under Section 302(a) or 303(a). Reg. § 1.355–2(d)(5).

In discussing evidence of *device* factors, the regulations provide that a sale of 20 percent or more of the stock of either the distributing or the controlled corporation negotiated or agreed upon before the distribution is substantial (but not conclusive) evidence of a prohibited device, which may be outweighed by sufficiently persuasive nondevice factors. In general, the larger the percentage of stock sold and the shorter the time between the distribution and the sale, the stronger is the evidence of device. Other device factors include the fact that the distribution is fully or substantially pro rata, the existence of assets such as cash and liquid assets not used in the business of the distributing or controlled corporation, and conduct by one of the corporations of a "secondary" business that can be sold without adversely affecting the business of the other corporation. Reg. § 1.355–2(d)(2). The regulations state that the strength of each device and nondevice factor depends on all of the facts and circumstances relating to the distribution. Reg. § 1.355–2(d)(2)(i) and (3)(i).

The list of *nondevice* factors includes, among others, (1) the existence of a corporate business purpose for the distribution, (2) the fact that the distributing corporation is publicly traded and widely held, and (3) the fact that the distribution is made to domestic corporate shareholders entitled to a dividends-received deduction. Reg. § 1.355–2(d)(3). The strength of the business purpose nondevice factor may be particularly important because all distributions that would otherwise qualify under Section 355 must have a corporate business purpose. The stronger the evidence of device, the stronger the corporate business purpose required to preclude a determination that the transaction is used principally as a device. The evaluation of the strength of a corporate business purpose will be based on all the facts and circumstances, such as

(1) the importance of achieving the purpose to the success of the business;

(2) the extent to which the transaction is prompted by a person having no proprietary interest in either corporation or by other factors beyond the control of the distributing corporation; and

(3) the immediacy of the conditions prompting the division.

Reg. § 1.355–2(d)(3)(ii).

[¶ 12,045]

4. CORPORATE BUSINESS PURPOSE AND CONTINUITY OF INTEREST

Prior to 1989, distributions under Section 355 were subject only to the business purpose and shareholder continuity of interest requirements via the judicial doctrines discussed in Chapter 9. In 1989, however, Treasury adopted regulations that added independent corporate business purpose and continuity of shareholder interest requirements. Reg. § 1.355–2(b) and (c). These are required to ensure that nonrecognition treatment is accorded only to "distributions that are incident to readjustments of corporate structures required by business exigencies and that effect only readjustments of continuing interests in property under modified corporate forms." Reg. § 1.355–2(b)(1) and (c)(1).

After the corporate business purpose requirement was added, practitioners sought further guidance on appropriate corporate business purposes. In response, the IRS issued Rev. Proc. 96–30, 1996–1 C.B 378, which identified several corporate business purposes that the IRS would accept for purposes of ruling requests. These included distributions to retain a key employee, to facilitate a stock offering, borrowing, cost savings, or an acquisition of or by the Distributing or Controlled corporations, to maintain superior "fit and focus" and competitive strength, or to reduce risk.

In recent years, the Service has been concerned about the volume of private letter ruling requests seeking guidance on the business purpose issue. Thus, in 2003, the IRS announced a pilot program to suspend the issuance of private letter rulings on, among other things, whether the business purpose for the distribution was sufficient to satisfy the corporate business purpose requirement. Instead, the IRS issued a number of revenue rulings designed to provide guidance on the business purpose issue. Rev. Rul. 2004–23 addresses the threshold question of distinguishing a shareholder business purpose from a corporate business purpose.

[¶ 12,050]

REVENUE RULING 2004–23
2004–1 C.B. 585

ISSUE

Whether a distribution that is expected to cause the aggregate value of the stock of a distributing corporation and the stock of a controlled corporation to exceed the pre-distribution value of the distributing corporation's stock satisfies the corporate business purpose requirement of § 355 * * * and § 1.355–2(b) of the Regulations when the increased value is expected to serve a corporate business purpose of either the distributing corporation or the controlled corporation (or both), even if it benefits the shareholders of the distributing corporation.

FACTS

D is a corporation that indirectly conducts Business 1 and Business 2 through its subsidiaries. Some subsidiaries engage only in Business 1 and others only in Business 2. *D*'s common stock is widely held and publicly traded.

The two businesses attract different investors, some of which are averse to investing in D because of the presence of the other business. Therefore, *D* believes, and *D*'s investment banker has advised *D*, that if each business were conducted in a separate and independent corporation, the stock of the two corporations likely would trade publicly for a higher price, in the aggregate, than the stock of *D* if it continued to represent an interest in both businesses. The expected increase in the aggregate trading price of the stock of *D* and *C* over the pre-distribution trading price of *D* would not, however, derive in any significant respect from any Federal tax advantage made available to either *D* or *C* by the transaction.

With the intent and expectation of increasing the aggregate trading price of the common stock representing Business 1 and Business 2, *D* transfers the subsidiaries that engage in Business 2 to a newly formed corporation, *C*, in exchange for all of the *C* stock and distributes the *C* stock to its common shareholders, *pro rata*. *D*'s remaining subsidiaries will continue to conduct Business 1.

Increasing the aggregate trading price of the *D* and *C* common stock over the trading price of the pre-distribution *D* common stock is expected to confer a benefit to existing shareholders. In deciding whether to undertake the distribution, *D*'s directors consider this expected benefit to the shareholders, as well as the expected benefits to the corporation described below. However, *D*'s directors do not effect the distribution to facilitate any particular shareholder's disposition of the stock of either *D* or *C*.

Apart from the issue of whether the business purpose requirement of § 1.355–2(b) is satisfied, the distribution meets the requirements of §§ 368(a)(1)(D) and 355.

Situation 1. D uses equity-based incentives as a significant part of its program to compensate a significant number of employees of both Business 1 and Business 2. *D*'s directors wish to enhance the value of employee compensation and have considered either granting additional equity-based incentives or making cash payments in lieu of additional equity incentives. However, granting additional equity-based incentives would unacceptably dilute *D*'s existing shareholders' interests, and making cash payments would be unduly expensive. Therefore, *D* undertakes the separation of Business 2 from Business 1 with the expectation that its stock value will increase and such increase will enhance the value of its equity-based compensation, providing *D* with a real and substantial benefit.

Situation 2. As part of its overall strategic planning, *D* has expanded both Business 1 and Business 2 through acquisitions of assets and the stock of other corporations. In some of these acquisitions, *D* has used its stock, either in whole or in part, as consideration. *D*'s directors expect to

¶ 12,050

continue expanding Business 1 as appropriate acquisition opportunities are identified in the future. *D* expects to offer its common stock as consideration, either in whole or in part, in connection with future acquisitions. Therefore *D* undertakes the separation of Business 2 from Business 1 with the expectation that its stock value will increase and such increase may permit *D* to effect such acquisitions in a manner that preserves capital with significantly less dilution of the existing shareholders' interests, providing *D* with a real and substantial benefit.

LAW

Section 355 provides that if certain requirements are met, a corporation may distribute stock and securities in a controlled corporation to its shareholders and security holders without causing the distributees to recognize gain or loss.

In addition to the statutory requirements, the regulations provide that § 355 will apply to a transaction only if it is carried out for one or more corporate business purposes. Section 1.355–2(b)(1). A transaction is carried out for a corporate business purpose if it is motivated, in whole or substantial part, by one or more corporate business purposes. *Id.* A corporate business purpose is a real and substantial non-Federal tax purpose germane to the business of the distributing corporation, the controlled corporation, or the affiliated group (as defined in § 1.355–3(b)(4)(iv)) to which the distributing corporation belongs. Section 1.355–2(b)(2). The principal reason for the business purpose requirement is to provide nonrecognition treatment only to distributions that are incident to readjustments of corporate structures required by business exigencies and that effect only readjustments of continuing interests in property under modified corporate forms. Section 1.355–2(b)(1). If a corporate business purpose can be achieved through a nontaxable transaction that does not involve the distribution of stock of a controlled corporation and that is neither impractical nor unduly expensive, then the separation is not carried out for that corporate business purpose. Section 1.355–2(b)(3).

A shareholder purpose (for example, the personal planning purposes of a shareholder) is not a corporate business purpose. Section 1.355–2(b)(2). Depending upon the facts of a particular case, however, a shareholder purpose for a transaction may be so nearly coextensive with a corporate business purpose as to preclude any distinction between them. *Id.* In such a case, the transaction is carried out for one or more corporate business purposes. *Id.* A transaction motivated in substantial part by a corporate business purpose does not fail the business purpose requirement merely because it is motivated in part by non-Federal tax shareholder purposes. *See* § 1.355–2(b)(5), Example (2).

ANALYSIS

Situation 1. Because *D* believes that the increased value of its stock expected to result from the separation will enhance the value of its

¶ 12,050

employee compensation, providing a real and substantial benefit to *D*, the distribution is motivated by a real and substantial non-Federal tax purpose germane to the business of *D*. Section 1.355–2(b)(1) and (2). Further, because this purpose cannot be achieved through another nontaxable transaction that is neither impractical nor unduly expensive, the distribution is carried out for a corporate business purpose. Section 1.355–2(b)(2) and (3). Although the increase in stock value is expected to benefit the shareholders by increasing the amount they would realize on a sale of their shares, this shareholder purpose is so nearly coextensive with the corporate business purpose as to preclude any distinction between them. Section 1.355–2(b)(2). Therefore, the distribution is treated as carried out for a corporate business purpose. *Id*.

Situation 2. Because *D* expects that the increased value of its stock expected to result from the separation may permit *D* to effect future acquisitions in a manner that preserves capital with significantly less dilution of the existing shareholders' interests, providing *D* with a real and substantial benefit, the distribution is motivated by a real and substantial non-Federal tax purpose germane to the business of *D*. Section 1.355–2(b)(1) and (2). Further, because this purpose cannot be achieved through another nontaxable transaction that is neither impractical nor unduly expensive, the distribution is carried out for a corporate business purpose. Section 1.355–2(b)(2) and (3). Although the increase in stock value is expected to benefit the shareholders by increasing the amount they would realize on a sale of their shares, this shareholder purpose is so nearly coextensive with the corporate business purpose as to preclude any distinction between them. Section 1.355–2(b)(2). Therefore, the distribution is treated as carried out for a corporate business purpose. *Id*.

HOLDING

A distribution that is expected to cause the aggregate value of the stock of a distributing corporation and the stock of a controlled corporation to exceed the pre-distribution value of the distributing corporation's stock satisfies the corporate business purpose requirement of § 355 and § 1.355–2(b) when the increased value is expected to serve a corporate business purpose of either the distributing corporation or the controlled corporation (or both), even if it benefits the shareholders of the distributing corporation.

* * *

[¶ 12,055]

Notes

1. As was true in Rev. Rul. 2004–23, a corporate business purpose often may be aligned with a shareholder business purpose without

disqualifying the distribution. This may be true even if the accompanying shareholder purpose accomplishes a personal objective for an individual shareholder, rather than a business purpose for all shareholders such as increasing share values. See Rev. Rul. 2003–52, 2003–1 C.B. 960 (approving the corporate business purpose even though it also satisfied the shareholder's estate planning goals). Citing Section 1.355–2(b)(2), Rev. Rul. 2003–52 explained

> A shareholder purpose (for example, the personal planning purposes of a shareholder) is not a corporate business purpose. Depending upon the facts of a particular case, however, a shareholder purpose for a transaction may be so nearly coextensive with a corporate business purpose as to preclude any distinction between them. In such a case, the transaction is carried out for one or more corporate business purposes. A transaction motivated in substantial part by a corporate business purpose does not fail the business purpose requirement merely because it is motivated in part by non-federal tax shareholder purposes.

Id.

2. A distribution will not be deemed to have a corporate business purpose if an alternative tax-free transaction that does not require distribution of stock of a controlled corporation and that is not unduly expensive or impractical could be used to achieve the result sought. For example, a spin-off of a controlled corporation (S) to the shareholders of the distributing corporation (P) for the purpose of insulating the business transferred by P to S from the risks of the other businesses of P will not satisfy the business purpose requirement because that insulation effect is achieved as soon as the business is transferred to S under Section 351. The distribution of S stock is unnecessary to achieve that purpose. Reg. § 1.355–2(b)(3) and (5), Exs. 3 and 4. Thus, the IRS may be expected to examine transactions closely to determine whether a taxpayer's business objective could have been satisfied without use of a Section 355 distribution.

3. A commonly cited business purpose for a distribution is to improve the fit and focus of the distributing and controlled companies. The prototypical example is the pesticide manufacturer's distribution of its baby food subsidiary to improve the market perception of the subsidiary's product. See Rev. Rul. 2003–110, 2003–2 C.B. 1083. Because of the ease in asserting the fit and focus justification, the IRS seeks to ensure that the separation is real and not a disguised bailout. In Rev. Rul. 2003–74, 2003–2 C.B. 77, a publicly held software company sought to spin off its wholly owned paper products subsidiary to allow the management of each company to focus their attention on the different needs of the two businesses. In finding the corporate business purpose to be legitimate, the IRS emphasized that (1) the software company was publicly held, where fit and focus is more necessary, (2) there was no significant

shareholder influencing the distribution, and (3) the management teams of the distributing and controlled companies would remain largely separate other than two directors of the distributing company who would remain on the controlled board after the spin-off to facilitate the transition and would constitute a small number of the total board. See also Rev. Rul. 2003–75, 2003–2 C.B. 79 (permitting a distribution despite the presence of certain transitional agreements between the distributing and controlled companies, including a working capital loan, since the agreements would expire within two years and were designed to facilitate rather than impede the separation of the businesses).

4.   Although the 1989 regulations codified a continuity of interest requirement at the same time as a corporate business purpose requirement, there has been little elaboration on the nature of this requirement. What is clear is that the new continuity of interest regulations described in Chapters 9 and 10 do not apply to 355 transactions. See ¶¶ 9100 and 10,040. At the time these new continuity of interest regulations were first released, Treasury stated that "[t]he IRS and Treasury Department continue to study the role of the COI requirement in section 368(a)(1)(D) reorganizations and section 355 transactions. Therefore, these final COI regulations do not apply to section 368(a)(1)(D) reorganizations and section 355 transactions. See § 1.355–2(c)." Preamble to T.D. 8760, 1998–1 C.B. 803, 805. Theoretically, this means that the pre–1998 rules governing continuity of interest, including the temporal requirement discussed at ¶ 10,040, still apply in the context of 355 transactions. At least in the context of the device requirement, however, the Code specifically exempts Section 355 transactions from any post-distribution holding requirement. See § 355(a)(1)(B).

[¶ 12,060]

Problems

Consider whether in the light of the Section 355 regulations the following transactions will qualify for nonrecognition of gain to the distributing corporation and the distributee shareholders under Section 355:

1.   Buildit Corporation has been involved in the construction business for six years. One half of its only class of stock is owned by an individual, Smith, and the other half, by an unrelated individual, Brown. Smith and Brown, who have been active in the business from the start, have become deadlocked on basic issues of business policy and, as a means of resolving their differences, they contemplate a transaction in which the business assets (including four existing contracts, fixed assets, and liquid assets) will be divided. One half will be contributed to a new wholly owned subsidiary of Buildit. Because the existing contracts have differing values, in order to equalize the value of Buildit and the subsidiary, the subsidiary will receive, in addition to two of the con-

tracts, 75 percent of the liquid assets, which exceeds the amount needed in connection with performance of the two contracts being transferred. All of the stock of the subsidiary will be distributed to Smith in exchange for all of Smith's Buildit stock.

2.   Fabulair Corporation has two divisions that have been engaged in the manufacture and sale of sailboards and small boats, respectively, during each of the past five years. Fabulair has 500 shares of stock outstanding, 400 of which are held by individual Smith and 100 by individual Brown. The value of the Fabulair stock has increased substantially in recent years, largely as a result of the efforts of Brown, a key employee and manager of Fabulair's sailboard division. Brown is seriously considering terminating employment with Fabulair if she is not offered the opportunity to acquire a controlling equity interest in the sailboard business. However, Brown lacks the funds to purchase any additional equity. In order to retain Brown's services for the sailboard division, Fabulair proposes to undertake the following two steps: (i) Fabulair will transfer to a new wholly owned subsidiary, solely in exchange for 500 shares of subsidiary stock, the assets, subject to liabilities, associated with the sailboard business; and (ii) Fabulair will then distribute 300 shares of the subsidiary's stock to Brown in exchange for all of Brown's 100 shares of Fabulair common stock, and Fabulair will distribute the remaining 200 shares of subsidiary common stock to Smith, without any surrender by Smith of Fabulair stock. The value of the subsidiary stock received by Brown will be equal to the value of the Fabulair stock that Brown surrenders.

3.   Assume that the facts are the same as in Problem 2, except that pursuant to an agreement entered into before the distribution of subsidiary stock, Brown buys 200 shares of subsidiary stock from Smith for cash.

4.   Cosmos Corporation, a publicly owned corporation, buys for cash in the over-the-counter market 25 percent of the shares of Orbit Corporation, which has conducted two separate businesses, a toy manufacturing business and a household appliance business, for five years. Six months after the stock acquisition, Orbit agrees with Cosmos that Orbit will transfer the toy business to a new wholly owned subsidiary in exchange for all of the subsidiary's stock and will then exchange the shares of the subsidiary for the Orbit shares owned by Cosmos.

5.   Assume the facts are the same as in Problem 4 except that Cosmos Corporation agrees with Orbit Corporation that Cosmos will have the option, exercisable for a six-month period beginning three years after Cosmos Corporation's acquisition of the Orbit shares, to put those shares to Orbit in exchange for Orbit's shares in the subsidiary or in exchange for cash.

6.   Individuals Smith and Brown own 40 percent and 60 percent, respectively, of the stock of Duality Corporation, which has been engaged

in the manufacture and sale of bicycles and the manufacture and sale of books on bicycle touring for more than five years. In order to protect the book business from the potential liabilities of the bicycle business, Smith and Brown contemplate a transaction in which the book business would be transferred to a newly formed subsidiary of Duality in exchange for all of its stock, and all of the stock of the subsidiary would then be distributed to Smith and Brown pro rata.

7. Hype Corporation, which is publicly owned, has been engaged in the advertising agency business for more than five years. Its principal office is owned by a wholly owned subsidiary, which leases the office to Hype on a long-term net lease basis (under which the lessee is responsible for all taxes and expenses and for managing the building). Flog Corporation, another publicly owned corporation, is interested in acquiring Hype in a tax-free acquisition but is not interested in acquiring the subsidiary. The plan under consideration calls for distribution of all the stock of the subsidiary pro rata to the shareholders of Hype followed by the merger of Hype into Flog in which shareholders of Hype will exchange their Hype shares solely for Flog shares.

8. Happyplay Corporation, a publicly owned corporation, has been engaged in the manufacture and sale of toys for more than 10 years. A division of Happyplay has been involved in doing market research, principally for Happyplay, but also for other toy manufacturers on a contract basis. In order to enable the market research division to compete more effectively for market research business from other toy manufacturers, some of which are competitors of Happyplay, it has been proposed that all of the assets and liabilities associated with the market research function be transferred to a new wholly owned subsidiary of Happyplay in exchange for all of the stock of the subsidiary and then the subsidiary stock be distributed pro rata to the shareholders of Happyplay. The subsidiary would continue rendering market research activities to Happyplay and others.

[¶ 12,065]

C. DIVISIONS INCIDENT TO "D" REORGANIZATIONS

As pointed out above, a corporate division under Section 355 may be effected through distribution of the stock of an existing controlled corporation to which no additional assets are transferred in connection with the readjustment transaction. If, however, any such transfer of assets is made by the transferor corporation to the controlled corporation, the transaction will qualify for nonrecognition treatment only if it falls within the definition of a "D" reorganization. Under Section 368(a)(1)(D), a "D" reorganization involves a transfer by a corporation of all or part of its assets to another corporation that is controlled by the transferor and/or its shareholders immediately after the transfer, but only if the stock and securities of the controlled corporation are distributed pursuant to the plan in a transaction that qualifies under Section 355 (and Section 356) or under Section 354 (and Section 356).

For purposes of the "D" reorganization definition when applied to a transaction including a qualifying Section 355 distribution, control was redefined by legislation enacted in 1997 to mean ownership of, not 80 percent as under prior law, but more than 50 percent of the voting power and value of the transferee (distributed) corporation. See ¶ 12,090.

If, prior to the distribution, the transferor corporation transfers less than substantially all of its assets to a single controlled corporation or transfers all of its assets to two or more controlled corporations, the requirements of Section 355, discussed above, must be met if the transaction is to be treated as a "D" reorganization qualifying for nonrecognition treatment. This is dictated by the fact that Section 355 contains the tests for nonrecognition that must be met in every case in which there is to be a division of the shareholders' investment between two or more corporations.

If, however, substantially all of the assets of the transferor corporation are transferred to a single controlled corporation and the transferor corporation then liquidates and distributes the shares of the controlled corporation in liquidation, the transaction also constitutes a "D" reorganization. However, in this case, because there is no division of the shareholders' investment, there is no reason for subjecting the transaction to the Section 355 requirements. With respect to this type of transaction, the "D" reorganization definition must be read in conjunction with Sections 354 and 356 because the distribution of stock or securities must qualify for nonrecognition of gain under these sections. See ¶ 11,085.

D. EFFECTS ON DISTRIBUTEES AND DISTRIBUTING CORPORATIONS

[¶ 12,070]

1. CONSEQUENCES TO DISTRIBUTEE SHAREHOLDERS

Section 355 itself provides for nonrecognition of gain realized by the distributee shareholder on the receipt of stock or securities of a controlled corporation if the statutory requirements are met. § 355(a)(1). If stock or securities are surrendered by the distributee shareholder or securityholder in exchange for securities of the controlled corporation having a larger principal amount than any securities surrendered, the value of the excess is treated as boot, and the distributee's gain is recognized to the extent of that boot's value. §§ 355(a)(3)(A), 356(d)(2)(C). Moreover, under the 1997 legislation, the value of nonqualified preferred stock, as defined in Section 351(g)(2), that is distributed in exchange for stock (except nonqualified preferred stock) is taxed as boot. § 355(a)(3)(D). All stock and securities received by a distributee for accrued interest are boot. § 355(a)(3)(C). If any property other than stock or securities of the controlled corporation is received by the distributee shareholder, it is also boot. § 356(a)(1). In addition, stock of a controlled corporation acquired by purchase within five years of its distribution is treated as boot. § 355(a)(3)(B).

The treatment of boot is governed by Section 356. § 355(a)(4). If boot is received in a spin-off (a distribution), Section 356(b) treats the amount of boot as a distribution to which Section 301 applies. If boot is received in a split-off or split-up (an exchange), Section 356(a) is the applicable provision. The IRS discusses the treatment of boot in a split-off exchange transaction under Section 356(a) in the following ruling.

[¶ 12,075]

REVENUE RULING 93–62

1993–2 C.B. 118.

Issue

Whether gain recognized on the receipt of cash in an exchange of stock that otherwise qualifies under section 355 * * * is treated as a dividend distribution under section 356(a)(2).

Facts

Distributing is a corporation with 1,000 shares of a single class of stock outstanding. Each share has a fair market value of $1x. *A*, one of five unrelated individual shareholders, owns 400 shares of Distributing stock. Distributing owns all of the outstanding stock of a subsidiary corporation, Controlled. The Controlled stock has a fair market value of $200x. Distributing distributes all the stock of Controlled plus $200x cash to *A* in exchange for all of *A*'s Distributing stock. The exchange satisfies the requirements of section 355 but for the receipt of the cash.

Law and Analysis

Section 355(a)(1) * * * provides, in general, that the shareholders of a distributing corporation will not recognize gain or loss on the exchange of the distributing corporation's stock or securities solely for stock or securities of a controlled subsidiary if the requirements of section 355 are satisfied.

Section 356(a)(1) * * * provides for recognition of gain on exchanges in which gain would otherwise not be recognized under section 354 (relating to tax-free acquisitive reorganizations) or section 355 if the property received in the exchange consists of both property permitted to be received without gain recognition and other property or money ("boot"). The amount of gain recognized is limited to the sum of the money and the fair market value of the other property.

Under section 356(a)(2) * * *, gain recognized in an exchange described in section 356(a)(1) that "has the effect of the distribution of a dividend" is treated as a dividend to the extent of the distributee's ratable share of the undistributed earnings and profits accumulated after February 28, 1913. Any remaining gain is treated as gain from the exchange of property.

Determinations of whether the receipt of boot has the effect of a dividend are made by applying the principles of section 302 * * *. *Commissioner v. Clark*, 489 U.S. 726 (1989) * * *. Section 302 contains rules for determining whether payments in redemption of stock are treated as payments in exchange for the stock or as distributions to which section 301 applies.

Under section 302(a) * * *, a redemption will be treated as an exchange if it satisfies one of the tests of section 302(b). Section 302(b)(2) provides exchange treatment for substantially disproportionate redemptions of stock. A distribution is substantially disproportionate if (1) the shareholder's voting stock interest and common stock interest in the corporation immediately after the redemption are each less than 80 percent of those interests immediately before the redemption, and (2) the shareholder owns less than 50 percent of the voting power of all classes of stock immediately after the redemption.

In *Clark*, the Supreme Court determined whether gain recognized under section 356 * * * on the receipt of boot in an acquisitive reorganization under section 368(a)(1)(A) and (a)(2)(D) should be treated as a dividend distribution. In that case, the sole shareholder of the target corporation exchanged his target stock for stock of the acquiring corporation and cash. In applying section 302 to determine whether the boot payment had the effect of a dividend distribution, the Court considered whether section 302 should be applied to the boot payment as if it were made (i) by the target corporation in a pre-reorganization hypothetical redemption of a portion of the shareholder's target stock, or (ii) by the acquiring corporation in a post-reorganization hypothetical redemption of the acquiring corporation stock that the shareholder would have received in the reorganization exchange if there had been no boot distribution.

The Supreme Court stated that the treatment of boot under section 356(a)(2) * * * should be determined "by examining the effect of the exchange as a whole," and concluded that treating the boot as received in a redemption of target stock would improperly isolate the boot payment from the overall reorganization by disregarding the effect of the subsequent merger. Consequently, the Court tested whether the boot payment had the effect of a dividend distribution by comparing the

¶ 12,075

interest the taxpayer actually received in the acquiring corporation with the interest the taxpayer would have had if solely stock in the acquiring corporation had been received in the reorganization exchange.

Prior to the decision in *Clark*, the Service considered the facts and issue presented in this revenue ruling in Rev. Rul. 74–516, 1974–2 C.B. 121. The determination of whether the exchange of Distributing stock for Controlled stock and boot under section 355 of the Code had the effect of a dividend distribution under section 356(a)(2) was made by comparing A's interest in Distributing prior to the exchange with the interest A would have retained if A had not received Controlled stock and had only surrendered the Distributing stock equal in value to the boot. The Court's decision in *Clark* does not change the conclusion in Rev. Rul. 74–516, because, like *Clark,* the ruling determined whether the exchange in question had the effect of a dividend distribution based on an analysis of the overall transaction.

The exchange of A's Distributing stock for stock of Controlled qualifies for non-recognition treatment under section 355 * * * in part because the overall effect of the exchange is an adjustment of A's continuing interest in Distributing in a modified corporate form. *See* section 1.355–2(c) of the * * * Regulations. The Controlled stock received by A represents a continuing interest in a portion of Distributing's assets that were formerly held by A as an indirect equity interest. The boot payment has reduced A's proportionate interest in the overall corporate enterprise that includes both Distributing and Controlled. Thus, the boot is treated as received in redemption of A's Distributing stock, and A's interest in Distributing immediately before the exchange is compared to the interest A would have retained if A had surrendered only the Distributing shares equal in value to the boot.

Under the facts presented here, before the exchange, A owned 400 of the 1,000 shares, or 40 percent, of the outstanding Distributing stock. If A had surrendered only the 200 shares for which A received boot, A would still hold 200 of the 800 shares, or 25 percent, of the Distributing stock outstanding after the exchange. This 25 percent stock interest would represent 62.5 percent of A's pre-exchange stock interest in Distributing. Therefore, the deemed redemption would be treated as an exchange because it qualifies as substantially disproportionate under section 302(b)(2) * * *.

HOLDING

In an exchange of stock that otherwise qualifies under section 355 * * *, whether the payment of boot is treated as a dividend distribution under section 356(a)(2) is determined prior to the exchange. This determination is made by treating the recipient shareholder as if the shareholder had retained the distributing corporation stock actually exchanged for controlled corporation stock and received the boot in exchange for distributing corporation stock equal in value to the boot.

[¶ 12,080]

Note

The distributee's basis in the stock of the distributing corporation is generally allocated between the stock of the distributing and the controlled corporations held by the distributee in proportion to their relative fair market values. § 358(c); Reg. § 1.358–2. The distributee's holding period for stock or securities of the controlled corporation held as capital assets that qualify as nonrecognition property is determined under Section 1223(1). It provides that their holding period includes the holding period of stock or securities of the distributing corporation retained (in a spin-off) or surrendered (in a split-off or split-up).

[¶ 12,085]

2. CONSEQUENCES TO DISTRIBUTING CORPORATION

Under Section 355(c), a distributing corporation generally does not recognize gain or loss on a distribution of "qualified property." "Qualified property" means the stock or securities of the controlled corporation, provided that Section 355 applies to the distribution. If the transaction also qualifies as a "D" reorganization, "qualified property" includes stock, securities, and any debt obligation of the controlled corporation, § 361(c)(2)(B). Gain, but not loss, is recognized on the distribution of other nonqualified property (i.e., boot). §§ 355(c)(2), 361(b)(1). Thus, gain is recognized to the distributing corporation if appreciated nonqualified property is distributed, as if the property were sold to the distributee for its fair market value. §§ 355(c)(2)(A), 361(c)(2). If the shareholder assumes liabilities or takes distributed property subject to liabilities, the fair market value of distributed boot is treated as at least equal to the amount of the liabilities. §§ 355(c)(2)(C), 361(c)(2)(C).

Appreciated stock of the controlled corporation which has been acquired by the distributing corporation in a taxable transaction during the five years prior to the distribution is treated as boot under Section 355(a)(3)(B), but not if the transaction is a "D" reorganization. Nonqualified preferred stock, as defined in Section 351(g)(2), is also treated as boot unless it is distributed in exchange for or with respect to other nonqualified preferred stock or unless the transaction is a "D" reorganization (subject to the possibility that yet to be issued regulations may provide to the contrary).

Normally, a corporation in a reorganization may avoid gain on the receipt of boot in the exchange if it transfers the boot property to its creditors as part of the plan of reorganization. § 361(b)(1), (3). In a "D" reorganization effected in connection with a Section 355 transaction, however, nonrecognition treatment with respect to boot property applies only to the extent that the sum of the money and the fair market value of other property transferred to creditors does not exceed the adjusted bases of the assets transferred. This limitation was enacted in 2004 to prevent the use of 355 transactions to avoid gain recognition under Section 357(c) by virtue of the application of Section 361(b)(1).

Section 355(d) and (e) contain special rules examined in the next section. These rules may require recognition of gain to the distributing corporation, but not to the distributee shareholder, and may apply when a Section 355 division is combined with certain taxable and tax-free acquisitions of the stock of the distributing or the controlled corporation.

E.   COMBINING A CORPORATE DIVISION WITH AN ACQUISITION

[¶ 12,090]

1. CORPORATE DIVISION COMBINED WITH A TAXABLE ACQUISITION

The general rule, now reflected in Section 355(c)(1), that a corporate division meeting the requirements of Section 355 is tax free to the distributing corporation is an exception to the repeal of the *General Utilities* doctrine in the 1986 Act. The exception proved a tempting avenue by which a party seeking, in effect, to purchase a subsidiary of a corporation could attempt to do so without any tax to the selling corporation on the disposition of its subsidiary. One variation of the technique involved a purchase by the prospective acquirer of stock in the parent corporation of the target subsidiary. After a period long enough to comply with the continuity of shareholder interest requirement of Reg. § 1.355–2(c), the stock of the target subsidiary would be distributed by the parent corporation to the acquirer in exchange for the stock the acquirer had purchased in the parent. This distribution would be structured to qualify for nonrecognition of gain to the parent corporation under Section 355.

This gambit eventually evoked a statutory response contained in Section 355(c)(2) and (d), enacted in 1990. Broadly speaking, these provisions require recognition of gain realized by a distributing corporation upon a distribution of stock or securities of a controlled subsidiary under Section 355, if, immediately following the distribution, a shareholder holds a 50 percent or greater stock interest in the distributing corporation or a distributed subsidiary that is attributable to stock or securities purchased within the prior five year period. Section 355(d) has no effect on qualification of the transaction as tax free to the distributee shareholders under Section 355(a); it applies only to impose tax on the gain realized by the distributing corporation. If the transaction otherwise qualifies for nonrecognition of gain at the distributee shareholder level, and even if gain is recognized to the distributing corporation, gain realized by the distributee shareholder remains free of tax.

The background to the enactment of Section 355(c)(2) and (d) is described as follows in the House Committee Report:

> Some corporate taxpayers may attempt, under present-law rules governing divisive transactions, to dispose of subsidiaries in transactions that resemble sales * * * without incurring corporate-level tax. The avoidance of corporate level tax is inconsistent with the repeal of the General Utilities doctrine as part of the Tax Reform Act of 1986.
>
> Under the present-law rules, individual purchasers, or corporate purchasers of less than 80 percent, of the stock of a parent corporation may attempt to utilize section 355 to acquire a subsidiary (or a division incorporated for this purpose) from the parent without the parent incurring any corporate-level tax. The purchaser may acquire stock of the parent equal in value to the value of the desired subsidiary or division, and later surrender that stock for stock of the subsidiary, in a transaction intended to qualify as a non-pro-rata tax-free divisive transaction. Alternatively, the transaction might be structured as a surrender of the parent stock by all shareholders other than the acquiror, in exchange for a distribution (intended to be tax-free) of all subsidiaries or activities other than those the acquiror desires.
>
> * * *
>
> The provisions for tax-free divisive transactions under section 355 were a limited exception to the repeal of the General Utilities doctrine, intended to permit historic shareholders to continue to carry on their historic corporate businesses in separate corporations. It is believed that the benefit of tax-free treatment should not apply where the divisive transaction, combined with a stock purchase resulting in a change of ownership, in effect results in the disposition of a significant part of the historic shareholders' interests in one or more of the divided corporations.
>
> The present-law provisions granting tax-free treatment at the corporate level are particularly troublesome because they may offer taxpayers an opportunity to avoid the general rule that corporate-level gain is recognized when an asset (including stock of a subsidiary) is disposed of. There is special concern about the possibility for the distributing corporation to avoid corporate-level tax on the transfer of a subsidiary. Therefore, although the provision does not affect shareholder treatment if section 355 is otherwise available, it does impose tax at the corporate level, in light of the potential avoidance of corporate tax on what is in effect a sale of a subsidiary.

¶ 12,090

H.R. Rep. No. 882, 101st Cong., 2d Sess. 90–92 (1990).

Under Section 355(d), nonrecognition of gain is denied to a "disqualified distribution." This term is defined in Section 355(d)(2) as a Section 355 distribution, if immediately after the distribution any person holds "disqualified stock" in the distributing corporation or in a controlled corporation, which constitutes a 50 percent or greater interest in the corporation concerned. "Disqualified stock," in turn, includes (i) any stock in the distributing corporation and any stock in any controlled corporation acquired by purchase during the five-year period ending on the date of the distribution and (ii) stock in a controlled corporation received in the distribution to the extent that the stock is attributable to distributions on stock or securities in the distributing corporation purchased during such period. § 355(d)(3). Detailed rules concerning the application of Section 355(d) are contained in Reg. § 1.355–6.

Acquisition by purchase includes the acquisition of property for cash, marketable stock, or securities, or a debt obligation of the transferor in a Section 351 exchange. § 355(d)(5)(B). In a carryover basis acquisition from a person who purchased the stock, the five-year period begins with the date of that purchase. § 355(d)(5)(C). The five-year period is suspended for any period during which the holder's risk of loss is substantially diminished through a device such as an option or a short sale. § 355(d)(6).

Related persons are treated as one person for purposes of Section 355(d). Thus, for example, in determining whether a person holds a 50 percent or greater interest, a corporation and its more than 50 percent owned subsidiary are treated as one person. The related person rules applied for this purpose are the rules of Sections 707(b)(1) and 267(b). § 355(d)(7). In addition, persons acting pursuant to a plan or arrangement with respect to acquisitions of stock or securities in the distributing or any controlled corporation are treated as one person for purposes of determining whether a shareholder holds a 50 percent or greater interest acquired by purchase. § 355(d)(7)(B).

In determining whether a person holds a 50 percent or greater interest in a distributing corporation or a distributed subsidiary that is attributable to stock or securities purchased during the prior five-year period, the from the entity attribution rules of Section 318(a)(2) are applied. However, in applying these rules, "10 percent" is substituted for the "50 percent" in Section 318(a)(2)(C). § 355(d)(8)(A).

Stock of the distributing or controlled corporation that is acquired directly or indirectly by a purchase within the five-year period ceases to be acquired by the purchase if the basis resulting from the purchase is eliminated (i.e., when the basis would no longer be taken into account by any person in determining gain or loss on a sale or exchange of any stock of such corporation). For example, a direct purchase by the distributing of all of the stock in a controlled corporation, followed by a distribution

¶ 12,090

of the controlled corporation stock, will result in elimination of the basis that resulted from the distributing corporation's purchase of the controlled stock, and so the controlled corporation's stock would no longer be treated as purchased. Reg. § 1.355–6(b)(2)(iii). Basis is not eliminated, however, if it is allocated between the stock of two corporations under Reg. § 1.358–2(a).

Section 355(d) does not apply to any distribution that does not violate its purposes. A distribution does not violate the purposes of Section 355(d) if the effect of the distribution is neither (i) to increase ownership (direct and indirect) in the distributing corporation or any controlled corporation by a disqualified person nor (ii) to provide a disqualified person with a purchased basis in the stock of any controlled corporation. Reg. § 1.355–6(b)(3)(i). A disqualified person is a person who holds (directly or indirectly), immediately after the distribution, disqualified stock in the distributing or controlled corporation. Reg. § 1.355–6(b)(3)(ii). In applying the purchased basis exception, any increase in direct or indirect ownership in the distributing corporation or any controlled corporation by a disqualified person because of a payment of cash in lieu of issuing fractional shares will be disregarded. Reg. § 1.355–6(b)(3)(iii). The following example of a spin-off transaction that does not violate the purposes of Section 355(d) is given in Reg. § 1.355–6 (b)(3)(iv), Ex. 1:

> D owns all of the stock of D1, and D1 owns all of the stock of C. A purchases 60 percent of the D stock for cash. Within five years of A's purchase, D1 distributes the C stock to D. A is treated as having purchased 60 percent of the stock of both D1 and C on the date A purchases 60 percent of the D stock under the attribution rules of section 355(d)(8) and paragraph (e)(1) of this section. The C stock received by D is attributable to a distribution on purchased D1 stock under section 355(d)(3)(B)(ii). Accordingly, the D1 and C stock each is disqualified stock under section 355(d)(3) and paragraph (b)(2) of this section, and A is a disqualified person under paragraph (b)(3)(iii) of this section. However, the purposes of this section 355(d) under paragraph (b)(3)(i) of this section are not violated. A did not increase direct or indirect ownership in D1 or C. In addition, D's basis in the C stock is not purchased basis under paragraph (b)(3)(iii) of this section because both the D1 and the C stock are treated as acquired by purchase solely under the attribution rules of section 355(d)(8) and paragraph (e)(1) of this section. Accordingly, D1's distribution of the C stock to D is not a disqualified distribution under section 355(d)(2) and paragraph (b)(1) of this section.

For purposes of Section 355(d), stock acquired in a qualified stock purchase with respect to which a Section 338 or Section 338(h)(10) election is made is not treated as purchased. However, any stock held by old target that is deemed purchased by new target is treated as acquired by purchase unless a Section 338 or Section 338(h)(10) election also is made with respect to that purchase. Reg. § 1.355–6(d)(2)(iv). See ¶ 8123.

[¶ 12,095]

Problems

1.   Assume that on January 15 of year 1 individual A purchased ten percent of the stock of P Corporation , which had owned 100 percent of the stock of T Corporation for more than five years at the time of A's purchase. Two years later, A purchases an additional 41 percent of the stock of P. How much, if any, of T's stock is A deemed to have acquired by purchase?

2.   Assume that on December 15 of year 1 individual A purchased a 20 percent interest in the stock of P Corporation and a ten percent interest in the stock of its wholly owned subsidiary, S Corporation, and that 45 percent of the stock of S is distributed to A within five years in exchange for A's 20 percent interest in P. (The remainder of the S stock distributed in the Section 355 distribution is distributed to other P shareholders.) Does corporation P have recognized gain?

3.   Assume that on January 15 of year 1 individual A purchased a 20 percent interest in P Corporation and P redeemed stock of other shareholders so that A's interest in P was increased to a 30 percent interest. Within five years of A's purchase, P distributes 50 percent of the stock of its wholly owned subsidiary, S Corporation, to A in exchange for A's 30 percent interest in P. (The remainder of the stock of S distributed in the Section 355 transaction is distributed to other P shareholders.) Does P have recognized gain?

4.   Assume that on January 15 of year 1, X Corporation purchased 25 percent of the stock of P Corporation. The following year P splits off unwanted subsidiaries to P shareholders other than X in transactions that qualify under Section 355(a)(1). Thereafter X owns 60 percent of the P stock. Does P have recognized gain on the distributions?

2.   CORPORATE DIVISION COMBINED WITH A TAX–FREE ACQUISITION

[¶ 12,100]

a.   Case Law and Administrative Developments Before the 1997 Legislation

Commissioner v. Morris Trust, 367 F.2d 794 (4th Cir.1966), involved the important question whether a tax-free division would be disqualified for nonrecognition of gain under Section 355 because, after distributing the stock of the controlled corporation, the distributing corporation was acquired in a tax-free statutory merger under Section 368(a)(1)(A). The distributing corporation (American) was a state-chartered bank which had an insurance business. An unrelated national bank (Security Nation-

¶ 12,100

al) wanted to acquire American but was prohibited by law from operating an insurance business. Therefore, American spun off pro rata to its shareholders a wholly owned subsidiary (Agency) to which the insurance business had been transferred. American then merged into Security National.

The IRS conceded that American's spin-off of its insurance business was a "D" reorganization, as defined in Section 368(a)(1)(D), if the distribution of Agency's stock qualified for nonrecognition of gain under Section 355. However, the IRS argued that the active business requirements of Section 355(b)(1)(A) were not met because American's banking business was not continued in unaltered corporate form. The IRS also argued that there was an inherent incompatibility in substantially simultaneous divisive and amalgamating reorganizations. The court rejected both of these contentions stating in part:

> The * * * [IRS] concedes that American's stockholders would have recognized no gain had American not been merged into Security after, but substantially contemporaneously with, Agency's spin-off. Insofar as it is contended that § 355(b)(1)(A) requires the distributing corporation to continue the conduct of an active business, recognition of gain to American's stockholders on their receipt of Agency's stock would depend upon the economically irrelevant technicality of the identity of the surviving corporation in the merger. Had American been the survivor, it would in every literal and substantive sense have continued the conduct of its banking business.
>
> Surely, the Congress which drafted these comprehensive provisions did not intend the incidence of taxation to turn upon so insubstantial a technicality. * * *
>
> * * *
>
> Nor can we find elsewhere in the Code any support for the Commissioner's suggestion of incompatibility between substantially contemporaneous divisive and amalgamating reorganizations. The 1954 Code contains no inkling of it; nor does its immediate legislative history. * * *

367 F.2d at 799.

In Rev. Rul. 68–603, 1968–2 C.B. 148, the IRS agreed to follow *Morris Trust,* to the extent it holds that (i) the active business requirements of Section 355(b)(1)(A) were satisfied even though the distributing corporation immediately after the spin-off was merged tax-free into another corporation, (ii) the control requirement of Section 368(a)(1)(D) implies no limitation upon a reorganization of the distributing corporation after the distribution of stock of the controlled corporation, and (iii) there was a business purpose for the spin-off and the merger.

¶ 12,100

Rev. Rul. 70–434, 1970–2 C.B. 83, reached a similar conclusion when all of the stock of the distributing corporation was acquired in exchange for voting stock of an unrelated acquiring corporation. In this ruling, Corporation X had been engaged in the active conduct of two businesses (toy manufacturing and hand tool manufacturing) for over five years. Corporation Z, an unrelated corporation, desired to acquire the stock of X but was only interested in having X conduct the hand tool manufacturing business. Corporation Z's objective was achieved pursuant to a plan under which X transferred its toy manufacturing business, representing 23 percent of the assets of X, to a newly created corporation, Y, in exchange for all of the stock of Y. The Y stock was distributed pro rata to the X shareholders in a transaction that qualified as a reorganization within the meaning of Section 368(a)(1)(D) because the distribution of the Y stock met all of the requirements of Section 355. Z then acquired all of the outstanding stock of X in exchange solely for voting common stock of Z. X remained in existence as a wholly owned subsidiary of Z. The IRS ruled that the exchange of the X stock for the Z stock qualified as a "B" reorganization.

A spin-off of an unwanted business by the acquired corporation followed by a putative "C" reorganization or a forward or reverse triangular merger would not qualify as a tax-free reorganization because the substantially all of the properties test would not be met. See ¶¶ 10,080 et seq.

By contrast to Rev. Ruls. 68–603 and 70–434, which involved acquisition of the distributing corporation, Rev. Rul. 70–225, 1970–1 C.B. 80, involved acquisition of the distributed controlled corporation. R, a corporation with one shareholder, A, had for many years operated a taxicab business and a car rental business. T, an unrelated widely held corporation, desired to acquire R's car rental business. Pursuant to a plan, R transferred the assets of its car rental business to a newly formed corporation, S, in exchange for all the stock of S and distributed the stock of S to its sole shareholder, A, in a transaction intended to qualify under Sections 368(a)(1)(D) and 355. As part of the pre-arranged plan, A immediately exchanged all his S stock for some of the outstanding voting stock of T in an exchange intended to meet the requirements of Section 368(a)(1)(B). The IRS ruled that the transfer by R of part of its assets to S in exchange for all the stock of S followed by the distribution of the S stock to A and by the transfer of the S stock to T by A in exchange for T stock involved a series of integrated steps under the step transaction doctrine. Accordingly, neither R nor its sole shareholder, A, was in control of S after the transfer of the S stock to T, and the transaction could not qualify as a reorganization under Section 368(a)(1)(D) or a transfer under Section 351. Section 368(a)(1)(B) did not apply to the transaction because in effect R transferred part of its assets to T in exchange for a part of the T stock, rather than T having acquired all the stock of a previously existing corporation solely in exchange for its own

¶ 12,100

voting stock. Accordingly, the receipt by A of the stock of T was not a distribution to which Section 355 applied. The fair market value of the stock of T was taxable to A as a distribution by R under Section 301. In addition, gain or loss was recognized to R on the transaction.

As a result of Rev. Ruls. 68–603 and 70–434, a spin-off transaction under Section 355 followed by an acquisition of the distributing corporation in an acquisitive direct "A" or "B" reorganization became a common method of handling the unwanted asset problem that arises when the acquiring corporation does not want to acquire one of the businesses of the acquired corporation. Rev. Ruls. 70–225 and 70–434 imply a distinction between using a Section 355 transaction, prior to an acquisitive reorganization, to spin off the wanted assets, on the one hand, and the unwanted assets, on the other. Is the basis for this distinction a persuasive one?

Another combination of a spin-off and a tax-free acquisition involved a wanted business conducted by a subsidiary for more than five years and a parent with an unwanted business. Here the spin-off did not have to qualify as a "D" reorganization and therefore the controlled corporation did not have to be controlled by the distributing corporation or its shareholders after the spin-off. In this situation, the spin-off corporation could be acquired in an acquisitive reorganization without forfeiting tax-free treatment of the spun-off corporation under Section 355. Rev. Rul. 75–406, 1975–2 C.B. 125.

The combination of a tax free spin-off of one business followed by a tax-free acquisition of the controlled corporation or the distributing corporation involved at least one serious policy concern. In the tax-free acquisitive reorganizations discussed in Chapter 10, tax-free treatment is usually accorded only if all, or substantially all, of the assets of the target corporation or enough of its stock to give the acquiring corporation 80 percent control under Section 368(c) is acquired in an "A," "C," or "B" reorganization. In these cases, the target is not subject to tax on the appreciation inherent in its assets. However, in the case of the Section 355 spin-off of the unwanted business in the controlled corporation followed by the acquisition of the distributing corporation (with the wanted business) in an "A" or "B" reorganization, it was possible to acquire only one business of the target corporation's two businesses without tax on the appreciation in any of the business assets of that corporation. This treatment represented a significant loophole in the repeal of *General Utilities*. If one of two businesses of a corporation is distributed as a dividend in kind or in redemption of the corporation's stock, the distributing corporation is taxed as if it had sold the assets to the distributees. But this was not the result in the case of the spin-off of the unwanted business and the acquisition of the distributing corporation in an "A" or "B" reorganization.

¶ 12,100

Concerned about the potential abuse in cases in which the acquisition of the controlled corporation was negotiated before the spin-off and as part of a plan contingent on the spin-off, the IRS issued Rev. Rul. 96–30, 1996–1 C.B. 36. This ruling held that if the acquisition of the spun-off controlled corporation were negotiated by the controlled corporation after it had been distributed by the distributing corporation, the merger of the controlled corporation into an unrelated corporation with the shareholders of the controlled corporation receiving stock in the acquiring corporation, the transaction would be respected as a tax-free spin off under Section 355 followed by a qualifying tax-free merger of the controlled corporation. The IRS respected the form of the transaction and cited the distinction between Commissioner v. Court Holding, 324 U.S. 331 (1945), and United States v. Cumberland Public Service Co., 338 U.S. 451 (1950), and implied that the result would have been different if the terms of the acquisition of the controlled corporation had been negotiated before its distribution.

The basic ground rules for the tax treatment of a distribution of a controlled corporation followed by a putative tax-free acquisition of the distributing or the controlled corporation were changed by tax legislation enacted in 1997 and 1998.

[¶ 12,105]

REVENUE RULING 98–27

1998–1 C.B.1159.

Purpose

This revenue ruling obsoletes Rev. Ruls. 96–30, 1996–1 C.B. 36, and 75–406, 1975–2 C.B. 125, modified by Rev. Rul. 96–30. This revenue ruling also modifies Rev. Rul. 70–225, 1970–1 C.B. 80.

Background

Rev. Rul. 96–30 applies the principles of Commissioner v. Court Holding Co., 324 U.S. 331 (1945), to a distribution of controlled corporation stock by a publicly traded parent, followed by a merger of the controlled corporation into an unrelated acquiring corporation. The former shareholders of the controlled corporation receive a 25 percent interest in the acquiring corporation. Based on all the facts and circumstances, the ruling concludes that the transaction satisfies the requirements of § 355 * * *. Rev. Rul. 96–30 also modifies the factually similar Rev. Rul. 75–406 by eliminating the implication that an independent, post-distribution shareholder vote to approve the acquisition of a controlled corporation is, by itself, enough to prevent application of the step transaction doctrine.

Section 1012(c) of the Taxpayer Relief Act of 1997 (the "Act") * * * amended the control requirements of §§ 351 and 368(a)(1)(D) to provide that, generally for transactions seeking qualification after August 5, 1997 under either provision and § 355, the shareholders of the distributing corporation must own stock possessing more than 50 percent of the voting power and more than 50 percent of the total value of the controlled corporation's stock immediately after the distribution. Sections 351(c) and 368(a)(2)(H). In addition, § 1012(a) of the Act amended § 355 by adding subsection (c), which provides rules for the recognition of gain on certain distributions of stock or securities of a controlled corporation in connection with acquisitions of stock representing a 50 percent or greater interest in the distributing corporation or any controlled corporation. Section 1012(a) of the Act generally applies to distributions after April 16, 1997, pursuant to a plan (or series of related transactions) that involves an acquisition described in § 355(e)(2)(A)(ii) occurring after such date.

The Conference Report accompanying the legislation states, in part, that:

> The House bill does not change the present law requirement under section 355 that the distributing corporation must distribute 80 percent of the voting power and 80 percent of each other class of stock of the controlled corporation. It is expected that this requirement will be applied by the Internal Revenue Service taking account of the provisions of the proposal regarding plans that permit certain types of planned restructuring of the distributing corporation following the distribution, and to treat similar restructurings of the controlled corporation in a similar manner. Thus, the 80–percent control requirement is expected to be administered in a manner that would prevent the tax-free spin-off of a less-than–80–percent controlled subsidiary, but would not generally impose additional restrictions on post-distribution restructurings of the controlled corporation if such restrictions would not apply to the distributing corporation. H.R.Rep. No. 105–220, at 529–30 (1997).

ANALYSIS

The application of Court Holding principles to determine whether the distributed corporation was a controlled corporation immediately before the distribution under § 355(a) imposes a restriction on postdistribution acquisitions or restructurings of a controlled corporation that is inconsistent with § 1012 of the Act. See § 1012(c) of the Act and H.R.Rep. No. 105–220, at 529–30. Accordingly, the Service will not apply Court Holding (or any formulation of the step transaction doctrine) to determine whether the distributed corporation was a controlled corporation immediately before the distribution under § 355(a) solely because of any postdistribution acquisition or restructuring of the distributed corporation, whether prearranged or not. In otherwise applying the step transaction doctrine, the Service will continue to consider all facts and circumstances. See, e.g., Rev. Rul. 63–260, 1963–2 C.B. 147. An independent shareholder vote is only one relevant factor to be considered.

HOLDING

Based on the enactment of § 1012 of the Act, the Service will not apply Court Holding (or any formulation of the step transaction doctrine) to determine whether the distributed corporation was a controlled corporation immediately before the distribution under § 355(a) solely because of any postdistribution acquisition or restructuring of the distributed corporation, whether prearranged or not.

EFFECT ON OTHER REVENUE RULINGS

* * * Rev. Rul. 70–225 is modified to the extent inconsistent with this revenue ruling.

[¶ 12,110]

Note

The IRS dropped the other shoe in Rev. Rul. 98–44, 1998–2 C.B. 315, and held Rev. Rul. 70–225, as modified by Rev. Rul. 98–27, to be obsolete as of August 5, 1997, as a result of the statutory changes in the 1997 Act.

[¶ 12,115]

b. Gain Recognition Triggered under Section 355(e) by a Section 355 Distribution Related to a Tax–Free or Taxable Acquisition

Under Section 355(e), enacted in 1997, gain recognition extends well beyond that mandated in Section 355(d) and contemplated in Rev. Rul. 96–30. Section 355(e) establishes a general rule that is analogous to that earlier enacted in Section 355(d) but that encompasses Section 355 distributions associated with tax-free, as well as taxable, acquisitions.

Section 355(e) provides that if pursuant to a plan or arrangement in existence on the date of distribution, either the controlled or distributing corporation is "acquired," gain is recognized by the distributing corporation as of the date of the distribution. Recognition of gain is triggered by excluding the stock or securities of the controlled corporation distributed from "qualified property" for purposes of Sections 355(c)(2) and 351(c)(2). § 355(e)(1). The amount of gain recognized is the amount that the distributing corporation would have recognized had the stock of the controlled corporation been sold for its fair market value on the date of the distribution. No adjustment to the basis of the stock or assets of either the distributing or controlled corporation is allowed to reflect this recognition of gain.

Whether a corporation is "acquired" for purposes of Section 355(e) is determined under rules similar to those of Section 355(d), except that acquisitions are not restricted to "purchase" transactions but also encompass tax-free acquisitions. Thus, an acquisition occurs if one or more persons acquire 50 percent or more of the vote or value of the stock of the controlled corporation or the distributing corporation pursuant to a plan or arrangement. For example, assume that P Corporation distributes the stock of its wholly owned subsidiary, S Corporation, to its shareholders. If, pursuant to a plan or arrangement, 50 percent or more of the vote or value of either P or S is acquired by one or more persons, gain recognition is required upon the distribution of the controlled corporation. Moreover, except as may be provided in Treasury regulations, if the assets of the distributing or controlled corporation are acquired by a successor in a tax-free "A," "C," or "D" reorganization, the shareholders (immediately before the acquisition) of the corporation acquiring such assets are treated as acquiring stock in the corporation from which the assets were acquired. § 355(e)(3)(B). Under Treasury regulations, other asset transfers also could be made subject to this rule.

Section 355(e) does not apply to distributions that would otherwise be subject to Section 355(d). § 355(e)(2)(D). As discussed at ¶ 12,090, Section 355(d) imposes corporate level tax on certain distributions of controlled corporations associated with purchases of 50 percent or more of the distributing or controlled corporation. Section 355(e) also does not apply to a distribution pursuant to a title 11 or similar case. § 355(e)(4).

Acquisitions occurring within the four-year period beginning two years before the date of distribution are presumed to have occurred pursuant to a plan or arrangement, unless it is established that the distribution and the acquisition are not pursuant to a plan or series of related transactions. § 355(e)(2)(B). Regulations have been issued to provide guidance on the existence of a plan and how the presumption can be rebutted. See ¶ 12,125.

Unless regulations provide otherwise, under Section 355(e)(3)(A) the following acquisitions will not trigger gain recognition, provided that the stock owned before the acquisition was not acquired pursuant to a plan or series of related transactions to acquire a 50 percent or greater ownership interest in either the distributing or the controlled corporations:

> (i) the acquisition of stock in any controlled corporation by the distributing corporation (e.g., in the case of a drop-down of property by the distributing corporation in exchange for the stock of the controlled corporation);

> (ii) the acquisition by a person of stock in any controlled corporation by reason of holding stock or securities in the distributing corporation (e.g., the receipt by a distributing corporation shareholder of controlled corporation stock in a distribution, including a split-off distribution, in which a shareholder that did not own 50

percent of the stock of the distributing corporation owns 50 percent or more of the stock of the controlled corporation);

(iii) the acquisition by a person of stock in any successor corporation of the distributing corporation or any controlled corporation by reason of holding stock or securities in such distributing or controlled corporation (e.g., the receipt by former shareholders of the distributing corporation of 50 percent or more of the stock of an acquiring corporation in a merger of the distributing corporation); and

(iv) the acquisition of stock in the distributing corporation or any controlled corporation to the extent that the percentage of stock owned (directly or indirectly) by each person owning stock in such corporation immediately before the acquisition does not decrease.

Under Section 355(e), a modified attribution rule has been adopted for determining when an acquisition has occurred. Rather than apply Section 355(d)(8)(A), which attributes stock owned by a corporation to a corporate shareholder only if that shareholder owns 10 percent of the corporation, Section 318(a)(2)(C) is here applied to any shareholder without regard to the percentage of stock owned. § 355(e)(4)(C)(ii).

[¶ 12,120]

c. *Regulations under Section 355(e)*

In April 2005, after a lengthy notice and comment period while temporary regulations were in use, final regulations were issued under Section 355(e). As with the temporary regulations, the final regulations provide that whether a distribution and an acquisition are part of a plan is determined on the basis of all the facts and circumstances, and they include nonexclusive lists of facts and circumstances to be considered in making this determination. Reg. § 1.355–7(b)(1).

In the case of an acquisition *after* a distribution, the regulations provide that, in general, the distribution and acquisition are considered part of a plan if the distributing corporation (DC), or the controlled corporation (CC) or any of their respective controlling shareholders intended, on the date of the distribution, that the acquisition or a similar acquisition occur in connection with the distribution. The reference to "a similar acquisition" ensures that changes in the terms of the acquisition intended at the time of the distribution (including the substitution of a new acquirer) do not prevent the distribution and the acquisition that actually occurs from being considered parts of a plan. Reg. § 1.355–7(b)(2).

In the case of an acquisition *before* a distribution, the regulations provide that, in general, the distribution and acquisition are considered part of a plan if the distributing or controlled corporation or any of their respective controlling shareholders intended, on the date of the acquisition, that a distribution occur in connection with the acquisition. Reg. § 1.355–7(b)(1).

In addition to the facts and circumstances test, the regulations contain nine safe harbor provisions that, when applicable, provide that the acquisition and distribution will not be considered to be part of a plan. Reg. § 1.355–7(d).

Under the regulations, the distributing corporation must test each acquisition of the distributing or controlled corporation stock to determine whether it is part of a plan that includes a distribution. The regulations aggregate all acquisitions of stock of a DC or CC that are pursuant to a plan including a particular distribution to determine whether the 50 percent threshold of Section 355(e)(2)(A)(ii) is met.

[¶ 12,125]

(i) Plan and Non-plan Factors

For those situations to which the safe harbor provisions do not apply, the regulations provide two nonexclusive lists of factors to consider in assessing whether an acquisition and a distribution are part of a plan. Reg. § 1.355–7(b)(1). One list of factors tends to demonstrate that a distribution and an acquisition are part of a plan and the other list tends to demonstrate that a distribution and an acquisition are not part of a plan. The weight of the factors depends on the particular case. The existence of a plan is not to be determined merely by comparing the number of factors tending to show that the acquisition and distribution are, or are not, part of a plan. Id.

Plan Factors. Many of the factors tending to show that a distribution and an acquisition are part of a plan focus on whether the distributing or controlled corporation or their respective controlling shareholders participated in discussions with outside parties regarding the second transaction of the pair being tested before the first transaction occurred (factors (i), (ii), (iii), and (iv)). Reg. § 1.355–7(b)(3). Such discussions provide evidence that DC, CC, or any of their respective controlling shareholders had an intent that the transactions occur in connection with each other. Factor (v) considers whether the distribution was motivated by a business purpose to facilitate the acquisition or a similar acquisition of DC or CC corporation.

The regulations also incorporate a set of operating rules to be applied under Section 355(e). Under the operating rule in Reg. § 1.355–7(c)(1), the fact that internal discussions or discussions with advisers occurred may be indicative of the business purpose that motivated the distribution. Similarly, Reg. § 1.355–7(c)(2) provides that, if, in the context of a hostile takeover defense, DC distributes CC stock intending, in whole or substantial part, to decrease the likelihood of the acquisition of DC or CC by separating it from another corporation that is likely to be acquired, DC is treated as having a business purpose to facilitate the acquisition of the corporation that is acquired. By contrast, the operating rules also indicate certain factors that should be disregarded. Under Reg. § 1.355–7(c)(3), the fact that the distribution will make CC's stock available for trading or will make DC's or CC's stock trade more actively is not taken into account. The same is true under Reg. § 1.355–7(c)(4) for the presence of a contractual indemnity by CC for the possible tax consequences under 355(e) to DC in the event of CC's acquisition.

Non-plan Factors. The regulations also provide a nonexclusive list of factors tending to show that a distribution and an acquisition are not part of a plan. Just as discussions with outside parties about the second transaction prior to the first transaction tend to show that DC, CC, or their respective controlling shareholders had an intent that the second transaction occur in connection with the first transaction, the absence of such discussions tends to show that the transactions did not occur in connection with each other. Reg. § 1.355–7(b)(4). Thus, there are non-plan factors that are analogous to the plan factors related to discussions (factors (i), (ii), and (iii)).

The existence of a corporate business purpose, other than a business purpose to facilitate the acquisition or a similar acquisition, that motivated DC, in whole or substantial part, to make the stock distribution tends to show that a distribution and an acquisition are not part of a plan (factor (v)). Analyzing whether there is another substantial corporate business purpose for the distribution in light of an acquisition-related purpose is similar to analyzing whether there is a corporate business purpose for a distribution in light of the potential avoidance of federal taxes. See Reg. § 1.355–2(b)(1) and (5), Ex. 8. Thus, another business purpose must be real and substantial.

Factor (iv) considers whether there was an identifiable, unexpected change in market or business conditions after the first of the two transactions being tested that resulted in the second, unexpected transaction. Factor (vi) considers whether the distribution would have occurred at approximately the same time and in similar form regardless of the acquisition or a previously proposed similar acquisition.

The following revenue ruling illustrates the application of the regulations' facts and circumstances test.

[¶ 12,130]

REVENUE RULING 2005–65

2005–2 C.B. 684

ISSUE

Under the facts described below, is a distribution of a controlled corporation by a distributing corporation part of a plan pursuant to which one or more persons acquire stock in the distributing corporation under § 355(e) * * * and § 1.355–7 of the * * * Regulations?

FACTS

Distributing is a publicly traded corporation that conducts a pharmaceuticals business. Controlled, a wholly owned subsidiary of Distributing, conducts a cosmetics business. Distributing does all of the borrowing for both Distributing and Controlled and makes all decisions regarding the allocation of capital spending between the pharmaceuticals and cosmetics businesses. Because Distributing's capital spending in recent years for both the pharmaceuticals and cosmetics businesses has outpaced internally generated cash flow from the businesses, it has had to limit total expenditures to maintain its credit ratings. Although the decisions reached by Distributing's senior management regarding the allocation of capital spending usually favor the pharmaceuticals business due to its higher rate of growth and profit margin, the competition for capital prevents both businesses from consistently pursuing development strategies that the management of each business believes are appropriate.

To eliminate this competition for capital, and in light of the unavailability of nontaxable alternatives, Distributing decides and publicly announces that it intends to distribute all the stock of Controlled pro rata to Distributing's shareholders. It is expected that both businesses will benefit in a real and substantial way from the distribution. This business purpose is a corporate business purpose (within the meaning of § 1.355–2(b)). The distribution is substantially motivated by this business purpose, and not by a business purpose to facilitate an acquisition. After the announcement but before the distribution, X, a widely held corporation that is engaged in the pharmaceuticals business, and Distributing begin discussions regarding an acquisition. There were no discussions between Distributing or Controlled and X or its shareholders regarding an acquisition or a distribution before the announcement. In addition, Distributing would have been able to continue the successful operation of its pharmaceuticals business without combining with X. During its negotiations with Distributing, X indicates that it favors the distribution. X merges into Distributing before the distribution but nothing in the merger agreement requires the distribution.

As a result of the merger, X's former shareholders receive 55 percent of Distributing's stock. In addition, X's chairman of the board and chief executive officer become the chairman of the board and chief executive officer, respectively, of Distributing. Six months after the merger, Distributing distributes the stock of Controlled pro rata in a distribution to which § 355 applies and to which § 355(d) does not apply. At the time of the distribution, the distribution continues to be substantially motivated by the business purpose of eliminating the competition for capital between the pharmaceuticals and cosmetics businesses.

LAW

Section 355(c) generally provides that no gain or loss is recognized to the distributing corporation on a distribution of stock in a controlled corporation to which § 355 (or so much of § 356 as relates to § 355) applies and which is not in pursuance of a plan of reorganization. Section 355(e) generally denies nonrecognition treatment under § 355(c) if the distribution is part of a plan (or series of related transactions) (a plan) pursuant to which one or more persons acquire directly or indirectly stock representing a 50–percent or greater interest in the distributing corporation or any controlled corporation.

Section 1.355–7(b)(1) provides that whether a distribution and an acquisition are part of a plan is determined based on all the facts and circumstances, including those set forth in § 1.355–7(b)(3) (plan factors) and (4) (non-plan factors). The weight to be given each of the facts and circumstances depends on the particular case. The determination does not depend on the relative number of plan factors compared to the number of non-plan factors that are present.

Section 1.355–7(b)(3)(iii) provides that, in the case of an acquisition (other than involving a public offering) before a distribution, if at some time during the two-year period ending on the date of the acquisition there were discussions by Distributing or Controlled with the acquirer regarding a distribution, such discussions tend to show that the distribution and the acquisition are part of a plan. The weight to be accorded this fact depends on the nature, extent, and timing of the discussions. In addition, the fact that the acquirer intends to cause a distribution and, immediately after the acquisition, can meaningfully participate in the decision regarding whether to make a distribution, tends to show that the distribution and the acquisition are part of a plan.

Section 1.355–7(b)(4)(iii) provides that, in the case of an acquisition (other than involving a public offering) before a distribution, the absence of discussions by Distributing or Controlled with the acquirer regarding a distribution during the two year period ending on the date of the earlier to occur of the acquisition or the first public announcement regarding the distribution tends to show that the distribution and the acquisition are not part of a plan. However, this factor does not apply to an acquisition where the acquirer intends to cause a distribution and, immediately after the acquisition, can meaningfully participate in the decision regarding whether to make a distribution.

Section 1.355–7(b)(4)(v) provides that the fact that the distribution was motivated in whole or substantial part by a corporate business purpose (within the meaning of § 1.355–2(b)) other than a business purpose to facilitate the acquisition or a similar acquisition tends to show that the distribution and the acquisition are not part of a plan.

Section 1.355–7(b)(4)(vi) provides that the fact that the distribution would have occurred at approximately the same time and in similar form regardless of the acquisition or a similar acquisition tends to show that the distribution and the acquisition are not part of a plan.

Section 1.355–7(h)(6) provides that discussions with the acquirer generally include discussions with persons with the implicit permission of the acquirer.

Section 1.355–7(h)(9) provides that a corporation is treated as having the implicit permission of its shareholders when it engages in discussions.

ANALYSIS

Whether the X shareholders' acquisition of Distributing stock and Distributing's distribution of Controlled are part of a plan depends on all the facts and circumstances, including those described in § 1.355–7(b). The fact that Distributing discussed the distribution with X during the two-year period ending on the date of the acquisition tends to show that the distribution and the acquisition are part of a plan. See § 1.355–7(b)(3)(iii). In addition, X's shareholders may constitute acquirers who intend to cause a distribution and who, immediately after the acquisition, can meaningfully participate (through X's chairman of the board and chief executive officer who become D's chairman of the board and chief executive officer) in the decision regarding whether to distribute Controlled. See id. However, the fact that Distributing publicly announced the distribution before discussions with X regarding both an acquisition and a distribution began suggests that the plan factor in § 1.355–7(b)(3)(iii) should be accorded less weight than it would have been accorded had there been such discussions before the public announcement.

With respect to those factors that tend to show that the distribution and the acquisition are not part of a plan, the absence of discussions by Distributing or Controlled with X or its shareholders during the two-year period ending on the date of the public announcement regarding the distribution would tend to show that the distribution and the acquisition are not part of a plan only if X's shareholders are not acquirers who intend to cause a distribution and who, immediately after the acquisition, can meaningfully participate in the decision regarding whether to distribute Controlled. See § 1.355–7(b)(4)(iii). Because X's chairman of the board and chief executive officer become the chairman and chief executive officer, respectively, of Distributing, X's shareholders may have the ability to meaningfully participate in the decision whether to distribute Controlled. Therefore, the absence of discussions by Distributing or Controlled with X or its shareholders during the two-year period ending on the date of the public announcement regarding the distribution may not tend to show that the distribution and the acquisition are not part of a plan.

Nonetheless, the fact that the distribution was substantially motivated by a corporate business purpose (within the meaning of § 1.355–2(b)) other than a business purpose to facilitate the acquisition or a similar acquisition, and the fact that the distribution would have occurred at approximately the same time and in similar form regardless of the acquisition or a similar acquisition, tend to show that the distribution and the acquisition are not part of a plan. See § 1.355–7(b)(4)(v), (vi). The fact that the public announcement of the distribution preceded discussions by Distributing or Controlled with X or its shareholders, and the fact that Distributing's business would have continued to operate successfully even if the merger had not occurred, evidence that the distribution originally was not substantially motivated by a business purpose to facilitate the acquisition or a similar acquisition. Moreover, after the merger, Distributing continued to be substantially motivated by the same corporate business purpose (within the meaning of § 1.355–2(b)) other than a business purpose to facilitate the acquisition or a similar acquisition (§ 1.355–7(b)(4)(v)). In addition, the fact that Distributing decided to distribute Controlled and announced that decision before it began discussions with X regarding the combination suggests that the distribution would have occurred at approximately the same time and in similar form regardless of Distributing's combination with X and the corresponding acquisition of Distributing stock by the X shareholders.

Considering all the facts and circumstances, particularly the fact that the distribution was motivated by a corporate business purpose (within the meaning of § 1.355–2(b)) other than a business purpose to facilitate the acquisition or a similar acquisition, and the fact that the distribution would have occurred at approximately the same time and in similar form regardless of the acquisition or a similar acquisition, the acquisition and distribution are not part of a plan under § 355(e) and § 1.355–7(b).

Holding

Under the facts described above, the acquisition and the distribution are not part of a plan under § 355(e) and § 1.355–7(b).

[¶ 12,135]

Note

While Reg. § 1.355–7(b)(1) indicates that the weight to be given to the plan and non-plan factors depends upon the case, Rev. Rul. 2005–65 places particular emphasis on the presence of the non-plan factors of a corporate business purpose and the evidence that the distribution would have occurred at approximately the same time and in similar form regardless of the acquisition.

[¶ 12,140]

(ii) Safe Harbors

Reg. § 1.355–7(d) includes nine safe harbor provisions. A distribution and an acquisition are not part of a plan if they are described in one of the safe harbors. Safe Harbors I, II and III address post-distribution acquisitions and Safe Harbors IV, V, and VI address pre-distribution acquisitions. Safe Harbor VII addresses open market acquisitions of publicly-traded stock and Safe Harbors VIII and IX address acquisitions by employees as part of compensation or retirement schemes.

Post-Distribution Acquisitions: Safe Harbor I applies to an acquisition more than six months after a distribution if (1) there was no agreement, understanding, arrangement, or substantial negotiations concerning the acquisition during the period starting one year prior to and ending six months after the distribution and (2) the distribution was motivated in whole or substantial part by a corporate business purpose other than a business purpose to facilitate an acquisition. The nonacquisition corporate business purpose for the distribution is considered in light of any business purpose to facilitate the acquisition, and the operating rules of Reg. § 1.355–7(c) apply.

Safe Harbor II, like Safe Harbor I, applies to acquisitions more than six months after a distribution for which there was no agreement, understanding, arrangement, or substantial negotiations concerning the acquisition that occurred during the period starting one year prior to and ending six months after the distribution. Safe Harbor II, however, only requires that the distribution not be motivated in whole or substantial part by a business purpose to facilitate an acquisition, rather than be motivated by a corporate business purpose as in Safe Harbor I, so long as no more than 25 percent of the stock of the acquired corporation (either DC or CC) was acquired or the subject of agreement, understanding, arrangement, or substantial negotiations during the period starting one year prior to and ending six months after the distribution (except for acquisitions covered by one of Safe Harbors VII, VIII, or IX).

Under Safe Harbor III, post-distribution acquisitions are not pursuant to a plan if there is no agreement, understanding, arrangement, or substantial negotiations concerning the acquisition at the time of the distribution or within one year thereafter.

Pre-Distribution Acquisitions: Under Safe Harbor IV, a pre-distribution acquisition is not part of a plan if the acquisition (other than a public offering) occurs prior to the first "disclosure event" regarding the distribution as long as the acquiring corporation is not a controlling shareholder or a 10 percent owner of the DC or CC during the period between the acquisition and distribution and as long as no more than 20 percent of the vote or value of the DC or CC is acquired in the acquisition. The rationale for the latter two provisions, which also apply to Safe Harbor V, is to exclude acquisitions in which the acquirer is in a position to influence the subsequent distribution. According to Reg. § 1.355–7(h)(5), a "disclosure event" is any communication to the acquirer by an officer, director, controlling shareholder, or employee of DC, CC, an affiliate, or an outside advisor to one of these entities regarding the distribution or the possibility thereof.

Under Safe Harbor V, an acquisition preceding a pro rata distribution is not part of a plan if it occurs prior to the date of the first "public announcement" and there were no discussions between DC or CC and the acquiring corporation before the public announcement. According to Reg. § 1.355–7(h)(10), a "public announcement" is any communication regarding the distribution by DC or CC that is generally available to the public.

Safe Harbor VI addresses a pre-distribution acquisition involving a public offering of stock. In the case of stock that is not listed on an established market after the transaction, then the acquisition will not be treated as part of a plan if it occurs prior to the first disclosure event regarding the distribution. In the case of stock that is listed on an established market after the transaction, then the acquisition will not be treated as part of a plan if it occurs prior to the date of the first public announcement regarding the distribution.

Open Market Acquisitions: Safe Harbor VII provides that an acquisition of DC or CC stock that is listed on an established market is not part of a plan unless the stock is transferred between DC, CC, an affiliate of either, or shareholders of DC or CC who are controlling or ten percent shareholders. In general, a person will be considered a five-percent shareholder if, immediately before or after each transfer, the person owns, directly or indirectly, or together with related persons (as described in Sections 267(b) and 707(b)), five percent or more of any class of stock of the corporation the stock of which is transferred.

Employee Benefit Acquisitions: Safe Harbor VIII provides that an acquisition of stock by an employee or director in connection with the performance of services, including an acquisition resulting from the exercise of certain compensatory stock options, is not part of a plan. Similarly, Safe Harbor IX provides that the acquisition of stock in connection with a retirement plan of DC or CC will not be considered as part of a plan unless it represents more than 10 percent of the vote or value of the acquired corporation's stock.

[¶ 12,145]

(iii) Agreement, Understanding, Arrangement, or Substantial Negotiations

The regulations do not define an agreement, understanding, arrangement, or substantial negotiations precisely. A binding contract clearly is included as an agreement but, depending on all relevant facts and circumstances, parties can have an agreement, understanding, or arrangement even though they have not reached agreement on all terms. Under certain circumstances, such as in public offerings or auctions of DC's or CC's stock, an agreement, understanding, arrangement, or substantial negotiations can exist regarding an acquisition even if the acquirer has not been specifically identified. Reg. § 1.355–7(h)(1).

[¶ 12,150]

(iv) Options

If stock of DC or CC is acquired pursuant to an option, the option is treated as an agreement to acquire stock on the date of writing unless DC establishes that, on the later of the date of the stock distribution or the writing of the option, the option was not more likely than not to be exercised. Reg. § 1.355–7(e)(1). Certain options are exempted from treatment as options unless they are written, transferred, or listed with a principal purpose of avoiding the application of Section 355(e) or the regulations. Reg. § 1.355–7(e)(4). The exceptions include certain commercially customary options, such as compensatory options or rights of first refusal in a shareholders' agreement.

If, pursuant to a plan, the stock of more than one controlled corporation is distributed and stock representing a 50 percent or greater interest is acquired in some, but not all, of the distributed controlled corporations, DC only recognizes gain on the stock of the distributed controlled corporations that were subject to 50 percent or greater acquisitions. Reg. § 1.355–7(f). If DC is the acquired corporation, it must recognize gain on all of the distributed controlled corporations.

[¶ 12,155]

Problems

1.   P Corporation contributes one of its three businesses to a newly formed S Corporation, in exchange for 100 percent of the stock of S. P then distributes the S stock to its shareholders in a transaction that otherwise meets the requirements for a tax free division under Section 355. Pursuant to a plan in existence on the date of the distribution, all of the stock of P is then acquired in exchange for the voting stock of X Corporation, which was previously unrelated to P and S, in a "B"

reorganization. Is the transaction taxable to P or its shareholders? Are the results altered if P is merged into X in an "A" reorganization?

2.   Individual A owns all the stock of P Corporation. P owns all the stock of S Corporation, which has been engaged in an active business for more than five years. All of the stock of S is distributed to A in a transaction that otherwise qualifies under Section 355. As part of a plan, which existed at the time of the distribution of the stock of S, P then merges with X Corporation, also owned entirely by A. Is the distribution of the S stock taxable? Would the result be the same if the stock of P were contributed to a holding corporation, all the stock of which is owned by A?

3.   Assume the facts are the same as in Problem 2 except that P Corporation and X Corporation are each owned in the same proportions by the same 20 individual (five percent) shareholders (rather than wholly by individual A). Would the transaction described in Problem 2 in which S is spun off by P to P's shareholders and P is then acquired by X, cause gain recognition to P?

4.   D Corporation is engaged in the soft drink distribution business. It owns 100 percent of the stock of S Corporation, which owns a number of computer software franchises. X Corporation, which is engaged in the soft drink distribution business, wants to acquire D Corporation but not S Corporation. On February 1, X Corporation and D Corporation initiate substantial negotiations relating to a possible acquisition of D Corporation by X Corporation, but no agreement, understanding, or arrangement is reached. On May 1, D Corporation distributes all of the stock of S Corporation pro rata to its shareholders in a distribution to which Section 355 applies and Section 355(d) does not. D Corporation's principal reason for the distribution is to facilitate its acquisition by X Corporation. Agreement between D Corporation and X Corporation concerning acquisition of D Corporation is reached on September 1, and on December 1, D Corporation merges into X Corporation, following which D Corporation's former shareholders own 48 percent of the stock of X Corporation. Under the circumstances, what is the likelihood that the distribution and acquisition will be considered to be part of a plan, which would result in the distribution of the S Corporation stock being taxable to D Corporation?

5.   Would the result in Problem 4 be different if, after the distribution, negotiations between D Corporation and X Corporation fall through, and negotiations are conducted and agreement reached on August 15 on a merger between D Corporation and Y Corporation, one of X Corporation's competitors. On September 15, D Corporation merges into Y Corporation and the former D Corporation shareholders receive 45 percent of the stock of Y Corporation.

6.   If the facts are as stated in Problem 4, except that D Corporation's principal purpose for distributing the stock of S Corporation was

to separate the software franchises, which are highly volatile businesses, from the more stable soft drink distribution business, would the result be different?

7. If the facts are as stated in Problem 6, except that the distribution of the S Corporation stock occurred on April 1, and there were no negotiations between D Corporation and X Corporation until November 1, would the result be different?

8. D Corporation and S Corporation are engaged in the businesses described in Problem 4. On January 15, D Corporation's management discusses with its investment bankers the possible sale of some of the stock of S Corporation to the public. On February 1, the board of directors of D Corporation discussed the distribution of all of the stock of S Corporation pro rata to D Corporation's shareholders primarily to facilitate the sale of S Corporation stock to the public. However, in the light of a sudden change in market conditions, D Corporation decides on February 15, to have S Corporation sell as promptly as possible to the public newly issued shares equal to 20 percent of S Corporation's outstanding shares, disclosing in the prospectus D Corporation's intent to distribute the remaining S Corporation shares to the D shareholders. At the time of the distribution, which occurred on April 1, there had been no negotiations concerning an acquisition. On August 1, S Corporation is approached unexpectedly regarding an opportunity for S Corporation to acquire X Corporation. After substantial negotiations, agreement is reached and X Corporation is merged on September 1 into S Corporation, and the X Corporation shareholders emerge with 32 percent of the S Corporation shares. Would the distribution of S Corporation shares be taxable? If negotiations between S Corporation and X Corporation begin on November 1, and X Corporation is merged into S Corporation on December 1, does the analysis change?

[¶ 12,160]

d. *Determination of "Control" in Divisions Involving Asset Transfers*

The 1997 Act also modified the rules for determining control immediately after a distribution in the case of certain corporate divisions in which assets are transferred to a controlled corporation in exchange for stock, the controlled corporation is distributed, and the transaction meets the requirements of Section 355. In such cases, for purposes of Section 351 and the definition of the "D" reorganization, under Section 368(a)(2)(H)(ii), those shareholders receiving stock in the distributed corporation are treated as in control of the distributed corporation immediately after the distribution if they hold stock representing a greater than 50 percent interest in the vote and value of the stock of the distributed corporation. § 351(c). The distribution will be taxable only if the more than 50 percent control test is not met. In any event, most transactions that result in a loss of 50 percent control would result in recognized gain to the distributing corporation under Section 355(e). Thus, the significance of the more than 50 percent control test is that if this test is not met, tax is also imposed at the shareholder level.

[¶ 12,165]

Problems

1.   P Corporation owns two businesses, A and B. It contributes business A to newly formed S Corporation in exchange for 100 percent of the only class of S stock. P then distributes the S stock to its shareholders in a transaction that otherwise meets the requirements for a tax-free division under Section 355. The shareholders, pursuant to a binding agreement in effect at the time of the distribution, sell 30 percent of the S stock to unrelated persons. Is the transaction tax-free to P and its shareholders?

2.   P Corporation contributes one of its two businesses to newly formed S Corporation in exchange for 100 percent of the only class of stock of S. P then distributes the S stock to its shareholders in a transaction which otherwise meets the requirements for a tax-free division under Section 355. Pursuant to a plan in existence at the time of the distribution, S then issues, in a private placement, a second class of stock to a third party. This second class of stock has 75 percent of the total value, but only 10 percent of the aggregate voting power, of all of the S stock. Is the transaction tax-free to P and its shareholders?

[¶ 12,170]

e.   *Consolidated Return Changes*

Another area of congressional concern addressed in the 1997 changes was the use of the consolidated return rules to produce results considered inappropriate on policy grounds. For a general discussion of consolidated returns, see Chapter 14. One series of transactions that attracted attention involved, as a first step, a borrowing of funds by a controlled corporation. The funds were then distributed as a tax-free dividend to its parent which filed a consolidated return with the subsidiary. The controlled corporation's stock was then distributed in a tax-free spin-off. Under the consolidated return regulations, (i) if the cash dividend exceeded the parent's basis in the controlled corporation's stock, an excess loss account[1] was created and this account was eliminat-

---

1.   Excess loss accounts in consolidation generally are created when a subsidiary corporation makes a distribution (or has a loss that is used by other members of the group) that exceeds the parent's basis in the stock of the subsidiary. See ¶ 14,080. In general, such excess loss accounts in consolidation are permitted to be deferred rather than causing immediate taxable gain. Nevertheless, they are recaptured when a subsidiary leaves the group or in certain other situations. However, such excess loss accounts are not recaptured in certain cases where there is an internal spin-off before the sub-

ed in connection with the tax-free spin-off. The parent could then sell the controlled corporation's stock to a third party without tax triggered by an excess loss account and retain the proceeds of the controlled corporation's borrowing (previously distributed as a dividend to it) tax-free.

Under new Section 355(f), except as provided in regulations, Section 355 does not apply to the distribution of stock from one member of an affiliated group of corporations (as defined in Section 1504(a)) to another member of such group (an "intragroup spin-off") if such distribution is part of a plan (or series of related transactions) described in Section 355(e)(2)(A)(ii). This is a plan pursuant to which one or more persons acquire directly or indirectly stock representing a 50 percent or greater interest in the distributing corporation or any controlled corporation. As an example, assume that P Corporation owns 100 percent of subsidiary corporation, S1, which owns 100 percent of subsidiary corporation S2. S1 distributes the stock of S2 corporation to P as part of a plan or series of related transactions in which P distributes the stock of S1 to its shareholders and then P is merged into unrelated Z Corporation. After the merger, former shareholders of Z own 50 percent or more of the voting power or value of the stock of P. Because the distribution of the stock of S2 by S1 is part of a plan or series of related transactions in which the S1 stock is distributed by P outside the P affiliated group and P is then "acquired" under Section 355(e), Section 355 does not apply to the intragroup spin-off of S2 to P. § 355(f). Also, the distribution of the stock of S1 by P is subject to Section 355(e).

In determining whether an acquisition described in Section 355(e)(2)(A)(ii) occurs, all the provisions of Section 355(e) are applied. For example, an intragroup spin-off in connection with an overall transaction that does not cause gain recognition under Section 355(e) (e.g., because it is described in Section 355(e)(2)(C)) is not subject to the rule of Section 355(f).

As noted above, after a tax-free spin-off transaction, the amount of a shareholder's basis in the stock of the distributing corporation is generally allocated between the stock of the distributing and the controlled corporations received by that shareholder in proportion to their relative fair market values. In the case of an affiliated group of corporations filing a consolidated return, this basis allocation rule generally eliminates any excess loss account in the stock of a controlled corporation that is distributed within the group, and its basis is generally determined with reference to the basis of the distributing corporation.

---

sidiary leaves the group. See Reg. § 1.1502–19(g). In addition, an excess loss account may not be created at all in certain cases that are similar economically to a distribu-tion that would reduce the stock basis of the distributing subsidiary corporation if the distribution from the subsidiary is structured as a Section 355 distribution.

¶ 12,170

A plan (or series of related transactions) described in Section 355(e)(2)(A)(ii) is not one that will cause gain recognition if, immediately after the completion of such plan or transactions, the distributing corporation and all controlled corporations are members of a single affiliated group of corporations (as defined in Section 1504 without regard to subsection (b) thereof). The Conference Committee Report, H.R. Conf. Rep. No. 220, 105th Cong., 1st Sess. 532 (1997), gives the following example:

> *Example 1*: P corporation is a member of an affiliated group of corporations that includes subsidiary corporation S and subsidiary corporation S1. P owns all of the stock of S. S owns all the stock of S1. P corporation is merged into unrelated X corporation in a transaction in which the former shareholders of X corporation will own 50 percent or more of the vote or value of the stock of surviving X corporation after the merger. As part of the plan of merger, S1 will be distributed by S to X, in a transaction that otherwise qualifies under Section 355. After this distribution, S, S1, and X will remain members of a single affiliated group of corporations under section 1504 * * *. Even though there has been an acquisition of P, S and S1 by X, and distribution of S1 by S that is part of a plan or series of related transactions, the plan is not treated as one that requires gain recognition of the distribution of S1 to X. This is because the distributing corporation S and the controlled corporation S1 remain within a single affiliated group after the distribution (even though the P group has changed ownership).

In the case of any distribution of stock of one member of an affiliated group of corporations to another member, regulations are authorized under Section 358(c) to provide adjustments to the basis of any stock in a corporation which is a member of the group to reflect appropriately the proper treatment of the distribution. For example, rules may be provided that require a carryover basis within the group for the stock of the distributed controlled corporation (including a carryover of an excess loss account, if any, in a consolidated return) and that also provide a reduction in the basis of the stock of the distributing corporation to reflect the change in the value and basis of the distributing corporation's assets. The aggregate stock basis of the distributing and the controlled corporations after the distribution may be adjusted to an amount that is less than the aggregate basis of the stock of the distributing corporation before the distribution to prevent inappropriate potential for artificial losses or reduction of gain on disposition of any of the corporations involved in the spin-off. The Conference Committee Report, H.R. Conf. Rep. No. 220, 105th Cong., 1st Sess. 535–36 (1997), describes as follows the concerns addressed by this authority:

> * * * First, under present law consolidated return regulations, it is possible that an excess loss account of a lower tier subsidiary may be eliminated. This creates the potential for the subsidiary to

leave the group without recapture of the excess loss account, even though the group has benefitted from the losses or distributions in excess of basis that led to the existence of the excess loss account.

Second, under present law, a shareholder's stock basis in its stock of the distributing corporation is allocated after a spin-off between the stock of the distributing and controlled corporations, in proportion to the relative fair market values of the stock of those companies. If a disproportionate amount of asset basis (as compared to value) is in one of the companies (including but not limited to a shift of value and basis through a borrowing by one company and contribution of the borrowed cash to the other), present law rules under section 358(c) can produce an increase in stock basis relative to asset basis in one corporation, and a corresponding decrease in stock basis relative to asset basis in the other company. Because the spin-off has occurred within the corporate group, the group can continue to benefit from high inside asset basis either for purposes of sale or depreciation, while also choosing to benefit from the disproportionately high stock basis in the other corporation. If, for example, both corporations were sold at a later date, a prior distribution can result in less gain being recognized than would have occurred if the two corporations had been sold together without a prior spin-off (or separately, without a prior spin-off).

Example 5: P owns all the stock of S1 and S1 owns all the stock of S2. P's basis in the stock of S1 is 50; the inside asset basis of S1's assets is 50; and the total value of S1's stock and assets (including the value of S2) is 150. S1's basis in the stock of S2 is 0; the inside basis of S2's assets is 0; and the value of S2's stock and assets is 100. If S1 were sold, holding S2, the total gain would be 100. S1 distributes S2 to P in a section 355 transaction. After this spin-off, under present law, P's basis in the stock of S1 is approximately 17 (50/150 times the total 50 stock basis in S1 prior to the spin-off) and the inside asset basis of S1 is 50. P's basis in the stock of S2 is 33 (100/150 times the total 50 stock basis in S1 prior to the spin-off) and the inside asset basis of S2 is 0. After a period of time, S2 can be sold for its value of 100, with a gain of 67 rather than 100. Also, since S1 remains in the corporate group, the full 50 inside asset basis can continue to be used. S1's assets could be sold for 50 with no gain or loss. Thus, S1 and S2 can be sold later at a total gain of 67, rather than the total gain of 100 that would have occurred had they been sold without the spin-off.

As one variation on the foregoing concern, taxpayers have attempted to utilize spin-offs to extract significant amounts of asset value and basis (including but not limited to transactions in which one corporation decreases its value by incurring debt, and increases the asset basis and value of the other corporation by contributing the proceeds of the debt to the other corporation) without creation of an excess loss account or triggering of gain, even when the extraction is in excess of the basis in the distributing corporation's stock.

The Treasury Department may promulgate any regulations necessary to address these concerns and other collateral issues. * * * The Treasury Department may provide separate regulations for corporations in affiliated groups filing a consolidated return and for affiliated groups not filing a consolidated return, as appropriate to each situation.

[¶ 12,172]

f. *Disqualified investment corporations*

Recently, Congress has become concerned about the use of split-offs by corporations seeking to dispose of appreciated portfolio investments in a tax-efficient transaction. In one example of such a transaction, a corporation (P) holding less than a controlling interest in another corporation (S) seeks to separate from S. As part of the plan for accomplishing this, S contributes primarily cash, but also the assets of a small trade or business actively conducted for the prior five years, to a newly-created corporation (S1). S then distributes the stock of S1 to P in exchange for P's stock in S. Effectively, S has redeemed P's stock in a tax-free reorganization for cash. Because of the contribution to S1 of the assets of a small actively conducted trade or business, though, the distribution qualifies as a split-off. There is no minimum percentage for the amount of assets devoted to an active trade or business and the transaction could not be characterized as a device to bail-out earnings and profits since it would be taxed as a redemption rather than a dividend in the absence of Section 355. Thus, through this plan, P is able to defer the tax on a redemption.

Section 355(g) was adopted to address these so-called "cash-rich" split-offs. Under this provision, Section 355 treatment is denied if (1) either the distributing or controlled corporation is a "disqualified investment corporation" immediately after the transaction, and (2) there is a change in the majority ownership (by vote or value) of such corporation as a result of the transaction, after applying the attribution rules in Section 318. A corporation is considered a "disqualified investment corporation" if the fair market value of its invested assets is three-quarters of the fair market value of all of its assets. Starting in May of 2007, the threshold for disqualified investment corporation status drops from three-quarters to two-thirds. Except when used in the active conduct of a financial or investment business, "investment assets" include cash, stock or securities in a corporation, a partnership interest, any debt instrument or other evidence of indebtedness, an option, forward contract or other derivative, foreign currency, or other similar asset. In the case of a corporation which holds a 20 percent or greater

¶ 12,172

stake in stock or securities of another corporation, the rules require a look-through to the ratable share of the corporation's assets rather than including the stock or securities themselves as investment assets.

[¶ 12,175]

F. CONSEQUENCES OF FAILURE OF CORPORATE DIVISION TO QUALIFY UNDER SECTION 355

If a corporate division fails to meet the requirements of Section 355, the consequences are potentially severe at the corporate and shareholder levels. At the level of the distributing corporation, if the transaction is a nonqualifying spin-off or split-off, the distribution of controlled corporation stock will give rise to recognition of gain but not loss under Section 311. If the transaction is a split-up, gain and loss will be recognized under Section 336(a), except that loss will not be recognized in the case of certain distributions covered by Section 336(d), discussed at ¶ 8025. Gain and loss will not be recognized under Section 337 if the distributee is a corporation that owns 80 percent of the voting power and value of the distributing corporation's stock.

At the shareholder level, the consequences also vary depending on the nature of the transaction. If a nonqualifying spin-off is involved, the transaction will be treated as a distribution in kind under Section 301. See Chapter 4. If the transaction is a nonqualifying split-off, the transaction should be treated as a redemption by the distributing corporation, the tax consequences of which are governed by Section 302. See Chapter 5. In the case of a nonqualifying split-up, the shareholder should be treated as receiving a liquidating distribution on which capital gain or loss would be recognized under Section 331(a). If the spin-off, split-off, or split-up follows a transfer of assets by the distributing corporation to the controlled corporation, Section 351 will preclude recognition of gain or loss to the distributing corporation on the transfer of assets to the controlled corporation.

[¶ 12,180]

G. DISTRIBUTION OF RIGHTS

Is a transaction outside the ambit of Section 355 if a corporation transfers a separate business conducted for more than five years to a newly formed subsidiary and then distributes rights or warrants to its shareholders to purchase shares of the new subsidiary at less than fair market value? This issue was considered in Redding v. Commissioner, 630 F.2d 1169 (7th Cir.1980), cert. denied, 450 U.S. 913 (1981).

This case involved distribution of warrants (or stock rights) as part of a series of transactions involving distribution by the Indianapolis

¶ 12,172

Water Company (Water Company) to its stockholders of all the stock of its wholly owned subsidiary, Shorewood Corporation (Shorewood). The distribution of warrants was made before the distribution of stock, which was distributed upon the exercise of the warrants. The Tax Court, applying the step transaction doctrine, treated the two distributions as being part of a single transaction, sheltered from taxation under Section 355. The court of appeals reversed, holding that the distribution of stock warrants to the taxpayers constituted a dividend to them and that Section 355 did not apply to render the transaction tax-free.

The court examined various formulations of the step transaction doctrine and found none of them applicable to justify telescoping the distribution of the warrants and their exercise into a single transaction. The court went on to state:

> Even were we to agree that the step transaction doctrine permits these transactions to be viewed as simply a distribution of Shorewood stock, the requirement of section 355(a)(1)(A) that this stock be distributed with respect to the stock of the Water Company has not been met. What has instead happened has been that the stock warrants have been distributed *with respect* to the stock of the Water Company, and the Shorewood stock has then been distributed with respect to the warrants * * *. It was the warrant distribution rather than the stock distribution which conformed to this statutory test.

> After the distribution of warrants to Water Company stockholders had taken place, the subsequent distribution of shares of Shorewood stock was made "with respect to" the holders of warrants—some Water Company shareholders and some not * * *. * * *

630 F.2d at 1178.

The court concluded that the distribution of the warrants was a taxable distribution of property to shareholders with respect to the distributing corporation's stock under Sections 301(a), 301(c), and 317(a). Consequently, there being ample E & P in the distributing corporation, the fair market value of the warrants was taxable as a dividend. In reaching this result, the court had to deal with celebrated Supreme Court dictum in *Palmer v. Commissioner*. It did so by reasoning as follows:

> It is argued, of course, that such a result contradicts the dictum of *Palmer v. Commissioner*. In that opinion Mr. Justice Stone said:

> > The mere issue of rights to subscribe and their receipt by stockholders, is not a dividend. No distribution of corporate assets or diminution of the net worth of the corporation results in any practical sense. Even though the rights have a market or exchange value, they are not dividends within the statutory definition * * *. They are at most options or continuing offers,

potential sources of income to the stockholders through sale or the exercise of their rights. Taxable income might result from their sale, but distribution of the corporate property could take place only on their exercise. 302 U.S. at 71 * * *.

But this analysis in the *Palmer* dictum was made under the Revenue Act of 1928, which did not contain the broad definition of "property" added in 1954 as section 317(a) of the Code.[24] Obviously, the Internal Revenue Code of 1954 must govern our decision. Although the superseding legislation and the congressional commentary it generated did not specifically discuss the *Palmer* dictum, several provisions of the 1954 Code governing corporate distributions seem incompatible with the principle that income never results from the mere issuance of stock rights. Whether, in enacting these provisions, Congress intended to "overrule" *Palmer* with respect to its famous dictum is left for us to intuit. We believe, though, that a "reasonable interpretation" of the corporate distribution provisions as a whole yields the conclusion that, even if the dictum was authoritative prior to 1954, it must now make way for a result consonant with the 1954 Code (and, incidentally, more reflective of economic reality).

In addition to the definition of "property" in section 317(a), which we find includes stock rights in the shares of a non-issuing corporation, the 1954 Code added a provision in section 305 which indicates another change in the law of tax-free receipt of stock rights. The general rule of section 305(a) excludes from taxability stock rights to acquire stock in the issuing corporation. However, one exception to this rule in section 305(b) is designed to tax distributions when they are effectively granted "in lieu of money." If the exception applies, the distribution of stock or of stock rights "shall be treated as a distribution of property to which section 301 applies." This exception precludes any inference that Congress intended to perpetuate the *Palmer* dictum. Thus, both section 305(b) and 317(a) vitiate the "no property" rationale of the *Palmer* dictum. * * *

Indeed, the Supreme Court itself has apparently done the next thing to explicitly rejecting the *Palmer* dictum in light of the 1954 Code. In *Commissioner v. Gordon*, [391 U.S. 83 (1968)] the Court discussed the relevant provisions of the Code and said that when a corporation sells its property to its stockholders or their assignees at less than fair market value, the transaction diminishes the net worth of the corporation and is a "distribution of property" within

---

24. As has been noted, "[T]he 1928 revenue statute, . . . defined a dividend as 'any distribution made by a corporation to its shareholders, whether in money or in other property, out of its earnings and profits.' The *Palmer* Court concluded that the issuance of an option did not constitute a distribution out of corporate profits, and so was not a dividend." * * *

section 316. In attempting to relate this statement to discussion of the same subject in *Palmer*, the Court made broader observations:

> In *Palmer*, rights were distributed entitling shareholders to purchase from the corporation shares of stock in another corporation. Finding that the sales price represented the reasonable value of the shares at the time the corporation committed itself to sell them, the Court found no dividend. It held that the mere issue of rights was not a dividend. *It has not, however, been authoritatively settled whether an issue of rights to purchase at less than fair market value itself constitutes a dividend, or the dividend occurs on the actual purchase.* 391 U.S. at 90 n. 4 * * *. (Emphasis supplied).

This statement in *Gordon*, which as we have noted was quite similar on its facts to the instant case, withdraws any compulsion which may previously have arisen from the dictum in *Palmer* to prohibit treating the receipt of stock rights as the receipt of a dividend. * * * We think the better interpretation under the provisions of the 1954 Code and the regulations construing them is that, in the case of stock rights, where the subscription price is lower than fair market value, there is a dividend at the time of issuance (and receipt) of the rights measured by the fair market value of the rights at the time of issuance.

* * *

To say that a distribution of rights to buy portfolio shares cannot be a dividend because it results in no diminution of corporate assets is in any event not a complete legal argument. In the first place, a corporation that has granted an option on its property has in a real economic sense parted with a valuable asset—the right to dispose of that property to others and thus to realize any spread between its market value and the option price—not to mention the sacrifice of its interest in any future increment in value while the option is outstanding. But more to the point, there is no rule that a dividend must diminish corporate assets, although that is usually its effect. * * *

We believe that we are required under the provisions of the 1954 Code to move beyond the dictum of *Palmer* * * *. A fair reading of the decision of the Supreme Court in *Commissioner v. Gordon* requires that *Palmer* be limited to its facts, namely, a situation where there was no spread between option (subscription) price and market value on the date the corporation adopted its plan of distribution. When a substantial spread between market and option price prevails at all relevant times, we perceive no requirement to follow rigidly the *Palmer* dictum. Since options (warrants) are "property" as defined in the 1954 Code, they fall easily within the scope of the statutory scheme for the taxation of dividends. Such

¶ 12,180

an approach better reflects economic reality since an option incorporating a spread is a thing of value capable of being actively traded in public markets. * * * Hence, based on careful analysis of relevant authority and a perception of the economic realities, we believe that the step we take here is fully justified. The time has come to put *Palmer* in perspective, and we do so with full confidence that our conclusion meets the most exacting standards of deference to the precedents of the Supreme Court * * *.

630 F.2d at 1181–84.

[¶ 12,185]

H. CARRYOVER OF CORPORATE ATTRIBUTES

Section 381, discussed at ¶¶ 13,005 et seq., which deals with the carryover of corporate attributes in specified reorganization and liquidation transactions, does not apply to corporate divisions. Section 312(h)(1), however, provides that E & P of the distributing and controlled corporations must be allocated pursuant to regulations. In the case of a divisive "D" reorganization in which the distributing corporation transfers part of its assets constituting an active trade or business to a controlled corporation and then distributes the latter's stock in a distribution to which Section 355 applies, the E & P of the distributing corporation immediately before the transaction must be allocated between the distributing corporation and the controlled corporation in accordance with the rules prescribed in Reg. § 1.312–10(a). This regulation provides that in the case of a newly created controlled corporation, E & P are allocated between the controlled and distributing corporation in proportion to the relative fair market values of the assets of the controlled and distributing corporations immediately after the transaction. In other cases, the allocation is made in proportion to the net basis (i.e., basis less liabilities assumed or to which the assets are subject) of the assets transferred and assets retained or by some other appropriate method.

If a distribution or exchange to which Section 355 applies is not in pursuance of a plan of a "D" reorganization, the E & P of the distributing corporation must be decreased by the lesser of:

(i) the amount by which the E & P of the distributing corporation would have been decreased if it had transferred the stock of the controlled corporation to a new corporation in a "D" reorganization and immediately thereafter distributed the stock of such new corporation or

(ii) the net worth (i.e., the sum of the basis of all properties, plus cash, minus all liabilities) of the controlled corporation.

Reg. § 1.312–10(b).

If the E & P of the controlled corporation immediately before the transaction are less than the amount of the decrease in E & P of the distributing corporation (even if the controlled corporation has a deficit), the E & P of the controlled corporation, after the transaction, are increased in the amount of the decrease in the distributing corporation's E & P. In the converse situation, the E & P of the controlled corporation remain unchanged. Reg. § 1.312–10(b). Under no circumstances can any part of a deficit of a distributing corporation in a Section 355 transaction be allocated to the controlled corporation. Reg. § 1.312–10(c).

The treatment of net operating losses in a Section 355 division is discussed in the following ruling.

[¶ 12,190]

REVENUE RULING 77–133

1977–1 C.B. 96.

Advice has been requested concerning the Federal income tax treatment of a net operating loss (NOL) incurred prior to a corporate reorganization under the circumstances described below.

A and *B*, both individuals, owned all of the stock of *M*, a domestic corporation engaged in farming. Serious disputes arose between *A* and *B* regarding the operation of the farming business that endangered the continued operation of the business. As a result, *M* formed *S*, also a domestic corporation, by transferring 50 percent of its assets and liabilities to *S* in exchange for all of the *S* stock. *M*, immediately thereafter, distributed all of the *S* stock to *B* in exchange for all of *B*'s stock in *M*. The non pro rata distribution was undertaken for reasons germane to corporate business problems and was necessary for the future conduct of the farming business. This split-off transaction, the formation of *S* followed by the distribution and exchange between *M* and *B*, qualified as a reorganization under section 368(a)(1)(D) * * * and satisfied the requirements of section 355. Prior to the split-off, *M* had incurred a NOL that was available to be carried forward to years subsequent to the split-off.

The specific questions presented are whether the entire NOL is available to *M* after the split-off and, if not, whether any portion of the NOL carries over to *S* under section 381 * * *.

Section 381(a)(2) * * * states, in part, that in the case of the acquisition of assets of a corporation by another corporation in a transfer to which section 361 (relating to nonrecognition of gain or loss to corporations) applies, but only if the transfer is in connection with a reorganization described in section 368(a)(1)(D) that satisfies the requirements of section 354(b)(1)(A) and (B), the acquiring corporation shall succeed to and take into account as of the close of the day of distribution, the items described in section 381(c).

Section 381(c) * * * states, in part, that one of the items to be taken into account under section 381(a) is a NOL of the transferor corporation.

Section 354(b)(1)(A) * * * provides, in part, that no gain or loss will be recognized in connection with certain exchanges of stock or securities pursuant to a reorganization within the meaning of section 368(a)(1)(D) if the corporation to which the assets are transferred in the reorganization acquires substantially all of the assets of the transferor of such assets.

Rev. Rul. 56–373, 1956–2 C.B. 217, holds that under section 381(a)(2) * * * where a corporate reorganization, to which sections 361 and 368(a)(1)(D) apply, is a 'split up' within the purview of section 355, an unused NOL carryover of the transferor corporation may not be taken into account by any of the successor corporations.

The split-off in the present transaction is similar in many respects to the split-up described in Rev. Rul. 56–373. Both a split-up and a split-off are divisive reorganizations but a split-off does not involve the liquidation of the transferor corporation, as does a split-up.

In the present situation, substantially all of the assets of M, the transferor corporation, have not been transferred to S, so that the requirements of section 354(b)(1)(A) * * * and section 381(a)(2) have not been met. Furthermore, the Congressional committee reports underlying section 381, * * * S. Rep. No. 1622, 83rd Cong., 2nd Sess. 52 (1954), state that section 381 does not apply in the case of split-ups, spin-offs or other divisive reorganizations.

* * *

Accordingly, the entire NOL is available to M following the split-off.

* * *

[¶ 12,195]

Notes

1. If the transaction is a split-up in which the loss corporation transfers separate businesses to two newly organized subsidiaries and distributes the shares of each to different shareholders in liquidation, neither of the successor corporations can use the distributing corporation's NOL carryover because the transaction is not described in Section 354(b)(1) and is not eligible for attribute carryover under Section 381(a)(2). See Rev. Rul. 56–373, 1956–2 C.B. 217. Thus, survival of an NOL carryover (in the distributing corporation) in a divisive "D" reorga-

nization appears to turn on whether the transaction is effected as a spin-off or a split-off, on the one hand, or a split-up, on the other. Is this distinction appropriate on policy grounds?

2.   The limitations on NOL carryforwards contained in Section 382, discussed in Chapter 13, apply to NOL carryforwards that survive a spin-off or a split-off.

Chapter 13

CARRYOVER AND CARRYBACK
OF TAX ATTRIBUTES

[¶ 13,000]

A. OVERVIEW

An issue that arises in connection with any reorganization involving a transfer of assets of one corporation to another is what effect the transfer will have on the tax attributes of the transferor and the transferee corporations. The same issue arises when an 80 percent owned subsidiary is liquidated into its parent corporation under Section 332.

One important attribute of the transferor is the basis of its assets. The carryover of basis of transferred assets is governed by Sections 362(b) and 334(b) and has been previously discussed. See, e.g., ¶¶ 9035 and 8040. This Chapter considers the carryover of tax attributes of the acquired corporation (other than basis of its assets) and the limitations that apply to the use of certain carryovers of net operating and other losses and certain excess tax credits after a substantial change in the stock ownership of a loss corporation. These limitations are the latest in a series of statutory measures designed to discourage the acquisition of a corporation primarily to obtain the use of its loss carryovers and other favorable tax attributes.

[¶ 13,005]

B. INTRODUCTION TO SECTION 381

When two or more corporate entities are combined as a result of an acquisitive tax free reorganization or a Section 332 liquidation, to what extent are tax attributes of an absorbed corporation, such as operating losses, earnings and profits (E & P), depreciation methods, capital losses, and accounting methods, carried over to the surviving entity? These issues are the focus of Section 381, which applies to the acquisition of the assets of one corporation by another in a liquidation of a subsidiary into its corporate parent under Section 332 or in an "A," "C," or "F" reorganization. It also applies to a "D" or "G" reorganization if substantially all of the assets of the transferor are acquired and if the transferor distributes all of the assets it owns after the transfer. Section 381 does not apply to corporate divisions under Section 355. See ¶ 12,185.

If assets are acquired in a covered transaction, Section 381(a) provides that the acquiring corporation succeeds to, and takes into account, as of the close of the day of transfer, the 26 items specified in Section 381(c), subject to the limitations set forth in Sections 381 through 384. Two of these items, E & P (or deficits in E & P) and net operating losses, are discussed below.

What is the effect of Section 381 when a transaction or a tax attribute not covered in Section 381 is involved? Reg. § 1.381(a)–1(b)(3) states only (and somewhat enigmatically) that no inference is to be drawn as to whether the acquiring corporation succeeds to any such noncovered attribute. Thus, the Section 381(c) list is apparently not exhaustive.

Reg. § 1.381(a)–1(b)(2) provides that in an acquisition or liquidation only one corporation may be an acquiring corporation that can succeed to the tax attributes of an acquired corporation for purposes of Section 381. Generally, the acquiring corporation is the corporation that, pursuant to the plan of reorganization or liquidation, ultimately acquires all of the assets of the transferor corporation. However, if no single corporation ultimately acquires all of the assets transferred by the transferor, the corporation that initially acquires the assets will be the acquiring corporation under Section 381, even though it ultimately retains none of the assets. Thus, if X Corporation acquires all of the assets of Z Corporation in a "C" reorganization and thereafter transfers all the acquired assets to a wholly owned subsidiary, the subsidiary succeeds to the attributes of Z Corporation. If, however, X Corporation transfers only one half of the assets to its subsidiary, retaining the other half, or if X Corporation divides the acquired assets between two wholly owned subsidiaries, X Corporation would remain the acquiring corporation for purposes of Section 381. See Reg. § 1.381(a)–1(b)(2)(ii), Exs. 2–4.

There are some important operating rules under Section 381 relating to the closing of the taxable year of the transferor or distributing (liquidating) corporation involved in a transaction covered by Section 381. Section 381(b)(1) provides that, unless the transaction constitutes an "F" reorganization, the taxable year of the transferor corporation terminates on the date of the transfer or distribution. The transferor must therefore file a return for the taxable year that ends at that point. If the transaction is an "F" reorganization (whether or not it also falls within the definition of one of the other types of reorganization under

¶ **13,005**

Section 368(a)(1)), the acquiring corporation is treated as the transferor would have been treated if there had been no reorganization. Reg. § 1.381(b)–1(a)(2). Accordingly, the "F" reorganization does not terminate the corporation's taxable year, its tax attributes are retained, and post-reorganization losses can be carried back and deducted against pre-reorganization income. See ¶ 11,055.

The date of transfer or distribution is the date on which the transfer or distribution is completed. § 381(b)(2). However, if the transferor or distributor and acquiring corporations file the statements called for in Reg. § 1.381(b)–1(b)(3), the date of transfer or distribution is the day as of which (i) substantially all of the properties concerned have been transferred or distributed and (ii) the transferor or distributor has completed all operations other than liquidating activities.

[¶ 13,010]

C. EARNINGS AND PROFITS

The general rule with respect to carryovers of E & P is that the distributing (liquidating) or transferor corporation's E & P or deficits in E & P are deemed to have been received or incurred by the acquiring corporation as of the close of the date of the distribution or transfer. § 381(c)(2)(A). However, a deficit in E & P of the distributing, transferor, or acquiring corporation can be used only to offset E & P of the acquiring corporation accumulated after the date of the transfer. § 381(c)(2)(B). For this purpose, the E & P for the taxable year of the acquiring corporation in which the distribution or transfer occurs are allocated to the period after the date of the distribution or transfer in the proportion that the number of days in the taxable year after that date bears to the number of days in the taxable year. § 381(c)(2)(B).

[¶ 13,015]

Problems

1. X Corporation has substantial E & P. On June 30, X transfers substantially all of its assets to Y Corporation in exchange solely for the latter's voting stock in a "C" reorganization. Both corporations have calendar year tax accounting periods. X is then liquidated. Are X's E & P carried over to Y? When does X's taxable year end? What if the transaction also constitutes an "F" reorganization?

2. X Corporation had a deficit in E & P on September 30 of year 1 of $400,000. Y Corporation had current E & P of $400,000 for that full year and current E & P of $250,000 for the next full year. Effective September 30 of year 1, X is merged into Y in a statutory merger with Y as the survivor. To what extent can the carryover of X's E & P deficit be

used to offset E & P of Y in years 1 and 2 assuming that both corporations have calendar year tax accounting periods?

3. X Corporation has assets with a fair market value of $800,000 and an adjusted basis of $200,000 and current and accumulated E & P of $600,000 as of December 31 of year 1. Suppose X adopts a plan of liquidation and thereafter transfers on December 31 of year 1 all its assets and liabilities to Y Corporation, an unrelated corporation with no current or accumulated E & P. Y issues in exchange Y voting stock and enough cash so that, when added to the liabilities assumed by Y, the transfer will not qualify as a "C" reorganization. After the transfer, X owns 75 percent of the only class of outstanding Y stock. X liquidates and three months later, Y makes a distribution of $500,000 to its shareholders. What are the tax consequences of this distribution by Y?

[¶ 13,020]

D.   NET OPERATING LOSS CARRYOVERS

The one attribute of the acquired corporation that has been the focus of most tax minimization planning and has generated the greatest volume of controversy and legislative activity over the years has been the net operating loss (NOL). In general, NOLs may, under current law, be carried back to the two (and in some cases three) tax years preceding the loss year and forward to as many as 20 years under Section 172(b)(1)(A).[1] Historically, corporations with sizeable operating losses have proved tempting acquisition targets for profitable corporations. Especially during the period before the enactment of the 1954 Code, but also to a somewhat diminished extent thereafter, a large amount of trafficking in loss corporations occurred. A major, if not the principal, purpose of the acquisition of the loss corporation was often to use the loss carryover to shelter post-acquisition earnings of the acquiring corporation from tax.

One potentially important weapon against tax-motivated acquisitions of loss corporations was Section 269, which was enacted in 1943 primarily to discourage the acquisition of corporate entities with little of value other than attractive tax attributes. Under Section 269, the IRS is authorized to disallow a deduction, credit, or other allowance if the principal purpose of certain acquisitions was evasion or avoidance of federal income tax by securing the benefit of such deduction, credit, or other benefit.

In 1954, however, Congress concluded that Section 269 had proved to be an inadequate weapon, primarily because of the necessity of

---

1. Under legislation enacted in 2002, NOLs arising in tax years ending in 2001 and 2002 may be carried back five years. § 172(b)(1)(h). Additionally, NOLs may not be used to offset domestic production gross receipts for purposes of Section 199. Notice 2005–14, 2005–1 C.B. 498.

proving that the *principal* purpose of the acquisition was tax avoidance. In an effort to plug the gap more effectively, Congress enacted Section 382. This provision also proved to be an inadequate deterrent to NOL trafficking abuses and it was amended in 1976. However, because of widespread dissatisfaction with the changes, their effective date was postponed repeatedly and the amendments were eventually repealed retroactively and never came into effect. Instead, the provisions of Section 382 now in effect were enacted in the Tax Reform Act of 1986.

[¶ 13,025]

1. OUTLINE OF SECTION 382

Under Section 382, if a specifically defined ownership change in a corporation (called here "a Section 382 ownership change") occurs, two potential limitations on the use of an existing NOL carryover come into play. If the first of these limitations applies, the pre-ownership change NOL carryover is eliminated altogether. Under the second, an annual limit (the Section 382 limitation) is imposed on the amount of a pre-ownership change NOL carryover that may be used by the corporation that succeeds to it. A Section 382 ownership change is, broadly speaking, a change or changes in the ownership of loss corporation stock totaling more than 50 percentage points occurring over a three-year period.

Following a Section 382 ownership change, the Section 382 limitation of the loss corporation or a successor corporation is generally reduced to zero for any post-change year unless a continuity of business enterprise requirement is satisfied for two calendar years after the ownership change. § 382(c). This is similar to the requirement that generally must be met if an acquisition transaction is to qualify as a tax-free reorganization. See ¶¶ 9105 & 10,060. The continuity of business enterprise requirement under Section 382(c) is met if the loss corporation (or a successor corporation) either (i) continues a significant historic line of the loss corporation's business or (ii) uses a significant portion of the loss corporation's historic business assets in a business (not necessarily the same as the loss corporation's historic business).[2]

Assuming that the continuity of business enterprise test is met, the amount of a loss corporation's NOL carryovers (pre-ownership change losses), including built-in losses (i.e., losses economically accrued but not yet recognized), is not reduced. However, the maximum amount of taxable income that can be offset by those NOL carryovers (or by built-in losses when recognized) in years ending after the Section 382 ownership change is subject to an annual limitation. § 382(a). The annual Section 382 limitation equals (i) the value of the stock of the loss corporation immediately before the Section 382 ownership change multiplied by (ii) a

---

2. Even if the loss corporation fails the continuity of business enterprise test, it can use NOL carryovers and recognized built-in losses to offset recognized built-in gains or gains resulting from a Section 338 election. § 382(c)(2).

prescribed interest rate fixed at the time of the ownership change equal to a long-term tax-exempt bond rate. § 382(b)(1). The excess of the NOL carryover over the Section 382 limitation for a given taxable year may be carried forward until the carryover expires.

The rationale of the 1986 changes is that the outgoing shareholders who owned the stock when the corporation's losses were incurred should be permitted to enjoy the economic benefit of those losses by in effect selling them to purchasers. The purchasers are, in turn, entitled to use those losses as benefits flowing from their investment but only at a rate equal to the long-term tax-exempt bond rate applied to the value of the acquired corporation. Thus, the use of losses by the loss corporation or the successor corporation is not generally precluded, but the rate at which the losses can be used is limited. Section 383 imposes limitations on capital loss carryovers and certain excess tax credit carryovers correlative to those imposed under Section 382.

For purposes of determining the value of the stock of the loss corporation at the time of a Section 382 ownership change, if at least one third of the loss corporation's assets consist of nonbusiness assets held for investment, the value of the loss corporation is reduced by the excess (if any) of the value of the nonbusiness assets of the loss corporation over the nonbusiness asset share of the corporation's debt. § 382(l)(4).

The Section 382 limitation applies to built-in losses that (i) were economically accrued at the time of a Section 382 ownership change and (ii) are recognized within five years after the ownership change. This limitation recognizes that built-in losses need only to be recognized to become part of an operating loss. Under a parallel rule, the Section 382 limitation is increased by the amount of built-in gains recognized within five years of the ownership change and by the amount of gain resulting from a Section 338 election. § 382(h). See ¶ 13,080.

[¶ 13,030]

STAFF OF JOINT COMM. ON TAX'N GENERAL EXPLANATION OF THE TAX REFORM ACT OF 1986

100th Cong., 1st Sess., 294–96 (1987).

[The amendments to Section 382 that were enacted in 1976 but never came into effect] reflect the view that the relationship of one year's loss to another year's income should be largely a function of whether and how much the stock ownership changed in the interim, while the *Libson Shops* [Libson Shops, Inc. v. Koehler, 353 U.S. 382 (1957)] business continuation rule measures the relationship according to whether the loss and the income were generated by the same business. The [1986] Act acknowledges the merit in both approaches, while

¶ **13,030**

seeking to avoid the economic distortions and administrative problems that a strict application of either approach would entail.

A limitation based strictly on ownership would create a tax bias against sales of corporate businesses, and could prevent sales that would increase economic efficiency. For example, if a prospective buyer could increase the income from a corporate business to a moderate extent, but not enough to overcome the loss of all carryovers, no sale would take place because the business would be worth more to the less-efficient current owner than the prospective buyer would reasonably pay. A strict ownership limitation also would distort the measurement of taxable income generated by capital assets purchased before the corporation was acquired, if the tax deductions for capital costs economically allocable to post-acquisition years were accelerated into pre-acquisition years, creating carryovers that would be lost as a result of the acquisition.

Strict application of a business continuation rule would also be undesirable, because it would discourage efforts to rehabilitate troubled businesses. Such a rule would create an incentive to maintain obsolete and inefficient business practices if the needed changes would create the risk of discontinuing the old business for tax purposes, thus losing the benefit of the carryovers.

Permitting the carryover of all losses following an acquisition, as is permitted under the 1954 Code if the loss business is continued following a purchase, provides an improper matching of income and loss. Income generated under different corporate owners, from capital over and above the capital used in the loss business, is related to a pre-acquisition loss only in the formal sense that it is housed in the same corporate entity. Furthermore, the ability to use acquired losses against such unrelated income creates a tax bias in favor of acquisitions. For example, a prospective buyer of a loss corporation might be a less efficient operator of the business than the current owner, but the ability to use acquired losses could make the loss corporation more valuable to the less efficient user and thereby encourage a sale.

Reflecting the policies described above, the Act addresses three general concerns: (1) the approach of prior law (viz, the disallowance or reduction of NOL and other carryforwards), which is criticized as being too harsh where there are continuing loss-corporation shareholders, and ineffective to the extent that NOL carryforwards may be available for use without limitation after substantial ownership changes, (2) the discontinuities in the prior law treatment of taxable purchases and tax-free reorganizations, and (3) defects in the prior law rules that presented opportunities for tax avoidance.

GENERAL APPROACH

After reviewing various options for identifying events that present the opportunity for a tax benefit transfer (*e.g.,* changes in a loss corporation's business), it was concluded that changes in a loss corporation's stock ownership continue to be the best indicator of a potentially abusive transaction. Under the Act, the special limitations generally apply when shareholders who bore the economic burden of a corporation's NOLs no longer hold a controlling interest in the corporation. In such a case, the possibility arises that new shareholders will contribute income-producing assets (or divert income opportunities) to the loss corporation, and the corporation will obtain greater utilization of carryforwards than it could have had there been no change in ownership.

To address the concerns described above, the Act adopts the following approach: After a substantial ownership change, rather than reducing the NOL carryforward itself, the earnings against which an NOL carryforward can be deducted are limited. This general approach has received wide acceptance among tax scholars and practitioners. This "limitation on earnings" approach is intended to permit the survival of NOL carryforwards after an acquisition, while limiting the ability to utilize the carryforwards against unrelated income.

The limitation on earnings approach is intended to approximate the results that would occur if a loss corporation's assets were combined with those of a profitable corporation in a partnership. This treatment can be justified on the ground that the option of contributing assets to a partnership is available to a loss corporation. In such a case, only the loss corporation's share of the partnership's income could be offset by the corporation's NOL carryforward. Presumably, except in the case of tax-motivated partnership agreements, the loss corporation's share of the partnership's income would be limited to earnings generated by the assets contributed by the loss corporation.

For purposes of determining the income attributable to a loss corporation's assets, the Act prescribes an objective rate of return on the value of the corporation's equity. Consideration was given to the arguments made in favor of computing the prescribed rate of return by reference to the gross value of a loss corporation's assets, without regard to outstanding debt. It was concluded that it would be inappropriate to permit the use of NOL carryforwards to shelter earnings that are used (or would be used in the absence of an acquisition) to service a loss corporation's debt. The effect of taking a loss corporation's gross value into account would be to accelerate the rate at which NOL carryforwards would be used had there been no change in ownership, because interest paid on indebtedness is deductible in its own right (thereby deferring the use of corresponding amount of NOLs). There is a fundamental difference between debt capitalization and equity capitalization: true debt represents a claim against a loss corporation's assets.

ANNUAL LIMITATION

The annual limitation on the use of pre-acquisition NOL carryforwards is the product of the prescribed [long-term federal bond] rate and

¶ 13,030

the value of loss corporation's equity immediately before a prescribed ownership change. The average yield for long-term marketable obligations of the U.S. government was selected as the measure of a loss corporation's expected return on its assets.

The rate prescribed by the Act is higher than the average rate at which loss corporations actually absorb NOL carryforwards. Indeed, many loss corporations continue to experience NOLs, thereby increasing—rather than absorbing—NOL carryforwards. On the other hand, the adoption of the average absorption rate may be too restrictive for loss corporations that out-perform the average. Therefore, it would be inappropriate to set a rate at the lowest rate that is theoretically justified. The use of the long-term rate for Federal obligations was justified as a reasonable risk-free rate of return a loss corporation could obtain in the absence of a change in ownership.

* * *

[¶ 13,035]

Note

The long-term interest rate for federal obligations is actually adjusted downward to a long-term tax-exempt rate. § 382(f). According to the Conference Report this adjustment was based on the following considerations:

> The use of a rate lower than the long-term Federal rate is necessary to ensure that the value of NOL carryforwards to the buying corporation is not more than their value to the loss corporation. Otherwise there would be a tax incentive for acquiring loss corporations. If the loss corporation were to sell its assets and invest in long-term Treasury obligations, it could absorb its NOL carryforwards at a rate equal to the yield on long-term government obligations. Since the price paid by the buyer is larger than the value of the loss company's assets (because the value of NOL carryforwards are taken into account), applying the long-term Treasury rate to the purchase price would result in faster utilization of NOL carryforwards by the buying corporation. * * *

H.R. Conf. Rep. No. 841, 99th Cong., 2d Sess. II–188 (1986). The long-term tax-exempt bond rate is published monthly by the Treasury.

[¶ 13,040]

2. TRIGGERING EVENT UNDER SECTION 382

The triggering event that brings into play the limits on NOL carryforwards under Section 382 is referred to in this Chapter as "a Section 382 ownership change." Such a change is deemed to occur if the percentage of the stock of the loss corporation owned by one or more five-percent shareholders exceeds by more than 50 percentage points the lowest total percentage holdings of those shareholders at any time during the "testing period" (generally three years). § 382(g). All changes in stock ownership during the testing period are counted even if they are isolated events and not part of a plan to acquire the loss corporation. In determining whether a Section 382 ownership change has occurred, any transaction that changes the percentage of stock owned by five-percent shareholders is counted, however that change is effected. Thus, transactions that may be counted include, in addition to purchases of stock by one shareholder from another, tax-free reorganizations or other corporate restructurings and redemptions or issuances of stock.

Section 382(g) identifies two types of ownership changes. The first is an owner shift that affects the percentage of stock owned by any five-percent shareholder, and the second is an "equity structure shift," which encompasses all reorganizations except divisive "D," "F," and "G" reorganizations. See Temp. Reg. § 1.382–2T(e)(1) and (2). The two categories overlap, however (e.g., in the case of a recapitalization), and whether a transaction falls in one or the other seems to have no significance in connection with the operation of the Section 382 rules. Because changes in stock ownership are measured in percentage terms, a pro rata redemption, exchange, or distribution of stock would not constitute or form part of a Section 382 ownership change.

Five percent shareholder. Changes in stock ownership are measured by aggregating increases in the ownership of stock by five-percent shareholders (i.e., owners of five percent or more of the value of the loss corporation's stock). § 382(g)(1). However, all owners of less than five-percent are aggregated and treated as a single five-percent shareholder (called a "public group"). § 382(g)(4)(A). Thus, any sale of stock by a five-percent shareholder to other shareholders will be counted as an increase in stock ownership by a five-percent shareholder regardless of the size of the holdings of the purchasing shareholders. The only sales that will not be counted are sales by one less than five percent shareholder to another less than five percent shareholder.

Public shareholders in acquisitive reorganizations. A tax-free reorganization in which a publicly owned loss corporation (Loss Corporation) is combined with a publicly held profitable corporation (Profit Corporation) can result in an ownership change because of the increase in the ownership of the stock of Loss Corporation by the public shareholders of Profit Corporation.

Stock offerings. In the case of a public offering of shares of a corporation that has public shareholders before the offering, the pre-offering group of public shareholders is segregated from the new group of public shareholders, with each group being treated as a different public group. As a result, the increase in ownership by the new public group would be counted in full in determining whether an ownership change has occurred.

Recapitalizations and redemptions. Different groups of public shareholders are also segregated in connection with recapitalizations and redemptions for cash.

Multiple transactions. In the case of open market purchases of stock following a tax-free reorganization (equity structure shift) or other transaction that results in the creation of two public groups, Section 382 provides that those purchases are deemed to have been made from each public group on a proportionate basis unless the actual source can be shown. § 382(g)(4)(B)(ii).

[¶ 13,045]

3. ATTRIBUTION RULES

Ultimate beneficial ownership. In determining whether five-percent shareholders have increased their ownership of Loss Corporation stock, the ownership attribution rules of Section 318(a) apply, subject to a number of exceptions. For example, under Section 381(a)(2)(C), stock owned by a corporation is attributed proportionately to all shareholders however small their interest. § 382(*l*)(3)(A). The effect of these rules is to ensure that only changes in ultimate beneficial ownership of stock are counted. For example, if Profit Corporation owns all of the stock of Loss Corporation and distributes the Loss Corporation stock pro rata to its shareholders, no Section 382 ownership change occurs because, for purposes of Section 382, shareholders of Profit Corporation are deemed to have held the Loss Corporation stock even before the distribution. There is also no Section 382 ownership change if Loss Corporation is owned equally by five shareholders and a holding company structure for Loss Corporation is adopted through the contribution of all of the stock of Loss Corporation to a newly organized holding company in exchange for the stock of the latter. Under the attribution rules, the former Loss Corporation shareholders are deemed to continue to own Loss Corporation stock held by the holding company.

Options and contingent payouts. Options (including warrants, convertible debt, contingent purchase price arrangements, puts, stock subject to a risk of forfeiture, and contracts to acquire stock) are generally treated as exercised if that treatment would result in a Section 382 ownership change. § 382(*l*)(3)(A)(iv) and (v). Inconsistent assumptions may apply to different options if that would result in a Section 382 ownership change. If an option is considered to have been exercised for purposes of determining whether a Section 382 ownership change has occurred, then an eventual actual exercise is disregarded. If a Section 382 limitation has been applied because an option was assumed to have been exercised and the option in fact expires unexercised, Loss Corporation may file an amended return for the relevant years, subject to the applicable statute of limitation.

[¶ 13,050]

4. "STOCK"

For purposes of determining whether the required change in ownership of stock has occurred, all stock, whether common or preferred, is treated as "stock" except for certain nonvoting, nonconvertible, nonparticipating preferred stock that is issued with a reasonable redemption premium. § 382(k)(6).

[¶ 13,055]

5. TESTING PERIOD

Generally, the testing period is a rolling three calendar year period. § 382(i). However, the testing period may be shorter than three years in two circumstances. First, following any Section 382 ownership change, the testing period for determining whether a *second* Section 382 ownership change has occurred starts on the day after the day on which the prior ownership change occurred. § 382(i)(2). Second, the testing period does not start before the earlier of the first day of the first taxable year in which the NOL carryovers (or built-in losses) that are subject to the Section 382 limitation arose or the taxable year in which the transaction being tested occurs. § 382(i)(3).

[¶ 13,060]

6. EFFECT OF A SECTION 382 OWNERSHIP CHANGE

Section 382 uses the term "Loss Corporation" to denote the corporation that succeeds to the NOL carryover and the term "Old Loss Corporation" to denote the corporation that generated the loss before the Section 382 ownership change in its stock. § 382(k)(1) and (2). In the event that Section 382 is triggered as a result of a Section 382 ownership change, then, for each taxable year ending after the date of such ownership change, the amount of Loss Corporation's taxable income that can be offset by the Old Loss Corporation's pre-change NOL carryovers is limited to the Section 382 limitation for that year.

The Section 382 limitation for any taxable year generally is an amount equal to the product of multiplying (i) the value of the stock of the Old Loss Corporation immediately before the ownership change by (ii) a fixed long-term tax-exempt bond rate determined at the time of the ownership change. See ¶ 13,035. The Section 382 limitation for any taxable year is increased by an excess Section 382 limitation from prior years. This excess is the amount, if any, by which the Section 382 limitation in a prior taxable year exceeded the amount of taxable income in that year that was offset by pre-Section 382 ownership change losses. § 382(b)(2).

[¶ 13,065]

7. VALUE OF STOCK OF OLD LOSS CORPORATION

The value of the stock of the Old Loss Corporation is generally the fair market value of its stock immediately before the Section 382 ownership change. § 382(e)(1). This includes the value of preferred stock not treated as stock for purposes of determining whether an ownership change has occurred. However, if a redemption or other corporate contraction by the Old Loss Corporation occurs in connection with an ownership change (either before or after the change), the value of the Old Loss Corporation is determined after taking into account the redemption or contraction. § 382(e)(2).

Under a special "anti-stuffing" rule, a capital contribution is not taken into account in determining the value of the Old Loss Corporation if the contribution is made to the Old Loss Corporation as part of a plan, a principal purpose of which is the avoidance of the effects of Section 382. § 382(*l*)(1). In the absence of such a rule there would be an obvious incentive to increase the value of the Old Loss Corporation by making contributions to its capital.

Another special rule comes into play if at least one third (by fair market value) of the Old Loss Corporation's gross assets consists of nonbusiness assets held for investment (for example, cash or marketable securities not held in connection with an active business). In this case, the Old Loss Corporation's value is reduced by the excess of the value of those nonbusiness assets over the portion of the Old Loss Corporation's indebtedness attributable to those assets (determined on the basis of the ratio of the fair market value of nonbusiness assets to the fair market value of all assets). § 382(*l*)(4)(D). Nonbusiness assets owned by a subsidiary that is at least 50 percent owned by the Old Loss Corporation are not treated in full as nonbusiness assets. Instead, the Old Loss Corporation is deemed to own its ratable share of the subsidiary's nonbusiness assets. § 382(*l*)(4)(E).

The following opinion involves the application of several of these rules in the context of a case where the new owner of a loss corporation sold an old loss corporation asset after the ownership change, but pursuant to an agreement entered into prior to the ownership change.

[¶ 13,070]

BERRY PETROLEUM CO. v. COMMISSIONER

United States Tax Court, 1995.
104 T.C. 584.

BEGHE, JUDGE: * * *.

* * *

III. ISSUE 3: EFFECTS OF SECTION 382 ON USEFULNESS
OF NET OPERATING LOSS CARRYOVERS

A. *Findings of Fact*

* * *

At all relevant times, petitioner and its subsidiaries were engaged in the exploration, development, production, and sale of oil and natural gas, including "heavy oil". "Heavy oil" has such high viscosity and low specific gravity that it will not flow at normal temperatures. Various capital-intensive "enhancement" techniques are required to extract heavy oil from the ground and to transport it to the refinery.

During the years 1981 through 1988, Tosco Corp. (Tosco) was engaged primarily in the business of refining petroleum. During 1981, Tosco organized Tosco Enhanced Oil Recovery Corp. (Teorco) to acquire and operate heavy-oil properties. By 1987, Teorco had become a relatively low-cost producer of heavy oil, but it was still only marginally profitable and would have required capital contributions from Tosco of at least $2 million per year over the next 3 years. Although the market for oil-producing properties was weak in 1987, Tosco decided to get out of its heavy-oil business, which then consisted primarily of Teorco's leasehold interests in four heavy-oil properties in the San Joaquin Valley of California (Placerita, McKittrick, Edison Grove, and Jasmin). Of these interests, only Placerita had generated significant gross receipts, and Tosco viewed McKittrick, Edison Grove, and Jasmin as liabilities.

Tenneco Oil Co. (Tenneco), a substantial operator of heavy-oil projects, owned most of the leasehold interests surrounding Placerita. Prior to November 1987, Tenneco offered to purchase Placerita from Teorco for $7.5 million. Tosco rejected this offer because it did not wish to sell Teorco's properties separately. Tosco did not wish to retain responsibility for any large, undiscovered contingent liabilities, nor did it wish to sell Teorco's "crown jewel"—Placerita—and get stuck with the "dogs". Tosco offered to sell Tenneco the Teorco stock, but Tenneco only wanted Placerita. Negotiations between Tosco and Tenneco ended prior to November 1987.

After surveying other heavy-oil producers to determine whether they were interested in purchasing Teorco, Tosco formulated a marketing

¶ 13,070

plan to sell Teorco. In addition to making many telephone calls to potential buyers, Tosco circulated a letter dated November 20, 1987, announcing that Teorco's business operations did not fit into Tosco's long-term business plan and that Tosco was prepared to sell Teorco for an acceptable price. * * *

By a letter dated December 11, 1987, Tosco announced the procedure for submitting bids for the Teorco stock. * * *

Even before petitioner received Tosco's November 20 letter, petitioner and Tenneco had informally discussed their mutual interests in Teorco. After petitioner received Tosco's December 11 letter, petitioner and Tenneco engaged in formal discussions. As a result, petitioner and Tenneco entered a letter agreement dated January 13, 1988, in which they agreed to act jointly in the bidding for Teorco. Pursuant to that letter agreement, petitioner and Tenneco entered an agreement dated February 18, 1988 (the acquisition agreement), in which petitioner agreed to sell Placerita to Tenneco if petitioner should be the successful bidder for Teorco. Although the agreement was between Tenneco and petitioner, it specifically identified Bush as a wholly owned subsidiary of petitioner, and described Bush's role in the acquisition.

The acquisition agreement provided that petitioner, through Bush, would submit a timely offer of $6.5 million for 100 percent of the stock of Teorco, would submit only offers that had been reviewed by Tenneco, would inform Tenneco of any communications or negotiations with Tosco, and, if Bush were the successful bidder, would cause Teorco to assign Placerita to Tenneco immediately after the closing of petitioner's acquisition of Teorco. As consideration for Teorco's assignment of Placerita, Tenneco agreed to pay $1,250,000 more than the final adjusted purchase price for all the Teorco stock, but not more than $7,750,000, and to assume all financial, environmental, and contractual obligations related to Placerita. The acquisition agreement was subject to Tenneco's right to review the terms and provisions of the stock purchase agreement between petitioner and Tosco.

By letter dated February 18, 1988 (the Bush offer), Bush offered to purchase 100 percent of the stock of Teorco for $6.5 million in cash, payable at closing. * * *

Throughout the process of acquiring Teorco, petitioner's board discussed the advantages of acquiring the stock of Teorco under the assumption that Bush would acquire the assets of Teorco. When Bush made its offer to purchase the Teorco stock from Tosco, petitioner and Bush intended to merge Teorco and Bush within a year of acquisition.

* * *

Tosco considered $6.5 million to be an adequate price, and by letter dated February 26, 1988, Tosco accepted the Bush offer, subject to minor modifications and amendments. Bush and Tosco executed a stock purchase agreement, stated to be effective at midnight April 30, 1988 (the stock agreement). * * *

Bush and Tenneco then executed an agreement, stated to be effective at 7 a.m., May 1, 1988, for the sale of Placerita to Tenneco (Placerita agreement). * * *

* * *

Bush and Tosco closed the Teorco stock purchase pursuant to the stock agreement. Immediately upon closing, Bush caused Teorco to change its name to C.J. Co. C.J. Co. and Tenneco then closed the Placerita sale pursuant to the Placerita agreement. Neither Tosco nor Teorco was a party to the Placerita agreement or any other agreement for the sale of Placerita to Tenneco.

At the time of Teorco's ownership change, its principal business was the acquisition, development, and holding of heavy-oil properties in California, and the production and sale of heavy oil from those properties.

Immediately prior to the stock closing on April 30, 1988, the gross values of Teorco's assets were as follows:

Placerita	$ 7,750,000
McKittrick (50–percent interest)	2,000,000
Jasmin	250,000
Jasmin equipment	385,000
Edison Grove (35–percent interest)	200,000
Jasmin note receivable	1,588,155
Accounts receivable	289,278
Inventory	165,787
Prepaid expenses	12,274
Total gross asset value	12,640,494

Known liabilities totaled $535,569, and after the transfer of stock, C.J. Co. reserved an additional $200,000 for unknown contingencies.

* * *

Immediately after Bush purchased Teorco, C.J. Co. had net operating loss carryovers of $8,109,272 and investment tax credit carryovers of $336,169, both arising in pre-acquisition years. In calculating the amount of C.J. Co.'s 1988 and 1989 taxable income that could be offset by those net operating loss carryovers, petitioner used $6.5 million as the value of Teorco. Petitioner's Federal consolidated income tax returns showed a $262,882 net operating loss deduction for 1988 and a $485,550 net operating loss deduction for 1989.

Pursuant to section 1.382–2T(a)(2)(ii) and (h)(4)(vi)(B), Temporary Income Tax Regs., * * * petitioner attached a disclosure statement to its 1988 income tax return, electing to treat April 30, 1988, as the date of the ownership change. Bush did not file a section 338 election under section 1.338–1T, Temporary Income Tax Regs. [Reg. § 1.338–1 of current law] * * * to treat the purchase of Teorco stock as a purchase of Teorco's assets.

For Federal income tax purposes, the basis of Placerita in the hands of C.J. Co. was unaffected by the ownership change, and petitioner's 1988 Federal consolidated income tax return showed a $79,068 gain from the sale of Placerita to Tenneco. * * *

On December 1, 1988, C.J. Co. advanced Bush $1 million, and, on March 6, 1989, C.J. Co. advanced Bush $2,625,946. Both advances were evidenced by demand notes bearing interest at the Wells Fargo Bank's prime rate, plus 1 percent. Bush made monthly interest payments on these notes through May 22, 1989.

On March 23, 1988, a court had ruled that Bush was in default on its $2,675,577 note payable to ABEG, which petitioner had guaranteed as part of its purchase of 80 percent of the stock of Norris (now Bush) from ABEG. In March 1989, Bush paid its note to ABEG (less a $50,000 discount) using the proceeds of the March 6 advance from C.J. Co.

Early in 1988, petitioner had realized that, if the major oil companies refused to buy or transport the heavy oil it was producing, it would not be able to transport its heavy oil out of the San Joaquin Valley. Although C.J. Co. did not currently need a blending facility, C.J. Co. expected that it would eventually need to blend and transport oil from McKittrick, and petitioner believed that it needed a blending facility to secure reliable transportation of oil from its other properties. In an attempt to solve these problems, petitioner negotiated with Enron to purchase a one-half interest in a blending facility in the San Joaquin Valley. Negotiations seemed to go well, and, as of May 19, 1989, C.J. Co. planned to purchase a one-half interest in the Enron blending facility on July 1, 1989.

Negotiations for purchase of an interest in the Enron blending facility were ultimately unsuccessful, and the planned purchase did not occur. However, in May 1989, in anticipation of that purchase, Bush distributed a dividend to petitioner by transferring all its stock in C.J. Co. to petitioner. C.J. Co. thereupon changed its name to Berry Oil Trading & Transportation Co. (for simplicity, we continue to refer to the acquired corporation as C.J. Co.). The shift of C.J. Co. to first-tier subsidiary of petitioner was intended to facilitate intercompany sales between petitioner and C.J. Co. after the purchase of the blending facility, and to allow C.J. Co. to pay dividends directly to petitioner if C.J. Co. should become more profitable. Immediately prior to Bush's distribution to petitioner, Bush caused C.J. Co. formally to distribute a $3,625,946 dividend to Bush by canceling the prior advances to Bush in that amount. The record contains no stated explanation of the reason for the dividend from C.J. Co. to Bush.

After the failure of petitioner's efforts to have C.J. Co. purchase an interest in a blending facility, petitioner decided to design and build a blending facility. On November 14, 1989, C.J. Co. and Shoreline Energy Corp. entered a joint venture to build and operate a blending facility in the San Joaquin Valley, which opened in May 1990.

Soon after Bush had purchased Teorco, C.J. Co. moved a steam generator, tanks, a water treatment facility, and insulated tubing from Jasmin to one of petitioner's properties. Petitioner did not pay C.J. Co. for the use of that equipment, and eventually C.J. Co. transferred ownership of the equipment to petitioner without consideration.

Soon after Bush had purchased Teorco, C.J. Co. also purchased its co-owner's 65–percent interest in Edison Grove, and thereafter upgraded the property and continued to produce oil from the property. On September 1, 1989, C.J. Co. sold Edison Grove, except "deep rights", to an unrelated party for $200,000. On September 6, 1989, C.J. Co. sold Jasmin, except one lease, to an unrelated party for $250,000. Between May 1, 1987, and September 6, 1988, C.J. Co. paid $123,693 for capital acquisitions, improvements, and selling expenses relating to Edison Grove and Jasmin.

When Bush acquired Teorco, Chevron USA, Inc. (Chevron), was the operator of McKittrick and was producing only enough oil therefrom to hold the lease. C.J. Co. wanted Chevron to develop McKittrick fully, but Chevron refused to do so. Because C.J. Co. was unhappy with the way Chevron was operating McKittrick, C.J. Co. offered to sell its interest in McKittrick to Chevron, or to buy Chevron's interest. As a result, in October 1991, C.J. Co. purchased Chevron's 50–percent interest in McKittrick for an amount not disclosed in the record. After C.J. Co. acquired Chevron's interest in McKittrick, C.J. Co. spent approximately $4 million drilling new wells, reworking existing wells, and installing new fixtures and equipment.

On December 31, 1988 and 1989, C.J. Co. held the remaining proceeds of the sale of Placerita in short-term commercial notes and short-term Government securities, which totaled $7,035,636 and $5,732,269, respectively. The reduction between December 1988 and 1989 is attributable primarily to C.J. Co.'s $2,625,946 advance to Bush, which was used by Bush to pay its note to ABEG. On December 31, 1987, 1988, and 1989, Bush's cash balances were $10,709,990, $2,782,234, and ($32,939), respectively. The reduction between December 1987 and 1988 is attributable primarily to Bush's payment of $6.5 million to purchase the Teorco stock. On December 31, 1987, 1988, and 1989, petitioner's consolidated cash and cash equivalents totaled $26,989,000, $25,618,000, and $49,505,000, respectively.

Petitioner never abandoned its intent to merge Teorco out of existence as a separate entity. At the end of 1991, C.J. Co. was merged into petitioner.

* * *

¶ **13,070**

B.   Opinion

1.   Background

* * *

Petitioner made two great deals, arranging to have Bush purchase Teorco and sell Placerita * * *. Those deals continued to play out favorably as C.J. Co. developed its three other properties, sold the two minor properties (Jasmin and Edison Grove), and then integrated the remaining, fully developed property (McKittrick) into petitioner's preexisting heavy-oil business.

Our task is to decide how section 382 affects petitioner's ability to use Teorco's net operating loss carryovers on its consolidated returns. What we have to work with is the most recent version of a complex, in parts ambiguous, statute, its legislative history, and the public comments, discussion, and debate that preceded its enactment, but no interpretative regulations. Cf. sec. 1.382–2T, Temporary Income Tax Regs. * * * (interpreting the ownership change provisions).

2.   Section 382—Net Operating Loss Carryovers Generally

Section 382 in its present form is the most recent statutory expression of a long-standing congressional perception that trafficking in loss carryovers must be regulated to prevent abuse. Section 382 of the 1954 Code subjected net operating loss carryovers to reduction or elimination under separate rules, whose application depended on whether the transfer of ownership was a purchase or a reorganization. In 1976, section 382 was amended in an effort to coordinate the treatment of purchases and reorganizations and to close perceived loopholes in the types of transactions that would trigger the limitations. Congress postponed the effective date of the 1976 amendments four times before repealing them retroactively; they never became operative, and were replaced with the amendments to section 382 in effect during the years in issue.

Section 382(a), as amended by the Tax Reform Act of 1986, * * * provides that, after certain significant changes in corporate ownership, the amount of income of a "new loss corporation" that may be offset by loss carryovers arising prior to the ownership change shall not exceed the "section 382 limitation". The section 382 limitation is equal to the "value of the old loss corporation" multiplied by the long-term tax exempt rate (plus certain gains and any excess section 382 limitation from the prior year). Sec. 382(b).

The section 382 limitation does not directly limit the amount of the loss carryovers of an old loss corporation. It limits only their continuing usefulness. * * * The section 382 limitation is intended to approximate the annual income that the business capital of the old loss corporation would have generated, and thereby prevent the new loss corporation from using the loss carryovers faster than the old loss corporation could have used them in the absence of a change in ownership. * * *

* * * Congress was concerned that the mechanical rules of section 382(b) would provide opportunities to structure transactions that would literally satisfy those rules but be inconsistent with their spirit and intent. * * * To address those concerns, section 382 includes a series of somewhat overlapping responses, which impose obstacles to a new loss corporation's use of the old loss corporation's net operating loss carryovers in various situations. See, e.g., sec. 382(c), (e), (*l*)(1), (4). The operations of three of those statutory responses are at issue in this case.

Petitioner calculated the section 382 limitation using a value for Teorco of $6.5 million (Bush's purchase price), resulting in net operating loss deductions of $262,882 and $485,550 for 1988 and 1989, respectively. In the statutory notice of deficiency, respondent disallowed both deductions in their entirety on the ground that petitioner had not substantiated the loss. Petitioner alleged in its petition that it had erroneously calculated the section 382 limitation and that it should have calculated the limitation using a value of $16,723,645. In respondent's trial memorandum, the issue was narrowed to whether sections 269 and 382(c), (e)(2), and (*l*)(4) prevent petitioner's affiliated group from deducting, in whole or in part, the net operating loss carryovers of Teorco. Respondent has conceded that section 269 does not apply.

The parties agree that Bush's acquisition of Teorco was an ownership change under section 382(g) and that the applicable long-term tax exempt rate under section 382(f) is 7.47 percent. The parties disagree whether C.J. Co. continued the business enterprise of Teorco during the 2 years after the ownership change. If we should find that C.J. Co. did not continue Teorco's business enterprise, the section 382 limitation would be zero under section 382(c). If we find that C.J. Co. did continue Teorco's business enterprise, we must decide what was the value of Teorco immediately prior to the ownership change and whether that value should be reduced under section 382(e)(2) by reason of the canceled advances from C.J. Co. to Bush and under section 382(*l*)(4) on the ground that C.J. Co. had enough nonbusiness assets to invoke that provision.

We hold that C.J. Co. continued Teorco's business enterprise at all times during the 2 years after the ownership change, that the fair market value of Teorco was $6.5 million immediately prior to the ownership change, and that value should be reduced by $3,625,946 (the canceled advances to Bush) under section 382(e)(2) and $1,520,866 (the Jasmin receivable less its share of Teorco's indebtedness) under section 382(*l*)(4).

3. *Continuity of Business Enterprise—Section 382(c)(1)*

Section 382(c)(1) provides that if a new loss corporation does not continue the business enterprise of the old loss corporation at all times during the 2 years following an ownership change, the section 382 limitation is equal to zero (except for certain recognized gains). This is

¶ 13,070

similar to the continuity-of-business requirement that a transaction must satisfy in order to qualify as a tax-free reorganization under section 368. * * *

The fact that an acquired corporation and the acquiring corporation are in the same line of business tends to establish continuity, but is not determinative. Sec. 1.368–1(d)(3), Income Tax Regs. The new loss corporation must retain a link to the business enterprise of the old loss corporation, either by continuing the old loss corporation's historic business or by using a significant portion of the old loss corporation's historic business assets in a business. Sec. 1.368–1(d)(2), Income Tax Regs. This continuity-of-business requirement is broader, more objective, and more lenient than the corresponding requirement under section 382(a)(1)(C) of the 1954 Code, which required the acquired corporation "to continue to conduct a trade or business 'substantially the same' as its historic business." * * * Thus, a new loss corporation may discontinue more than a minor portion of the old loss corporation's historic business, or dispose of more than a minor portion of the old loss corporation's historic assets, and still satisfy the continuity-of-business requirement. * * *

At all relevant times, petitioner was engaged in the exploration, development, production, and sale of domestic heavy oil. Teorco had acquired and operated heavy-oil properties while it was owned by Tosco. Throughout the 2–year period after the ownership change, C.J. Co. continued to acquire and hold heavy-oil properties. Although C.J. Co. sold Placerita, the most valuable property owned by Teorco, C.J. Co. continued to hold, and tried to develop, McKittrick, its second most valuable property, and it acquired its coowner's interest in Edison Grove, which it developed and operated and then sold.

Respondent contends we should conclude that petitioner intended to dispose of all the assets of Teorco, particularly in view of C.J. Co.'s contingent offer to sell its interest in McKittrick to Chevron. However, neither the statute, the regulations, nor the legislative history provides persuasive support for respondent's contention; we consider only what actually happened during the 2 years following the ownership change, not what might have happened. * * *

Although the sale of Placerita substantially reduced what had been Teorco's historic business enterprise, C.J. Co. continued that business enterprise at all times during the 2–year period after the ownership change. Therefore, section 382(c)(1) does not reduce the section 382 limitation to zero, and the section 382 limitation must be calculated under section 382(a).

4. *Fair Market Value of Teorco*

The calculation of the section 382 limitation starts with "the value of the old loss corporation", sec. 382(a)(1), which in turn depends on the fair market value of the stock of the old loss corporation immediately

¶ 13,070

prior to the ownership change, sec. 382(e), (k)(5). The fair market value of that stock is the price at which it "would change hands between a willing buyer and a willing seller, neither being under any compulsion to buy or to sell and both having reasonable knowledge of relevant facts." * * *

"[T]he best evidence of that value is, in general, actual sales made in reasonable amounts and at arm's length within a reasonable time before or after the date for which a value is sought." *Morris v. Commissioner*, [70 T.C. 959 (1978)] at 988. However, prices obtained at forced sales, at public auctions, or in restricted markets may not be the best criteria of value, particularly when other evidence shows that the property would sell at a higher price under different circumstances. * * *

Although petitioner originally calculated the section 382 limitation using a value of $6.5 million, petitioner contends on brief that the value of the Teorco stock should not be limited to $6.5 million

> because (i) the Teorco Stock was sold by Tosco to Petitioner in a restricted market, (ii) Tosco's sale of Teorco should be viewed as a forced bargain sale, and (iii) the record clearly establishes that the net fair market value of Teorco's assets was $11,909,865, and this value indicates that the value of the Teorco Stock was at least $11,909,865 rather than the distorted below-market value resulting from the forced auction sale of Teorco.

Tosco sent its bid solicitation letter to only about 20 companies. However, Tosco had targeted those companies after investigating which companies might be interested in buying Teorco. Market forces may have limited the number of potential buyers, but those same market forces set the value of the stock in Teorco. Unfortunately for Tosco, the market for oil-producing properties (including heavy-oil properties) was weak, as reflected by the paucity of responses to its request for bids.

There is no evidence that Bush knew there would be no other responsive bidders and that it therefore set its bid artificially low. Bush presumably set its bid as low as it thought it could and still acquire Teorco. Although there were no other bids that Tosco considered responsive, the bidding process was open, and Tosco reserved the right to reject any and all offers for Teorco.

Petitioner contends that Tosco's decision to sell Teorco should be viewed as a forced bargain sale, equating Tosco's business judgment that Teorco did not fit into its long-term business plan with the exigencies imposed by bankruptcy or foreclosure. Although Tosco wished to divest itself of Teorco, Tosco was not forced to do so. Tosco had alternative plans and access to the capital necessary to continue Teorco's business if it had not been sold. Tosco's decision to sell Teorco is not the equivalent of a sale imposed by outside forces.

Petitioner contends that the value of the stock of Teorco is "the net fair market value of Teorco's assets", and not the price that Bush paid for the stock of Teorco. Although the underlying asset value may be significant, * * * a perceived risk of undisclosed and contingent liabilities depressed the fair market value of the Teorco stock * * *. We find that the value of the stock of Teorco is more clearly shown by the price that Bush paid for 100 percent of that stock than by the value of the underlying assets. We therefore find that, immediately prior to the ownership change, the fair market value of the stock of Teorco was $6.5 million.

Tosco must have believed that $6.5 million was an adequate price for Teorco. Tenneco had offered Tosco $7.5 million to buy Placerita, but Tosco had rejected that offer. We do not believe that Tosco, as owner and fully informed seller of Teorco, would have accepted Bush's offer unless Tosco thought that avoiding the risks and burdens of potential liabilities (environmental and otherwise) outweighed the advantage of immediately receiving an additional $1 million.

Tenneco also appears to have thought that avoiding those risks and burdens justified an immediate expenditure of $1,250,000. Tenneco was willing to spend $7,750,000 to acquire Placerita but was not willing to accept McKittrick, Edison Grove, and Jasmin in addition to Placerita. Even though Placerita may have been worth $7,750,000 to Tenneco, Teorco as a whole was not.

There is nothing in the record to suggest that petitioner or Bush had access to any relevant facts that Tenneco or Tosco did not have. The unwillingness of either Tosco or Tenneco to accept the perceived risks and burdens associated with McKittrick, Edison Grove, and Jasmin indicates that those perceived risks and burdens reduced the value of Teorco as a whole. Both Tenneco and Tosco were willing, in effect, to pay Bush approximately $1 million to assume those risks and burdens.

In hindsight, petitioner's purchase of Teorco and the sale of Placerita were great deals. However, hindsight is 20/20, and the actions of the willing buyer and seller of Teorco have established that, at the time of the ownership change, the value of the stock of Teorco was $6.5 million.

5. *Redemption or Other Corporate Contraction—Section 382(e)(2)*

To limit bootstrap acquisitions of loss corporations' net operating loss carryovers, section 382(e)(2) provides that the value of the old loss corporation (and therefore the amount of the section 382 limitation) is determined after taking into account any "redemption or other corporate contraction [that] occurs in connection with an ownership change". * * * A redemption or corporate contraction can occur in connection with an ownership change regardless of whether it occurs before or after the ownership change. * * * Although section 382(e)(2), as enacted by TRA 1986, did not explicitly include "other corporate contraction", the

Technical and Miscellaneous Revenue Act of 1988, added that phrase to section 382(e)(2) for ownership changes after June 10, 1987.

The rule of section 382(e)(2) applies to a "redemption or *other* corporate contraction" (emphasis added). The focus of section 382(e) is on the value of the loss corporation, and the use of the adjective "other" indicates that a redemption is a corporate contraction. As a result, the term "corporate contraction" has a broader meaning than it had in the context of partial liquidations under the 1939 and 1954 Codes, in which the courts stressed the need for a curtailment of business activities. It therefore follows that a distribution not amounting to a partial liquidation under prior law can be a corporate contraction under section 382(e)(2).

The example provided in the House and Senate reports that accompanied the amendment to section 382(e)(2) supports this interpretation of "corporate contraction":

> [A] "bootstrap" acquisition, in which aggregate corporate value is directly or indirectly reduced or burdened by debt to provide funds to the old shareholders, could generally be subject to the provision. This may include cases in which debt used to pay the old shareholders remains an obligation of an acquisition corporation or an affiliate, where the acquired loss corporation is directly or indirectly the source of funds for repayment of the obligation. [H. Rept. 100–795, * * * at 43; S. Rept. 100–445, * * * at 45.]

The example focuses on reduction of the loss corporation's value by reason of its use as a source of funds in a bootstrap acquisition. It does not consider reduction of the loss corporation's business activities as such.

Respondent contends that the advances from C.J. Co. to Bush, which were subsequently distributed as a formal dividend to Bush by cancellation, were a "corporate contraction" because Bush never intended to repay them and that the advances therefore had no economic substance. Respondent contends further that the advances were made "in connection with the ownership change" because Bush would not have needed to borrow substantial funds if it had not paid for Teorco with cash.

Petitioner contends that "corporate contraction" does not include loans or distributions between members of an affiliated group that files a consolidated return because such loans and distributions do not transfer equity value out of the affiliated group. Petitioner also contends that, if the canceled advances amounted to a corporate contraction, it did not occur in connection with the ownership change.

If we were to accept petitioner's contention that "corporate contraction" does not include distributions between members of an affiliated group, a corporation could acquire a loss corporation (without suffering a reduction in its value for the purposes of section 382) by causing the loss corporation to redeem some of its stock or pay a substantial dividend immediately after the ownership change and then use the proceeds of the distribution to pay the old shareholders. An acquisition so structured is the kind of bootstrap acquisition that section 382(e)(2) is intended to inhibit. Structuring the payment to the acquiror as a loan that is intended to be forgiven would reduce the loss corporation's assets in the same way as a redemption or formal dividend.

When a controlling shareholder withdraws funds from its controlled corporation, the relationship invites special scrutiny to determine whether the withdrawal is a bona fide loan, or a dividend at its inception or some later time. * * * This is a factual question, which depends in the first instance upon the shareholder's intent to repay at the time of the withdrawal, and the intention of the corporation to enforce collection. * * * The parties' intent must be inferred from all the facts and circumstances. * * *

When Bush received the advances from C.J. Co., Bush executed unsecured demand notes providing a market rate of interest. Although interest was paid monthly, no principal payment was ever demanded or made, and the advances were discharged by cancellation less than 6 months after the first payment and less than 3 months after the second payment. The cancellation so soon after the advances were made is strong evidence that, when C.J. Co. made the advances to Bush, neither Bush nor C.J. Co. intended them to be repaid.

Bush's financial position during 1987, 1988, and 1989, including its dwindling year-end cash balances ($10,709,990, $2,782,234, and ($32,-939), respectively) and its obligations under the note to ABEG ($2,675,-577) and the joint-venture agreement with Tenneco ($15.5 million), also indicate that Bush had no intention or ability to repay the advances from its own resources at the times they were received from C.J. Co.

Even if the advances standing alone did not amount to corporate contractions, C.J. Co.'s formal payment of a dividend by canceling the notes from Bush was a corporate contraction. C.J. Co.'s cancellation of the notes completed the process that the advances initiated, reimbursing Bush for a substantial portion of its investment in C.J. Co.

Because we find that Bush did not intend to repay the advances, and that these advances and their cancellation reduced the equity capital and value of C.J. Co., these events amounted to a corporate contraction. We must therefore determine whether the contraction occurred in connection with the ownership change.

Immediately prior to the ownership change, Bush had approximately $9 million of cash, which was sufficient to fund its projected operating losses for the next year, to pay off the $2,675,577 ABEG note, which a court had recently found to be in default, and to maintain a significant reserve. However, after purchasing Teorco, Bush had only approximately

$3.4 million of cash, enough to pay off the ABEG note and to fund a few months of losses. The ownership change caused Bush to need a cash infusion, a need that was foreseeable in April 1988 and that would not have continued through March 1989 but for the acquisition of Teorco. Bush's needs for cash were satisfied by the advances from C.J. Co., making the advances a direct and foreseeable result of Bush's acquisition of Teorco.

When Bush distributed the stock of C.J. Co. to petitioner, Bush still needed cash and was not in a position to repay the advances. We think that Bush's need for cash continued to be caused by its acquisition of Teorco, and that the advances were canceled in connection with the ownership change. Although the advances and the formal dividend in this case were not as closely connected to the ownership change as they would have been if a portion of the proceeds of the Placerita sale had been paid directly to Tosco, Bush would not have received or needed the funds represented by the advances if it had not acquired Teorco.

* * *

The question in the case at hand is * * * whether one transaction— the contraction of C.J. Co.—occurred in connection with a prior transaction—the ownership change of Teorco. In this case, Bush's need for cash and its ability to borrow from C.J. Co. had their origins in, and were connected causally with, Bush's acquisition of Teorco and C.J. Co.'s sale of Placerita. We conclude that the canceled advances occurred in connection with the ownership change for the purpose of section 382(e).

The value of Teorco is to be determined after taking into account the corporate contraction caused by the advances and their cancellation in the amount of $3,625,946.

6.   *Substantial Nonbusiness Assets—Section 382(l)(4)*

To discourage "stuffing" a loss corporation with liquid assets or liquidating its active business assets before an ownership change, the value of the *old* loss corporation is reduced by the value of its nonbusiness assets (adjusted for their share of indebtedness), but only if the *new* loss corporation has substantial nonbusiness assets immediately after the ownership change. Sec. 382(l)(4)(A); * * * see also sec. 382(l)(1) (certain capital contributions not included in value).

Although a loss corporation may be both the old loss corporation and the new loss corporation, it cannot be both at the same time. Sec. 382(k)(1), (2), and (3). Upon the ownership change, the old loss corporation becomes the new loss corporation.

The parties adopt opposing "all or nothing" approaches to the interpretation of section 382(l)(4). Petitioner asserts that section 382(l)(4)(A) does not become operative and that therefore the value of Teorco's stock is not reduced thereby. Respondent asserts that section 382(l)(4)(A) does operate and that the entire value of Teorco's stock is eliminated by its nonbusiness assets. Our approach leaves us standing on middle ground.

Petitioner asserts that "both the plain language of the statute and the legislative history indicate that the Section 382(l)(4) nonbusiness asset limitation only applies if the old loss corporation has nonbusiness assets *prior* to the ownership change", and that "Section 382(l)(4) was enacted solely to prevent the *seller* of a loss corporation from liquidating the loss corporation's assets and then selling a shell corporation". Petitioner concludes that section 382(l)(4)(A) focuses solely on the assets of the old loss corporation, and that for section 382(l)(4) to apply, we must reorder the sequence of the purchase of the Teorco stock and the sale of Placerita. We disagree.

We do not find the language of section 382(l)(4) to be "plain"; it seems to us that the paragraph includes what might be taken to be conflicting references to "the new loss corporation" and "the old loss corporation". The reduction in the value of the old loss corporation is triggered by the substantial nonbusiness assets of the *new* loss corporation, but the amount of the reduction is measured by the value of the nonbusiness assets of the *old* loss corporation. Sec. 382(l)(4)(A). In addition, "substantial nonbusiness assets" of the *new* loss corporation is defined by reference to the nonbusiness assets of the *old* loss corporation. Sec. 382(l)(4)(B)(i).

Although section 382(l)(4) is not a model of clarity, its focus does not appear to us to be solely on the assets of the old loss corporation, as petitioner contends. Section 382(l)(4)(A) uses the terms "old" and "new", focusing on the assets of both the old loss corporation and the new loss corporation. H. Conf. Report 99–841, at II–190 (1986), * * * supports this interpretation, referring to "a corporation's assets" and "the loss corporation", not merely to the old loss corporation. Although in most cases neither the value nor the character of the loss corporation's assets will change when the loss corporation is the subject of an ownership change, in this case Placerita was changed from a business asset to a nonbusiness asset when Bush purchased the Teorco stock, and, pursuant to prearrangement, caused C.J. Co. to sell Placerita to Tenneco.

Nonbusiness assets are defined as "assets held for investment". Sec. 382(l)(4)(C). H. Conf. Report 99–841, * * * at II–190, * * * states that assets held for investment include cash and marketable securities that are not held as an integral part of the conduct of a trade or business, and the report cites the reserves of an insurance company or bank as examples of cash and securities held as an integral part of the business.

* * *

We think Congress recognized that it could not foresee all the ways that transactions could be structured, and that, to prevent avoidance of the mechanical rules of section 382(b), Congress provided a flexible, general definition of nonbusiness assets. We interpret the definition of nonbusiness assets so as to implement the antiavoidance purpose of section 382(l)(4). See H. Conf. Rept. 99–841, * * * at II–172.

Neither petitioner, Bush, nor C.J. Co. was ever interested in acquiring or retaining Placerita and the benefits associated with its operation, nor was any of them ever at risk with respect thereto. C.J. Co. did not earn any income or incur any expenses with respect to the operation of Placerita. C.J. Co. never had an operating interest in Placerita because it was immediately bound, through Bush's commitment, to sell Placerita to Tenneco upon Tosco's sale of Teorco to Bush. We see no practical difference between a corporation's acquiring a corporation that has converted its business assets to investment assets before being sold, and an acquiring corporation's obligating itself, before it contracts to purchase the acquired corporation, to convert those business assets to investment assets immediately after it acquires control of them.

As petitioner contends, "it can hardly be said that Petitioner converted Teorco's operating assets to nonbusiness assets * * * *and then* sold the stock of Teorco as a corporate shell". What can be said, however, is that petitioner bound itself to convert Teorco's most important business asset to a nonbusiness asset, purchased the stock of Teorco, and then effected the conversion pursuant to the preexisting, binding obligation.

We look to the definition of "immediately after" as that phrase is used in the regulations under section 351 as "a situation where the rights of the parties have been previously defined and the execution of the agreement proceeds with an expedition consistent with orderly procedure." Sec. 1.351–1(a)(1), Income Tax Regs. Momentary ownership of what might otherwise be a business asset is insufficient where the owner's rights and obligations with respect to that asset have been previously defined, and must be subsequently carried out, pursuant to a prearrangement, in this case, an agreement whose enforceability was triggered by the ownership change. * * *

We stress that the Teorco and Placerita transactions made good business sense, regardless of the net operating loss carryovers. As respondent has conceded, petitioner did not arrange those transactions with the principal purpose of evading or avoiding Federal income tax. See sec. 269(a). However, immediately after the ownership change, C.J. Co. held Placerita as the functional equivalent of the cash proceeds from its impending sale.

Petitioner, assuming for the sake of argument that we might reorder the purchase of Teorco's stock and the sale of Placerita and treat the cash proceeds from the Placerita sale as assets of Teorco (we have not done so), asserts that Congress did not intend cash and marketable securities to be per se nonbusiness assets, and suggests that we adopt a "reasonable needs of the business" test similar to section 537. We agree that, when cash and marketable securities are held as an integral part of the taxpayer's business, they will not be characterized as nonbusiness assets. * * * However, considering that the examples cited in H. Conf. Report 99–841 (insurance company and bank reserves) are reserves required by law, we think that Congress intended a more stringent test of need. *Id.* Although future acquisitions and other business needs of a subsidiary's parent may be reasonable needs for the subsidiary to hold cash under section 537, see Secs. 1.537–1(a)(2), 1.537–3, Income Tax Regs., we find that neither Placerita nor the proceeds of its sale was an integral part of C.J. Co.'s heavy-oil business immediately after the ownership change.

The Jasmin receivable was also a nonbusiness asset. The primary purpose of section 382(l)(4) is to discourage the conversion of a loss corporation's active business assets into passive assets prior to a change in ownership of the corporation. * * * The Jasmin receivable was created as part of just such a transaction, and resulted, prior to the ownership change, in the conversion of one of Teorco's business assets into a passive investment asset.

Placerita and the Jasmin receivable were nonbusiness assets immediately after the ownership change, and therefore C.J. Co. had substantial nonbusiness assets immediately after the ownership change. Because C.J. Co. had substantial nonbusiness assets immediately after the ownership change, the value of Teorco immediately prior to the ownership change must be reduced by the value of the nonbusiness assets owned by Teorco immediately prior to the ownership change.

Although immediately after the ownership change C.J. Co. held Placerita as a nonbusiness asset, immediately prior to the ownership change, Teorco held Placerita as a business asset. Teorco, unlike C.J. Co., had earned income and incurred expenses with respect to Placerita. We do not impute Bush's or C.J. Co.'s intent or contractual obligation to sell Placerita to Tosco or Teorco because neither Tosco nor Teorco was a party to the Placerita agreement or any other agreement for the sale of Placerita. Tosco and Teorco were not interested in selling Placerita. Neither Tosco nor Teorco was obligated to convert Placerita to cash, and the sale of Teorco to Bush was not dependent on Bush's being able to sell Placerita. Because Placerita was not a nonbusiness asset of Teorco immediately prior to the ownership change, the value of Teorco immediately prior to the ownership change is not reduced by the value of Placerita.

Because Placerita was a nonbusiness asset immediately after the ownership change, it triggers section 382(l)(4). However, because Placerita was not a nonbusiness asset immediately before the ownership change, it does not reduce the value of Teorco immediately before the ownership change for the purposes of section 382. The only nonbusiness asset that Teorco held immediately before the ownership change was the Jasmin note receivable, which had a value of $1,588,155. Therefore, for the purposes of section 382, the value of Teorco immediately before the ownership change, $6,500,000, must be reduced by $1,520,866 ($1,588,-155–(($1,588,155/$12,640,494) × $535,569)), the amount by which value of the Jasmin note receivable exceeds its proportionate share of the $535,569 of debt for which Teorco was liable. Sec. 382(l)(4)(A)(i) and (ii).

The amount of petitioner's section 382 limitation with respect to C.J. Co. will be calculated using a "value of the old loss corporation" of $1,353,188 ($6,500,000–$3,625,946–$1,520,866) and a "long-term tax exempt rate" of 7.47 percent.

* * *

[¶ 13,075]

Note

The Tax Court looks to the definition of "immediately after" in Section 351 for guidance in interpreting the same phrase in Section 382(l)(4)(A) for purposes of determining whether the new loss corporation has substantial nonbusiness assets. The prearranged sale of Placerita might be characterized as falling under the "binding commitment" test of the step transaction doctrine used in that context. Would the result have been different if a sale of Placerita had been merely contemplated but not arranged prior to the ownership change?

[¶ 13,080]

8. BUILT–IN GAINS AND LOSSES

The Section 382 limitation for any taxable year that falls in whole or in part within what is called the "recognition period" is increased by the amount of "recognized built-in gains" for that year. Any "recognized built-in losses" for any such period are subject to the Section 382 limitation in the same manner as NOL carryovers. The "recognition period" is the five calendar year period beginning on the date of the Section 382 ownership change. § 382(h).

Built-in gain rules. The Loss Corporation can have recognized built-in gains only if the Old Loss Corporation had a "net unrealized built-in gain." The Old Loss Corporation's net unrealized built-in gain generally is the excess, if any, of the fair market value of all of its assets over their basis at the time of a Section 382 ownership change. § 382(h)(3). (This calculation reflects a netting of unrealized gains and losses.) However, under a threshold de minimis rule, if net unrealized built-in gain does not exceed the lesser of $10 million or 15 percent of the fair market value of the Old Loss Corporation's assets at the time of the ownership change, the net unrealized built-in gain is considered to be zero. § 382(h)(3)(B)(i). For this purpose, assets do not include cash,

cash items, and any marketable security if the value of such security does not differ substantially from its adjusted basis. § 382(h)(3)(B)(ii).

Gain recognized upon disposition of an asset is recognized built-in gain to the extent the taxpayer can demonstrate that such gain existed economically on the date of the Section 382 ownership change. However, the total amount of recognized built-in gains for any taxable year cannot exceed the net unrealized built-in gain, as defined above, less the aggregate amount of recognized built-in gains for all prior taxable years. A special rule increases the Section 382 limitation by the amount of gain recognized as a result of a Section 338 election (to the extent not already taken into account in computing recognized built-in gains for the taxable year). § 382(h)(1)(C). Accordingly, while the repeal of *General Utilities* under the 1986 Act will usually make the exercise of a Section 338 election uneconomic, it may be advantageous to make the election for an acquired corporation with NOL carryovers in order to obtain a stepped-up basis while sheltering any gain to the extent of pre-acquisition losses, which are not subject to limitation under Section 382.

Built-in loss rules. The Loss Corporation can have recognized built-in losses only if the Old Loss Corporation had a "net unrealized built-in loss." The definition of "net unrealized built-in loss" parallels the definition of "net unrealized built-in gain," including a similar threshold de minimis rule. § 382(h)(3). The definition of "recognized built-in loss" for a taxable year is parallel to the definition of "recognized built-in gain." The burden is on the taxpayer to show that a recognized loss is not a recognized built-in loss. Expenses that accrue before the date of a Section 382 ownership change but that are not deductible until a later date and built-in deductions for depreciation, amortization, or depletion allowable during the recognition period may be subject to the built-in loss rules of Section 382. § 382(h)(2)(B).

Recognized built-in losses are subject to the same limitations as NOL carryovers. Amounts disallowed because of the operation of the Section 382 limitation may be carried over to succeeding taxable years under rules similar to the rules for the carryover of NOLs.

Determination of built-in gains and losses. For many years, there was confusion over the method of determining the amount of built-in gains and losses for purposes of Section 382(h). In the absence of regulatory guidance, the Service eventually issued Notice 2003–65 as an interim measure. The Notice instructs taxpayers to compute the amount of built-in gains and losses using a "hypothetical sale" approach. Under this approach, the taxpayer computes an amount realized as if, immediately prior to the ownership change, the Loss Corporation had sold all of its assets at fair market value to a third party that assumed all of its liabilities. The taxpayer can then elect to compute the recognized built-in gain or loss under either the "Section 1374 Approach," which uses the accrual method, or the "Section 338 Approach," which uses the Loss Corporation's actual method of accounting.

[¶ 13,085]

9. SECTION 383 RESTRICTIONS ON USE OF CARRYOVERS OF VARIOUS EXCESS CREDITS AND CAPITAL LOSSES

Under Section 383, if a Section 382 ownership change occurs with respect to a transferor corporation, the Section 382 limitation and a special Section 383 credit limitation apply. These limitations apply to the amount of taxable income and regular tax liability, respectively, that can be offset by pre-change capital losses and certain pre-change excess credits, such as excess general business credits and excess foreign tax credits.

Use of capital loss carryforwards is subject to the Section 382 limitation, and such carryforwards reduce the Section 382 limitation applied to pre-change NOLs. § 383(b) and Reg. § 1.383–1. Section 383(a) limits use of excess general business credits and foreign tax credits after a Section 382 ownership change. The amount of any such excess credit that may be carried forward to any taxable year following a Section 382 ownership change is limited to the "Section 382 credit limitation." This limitation is in essence the amount of tax liability for the post-change year that is attributable to the amount of the applicable Section 382 limitation (after accounting for the post-change use of pre-change losses). Reg. § 1.383–1.

The regulations contain ordering rules that specify how the use of pre-change capital losses and pre-change excess credits are applied to reduce the Section 382 and Section 383 limitations. See Reg. § 1.383–1(d).

[¶ 13,090]

10. SECTION 384 RESTRICTIONS ON USE OF PRE–ACQUISITION LOSSES OF ACQUIRING CORPORATION AGAINST BUILT–IN GAINS OF ACQUIRED CORPORATION

Section 384 was enacted to prevent an acquiring corporation with losses (and members of an affiliated group that have losses) from using those losses to shelter built-in gains of an acquired corporation recognized within five years of the acquisition. This represented a departure from the longstanding prior policy of not restricting an acquiring loss corporation in the use of its own losses against profits of an acquired business. The limitation applies in the case of an acquisition of stock or an acquisition of assets through a reorganization under Section 368(a)(1)(A), (C), or (D), but it does not apply in the case of an acquisition involving two or more corporations previously under common control for five years.

Section 384 applies even though Section 382 also applies. Apparently, Section 382 is applied first, and, to the extent that it does not preclude use of losses, Section 384 may be applied to do so.

[¶ 13,095]

11.   RULES TO PREVENT AVOIDANCE OF SECTION 382

With respect to possible taxpayer efforts to avoid the impact of Section 382, the Conference Committee Report on the 1986 Tax Reform Act, H.R. Conf. Rep. No. 841, 99th Cong., 2d Sess. II–1194–95 (1986), states:

> The conference agreement does not alter the continuing application of section 269, relating to acquisitions made to evade or avoid taxes, as under present law. Similarly, the SRLY and CRCO principles under the regulations governing the filing of consolidated returns [discussed at ¶ 13,115] will continue to apply. The conferees intend, however, that the *Libson Shops* doctrine will have no application to transactions subject to the provisions of the conference agreement.

> The conference agreement provides that the Treasury Department shall prescribe regulations preventing the avoidance of the purposes of section 382 through the use of, among other things, pass-through entities. For example, a special allocation of income to a loss partner should not be permitted to result in a greater utilization of losses than would occur if the principles of section 382 were applicable.

> In the case of partnerships, for example, the conferees expect the regulations to limit the tax benefits that may be derived from transactions in which allocations of partnership income are made to a loss partner or to a corporation that is a member of a consolidated group with NOL carryovers (a "loss corporation partner") under an arrangement that contemplates the diversion of any more than an insignificant portion of the economic benefit corresponding to such allocation (or any portion of the economic benefit of the loss corporation partner's NOL) to a higher tax bracket partner.

[¶ 13,100]

Problems

1.   On January 1 of year 1, Loss Corporation is owned equally by four shareholders: A, B, C, and D. On that date, A buys B's 25–percent interest. On July 1 of year 3 in a transaction unrelated to A's purchase of B's stock, E buys the stock held by C and D. Is there a Section 382 ownership change on the July 1 date?

¶ 13,090

2.   Loss Corporation is wholly owned by a single shareholder, A. In a public stock offering by Loss Corporation public investors buy newly issued stock that represents 60 percent of the stock of Loss Corporation outstanding after the offering. No investor acquires as much as five percent of the Loss Corporation stock. Would this constitute a Section 382 ownership change?

3.   If following the stock offering described in Problem 2, one public shareholder sold stock to another, would that sale count toward a subsequent Section 382 ownership change?

4.   What if A sold stock to one or more public shareholders?

5.   Profit Corporation and Loss Corporation are each publicly owned with no individual five-percent shareholders. On January 10, the two corporations merge, forming P–L Corporation. Profit Corporation's former shareholders receive 60 percent of the stock of P–L Corporation in the merger transaction and Loss Corporation's former shareholders receive 40 percent. Is there a Section 382 ownership change with respect to Loss Corporation?

6.   Loss Corporation is widely held with no individual five-percent shareholders. The value of the Loss Corporation stock is $500 million. On January 10, Loss Corporation issues stock with a value of $750 million in a public offering to shareholders each of whom acquires less than a five-percent interest. Has a Section 382 ownership change occurred?

7.   Would the result in Problem 6 be different if the public offering on January 10 involved $350 million?

8.   Loss Corporation is widely held with no person owning five-percent of its stock. Sixty percent of the Loss Corporation's stock is redeemed for preferred stock that is not treated as "stock" for purposes of the definition of a Section 382 ownership change. Has a Section 382 ownership change occurred?

9.   Loss Corporation and Profit Corporation are each widely held with no shareholder owning as much as five-percent. On January 10, the two corporations merge, forming P–L Corporation. Profit Corporation shareholders receive 40 percent of the stock of P–L Corporation in the merger, while Loss Corporation shareholders receive 60 percent. On July 31 of the same year, A, an individual, purchases 15 percent of the P–L Corporation's stock on the New York Stock Exchange. Has a Section 382 ownership change occurred?

10.   Assume the same facts as in Problem 9, except that Profit Corporation had been owned entirely by an individual, B, and none of A's stock is bought from B. Has a Section 382 ownership change occurred?

11.   Loss Corporation has outstanding 1,000 shares of common stock which are equally owned by A and B. Loss Corporation grants identical options to purchase 1,100 shares of newly issued common stock

to each of A and an unrelated investor, C. Has a Section 382 ownership change occurred?

12.   X Corporation wishes to sell its subsidiary, Loss Corporation, to Profit Corporation. Loss Corporation issues to X Corporation a straight nonvoting, nonqualified preferred stock that represents more than 50 percent of the value of Loss Corporation. X Corporation sells to Profit Corporation the common stock of Loss Corporation (representing less than 50 percent of the Loss Corporation stock if the preferred stock is counted as stock), and retains the preferred stock. Has a Section 382 ownership change occurred?

[¶ 13,105]

12. LIMITATIONS ON NOL CARRYFORWARDS AFTER WORTHLESS STOCK LOSS DEDUCTION

A deduction is allowed for any loss sustained during the taxable year as a result of securities held by the taxpayer becoming worthless. § 165(g). Moreover, it has been held that, notwithstanding the fact that a worthless stock deduction has been claimed by a parent corporation with respect to stock of a nonconsolidated subsidiary, the net operating loss carryforwards of the subsidiary survive and may be used to offset future income of the subsidiary. Textron, Inc. v. United States, 561 F.2d 1023 (1st Cir.1977). This double counting is the target of Section 382(g)(4)(D).

If a worthless securities deduction is claimed for a taxable year by a 50–percent shareholder with respect to stock of a loss company, for purposes of determining whether a Section 382 ownership change occurs after the close of that taxable year, the shareholder is treated as having acquired the stock as of the first day of the succeeding taxable year and as not having owned such stock during any prior period. A "50–percent shareholder" means any person owning 50 percent or more of the corporation during the three year period ending on the last day of the year in which the stock is treated as acquired. Accordingly, if a worthless stock deduction is claimed during year one by a person holding 50 percent or more of a loss corporation's stock, net operating loss carryovers of the corporation arising before the constructive stock ownership change at the end of year one are subject to the Section 382 limitations. § 382(g)(4)(D).

[¶ 13,110]

13. ONGOING SIGNIFICANCE OF SECTION 269

Under Section 269, NOL carryovers can be disallowed in part or in full if the "principal purpose" of an acquisition of control of a loss corporation is the avoidance of federal income tax by securing the benefit of a deduction that the acquiror would not otherwise enjoy. The "principal purpose" of an acquisition is the purpose that exceeds in importance any other single purpose. For purposes of Section 269, the acquisition of "control" of a loss corporation means the acquisition of 50 percent or more of the total combined voting power or the total value of all classes of stock (including stock which does not qualify as stock for purposes of Section 382). § 269(a). Section 269 also is triggered by an acquisition of the property of a loss corporation in certain tax-free reorganizations. § 269(a)(2).

However, Sections 382 and 383 could apply to virtually every acquisition of control or property to which Section 269 could apply. Therefore, it is unlikely that an acquisition of control of a loss corporation would be found in fact to be undertaken for the principal purpose of securing the benefit of the loss corporation's carryovers, given the limitations of Sections 382 and 383. Reg. § 1.269–7 confirms that Section 269 may apply in circumstances in which Sections 382 and 383 also apply. However, the fact that the deduction or credit is limited under Section 382(a) or 383 will be relevant in determining whether the principal purpose of an acquisition is tax avoidance.

[¶ 13,115]

14. CONSOLIDATED RETURN REGULATIONS

As discussed at ¶ 14,060, in calculating the consolidated taxable income of an affiliated group of corporations filing a consolidated return, losses of one member may generally be offset against profits of another member or members. If an acquired corporation joins an acquiring corporation in the filing of a consolidated return, however, use of the acquired corporation's pre-acquisition losses to offset income generated by other members of the group is limited by the "separate return limitation year" (SRLY) rules discussed at ¶ 13,125. In addition, Sections 382 and 383 may apply to the losses carried from the new member's SRLYs to the group's consolidated return years. Final regulations were adopted on June 25, 1999, to govern the application of Sections 382 and 383 to groups of corporations filing consolidated returns. In general, Reg. §§ 1.1502–91 through 1.1502–93 adopt a single entity approach to determine ownership changes and the Section 382 limitations with respect to such losses. The final regulations also extend the single entity approach to loss subgroups within consolidated groups. A second set of rules, set forth in Reg. §§ 1.1502–94 and 1.1502–95, apply to corporations that join or leave a consolidated group with respect to certain attributes. In general, Section 382 is applied separately with respect to those attributes because other members cannot use them.

[¶ 13,120]

a. Application of Sections 382 and 383 to Consolidated Groups

The final consolidated return regulations contain rules for determining whether a consolidated loss group of affiliated corporations has undergone a Section 382 ownership change; for computing the applicable Section 382 limitation for consolidated groups; and for applying Sections 382 and 383 to corporations that join or leave a consolidated group. The final regulations replace the former consolidated return change of ownership (CRCO) rules.

If a consolidated loss group (or loss subgroup) is involved, a Section 382 ownership change and the resultant Section 382 limitation are determined for the consolidated loss group (or loss subgroup) on a single entity basis and not for its members separately. Reg. § 1.1502–91(a)(1). After a Section 382 ownership change with respect to a consolidated loss group (or loss subgroup) the amount of consolidated taxable income for any post-change year that may be offset by pre-change consolidated losses or other attributes (or pre-change subgroup attributes) may not exceed the consolidated group Section 382 limitation (or subgroup Section 382 limitation) for such year as determined under Reg. § 1.1502–93. The final regulations prohibit the use of recognized built-in gains to increase the amount of consolidated taxable income that can be offset by recognized built-in losses. Reg. § 1.1502–93(c)(2). For the definitions of consolidated loss group and subgroup, see Reg. § 1.1502–91(c)(1) and (d)(1).

A consolidated loss group is considered to have a Section 382 ownership change if the loss group's common parent has a Section 382 ownership change. Reg. § 1.1502–92(b)(1)(i). Similarly, a loss subgroup has a Section 382 ownership change if its parent does. Reg. § 1.1502–92(b)(1)(ii). The final regulations make several clarifications with respect to circumstances that require an adjustment to the value of a loss group or loss subgroup under Reg. § 1.1502–93 and add a new Reg. § 1.1502–93(c)(2). This new section provides that appropriate adjustments must be made so that any recognized built-in gain of a member that increases more than one Section 382 limitation (whether consolidated, subgroup, or separate) does not effect a duplication in the amount of consolidated taxable income that can be offset by pre-change net operating losses.

The Section 382 limitation is an amount equal to the value of the consolidated loss group (or loss subgroup) multiplied by the long-term tax-exempt federal bond rate. The value of the loss group (or loss subgroup) is the aggregate value of the stock of all members, other than stock that is owned (directly or indirectly) by another member immediately before the Section 382 ownership change. Reg. § 1.1502–93(b).

When a new loss member joins a consolidated group, Section 382 is applied to the new member as a separate entity. This is done to determine to what extent a Section 382 limitation applies to limit the amount of consolidated taxable income that may be offset by the new loss member's pre-change separate attributes, including any NOL carryover and any recognized built-in loss of the new loss member. Thus, if a Section 382 ownership change with respect to the new loss member occurs, the amount of consolidated taxable income for any post-change year that may be offset by the new loss member's pre-change separate NOL and other attributes may not exceed the Section 382 limitation as determined separately under Section 382(b) with respect to that member for the year concerned. Reg. § 1.1502–94(b)(1). The limitation is calculated by multiplying the value of the new loss member's stock at the time of the Section 382 ownership change by the long-term tax-exempt federal bond rate. Reg. § 1.1502–94(b).

If a loss corporation leaves a consolidated return group which was subject to a Section 382 ownership change while the loss corporation was a member, losses apportioned to the member continue to be subject to the Section 382 limitation. The common parent may elect to apportion all or any part of a consolidated Section 382 limitation to a departing member. Reg. § 1.1502–95(c).

[¶ 13,125]

b.   *Separate Return Limitation Year (SRLY) Rules*

Under the current SRLY rules, if a loss corporation (or loss group) becomes a member of a consolidated group, the pre-acquisition NOL carryovers of the loss corporation (or loss group) arising in SRLYs may not be used to reduce the income of the other members of the consolidated group. Those carryovers may be used, however, to offset the loss corporation's (or loss group's) own allocable share of post-acquisition consolidated taxable income (subject to the possible application of Sections 382, 383, and 269). Reg. § 1.1502–21(c).

Under the prior regulations, the SRLY limitation was determined separately for each member and for each year. The SRLY limitation was based on the member's contribution to consolidated taxable income for the year, with the contribution being determined by measuring the difference between the group's income with and without that member's income and deductions.

This approach produced some anomalies. For example, if the member produced income in a consolidated return year, but the group had no positive consolidated taxable income for that year (e.g., because losses of other members offset the income), the member's SRLY losses could not be absorbed in that year. Because the amount of the member's contribution in one year was not carried over to later years, the SRLY losses could not be absorbed in a later consolidated return year unless the member contributed to consolidated taxable income again in that year.

The SRLY rules limit a member's SRLY losses based on the member's contribution to consolidated taxable income. However, the member's contribution to consolidated taxable income is measured cumulatively over the entire period during which the corporation is a member of the consolidated group. Therefore, a member's SRLY losses may be absorbed in a consolidated return year in which the member does not contribute to consolidated taxable income to the extent of the member's cumulative net contribution to consolidated taxable income in prior consolidated return years of the group. Reg. § 1502–21(c).

Using a cumulative measurement of a member's contribution to consolidated taxable income also permits better coordination with the application of the Section 382 limitation to NOL carryovers as applied to consolidated groups than would be permitted under the prior rules. Under the prior rules, if a member's contribution to consolidated taxable income in a particular year was sufficient to absorb a loss carryover from a SRLY, but the loss could not be absorbed because of a limitation under Section 382, the excess contribution could not be taken into account for purposes of applying the SRLY limitation in subsequent years. The cumulative measurement approach allows any excess contribution in one year to be taken into account in a subsequent year for purposes of the SRLY limitation.

Under the prior regulations, the SRLY limitation operated on a member-by-member basis—an approach often referred to as "fragmentation." Fragmentation was largely inconsistent with the single entity approach to the use of losses adopted under the temporary consolidated return regulations. The single entity approach reduces the tax distinctions between separate affiliated corporations and separate divisions within a single corporation and reflects two principles. First, corporations that file a consolidated return should be able to use each other's losses as if they were divisions of a single corporation rather than separate corporations. Second, the tax laws should be neutral with respect to changes in ownership so that losses arising among members of a group can be used among the members following an ownership change, subject only to the restrictions imposed on a single entity in similar circumstances.

In order to better implement these principles, the temporary regulations eliminate fragmentation in certain cases and apply the SRLY limitation on a subgroup basis rather than separately to the members of the subgroup. In the case of a SRLY subgroup, the SRLY limitation is based on the aggregate contribution to consolidated taxable income by the members included in that subgroup, rather than on contributions on a member-by-member basis. Reg. § 1.1502–21(c)(2).

[¶ 13,130]

c.　*SRLY Limitation on Built–In Losses*

Reg. § 1.1502–15 provides rules limiting deductions if they accrued economically in SRLYs but are recognized in consolidated return years. Generally, these deductions are treated as a hypothetical NOL arising in a SRLY rather than as a deduction in the year recognized and are subject to the SRLY limitations in the year the loss is recognized and thereafter. Reg. § 1.1502–15(a)(1).

Section 382(h) provides comparable rules regarding built-in losses that are attributable to the period before a Section 382 ownership change and are recognized during a five year recognition period following the ownership change. Because a group's acquisition of assets often results in the application of both sets of rules, Reg. § 1.1502–15 conforms certain aspects of the SRLY rules for built-in losses to the rules provided under Section 382(h). Reg. § 1.1502–15(b)(1).

The final regulations provide an overlap rule which eliminates the application of the SRLY rules when the date a corporation becomes a member of a consolidated group is the same date as the "change date" defined in § 382(j). As a result, the final regulations remove the burden of determining two limitations, and simplify the loss limitation rules applicable to consolidated groups in most instances in which both the SRLY and the § 382 limitations would otherwise arise.

The built-in loss rules apply to a new consolidated group member that has a net unrealized built-in loss under Section 382(h)(3) when it becomes a member, determined as if the member had a Section 382 ownership change at that time. Deductions are treated as subject to the SRLY limitation to the extent they would be treated as recognized built-in losses under Section 382(h)(2)(B) during the five year recognition period after the member joins the group. Thus, the rules generally adopt the built-in loss rules of Section 382, including the threshold requirements of Section 382(h)(3)(B). Reg. § 1.1502–15(b)(1).

The regulations adopt a subgroup principle that is generally consistent with the SRLY subgroup rules described above and the rules relating to subgroups for purposes of Section 382. Reg. § 1.1502–15(c)(1). Under the built-in loss rules, a subgroup is composed only of those members that have been continuously affiliated with each other during the 60 month period ending on the date they become members of the group in which the loss is recognized. Reg. § 1.1502–15(c)(2). In order for the SRLY limitation to be determined on a subgroup basis, the members of a SRLY subgroup with respect to the loss must remain affiliated until the year the loss is absorbed.

The final regulations provide that after a corporation joins a group in an overlap transaction, it is deemed to have been affiliated with the common parent of the acquiring group for 60 consecutive months. Those corporations that join the group in the same transaction, but that were not part of a subgroup eligible for the overlap rule, begin measuring the period of their affiliation immediately after joining the group, notwithstanding their actual affiliation history.

If the built-in loss is not allowable by reason of a SRLY limitation, the loss is treated as a separate loss of the group that remains subject to the SRLY limitation and that may be carried over or back to consolidated or separate return years under the principles of Reg. § 1.1502–21(b). Reg. § 1.1502–15(c)(2).

[¶ 13,135]

E. NET OPERATING LOSS CARRYBACKS

1. GENERAL RULES

The general rule of Section 381(b)(3) is that there is to be no carryback by the acquiring corporation of a post-acquisition net operating loss or net capital loss against the income of a prior taxable year of the transferor corporation. There are a number of exceptions to the general rule. First, if stock of a corporation is acquired and the acquired corporation is kept in existence, a post-acquisition loss of the acquired corporation can be carried back to offset pre-acquisition income of the acquired corporation itself. Since the acquired corporation is regarded as a single taxable entity, this carryback is available under the general rules of Section 172 and is not affected by Section 381(b). Also, for the same reason, if the corporate adjustment involves only a single corporation, such as an "E" reorganization, the carryback is available. Under Section 381(b), the same principle has been applied in the case of the "F" reorganization. See Estate of Stauffer v. Commissioner, 403 F.2d 611 (9th Cir.1968); Associated Machine v. Commissioner, 403 F.2d 622 (9th Cir.1968), discussed at ¶ 11,060; and Rev. Rul. 75–561, 1975–2 C.B. 129.

[¶ 13,140]

2. LIMITATION OF NOL CARRYBACKS FOLLOWING CORPORATE EQUITY–REDUCING TRANSACTION (CERT)

One of the tax incentives to leveraged buyouts and buybacks that burgeoned in popularity in the 1980s was the capacity of the corporation concerned to obtain refunds of taxes paid in prior years by carrying back NOLs generated by the large interest payments on the debt incurred to finance the buyout or buyback. Congressional concern over using tax refunds generated by NOL carrybacks to help finance such transactions led to the enactment in 1989 of Section 172(h) relating to a corporate equity reduction transaction (CERT). A corporation may not carry back a part of its NOL if $1 million or more of its interest expense is allocable to a CERT.

A CERT includes either a "major stock acquisition" or an "excess distribution" by a corporation. A major stock acquisition is an acquisition by a corporation (or any group of persons acting in concert with such corporation) of at least 50 percent of the vote or value of the stock of another corporation. § 172(h)(3)(B). All acquisitions made during any 24 month period are aggregated for these purposes. A major stock acquisition does not include an acquisition in which the acquiring corporation has made a Section 338 election.

An excess distribution is the excess of the aggregate distributions and redemptions made by a corporation during the taxable year with respect to its stock (other than stock described in Section 1504(a)(4)) over 150 percent of the annual average of such distributions and redemptions for the prior three taxable years. However, a distribution or redemption (or series thereof) is not treated as an excess distribution if it does not exceed 10 percent of the value of the corporation's outstanding stock (other than stock described in Section 1504(a)(4)) measured at the beginning of the corporation's taxable year. § 172(h)(3)(C). The amount of distributions and redemptions made by a corporation during a taxable year is reduced by consideration (other than stock) received in exchange for stock (other than stock described in Section 1504(a)(4)) issued by the corporation during that year.

If a corporation has an NOL in the taxable year in which it is involved in a CERT or in the following two taxable years, the corporation may be limited in its ability to carry back some portion of the loss. A corporation is treated as being involved in a CERT if it is either the acquired or acquiring corporation or the successor thereto (in the case of a major stock acquisition) or the distributing or redeeming corporation or the successor thereto (in the case of an excess distribution).

The portion of the corporation's NOL from the taxable year in which the CERT occurred or in any of the two following years that can be carried back is limited to the lesser of (1) the corporation's interest expense for that year that is allocable to the CERT or (2) the excess of the corporation's interest expense in that year over the average of the corporation's interest expense for the three taxable years prior to the taxable year in which the CERT occurred. However, under a de minimis rule, if the lesser of these two amounts is less than $1 million, Section 172(h) does not apply. Any portion of an NOL that cannot be carried back due to the operation of this provision may be carried forward to the corporation's future taxable years, as otherwise permitted.

A key issue under the CERT provisions is how a corporation's interest expense is to be allocated to a CERT. The House Ways and Means Committee Report elaborates on this as follows:

> The Secretary of the Treasury is authorized to specify the method of allocating a corporation's interest expense to a CERT. Until regulations are promulgated, however, a corporation's indebtedness is allocable to a CERT to the extent that the corporation's indebtedness could have been reduced if the CERT had not occurred, in the manner prescribed under section 263A(f)(2)(A)(ii) (without regard to clause (i) thereof). The interest expense associated with such allocable indebtedness is equal to a pro rata portion of the corporation's total interest expense.

¶ 13,140

For purposes of determining whether a corporation's interest expense exceeds the prior 3–year average, it is expected that regulations would provide that increases attributable solely to fluctuations in interest rates would not be taken into account.

H.R. Rep. No. 247, 101st Cong., 1st Sess. 1907 (1989).

The Conference Committee states:

The conferees are aware of the complexity of the legal issues involved in this matter and the possible evolution of the international standards for identifying thin capitalization. The conferees have therefore granted authority to the Treasury to make appropriate adjustments, by regulation, to the definitions applicable to debt, equity, net interest expense, and adjusted taxable income so that the application of the statute will be consistent with the concept of thin capitalization * * *.

H.R. Conf. Rep. No. 386, 101st Cong., 1st Sess. 386 (1989).

[¶ 13,145]

Problem

Assume that profitable P Corporation, a calendar year corporation, is capitalized with $150 million of debt and $50 million of equity. P's average annual interest expense has been $15 million for the past three years. P has paid a one-percent annual dividend to its shareholders, or an average of $500,000, for each of the past three years. On January 1 of the current year, P borrows $50 million and distributes the proceeds to its shareholders. Due to an increased interest deduction of $5 million, P incurs an NOL in the current year of $4 million. Was P involved in a CERT? If so, how much of its $4 million NOL can be carried back under Section 172(h)?

Chapter 14

MULTIPLE CORPORATIONS

[¶ 14,000]

A. INTRODUCTION

On occasion business managers decide that if one corporation is a good idea, two—or more—would be even better. Sometimes they are right. The use of multiple corporations, owned by the same or nearly the same shareholders, to conduct business may serve a variety of nontax objectives. Most obviously, the assets of one segment of the business may often be insulated from liabilities generated by another segment if the two segments are separately incorporated. Similarly, if one portion of a business is subject to burdensome regulatory or reporting requirements, or labor agreements, the separate incorporation of that portion may eliminate the need for the remainder of the business to comply with those requirements. Also, the separate incorporation of portions of a business may assist in the estate planning needs of the founder of the business.

In addition, multiple corporations may facilitate achieving a wide range of income tax advantages. Separate corporations, although owned by the same interests, may make different elections on such tax issues as accounting methods and rates of depreciation. Indeed, a separate corporation may be eligible to elect under Subchapter S or another specialized tax regime. Ultimately, the separate incorporation of a business may allow the disposition of that business, either through a sale of stock or a liquidation, at a lower tax cost than would be incurred on the disposition of a division.

For these and many other tax and nontax reasons, it has not been uncommon for the owners of a business enterprise to divide their holdings among numerous corporate entities. In general, Congress has made no attempt to prevent this use of multiple corporations or to deny the tax benefits that multiple corporations achieve. The general rule is that the owners of a business are entitled to operate that business through as many different entities as they wish. On the other hand, Congress often has been unwilling to allow taxpayers to multiply the benefits of specific tax allowances through the use of multiple corporations or to engage in manipulative transactions. This Chapter provides an overview of the principal restrictions on the tax advantages of multiple corporations.

A more complex aspect of the taxation of groups of related corporations is the ability of the group to file a single consolidated income tax return. While a thorough examination of consolidated returns would consume an entire course, this Chapter also summarizes the concepts embodied in the consolidated return regulations.

[¶ 14,005]

B. RESTRICTIONS ON MULTIPLE ALLOWANCES

Numerous Code provisions impose dollar limitations on tax benefits or exemptions from tax burdens. Those benefits might be unduly extended if each newly formed, but commonly controlled, corporation were entitled to a full allowance. To prevent that result, one of the principal restrictions on the use of multiple corporations is the requirement that a group of corporations under common control share a single such tax allowance. The principal Code section imposing that limitation is Section 1561.

Under that section, for the allowances specified, a single allowance must be shared among all members of the group. The most commonly encountered limitation in Section 1561 prevents the members of a controlled group of corporations from multiplying the benefits of the progressive rate structure extended by Section 11(b). The entire group must share the amount of income that is eligible for taxation at each of the lower rates. As a result and regardless of the number of members of the group, only $50,000 of the combined income of the group is taxed at the 15–percent rate and only $25,000 is taxed at the 25–percent rate. In addition, the corporate group must share a single accumulated earnings tax minimum credit under Section 535(c), a single alternative minimum tax exemption under Section 55(d), and a single exemption from the environmental tax imposed by Section 59A.

While Section 1561 imposes the most significant restrictions on multiple allowances, it is not the only section to do so. Several additional sections of the Code that contain fixed dollar allowances require that a controlled group share a single allowance. See, e.g., § 179(d)(6) (limit on expensing certain acquisition costs). Moreover, the predecessor to Section 1561, Section 1551, still exists. Section 1551 limits the use of the same allowances that Section 1561 addresses and on rare occasion may apply even though the more recently enacted section does not.

The cumulative effect of Section 1561 and related sections has been to eliminate substantially any direct reduction in income tax liability attributable to the dispersal of business activities among different corporate entities. Today, therefore, the decision to use multiple corporate entities is more likely than in the past to be dictated by nontax considerations which, of course, is as it should be.

The prerequisite to the application of Section 1561 is the existence of a "controlled group of corporations." That concept is defined in a startlingly complex manner in Section 1563 and includes both parent-subsidiary and brother-sister groups. A parent-subsidiary group is one that has a "common parent" which is defined as a corporation which owns 80 percent of the stock, measured by vote or value, of one other corporation. The controlled group includes the corporations in the chains leading from the common parent as long as 80 percent of the stock of each corporation (other than the common parent) is owned by one or more other corporations in the group.

A brother-sister group consists of the corporations in which five or fewer unincorporated persons own 50 percent of the stock of each corporation, measured by either vote or value, in identical proportions. If one member of a brother-sister group is a common parent of a parent-subsidiary group, then all members of both groups are treated as a single controlled group of corporations. The application of the brother-sister group definition is helpfully illustrated in the examples to Reg. § 1.1563–1(a)(3). For the purposes of determining whether five or fewer persons own a corporation, stock attribution rules, similar but not identical to the rules of Section 318, are applied. § 1563(d) and (e).

When the Section 1563 definition of a controlled group of corporations is applied by cross-reference to other sections, it may be modified by the addition of the requirement that 80 percent of the stock of an includible corporation must be owned by one or more of the same persons who meet the 50–percent test. § 1563(f)(5).

[¶ 14,010]

C. REALLOCATION OF INCOME

Even though the income tax rates applicable to corporations appear relatively flat, the effective marginal rate of tax on corporations varies widely. Some corporations are taxed at preferential rates. Others have operating loss or foreign tax credit carryovers that offset any income tax liability. Still others may benefit from the reduced rates on lower levels of income. And, many corporations are incorporated under foreign law and are not subject to U. S. tax at all. For all those reasons and others, it

¶ 14,010

may matter a great deal which corporation in a group of related corporations reports an item of income or expense.

To prevent taxpayers from improperly reducing their income tax liabilities by arbitrarily shifting income among members of a group, the IRS has long had statutory authority to reallocate income in order "clearly to reflect" the income of a business. § 482. In recent years, however, the IRS has become increasingly aggressive in exerting that authority. Much of the pressure to reallocate income derives from the increasing levels of international trade and the resulting ability of multinational taxpayers to shift income outside the taxing jurisdiction of the United States. However, the rules that have evolved under Section 482 remain fully applicable to purely domestic transactions.

[¶ 14,015]

1. THE "ARM'S LENGTH" STANDARD

In principle, at least, the fundamental standard that controls all allocations and reallocations of income is the familiar rule that related taxpayers are required to deal with each other in the same manner as they would deal with an unrelated party—the arm's length standard. Reg. § 1.482–1(b)(1). However, over time, that standard has evolved into a series of more specific rules applicable to different types of transactions. Thus, specific, detailed rules implement the general requirement that when one business lends money or sells or rents property to, or performs services for, a related business, an arm's length charge must be made for the benefit provided. If such a charge is not made, the regulations to Section 482 authorize the IRS to adjust the taxable incomes of both the provider and the recipient businesses to the levels they would have attained if an arm's length charge had been made. See Reg. § 1.482–2.

[¶ 14,020]

2. TRANSFERS OF TANGIBLE PROPERTY

In certain areas, however, a third generation of regulatory provisions have evolved quite highly developed tests for determining whether an arm's length charge has been made. The first such area consists of the rules governing the transfer of property between related taxpayers. Since those rules control the appropriate transfer price on sales of inventory between manufacturers and their affiliated distributors, they assume enormous importance. The *Texaco* case set forth below, while arising for an unusual reason, illustrates both the nature of the transactions in question and the magnitude of the potential tax reduction. Comparable regulations have been issued governing the transfer of intangible property and have been proposed governing the transfer of services.

¶ 14,010

The regulations governing the sale of tangible property set forth a series of quite distinct, alternative approaches to determining an arm's length charge. Reg. § 1.482–3(a). The traditional approach to transfer pricing is reflected in the comparable uncontrolled price or CUP method. Under that method, an arm's length selling price is the price that the seller would charge in a comparable sale to an unrelated purchaser. Since transactions with affiliates are apparently never identical to transactions with strangers, most of the dispute in the application of this method is over what differences may exist before transactions are no longer comparable and what adjustments can be made to reflect the lack of absolute identity. Reg. § 1.482–3(b). Two additional methods focus on the comparability of the gross profit earned on the transaction to the gross profit earned on transactions with unrelated companies rather than on the comparability of the price charged. The resale price method of Reg. § 1.482–3(c) examines the profit margin earned by the distributor while the cost-plus method of Reg. § 1.482–3(d) addresses the gross profit of the manufacturer. Under these methods, the arm's length transfer price becomes the price required to produce the appropriate level of profit.

A further method, the comparable profits method, extends the notion of profit, rather than price, comparisons to a comparison of the overall profitability of the controlled entity with the overall profitability of a similar but uncontrolled entity. Reg. § 1.482–5. This method abandons the transaction based analysis of the first three methods, which has been the traditional focus of Section 482, in favor of a more generalized, rough justice approach. This method was adopted presumably in response to the difficulty of developing the reliable comparative data with respect to particular transactions required by the more traditional approaches.

The final method authorizes a transfer price that results in a division of profits among the parties to the transaction that is proportional to the value of each party's contribution to the generation of that profit. Reg. § 1.482–6. The adoption of the profit split method was controversial because it moved the furthest from the traditional arm's length approach to intercompany transactions. Indeed, the approach seems to substitute a formula approach to the allocation of taxable income that is geared to the value of property used in the production of income for the valuation approach taken by the traditional CUP method. Nevertheless, because this method is often easier than the others to apply, and has intuitive appeal, it has in fact been applied by the courts from time to time. See, e.g., Eli Lilly & Co. v. Commissioner, 84 T.C. 996 (1985), aff'd in part, 856 F.2d 855 (7th Cir.1988).

The regulations do not provide a very clear rule for selecting the method that a taxpayer may use. Rather, under the so-called "best method" rule, the method to be used is the one that results in the most reliable measure of an arm's length result. Reg. § 1.482–1(c). While the flexibility of this approach is generally applauded, the most important issue in a transfer pricing controversy may become the selection of the best method!

[¶ 14,025]

3. TRANSFERS OF INTANGIBLE PROPERTY

The determination of an arm's length price for the transfer of intangibles has been especially troublesome. At an early stage in the development of a product, such as a new drug, the usefulness of the product will be unproven and its value, accordingly, will be low. Some relatively predictable percentage of those drugs, however, will in time prove to hugely profitable. If a low valuation for the transfer of intangible property rights is accepted, the tax liability for those huge profits may be shifted from the inventor/manufacturer to its distributor—which may be a foreign subsidiary not subject to U.S. tax.

To address that problem, Congress added just one substantive rule to Section 482 which, in somewhat vague language, requires that the income reported by the transferor of an intangible be "commensurate with the income attributable to the intangible." The regulations interpret that language to require that in general royalties paid for the right to use an intangible must be reevaluated annually to ensure that the royalty paid reflects the actual profits derived by the transferee from the exploitation of the intangible. Reg. § 1.482–4(f)(2). As a result, additional royalty income from a successful product will be allocated to the manufacturer/transferor even though the original transfer price for the unproven product was not unreasonable at the time it was established. Of course, the appropriate royalty level must be established under one or another of the comparative methods used to determine an arm's length price on the transfer of tangible property.

[¶ 14,030]

4. EFFECT OF INCONSISTENT LEGAL RESTRICTIONS

The rules of Section 482 constitute one aspect of a regulatory framework that is designed to ensure that each component in a business organization pay an appropriately computed income tax. Needless to say, all businesses are also subject to other sets of nontax regulations that have other objects entirely. Sometimes the obligations imposed by one set of regulations conflicts with the obligations of a taxpayer under a provision like Section 482. As the following case discloses, that seeming conflict has been litigated repeatedly in connection with the application of assignment of income principles, including Section 482. For years after those involved in *Texaco*, a revised set of regulations seeks to achieve a compromise to the controversy. One provision would allow a taxpayer to treat an item, the payment of which is illegal under foreign law, as a deferred item to be taken into income when the payment is no longer illegal. Reg. § 1.482–1(h)(2). As you read the following opinion, consider whether the Fifth Circuit would accept that compromise.

[¶ 14,035]

TEXACO, INC. v. COMMISSIONER

United States Court of Appeals, Fifth Circuit, 1996.
98 F.3d 825, cert. denied, 520 U.S. 1185 (1997).

DAVIS, CIRCUIT JUDGE:

The Commissioner of Internal Revenue challenges the Tax Court's legal conclusion that Letter 103/z, a 1979 pronouncement of Saudi Arabian oil policy by the Saudi Arabian Oil Minister, prohibits the Commissioner from exercising her authority to reallocate income under * * * §§ 482 and 61. We affirm.

I.

Texaco, Inc. is the parent corporation of a group of entities engaged in the production, refining, transportation, and marketing of crude oil and refined products in the United States and abroad. Texaco has a number of subsidiary/affiliate corporations under its umbrella. One of those affiliates is Texaco International Trader, Inc. (Textrad), which acted as the international trading company for the worldwide Texaco refining and marketing system during the period in question. As the trading company, Textrad purchased Saudi crude oil from the Saudi government by way of the Arabian American Oil Company (Aramco) and resold that crude to both affiliates and unrelated customers.

* * *

A.

From early 1979 through late 1981, Saudi Arabia permitted Texaco and the other Aramco participants to buy Saudi Arabian crude oil at below market prices. The Saudi government also established the official selling price (the OSP) for Saudi Arabian crude below the market price. The Saudi government took these actions in response to requests by the United States and other consuming countries to moderate the price of crude oil. To ensure its price regulation had its intended effect, the Saudi government prohibited Texaco and other participants in Aramco from re-selling Saudi crude at prices higher than the OSP. As the Tax Court found, these restrictions were authorized by the King and communicated to Aramco by Minister Yamani in Letter 103/z, dated January 23, 1979. Except in instances where it was excused from doing so, Textrad complied with Letter 103/z and resold the Saudi crude at the OSP.

¶ 14,035

During the period in question, Textrad sold approximately 34 percent of its Saudi crude or about 780,000,000 barrels to its refining affiliates. Of these, approximately 275,000,000 barrels were sold to Texaco's domestic refining company and 505,000,000 barrels to Texaco's foreign refining affiliates. Textrad also sold 15–20 percent of its Saudi oil at the below market OSP to customers that were completely unrelated to Texaco. This was consistent with the pattern and volume of Textrad's sales to unrelated customers in earlier years. Moreover, the Tax Court specifically found that any changes in Textrad's sales to both its affiliates and its unrelated customers during this period were not related to the Saudi price restrictions.

The restrictions in Letter 103/z, however, applied only to Saudi crude, not to the sale of products refined from Saudi crude. As a result, the companies that bought Saudi crude from Textrad at the below market OSP, including Texaco's refining affiliates, earned large profits from the sale of refined products. Unlike its domestic affiliates, Texaco's foreign refining affiliates reported no taxable income in the United States.

B.

The Commissioner alleges that Textrad shifted profits attributable to the lower cost of Saudi crude out of Texaco's U.S. taxable income when it sold Saudi crude at the OSP to its foreign refining affiliates. The Commissioner reallocated over $1.7 billion in income to Textrad for taxable years 1979, 1980, and 1981. Following a five-week trial, the Tax Court issued a detailed opinion. The Tax Court held that the Commissioner was precluded from allocating income to Texaco under §§ 482 and 61 because the price restrictions in Letter 103/z were the "virtual equivalent of law," which Texaco was required to obey.

The Tax Court supported this conclusion with a number of factual findings, including the following:

1. The Saudi government, with the approval of the King, issued Letter 103/z prohibiting the resale of Saudi crude at amounts exceeding the OSP.

2. Texaco was subject to that restriction and faced severe economic repercussions, including loss of its supply of Saudi crude and confiscation of its assets, if it violated Letter 103/z.

3. This mandatory price restriction applied to all sales of Saudi crude, including sales to affiliated entities.

4. Neither Texaco nor any other Aramco participant had any power to negotiate or alter the terms of this restriction.

Based on its findings that Texaco was obligated to comply, and did comply, with the Saudi government's price restrictions, the Tax Court concluded that Texaco's pricing policy as to its foreign affiliates as well

¶ 14,035

as its unrelated customers was due to these restrictions and not to any attempt to distort its true income for tax purposes. The Commissioner has appealed the order disallowing the allocation.

II.

A.

Based on the Tax Court's factual findings, which are not clearly erroneous, we agree that Letter 103/z had the effect of a legal restriction in Saudi Arabia. The 1979 pricing requirements were authorized by the King and issued by Minister Yamani on behalf of the Saudi government as mandatory restrictions. These restrictions applied to all sales of Saudi crude by the Aramco participants and others. The restrictions were in effect during the period at issue and were followed by Texaco. The Tax Court's findings of fact fully support its conclusion that Letter 103/z should be given the effect of law for purposes of §§ 482 and 61.

We also agree with the Tax Court's legal conclusion that the teaching of *Commissioner v. First Security Bank*, 405 U.S. 394, * * * (1972), bars the Commissioner from allocating income to Textrad on its sales of Saudi crude under § 482. Because the sales price of the crude is governed by Letter 103/z, Texaco did not have the power to control the sales price of the oil.

Section 482 of the Internal Revenue Code authorizes the Secretary to apportion or allocate income between organizations controlled by the same interests "if he determines that such distribution, apportionment, or allocation is necessary in order to prevent evasion of taxes or clearly to reflect the income of any such organizations." * * * The relevant IRS regulation explains that the purpose of § 482 is "to place a controlled taxpayer on a tax parity with an uncontrolled taxpayer" and to ensure that controlling entities conduct their subsidiaries' transactions in such a way as to reflect the "true taxable income" of each controlled taxpayer. 26 C.F.R. § 1.482–1A(b)(1) (1996). The regulation further explains that "[t]he standard to be applied in every case is that of an uncontrolled taxpayer dealing at arm's length with another uncontrolled taxpayer." *Id.*

In *First Security*, the Court held that § 482 did not authorize the Commissioner to allocate income to a party prohibited by law from receiving it. 405 U.S. at 404 * * *. In that case, two related banks offered credit life insurance to their customers. Federal law prohibited the banks from acting as insurance agents and receiving premiums or commissions on the sale of insurance. The banks referred their customers to an unrelated insurance company to purchase this insurance. The insurance company retained a small percent of the premiums for administrative services and transferred the bulk of the premiums through a reinsurance agreement to an insurance company affiliated with the banks, which reported all of the reinsurance premiums it received as

¶ 14,035

income. The Commissioner reallocated 40 percent of the related insurance company's income from these reinsurance premiums to the banks as compensation for originating and referring the insurance business. *Id.* at 396–99 * * *.

The Court concluded that due to the restrictions of federal banking law, the holding company that controlled the banks and the insurance affiliate did not have the power to shift income among its subsidiaries. In so holding, the Court emphasized that the Commissioner's authority to allocate income under § 482 presupposes that the taxpayer has the power to control its income: "The underlying assumption always has been that in order to be taxed for income, a taxpayer must have complete dominion over it." *Id.* at 403 * * *. Indeed, as the Court noted, the Commissioner's own regulations for implementing § 482 contemplate that the controlling interest "must have 'complete power' to shift income among its subsidiaries." *Id.* at 404–05 * * *.

* * *

The Sixth Circuit decision in *Procter & Gamble Co. v. Commissioner*, 961 F.2d 1255 (6th Cir.1992), also supports the Tax Court's conclusion. In that case, the court held that a Spanish law prohibiting a foreign affiliate from paying royalties for the use of patents was sufficient to preclude the Commissioner from reallocating income to account for a reasonable royalty. The court stated that "the purpose of § 482 is to prevent *artificial* shifting of income between related taxpayers." *Id.* at 1259 (emphasis added). Again the deciding issue was one of control: "Because Spanish law prohibited royalty payments, [the controlling company] could not exercise the control that § 482 contemplates, and allocation under § 482 is inappropriate." *Id.* at 1259. *See also L.E. Shunk Latex Products, Inc. v. Commissioner*, 18 T.C. 940 * * * (1952) (holding that Commissioner could not allocate additional income to condom manufacturer where manufacturer sold condoms to its affiliate at price set by Office of Price Administration, even though affiliate made substantial profits on the transactions).

It is precisely this ability to control the flow of its income that Texaco lacked. The Tax Court found, and we agree, that Letter 103/z had the force and effect of law, that Textrad was obligated to comply with its requirements, and that it did so comply. Because Textrad lacked the power to sell Saudi crude above the OSP, reallocation under § 482 is inappropriate.

* * *

C.

Nor would the Commissioner's proposed allocation be consistent with § 482's goal of achieving tax parity between controlled and uncontrolled taxpayers. As the *First Security* Court and the regulations make clear, the "purpose of § 482 is to place a controlled taxpayer on a tax parity with an uncontrolled taxpayer." 405 U.S. at 407 * * *. Thus, "[t]he standard to be applied in every case is that of an uncontrolled taxpayer dealing at arm's length with another uncontrolled taxpayer." 26 C.F.R. § 1.482–1A(b)(1) (1996).

The record evidence fully supports the Tax Court's findings that Textrad sold significant amounts of Saudi crude to unrelated customers at the same OSP it sold to its affiliates, that the volume of Textrad's sales of Saudi crude to unrelated customers during this period remained generally consistent with historic levels, and that any changes in Textrad's sales to its affiliates and its unrelated customers during this period had no nexus with the restrictions imposed by Letter 103/z. Therefore, the Tax Court did not err in concluding that the Commissioner failed to demonstrate any disparity between Texaco's treatment of its affiliates and its unrelated customers as a result of the Saudi price restrictions. Thus, under the regulation's tax parity standard, the Commissioner's allocation of Texaco's income under § 482 is improper.

In sum, the Tax Court did not err in concluding that Textrad sold the Saudi crude to both its affiliates and its unrelated customers at the below market OSP to avoid violating Letter 103/z and the severe economic reprisal that would have flowed from such a violation. Accordingly, the Commissioner had no authority to allocate the income under § 482.

* * *

[¶ 14,040]

Notes

1. Assume that under the law of a hypothetical foreign country in which Texaco purchased crude oil, it was illegal for Texaco to resell petroleum products at any price to purchasers in certain designated countries. If Texaco ignored that foreign law and engaged in the prohibited sale, there could be no question but that the United States could tax any profit on the illegal sale. What if, instead, Texaco sold the petroleum to the prohibited purchaser but, to avoid violating the foreign country law, stipulated that payment was to be made to a wholly owned German subsidiary of Texaco—the profits of which could not be subject to U. S. tax. Could there now be any question of the right of the IRS to tax the income from this sale to Texaco? How, if at all, does that differ from the principal case?

2. Both the Tax Court and the court of appeals in *Texaco* seem to have assumed that the reason that property is sold for less than its value is relevant to the propriety of an allocation under Section 482. Why should that be the case? Compare Reg. § 1.482–1(f).

3. Does a decision like *Texaco* encourage multinational corporations to conspire with foreign governments to enact legislation such as the Saudi Arabian extraterritorial pricing restriction to undermine Section 482?

[¶ 14,045]

5. COMMON CONTROL

The prerequisite for the application of Section 482 is that two or more businesses are owned or controlled "by the same interests." While the definition of the separate business to which the section may be applied has remained somewhat unsettled in the context of transactions between a corporation and its individual owner/employee, a matter raised in Chapter 1, in general the application of Section 482 has not turned on the hairsplitting distinctions that have burdened other Code definitions. By contrast to the precise statutory definitions of controlled groups of corporations found in such Code provisions as Section 1563, Section 482 does not contain a definition of common control and the regulations have adopted a broad and flexible approach to the definition. See Reg. § 1.482–1(i)(4) through (6). Those provisions define control in practical, rather than technical, terms. "It is the reality of the control that is decisive, not its form or the mode of its exercise." Reg. § 1.482–1(i)(4). Indeed, the same regulation would further diminish the role of control by providing that the mere existence of a shifting of income raises a presumption of control.

One issue of control that has arisen under Section 482 is where two unrelated corporations each own 50 percent of the stock of a third and the issue is whether one or both of the stockholders can be said to be in control of the subsidiary. In B. Forman Co. v. Commissioner, 453 F.2d 1144 (2d Cir.), cert. denied, 407 U.S. 934 (1972), the court held that at least where the shareholders were acting in concert to manipulate the income of the subsidiary, the subsidiary and its corporate shareholders would be regarded as controlled by the same interests. As a result of such pragmatic decisions as *B. Forman*, the issue of control has not played a major role in the application of Section 482.

[¶ 14,050]

D. CONSOLIDATED RETURNS

Larger businesses tend to conduct their affairs through large numbers of subsidiary corporations, all of which are owned directly or through other subsidiaries by a single common parent corporation. Each of these corporations may be taxed as a separate entity, subject, of course, to the rules governing transactions among related corporations discussed earlier in this Chapter. That treatment, however, may seem unrealistic. Transactions between two wholly owned subsidiaries can more nearly resemble transactions between two divisions of a single corporation than they resemble transactions between distinct corporate entities. Responding to that reality, Section 1501 allows groups of closely related corporations to file a single consolidated income tax return. The consolidation of the income of a group of corporations, however, has proven to be far more complicated than merely ignoring their separate incorporation, partly because the ownership of a subsidiary may pass freely in or out of the group.

Other than defining, in Section 1504, the degree of relationship required for the filing of a consolidated return, the Code itself contains no guidance at all concerning how the income of separate corporations should be consolidated. Rather, acting pursuant to the authority granted in Section 1502, the Treasury Department has issued highly elaborate legislative regulations, now in their third generation, that govern all aspects of consolidation. Those regulations frequently override the tax rules prescribed for corporations by the Code itself.

[¶ 14,055]

1. DEFINING THE "AFFILIATED GROUP"

If the election to file a consolidated return is made, all "includible" corporations falling within the "affiliated group" must be included in the return. § 1504(a). All domestic corporations except those subject to special tax regimes, such as insurance companies, are includible corporations. The affiliated group consists of the common parent company and all subsidiaries in which stock possessing at least 80 percent of both the voting power and value is owned by the common parent or one or more other subsidiaries included within the group. To prevent the exclusion of some corporations from the group too easily, the stock taken into account for these purposes does not include certain nonvoting preferred stock.

[¶ 14,060]

2. CONSOLIDATED INCOME AND LOSS

The computation of consolidated income begins with the computation of the income of each separate corporation as if separate returns were to be filed and then sums the results to arrive at consolidated income. Reg. §§ 1.1502–11(a) and–12. However, a few significant items, including income or loss attributable to intercompany transactions, net operating losses, and capital gains, are separated from this general consolidation and combined under more specific rules. As a general result, the filing of a consolidated return has little effect upon the income tax liabilities of profitable corporations generating ordinary business income from transactions with persons outside the group.

¶ 14,060

Rather, consolidation has its principal significance in three areas: (a) operating losses, (b) intercorporate transactions, and (c) investments in, and withdrawals from, subsidiaries.

One of the principal advantages of the filing of a consolidated income tax return is that any net operating loss generated by one member of the group may be applied in the current year against the profits of other, separately incorporated, members of the group. Reg. §§ 1.1502–11 and–21. The ability to use those losses currently rather than carry them forward against the future profits, if any, of the corporation generating the loss is of substantial value. However, if the loss was accrued in economic terms, whether or not it was realized for income tax purposes, before the corporation generating the loss became a member of the group, the ability to apply the loss against the consolidated income becomes subject to special limitations. Since that circumstance normally accompanies an acquisition, those limitations are described in Chapter 13.

[¶ 14,065]

3. INTERCOMPANY TRANSACTIONS

The core of the consolidated return regulations is the treatment of intercompany transactions, where one member (referred to in the regulations as S, the selling member) sells property or provides services or lends capital to another (B, the buying member). The general objective of the regulations is to treat those transactions to the maximum extent possible as if they occurred within a single entity, rather than between separate entities, while recognizing that the cumulative tax position of the individual members of the group must be maintained. To achieve that balance, the regulations adopt what has been referred to as a "deferred sale" approach to intercompany transactions. See Reg. § 1.1502–13(a)(2).

Under this approach, both S and B, as an initial matter, reflect their transaction as if they were separate entities. However, the income or loss from the transaction is not reported for income tax purposes until the time in which income would be reported if S and B were divisions of a single corporation. Thus, for example, assume that S creates property at a cost of $50 and sells it to B in year one for $70. B resells the property outside the group in year two for $100. B is treated as having a cost basis for the property of $70 and thus a gain of $30 in year two. S is treated as having a gain of $20 in year one but the reporting of the gain is deferred until the time of the resale out of the group, i.e., year two.

In addition to timing, the other attributes of the income, other than the amount attributable to S and B, are also determined in a manner designed to approximate the treatment of a single entity. Thus, the character of the income as ordinary or capital and its source for foreign tax credit purposes, are determined in the manner applicable to single entities. Thus, in the above example, if the property were a capital asset in S's hands but were held by B as inventory, the entire $50 of income presumably would be ordinary.

These results are reached under the regulations through just two general rules, referred to as the "matching rule" and the "acceleration rule." The matching rule is the heart of the rules governing intercompany transactions. That rule, in quite general terms, requires that the income and loss items of both S and B must be "redetermined to the extent necessary to produce the same effect on consolidated taxable income * * * as if S and B were divisions of a single corporation * * *." Reg. § 1.1502–13(c)(1)(i).

When B engages in a transaction, the income tax consequences of which would be different if S and B were divisions of a single corporation, the matching rule requires that an amount of the deferred income or loss of S be reported that will bring the results into line with the treatment of a single corporate entity. The regulations explain that rule with an example which assumes that S holds land for investment purposes with a basis of $70 which is sold to B in year one for $100. In year three B sells the land outside the group for $90.

In year one S incurs an intercompany gain of $30. However, if S and B were divisions of a single corporation, no income would be recognized for tax purposes. Accordingly, none of the gain is reportable in year one. In year three B has a loss of $10. However, if S and B were divisions, B would have succeeded to S's basis of $70 and thus would have a gain of $20. The matching rule thus requires that an amount of gain from S's intercompany sale be reported to produce a net gain of $20. Thus, all $30 of S's gain must be reported in year three. On a consolidated basis, the group will report a gain of $20. Reg. § 1.1502–13(c)(7)(ii), Ex. 1(f).

If B held all of the stock of S and the property were distributed from S to B as a dividend having a value of $100, under Section 311(b), S would have a gain of $30. That gain would be an intercompany gain reportable in accordance with the rules just described. By contrast to Section 311, however, the consolidated return regulations require the recognition of loss on the distribution of depreciated property but the reporting of that loss is deferred under the matching rule.

Under certain conditions the matching rule would allow the permanent deferral of the income realized by S. That would occur, for example, if the property sold by S to B left the group in a transaction that did not result in taxing the gain or loss in the property to B. That would be the result if the stock of B were sold outside the group before B resold the property. Such an exemption from tax is prevented by the so-called acceleration rule. Again in quite general terms, that rule provides that, if as a result of any transaction (such as deconsolidation of B) it is no longer possible to report S's deferred gain under the matching rule, it will become reportable immediately.

¶ 14,065

In general, the matching rule permits the deferral of the reporting of income from an intercompany sale of property until the property leaves the group (including by being consumed by B). That rule normally will be more favorable to taxpayers than would be the reporting of income on an unconsolidated, separate entity approach. However, the deferred sale approach is not always as favorable as if the group were in fact a single corporation. If, for example, B does not resell the property but transfers it in a Section 351 nonrecognition transaction to a corporation that is not a member of the group, S's deferred gain would become taxable under the acceleration rule even though, if S and B were divisions, no gain would be recognized as a result of the Section 351 exchange.

When a transaction would result in ordinary income to one member and an ordinary deduction to another, the matching rule will require that the income from the intercompany transaction be taken into account to eliminate the effect of the deduction. That will be the result on the provision of services, the rental of property, or the payment of interest on a loan. If, on the other hand, the payment is not deductible, the effect of the matching rule depends upon the treatment of the expense. For example, if the payment for services must be capitalized and recovered through depreciation, the income derived by S will be reported as depreciation is claimed by B. Reg. § 1.1502–13(c)(7), Ex. 7. In each instance, the general effect of the rule is to replicate the tax payable by a single entity as a result of purely internal transactions.

[¶ 14,070]

4.   INVESTMENT ADJUSTMENTS

Because corporations may leave the consolidated return world and return to the normal Subchapter C world, the consolidated return regulations contain elaborate rules governing the effect of consolidated transactions on the basis of the stock in members of the group as well as on earnings and profits (E & P). In several important respects, the consolidated return rules are not only different from the normal Subchapter C rules but are superior to those rules in terms of their implementation of corporate tax policy. They are, for that reason, worth examination. Students with some knowledge of the taxation of conduit entities, partnerships or S corporations, will find much in the investment adjustment rules that is familiar.

[¶ 14,075]

a.   *Stock Basis Adjustments*

By sharp contrast to the taxation of separate corporate entities under Subchapter C, the basis of the stock in a member of the group (S, or subsidiary) which is held by another member (P, or parent) is adjusted annually by the amount of the income and loss of S. Reg. § 1.1502–32(a). Stock basis is increased by items of income and decreased by items of loss that are actually reflected in consolidated taxable income (i.e., is not deferred) or that are exempt from tax. The salutary effect of that rule is to prevent the imposition of a second (or more) corporate level tax attributable to S's income upon the sale or other disposition of the stock in S. This special consolidated return rule thus avoids one of the deficiencies in the normal Subchapter C scheme which plagues unconsolidated corporate families.

In addition, these basis adjustments are "tiered up" the chain of stock ownership to the common parent (CP). Reg. § 1.1502–32(a)(3)(iii). To illustrate, assume that P owns all of the stock of S and has a basis of $150 in that stock. All of the stock of P is owned by CP. S has net taxable income of $100 for the year. As a result, P increases the basis of its stock in S by that $100 to $250. In addition, CP also increases the basis of its stock in P by the same $100. Thus, multiple tiers of taxation on the income of S are avoided regardless of whether the stock of S or the stock of P is sold.

Pursuant to the same policy, all distributions subject to Section 301 from S to P are permanently excluded from P's income. The exclusion applies both to distributions that are dividends and to distributions that exceed S's E & P. However, the basis for P's stock in S must be reduced by the amount of the tax-free distribution. Reg. § 1.1502–32(b)(2).

[¶ 14,080]

b. *Excess Loss Accounts*

One striking feature of this stock basis adjustment is that negative adjustments attributable to losses or distributions may exceed the basis of the S stock. In that event, basis is in fact reduced to below zero. The negative amount is referred to as S's "excess loss account" and may be the only place in the Code in which negative basis is sanctioned. Reg. § 1.1502–19(a)(2).

In transactions involving the stock of S, the excess loss account operates very much as negative basis would be expected to operate. Thus, for example, on a sale of the stock of S outside the group, the gain to P would be the sum of the payment from the purchaser plus the amount of the excess loss account. Because the excess loss account represents losses made available to the group in excess of their investment in S, the amount of the account must be recaptured, i.e., taxed, when S leaves the group even if the disposition of S would not otherwise be taxable. Reg. § 1.1502–19(b)(2)(ii) and (c). Note that here, as elsewhere, the consolidated return regulations override the specific nonrecognition rules of such Code provisions as Section 351.

[¶ 14,085]

c. Earnings and Profits

Each member of the group must compute its E & P in the same manner as it would as an unconsolidated corporation except that deferred intercompany items are not reflected in E & P until they are reported in consolidated taxable income. However, to approximate the treatment of distributions from single entities, the consolidated return regulations require that the E & P of all members of the group support dividend treatment of distributions by the common parent. That result is reached by requiring the tiering up of E & P. Reg. § 1.1502–33(a). Thus, for example, if S derives E & P of $75 in a year, its E & P account is increased by that amount and the E & P account of P is increased by the same $75 as is the E & P account of P's parent. As a result, the E & P account of the common parent will include all of the increases to the E & P accounts of all of its consolidated subsidiaries.

If a corporation leaves the group, its E & P generally remains with the group and does not remain with the former group member. Thus, for example, if the stock of S were sold outside the group, its E & P account would be reduced to zero immediately before the sale but the E & P account of P would not be reduced. Reg. § 1.1502–33(e).

[¶ 14,090]

Problems

1. At a cost to it of $700, CP provides engineering assistance to S for which it charges S $1,000. The assistance is in connection with the construction of a new factory building for S's use. Assume that S is entitled to depreciate the building on a straight-line basis over 10 years. If CP and S were divisions of a single corporation, the corporation would not be entitled to deduct the cost of providing the services but would be required to amortize that amount over the depreciable life of the building. How should that result be reached if CP and S file consolidated returns?

2. CP owns all of the stock of P, which owns all of the stock of S. Assume that in year 1 all stock basis and E & P accounts have a zero balance. In year 2, S earns taxable income of $100 but its E & P for the year increases by $120. In year 3, S distributes $75 to P, which redistributes it to CP, which further redistributes it to the shareholders. In year 4, P sells all of the stock of S to a partnership of individuals for $60.

For each of the three years, what will be the effect of these events on the basis of the S, P, and CP stock? What will be the effect on the E & P accounts of the three corporations?

Chapter 15

S CORPORATIONS AND THEIR SHAREHOLDERS

[¶ 15,000]

A. INTRODUCTION TO CONDUIT TAXATION

The preceding chapters have examined the dual tax regime of Subchapter C. In this Chapter, coverage now shifts to the pass-through or conduit systems of taxation of business enterprises. These pass-through methods require owners of the business enterprise to account for business operations on their own tax returns. Most unincorporated businesses do in fact so report, with the exception of publicly traded partnerships and those noncorporate businesses that under the check-the-box regulations elect to be taxed as C corporations. For example, a sole proprietorship or other unincorporated business enterprise with a single owner (including a single owner limited liability company) that either cannot or does not elect corporate status for tax purposes is called a "disregarded entity" under current law and is not treated as separate from its owner; hence, the income and deductions of the business are reported on the owner's tax return. The Code provides two other principal pass-through regimes that may apply to a business enterprise that is not a disregarded entity for tax purposes: Subchapter K applies to partnerships (including limited liability companies with more than one owner that elect to be taxed as partnerships) and Subchapter S applies to a corporation that qualifies for and elects S corporation status. These two pass-through regimes are similar in that, under both regimes, generally only one level of tax is imposed on the net income of the business enterprise at the owner level, and the income and deductions of the business enterprise flow through to the owners and are reported on the owners' own tax returns. However, as the material in the following chapters will demonstrate, the similarity between the pass-through regime in Subchapter S and the pass-through regime in Subchapter K is more apparent than real. In Subchapter S, Congress has created a

¶ 15,000

system of taxing business entities that differs from the taxation of either partnerships or C corporations, and is replete with highly technical procedural requirements that have brought some taxpayers and their tax advisers to grief.

A corporation governed for tax purposes by Subchapter S bears the label, logically enough, of an "S corporation," by contrast to the so-called "C corporation" subject to the provisions of Subchapter C. § 1361(a). An S corporation is strictly a creature of congressional legislation; the S corporation status has no relevance outside of the tax law. For all nontax purposes an S corporation is indistinguishable from a corporation that has not made an S election. The end result is that the S corporation imparts the practical nontax advantage of limited liability and other nontax corporate attributes but without the disadvantageous imposition of the dual tax regime of Subchapter C.

[¶ 15,005]

1.   HISTORICAL BACKGROUND TO SUBCHAPTER S

The origins of Subchapter S trace back to 1958, many years before the advent of limited liability companies. Congress added Subchapter S to the Code for the purpose of neutralizing tax considerations for small businesses in choosing an appropriate organizational form for operations. As indicated in Chapter 1, the alternative of attempting to limit the liability of owners through a limited partnership arrangement was often unsuccessful. Active participation in management converted one's status from a limited partner to a general partner with corresponding unlimited liability, at least under the limited partnership law in effect at that time. The original congressional purpose in enacting Subchapter S was to enable small businesses to obtain the nontax advantages of incorporation while retaining the income tax consequences of operating through a partnership.

A serious challenge to the unique utility of S corporations, with their combined pass-through treatment and limited liability for owners, emerged during the early 1990s when all 50 states and the District of Columbia in rapid succession enacted enabling legislation on limited liability companies (LLCs). As their name implies, LLCs offer even active participants the promise of limited liability. They achieve this while concurrently permitting conduit tax treatment modeled on the partnership system. In addition, a new form of partnership—the limited liability partnership (LLP), in which no partner is unconditionally liable for all partnership debts—also entered the scene and likewise offered the twin benefits of a form of limited liability and pass-through treatment for federal income tax purposes.

Yet S corporations continue to thrive in number, primarily for reasons noted in the next section. At the least it is too early to dismiss Subchapter S as of historical interest only.

¶ 15,000

2. COMPARISON OF PARTNERSHIPS, LLCs, C CORPORA-TIONS, AND S CORPORATIONS

[¶ 15,010]

a. S Corporations Contrasted with Partnerships and LLCs

Ironically, although S corporations were meant to eliminate tax considerations in choosing an organizational structure for business, their perpetuation as a vehicle to conduct business operations is in large measure tax-driven. For a business already in corporate form, the S election makes it possible to achieve pass-through treatment without incurring costly taxes to liquidate and convert to partnership or LLC status. A further advantage even for new businesses is the likelihood of relatively lower payroll taxes in an S corporation's operation, for these taxes tend to be imposed only on the salaries of an S corporation's owners rather than on the totality of business earnings as is common with partnerships or LLCs. An S corporation could also yield greater discounts when valuing owners' interests for purposes of estate taxation, reflecting the comparatively greater difficulty of forcing a dissolution to reach the assets of a business enterprise conducted as a corporation as contrasted with one conducted as a partnership or LLC.

On balance, however, at least for a newly organized business enterprise, tax considerations favor a partnership or LLC over an S corporation. The major reasons are an S corporation's: (1) relative rigidity in allocations of taxable income and losses; (2) nonattribution to owners of basis from entity level borrowings; and (3) qualification for pass-through status only upon compliance with election procedure requirements and strict restrictions on the nature of the business and its owners. For additional tax considerations, see generally ¶ 1055.

Nontax features likewise tend to favor partnerships and LLCs over S corporations. That is, partnerships and LLCs enjoy freedom from the usual broad range of corporate regulations and restrictions (such as statutory dissenters' rights, reporting requirements, prohibitions on permissible consideration for which stock can be issued, and rights to distributions).[1]

In view of the numerous relative advantages enjoyed by LLCs, partnerships, and LLPs, what then accounts for the continuing appeal of S corporations, not simply for existing but for new businesses as well? The answer appears to be the discomfiting novelty inherent in the LLC/LLP structure. Experience over time will no doubt reduce the uncertainties and resulting reservations about use of LLCs. In the

---

1. Note, however, that a partnership or LLC that elects to be classified as a corporation for federal income tax purposes should be able to elect Subchapter S status (see Problem 12 at ¶ 16,077), assuming that the entity meets the eligibility requirements in § 1361(b), and obtain the nontax attributes of partnership or LLC status, but the tax features of Subchapter S status (at least for federal tax purposes).

¶ 15,010

interim, many new businesses continue to elect the treatment of Subchapter S of the Code. Thus, it is too important an area of corporate tax to ignore.

[¶ 15,015]

b. S Corporations Contrasted with C Corporations

For businesses that in fact choose to operate in corporate form for nontax reasons, the option of Subchapter K (partnership) pass-through tax treatment under the check-the-box regulations is simply not available. Alternatively, the dual taxation of corporate earnings under the Subchapter C corporate tax regime may be somewhat reduced through deductible salary, rent, royalty, and interest payments, but a far greater reduction may be achieved by electing and maintaining S corporate status. The major factors that inform the choice between S and C corporation status are discussed at ¶ 1055.

The most prominent influence from a tax perspective is that an S corporation, unlike a C corporation, is a pass-through entity the income and losses of which are reportable by its shareholders currently. In lieu of a dual level of tax on corporate operations, typical of C corporations, a single level of tax applies to corporate income and is assessed at the shareholders' own marginal rates. (As will be discussed later in the Chapter, there are some exceptions to this rule, whereby an S corporation does bear tax at the entity level.) Thus, the S corporation election is most advantageous when the corporation cannot otherwise reduce or eliminate the double tax on corporate earnings through deductible payments to the shareholders in the form of salaries, rents, or royalties, and when the rate of tax that would apply at the shareholder level on the income is less than the rate of tax that would apply at the corporate level if the corporation were a C corporation. Moreover, an S corporation election is more advantageous for a corporation that intends to distribute its net earnings currently to its shareholders, than for one that intends to retain and reinvest those earnings in the corporate business. In such a case, given the time value of money, the double tax on corporate earnings if C corporation status applies is immediate and has a greater sting than if the second, shareholder level tax can be deferred well into the future.

The analysis changes if the corporation is generating current losses, such as the start-up losses of a new business. Losses of S corporations directly and immediately reduce the taxable incomes of the shareholders, while comparable losses of C corporations produce operating loss carryovers only at the corporate level (albeit with a potential loss eventually on the shareholders' stock upon disposition to the extent that the value of the stock decreases to reflect the corporation's operating losses). Unless the corporation has a recent history of profits against which those losses may be carried back, the current losses will offset the

¶ 15,010

taxable income of the corporation only in future years. The immediate use of losses by S corporation shareholders is normally far more valuable than are deferred losses, given the time value of money. Particularly this is so when the eventual corporate income, against which the losses of a C corporation could be offset through net operating loss carryovers, is taxable at lower rates than is the income of S shareholders against which operating losses of S corporations apply. As you will see, however, the ability of shareholders to report the losses of S corporations is subject to several limitations that do not apply to the reporting of operating losses by C corporations. If shareholders cannot currently use losses allocated to them by their S corporation, the desirability of the election for a corporation with current losses quickly vanishes.

A computation of the immediate tax burdens and benefits of an S corporation election is, however, only part of the picture. By contrast to both C corporations and partnerships, an S corporation is by design severely restricted. Such factors as the statutory limitations on the corporation's capital structure and on the nature of permissible S corporation shareholders curtail both tax and nontax planning options of the shareholders, or at the least require costly adaptations of those planning options. Furthermore, the very complexity of S corporations require that the corporation obtain more frequent and more sophisticated tax advice than might be required for the routine operations of either C corporations or partnerships.

On the other hand, the Subchapter S election makes possible the avoidance of common tax pitfalls that confront C corporations. Penalty taxes on both unreasonable accumulations of earnings and the income of personal holding companies do not apply to an S corporation, and the threat of disallowed corporate deductions for unreasonable compensation or of constructive dividend income to the shareholders loses much of its sting for an S corporation. Furthermore, in the event that the business has cancellation-of-debt income governed by Section 108, the unfavorable adjustments in tax attributes called for by that provision are no more applicable at the shareholder level than if the income were that of a C corporation. § 108(d)(7). Therefore, many small businesses that have chosen to incorporate may still benefit by making a Subchapter S election.

[¶ 15,017]

c. *Overview of Policy Issues Raised by Subchapter S*

Given the distinctiveness of its tax results as contrasted with those of a C corporation, Subchapter S raises substantial questions of income tax policy. Should Subchapter S be viewed as a tax expenditure—an erosion of the corporate income tax base to subsidize small business? Or should Subchapter S be viewed as one manifestation of the notion that the double taxation of small business is unnecessary or even improper, or at least ought not depend on access to check-the-box entity classification treatment (see ¶¶ 1085 and 16,070) or the adequacy of a taxpayer's resources to obtain the tax expertise necessary to eliminate a dual level of tax? If so, are the remaining restrictions on qualifying for Subchapter S relief and its unique system of taxation justified? Consider, as you work through these materials, which of the restrictions ought to be eliminated on policy grounds.

[¶ 15,020]

3.   ILLUSTRATIVE EXAMPLE

It may help in evaluating the utility of an S election, and in understanding the procedural restrictions imposed on S corporations, to examine how the shareholders are taxed in the simplest of cases. While an S election commonly is made by an existing corporation, the purest treatment applies to newly formed corporations.

Able and Baker are co-owners of a business. Their business has a value of $100,000 and an aggregate tax basis for its assets of $30,000. Each co-owner has a $15,000 basis for his or her interest in that business. Able and Baker contribute the business to a newly formed corporation in a transaction governed by Section 351. Each partner receives 500 shares of the same class of common stock. If no debt is assumed by the corporation, Able and Baker will each have a substituted basis of $15,000 for that stock under Section 358, while the corporation will have an aggregate $30,000 carryover basis for its assets under Section 362(a)(1).

In year 1, the corporation derives gross income of $20,000 and incurs deductible expenses of $10,000. If an S election has been made for the corporation, it will not be subject to tax; rather, each shareholder's personal income tax return will include $5,000 of income (i.e., $10,000 of gross income less $5,000 of deductible expense). In addition, the basis for each shareholder's stock will be increased by the same $5,000, resulting in a year-end basis of $20,000 each.

In year 2, income equals expenses, and the corporation distributes a dividend of $3,000 to each shareholder of accumulated earnings on which each has already been taxed. That distribution constitutes a nontaxable return of capital that reduces each shareholder's stock basis by $3,000 to $17,000. If that basis were reduced to zero by either future losses or distributions, further distributions would become taxable and further losses would not be deductible until an increase in basis occurred.

For additional assistance concerning the provisions of Subchapter S of the Code, see the following helpful reference materials: J. Eustice & J. Kuntz, Federal Income Taxation of S Corporations (4th ed. 2001); J. McNulty, Federal Income Taxation of S Corporations (1992); and D. Schenk, Federal Taxation of S Corporations (1985).

B. CREATION OF AN S CORPORATION

[¶ 15,025]

1. APPLICABILITY OF SUBCHAPTER C PROVISIONS ON FORMATION

Although an S corporation is unlike a C corporation for purposes of reporting income and losses, in most other respects an S corporation remains subject to Subchapter C of the Code. § 1371(a). For example, Section 351 and the related tax provisions on corporate formation (discussed in Chapter 2) apply to an S corporation. This has on more than one occasion proven to be a trap for the unwary, as the following case illustrates.

[¶ 15,030]

WIEBUSCH v. COMMISSIONER

United States Tax Court, 1973.
59 T.C. 777, aff'd per curiam, 487 F.2d 515 (8th Cir.1973).

STERRETT, JUDGE: * * *.

* * *

Petitioners transferred assets with an adjusted basis of $119,219.08 and a fair market value of $292,975 to L & C, a subchapter S corporation, in exchange for L & C stock. The assets were subject to liabilities in the amount of $180,441.33. During 1964, 1965, and 1966, the first 3 years of operation, petitioners' share of L & C losses were $13,496.05, $21,779.90, and $13,759.73, respectively. They deducted these losses in determining their personal tax liability for each year.

The first issue we must decide is whether the petitioners must recognize as gain the excess of the liabilities assumed over the adjusted basis of property transferred to their corporation pursuant to section 357(c).

* * *

The petitioners admit that their transfer falls within the express language of section 357(c). However they attack the constitutionality of the statute. [The court rejected the argument.] * * *

* * *

The second issue we must face is whether section 1374(c)(2) [Section 1366(d)(1) of current law] precludes the deduction of losses of L & C, a subchapter S corporation, against the petitioners' personal income tax liability.

* * *

¶ 15,030

Applying the statute to the facts of the instant case, the petitioners' basis in their L & C stock is $119,219.08 decreased by liabilities of $180,441.33 (which is treated as money) and increased by the amount of gain recognized on the exchange of $61,222.25, which equals a basis of zero. The foregoing can be reflected as follows:

$119,219.08 . . . . Basis of property exchanged
− 180,441.33 . . . . Liabilities assumed (money)
+   61,222.25 . . . . Gain recognized
=   0

While section 1374(b) [Section 1366(a) of current law] allows a shareholder to offset his portion of a properly electing small business corporation loss against his personal income, section 1374(c)(2) [Section 1366(d)(1) of current law] limits this carry-through effect * * * [to the amount of the shareholder's tax basis].

Since the petitioners' basis in their stock did not increase in the years in question, and further because there was no apparent L & C indebtedness to the petitioners, their basis remained a constant zero. Hence they are not entitled to any carry-through of any portion of L & C losses. * * *

We are not without sympathy for the petitioners, for this case is simply another illustration of the frequently heard statement that subchapter S can be a bitter trap for the unwary. As exemplified here the petitioners, by the simple act of shifting their business assets from a sole proprietorship to a subchapter S corporation, incurred a statutorily created gain on the transfer and, at the same time, forfeited the right to deduct the business's subsequent losses, which would otherwise have been available to them, on their own personal tax returns. Taxwise it might be * * * said that petitioners should have "stayed in bed."

* * *

[¶ 15,035]

Notes

1. Had the petitioners "stayed in bed" and perpetuated the sole proprietorship operation, what practical disadvantages might they have faced? Could the sole owner of the proprietorship have achieved limited liability yet avoided the Subchapter C rules by converting to a limited partnership or LLC?

2. See ¶ 15,040 on the possibility of Wiebusch avoiding his zero basis problem by personally borrowing and then contributing the funds to the corporation. However, is this a practical way to proceed if someone in Wiebusch's position wishes to limit the risk of his economic losses to a lesser amount of investment?

3.   Consider how the provisions of Section 362(e)(2), enacted as part of the American Jobs Creation Act of 2004 and discussed at ¶ 2150, apply in the context of a Subchapter S corporation. If a taxpayer transfers properties to an S corporation in a transaction to which Section 351 applies and the contributed properties have an aggregate built-in loss (i.e., the total adjusted bases of the contributed properties exceed the total fair market value of the contributed properties), the S corporation's basis in the contributed properties under Section 362(a) must be reduced by the amount of the aggregate built-in loss. If the transferor transfers more than one property to the S corporation, the basis reduction required by Section 362(e)(2) will be allocated among the contributed properties in proportion to their relative amounts of built-in loss immediately before the transfer. This provision was aimed at preventing the double deduction of losses in a C corporation context, but in an S corporation context it will have the effect of deferring or limiting the deduction of built-in losses in an S corporation's contributed properties in ways that make little or no policy sense. For example, suppose that a taxpayer organizes a wholly owned S corporation by contributing property with an adjusted basis of $100,000 and a fair market value of $60,000. Under Section 362(e)(2), the S corporation's adjusted basis in the property will be reduced to $60,000; the shareholder's adjusted basis in the S corporation stock will be $100,000 under Section 358. If the S corporation sells the property a few months later for $60,000, its then fair market value, it will have no loss and the $40,000 built-in loss inherent in the stock will be deferred until the shareholder sells her stock or the corporation liquidates. It is difficult to see what policy objective is achieved by deferring the deduction of the built-in loss in this way.

As an alternative, the corporation and the shareholder could both elect under Section 362(e)(2)(C), at the time of the incorporation exchange, to instead reduce her Section 358 adjusted basis in the stock to $60,000, in which event the corporation's adjusted basis in the property transferred to it will be a carryover basis of $100,000. The S corporation then will have a $40,000 loss when it sells the property a few months later and that loss will flow through to the shareholder. The shareholder's basis in the stock will be reduced to $20,000 to reflect the flow-through of the $40,000 loss and if the shareholder sells the stock for its fair market value of $60,000, she would have a gain of $40,000 on its sale. However, there is no economic gain here and the effect of Section 362(e)(2), working together with the provisions of Subchapter S, is to eliminate (not just defer) the shareholder's economic loss of $40,000 on the contributed property (i.e., the combination of a $40,000 loss flowing through when the S corporation sells the property and a $40,000 gain when the shareholder sells her stock, which nets to zero). This is an even more questionable policy result than merely deferring the $40,000 built-in loss to the time when the shareholder sells her stock.

¶ 15,035

[¶ 15,040]

2. PLANNING THE CAPITAL STRUCTURE

Although the same statutory provisions of Subchapter C on corporate formation govern both C and S corporations, the planning principles on capital structure sharply diverge. With respect to equity interests, for example, a single class of stock is mandatory for an S corporation. See ¶¶ 15,180 et seq. Multiple classes of stock, including those resulting from debt obligations treated as a second class of stock, spell automatic ineligibility for S status. Hence, the diversified stockholdings and hybrid debt instruments commonplace and useful for a C corporation have no place in the capital structure of an S corporation.

For tax purposes it may also be inadvisable, in the S (as contrasted with the C) context, for the corporation to do the borrowing rather than the shareholders. *Wiebusch* (at ¶ 15,030) furnished one illustration of why this is so. True, its implicit lesson, about avoiding reportable gain under Section 357(c) by having the shareholders borrow and contribute added equity capital, can also be apt for a C corporation. See ¶ 2190. But this is potentially a more costly tax strategy in the long run for shareholders of a C than of an S corporation; later withdrawals from the corporation to finance the repayment of the loan will most likely constitute taxable dividends for shareholders of the C but not of the S corporation.

Another reason unique to the S corporation for involving shareholders in borrowings for corporate purposes is to increase the potential amount of corporate losses that can be passed through and deducted currently by the shareholder. This consideration is irrelevant in the Subchapter C area because a C corporation's losses do not pass through to its shareholders. See ¶¶ 15,290 et seq.

3. MAKING THE ELECTION

[¶ 15,045]

a. *A Timely Filing*

A consent to an S election, signed by the corporation and all of its shareholders and submitted before, or within two and one-half months after the start of, the year to which the election pertains is all that Section 1362(a) and (b) procedurally requires. Sounds simple, does it not?

[¶ 15,050]

LETTER RULING 8807070

* * *

¶ 15,040

The information submitted discloses that on March 4, 1987, X filed a Form 2553 (Election by a Small Business Corporation) to elect to be taxed under subchapter S * * *. On March 17, 1987, State issued a certificate of incorporation for X. Thus, X's election to be taxed as an S corporation was filed before the issuance of a certificate of incorporation by State.

* * *

In this case, X was not a domestic corporation under State law at the time X's election to be taxed as an S corporation was filed. Under analogous circumstances the Tax Court has held that an election to be taxed as an S corporation made prior to incorporation under state law is void. * * * Accordingly, we conclude that X's election to be treated as an S corporation * * * is not valid and X is not an S corporation as defined in section 1361 (formerly section 1371) * * *. * * *

[¶ 15,055]

Notes

1.   As the above ruling illustrates, for a newly formed corporation, the early bird gets a totally invalid election. See also Reg. § 1.1362–6(a)(2)(iii), Ex. 1. Facts like these tend to arise because the parties followed the perfectly logical procedure of executing all documents in a single visit to their attorney's office. Would the election have been valid—and the parties' conduct ethical—if the parties had executed the election form on March 4 but dated it March 20 and filed it on the latter date?

2.   Incidentally, when exactly does the taxable year of a new corporation begin? The regulations provide that the year begins when the corporation has shareholders, acquires assets, or begins doing business, whichever occurs first, Reg. § 1.1362–6(a)(2)(ii)(C), but when is that? If the incorporator pays a $25 fee to obtain the certificate of incorporation, does the corporation have assets?

3.   Until recent years, an election filed too late was not nearly as unpleasant as one filed too early. The tardy election might at least apply to the following taxable year, and could even take effect retroactively with a favorable private ruling from IRS. Now, under revised Section 1362(b)(5), not only premature and tardy defective elections but the absence of any election at all can be cured simply with the concurrence of the IRS. This statutory revision came about in 1996 when Congress deliberately relaxed various procedural and even some substantive restrictions in order to eliminate traps for the unwary. However, the lack or tardiness of filing must be attributable to "reasonable cause," not an attempt through a deferred election to reverse the negative tax consequences exposed through the lens of hindsight. Do the procedures

authorized in Rev. Proc. 97–48, Rev. Proc. 2003–43, and Rev. Proc. 2004–48, below, furnish appropriate conditions?

[¶ 15,060]

REVENUE PROCEDURE 97–48

1997–2 C.B. 521.

SECTION 1.   PURPOSE

This revenue procedure grants automatic relief under § 1362(b)(5) * * * for certain late S corporation elections.

* * *

SECTION 4.   AUTOMATIC RELIEF FOR LATE S CORPORATION ELECTIONS UNDER THIS REVENUE PROCEDURE

.01 *Situation 1: Automatic Relief Where Return Filed as an S Corporation.*

(1) *Eligibility for Automatic Relief.* Automatic relief is available in situation 1 if all of the following conditions are met:

(a) The corporation fails to qualify as an S corporation solely because the Form 2553 (Election by a Small Business Corporation) was not filed timely;

(b) The corporation and all of its shareholders reported their income consistent with S corporation status for the year the S corporation election should have been made, and for every subsequent taxable year (if any);

(c) At least 6 months have elapsed since the date on which the corporation filed its tax return for the first year the corporation intended to be an S corporation; and

(d) Neither the corporation nor any of its shareholders was notified by the Internal Revenue Service of any problem regarding the S corporation status within 6 months of the date on which the Form 1120S for the first year was timely filed.

(2) *Procedural Requirements for Automatic Relief.* The corporation must file with the applicable service center (or district director if under examination) a completed Form 2553, signed by an officer of the corporation authorized to sign and all persons who were shareholders at any time during the period that the corporation intended to be an S corporation. The Form 2553 must state at the top of the document "FILED PURSUANT TO REV. PROC. 97–48." Attached to the Form 2553 must be a dated declaration signed by an officer of the corporation authorized to sign and all persons who were shareholders at any time during the period that the corporation intended to be an S corporation, attesting

(but, in the case of a shareholder, only with respect to that shareholder) that:

(a) the corporation and the shareholder reported their income (on all affected returns) consistent with S corporation status for the year the S corporation election should have been made, and for every subsequent taxable year; and

(b) "Under penalties of perjury, to the best of my knowledge and belief, the facts presented in support of this election are true, correct, and complete."

* * *

[¶ 15,062]

REVENUE PROCEDURE 2003–43

2003–1 C.B. 998.

SECTION 1. PURPOSE

This revenue procedure provides a simplified method for taxpayers to request relief for late S corporation elections, Electing Small Business Trust (ESBT) elections, Qualified Subchapter S Trust (QSST) elections and Qualified Subchapter S Subsidiary (QSub) elections. Generally, this revenue procedure provides that certain eligible entities may be granted relief for failing to file these elections in a timely manner if the request for relief is filed within 24 months of the due date of the election. * * *

* * *

SECTION 3. SCOPE

.01 *In General.* This revenue procedure supersedes Rev. Proc. 98–55, 1998–2 C.B. 643, and provides relief for a late Election Under Subchapter S (as defined in section 4.01(1) of this revenue procedure.)

* * *

This revenue procedure provides procedures in lieu of the letter ruling process ordinarily used to obtain relief for a late Election Under Subchapter S filed pursuant to § 362(b)(5), § 1362(f), or § 301.9100–1 and § 301.9100–3. Accordingly, user fees do not apply to corrective actions under this revenue procedure.

.02 *Entities That Fail to Qualify for Relief Under This Revenue Procedure.*

(1) *Letter Rulings.* A corporation or trust that does not meet the requirements for relief or is denied relief under this revenue procedure may request inadvertent termination, inadvertent invalid election, or late election relief (as appropriate) by requesting a letter ruling. The

Service will not ordinarily issue a letter ruling if the period of limitations on assessment under § 6501(a) has lapsed for any taxable year for which an election should have been made or any taxable year that would have been affected by the election had it been timely made. * * *

(2) *Rev. Proc. 97–48.* Certain corporations may be eligible for automatic late S corporation election relief pursuant to Rev. Proc. 97–48, 1997–2 C.B. 521. Rev. Proc. 97–48 provides special procedures to obtain automatic relief for certain late S corporation elections. Generally, relief is available in situations in which a corporation intends to be an S corporation, the corporation and its shareholders reported their income consistent with S corporation status for the taxable year the S corporation election should have been made and for every subsequent year, and the corporation did not receive notification from the Service regarding any problem with the S corporation status within 6 months of the date on which the Form 1120S for the first year was timely filed. Rev. Proc. 97–48 does not provide relief for late ESBT, QSST or QSub elections.

SECTION 4.   RELIEF FOR LATE S CORPORATION, ESBT, QSST AND QSUB ELECTIONS UNDER THIS REVENUE PROCEDURE

.01 Definitions.

(1) *Election Under Subchapter S*: For purposes of this revenue procedure, Election Under Subchapter S refers to the filing of a Form 2553 by a corporation to be treated as a subchapter S corporation under § 1362, an election by a trustee to treat a trust as an ESBT under § 1361(e), an election by a trust beneficiary to treat a trust as a QSST under § 1361(d), or the filing of a Form 8869 by a parent S corporation to treat a subsidiary as a QSub under § 1361(b)(3).

(2) *Due Date of Election Under Subchapter S*: The Due Date of the Election Under Subchapter S will vary depending on the type of election sought. For a corporation that requests to be treated as a subchapter S corporation, the Due Date of the Election Under Subchapter S is specified by § 1362(b). For ESBT or QSST elections, the Due Date of the Election Under Subchapter S is specified by § 1.1361–1(m)(2)(iii) or § 1.1361–1(j)(6)(iii), respectively. The Due Date of the Election Under Subchapter S for a parent S corporation to make an election to treat a subsidiary as a QSub on a specific date is specified by § 1.1361–3(a)(3).

.02 *Eligibility for Relief.* Relief is available under section 4.04 of this revenue procedure if the following requirements are met:

(1) The entity fails to qualify for its intended status as an S corporation, ESBT, QSST, or QSub on the first day that status was desired solely because of the failure to file the appropriate Election Under Subchapter S timely with the applicable service center;

(2) Less than 24 months have passed since the original Due Date of the Election Under Subchapter S;

(3) Either,

(a) the entity is seeking relief for a late S corporation or QSub election and the entity has reasonable cause for its failure to make the timely Election Under Subchapter S, or

(b) the S corporation and the entity are seeking relief for an inadvertent invalid S corporation election or an inadvertent termination of an S corporation election due to the failure to make the timely ESBT or QSST election and the failure to file the timely Election Under Subchapter S was inadvertent; and

(4) Either,

(a) all of the following requirements are met: (i) the entity seeking to make the election has not filed a tax return (in the case of QSubs, the parent has not filed a tax return) for the first year in which the election was intended, (ii) the application for relief is filed under this revenue procedure no later than 6 months after the due date of the tax return (excluding extensions) of the entity seeking to make the election (in the case of QSubs, the due date of the tax return of the parent) for the first year in which the election was intended, and, (iii) no taxpayer whose tax liability or tax return would be affected by the Election Under Subchapter S (including all shareholders of the S corporation) has reported inconsistently with the S corporation election (as well as any ESBT, QSST or QSub elections), on any affected return for the year the Election Under Subchapter S was intended; or

(b) all of the following requirements are met: (i) the entity seeking to make the election has filed a tax return (in the case of QSubs, the parent has filed a tax return) for the first year in which the election was intended within 6 months of the due date of the tax return (excluding extensions), and (ii) all taxpayers whose tax liability or tax returns would be affected by the Election Under Subchapter S (including all shareholders of the S corporation) have reported consistently with the S corporation election (as well as any ESBT, QSST or QSub elections), on all affected returns for the year the Election Under Subchapter S was intended, as well as for any subsequent years.

.03 Procedural Requirements for Relief.

(1) *Procedural Requirements When a Tax Return Has Not Been Filed for the First Year of the Intended Election Under Subchapter S.* If the entity seeking the election has not filed a tax return for the first taxable year of the intended Election Under Subchapter S, the entity may request relief for the late Election Under Subchapter S by filing with the applicable service center the properly completed election form(s). The election form(s) must be filed within 18 months of the original Due Date of the intended Election Under Subchapter S (but in

¶ 15,062

no event later than 6 months after the due date of the tax return (excluding extensions) of the entity (in the case of QSubs, the due date of the tax return of the parent) for the first year in which the election was intended) and must state at the top of the document "FILED PURSU-ANT TO REV. PROC. 2003–43." Attached to the election form must be a statement establishing either reasonable cause for the failure to file the Election Under Subchapter S timely (in the case of S corporation or QSub elections), or a statement establishing that the failure to file the Election Under Subchapter S timely was inadvertent (in the case of ESBT or QSST elections.)

(2) *Procedural Requirements When a Tax Return Has Been Filed for the First Year of the Intended Election Under Subchapter S.* If the entity seeking the election has filed a tax return for the first taxable year of the intended Election Under Subchapter S within 6 months of the due date of that tax return (excluding extensions), then the entity may request relief for the late Election Under Subchapter S by filing with the applicable service center the properly completed election form(s) and the supporting documents described below. The election form(s) must be filed within 24 months of the original Due Date for the Election Under Subchapter S and must state at the top of the document "FILED PURSUANT TO REV. PROC. 2003–43." Attached to the election form must be a statement establishing either reasonable cause for the failure to file the Election Under Subchapter S timely (in the case of S corporation or QSub elections), or a statement establishing that the failure to file the Election Under Subchapter S timely was inadvertent (in the case of ESBT or QSST elections.) The following additional documents must be attached to the election form (if applicable):

(a) *S Corporations.* An entity seeking relief for a late S corporation election must file a completed Form 2553, signed by an officer of the corporation authorized to sign and all persons who were shareholders at any time during the period that began on the first day of the taxable year for which the election is to be effective and ends on the day the election is made. The completed election form must include the following material:

(i) Statements from all shareholders during the period between the date the S corporation election was to have become effective and the date the completed election was filed that they have reported their income (on all affected returns) consistent with the S corporation election for the year the election should have been made and for all subsequent years; and

(ii) A dated declaration signed by an officer of the corporation authorized to sign which states: "Under penalties of perjury, I declare that, to the best of my knowledge and belief, the facts presented in support of this election are true, correct, and complete."

* * *

¶ 15,062

.04 *Relief for Late Election Under Subchapter S.* Upon receipt of a completed application requesting relief under section 4.03 of this revenue procedure, the Service will determine whether the requirements for granting additional time to file the Election Under Subchapter S have been satisfied and will notify the entity of the result of this determination.

* * *

[¶ 15,063]

REVENUE PROCEDURE 2004–48

2004–2 C.B. 172.

SECTION 1. PURPOSE

This revenue procedure provides a simplified method for taxpayers to request relief for a late S corporation election and a late corporate classification election which was intended to be effective on the same date that the S corporation election was intended to be effective. Generally, this revenue procedure provides that certain eligible entities may be granted relief if the entity satisfies the requirements of section 4 of this revenue procedure.

* * *

SECTION 3. SCOPE

.01 *In General.* An eligible entity that seeks to be classified as a subchapter S corporation must elect to be classified as an association under § 301.7701–3(c)(1)(i) by filing Form 8832 and must elect to be an S corporation under § 1362(a) by filing Form 2553, *Election by a Small Business Corporation.* In many situations, an entity may timely file Form 2553 but fail to file the Form 8832. Section 301.7701–3T(c)(1)(v)(C) applies to these situations and deems an eligible entity that timely files a Form 2553 to also have filed a Form 8832. In other situations, an eligible entity fails to file a timely Form 2553. In these situations, § 301.7701–3T(c)(1)(v)(C) does not apply and the entity would be required to obtain relief in a letter ruling. This revenue procedure provides a simplified method for requesting relief for those situations not covered by § 301.7701–3T, provided that the requirements of sections 4.01 and 4.02 of this revenue procedure are satisfied. The method provided in this revenue procedure is in lieu of the letter ruling process ordinarily used to obtain relief for late elections under §§ 1362(b)(5), 301.9100–1, and 301.9100–3. Accordingly, user fees do not apply to corrective action under this revenue procedure.

.02 *Relief if this Revenue Procedure is not Applicable.* An entity that does not meet the requirements for relief or is denied relief under this revenue procedure may seek relief by requesting a letter ruling. * * *

¶ 15,063

SECTION 4. RELIEF FOR LATE S CORPORATION ELECTION AND LATE CORPORATE CLASSIFICATION ELECTION

.01 *Eligibility for Relief.* An entity may request relief under this revenue procedure if the following requirements are met:

(1) The entity is an eligible entity as defined in § 301.7701–3(a);

(2) The entity intended to be classified as a corporation as of the intended effective date of the S corporation status;

(3) The entity fails to qualify as a corporation solely because Form 8832 was not timely filed under § 301.7100–3(c)(1)(i), or Form 8832 was not deemed to have been filed under § 301.7701–3T(c)(1)(v)(C);

(4) In addition to section 4.01(3) of this section, the entity fails to qualify as an S corporation on the intended effective date of the S corporation status solely because the S corporation election was not filed timely pursuant to § 1362(b); and

(5) The entity has reasonable cause for its failure to file timely the S corporation election and the entity classification election.

.02 *Procedural Requirements for Relief.* Within 6 months after the due date for the tax return, excluding extensions, for the first year the entity intended to be an S corporation), the corporation must file a properly completed Form 2553 with the applicable service center. The Form 2553 must state at the top of the document "FILED PURSUANT TO REV. PROC. 2004–48." Attached to the Form 2553 must be a statement explaining the reason for the failure to file timely the S corporation election and a statement explaining the reason for the failure to file timely the entity classification election.

.03 *Relief for Late S Corporation Election and Relief for a Late Corporate Classification Election.* Upon receipt of a completed application requesting relief under section 4 of this revenue procedure, the Service will determine whether the requirements for granting additional time to file the elections have been satisfied and will notify the entity of the result of this determination. An entity receiving relief under this revenue procedure is treated as having made an election to be classified as an association taxable as a corporation under § 301.7701–3(c) as of the effective date of the S corporation election.

* * *

[¶ 15,064]

Note

The regulations now provide that if an entity eligible to elect its classification for federal income tax purposes files a timely election to be an S corporation, it will be deemed to have made an election to be classified as a corporation as of the effective date of the S election, provided that the entity meets all of the other requirements for making an S election. Reg. § 301.7701–3(c)(1)(v)(C).

[¶ 15,065]

Problems

1.   A calendar year C corporation, wishing to make a Subchapter S election for year 1, filed its election on April 1 of that year, together with the consents of all of its shareholders. Can it utilize the procedure outlined in Rev. Proc. 2003–43, at ¶ 15,062, to cure the tardiness of its election, or must it instead apply for a favorable private ruling under Section 1362(f) and incur the attendant costs? What must the taxpayer show?

2.   A calendar year C corporation intended to make a Subchapter S election for year 1 and obtained consents to the election from all of its shareholders but did not file a timely election form. On March 15 of year 2, the corporation files a Form 1120S (an S corporation income tax return) for the year 1 taxable year, and all of its shareholders file their individual returns reporting their shares of the corporation's income and deductions as if the corporation were an S corporation. In October of year 2, the corporation realizes that an S corporation election was not timely filed. Neither the corporation nor its shareholders received any notification from the IRS of any problem regarding the corporation's status as an S corporation. Can the corporation utilize the procedure outlined in Rev. Proc. 97–48, at ¶ 15,060, to cure the tardiness of its election?

3.   A calendar year LLC, which is an eligible entity, intended to make an election to be classified as a corporation for year 1 and also intended to make a Subchapter S election for year 1. The LLC obtained consents to the election from all of its members to make the S election but did not file a timely association election form or an entity classification election form. On March 15 of year 2, the corporation files a Form 1120S (an S corporation income tax return) for the year 1 taxable year, and all of its shareholders file their individual returns reporting their shares of the corporation's income and deductions as if the corporation were an S corporation. In June of year 2, the LLC realizes that it had not timely filed either election form. Can the LLC utilize the procedure outlined in Rev. Proc. 2004–48, at ¶ 15,063, to cure the tardiness of the elections?

[¶ 15,070]

b.   Effective Date of Election

An election of S status may be filed by an existing corporation at any time prior to the year for which it is to be effective, or instead, for both new and existing corporations, at any time during the first two and one-

¶ 15,070

half months of the year for which the election is to be effective. § 1362(b)(1). The latter filing, if valid, becomes retroactively effective to the beginning of that year. For the election to be given effect, the corporation must meet the definitional requirements of Subchapter S during each day of the year to which the election applies, and the election must be accompanied by the consents of all shareholders on the filing date, § 1362(a)(2), and also by all who were shareholders during the portion of the year preceding the filing, § 1362(b)(2)(B)(ii)—the obvious reason being that all such shareholders would be affected by an election of pass-through treatment for that period.

If stock in a corporation is acquired more than two and one-half months after the beginning of its taxable year, the new owners generally cannot cause the corporation to elect Subchapter S treatment until the beginning of the following year. However, under the consolidated return regulations, if a corporation leaves a consolidated group, its first separate year begins on the day following deconsolidation. See Reg. § 1.1502–76(b). Thus, if the acquired corporation had been a member of a consolidated group immediately before the acquisition, the new owners could immediately elect Subchapter S status. See Letter Ruling 8443039. If a taxpayer wishes to acquire a corporation that is not a member of an affiliated group and to elect under Subchapter S immediately, how must the acquisition be structured?

A tardy S election attempted more than two and one-half months after the beginning of the corporation's taxable year, and that is otherwise valid, will at the least be effective the following year if all eligibility requirements are then still met. § 1362(b)(3). It may even be effective retroactively, as indicated above, if reasonable cause existed for the tardiness. Whether other defects beyond timing can be cured retroactively depends on the nature of and reason for the defect in the election. Under limited conditions, Section 1362(f) now permits retroactive correction both of the failure to obtain a shareholder's consent and the failure of the corporation to comply with the eligibility requirements of Section 1361(b), discussed below. The cure to an election defective for these reasons necessitates (i) that within a reasonable time after discovering the defects, curative action be taken; (ii) inadvertence as the cause of the defect; and (iii) agreement by the corporation and all potentially affected shareholders to adjustments in tax reporting consistent with corrective actions.

c. *Who Must Consent to the Election*

[¶ 15,075]

KEAN v. COMMISIONER

United States Court of Appeals, Ninth Circuit, 1972.
469 F.2d 1183.

WM. MATTHEW BYRNE, JR., DISTRICT JUDGE:

Appellants, petitioners in the Tax Court, were shareholders in Ocean Shores Bowl, Inc., hereinafter referred to as Bowl, a Washington corporation. They appeal from a judgment of the Tax Court, * * * invalidating Bowl's election, under Subchapter S, * * * and disallowing petitioners' deductions on their personal tax returns of their pro rata shares of Bowl's 1962 and 1963 net operating losses.

Bowl was formed on March 20, 1962 and had only one class of stock issued and outstanding. On October 30, 1962 Bowl filed a timely election to be taxed as a small business corporation pursuant to § [1362] * * *. Consents to such election were contemporaneously filed by all of the shareholders of record and their wives. As a result of the election, Bowl's net operating losses of $15,316 for the short taxable year 1962 and $56,638.28 for 1963 were deducted in pro rata shares by petitioners on their 1962 and 1963 personal income tax returns.

Some Bowl debentures and 125 shares of Bowl stock were held in the name of petitioner, William MacPherson. He and his brother, petitioner Murdock MacPherson, were engaged in the real estate business in a company called MacPhersons, Inc. Each brother owned 45% of the stock of MacPhersons, Inc. with the remaining 10% being held by their mother. William and Murdock MacPherson had many joint investments which were conducted without any written agreement. Whoever initiated the investment would normally be responsible for its management. Neither held a power of attorney for the other. The books and records of MacPhersons, Inc. were maintained by its employee, Donald Minkler.

On their 1962 joint income tax return William MacPherson and his wife deducted the net operating loss of Bowl accruing to the 125 shares in William's name. In 1963 William MacPherson and his wife deducted one half of the net operating loss for that year attributed to said shares while Murdock MacPherson and his wife deducted the other one half on their joint return. In 1964 the William MacPhersons and the Murdock MacPhersons each reported the sale of one half of the 125 shares of Bowl stock and one half of the Bowl debentures. All of these returns were prepared by Donald Minkler.

A 1965 Internal Revenue Service audit disclosed that the 125 shares of Bowl stock and Bowl debentures, issued to William MacPherson in 1962, were purchased with a MacPhersons, Inc. check. The cost of the

¶ 15,075

purchase was charged on the books of MacPhersons, Inc. equally against the drawing accounts of William and Murdock. Murdock MacPherson has never been repaid by William MacPherson for the amounts taken out of his drawing account to pay for the stock and debentures.

Murdock MacPherson was not a shareholder of record of Bowl. Neither he nor his wife were mentioned in the Subchapter S election filed with the Internal Revenue Service in October, 1962; nor did they file a consent to the election. None of the other shareholders knew that Murdock MacPherson was involved in any way with Bowl until the 1965 audit.

The Tax Court held that Bowl's Subchapter S election was invalid because Murdock MacPherson, as a beneficial owner of Bowl stock, was a shareholder within the meaning of § [1361] and had not consented to the corporation's election. Based on this finding, the court disallowed petitioners' deduction of their pro rata shares of the corporation's net operating losses.

* * * Section [1362] provides that the corporation's election is "valid only if all persons who are shareholders ... consent to such election."

Petitioners contend that since Murdock MacPherson was not a shareholder of record and was not able to exercise any rights as a shareholder under Washington law, he was not a "shareholder" under § [1362]. We disagree. The question of who is a shareholder as the term is used in Subchapter S must be determined by federal rather than state law. * * * [Former] Treasury Regulation § 1.1371–1(d)(1), implementing Subchapter S, states that "Ordinarily, the persons who would have to include in gross income dividends distributed with respect to the stock of the corporation are considered to be shareholders * * *."

* * *

Subchapter S allows shareholders of a small business corporation to elect alternative tax consequences resulting from stock ownership. Without a Subchapter S election the corporation is liable for corporate taxes, the shareholders cannot deduct corporate losses, and only distributed dividends are subject to the personal income tax. If the election is made, the corporation is exempt from corporate taxes and the shareholders may deduct corporate net operating losses but must pay personal income tax on all corporate income whether distributed or not. The desirability of a Subchapter S election depends upon the individual tax considerations of each shareholder. The final determination of whether there is to be an election should be made by those who would suffer the tax consequences of it. Therefore, "shareholders" who must file a consent are not necessarily "shareholders of record" but rather beneficial owners of shares "who would have to include in gross income dividends distributed with respect to the stock of the corporation." [Former] Treas.Reg. § 1.1371–1(d)(1)* * *.

A treasury regulation which supplies the definition that Congress omitted must be sustained unless unreasonable and obviously inconsistent with the statute. * * * [Former] Treasury Regulation § 1.1371–1(d)(1) is consistent with the basic purpose of Subchapter S and reasonably implements the legislative mandate.

We conclude, as did the Tax Court, that William and Murdock MacPherson jointly invested in the 125 shares of Bowl stock issued to William MacPherson. Murdock MacPherson was the beneficial owner of one half of that stock in William MacPherson's name and must be considered a "shareholder" for the purpose of § [1362]. Murdock MacPherson's failure to file a consent invalidates Bowl's Subchapter S election. Therefore, petitioners were not entitled to deduct their pro rata shares of Bowl's net operating loss for 1962 and 1963.

* * *

Finally, petitioners contend that the District Director abused the discretion reposed in him [to extend the time for filing consents to the Subchapter S election] and that the Tax Court erred in refusing to review the exercise of the District Director's discretion.

* * *

* * * There was reasonable cause for Murdock MacPherson's failure to file a timely consent. Murdock MacPherson was not a shareholder of record. He believed that whatever ownership interest he had in the shares did not necessitate his consent to Bowl's election. When the Internal Revenue Service disagreed with this position, the petitioners sought a judicial determination. Until the Tax Court issued its opinion, Murdock MacPherson did not know that his consent was required to consummate Bowl's election under § [1362]. Furthermore, there is nothing to indicate that any government interest is jeopardized by now validating the Subchapter S election.

At the time of the Subchapter S election, petitioners, other than possibly the MacPhersons, did not know or have reason to suspect that Murdock MacPherson had any ownership interest in Bowl's stock. The District Director's failure to exercise his discretion so as to allow petitioners to file their consents deprives eight taxpayers of deductions taken in good faith ten years earlier and saddles each taxpayer with a substantial liability for back taxes. * * *

The District Director abused his discretion by arbitrarily refusing to allow petitioners an extension of time in which to file their consent to Bowl's Subchapter S election. * * *

We * * * order the District Director to grant petitioners an extension of time to file the consents [for the years 1962 and 1963]* * *.

¶ **15,075**

[¶ 15,080]

Notes

1. As discussed in the *Kean* case, in addition to the consent required by an authorized corporate official on behalf of the corporation, all actual and deemed shareholders of an S corporation must consent to the S election, including certain shareholders not counted toward the now 100–shareholder ceiling (Reg. § 1.1362–6(b)(2)). This includes, for example, all members of the same family who own stock in the S corporation at the time of the election, even though all such family members may be treated as one shareholder for purposes of the 100–shareholder ceiling under Section 1361(c)(1)(A)(ii), discussed below in Note 2 at ¶ 15,105. Does this seem reasonable, given the impact of an election on all such parties?

Note that under current law, a new shareholder of a corporation that already has properly made an S election does not have to consent to the election. Reg. § 1.1362–6(a)(2)(i) and (b)(3)(ii), Ex. 2. Thus, once a corporation's S election has been properly made, it continues until it is terminated by voluntary revocation, the corporation failing to meet the shareholder level or corporate level definitional requirements on any day, or the corporation deriving an excessive amount of passive income and the election terminating under Section 1362(d)(3). See ¶ 15,455.

2. Reg. § 1.1361–1(e)(1) provides that "[o]rdinarily, the person who would have to include in gross income dividends distributed with respect to the stock of the corporation (if the corporation were a C corporation)" is treated as the shareholder of the stock for S election purposes.

3. The defective election in *Kean* could not be cured by the procedure outlined above in Rev. Proc. 97–48, due to the failure of all of the corporation's shareholders (i.e., Murdock MacPherson) to file their individual returns consistent with S corporation status, or by the procedure outlined above in Rev. Proc. 2003–43, due to the delayed date of discovery. However, the facts do seem amenable to a showing that the defect was attributable to inadvertence and hence qualified for relief pursuant to Section 1362(f). In such case, rectification of the defect can be sought through a request for a favorable private ruling. Why the difference in procedures?

4. Regardless of whether Murdock MacPherson was an undisclosed shareholder or an impermissible partner, how is an S corporation to protect its eligibility? Would restrictions on the transferability of the stock involved in *Kean* have helped? In American Nurseryman Publishing Co. v. Commissioner, 75 T.C. 271 (1980), aff'd without published opinion, 673 F.2d 1333 (7th Cir.1981), the court found an S election invalidated by a stock transfer which the state courts had held to be void ab initio—but the facts have the unmistakable odor of attempted retroactive tax planning.

¶ 15,080

[¶ 15,085]

Problems

For each of the following situations, determine who must consent to the making of a new Subchapter S election.

1. X and Y are the original incorporators of XYZ Corporation. Each receives 1,000 shares at the time of incorporation in exchange for capital contributions of property. Z receives 1,000 shares of restricted stock which will vest indefeasibly once Z works for the corporation for three years. See Reg. § 1.1361–1(b)(3).

2. Now assume that X and Y are a married couple, each owning 1,000 shares of stock in his and her individual names. See Reg. § 1.1361–1(e)(2).

3. H dies and the stock passes to his estate, of which individual X is the executor and A, B, and C are the beneficiaries. See Reg. § 1.1361–1(e)(1) (last sentence).

[¶ 15,090]

C. ELIGIBILITY TO ELECT/MAINTAIN ELECTION

Only corporations that meet a precise list of definitional tests are eligible for S corporation status. This list raises critical policy questions. On the one hand, procedural restrictions along the lines discussed above serve an obvious function of assuring notice to and consent by those who would be affected by the pass-through treatment, as well as protection of the government's interests against taxpayers benefitting from hindsight. By contrast, which of the substantive restrictions of Subchapter S are essential to a system of conduit taxation for small businesses? Is the availability of partnership tax treatment for LLCs relevant to the requirements that should be imposed by Subchapter S?

As you proceed through the following materials, note that the definitional requirements on eligibility to elect S status have a dual role. Each must be met in order to elect S status, and subsequent failure to satisfy any of the tests can cause the status to terminate.

While only a so-called small business corporation, as defined in Section 1361(b), may make an S election, there are no definitional tests concerning either the income or net worth of the corporation. Compare the limitations on the size of "qualified small businesses" eligible for special preferential tax treatment under Section 1202, discussed in Chapter 3. Do differences in the respective underlying statutory purposes explain, and even justify, the distinctive statutory definitional requirements?

¶ 15,090

1. SHAREHOLDER LEVEL REQUIREMENTS

[¶ 15,095]

a. 100–Shareholder Limit

In keeping with the basic legislative purpose of Subchapter S, of providing tax relief for "small corporations," the Code originally permitted only 10 shareholders. The authorized number was later increased to 35 to correspond with the cutoff between public and private securities offerings. The 1996 Act raised it to 75. Reg. § 1.1361–1(e)(1). The American Jobs Creation Act of 2004 further increased the limit to 100 and, as more fully described below, added a provision that treats all members of the same family as one shareholder for purposes of this limit. § 1361(b)(1)(A) and (c)(1). The express purpose was to modernize the S corporation rules and in general to eliminate undue restrictions on the availability of Subchapter S so that a greater number of corporations and shareholders are able to obtain the benefits of Subchapter S status. See H.R. Rep. No. 548, pt. 1, 108th Cong., 2d Sess. 128 (2004).

Are there any practical limits now on the maximum number of shareholders in view of these changes to the statutory rules and the following ruling? What tax policy purpose is being served by retaining this expanded shareholder limit?

[¶ 15,100]

REVENUE RULING 94–43

1994–2 C.B. 198.

In Rev. Rul. 77–220, 1977–1 C.B. 263, thirty unrelated individuals entered into the joint operation of a single business. The individuals divided into three equal groups of ten individuals and each group formed a separate corporation. The three corporations then organized a partnership for the joint operation of the business. The principal purpose for forming three separate corporations instead of one corporation was to avoid the 10 shareholder limitation of § 1371 of the Internal Revenue Code of 1954 (the predecessor of § 1361) and thereby allow the corporations to elect to be treated as S corporations under Subchapter S.

Rev. Rul. 77–220 concluded that the three corporations should be considered to be a single corporation, solely for purposes of making the election, because the principal purpose for organizing the separate corporations was to make the election. Under this approach, there would be 30 shareholders in one corporation and the election made by this corporation would not be valid because the 10 shareholder limitation would be violated.

The Service has reconsidered Rev. Rul. 77–220 and concluded that the election of the separate corporations should be respected. The purpose of the number of shareholders requirement is to restrict S corporation status to corporations with a limited number of shareholders so as to obtain administrative simplicity in the administration of the corporation's tax affairs. In this context, administrative simplicity is not affected by the corporation's participation in a partnership with other S corporation partners; nor should a shareholder of one S corporation be considered a shareholder of another S corporation because the S corporations are partners in a partnership. Thus, the fact that several S corporations are partners in a single partnership does not increase the administrative complexity at the S corporation level. As a result, the purpose of the number of shareholders requirement is not avoided by the structure in Rev. Rul. 77–220 * * *.

* * *

Rev. Rul. 77–220 is hereby revoked.

[¶ 15,105]

Notes

1. The positive result announced in the above ruling is the culmination of a series of favorable private rulings in which the IRS approved organizational structures that effectively allowed more than the then permissible 35 beneficial owners of an S corporation. In each of those private rulings the IRS noted the presence of a business purpose beyond mere avoidance of the 35–shareholder limit. To the surprise of observers, however, the justification relied on in Rev. Rul. 94–43 seems to be a revisionist explanation of the alleged congressional purpose for the original limit imposed on the permissible number of shareholders.

2. For purposes of applying the 100–shareholder limit of current law, a husband and wife (and their estates) are treated as one shareholder. § 1361(c)(1)(A)(i); Reg. § 1.1361–1(e)(2). In addition, under a statutory provision added to the Code in 2004 and revised in 2005, all members of a family (and their estates) are treated as one shareholder for purposes of this limit. § 1361(c)(1)(A)(ii). The term "members of the family" is defined for this purpose to mean the common ancestor, any lineal descendant of the common ancestor, and any spouse or former spouse of the common ancestor or any such lineal descendant. The common ancestor cannot be more than six generations removed from the youngest generation of shareholders on the "applicable date," which is the date that is the later of (i) the date that the Subchapter S election is made, (ii) the earliest date that a member of the family holds stock in the S corporation, or (iii) the effective date of this statutory change (October 22, 2004). In applying this rule, a spouse or former spouse is treated as being of the same generation as the individual to whom such spouse is or was married. § 1361(c)(1)(B). A legally adopted child, a child placed with an individual for legal adoption by the individual, and any eligible foster child of an individual is treated as a child of the individual

for purposes of this rule. § 1361(c)(1)(C). (The Treasury and the IRS provided their initial guidance under this provision in IRS Notice 2005–91, 2005–2 C.B. 1164.) Note that this provision, combined with the expanded 100–shareholder limit, makes it far less likely that taxpayers will have to use partnership arrangements of the type sanctioned in Rev. Rul. 94–43 to qualify for Subchapter S status.

3.   As discussed below at ¶ 15,145, Section 1361(c)(2)(A)(v) permits an "electing small business trust" to serve as an eligible shareholder of an S corporation, although Section 1361(c)(2)(B)(v) requires that each potential current beneficiary of such trust "be treated as a shareholder * * *." Reg. § 1.1361–1(m)(4)(i) provides that a potential current beneficiary "generally is, with respect to any period, any person who at any time during such period is entitled to, or in the discretion of any person may receive, a distribution from the principal or income of the trust." The IRS's position, expressed in Reg. § 1.1361–1(m)(4)(i) and (vii) and IRS Notice 97–12, discussed at ¶ 15,145, is that this separate counting of beneficiaries pertains both to determining who by nature is an eligible shareholder and whether the limit on the permissible number of shareholders has been exceeded. If this is a correct interpretation, might the 100–shareholder limitation be skirted in the case of 120 beneficiaries by, for example, creating three electing small business trusts each with 40 beneficiaries, each of which would in turn create a separate S corporation to serve as a partner of the other corporations in operating a single business?

4.   For purposes of this limit, Reg. § 1.1361–1(m)(4)(vii) takes the position that a person is counted as only one shareholder of an S corporation even though the person may both directly own stock in the corporation and own stock in the corporation through one or more eligible trusts described in Section 1361(c)(2)(A). For example, if a person owns stock directly in an S corporation and also is a potential current beneficiary of an electing small business trust owning stock in the same S corporation, that person is counted as only one shareholder.

[¶ 15,110]

b.   Nature of Authorized Shareholders, In General

Only a rigidly screened group of taxpayers can serve as shareholders of an S corporation. The austere listing under Section 1361(b)(1)(B) and (C) rules out many forms of trusts as well as all partnerships, LLCs, foreign taxpayers, and most corporations and tax-exempt entities. Those who remain as eligible shareholders are individuals, other than nonresident aliens, § 1361(b)(1)(C); estates (of both bankrupts and decedents, the latter for a limited time period only), § 1361(b)(1)(B) and (c)(3); certain trusts described in Section 1361(c)(2) (some also eligible for only a limited time period); and a severely limited group of corporate entities and tax-exempt organizations, § 1361(b)(1)(B) and (c)(6).

¶ 15,105

What prompted Congress's original restrictive approach was a desire to facilitate the application and operation of the conduit regime while maintaining the integrity of the tax base. To these ends it authorized the pass-through of an S corporation's income and losses only if this could be accomplished with relatively minimal administrative complexity, in strict proportion to stockholdings, but without a loss of revenues on the passed-through income. The consequence was the ineligibility of trusts and other entities as shareholders due to their potential to allocate passed-through items among their owners or beneficiaries in complex and varying ratios, or to accumulate income for those owners but within the shelter of the entity's own tax rates. The disqualification of nonresident aliens stemmed from fears about difficulty or inability to collect the tax due on passed-through items—a concern that has not, however, affected eligibility of nonresident aliens as partners for purposes of Subchapter K.

[¶ 15,115]

2. TRUSTS AND OTHER (IN)ELIGIBLE SHAREHOLDERS

A compromising tolerance has spread into Congress's once-hostile attitude toward trusts as shareholders of S corporations. The change reflects a combination of increased deference to common estate planning techniques, and an interest in liberalizing access to Subchapter S treatment for small businesses and in eliminating previous traps for the unwary. How much more liberalization would be appropriate?[2]

[¶ 15,120]

a. *Grantor and Grantor–Like Trusts*

Not all forms of trust occasion the risks of complexity and tax avoidance that Congress originally sought to avoid by its restrictions on permissible shareholders. For example, a so-called "grantor trust" described by Sections 671–677 holds the settlor responsible for reporting all trust items by virtue of that settlor's retained broad interests or controls. Such a trust automatically eliminates any potential for income allocation or replacement of the beneficiary's tax rate with that of the trust. The same is true of a grantor-like trust covered by Section 678, for there a person other than the settlor possesses the right to divert the income or corpus to his or her own favor and accordingly must report all

---

2. In a further "liberalizing" move by Congress in 2004, a trust constituting an individual retirement account is eligible to hold stock in an S corporation that is a bank, but only to the extent of the stock held by the trust in the banking corporation on the date of enactment of the provision (i.e., October 22, 2004). § 1361(c)(2)(A)(vi). In this case, the individual for whose bene- fit the trust was created is treated as the shareholder of the S corporation. § 1361(c)(2)(B)(vi). The limited applicability of this provision to pre-existing IRA stock held in banking corporations suggests that it is a special interest provision designed to apply to only a targeted group of taxpayers.

items of the trust. Consequently, both a grantor and grantor-like trust are eligible shareholders. § 1361(c)(2)(A)(i); Reg. § 1.1361–1(h)(1)(i). Similar reasons justify the eligibility status of a Qualified Subchapter S Trust, discussed immediately below. § 1361(d).

[¶ 15,125]

b.   *Qualified Subchapter S Trusts*

Unlike a grantor trust, the trust known as a "Qualified Subchapter S Trust" (QSST) does not by its nature require all its income to be reported by its beneficiary, although by election of the beneficiary that can be the result. In the event of such election, Section 1361(d)(1)(B) treats the beneficiary as the owner of the portion of the trust that consists of the S corporation stock. In turn Section 678(a) assures that the items of income and loss of the trust attributable to the S corporation are taxed directly to the beneficiary. Other requirements of a QSST further ensure that this beneficiary, who must be a citizen or resident of the United States, will be taxed on the trust income. See § 1361(d)(3).

The addition of this type of trust to the roster of eligible shareholders permits some estate planning flexibility as to the shareholders of an S corporation. It in effect tolerates having S corporate stock held in the corpus of three types of trusts commonly used in transfer tax planning: both the marital deduction power of appointment trust (Section 2056(b)(5)) and the QTIP trust (Section 2056(b)(7)), as well as the Section 2503(c) trust for a minor. All three can be drafted to qualify as QSSTs.

[¶ 15,130]

Notes

1.   Upon a shift in a QSST's beneficiaries, any successor income beneficiary can affirmatively refuse to consent to the election. § 1361(d)(2)(B)(ii); Reg. § 1.1361–1(j)(9) and (10). Could such a successor, by threatening to withhold a consent that would implicitly terminate the QSST election and thereby the Subchapter S election, use that power to extort payment from the other S corporation shareholders? How can the corporation protect itself against such a possibility? See Note 4 at ¶ 15,210.

2.   In view of the requirement of Section 1361(d)(3)(B), that all the "income" of a QSST must be "distributed (or required to be distributed) currently," would a trust fail to qualify as a QSST if the S corporation in which it holds stock deliberately retains some of its taxable income for the year rather than distributing it all to its shareholders? See Reg. § 1.1361–1(j)(1)(i) and Letter Ruling 8839006. Based on Section 643(b) and Reg. § 1.643(b)–1, which construe the word "income" to refer to income in the trust accounting sense (i.e., as determined under the

¶ 15,120

terms of the governing instrument and applicable local law), the ruling concludes that the distribution requirement of Section 1361(d)(3)(B) will not be violated if the corporation's undistributed income does not constitute accounting income under the terms of the governing instrument. Moreover, as the ruling observes, if the corporation is an S corporation, its income will be reported directly by its shareholders whether or not distributed.

3. Rev. Proc. 2003–43, §§ 2.03, 4, 2003–1 C.B. 998, provides relief for certain late QSST elections.

4. If not all income of a trust is required to be distributed currently, and that trust is neither a grantor nor grantor-like trust, the "Electing Small Business Trust," discussed below at ¶ 15,145, presents another possibility for achieving eligible shareholder status.

[¶ 15,135]

c. Trusts in the Two-Year, Post–Death Period

For a brief two-year, post-death grace period, the statutory list of permissible shareholders temporarily expands to accommodate certain trusts that would otherwise be ineligible shareholders of an S corporation. This suspension of the usual eligibility rules permits an orderly transition of wealth to occur without a disruption of S status as interests in S corporate stock change hands at the death of a qualified shareholder. Instead of forfeiture of S status after the death of the deemed owner of a grantor or grantor-like trust, including a QSST, or following the distribution from an estate to a testamentary trust of a deceased shareholder's stock, the trusts holding such stock enjoy two years during which to make substitute arrangements for qualified shareholders in compliance with the usual list of eligible shareholders. See § 1361(c)(2)(A)(ii) and (iii); Reg. § 1.1361–1(h)(1)(ii) and (iv).

[¶ 15,140]

Problems

1. Emma transfers the shares in her wholly owned corporation to a revocable trust, of which her attorney Y is trustee, for the benefit of her three children, one of whom is a nonresident alien.

a. Determine whether the corporation would be eligible to make an S election, who would be counted toward the 100–shareholder ceiling, and who must consent to the election. See §§ 676 and 1361(c)(1), (c)(2)(A)(i), and (B)(i).

b. What if, before making the election, Emma had released all of her powers over the trust, and one of her daughters who was a U.S. citizen had the power annually to withdraw all of the trust income? See § 678.

c. What would become of the S corporate status at the death of Emma in Problem 1.a., or of her daughter in Problem 1.b.?

2. Marcus, who was the sole proprietor of a residential roofing business, has just died. In his will, he directs his executor to incorporate his business and transfer the stock to a trust that he had previously established for his minor daughter. That trust is to terminate when his daughter reaches age 21, and until then the trustee may accumulate or distribute income and corpus as he deems desirable for the benefit of the daughter.

a. Upon incorporation, may the executor make an S election? See § 1361(c)(2)(A)(iii) and (B)(iii).

b. If so, what will happen when the stock is transferred to the trust? See § 1361(d).

c. How long can the estate avoid a distribution to the trust? See Reg. § 1.641(b)–3(a). One court found that an S election terminated because the administration of the estate that was its shareholder was unduly prolonged and became a trust for federal income tax purposes, which was not a permitted S corporation shareholder. Old Virginia Brick Co. v. Commissioner, 44 T.C. 724 (1965), aff'd, 367 F.2d 276 (4th Cir.1966).

3. Trust X has just acquired stock in a corporation that has heretofore qualified as an S corporation. The corporation is profitable, and taxable income of $50,000 earned by the corporation is attributable to the shares held by Trust X. However, the corporation does not make any actual distributions during the year.

a. If the S status of the corporation is to continue, what amount must be distributed by Trust X to the trust's sole beneficiary if this is a grantor or grantor-type trust? What if it is a trust seeking status as a QSST?

b. Assume that Trust X holds other income-producing assets which yield $20,000 of taxable interest and dividend income for the year. Now what income must be distributed to the beneficiary? Is this sensible in view of your answer in Problem 3.a.?

4. Decedent left stock in an S corporation to a trust, the income of which was payable to his wife for her life, then to their four children until the youngest reaches 21 years of age, with the corpus of the trust distributable at that time among the then surviving children. Such a trust would qualify for the estate tax marital deduction under Section 2056(b)(7) and could be a QSST. Assume that W so elects.

a. When the wife dies, what must be done to preserve the S election, and when, if all the children are at that time alive and more than 21 years of age? See § 1362(c).

¶ 15,140

b.   If one of the children at wife's death is then only 18 years of age, and the trustee has power to sprinkle income among the children or accumulate it until the youngest reaches age 21, once wife dies would the trust necessarily become an ineligible shareholder? (See the discussion immediately below of the Electing Small Business Trust.)

[¶ 15,145]

d.   *Electing Small Business Trust (ESBT)*

If either the accumulation of income or the "sprinkling" of it among one or more of several beneficiaries is a desired goal, a vehicle other than the QSST must be used if the trust is to be an S shareholder. Before the 1996 Act, a trust containing such fiduciary powers could not qualify as a shareholder of an S corporation, notwithstanding that such powers were heralded features in estate planning and wealth administration and were of a sort commonly utilized and often for reasons totally unrelated to tax planning. Disallowance of S status to a corporation whose stock was held in the corpus of such a trust could thus be an anathema to the orderly management and planning of a corporate owner's wealth. The restriction forced the corporate owner to the distasteful choice of either abandoning S corporation treatment for the business or abandoning the vehicle of choice (i.e., the trust) for administering her wealth.

Motivated by a twofold purpose—of deferring to common estate planning techniques plus enlarging access to S treatment by small businesses—Congress in 1996 expanded the range of trusts eligible as S shareholders to include the "Electing Small Business Trust" (ESBT). § 1361(c)(2)(A)(v) and (e). This authorization makes it possible for a trust owning S corporation stock to have multiple beneficiaries, and without the predetermination of which if any of those beneficiaries will receive the income currently. What the statute requires, however, consistent with Congress's motivating purpose of accommodating estate planning goals, is that the beneficial interests in such a sprinkling or accumulation trust be acquired by means other than purchase—i.e., by gift or bequest. See § 1361(e)(1)(A)(ii) and (C).

The liberalized right of election comes at a significant price, however. Income from the S corporate stock is automatically taxed at the highest marginal rate. § 641(c). This has the effect of preventing administrative complexities that might otherwise result were the tax rate to fluctuate according to which beneficiaries were actually favored by the exercise of the sprinkling or accumulation power.

There are, of course, some positive aspects to this levy. First, taxation of the income to the trust relieves the beneficiaries of further tax upon eventual income distributions. Second, according to IRS Notice 97–12, 1997–1 C.B. 385, with the tax imposed on the trust itself, it is only the trustee who need consent to the S corporation election. This same Notice and Reg. § 1.1361–1(m)(4)(vii) and (m)(5)(iii) conclude,

¶ 15,145

however, that with all actual or potential current beneficiaries of the ESBT treated as shareholders by Section 1361(c)(2)(B)(v), all such beneficiaries must meet the tests of Section 1361(b)(1) on the number and nature of eligible shareholders.[3] The expansion of the shareholder limit to 100 shareholders, and the treatment of all members of the same family as one shareholder for purposes of this limit, should make this task easier.

[¶ 15,147]

Notes

1.   Rev. Proc. 2003–43, §§ 2.03, 4, 2003–1 C.B. 998, provides relief for certain late ESBT elections.

2.   Rev. Proc. 98–23, 1998–1 C.B. 662, and Reg. §§ 1.1361–1(j)(12) and (m)(7), provide guidance on how to convert a QSST to an ESBT and how to convert an ESBT to a QSST.

[¶ 15,150]

Problems

1.   On December 1 of year 1, by inter vivos gift Samantha transfers the stock of her wholly owned corporation to a discretionary trust for the benefit of her three children, one of whom is a nonresident alien. She directs the trustee to cause the corporation to obtain Subchapter S status for the following year. Can it? Who would be counted toward the 100–shareholder ceiling and who must consent to the election? At what rate would the income of the trust be taxed?

2.   How would your answers in Problem 1 change if the terms of the testamentary trust dictated the mandatory accumulation of all income for three years?

[¶ 15,155]

e. Nonresident Aliens: Ineligibility as Shareholders and Trust Beneficiaries

Despite other liberalizations in the roster of authorized shareholders, Congress continues to deny that status to nonresident aliens as well as to trusts having a nonresident alien as an income beneficiary. § 1361(b)(1)(C) and (c)(2)(A)(i); Reg. § 1.1361–1(g). This prohibition

---

3.   Accord IRS Notice 97–49, 1997–2 C.B. 304. However, as clarified in this Notice and Reg. § 1.1361–1(m)(1)(ii)(C), the term "beneficiary" is not so broad as to include a person in whose favor a power of appointment could be exercised, nor a person whose contingent interest is so remote as to be negligible, such as the contingent interest of a State under its laws pertaining to escheat. Congress confirmed this interpretation in 2004 by adding language to Section 1361(e)(2) that makes clear that the determination of whether a person is a potential current beneficiary of an ESBT for any period is made without regard to any power of appointment to the extent that it remains unexercised at the end of the period.

avoids the necessity of meshing the taxation of S corporation shareholders under the pass-through regime with the general invulnerability of nonresident aliens to tax assessments by the United States. Repeated legislative proposals for curing the problem, by utilizing a system of withholding U.S. taxes analogous to that used with foreign owners of a partnership (see § 1446), have failed to be enacted.

Is it possible that the same structural technique approved in Rev. Rul. 94–43, at ¶ 15,100, would permit avoidance of restrictions on who can be shareholders of S corporations, including the ban on nonresident alien shareholders? For example, could a nonresident alien join with an S corporation to operate a business in partnership form, so that in end result all earnings of the business would flow through to the nonresident alien along with the shareholders of the S corporation? How would this differ from having the S corporation itself conduct the operations, with the nonresident alien as one of the shareholders of the S corporation?

[¶ 15,160]

f. *Qualified Exempt Organizations and Select S Corporations as Eligible Shareholders*

In the 1996 legislation another philosophical shift as to permissible shareholders became manifest with the recognition of select exempt organizations as authorized shareholders. Earlier, contributions of an S corporation's stock to a charity automatically disqualified the corporation from an ongoing S status. Likewise, tax-exempt qualified retirement plan trusts could not hold such stock. In the interest of eliminating either the discouragement of charitable gifts or employee ownership of S stock, the 1996 Act extended the eligibility rules to cover both such classes of organizations. § 1361(c)(6).

Furthermore, the 1996 legislation for the first time tolerated the ownership of S stock by another corporation, albeit only if the corporate shareholder were another S corporation and one holding all of the subsidiary's stock. At the heart of this change was Congress's recognition of the nontax virtues and desirability of vertically integrated businesses, hence the approval of a parent-subsidiary S corporate structure but only if the S corporate subsidiary were wholly owned by another S corporation. See ¶¶ 15,170 and 15,175.

[¶ 15,165]

3. CORPORATE LEVEL ELIGIBILITY REQUIREMENTS

The corporate level requirements for a Subchapter S election are fewer than the shareholder level requirements but can be just as important. The corporation must be a domestic corporation, § 1361(b)(1), although it may derive any amount of its income from foreign sources. It may own stock in other corporations, and even controlling interests. See ¶ 15,170. It cannot be an "ineligible" corporation (i.e., engaged in certain proscribed lines of business, or subject to certain specialized tax regimes). § 1361(b)(2). Nor, the cruncher, can the corporation have more than one class of stock outstanding. § 1361(b)(1)(D).

[¶ 15,170]

a. Permissible Affiliate Status

At one time, under former Section 1361(b)(2)(A), corporations that were members of affiliated groups could not be S corporations. Together with the general statutory prohibition that still appears in Subchapter S against any corporate shareholders, this added ban on affiliate status had to mean that an S corporation could not itself own 80 percent of the stock of another corporation. One purpose was to prevent the S corporation from dropping a portion of its operations down to a controlled subsidiary and allowing the income therefrom to accumulate without current tax to the parent's own shareholders. See Haley Bros. Construction Corp. v. Commissioner, 87 T.C. 498 (1986). Another purpose was to prevent the S corporation from deflecting its income away from its owners, and having it taxed other than in proportion to stockholdings through consolidated reporting of that income with affiliated companies.

Nothing, however, has ever prevented an S corporation from owning 79 percent of another corporation. Moreover, under former Section 1361(c)(6), wholly inactive subsidiaries that had never engaged in business and had no gross income for the year in question were ignored in determining the S corporation eligibility of the parent.

With the disqualification of affiliate corporate status removed (as part of Congress's program to expand the availability of Subchapter S status and to facilitate the raising of capital by small business), an S corporation may now own any amount of stock in another corporation, from a minority to a controlling interest. If, however, it is to own stock in another S corporation, it must own 100 percent of that subsidiary in order not to jeopardize the subsidiary's ongoing S status. See § 1361(b)(3). Although affiliate status is now permitted, an S corporation still cannot participate in a consolidated filing of its income with others. § 1504(b)(8).

The ability of an S corporation to own a controlling interest in another corporation is of significant practical import, for it facilitates that corporation's engaging in a corporate takeover yet maintaining its S status throughout. True, before this legislative change, the IRS had quite liberally ignored an S corporation's transitory affiliation with a second corporation in various acquisitive and other restructuring transactions. Nonetheless, literally such momentary ownership violated the statute and, no doubt, deterred some S corporate takeovers. Repeal of the ban on

¶ 15,165

affiliate status should cure any such reticence. It also makes obsolete numerous earlier published and private rulings on this matter.

[¶ 15,175]

b. *The Wholly Owned "Qualified Subchapter S Subsidiary"*

One particular form of affiliate status enjoys explicit statutory recognition: the ownership by an S corporation of 100 percent of the stock in an S subsidiary. § 1361(b)(3). To repeat, underlying this provision is congressional approval of S corporations engaging in vertically integrated operations without forfeiting their S status. Presumably chains of interlinked S corporations can operate as brother-sister and parent-subsidiary entities, provided all subsidiaries are wholly owned by a parent that is itself an S corporation. See Reg. § 1.1361–2(d), Ex. 1. This makes it possible for an S corporation to structure its organization for risk and regulatory purposes into a format in which some operations are relegated to subsidiaries and others conducted by the parent, according to what achieves the greatest nontax efficiencies.

By election of the parent corporation, a wholly owned subsidiary becomes a "qualified subchapter S subsidiary" (QSSS).[4] Like the parent, the subsidiary must meet all the standard corporate level eligibility requirements for an S corporation. § 1361(b)(3)(B); Reg. § 1.1361–2(a). Once the parent makes the election, the subsidiary constructively liquidates into the parent tax-free under Sections 332 and 337 (discussed in Chapter 8). See Reg. § 1.1361–4. The two corporations are thereafter regarded as a single entity for tax purposes. § 1361(b)(3)(A); Reg. § 1.1361–2(b).

The panoply of advantages of such an election are still unfolding. One potential advantage is that an S corporation might become a party to a reorganization in which another S corporation ends up in the position of owning up to a 100 percent interest as a parent. This could be the result, for example, of the takeover of a target company through the technique of a forward triangular merger in which the QSSS is to become the surviving subsidiary.

But there are also potential disadvantages. Thus, once the subsidiary ceases its QSSS status it is treated as becoming a new corporation, presumably in a Section 351 transaction. § 1361(b)(3)(C); Reg. § 1.1361–5(b). This could trigger recognition of gain under Section 357(c), discussed at ¶ 2190, depending on the relative amounts of the corporation's debt and adjusted bases in its assets. Moreover, once the QSSS election terminates, the subsidiary may neither make an S corporate election nor

---

4. Rev. Proc. 2003–43, §§ 2.02, 4, 2003–1 C.B. 998, provides relief for certain late QSSS elections.

again assume a QSSS status for five years after this termination unless the IRS consents to the election. § 1361(b)(3)(D); Reg. § 1.1361–5(c).

[¶ 15,180]

c. *One Class of Stock*

A serious structural limitation for S corporations is the requirement that there be but one class of stock. § 1361(b)(1)(D). Shares can be differentiated only in voting rights. § 1361(c)(4). Other benefits from using multiple classes of stock, as discussed in Chapter 3, are unavailable to S corporations.

The restriction is not arbitrary, although it may prove chafing. The historical purpose for limiting the stock of S corporations to a single class was to avoid administrative complexity in allocating income and loss among shareholders whose rights thereto were of differing priorities; the limit effectively assured that income would be received by the shareholders to whom taxed. As described in Portage Plastics Co. v. United States, 486 F.2d 632, 637 (7th Cir.1973) (footnote omitted):

> As can best be divined, the purpose of the single class of stock requirement was none other than to avoid the administrative complexity in the allocation of income which would result with more than one class of stock when preferred dividends were paid in excess of current earnings from undistributed but taxed prior earnings. Because the shareholders of a Subchapter S corporation are pro rata taxed on the corporation's undistributed taxable income for any year, if in a subsequent year dividends in excess of current earnings are distributed to preferred shareholders, the common stockholders will have already been taxed on the excess going to the preferred shareholders. But under the existing provisions of the Code, the common shareholders could only receive a capital loss benefit for the previously taxed income which they did not receive. [Former] Section 1376(a). Consequently, some sort of refund mechanism would be necessary to prevent the inequity to the common shareholders, and that is the administrative problem Congress evidently sought to avoid through the single class of stock requirement.

Such reasoning is obviously inapposite to differentiated voting rights which, to repeat, the statute permits. § 1361(c)(4).

Exactly what differences in rights among the shares of stock will constitute a different class of stock for the purposes of this rule remains unsettled although the regulations do provide considerable guidance. They confirm that the one class of stock rule will be satisfied if each share of stock has identical economic rights even if not identical control rights. Thus, some of an S corporation's common stock may be nonvoting or limited to voting on only certain issues, such as the election of directors, or some shareholders may grant irrevocable proxies, all without violating the requirement of a single class of stock. See Reg. § 1.1361–1(*l*)(1).

In general, a corporation will be regarded as issuing only a single class of stock if each share of stock has identical rights to distribution and liquidation proceeds. Reg. § 1.1361–1(*l*)(1). Whether this identity exists is determined under the corporate charter and bylaws, state law, and binding agreements relating to distribution and liquidation proceeds, in the aggregate referred to in the regulations as the "governing provisions." Reg. § 1.1361–1(*l*)(2)(i).

Limiting the scope of the inquiry as to respective rights to the contents of relatively formal governing provisions has a benign effect. It permits the corporation to enter into a broad range of routine commercial contracts (loan agreements, employment contracts, and the like) which alter shareholders' respective economic rights to distributions, and without jeopardizing the Subchapter S status, unless, however, the principal purpose of the agreement was to circumvent the one class of stock requirement. Reg. § 1.1361–1(*l*)(2)(i).

For example, a prohibition against the distribution of dividends to controlling shareholders contained in a loan agreement with a commercial bank would not create a second class of stock because the loan agreement is not a governing provision. Reg. § 1.1361–1(*l*)(2)(i). By contrast, a similar prohibition imposed by a State Corporation Commission as a condition upon the sale of stock within the state would create a second class of stock. See Reg. § 1.1361–1(*l*)(2)(vi), Ex. 1, and Paige v. United States, 580 F.2d 960 (9th Cir.1978). Similarly, the imputed dividend created by Section 7872 upon the corporation making a below-market loan to a shareholder does not create a second class of stock because the loan agreement is not a governing provision. Reg. § 1.1361–1(*l*)(2)(vi), Ex. 5.

The governing provision limitation also prevents the accidental loss of Subchapter S status that a constructive distribution might otherwise produce. For example, neither the payment of differing premiums on health insurance for shareholder-employees nor the payment of excessive compensation to certain shareholder-employees creates a second class of stock because an employment agreement is not a governing provision. Reg. § 1.1361–1(*l*)(2)(vi), Exs. 3 and 4.

Because a corporation will not be treated as having a second class of stock if the governing provisions confer identical distribution rights on all shares of stock, S status will not be lost if current distributions in fact are not pro rata as long as the disparity in timing is not intended to avoid the one class of stock requirement. See Reg. § 1.1361–1(*l*)(2)(vi), Ex. 2. However, if disproportionate distributions are made to one group of shareholders at a materially earlier time than distributions are made to other shareholders, the transaction may have other tax consequences under Section 7872 or other recharacterization provisions (e.g., the

¶ 15,180

shareholder receiving the earlier distribution may be in receipt of a gift or taxable compensation). Id.

Nor are instruments representing "disguised equity" under general principles of the tax law (see Chapter 3) automatically treated as a second class of stock. Instead, Reg. § 1.1361–1(*l*)(4) and (5)(iv) and (v) posits specific rules as to when this treatment will result. Not surprisingly, a second class of stock will be found where a "principal purpose [underlying the instrument or arrangement] * * * is to circumvent the rights to distribution or liquidation proceeds conferred by the outstanding shares of stock or to circumvent the limitation on eligible shareholders." Reg. § 1.1361–1(*l*)(4)(ii)(A)(*2*).

The regulations are even more lax in their attitude toward agreements to redeem stock and buy-sell agreements. Differences among shareholders are ignored unless the arrangement is intended to avoid the one class of stock rule, and even then only if the price established is significantly greater or less than the fair market value of the stock. Reg. § 1.1361–1(*l*)(2)(iii)(A). Moreover, for that purpose, book value is not regarded as significantly different from fair market value. In addition, agreements to redeem stock upon death, disability, or termination of employment apparently are always disregarded regardless of the redemption price. Reg. § 1.1361–1(*l*)(2)(iii)(B). As a result of these rules, shareholder agreements governing the disposition of stock will rarely, if ever, involve risk of creating a second class of stock. See, e.g., Reg. § 1.1361–1(*l*)(2)(vi), Exs. 8 and 9.

The following ruling illustrates one common arrangement that would be approved automatically under the regulations.

[¶ 15,185]

REVENUE RULING 85–161

1985–2 C.B. 191, declared obsolete by Rev.Rul. 95–71, 1995–2 C.B. 323.

ISSUE

Will the stock purchase agreement described below cause a corporation to be treated as having more than one class of stock within the meaning of section 1361(b)(1)(D) * * *?

FACTS

Corporation *X* has two classes of stock issued and outstanding: voting common stock and nonvoting common stock. The nonvoting stock is held by *A*, *B*, and *C*, siblings, and by *D*, an unrelated individual who is an officer of the corporation. *A* and *B* own all the voting stock. The voting and nonvoting shares are identical other than with respect to voting rights and other than as provided in a shareholder's agreement described below.

X and all the shareholders of *X* have entered into an agreement with respect to the transfer of *D*'s stock. Under the agreement, *D* may transfer *D*'s stock only after obtaining the consent of the holders of voting stock in *X*. If such consent cannot be obtained, *D* may sell the stock only to the corporation or the other shareholders at book value. Other provisions of the agreement give *X* or the other shareholders the right to purchase *D*'s stock in the event of *D*'s termination of employment or disability and upon *D*'s death.

X filed an election to be an S corporation under section 1362 * * * with respect to its taxable year beginning January 1, 1984.

LAW AND ANALYSIS

Section 1361(b)(1)(D) * * * provides that the term "small business corporation" means a corporation that does not have more than one class of stock.

* * *

Although there may be differences in voting rights among the shares of common stock, the outstanding shares of a corporation must be identical as to the rights of the holders in the profits and in the assets of the corporation. S. Rep. No. 97–640, 97th Cong., 2d Sess. 8 (1982) * * *.

In this case, all shares of *X*'s stock are equal with respect to rights to profits and rights in the assets of the corporation. The agreement restricting the transfer of *D*'s stock does not affect *D*'s interest in corporate profits or corporate assets while *D* is a shareholder. Therefore, *X* does not have more than one class of stock within the meaning of section 1361(b)(1)(D) * * *.

* * *

[¶ 15,190]

Notes

1.   Do you agree with the conclusion of the ruling, and implicitly a similar conclusion in the regulations, to the effect that all shares of *X*'s stock are equal with respect to rights in the assets of the corporation notwithstanding that "book value" rather than "fair market value" is the price set for *D*'s stock by the agreement? In answering this question, note that if the redemption price paid were limited to book value, the excess of fair market value over book value would necessarily redound to the remaining shareholders who continued to own the entire corporation (at its full value). Yet, the payment of book value does assure that corporate income that had been formerly allocated to and taxed to the outgoing shareholder *D* eventually will find its way to that shareholder through the redemption proceeds. Is that adequate to prevent the evil at which the one class of stock requirement was directed?

¶ 15,190

2.   Warrants or options to acquire stock are generally not treated as a second class of stock, whether issued as compensatory or investment options to acquire an S corporation's stock. However, if a noncompensatory option is substantially certain to be exercised and requires a payment that is substantially less than the value of the underlying stock, the warrant or option will be regarded as a second class of stock. Reg. § 1.1361–1(l)(4)(iii).

3.   Stock subject to restrictions that are "substantial risks of forfeiture" which, under Section 83, prevent current taxation will not count as outstanding or as a second class of stock unless the employee elects under Section 83(b) to be taxed currently. Reg. § 1.1361–1(l)(3).

4.   ***Safe-Harbor Debt.*** In the past, the difficulties with the one class of stock requirement have stemmed not so much from the disproportionate treatment of acknowledged shareholders as from the characterization of purported "debt" holders. To alleviate the problem, Section 1361(c)(5) provides a statutory safe harbor for assuring that certain debt—"straight debt"—not count as a second class of stock.

By definition, "straight debt" is that: (i) created by a written and unconditional promise to repay; (ii) repayable in money; (iii) carrying a fixed, noncontingent interest rate and interest payment dates; (iv) not convertible into stock; and (v) having as its creditor either an individual, estate, or trust that is eligible to qualify as an S shareholder, or a person in the active and regular business of loaning funds. § 1361(c)(5)(B) and Reg. § 1.1361–1(l)(5)(i). "Straight debt" does not run afoul of the ban on a second class of stock even if it is subordinated to other debt of the corporation, carries an unreasonably high interest rate, or is treated as equity for other purposes of the Code.[5] Reg. § 1.1361–1(l)(5)(ii) and (iv).

d.   Avoiding Corporate Limitations by Multi–Tier Structures and Partnerships

[¶ 15,195]

LETTER RULING 8819040

This is in reply to a letter of August 21, 1987, written on your behalf by your authorized representative, requesting a ruling under subchapter S * * *.

The information submitted discloses that X is an S corporation in the business of managing hotels. In order to expand its operations X proposes to enter into a Joint Venture Limited Partnership with Y, a C corporation. X will be a general partner and Y will be the limited partner. It is proposed that X will contribute its management contracts,

---

5.   However, Reg. § 1.1361–1(l)(5)(iv) provides that unreasonably high interest on a safe-harbor debt may cause the excess amount to be recharacterized as a distribution to which Section 1368 applies (discussed at ¶¶ 15,330 et seq.).

employees, cash, and miscellaneous property and liabilities to the partnership for an 84 percent interest in profits and losses of the partnership. Y will contribute cash and agree to provide funding or cause an affiliate to provide funding in the form of short term loans to the partnership for a 16 percent interest in the profits and losses of the partnership.

The partnership will continue the existing business of X and will expand the business with the additional funding provided by Y.

X will continue and enter into other businesses separate from its activities in the partnership. X currently receives purchasing fees for making bulk purchases of supplies, furniture, fixtures and equipment for various hotels.

It is represented that Y will have no right to participate in the profit or loss of the other business activities that X is involved in. Y also wishes to avoid ownership interest in X for liability purposes as well as not being interested in participating in the other activities of X. The partnership was formed to create an independent business separate and apart from both X and Y.

We have been requested to rule that following the formation of the partnership X will continue to be treated as an S corporation and as having met the definition of a "small business corporation" under Section 1361(b)(1) * * *.

* * *

The formation of a partnership and the subsequent ownership of an interest in such partnership will not, in and of itself, cause an S corporation to lose its status. For example, in Rev. Rul. 71–455, 1971–2 C.B. 318, an S corporation was a partner in a joint venture that operated a movie theatre. Another example may be found in *Patterson v. Commissioner*, T.C. Memo. 1984–58, where the court concluded that the taxpayer could not ignore the separate existence of his wholly owned S corporation in an attempt to pass through losses from a partnership in which the S corporation was a partner.

In Rev. Rul. 77–220, 1977–1 C.B. 263, S corporation status was denied to three companies that formed a partnership because the transaction lacked economic substance and was only arranged to circumvent the limitation under subchapter S * * * of the number of permissible shareholders.

This case is distinguishable from Rev. Rul. 77–220 in that there exists a valid business purpose for the transaction other than the circumvention of the shareholder limitation rules under subchapter S * * *.

Accordingly, we conclude that consummation of the proposed transaction will neither affect X's S corporation status nor cause X not to be considered a "small business corporation" within the meaning of section 1361(b)(1) * * *.

* * *

[¶ 15,200]

Note

Apparently, as evident from this ruling, S corporations can participate as partners in a business operation with other partners that include C corporations or with partners having rights senior or subordinate to those of the S corporation. Therefore, to what extent can multi-tier structures or partnerships among S corporations be used to accomplish, indirectly, differentiated interests among shareholders in income and losses of S operations? What other restrictive requirements in Subchapter S may be avoided through multi-tier structures combining partnerships, S corporations, and C corporations: the prohibition against corporate or nonresident alien shareholders? The requirement that income be allocated in strict proportion to stockholdings? The 100–shareholder limit? Recall the material discussed at ¶¶ 15,100–15,105. In which cases is a business purpose vital to the outcome? Consider the impact of the "anti-abuse" regulation in the partnership area. Reg. § 1.701–2, discussed at ¶ 16,085. How, if at all, does this regulation limit the viability of using partnership structures to circumvent Subchapter S restrictions? See Reg. § 1.701–2(d), Ex. 2 (use of a partnership with an S corporation and a nonresident alien individual as its partners to conduct a bona fide business treated as consistent with the intent of Subchapter K and the partnership treated as having a form consistent with its substance; accordingly, the IRS cannot invoke the partnership anti-abuse rule to recast the transaction and invalidate the corporate partner's S election).

4. IMPACT OF INELIGIBLE AND QUASI–INELIGIBLE SHAREHOLDERS

[¶ 15,205]

LETTER RULING 8814042

This is in reply to a letter dated June 5, 1987, and subsequent correspondence, submitted on behalf of Company by its authorized representative, requesting a ruling under Section 1362(f) * * *.

Company filed an election to be treated as an S corporation for its tax year beginning D1. On D1, one of the shareholders of Company stock was A's estate. The executrix of A's estate consented to Company's S corporation election on behalf of A's estate.

On D2, pursuant to the terms of A's last will and testament, the one share of Company stock held by A's estate was transferred to Trust.

Trust held the share of Company stock beyond D3, i.e., more than 60 days [now 2 years] after D2. Neither Company nor its officers were aware that Company's S corporation election would be terminated because Trust held the share of Company stock beyond the 60 day [now 2–year] period following D2.

In D4, during the preparation of Company's D5 federal income tax return, Company's accountant became aware of the transfer of the share of Company stock from A's estate to Trust. Shortly thereafter, Company's accountant advised B, the president of Company, that Trust was an ineligible shareholder, and as a consequence, Company's S corporation election was automatically terminated. On advice of the accountant, B promptly took steps to purchase the share of Company stock from Trust so that Company would qualify as a small business corporation. In connection with B's action, Trust transferred the share of Company's stock to B on D6.

It is represented that at all times since D3, Company has viewed and treated itself as an S corporation and that the transfer to Trust was not part of a plan to terminate the S corporation election and was not motivated by tax avoidance.

Company, and each person who was a shareholder of Company at any time during the period specified pursuant to section 1362(f) * * *, have agreed to make any adjustments (consistent with the treatment of Company as an S corporation) as may be required by the Secretary with respect to such period.

* * *

S. Rep. No. 97–640, 97th Cong., 2d Sess. 12 (1982) * * *, in discussing section 1362(f) * * *, provides that if the Internal Revenue Service determines that a corporation's subchapter S election is inadvertently terminated, the Service can waive the effect of the terminating event for any period if the corporation and the shareholders agree to be treated as if the election had been in effect for such period. The committee intends that the Internal Revenue Service be reasonable in granting waivers, so that corporations whose subchapter S eligibility requirements have been inadvertently violated do not suffer the tax consequences of a termination if no tax avoidance would result from the continued subchapter S treatment. In granting a waiver, it is hoped that taxpayers and the government will work out agreements that protect the revenue without undue hardship to the taxpayers. It is expected that the waiver may be made retroactive for the period in which the corporation again became eligible for subchapter S treatment, depending on the facts.

In Rev. Rul. 86–110, 1986–2 C.B. 150, the Service ruled that a small business corporation whose election was terminated because it inadvertently had one or more ineligible shareholders for a limited period of time before discovery and correction will be treated as continuing to be an S corporation under section 1362(f) of the Code for the period specified by the Service during which the stock was held by ineligible shareholders.

Based solely on the information submitted and the representations set forth above, we conclude that (1) the termination of the election of Company which occurred because Trust held a share of Company stock while an ineligible shareholder constituted an "inadvertent termination" within the meaning of section 1362(f) * * *, (2) no later than a reasonable period of time after discovery of the terminating event, steps were taken so that Company once more was a small business corporation, and (3) no tax avoidance would result from the continued treatment of Company as an S corporation.

Accordingly, pursuant to the provisions of section 1362(f) * * *, Company will be treated as continuing to be an S corporation during the period from D3 to D6 and thereafter provided that Company's election is not otherwise terminated. During the period from D3 to D6, Trust will be treated as a shareholder of S corporation stock and therefore must, in determining its income tax liability, include its pro rata share of the separately and nonseparately computed items of Company as provided in section 1366, make any adjustments to stock basis as provided in section 1367, and take into account any distributions made by Company to Trust as provided in section 1368. This ruling shall be null and void should Trust fail to comply with these adjustments.

* * *

[¶ 15,210]

Notes

1. Apparently there is no flexibility in the permissible shareholder requirement for the purpose of qualifying a corporation either initially to make or later to perpetuate a Subchapter S election. However, as indicated earlier and in Letter Ruling 8814042 above, Section 1362(f) does provide leeway for the IRS temporarily to overlook irregularities even in eligibility requirements, if, for example, the presence of an ineligible shareholder came about inadvertently and steps are promptly taken to rectify the error once discovered.

In the past the IRS has been remarkably generous in exercising its discretion under Section 1362(f) to relieve corporations from the consequences of the transfer of stock in an existing S corporation to an ineligible shareholder. The IRS has treated as inadvertent, and thus not causing a termination of the Subchapter S election, the transfer of stock to every possible variety of ineligible shareholder. See, e.g., Letter Rulings 8621013 (corporate shareholder), 8846013 (partnership), and

8821020 (individual retirement account). There is no reason to think that it will be any less generous now that Congress has extended relief under Section 1362(f) even further to the curing of inadvertent procedural defects causing ineffective elections.

2.   When stock in an existing S corporation is transferred to a trust that is intended to be a QSST but the beneficiary unintentionally fails to make the appropriate election, the prompt curing of the defect after discovery will cause the IRS to rule that the election terminated inadvertently and that, accordingly, S corporation status will not be lost. See Rev. Proc. 2003–43, § 4, 2003–1 C.B. 998, specifying the procedures for qualifying for automatic relief in the event of an inadvertent termination.

3.   What kinds of terminating events should be treated as "inadvertent?" At least it seems clear that "ignorance of the law" is a perfectly good excuse. It also seems clear that ignorance of fact (e.g., the ineligibility of a shareholder) may also be treated as inadvertent. What if knowledge of the defect is present? For example, what should be the result if the sole income beneficiary of a QSST dies, causing the income interest to pass to three individuals, and the trustee is unable to distribute the stock for 25 months? Cf. Reg. § 1.1362–5(a) (events not within the control of the corporation may be inadvertent).

The IRS has refined the definition of "inadvertent" in private letter rulings. In one, inadvertent termination relief was denied when the election terminated because of excess passive investment income. The corporation had paid the "sting" tax imposed by Section 1375 (discussed below at ¶ 15,440) and thus, the IRS concluded, was aware that termination would result. Accordingly, the termination could not have been inadvertent. Letter Ruling 9224027. However, the IRS has continued to rule that a termination attributable to excess passive income is inadvertent if the shareholders represent that they did not know that the passive income would cause a termination of the election. In those rulings, it is not always clear whether the sting tax has been paid or not. Indeed, sometimes that fact may have been concealed. See, e.g., Letter Ruling 9241035 ("As an adjustment under Section 1362(f)(4), X must send a payment of $Y . . . to the following address. . . .").

4.   Might the risk of a transfer to an ineligible shareholder be reduced by a shareholders' agreement that prohibited stock transfers to ineligible shareholders and that explicitly provided that any such transfers would be void ab initio? See Letter Ruling 9452037, approving the efficacy of such an agreement where its effect under state law was to preclude the transferee from ever becoming the owner of stock in the S corporation.

¶ 15,210

[¶ 15,215]

D. REPORTING OF NET INCOME FROM OPERATIONS

An S corporation is not subject to the corporate income tax or the alternative minimum tax imposed by Section 55. § 1363(a); Reg. § 1.1363–1(a)(1). Rather, the items of income and expense derived by the corporation are included directly on the tax returns of its shareholders. § 1366(a); Reg. § 1.1366–1(a)(1). However, by contrast to a partnership which is also a pass-through entity, an S corporation may at times itself be subject to tax. See Reg. § 1.1363–1(a)(2) and ¶¶ 15,400 et seq.

1. CORPORATE LEVEL COMPUTATIONS AND DETERMINATIONS

[¶ 15,220]

a. *Computations, In General*

The one point at which the taxation of S corporations closely parallels the taxation of partnerships is in the computation of taxable income. Consistent with the conduit nature of each, the income of S corporations and of partnerships is generally computed in the same manner as individuals, and not as corporations compute their income. See §§ 703(a) and 1363(b). Thus, for example, C corporations are expressly disqualified from the benefits of Section 1237, unlike individuals, partnerships, and S corporations. See § 1237(a). Likewise, individuals, partnerships, and S corporations cannot avail themselves of the dividends-received deduction of Section 243, which is available only to C corporations.

On the other hand, an S corporation remains a corporation for most purposes under the Internal Revenue Code other than income reporting. § 1371(a). So, for example, as mentioned at ¶ 15,025, the provisions of Subchapter C on incorporation (see Chapter 2) apply equally to an S or C corporation, including the limitations on the corporate transferee's adjusted basis in the contributed property in Section 362(e)(2) (which was added to the Code in 2004). Furthermore, an S corporation may avail itself of corporate tax provisions providing nonrecognition treatment for reorganizations or restructurings of corporate ownership, such as Sections 332, 338, and 368, presumably for the same policy reasons that justify applying these provisions to C corporations.

Sometimes, however, it is unclear whether the individual or the corporate tax regime controls. If an S corporation incurs a nonbusiness bad debt, must it treat this as a short-term capital loss under Section 166(d) rather than ordinary loss under Section 166(a) as does an individual? Yes, according to Rev. Rul. 93–36, 1993–1 C.B. 187, in that Section

1363(b) does not list Section 166 as an exception to the rule on an S corporation reporting as an individual. Therefore, upon incurring a loss on an investment in stock of another corporation, is the S corporation entitled to an ordinary loss under Section 1244? No, according to Rath v. Commissioner, 101 T.C. 196 (1993), on the ground that an S corporation is not an individual. Compare Section 1202(g), which explicitly extends the benefits of the Section 1202 exclusion to individual owners of an S corporation or other pass-through entity which, in turn, sells the qualified small business stock, notwithstanding the denial of the benefits to corporations under Section 1202(a).

[¶ 15,225]

b. *Nature of Passed-Through Items*

As is true under the conduit tax regime applicable to partnerships, the character of items of income or loss that pass through to shareholders from the S corporation is generally determined at the corporate level and retains that character in the hands of the shareholder. § 1366(b); Reg. § 1.1366–1(b)(1). Thus, under this general rule, if an item of income would be entitled to capital gains treatment or would be exempt from tax altogether at the corporate level, that character is preserved in the hands of the shareholders. For example, if an S corporation has capital gain from the sale or exchange of property, a shareholder's pro rata share of that gain also will be characterized as capital gain under Section 1366(b), regardless of whether the shareholder is dealer in that type of property. Reg. § 1.1366–1(b)(1).

However, Reg. § 1.1366–1(b)(2) provides an exception to this general rule if the S corporation "is formed or availed of by any shareholder or group of shareholders for a principal purpose of selling or exchanging contributed property that in the hands of the shareholder or shareholders would not have produced capital gain if sold or exchanged" by those shareholders. In such a case, the gain recognized by the corporation is treated as ordinary income. Likewise, Reg. § 1.1366–1(b)(3) provides an anti-abuse exception if the S corporation "is formed or availed of by any shareholder or group of shareholders for a principal purpose of selling or exchanging contributed property that in the hands of the shareholder or shareholders would have produced capital loss if sold or exchanged" by those shareholders. In such a case, the corporation's recognized loss on the sale or exchange of the property is treated as a capital loss, but only to the extent of the shareholders' precontribution loss with respect to the property, i.e., to the extent that, immediately before the contribution of the property to the corporation, the adjusted basis of the property in the hands of the shareholders exceeded the fair market value of the property.

To permit the character of items of income and expense to pass through to the shareholders, each item that receives special tax treatment is passed through separately. §§ 1363(b)(1) and 1366(a)(1); Reg. § 1.1366–1(a)(2). Thus, for example, the corporation does not pass through a net capital gain but rather its components (i.e., comprised of the nature and holding periods of the underlying capital gains and capital losses and Section 1231 gains and losses). Similarly, investment interest expense must be stated separately from interest expense attributable to tax-exempt income, and both must be separated from general business interest expense.

Under Section 1363(b)(2), certain expenditures are not deductible by S corporations. That provision, however, is of little significance. To the extent that the items specified would ever be properly allowable as a deduction to a corporation, the expenditures pass through to the shareholders and are deductible by them. § 1366(a)(1).

[¶ 15,230]

c. *Accounting Methods and Other Elections*

An S corporation may use either the cash or the accrual method of accounting, and the method that it selects may differ from the methods used by its shareholders. However, under Section 267(a)(2) and (e), an S corporation may not deduct a payment made to a shareholder or a person related to a shareholder before the day on which the payee is required to report the payment in income. In effect, Section 267 places an S corporation on the cash method of accounting with respect to all payments to its shareholders or related persons.

Furthermore, to ensure the uniform treatment of all S corporation shareholders, all elections that taxpayers are entitled to make, with the two exceptions mentioned by statute, must be made by the S corporation and bind all of its shareholders. § 1363(c); Reg. § 1.1363–1(c). This replicates the partnership approach.

[¶ 15,235]

d. *Fringe Benefits*

Shareholders of S corporations who, actually or constructively, own more than two percent of the outstanding stock of their corporation are regarded for purposes of the fringe benefit rules as owners rather than employees. § 1372. Thus, the S corporation cannot deduct amounts paid to them under employee death benefit plans, accident and health plans, or group term life insurance plans. Similarly, shareholders apparently are not eligible for the exclusion of the value of employer-provided meals and lodging under Section 119. See Dilts v. United States, 845 F.Supp. 1505 (D.Wyo.1994), disapproving the exclusion allowed in Wilhelm v. United States, 257 F.Supp. 16 (D.Wyo.1966), and distinguishing the exclusion allowed to a partner in Armstrong v. Phinney, 394 F.2d 661

(5th Cir.1968). Expenditures for fringe benefits payable to less than two percent shareholders continue to be deductible by the S corporation.

[¶ 15,240]

e. *Distributions of Property in Kind*

As is true of a C corporation, an S corporation on distributing appreciated property to its shareholders is treated as if it had sold the property for its fair market value. § 311(b). Distributions of loss properties by S corporations are likewise governed by the rules applicable to comparable distributions by C corporations. That is, loss is not recognized on a nonliquidating distribution although it may be recognized on distributions in complete liquidation (subject to several limitations). See §§ 311(a) and 336. At the shareholder level, whether gain or loss property is distributed by a C or an S corporation to a shareholder, the shareholder's basis in the property will be its fair market value. § 301(d). A correlative decrease occurs in the basis for the recipient's S corporation stock, together with an increase in that basis to the extent of the recipient shareholder's pro rata share of the taxable income created at the corporate level by distributions of appreciated property (which flows through to and is included in the income of the recipient shareholder under Section 1366). See ¶ 15,280.

In the case of a C corporation, imposition of a tax on the appreciation inherent in the distributed property preserves the integrity of a corporate-level tax. What purpose and effect does corporate recognition of income achieve in the context of an entity such as an S corporation which is not itself subject to tax on the distribution? (But see ¶ 15,410, as to possible corporate-level tax on "built-in gain.") As with property distributions by a partnership under Sections 731 and 732 (discussed in Chapter 22), would a tax-free distribution with a carryover basis be correct in theory?

[¶ 15,245]

Problems

1. Marguerita in her individual capacity is engaged in the development and sale of real estate and would be regarded as a dealer in real property. In theory, she could hold other real property as an investment, but proof of investment intent can be difficult. Instead, Marguerita joined with other members of her family to form an S corporation for the purpose of purchasing and holding for appreciation an undeveloped tract of real property. On a later sale of that land by the S corporation, will Marguerita be entitled to capital gains treatment? See §§ 1237(a)(2)(A) and 1366(b); Reg. § 1.1366–1(b).

2. What would be the result in Problem 1 if Marguerita had individually owned the land and contributed it to the S corporation in a transaction qualifying for nonrecognition treatment under Section 351?

¶ 15,245

3. An S corporation's stock is equally owned by Tom, Dick, and Mary. The corporation has always been an S corporation and has no earnings and profits. It now distributes Asset X, which has a fair market value of $800 and a basis of $200, to Tom; distributes Asset Y, which has a fair market value of $800 and a basis of $1,100, to Dick; and distributes cash of $800 to Mary. Asset X is a capital asset in the S corporation's hands but will be a noncapital asset in Tom's hands. Asset Y is an ordinary income asset in the S corporation's hands but will be a capital asset in Dick's hands (assume that the property had a fair market value of $900 and a basis of $1,100 at the time of its contribution to the S corporation by Mary). What effect will these distributions have on the corporation? What basis will Tom, Dick, and Mary each take for the asset received?

2. SHAREHOLDERS' REPORTING OF CORPORATE INCOME AND EXPENSES

[¶ 15,250]

a. *Date Includible*

Shareholders of S corporations must include the income of the corporation in their individual returns for the year in which the taxable year of the corporation ends. § 1366(a)(1); Reg. § 1.1366–1(a)(1). Under prior law, shareholders were able to use that rule to defer the taxation to them of corporate income by causing the corporation to elect a taxable year other than the calendar year. All S corporations now are required to use a "permitted" year as their taxable year. § 1378(a). That requirement means that the corporation must use the calendar year unless it is able to establish to the satisfaction of the IRS a business purpose for the use of a different taxable year. § 1378(b). A similar rule applies to partnerships. See § 706(b), discussed at ¶ 18,015.

Notwithstanding Section 1378, to ease the burden on tax return preparers, the S corporation (or partnership) may elect under Section 444 to use a taxable year other than a permitted year, but at a cost. If an S corporation elects a taxable year under Section 444, it becomes subject to a special tax under Section 7519 that is designed to eliminate any deferral benefit from the election. Under this highly unusual provision, the S corporation, not its shareholders, is required to have on deposit with the Treasury Department by April 15 of each year an amount roughly equal to the tax that would be due on the deferred income for the prior year. When the corporation terminates its S election or its election under Section 444, the amount deposited is to be refunded in full. Thus, the net effect of Section 7519 is to require the S corporation to forfeit an amount equal to an interest charge on the deferred tax liability.

¶ 15,245

Paraphrasing the pointlessly obscure statutory language, in general the amount of the deposit, or "required payment," will equal (a) the highest marginal rate for individuals in Section 1 plus one percentage point, multiplied by (b) the corporation's net income for the prior year, with some adjustments, multiplied by (c) the number of months of deferral divided by 12 less (d) the required payment for the prior year.

[¶ 15,255]

b. Allocation in Proportion to Stock Ownership

The items of income and expense of an S corporation must be allocated to its shareholders in strict proportion to their ownership of stock in the corporation, by sharp contrast with the tax provisions that permit, and sometimes require, partners to allocate items of income and loss among themselves in differing ratios. Compare §§ 1366(a)(1) and 1377(a)(1) with § 704(b) and (c) (discussed at ¶¶ 18,065 et seq.). This lack of flexibility in income and loss allocations is one of the salient comparative tax disadvantages of an S corporation. Furthermore, a shareholder may deduct the losses so allocated only up to basis of that shareholder's actual stock and debt investments in the S corporation. See ¶ 15,280. Although a partner likewise cannot deduct losses currently in excess of the basis in the partnership interest, such basis includes the partner's allocable share of partnership debt owed to others; by contrast, a shareholder's basis does not include the S corporation's obligations owed to others. See ¶ 15,290.

[¶ 15,260]

Problems

1. Father and his two children form an S corporation with Father obtaining 50 percent of the stock and each child obtaining 25 percent. The children contribute $25,000 each in cash for their shares, and Father contributes real property with a tax basis in his hands of $10,000 and a fair market value of $50,000, which the corporation shortly thereafter sells. (In a partnership of the same individuals, the entire precontribution gain would have to be allocated to Father under Section 704(c).) How would the gain from the sale of this real property be allocated among and reported by the S corporation's shareholders? Is the potential shifting of the taxable gain among family members in the Subchapter S context contrary to what the tax law permits in general under the assignment of income doctrine, or is it consistent with the general results under Subchapter C? Should the Subchapter C or partnership tax model prevail in the Subchapter S context?

2. On the formation of an S corporation, Abel contributes $30,000 in exchange for 30 shares of stock (worth $30,000) and Bakker contributes $30,000 in exchange for 10 shares of stock (worth $10,000) and $20,000 of the S corporation's debt. As we will see, S corporation losses

may be claimed by Bakker up to his $10,000 basis for the stock as well as his $20,000 basis in the debt owed to him by the corporation. However, if the corporation did incur losses of $40,000, how much of the loss would be allocated to each shareholder and reported by each? In view of this result, why does it matter to Bakker that he can report passed-through losses of another $20,000 (i.e., up to the amount of debt still owed to him by the corporation)?

[¶ 15,265]

c.   *Family Owned S Corporations*

Congress has always displayed a special concern that conduit business entities not be used to achieve an improper shifting of income among family members. As one result, the provisions governing both partnerships and S corporations specifically authorize the IRS to reallocate the income of the entity from one family member to another. Before reaching those provisions, however, family owned S corporations have an additional hurdle.

[¶ 15,270]

SPECA v. COMMISSIONER

United States Court of Appeals, Seventh Circuit, 1980.
630 F.2d 554.

NOLAND, DISTRICT JUDGE:

This is an appeal from a finding by the Tax Court of a deficiency in income taxes by appellants Gino A. Speca and Joseph F. Madrigrano for the year 1971. The sole issue for review is whether the Tax Court erred in holding that certain transfers of stock by appellants to their children lacked sufficient economic reality to permit income from the stock to be taxed to the transferee-children rather than the transferor-parents. A review of the record reveals the following undisputed facts.

Appellants are executives of Triangle Wholesale Company, Inc. (Triangle), a beer wholesaler and distributor operating in Wisconsin. Since 1969, Triangle has operated as a Subchapter S corporation. As of 1968, stock ownership in Triangle was completely within the Speca and Madrigrano families. * * *

At all times relevant to these proceedings, Madrigrano was president, secretary, and a director of Triangle. Speca was also a director of Triangle in addition to serving in the capacity of vice-president and treasurer. Both Madrigrano and Speca received salaries of approximately $42,000 for each of the years 1971 through 1975.

On March 31, 1971, the date of the transfer at issue, Madrigrano conveyed all of his remaining 376 shares of Triangle stock to his sons,

¶ 15,260

Joseph and Glenn. In exchange for the stock, Joseph and Glenn each executed a non-interest bearing promissory note in the amount of $7,110.97. The notes were made payable on March 31, 1972.

At the time of the above transfer, Joseph was 23 years of age and a full-time, second-year law student who worked part-time during the school year and during summer vacations as an employee of Triangle. Glenn was 21 years of age, and a full-time undergraduate student. Like Joseph, Glenn also worked on weekends and during summer vacations for Triangle.

On March 31, 1971, appellant Speca also conveyed all of his remaining shares of Triangle stock to his sons, Peter and Gene, who were 10 and 7 years of age, respectively, at the time. Speca's sons were also expected to pay $7,110.97 in exchange for the stock received from their father. However, unlike the Madrigrano transfer, there were no sale documents or notes evidencing a stock sale between Speca and his children. Speca expected payment of the $7,110.97 due from each child to be made from Triangle's profits. Although minors, Peter and Gene received Triangle stock certificates without benefit of a named custodian, guardian, or trustee. * * *

In a subsequent audit of appellants' federal income tax returns for the year 1971, respondent determined that the transfers of stock on March 31, 1971, were not bona fide and lacked economic substance. Therefore, that income from the transferred stock was included in the taxpayers-appellants' gross income. Respondent's position was upheld by the Tax Court and this appeal followed.

* * *

The issue of shareholder status in subchapter S corporations is not a new one. Examination of prior decisions reveals a consistent pattern of analysis involving the use of four specific factors. Those factors include: (1) Are the transferees within the family able to effectively exercise ownership rights of their shares; (2) Did the transferor continue to exercise complete dominion and control over the transferred stock; (3) Did the transferor continue to enjoy economic benefits of ownership after conveyance of the stock; and (4) Did the transferor deal at arm's length with the corporation involved. See *Duarte v. Commissioner* 44 T.C. 193 (1965); * * * and *Kirkpatrick v. Commissioner*, 36 T.C.M. (CCH) 1122 (1977).

In addition to the foregoing factors, [former] Section 1.1373–(a)(2), Income Tax Regulations, provides as follows:

> A donee or purchaser of stock in the corporation is not considered a shareholder unless such stock is acquired in a bona fide transaction and the donee or purchaser is the real owner of such stock. The circumstances, not only as of the time of the purported transfer but also during the periods preceding and following it, will be taken into

¶ 15,270

consideration in determining the bona fides of the transfer. Transactions between members of a family will be closely scrutinized.

* * *

For purposes of analysis, the instant case invites comparison to the decision rendered in *Kirkpatrick, supra.* In that case, petitioners Donald D. and Carolyn Kirkpatrick owned 52 percent of the outstanding shares of Quality Poultry and Egg Co., Inc., an Arkansas subchapter S corporation. The remaining 48 percent of Quality's shares were owned by the four Kirkpatrick children. After making use of the four factor analysis, the Tax Court determined that the ownership of 48 percent of the stock of Quality by the children did not lack economic reality and, for tax purposes, each child owned 12 percent of the common stock of Quality.

* * *

I.

First to be considered is whether appellants' transfer of stock on March 31, 1971, gave the intended transferees the ability to effectively exercise their ownership rights. Appellant Speca transferred his remaining eighteen percent share ownership equally to his sons, Gene and Peter, ages ten and seven. As minors, neither child exercised any influence in the operation of Triangle. The Tax Court found no evidence that a custodian, guardian, or legally designated representative was ever appointed to represent the children's interests. These facts differ substantially from those in *Kirkpatrick.* There, the wife was named custodian for the children and was present at all corporate meetings. She fully participated in corporate decisions, acted independently, and exercised considerable influence over the affairs of "Quality." * * * This was unlike the present situation where no independent person represented the interests of the minor transferee-children who were too young to adequately represent themselves. *Duarte v. Commissioner*, 44 T.C. at 197. Therefore, we conclude that stock transferees Gene and Peter Speca were unable to effectively exercise their ownership rights.

Likewise, we find that stock transferees Glenn and Joseph Madrigrano were unable to exercise their ownership rights. Although adults, both Glenn and Joseph were full-time students. In 1971, their contact with Triangle was limited to part-time employment during summers and on weekends. The record reflects no specific instance in which either Glenn or Joseph actually exercised their judgment with respect to a corporate decision. The absence of any corporate activity by either Glenn or Joseph in addition to the circumstances detailed below, lead us to believe that they also possessed no effective ownership rights.

II.

The next factor for consideration involves the extent to which the transferor continues to exercise dominion and control over the transferred stock. The actions of appellant Speca evidence a retention of control in the transferred stock to the detriment of the transferees' supposed rights. Acting for his sons, Peter and Gene, Speca signed a waiver of notice as to the 1972 shareholders' meeting and also approved the minutes of said meeting. The minutes of the 1974 shareholder meeting indicate that Peter and Gene were present by "proxy" without stating who the proxy was. However, Speca's signature again appears approving the minutes even though he was not on record as a sharehold-er. In contrast to *Kirkpatrick*, the presence of a custodian or legal representative acting on behalf of the Speca children is noticeably absent. Instead, we find appellant Speca in "control" of those shares purportedly sold.

The "control" exercised by appellant Madrigrano was accomplished through different means. Since its formation, Triangle operated as a beer distributor and wholesaler for the Joseph Schlitz Brewing Company (Schlitz). The relationship between Triangle and Schlitz consisted of an unwritten declaration of terms by which each party was free to buy or sell on an order-to-order basis. In October of 1972, Schlitz first learned that Madrigrano was no longer a shareholder of Triangle. Subsequently, Schlitz requested a meeting with Madrigrano to insure his continued participation in Triangle operations. Schlitz, through its sales manager Donald Hucko, informed Madrigrano that it wanted him to enter into an employment contract of at least a 5 or 10–year duration to insure his continued direction of Triangle's day-to-day operations. This request was based upon the fact that Mr. Madrigrano was no longer a Triangle shareholder.

* * *

The provisions of the resulting employment contract between Madrigrano and Triangle expressly stated that Madrigrano was hired "for a period beginning October 1, 1972 and ending September 30, 1982 as general manager, advisor, and consultant to management on all matters pertaining to the business of the Company." The contract itself was discussed at the January 11, 1972 shareholders' meeting. The minutes of the meeting stated that: "Schlitz made it emphatic since he (Madrigrano) was not a stockholder he must have a five year employment contract. Without this Triangle would be a shell and worthless corporation."

Based upon the record before us, we are convinced that Madrigrano's "presence" within Triangle was greater than that which normally flows from occupying an executive position. Madrigrano was the dominant figure who controlled corporate policy. As far as Schlitz was concerned, Madrigrano himself was the distributor of Schlitz products.

The March 31, 1971, transfer of stock was simply a paper transaction. It is evident that because Triangle depended for its business existence upon Schlitz, and Schlitz dealt with Triangle only because of Madrigrano's presence, neither Glenn nor Joseph could effectively chal-

¶ 15,270

lenge their father's judgment. As noted earlier, no specific instances can be found where either son exercised their judgment as shareholders with respect to a corporate decision. Thus, it is apparent that Madrigrano continued to effectively exercise complete dominion and control over the transferred stock as well as the corporation.

III.

We now turn to the question of whether appellants retained economic enjoyment of the benefits of ownership in the transferred shares of Triangle stock, and whether they dealt at arm's length with the corporation. To answer the first part of the above question is to determine whether the transferee-children were deprived of the economic incidents of ownership in their Triangle stock. In the case of the Speca children, the dividends distributed in cash were approximately equal to the increase in their tax liability due to the inclusion of Triangle's income on their returns. The same was true as to cash dividends distributed to Glenn and Joseph Madrigrano. In fact, an examination of the business records of Triangle reveals that the dividends actually received were in no way commensurate to the profits being made by Triangle. Moreover, the record reflects the failure of appellants to adequately explain the retention of large amounts of corporate income in the year 1971 and thereafter.

Further analysis reveals that during the same time period appellants were the recipients of sizeable unsecured, interest-free loans from Triangle. These loans remained outstanding long after appellants ceased ownership in Triangle. The payment of the loans was accomplished in part by appellants' use of their children's non-cash dividends. The non-cash dividends were taken by appellants as part payment for the stock "sold" to their children in March of 1971. The dividends were then applied by appellants against the balance owing Triangle on their loans.

The situation in the instant case is again clearly distinguishable from *Kirkpatrick*. In that case, the transferee-children also received insignificant corporate distribution amounts. However, the undistributed corporate income was eventually used for legitimate investment and expansion purposes. Any explanation proffered in the present case lacked such legitimacy. Although in both instances the children's dividends were tapped by a transferor-parent, only the *Kirkpatrick* children enjoyed the benefit of a custodian to insure a legitimate transaction. Taking these facts into consideration, it is our opinion that appellants retained the economic benefits of Triangle stock ownership to the detriment of their children. We also find that appellants failed to "deal at arm's length ... either in obtaining [their loans] or paying them back." *Beirne v. Commissioner*, 61 T.C. at 277.

* * *

¶ 15,270

VI.

Having reviewed the evidence in its entirety, we necessarily conclude that the decision of the Tax court is not clearly erroneous. Substantial evidence exists to support the Tax court's finding that appellants' purported transfer of stock lacked sufficient economic substance and therefore appellants are the beneficial owners of the transferred stock for income tax purposes. Accordingly, the judgment appealed from is AFFIRMED.

[¶ 15,275]

Notes

1. Were the taxpayers' problems substantive or merely formal? What steps might they have taken to ensure that the stock transfers would be respected?

2. All other things being equal, would a transferee-child be more likely to be respected as the owner of a business interest, as a partner, or as an S corporation shareholder? Note that Subchapter S lacks a provision like Section 704(e)(1).

3. If the stock transfer is respected, the taxpayers must still avoid a reallocation of income by the IRS under the authority of Section 1366(e). What factors would be likely to cause the IRS to seek a reallocation? Consider the following observation by the court in Krahenbuhl v. Commissioner, T.C. Memo. 1968–34 (1968) (acq.):

> The task of the Commissioner in protecting the revenue under section [1366(e)] apparently acquires a different emphasis from the responsibility which he has under Section 162(a)(1) for determining a reasonable allowance for salaries or compensation for services. Here the emphasis is on keeping salaries *up* to a reasonable limit; under Section 162(a)(1) it is on keeping salaries *down* to a reasonable figure. There is, however, no shifting of the burden of proof from petitioners to the Commissioner and the burden to show error in the Commissioner's determination is still on the petitioners.

4. If a reallocation is deemed appropriate, how is it to be made? The Code does not appear to authorize the IRS to increase the salary of the undercompensated shareholder-employee, which would create an equal deduction for the shareholders. If a fraction of the "items" of corporate income and expense are reallocated, is their character (as a capital gain, for example) preserved?

5. Section 1366(e) seems to apply even if the employee is not a shareholder so long as members of the employee's family are shareholders. See Reg. § 1.1366–3(a) and (b), Ex. 2. In that event, how is the reallocation to be made? What would be the effect of any such reallocation on the basis of the shareholder's stock?

6. What is the scope of the authority of the IRS if a shareholder receives *excessive* compensation for services or capital?

3. IMPACT OF OPERATIONS ON SHAREHOLDERS' BASIS

[¶ 15,280]

a. *In General*

The heart of a conduit system of taxation in which income is to be subject to only one level of taxation is the computation of the basis of the owner's interest in the entity. In the case of an S corporation, that ownership interest is the S corporation stock. Under a conduit system of taxation, if the corporate income is to be subject to one, but only one, level of tax, it becomes essential to track what income has already been taxed to the shareholder on a flow-through basis. Upward adjustments in the basis of a shareholder's stock equal to the amount of passed-through income accomplish that purpose. These upward adjustments, when added to the basis of the stock resulting from the owner's equity contributions, measure the total of tax-free distributions from the corporation to which the shareholder is entitled. Likewise, if corporate losses are to pass through and be reported directly by the shareholders, it is essential that the shareholder's remaining tax investment/basis in the S corporation stock be correlatively decreased so as not to duplicate the losses that have been reported earlier or the withdrawals already recouped tax-free.

Basis in S corporation stock (and debt) thus plays two key roles in the taxation of the shareholders. As in any investment, basis limits not only the amounts that may be returned free of tax to a shareholder but also the amounts that the shareholder may claim as losses on that investment. Thus, Section 1366(d)(1) limits the total amount of loss and deduction that an S corporation shareholder can currently deduct to the sum of the shareholder's basis in the S corporation stock and the basis of any indebtedness by the corporation to the shareholder. See Reg. § 1.1366–2(a)(1). Losses that may not be deducted currently because they exceed basis may be carried forward and deducted in the first year thereafter of the S corporation in which the shareholder's basis becomes adequate to cover such losses. § 1366(d)(2)(A); Reg. § 1.1366–2(a)(2). They may even be carried over and deducted after the corporation terminates its S election, provided the requisite increase in the shareholder's basis occurs by the last day of the "post-termination transition period." § 1366(d)(3); Reg. § 1.1366–2(b). See ¶ 15,470.

In general, a shareholder's initial basis in S corporation stock is increased by the amount of all items of income derived by the corporation during the taxable year and included in the income of the shareholder, as well as the shareholder's pro rata share of the corporation's income that is not subject to tax. § 1367(a)(1); Reg. § 1.1367–1(b). If the shareholder's stock basis were not increased by items of tax-exempt income, that income would be taxed to the S corporation shareholder when it is distributed to the shareholder in violation of the legislative policy supporting exemption of the income from tax. Similarly, the basis for S corporation stock is reduced by the amount of the items of loss and deduction allocated to the shareholder, but such basis reduction may not decrease the shareholder's basis in the S corporation stock below zero. § 1367(a)(2); Reg. § 1.1367–1(c)(1). In addition, a shareholder's stock basis is reduced by any expense for which a deduction is permanently disallowed but which also is not properly capitalized, such as illegal bribes and kickbacks, fines and penalties, and the portion of meals and entertainment disallowed by Section 274. § 1367(a)(2)(D). A shareholder's stock basis is not reduced by a deduction of the S corporation that is merely deferred to a later taxable year nor is it reduced by any expenditures of the corporation that are required to be capitalized. Reg. § 1.1367–1(c)(2). What is the effect of reducing a shareholder's stock basis for such nondeductible, noncapital expenses? What will be the eventual effect on stock basis of amounts that are capitalized but that do not currently reduce the shareholder's basis in the stock? Finally, of course, a shareholder's stock basis is reduced by the amount of all distributions to the shareholder from the S corporation that are not taxable to the shareholder (see ¶¶ 15,340 et seq.). § 1367(a)(2)(A); Reg. § 1.1367–1(c)(1).

Sperl v. Commissioner, T.C. Memo. 1993–515 (1993), illustrates the basis adjustments that can result from the informal transfers that not uncommonly occur between S corporations and their shareholders. The payment of corporate expenses by the shareholder resulted in an increase in the basis of his stock. On the other hand, the rent-free use of corporate property by the shareholder was treated as a reduction in the amount of the corporation's debt to the shareholder and thus reduced the shareholder's basis in the loan.

In principle, the Section 1367 regulations adopt a share-by-share approach to the basis of S corporations' stock that is consistent with the rules of Subchapter C and do not permit the aggregation of the basis of different blocks of stock. However, the potential harshness of that rule is virtually eliminated by the special rule in Reg. § 1.1367–1(c)(3)—if an allocated loss or a distribution exceeds the basis of a share, it may be applied against the basis of other shares owned by the taxpayer.

Increases and decreases of stock basis in general are made as of the end of the S corporation's taxable year. However, if all or a portion of a shareholder's stock interest is transferred during the year, the adjustments to the basis of that stock are effective immediately before the transfer. Reg. § 1.1367–1(d)(1).

The order in which basis adjustments generally are made is prescribed by Reg. § 1.1367–1(f), as follows:

(1) increases under Section 1367(a)(1);

¶ 15,280

(2) decreases attributable to nontaxable distributions under Section 1367(a)(2)(A);

(3) decreases attributable to nondeductible, noncapital expenses under Section 1367(a)(2)(D) (and for certain depletion deductions); and

(4) decreases attributable to losses or deductions under Section 1367(a)(2)(B) and (C).

The regulations also contain a special elective ordering rule that allows a taxpayer to elect to reduce basis first by any losses or deductions under Section 1367(a)(2)(B) and (C). Reg. § 1.1367–1(g)

[¶ 15,285]

Problems

1. How do the following items affect a sole shareholder of an S corporation whose initial basis for the S corporation stock was $1,000?

Income from operations	$2,000
Tax-exempt interest	500
Salary expense	600
Fine for speeding	50
Shareholder's medical expense	100
Purchase of land	1,000
May 31 distribution to shareholder	2,300

2. At the beginning of the year, a shareholder's basis for her S corporation stock was $15,000. On July 1, she gave the stock to her son Mark. The S corporation income for the year allocable to that stock was $4,000. What should be Mark's basis in the stock at the end of the year, assuming that the gift of stock to Mark is respected for purposes of Subchapter S?

3. Tom, Dick, and Mary received the distributions of property from their S corporation described in Problem 3 at ¶ 15,245. How did the distributions affect the basis of each shareholder's stock?

4. Byrned is the sole shareholder in Xcessive Toys, Inc. and has a basis of $1,000 for his stock, which he has held since he caused the incorporation of Xcessive in 1952. The value of his stock, however, is $1 million. Xcessive has a basis for its assets of $750,000. Last year Xcessive elected to be taxed as an S corporation and in that first year incurred a net loss of $10,000.

a. How much of that loss may be claimed by Byrned? See Byrne v. Commissioner, 361 F.2d 939 (7th Cir.1966).

b. Incidentally, how is it possible for Byrned to have a basis of only $1,000 for his shares while the corporation has a basis of $750,000 for its assets? Also, how can the stock be worth $1 million in view of the bases to Byrned and the corporation for their respective holdings?

¶ 15,280

c. How might Byrned arrange to claim all $10,000 of the loss currently without making any added capital contributions to the corporation? See the discussion at ¶ 15,290.

[¶ 15,287]

b. *Effect of Cancellation-of-Debt Income at the Corporate Level*

As discussed above, Section 1366(a)(1)(A) and 1367(a)(1)(A) authorize an increase in a shareholder's basis for S corporation stock by the shareholder's share of the corporation's "tax-exempt income." Neither the statute nor regulations define what is tax-exempt income for this purpose. Does it apply to an S corporation's income from the discharge of indebtedness, which may be excludable at the corporate level under Section 108? See § 108(d)(7)(A). However, Section 108 often works as merely a deferral of income because a debtor must reduce its tax attributes (if any) under Section 108(b) by the amount of cancellation-of-debt income excluded under Section 108(a). Is income excluded at the S corporation level under Section 108 "tax-exempt income" that increases the shareholder's basis under Section 1367(a)(1)(A)?

That issue was the subject of the Supreme Court's decision in Gitlitz v. Commissioner, 531 U.S. 206 (2001), which, as explained below, was ultimately reversed by Congress in a legislative change made in 2002. The Court majority in *Gitlitz* used the textualist approach to statutory interpretation and held in favor of the taxpayer, resolving a split among the circuits on this issue. The Court majority reasoned, as follows (531 U.S. at 212–16 (some footnotes omitted)):

> * * * The Commissioner argues that the discharge of indebtedness of an insolvent S corporation is not an "item of income" and thus never passes through to shareholders. Under a plain reading of the statute, we reject this argument and conclude that excluded discharged debt is indeed an "item of income," which passes through to the shareholders and increases their bases in the stock of the S corporation.

> Section 61(a)(12) states that discharge of indebtedness generally is included in gross income. Section 108(a)(1) provides an express exception to this general rule:

>> "Gross income does not include any amount which (but for this subsection) would be includible in gross income by reason of the discharge ... of indebtedness of the taxpayer if—

>> * * *

>> "(B) the discharge occurs when the taxpayer is insolvent."

¶ 15,287

The Commissioner contends that this exclusion from gross income alters the character of the discharge of indebtedness so that it is no longer an "item of income." However, the text and structure of the statute do not support the Commissioner's theory. Section 108(a) simply does not say that discharge of indebtedness ceases to be an item of income when the S corporation is insolvent. Instead it provides only that discharge of indebtedness ceases to be included in gross income. Not all items of income are included in gross income, see § 1366(a)(1) (providing that "items of income," including "tax-exempt" income, are passed through to shareholders), so mere exclusion of an amount from gross income does not imply that the amount ceases to be an item of income. Moreover, §§ 101 through 136 employ the same construction to exclude various items from gross income: "Gross income does not include...." The consequence of reading this language in the manner suggested by the Commissioner would be to exempt all items in these sections from pass-through under § 1366. However, not even the Commissioner encourages us to reach this sweeping conclusion. Instead the Commissioner asserts that discharge of indebtedness is unique among the types of items excluded from gross income because no economic outlay is required of the taxpayer receiving discharge of indebtedness. But the Commissioner is unable to identify language in the statute that makes this distinction relevant, and we certainly find none.

On the contrary, the statute makes clear that § 108(a)'s exclusion does not alter the character of discharge of indebtedness as an item of income. Specifically, § 108(e)(1) reads:

> "Except as otherwise provided in this section, there shall be no insolvency exception from the general rule that gross income includes income from the discharge of indebtedness."

This provision presumes that discharge of indebtedness is always "income," and that the only question for purposes of § 108 is whether it is includible in gross income. If discharge of indebtedness of insolvent entities were not actually "income," there would be no need to provide an exception to its inclusion in gross income; quite simply, if discharge of indebtedness of an insolvent entity were not "income," it would necessarily not be included in gross income.

Notwithstanding the plain language of the statute, the Commissioner argues, generally, that excluded discharge of indebtedness is not income and, specifically, that it is not "tax-exempt income" under § 1366(a)(1)(A).[6] First, the Commissioner argues that § 108

---

6. The Commissioner also contends, as does the dissent, that because § 108(d)(7)(A) mandates that the dis- charged debt amount be determined and applied to reduce tax attributes "at the corporate level," rather than at the share-

merely codified the "judicial insolvency exception," and that, under this exception, discharge of indebtedness of an insolvent taxpayer was not considered income. The insolvency exception was a rule that the discharge of indebtedness of an insolvent taxpayer was not taxable income. * * * But the exception has since been limited by § 108(e). Section 108(e) precludes us from relying on any understanding of the judicial insolvency exception that was not codified in § 108. And as explained above, the language and logic of § 108 clearly establish that, although discharge of indebtedness of an insolvent taxpayer is not included in gross income, it is nevertheless income.

* * *

Second, the Commissioner argues that excluded discharge of indebtedness is not "tax-exempt" income under § 1366(a)(1)(A), but rather "tax-deferred" income. According to the Commissioner, because the taxpayer is required to reduce tax attributes that could have provided future tax benefits, the taxpayer will pay taxes on future income that otherwise would have been absorbed by the forfeited tax attributes. Implicit in the Commissioner's labeling of such income as "tax-deferred," however, is the erroneous assumption that § 1366(a)(1)(A) does not include "tax-deferred" income. Section 1366 applies to "items of income." This section expressly includes "tax-exempt" income, but this inclusion does not mean that the statute must therefore exclude "tax-deferred" income. The section is worded broadly enough to include any item of income, even tax-deferred income, that "could affect the liability for tax of any shareholder." § 1366(a)(1)(A). Thus, none of the Commissioner's contentions alters our conclusion that discharge of indebtedness of an insolvent S corporation is an item of income for purposes of § 1366(a)(1)(A).

[The Court majority went on to hold that basis increase for the pass-through of the tax-exempt cancellation of indebtedness income

holder level, the discharged debt, even if it is some type of income, simply cannot pass through to shareholders. In other words, the Commissioner contends that § 108(d)(7)(A) excepts excluded discharged debt from the general pass-through provisions for S corporations. However, § 108(d)(7)(A) merely directs that the exclusion from gross income and the tax attribute reduction be made at the corporate level. Section 108(d)(7)(A) does not state or imply that the debt discharge provisions shall apply *only* "at the corporate level." The very purpose of Subchapter S is to tax at the shareholder level, not the corporate

level. Income is determined at the S corporation level, see § 1363(b), not in order to tax the corporation, see § 1363(a) (exempting an S corporation from income tax), but solely to pass through to the S corporation's shareholders the corporation's income. Thus, the controlling provision states that, in determining a shareholder's liability, "there shall be taken into account the shareholder's pro rata share of the corporation's . . . items of income (including tax-exempt income). . . ." § 1366(a)(1). Nothing in § 108(d)(7)(A) suspends the operation of these ordinary pass-through rules.

¶ 15,287

occurs before the S corporation reduces its attributes under Section 108(b).]

* * *

Justice Breyer wrote a vigorous dissenting opinion in *Gitlitz* in which he stated (531 U.S. at 221–24 (footnotes omitted)):

> If one reads this language literally as exclusive, both the COD exclusion (§ 108(a)) and the tax attribute reduction (§ 108(b)) would apply only "at the corporate level." Hence the COD income would not flow through to S corporation shareholders. Consequently, the insolvent S corporation's COD income would not increase the shareholder's basis and would not help the shareholder take otherwise unavailable deductions for suspended losses.
>
> The Commissioner argues that we should read the language in this way as preventing the flow-through of the corporation's COD income. * * * He points to the language of a House Committee, which apparently thought, when Congress passed an amendment to § 108, that the Commissioner's reading is correct. H. R. Rep. No. 103–111, pp. 624–625 (1993) * * *. * * *
>
> The Commissioner finds support for his literal, exclusive reading of § 108(d)(7)(A)'s language in the fact that his reading would close a significant tax loophole. That loophole—preserved by the majority—would grant a *solvent* shareholder of an insolvent S corporation a tax benefit in the form of permission to take an otherwise unavailable deduction, thereby sheltering other, unrelated income from tax. See *Witzel v. Commissioner*, 200 F.3d 496, 497 (C.A.7 2000) (Posner, C. J.) ("It is hard to understand the rationale for using a tax exemption to avoid taxation not only on the income covered by the exemption but also on unrelated income that is not tax exempt"). Moreover, the benefit often would increase in value as the amount of COD income increases, a result inconsistent with congressional intent to impose a "price" (attribute reduction), * * *, on excluded COD. Further, this deduction-related tax benefit would have very different tax consequences for identically situated taxpayers, depending only upon whether a single debt can be split into segments, each of which is canceled in a different year. For example, under the majority's interpretation, a $1 million debt canceled in one year would permit Taxpayer A to deduct $1 million of suspended losses in that year, thereby permitting A to shelter $1 million of unrelated income in that year. But because § 108 reduces tax attributes after the first year, five annual cancellations of $200,000 will not create a $1 million shelter. Timing is all important.
>
> The majority acknowledges some of these policy concerns and confesses ignorance of any "other instance in which § 108 directly benefits a solvent entity," but claims that its reading is mandated by

the plain text of § 108(d)(7)(A) and therefore that the Court may disregard the policy consequences. * * * It is difficult, however, to see why we should interpret that language as treating different solvent shareholders differently, given that the words "at the corporate level" were added "[i]n order to treat all shareholders in the same manner." H. R. Rep. No. 98–432, pt. 2, p. 1640 (1984). And it is more difficult to see why, given the fact that the "plain language" admits either interpretation, we should ignore the policy consequences. * * *

The arguments from plain text on both sides here produce ambiguity, not certainty. And other things being equal, we should read ambiguous statutes as closing, not maintaining, tax loopholes. Such is an appropriate understanding of Congress' likely intent. Here, other things are equal, for, as far as I am aware, the Commissioner's literal interpretation of § 108(d)(7)(A) as exclusive would neither cause any tax-related harm nor create any statutory anomaly. * * *

* * * I do not contend that § 108(d)(7)(A) *must* be read as having exclusive effect, only that, given the alternative, this interpretation provides the best reading of § 108 as a whole. And I can find no "clear declaration of intent by Congress" to support the majority's contrary conclusion regarding § 108(d)(7)(A)'s effect. It is that conclusion from which, for the reasons stated, I respectfully dissent.

The regulations take the position that income excluded by an S corporation under Section 108 is not "tax-exempt income," because it is not "permanently excludible from gross income in all circumstances in which * * * [Section 108] applies." Reg. § 1.1366–1(a)(2)(viii). Accordingly, an S corporation shareholder obtains no basis increase for such income under Section 1367(a)(1)(A).

Of greater importance, as mentioned above, Congress amended the statute in 2002 to reverse the *Gitlitz* decision for discharges of indebtedness occurring after October 11, 2001, in taxable years ending after that date. Revised Section 108(d)(7)(A) now provides that cancellation-of-indebtedness income that is excluded under Section 108(a) will not be taken into account under Section 1366(a). Consequently, such excluded cancellation-of-indebtedness income will not result in an adjustment to the S corporation shareholder's stock basis under Section 1367.

[¶ 15,288]

Notes

1. Does the *Gitlitz* majority reach the correct conclusion based on the language of the statute, i.e., is the majority's conclusion mandated from a plain textual reading of the statute? Stated differently, does the

majority's conclusion reflect a logical, rational, and commonsense interpretation of the statute?

2. Why does the *Gitlitz* majority feel compelled to ignore policy concerns in interpreting the meaning of the words in the statute? Should policy concerns be taken into account in determining which of two possible meanings of statutory language was intended by Congress?

3. Has the Internal Revenue Code in general and the Subchapter S provisions in particular become so complex that the Court cannot trust its own understanding of the internal logic of the tax law?

[¶ 15,290]

c. *Relevance of Loans by Shareholders*

As mentioned earlier, one of the more significant distinctions between the taxation of S corporations and the taxation of partnerships is that an S corporation's borrowing at the entity level is not reflected in the shareholders' stock basis. Whereas a partner can deduct passed-through losses up to the sum of that partner's equity interest plus the partner's allocable share of borrowings by the partnership, in the case of an S corporation the ability to deduct losses incurred by the entity is far more limited. Compare § 1367(a)(1) with § 752. One common result is that losses incurred by an S corporation attributable to the use of funds borrowed by the corporation cannot be currently deducted by the shareholders. For example, assume that a sole shareholder contributes $10,000 to an S corporation. The corporation then borrows $90,000 and purchases depreciable property for $100,000. If the corporation generates operating losses for its first few years, the shareholder will not be able to deduct currently losses in excess of the $10,000 basis in the stock.

On the other hand, it is not only a shareholder's stock investment in an S corporation that entitles the shareholder to a pass-through of the corporation's losses; loans made by the shareholder to the corporation can also be used with like effect. § 1366(d)(1)(B); Reg. § 1.1366-2(a)(1)(ii). In both cases the passed-through losses appear on the shareholder's own return, limited however to the shareholder's total basis in the stock and loan. (Passed-through losses and deductions first reduce a shareholder's basis in her S corporation stock and then, if in excess of that basis, are applied to reduce her basis in a loan made by the shareholder to the corporation. § 1367(b)(2)(A); Reg. § 1.1367-2(b).) With basis in shareholder-held debt and stock equally available to support the deduction of passed-through losses, what is the tax significance, if any, to whether the corporation issues debt or stock instruments in exchange for a cash payment from a shareholder? Recall the material at ¶ 15,040.

¶ 15,288

The following authorities discuss when a shareholder will be viewed as having borrowed from an outside lender and then having contributed the loan proceeds to the S corporation.

[¶ 15,295]

BOLDING v. COMMISSIONER

United States Court of Appeals, Fifth Circuit, 1997.
117 F.3d 270.

GARWOOD, CIRCUIT JUDGE:

This appeal involves disputed deficiencies in the income tax returns of appellants Dennis and Dixie Bolding, husband and wife, for the taxable years 1988, 1989, and 1990. The Boldings filed a petition contesting the deficiencies in the United States Tax Court. The court entered a memorandum opinion, * * * rendering a decision in favor of the Commissioner of Internal Revenue (Commissioner). We reverse.

FACTS AND PROCEEDINGS BELOW

In the late 1970s, Dennis Bolding (Taxpayer) began a cattle ranch operation, breeding and selling cattle for the meat market. Taxpayer was advised by his accountant that he should conduct his cattle ranching operation through a corporation for liability purposes. Accordingly, in August 1983 Taxpayer formed Three Forks Land & Cattle Company (Three Forks), a Texas corporation * * *. The corporation was structured as a Subchapter S corporation, and at all times was wholly owned by Taxpayer, who was its president.

* * *

At the beginning of 1990, Taxpayer leased a ranch known as the Hopper Ranch. He needed additional funds to purchase cattle to stock his ranching operation. He contacted the Citizens State Bank of Lometa * * *. The Bank required Taxpayer to submit a personal financial statement and a proposed operating statement showing the planned use of the funds. Pursuant to the Bank's request, * * * [t]he proposed operating statement indicated that Taxpayer wanted the loan to fund a "cow-calf operation" in which he would purchase 400 cows and 20 bulls and graze them on 4,800 acres. He asked for a line of credit from the Bank in the amount of $250,000. No financial information with respect to Three Forks was asked for or submitted.

The Bank approved the $250,000 line of credit and prepared a promissory note, which Taxpayer signed, naming "Dennis E. Bolding d/b/a Three Forks Land & Cattle Co." as the maker-borrower. The Bank also required the filing of a security agreement and a UCC–1 financing statement. The security agreement was signed "Dennis E. Bolding d/b/a Three Forks Land & Cattle Co.," and provided the Bank with a security interest in the cows and bulls that were to be acquired with the funds borrowed under the line of credit. The UCC–1 statement, however, was signed by Taxpayer simply as "Dennis E. Bolding."

Taxpayer believed that he was borrowing the funds in his personal capacity and not on behalf of Three Forks. Also, the Bank indicated that it was making the loan to Taxpayer alone and based upon his personal credit. None of the loan documents prepared by the Bank was prepared for Three Forks as debtor, nor were any signed by anyone on behalf of the corporation.

The funds were disbursed directly from the Bank to Three Forks' corporate account and were used by Three Forks to purchase cattle. Principal and interest payments were made to the Bank from time to time with respect to the $250,000 line of credit. Such principal and interest payments to the Bank were made by checks drawn on Three Forks' account.

By the end of 1990, the total amount outstanding on the line of credit, net of all repayments, was $223,000. The line of credit was rolled over into later years, after its initial maturity, but ultimately went into default in March 1994 with an outstanding balance. The Bank sued Taxpayer for repayment on the outstanding balance of the loan; no action was taken against Three Forks.

Three Forks reported an ordinary loss for its 1990 year of $93,769. Taxpayer deducted, among other things, that amount on his 1990 income tax return as his share of the S corporation's loss. Also, Taxpayer deducted a carryover loss from the corporation's 1989 tax return in the amount of $25,454, for a total loss of $119,223. After reporting a capital gain of $19,681 from the corporation in the corporation's 1990 tax return, the net loss from the corporation claimed in Taxpayer's 1990 tax return was $99,542. * * *

The Commissioner disagreed with Taxpayer's deductions, and issued a statutory notice of deficiency in July 1993. The Commissioner disallowed the entire $99,542 net loss claim for 1990 on the grounds that Taxpayer had insufficient basis in Three Forks' stock to support such an allowance. * * *

* * * Although corporate losses deducted prior to 1990 had exhausted his adjusted basis in Three Forks, Taxpayer maintained that his basis in the corporation increased during 1990 as a result of the $250,000 line of credit obtained from the Bank. According to Taxpayer, he, solely in his individual capacity, borrowed the funds under the $250,000 credit from the Bank and, in turn, he lent those funds to Three Forks. * * *

The Commissioner, on the other hand, maintained that Three Forks, rather than Taxpayer, was the true borrower * * *. * * *

Following a one-day trial, the Tax Court entered a memorandum opinion holding that Taxpayer was not entitled to deduct the corporation's net operating loss. The Tax Court found as a fact that Taxpayer, rather than Three Forks, was the true borrower from the Bank with respect to the funds disbursed under the $250,000 line of credit. The court, however, ultimately agreed with the Commissioner that Taxpayer did not have sufficient basis in Three Forks' stock or debt to entitle him to deduct any of the corporation's $99,542 net operating loss. According to the court, the evidence showed that the funds from the loan were deposited sometimes directly from the Bank to Three Forks' accounts, and sometimes to Taxpayer's personal account, and Taxpayer had failed to show how much went to Three Forks.[6] * * *

DISCUSSION

The key issue in this case centers around the nature of the $250,000 line of credit. If, as the Commissioner contends, the loan was one from the Bank to Three Forks, Taxpayer could not have invested the proceeds of the loan in the corporation, and thus his basis in the corporation would not have increased and would not suffice to allow him to deduct its operating losses. On the other hand, if the line of credit was actually a loan from the Bank to Taxpayer, who then invested the funds in or loaned them to his corporation, the Taxpayer's basis in the corporation would be correspondingly increased and sufficient to allow him to deduct its referenced losses. *See In re Breit*, 460 F.Supp. 873, 875 (E.D.Va.1978). In other words, we must determine whether the $250,000 line of credit was a loan from the Bank to Three Forks or whether it was a loan to Taxpayer, who in turn furnished it to Three Forks as either a loan or a capital contribution. *See Estate of Leavitt v. Commissioner*, 875 F.2d 420, 422 (4th Cir.), *cert. denied*, 493 U.S. 958 * * * (1989).

* * * The question presented here—whether the $250,000 line of credit was a loan to Taxpayer or to Three Forks—is one of fact, and the Tax Court's findings of fact will not be overturned unless clearly erroneous. * * * After examining the record in this case, we are convinced that the Tax Court's finding that the $250,000 line of credit was a loan from the Bank to Taxpayer is not clearly erroneous.

"Ordinarily, taxpayers are bound by the form of the transaction they have chosen; taxpayers may not in hindsight recast the transaction as one that they might have made in order to obtain tax advantages." *Harris v. United States*, 902 F.2d 439, 443 (5th Cir.1990) * * *. In this case, the "form" of the $250,000 line of credit is consistent with a loan from the Bank to Taxpayer, not to Three Forks. The promissory note was signed by Taxpayer, not in his representative capacity on behalf of Three Forks, but rather as an individual borrower. Taxpayer did not sign the note, or for that matter any other document associated with the $250,000 line of credit, as "President" of Three Forks or in some other

---

6. As discussed below, the Commissioner does not defend the Tax Court's decision on this basis, and concedes that all the $250,000 advanced on the line of credit went to Three Forks.

¶ 15,295

representative capacity. *Cf. Reser*, 112 F.3d at 1264 (explaining that one of the relevant factors in determining whether a bank loaned money to a taxpayer individually is whether the promissory note was executed by taxpayer alone or with his corporation). Moreover, instead of including Three Forks' identification number on the note—which the Bank would have done had Three Forks been the borrower—the note contained only Taxpayer's personal social security number. Finally, Taxpayer signed both the security agreement and UCC–1 financing statement in his individual capacity. Clearly, all of the loan documents, in form, establish that Taxpayer was the true borrower of the line of credit.

* * *

Although not directly on point, this Court's decisions in *Harris* and *Reser* are instructive. The taxpayers in *Harris*, J.H. Harris (Harris) and William Martin (Martin), wanted to convert a pornographic theater into a wedding hall and approached Hibernia National Bank (Hibernia) to obtain a $700,000 loan to fund their project. To shield themselves from liability, the taxpayers formed Harmar, a Louisiana corporation which elected to be taxed pursuant to Subchapter S of the Internal Revenue Code. The taxpayers were the sole shareholders of Harmar. Hibernia agreed to make the loan, and Harmar executed two promissory notes payable to Hibernia for $350,000 each. One of the notes was secured by certificates of deposit of Harris individually and of his wholly-owned corporation, Harris Mortgage Corporation. Harmar secured both notes by using the mortgage on the theater as collateral. Harris and Martin also executed personal guarantees of the notes in the amount of $700,000 each in favor of Hibernia. *Id.* at 440.

The taxpayers sought to deduct on their 1982 income tax returns Hamar's 1982 net operating loss of $104,013. * * * The district court granted summary judgment for the IRS, rejecting the taxpayers' argument that the Hibernia loan should be recharacterized to reflect what taxpayers contended was its true substance, namely a loan from Hibernia to taxpayers followed by a loan of the same funds from taxpayers to Hamar. *Id.* at 440–41. In affirming the district court's order, this Court looked to all of the facts and circumstances surrounding the loan agreement, and in particular, undisputed evidence that:

> "Each of the two $350,000 promissory notes was executed by and only in the name of Harmar.... Hibernia, an independent party, in substance earmarked the loan proceeds for use in purchasing the subject property to which Harmar took title, Harmar contemporaneously giving Hibernia a mortgage to secure Harmar's debt to Hibernia. The bank sent interest due notices to Harmar, and all note payments were made by checks to Hibernia drawn on Harmar's corporate account. Harmar's books and records ... reflect the $700,000 loan simply as an indebtedness of Harmar to Hibernia.... Hibernia's records showed Harmar as the 'borrower' in respect to

the $700,000 loan and the renewals of it. Harmar's 1982 tax return, ... indicates that Harmar deducted $12,506 in interest expenses. Because only the Hibernia loan generated such expenses for that period, it is reasonably inferable that the deduction corresponded to that loan. The 1982 Harmar return showed no distribution to Taxpayers, as it should have if the $700,000 Hibernia loan on which Harmar paid interest was a loan to the Taxpayers. Further, the return shows the only capital contributed as $2,000 and the only loan from stockholders as $68,000, but shows other indebtedness of $675,000. In short, Harmar's 1982 income tax return is flatly inconsistent with Taxpayers' present position. Moreover, there is no indication that Taxpayers treated the loan as a personal one on their individual returns by reporting Harmar's interest payments to Hibernia as constructive dividend income. In sum, the parties' treatment of the transaction, from the time it was entered into and for years thereafter, has been wholly consistent with its unambiguous documentation and inconsistent with the way in which Taxpayers now seek to recast it." *Id.* at 443–44.

In *Reser*, Don Reser (Don) was the sole shareholder of Don C. Reser, P.C. (DRPC), a Subchapter S professional corporation formed to broker large real estate projects. Don and DRPC approached Frost Bank and requested a line of credit for operating capital. Frost Bank approved the line of credit and documented the loan with fourteen promissory notes executed jointly by Don and DRPC in favor of Frost Bank during the years 1985 through 1989. Don and DRPC were jointly and severally liable for repayment of the loan; however, the loan was not collateralized with any property belonging to either Don or DRPC. Whenever DRPC needed funds from the line of credit, Don would have Frost Bank directly deposit the funds into DRPC's corporate account. The funds were used by Don for DRPC's operating capital and for his own personal use.

The IRS disallowed Don's attempt to deduct DRPC's losses on his 1987 and 1988 income tax returns because his basis in DRPC was insufficient. * * * The Tax Court, following trial on the merits, agreed with the IRS, and we affirmed. We held that the Tax Court was not clearly erroneous in its finding that the loan was one by Frost Bank to DRPC, rather than one by Frost Bank to Don, with Don in turn loaning to DRPC. We observed:

"First, the promissory notes payable to Frost Bank were executed by Don and DRPC together, indicating on their face that Frost Bank did not lend the money to Don alone. Second, Frost Bank always deposited the loan proceeds directly into DRPC's account. Third, Don, individually, did not make any repayments on the loan to Frost Bank, but DRPC made both principal and interest payments to Frost Bank. Finally, DRPC's corporate tax returns reflected the notes as payable to Frost Bank, not to Don, even though the returns

¶ 15,295

listed other notes payable to Don...." * * * *Reser*, 112 F.3d at 1264–65 * * *.

Applying the factors relied on by this Court in *Harris* and *Reser* to the case at bar, we conclude that the Tax Court did not clearly err in finding that the $250,000 line of credit was a loan from the Bank to Taxpayer individually. As discussed earlier, the promissory note, security agreement, and UCC–1 financing statement were all signed by and only in the name of Taxpayer individually. Taxpayer did not sign the loan documents as "President" (or otherwise as agent) of Three Forks, nor were these documents signed by any other representative of the corporation.

It is uncontroverted the Bank intended and understood that Taxpayer, and not Three Forks, was the borrower in the loan. Jerry Albright, the Bank's vice-president and one of the loan officers responsible for approving the $250,000 line of credit, testified at trial that he intended the loan to be one to Taxpayer, that the Bank looked to Taxpayer as the obligor, that in deciding whether to approve the loan, the Bank requested financial information only from Taxpayer personally and not from Three Forks, and that when the loan went into default in March 1994, the Bank looked solely to Taxpayer for repayment. In fact, it appears that neither Albright nor any other Bank official even knew of Three Forks' existence as a corporate entity when the Bank extended the line of credit to Taxpayer, as the Bank never asked for any financial information respecting Three Forks or, for that matter, any proof of Three Forks' corporate status, such as a corporate certificate of good standing or articles of incorporation.[10] *See Harris*, 902 F.2d at 444 n.12.

Three Forks' 1990 corporate year-end balance sheet reflected the loan as one from Taxpayer to the corporation, and Three Forks' 1990 corporate tax return shows the line of credit as a loan from Taxpayer, appearing as "loans from stockholders." *Cf. Reser*, 112 F.3d at 1265 (discussing relevance of corporation reporting loan as indebtedness to taxpayer). Moreover, unlike the loan transaction in *Harris*, where Hibernia furnished the $700,000 on the same day the purchase of the theater closed, the cattle which acted as collateral on the loan were purchased by Three Forks *after* the Bank loan closed.

As the Commissioner aptly points out, however, Taxpayer failed to include as income on his 1990 tax return the interest payments made to him by Three Forks, on the loan from him to Three Forks, a factor the *Harris* and *Reser* Courts found to be of some importance. Taxpayer testified that he did not include any of the interest payments on his 1990 tax return—either those to him by Three Forks or those by him to the

---

10. Albright testified that had the loan been made to the corporation, there would have been a signature line for the corporation, the corporation's taxpayer identification number would have appeared on the note, and the Bank would have required a corporate good standing certificate and corporate financial documents.

Bank—because he charged Three Forks the exact same amount of interest that the Bank charged him on the $250,000 line of credit. Thus, the interest payments from Three Forks to Taxpayer and the interest payments from Taxpayer to the Bank essentially canceled each other out. We agree with the Commissioner that Taxpayer should have reported on his 1990 tax return the interest payments that he received from Three Forks. * * *

Based on our assessment of the totality of the circumstances surrounding the $250,000 line of credit, we conclude that the Tax Court did not commit clear error in finding that the Bank loan was solely to the Taxpayer individually.

* * *

* * * [However,] [t]he court mistakenly overlooked the parties' stipulation of facts, which expressly provided that all of the proceeds from the $250,000 line of credit were deposited into Three Forks' corporate account. * * *

* * *

REVERSED.

[¶ 15,300]

Notes

1. What facts in *Bolding* were critical to the trial court's conclusion that in substance the borrowing had been by the shareholders who then in turn loaned the proceeds to the corporation? Had the trial court's finding been that the loan was made to the corporation rather than to the shareholders, would the appellate court have reversed?

2. Would the shareholder in *Bolding* likewise have prevailed had the bank loaned funds to the S corporation on a guarantee of the loan by the shareholder? The cases have nearly uniformly held against the shareholder on such facts, the leading authority being Estate of Leavitt v. Commissioner, 90 T.C. 206 (1988), aff'd, 875 F.2d 420 (4th Cir.), cert. denied, 493 U.S. 958 (1989). The court there held that, as a matter of law, shareholder guarantees did not result in constructive contributions with correlative adjustments to the basis of stock.

By contrast, in Selfe v. United States, 778 F.2d 769 (11th Cir.1985), the Eleventh Circuit remanded the district court's summary judgment in favor of the government with direction to apply the principles of Plantation Patterns, Inc. v. Commissioner, 462 F.2d 712 (5th Cir.), cert. denied, 409 U.S. 1076 (1972), excerpted at ¶ 3065, to determine to which party in substance the loan had been made. The Eleventh Circuit held that an S corporation shareholder who personally guarantees a debt of the S corporation may increase her basis in the corporation by the amount of the debt "where the facts demonstrate that, in substance, the sharehold-

¶ 15,300

er has borrowed funds and subsequently advanced them to her corporation." 778 F.2d at 773. In the court's view, an S corporation shareholder's guarantee of a loan to the corporation "may be treated for tax purposes as an equity investment in the corporation where the lender looks to the shareholder as the primary obligor." Id. at 774.

In Sleiman v. Commissioner, 187 F.3d 1352 (11th Cir.1999), however, another case involving S corporation shareholders' guarantees of loans made to the corporation, the Eleventh Circuit distinguished *Selfe* and acknowledged the limited applicability of its holding in that case. The court held that the taxpayers in *Sleiman* had "not presented one of the unusual sets of facts that would lead us to conclude that the substance of the loans did not equal their form." Id. at 1359. The court, therefore, did not allow the shareholders to include the amounts of the guaranteed loans in their bases in the S corporations. The principle that an S corporation shareholder does not obtain a basis increase in the corporation by guaranteeing a third party loan to the corporation was affirmed in the recent case of Maloof v. Commissioner, T.C. Memo. 2005–75 (2005).

3.   Economically, what is the practical difference to the shareholder between the shareholder borrowing and contributing the proceeds to the corporation as opposed to merely guaranteeing a loan made directly to the corporation by a third party?

In Grojean v. Commissioner, 248 F.3d 572 (7th Cir.2001), the Seventh Circuit treated an S corporation shareholder's loan participation in a bank loan to the S corporation as, in substance, a guarantee of the loan made to the corporation, which did not provide the shareholder with additional basis to absorb the deduction of passed-through losses from the corporation. In his opinion for the court, Judge Posner provided the following analysis:

> The difference between a loan and a guaranty may seem a fine one, since, when the amount is the same, the lender and guarantor assume the same risk (subject to a possible wrinkle, concerning bankruptcy * * *). The difference between the two transactional forms may seem to amount only to this: the loan supplies funds to the borrower, and the guaranty enables funds to be supplied to the borrower. That is indeed the main difference, but it is not trivial or nominal ("formal"). * * * [T]he three-cornered arrangement (borrower, lender, guarantor) created by a guaranty makes economic sense only if the lender has a comparative advantage in liquidity (that is, in being able to come up with the money to lend the borrower) and the guarantor a comparative advantage in bearing risk. Otherwise the additional transaction costs of the more complex arrangement would be uneconomical.

> At a high level of abstraction, it is true, the difference between providing and enabling the provision of funding may disappear.

¶ 15,300

Indeed, at that level, the difference between equity and debt, as methods of corporate financing, disappears. * * * But at the operational level, because of various frictions that some economic models disregard, such as transaction and liquidity costs, there really is a substantive and not merely a formal difference between lending and guaranteeing. In contrast, the difference between a guaranty and the form that Grojean's [the taxpayer's] loan participation assumed was nothing but the label. It was a purely formal difference, and in federal taxation substance prevails over form.

248 F.3d at 573–74.

4. If a shareholder as guarantor is called upon to honor the guarantee and pays off the corporation's loan either with cash or with the shareholder's own note, is the shareholder then entitled to claim a pass-through of the corporation's losses? See the following revenue ruling.

[¶ 15,305]

REVENUE RULING 75–144
1975–1 C.B. 277.

The Internal Revenue Service has been asked to amplify Rev. Rul. 70–50, 1970–1 C.B. 178, which discusses the computation of a net operating loss deduction allowed to a shareholder * * * under [former] Section 1374(c)(2) * * *.

The facts presented in Rev. Rul. 70–50 are that an electing small business corporation incurred net operating losses for two consecutive years and that the shareholder's portion of the loss for the second year was greater than the adjusted basis of his stock in the corporation. In the third year, the corporation defaulted on a bank loan guaranteed by the shareholder under the guaranty. The shareholder paid the bank loan in satisfaction of his guaranty.

Rev. Rul. 70–50 holds that although the shareholder's guaranty of the corporation's indebtedness did not create an indebtedness of the corporation to the shareholder, when the shareholder later paid the corporation's creditor in satisfaction of his guaranty, the corporation became indebted to the shareholder under the doctrine of subrogation. This conclusion was based on the general rule, as observed by the Supreme Court of the United States in *Putnam v. Commissioner*, 352 U.S. 82 (1956), * * * that after the guarantor performs on his contract of guaranty the debtor's indebtedness to the creditor becomes an indebtedness owed to the guarantor.

Rev. Rul. 70–50 concludes that the amount paid by the shareholder as a result of the satisfaction of his obligation as guarantor of the debt of the electing small business corporation is treated as an indebtedness of the corporation to the shareholder for the purpose of computing the net operating loss allowable to him * * * in accordance with [former] Section 1374 * * *.

Rev. Rul. 70–50 was clarified by Rev. Rul. 71–288, 1971–2 C.B. 319, to provide that the indebtedness of the corporation to the shareholder arising in the third year upon payment by the shareholder under his guaranty did not relate back to the second year, and would not entitle the shareholder to deduct any portion of the corporation's losses in the second year in excess of the adjusted basis of his stock in that year.

The Service has been asked to state its position where the facts are the same as in Rev. Rul. 70–50, as clarified, except that instead of actually paying money to the bank in satisfaction of his guaranty, the shareholder, in the third year, executed his own promissory note for the full amount due and substituted it for the note of the corporation. The bank accepted the note in satisfaction of the guaranty and relieved the corporation of its liability on the old note. The shareholder made no payment on his own note until the fourth year.

The specific questions raised are (1) whether the execution of the shareholder's own note, and its acceptance by the bank, constitute a payment of the debt that would cause the indebtedness of the corporation to accrue to the shareholder under the doctrine of subrogation, and (2) whether the shareholder would have a basis in such indebtedness as of the end of the third year so that he would be entitled to deduct from his income his share of net operating losses of the corporation, if any, in that year, or in any subsequent year, under [former] Section 1374 * * *.

As the *Putnam* case explained, after actual performance by the guarantor on his contract of guaranty, the corporation's obligation to the bank generally becomes an obligation to the guarantor under the doctrine of subrogation. Whether the subrogation occurs is determined by State law. If subrogation occurs, a guarantor who has discharged his obligation by giving his own promissory note which the creditor has accepted in full satisfaction becomes a creditor of the principal even though the guarantor's note remains unpaid. In such a case the guarantor's basis in the corporation's indebtedness is its cost to him, which includes the face amount of the note he gave up.

Accordingly, the execution of a note by a shareholder, together with the acceptance of the note by a bank, under the circumstances described above, caused the indebtedness of the corporation to accrue to the shareholder, and created a basis in the indebtedness for purposes of computing his share of net operating losses of the corporation, if any, in the third year, or in any subsequent taxable year of the corporation, under [former] Section 1374 * * *.

Rev. Rul. 70–50 is amplified.

¶ 15,305

[¶ 15,310]

Note

On facts similar to those in Rev. Rul. 75–144, the Tax Court has refused to allow a basis increase to shareholders who substituted their note for that of the S corporation. Ellis v. Commissioner, T.C. Memo. 1989–280 (1989), aff'd without published opinion, 937 F.2d 602 (4th Cir.1991), and Underwood v. Commissioner, 63 T.C. 468 (1975), aff'd, 535 F.2d 309 (5th Cir.1976). Apparently the court's position is that a shareholder's basis in an S corporation's stock requires an actual economic outlay and that the issuance of a note does not constitute such an outlay. Is that position defensible?

[¶ 15,315]

d. Restoration of Basis

Generally, the ability of shareholders to claim S corporation losses against the basis of the debt obligations owed to them by the corporation is highly favorable. The rule permits greater flexibility in the design of the capital structure of an S corporation than would otherwise be possible.

At one time, there was a serious risk that, because of the reduction in the basis of debt caused by passed-through losses, the shareholder-creditor would face reportable income upon receiving principal repayments on the debt. Now Section 1367(b)(2)(B) minimizes the risk of such income. Under that provision, if a shareholder's basis in S corporation debt has been reduced by losses, any net increase in basis for any subsequent taxable year first increases the basis of the debt. See Reg. § 1.1367–2(c). Only after the debt basis is completely restored is the basis of the shareholder's stock increased. Furthermore, although in general the basis of debt is restored as of the end of the corporation's taxable year according to Reg. § 1.1367–2(d)(1), if the debt is disposed of or repaid in whole or in part during the year, the restoration is effective immediately before the transfer or repayment.

While Section 1367(b)(2)(B) protects against payments on a debt exceeding the basis remaining in that debt after a pass-through of losses, this provision correlatively increases the probability that returns on stock will be taxable for exceeding the basis in that stock. For example, assume that in year 1 losses allocated to an S corporation shareholder eliminated the basis of her stock and reduced the basis of her $10,000 debt to $6,000. In year 2 the corporation derived a profit, and the $4,000 of income allocated to the shareholder completely restored the basis of her debt. In year 3 the corporation broke even but made a dividend distribution to all shareholders out of the income from the prior year. Is the shareholder subject to a second tax because the distribution exceeds the zero basis of her stock?

4. OTHER LIMITS ON SHAREHOLDERS' REPORTABLE LOSSES

[¶ 15,320]

a. *Worthlessness*

If stock or debt become worthless during a taxable year, a shareholder is entitled to a loss equal to the remaining basis in the security under either Section 165(g) or Section 166(d). Those losses reduce the basis of the stock or debt to zero. What tax result should occur if the stock or debt of a shareholder in an S corporation becomes worthless during the taxable year, but the corporation incurs operating losses that are allocated to the shareholder as of the last day of the taxable year? Why would it matter to the shareholder whether she was entitled to a loss from operations or from worthlessness? Under Section 1367(b)(3), the shareholder is entitled to claim the operating loss before the worthlessness loss. If a shareholder does incur a loss from worthlessness with respect to stock in an S corporation, the loss may nevertheless be an ordinary loss under Section 1244. But cf. Peterson v. Commissioner, T.C. Memo. 1997–377 (1997), confining the guarantor-shareholder to a capital loss upon honoring a guarantee of the corporation's worthless debt.

[¶ 15,325]

b. *Tax Shelter Limitations*

Under Section 465, noncorporate taxpayers may not deduct losses with respect to an activity in excess of the amount for which they are "at risk." In general, this provision bars claiming deductions with respect to nonrecourse and similar borrowings. Section 465 does not apply to S corporations at the corporate level. However, this provision does apply to the shareholders of an S corporation with respect to losses allocated to them by the corporation. As a result, losses may be allocated to a shareholder, thereby reducing the basis in the shareholder's S corporation stock or debt, which the shareholder nevertheless may not deduct currently. Does this jeopardize a shareholder's future ability to currently deduct losses for which the taxpayer is at risk?

Losses or deductions disallowed under the at risk rules may be carried forward and deducted in the first year in which the taxpayer regains an amount at risk, provided this occurs either while the corporation remains an S corporation or by the last day of the post-termination transition period. § 1366(d)(2) and (3). Because the basis of S corporation stock is not adjusted for a corporate level borrowing, the at risk limitations do not commonly affect S corporation shareholders unless the stock itself was purchased with the proceeds of a nonrecourse borrowing.

In a similar manner, Section 469 disallows the current deduction of losses attributable to the conduct of a trade or business in which an individual taxpayer does not materially participate to the extent that the loss exceeds the aggregate income from all such passive activities. Section 469 also does not apply to S corporations at the corporate level but rather applies to S corporation shareholders with respect to items of income and expense allocated to the shareholder from the corporation.[6]

[¶ 15,330]

E.   DISTRIBUTIONS

One of the basic concepts of conduit entity taxation as employed in Subchapters K and S is that the owner of a partnership or S corporation should be permitted to make tax-free withdrawals from the business equal to the net amount on which the owner has already been subjected to tax. Section 1368 undertakes to implement that concept for S corporations. In so doing, it creates special treatment for those S corporations with accumulated earnings and profits dating from a period when the entity was a C corporation with earnings and profits on which the shareholders have not yet been taxed.

[¶ 15,335]

1.   EARNINGS AND PROFITS

Section 1368 applies to distributions by an S corporation in which there may be earnings and profits on which the shareholders have not yet been taxed and that date from an era of corporate operations in C status. In such a case, Section 1368 undertakes to provide special tax treatment appropriate to the corporation's current S status but moderated to cover the presence of the previously untaxed earnings and profits.

As a result of the 1982 revision of Subchapter S, S corporations generally do not generate or accumulate "earnings and profits." However, an S corporation may have earnings and profits that are traceable to a period when the S corporation itself formerly operated as a C corporation. Moreover, before 1983, even S corporations generated earnings and profits. Indeed, most pre–1983 S corporations accumulated a significant earnings and profits account.

Furthermore, it is even possible for a corporation formed after 1982 and that has always been an S corporation to have earnings and profits potentially taxable to distributee-shareholders if that corporation has acquired the business of a second corporation in a transaction, such as a reorganization, in which earnings and profits carry over to the acquirer. Accordingly, many S corporations today do or will in the future have

---

6. Under a statutory change made in 2004, the disposition of stock in an S corporation by a trust that has elected to be a QSST is treated as a disposition of the stock by the beneficiary of the QSST for purposes of applying Sections 465 and 469 to that beneficiary. § 1361(d)(1)(C).

accumulated earnings and profits that can and should be taxed when withdrawn from the corporation, notwithstanding an adequate basis in the shareholder's stock to cover the amounts withdrawn. Section 1368 covers this situation as well.

[¶ 15,340]

2.   CORPORATIONS LACKING EARNINGS AND PROFITS

The taxation of distributions from S corporations that do not have any earnings and profits is straightforward. Under Section 1368(b)(1), distributions from such corporations are not subject to tax so long as the cash distributed and the fair market value of the property distributed together do not exceed the basis for the shareholder's stock. Under Section 1367(a)(2)(A), the amount of such a nontaxable distribution reduces the basis of the stock. Once the basis of the shareholder's stock has been reduced to zero, further distributions become taxable. § 1368(b)(2). As in the case of C corporations, the income produced by such a distribution is treated as gain from the sale or exchange of the stock and, as such, normally will be entitled to capital gain treatment. Id.

[¶ 15,345]

3.   CORPORATIONS HAVING EARNINGS AND PROFITS

The taxation of distributions from S corporations that do have earnings and profits can also be straightforward in simple situations. Unfortunately, under Subchapter S, situations rarely remain simple.

The general concept of Section 1368(c) is that the shareholders of an S corporation should be entitled to withdraw from the corporation without tax an amount equal to the income of the corporation on which they have been subject to tax. Distributions in excess of that amount are treated as distributions of earnings and profits and are taxable to the shareholder in the same manner as are dividends from C corporations. Only after the entire earnings and profits account has been distributed as a dividend will the shareholders again be entitled to receive nontaxable distributions to the extent of the remaining basis in their S corporation stock. The implementation of this three-tier system, however, has turned out to be more complicated than it sounds.

[¶ 15,350]

a.   Accumulated Adjustments Account

The so-called accumulated adjustments account of Section 1368(e)(1) is a bookkeeping concept that measures how much an S corporation may distribute tax-free to shareholders, representing net income already taxed to them, before the corporation is treated as making a taxable distribution of earnings and profits. This corporate level account is not specifically allocable to any individual shareholder. Reg. § 1.1368–2(a)(1). In that sense, it is reminiscent of a C corporation's earnings and profits account. In general, its balance increases as a result of the same items of income that increase a shareholder's basis and declines concomitantly with the same items of expense or tax-free distributions that reduce a shareholder's basis. Reg. § 1.1368–2(a)(2) and (a)(3). The account includes adjustments only from S corporation years after 1982. However, unlike the basis adjustments in Section 1367, the accumulated adjustments account does not include tax-exempt income or expenses related to that income. What is the purpose and effect of the exclusion for tax-exempt income? Note also that, unlike basis, the accumulated adjustments account might have a negative balance. How might that occur?

Like current earnings and profits, the accumulated adjustments account is computed at the end of the year without regard to distributions during the year. Reg. §§ 1.1368–1(e)(2)(ii), –2(a)(5), and –3, Ex. 8; Letter Ruling 8842024. Under Section 1368(c) (last sentence), if the total of the distributions during the year exceeds the amount in the account, the account is allocated over all distributions in proportion to their relative amounts. The particulars of this allocation rule appear in Reg. § 1.1368–2(b). Distributions treated as redemptions affect the accumulated adjustment account under Section 1368(e)(1)(B) and the regime detailed in Reg. § 1.1368–2(d).

[¶ 15,355]

b. Three–Tier Distribution Scheme

Section 1368 creates a three-tier scheme for determining whether distributions by a corporation having accumulated earnings and profits are of earnings already taxed to the shareholder. Its approach in general is to treat distributions as coming first from earnings previously taxed to the shareholders (i.e., up to the balance in the accumulated adjustments account), with the excess relegated to tiers two and three. Stated differently, under Section 1368(c), distributions from S corporations having accumulated earnings and profits are to be taxed in exactly the same manner as distributions by S corporations lacking such earnings and profits, to the extent the distribution does not exceed the accumulated adjustments account. Such distributions reduce the balance in the accumulated adjustments account. They are tax-free to shareholders so long as they do not exceed the basis in a recipient's stock; if they do, the excess is taxable as a capital gain (just as with distributions by S corporations that have no accumulated earnings and profits). Distributions in excess of this first-tier distribution are second-tier distributions out of earnings and profits and thus are taxable as dividends. Once the earnings and profits account is exhausted, further distributions become third-tier distributions. Since the corporation now lacks earnings and profits, third-tier distributions are taxed in precisely the same way as are all distributions from S corporations lacking earnings and profits (i.e., first, as a nontaxable return of capital up to the amount of the shareholder's remaining basis in the S corporation stock and, second, any excess as a capital gain from the sale or exchange of the stock).

[¶ 15,360]

c. Elective Second-Tier Distributions

All distributions during a taxable year may, by corporate election coupled with the unanimous concurrence of the shareholders receiving such distributions, be treated as though there were no accumulated adjustments account warranting first-tier treatment. The effect is to subject the distributions to second-tier treatment up to the amount of accumulated earnings and profits, and then first-tier treatment on exhaustion of the second tier up to the balance in the accumulated adjustments account, and, finally, to third-tier treatment under Section 1368(b). § 1368(e)(3); Reg. §§ 1.1368–1(f)(2)(i) and –3, Ex. 7. Why might the shareholders so consent? See ¶¶ 15,435–15,450 on the problems that might be encountered for S corporations having accumulated earnings and profits.

The regulations permit the elimination of earnings and profits through a deemed dividend distribution. Reg. § 1.1368–1(f)(3). If all shareholders so elect, the corporation will be treated as if it distributed a dividend in cash on the last day of the year and received the same amount back from the shareholders as reinvestments in the corporation's stock. For no very obvious reason, this deemed distribution is limited to distributions of Subchapter C earnings and profits.

[¶ 15,365]

d. Pre–1983 S Corporations

Before 1983, Subchapter S used a very different concept in seeking to arrive at a result similar to Section 1368. Under prior law, the accumulated Subchapter S income that could be distributed tax-free did not create a corporate level account but rather created an individual account for each shareholder. These so-called previously taxed income accounts survived the 1982 revision of Subchapter S. Bearing in mind that an S corporation may have some shareholders who have previously taxed income accounts and some shareholders who do not have such accounts, where in the three-tier scheme of Section 1368 should distributions from these accounts fit? Reg. § 1.1368–1(d)(2) indicates that distributions of previously taxed income fall between first-tier and second-tier distributions.

¶ 15,355

[¶ 15,370]

Problems

1. An S corporation has two equal shareholders, High and Low. At the beginning of the taxable year, High had a basis for his stock of $1,000 and Low had a basis for her stock of $125. The corporation has no earnings and profits. What are the consequences if the corporation makes a midyear distribution of $175 to each shareholder and the corporate operations break even for the year? See § 1368(b); Reg. §§ 1.1368–1(c) and –3, Ex. 2.

2. How would the results change if during the year the corporation earned income of $200? See Reg. § 1.1368–1(e)(2).

3. Returning to the facts of Problem 1, assume now that the S corporation has an earnings and profits account of $200 and an accumulated adjustments account of $350. What now would be the consequences of distributing $175 to each shareholder? See Reg. § 1.1368–2(a)(3)(iii), indicating that a reduction occurs in the accumulated adjustments account balance for all first-tier distributions, even where the distribution exceeds the basis in the recipient's stock and is therefore taxable to her.

4. An S corporation has earnings and profits of $5,000. Since 1982 the corporation has made no distributions. It has earned net taxable income of $3,000 and net tax-exempt interest income of $12,000. If the corporation now distributes $9,000 to its sole shareholder, whose basis for his stock is $20,000, how will the distribution be taxed? What will be the shareholder's basis for his stock following the distribution?

5. An S corporation has an accumulated adjustments account of $120,000 and earnings and profits of $200,000. Two individuals each own 500 of the 1,000 shares outstanding. During the year, the corporation raises additional capital by selling 500 shares of stock to a third individual. What is the amount that may be distributed tax-free to each of the shareholders immediately before the stock issuance? Immediately after? Is that sensible?

e. *Redemptions*

[¶ 15,375]

REVENUE RULING 95–14

1995–1 C.B. 169.

ISSUE

If an S corporation shareholder receives proceeds in a redemption that is characterized as a distribution under § 301 * * *, is the redemption treated as a distribution for purposes of § 1368 that reduces the corporation's accumulated adjustments account?

¶ 15,375

FACTS

A, and *A*'s child *B,* together own all of the stock of *X,* a corporation that files returns for a calendar year. *X* has a valid S election in effect. *X* redeems for cash a portion of *A*'s stock at fair market value. There are no facts present that cause the redemption to be treated as a sale or exchange under § 302(a) or § 303(a). *X* makes no other distributions during the taxable year.

At the end of the year, *A* has a basis in *X* stock in excess of the amount of the distribution made by *X* during the year. In addition, *X* has an accumulated adjustments account (AAA) in excess of that distribution. *X* also has subchapter C earnings and profits.

LAW AND ANALYSIS

Section 1371(a)(1) provides that except as otherwise provided in the Code, and except to the extent inconsistent with subchapter S, subchapter C applies to an S corporation and its shareholders.

Under the rules of subchapter C, * * * [b]ecause the redemption of *A*'s stock is not treated as a sale or exchange under § 302(a) or § 303(a), the redemption is treated, under § 302(d), as a distribution of property to which § 301 applies.

* * *

Section 301(c) provides that, in the case of a distribution to which § 301(a) applies: (1) the portion of the distribution that is a dividend (as defined in § 316) is included in gross income; and (2) the portion of the distribution that is not a dividend is applied against and reduces the adjusted basis of the stock. The portion of the distribution that is not a dividend, to the extent that it exceeds the adjusted basis of the stock, is treated as gain from the sale or exchange of property.

* * *

Section 1368(b) provides that, in the case of a distribution * * * by an S corporation that has no accumulated earnings and profits, the distribution is not included in gross income to the extent that it does not exceed the adjusted basis of the stock. If the amount of the distribution exceeds the adjusted basis of the stock, the excess is treated as gain from the sale or exchange of property.

Section 1368(c) provides that, in the case of a distribution * * * by an S corporation that has accumulated earnings and profits: (1) that portion of the distribution that does not exceed AAA is treated in the manner provided by § 1368(b); (2) that portion of the distribution that remains after the application of § 1368(c)(1) is treated as a dividend to the extent it does not exceed the accumulated earnings and profits of the S corporation; and (3) any portion of the distribution remaining after the application of § 1368(c)(2) is treated in the manner provided by § 1368(b).

* * *

An S corporation's AAA tracks the amount of undistributed income that has been taxed to the shareholders, similar to the manner in which earnings and profits generally track a C corporation's undistributed income (whether or not taxable). AAA is the mechanism that allows previously taxed but undistributed income to be distributed tax-free to S corporation shareholders. It is an account of the S corporation and is not apportioned among shareholders. Section 1.1368–2(a).

Section 1368(c)(1)(B) provides a special rule to determine the adjustment to AAA in the case of a redemption that is treated as an exchange. In the case of any redemption that is treated as an exchange under § 302(a) or § 303(a), the adjustment to AAA is an amount that bears the same ratio to the balance in the account as the number of shares redeemed bears to the number of shares of stock in the corporation immediately before the redemption. Section 1368(e) does not provide a specific rule for adjusting AAA in the case of a redemption treated as a § 301 distribution.

Because *X* has subchapter C earnings and profits, [and] * * * *A* has an adjusted basis in *X* stock in excess of the amount of the distribution * * * and *X* has AAA in excess of the amount of that distribution * * *, under § 1368(c)(1), the distribution is not included in *A*'s income.

* * * Section 1.1368–2(a)(3)(iii) provides that AAA is decreased (but not below zero) by any portion of a distribution to which § 1368(b) or § 1368(c)(1) applies. Because, under these facts, § 1368(b) and § 1368(c)(1) apply to the entire distribution, *X*'s AAA is reduced by the full amount of *X*'s distribution in redemption of *A*'s stock. The provision of § 1368(e)(1) that refers to redemptions does not apply on these facts because this is not a redemption that is treated as an exchange under § 302(a) or § 303(a).

HOLDING

When an S corporation shareholder receives proceeds in a redemption that is characterized as a distribution under § 301, the entire redemption is treated as a distribution for purposes of § 1368 that reduces the corporation's AAA.

* * *

[¶ 15,380]

Problems

All of the stock of an S corporation is divided equally between Mother and Son, each of whom has a basis of $500 for the stock. The corporation has earnings and profits of $200 and an accumulated adjustments account of $700. Assume that one-half of Mother's stock is redeemed by the corporation for $1,000.

1. Assuming for purposes of comparison that the redemption qualifies as a sale or exchange under Section 302, what would be the tax consequences to Mother and to the corporation? See § 1368(e)(1)(B); Reg. §§ 1.1368–2(d)(1) and –3, Ex.9.

2. Assuming now that the redemption fails the tests of Section 302 and thus would be taxable under Section 301 if the corporation were not an S corporation, what will be the tax consequences of the redemption to Mother and to the corporation?

F. DISPOSITIONS OF STOCK

[¶ 15,385]

1. GENERAL CONSEQUENCES

Subchapter S addresses only a select few of the principal tax consequences affecting the transferor and transferee of stock in an S corporation. Such basics as the computation of gain or loss to the transferor and of basis to the transferee are governed by basic tax principles. Moreover, the character of the gain is determined by reference to the stock being sold and not to the character of the assets of the S corporation. Normally, therefore, the gain will be taxed as capital gain.[7] In these respects, S corporations are subject to the same, simpler, entity-based rules that apply to C corporations rather than to the more complex, aggregate-based rules that apply to partnerships.

Subchapter S does, however, contain provisions governing the allocation of income and expense among shareholders for a year in which a change in ownership occurs. See § 1377(a). In other words, a type of conduit approach continues to apply to the allocation of income and expense of the S corporation during a year in which shareholders'

---

7. As discussed in more detail at ¶ 18,030, the Taxpayer Relief Act of 1997 added substantial complexity to the tax treatment of capital gains and losses by creating in Section 1(h) several different categories of long-term capital gain, each having its own preferential rate, including long-term capital gain from the sale of "collectibles," long-term capital gain attributable to prior depreciation deductions taken with respect to depreciable real estate (so-called "unrecaptured Section 1250 gain"), and all other long-term capital gain (the latter category qualifying for the most favorable preferential rate). The statute specifically authorizes the Treasury to issue appropriate regulations to apply the provisions of Section 1(h) to sales and exchanges by flow-through entities (including S corporations) and of interests in such entities. § 1(h)(9). In 2000, the Treasury and the IRS issued regulations relating to gain from the sale of stock in an S corporation and other flow-through entities, which generally take a look-through approach for determining the portion of a taxpayer's long-term capital gain from the sale of stock in an S corporation that will be treated as "collectibles gain" not qualifying for the most favorable preferential capital gains rates. See Reg. § 1.1(h)–1. These regulations are discussed in more detail in the context of the sale of partnership interests at ¶ 21,092.

¶ 15,380

interests change. To this extent the approach is closer to that of partnerships.

Under the rules on how the income and expenses of an S corporation are to be reported when the proportionate interest of a shareholder in an S corporation changes for any reason during the taxable year, the corporation must adjust the income allocation among the shareholders under one of two specified methods. The general rule is a pro rata approach that disregards when the tax item actually arose; the other more closely attributes tax reporting responsibility to shareholders in accordance with their shareholdings when the tax items arose.

Under the general rule (i.e., the pro rata approach), the S corporation first prorates each item of income and expense for the year ratably to each day in the taxable year, without regard to when the item in fact arose. In turn, each daily allocation is attributed to and among the shareholders in proportion to the stock that each owned on each day. § 1377(a)(1); Reg. § 1.1377–1(a). Alternatively, in the event that a shareholder completely terminates her interest in the corporation during the taxable year, an interim closing method of reporting may be elected under which the tax items will be allocated throughout the year pursuant to normal tax accounting rules, as if the corporation had closed its books on the day the interest terminated. § 1377(a)(2); Reg. § 1.1377–1(b). For the interim closing method rather than the pro rata method to apply, all the shareholders who would be affected must consent to the election.

If the selling shareholder of stock in an S corporation has a zero basis in her stock and losses from the S corporation that were suspended under Section 1366, her gain from the sale of the S corporation stock does not increase her basis in the stock for purposes of absorbing the suspended losses. Thus, in such a case, those suspended losses will not be deductible by the selling shareholder or anyone else and are permanently lost (except to the extent of the selling shareholder's share of S corporation net income for the year of sale). Such suspended losses are personal to the selling shareholder and the buyer of the stock does not acquire any portion of the seller's disallowed losses. Reg. § 1.1366–2(a)(5).[8] For example, suppose that the selling shareholder has a zero

---

8. However, under a change to the statute made in 2004, in the case of a transfer of S corporation stock between spouses or former spouses incident to divorce to which nonrecognition treatment under Section 1041 applies, Section 1366(d)(2)(B) treats the suspended losses attributable to the transferred stock as incurred by the corporation in the next taxable year with respect to the transferee. Accordingly, the transferee will be able to deduct those losses as the transferee's carryover basis in the S corporation stock under Section 1041(b) is in-

creased by reason of the items listed in Section 1367(a)(1). It is unclear, however, how this provision will apply in a case where the transferor transfers only some shares of the S corporation stock to the transferee and retains the remaining shares. Will a proportionate amount of the transferor's suspended S corporation losses follow the transferred portion of the stock in the hands of the transferee or will all of the suspended losses remain with the transferor by reason of his or her retention of part of the S corporation stock?

¶ 15,385

basis for her S corporation stock (which she has held for five years), has $50,000 of suspended losses from years before the sale and $10,000 of loss allocable to her for the year of sale, and sells her stock for $40,000. She has taxable long-term capital of $40,000 from the sale of the stock and neither she nor anyone else will ever be able to deduct the $60,000 of losses suspended because she had insufficient basis in her stock to absorb them.

[¶ 15,390]

Problems

1. Connie and Dan are equal shareholders in an S corporation. Each has an adjusted basis of $15,000 in the stock. In each month during the year, which is the calendar year, the corporation has incurred an operating loss of $1,000.

a. If, on December 1, Connie sells all of her stock to Dan for $25,000, what amount of loss will be allocated to each of them? How much of that loss may Connie and Dan each deduct?

b. How would your answers change if each had an adjusted basis of zero in the stock?

c. How would your answers change if the entire loss occurred during the month of December?

2. Assume that a calendar year S corporation is operated at the break-even point for each month in the year, except that in May the corporation sold a Section 1231 asset at a loss of $200,000. Greg owned 10 percent of the stock in the corporation and had a basis for his stock of $40,000. On July 1, Greg sold all of his stock to Herma for $60,000.

a. What difference does it make to Greg whether the S corporation uses the pro rata or interim closing method of allocating the corporate loss? In answering that question, do not overlook the effect of losses on Greg's basis for his stock and thus on his gain from the sale.

b. What difference does it make to Herma which method is selected? If the contract for the sale of the stock is silent on the question, would Herma be willing to consent to the use of the interim closing method? Would there be any objection to Greg's paying Herma for her consent? What amount should Herma demand? If the contract of sale had required Herma to consent to the election of the interim closing method, what effect would that provision have had on the purchase price for the stock?

c. What difference does the method of allocation make to the nonselling shareholders? Does that explain why their consent to the election of the interim closing method is unnecessary?

¶ 15,385

3.   Edley is the sole shareholder of a calendar year S corporation, the only asset of which is an airplane that is leased to others and has a tax basis of $180,000. On April 1, he sold one-half of his stock in the corporation to Fran for $250,000. On July 1, the corporation sold the airplane for $500,000. What amount of the resulting gain will be allocable to Fran? What will be the basis of Fran's stock at year's end?

4.   A wholly owned S corporation has an accumulated adjustments account of $10,000 and earnings and profits of $15,000. Seller has a basis for her stock of $12,000.

a.   If Seller on December 30 sells her stock to Buyer for $30,000, how will she report the proceeds? How will Buyer report a corporate distribution to him of $10,000 on December 31?

b.   Anticipating a sale of the stock, suppose that Seller causes the corporation to distribute $10,000 to her on December 30, and then sells all of the stock to Buyer the next day for $20,000. Ignoring the effect of income during the year, now what are the consequences of the distributions and of the sale? Will Seller be entitled to treat the entire $10,000 distribution as coming out of the accumulated adjustments account? See Reg. § 1.1368–1(g); see also Rev. Rul. 95–14, at ¶ 15,375.

[¶ 15,395]

2.   DISPOSITIONS AT DEATH

When a shareholder dies and bequeaths her stock in an S corporation to another, the legatee may fail to receive a full stepped-up basis for the stock under Section 1014. This is because any income in the corporation that was earned but not yet includible in the income of the decedent (such as an installment obligation resulting from the S corporation's sale of property on the installment method under Section 453), becomes an item of "income in respect of a decedent" under Section 691. Accordingly, the stepped-up basis allowed to the stock is correlatively limited. § 1367(b)(4).

[¶ 15,400]

G.   COMPLICATIONS TO CORPORATION FROM MIDSTREAM ELECTIONS

When a C corporation elects Subchapter S status, thereby eliminating double taxation of future corporate income, the effect is tantamount to a liquidation of the C corporation. In the absence of some corrective measure, the assets of the C corporation would in effect be removed tax-free from "corporate solution" in the sense that the income from the assets would no longer be subject to the corporate income tax. Following the repeal of the *General Utilities* doctrine in 1986, the removal of assets

¶ 15,400

from corporate solution in any other manner precipitates significant income tax consequences at both the corporate and shareholder levels. However, the making of a Subchapter S election in general does not occasion tax at either level—a very generous result.

In lieu of taxing a midstream S election as a constructive liquidation, the Code does, however, cause certain of the tax attributes of the C corporation to carry over and lurk within the nascent S corporation. This may in fact prove even more costly than if a liquidation-reincorporation without carryover of attributes had taken place. The taxation of distributions from S corporations is one example, discussed above at ¶¶ 15,345 et seq. The C corporation attribute of earnings and profits is preserved within the S corporation. The following materials examine three additional sets of rules that are made necessary by the absence of tax consequences on the making of a midstream Subchapter S election. These materials also examine another complication that may arise on the conversion of a C corporation with net operating loss carryforwards or suspended losses into an S corporation.

[¶ 15,405]

1. LIFO INVENTORY

There is one significant exception to the exemption of S corporations from tax on the making of the Subchapter S election: the mandatory recapture of LIFO inventory benefits at the time of election. (That is, a corporation using the LIFO inventory method benefits during a period of rising inventory prices by calculating its cost of goods sold as though the newer more expensive inventory—i.e., the "Last–In"—were the first sold—i.e., "First–Out," contrasted to the older and cheaper inventory deemed sold under the FIFO method of "First–In–First–Out.") In general, an amount equal to the excess of the cost of the inventory computed under the FIFO method over the cost of the inventory computed under the LIFO method becomes includible in the income of the C corporation for its last taxable year. § 1363(d).[9]

For many kinds of corporations, this LIFO recapture tax imposes a significant toll charge on the making of a Subchapter S election. The sting is somewhat diminished by permitting the resulting tax to be paid in four equal annual installments, without interest. Reg. § 1.1363–2 describes the circumstances causing the recapture of LIFO benefits under Section 1363(d), when a C corporation either elects to become an S corporation or transfers LIFO inventory to the latter in a tax-free reorganization transaction.

---

9. Under a provision added to the statute in 2005, (1) the requirement in Section 1367(a)(2)(D) that the S corporation's stock basis be reduced by nondeductible, noncapital expenses of the corporation and (2) the prohibition in Section 1371(c)(1) against making adjustments to an S corporation's earnings and profits do not apply to any corporate tax imposed by Section 1363(d). See § 1363(d)(5).

[¶ 15,410]

2. BUILT–IN GAINS

In general, although the making of a Subchapter S election is not treated as a constructive distribution of corporate property that causes corporate gain, Section 1374 does preserve a possible corporate level tax on the net accrued appreciation inherent in properties owned by the C corporation at the date of a Subchapter S election. The Section 1374 tax on built-in gains, if applicable, is imposed on the S corporation itself when it ultimately disposes of those appreciated assets or their substitutes. This tax thus constitutes a major exception to the exemption of S corporations from the corporate income tax. Moreover, the application of the Section 1374 tax imposes an indirect assessment on the shareholders of the S corporation due to the usual consequence of their being subject to tax whenever their corporation derives a recognized gain. Thus, Section 1374 preserves not only the corporate tax but also the double taxation of C corporations. However, the amount of the Section 1374 tax paid by an S corporation is deducted as a loss from the amount of gain that is taxable to the shareholders. § 1366(f)(2); Reg. § 1.1366–4(b).

The total amount of gain subject to tax under Section 1374 is the excess of the aggregate fair market value of the corporate properties as of the beginning of the first taxable year for which the S election is in effect over the aggregate adjusted bases for those properties. § 1374(d)(1); Reg. § 1.1374–3. Thus, the total built-in gain is reduced by the total built-in loss. Moreover, if the C corporation had a net operating loss carryforward at the time of making a Subchapter S election, the amount of the loss carryforward may be offset against the gain subject to tax. § 1374(b)(2).

Corporations that have always been S corporations generally are not subject to the Section 1374 tax. § 1374(c)(1). However, if such a corporation acquires any assets from a C corporation (or from a successor S corporation) in a carryover basis transaction, that property becomes subject to the potential tax. In that event, the amount of the built-in gain is determined on the date the properties are acquired. § 1374(d)(8); Reg. § 1.1374–8.

The Section 1374 tax applies only to gain recognized during the 10–year (120–month) period starting on the first day that the S corporation election is in effect. § 1374(d)(7); Reg. § 1.1374–1(d). As a result, if the S corporation delays for at least 10 years the disposition of an asset that it held on the date that its S election first went into effect, the gain in that asset escapes the Section 1374 tax. The tax will also be avoided if the corporation retains the asset and merely consumes it in the conduct of its business. While these rules may appear to put significant limitations on the scope of Section 1374, those limitations may be largely illusory because of the manner in which the gain subject to the tax is defined.

Under Section 1374(d)(3), the gain subject to the Section 1374 tax is any gain recognized by the S corporation on the disposition of any asset, unless the S corporation is able to establish either that it did not own the asset as of the start of its first taxable year for which it was an S corporation or that the asset was sold for an amount that exceeded its fair market value on the date that the S election first went into effect, § 1374(d)(3); see also Reg. §§ 1.1374–2 and–4. How is the latter demonstration to be made? In order to minimize exposure to the tax, will corporations be required to obtain an independent appraisal of each of its assets on making a Subchapter S election? Such an appraisal might be persuasive evidence of the value of the assets, but it would not be binding on the IRS. And, which would be more expensive to the S corporation: permitting liability for the Section 1374 tax to be accelerated or paying for an adequate appraisal?

The gain taxed under Section 1374 is reduced by any built-in loss recognized during the year if the taxpayer can establish that the loss does not exceed the excess of the adjusted basis for the property over its fair market value as of the first day of the first taxable year for which the corporation was an S corporation. § 1374(d)(2)(A)(i) and (d)(4). However, if the net built-in gain exceeds the taxable income of the corporation computed as if it were a C corporation (but ignoring the intercorporate dividends-received deduction), only the lesser amount is taxed. § 1374(d)(2)(A)(ii). The excess is carried over and taxed in the following year. § 1374(d)(2)(B).

[¶ 15,415]

Problems

1. Compare the outcomes under Sections 1368 and 1374 if built-in gains are recognized before rather than after making the Subchapter S election. Assume, for example, that a C corporation holds an asset with an adjusted basis of $100 but a fair market value of $1,000. Assume further that the corporation plans to make a Subchapter S election and to continue its policy of not making distributions to its shareholders. Would you advise the corporation to sell the asset immediately before, or immediately after, the making of the Subchapter S election? If that result does not seem sensible, how else might Section 1374 have been drafted to produce a more sensible result?

2. If the Section 1374 tax is imposed, it is imposed at "the highest rate of tax specified in section 11(b)." § 1374(b)(1). Assume the corporation would have had taxable income as a C corporation of $110,000. What is that rate?

3. Assume that at the time of making a Subchapter S election in year 1, a corporation owns two assets. Asset A has a fair market value of $500 and an adjusted basis of $100. Asset B has a fair market value of $100 and an adjusted basis of $300. In year 3, when the corporation

incurs an operating loss of $350, the corporation sells asset A for $600. What is the amount subject to the Section 1374 tax? What would be the tax consequences to the sole shareholder of the S corporation for year 3?

4.   Alpha, Inc., was incorporated on February 1 of year 1, and two weeks later the appreciated assets of a partnership were contributed to Alpha in exchange for stock in a Section 351 transaction. On March 1 of that same year, the corporation filed a Subchapter S election that would be effective on the first day of the following calendar year (i.e., January 1 of year 2). Will the full gain in the Alpha assets on January 1 of year 2 be subject to the Section 1374 tax?

5.   Assume that three years after electing S corporation status, the corporation sells an asset that it owned on the date of the election in exchange for a note. The note calls for a single payment at maturity in 10 years and the corporation reported the sale on the installment method under Section 453. How should Section 1374 apply to such a sale? See Reg. § 1.1374–4(h). Incidentally, does the retention of an asset for 10 years justify excusing the Section 1374 tax as a matter of substantive tax policy? As a matter of administrative convenience?

[¶ 15,420]

LETTER RULING 8849015

This is in reply to a letter of May 20, 1988, written on behalf of Distributing and other interested parties, requesting rulings under subchapter S * * *.

The information submitted discloses that Distributing, an S corporation since July 1, 1984, currently is owned by two shareholders. A, an individual, owns 37.84 percent of the stock of Distributing with the balance being owned by Trust M.

Distributing is comprised of at least two separate and distinct operating businesses, Division I and Division II.

The two shareholders of Distributing presently have different reasons and objectives for holding stock in Distributing. Since they are unable to reconcile these differences they propose to split-off Division I from Division II in a transaction intended to meet the requirements of sections 368(a)(1)(D) and 355 * * *.

With respect to the proposed transaction the following steps will be taken:

1.   Either the attorney for Distributing or the Chief Financial Officer of Distributing, neither of whom have an ownership interest in Distributing, and neither of whom is related to any of the affected taxpayers, will prepare and submit documents to create Controlled in advance of the transaction which is the subject of this ruling. It is

contemplated that the appropriate Secretary of State will process the application in the normal course of such proceedings and approve the Articles of Incorporation for Controlled prior to the date contemplated for the transaction.

2.   No property will be contributed and no shares of Controlled stock will be issued from the date of incorporation prior to the day on which the contemplated transaction is to occur. On that day, Controlled will issue 5,000 shares of its stock to Distributing in exchange for all the assets of Division I (subject to its liabilities); Distributing, will, in turn, distribute all 5,000 shares of Controlled stock to Distributing's shareholder, A, in exchange for his 1,824 shares of stock of Distributing.

3.   Immediately after the distribution, both corporations will continue to operate in the same manner as they operated prior to the distribution.

4.   Controlled will elect to be treated as an S corporation effective as of the beginning of its first tax year.

5.   Distributing will maintain its status as an S corporation.

* * *

Section 1374 * * *, as amended by the Tax Reform Act of 1986 * * * (the "Act"), provides, generally, that S corporations will be subject to a corporate level tax on "built-in gains" following the conversion to S corporation status. The new provisions are generally applicable to corporations that were formerly C corporations and filed an S corporation election after December 31, 1986. Section 1374, as amended by the Act, generally does not apply to a corporation that has always been an S corporation.

Announcement 86–128, 1986–51 I.R.B. 22, states that the Service is concerned about the possible use of certain reorganization provisions in the Code to circumvent the application of the "built-in gains" tax. The Announcement further states that regulations when issued will provide that transferred basis property acquired by an S corporation from a C corporation such as in a tax-free merger generally will be treated as subject to the "built-in gains" tax notwithstanding the fact that the transferee corporation either was always an S corporation or did not hold those assets as of its first day as an S corporation. Similarly, when an S corporation subject to the "built-in gains" tax transfers property in a reorganization transaction to another S corporation, the "built-in gains" tax will apply to such transferred assets in the hands of the transferee S corporation.

* * *

¶ 15,420

Because Distributing, the predecessor of Controlled, has had its election in effect since July 1, 1984, and Controlled will elect S status for its first tax year, Controlled will not be subject to section 1374(a) * * *.

Controlled, as a result of the split-off from Distributing will only be receiving assets with a transferred basis from a corporation that is not subject to the "built-in gains" tax under Section 1374 * * *. Therefore, Announcement 86–128 does not apply to this transaction and Controlled will not be subject to the provisions of new section 1374 with respect to such transferred assets.

Provided that the proposed transaction meets the requirements of sections 368(a)(1)(D) and 355 * * * we conclude as follows:

* * *

2. An S election made by Controlled, within two months and 15 days after the earliest of the day it first has shareholders, assets, or begins doing business will be effective as of the first day of Controlled's first tax year and will not require the consent of Distributi[ng]. However, the validity of such election and the sufficiency of the shareholder consents will be determined by the Director of the Internal Revenue Service Center with whom the election is filed.

3. Controlled will not be subject to section 1374. In addition, Controlled will not be subject to section 1374 of the 1986 Code with respect to the assets transferred to Controlled by Distributing.

4. The transfer of appreciated Controlled stock by Distributing to A in exchange for his Distributing stock under section 355 * * * will not subject Distributing to the provisions of section 1363(d) by virtue of section 1363(e).

* * *

[¶ 15,425]

Notes

1. When it has not been feasible for a corporation to avoid the corporate income tax by electing under Subchapter S, many corporations have sought partial victory by separately incorporating a part of the business, distributing the stock in that corporation to all or a portion of its shareholders free of tax under Section 355, and causing the new corporation to elect under Subchapter S. If, unlike the facts in Letter Ruling 8849015, the parent is a C corporation, the subsidiary it creates can elect S status from the moment that it is created only by virtue of a ruling that disregards the transitory ownership of the subsidiary by the other corporation. As this ruling suggests and illustrates, the IRS has been willing to rule favorably to taxpayers on such an issue. Understandably, however, neither the IRS nor Congress will permit the use of this

technique also to avoid the impact of the repeal of the *General Utilities* doctrine. Rather, Section 1374(d)(8) applies the built-in gains tax to assets held by an S corporation with a basis traceable, in whole or in part, to a C corporation (i.e., resulting either from the corporation having converted to S from C status or having acquired assets with a carryover basis incident to a tax-free reorganization). The regulations implement this concept. See Reg. §§ 1.1374–1(e) and 1.1374–8.

2. A separate determination of the Section 1374 built-in gains tax is made for the assets that an S corporation acquires in each Section 1374(d)(8) transaction involving a transfer from a C corporation and for the assets the S corporation held when it became an S corporation. This means that an S corporation's Section 1374 attributes when it became an S corporation may only be used to reduce the Section 1374 built-in gains tax on dispositions of assets that it held at that time and may not be used to reduce the built-in gains tax on assets that it acquired in any Section 1374(d)(8) transaction. This also means that the Section 1374 attributes that an S corporation acquires in a particular Section 1374(d)(8) transaction involving a transfer from a C corporation may only be used by it to reduce the built-in gains tax imposed on dispositions of assets that it acquired in that same transaction and not in any other Section 1374(d)(8) transaction. Reg. § 1.1374–8(c).

3. When the distributing corporation is an S corporation, as in the above ruling, the IRS on a number of occasions has concluded that S corporations should be allowed to engage in both divisive and acquisitive reorganizations, utilizing the corporate tax provisions pertinent thereto. This was so even before: (i) the statutory change permitting affiliate status by an S, or (ii) the enactment of Section 1361(b)(3) in which Congress approved a parent S corporation, and thereby implicitly gave its blessing to a parent S corporation utilizing Section 332 for constructive liquidation of its qualified Subchapter S subsidiary.

4. Suppose that instead of a corporate division, an S corporation makes a "qualified stock purchase" of at least 80 percent of the stock of a target corporation within 12 months. The acquiring corporation may by election under Section 338(g) obtain a basis in the target corporation's assets geared to the amount it paid for the target's stock. The election makes it unnecessary to purchase the target's assets directly in order to effect a change in their basis, but it does impose a taxable outcome on the target as though that corporation had in fact sold its assets to the acquirer. Consequently, whether a Section 338 election is economically sound depends upon whether the tax burden of current income recognition by the target corporation is outweighed by the present value of the tax benefits from increased bases that may in the future pass through to the shareholders of the acquiring S corporation if the latter remains an S corporation (i.e., higher depreciation deductions, and smaller gains and larger losses on future dispositions of assets).

¶ 15,425

If the acquiring S corporation chooses not to make the election, gain on the target's appreciated assets becomes subject to the Section 1374 tax in the event that the gain accrued in the hands of a C corporation (i.e., in the hands either of the target company itself if it was a C corporation or in the hands of a predecessor C corporation if the target was itself an S corporation). See § 1374(d)(8).

[¶ 15,435]

3. PASSIVE INVESTMENT INCOME

The tax avoidance potential of a midstream Subchapter S election can be greatly magnified if the C corporation making the election is concurrently disposing of all of its active business assets. Absent the availability of Subchapter S, such a corporation, which would have been subject to a full corporate level tax, would normally liquidate, thereby subjecting the shareholders to a full tax on the appreciation in the value of their stock. While the corporation need not liquidate, if it remains in existence it could be somewhat needlessly subjecting its shareholders to double taxation on the income derived from investing the proceeds of sale and would be risking personal holding company classification or the imposition of the accumulated earnings tax. If such a corporation could instead elect Subchapter S, it could avoid: (1) the corporate level tax on the investment of the proceeds of sale without subjecting its shareholders to a tax on liquidation, and (2) all difficulties with the personal holding company and accumulated earnings tax provisions. Not surprisingly, Congress has sought to prevent a C corporation from gaining these two benefits by a midstream S election—a congressional deterrent which does not apply to a corporation that has always operated in S status and has always been exempt from such operating and penalty taxes.

[¶ 15,440]

a. Stage One: Double Taxation

Congress has adopted a two-tiered approach to discouraging this use of S corporations. The first stage of the attack is the imposition of a tax if too great a proportion of the corporation's gross receipts consists of passive investment income. § 1375. This tax, however, is imposed only on an S corporation that has earnings and profits accumulated from a period of time in which it, or a predecessor, was a C corporation.

As in the case of the Section 1374 tax, the Section 1375 tax is imposed on the S corporation. The shareholders are also subject to tax on the investment income subject to the Section 1375 tax, but the amount of the Section 1375 tax reduces the amount of investment income taxed to the shareholders. § 1366(f)(3).

The "excess net passive income" that is subject to tax under this provision is computed under a formula that is intended to permit the taxable passive income to be reduced by an allocable portion of the expenses incurred by the corporation in generating this income. Moreover, the amount taxed is not all of the passive investment income of the corporation but only the amount of passive income that exceeds 25 percent of the gross receipts of the S corporation. Under the statutory formula, the excess net passive income is passive income less expenses attributable to that income multiplied by a fraction obtained by dividing (i) passive investment income less 25 percent of gross receipts by (ii) passive investment income. § 1375(b).

One of the more dangerous aspects of Section 1375 is that the tax may be imposed if the S corporation has as little as $1 of C corporation earnings and profits. Since the computation of earnings and profits is as much an art as a science, a corporation may encounter Section 1375 even though the corporation in good faith believed that it did not have any earnings and profits. In those circumstances, the IRS is authorized to waive the application of Section 1375. § 1375(d).

[¶ 15,445]

b. *Stage Two: Termination*

If the Section 1375 tax did not get the S corporation's attention, Congress provided a second stage attack. The Subchapter S election will be involuntarily terminated if an S corporation that has C corporation earnings and profits derives over 25 percent of its gross receipts from passive investment sources in each of three consecutive taxable years. § 1362(d)(3). Can an S corporation be subject to the termination provision even though it has not been subject to the Section 1375 tax? That tax is imposed on passive income reduced by related expenses, while a termination can occur only if the gross investment income exceeds 25 percent of gross receipts.

A termination under Section 1362(d)(3) can be inadvertent. As a condition to excusing the termination under Section 1362(f), what conditions should be attached to the relief? See Letter Ruling 8848065 (distribution of earnings and profits). Normally, an inadvertent termination will be caused by an erroneous computation of earnings and profits. In Letter Ruling 8848065, however, the inadvertence was that the transferee shareholders did not know that an S election had been made!

[¶ 15,450]

c. *Defining Passive Investment Income*

The term "passive investment income" is defined both for purposes of Sections 1362 and 1375 in Section 1362(d)(3)(C)(i) to mean "gross receipts derived from royalties, rents, dividends, interest, annuities, and sales or exchanges of stock or securities (gross receipts from such sales or exchanges being taken into account for purposes of this paragraph only to the extent of gains therefrom).''

Reg. § 1.1362–2(c)(5)(ii)(A)(*1*), in turn, defines "royalties" to mean "all royalties, including mineral, oil, and gas royalties, and amounts received for the privilege of using patents, copyrights, secret processes and formulas, good will, trademarks, trade brands, franchises, and other like property." However, royalties for this purpose do not include royalties derived in the ordinary course of the business of franchising or licensing property, nor copyright royalties or mineral or oil and gas royalties if the royalties would not be treated as personal holding company income under Section 543(a)(3) and (a)(4). Reg. § 1.1362–2(c)(5)(ii)(A)(*2*), (*3*).

Reg. 1.1362–2(c)(5)(ii)(B)(*1*) defines the term "rents" as "amounts received for the use of, or right to use, property (whether real or personal)" of a corporation. However, payments for the use of property do not constitute rents if they are derived from the active business of renting property. Reg. 1.1362–2(c)(5)(ii)(B)(*2*). Rents are treated as derived from an active business only if significant services are rendered or substantial costs incurred in connection with the rental business. Id. Thus, under this test, the owner of an apartment house might have passive income while the owner of a hotel likely would not. Thus, in Feingold v. Commissioner, 49 T.C. 461 (1968), the Tax Court held that the taxpayers' rental income from furnished summer bungalows constituted passive investment income under an earlier version of these regulations because the taxpayers had not provided "significant services" of a type comparable to those provided by an operator of a hotel or motel.

Passive investment income apparently includes tax-exempt interest. However, the taxable excess net passive income cannot exceed the corporation's taxable income computed as if it were a C corporation. § 1375(b)(1)(B). Is this limitation of any significance if less than 25 percent of the corporation's gross receipts consist of tax-exempt income?

Passive investment income does not include interest on debt obligations from the sale of inventory or other "dealer" property. § 1362(d)(3)(C)(ii). Nor does it include gross receipts from the active and regular conduct of a lending or financing business, if certain additional requirements are met. See § 1362(d)(3)(C)(iii). In addition, there is a special rule that applies to options and commodities dealers, which excludes from passive investment income gains or losses from Section 1256 contracts or property related to such contracts. See § 1362(d)(3)(D).

Note that the statute does not include gains from the sale or exchange of unimproved real property or other property (other than sales or exchanges of stock or securities or annuities) within the term "passive investment income." Authorities under an earlier version of this provision held that such omission means that the gains from the sale of such property are not passive investment income. See Howell v. Commissioner, 57 T.C. 546 (1972) (acq.); Rev. Rul. 75–188, 1975–1 C.B. 276.

Passive investment income also does not include dividends received from a controlled C corporate subsidiary when those dividends are attributable to earnings and profits derived by the C corporation from the active conduct of a trade or business. § 1362(d)(3)(E).

Finally, under a provision added to the Code in 2004 and amended in 2005, in the case of an S corporation that is a bank, passive income does not include interest income or dividends on assets required to be held by the banking corporation. The latter assets include stock in the Federal Reserve Bank, Federal Home Loan Bank, or the Federal Agricultural Mortgage Bank, as well as participation certificates issued by a Federal Intermediate Credit Bank. § 1362(d)(3)(F).

Both the Section 1375 tax and the termination provision are geared to a fraction of gross receipts. What are gross receipts as distinguished from gross income? Is it easier for a corporation to generate gross receipts than gross income? Note that, under Section 1362(d)(3)(C)(i), gross receipts are defined to include only gains from the sale of stock or securities. What about from the sale of used cars? Note also that termination is caused only by failing the gross receipts test in three consecutive years.

What is the relationship between the "passive" income penalized by Section 1375, the "personal holding company" income penalized by Section 541, and the "passive activity" and "portfolio" income addressed by Section 469? Are the definitional distinctions justified as a matter of tax policy?

[¶ 15,453]

4. NO CARRYFORWARD OR CARRYBACK OF LOSSES FROM C CORPORATION YEAR TO S CORPORATION YEAR

Another coordination issue that may arise from the conversion of a C corporation to an S corporation or from the termination of an S corporation election concerns net operating losses and other losses that arose while the corporation was operating as a C corporation but were suspended under Section 172 (net operating losses) or some other provision. Section 1371(b)(1) provides that no carryforward or carryback arising for a taxable year for which a corporation is a C corporation may be carried to a taxable year for which the corporation is an S corporation. For example, this means that a net operating carryforward of a C corporation may not be carried forward to a taxable year during which the corporation has properly elected S status and deducted by that corporation's shareholders under Section 1366. However, Section

1371(b)(3) makes clear that this rule does not prevent a taxable year during which a corporation is an S corporation from counting as a taxable year for purposes of determining the number of years to which an item may be carried back or carried forward. For example, if a C corporation incurs a net operating loss in year 1, which may be carried forward for 20 years under Section 172(b), makes an S election in year 2, and the S election continues for at least the next 19 years (i.e., years 3 through 21), the net operating loss from year 1 will expire in year 21, 20 years after it arose (notwithstanding the fact that Section 1371(b)(1) prevented the corporation from carrying forward the year 1 loss to any of the years for which the S election was in effect). (Note also that Section 1371(b)(2) prevents any net operating loss carryover or carryback from arising at the corporate level while the corporation has an S election in effect.)

Suppose that a closely held C corporation has passive activity losses that are suspended under Section 469(b), makes an S election, and thereafter sells the passive activity that generated the loss. Does Section 1371(b)(1) prevent the S corporation (and, hence, ultimately, its shareholders) from deducting the suspended losses under Section 469(g) on disposition of its entire interest in the passive activity? In St. Charles Investment Co. v. Commissioner, 232 F.3d 773 (10th Cir.2000), the Tenth Circuit reversed the Tax Court and held that the S corporation could deduct the suspended losses. Although the court of appeals recognized the potential windfall arising from the ability of one taxpayer (the shareholder of the S corporation) to deduct a loss realized by another separate taxpayer (the corporation while it was a C corporation), it concluded that the "plain language" of Section 469 unequivocally required that result. Is the appellate court correct that its holding in this case is required by the plain language of Section 469? Or, instead, is the statute ambiguous on the issue raised in the case, so that a court should properly consider the policy of the statutory provision involved and the internal logic of the tax law in resolving the ambiguity in such a way as to prevent taxpayers from obtaining an unintended windfall? Recall that these questions concerning the proper approach to interpreting tax statutes were also considered in the excerpt from the *Gitlitz* case, at ¶ 15,287, and the Notes following that excerpt at ¶ 15,288.

H. TERMINATION OF THE S ELECTION

[¶ 15,455]

1. METHODS OF TERMINATING THE ELECTION

A Subchapter S election can be terminated in any of three different ways (Section 1362(d)):

(1) Paradoxically, the voluntary revocation of the election is the most exacting method, requiring as it does the consent to the revocation

by the holders of more than one-half of the number of shares of stock outstanding in the corporation. § 1362(d)(1)(A) and (B); Reg. § 1.1362–6(a)(3)(i). Such a revocation may be prospective to any day specified. In addition, if the revocation is made during the first two and one-half months of the taxable year, the revocation will be retroactive to the first day of the year unless a prospective date is specified. § 1362(d)(1)(C).

(2) Alternatively, if the corporation fails to meet any of the shareholder level or corporate level definitional requirements on any day, the election automatically terminates on that day. § 1362(d)(2). The termination occurs regardless of whether the disqualifying act was deliberately undertaken for the purpose of terminating the election or was entirely inadvertent. (Recall, however, the authority of the IRS to disregard inadvertent terminations under Section 1362(f), discussed at ¶¶ 15,205 et seq.)

(3) Finally, for those S corporations which previously had been C corporations, and which derive an excessive amount of passive investment income, the Subchapter S election may be terminated under a complex rule, § 1362(d)(3), as discussed at ¶ 15,445.

[¶ 15,460]

2. IMPACT OF TERMINATION ON REPORTING INCOME

Upon the termination of a Subchapter S election during a taxable year, an "S short year" and a "C short year" arise. § 1362(e). The corporation's income for the termination year is then allocated between the two short years under one of the same two statutory methods that also apply when a shareholder in an ongoing S corporation disposes of her complete stock interest during the year. See ¶ 15,385. While contained in a different Code section, these rules on the midyear termination closely resemble the rules of Section 1377(a) for allocating income and expense among shareholders for a year in which a change in ownership occurs, and they create similar problems.

Income allocated to the S short year is taxable to the shareholders under the usual rules of Subchapter S while income allocated to the C short year becomes subject to the corporate income tax. To repeat, under the pro rata method of allocation, each item of income or loss of the S corporation for the termination year is allocated ratably to each day in the termination year. § 1362(e)(2); Reg. § 1.1362–3(a). Under the alternative interim closing method, the corporation allocates items of income and loss between the short years under its normal tax accounting rules. § 1362(e)(3); Reg. § 1.1362–3(b). Generally, this latter method of allocation requires a corporate election plus the consent of every shareholder during the S short year and all shareholders on the first day of the C short year. (Is it rational to permit the termination of the S election by majority vote but to require unanimous consent to the use of the interim closing method of allocating income?) Note, however, that the interim

¶ 15,455

closing method must be used if there has been a sale of 50 percent or more of the stock of the corporation during the termination year. § 1362(e)(6)(D).

In order to prevent taxpayers from moving in and out of Subchapter S, once an S election has been terminated, the corporation cannot re-elect Subchapter S status within five years without the consent of the IRS. § 1362(g). In general, the IRS will consent to an early re-election only when there has been a substantial change in the ownership of the corporation. Reg. § 1.1362–5(a).

[¶ 15,465]

Problems

1. Robert owns 250 of 1,000 outstanding shares in an S corporation. For the purpose of precipitating an involuntary termination of the election, he transferred one share of his stock to his uncle, a nonresident alien. Per pre-arrangement, three weeks later the uncle retransferred the stock to him.

a. Has the election terminated? See Hook v. Commissioner, 58 T.C. 267 (1972) (sham transfer not effective in terminating Subchapter S election).

b. If no retransfer took place, the election would, of course, terminate. By what planning might this be avoided?

c. Depending on the applicable state corporate law, is there any legal theory that the other shareholders of a corporation might use to prevent a minority shareholder from intentionally terminating a Subchapter S election? See A.W. Chesterton Co. v. Chesterton, 128 F.3d 1 (1st Cir.1997) (court enjoined a minority shareholder from transferring some of his shares in an S corporation to two shell C corporations wholly owned by him because the transfer would have terminated the S corporation's election in breach of the shareholder's fiduciary duty, under Massachusetts law, of utmost good faith and loyalty owed to the corporation and the other shareholders).

d. As a policy matter, should one shareholder have the power at will to terminate the election, and thus control the fate of an S corporation in contravention of the desires of all other shareholders, by a simple deliberate transfer of one share of stock to an ineligible shareholder?

2. An S corporation has outstanding 100 shares of voting stock and 300 shares of nonvoting stock. May the holders of 201 shares of nonvoting stock voluntarily revoke the Subchapter S election? See Reg. § 1.1362–6(a)(3)(i).

3. How much flexibility do the shareholders of an S corporation have in allocating items of income and expense between the two short taxable years when the interim closing method is elected? For example, could a cash method corporation accelerate the payment of deductible

expenses, such as rent, in anticipation of the termination of the election? (Compare Section 706(d), discussed at ¶ 18,205, which provides very precise rules for allocating items of income and expense during the year of a partnership in which ownership interests change.)

4. Assume that an S corporation derived net income of $10,000 during each month of the taxable year except that, during March, the corporation incurred a $100,000 loss attributable to the abandonment of a trademark. On July 1, the Subchapter S election was voluntarily terminated. What difference does it make to the shareholders whether the pro rata or the interim closing method is elected?

[¶ 15,470]

3. POST–TERMINATION TRANSITION PERIOD

Once the S status terminates and is replaced by a C corporation, a grace period known as the "post-termination transition period" emerges. § 1377(b); Reg. § 1.1377–2. The period lasts for at least one year from the termination of the election and at least as long as 120 days after determination of certain disputed tax matters. During this period two sorts of relief become available. First, cash distributions made by the former S corporation to a shareholder will produce a reduction in the basis of the distributee's stock in lieu of what might otherwise be dividend income, but not in excess of the accumulated adjustments account. § 1371(e). Second, any disallowed losses carried over from the S period (due either to the at risk rules or the inadequate basis in the shareholder's stock and debt interests) can be utilized during the post-termination transition period, but only in an amount not in excess of that shareholder's basis in her stock. § 1366(d)(3).

Note that a distribution made after this grace period will be governed by the rules on corporate distributions in Subchapter C, i.e., it will result in taxable dividend income to the shareholder if the distribution is a Section 301 distribution and the distributing corporation has sufficient earnings and profits to cover the distribution. This means that a shareholder counting on receiving a tax-free distribution of amounts representing earnings that have already been taxed at the shareholder level under the Subchapter S election will instead be taxed on the receipt of a dividend under Section 301. Note also that any disallowed losses at the corporate level remaining after the expiration of the post-termination transition period do not flow through to the corporation's shareholders and are permanently disallowed. See Reg. § 1.1366–2(b)(2).

Under a provision added to Section 1377 in 2004, special rules apply to the 120–day post-termination transition period triggered by an audit adjustment. First, this 120–day grace period does not apply for purposes of allowing suspended losses to be deducted under Section 1366(d)(3). § 1377(b)(3)(A). Second, Section 1377 allows a tax-free distribution of money by the corporation during this 120–day grace period under

Section 1371(e) only to the extent of any aggregate increase in the accumulated adjustments account because of adjustments from the audit. § 1377(b)(3)(B).

Why is relief limited in time to this post-termination transition period? Does this resemble the inability of a former partner to extract tax-favored distributions from a partnership? Is it a fair compromise with the rules applicable to shareholders of a C corporation?

¶ 15,470

Chapter 16

INTRODUCTION AND DEFINITION
OF PARTNERSHIPS

[¶ 16,000]

A. INTRODUCTION

As you have seen in the prior chapters of this book, under the Internal Revenue Code, corporations generally are quite rigorously treated as entities separate and apart from their shareholders. Moreover, unless the corporation has elected to be taxed as an S corporation, both the corporate entity and its shareholders are subject to separate levels of taxation on their respective incomes. One consequence of that approach to the incorporated business is the double tax system explored above in Chapters 1 through 13. By contrast, two or more individuals may own property as tenants in common, dividing among themselves the income and expense attributable to the property. In that event, the tax law does not recognize the existence of an entity apart from the owners of the property and apportions a single level of tax among the aggregate of co-owners.

In the design of the taxation of partnerships, the critical and recurring question is whether the partnership should be treated as a separate entity or as a mere aggregation of co-owners. This and the succeeding chapters examine the sophisticated and complex answers to that question provided by Subchapter K in Sections 701 through 761.

In one key respect the partnership entity is plainly ignored: partnerships are not taxpayers. Rather, the items of income and expense derived by a partnership are reported by the partners on their own returns and are subject to only a single level of tax at the partner level. Moreover, by sharp contrast to the taxation of C corporations, partnership losses may be claimed by the partners on their individual returns. As important as those aspects of Subchapter K may be, however, they are only pieces of a very large puzzle. The income tax consequences of virtually every aspect and transaction of a partnership will be affected by whether the entity or the aggregate model is controlling.

In addressing these issues of partnership taxation, Subchapter K does not uniformly adopt either an aggregate or an entity approach but rather synthesizes elements of each. In some instances, such as the routine computation of income and the filing of informational returns, an entity approach is employed; in others, such as the reporting of that income or loss by the partners, an aggregate approach is used. In still other circumstances, the partners may elect between an aggregate or an entity approach. And, finally, in its most complex provisions, Subchapter K creates a blend of both approaches. Thinking about the taxation of partnerships in terms of entity and aggregate approaches may at first seem overly abstract. However, Subchapter K can be thoroughly understood only in terms of the alternating or blended application of these two distinct approaches.

[¶ 16,005]

1. THE STATUTORY FRAMEWORK AND ITS HISTORICAL EVOLUTION

Subchapter K was enacted in 1954 in an attempt to bring rationality and predictability to an area of the law that had been remarkably deficient in those qualities. At that time the prototypical partnership was, or was envisioned as being, a small business that had a relatively few individual owners, many of whom were actively engaged in the partnership business, and that was conducted pursuant to a version of the Uniform Partnership Act. Reflecting that image and the Uniform Act, the hallmarks of the 1954 legislation were flexibility and minimal impact of taxation on partnership business activities. In their transactions with the partnership, partners were granted substantial freedom to select between the entity and the aggregate approaches to characterization of the transaction, and the imposition of tax was deferred to the maximum extent possible.

By the early 1980s, however, Congress faced a radically different investment vehicle. The features of partnership taxation tailored for the conditions in 1954 became targets for exploitation by the booming tax shelter industry; the flexibility and tax deferral opportunities inherent in Subchapter K became the vehicles for tax shelters and other tax avoidance transactions. Predictably, Congress and the Treasury Department responded to the perceived abuses by adopting new statutory and regulatory provisions that, although directed at tax avoidance transactions, materially complicate the conduct of all business in partnership form.

Moreover, in recent years, tax results perceived as inappropriate have flowed from the partnership rules faster than the response rate of Congress or the Treasury Department. As discussed at ¶ 16,085, the

¶ 16,005

Treasury has responded by asserting broad authority to attack partnership transactions regarded as abusive. See, e.g., Reg. § 1.701–2.

Subchapter K is thus a challenging mixture of rules both simple and complex, elective and mandatory, and favorable and unfavorable to tax deferral. Relative to other areas of the tax law, these rules have been the subject of scant judicial construction. Indeed, except for a few important provisions such as Sections 704, 707, 731, 737, 751, and 752, the rules have not been the subject of extensive administrative interpretation. As a result, Subchapter K itself represents the principal source of the rules governing the taxation of partnerships and thus presents a rare opportunity to examine the legislative process as the matrix of law.

[¶ 16,010]

2. THE BASIC RULES OF SUBCHAPTER K

The basic rules of Subchapter K remain relatively simple. The partnership is not a taxpayer. § 701. The act of establishing a partnership, including the contribution of property by the partners to the partnership, is normally not a taxable event either to the partners or the partnership. § 721. The basis of contributed property is not affected by the transfer; the contributing partner's basis carries over to the partnership. § 723. The allocation of income, gains, deductions, and losses to partners will reflect the provisions of the partnership agreement and applicable state law. § 704. Each partner is responsible for including income, gains, deductions, and losses properly allocated to him or her in determining income tax liability for the appropriate taxable year. §§ 701 and 702. Because a partner will already have paid income tax on the amount of income so attributed, the distribution of property by the partnership to the partner will not generally be a taxable event, although there are a growing number of exceptions to this general rule. §§ 731 and 736.

The establishment of a partnership or the acquisition of a partnership interest means that the partner has a new asset—his or her interest in the partnership. The partner's adjusted basis in the partnership interest will be measured initially by the cost of the partnership interest or the adjusted basis of properties transferred by the partner to the partnership. § 722. The partner's adjusted basis in the partnership interest will be increased by partnership income and gains, and be reduced by partnership deductions and losses, allocated to the partner. The partner's adjusted basis in the partnership interest will also be reduced when the partnership distributes property to the partner. § 705. The partner is likely to realize a gain or loss upon the sale or exchange of the partnership interest to another. § 741. The partners will recognize a gain or loss upon the liquidation of a partnership only in limited circumstances. §§ 731 and 736.

[¶ 16,015]

3.   A SIMPLIFIED ILLUSTRATION

Smith and Jones decided to establish a law partnership. On January 1 of year 1, each contributed $25,000 to a partnership account to finance start-up costs. The partnership agreement provided that they would share profits and losses equally and that distributions would be determined periodically in the light of the business needs of the enterprise. During year 1, the partnership received $100,000 in fees and paid $60,000 in deductible expenses, including rental payments for the first year of a five-year lease of office space. Both Smith and Jones drew $10,000 from the partnership account to cover their personal needs.

The tax consequences for year 1 were:

a.   Both Smith and Jones had to report $20,000 of income (one-half each of the partnership's net business income for year 1 of $40,000, i.e., $100,000 of fee income minus the deductible expenses of $60,000).

b.   Each had an adjusted basis in the partnership interest at the end of year 1 of $35,000 ($25,000 initial basis plus $20,000, each partner's distributive share of the partnership's year 1 net income, less $10,000, the amount of each partner's draw that is treated as a distribution).

During year 2, the partnership received fees of $200,000 and paid deductible expenses of $100,000. Both partners drew $20,000 from the partnership account.

The tax consequences for year 2 were:

a.   Both Smith and Jones had to report $50,000 of income (one-half each of the partnership's net business income for year 2 of $100,000, i.e., $200,000 of fee income minus the deductible expenses of $100,000).

b.   Both Smith and Jones had an adjusted basis in the partnership interest at the end of year 2 of $65,000 ($35,000 basis at the end of year 1 plus $50,000, each partner's distributive share of the partnership's year 2 income, less $20,000, the amount of each partner's draw that is treated as a distribution).

The first week of year 3 was marked by a highly emotional debate about the future of the firm. The partners agreed to terminate their relationship. They assigned the remainder of their lease for $10,000 and ended the operation. Expenses for the few weeks of year 3 were just equal to revenues.

The tax consequences for year 3 are:

a. Both Smith and Jones must report $5,000 of capital gain (one-half each of the $10,000 of capital gain deriving from the sale of the leasehold interest).

b. Both Smith and Jones have an adjusted basis in the partnership interest at this point of $70,000 ($65,000 basis at the end of year 2 plus $5,000, each partner's distributive share of the partnership's capital gain of $10,000).

c. When the partnership makes a liquidating distribution of $70,000 to each partner, there is no gain or loss to the partnership, Smith, or Jones.

[¶ 16,020]

4. SOME USEFUL REFERENCES

The following reference materials will be helpful in addressing the issues raised in this and the succeeding chapters on partnership taxation: Federal Income Tax Project: Subchapter K: Proposals on the Taxation of Partners (A.L.I. 1984); L. Cunningham & N. Cunningham, The Logic of Subchapter K—A Conceptual Guide to the Taxation of Partnerships (3d ed. 2006); Jerold A. Friedland, Understanding Partnership and LLC Taxation (2000); A. Gunn & J. Repetti, Partnership Income Taxation (4th ed. 2005); W. McKee, W. Nelson & R. Whitmire, Federal Taxation of Partnerships and Partners (3d ed. 1997, plus supplements); and A. Willis, J. Pennell & P. Postlewaite, Partnership Taxation (6th ed. 1999, plus supplements).

[¶ 16,025]

B. DEFINING A PARTNERSHIP FOR TAX PURPOSES: BUSINESS ENTERPRISE CLASSIFICATION

For state law purposes, a business enterprise involving more than one equity owner may be treated as conducted by an entity, such as a corporation, a partnership, or a trust, or merely by individuals acting in concert. However, whether that enterprise will be subject to the income tax rules governing corporations, or the rules governing partnerships, or trusts, or individuals, is determined by federal law. While state law generally establishes the legal relationships among the owners of the business, the state law characterization of an enterprise does not control its classification for income tax purposes. Rather, that definition is supplied by the tax law itself. As a result, Subchapter K applies to some enterprises that are not treated as partnerships for state law purposes and does not apply to other enterprises that are so treated.

Somewhat confusingly, the Code contains two separate definitions of what will be treated as a partnership. Those definitions, however, serve two separate purposes. Section 761(a) distinguishes partnerships from joint activities that do not amount to the creation of an entity for tax purposes (although the regulations on that issue are now at Reg. § 301.7701–1(a)(2)). Section 7701(a)(2), on the other hand, distinguishes partnerships from other business entities. As discussed below, the current entity classification regulations, sometimes called the "check-the-box" regulations, allow many types of business entities to elect to be treated either as partnerships or as associations taxable as corporations for federal tax purposes. The first issue under these regulations is to determine whether a separate entity exists.

1. PARTNERSHIP VERSUS NONENTITY

[¶ 16,030]

REVENUE RULING 75–374

1975–2 C.B. 261.

Advice has been requested whether, under the circumstance described below, the coowners of an apartment project would be treated as a partnership for Federal income tax purposes.

X, a life insurance company, and *Y*, a real estate investment trust, each own an undivided one-half interest in an apartment project. *X* and *Y* entered into a management agreement with *Z*, an unrelated corporation, and retained it to manage, operate, maintain, and service the project.

Generally, under the management agreement *Z* negotiates and executes leases for apartment units in the project; collects rents and other payments from tenants; pays taxes, assessments, and insurance premiums payable with respect to the project; performs all other services customarily performed in connection with the maintenance and repair of an apartment project; and performs certain additional services for the tenants beyond those customarily associated with maintenance and repair. *Z* is responsible for determining the time and manner of performing its obligations under the agreement and for the supervision of all persons performing services in connection with the carrying out of such obligations.

Customary tenant services, such as heat, air conditioning, hot and cold water, unattended parking, normal repairs, trash removal, and cleaning of public areas are furnished at no additional charge above the basic rental payments. All costs incurred by *Z* in rendering these customary services are paid for by *X* and *Y*. As compensation for the customary services rendered by *Z* under the agreement, *X* and *Y* each pay *Z* a percentage of one-half of the gross rental receipts derived from the operation of the project.

¶ 16,030

Additional services, such as attendant parking, cabanas, and gas, electricity, and other utilities are provided by Z to tenants for a separate charge. Z pays the costs incurred in providing the additional services, and retains the charges paid by tenants for its own use. These charges provide Z with adequate compensation for the rendition of these additional services.

Section 761(a) * * * provides that the term "partnership" includes a syndicate, group, pool, joint venture or other unincorporated organization through or by means of which any business, financial operation, or venture is carried on, and which is not a corporation or a trust or estate.

[Section 301.7701–1(a)(2)] * * * of the * * * Regulations provides that mere coownership of property that is maintained, kept in repair, and rented or leased does not constitute a partnership. Tenants in common may be partners if they actively carry on a trade, business, financial operation, or venture and divide the profits thereof. For example, a partnership exists if coowners of an apartment building lease space and in addition provide services to the occupants either directly or through an agent.

The furnishing of customary services in connection with the maintenance and repair of the apartment project will not render a coownership a partnership. However, the furnishing of additional services will render a coownership a partnership if the additional services are furnished directly by the coowners or through their agent. In the instant case by reason of the contractual arrangement with Z, X and Y are not furnishing the additional services either directly or through an agent. Z is solely responsible for determining the time and manner of furnishing the services, bears all the expenses of providing these services, and retains for its own use all the income from these services. None of the profits arising from the rendition of these additional services are divided between X and Y.

Accordingly, X and Y will be treated as coowners and not as partners for purposes of section 761 * * *.

[¶ 16,035]

REVENUE RULING 77–332

1977–2 C.B. 484.

Advice has been requested whether the individuals described below are partners for Federal tax purposes.

In order to provide greater incentives for certain of its management consulting personnel, a certified professional accounting partnership established the category of "principal." Under state law, since these individuals are not certified public accountants, they are not recognized as partners of the partnership. Nevertheless, for certain purposes, the principals are treated as partners by the firm. The partnership formalized the status of a principal under a written partnership agreement among all the partners and the principals of the firm.

Article I of the partnership agreement provides, in part, as follows:

"Principals" means the parties hereto who are not partners solely because they are not certified under state law. Except with respect to any provisions of these Articles specifically designated as being applicable solely to certified members, principals shall enjoy all of the rights, privileges and liabilities of partners. Principals are prohibited from (i) being held out, or holding themselves out to the public as partners; their separate title must accompany all mention of their names in directories and in other publications so that it is clear that they are not partners of the firm; (ii) signing the firm name on any report that relates to expressing an opinion on a client's financial statements; (iii) being designated as managing partner of any operating office of the firm from which opinions on financial statements are issued; (iv) contributing or having any interest in the capital of the firm other than making subordinated loans to the firm in the form of deposit accounts; and (v) being elected to the position of senior partner and deputy senior partner.

Instead of contributing to the capital of the firm to acquire units of interest as the partners do, principals deposit with the firm an amount per unit of interest equal to the capital requirements of a partner. Article I of the agreement further provides that "units of interests" means the shares in the firm for the purposes of voting and profit and loss sharing. After deducting salaries and interest payments to partners and principals, and retirement payments, the remainder of profits and losses will be shared by the partners and principals in proportion to their respective units of interest outstanding.

Under the provisions of Article II of the agreement, principals are given the right to vote in all matters coming before the firm other than matters of a professional nature that, by law, can only be performed by certified members. In addition, principals can be elected to the executive committee. The executive committee of the firm has general direction over the affairs of the firm.

Under Article III of the agreement, the decision of two-thirds of the partners and principals is necessary in all matters relating to the practice, business and affairs of the firm. However, at least 95 percent of the partners and principals must authorize any change in the agreement or any significant departure from the manner in which the practice of the firm is conducted.

Under Article IV of the agreement, any partners or principals may retire from the firm and surrender their units of interest upon six months written notice unless such notice is waived by the executive committee. Upon retirement of a partner or principal, the firm shall

¶ 16,035

terminate as to such retiring partner or principal. In the event of the death of any of the partners or principals prior to their retirement, the balance of the capital, drawing, and unrealized receivables accounts of the deceased partner, or the deposit, drawing, and deferred compensation accounts of the deceased principal, and the deceased's share of the firm's net profits, will be paid according to the terms of the deceased's will, or if no applicable terms or if no will, to the deceased's spouse or, if no surviving spouse, to the deceased's legal representative.

Under Article V of the agreement neither the death nor retirement of a partner or a principal shall effect a dissolution or termination of the firm, except as to that partner or principal, or the creation of a new partnership.

Under Article VI of the agreement, additional partners and principals may be admitted to the firm by unanimous vote of the partners and principals.

Other facts disclose that (1) although the principals' accounts are denominated subordinated loans in the form of deposits, in every respect, save name, the deposit accounts are identical to the capital accounts of the partners; (2) upon liquidation of the firm, there will be no distinction between principals and partners as to their rights in the assets of the firm, except that the deposit accounts would be divided among the principals and the capital accounts among the partners; (3) in the event of a suit by a third party against the individual members of the firm, principals would be treated as partners; (4) except for functions restricted by law to the certified members, principals can bind the firm in the same manner as partners; and (5) in the event that losses of the firm have to be covered and the assets of the firm are insufficient to do so, each partner and principal will be required to make a proportionate contribution.

Even though state law does not recognize principals as partners, the rights and obligations of principals, as described above, are enforceable under applicable state law.

Section 7701(a)(2) * * * states, in part, that the term "partnership" includes a syndicate, group, pool, joint venture or other unincorporated organization through or by means of which any business, financial operation, or venture is carried on, and which is not a trust, estate, or a corporation; and the term "partner" includes a member in such a syndicate, group, pool, joint venture, or organization. Section 761 contains language that is similar to the above.

* * *

Therefore, since a partner, for Federal income tax purposes, is defined as a member of a partnership and the Internal Revenue Code establishes the tests or standards for classifying an organization as a partnership for Federal tax purposes, it follows that the standards for

¶ 16,035

determining who is a partner, for Federal tax purposes, must be made under Federal law.

The Supreme Court of the United States in *Commissioner v. Tower*, 327 U.S. 280, 286 (1946), * * * and again in *Commissioner v. Culbertson*, 337 U.S. 733, 740 (1949), * * * stated that a partnership is created, for Federal income tax purposes, "when persons join together their money, goods, labor or skill for the purpose of carrying on a trade, profession or business and when there is a community of interest in the profit and losses."

The Tax Court of the United States in *Beulah H. Nichols*, 32 T.C. 1322 (1959), acq., * * * cited the standard expressed above in *Tower* and *Culbertson* in holding that a partnership, for Federal income tax purposes, existed between a medical doctor specializing in radiology and a non-doctor spouse for the purpose of carrying on a medical business even though the non-doctor spouse could not legally be a partner under state law.

Rev. Rul. 58–243, 1958–1 C.B. 255, concludes that the fact that a husband and wife cannot legally be partners under state law does not necessarily prevent recognition of such a partnership for Federal income tax purposes.

Thus, whether a person qualifies as a partner within the meaning of sections 7701 and 761(a) * * * depends on whether the facts, as manifested in the agreement and the execution of the agreement, reveal that the person has contributed money, goods, labor or skill for the purpose of carrying on a trade, profession or business, and participates in the community of interest in the profits and losses. In the instant case, both the principals and the partners meet the above qualifications.

Accordingly, the members of the certified professional accounting partnership designated as "principals" are considered to be partners of the firm for Federal tax purposes.

[¶ 16,040]

**MADISON GAS & ELECTRIC
CO. v. COMMISSIONER**

United States Court of Appeals, Seventh Circuit, 1980.
633 F.2d 512.

CUMMINGS, CIRCUIT JUDGE:

* * * The question is whether certain training and related expenses incurred by a public utility in the expansion of its generating capacity through the joint construction and operation of a nuclear plant with two other utilities are deductible as ordinary and necessary expenses in the years of payment or are non-deductible pre-operating capital expenditures of a new partnership venture. The Tax Court * * * held that they are nondeductible capital expenditures. We affirm.

¶ 16,040

I

* * * Taxpayer Madison Gas and Electric Co. (MGE), a Wisconsin corporation, is an operating public utility which has been engaged since 1896 in the production, purchase, transmission and distribution of electricity and the purchase and distribution of natural gas. * * *

* * *

MGE has over the years kept pace with the increasing demand for electrical power and provided it at reasonable rates by expanding the generating capacity of its facilities, contracting for the purchase and sale of excess electrical power, interconnecting transmission facilities with those of other Wisconsin utilities, and finally by building and operating additional facilities in conjunction with other utilities. Expenses incurred in connection with one of these joint ventures is the subject of the present suit.

On February 2, 1967, MGE entered into an agreement, entitled "Joint Power Supply Agreement" (Agreement) * * *, with Wisconsin Public Service Corporation (WPS) and Wisconsin Power and Light Co. (WPL) under which the three utilities agreed, *inter alia*, to construct and own together a nuclear generating plant now known as the Kewaunee Nuclear Power Plant (Plant). Under the Agreement, the Plant is owned by MGE, WPS and WPL as tenants-in-common with undivided ownership interests of 17.8%, 41.2% and 41.0% respectively. Electricity produced by the Plant is distributed to each of the utilities in proportion to their ownership interests. Each utility sells or uses its share of the power as it does power produced by its own individually owned facilities, and the profits thereby earned by MGE contribute only to MGE's individual profits. No portion of the power generated at the Plant is offered for sale by the utilities collectively, and the Plant is not recognized by the relevant regulatory bodies as a separate utility licensed to sell electricity. Each utility also pays a portion of all expenditures for operation, maintenance and repair of the Plant corresponding exactly to its respective share of ownership. Under utility accounting procedures mandated by the PSC and the FERC, these expenses are combined with and treated in the same manner by MGE as expenses from its individually owned facilities. The ownership and operation of the Plant by MGE, WPS and WPL is regarded by the PSC and the FERC as a tenancy-in-common. It was the intention of the utilities to create only a co-tenancy and not a partnership and to be taxed as co-tenants and not as partners.

In its 1969 and 1970 taxable years, MGE incurred certain expenses relating to the nuclear training of WPS employees, the establishment of internal procedures and guidelines for plant operation and maintenance, employee hiring activities, nuclear field management, environmental activities and the purchase of certain spare parts * * *. MGE had to incur these expenses in order to carry out its Plant activities. * * *

MGE's position was, and is, that the claimed expenses were current-ly deductible under Section 162(a) * * * as ordinary and necessary business expenses. The Commissioner's position was, and is, that the claimed expenses were non-deductible capital expenditures. The Tax Court agreed with the Commissioner, holding that the operation of the Plant by MGE, WPS and WPL is a partnership within the meaning of Section 7701(a)(2) * * *, that the expenses in question were incurred not in the carrying out of an existing business but as part of the start-up costs of the new partnership venture, and that the expenses were therefore not currently deductible but must be capitalized under Section 263(a) * * *. MGE appeals from this judgment, arguing that its arrange-ment with WPS and WPL is not a partnership within the meaning of the Code and, alternatively, that even if it is a partnership the expenses are currently deductible.

II

The threshold issue is whether MGE's joint venture with WPS and WPL is a tax partnership. The Commissioner concedes that if it is not, the expenses are currently deductible under Section 162(a). A partner-ship for federal tax purposes is defined * * * in Section 7701(a)(2), which provides in pertinent part:

> "The term 'partnership' includes a syndicate, group, pool, joint venture, or other unincorporated organization, through or by means of which any business, financial operation, or venture is carried on, and which is not, within the meaning of this title, a trust[,] estate or a corporation."

MGE's arrangement with WPS and WPL in connection with the Plant clearly establishes an unincorporated organization carrying on a "busi-ness, financial operation, or venture" and therefore falls within the literal statutory definition of a partnership. The arrangement is, of course, not taken out of this classification simply because the three utilities intended to be taxed only as a co-tenancy and not as a partner-ship. While it is well-settled that mere co-ownership of property does not create a tax partnership, * * * co-owners may also be partners if they or their agents carry on the requisite "degree of business activities." * * *

MGE's argument is that a co-tenancy does not meet the business activities test of partnership status unless the co-tenants anticipate the earning and sharing of a single joint cash profit from their joint activity. Because its common venture with WPS and WPL does not result in the division of cash profits from joint marketing, MGE contends that the venture constitutes only a co-tenancy coupled with an expense-sharing arrangement and not a tax partnership. The Tax Court held that the Code definition of partnership does not require joint venturers to share in a single joint cash profit and that to the extent that a profit motive is

¶ 16,040

required by the Code it is met here by the distribution of profits in kind. We agree.

The definition of partnership in Section 7701(a)(2) was added to the Code by Section 1111(a) of the Revenue Act of 1932 and first appeared in Section 3797(a)(2) of the 1939 Code. The Congressional Reports accompanying the 1932 Act make clear, in largely identical language, that Congress intended to broaden the definition of partnership for federal tax purposes to include a number of arrangements, such as joint ventures, which were not partnerships under state law. H.R.Rep. No. 708, 72d Cong., 1st Sess., 53 (1932); S.Rep. No. 665, 72d Cong., 1st Sess., 59 (1932). In so doing, they briefly discuss the advantages of requiring a partnership return for joint venturers rather than leaving the sole responsibility for reporting annual gains and losses on the individual members. MGE invites us to infer from these discussions that Congress contemplated inclusion only of those joint ventures that are capable of producing joint cash gains and losses. But even if we were inclined to narrow the statutory language on the basis of such slender evidence, the subsequent legislative history would dissuade us from reaching MGE's suggested construction.

In *Bentex Oil Corp. v. Commissioner*, 20 T.C. 565 (1953), the Tax Court held that an unincorporated organization formed to extract oil under an operating agreement which called for distribution of oil in kind was a partnership within the meaning of Section 3797(a)(2) of the 1939 Code. The Bentex joint venture is not distinguishable from that presented here in any meaningful way. The co-owners there, as here, shared the expenses of production but sold their shares of the production individually. Following *Bentex*, Congress reenacted the definition of partnership in Section 3797(a)(2) of the 1939 Code without change as Section 7701(a)(2) of the 1954 Code. In addition, it repeated the definition verbatim in Section 761(a), which permits certain qualifying organizations to elect to be excluded from application of some or all of the special Subchapter K partnership provisions. A qualifying corporation is one which is used

> "(1) for investment purposes only and not for the active conduct of a business,["]

> or

> "(2) for the joint production, extraction, or use of property, but not for the purpose of selling services or property produced or extracted, if the income of the members of the organization may be adequately determined without the computation of partnership taxable income."

In short, Section 761(a) allows unincorporated associations such as the Bentex venture and the one in issue here, which fall within the statutory definition of partnership, to elect out of Subchapter K.[2] The Section has

2. * * *

The three utilities here in fact did file a partnership return and election-out of Sub-

generally been interpreted, in the absence of any legislative history, as approving the *Bentex* decision while providing relief from certain resulting hardships. * * * This interpretation is surely correct for, as the Tax Court observed:

"[i]f distribution in kind of jointly produced property was enough to avoid partnership status, we do not see how such distribution could be used as a test for election to be excluded from the partnership provisions of subchapter K" (72 T.C. at 563).

MGE also relies on [now former] Treasury Regulation Sections 301.7701–3 and 1.761–1(a) * * * to support its argument that joint marketing is a *sine qua non* of partnership status. These Sections state in identical language that tenants in common

"may be partners if they actively carry on a trade, business, financial operations, or venture and divided the profits thereof."

In addition, MGE cites to us case law referring to a joint profit motive as a characteristic of partnerships.[3] See, *e.g.*, *Commissioner v. Tower*, 327 U.S. 280, 286 * * * ("community of interest in the profits and losses"); *Ian Allison v. Commissioner*, 35 T.C.M. 1069 (1976) ("an agreement to share profits"). Neither the above-quoted Treasury Regulation Sections nor the case law distinguish between the division of cash profits and the division of in-kind profits, and none of the cited cases involved in-kind profits. Moreover, while distribution of profits in-kind may be an uncommon business arrangement, recognition of such arrangements as tax partnerships is not novel. * * *

The practical reality of the venture in issue here is that jointly produced electricity is distributed to MGE and the other two utilities in direct proportion to their ownership interest for resale to consumers in their service areas or to other utilities. The difference between the market value of MGE's share of that electricity and MGE's share of the cost of production obviously represents a profit. Just as obviously, the three utilities joined together in the construction and operation of the Plant with the anticipation of realizing these profits. The fact that the profits are not realized in cash until after the electricity has been

chapter K * * *. The Tax Court held that the filing of a partnership return and election-out under Section 761(a) are not admissions of partnership status * * *. MGE did not argue below that election-out caused the organization not to be a partnership for non-Subchapter K tax purposes, and the Tax Court declined to decide this possible issue * * *. In its alternative position here, however MGE contends that the holding below is "inconsistent with the purpose" of Section 761(a) * * *. This argument is indistinguishable from an argument that election-out under Section 761(a) negates partnership status except where the Code explicitly provides to the contrary.

Since the issue was not raised and decided below, we do not address it here. We note, however, that Section 7701(a)(2) explicitly states that an organization which is a partnership as defined in that Section is a partnership for the purposes of the entire Code, whereas Section 761(a) provides only for election-out of Subchapter K.

3. The Commissioner takes the position that the presence of a joint profit motive is merely one factor to be considered in determining partnership status, while MGE argues that it is a necessary element. Because we find a joint profit motive here, albeit for in-kind profits, we need not resolve this dispute.

channeled through the individual facilities of each participant does not negate their joint profit motive nor make the venture a mere expense-sharing arrangement.[5] We hold therefore that MGE's joint venture with WPS and WPL constitutes a partnership within the meaning of Sections 7701 (a)(2) and 761(a) * * *.

III

On the ultimate issue in this case, the Tax Court held that the claimed expenses were incurred as pre-operational costs of the partnership venture and therefore under settled law were non-deductible capital expenditures. See *Richmond Television Corp. v. United States*, 345 F.2d 901 (4th Cir.1965), vacated on other grounds, 382 U.S. 68 * * *. MGE argues that this holding elevates form over substance in that even if the operating arrangement is technically a tax partnership, the claimed expenses were in actuality simply ordinary and necessary expenses of expanding its existing business. MGE asks us therefore to ignore the partnership entity as lacking economic substance.

* * *

Here MGE, WPS and WPL are engaged in the joint production of electricity for resale, a joint venture for profit. Because they were each already in the business of selling electricity, it can, of course, be argued that the partnership venture itself is an extension or expansion of their existing businesses. It does not follow from this though that we should ignore the partnership as lacking economic substance. Such reasoning would lead to the absurd conclusion that any partnership established to do collectively what its participants formerly did individually or continue to do individually outside the partnership lacks economic substance and should not be treated as a partnership for tax purposes.

At bottom, MGE's position is that it is not sound policy to treat the entity here as a partnership. But we are not free to rewrite the tax laws, whatever the merits of MGE's position. Under the Internal Revenue Code the joint venture here is a partnership and the expenses were non-deductible, pre-operational start-up costs of the partnership venture. Accordingly, the judgment of the Tax Court is affirmed.

[¶ 16,043]

REVENUE PROCEDURE 2002–22

2002–1 C.B. 733.

Section 1. Purpose

This revenue procedure specifies the conditions under which the Internal Revenue Service will consider a request for a ruling that an

---

5. Treasury Regulation Sections 301.7701–3 and 1.761–1(a) * * * [now Section 301.7701–1(a)(2)] state that a "joint undertaking merely to share expenses is not a partnership," and go on to give the example of neighboring landowners who jointly construct a ditch "merely to drain surface water from their properties." We agree with the Tax Court that the venture here is "in no way comparable to the joint construction of a drainage ditch" * * *.

undivided fractional interest in rental real property (other than a mineral property as defined in section 614) is not an interest in a business entity, within the meaning of § 301.7701–2(a) of the * * * Regulations.

* * *

SECTION 2. BACKGROUND

* * *

The central characteristic of a tenancy in common, one of the traditional concurrent estates in land, is that each owner is deemed to own individually a physically undivided part of the entire parcel of property. Each tenant in common is entitled to share with the other tenants the possession of the whole parcel and has the associated rights to a proportionate share of rents or profits from the property, to transfer the interest, and to demand a partition of the property. These rights generally provide a tenant in common the benefits of ownership of the property within the constraint that no rights may be exercised to the detriment of the other tenants in common. * * *

Rev. Rul. 75–374, 1975–2 C.B. 261, concludes that a two-person co-ownership of an apartment building that was rented to tenants did not constitute a partnership for federal tax purposes. In the revenue ruling, the co-owners employed an agent to manage the apartments on their behalf; the agent collected rents, paid property taxes, insurance premiums, repair and maintenance expenses, and provided the tenants with customary services, such as heat, air conditioning, trash removal, unattended parking, and maintenance of public areas. The ruling concludes that the agent's activities in providing customary services to the tenants, although imputed to the co-owners, were not sufficiently extensive to cause the co-ownership to be characterized as a partnership. See also Rev. Rul. 79–77, 1979–1 C.B. 448, which did not find a business entity where three individuals transferred ownership of a commercial building subject to a net lease to a trust with the three individuals as beneficiaries.

Where a sponsor packages co-ownership interests for sale by acquiring property, negotiating a master lease on the property, and arranging for financing, the courts have looked at the relationships not only among the co-owners, but also between the sponsor (or persons related to the sponsor) and the co-owners in determining whether the co-ownership gives rise to a partnership. For example, in *Bergford v. Commissioner*, 12 F.3d 166 (9th Cir. 1993), seventy-eight investors purchased "co-ownership" interests in computer equipment that was subject to a 7–year net lease. As part of the purchase, the co-owners authorized the manager to arrange financing and refinancing, purchase and lease the equipment, collect rents and apply those rents to the notes used to finance the equipment, prepare statements, and advance funds to participants on an interest-free basis to meet cash flow. The agreement allowed the co-owners to decide by majority vote whether to sell or lease the equipment at the end of the lease. Absent a majority vote, the manager could make that decision. In addition, the manager was entitled to a remarketing fee of 10 percent of the equipment's selling price or lease rental whether or not a co-owner terminated the agreement or the manager performed any remarketing. A co-owner could assign an interest in the co-ownership only after fulfilling numerous conditions and obtaining the manager's consent.

The court held that the co-ownership arrangement constituted a partnership for federal tax purposes. Among the factors that influenced the court's decision were the limitations on the co-owners' ability to sell, lease, or encumber either the co-ownership interest or the underlying property, and the manager's effective participation in both profits (through the remarketing fee) and losses (through the advances). *Bergford*, 12 F.3d at 169–170. *Accord Bussing v. Commissioner*, 88 T.C. 449 (1987), *aff'd on reh'g*, 89 T.C. 1050 (1987) * * *.

Under § 1.761–1(a) and §§ 301.7701–1 through 301.7701–3, a federal tax partnership does not include mere co-ownership of property where the owners' activities are limited to keeping the property maintained, in repair, rented or leased. However, as the above authorities demonstrate, a partnership for federal tax purposes is broader in scope than the common law meaning of partnership and may include groups not classified by state law as partnerships. *Bergford*, 12 F.3d at 169. Where the parties to a venture join together capital or services with the intent of conducting a business or enterprise and of sharing the profits and losses from the venture, a partnership (or other business entity) is created. *Bussing*, 88 T.C. at 460. Furthermore, where the economic benefits to the individual participants are not derivative of their co-ownership, but rather come from their joint relationship toward a common goal, the co-ownership arrangement will be characterized as a partnership (or other business entity) for federal tax purposes. *Bergford*, 12 F.3d at 169.

SECTION 3. SCOPE

* * *

This revenue procedure provides guidelines for requesting advance rulings solely to assist taxpayers in preparing ruling requests and the Service in issuing advance ruling letters as promptly as practicable. The guidelines set forth in this revenue procedure are not intended to be substantive rules and are not to be used for audit purposes.

SECTION 4.   GUIDELINES FOR SUBMITTING RULING REQUESTS

The Service ordinarily will not consider a request for a ruling under this revenue procedure unless the information described in section 5 of this revenue procedure is included in the ruling request and the conditions described in section 6 of this revenue procedure are satisfied. Even if sections 5 and 6 of this revenue procedure are satisfied, however, the Service may decline to issue a ruling under this revenue procedure whenever warranted by the facts and circumstances of a particular case and whenever appropriate in the interest of sound tax administration.

* * *

For purposes of this revenue procedure, the following definitions apply. The term "co-owner" means any person that owns an interest in the Property as a tenant in common. The term "sponsor" means any person who divides a single interest in the Property into multiple co-ownership interests for the purpose of offering those interests for sale. The term "related person" means a person bearing a relationship described in § 267(b) or 707(b)(1), except that in applying § 267(b) or 707(b)(1), the co-ownership will be treated as a partnership and each co-owner will be treated as a partner. The term "disregarded entity" means an entity that is disregarded as an entity separate from its owner for federal tax purposes. Examples of disregarded entities include * * * qualified subchapter S subsidiaries (within the meaning of § 1361(b)(3)(B)), and business entities that have only one owner and do not elect to be classified as corporations. The term "blanket lien" means any mortgage or trust deed that is recorded against the Property as a whole.

SECTION 5.   INFORMATION TO BE SUBMITTED

* * *

SECTION 6.   CONDITIONS FOR OBTAINING RULINGS

The Service ordinarily will not consider a request for a ruling under this revenue procedure unless the conditions described below are satisfied. Nevertheless, where the conditions described below are not satisfied, the Service may consider a request for a ruling under this revenue procedure where the facts and circumstances clearly establish that such a ruling is appropriate.

.01 *Tenancy in Common Ownership.* Each of the co-owners must hold title to the Property (either directly or through a disregarded entity) as a tenant in common under local law. Thus, title to the Property as a whole may not be held by an entity recognized under local law.

.02 *Number of Co–Owners.* The number of co-owners must be limited to no more than 35 persons. For this purpose, "person" is defined as in § 7701(a)(1), except that a husband and wife are treated as a single person and all persons who acquire interests from a co-owner by inheritance are treated as a single person.

.03 *No Treatment of Co–Ownership as an Entity.* The co-ownership may not file a partnership or corporate tax return, conduct business under a common name, execute an agreement identifying any or all of the co-owners as partners, shareholders, or members of a business entity, or otherwise hold itself out as a partnership or other form of business entity (nor may the co-owners hold themselves out as partners, shareholders, or members of a business entity). The Service generally will not issue a ruling under this revenue procedure if the co-owners held interests in the Property through a partnership or corporation immediately prior to the formation of the co-ownership.

.04 *Co-Ownership Agreement.* The co-owners may enter into a limited co-ownership agreement that may run with the land. For example, a co-ownership agreement may provide that a co-owner must offer the co-ownership interest for sale to the other co-owners, the sponsor, or the lessee at fair market value (determined as of the time the partition right is exercised) before exercising any right to partition * * *; or that certain actions on behalf of the co-ownership require the vote of co-owners holding more than 50 percent of the undivided interests in the Property * * *.

.05 *Voting.* The co-owners must retain the right to approve the hiring of any manager, the sale or other disposition of the Property, any leases of a portion or all of the Property, or the creation or modification of a blanket lien. Any sale, lease, or re-lease of a portion or all of the Property, any negotiation or renegotiation of indebtedness secured by a blanket lien, the hiring of any manager, or the negotiation of any management contract (or any extension or renewal of such contract) must be by unanimous approval of the co-owners. For all other actions on behalf of the co-ownership, the co-owners may agree to be bound by the vote of those holding more than 50 percent of the undivided interests in the Property. A co-owner who has consented to an action in conformance with this section 6.05 may provide the manager or other person a power of attorney to execute a specific document with respect to that action, but may not provide the manager or other person with a global power of attorney.

.06 *Restrictions on Alienation.* In general, each co-owner must have the rights to transfer, partition, and encumber the co-owner's undivided interest in the Property without the agreement or approval of any person. However, restrictions on the right to transfer, partition, or encumber interests in the Property that are required by a lender and that are consistent with customary commercial lending practices are not prohibited. * * * Moreover, the co-owners, the sponsor, or the lessee may have a right of first offer (the right to have the first opportunity to offer to purchase the co-ownership interest) with respect to any co-owner's exercise of the right to transfer the co-ownership interest in the Property. In addition, a co-owner may agree to offer the co-ownership

¶ 16,043

interest for sale to the other co-owners, the sponsor, or the lessee at fair market value (determined as of the time the partition right is exercised) before exercising any right to partition.

.07 *Sharing Proceeds and Liabilities upon Sale of Property.* If the Property is sold, any debt secured by a blanket lien must be satisfied and the remaining sales proceeds must be distributed to the co-owners.

.08 *Proportionate Sharing of Profits and Losses.* Each co-owner must share in all revenues generated by the Property and all costs associated with the Property in proportion to the co-owner's undivided interest in the Property. Neither the other co-owners, nor the sponsor, nor the manager may advance funds to a co-owner to meet expenses associated with the co-ownership interest, unless the advance is recourse to the co-owner (and, where the co-owner is a disregarded entity, the owner of the co-owner) and is not for a period exceeding 31 days.

.09 *Proportionate Sharing of Debt.* The co-owners must share in any indebtedness secured by a blanket lien in proportion to their undivided interests.

.10 *Options.* A co-owner may issue an option to purchase the co-owner's undivided interest (call option), provided that the exercise price for the call option reflects the fair market value of the Property determined as of the time the option is exercised. For this purpose, the fair market value of an undivided interest in the Property is equal to the co-owner's percentage interest in the Property multiplied by the fair market value of the Property as a whole. A co-owner may not acquire an option to sell the co-owner's undivided interest (put option) to the sponsor, the lessee, another co-owner, or the lender, or any person related to the sponsor, the lessee, another co-owner, or the lender.

.11 *No Business Activities.* The co-owners' activities must be limited to those customarily performed in connection with the maintenance and repair of rental real property (customary activities). See Rev. Rul. 75–374, 1975–2 C.B. 261. * * * In determining the co-owners' activities, all activities of the co-owners, their agents, and any persons related to the co-owners with respect to the Property will be taken into account, whether or not those activities are performed by the co-owners in their capacities as co-owners. * * *

.12 *Management and Brokerage Agreements.* The co-owners may enter into management or brokerage agreements, which must be renewable no less frequently than annually, with an agent, who may be the sponsor or a co-owner (or any person related to the sponsor or a co-owner), but who may not be a lessee. The management agreement may authorize the manager to maintain a common bank account for the collection and deposit of rents and to offset expenses associated with the Property against any revenues before disbursing each co-owner's share of net revenues. In all events, however, the manager must disburse to the co-owners their shares of net revenues within 3 months from the date of receipt of those revenues. The management agreement may also authorize the manager to prepare statements for the co-owners showing their shares of revenue and costs from the Property. In addition, the management agreement may authorize the manager to obtain or modify insurance on the Property, and to negotiate modifications of the terms of any lease or any indebtedness encumbering the Property, subject to the approval of the co-owners. * * * The determination of any fees paid by the co-ownership to the manager must not depend in whole or in part on the income or profits derived by any person from the Property and may not exceed the fair market value of the manager's services. Any fee paid by the co-ownership to a broker must be comparable to fees paid by unrelated parties to brokers for similar services.

.13 *Leasing Agreements.* All leasing arrangements must be bona fide leases for federal tax purposes. Rents paid by a lessee must reflect the fair market value for the use of the Property. The determination of the amount of the rent must not depend, in whole or in part, on the income or profits derived by any person from the Property leased (other than an amount based on a fixed percentage or percentages of receipts or sales). * * * Thus, for example, the amount of rent paid by a lessee may not be based on a percentage of net income from the Property, cash flow, increases in equity, or similar arrangements.

.14 *Loan Agreements.* The lender with respect to any debt that encumbers the Property or with respect to any debt incurred to acquire an undivided interest in the Property may not be a related person to any co-owner, the sponsor, the manager, or any lessee of the Property.

.15 *Payments to Sponsor.* Except as otherwise provided in this revenue procedure, the amount of any payment to the sponsor for the acquisition of the co-ownership interest (and the amount of any fees paid to the sponsor for services) must reflect the fair market value of the acquired co-ownership interest (or the services rendered) and may not depend, in whole or in part, on the income or profits derived by any person from the Property.

* * *

[¶ 16,045]

Note

Since partnerships are not subject to tax, what difference does it make whether a partnership has been formed? Do not attempt to answer this question now, but keep it in mind as you examine the following materials. For one example of the difference that classification can make, see the *Demirjian* case, at ¶ 18,035.

[¶ 16,050]

Problem

By devise under their father's will, A and B have acquired title to an apartment building as tenants in common. The building includes 50 apartments and they have retained a full-time resident agent to manage and supervise the property. The agent regularly employs four full-time employees to render janitorial and maintenance services. The agent executes the leases, collects rents, supervises maintenance, pays expenses, and remits the net proceeds to A and B. A regularly files her personal income tax return by the cash method on a calendar year basis; B, who is in a retail business, has filed her tax return for many years by the accrual method on the basis of a fiscal year ending March 31.

Are A and B partners? See Reg. § 301.7701–1(a)(1) and (2). If A and B are not partners, what is their relationship?

[¶ 16,055]

2.   ELECTING OUT OF SUBCHAPTER K

In limited circumstances, an entity that is classified as a partnership for tax purposes may nevertheless elect not to be subject to the provisions of Subchapter K. § 761(a). If that election is made, the participants in the activity are taxed directly on their share of the income and expense of the venture, and all tax elections are made by the individual participants rather than by the partnership entity.

In general, this election is available to ventures that are not engaged in the active conduct of a business either because the venture is engaged only in investment activities or because it is engaged in the production, but not the sale for joint profit, of property. The key to qualification for the election is that the venturers must reserve the right to take in kind or sell their own share of production (thus avoiding a joint profit), although each venturer may authorize one of their number to sell its share of the production for that venturer's own account provided that the delegation is for no longer than one year. See Reg. § 1.761–2(a). In some cases, quite substantial business ventures have been permitted to make this election. See, e.g., Madison Gas & Electric Co. v. Commissioner, at ¶ 16,040, (electric generating facility jointly owned by several utilities). In general, this election only affects the application of the rules of Subchapter K; for most other tax purposes, the venture is treated as a partnership. For a statutory exception to this general rule, see Section 1031(a)(2), which requires ignoring a partnership for which a Section 761(a) election has been made.

[¶ 16,060]

3.   LIMITED PARTNERSHIP VERSUS CORPORATION: FORMER ASSOCIATION REGULATIONS

Under former Reg. § 301.7701–2, the so-called "association regulations," any entity, whether or not incorporated under state law, was

¶ 16,060

subject to classification as an "association taxable as a corporation" for income tax purposes. A trust that had more than one beneficiary and was engaged in business, for example, normally was so classified. See ¶ 1080. Nevertheless, the most common, and controversial, use of the association regulations had been the attempt by the IRS to treat limited partnerships engaged in tax sheltering activities as associations and thus taxable under Subchapter C rather than Subchapter K. By treating the limited partnership as a C corporation for federal tax purposes, the government sought to prevent the flow-through of losses from the partnership to the partners since a C corporation's losses do not pass through to its shareholders. The association regulations thus became one of the government's weapons against tax shelter abuses.

Former Reg. § 301.7701–2(a)(1) listed six characteristics ordinarily found in a corporation: (1) associates; (2) objective to carry on a business and divide the profits therefrom (i.e., a joint profit objective); (3) centralization of management; (4) continuity of life; (5) free transferability of interests; and (6) limited liability. To classify an entity for tax purposes, the former regulations used a mechanical test in which each characteristic was equally weighted; an entity was treated as a corporation only if it possessed a majority of corporate characteristics. However, in classifying an entity as either a corporation or partnership, the first two characteristics—associates and joint profit objective—were disregarded since such characteristics are common to both types of business entities. Thus, a business entity was treated as a partnership rather than a corporation under these association regulations unless it possessed at least three out of the four remaining corporate characteristics.

These association regulations made it very difficult for the IRS to succeed in classifying partnerships as corporations for federal tax purposes, even in the case of a limited partnership in which only the general partners have liability for the debts of the partnership and which often has freely transferable interests. For example, in one leading case under the association regulations, the IRS sought to classify two limited partnerships as corporations, where their interests were freely transferable, they had centralized management, and they each had as their only general partner a corporation with no substantial assets and which was subject to removal by the limited partners (thus leading the IRS to argue that the partnerships also possessed the corporate attribute of limited liability). The Tax Court, however, held that the limited partnerships lacked limited liability because the sole corporate general partner was not a mere "dummy" for the limited partners and lacked continuity of life because they could be dissolved on the bankruptcy of the corporate general partner (regardless of how unlikely that event was to occur). Accordingly, the limited partnerships possessed only two of the four requisite corporate characteristics and were classified as partnerships for federal tax purposes. Larson v. Commissioner, 66 T.C. 159 (1976) (acq.).

¶ 16,060

[¶ 16,065]

4. THE RISE OF LIMITED LIABILITY COMPANIES

The classification criteria in the association regulations had been based on the historical differences between partnerships and corporations under state law. However, those differences became increasingly blurred as states revised their business enterprise laws to allow partnerships and other unincorporated entities to possess attributes that had been traditionally associated with corporations, such as limited liability for all equity owners. See IRS Notice 95–14, 1995–1 C.B. 297. One such development involved the modification of partnership statutes in some states to create a so-called limited liability partnership (LLP) and a limited liability limited partnership (LLLP) in which no partner was unconditionally liable for all partnership debts. See, e.g., Rev. Rul. 95–55, 1995–2 C.B. 313 (New York limited liability partnership classified as a partnership for federal tax purposes). An even more important development was the rise in the United States of a hybrid entity—the limited liability company (LLC).

The LLC is an entity created under state law that has the corporate attribute of limited liability under state law for all owners of the entity and the partnership attribute of pass-through treatment of income and losses for federal tax purposes. Although the LLC has existed in civil law countries for many years, Wyoming became the first state in the United States to enact a limited liability company statute in the 1970s. The LLC's early use in the United States was largely confined to natural resource ventures, but, since the late 1980s, the use of LLCs in a wide variety of business ventures has grown tremendously as all states and the District of Columbia have enacted their own LLC statutes. One reason for the increased use of LLCs in the United States is that foreign investors may invest in U.S. business activities through an LLC whereas they cannot do so through an S corporation.

An LLC has a number of advantages over limited partnerships and S corporations, the other two types of business entities that offer limited liability for their owners and pass-through treatment for tax purposes. The LLC's main advantage over a limited partnership is that a member of an LLC can participate in the management of the LLC without causing that member to lose the limited liability shield under state law. By contrast, under state law, a limited partner's participation in the control of the limited partnership can cause the partner to become liable for the partnership's obligations. However, changes in the limited partnership law of many states have significantly limited the circumstances under which the exercise of control by a limited partner could lead to loss of the limited partner's liability shield, thus reducing (but not eliminating) this advantage of the LLC over a limited partnership.

¶ 16,065

As discussed at ¶ 15,010, the LLC has three main advantages over S corporations. First, assuming, as is usually the case, that an LLC is treated as a partnership for federal tax purposes, its members have the flexibility under the partnership provisions of the Code to make special allocations of income and deductions among themselves. See § 704. By contrast, the income and losses of an S corporation generally are allocated pro rata to the corporation's shareholders in accordance with their stock holdings. See § 1366. Second, members of an LLC, like partners in a partnership, can include their share of the LLC's liabilities in their adjusted basis for the LLC interest. See § 752. By contrast, the shareholders of an S corporation generally cannot include their share of the corporation's liabilities in their adjusted basis for the corporation's stock. Third, an LLC is not subject to special tax rules limiting the identity or number of its shareholders or classes of ownership interests. By contrast, an S corporation cannot have a nonresident alien shareholder and must meet a 100–shareholder limit, a one class of stock requirement, and certain other eligibility requirements in order to elect and maintain S corporation status. See § 1361.

The main disadvantage of the LLC over the other pass-through entities is that since the LLC is a relatively new entity under state law, the law, both tax and nontax, concerning LLCs is not as well developed as it is with S corporations and partnerships. For example, although there is a large body of case law addressing the limits of corporate shareholder liability, there is not yet any such body of law delineating the limits of LLC member liability. Consequently, the nontax and tax legal consequences of operating the LLC are less certain than for S corporations and partnerships. Another disadvantage of the LLC over the limited partnership form is that it is more likely that an unwanted dissolution of the LLC will occur, since the LLC typically terminates on the death, resignation, expulsion, bankruptcy, or dissolution of any member. By contrast, a limited partnership generally dissolves only upon an event of dissolution occurring with respect to a general partner.

It was not until 1988 that the IRS announced its position on the classification of the Wyoming LLC for federal tax purposes under the former association regulations. In Rev. Rul. 88–76, 1988–2 C.B. 360 (declared obsolete by Rev. Rul. 98–37, 1998–2 C.B. 133), the IRS applied former Reg. § 301.7701–2 and classified a Wyoming LLC as a partnership for federal tax purposes because while the LLC had the corporate attributes of limited liability and centralized management, it lacked the corporate characteristics of continuity of life and free transferability of interests. In the succeeding years, the IRS issued a series of revenue rulings that classified LLCs formed under various other state statutes as partnerships for federal tax purposes. Rev. Rul. 93–38, 1993–1 C.B. 233 (also declared obsolete by Rev. Rul. 98–37, 1998–2 C.B. 133), was typical of the approach taken by the IRS in these rulings. If, as is true in many states, the LLC statute allowed its provisions to be modified by an LLC

¶ 16,065

agreement, Rev. Rul. 93–38 made clear that resolution of the classification issue depended on the provisions of the particular LLC agreement. Note that since LLCs typically have the corporate characteristic of limited liability, this meant that an LLC was classified as a partnership under the former association regulations, provided that it had no more than one additional corporate characteristic (i.e., centralized management, continuity of life, or free transferability of interests). Finally, in Rev. Proc. 95–10, 1995–1 C.B. 501, the IRS set forth its requirements for issuing a private ruling classifying a domestic or foreign LLC as a partnership for federal tax purposes and set the stage for the next major development in the entity classification area—promulgation of more explicitly elective entity classification regulations.

[¶ 16,070]

5. "CHECK–THE–BOX" ENTITY CLASSIFICATION REGULATIONS

As discussed above, the burgeoning LLC movement and other state law developments in the business enterprise area (such as the development of LLPs and LLLPs) undercut the traditional nontax distinctions between corporations and other types of business entities. Taxpayers and their advisers often could structure the business organization to achieve partnership classification for tax purposes even though the business organization resembled a corporation in all material respects. This classification process involved considerable expense for taxpayers and for the government which had to administer these entity classification standards and process taxpayer requests for classification rulings. In particular, the government was concerned that small businesses might not have the requisite expertise and resources to achieve the tax classification they wanted under the association regulations. See IRS Notice 95–14, 1995–1 C.B. 297. Thus, the Treasury concluded that the traditional entity classification regulations were formalistic and inefficient and, in 1996, replaced those regulations with an elective classification system (often called the "check-the-box" system).

Determining whether an entity exists. As discussed at ¶ 16,030, under the check-the-box entity classification regulations, the first step in the classification process is to determine whether a separate entity exists for federal tax purposes. This determination is a question of federal tax law and does not depend on whether the organization is recognized as a separate entity under local law. Reg. § 301.7701–1(a)(1). A joint venture or other contractual arrangement may create a separate entity for federal tax purposes if the participants carry on a joint business and divide the profits therefrom. By contrast, a mere cost sharing arrangement or mere co-ownership of property does not by itself create a separate entity for federal tax purposes. Reg. § 301.7701–1(a)(2).

¶ 16,070

Distinguishing between trusts and business entities. If a separate entity exists, the second step in the classification process is to determine whether the entity is a trust or a business entity. The check-the-box regulations basically retain the rules contained in the prior regulations on this issue, as discussed at ¶ 1090. If the entity is a trust, it will be taxed under the Code rules applicable to trusts. If the entity is a business entity, it may elect to be taxed as a corporation or as a partnership if it has two or more owners, or disregarded and not treated as separate from its owner if it has only one owner.

Per se corporations. Under the check-the-box regulations, certain business entities will be classified automatically as corporations for federal tax purposes; thus, these entities are not allowed to elect their classification. Reg. § 301.7701–2(b). Most importantly, these per se corporations include business entities incorporated under a federal or state statute. Also included in the per se corporation category are insurance companies, state-chartered business entities that conduct certain banking activities, and organizations wholly owned by a state. Publicly traded partnerships taxable as corporations under Section 7704 also are treated as per se corporations and may not elect their classification under these regulations. See ¶ 16,080.

In addition, the check-the-box regulations classify certain foreign business entities as per se foreign corporations for federal tax purposes. The list of such entities is set forth in the regulations. Reg. § 301.7701–2(b)(8). This list is updated and revised from time to time by the Treasury and the IRS.

"Eligible" entities may elect classification. If an entity is not a per se corporation under the above rules, it is called an "eligible entity" in the regulations and may elect its classification for federal tax purposes. An eligible entity with two or more members may elect to be classified as a corporation or a partnership for federal tax purposes. An eligible entity with a single member may elect to be classified as a corporation, or disregarded and not treated as separate from its owner (in tax parlance, often referred to by the oxymoronic term "disregarded entity"). Reg. § 301.7701–3(a). If the entity is disregarded, the regulations treat its activities in the same manner as a sole proprietorship, branch, or division of the owner. Reg. § 301.7701–2(a).

Default rules. For eligible entities that fail to make an election, the check-the-box regulations have default rules, which provide the classification that such entities could be expected to choose if they filed an election. If the eligible entity was not in existence before 1997, the default rules provide that a domestic entity with two or more members is classified as a partnership. A domestic entity with a single owner is disregarded as an entity separate from its owner under the default rules. Reg. § 301.7701–3(b)(1). An eligible foreign entity with two or more members is classified as a partnership if at least one member does not

¶ 16,070

have limited liability, or a corporation if all members have limited liability. A foreign entity with a single owner is treated as a corporation if the single owner has limited liability, and disregarded as an entity separate from its owner if the owner does not have limited liability. Reg. § 301.7701–3(b)(2).

Election mechanics. An eligible entity may affirmatively elect its classification or change its classification on Form 8832. The regulations require that the election be signed by each member of the entity or any officer, manager, or member of the entity who is authorized to make the election and who represents under penalties of perjury to have such authorization. The election form may specify an effective date that is not more than 75 days before or 12 months after the date on which the election is filed. If the election form specifies no effective date, the election will be effective on the date it is filed. If the election form specifies an effective date that is more than 75 days before the date the election is filed, the election will be effective 75 days before the date on which it is filed. If the election form specifies an effective date that is more than 12 months after the date the election is filed, the election will be effective 12 months after the date on which it was filed. Reg. § 301.7701–3(c).

Changes in entity classification. Under the check-the-box regulations, an eligible entity may elect to change its classification for federal tax purposes by filing an election on Form 8832. If an eligible entity makes an election to change its classification, it generally cannot change its classification again during the 60 months following the effective date of the election, unless the IRS consents to another change within the 60–month period. Reg. § 301.7701–3(c)(1)(iv).

A change in classification of an entity for federal tax purposes may have federal tax consequences. See Reg. § 301.7701–3(g). For example, a change in classification from a corporation to a partnership is treated as a liquidation of the corporation that will be analyzed under the rules discussed in Chapter 8 and a contribution by the shareholders of the liquidated corporation of all of the distributed assets and liabilities to a newly formed partnership. Reg. § 301.7701–3(g)(1)(ii). A change in classification from a partnership to a corporation is treated as a contribution by the partnership of all its assets and liabilities to the corporation in exchange for stock in the corporation and followed, immediately thereafter, by a liquidation of the partnership in which the partnership distributes the corporate stock to its partners. Reg. § 301.7701–3(g)(1)(i). That deemed liquidation of the partnership will be governed by the tax rules discussed in Chapters 23 and 24. If an eligible entity that is classified as a corporation elects to be disregarded as an entity separate from its owner, the regulations treat the corporation as having distributed all of its assets and liabilities to its single owner in liquidation of the corporation. Reg. § 301.7701–3(g)(1)(iii). That liquidation will be analyzed under the rules discussed in Chapter 8. If an eligible entity that is disregarded as an entity separate from its owner elects to be classified as a corporation, the regulations treat the owner of the eligible entity as having contributed all of the entity's assets and liabilities to the corporation in exchange for its stock. Reg. § 301.7701–3(g)(1)(iv). That exchange will be analyzed under the rules in Section 351 and the related provisions discussed in Chapter 2.

The regulations provide that classification of an eligible entity as a corporation is not affected by a change in the number of its members. On the other hand, a single member eligible entity that is disregarded as an entity separate from its owner is classified as a partnership as of the date the entity has more than one member. An eligible entity that is classified as a partnership is disregarded as an entity separate from its owner as of the date the entity has only one member. Reg. § 301.7701–3(f).

Treatment of entities in existence on effective date of check-the-box regulations. Under the check-the-box regulations, an eligible entity in existence before January 1, 1997, the effective date of the regulations, generally retains the same classification that it claimed under the former association regulations unless it properly elects to change that classification. However, an eligible entity with a single owner that claimed to be a partnership under the prior regulations will be disregarded as an entity separate from its owner. Reg. § 301.7701–3(b)(3).

[¶ 16,075]

Notes

1.   Did the Treasury Department have the legal authority to issue regulations that so dramatically changed the classification of business entities for federal tax purposes without obtaining specific legislative direction from the Congress? Even if it had such authority, was it sound as an administrative policy matter for the Treasury to issue these regulations without obtaining prior legislative approval? Note that in the *Littriello* case, excerpted at ¶ 1082, a federal district court applied the Supreme Court's decision in Chevron, U.S.A., Inc. v. Natural Resources Defense Council, Inc., 467 U.S. 837 (1984), and upheld the validity of the check-the-box regulations.

2.   Some states allow organizations with only one owner to form an LLC. Under the check-the-box regulations, a single member LLC is allowed to affirmatively elect to be treated as a corporation for federal tax purposes or be disregarded as an entity separate from its owner under the default rules.

What about an individual who conducts his or her business as a sole proprietorship? Can such an individual affirmatively elect to treat the sole proprietorship as a corporation for federal tax purposes without actually incorporating the business under state law? Does such a sole proprietorship constitute an "entity" with the meaning of the check-the-box regulations? Similar questions arise concerning a corporation's unincorporated branch. Does such an unincorporated branch constitute an "entity" that is eligible to elect its classification under the check-the-box rules?

3.   For the reasons discussed above, an LLC generally will elect to be classified as a partnership for federal tax purposes and thus will be governed by the provisions of Subchapter K of the Code. For purposes of applying the partnership provisions of the Code (including Sections 704(b) and 752), should manager-owners of the LLC be treated as general partners and all other owners of the LLC treated as limited partners?

4.   What are the tax policy implications of the burgeoning LLC movement? One obvious result of the LLC movement is a smaller number of business enterprises paying a corporate level income tax, thus further reducing the significance of Subchapter C. In effect, business enterprises that want both the corporate attribute of limited liability and only one level of income tax on the earnings of the business can achieve de facto corporate integration through the use of an LLC. Is this a desirable or undesirable result from a tax policy point of view? Does the increasing use of the LLC as a business entity represent an abuse of the tax system that Congress should correct by legislation? Or is the LLC movement a welcome development that should help lead to serious congressional consideration of more comprehensive corporate integration proposals beyond the "rough justice" partial integration approach Congress adopted in 2003 in Section 1(h)(11) of the Code?

[¶ 16,077]

Problems

1.   Tony is an individual taxpayer who operates his business as a sole proprietorship. What choices does he have concerning the classification of the business enterprise for federal income tax purposes?

2.   Emil and Betty are co-owners of a new unincorporated business that is just about to start its operations. What choices do they have concerning the classification of the business enterprise for federal income tax purposes?

3.   In Problem 2, if the business entity makes no affirmative classification election, how will it be classified for federal income tax purposes?

4.   Would your answer in Problem 2 change if Emil and Betty incorporated the business under state law?

5.   Would your answers in Problems 2 and 3 change if Emil and Betty organized the business as a limited liability company under state law?

6. Assume in Problem 2 that the entity elects in year 1 to be classified as a corporation for federal income tax purposes. May the entity elect to change its classification to a partnership in year 4? What would be the tax consequences of that change in entity classification?

7. In Problem 6, Emil and Betty change their minds and in year 7 would like the entity to change again its classification to a corporation for federal income tax purposes. May the entity do so?

8. Assume in Problem 2 that the entity elects in year 1 to be classified as a partnership for federal income tax purposes. Would the admission of a new partner in year 3 affect the classification of the business enterprise? What if the new partner, but not Emil and Betty, wants to change the classification of the entity for federal income tax purposes?

9. Diane is a U.S. citizen and the sole owner of a business that she organizes as a single member limited liability company under state law in year 1. What choices does she have concerning the classification of the entity for federal income tax purposes?

10. In Problem 9, if the entity makes no affirmative election, how will it be classified for federal income tax purposes?

11. Assume in Problem 9 that the limited liability company elects to be classified as a disregarded entity for federal income tax purposes. What happens to the classification of the entity if Diane sells part of her interest in the limited liability company to a buyer who becomes its second member? See also Rev. Rul. 99–5, at ¶ 17,007.

12. Assume in Problem 9 that the limited liability company files an election be an S corporation under Section 1362 but makes no explicit entity classification election. How will the entity be classified for federal income tax purposes? Is the entity eligible to file an election to be an S corporation even though it is not incorporated under state or federal law? See § 1361(b); Reg. § 301.7701–3(c)(1)(v)(C); and Rev. Proc. 2004–48, at ¶ 15,063.

[¶ 16,080]

6. PUBLICLY TRADED PARTNERSHIPS

In a 1983 report prepared by the Staff of the Senate Finance Committee, it was proposed that limited partnerships with publicly traded interests be taxed as corporations. This proposal had the support of the American Law Institute. It was premised on the inherent inequity of extending tax exemption to these large centralized business organizations while the ordinary corporate business is subjected to the corporate income tax as a separate taxable entity. Moreover, it was argued that such limited partnerships should be classified as corporations because the method of raising capital and marketing of the partnership interests closely resembled the methods customarily used by corporations and the partnership interests were freely transferable. See Larson v. Commissioner, 66 T.C. 159, 194–95 (1976) (acq.) (dissenting opinion of Judge Simpson).

The Treasury Department in its 1984 report on *Tax Reform for Fairness, Simplification and Economic Growth* recommended a somewhat broader change. Under the Treasury proposal, limited partnerships with more than 35 partners would have been taxed as corporations. This rule would have paralleled the then existing 35–shareholder limitation that was applicable to S corporations (under current law, the limit is 100 shareholders). Although this proposal was not enacted as part of the Tax Reform Act of 1986, action was taken with respect to publicly traded partnerships in 1987.

One consequence of the 1986 Act's reduction in the maximum federal income tax rate on individuals was the proliferation of so-called master limited partnerships. These are limited partnerships organized to carry on major business activities, such as natural resource exploration and exploitation, equipment leasing, and real estate operations, with large numbers of limited partners and with public trading of the limited partnership interests. The objective of the master limited partnerships was to achieve limited liability and free transferability of equity interests comparable to those of a corporation but free of the imposition of the corporate income tax. In the case of master limited partnerships engaged in natural resource activities, another objective was the pass-through of tax incentives to the limited partners.

Concerned that the burgeoning of master limited partnerships would result in a serious erosion of the corporate income tax base, Congress enacted Section 7704 as part of the Revenue Act of 1987, under which "publicly traded partnerships" are to be treated as corporations. A "publicly traded partnership" is defined in Section 7704(b) as any partnership if—

> "(1) interests in such partnership are traded on an established securities market, or
>
> (2) interests in such partnership are readily tradable on a secondary market (or the substantial equivalent thereof)."

An exception is made in Section 7704(c), however, for a publicly traded partnership if, for each taxable year starting after 1987 during which it was in existence, 90 percent or more of its gross income constitutes "qualifying income." Qualifying income is defined in Section 7704(d) to include, for example, interest, dividends, real property rents, gain from the disposition of real property, capital assets, or Section 1231(b) property, and certain mineral or natural resource income. The qualifying income exception does not apply to a partnership that would qualify as a regulated investment company under Section 851 if it were a domestic corporation. § 7704(c)(3). The qualifying income exception will be available, to the extent provided in regulations, to a partnership that

¶ 16,080

has, as a principal activity, the buying and selling of commodities or options, futures or forward contracts with respect to commodities. Id.

If the IRS determines that the partnership's failure to meet the 90 percent qualifying income test during any taxable year was inadvertent, the partnership will not be treated as a corporation provided that—

(1) no later than a reasonable time after the discovery of such failure, steps are taken so that such partnership once more meets that test, and

(2) the partnership agrees to make such adjustments as may be required by the IRS with respect to such period.

§ 7704(e).

The regime for publicly traded partnerships did not apply until taxable years starting after 1997 to partnerships that were "existing partnerships" on December 17, 1987, including, for example, a partnership that was publicly traded or had a registration statement on file with the SEC on that date. Moreover, under Section 7704(g), enacted as part of the Taxpayer Relief Act of 1997, a grandfathered partnership may elect to continue its "existing partnership" status for taxable years starting after 1997, but it is subject to a tax of 3.5 percent of its gross income from any active trades or businesses.

A partnership not grandfathered as an "existing partnership" on December 17, 1987, will be treated as a corporation on the first day it is publicly traded. On that day it will be treated as having transferred all of its assets (subject to all of its liabilities) to a newly formed corporation in exchange for that corporation's stock and as having distributed the stock to the partners in liquidation of their interests in the partnership. § 7704(f).

Note that, under Section 7704, a partnership will be treated as a corporation and will not be eligible to elect its classification under the check-the-box regulations if it possesses just one of the corporate criteria contained in the former association regulations: freely transferable interests. Does that sole attribute justify taxation of the entity under Subchapter C rather than under Subchapter K?

[¶ 16,085]

C. ANTI–ABUSE RULES: IRS DISREGARD OF THE PARTNERSHIP FORM

Since the enactment of Subchapter K in 1954, there has been a substantial increase in the use of the partnership form as a vehicle for conducting legitimate business enterprises. This increased use of the partnership form is consistent with congressional intent in enacting Subchapter K to provide "simplicity, flexibility, and equity as between the partners" for businesses conducted through the partnership form. H.R. Rep. No. 1337, 83d Cong., 2d Sess. 65 (1954); S. Rep. No. 1622, 83d Cong., 2d Sess. 89 (1954). Unfortunately, however, during the ensuing years, there also has been an increase in the use of the partnership as a tax avoidance device. Some tax planners have structured transactions that use a partnership to attempt to circumvent other provisions of the Code or to create tax advantages that are inconsistent with the substance of the transaction, a use that contravenes the legislative intent underlying the enactment of Subchapter K. See T.D. 8588, 1995–1 C.B. 109. As will be discussed throughout the succeeding chapters, at times, Congress has responded to these perceived abuses by enacting changes in the statute that respond to the abuses, often in conjunction with a broad delegation of regulatory authority to the Treasury Department to craft regulations that deal specifically with those abuses. However, during the past fifteen years or so, inappropriate tax results from the misuse of the partnership form have outpaced the capacity of Congress or the Treasury to respond adequately. To deal with this problem, the Treasury has been asserting broad authority to attack abusive partnership transactions. There are at least six major developments that should be mentioned in this respect.

First, in 1993, Congress added Section 7701(l) to the Code, which broadly authorizes the Treasury Department to issue regulations "recharacterizing any multiple-party financing transaction as a transaction directly among any 2 or more of such parties" where the Treasury determines that such recharacterization is appropriate to prevent tax avoidance. The first set of regulations issued under the authority of Section 7701(l), released in final form in 1995, appropriately dealt with international tax issues under Sections 871, 881, 1441, and 6038A, which were a prime congressional concern underlying the enactment of Section 7701(l). These regulations did not directly deal with financing transactions involving the use of a partnership. The other sets of proposed and final regulations that have been issued to date under Section 7701(l), which have dealt with the recharacterization of various other types of financing arrangements, also have not focused on transactions involving the use of a partnership. However, it is possible that future regulations under Section 7701(l) will allow the IRS to disregard or recast some financing arrangements using partnerships where necessary to prevent tax avoidance.

Second, from time to time, the IRS has issued guidance about particular transactions involving partnerships the form of which it will not respect for federal income tax purposes. For example, in IRS Notice 94–48, 1994–1 C.B. 357, the IRS indicated that it would scrutinize and recast certain financing transactions involving partnerships even without the assistance of Section 7701(l). Of particular concern to the IRS in this Notice were transactions designed to provide a corporation with the tax benefits of issuing debt even though the corporation actually issues stock. As an example, the Notice described a transaction in which a corporation creates a partnership to achieve its financing objectives and contributes money to the partnership in return for a limited partnership interest. A general partner then also contributes money to the partnership. The partnership issues debt instruments to third-party investors and a significant portion of the capital raised by the partnership in this transaction is thereafter used to purchase newly issued preferred stock of the corporation. As a limited partner in the partnership, the corporation attempts to deduct its distributive share of the interest paid by the partnership on its debt instruments. The IRS, however, indicated that it would attack transactions of this type and recast them in accordance with their overall economic substance—a simple issuance of preferred stock by the corporation with no corporate interest deduction.

Third, the Treasury has issued regulations under some provisions of Subchapter K that have their own anti-abuse rules. Thus, for example, as discussed at ¶ 22,090, in the case of a transaction a principal purpose of which is to achieve tax results inconsistent with Section 704(c)(1)(B), the regulations under that provision broadly authorize the IRS to recast a transaction as appropriate to achieve results consistent with the purpose of Section 704(c)(1)(B). Reg. § 1.704–4(f)(1). A similar anti-abuse rule has been issued under Section 737, discussed at ¶ 22,095. Reg. § 1.737–4(a).

Fourth, most significantly, in a regulation issued under Section 701, the IRS has asserted authority to recast a transaction for federal tax purposes where "a partnership is formed or availed of in connection with a transaction a principal purpose of which is to reduce substantially the present value of the partners' aggregate federal tax liability in a manner that is inconsistent with the intent of subchapter K." Reg. § 1.701–2(b). If the requisite use of the partnership in a manner inconsistent with the intent of Subchapter K exists, the regulation authorizes the IRS, where appropriate, to (i) disregard the purported partnership and treat the partnership's assets and activities as owned and conducted by one or more of its purported partners; (ii) treat one or more of the purported partners as not a partner; (iii) adjust the partnership's or a partner's method of tax accounting to clearly reflect income; (iv) reallocate an item of partnership income, gain, loss, deduction, or credit; or (v) otherwise adjust or modify the claimed tax treatment.

In addition, the regulation broadly authorizes the IRS to treat a partnership as an aggregate of its partners (in whole or in part) as appropriate to carry out the purpose of any provision of the Code or regulations. However, this aggregation authority does not apply to the extent that (i) a provision of the Code or regulations prescribes entity treatment for the partnership and (ii) that entity treatment and the ultimate tax results are "clearly contemplated" by the Code or regulation provision. Reg. § 1.701–2(e).

¶ 16,085

In applying this regulation, the purposes for structuring a partnership transaction are to be determined based on all of the facts and circumstances, "including a comparison of the purported business purpose for a transaction and the claimed tax benefits resulting from the transaction." Reg. § 1.701–2(c). The regulation contains a list of illustrative (nonexclusive) factors that indicate that the partnership was used in a manner inconsistent with the intent of Subchapter K. Id. The regulation also contains a number of examples that illustrate the application of the principles of these anti-abuse rules. See Reg. § 1.701–2(d) and (f).

As would be expected, this anti-abuse regulation received a heated response from the practicing bar when it was first issued in proposed form in May 1994. Questions were raised about the Treasury's authority to issue such a broad anti-abuse rule without obtaining legislative approval and about the wisdom of issuing such a broad anti-abuse rule that contains no safe harbors (other than by way of example) or de minimis rules exempting transactions from the application of the rule. Further, many practitioners claimed that the regulation would have a chilling effect on legitimate business transactions involving the use of a partnership because of the cloud the regulation casts over the certainty of tax results for all partnership transactions (an unsubstantiated claim often made by the bar about anti-abuse rules in the federal tax area). By contrast, other commentators (including many tax academics) argued that the anti-abuse rule was an appropriate response by the Treasury to the misuse of partnership provisions by overly aggressive tax practitioners.

Some twelve years after it was first proposed, there is scant evidence that this anti-abuse rule has had the dramatic effect on the legitimate business use of the partnership form that its detractors predicted it would. In fact, one could argue that given the rise in the marketing of corporate and other tax shelter transactions during the past 10 years, many of which involve the use of partnerships, it is not clear that this anti-abuse regulation has been anywhere near as effective as its drafters had hoped it would be in stemming abuse of the provisions of Subchapter K. At a minimum, however, one can safely say that the rule makes life even more complicated for the tax planner in the partnership tax area.

Fifth, as the anti-abuse regulation itself makes clear, the IRS can continue to use judicial doctrines like substance over form, business purpose, and step transaction to challenge abusive partnership transactions; the regulatory anti-abuse rule is merely intended to provide the IRS with another weapon in its arsenal. See Reg. § 1.701–2(i). Thus, the IRS has been active in litigating partnership transactions that it views as abusive in nature and arguing that literal interpretations of the statute or regulations in certain situations achieve grossly erroneous tax results. For example, in appropriate circumstances, the IRS has successfully asserted that a partner's share of losses realized by a partnership should be disallowed because the transaction lacks economic substance and serves no substantial nontax business purpose. See, e.g., ACM Partnership v. Commissioner, T.C. Memo. 1997–115, aff'd in part, rev'd in part, 157 F.3d 231 (3d Cir.1998), cert. denied, 526 U.S. 1017 (1999) (corporate partner's deduction for its share of foreign partnership's capital losses realized in complex series of transactions disallowed because the transactions lacked economic substance and served no business purpose); ASA Investerings Partnership v. Commissioner, T.C. Memo. 1998–305, aff'd, 201 F.3d 505 (D.C.Cir.), cert. denied, 531 U.S. 871 (2000) (involving similar transactions to those in the *ACM* case and holding that a partnership formed in these transactions was organized solely to reduce domestic corporate taxpayer's tax liability and therefore was not a separate entity and its income was attributed to the domestic corporation). In another recent case involving a somewhat complicated cross-border transaction using a partnership, the IRS was successful in having the transaction recast in accordance with its economic substance and deduction of the claimed losses disallowed. See Long Term Capital Holdings v. United States, 330 F. Supp. 2d 122 (D. Conn. 2004), aff'd without published opinion, 2005–2 U.S.T.C. (CCH) ¶ 50,575, 96 A.F.T.R.2d (RIA) 6344 (2d Cir. 2005).

Finally, another approach Congress, the Treasury, and the IRS have taken to deal with certain abusive transactions that fall within the "tax shelter" category, including those involving the use of partnerships, is to require disclosure by taxpayers and their "material advisors" with respect to transactions that fall within the definition of "reportable transactions." See §§ 6011 and 6111; Reg. § 1.6011–4. The statute defines reportable transactions as certain transactions that the Treasury and the IRS identify in regulations as of a type having a potential for tax avoidance or evasion. See § 6707A(c)(1). This disclosure regime also requires material advisors to maintain lists identifying each person with respect to whom they acted as a material adviser for a reportable transaction. See § 6112. One aspect of these provisions that has drawn the close attention of tax practitioners is that the statute imposes significant monetary penalties on taxpayers and their material advisors who do not follow the disclosure and list maintenance requirements. See §§ 6707A and 6708. Keep in mind that tax attorneys and accountants who advise taxpayers with respect to "reportable transactions" may be "material advisors" subject to these requirements and the serious monetary penalties for noncompliance. It is fair to say that these provisions increase substantially the financial risks for tax advisers who engage in abusive tax planning activities.

[¶ 16,090]

D. CHOICE OF ENTITY CONSIDERATIONS

As suggested by the material in this Chapter, a crucial question in planning for the formation of any business enterprise is whether the business should be conducted through a C corporation, S corporation, partnership, or LLC. The resolution of that planning question will depend on a wide range of legal and financial considerations, of both a tax and nontax nature. Introductory discussions of these considerations are set forth at ¶ 1055 and at ¶¶ 15,010–15,015.

In helping a client to resolve the choice of entity issue, the tax adviser must consider each of the three distinct patterns of taxation applicable to partnerships and LLCs (in Subchapter K), S corporations (in Subchapter S), and C corporations (in Subchapter C). As you progress through your study of partnership taxation in the succeeding chapters, compare the tax consequences produced by Subchapter K with the consequences that would have been produced by the other two regimes for taxing business entities.

Chapter 17

PARTNERSHIP FORMATION

[¶ 17,000]

A. INTRODUCTION

One of the fundamental principles of Subchapter K is that a transfer of property between a partner and the partnership will not be a taxable event. In the context in which that principle is about to be examined, i.e., the transfer of property to partnerships, its application is not surprising from either the technical or the policy perspective. Property transfers to partnerships are nonrecognition/carryover basis transactions very much like other transactions that are entitled to nonrecognition treatment under the Code. From a policy perspective, the nontaxability of the formation of a partnership closely resembles the tax consequences of the formation of a corporation under Section 351 and appears to reflect the same premise: that the creation of a business entity represents a mere change in the form of ownership of business assets and ought not be impeded by the imposition of tax. Significantly, however, the scope of Section 721 is far broader than the scope of Section 351.

B. CONTRIBUTIONS OF CAPITAL

[¶ 17,005]

1. TAXATION OF THE TRANSFER

Under Section 721, neither gain nor loss is recognized by a partner or by a partnership upon the transfer of property to the partnership in exchange for a partnership interest. To preserve that deferred gain or loss for possible future recognition, Section 723 provides that the partnership's adjusted basis in the contributed property normally will be the same as the adjusted basis of the property in the hands of the partner (a "carryover basis"). In addition, Section 722 provides that the basis of the partnership interest received by the transferor partner will be the same as the transferor's adjusted basis in the contributed property (a "substituted basis").

Under Section 1223(2), the partnership's holding period for contributed property includes the holding period of the partner. However, the partner's holding period for the partnership interest will include the holding period of contributed property only to the extent that the property was a capital asset or an asset described in Section 1231. § 1223(1).

The net effect of these provisions is similar to results that obtain for certain contributions of property to corporations. See §§ 351, 358, and 362. The application of the rules for contributions to partnerships are not, however, conditioned on the satisfaction of a "control" requirement, such as that imposed by Section 351 in respect of corporations. See ¶ 2040. As a result, Section 721 is much broader than Section 351. The transfer of a single asset to the partnership by one partner owning a minor interest in the partnership will qualify for nonrecognition treatment. Why would the nonrecognition provisions for contributions to partnerships be broader than those for contributions to corporations?

There are two statutory exceptions to the general rule of nonrecognition in Section 721. The first exception in Section 721(b) denies nonrecognition treatment to gain realized on a transfer of property to a partnership that would be treated as an investment company (as defined in Section 351) if the partnership were incorporated. This exception parallels an exception to nonrecognition treatment on incorporation transfers in Section 351(e) (see ¶ 2100) and is based on the theory that the diversification in the taxpayer's investment assets resulting from a transfer to an investment partnership is a change in the substance (not merely the form) of the taxpayer's investment and thus falls outside the intended scope of Section 721.

The second exception in Section 721(c) was added in legislation enacted in 1997 and denies nonrecognition treatment to a gain realized on a transfer to a partnership (to the extent provided in regulations) if the gain when recognized by the partnership will be includible in the gross income of a foreign partner. The purpose of this provision is to preserve U.S. taxing jurisdiction over the precontribution gain in the property by triggering gain recognition to the contributing partner at the time of contribution if such gain on later recognition by the partnership would be allocable to a foreign partner who would not be subject to U.S. tax on such gain.

These principles are applied in the following ruling. The ruling involves a single member limited liability company classified as a disregarded entity that becomes an entity with more than one member classified as a partnership for federal income tax purposes.

¶ **17,005**

[¶ 17,007]

REVENUE RULING 99–5

1999–1 C.B. 434.

ISSUE

What are the federal income tax consequences when a single member domestic limited liability company (LLC) that is disregarded for federal tax purposes as an entity separate from its owner under section 301.7701–3 of the * * * Regulations becomes an entity with more than one owner that is classified as a partnership for federal tax purposes?

FACTS

In each of the following two situations, an LLC is formed and operates in a state which permits an LLC to have a single owner. Each LLC has a single owner, A, and is disregarded as an entity separate from its owner for federal tax purposes under § 301.7701–3. In both situations, the LLC would not be treated as an investment company (within the meaning of section 351) if it were incorporated. All of the assets held by each LLC are capital assets or property described in section 1231. For the sake of simplicity, it is assumed that neither LLC is liable for any indebtedness, nor are the assets of the LLCs subject to any indebtedness.

Situation 1. B, who is not related to A, purchases 50% of A's ownership interest in the LLC for $5,000. A does not contribute any portion of the $5,000 to the LLC. A and B continue to operate the business of the LLC as co-owners of the LLC.

Situation 2. B, who is not related to A, contributes $10,000 to the LLC in exchange for a 50% ownership interest in the LLC. The LLC uses all of the contributed cash in its business. A and B continue to operate the business of the LLC as co-owners of the LLC.

After the sale, in both situations, no entity classification election is made under § 301.7701–3(c) to treat the LLC as an association for federal tax purposes.

LAW AND ANALYSIS

Section 721(a) generally provides that no gain or loss shall be recognized to a partnership or to any of its partners in the case of a contribution of property to the partnership in exchange for an interest in the partnership.

Section 722 provides that the basis of an interest in a partnership acquired by a contribution of property, including money, to the partnership shall be the amount of the money and the adjusted basis of the property to the contributing partner at the time of the contribution increased by the amount (if any) of gain recognized under § 721(b) to the contributing partner at such time.

Section 723 provides that the basis of property contributed to a partnership by a partner shall be the adjusted basis of the property to the contributing partner at the time of the contribution increased by the amount (if any) of gain recognized under § 721(b) to the contributing partner at such time.

Section 1001(a) provides that the gain or loss from the sale or other disposition of property shall be the difference between the amount realized therefrom and the adjusted basis provided in § 1011.

Section 1223(1) provides that, in determining the holding period of a taxpayer who receives property in an exchange, there shall be included the period for which the taxpayer held the property exchanged if the property has the same basis in whole or in part in the taxpayer's hands as the property exchanged, and the property exchanged at the time of the exchange was a capital asset or property described in § 1231.

Section 1223(2) provides that, regardless of how a property is acquired, in determining the holding period of a taxpayer who holds the property, there shall be included the period for which such property was held by any other person if the property has the same basis in whole or in part in the taxpayer's hands as it would have in the hands of such other person.

HOLDING(S)

Situation 1. In this situation, the LLC, which, for federal tax purposes, is disregarded as an entity separate from its owner, is converted to a partnership when the new member, *B*, purchases an interest in the disregarded entity from the owner, *A*. *B*'s purchase of 50% of *A*'s ownership interest in the LLC is treated as the purchase of a 50% interest in each of the LLC's assets, which are treated as held directly by *A* for federal tax purposes. Immediately thereafter, *A* and *B* are treated as contributing their respective interests in those assets to a partnership in exchange for ownership interests in the partnership.

Under § 1001, *A* recognizes gain or loss from the deemed sale of the 50% interest in each asset of the LLC to *B*.

Under § 721(a), no gain or loss is recognized by *A* or *B* as a result of the conversion of the disregarded entity to a partnership.

Under § 722, *B*'s basis in the partnership interest is equal to $5,000, the amount paid by *B* to *A* for the assets which *B* is deemed to contribute to the newly-created partnership. *A*'s basis in the partnership interest is equal to *A*'s basis in *A*'s 50% share of the assets of the LLC.

Under § 723, the basis of the property treated as contributed to the partnership by *A* and *B* is the adjusted basis of that property in *A*'s and *B*'s hands immediately after the deemed sale.

¶ 17,007

Under § 1223(1), *A*'s holding period for the partnership interest received includes *A*'s holding period in the capital assets and property described in § 1231 held by the LLC when it converted from an entity that was disregarded as an entity separate from *A* to a partnership. *B*'s holding period for the partnership interest begins on the day following the date of *B*'s purchase of the LLC interest from *A*. See Rev. Rul. 66–7, 1966–1 C.B. 188, which provides that the holding period of a purchased asset is computed by excluding the date on which the asset is acquired. Under § 1223(2), the partnership's holding period for the assets deemed transferred to it includes *A*'s and *B*'s holding periods for such assets.

Situation 2. In this situation, the LLC is converted from an entity that is disregarded as an entity separate from its owner to a partnership when a new member, *B*, contributes cash to the LLC. *B*'s contribution is treated as a contribution to a partnership in exchange for an ownership interest in the partnership. *A* is treated as contributing all of the assets of the LLC to the partnership in exchange for a partnership interest.

Under § 721(a), no gain or loss is recognized by *A* or *B* as a result of the conversion of the disregarded entity to a partnership.

Under § 722, *B*'s basis in the partnership interest is equal to $10,000, the amount of cash contributed to the partnership. *A*'s basis in the partnership interest is equal to *A*'s basis in the assets of the LLC which *A* was treated as contributing to the newly-created partnership.

Under § 723, the basis of the property contributed to the partnership by *A* is the adjusted basis of that property in *A*'s hands. The basis of the property contributed to the partnership by *B* is $10,000, the amount of cash contributed to the partnership.

Under § 1223(1), *A*'s holding period for the partnership interest received includes *A*'s holding period in the capital and § 1231 assets deemed contributed when the disregarded entity converted to a partnership. *B*'s holding period for the partnership interest begins on the day following the date of *B*'s contribution of money to the LLC. Under § 1223(2), the partnership's holding period for the assets transferred to it includes *A*'s holding period.

* * *

[¶ 17,008]

Note

A partner's holding period for a partnership interest will be divided if the partner acquires portions of the interest at different times or if the partner acquired portions of the interest in exchange for items of property transferred at the same time but that result in different holding periods (e.g., only some of the items of property transferred result in the tacking of holding period(s) under Section 1223(1)). Regulations issued in 2000 provide rules for determining the holding periods of a partner's interest in a partnership when such a holding period is divided. Under the general rule, the portion of a partnership interest to which a holding period relates is determined by reference to a fraction—the numerator of the fraction is the fair market value of the portion of the partnership interest received in the transaction to which the holding period relates and the denominator of the fraction is the fair market value of the partner's entire partnership interest (determined immediately after the transaction). Reg. § 1.1223–3(b)(1). Accordingly, a partner will be able to tack holding period(s) under Section 1223(1) only with respect to the portions of the partnership interest attributable to the fair market values of the capital and Section 1231 assets contributed by the partner to the partnership (determined at the time of contribution); Section 1223(1) tacking of holding period(s) generally will not apply to the portion of the partnership interest attributable to cash or the fair market value of ordinary income assets contributed by the partner to the partnership (also determined at the time of contribution). This general rule is illustrated by the following two examples drawn in substantial part from the regulations:

Example 1. X contributes the following assets to a partnership in exchange for a 50–percent interest in the partnership: $10,000 of cash and a nondepreciable capital asset held by X for 14 months which has a fair market value of $30,000 and in which X has an adjusted basis of $2,000. After the exchange, under Section 722, X's basis in the partnership interest is equal to $12,000, the amount of cash contributed plus the adjusted basis of the capital asset contributed to the partnership, and the fair market value of the partnership interest is $40,000. X received one-fourth of the interest in the partnership for the $10,000 of cash contributed ($10,000/$40,000) and three-fourths of the interest in exchange for the capital asset contributed ($30,000/$40,000). Accordingly, X's holding period in one-fourth of the partnership interest starts on the day after the contribution and X's holding period in the other three-fourths of the partnership interest is 14 months under Section 1223(1) (i.e., X tacks the holding period for the capital asset on to the holding period for the partnership interest). See Reg. § 1.1223–3(f), Ex. 1.

Example 2. M, N, and O are equal partners in a partnership that was formed on January 2 of year 1, with cash contributions by each partner. The initial holding period for each partner in the partnership interest starts on January 3 of year 1. On February 1 of year 4, each partner contributes an additional $20,000 cash to partnership capital, thereby increasing each partner's basis in the partnership interest by $20,000 under Section 722 and increasing the fair market value of each partner's partnership interest to $100,000. As a result of the additional cash contribution, each partner has a new holding period starting on February 2 of year 4 in the one-fifth portion of the partnership interest attributable to the additional contribution ($20,000/$100,000). Each partner's holding period in the remaining four-fifths portion of the partnership interest still starts on January 3 of year 1. See Reg. § 1.1223–3(f), Ex. 4.

Under these regulations, if a partner sells or exchanges the partner's entire interest in a partnership, any capital gain or loss recognized on the transaction is divided between long-term and short-term capital gain or loss in the same proportions as the selling partner's holding period of the partnership is divided between the portion of the interest held for more than one year and the portion held for one year or less. Reg. § 1.1223–3(c)(1). If a partner has taxable capital gain or loss on account of a distribution from the partnership, the capital gain or loss recognized is divided between long-term and short-term capital gain or loss in the same proportion as the long-term or short-term capital gain or loss that the distributee partner would realize if her entire partnership interest were transferred in a fully taxable transaction immediately before the distribution. Reg. § 1.1223–3(d)(2).

[¶ 17,010]

2. TAX VERSUS FINANCIAL ACCOUNTING: THE "CAPITAL ACCOUNT"

Because contributions of property to a partnership are carryover basis transactions, the tax books of the partnership will reflect the partnership properties at an adjusted basis that will almost always differ from the value of those properties at the time of the contribution. The practical consequences of such differences may be illustrated with the following simple example.

Assume that Al and Bea formed a partnership. Al contributed property having a basis of $40 and a value of $100; Bea contributed cash of $100. Al would have a basis for his partnership interest of $40; Bea would have a basis of $100. The partnership would have a total basis in its properties of $140 ($40 basis in the property contributed by Al plus the $100 cash contributed by Bea), even though the value of the properties was $200. The bases of the properties for tax purposes obviously do not reflect either the economic posture of the partnership or the respective interests of the partners. For example, if the partnership were immediately liquidated, Al and Bea would each expect to receive distributions of $100. Al would presumably not be enthusiastic about a distribution in which he received an amount equal to his basis of $40 and the $60 gain was split between him and Bea (so that he received only $70 while she received $130).

In order to reflect accurately their economic interests in the partnership, Al and Bea will have to keep a separate set of books. See Reg. § 1.704–1(b)(2)(ii)(*b*)(*1*). These books, referred to generally as the "capital accounts," would reflect the fair market value of contributed property rather than the tax basis of that property. Reg. § 1.704–1(b)(2)(iv)(*b*) and (*d*). As the partnership derives income and losses, these capital accounts will be adjusted by the amounts thereof allocated to each partner. Reg. § 1.704–1(b)(2)(iv)(*b*). If the partnership distributes cash or other property to partners, their respective capital accounts will be reduced by the value of the distributions. See Reg. § 1.704–1(b)(2)(iv)(*b*) and (*e*).

[¶ 17,015]

Problems

1.   The ABCD partnership is formed by four friends. In exchange for the following properties, each partner obtained a 25–percent interest in the partnership:

Able   Cash of $50,000

Baker   Section 1245 property (i.e., equipment) originally purchased five years ago for $100,000 but having a basis of $20,000 and a value of $50,000

Cathy   Lots held by her as inventory having a basis of $15,000 and a value of $30,000, and Accounts Receivable having no tax basis and a value of $20,000, all of which Cathy acquired 14 months ago

Donna   Land having a basis of $70,000 and a value of $50,000, which Donna acquired three years ago.

   a.   How much gain or loss will be recognized on the exchange by each partner and the partnership?

   b.   What is each partner's basis and initial holding period in his or her partnership interest?

   c.   What is each partner's initial capital account in the partnership?

   d.   What is the partnership's basis and initial holding period in each asset transferred to it?

2.   The Investco Group is a partnership in which three individuals hold equal interests. The partnership has assets worth $75,000 and no liabilities. Nancy has agreed to contribute to the partnership her portfolio of publicly traded stock, which is worth $25,000 and has a basis of $10,000. Nancy will receive a 25–percent interest in the partnership capital and profits. What are the tax consequences of the transaction to Nancy and the partnership? Would the consequences differ if some stocks had declined in value since their acquisition? How do these results compare to those that would apply if Investco were a corporation?

[¶ 17,020]

3.   CAPITAL CONTRIBUTION OR SALE?

Because of the breadth of Section 721, virtually all transfers of property by a partner to a partnership may qualify for nonrecognition.

On the other hand, Section 707(a) permits a partner to act as a nonpartner in dealing with the partnership. Accordingly, whenever a partner transfers property to a partnership and the partnership thereafter transfers cash or property to the partner, the transfers must be classified either as a contribution and distribution, the tax consequences of which are determined under Sections 721 and 731, or as a fully taxable sale. What factors should govern that characterization issue?

In prior years, the courts had great difficulty in drawing the line between contributions and sales—just as they have experienced great difficulty in resolving the similar issue when a shareholder transfers property to a corporation. In an attempt to defuse this issue, in 1984, Congress amended Section 707(a) to authorize the Treasury to issue regulations defining sales by partners. That legislation, the case law history that led to it, and the regulations issued under amended Section 707(a) are examined in Chapter 20.

[¶ 17,025]

C. EFFECT OF PARTNERSHIP DEBT ON PARTNERS' BASIS

If a partner borrows cash to invest in a partnership, the amount borrowed and invested will, of course, increase the adjusted basis of that partner's partnership interest. Often, however, the partners will prefer that the partnership itself borrow the funds to be used in the business. If such a partnership level borrowing did not likewise increase the basis of the partnership interests, a serious trap for the partners would be created. While the borrowing would result in an increase in the basis of the partnership's properties, losses attributable to the exhaustion of that basis might well exceed the basis of the partnership interests and thus could not be claimed currently by the partners. That result is avoided by the aggregate approach embodied in Section 752, which effectively treats a partnership borrowing as if it were a borrowing by the partners themselves followed by a contribution by them of the loan proceeds to the partnership. In this respect, the taxation of partnerships is vastly more favorable to their owners than is the taxation of S corporations. The shareholders of an S corporation generally cannot include their share of the corporation's liabilities in their adjusted basis for the corporation's stock. See ¶¶ 15,290 et seq.

[¶ 17,030]

1. THE GENERAL SCHEME OF SECTION 752

Section 752(a) provides that any increase in a partner's share of partnership liabilities, as would occur when the partnership borrows, is to be treated as a "contribution of money" by the partner to the partnership. Correspondingly, Section 752(b) provides that any decrease in partnership liabilities is treated as a "distribution of money" by the partnership to the partners to the extent of the reduction in their respective shares of the liabilities. Accordingly, any increase in the liabilities of the partnership will result in an increase in the adjusted bases of the partnership interests (Section 722) while any decrease in the liabilities of the partnership will result in a reduction of the bases of the partnership interests. § 705(a)(2).

To illustrate, using the Al–Bea partnership (at ¶ 17,010), assume that the partnership itself borrowed $20,000 from a local bank to provide funds for the start of business. Because Al and Bea were equal partners, the increase in their share of partnership liabilities would result in an increase in the basis of Al's partnership interest to $10,040 and Bea's partnership interest to $10,100. When the partnership repaid the loan, the reduction in their share of partnership liabilities would be treated as a constructive cash distribution resulting in a $10,000 reduction in each of the bases of their partnership interests. In the unlikely event that nothing else had occurred, Al's basis would be returned to $40 and Bea's would be returned to $100.

For Section 752 purposes, accrued but unpaid expenses and accounts payable of a cash basis partnership are not "partnership liabilities." See Reg. § 1.752–1(a)(4)(i); Rev. Rul. 88–77, 1988–2 C.B. 128. Why not? Notice that this result is consistent with the treatment of such liabilities under Section 357(c)(3) in the case of the incorporation of an existing cash basis business, discussed at ¶¶ 2190–2195.

Further, a partnership liability is disregarded for Section 752 purposes if the liability is subject to contingencies that make it unlikely that it will ever be discharged. See, e.g., Reg. § 1.752–2(b)(4). If the partnership's obligation to pay a liability would arise at a future time only after the occurrence of an event not determinable with reasonable certainty, the liability is ignored for Section 752 purposes until the event occurs. Id.

[¶ 17,035]

2. ALLOCATION OF PARTNERSHIP DEBT AMONG THE PARTNERS

The allocation among the partners of the increased basis attributable to a partnership borrowing raises troublesome conceptual issues. In an attempt to resolve some of those issues, in 1991, the Treasury Department promulgated a greatly revised version of the regulations under Section 752. The general underlying theme of these regulations is that the basis increase attributable to a partnership level borrowing should be allocated among the partners in the same proportion that the losses attributable to the exhaustion of the proceeds of the borrowing would be allocated. As under the prior regulations, the basis increase attributable to recourse and nonrecourse debt is allocated pursuant to quite different rules.

The following discussion of the Section 752 regulations is intended to be introductory in nature. A more detailed discussion of these regulations is contained at ¶¶ 18,165 et seq.

[¶ 17,040]

a. *Recourse Debt*

In general, the basis increase attributable to a partnership level borrowing that at least one partner is personally obligated to repay is allocated to the partners responsible for repayment in proportion to their obligation to repay the borrowing should the partnership assets prove insufficient.

For each separate partnership liability, under Reg. § 1.752–2, the basis increase is allocated to the partners in proportion to their obligation to bear the ultimate risk of economic loss on the liability. To determine which partners would bear that ultimate risk, the regulations create the concept of a "constructive liquidation," in which several steps are deemed to occur (subject to certain exceptions, of course): (i) all of the partnership assets, including money, become worthless and are disposed of in a taxable transaction for no consideration, (ii) the items of income and loss for the year are allocated among the partners and reflected in the partners' bases and capital accounts, (iii) the partners' interests in the partnership are liquidated, and (iv) all of the partnership liabilities become immediately due and payable in full.

The basis increase attributable to a particular loan is then allocated to the partners in proportion to their obligation, in the constructive liquidation, to make a payment to the partnership, another partner, or a creditor of the partnership to permit the discharge of that loan. In determining which partners would be obligated to make such a payment, it is immaterial whether the obligation arises under the partnership agreement, the loan agreement, state law, or a side agreement such as a guarantee or indemnity. Further, the amount of any partner's obligation is reduced by the amount of any right to a reimbursement from another partner. For the purpose of these determinations, it is assumed that all partners will, in fact, discharge their legal obligations without regard to their actual net worth.

Consider the following example: Gerry and Linda form a partnership to which each contributes $200. The partnership borrows $600 on a recourse basis and purchases land. In a constructive liquidation, each partner would have a personal liability to contribute to the partnership an amount sufficient to repay the partnership debt. If Gerry was required to pay more than his share, he would be entitled to recover against Linda. Thus, Gerry and Linda would share equally in the basis

¶ 17,035

increase attributable to the borrowing. The basis of each would increase by $300.

Assume instead that Linda is a limited partner and has no further obligation to contribute to the capital of the partnership. In a constructive liquidation, only Gerry would have an obligation to contribute. All of the $600 basis increase would be allocated to Gerry.

Now assume that the limited partner (Linda) enters into an agreement with the lender pursuant to which she personally guarantees repayment of the loan. If, in a constructive liquidation, Linda made any payment on her guarantee, she would be subrogated under state law to the rights of the lender against the partnership. Thus, the partnership would have an obligation to repay Linda, and Gerry would be obligated to make a contribution to the partnership sufficient to discharge that obligation. Linda therefore would have a right to a reimbursement from a partner and bear no ultimate risk of loss. The entire basis increase would again be allocated to Gerry.

If Linda had merely indemnified the lender against loss and did not have a right to reimbursement from the partnership, it might appear that she would be exposed to a risk of loss. However, Linda would only bear that loss if Gerry did not discharge his obligation as general partner to contribute to the partnership. Since Gerry is assumed to satisfy his obligations, the entire risk of loss, and basis increase, remain with him.

[¶ 17,045]

b. Nonrecourse Debt

In the case of a nonrecourse partnership liability, no partner bears the economic risk of loss for such liability. The regulations provide that the basis increase attributable to liabilities for which no partner bears an economic risk of loss is allocated among the partners, limited as well as general, in proportion to the partnership profit-sharing ratio. The highly complex, three-tiered definition of the profit-sharing ratio contained in the regulations, however, is geared to the rules governing the allocation of profits and loss contained in the regulations under Section 704(b) and (c). Accordingly, the examination of those basis allocation rules must be deferred until after we have studied Section 704(b) and (c) and will be covered at ¶ 18,175.

[¶ 17,050]

3. CONTRIBUTIONS OF ENCUMBERED PROPERTY

When a partnership assumes an individual liability of a partner, to the extent that the partner is thereby relieved of the burden of the debt, the economic effect of the transaction is identical to the distribution of cash to the partner and is so treated by Section 752(b). Accordingly, the basis of the benefited partner's partnership interest must be reduced by the amount of any such liability assumed. However, as discussed above, under Section 752(a), any increase in the liabilities of a partnership is treated as a contribution of money by the partners to the partnership. Thus, the assumption of a liability by a partnership also results in an increase in the basis of the partnership interests, including the interest held by the partner from whom the liability was assumed. When a partnership assumes a liability of a partner, both of these adjustments must be made—the basis of the partner's interest is increased by the share of the liability assumed that is allocable to the partner under the regulations and is reduced by the full amount of that liability.

The assumption by a partnership of a partner's liability is most likely to occur in connection with the transfer of encumbered property to the partnership. When a partner transfers property to the partnership and the property is subject to a liability that the partnership assumes, a constructive distribution to the transferor partner will occur. Assume, for example, that Bonnie and Clyde form a partnership in which they will share equally partnership profits and losses. Bonnie contributes cash of $50,000. Clyde contributes real property having a basis of $20,000 and a value of $60,000. The property is subject to a mortgage of $10,000 to secure a debt that the partnership assumes. Under the Section 752 regulations, Bonnie and Clyde would share equally in the basis increase attributable to the debt assumed by the partnership. Thus, Bonnie's basis is increased to $55,000 by her share of the new partnership debt. Clyde's basis is the substituted basis of $20,000, increased by his $5,000 share of the partnership debt and reduced by the $10,000 constructive distribution resulting from the partnership's assumption of his debt. Since the amount of the constructive distribution does not exceed Clyde's basis in the partnership interest, Clyde recognizes no gain; the basis in his partnership interest is $15,000.

Considerable significance attaches to the fact that the assumption of a partner's liability in connection with the contribution of encumbered property is treated as a constructive distribution and is not treated as a payment in exchange for the property transferred. The transferor partner will not recognize gain merely because the amount of the liability assumed exceeds the basis of the property transferred.[1] Rather, gain will be recognized by the contributing partner only if the amount of the constructive distribution exceeds the total basis of the partner's interest in the partnership. § 731(a)(1). Moreover, the character of the gain is not determined by the nature of the property transferred; it is treated as gain from the sale of a partnership interest under Sections 731 and 741. Finally, the partner's recognition of such gain does not enable the partnership to increase its adjusted basis in the contributed property.[2]

1. Compare the different rules under Section 357(b) and (c) for shareholder transfers of encumbered property to corporations, discussed at ¶¶ 2170 et seq.

2. Compare § 362(a) in the context of gain recognition by a transferor of encum-

bered property in an incorporation exchange governed by § 351, discussed in Chapter 2.

¶ 17,050

[¶ 17,055]

Problems

1. Erik obtained a 25–percent interest in an existing partnership in exchange for the transfer of depreciable property having a value of $1,000 and a tax basis of $400. The property was, however, subject to a debt of $800, which was assumed by the partnership. Determine all of the federal income tax consequences to Erik and the partnership.

2. How would your answer in Problem 1 change if Erik were a partner at the time of the transfer and had a $300 existing basis for his partnership interest before his transfer of the property to the partnership?

[¶ 17,060]

D.   CONTRIBUTION OF SERVICES

The nonrecognition rule of Section 721 is limited to contributions of property. It is not intended to defer the taxation of compensation for services received in the form of a partnership interest. When a partner obtains an interest in a partnership in exchange for the performance of services, Section 721 does not apply to the transaction. The tax consequences to the partner and the partnership are controlled by the more general rules of the Code that determine the taxation of compensation arrangements, including Sections 61, 83, and 162. While the basic principles are clear, many questions concerning the transfer of a partnership interest to a service partner are difficult to answer.

An example will illustrate some of the problems. Assume that some years ago Cap and Tal each contributed $50,000 to form a partnership that purchased investment assets. The value of the partnership assets is now $200,000. Service Provider is to be admitted as a 10–percent partner. Service Provider will make no capital contribution. She will assume responsibility for managing the partnership investments.

Service Provider might receive an interest in 10 percent of the existing partnership properties as well as the right to receive 10 percent of future partnership profits and losses. In that event, Service Provider will have received a capital interest in the partnership that has a clear and immediate value of at least $20,000. Alternatively, Service Provider might be given only a 10–percent interest in partnership profits generated after her admission to the partnership. In that event, Service Provider will have received only a right to future profits having an uncertain value. Not surprisingly, historically the income tax consequences of the receipt of a profits interest have been less clear than the consequences of receiving a capital interest. However, in 2005, the Treasury and the IRS

¶ 17,060

issued proposed regulations that would apply the same rules to all transfers of partnership interests in exchange for services, without regard to whether the interest transferred is a capital interest or a profits interest. See Prop. Reg. §§ 1.83–3(e) and 1.721–1(b)(1); REG–105346–03, 2005–1 C.B. 1244, 1246.

[¶ 17,065]

1. RECEIPT OF CAPITAL INTEREST

The receipt of an interest in partnership capital in exchange for services is fully taxable as ordinary income. The timing of the tax is controlled by Section 83, which governs all transfers of property as compensation for services. The service partner will be taxed immediately on the fair market value of the capital interest (less any amount paid for the interest), unless the interest is subject to a substantial risk of forfeiture and is nontransferable. § 83(a); Reg. § 1.721–1(b)(1), and Prop. Reg. §§ 1.83–3(e) (the definition of property for Section 83 purposes includes a partnership interest) and 1.721–1(b)(1).[3] Since there are no such restrictions on Service Provider's partnership interest in the foregoing example, she would be taxed on the $20,000 value of the capital interest that she receives.[4]

Possible compensation deduction for compensatory partnership interest transfer. The partnership in the Example has paid compensation and should be entitled to the same tax benefit as would arise from the payment of compensation in cash or any other form. The treatment of compensation to a partner under Subchapter K raises a number of complexities that are addressed at ¶ 17,075. It is, in any event, clear that the partnership should be entitled either to deduct or capitalize an amount equal to the compensation taxed to the service partner, depending upon the nature of the services performed (i.e., depending, for example, on whether the service expense is an ordinary and necessary business expense or, instead, is a capital expenditure). As mentioned above, the timing and amount of that deduction is governed by the timing rules in Section 83(h) and the regulations issued under

---

3. Under the proposed regulations issued in 2005, a transfer of a partnership interest, whether a capital interest or a profits interest, in connection with the performance of services would be treated as a guaranteed payment. See Prop. Reg. § 1.721–1(b)(4)(i). (The federal tax treatment of guaranteed payments is discussed in Chapter 20.) However, these proposed regulations provide that the timing rules in Section 83 would override the timing rules of Section 706(a) and Reg. § 1.707–1(c) to the extent of any inconsistency. Thus, the timing rules of Section 83(a) and the regulations under Section 83 would determine the timing and amount of the service partner's income inclusion and the timing and amount of the partnership's deduction for the service payment (assuming that such payment is not a capital expenditure). See Prop. Reg. § 1.707–1(c).

4. Under the proposed regulations issued in 2005, a partnership interest received in connection with the performance of services may be valued based on its liquidation value, if certain requirements are met. See Prop. Reg. § 1.83–3(*l*); IRS Notice 2005–43, excerpted at ¶ 17,085.

that provision. See Prop. Reg. §§ 1.707–1(c) and 1.721–1(b)(4)(i); REG–105346–03, 2005–1 C.B. 1244, 1247. If the services are provided to another partner, rather than the partnership, that other partner may be entitled to a deduction for the service expense (unless the expense constitutes a capital expenditure). See Prop. Reg. § 1.721–1(b)(4)(ii).

Which partners should be entitled to the tax benefit from the payment of that compensation is somewhat less clear. If the compensation is for services performed in the past (when Service Provider was not a partner) and the amount is not required to be capitalized, Section 706 will require that any deduction claimed by the partnership be allocated between Cap and Tal. However, if the amount must be capitalized (e.g., the amount is for services to be performed in the future), Service Provider may be entitled to her proportionate share of the future deductions.

Compensatory partnership interest subject to a substantial risk of forfeiture. Suppose that Service Provider's receipt of the partnership interest is subject to a substantial risk of forfeiture and is nontransferable (as both such terms are defined in Section 83 and the regulations issued under that provision). For example, assume that Service Provider's receipt of the partnership interest is subject to the restriction that Service must perform services for the next three years for the partnership or forfeit the partnership interest. If one ignores the effect of the restriction on the value of the partnership interest, the interest has a fair market value of $20,000 on the date of its receipt by Service Provider, and the interest has a fair market value of $50,000 at the end of year 3, when the forfeiture restriction will lapse. How does the existence of the forfeiture restriction affect the timing and amount of Service Provider's compensation income? What if Service Provider elects under Section 83(b) to report the fair market value of the partnership interest as ordinary compensation income at the time of its receipt, notwithstanding the presence of the forfeiture restriction?

Under the timing rules in Section 83, unless Service Provider makes the election under Section 83(b), Service would have to include $50,000 as ordinary compensation income in year 3, the fair market value of the partnership interest when the restriction lapses. In the words of the Section 83 regulations, the partnership interest in this example is "substantially nonvested" at the time of its receipt, unless Service Provider makes the Section 83(b) election. In such a situation, the proposed regulations issued in 2005 would not treat the holder of the partnership interest as a partner for Subchapter K purposes until the end of year 3 when the property is no longer subject to the restriction and Service Partner reports its value as compensation income under Section 83 (i.e., at that time, the partnership interest becomes "substantially vested" and Service is treated as a partner for Subchapter K purposes). Prop. Reg. § 1.761–1(b). By contrast, if Service Provider properly makes the Section 83(b) election within 30 days after the transfer of the interest, Service would include $20,000 as ordinary compensation income in year 1, the fair market value of the interest at the time of its receipt by Service (ignoring the effect of any restriction on the value of the interest, except certain restrictions that will never leave the property, called "nonlapse restrictions"). Service Provider would be treated as a partner during the period that the restriction remains on the partnership interest, notwithstanding the fact that Service might end up forfeiting the interest if the restriction is not fulfilled. See Prop. Reg. § 1.761–1(b).

Capital account adjustments to reflect compensatory partnership interest. Under Prop. Reg. § 1.704–1(b)(2)(iv)(*b*)(*1*), the service partner increases his or her capital account by the amount included in gross income under Section 83 on account of receiving the interest, plus any amount paid for the interest. Thus, for example, if a service provider pays $20 for a "substantially vested" compensatory partnership interest having a fair market value of $100, the service provider must include $80 ordinary income under Section 83 and increase her capital account by $100 (the $80 included in income under Section 83, plus the $20 paid for the interest).

Nonrecognition of gain or loss to the partnership on the transfer of the compensatory partnership interest. There is one further interesting question to the partnership arising from the transfer of a capital interest. If the Cap–Tal partnership had compensated Service Provider by transferring to her securities having a value of $20,000 and a tax basis of $10,000, the partnership would clearly be taxable on a gain of $10,000 as if it had sold the property to Service Provider. If, instead, a partnership interest is transferred, should the partnership similarly be required to recognize the same $10,000 gain? That would characterize the transaction as a transfer by the partnership of an undivided 10–percent interest in the partnership properties to Service Provider and a contribution by Service of those properties back to the partnership in exchange for the partnership interest. In that event, the partnership would be entitled to increase the basis for its properties by the gain recognized, and the partners to whom the gain is taxed would be entitled to increase the bases of their partnership interests.

If this view of the transaction is adopted, must the partnership be treated as constructively transferring to Service Provider an undivided interest in each of its assets? For example, if the partnership in fact had cash of $20,000 on hand when Service Provider was admitted, could the partnership avoid gain by treating that cash as the property constructively distributed to Service? If the partnership had actually paid cash to Service Provider, would the payment and recontribution be ignored as a step transaction?

Alternatively, the transaction might be viewed as if the partnership had constructively paid Service Provider cash compensation for her

¶ 17,065

services and Service then recontributed the cash to the partnership in exchange for her partnership interest. Under this formulation, the partnership would not recognize any gain and would not be entitled to adjust the basis of its properties.

Is any of the foregoing descriptions of the essential transaction more consistent with the underlying premises of Subchapter K? Does any seem more potentially abusive? The proposed regulations issued in 2005 take the position that a partnership generally does *not* recognize gain or loss on the transfer of a partnership interest in return for services. See Prop. Reg. § 1.721–1(b)(2). In effect, these proposed regulations treat the transaction as if the partnership had paid the service provider cash for her services equal to the value of the partnership interest and then she contributed the cash back to the partnership in return for the partnership interest. See L. Cunningham & N. Cunningham, The Logic of Subchapter K 136 (3d ed. 2006). In the preamble to these proposed regulations, the Treasury and the IRS reasoned that such "a rule is more consistent with the policies underlying section 721—to defer recognition of gain and loss when persons join together to conduct a business—than would be a rule requiring the partnership to recognize gain on the transfer of these types of interests." REG–105346–03, 2005–1 C.B. 1244, 1249.[5]

2. RECEIPT OF PROFITS INTEREST

[¶ 17,070]

DIAMOND v. COMMISSIONER

United States Tax Court, 1971.
56 T.C. 530, aff'd, 492 F.2d 286 (7th Cir.1974).

* * *

RAUM, JUDGE: * * *.

* * *

2. *201–207 W. Monroe Street property.*—Petitioner performed services for Kargman in obtaining a $1,100,000 mortgage loan for the Monroe Street property which Kargman was in the process of purchas-

---

5. This nonrecognition rule would not apply to the transfer or substantial vesting of an interest in an eligible entity (as defined in Reg. § 301.7701–3(a)) that becomes a partnership as result of the transfer or substantial vesting of the interest. See REG–105346–03, 2005–1 C.B. 1244, 1249 (citing McDougal v. Commissioner, 62 T.C. 720 (1974), where the Tax Court required the service recipient to recognize gain on the transfer of a 50–percent interest in an appreciated racehorse to the service provider, immediately before the service recipient and the service provider contributed their interests in the racehorse to a newly organized partnership); L. Cunningham & N. Cunningham, The Logic of Subchapter K 136 (3d ed. 2006) (stating that this nonrecognition rule does not apply to "the transfer of a partnership interest that initially creates a partnership").

¶ 17,070

ing. The loan was in the full amount of the purchase price. As compensation for his services Kargman agreed to give petitioner an interest in the venture whereby for 24 years petitioner would become entitled to 60 percent of the earnings from the property and would be chargeable with losses in the same proportion; also, in the event of future sale of the property petitioner would become entitled to 60 percent of the net proceeds after Kargman had been reimbursed in full for the funds expended by him in the acquisition of the property. Petitioner in fact acquired that interest on February 18, 1962, when title was finally transferred to The Exchange National Bank under a so-called Illinois land trust, and he thereby became a 60–percent beneficiary of that land trust. On March 8, 1962, less than three weeks after he had acquired that interest, he sold it for $40,000. The Commissioner argues that the interest had a fair market value of $40,000 when petitioner got it on February 18, 1962, and that since it was received by him as compensation for services it represented ordinary income to him under section 61(a)(1) * * * and regs. sec. 1.61–2(d)(1). We agree.

Petitioners do not appear to challenge the basic argument that the fair market value of property received for services must be treated as ordinary income. They seek to avoid the consequences of that result here, however, by contending that petitioner received only an interest in a partnership (limited to a percentage of its future earnings) for his services and that he realized no income thereby by reason of section 721, * * * as interpreted by regs. sec. 1.721–1(b)(1); that in any event the interest had no value when received; and finally that when petitioner sold his interest there was a termination of the alleged partnership and that he is entitled to an "offset deduction" for his share of an alleged loss of the partnership. We think that none of these points is sound.

(a) Although the relationship between petitioner and Kargman was referred to in some of the documents in evidence as a "partnership," it is by no means clear that petitioner's 60–percent beneficial interest in the land trust was that of a partner. However, we need not pass upon the matter, because we think that even if it were a partnership interest, its fair market value must nevertheless be included in income under section 61 and that neither section 721 nor the regulations construing it render section 61 inapplicable here.

* * *

As its terms plainly indicate, [section 721] provides merely that no gain or loss shall be recognized to a partner who contributes property to a partnership in exchange for an interest therein. The present case simply does not come within those provisions, for it is clear that a contribution of services is not a contribution of "property."[14]

---

14. Cognate provisions of the 1954 Code in sec. 351, relating to nonrecognition of gain or loss in respect of contributions of property to a corporation in return for its

In construing section 721, the regulations state:

Sec. 1.721–1 Nonrecognition of gain or loss on contribution.

(b)(1) Normally, under local law, each partner is entitled to be repaid his contributions of money or other property to the partnership (at the value placed upon such property by the partnership at the time of the contribution) whether made at the formation of the partnership or subsequent thereto. To the extent that any of the partners gives up any part of his right to be repaid his contributions (as distinguished from a share in partnership profits) in favor of another partner as compensation for services (or in satisfaction of an obligation), section 721 does not apply. The value of an interest in such partnership capital so transferred to a partner as compensation for services constitutes income to the partner under section 61.

* * *

Relying upon these provisions, petitioners contend that when a taxpayer receives a partnership interest as compensation for services he is required to account for that interest at once as ordinary income if he acquires an interest in partnership capital, but not if he receives only the right to share in the partnership's future profits and losses. It is true that the regulations make section 721 inapplicable in the case of a taxpayer who has received an interest in the capital contribution made by another partner. Cf. *United States v. Frazell*, 339 F.2d 885 (C.A.5), denying petition for rehearing of 335 F.2d 487, certiorari denied 380 U.S. 961. But the effect of the first parenthetical clause in the second sentence of these regulations, "(as distinguished from a share in partnership profits)," upon which petitioners place their sole reliance, is obscure. Certainly, unless section 721 of the Code grants the relief which petitioners seek, they are left subject to section 61. Yet nothing in the foregoing regulations explicitly states that a partner who has received a partnership interest like the one before us in exchange for services already performed comes within the provisions of section 721. The parenthetical language does not so state. At most, it excludes that type of situation from the rule which the regulations affirmatively set forth in respect of readjustments of capital interests; but it does not deal one way or the other with situations described in the parenthetical clause. The reason for this kind of opaque draftsmanship in the regulations is by no means clear to us. However, what is plain is that the regulations do not call for the applicability of section 721 where a taxpayer has performed services for someone who has compensated him therefor by giving him an interest in a partnership that came into being at a later date.

stock or securities explicitly state that for purposes of that section "stock or securities issued for services shall not be considered as issued in return for property." However, the quoted language simply codified what was implicit in prior case law; under the predecessor of sec. 351 in the 1939 Code, which contained no such language, there was no suggestion that services might be included within the meaning of "property." * * *

¶ 17,070

Regardless of whether there may be some kind of equitable justification for giving the parenthetical clause some limited form of affirmative operative scope, as perhaps where there is a readjustment of partners' shares to reflect services being performed by one of the partners, we cannot believe that the regulations were ever intended to bring section 721 into play in a situation like the one before us. The Commissioner disavows such intention, and we agree with him. To apply section 721 here would call for a distortion of statutory language, and we cannot believe that the regulations were ever intended to require that result. Certainly, in the absence of a clearer statement to that effect, we will not approve any such interpretation of them as is requested by petitioners.

(b) The alternative argument that petitioner's interest in the venture had no value at the time he acquired it is unconvincing. To be sure, as he points out, the December 15, 1961, agreement between him and Kargman provided that neither party could assign it without the consent of the other. But even if that restriction on assignment carried over to the interests in the land trust, which were explicitly declared to be assignable, such restriction would not deprive petitioner's interest of any fair market value. It was a conditional, not an absolute restriction, and, at most, it would merely be a factor to be taken into account in determining the amount of such value. * * * In the present case petitioner sold his interest to Liederman less than 3 weeks after he received it for $40,000. Presumably—and petitioner has not shown otherwise—Liederman acquired the interest subject to the same restriction (if any); yet he was willing to pay $40,000 for it. On this record, we cannot say that Commissioner erred in valuing petitioner's interest at that amount.[16]

(c) Petitioners have also urged that they are entitled to a deduction for petitioner's share of partnership loss stemming from the "termination" of the partnership. They rely upon sections 708 and 752 * * *. * * * Petitioners urge that on termination of the partnership, each partner was entitled to take into account, in determining his distributive share of the partnership's taxable income or loss, his distributive share of the partnership's unamortized loan expense of $33,000. See sec. 702(a)(9) * * *. However, regardless of whatever validity their argument may have, they have produced no evidence of the venture's income for the period during which Kargman and petitioner were associated. Consequently they have failed to carry their burden of proof in establishing

---

16. Even if one of petitioners' two foregoing arguments had prevailed, it would still not be altogether clear that the $40,000 petitioner received on the sale of his interest in the land trust would qualify as a short-term capital gain. Although sec. 741 * * * provides for capital gain treatment on the sale of an "interest in a partnership," it is not at all clear that it contemplates the sale of a right to receive income in the future in return for a lump sum payment which would enable a taxpayer to convert what would otherwise be taxable as ordinary income into capital gain. Cf. *Commissioner v. Gillette Motor Transport, Inc.*, 364 U.S. 130, 134–135; *Commissioner v. P.G. Lake, Inc.*, 356 U.S. 260, 265–266; *Hort v. Commissioner*, 313 U.S. 28 * * *. In view of our disposition of this case, however, we need not reach this question.

¶ 17,070

the purported partnership loss. We uphold the Commissioner's determination.

Reviewed by the Court.

* * *

[¶ 17,075]

Notes

1. In its decision affirming the Tax Court, the Seventh Circuit observed that "in the absence of regulation, we think it sound policy to defer to the expertise of the Commissioner and the Judges of the Tax Court, and to sustain their decision that the receipt of a profit-share with determinable market value is income." Diamond v. Commissioner, 492 F.2d 286, 291 (7th Cir.1974).

2. Under the rule of the *Diamond* case, a service partner who is compensated by the transfer of a profits interest would be taxed on the income earned thereafter by the partnership and allocated to the service partner. Thus, taxing the receipt of the profits interest not only accelerates the tax but suggests the possibility of double taxation. However, taxing the receipt of the interest establishes a "tax cost" basis under Section 1012 for the interest equal to the value of the interest included in the service partner's gross income. How and when would the service partner recover her basis in the partnership interest? Would she be able to amortize the basis against her share of the partnership income as it is earned? Is the issue solely one of timing?

3. Taxing the receipt of a profits interest that cannot readily be liquidated may appear harsh; but does the effect differ materially from that attending the taxation of the receipt of a capital interest? After all, a capital interest merely comprises an interest in both existing capital and a share of the future stream of partnership earnings.

4. Is the troublesome issue in *Diamond* in fact the question of timing or is it the character of income? If the latter, could the Tax Court have reached the same result without taxing the receipt of the interest?

5. If the receipt of a mere profits interest is taxable, it will be necessary to establish the value of the interest. How often will a profits interest be capable of valuation, considering the difficulties of predicting the timing and magnitude of future income? Some later cases have acknowledged the applicability of the *Diamond* analysis but have found the profits interest incapable of valuation. See St. John v. United States, 84–1 U.S.T.C. (CCH) ¶ 9158, 53 A.F.T.R.2d (RIA) 718 (C.D.Ill.1983); see also Kenroy, Inc. v. Commissioner, T.C. Memo. 1984–232 (1984) (taxpayer's profits interest was worthless on the date of its receipt and hence not taxable); Kobor v. United States, 88–2 U.S.T.C. (CCH) ¶ 9477, 62 A.F.T.R.2d (RIA) 5047 (C.D.Cal.1987) (profits interest received by taxpayer for future services to be performed was too speculative in value to

be taxable at time of receipt of the interest, where interest was subject to a substantial risk of forfeiture and was nontransferable).

6. Should a distinction be drawn between the receipt of a profits interest in a partnership where capital is a material income-producing factor and the receipt of an interest in a service partnership? Would the distinction be one of principle or of valuation?

7. The present status of the *Diamond* rule is very much in doubt. After a period of dormancy, and very much to the surprise of the practicing bar, the Tax Court reaffirmed its decision in Campbell v. Commissioner, T.C. Memo. 1990–162 (1990), and held that the receipt of the profits interest was currently taxable under Section 83. Adding to the surprise, on appeal the government conceded that the Tax Court decision was in error and unsuccessfully sought to sustain its victory on an alternative ground, 943 F.2d 815 (8th Cir.1991). Rather than simply accept that concession, however, the appellate court reviewed the lower court decision. Relying on a distinction drawn in Section 707, the court suggested that whether the profits interest was taxable might depend on whether the services were provided by the taxpayer in the capacity of partner or in another capacity. Is that a meritorious distinction? Finally, the court held that the value of the interest was too speculative to be taxable and reversed the Tax Court decision.

Moreover, in many cases, the proposed regulations issued in 2005, if and when they become finalized, may provide relative certainty regarding the taxation of a service provider's receipt of a partnership profits interest in return for services performed or to be performed for the partnership. Under those regulations, the service partner's receipt of a partnership profits interest potentially would be taxable as ordinary compensation income under Sections 61 and 83. See Prop. Reg. §§ 1.83–3(e) and 1.721–1(b)(1). However, as mentioned in an earlier footnote in this Chapter, if certain requirements are met, those proposed regulations would allow the partnership and all of its partners, including the service partner, to elect to treat the value of a compensatory partnership interest, whether a capital interest or a mere profits interest, as equal to its liquidation value. For this purpose, the liquidation value of a partnership interest is the amount of cash that the holder of the interest would receive if, immediately after the transfer of the interest to the service provider, the partnership sold all of its assets (including goodwill and any other intangibles related to the partnership's operations) for an amount of cash equal to the fair market value of those assets, and then liquidated. See REG–105346–03, 2005–1 C.B. 1244, 1249; IRS Notice 2005–43, excepted below at ¶ 17,085. Under this liquidation valuation method, a profits interest may have a zero value because the holder of such interest would not be entitled to receive any cash on a liquidation of the partnership shortly after the transfer and, thus, the service partner may not have to report any income on receipt of the profits interest.

¶ 17,075

8. Even before the issuance of the proposed regulations in 2005, the Treasury and the IRS had signaled their retreat on the enforcement of the *Diamond* rule in two revenue procedures issued in 1993 and 2001. In Rev. Proc. 93–27, excerpted below, the IRS announced its position on the tax treatment of the receipt of a partnership profits interest for services provided to the partnership. In Rev. Proc. 2001–43, also excerpted below, the IRS clarified its earlier position in Rev. Proc. 93–27. The latter revenue procedure deals with the situation where at time of the service provider's receipt of the profits interest, the interest is subject to a substantial risk of forfeiture (within the meaning of Section 83(c)(1) and Reg. § 1.83–3(c)) and is nontransferable (within the meaning of Section 83(c)(2) and Reg. § 1.83–3(d)). These two revenue procedures will be declared obsolete if and when the 2005 proposed regulations become finalized and a new proposed revenue procedure is issued containing rules that a partnership and all of its partners must follow in order to be able to elect to value the compensatory partnership interest under the liquidation value method of valuation in Prop. Reg. § 1.83–3(*l*). That proposed revenue procedure is set forth in IRS Notice 2005–43, excerpted at ¶ 17,085.

[¶ 17,080]

REVENUE PROCEDURE 93–27

1993–2 C.B. 343.

[Sec.] 1. Purpose

This revenue procedure provides guidance on the treatment of the receipt of a partnership profits interest for services provided to or for the benefit of the partnership.

Sec. 2. Definitions

The following definitions apply for purposes of this revenue procedure.

.01 A capital interest is an interest that would give the holder a share of the proceeds if the partnership's assets were sold at fair market value and then the proceeds were distributed in a complete liquidation of the partnership. This determination generally is made at the time of receipt of the partnership interest.

.02 A profits interest is a partnership interest other than a capital interest.

Sec. 3. Background

Under section 1.721–1(b)(1) of the * * * Regulations, the receipt of a partnership capital interest for services provided to or for the benefit of the partnership is taxable as compensation. On the other hand, the issue of whether the receipt of a partnership profits interest for services is taxable has been the subject of litigation. Most recently, in *Campbell v. Commissioner*, 943 F.2d 815 (8th Cir.1991), the Eighth Circuit in dictum suggested that the taxpayer's receipt of a partnership profits interest received for services was not taxable, but decided the case on valuation. Other courts have determined that in certain circumstances the receipt of a partnership profits interest for services is a taxable event under section 83 of the Internal Revenue Code. *See, e.g., Campbell v. Commissioner*, T.C.M. 1990–[162], rev'd, 943 F.2d 815 (8th Cir.1991); *St. John v. United States*, No. 82–1134 (C.D.Ill. Nov.16, 1983). The courts have also found that typically the profits interest received has speculative or no determinable value at the time of receipt. *See Campbell*, 943 F.2d at 823; *St. John*. In *Diamond v. Commissioner*, 56 T.C. 530 (1971), aff'd, 492 F.2d 286 (7th Cir.1974), however, the court assumed that the interest received by the taxpayer was a partnership profits interest and found the value of the interest was readily determinable. In that case, the interest was sold soon after receipt.

Sec. 4. Application

.01 Other than as provided below, if a person receives a profits interest for the provision of services to or for the benefit of a partnership in a partner capacity or in anticipation of being a partner, the Internal Revenue Service will not treat the receipt of such an interest as a taxable event for the partner or the partnership.

.02 This revenue procedure does not apply:

(1) If the profits interest relates to a substantially certain and predictable stream of income from partnership assets, such as income from high-quality debt securities or a high-quality net lease;

(2) If within two years of receipt, the partner disposes of the profits interest; or

(3) If the profits interest is a limited partnership interest in a "publicly traded partnership" within the meaning of section 7704(b) * * *.

[¶ 17,082]

REVENUE PROCEDURE 2001–43

2001–2 C.B. 191.

Section 1. Purpose

This revenue procedure clarifies Rev. Proc. 93–27 * * *, by providing guidance on the treatment of the grant of a partnership profits interest that is substantially nonvested for the provision of services to or for the benefit of the partnership.

* * *

¶ 17,080

SECTION 3. SCOPE

This revenue procedure clarifies Rev. Proc. 93–27 by providing that the determination under Rev. Proc. 93–27 of whether an interest granted to a service provider is a profits interest is, under the circumstances described below, tested at the time the interest is granted, even if, at that time, the interest is substantially nonvested (within the meaning of § 1.83–3(b) of the * * * Regulations). Accordingly, where a partnership grants a profits interest to a service provider in a transaction meeting the requirements of this revenue procedure and Rev. Proc. 93–27, the Internal Revenue Service will not treat the grant of the interest or the event that causes the interest to become substantially vested (within the meaning of § 1.83–3(b) of the * * * Regulations) as a taxable event for the partner or the partnership. Taxpayers to which this revenue procedure applies need not file an election under section 83(b) of the Code.

SECTION 4. APPLICATION

This revenue procedure clarifies that, for purposes of Rev. Proc. 93–27, where a partnership grants an interest in the partnership that is substantially nonvested to a service provider, the service provider will be treated as receiving the interest on the date of its grant, provided that:

.01 The partnership and the service provider treat the service provider as the owner of the partnership interest from the date of its grant and the service provider takes into account the distributive share of partnership income, gain, loss, deduction, and credit associated with that interest in computing the service provider's income tax liability for the entire period during which the service provider has the interest;

.02 Upon the grant of the interest or at the time that the interest becomes substantially vested, neither the partnership nor any of the partners deducts any amount (as wages, compensation, or otherwise) for the fair market value of the interest; and

.03 All other conditions of Rev. Proc. 93–27 are satisfied.

* * *

[¶ 17,083]

Notes

1. Rev. Proc. 93–27, as clarified by Rev. Proc. 2001–43, considerably reduces the uncertainty concerning the taxability of a partnership profits interest received in exchange for the rendition of services. In many circumstances, the safe harbor in Rev. Proc. 93–27 will apply, and the receipt of the profits interest will not be a taxable event to either the recipient or the partnership unless one of the three exceptions in the revenue procedure applies.

¶ 17,083

2. However, the safe harbor in Rev. Proc. 93–27, by its terms, applies only if the services rendered in exchange for the partnership profits interest are rendered "to or for the benefit of a partnership in a partner capacity or in anticipation of being a partner." Thus, the position of the IRS seems to be that the service partner's receipt of the profits interest may be a taxable event if the service partner is rendering the services for the benefit of another partner or some other third party (rather than the partnership itself), or if the service partner is otherwise rendering the services in a nonpartner capacity. What is the policy underlying this limitation on the application of the safe harbor in Rev. Proc. 93–27? Note that Section 707 and the regulations issued under that provision, discussed in Chapter 20, provide rules for determining whether a partner is acting in a partner or nonpartner capacity in her transactions with the partnership.

3. Why does Rev. Proc. 93–27 contain an exception to the safe harbor if the service partner disposes of the profits interest within two years of receipt? If that exception applies, when is the service partner taxed on account of her receipt of the profits interest—at the time of receipt of the interest or upon disposition? Does this exception apply if the service partner disposes of the interest by inter vivos or testamentary gift or in a nonrecognition transfer to a corporation or other entity?

4. Given the current state of the case law on the issue of the taxability of a service partner's receipt of a profits interest and the existence of the liquidation value safe harbor in the 2005 proposed regulations (discussed in IRS Notice 2005–43, at ¶ 17,085), what are the practical consequences of a service partner's failure to qualify for the safe harbor in Rev. Proc. 93–27? What is the significance of the clarification in Rev. Proc. 2001–43 treating the service provider as receiving the profits interest on the date of its grant even though it is substantially nonvested (within the meaning of Reg. § 1.83–3(b))?

5. The proposed regulations and the other Treasury and IRS guidance on the exchange of services for partnership equity interests appear to be focused primarily on whether the issuance of the partnership interest for services results in inappropriate deferral of the tax on the service partner's compensation income. However, do these proposed regulations properly consider the potential for a service partner to alter the character of his or her income from ordinary compensation income to long-term capital gain through the use of a services for partnership interest arrangement? For example, suppose a taxpayer performs services for a hedge fund partnership in return for a partnership profits interest (having a zero liquidation value under the liquidation value safe harbor) and the hedge fund's later income consists largely of long-term capital gain income. Do the proposed regulations allow the service partner to essentially convert ordinary service income into long-term capital income by not requiring the service partner to report any

¶ 17,083

compensation income on the receipt of the profits interest (assuming that the requirements for the liquidation value safe harbor are met)?

[¶ 17,084]

3. 2005 PROPOSED REGULATIONS AND THE LIQUIDATION VALUE SAFE HARBOR

As discussed above, the 2005 proposed regulations would apply the same tax rules to the receipt of compensatory partnership capital interests and compensatory partnership profits interests. Those rules would attempt to coordinate the taxation of the service partner's compensation income on the receipt of the interest under Sections 61 and 83 with the taxation of the service partner's distributive share of partnership profits and losses under Sections 702 and 704. Those rules also would provide the partnership and its partners with an election to treat the fair market value of the compensatory partnership interest as equal to its liquidation value.

The following IRS Notice contains a proposed revenue procedure that summarizes various provisions in the 2005 proposed regulations discussed above and illustrates those provisions with a series of Examples. This proposed revenue procedure also contains some additional rules that the partnership and all of its partners must follow in order to elect the liquidation value safe harbor in the proposed regulations.

[¶ 17,085]

IRS NOTICE 2005–43

2005–1 C.B. 1221.

PURPOSE

This notice addresses the taxation of a transfer of a partnership interest in connection with the performance of services. In conjunction with this notice, the Treasury Department and the Internal Revenue Service are proposing regulations under § 83 * * *. The proposed regulations grant the Commissioner authority to issue guidance of general applicability related to the taxation of the transfer of a partnership interest in connection with the performance of services. This notice includes a proposed revenue procedure under that authority. The proposed revenue procedure provides additional rules for the elective safe harbor under proposed § 1.83–3(l) for a partnership's transfers of interests in the partnership in connection with the performance of services for that partnership. The safe harbor is intended to simplify the application of § 83 to partnership interests and to coordinate the provisions of § 83 with the principles of partnership taxation. Upon the finalization of the proposed revenue procedure, Rev. Proc. 93–27, 1993–2 C.B. 343, and Rev. Proc. 2001–43, 2001–2 C.B. 191, (described below) will be obsoleted. Until that occurs, taxpayers may not rely upon the safe harbor set forth in the proposed revenue procedure, but taxpayers may continue to rely upon current law, including Rev. Proc. 93–27, 1993–2 C.B. 343, and Rev. Proc. 2001–43, 2001–2 C.B. 191.

Effective Date

The Treasury Department and the Service intend for the revenue procedure proposed in this notice to be finalized and made effective in conjunction with the finalization of the related proposed regulations under § 83 and subchapter K of chapter 1 of the Internal Revenue Code (subchapter K).

* * *

PROPOSED REVENUE PROCEDURE

Section 1. Purpose

Proposed § 1.83–3(*l*) of the * * * Regulations allows taxpayers to elect to apply special rules (the Safe Harbor) to a partnership's transfers of interests in the partnership in connection with the performance of services for the partnership. The Treasury Department and the Internal Revenue Service intend for the Safe Harbor to simplify the application of § 83 * * * to partnership interests transferred in connection with the performance of services and to coordinate the principles of § 83 with the principles of partnership taxation. This revenue procedure sets forth additional rules for the elective safe harbor under proposed § 1.83–3(*l*) for a partnership's transfer of interests in the partnership in connection with the performance of services for that partnership.

Section 2. Law and Discussion

Section 83(a) provides that if, in connection with the performance of services, property is transferred to any person other than the person for whom such services are performed, the excess of (1) the fair market value of such property (determined without regard to any restriction other than a restriction which by its terms will never lapse) at the first time the rights of the person having the beneficial interest in such property are transferable or are not subject to a substantial risk of forfeiture, whichever occurs earlier, over (2) the amount (if any) paid for such property, is included in the gross income of the person who performed such services in the first taxable year in which the rights of the person having the beneficial interest in such property are transferable or are not subject to a substantial risk of forfeiture, whichever is applicable.

Section 1.83–3(e) provides that, for purposes of § 83 and the regulations thereunder, the term property includes real and personal property other than either money or an unfunded and unsecured promise to pay money or property in the future. For these purposes, under proposed

§ 1.83–3(e) property includes a partnership interest. Generally, a mere right to allocations or distributions described in § 707(a)(2)(A) is not a partnership interest. Proposed § 1.83–3(e) also provides that, in the case of a transfer of a partnership interest in connection with the performance of services, the Commissioner may prescribe generally applicable administrative rules to address the application of § 83 to the transfer.

Section 83(b) provides that a service provider may elect to include in his or her gross income, for the taxable year in which substantially nonvested property is transferred, the excess of (1) the fair market value of the property at the time of the transfer (determined without regard to any restriction other than a restriction which by its terms will never lapse), over (2) the amount (if any) paid for the property. If such an election is made, § 83(a) does not apply with respect to the transfer of the property upon vesting and, if the property is subsequently forfeited, no deduction is allowed to the service provider in respect of the forfeiture.

Section 1.83–2(b) provides that an election under § 83(b) must be filed not later than 30 days after the date the property was transferred and may be filed prior to the date of the transfer. Section 1.83–2(c) provides that the election is made by filing one copy of a written statement with the Internal Revenue Service Center with which the service provider files his or her return. In addition, one copy of such statement must be submitted with the service provider's income tax return for the taxable year in which the property was transferred.

Section 1.83–1(a) provides that, unless an election under § 83(b) is made, the transferor is regarded as the owner of substantially nonvested property transferred in connection with the performance of services until such property becomes substantially vested, and any income from such property received by the service provider (or beneficiary thereof), or the right to the use of such property by the service provider, constitutes additional compensation and is included in the gross income of the service provider for the taxable year in which the income is received or the use is made available. Under this rule, a partnership must treat as unissued any substantially nonvested partnership interest transferred in connection with the performance of services for which an election under § 83(b) has not been made. If the service provider who holds such an interest receives distributions from the partnership with respect to that interest while the interest is substantially nonvested, the distributions are treated as compensation in the capacity in which the service provider performed the services. For example, if a service provider that is not a pre-existing partner holds a substantially nonvested partnership interest that the service provider received in connection with the performance of services and the service provider did not make an election under § 83(b) with respect to that interest, then any distributions made to the service provider on account of such interest are treated as additional compensation and not partnership distributions. If, instead, the service provider who receives a substantially nonvested partnership interest in connection with the performance of services makes a valid election under § 83(b), then the service provider is treated as the owner of the property. See Rev. Rul. 83–22, 1983–1 C.B. 17. The service provider is treated as a partner with respect to such an interest, and the partnership must allocate partnership items to the service provider as if the partnership interest were substantially vested.

Section 1.83–3(b) provides that property is substantially nonvested for § 83 purposes when it is subject to a substantial risk of forfeiture and is nontransferable. Property is substantially vested for § 83 purposes when it is either transferable or not subject to a substantial risk of forfeiture.

Section 1.83–3(c) provides that, for § 83 purposes, whether a risk of forfeiture is substantial or not depends upon the facts and circumstances. A substantial risk of forfeiture exists where rights in property that are transferred are conditioned, directly or indirectly, upon the future performance (or refraining from performance) of substantial services by any person, or the occurrence of a condition related to a purpose of the transfer, and the possibility of forfeiture is substantial if such condition is not satisfied.

Section 1.83–3(d) provides that, for § 83 purposes, the rights of a person in property are transferable if such person can transfer any interest in the property to any person other than the transferor of the property, but only if the rights in such property of such transferee are not subject to a substantial risk of forfeiture.

Proposed § 1.83–3(*l*) provides that, subject to such additional conditions, rules, and procedures that the Commissioner may prescribe in regulations, revenue rulings, notices, or other guidance published in the Internal Revenue Bulletin, a partnership and all of its partners may elect a safe harbor under which the fair market value of a partnership interest that is transferred in connection with the performance of services is treated as being equal to the liquidation value of that interest for transfers on or after the date final regulations are published in the Federal Register if the following conditions are satisfied: (1) the partnership must prepare a document, executed by a partner who has responsibility for federal income tax reporting by the partnership, stating that the partnership is electing, on behalf of the partnership and each of its partners, to have the safe harbor apply irrevocably as of the stated effective date with respect to all partnership interests transferred in connection with the performance of services while the safe harbor election remains in effect and attach the document to the tax return for the partnership for the taxable year that includes the effective date of the election; (2) except as provided below, the partnership agreement must contain provisions that are legally binding on all of the partners stating that (a) the partnership is authorized and directed to elect the

¶ 17,085

safe harbor, and (b) the partnership and each of its partners (including any person to whom a partnership interest is transferred in connection with the performance of services) agrees to comply with all requirements of the safe harbor with respect to all partnership interests transferred in connection with the performance of services while the election remains effective; and (3) if the partnership agreement does not contain the provisions described in clause (2) of this sentence, or the provisions are not legally binding on all of the partners of the partnership, then each partner in a partnership that transfers a partnership interest in connection with the performance of services must execute a document containing provisions that are legally binding on that partner stating that (a) the partnership is authorized and directed to elect the safe harbor, and (b) the partner agrees to comply with all requirements of the safe harbor with respect to all partnership interests transferred in connection with the performance of services while the election remains effective. The specified effective date of the safe harbor election may not be prior to the date that the safe harbor election is executed. Proposed § 1.83–3(*l*) provides that the partnership must retain such records as may be necessary to indicate that an effective election has been made and remains in effect, including a copy of the partnership's election statement under this paragraph (*l*), and, if applicable, the original of each document submitted to the partnership by a partner under this paragraph (*l*). If the partnership is unable to produce a record of a particular document, the election will be treated as not made, generally resulting in termination of the election. The safe harbor election also may be terminated by the partnership preparing a document, executed by a partner who has responsibility for federal income tax reporting by the partnership, which states that the partnership, on behalf of the partnership and each of its partners, is revoking the safe harbor election on the stated effective date, and attaching the document to the tax return for the partnership for the taxable year that includes the effective date of the revocation.

Section 83(h) provides that, in the case of a transfer of property in connection with the performance of services or a cancellation of a restriction described in § 83(d), there is allowed as a deduction under § 162, to the person for whom the services were performed (the service recipient), an amount equal to the amount included under § 83(a), (b), or (d)(2) in the gross income of the service provider. The deduction is allowed for the taxable year of the service recipient in which or with which ends the taxable year in which such amount is included in the gross income of the service provider. Under § 1.83–6(a)(3), if property is substantially vested upon the transfer, the deduction is allowed to the service recipient in accordance with its method of accounting (in conformity with §§ 446 and 461).

Section 1.83–6(c) provides that if, under § 83(h) and § 1.83–6(a), a deduction, an increase in basis, or a reduction of gross income was allowable (disregarding the reasonableness of the amount of compensation) in respect of a transfer of property and such property is subsequently forfeited, the amount of such deduction, increase in basis, or reduction of gross income shall be includible in the gross income of the person to whom it was allowable for the taxable year of the forfeiture. The basis of such property in the hands of the person to whom it is forfeited shall include any such amount includible in the gross income of such person, as well as any amount such person pays upon forfeiture.

* * *

Proposed § 1.704–1(b)(2)(iv)(*b*)(*1*) provides that a partner's capital account includes the amount contributed by that partner to the partnership, and, in the case of a compensatory partnership interest that is transferred on or after the date final regulations are published in the Federal Register, the amount included on or after that date as the partner's compensation income under § 83(a), (b), or (d)(2). For these purposes, a compensatory partnership interest is an interest in the transferring partnership that is transferred in connection with the performance of services for that partnership (either before or after the formation of the partnership), including an interest that is transferred on the exercise of a compensatory partnership option. A compensatory partnership option is an option to acquire an interest in the issuing partnership that is granted in connection with the performance of services for that partnership (either before or after the formation of the partnership). See proposed § 1.721–1(b)(4).

* * *

Section 721(a) provides that no gain or loss is recognized to a partnership or to any of its partners in the case of a contribution of property to the partnership in exchange for an interest in the partnership.

Proposed § 1.721–1(b)(1) provides that § 721 generally does not apply to the transfer of a partnership interest in connection with the performance of services. Such a transfer constitutes a transfer of property to which § 83 and the regulations thereunder apply. However, under proposed § 1.721–1(b)(2), except as provided in § 83(h) or § 1.83–6(c), no gain or loss is recognized by a partnership upon: (i) the transfer or substantial vesting of a compensatory partnership interest, or (ii) the forfeiture of a compensatory partnership interest.

Proposed § 1.761–1(b) provides that if a partnership interest is transferred in connection with the performance of services, and that partnership interest is substantially nonvested (within the meaning of § 1.83–3(b)), then the holder of the partnership interest is not treated as a partner solely by reason of holding the interest, unless the holder makes an election with respect to the interest under § 83(b).

¶ 17,085

Rev. Proc. 93–27 * * * [excerpted at ¶ 17,080] provides generally that if a person receives a profits interest for the provision of services to or for the benefit of a partnership in a partner capacity or in anticipation of becoming a partner, the Service will not treat the receipt of such an interest as a taxable event for the partner or the partnership. The revenue procedure does not apply if (1) the profits interest relates to a substantially certain and predictable stream of income from partnership assets, such as income from high-quality debt securities or a high-quality net lease; (2) within two years of receipt, the partner disposes of the profits interest; or (3) the profits interest is a limited partnership interest in a "publicly traded partnership" within the meaning of § 7704(b).

Rev. Proc. 2001–43 * * * [excerpted at ¶ 17,082] clarifies Rev. Proc. 93–27 and provides that, for purposes of Rev. Proc. 93–27, if a partnership grants a substantially nonvested profits interest in the partnership to a service provider, the service provider will be treated as receiving the interest on the date of its grant, provided that: (1) the partnership and the service provider treat the service provider as the owner of the partnership interest from the date of its grant and the service provider takes into account the distributive share of partnership income, gain, loss, deduction and credit associated with that interest in computing the service provider's income tax liability for the entire period during which the service provider has the interest; (2) upon the grant of the interest or at the time that the interest becomes substantially vested, neither the partnership nor any of the partners deducts any amount (as wages, compensation, or otherwise) for the fair market value of the interest; and (3) all other conditions of Rev. Proc. 93–27 are satisfied.

Section 3. Scope

.01 *In General.* The Safe Harbor in section 4 of this revenue procedure applies to any Safe Harbor Partnership Interest transferred by a partnership if the transfer is made during the period in which the Safe Harbor Election is in effect (whether or not the Safe Harbor Partnership Interest is substantially vested on the date of transfer). Thus, for example, sections 4.02 through 4.04 of this revenue procedure apply to a Safe Harbor Partnership Interest that is transferred during the period in which the Safe Harbor Election is in effect, even if that Safe Harbor Partnership Interest does not become substantially vested until after the Safe Harbor Election is terminated, a § 83(b) election is made after the Safe Harbor Election is terminated, or that Safe Harbor Partnership Interest is forfeited after the Safe Harbor Election is terminated. Further, a Safe Harbor Election is binding on the partnership, all of its partners, and the service provider. The Safe Harbor includes all of the rules set forth in section 4 of this revenue procedure, and a partnership, its partners, and the service provider may not choose to apply only certain of the rules in section 4 of this revenue procedure or

¶ 17,085

to apply the Safe Harbor only to certain partners, service providers, or partnership interests.

.02 *Safe Harbor Partnership Interest.* (1) Except as otherwise provided in section 3.02(2) of this revenue procedure, a Safe Harbor Partnership Interest is any interest in a partnership that is transferred to a service provider by such partnership in connection with services provided to the partnership (either before or after the formation of the partnership), provided that the interest is not (a) related to a substantially certain and predictable stream of income from partnership assets, such as income from high-quality debt securities or a high-quality net lease, (b) transferred in anticipation of a subsequent disposition, or (c) an interest in a publicly traded partnership within the meaning of § 7704(b). Unless it is established by clear and convincing evidence that the partnership interest was not transferred in anticipation of a subsequent disposition, a partnership interest is presumed to be transferred in anticipation of a subsequent disposition for purposes of the preceding clause (b) if the partnership interest is sold or disposed of within two years of the date of receipt of the partnership interest (other than a sale or disposition by reason of death or disability of the service provider) or is the subject, at any time within two years of the date of receipt, of a right to buy or sell regardless of when the right is exercisable (other than a right to buy or sell arising by reason of the death or disability of the service provider). For the purposes of this revenue procedure, "disability" means a condition which causes a service provider to be unable to engage in any substantial gainful activity by reason of a medically determinable physical or mental impairment expected to result in death or to last for a continuous period of not less than 12 months.

(2) An interest in a partnership is not a Safe Harbor Partnership Interest unless at the date of transfer the requirements of section 3.03 of this revenue procedure are satisfied and a Safe Harbor Election has not terminated pursuant to section 3.04 of this revenue procedure. For the first taxable year that a partnership is subject to a Safe Harbor Election, a partnership interest may be a Safe Harbor Partnership Interest if a Safe Harbor Election is attached to the partnership tax return for the taxable year including the date of transfer, provided that the other requirements of section 3.03 of this revenue procedure are satisfied on or before the date of such transfer.

.03 *Required Conditions for Safe Harbor Election.* In order to effect and maintain a valid Safe Harbor Election the following conditions must be satisfied:

(1) The partnership must prepare a document, executed by a partner who has responsibility for federal income tax reporting by the partnership, stating that the partnership is electing, on behalf of the partnership and each of its partners, to have the Safe Harbor described in Rev. Proc. 200X–XX apply irrevocably with respect to all partnership

interests transferred in connection with the performance of services while the Safe Harbor Election remains in effect. The Safe Harbor Election must specify the effective date of the Safe Harbor Election, and the effective date for the Safe Harbor Election may not be prior to the date that the Safe Harbor Election is executed. The Safe Harbor Election must be attached to the tax return for the partnership for the taxable year that includes the effective date of the Safe Harbor Election.

(2) Except as provided in section 3.03(3) of this revenue procedure, the partnership agreement must contain provisions that are legally binding on all of the partners stating that (a) the partnership is authorized and directed to elect the Safe Harbor described in this revenue procedure, and (b) the partnership and each of its partners (including any person to whom a partnership interest is transferred in connection with the performance of services) agrees to comply with all requirements of the Safe Harbor described in this revenue procedure with respect to all partnership interests transferred in connection with the performance of services while the election remains effective. If a partner that is bound by these provisions transfers a partnership interest to another person, the requirement that each partner be bound by these provisions is satisfied only if the person to whom the interest is transferred assumes the transferring partner's obligations under the partnership agreement. If an amendment to the partnership agreement is required, the amendment must be effective before the date on which a transfer occurs for the Safe Harbor to be applied to such transfer.

(3) If the partnership agreement does not contain the provisions described in section 3.03(2) of this revenue procedure, or the provisions are not legally binding on all of the partners of the partnership, then each partner in a partnership that transfers a partnership interest in connection with the performance of services must execute a document containing provisions that are legally binding on each partner stating that (a) the partnership is authorized and directed to elect the Safe Harbor described in this revenue procedure, and (b) the partner agrees to comply with all requirements of the Safe Harbor described in this revenue procedure with respect to all partnership interests transferred in connection with the performance of services while the election remains effective. Each person classified as a partner must execute the document required by this paragraph (3), and the document must be effective, before the date on which a transfer occurs, for the Safe Harbor to be applied to such transfer. If a partner who has submitted the required document transfers a partnership interest to another person, the condition that each partner submit the necessary document is satisfied only if the person to whom the interest is transferred either submits the required document or assumes the transferring partner's obligations under a document required by this paragraph that was previously submitted with respect to the transferred interest.

¶ 17,085

.04 *Termination of Safe Harbor Election.* A Safe Harbor Election continues in effect until terminated. A Safe Harbor Election terminates automatically on the date that a partnership fails to satisfy the conditions and requirements described in sections 3.02 and 3.03 of this revenue procedure. A Safe Harbor Election also terminates automatically in the event that the partnership, a partner, or service provider reports income tax effects of a Safe Harbor Partnership Interest in a manner inconsistent with the requirements of this revenue procedure, including a failure to provide appropriate information returns. A partnership may affirmatively terminate a Safe Harbor Election by preparing a document, executed by a partner who has responsibility for federal income tax reporting by the partnership, indicating that the partnership, on behalf of the partnership and each of its partners, is revoking its Safe Harbor Election under Rev. Proc. 200X–XX and the effective date of the revocation, provided that the effective date may not be prior to the date the election to terminate is executed. Such termination election must be attached to the tax return for the partnership for the taxable year that includes the effective date of the election. The rules of the Safe Harbor in section 4 of this revenue procedure do not apply to any partnership interests transferred on or after the date of a termination of the Safe Harbor Election under this paragraph but continue to apply to any Safe Harbor Partnership Interests transferred while the Safe Harbor Election was in effect.

.05 *Election After Termination.* If a partnership has made a Safe Harbor Election and if such Safe Harbor Election has been terminated under section 3.04 of this revenue procedure, then, absent the consent of the Commissioner, the partnership (and any successor partnerships) are not eligible to make a Safe Harbor Election for any taxable year that begins before the fifth calendar year after the calendar year during which such termination occurs. For purposes of this paragraph, a successor partnership is any partnership that (1) on the date of termination, is related (within the meaning of § 267(b) or § 707(b)) to the partnership whose Safe Harbor Election has terminated (or, if the partnership whose Safe Harbor Election has terminated does not exist on the date of termination would be related if it existed on such date), and (2) acquires (either directly or indirectly) a substantial portion of the assets of the partnership whose Safe Harbor Election has terminated.

.06 *Recordkeeping Requirement.* Under proposed § 1.83–3(*l*), the partnership is required to keep as records: (1) a copy of the Safe Harbor Election submitted by the partnership to the Service under section 3.03(1) of this revenue procedure, and (2) if applicable, the original of each document submitted to the partnership by a partner under section 3.03(3) of this revenue procedure. If the partnership is unable to produce a record of a particular document, the election will be treated as not made, generally resulting in termination of the Safe Harbor Election under section 3.04 of this revenue procedure.

¶ **17,085**

SECTION 4. SAFE HARBOR

.01 *Safe Harbor.* For purposes of § 83, the rules in sections 4.02 through 4.04 of this revenue procedure apply to any Safe Harbor Partnership Interest for which a Safe Harbor Election is in effect.

.02 *Liquidation Value.* Under the Safe Harbor, the fair market value of a Safe Harbor Partnership Interest is treated as being equal to the liquidation value of that interest. For this purpose, liquidation value is determined without regard to any lapse restriction (as defined at § 1.83–3(i)) and means the amount of cash that the recipient of the Safe Harbor Partnership Interest would receive if, immediately after the transfer, the partnership sold all of its assets (including goodwill, going concern value, and any other intangibles associated with the partnership's operations) for cash equal to the fair market value of those assets and then liquidated.

.03 *Vesting.* Under the Safe Harbor, a Safe Harbor Partnership Interest is treated as substantially vested if the right to the associated capital account balance equivalent is not subject to a substantial risk of forfeiture or the interest is transferable. A Safe Harbor Partnership Interest is treated as substantially nonvested only if, under the terms of the interest at the time of the transfer, the interest terminates and the holder may be required to forfeit the capital account balance equivalent credited to the holder under conditions that would constitute a substantial risk of forfeiture, and the interest is not transferable. For these purposes, the capital account balance equivalent is the amount of cash that the recipient of the Safe Harbor Partnership Interest would receive if, immediately prior to the forfeiture, the interest vested and the partnership sold all of its assets (including goodwill, going concern value, or any other intangibles associated with the partnership's operations) for cash equal to the fair market value of those assets and then liquidated. Notwithstanding the previous sentence, a Safe Harbor Partnership Interest will not be considered substantially nonvested if the sole portion of the capital account balance equivalent forfeited is the excess of the capital account balance equivalent at the date of termination of services over the capital account balance equivalent at the end of the prior partnership tax year or any later date before the date of termination of services.

.04 *Forfeiture Subsequent to § 83(b) Election.* If a Safe Harbor Partnership Interest with respect to which a § 83(b) election has been made is forfeited, the service provider must include as ordinary income in the taxable year of the forfeiture an amount equal to the excess, if any, of (1) the amount of income or gain that the partnership would be required to allocate to the service provider under proposed § 1.704–1(b)(4)(xii) if the partnership had unlimited items of gross income and gain, over (2) the amount of income or gain that the partnership actually allocated to the service provider under proposed § 1.704–1(b)(4)(xii).

¶ 17,085

.01 *Application of Safe Harbor to the Service Provider.* Under the Safe Harbor, the service provider recognizes compensation income upon the transfer of a substantially vested Safe Harbor Partnership Interest in an amount equal to the liquidation value of the interest, less any amount paid for the interest. If the service provider receives a Safe Harbor Partnership Interest that is substantially nonvested, does not make an election under § 83(b), and holds the interest until it substantially vests, the service provider recognizes compensation income in an amount equal to the liquidation value of the interest on the date the interest substantially vests, less any amount paid for the interest. If the service provider receives a Safe Harbor Partnership Interest that is substantially nonvested and makes an election under § 83(b), the service provider recognizes compensation income on the date of transfer equal to the liquidation value of the interest, determined as if the interest were substantially vested, pursuant to the rules of § 83(b) and § 1.83–2, less any amount paid for the interest.

.02 *Application of Safe Harbor to the Service Recipient.* Under § 83(h), the service recipient generally is entitled to a deduction equal to the amount included as compensation in the gross income of the service provider under § 83(a), (b), or (d)(2), but only to the extent the amount meets the requirements of § 162 or § 212. Under the Safe Harbor, the amount included in the service provider's gross income in accordance with section 4.02 of this revenue procedure is considered the amount included as compensation in the gross income of the service provider under § 83(a) or (b) for purposes of § 83(h). The deduction generally is allowed for the taxable year of the partnership in which or with which ends the taxable year of the service provider in which the amount is included in gross income as compensation. However, in accordance with § 1.83–6(a)(3), where the deduction relates to the transfer of substantially vested property, the deduction is available in accordance with the service recipient's method of accounting.

SECTION 6.   EXAMPLES

The following facts apply for all of the examples below:

SP is an individual with a calendar year taxable year. *PRS* is a partnership with a calendar year taxable year. Except as otherwise stated, *PRS*'s partnership agreement provides for all partnership items to be allocated to the partners in proportion to the partners' interests in the partnership. *PRS*'s partnership agreement provides that the partners' capital accounts will be determined and maintained in accordance with § 1.704–1(b)(2)(iv), that liquidation proceeds will be distributed in accordance with the partners' positive capital account balances, and that any partner with a deficit balance in the partner's capital account following the liquidation of the partner's interest must restore that deficit to the partnership. All allocations and distributions to all parties are not recast under § 707(a)(2), and § 751(b) does not apply to any distribution. The partnership, its members, and the service providers elect the Safe Harbor provided in section 4 of this revenue procedure and file all affected returns consistent with the Safe Harbor, and each partnership interest transferred constitutes a Safe Harbor Partnership Interest under section 3.02 of this revenue procedure. The issuance of the partnership interest in each example is not required to be capitalized under the rules of § 263 or other applicable provision of the Code. In examples in which the partnership interest transferred to the service provider is not substantially vested, there is not a plan that the service provider will forfeit the partnership interest.

(1) *Example 1: Substantially Vested Profits Interest*

Facts: *PRS* has two partners, *A* and *B*, each with a 50% interest in *PRS*. On March 1, 2005, *SP* agrees to perform services for the partnership in exchange for a partnership interest. Under the terms of the partnership agreement, *SP* is entitled to 10% of the future profits and losses of *PRS*, but is not entitled to any of the partnership's capital as of the date of transfer. Although *SP* must surrender the partnership interest upon termination of services to the partnership, *SP* will not surrender any share of the profits accumulated through the end of the partnership taxable year preceding the partnership taxable year in which *SP* terminates services.

Conclusion: Under section 4.03 of this revenue procedure, *SP*'s interest in *PRS* is treated as substantially vested at the time of transfer. Under section 4.02 of this revenue procedure, the fair market value of the interest for purposes of § 83 is treated as being equal to its liquidation value (zero). Therefore, *SP* does not recognize compensation income under § 83(a) as a result of the transfer, *PRS* is not entitled to a deduction, and *SP* is not entitled to a capital account balance.

(2) *Example 2: Substantially Vested Interest*

Facts: *PRS* has two partners, *A* and *B*, each with a 50% interest in *PRS*. On March 1, 2005, *SP* pays the partnership $10 and agrees to perform services for the partnership in exchange for a 10% partnership interest that is treated as substantially vested under section 4.03 of this revenue procedure. Immediately before *SP*'s $10 payment to *PRS* and the transfer of the partnership interest to *SP* in connection with the performance of services, the value of the partnership's assets (including goodwill, going concern value, and any other intangibles associated with the partnership's operations) is $990.

Conclusion: Under section 4.02 of this revenue procedure, the fair market value of *SP*'s interest in *PRS* at the time the interest becomes substantially vested is treated as being equal to its liquidation value at that time for purposes of § 83. Therefore, in 2005, *SP* includes $90 ($100 liquidation value less $10 amount paid for the interest) as compensation income under § 83(a), *PRS* is entitled to a deduction of $90 under § 83(h), and *SP*'s initial capital account is $100 ($90 included in income plus $10 amount paid for the interest).

(3) *Example 3: Substantially Nonvested Interest; No § 83(b) Election; Pre–Existing Partner*

Facts: *PRS* has two partners, *A* and *SP*, each with a 50% interest in *PRS*. On December 31, 2004, *SP* agrees to perform services for the partnership in exchange for a 10% increase in *SP*'s interest in the partnership from 50% to 60%. *SP* is not required to pay any amount in exchange for the additional 10% interest. Under the terms of the partnership agreement, if *SP* terminates services on or before January 1, 2008, *SP* forfeits any right to any share of accumulated, undistributed profits with respect to the additional 10% interest. The partnership interest transferred to *SP* is not transferable and no election is made under § 83(b). *SP* continues performing services through January 1, 2008. *PRS* has taxable income of $500 in 2005 and $1,000 in each of 2006 and 2007. No distributions are made to *A* or *SP* during such period. On January 1, 2008, the value of the partnership's assets (including goodwill, going concern value, and any other intangibles associated with the partnership's operations) is $3,500.

Conclusion: Under section 4.03 of this revenue procedure, the 10% partnership interest transferred to *SP* on December 31, 2004, is treated as substantially nonvested at the time of transfer. Because a § 83(b) election is not made, *SP* does not include any amount as compensation income attributable to the transfer, and correspondingly, *PRS* is not entitled to a deduction under § 83(h).

In accordance with the partnership agreement, *PRS*'s taxable income for 2005 is allocated $250 to *A* and $250 to *SP*, and *PRS*'s taxable income for each of 2006 and 2007 is allocated $500 to *A* and $500 to *SP*.

On January 1, 2008, *SP*'s additional 10% interest in *PRS* is treated as becoming substantially vested under section 4.03 of this revenue procedure. At that time, the additional 10% interest in the partnership has a liquidation value of $350 (10% of $3,500). Under section 4.02 of this revenue procedure, the fair market value of the interest at the time it becomes substantially vested is treated as being equal to its liquidation value at that time for purposes of § 83. Therefore, in 2008, *SP* includes $350 as compensation income under § 83(a), *PRS* is entitled to a deduction of $350 under § 83(h), and *SP*'s capital account is increased by $350.

(4) *Example 4: Substantially Nonvested Interest; No § 83(b) Election*

Facts: *PRS* has two partners, *A* and *B*, each with a 50% interest in *PRS*. On December 31, 2004, *SP* pays the partnership $10 and agrees to perform services for the partnership in exchange for a 10% partnership interest. Under the terms of the partnership agreement, if *SP* terminates services on or before January 1, 2008, *SP* forfeits any rights to any share of accumulated, undistributed profits, but is entitled to a return of *SP*'s $10 initial contribution. *SP*'s partnership interest is not transferable and no election is made under § 83(b). *SP* continues performing services through January 1, 2008. *PRS* earns $500 of taxable income in 2005, and $1,000 in each of 2006 and 2007. *A* and *B* each receive distributions of $225 in 2005, but neither *A* nor *B* receive distributions in 2006 and 2007. *PRS* transfers $50 to *SP* in 2005, but does not make any transfers to *SP* in 2006 or 2007. On January 1, 2008, *SP*'s partnership interest has a liquidation value of $300 (taking into account the unpaid partnership income credited to *SP* through that date).

Conclusion: Under section 4.03 of this revenue procedure, *SP*'s partnership interest is treated as substantially nonvested at the time of transfer. Because a § 83(b) election is not made, *SP* does not include any amount as compensation income attributable to the transfer and, correspondingly, *PRS* is not entitled to a deduction under § 83(h). Under proposed § 1.761–1(b), *SP* is not a partner in *PRS*; therefore, none of *PRS*'s taxable income for the years in which *SP*'s interest is substantially nonvested may be allocated to *SP*. Rather, *PRS*'s taxable income is allocated exclusively to *A* and *B*. In addition, the $50 paid by *PRS* to *SP* in 2005 is compensation income to *SP*, and *PRS* is entitled to a deduction of $50 under § 162 in accordance with its method of accounting.

On January 1, 2008, *SP*'s interest in *PRS* is treated as becoming substantially vested under section 4.03 of this revenue procedure. Under section 4.02 of this revenue procedure, the fair market value of the interest at the time the interest becomes substantially vested is treated as being equal to its liquidation value at that time for § 83 purposes. Therefore, in 2008, *SP* includes $290 ($300 liquidation value less $10 amount paid for the interest) as compensation income under § 83(a), *PRS* is entitled to a $290 deduction, and *SP*'s capital account is increased to $300 ($290 included in income plus $10 amount paid for the interest).

(5) *Example 5: Substantially Nonvested Interest; § 83(b) Election*

Facts: The facts are the same as in Example 4, except that *SP* makes an election under § 83(b) with respect to *SP*'s interest in *PRS*. The liquidation value of the interest is $100 at the time the interest in *PRS* is transferred to *SP*. *SP* continues performing services through January 1, 2008.

Conclusion: Under section 4.02 of this revenue procedure, the fair market value (disregarding lapse restrictions) of *SP*'s interest in *PRS* at the time of transfer is treated as being equal to its liquidation value (disregarding lapse restrictions) at that time for § 83 purposes. Because a § 83(b) election is made, in 2004 *SP* includes $90 ($100 liquidation

¶ 17,085

value less $10 amount paid for the interest) as compensation income, *PRS* is entitled to a $90 deduction, and *SP*'s initial capital account is $100 ($90 included in *SP*'s income plus $10 amount paid for the interest). Under proposed § 1.761–1(b), as a result of *SP*'s election under § 83(b), *SP* is treated as a partner starting from the date of the transfer of the interest to *SP*. Accordingly, *SP* includes in 2005 taxable income *SP*'s $50 distributive share of *PRS* income, and the $50 payment to *SP* by *PRS* in 2005 is a partnership distribution under § 731. *SP* includes in 2006 and 2007 taxable income *SP*'s $100 distributive shares of *PRS* income for those years.

* * *

Section 7. Effect on Other Documents

Rev. Proc. 93–27, 1993–2 C.B. 343, and Rev. Proc. 2001–43, 2001–2 C.B. 191, are obsoleted.

[¶ 17,090]

Problems

1. The LM Partnership has two equal partners, Larry and Martha, each with a 50% interest in the partnership. On January 1 of year 2, Felix pays the partnership $40 and agrees to perform services for the partnership in exchange for a 10% partnership interest that is not subject to any restrictions. Assume that immediately before Felix's $40 payment to the partnership and the transfer of the compensatory partnership interest to Felix, the value of the partnership's assets (including goodwill and any other intangibles associated with the partnership's operations) is $960. What are the tax consequences to Felix and the LM Partnership on account of the transfer of the compensatory partnership interest to Felix?

2. Assume that the facts are the same as in Problem 1, except that under the terms of the partnership agreement, if Felix terminates services on or before December 31 of year 6, he will forfeit any rights to any share of accumulated, undistributed profits, but is entitled to a return of his $40 initial contribution. Assume further that Felix's partnership interest is not transferable and he makes no election under Section 83(b). On December 31 of year 6, the value of the partnership's assets (including goodwill and any other intangibles associated with the partnership's operations) is $4,000. How would your answer in Problem 1 change on account of these additional facts?

3. How would your answer in Problem 2 change if Felix makes a Section 83(b) election on January 1 of year 2?

4. Partytime is a partnership that owns a resort hotel in Naples, Florida, which has a value of $1 million. The resort is profitable and well established and has a stable history of earning $100,000 annually before

depreciation. As compensation for negotiating the acquisition of the adjoining beach-front property, Alexandra, who was not previously a partner, was given a five-percent interest in the future profits of the partnership. Is Alexandra taxable now? Assuming that she is, are there any tax consequences to the partnership?

5. Would your answer in Problem 4 change if Alexandra sold her interest in partnership profits for $80,000 one year after her receipt of it? Assume that she did not receive any partnership profits before the sale.

6. After eight long years in the trenches, Patricia has been made a partner in her law firm. She will not be required to make any capital contribution to the partnership, and she will not obtain any interest in the existing equity of the partnership. She will receive five percent of all future partnership net profits. Is she taxed on her admission to the partnership?

4. SERVICES OR PROPERTIES CONTRIBUTED?

[¶ 17,095]

UNITED STATES v. STAFFORD

United States Court of Appeals, Eleventh Circuit, 1984.
727 F.2d 1043.

R. LANIER ANDERSON, III, CIRCUIT JUDGE:

Taxpayers DeNean and Flora Stafford appeal the district court's summary judgment in favor of the government on their refund action for allegedly overpaid taxes. The refund action involves the Staffords' 1969 tax return, in which they did not account for their receipt of a limited partnership interest valued at $100,000. The taxpayers argue that the partnership share qualified for nonrecognition treatment under I.R.C. § 721(a) because it was received in "exchange" for "property" they contributed to the partnership. The district court held that nonrecognition was not available because the taxpayers' contribution of a letter of intent to the partnership did not meet the exchange and property requirements of the statute. We conclude that the district court applied an improper legal standard and under the proper legal test several issues should have been decided in favor of the taxpayers. With regard to additional issues, we conclude that genuine issues of fact remain such that summary judgment for the government was inappropriate. We therefore reverse and remand.

I. HISTORY OF THE CASE

The commercial transaction that underlies the current tax dispute has been discussed in previous tax opinions. *See Stafford v. United*

States, 435 F.Supp. 1036 (M.D.Ga.1977), *rev'd*, 611 F.2d 990 (5th Cir. 1980), *on remand*, 552 F.Supp. 311 (M.D.Ga.1982) * * *.

Throughout the 1960's, DeNean Stafford worked as a real estate developer, often in projects involving hotel property. At least two of Stafford's projects had used financing from the Life Insurance Company of Georgia ("LOG"). The business relationship between Stafford and LOG had taken various forms depending on the project. The hotel development involved in the present case, however, was somewhat unique.

In the early 1960's, LOG acquired property in Atlanta and constructed its corporate headquarters. LOG also owned the land adjacent to the headquarters, which at the time was undeveloped. LOG officials, in particular Mr. H. Talmadge Dobbs, who was then an executive vice president and member of the finance committee, approached Stafford and began negotiations for construction of a hotel complex on the unused land. In February of 1967, the LOG finance committee officially authorized continued discussions with Stafford on the hotel development.

Negotiations between Stafford and LOG led to a July 2, 1968, letter from Mr. Dobbs to Stafford, setting forth the numerous points of agreement as of that date and additional details in need of future resolution. In particular, the letter promised 6¾% interest on the loan financing for the hotel and it specified lease terms; both the interest rate and lease terms were very favorable to Stafford given then existing market conditions. Mr. Dobbs sent additional correspondence to Stafford on July 3, 1968, indicating that the favorable conditions described in the July 2 letter would be open for Stafford's consideration for a period of 60 days.

Under the terms of the July 2 letter, Stafford or his designee were to provide 25% equity for the hotel development. With letter in hand, Stafford contacted attorneys and business acquaintances and investigated the formation of a limited partnership to provide that equity share. On August 30, 1968, he responded to the LOG letter of July 2, accepting the general terms set forth in the letter and proposing further negotiations on additional details.

On October 30, 1968, Mr. A.F. Irby, a business associate of Stafford's, contacted potential investors with a draft of a limited partnership agreement and details regarding the proposed development. The letter stated:

> You will note in this file that Mr. Stafford is delivering the lease, which is highly economic, the construction loan and the permanent financing to the partners for what amounts to $100,000 of additional participation. The cost in the open market of procuring these three items would be in excess of $250,000 * * *

¶ 17,095

The Life of Georgia will supply all of the construction funds but will require that $2,000,000 of equity be invested prior to their own advancement of construction monies.

When you consider the fact that this is a very favorable tax arrangement, that the permanent loan is for 30 years at an interest of 6¾% and that the cost of the development is at least $1,500,000 less than it would be under ordinary circumstances this would appear to be an excellent deal.

In January of 1969, Stafford and a number of investors formed Center Investments, Ltd., a Georgia limited partnership, to pursue the development. Stafford was designated the sole general partner. He purchased two $100,000 shares and received a third limited partnership share for contributing to the partnership the letter of intent and the agreement with LOG contained therein.[6] In all, the partnership sold 20 units for $100,000 each, which together with the unit Stafford received for his capital contribution made a total of 21 units. Some eighteen months later, the partnership voted to amend the partnership agreement to provide Stafford a salary for his duties as general manager.

By mid–1970 the necessary capital had been raised and plans for the hotel development were set and approved. LOG and Center Investments executed formal lease and loan documents. The hotel project had expanded to a 550 room facility. This expansion, and unforeseen construction problems, had escalated the cost to over $9,000,000. LOG increased the amount of its loan to $7,127,500, but it substantially abided by the terms set forth in the July 2, 1968, letter to DeNean Stafford. LOG maintained the 6¾% interest rate on the first $5,000,000 it loaned to Center Investments. (The remaining $2,127,500 was financed at 9¾% interest, the market rate in 1970.) LOG and Center Investments also followed the formula set forth in the July 2 letter as the method for calculating lease payments. These terms had become even more favorable to Center Investments than when first proposed, owing to changed market conditions.

---

6. The letter of assignment provided:

In consideration of initial ½₁ interest in Center Investments, Ltd., a limited partnership formed under the laws of the State of Georgia (hereinafter referred to as the "partnership"), the undersigned hereby contributes to the partnership as a capital contribution, and does assign and transfer to the partnership all of his right, title and interest in and to the following property, agreed to be worth $100,000:

1. Preliminary drawings dated June 19, 1968, prepared by Lamberson, Plunkett and Shirley, Architects.

2. Budget estimates and documents dated September 6, 1968, of McDonough Construction Company.

3. Agreement to lease and loan commitment by Life Insurance Company of Georgia, dated July 2, 1968.

This January 21, 1969.

DeNean Stafford

As noted in the previous panel opinion, * * * "Stafford does not argue that the architects' renderings or contractors' estimates constitute property within the meaning of § 721." The July 2 letter of intent is the only item in the assignment that Stafford now argues was property for purposes of nonrecognition treatment.

¶ 17,095

On their 1969 joint federal tax return, the Staffords did not report as income their receipt of the third partnership share. The Commissioner audited that return and determined that the Staffords should have treated the partnership share as compensation for services that Stafford rendered to the partnership in negotiating and developing the investment. The Commissioner thus concluded that the nonrecognition principles of § 721 did not apply to the third partnership share and assessed a deficiency of $64,000 plus interest. The Staffords paid the assessment and filed a claim for a refund.

After the Internal Revenue Service denied the refund claim, the taxpayers filed the present action in January of 1976. In 1977, after considering summary judgment motions by the government and the Staffords, the district court granted summary judgment to the Staffords on grounds that the taxpayers' 1969 receipt of the third limited partnership share qualified for nonrecognition treatment under I.R.C. § 721. * * * [In 1980, the] former Fifth Circuit reversed, * * * and remanded for resolution of an underlying factual dispute.

On remand, the parties supplemented the record in a June 24, 1981, evidentiary hearing. The district court, after considering cross-motions for summary judgment, granted summary judgment in favor of the government. * * * The taxpayers appealed to this court.

II. Issues on Appeal and Standard of Review

The issues we now consider are easily stated. We must determine the proper tax characterization of the third partnership interest Stafford received. As was the situation when this case was last on appeal, we also consider the narrower issue of whether the district court properly granted a summary judgment.

With regard to this narrower issue, we cannot affirm the district court's summary judgment unless there are no remaining disputes of material fact * * *. We conclude that the government has not met this high burden.

III. Exchange and Property Requirements

To qualify for nonrecognition treatment on the receipt of a partnership share, the partner must establish that he made a contribution of "property" in "exchange" for that share. I.R.C. § 721(a). Contrary to the district court's holding that the exchange and property requirements were not met, we conclude that these issues should have been decided in the taxpayers' favor. We will first state the proper resolution of the issues at hand.[8] In the final section of the opinion, we highlight the remaining factual issues that must be decided on remand.

8. In its holding the previous panel deciding this case noted but a single fact issue remaining in the record before it, namely, "What was the *quid pro quo* for Stafford's receipt of the twenty-first partnership interest?" * * * The panel concluded, based

A. The Exchange Requirement

1. Generally

The district court held that Stafford's contribution of the letter of intent to the limited partnership was not an "exchange" for purposes of § 721. * * *

* * *

The district court opinion focused on the lack of agreement between Stafford and the limited partners. Viewed properly, the exchange that took place was between Stafford and the partnership, not the limited partners as individuals. * * * The assignment of January 21, 1969, *see supra* note 6, tends to establish that such an exchange occurred. Stafford contributed the letter of intent and other items; the partnership issued the third share to Stafford. Again, that this exchange occurred at the formation of the partnership and without a formal partnership vote does not alter our conclusion that an exchange took place.

2. Whether Stafford Owned the Letter of Intent

* * *

The facts in the record are not in dispute and compel a holding that Stafford owned the letter and was free to contribute it to the investment vehicle of his choice. Having thus concluded that Stafford owned the letter of intent and that his assignment of it met the exchange requirement of § 721, we turn to a discussion of the property requirement.

B. The Property Requirement

The district court alternatively held that Stafford had not received his third partnership share as the result of a contribution of "property." The court correctly stated that "the key to the benefit of nonrecognition afforded by I.R.C. § 721(a) is that *property must be exchanged for an interest in the partnership*." * * * The district court then stated as its test for property under § 721:

> After having carefully considered the arguments of counsel in conjunction with the opinion of the court of appeals, it is the opinion of the court that both *value* and *enforceability* are necessary to a conclusion that a document is "property" for purposes of § 721.

on conflicting testimony in the depositions, that a factfinder might determine that Stafford received his third partnership share in whole or in part as compensation for services he was to provide to the partnership. Finding a genuine issue of material fact in this regard, the court held that summary judgment for Stafford was inappropriate. This fact question remains disputed on the record before us and must be resolved by the factfinder on remand pursuant to the instructions set out in Section IV, *infra*.

The panel opinion went on to discuss several of the legal issues in the case. It did not, however, designate additional issues appropriate only for a factfinder. In this opinion, finding few disputes of material fact in the record before us, we rely upon the previous panel opinion to resolve many of the legal disputes in the case.

¶ 17,095

* * * Finding as a matter of law that the letter of intent was not enforceable, the court concluded that it was not property and the taxpayers were not eligible for nonrecognition under § 721.

We agree with the district court's conclusion that the letter of intent was not enforceable. Under Georgia law an agreement becomes enforceable when there is a meeting of the parties' minds "at the same time, upon the same subject matter, and in the same sense." * * *

The agreement in the present case unambiguously contemplated resolution of additional items before execution of the final contract. [Under Georgia law,] "An agreement to reach an agreement is a contradiction in terms and imposes no obligations on the parties thereto." * * *; as such, the agreement between Stafford and LOG embodied in the letter of intent and acceptance letter was unenforceable. * * * Stafford's contention that the parties intended to carry through with the terms of agreement set forth in the letter of intent is unavailing. Where, as here, the parties' written documents clearly and definitely make final agreement subject to mutually satisfactory future negotiations, we must decide as a matter of Georgia law that "the parties did not intend the letter agreement to be a binding, enforceable contract." * * *

Nevertheless, notwithstanding its lack of legal enforceability, we still must determine whether the letter of intent was "property" within the meaning of § 721. The previous panel opinion stated that "enforceability of any agreement evidenced by the letter of intent, while perhaps not dispositive of the question, is important and material." * * * We agree. An enforceable contract would perhaps be assured of property status; but the absence of enforceability does not necessarily preclude a finding that a document, substantially committing the parties to the major terms of a development project, is property.

Several nonenforceable obligations may rise to the level of property for purposes of § 721 or § 351. Unpatented know-how, which results from services and is not enforceable, nevertheless can be deemed property. *See generally* [W. McKee, W. Nelson & R. Whitmire,] *Taxation of Partnerships*, * * * ¶ 4.02[1], n.17 (citing Rev. Rul. 64–56, 1964–1 (Part 1) C.B. 133 (the term property under § 351 includes unpatented secret processes and formulas); Rev. Rul. 71–564, 1971–2 C.B. 179 (transfer of exclusive right to use trade secret is property under § 351)).

The instant transfer of the letter of intent outlining the major terms of a proposed loan and lease agreement to which both parties felt morally bound is closely analogous to a transfer of goodwill, which, although clearly unenforceable, nevertheless has been treated as property. *See* [W. McKee, W. Nelson & R. Whitmire,] *Taxation of Partnerships*, * * * ¶ 4.02[1], n.18:

> If goodwill is associated with a going business that is transferred to a partnership, there should be no question about the applicability of § 721. Furthermore, even if goodwill is associated

with an individual who will remain active in the transferred business, an effective contribution of goodwill may be made.

Citing Rev. Rul. 70–45, 1970–1 C.B. 17 (for the proposition that a professional person realizes capital gain on partial sale of goodwill to newly admitted partners); *See also* Rev. Rul. 79–288, 1979–2 C.B. 139 (transfer of trade name and goodwill to newly formed foreign corporation is transfer of property for purposes of Section 351); Rev. Rul. 70–45, 1970–1 C.B. 17 (goodwill of a one-man personal service business can be capital asset; whether it is an anticipatory assignment of income or a transfer of goodwill is a question of fact).

Thus, we conclude that the district court's requirement of legal enforceability as an absolute prerequisite to finding property status under § 721 was improper.

For purposes of our discussion as to whether the instant letter of intent is "property," we will assume arguendo that the factfinder on remand determines that the letter had value. Under the appropriate legal standard and the circumstances peculiar to this case, we conclude that the letter of intent encompassed a sufficient bundle of rights to constitute "property" within the meaning of § 721.

* * *

In the present case, the letter of intent of July 2 played a unique role. LOG officials have testified that it is the only commitment of this type the company has ever issued and that the letter was part of what they viewed to be a special project. Because the hotel was adjacent to LOG headquarters, officials of the company were willing to provide both construction financing, a permanent mortgage, and a lease for land and airspace, all at terms very favorable to the developer. When Stafford and LOG had reached agreement on these terms, the company offered the letter of intent because "this was a very peculiar transaction and I think because the way it developed, and the way the negotiations went on, this was a proper instrument to put the intent of the parties into something that would be—that we could rely on." August 16, 1976, deposition of Jason Gilliland (corporate counsel for LOG), at p. 8.

Although not enforceable in a strict legal sense, the written documents—*i.e.*, the terms of the July 2 letter, together with the July 3 letter limiting availability of those terms to acceptance within 60 days, and Stafford's August 30 letter of acceptance wherein he agreed to the essential terms of the letter of intent, including the interest on the loan and the lease terms—represented an agreement on the major terms that was quite firm in the view of the parties. Both of the principals have testified that they felt bound by the terms of the letter. *See* Gilliland deposition at 41; Dobbs deposition at 16; Oct. 14, 1976 deposition of DeNean Stafford at 41, 46. Two years subsequent to the letter, when market conditions made those terms very favorable to the partnership, the parties substantially adhered to the terms stated in the letter of intent. The letter clearly was transferable. The letter itself evidenced a commitment to Stafford "or his designee." * * * The principals have testified that from the outset they anticipated Stafford would transfer the letter to an investment group formed to develop the hotel. LOG officials attended meetings of the prospective partners and were aware that the letter would be transferred. Again, we note that even though Stafford transferred the letter to the partnership, LOG officials were willing to abide by the terms of the letter in subsequent dealing. If property "encompasses whatever may be transferred," *Matter of Chromeplate*, 614 F.2d at 995, then the letter of intent meets this test. In addition, the letter of intent that Stafford transferred to the partnership embodied his entire interest in the hotel development venture; he held nothing back.

A conclusion that the letter of intent is "property" under the instant circumstances comports with the purpose of § 721. Stafford exerted personal efforts on his own behalf in negotiating with LOG. When LOG and Stafford exchanged the letter of intent and acceptance in 1968, the government had not suggested that Stafford recognized taxable income. He could have completed the project as a sole proprietor without recognition of income based on his receipt of the letter. The purpose of §§ 721 and 351 is to permit the taxpayer to change his individual business into partnership or corporate form; the Code is designed to prevent the mere change in form from precipitating taxation. In keeping with this purpose, we can discern no reason to exclude Stafford's transfer of the letter of intent from the protective characterization as "property."

Stafford through his business reputation and work efforts was able to negotiate a very promising development project with LOG. He obtained from LOG officials a written document, morally, if not legally, committing LOG to the major terms of a proposed loan and lease. The transferability of the letter is undisputed and Stafford transferred his full interest in the project to the partnership. We conclude that the letter encompassed a sufficient bundle of rights and obligations to be deemed property for purposes of § 721.

For the foregoing reasons, we have concluded that Stafford's transfer of the letter of intent to the partnership met both the "exchange" and "property" requirements of § 721. However, the factual dispute identified by the previous panel remains unresolved on the record before us and, accordingly, we must remand.

IV.   THE *QUID PRO QUO* FOR STAFFORD'S RECEIPT OF THE PARTNERSHIP SHARE

The previous panel remanded for the factfinder to determine: "what was the quid pro quo for Stafford's receipt of the twenty-first partnership interest?" * * * The panel was concerned that a jury might find that Stafford received the partnership share wholly or partially in exchange for the services he was to provide as general partner. *Id*. Thus, even though Stafford contributed the letter to the partnership, the panel was unable to conclude that Stafford's contribution of the letter was responsible for his receipt of the third partnership share. This dispute remains; from the record we cannot ascertain whether the partnership was compensating Stafford for services to be rendered or for contribution of the letter of intent, or partially for both.

* * *

[¶ 17,100]

Problems

1.   If Stafford had been a partner of an existing partnership at the time he negotiated the letter of intent and received an increased interest because of his success, would the result have been the same?

2.   Assume that the partnership had not been formed at the time the letter of intent was obtained, but that the five prospective partners had been identified and Stafford had discussed his negotiations with them. Would the result have been the same?

[¶ 17,105]

E.   ORGANIZATION AND SYNDICATION EXPENSES

In the formation of a partnership and the commencement of its business activities, the partnership will incur a variety of expenses. In principle, most, if not all, of those expenses create an asset with a life of indefinite length but extending substantially beyond the year in which the expenses are paid or incurred. Thus, under normal income tax principles, such expenditures should be capitalized by the partnership rather than currently deducted. In practice, the precise treatment of those expenses is now controlled by two Code provisions and depends on the category to which the expense is assigned.

Costs incident to the formation of the partnership itself are governed by Section 709 which, in turn, distinguishes between organization and syndication expenses. Organization expenses are defined as those (i) incurred incident to the creation of the partnership, (ii) chargeable to capital account, and (iii) of a character that would be amortizable over the life of the partnership if the life were ascertainable. § 709(b)(3) and Reg. § 1.709–2(a). Such expenses would include the legal costs of negotiating and drafting the partnership agreement and filing fees. Reg. § 1.709–2(a). If it so elects, the partnership may currently deduct as much as $5,000 of its actual organizational expenditures, but such

¶ **17,105**

$5,000 limit is reduced by the amount by which the organizational expenditures exceed $50,000. Thus, if the organizational expenditures reach $55,000 or more, no current deduction is available. The remaining organizational expenditures are deductible by the partnership ratably over a 15–year period, starting with the month in which the partnership begins business. § 709(b)(1). The date when the partnership begins business for this purpose is a question of fact that must be resolved on the basis of all the surrounding facts and circumstances. Reg. § 1.709–2(c). If the partnership is liquidated before the end of the 15–year period, any remaining organizational expenditures that have not yet been allowed as a deduction under Section 709(b)(1) may be deducted as a loss under Section 165. § 709(b)(2).

Prior to 2004, no current deduction of such organizational expenditures was permitted, but all such expenditures were deductible over a five-year period at the election of the partnership. As discussed at ¶ 2305 in connection with a similar change made in the tax treatment of a corporation's organizational expenditures, the change in 2004 brings the deductibility of organizational expenses other than the first $5,000 in line with the time period available for amortization of intangibles under Section 197. If a partnership does not elect to amortize its organizational expenditures under Section 709(b), the partnership may not deduct such expenditures, § 709(a), except, presumably, as a loss in the year in which it liquidates.

Syndication expenses are those incurred in connection with the issuance and marketing of the partnership interests, including legal, accounting, underwriting, and registration costs. Reg. § 1.709–2(b); see Rev. Rul. 85–32, 1985–1 C.B. 186. Under Section 709, those expenses must also be capitalized but may not be amortized. Thus, such expenses provide no tax benefit until a partnership interest is sold or liquidated.

Finally, the tax treatment of business start-up expenses of all taxpayers is governed by Section 195. In general, when incurred by a new business venture, the costs of creating or investigating the creation or acquisition of an active trade or business are start-up expenses that must be capitalized. However, like organizational expenses, as a result of a change made in 2004, the first $5,000 of start-up expenses are currently deductible at the taxpayer's election, but such $5,000 limit is reduced by the amount by which the start-up expenses exceed $50,000. The remaining start-up expenses are deductible ratably over a 15–year period, starting with the month in which the taxpayer's active trade or business begins. § 195(b)(1). By contrast, under general tax principles, costs incurred in connection with the acquisition of business assets must be capitalized as part of the purchase price of those assets and may not be currently deducted or amortized under Section 195.

¶ 17,105

Chapter 18

OPERATION OF THE PARTNERSHIP

[¶ 18,000]

A. REPORTING AND TAXING PARTNERSHIP INCOME

Subchapter K's principles for taxing partnership operations reflect an amalgam of the aggregate and entity approaches to partnership taxation. On the one hand, under Section 701, a partnership is not itself a taxable entity but merely serves as a conduit for transmission of various items of income and expense to the respective partners, thus reflecting an aggregate approach to partnership taxation. The partners are liable in their individual capacities for income tax on the partnership's income, and each partner reports his or her distributive share of partnership income, losses, deductions, and credits for the taxable year of the partnership ending within or with the partner's taxable year, whether there is or is not an actual distribution or a right to current distribution. See §§ 701, 702, 704, and 706(a); Reg. §§ 1.701–1 and 1.702–1(a); and *Basye,* at ¶ 18,005.

On the other hand, the partnership generally is treated as an entity for purposes of reporting tax information and determining the partnership income or loss. See §§ 701 and 703. Thus, a partnership is required to file an information return for its taxable year, which is due the fifteenth day of the fourth month following the close of the partnership taxable year. §§ 701, 6031(a), and 6072(a). Under Section 703(a), the partnership computes its taxable income on the information return in the same manner as an individual taxpayer, subject to certain exceptions. Section 703(b) requires that elections affecting the computation of partnership income be made at the partnership level, also subject to certain exceptions. Moreover, Section 702 contains rules that attempt to preserve the character of items of partnership income, deduction, loss, or credit as they flow through to the partners. Finally, the partnership is

¶ 18,000

generally treated as an entity for administrative and judicial procedure purposes. See §§ 6221 through 6255.

1. COMPUTATION OF PARTNERSHIP INCOME

[¶ 18,005]

UNITED STATES v. BASYE

Supreme Court of the United States, 1973.
410 U.S. 441.

[The taxpayers were members of Permanente Medical Group, a medical partnership that contracted to provide medical services for the members of Kaiser Foundation Health Plan, Inc., a nonprofit health organization. Kaiser had established a prepaid medical and hospital expense plan. Under the agreement, Kaiser paid the partnership a flat monthly fee of $2.61 per member and, in addition, paid 12 cents per month per member directly to an independent trustee to fund a retirement program for the partnership. None of the individual partners acquired a vested interest in the retirement program before death, disability, or retirement. At retirement, the balance credited to a partner's account would be applied to the purchase of a retirement income contract. If a partner withdrew from the firm, he forfeited his interest in the fund, and it was redistributed among the remaining partners. None of the contributions were repayable to Kaiser. The partnership reported income by the accrual method and the taxpayers reported income by the cash method. Neither the partnership nor the partners reported the payments to the trust as income. The IRS contended that the payments to the trust were income to the partnership, and thus includible in each partner's distributive share of partnership income. Suits for refund were brought by the taxpayers following payment of deficiency assessments. Both the district court and the Ninth Circuit held for the taxpayers on the ground that the partnership did not receive the payments made to the trust and never had a "right to receive" such payments.]

MR. JUSTICE POWELL delivered the opinion of the Court.

* * *

Section 703 * * *, insofar as pertinent here, prescribes that "[t]he taxable income of a partnership shall be computed in the same manner as in the case of an individual." * * * § 703(a). Thus, while the partnership itself pays no taxes, * * * § 701, it must report the income it generates and such income must be calculated in largely the same manner as an individual computes his personal income. For this purpose, then, the partnership is regarded as an independently recognizable entity apart from the aggregate of its partners. Once its income is ascertained and reported, its existence may be disregarded since each partner must pay a tax on a portion of the total income as if the

¶ 18,000

partnership were merely an agent or conduit through which the income passed.[8]

In determining any partner's income, it is first necessary to compute the gross income of the partnership. One of the major sources of gross income, as defined in § 61(a)(1) * * *, is "[c]ompensation for services, including fees, commissions, and similar items." * * * There can be no question that Kaiser's payments to the retirement trust were compensation for services rendered by the partnership under the medical service agreement. These payments constituted an integral part of the employment arrangement. The agreement itself called for two forms of "base compensation" to be paid in exchange for services rendered—direct per-member, per-month payments to the partnership and other, similarly computed, payments to the trust. Nor was the receipt of these payments contingent upon any condition other than continuation of the contractual relationship and the performance of the prescribed medical services. Payments to the trust, much like the direct payments to the partnership, were not forfeitable by the partnership or recoverable by Kaiser upon the happening of any contingency.

Yet the courts below, focusing on the fact that the retirement fund payments were never actually received by the partnership but were contributed directly to the trust, found that the payments were not includable as income in the partnership's returns. The view of tax accountability upon which this conclusion rests is incompatible with a foundational rule, which this Court has described as "the first principle of income taxation: that income must be taxed to him who earns it." *Commissioner v. Culbertson*, 337 U.S. 733, 739–740 (1949). The entity earning the income—whether a partnership or an individual taxpayer—cannot avoid taxation by entering into a contractual arrangement whereby that income is diverted to some other person or entity. Such arrangements, known to the tax law as "anticipatory assignments of income," have frequently been held ineffective as means of avoiding tax liability. The seminal precedent, written over 40 years ago, is Mr. Justice Holmes' opinion for a unanimous Court in *Lucas v. Earl*, 281 U.S. 111 (1930). * * *

* * * The principle of *Lucas v. Earl*, that he who earns income may not avoid taxation through anticipatory arrangements no matter how clever or subtle, has been repeatedly invoked by this Court and stands

---

8. There has been a great deal of discussion in the briefs and in the lower court opinions with respect to whether a partnership is to be viewed as an "entity" or as a "conduit." We find ourselves in agreement with the Solicitor General's remark during oral argument when he suggested that "[i]t seems odd that we should still be discussing such things in 1972." * * * The legislative history indicates, and the commentators agree, that partnerships are entities for purposes of calculating and filing informational returns but that they are conduits through which the taxpaying obligation passes to the individual partners in accord with their distributive shares. See, *e.g.*, H.R. Rep. No. 1337, 83d Cong., 2d Sess. 65–66 (1954); S. Rep. No. 1622, 83d Cong., 2d Sess., 89–90 (1954) * * *.

today as a cornerstone of our graduated income tax system. * * * And, of course, that principle applies with equal force in assessing partnership income.

Permanente's agreement with Kaiser, whereby a portion of the partnership compensation was deflected to the retirement fund, is certainly within the ambit of *Lucas v. Earl*. The partnership earned the income and, as a result of arm's-length bargaining with Kaiser, was responsible for its diversion into the trust fund. * * *

* * *

Since the retirement fund payments should have been reported as income to the partnership, along with other income received from Kaiser, the individual partners should have included their shares of that income in their individual returns. * * * §§ 61(a)(13), 702, 704. For it is axiomatic that each partner must pay taxes on his distributive share of the partnership's income without regard to whether that amount is actually distributed to him. *Heiner v. Mellon*, 304 U.S. 271 (1938), decided under a predecessor to the current partnership provisions of the Code, articulates the salient proposition. After concluding that "distributive" share means the "proportionate" share as determined by the partnership agreement, *id.*, at 280, the Court stated:

> "The tax is thus imposed upon the partner's proportionate share of the net income of the partnership, and the fact that it may not be currently distributable, whether by agreement of the parties or by operation of law, is not material." *Id.*, at 281.

Few principles of partnership taxation are more firmly established than that no matter the reason for nondistribution each partner must pay taxes on his distributive share. * * *

The courts below reasoned to the contrary, holding that the partners here were not properly taxable on the amounts contributed to the retirement fund. This view, apparently, was based on the assumption that each partner's distributive share prior to retirement was too contingent and unascertainable to constitute presently recognizable income. It is true that no partner knew with certainty exactly how much he would ultimately receive or whether he would in fact be entitled to receive anything. But the existence of conditions upon the actual receipt by a partner of income fully earned by the partnership is irrelevant in determining the amount of tax due from him. The fact that the courts below placed such emphasis on this factor suggests the basic misapprehension under which they labored in this case. Rather than being viewed as responsible contributors to the partnership's total income, respondent-partners were seen only as contingent beneficiaries of the trust. * * *

* * * Indeed, as the Government suggests, the result would be quite the same if the "potential beneficiaries included no partners at all, but

were children, relatives, or other objects of the partnership's largesse." The sole operative consideration is that the income had been received by the partnership, not what disposition might have been effected once the funds were received.

* * *

In summary, we find this case controlled by familiar and long-settled principles of income and partnership taxation. There being no doubt about the character of the payments as compensation or about their actual receipt, the partnership was obligated to report them as income presently received. Likewise, each partner was responsible for his distributive share of that income. We, therefore, reverse the judgment and remand the case with directions that judgment be entered for the United States.

* * *

[¶ 18,010]

Note

Is the decision in *Basye* consistent with established concepts of realization of income and principles of accounting for income under either the accrual or cash methods of tax accounting?

[¶ 18,015]

2. TAXABLE YEAR OF THE PARTNERSHIP

Section 706(a) provides that the "income, gain, loss, deduction, or credit" of a partnership is to be reflected by a partner in the partner's taxable year within, or with, which the partnership taxable year ends. This provision standing alone afforded a substantial opportunity to defer the taxation of partnership income by adopting a partnership year different from that of the partners. For example, in the case of partners reporting on a calendar year basis and a partnership on a fiscal year ending January 31, there was a continuous deferral of taxation of partnership income. In such circumstances, the income of the partnership would not be reflected on the tax return of a partner for as long as 14 1/2 months following the close of the partnership year.

Section 706(b), as amended by the Tax Reform Act of 1986, limits the alternative reporting periods available to a partnership. The partnership will generally have the same taxable year as "1 or more partners having * * * an aggregate interest * * * of more than 50 percent." If this standard cannot be met in the particular circumstances of a partnership, the taxable year of the partnership must be the same as all partners having at least a five-percent interest in partnership profits or capital. If that standard cannot be met, the taxable year of the partnership will generally be the calendar year.

The general restrictions can be avoided if the partnership satisfies the IRS that a business purpose (other than tax deferral) justifies some other taxable year. § 706(b)(1)(C). Also, Section 444 provides a limited opportunity for a partnership to adopt another taxable year if it makes the payments prescribed by Section 7519 to mitigate the advantage of deferral. These provisions, which also apply to S corporations, are described at ¶ 15,250.

One clear effect of the requirements of Section 706(b) is that partnerships with primarily individual partners often will have to use the calendar year as their taxable year.

[¶ 18,020]

3. CLASSIFICATION AND DETERMINATION OF PARTNER-SHIP INCOME AND EXPENSES

Subchapter K also applies the aggregate or conduit principle to the character of items of partnership income and expense allocable to the respective partners. Section 702(a) provides that each partner shall take into account separately the partner's share of long-term and short-term capital gains and losses, gains and losses from Section 1231 transactions, charitable contributions, dividends with respect to which there is a dividends-received deduction, foreign taxes, taxable income or loss exclusive of the items requiring separate computation (so-called bottom line income or loss), and any other items required by the regulations to be separately stated.

The items that the regulations require be separately stated include tax benefit recoveries under Section 111, exploration expenditures under Section 615, intangible drilling and development costs under Section 263(c), soil and water conservation expenditures under Section 175, wagering gains and losses under Section 165(d), and any items which are subject to special allocation under the partnership agreement in a manner different from the general allocation of partnership income or loss. Reg. § 1.702–1(a)(8)(i). Consequently, a partner's distributive share of the various items of partnership income and expense retains the same character as if realized or incurred directly by the partner. § 702(b). Similarly, each partner must account for the partner's share of various items subject to special rules and restrictions.

The aggregate or conduit principle also applies to the partnership's gross income. Section 702(c) provides that "[i]n any case where it is necessary to determine the gross income of a partner for purposes of this title, such amount shall include his distributive share of the gross income of the partnership." This rule applies, for example, in ascertaining whether a return must be filed by the partner, in determining the applicability of the extended six-year period of limitations under Section 6501(e) relating to the omission of an item constituting more than 25

¶ 18,015

percent of gross income, and in computing the limit on the allowance of soil and water conservation expenses under Section 175(b).

After excluding the various classes of income and expense that must be separately stated, the taxable income (bottom line income or loss) of the partnership is computed under Section 703 in the same manner as in the case of an individual with certain exceptions. The partnership is not allowed the deductions that are especially provided for individuals since these are taken by the partners on their respective individual returns. These include the personal exemption deductions and deductions for nonbusiness expenses, such as medical expenses, alimony, and charitable contributions. The net operating loss deduction (Section 172) is also applied separately for each partner. This deduction is not allowed to the partnership since the individual partners take their respective shares of net losses of the partnership into account in determining income (or loss) on their individual returns.

Section 703(b) provides that, with certain exceptions, "[a]ny election affecting the computation of taxable income derived from a partnership shall be made by the partnership." In this respect, Section 703(b) adopts the entity concept of partnership taxation, which has important practical consequences for the individual partners. These elections include, among others, the selection of accounting methods, methods of depreciation, and the treatment of soil and water conservation expenses and intangible drilling and development costs. Reg. § 1.703–1(b)(1). The election to use Section 179 to expense the cost of tangible personal property in the year placed in service must be made by the partnership, but the limits on the amount of the Section 179 deduction apply at both the partnership and partner level. § 179(d)(8). In Rev. Rul. 89–7, 1989–1 C.B. 178, the IRS ruled that a partner's basis in the partnership interest must be reduced by the share of expense items allocable to the partner, even though the partner cannot deduct the entire amount because it exceeds the statutory limit.

[¶ 18,025]

REVENUE RULING 68–79
1968–1 C.B. 310.

Advice has been requested whether a partner's distributive share of partnership capital gains resulting under the circumstances described below is long-term capital gain.

A, B and C were equal partners in ABC partnership. On June 1, 1966, the partnership acquired 300 shares of X corporation stock as an investment. On February 1, 1967, A sold his partnership interest to new partner D. On May 1, 1967, the partnership sold at a gain the 300 shares of X stock (at which time D's holding period for his partnership interest was not more than six months).

¶ 18,025

Section 1222(1) * * * defines the term "short-term capital gain" as gain from the sale or exchange of a capital asset held for not more than six months [one year under current law], if and to the extent such gain is taken into account in computing gross income.

Section 1222(3) * * * defines the term "long-term capital gain" as gain from the sale or exchange of a capital asset held for more than six months [one year under current law], if and to the extent that such gain is taken into account in computing gross income.

Section 702(a) * * * provides that in determining his income tax, each partner shall take into account separately his distributive share of the partnership's gains and losses from sales or exchanges of capital assets held for more than six months [one year under current law].

Section 702(b) * * * provides that the character of any item of income, gain, loss, deduction, or credit included in a partner's distributive share under paragraphs (1) through (8) of subsection (a) shall be determined as if such item were realized directly from the source from which realized by the partnership, or incurred in the same manner as incurred by the partnership.

The character of any item of income, gain, loss, deduction, or credit included in a partner's distributive share under paragraphs (1) through (8) of section 702(a) * * * is determined at the partnership level. * * *

Since the *ABC* partnership held the *X* stock for more than six months, the gain realized by the partnership is long-term capital gain.

Accordingly, in computing his gross income, *D* should take into account separately in his return, as long-term capital gain, his distributive share of the partnership's long-term capital gain arising from the sale by the partnership of *X* corporation stock held by it as an investment for more than six months, notwithstanding that *D* has a holding period for his partnership interest of not more than six months.

[¶ 18,030]

Note

The Taxpayer Relief Act of 1997 added substantial complexity to the tax treatment of capital gains and losses. The 1997 Act and subsequent legislation lowered the top rate in Section 1(h) to 20 percent for long-term capital gains from capital assets held more than one year, and lowered the top rate on long-term capital gains to 18 percent for capital assets acquired after the year 2000 and held for more than five years. However, the 20 percent and 18 percent rates do not apply to long-term capital gains from the sale of "collectibles," or capital gain attributable to prior depreciation deductions taken with respect to depreciable real estate held more than 12 months (so-called "unrecaptured Section 1250 gain"). Long-term capital gain from collectibles is taxed at a preferential rate of 28 percent and unrecaptured Section 1250 gain is taxed at a preferential rate of 25 percent. For taxpayers who are in the 15 percent tax bracket or below, the 1997 Act also created preferential top rates of 10 percent for such taxpayers' long-term capital gains from the sale of capital assets held for more than one year and, for taxable years starting after 2000, eight percent for gains from the sale of capital assets held more than five years; however, there is no preferential rate for these taxpayers' collectibles gain and unrecaptured Section 1250 gain. Legislation enacted in 2003, and extended in 2006, reduced the 20 percent rate to 15 percent and the 10 percent rate to five percent (0 percent for taxable years starting after 2007) and eliminated the 18 percent and eight percent preferential rates that applied to gains from the sale or exchange of capital assets held for more than five years. The 2003 legislation did not change the treatment of collectibles gain or unrecaptured Section 1250 gain. Moreover, the changes enacted in 2003 and extended in 2006 will sunset for taxable years starting after 2010, unless Congress extends or makes permanent the changes made by the 2003 legislation. This means that the rules in place after the enactment of the Taxpayer Relief Act of 1997 may again become the law in 2011.

By creating all of these different categories of capital gains and losses, the 1997 and 2003 legislation made more difficult the record keeping and reporting burdens for flow-through entities such as partnerships, which presumably must separate out and report each partner's share of each category of the partnership's capital gains and losses. The statute specifically authorizes the Treasury to issue appropriate regulations to apply the provisions of Section 1(h) to sales and exchanges by flow-through entities (including partnerships) and of interests in such entities. § 1(h)(9). The Treasury and the IRS have issued regulations governing the sale of interests in partnerships and other flow-through entities, which are discussed at ¶ 21,092.

[¶ 18,035]

DEMIRJIAN v. COMMISIONER

United States Court of Appeals, Third Circuit, 1972.
457 F.2d 1.

[A and M were equal partners in a partnership whose sole operating asset was an office building. In September 1962, this property was taken by the Newark Housing Authority in condemnation proceedings. As stated in the stipulation of facts, the property was conveyed to the Authority by A and M as "partners trading as Kin–Bro Real Estate Company." The net proceeds of the sale were distributed by the partnership in equal shares to A and M. A and M, as individuals and in reliance upon Section 1033, reinvested most of their respective portions of the proceeds of the sale in separately owned parcels of real estate. A purchased qualifying replacement property in April 1963. M was unable to obtain suitable property within the statutory replacement period and, on January 16, 1964, she obtained a formal extension of time from the IRS. Thereafter, on February 7, 1964, M consummated the purchase of other real estate. A and M reported only the excess of their portion of the proceeds of the condemnation over the cost of the replacement real estate as taxable gain. The Commissioner asserted a deficiency, treating the entire gain as taxable income on the ground that, under Section 703(b), an election under Section 1033 and replacement with equivalent property can be made only by the partnership. The Tax Court sustained the Commissioner.]

VAN DUSEN, CIRCUIT JUDGE:

* * *

In reviewing a decision of the Tax Court, this court is normally limited in its scope of review by the clearly erroneous test of Rule 52(a), F.R. Civ. P. However, in cases such as the instant action, where the facts have been fully stipulated and no testimony was taken, the Court of Appeals may, within certain limits, substitute its factual conclusions and inferences for those of the Tax Court.

Petitioners' first contention on this appeal is that the Newark office building was owned by Anne and Mable as tenants in common, not as partners, and that, therefore, the § 1033 nonrecognition of gain election and replacement was properly made by them in their individual capacities as co-tenants. On the basis of the record before the Tax Court, we find that the property in question was owned by Kin–Bro Realty, a partnership, composed of Anne and Mabel Demirjian. It is noted that several federal cases have ruled that taxpayers such as petitioners who represent, in their dealings with the Internal Revenue Service, that property is owned by a partnership are bound by such representations.

Petitioners next contend that even if the office building was owned by the partnership, the election and replacement with equivalent property under * * * § 1033(a)(3) were properly made by them in their capacity as individual partners. We agree with the Tax Court's determination that * * * § 703(b) requires that the election and replacement under § 1033 be made by the partnership and that replacement by individual partners of property owned by the partnership does not qualify for nonrecognition of the gain. Section 703(b) provides, with exceptions not relevant here, that any election which affects the computation of taxable income derived from a partnership must be made by the partnership. The election for nonrecognition of gain on the involuntary conversion of property would affect such computation and is the type of election contemplated by § 703(b). The partnership provisions of the Internal Revenue Code treat a partnership as an aggregate of its members for purposes of taxing profits to the individual members and as an entity for purposes of computing and reporting income.[23] In light of this entity approach to reporting income, Congress included § 703(b) to avoid the possible confusion which might result if each partner were to determine partnership income separately only on his own return for his own purposes. To avoid the possible confusion which could result from separate elections under § 1033(a), the election must be made by the partnership as an entity, and the failure of the partnership to so act results in the recognition of the gain on the sale of partnership property.

Petitioners' final contention is that the Commissioner is estopped from denying that a valid election and replacement were made under § 1033. Two separate grounds for estoppel are alleged. The first ground, that the petitioners have conformed their conduct to existing interpretations of the law and the Commissioner may not "invoke a retroactive interpretation to the taxpayer's detriment," is clearly without merit. The second alleged ground is that the Commissioner is estopped by the implicit approval of the individual partner's election and replacement by the District Director for Newark in his letter of January 16, 1964. Even if we were to accept the letter as a justifiable basis for detrimental reliance, petitioners have demonstrated no such reliance[27] and, furthermore, the doctrine of estoppel does not prevent the Commissioner from correcting errors of law.

For the foregoing reasons, the September 1, 1970, orders of the Tax Court, in accordance with its opinion of that date, will be affirmed.

[¶ 18,040]

Notes

1. Is the decision in *Demirjian* consistent with both the basic premises of Subchapter K and the legislative purposes served by Section 1033? Does the result in *Demirjian* serve a valid tax policy objective? How might you plan the transaction to avoid the result reached in *Demirjian*?

Demirjian was followed in McManus v. Commissioner, 65 T.C. 197 (1975), aff'd, 583 F.2d 443 (9th Cir.1978), cert. denied, 440 U.S. 959 (1979), and Fuchs v. Commissioner, 80 T.C. 506 (1983).

2. Brown Group, Inc. v. Commissioner, 104 T.C. 105 (1995), rev'd, 77 F.3d 217 (8th Cir.1996) (nonacq.), involved an application of the

---

23. Petitioners contend that since a partnership is not a "taxpayer," * * * § 7701(a)(14), it cannot make an election under § 1033, which provides that an election must be made by a taxpayer. It seems clear that in adopting the entity approach to reporting income, Congress intended that a partnership be considered a taxpayer for purposes of computing and reporting income.

27. Anne and Mabel had already received their distributive shares prior to the date of the District Director's letter and had decided to make individual replacements. Also, the time for replacement by the partnership had already expired by the time the letter was received.

complex controlled foreign corporation provisions of Subpart F of the Code to a foreign corporate partner's share of income earned by a partnership. In opting to emphasize the aggregate theory of partnership taxation in resolving the specific international tax issue in the case, Judge Halpern set forth the following analysis of the aggregate versus entity views of partnership taxation (104 T.C. at 116–18):

> Authorities on partnership taxation have stated that subchapter K does not espouse either the aggregate or the entity theory of partnerships, but rather blends the two theories. * * * We agree. * * * Moreover, for purposes of interpreting provisions of the Code not contained in subchapter K, a partnership also may be treated either as an aggregate of its partners or as an entity distinct from its partners. * * * The treatment of partnerships in each context must be determined on the basis of the characterization most appropriate for the situation. See H. Conf. Rept. 2543, 83d Cong., 2d Sess. (1954) * * *.

* * *

> * * * The relationship between the entity approach to the computation of partnership income found in sections 703 and 706 and the aggregate approach applied to the taxation of that income found in sections 701, 702, and 704 has been described by the Supreme Court as follows:

> > For * * * [the purpose of calculating partnership income], the partnership is regarded as an independently recognizable entity apart from the aggregate of its partners. Once its income is ascertained and reported, its existence may be disregarded since each partner must pay a tax on a portion of the total income as if the partnership were merely an agent or conduit through which the income passed. [*United States v. Basye*, 410 U.S. 441, 448 (1973); fn. ref. omitted.]

* * *

> Indeed, an examination of cases requiring an entity (partnership) level determination of income shows that, once such determination is made, the partnership is ignored and the individual partners take account of such income as if they had earned it directly. * * *

> Notwithstanding such shift in emphasis from an entity view at the partnership level to an aggregate view at the partner level, any characterization of the partnership's activities with regard to an item generally persists. * * *

> Pertinent to the question at hand, we, and other courts, have attributed to a partner the activities and even the property of a partnership to determine whether, by virtue of such activity or

¶ 18,040

property, the partner had a particular status important for determining some aspect of the partner's Federal income tax status. * * *

3.   Suppose that a partnership has cancellation-of-indebtedness income within the meaning of Section 108. At what level (partnership or partner level) should the exclusions in Section 108(a) be applied and the reductions of tax attributes contemplated by Section 108(b) be made? At what level should the elections to reduce the basis of depreciable property in Section 108(b)(5) and to treat debt as "qualified real property business indebtedness" in Section 108(c)(3) be made?

Section 703(b)(1) explicitly states that elections under Section 108(b)(5) (to reduce the basis of depreciable property) and 108(c)(3) (to treat qualifying debt as "qualified real property business indebtedness") are to be made by each partner separately. Furthermore, Section 108(d)(6) provides that the exclusions in Section 108(a) and the corresponding reduction of tax attributes required by Section 108(b) (as well as certain other provisions in Section 108) are to be applied at the partner level. Thus, the current statute reflects the aggregate approach to partnership taxation with respect to cancellation-of-indebtedness income realized by a partnership.

Should a partner's distributive share of cancellation-of-indebtedness income result in an increase in the basis of the partner's partnership interest under Section 705(a)(1)? Does the answer to this question depend on whether one of the exclusions in Section 108(a) applies to the partner's share of the partnership's cancellation-of-indebtedness income? See Rev. Rul. 92–97, at ¶ 18,100. Would your answer to this question be affected by the Supreme Court's decision in *Gitlitz v. Commissioner*, excerpted at ¶ 15,287? Think about these questions as you consider the materials in Chapter 19.

[¶ 18,045]

4.   ASSIGNMENT OF INCOME

One fundamental principle underlying the provisions of Subchapter K is that the partners of a partnership will be allowed to pool their earnings and allocate items of partnership income or loss without regard to who contributed these items into the pool, provided that the allocations have substantial economic effect. This principle is reflected in Section 704(b), discussed at ¶¶ 18,065 et seq., and is subject to certain exceptions such as Section 704(c) (allocations with respect to contributed property with built-in gain or loss), discussed at ¶¶ 18,135 et seq., and Section 704(e) (allocations with respect to a partnership interest acquired by gift or from certain family members in a partnership in which capital is a material income-producing factor), discussed at ¶¶ 18,220 et seq. Recall, however, that under the anticipatory assignment of income doctrine enunciated in Lucas v. Earl, 281 U.S. 111 (1930), and its progeny, income is taxed to the person who earns the income even if the person has agreed to assign the income to someone else. Is the pooling principle underlying Subchapter K inconsistent with the assignment of income doctrine so that the Subchapter K pooling concept should be viewed conceptually as an exception to the assignment of income doctrine? Or, alternatively, is there some way to reconcile the pooling principle of Subchapter K with the assignment of income doctrine? Under what circumstances can the assignment of income doctrine apply to require a partner who performs the services that earn income to report the income on her own return even though she has entered into a partnership agreement that requires that the income be paid to the partnership? The following Tax Court decision considers these questions.

[¶ 18,050]

SCHNEER v. COMMISSIONER

United States Tax Court, 1991.
97 T.C. 643.

[Schneer, the taxpayer, had been employed as an associate with a law firm, BSI. During his employment by BSI, he referred clients to the firm and received a fixed salary and a percentage of fees generated by the referred clients. The taxpayer then left BSI and became a partner in two other law firms, B&K and SSG&M. Under both firms' partnership agreements, the taxpayer agreed to turn over to each partnership all legal fees received by him after joining the partnership, regardless of whether the fees were earned in the partnership's name or from the partnership's contractual relationship with the client. After the taxpayer became a partner in B&K and SSG&M, he continued to perform consulting work with respect to clients he had referred to BSI. He was paid by BSI a percentage of the fees that BSI received from clients that he had referred to BSI when he was an associate with BSI. (With one exception, these fees were for work performed after the taxpayer left BSI.) The taxpayer turned over the fees received from BSI to B&K and SSG&M in accordance with those firms' partnership agreements. B&K and SSG&M reported these fees on their partnership returns as partnership income, which was distributed to each partner (including the taxpayer) according to the partner's percentage share of partnership profits. The IRS asserted that the taxpayer was taxable on the fees paid by BSI, notwithstanding the partnership agreements with B&K and SSG&M, because he was the earner of the income.]

GERBER, JUDGE: * * *.

* * *

Opinion

* * * There is agreement that the amounts paid to petitioner by his former employer-law firm are income in the year of receipt. The question

is whether petitioner (individually) or the partners of petitioner's partnerships (including petitioner) should report the income in their respective shares.

The parties have couched the issue in terms of the anticipatory assignment-of-income principles. See *Lucas v. Earl*, 281 U.S. 111 (1930). Equally important to this case, however, is the viability of the principle that partners may pool their earnings and report partnership income in amounts different from their contribution to the pool. See sec. 704(a) and (b). The parties' arguments bring into focus potential conflict between these two principles and compel us to address both.

First, we examine the parties' arguments with respect to the assignment-of-income doctrine. Respondent argues that petitioner earned the income in question before leaving BSI, despite the fact that petitioner did not receive that income until he was a partner in B&K and, later, SSG&M. According to respondent, by entering into partnership agreements requiring payment of all legal fees to his new partnerships, petitioner anticipatorily assigned to those partnerships the income earned but not yet received from BSI.

* * *

Petitioner contends that the income in question was not earned until after he left BSI and joined B&K and SSG&M. He argues that the income received from BSI is reportable by the partners of the B&K and SSG&M partnerships (including petitioner) in their respective shares. * * *

The principle of assignment of income, in the context of Federal taxation, first arose in *Lucas v. Earl*, *supra*, where the Supreme Court, interpreting the Revenue Act of 1918, held that income from a husband-taxpayer's legal practice was taxable to him, even though he and his wife had entered into a valid contract under State law to split all income earned by each of them. In so holding, Justice Holmes, speaking for the Court, stated:

> There is no doubt that the statute could tax salaries to those who earned them and provide that the tax could not be escaped by anticipatory arrangements and contracts however skillfully devised to prevent the salary when paid from vesting even for a second in the man who earned it. [281 U.S. at 114–115.]

From that pervasive and simply stated interpretation, a plethora of cases and learned studies have sprung forth. Early cases reflected the use of the assignment-of-income principle only with respect to income not yet earned. The theory behind those interpretations was that income not yet earned is controlled by the assignor, even if assigned to another. Such income is necessarily generated by services not yet performed. Because the assignor may refuse to perform services, he necessarily has control over income yet to be earned. See * * * *Helvering v. Horst*, 311 U.S. 112,

¶ 18,050

118 (1940). This early rationale left open the possibility of successful assignments, for tax purposes, of income already earned. That possibility was foreclosed in *Helvering v. Eubank*, 311 U.S. 122 (1940), where the Supreme Court held that income already earned would also fall within the assignment-of-income doctrine of *Lucas v. Earl, supra*.

Respondent contends that *Helvering v. Eubank, supra*, is controlling in this case because petitioner had already earned the income in question at the time he entered into the partnership agreements. In that case, the taxpayer was an insurance agent who switched jobs and then assigned the future renewal commissions from policies already written. The taxpayer had written the policies and completed all work on them before leaving that job. The renewals and commissions were realized by the taxpayer solely due to the initiative and action of policyholders. " 'At the time of assignment there was nothing contingent in the * * * [taxpayer's] right' "to collect the money. See *Helvering v. Eubank, supra* at 126 (McReynolds, J., dissenting and quoting the lower court at 110 F.2d 737, 738 (2d Cir.1940)).

In this case, petitioner was not entitled to the referral fees unless the work for the referred clients had been successfully completed. On the other hand, petitioner would be entitled to the fees if the work was completed or if at the time of the assignment there was nothing contingent in petitioner's right to collect his percentage of the fees. Additionally, the majority of the services had not been performed prior to petitioner's leaving BSI. In this regard services had been performed with respect to $1,250 prior to 1984. With respect to $3,325 of the $21,329 of fees received in 1984, petitioner did not consult and was not required to do anything subsequent to leaving BSI to be entitled to those fees. With respect to the remainder of the $21,329 for 1984 and all of the 1985 fees, petitioner was called upon to and did consult while he was a partner of B&K or SSG&M.

We must decide whether petitioner had earned the fees in question prior to assigning them to the B&K or the SSG&M partnerships. Although petitioner was on the cash method, the principles that control use of the cash method are not suited to this inquiry. For purposes of the assignment-of-income doctrine, it must be determined whether the income was earned prior to an assignment. * * *

* * *

The record in this case reflects that, with the exception of $1,250 of services performed in prior years, the billings and payments in question were performed and collected subsequent to the time of assignment of the income. * * *

With these principles as our guide, we hold that petitioner had not earned the fees in question prior to leaving BSI, with the exception of the $1,250 received for services performed in an earlier year. More

¶ 18,050

specifically, we hold that petitioner earned the income in question while a partner of a partnership to which he had agreed to pay such income. With respect to substantially all of the fees in issue, BSI records reflect that clients were billed and payment received during the years in issue. Moreover, if petitioner had refused a request for his consultation, it was, at very least, questionable whether he would have received his share of the fee if the work had been successfully completed without him. Petitioner was requested to and did provide further services with regard to clients from which about 90 percent of the fees were generated. We note that BSI did not request consultation with respect to $3,325 remitted during 1984. However, that amount was not earned as of the time of the assignment because the work had not yet been performed for the BSI clients (irrespective of whether or not petitioner would be called upon to consult). Accordingly, with the exception of $1,250 for petitioner's 1984 taxable year, we hold that petitioner had not earned the income in question prior to leaving BSI and did not make an anticipatory assignment of income which had been earned.

Two additional related questions remain for our consideration. First, respondent argues that irrespective of when petitioner earned the income from BSI, "there was no relationship * * * [between] the past activity of introducing a client to * * * [BSI], and the petitioner's work as a partner with * * * [B&K or SSG&M]." According to respondent, petitioner should not be allowed to characterize as partnership income fees that did not have a requisite or direct relationship to a partnership's business. In making this argument, respondent attempts to limit and modify his longstanding and judicially approved position in Rev. Rul. 64–90, 1964–1 C.B. (Part 1) 226. * * * Second, while we generally hold that petitioner did not make an assignment of income already earned, the possibility that this was an assignment of unearned income was not foreclosed.

These final two questions bring into focus the true nature of the potential conflict in this case—between respondent's revenue ruling and the assignment-of-income doctrine. Both questions, in their own way, ask whether any partnership agreement—under which partners agree in advance to turn over to the partnership all income from their individual efforts—can survive scrutiny under the assignment-of-income principles.

Rev. Rul. 64–90, 1964–1 C.B. (Part 1) at 226–227, in pertinent part, contains the following:

* * *

Advice has been requested regarding the Federal income tax consequences of a change in the terms of a partnership agreement to provide that all compensation received by the partners will be paid over to the partnership immediately upon receipt.

¶ 18,050

In the instant case, several individuals formed a partnership for the purpose of engaging in the general practice of law. Aside from the partnership business, each of the partners has performed services from time to time in his individual capacity and not as a partner. The several partners have always regarded the fees received for such services as compensation to the recipient as an individual.

The partnership which was formed in 1954 and uses the cash receipts and disbursements method of accounting files its Federal income tax returns for fiscal years ending January 31, and the partners file their individual returns on the cash method for calendar years. Each partner reports his distributive share of the partnership income, gain, loss, deduction or credit for the partnership fiscal year ending within the calendar year for which his individual return is filed. All compensation received by each partner for services performed in his individual capacity is reported in that partner's return for the calendar year when received.

It is proposed to amend the partnership agreement as of the beginning of the partnership's next fiscal year to provide that all compensation received by the partners be paid over to the partnership immediately upon receipt.

The question in the instant case is whether compensation remitted to the partnership pursuant to this provision will constitute partnership income.

Similar inquiries were previously considered by the Internal Revenue Service. * * * In both instances, it was pointed out that a partnership could not exist for the purpose of performing the services for which the compensation and allowances were received, and, thus, the recipient partner would be required to report the taxable portion of the compensation and allowances in his individual return, even though these items were pooled with partnership earnings. * * *

In the instant case, the general practice of the partnership consists of rendering legal advice and services. Consequently, fees received by a partner for similar services performed in his individual capacity will be considered as partnership income if paid to the partnership in accordance with the agreement. Those fees need not be reported separately by the partner on his individual return. However, the partner's distributive share of the partnership's taxable income which he must report on his individual return will include a portion of such fees. [Emphasis supplied.]

A key requirement of this ruling is that the services for which fees are received by individual partners must be *similar* to those normally performed by the partnership. * * * Respondent now attempts to add to this requirement by arguing that the fees here in question were earned through activity, which was admittedly legal work, but was not suffi-

¶ 18,050

ciently related to the work of petitioner's new partnerships. In other words, respondent argues that the income here was earned in BSI's business activity and not B&K's or SSG&M's business activity.

* * *

There is no need for us to adopt a broader view of petitioner's partnership in this case. His referral fee income was clearly earned through activities "within the ambit" of the business of his new partnerships. Their business was the practice of law as was petitioner's consulting activity for BSI. His work was incident to the conduct of the business of his partnerships. We decline to adopt respondent's more narrow characterization of the business of petitioner's new partnerships. Neither the case law nor respondent's rulings support such a characterization.

Thus, we arrive at the final question in this case. We have already held that petitioner had not yet earned the majority of the income in question when he joined his new partnerships. Additionally, petitioner's fee income for his BSI clients qualifies, under the case law and respondent's rulings, as income generated by services sufficiently related to the business conducted by petitioner's new partnerships. If we decide that petitioner's partnerships should report the income in question, petitioner would be taxable only to the extent of his respective partnership share. This would allow petitioner, through his partnership agreements with B&K and SSG&M, to assign income not yet earned from BSI. Thus, the case law and respondent's rulings permit (without explanation), in a partnership setting, the type of assignment addressed by *Lucas v. Earl*, 281 U.S. 111 (1930). We must reconcile the principle behind Rev. Rul. 64–90, * * * with *Lucas v. Earl, supra*. The question is whether income not yet earned and anticipatorily assigned under certain partnership agreements are without the reach of the assignment-of-income principle.

The Internal Revenue Code of 1954 provided the first comprehensive statutory scheme for the tax treatment of partners and partnerships. No section of the 1954 Code, successive amendments or acts, nor the legislative history specifically addresses the treatment of income earned by partners in their individual capacity but which is pooled with other partnership income. It is implicit in subchapter K, however, that the pooling of income and losses of partners was intended by Congress. This question is more easily answered where the partnership contracts with the client for services which are then performed by the partner. The question becomes more complex where the partner contracts and performs the services when he is a partner.

Moreover, no opinion contains a satisfactory rationale as to why partnership pooling agreements do not come within the holding of *Lucas v. Earl, supra*. * * *

¶ 18,050

The fundamental theme penned by Justice Holmes provides that the individual who earns income is liable for the tax. It is obvious that the partnership, as an abstract entity, does not provide the physical and mental activity that facilitates the process of "earning" income. Only a partner can do so. The income earned is turned over to the partnership due solely to a contractual agreement, i.e., an assignment, in advance, of income.

The pooling of income is essential to the meaningful existence of subchapter K. If partners were not able to share profits in an amount disproportionate to the ratio in which they earned the underlying income, the partnership provisions of the Code would, to some extent, be rendered unnecessary. See S. Rept. 1622, 83d Cong., 2d Sess., 89 (1954) (Finance Committee listing "flexibility" among partners as one of prime objectives of 1954 subchapter K reforms). See also *United States v. Basye*, 410 U.S. 441, 448–449 (1973), where the Supreme Court acknowledges partnerships as "independently recognizable [entities] apart from the aggregate of its partners" and that a partnership can, as an entity, earn income.

The provisions of subchapter K tacitly imply that the pooling of income is permissible. Said implication may provide sufficient reason to conclude that a partnership should be treated as an entity for the purpose of pooling the income of its partners. Under an entity approach, the income would be considered that of the partnership rather than the partner, even though the partner's individual efforts may have earned the income. If the partnership is treated as an entity earning the income, then assignment-of-income concepts would not come into play.

* * *

The theory concerning partnerships as entities is not easily defined. It is well established that the partnership form is a hybrid—part separate entity, part aggregate. * * * The difficulty lies in deciding whether a particular set of circumstances relate to one end or the other of the partnership hybrid spectrum. The Supreme Court in *Basye* stated that "partnerships are entities for purposes of calculating and filing informational returns but * * * they are conduits through which the taxpaying obligation passes to the individual partners in accord with their distributive shares." *United States v. Basye*, 410 U.S. at 448 n.8. This analysis provides some foundation for the idea that partners should report their distributive share, rather than the fruits of their personal labors. But it does not provide any guidance concerning the type of income or service that should be brought within the entity concept as it relates to partnerships.

The principle we must analyze in this case involves the role of the partnership with respect to the function of earning income. A general

¶ 18,050

partnership[28] is "an association of two or more persons to carry on as co-owners a business for profit." Uniform Partnership Act sec. 6(1). Either a partnership or a corporation may enter into a contract with clients to perform services. In a partnership, however, either the entity or the individual may enter into contracts. The question we seek to answer is whether this distinction should be treated differently.

For purposes of an entity concept approach to partnerships, we must consider the type and source of income which should be included. Because we have already determined that the type of activity generating the income is relevant to an assignment-of-income analysis in the partnership setting, we focus our analysis of partnerships as entities on situations where the income is of a type normally earned by the partnership. Only in such situations has a partner acted as part of the partnership entity.

The entity concept as it relates to partnerships is based, in part, on the concept that a partner may further the business of the partnership by performing services in the name of the partnership or individually. The name and reputation of a professional partnership plays a role in the financial success of the partnership business. If the partners perform services in the name of the partnership or individually they are, nonetheless, associated with the partnership as a partner. This is the very essence of a professional service partnership, because each partner, although acting individually, is furthering the business of the partnership. * * * The lack of structure inherent in the partnership form does not lend itself to easy resolution of the assignment-of-income question. A partnership's characteristics do, however, militate in favor of treating a partner's income from services performed in an individual capacity, which are contractually obligated to the partnership for allocation in accord with the preestablished distributive shares, in the same manner as income earned through partnership engagement.

Accordingly, in circumstances where individuals are not joining in a venture merely to avoid the effect of *Lucas v. Earl, supra*, it is appropriate to treat income earned by partners individually, as income earned by the partnership entity, i.e., partnership income, to be allocated to partners in their respective shares. To provide the essential continuity necessary for the use of an entity concept in the partnership setting, the income should be earned from an activity which can reasonably be associated with the partnership's business activity. In the setting of this case, with the exception of $1,250 in 1984, petitioner was a partner of B&K or SSG&M when the fees were earned. Additionally, about 90 percent of the fees were, in part, earned through petitioner's efforts while he was a partner of B&K or SSG&M.

28. Our discussion focuses upon professional partnerships composed of general partners who are actively engaged in a business venture. The principles here may not apply to limited or general partners who are mere passive investors and are not involved in the income earning process of the partnership.

¶ 18,050

There is no apparent attempt to avoid the incidence of tax by the formation or operation of the partnerships in this case. Petitioner, in performing legal work for clients of another firm, was a partner with the law firms of B&K and SSG&M. In view of the foregoing, we hold that, with the exception of $1,250 for 1984, the fee income from BSI was correctly returned by the two partnerships in accord with the respective partnership agreements.

* * *

Reviewed by the Court.

* * *

[The concurring opinion of Judge Beghe and the dissenting opinion of Judge Wells have been omitted.]

HALPERN, J., dissenting: The majority perceives a conflict between the anticipatory assignment-of-income doctrine, see *Lucas v. Earl*, 281 U.S. 111 (1930), and the principle that partners may pool their earnings and report partnership income in amounts different from their contribution to the pool. With respect, I believe the conflict to be illusory, except insofar as the majority here today creates one where heretofore none existed.

According to the majority, the mere redistribution of income within a partnership is inconsistent with the assignment-of-income doctrine. "In partnerships and personal service corporations an individual performs the services that earn income. In both, a separate entity—the partnership or personal service corporation—is cast as the 'earner' for tax purposes. That characterization in both situations is, in essence, an assignment of income." * * *

This analysis wholly ignores the doctrine of agency. When a partner, *acting as agent for the partnership*,[1] performs services for a client, the partnership is the earner of the income: the instrumentality (in this case the partner) through which the partnership has earned its fee is of no consequence. Therefore, the focus of the anticipatory assignment-of-income analysis ought to be on whether the partner acted for himself individually or as agent of the partnership. This is entirely consistent with the latitude accorded partnerships to disproportionately distribute partnership income: the pertinent requirement is merely that the partnership income so distributed have been earned *by the partnership*. In this case, it is quite clear that petitioner earned the fees in question pursuant to an agreement he entered into, on his own behalf, with

---

1. The Uniform Partnership Act, sec. 9(1), provides that a (general) partner is an agent of the partnership. Moreover, a partner has the power to bind the partnership to any act that is "for apparently carrying on in the usual way the business of the partnership of which he is a member," unless the third party knows of some restriction on that power. * * *

¶ 18,050

[BSI]—an agreement that was consummated before petitioner's relationship with [B&K].[2] Consequently, petitioner is the true earner of the income and should not escape taxation by means of an anticipatory assignment. *Lucas v. Earl*, 281 U.S. 111 (1930).

The majority's "resolution" of the perceived conflict is unsatisfactory. The majority considers the determinative question to be whether the income is "of a type normally earned by the partnership. Only in such situations has the partner acted as part of the partnership entity." * * * The majority requires merely that income "be earned from an activity which can reasonably be associated with the partnership's business activity." * * * Thus, the majority would allow a partner to assign fees to the partnership if the work performed for such fees is similar to that performed by the partnership, but not if the work is different. * * *

The majority's distinction is unprincipled.[3] The majority observes that "The name and reputation of a professional partnership plays a role in the financial success of a partnership business" suggesting that partners, even acting individually, can further the business of the partnership by adding to its reputation. * * * But, that may be so even if the partner acts individually, doing work entirely dissimilar to that normally performed by the partnership. In any event, the majority fails to explain why such an obviously incidental benefit to the partnership should permit us to frustrate the assignment-of-income doctrine. The majority asserts that "The lack of structure inherent in the partnership form does not lend itself to easy resolution of the assignment-of-income question." * * * I must respectfully disagree. The lack of structure of the partnership form is irrelevant. All that matters is whether the partner has acted on his own behalf or on behalf, and as agent of, the partnership. Moreover, even if the lack of structure were relevant, the majority fails to explain why such would mandate the distinction between the type of income normally earned by the partnership and the type of income that is not. It would make far more sense to ask, with agency principles in mind, whether the income in question was earned by the partnership or by the partner acting as an individual.

* * *

2. Had there been a novation, substituting the partnership for petitioner, then the partnership could properly be considered the earner of the income. In this case, however, there is no basis set forth in the majority opinion for concluding that a novation has taken place or that a substitution of [B&K] for petitioner had been even discussed with [BSI]. We are not privileged to simply assume a novation, since petitioner bears the burden of proof. * * *

3. The majority fails to explain why the similarity of the work done by the partner to earn the fees to the work of the partnership is determinative. That failure not only casts doubt upon the correctness of this decision, but foreshadows the difficulty future courts will have in resolving the question: how similar is similar enough? Without any inkling of why similarity has been deemed important, future courts will lack any effective guidelines for answering that question.

¶ 18,050

[¶ 18,055]

Notes

1. What tax abuse was the government trying to prevent in asserting that the assignment of income doctrine applied to tax Schneer on the earnings that he was required to pay over to B&K and SSG&M under his partnership agreements with those firms?

2. More generally, should the assignment of income doctrine of *Lucas v. Earl* and its progeny apply to transfers for value such as those made by Schneer? To what extent do such transfers undermine the vertical equity (i.e., desired progressivity) of the income tax system?

3. Could the transaction in *Schneer* be properly characterized as a transfer by Schneer to the partnership of accounts receivable with a value in excess of their zero basis? If so, does Section 704(c)(1)(A), discussed at ¶ 18,135, require that the partnership's gain from collection of those accounts receivable be allocated to Schneer, the contributing partner? Consider these questions as you read the material concerning Section 704(c)(1)(A).

B.   PARTNERSHIP ALLOCATIONS

[¶ 18,065]

1.   FLEXIBLE APPROACH PERMITTED BY LOCAL LAW

Under state partnership laws, items of income and expense incurred by a partnership generally do not have to be allocated among the partners in any prescribed ratio, such as in proportion to invested capital. Different items of income and expense may, in fact, be allocated among the partners pursuant to different ratios. Moreover, allocation ratios may be modified by the partners from year to year. State laws governing limited liability companies (LLCs) typically provide similar flexibility concerning the allocation of items of income and expense among members of an LLC. The considerable flexibility of the state law rules governing allocations is one of the primary advantages of conducting business in partnership or LLC, rather than corporate, form.

The income tax rules dealing with the allocation of income and deductions among partners (or members of an LLC classified as a partnership for federal tax purposes) generally follow the state law rules governing economic, or financial, allocations. Thus, Section 704(a) provides that a partner's distributive share of partnership income and expense is to be determined under the terms of the partnership agreement. The resulting flexibility, while creating a favorable tax climate for partnership or LLC operations, also provides substantial opportunities for abuse. Concern about such abuse has, over time, resulted in the evolution of highly complex provisions intended to establish boundaries on the extent to which partnership allocation arrangements, as reflected

¶ 18,055

in state law and the partnership agreement, will govern for federal income tax purposes.

These boundaries are established by a series of statutory provisions. Section 704(c) requires that income, gain, loss, and deduction with respect to contributed property be allocated among the partners to reflect the precontribution gain or loss in the property. Section 704(b) requires that tax allocations conform to the economic allocations made by the partnership. Section 704(e) governs the allocation of income in a family owned partnership. Section 706(c) and Section 706(d) govern the allocation of income in a year in which the capital interests of the partners change. The relationship among these several overlapping rules is not clearly defined by the statute.

The degree of complexity of the rules governing tax allocations suggests that, perhaps, the tax rules should not purport to afford the same flexibility as state laws do in providing for economic allocations. Would it be reasonable to require partnerships to establish a single profit-and loss-sharing ratio and require each partner to report the same fraction of each item of partnership income and expense pursuant to that ratio? Under what circumstances would the allocation of an item of income or expense under a different arrangement be justifiable as a matter of sound income tax policy?

[¶ 18,070]

2. ECONOMIC ALLOCATIONS

Before addressing the regulatory requirements for effecting valid allocations of taxable income, it is useful to reflect on the way in which the economic consequences of partnership operations are allocated. We have noted that capital accounts for the partners will be established to reflect the value of their contributions to the partnership and that these capital accounts may well differ from tax basis. Allocations of income and loss among the partners are then reflected by adjustments to the capital accounts. Distributions of cash or other property to partners are charged to their respective capital accounts. Partnership distributions, like income and expense allocations, need not be made in proportion to the partners' interests. Thus, if partners are to have an accurate record of the value of their economic interests in the partnership, distributions must be reflected in the capital accounts in terms of the market value of properties distributed.

Capital accounts are not normally affected by borrowings or repayments of loans by a partnership in the same way that basis adjustments of partnership interests are. Neither the proceeds of partnership borrowing nor the repayment necessarily affects the relative capital accounts of the partners. As a result, partners may have deficits in their capital accounts (losses or distributions allocated to the partners in an amount that exceeds the capital account balances). While positive capital accounts would normally control the distribution of partnership assets upon liquidation, the effect of a negative account is not necessarily self-evident.

Can a partner receive a liquidating distribution that is less than zero? The answer may be "yes"—depending upon the terms of the partnership agreement and applicable state law. Upon a liquidation, some or all of the partners may be required to pay to the partnership an amount equal to the deficit in their capital accounts. If a partner is required to restore a capital account deficit, that partner will, in a real sense, receive "less than zero." Even a negative capital account will thus control the distribution of partnership assets.

In a very simple partnership, the partners might be able to dispense with separate capital account practices. Such a record would not be needed if the partners allocated all income, expense, and distributions in accordance with a single, unchanging, ratio for both tax and financial purposes. Such a partnership could thus avoid entanglement with the regulations under Section 704(b), but much of the flexibility that the partnership vehicle provides would be sacrificed.

At one time the nature of the required linkage between the economic allocation formulae reflected in capital accounts and the tax allocations permitted by Section 704(b) was quite unclear. Some taxpayers took the position that the allocations for tax purposes did not have to correspond to economic allocations. That issue was addressed in the widely cited *Orrisch* case that served as a conceptual basis for the development of regulations governing these questions.

3. JUDICIAL ANALYSIS

[¶ 18,075]

ORRISCH v. COMMISSIONER

United States Tax Court, 1970.
55 T.C. 395, aff'd per curiam by memorandum decision, 73–1 U.S.T.C.
(CCH) ¶ 9330, 31 A.F.T.R.2d (RIA) 1069 (9th Cir.1973).

FEATHERSTON, JUDGE: * * *. The only issue for decision is whether an amendment to a partnership agreement allocating to petitioners the entire amount of the depreciation deduction allowable on two buildings owned by the partnership was made for the principal purpose of the avoidance of tax within the meaning of section 704(b).

* * *

ULTIMATE FINDING OF FACT

The principal purpose of the special allocation to petitioners of all of the deductions for depreciation taken by the Orrisch–Crisafi partnership for 1966 and 1967 was the avoidance of income tax.

¶ 18,070

Opinion

The only issue presented for decision is whether tax effect can be given the agreement between petitioners and the Crisafis that, beginning with 1966, all the partnership's depreciation deductions were to be allocated to petitioners for their use in computing their individual income tax liabilities. In our view, the answer must be in the negative, and the amounts of each of the partners' deductions for the depreciation of partnership property must be determined in accordance with the ratio used generally in computing their distributive shares of the partnership's profits and losses.

Among the important innovations of the 1954 Code are limited provisions for flexibility in arrangements for the sharing of income, losses, and deductions arising from business activities conducted through partnerships. The authority for special allocations of such items appears in section 704(a), which provides that a partner's share of any item of income, gain, loss, deduction, or credit shall be determined by the partnership agreement. That rule is coupled with a limitation in section 704(b), however, which states that a special allocation of an item will be disregarded if its "principal purpose" is the avoidance or evasion of Federal income tax. * * * In case a special allocation is disregarded, the partner's share of the item is to be determined in accordance with the ratio by which the partners divide the general profits or losses of the partnership. Sec. 1.704–1(b)(2), Income Tax Regs.

The report of the Senate Committee on Finance accompanying the bill finally enacted as the 1954 Code (S. Rept. No. 1622, * * * 83d Cong., 2d Sess., p. 379 (1954)) explained the tax-avoidance restriction prescribed by section 704(b) as follows:

> Subsection (b) * * * provides that if the principal purpose of any provision in the partnership agreement dealing with a partner's distributive share of a particular item is to avoid or evade the Federal income tax, the partner's distributive share of that item shall be redetermined in accordance with his distributive share of partnership income or loss described in section 702(a)(9) [i.e., the ratio used by the partners for dividing general profits or losses]. * * *

> Where, however, a provision in a partnership agreement for a special allocation of certain items has substantial economic effect and is not merely a device for reducing the taxes of certain partners without actually affecting their shares of partnership income, then such a provision will be recognized for tax purposes. * * *

This reference to "substantial economic effect" did not appear in the House Ways and Means Committee report (H. Rept. No. 1337, * * * 83d Cong., 2d Sess., p. A223 (1954)) discussing section 704(b), and was apparently added in the Senate Finance Committee to allay fears that special allocations of income or deductions would be denied effect in

¶ 18,075

every case where the allocation resulted in a reduction in the income tax liabilities of one or more of the partners. The statement is an affirmation that special allocations are ordinarily to be recognized if they have business validity apart from their tax consequences. * * *

In resolving the question whether the principal purpose of a provision in a partnership agreement is the avoidance or evasion of Federal income tax, all the facts and circumstances in relation to the provision must be taken into account. Section 1.704–1(b)(2), Income Tax Regs., lists the following as relevant circumstances to be considered:

> Whether the partnership or a partner individually has a business purpose for the allocation; whether the allocation has "substantial economic effect", that is, whether the allocation may actually affect the dollar amount of the partners' shares of the total partnership income or loss independently of tax consequences; whether related items of income, gain, loss, deduction, or credit from the same source are subject to the same allocation; whether the allocation was made without recognition of normal business factors and only after the amount of the specially allocated item could reasonably be estimated; the duration of the allocation; and the overall tax consequences of the allocation. * * *

Applying these standards, we do not think the special allocation of depreciation in the present case can be given effect.

The evidence is persuasive that the special allocation of depreciation was adopted for a tax-avoidance rather than a business purpose. Depreciation was the only item which was adjusted by the parties; both the income from the buildings and the expenses incurred in their operation, maintenance, and repair were allocated to the partners equally. Since the deduction for depreciation does not vary from year to year with the fortunes of the business, the parties obviously knew what the tax effect of the special allocation would be at the time they adopted it. Furthermore, as shown by our Findings, petitioners had large amounts of income which would be offset by the additional deduction for depreciation; the Crisafis, in contrast, had no taxable income from which to subtract the partnership depreciation deductions, and, due to depreciation deductions which they were obtaining with respect to other housing projects, could expect to have no taxable income in the near future. On the other hand, the insulation of the Crisafis from at least part of a potential capital gains tax was an obvious tax advantage. The inference is unmistakably clear that the agreement did not reflect normal business considerations but was designed primarily to minimize the overall tax liabilities of the partners.

Petitioners urge that the special allocation of the depreciation deduction was adopted in order to equalize the capital accounts of the partners, correcting a disparity ($14,000) in the amounts initially contributed to the partnership by them ($26,500) and the Crisafis ($12,500).

¶ 18,075

But the evidence does not support this contention. Under the special allocation agreement, petitioners were to be entitled, in computing their individual income tax liabilities, to deduct the full amount of the depreciation realized on the partnership property. For 1966, as an example, petitioners were allocated a sum ($18,904) equal to the depreciation on the partnership property ($18,412) plus one-half of the net loss computed without regard to depreciation ($492). The other one-half of the net loss was, of course, allocated to the Crisafis. Petitioners' allocation ($18,904) was then applied to reduce their capital account. The depreciation specially allocated to petitioners ($18,412) in 1966 alone exceeded the amount of the disparity in the contributions. Indeed, at the end of 1967, petitioners' capital account showed a deficit of $25,187.11 compared with a positive balance of $405.65 in the Crisafis' account. By the time the partnership's properties are fully depreciated, the amount of the reduction in petitioners' capital account will approximate the remaining basis for the buildings as of the end of 1967. The Crisafis' capital account will be adjusted only for contributions, withdrawals, gain or loss, without regard to depreciation, and similar adjustments for these factors will also be made in petitioners' capital account. Thus, rather than correcting an imbalance in the capital accounts of the partners, the special allocation of depreciation will create a vastly greater imbalance than existed at the end of 1966. In the light of these facts, we find it incredible that equalization of the capital accounts was the objective of the special allocation.[5]

Petitioners rely primarily on the argument that the allocation has "substantial economic effect" in that it is reflected in the capital accounts of the partners. Referring to the material quoted above from the report of the Senate Committee on Finance, they contend that this alone is sufficient to show that the special allocation served a business rather than a tax avoidance purpose.

According to the regulations, an allocation has economic effect if it "may actually affect the dollar amount of the partners' shares of the total partnership income or loss independently of tax consequences." The agreement in this case provided not only for the allocation of depreciation to petitioners but also for gain on the sale of the partnership property to be "charged back" to them. The charge back would cause the gain, for tax purposes, to be allocated on the books entirely to

---

5. We recognize that petitioners had more money invested in the partnership than the Crisafis and that it is reasonable for the partners to endeavor to equalize their investments, since each one was to share equally in the profits and losses of the enterprise. However, we do not think that sec. 704(a) permits the partners' prospective tax benefits to be used as the medium for equalizing their investments, and it is apparent that the economic burden of the depreciation (which is reflected by the allowance for depreciation) was not intended to be the medium used.

This case is to be distinguished from situations where one partner contributed property and the other cash; in such cases sec. 704(c) may allow a special allocation of income and expenses in order to reflect the tax consequences inherent in the original contributions.

petitioners to the extent of the special allocation of depreciation, and their capital account would be correspondingly increased. The remainder of the gain, if any, would be shared equally by the partners. If the gain on the sale were to equal or exceed the depreciation specially allocated to petitioners, the increase in their capital account caused by the charge back would exactly equal the depreciation deductions previously allowed to them, and the proceeds of the sale of the property would be divided equally. In such circumstances, the only effect of the allocation would be a trade of tax consequences, i.e., the Crisafis would relinquish a current depreciation deduction in exchange for exoneration from all or part of the capital gains tax when the property is sold, and petitioners would enjoy a larger current depreciation deduction but would assume a larger ultimate capital gains tax liability. Quite clearly, if the property is sold at a gain, the special allocation will affect only the tax liabilities of the partners and will have no other economic effect.

To find any economic effect of the special allocation agreement aside from its tax consequences, we must, therefore, look to see who is to bear the economic burden of the depreciation if the buildings should be sold for a sum less than their original cost. There is not one syllable of evidence bearing directly on this crucial point. We have noted, however, that when the buildings are fully depreciated, petitioners' capital account will have a deficit, or there will be a disparity in the capital accounts, approximately equal to the undepreciated basis of the buildings as of the beginning of 1966.[7] Under normal accounting procedures, if the building were sold at a gain less than the amount of such disparity petitioners would either be required to contribute to the partnership a sum equal to the remaining deficit in their capital account after the gain on the sale had been added back or would be entitled to receive a proportionately smaller share of the partnership assets on liquidation. Based on the record as a whole, we do not think the partners ever agreed to such an arrangement. On dissolution, we think the partners contemplated an equal division of the partnership assets which would be adjusted only for disparities in cash contributions or withdrawals.[8] Certainly there is no evidence to show otherwise. That being true, the special allocation does not "actually affect the dollar amount of the partners' shares of the total partnership income or loss independently of tax consequences" within the meaning of the regulation referred to above.

Our interpretation of the partnership agreement is supported by an analysis of a somewhat similar agreement, quoted in material part in our Findings, which petitioners made as part of a marital property settlement agreement in 1968. Under this agreement, Orrisch was entitled to

---

7. This assumes, of course, that all partnership withdrawals and capital contributions will be equal.

8. We note that, in the course of Orrisch's testimony, petitioners' counsel made a distinction between entries in the taxpayers' capital accounts which reflect actual cash transactions and those relating to the special allocation which are "paper entries relating to depreciation."

deduct all the depreciation for 1968 in computing his income tax liability, and his wife was to deduct none; but on the sale of the property they were to first reimburse Orrisch for "such moneys as he may have advanced," and then divide the balance of the "profits or proceeds" of the sale equally, each party to report one-half of the capital gain or loss on his income tax return. In the 1969 amendment to this agreement the unequal allocation of the depreciation deduction was discontinued, and a provision similar to the partnership "charge back" was added, i.e., while the proceeds of the sale were to be divided equally, only Orrisch's basis was to be reduced by the depreciation allowed for 1968 so that he would pay taxes on a larger portion of the gain realized on the sale. Significantly, in both this agreement and the partnership agreement, as we interpret it, each party's share of the sales proceeds was determined independently from his share of the depreciation deduction.

In the light of all the evidence we have found as an ultimate fact that the "principal purpose" of the special allocation agreement was tax avoidance within the meaning of section 704(b). Accordingly, the deduction for depreciation for 1966 and 1967 must be allocated between the parties in the same manner as other deductions.

* * *

[¶ 18,080]

4. THRUST OF THE REGULATIONS

The principle of *Orrisch* is the core of the regulations promulgated under the current version of Section 704(b)(2). The length and complexity of the regulations may conceal the fact that they are based on a simple, almost self-evident principle: the tax consequences attributable to an item of income or expense must attend the partner to whom the item is allocated for economic (or capital account) purposes.

A part of the complexity of the regulations may be attributable to the decision of the drafters (mostly tax lawyers) to reverse horse and cart. Instead of defining the tax consequences of economic allocations, the regulations endeavor to define when a tax allocation is valid; a tax allocation will be valid where it has "substantial economic effect." Since tax allocations have no economic effect (except between a taxpayer and the Treasury), the essential premise of the regulations is that the tax allocation must be accompanied by an identical economic allocation. The regulations describe the steps that must be taken to ensure that the allocation provisions of the partnership agreement in fact affect the financial interests of the various partners and, thus, have "substantial economic effect." If appearances do not reflect economic reality, the tax allocation must be altered to follow economic consequences.

[¶ 18,085]

5. ILLUSTRATIVE EXAMPLES—THE STAKES

Before confronting the complex structure of the regulations, it is useful to trace the effect of a special allocation for tax purposes under different economic arrangements. For the illustration, return again to the Al–Bea partnership (¶ 17,010). Recall that on the formation of their partnership, each partner contributed cash or property that had a value of $100. In each example, assume that cash income equals cash expense. The partnership losses are attributable to depreciation deductions. The partnership agreement provides that, for tax purposes, 75 percent of the losses are allocated to Al and 25 percent are allocated to Bea. The partnership has claimed depreciation deductions over several years totaling $40 and the value of the partnership properties has declined from $200 to $160. At that point the partnership liquidates and distributes all of its assets to Al and Bea.

Example 1. Notwithstanding the tax allocation, the partners have agreed that, upon liquidation, partnership assets will be distributed equally, as in *Orrisch*. Their capital accounts would be adjusted as follows:

	Al	Bea
Initial account	100	100
Losses	(30)	(10)
Adjusted account	70	90
Actual liquidation proceeds	80	80
Net economic loss	20	20

Because of the agreement to share in the proceeds of the liquidation equally, Al and Bea will bear the economic burden of the partnership losses equally. Since Al, in fact, bore only half of the loss (not 75 percent), the tax allocation of losses does not reflect the partners' economic deal and will not qualify under the Section 704(b) regulations.

Example 2. Now assume that Al and Bea have agreed that the proceeds of any liquidation (or other distribution) will be governed by the relative balances in their capital accounts:

	Al	Bea
Initial account	100	100
Losses	(30)	(10)
Adjusted account	70	90
Actual liquidation proceeds	70	80
Net economic loss	30	10

Under this economic arrangement, Al bore 75 percent of the economic loss, and the tax allocation accurately reflected that economic reality.

¶ 18,085

Example 3. Now assume that the partnership borrows $800 and purchases a depreciable asset for $1,000. The partnership claims a depreciation deduction of $200 and the value of the asset falls to $800. At that point, the partnership sells the asset (realizing no gain or loss), repays the loan, and liquidates. As before, 75 percent of the tax loss is allocated to Al. As in *Example 2*, the capital accounts control distributions to the partners, but the partners do not have any obligation to restore deficits in their account balances.

	Al	*Bea*
Initial account	100	100
Losses	(150)	(50)
Adjusted account	(50)	50
Actual liquidation proceeds	0	0
Net economic loss	100	100

Because Al was not required to restore his capital account deficit, he was not required to bear an economic loss in excess of his $100 capital contribution to the partnership. Thus, on liquidation, any loss allocated to Al in excess of $100 had to be borne by Bea. Even if the positive capital accounts would have controlled distributions, the tax allocation did not reflect the economic allocation once a capital account deficit arose.

Example 4. Now assume that the partners are obligated to restore capital account deficits on liquidation. Otherwise the facts are the same as in *Example 3*.

	Al	*Bea*
Initial account	100	100
Losses	(150)	(50)
Adjusted account	(50)	50
Actual liquidation proceeds	(50)	50
Net economic loss	150	50

Because Al was required to restore his capital account deficit, the partnership ended up with sufficient assets to permit repayment of Bea's capital account. Al actually bore the loss allocated to him.

Some clear principles are reflected by these examples. A partner will not in fact bear an economic loss unless:

(a) the partners maintain accurate capital accounts that reflect the allocations made for tax purposes;

(b) the capital accounts actually control the economic distributions made to the partners; and

(c) any capital account deficit must be restored by the partner affected upon liquidation.

¶ 18,085

Not surprisingly, the primary test set forth in the Section 704(b) regulations for sustaining the validity of a tax allocation requires that the partnership be governed by these three rules.

[¶ 18,090]

6. "SUBSTANTIAL ECONOMIC EFFECT" UNDER THE ALLOCATION REGULATIONS

The regulations under Section 704(b) begin by describing in great detail a safe harbor rule for sustaining the validity of a partnership's allocation for income tax purposes. The allocation will be sustained if it has "substantial economic effect." Reg. § 1.704–1(b)(1)(i) and (2)(i). There are two distinct parts to this safe harbor test: the allocation must have an economic effect, and the effect must be substantial. Reg. § 1.704–1(b)(2)(i).

[¶ 18,095]

a. Economic Effect

As the foregoing Al–Bea illustration demonstrated, an allocation may be regarded as having economic effect under Reg. § 1.704–1(b)(2)(ii) if three tests are met:

1. The partnership must maintain capital accounts for the partners in accordance with the rules of Reg. § 1.704–1(b)(2)(iv). Much of the regulation is devoted to the elaboration of these rules in complex situations. In general, however, the requirements of the regulation are unsurprising. The capital accounts must reflect all allocations to the partners of income and expense and of contributions and distributions. Contributions of property to and distributions from the partnership must be recorded at market value rather than tax basis. Moreover, the capital accounts may be restated to reflect current market values in limited circumstances in which the partnership is effectively restructured, such as the admission or retirement of a partner (though apparently not upon the transfer of a partnership interest). Such revaluations, however, must be made principally for a substantial nontax business purpose and may not be used to circumvent the limits on special allocations.

2. Upon the liquidation of any partner's interest, or of the partnership, all distributions to the partners must be made promptly and in accordance with the positive balances in the capital accounts.

3. If, upon such a liquidation of a partner's interest, the partner's capital account shows a deficit, the partner must be unconditionally obligated to restore promptly that amount to the partnership. The partnership must in turn repay creditors or make distributions to the partners who have positive capital account balances.

¶ 18,085

The first two of these requirements may impose burdensome accounting requirements on the partnership, but they are unlikely to have a substantive effect on the partners. Compliance with the third requirement, however, could well alter the economic arrangement of the partners. In particular, the very concept of a limited partner is inconsistent with the notion of a mandatory additional investment in the partnership. Accordingly, many partnerships will not comply with the deficit restoration requirement. However, those partnerships are not necessarily deprived of all safe harbor protection for their allocations.

Even though a partner is not subject to an obligation to restore an account deficit, an allocation to that partner will nevertheless be valid for tax purposes so long as alternative safeguards are present to assure that the allocation does not and will not create such a deficit. Reg. § 1.704–1(b)(2)(ii)(*d*). This alternate test for economic effect, however, contains troublesome requirements of its own. The drafters of the regulations were properly concerned that taxpayers could manipulate capital account balances, for example, by deferring distributions and thus capital account deficits so as to preserve a special allocation. Therefore, in testing for the existence of an account deficit for a given year, the account must be treated as reduced by certain allocations of loss or distributions that are anticipated as of year end. Moreover, the partnership agreement must provide that, if such an unanticipated loss or distribution in fact occurs to create an account deficit, the partnership will allocate items of gross income to the partner sufficient to eliminate the deficit. The regulations refer to that obligation as a "qualified income offset."

However, for partnerships lacking qualified income offset provisions, there is an alternative safe harbor. The tax allocation will nevertheless be valid to the extent that it is accompanied by an economic allocation that actually affects the amount that a partner would receive upon an immediate liquidation of the partnership. Reg. § 1.704–1(b)(3)(iii). Thus, so long as the partnership complies with the first two requirements of the regulations and the partners do not, in fact, have capital account deficits, tax allocations will generally be valid even if the agreement does not contain a qualified income offset.

The following rulings illustrate the application of the economic effect safe harbors in the Section 704(b) regulations. The first ruling examines the validity of a special allocation of cancellation of indebtedness income to a partner that differs from the partner's share of the cancelled partnership debt under Section 752(b). The second ruling discusses the calculation of the amount of a partner's limited deficit restoration obligation when the partner is treated as having such an obligation under the regulations by reason of the partner's liability to the partnership's creditors.

¶ 18,095

[¶ 18,100]

REVENUE RULING 92–97

1992–2 C.B. 124.

ISSUE

If a partner is allocated a share of the partnership's cancellation of indebtedness (COD) income that differs from the partner's share of the cancelled debt under section 752(b) * * *, does the allocation of COD income have substantial economic effect under section 704(b)?

FACTS

Situation 1. In year 1, *A* contributes $10x$ and *B* contributes $90x$ to form *AB*, a general partnership. *A* and *B* share the partnership's losses 10 percent and 90 percent, respectively, and share the partnership's income 50 percent each (*i.e.*, income allocations do not first restore previous losses). The partnership maintains capital accounts under the rules of section 1.704–1(b)(2)(iv) of the * * * Regulations, and the partners agree to liquidate according to positive capital account balances under the rules of section 1.704–1(b)(2)(ii)(*b*)(*2*).

Under applicable state law, *A* and *B* are jointly and severally liable to creditors for all partnership recourse liabilities. However, *A* and *B* do not agree to unconditional deficit restoration obligations as described in section 1.704–1(b)(2)(ii)(*b*)(*3*) of the regulations; they are obligated to restore deficit capital accounts only to the extent necessary to pay creditors. Thus, if *AB* were to liquidate after paying all creditors, and one partner had a positive capital account balance, the other partner would not be required to restore a deficit capital account to permit a liquidating distribution to the partner with a positive capital account balance.

Because the partners do not have unconditional deficit restoration obligations, the economic effect test of section 1.704–1(b)(2)(ii)(*b*) of the regulations is not met. However, *A* and *B* agree to a qualified income offset and are treated under section 1.704–1(b)(2)(ii)(*c*) as having a limited obligation to restore deficit capital accounts by reason of their liability to *AB*'s creditors. Accordingly, the requirements of the alternate test for economic effect of section 1.704–1(b)(2)(ii)(*d*) are met.

AB purchases property for $1000x$ from an unrelated seller, paying $100x$ in cash and borrowing the $900x$ balance from an unrelated bank that is not the seller of the property. The note is a general obligation of the partnership, and no partner has been relieved from personal liability. The principal of the loan is due in 6 years; interest is payable semi-annually at the applicable federal rate.

A and *B* bear an economic risk of loss equal to $90x$ and $810x$, respectively, for the partnership's $900x$ recourse liability and each increases basis in the partnership interest (outside basis) accordingly. *See* section 1.752–2 of the regulations.

The property generates $200x of depreciation each year for 5 years. All other partnership deductions and losses exactly equal the partnership's income, so that in each of its first 5 taxable years *AB* has a net loss of $200x. Under the partnership agreement, these losses are allocated 10 percent to *A* and 90 percent to *B*. The losses reduce *A*'s capital account to negative $90x and *B*'s capital account to negative $810x. At the beginning of year 6, after the fair market value of *AB*'s property has substantially declined, the creditor cancels the debt as part of a work-out arrangement. Because of the cancellation of the debt, *A* and *B* are no longer treated as obligated to restore their deficit capital accounts.

Situation 2. The facts are the same as *Situation 1*, except that *A* and *B* agree to unconditional deficit restoration obligations as described in section 1.704–1(b)(2)(ii)(*b*)(*3*) of the regulations. *A* and *B* thus have an obligation to restore deficit capital accounts not only to pay creditors, but to satisfy the other partner's positive capital account balance on liquidation.

LAW AND ANALYSIS

Section 61(a)(12) * * * requires the amount of a taxpayer's discharged debt to be included in gross income.

Under section 108(a) * * *, COD income is excluded from gross income if the debt is discharged in a title 11 case, if the taxpayer is insolvent, or if the debt discharged is qualified farm indebtedness. If a partnership's liability is discharged, the partnership recognizes income equal to the amount of debt cancelled and must allocate that income to the partners as a separately stated item under section 702(a). Under section 108(d)(6), the section 108(a) exclusions are applied at the partner level to the COD income.

If an allocation of a share of a partnership's COD income is made to a partner, and the allocation has substantial economic effect, the partner increases outside basis under section 705(a)(1)(A) * * *, receives a capital account increase under section 1.704–1(b)(2)(iv)(*b*)(*3*) of the regulations, and must determine, based on the partner's own circumstances, if all or part of the distributive share may be excluded from gross income under section 108(a).

Under section 722 * * *, a partner's outside basis is increased by the amount of money and the adjusted basis of property contributed to the partnership. Under section 731(a), a partner recognizes gain from the sale or exchange of a partnership interest to the extent the partner receives a distribution of money from the partnership that exceeds the partner's outside basis immediately before the distribution. Under section 733, a partner's outside basis is decreased (but not below zero) by the amount of any distribution of money from the partnership. Under section 752(a), an increase in a partner's share of partnership liabilities is treated as a contribution of money by the partner to the partnership. Under section 752(b), a decrease in a partner's share of partnership liabilities is treated as a distribution of money by the partnership to the partner.

Although section 731(a) * * * requires gain recognition if a distribution of money exceeds the distributee partner's outside basis immediately before the distribution, section 1.731–1(a)(1)(ii) of the regulations treats certain distributions as occurring at the end of the partnership's taxable year. Under section 1.731–1(a)(1)(ii), advances or drawings of money or property against a partner's distributive share of income are treated as current distributions made on the last day of the partnership taxable year.

Under section 704(b) * * * and the regulations thereunder, allocations of a partnership's items of income, gain, loss, deduction, or credit provided for in the partnership agreement will be respected if the allocations have substantial economic effect. Allocations that fail to have substantial economic effect will be reallocated according to the partners' economic interests in the partnership. The fundamental principles for establishing economic effect require an allocation to be consistent with the partners' underlying economic arrangement. A partner allocated a share of income should enjoy any corresponding economic benefit, and a partner allocated a share of losses or deductions should bear any corresponding economic burden. *See* section 1.704–1(b)(2)(ii)(*a*) of the regulations.

To come within the safe harbor for establishing economic effect in section 1.704–1(b)(2)(ii) of the regulations, partners must agree to maintain capital accounts under the rules of section 1.704–1(b)(2)(iv) and liquidate according to positive capital account balances; in addition, any partner with a deficit capital account must either agree to an unconditional deficit restoration obligation as described in section 1.704–1(b)(2)(ii)(*b*)(*3*) (as in *Situation 2*) or satisfy the requirements of the alternate test for economic effect provided in section 1.704–1(b)(2)(ii)(*d*) (as in *Situation 1*).

In *Situations 1 and 2*, the allocations of losses to A and B in years 1 through 5 meet the economic effect requirements under sections 1.704–1(b)(2)(ii)(*d*) and 1.704–1(b)(2)(ii)(*b*) of the regulations. These allocations are thus within the economic effect safe harbor provided by the regulations under section 704 * * *.

In year 6, when the $900x recourse liability is cancelled, the partnership recognizes $900x of COD income that must be allocated to A and B as a separately stated item under section 702(a) * * *. In both *Situations 1 and 2*, A and B receive a deemed distribution of money equal to $90x and $810x, respectively, because of the decrease in their shares of the liability when the debt is cancelled. See section 752(b) and section

¶ 18,100

1.752–1(c) of the regulations. Under section 733, A and B reduce outside bases (but not below zero) by $90x$ and $810x$, respectively, and under section 731(a), A and B recognize gain to the extent their respective distributions exceed their outside bases at the end of year 6.

Situation 1 Analysis

The AB partnership agreement provides for income to be allocated equally between A and B. However, in [S]ituation 1, the allocation of the partnership's COD income $450x$ to A and $450x$ to B, which would cause A's capital account to equal $360x$ (negative $90x$ plus $450x$) and B's capital account to equal negative $360x$ (negative $810x$ plus $450x$), cannot have economic effect even though the partners maintain capital accounts and liquidate according to positive capital accounts. The cancellation of the debt eliminates both partners' obligations to restore a deficit capital account, and neither partner has an independent deficit restoration obligation that could be invoked to satisfy the other partner's positive capital account. Because the partners' deficit restoration obligations were dependent on the cancelled debt, A can neither enjoy the economic benefit of an allocation of COD income exceeding $90x$ nor bear the economic burden of an allocation of COD income of less than $90x$. Similarly, B can neither enjoy the economic benefit of an allocation of COD income exceeding $810x$ nor bear the economic burden of an allocation of COD income of less than $810x$. See section 1.704–1(b)(5), *Example 15(iii)*, of the regulations. Thus, for the partnership's allocations of the COD income to have economic effect, the COD income must be allocated $90x$ to A and $810x$ to B, which is the same ratio as the decrease in A's and B's shares of partnership liability.

When the COD income is properly allocated, the outside bases of A and B are increased under section 705(a)(1)(A) * * * by $90x$ and $810x$, respectively, for their distributive shares of the partnership's COD income. Under section 108(d)(6), A and B individually determine if any portion of their distributive shares is excluded from gross income. Under section 705(a)(2), the outside bases of A and B are decreased by $90x$ and $810x$, respectively, for their distributions of money under section 752(b) resulting from the cancellation of the debt. A and B recognize no gain under section 731 in year 6 because the distributive shares of COD income provide an outside basis increase for each partner sufficient to cover the distribution of money to that partner. Because of the integral relationship between the COD income and the section 752(b) distribution of money from the cancelled debt, section 1.731–1(a)(1)(ii) of the regulations treats the distribution of money to each partner from the cancellation of the debt as occurring at the end of AB's taxable year as an advance or drawing against that partner's distributive share of COD income.

¶ 18,100

Situation 2 Analysis

In *Situation 2*, the allocation of the partnership's COD income $450x to A and $450x to B, which causes A's capital account to equal $360x and B's capital account to equal negative $360x, has economic effect and, therefore, meets the substantial economic effect safe harbor if substantiality is independently established. Because B's deficit restoration obligation is not dependent on the cancelled debt and can be invoked to satisfy A's positive capital account, the allocation of COD income results in B incurring an obligation to contribute $360x to satisfy A's $360x positive capital account. Similarly, if the COD income were allocated so that A had a deficit capital account balance, A would incur an obligation to contribute the amount of the deficit to satisfy B's positive capital account.

Under section 705(a)(1)(A) * * *, the outside bases of A and B are increased by $450x each, for their distributive shares of the partnership's COD income. Under section 108(d)(6), A and B individually determine if any portion of their distributive shares is excluded from gross income. This allocation, which is not in proportion to the partners' shares of the cancelled debt under section 752(b), causes B to recognize a $360x capital gain under sections 752(b) and 731(a). Although B's outside basis is increased under section 705(a)(1)(A) for B's $450x distributive share of COD income, the $810x distribution of money resulting from the decrease in B's share of the partnership liability exceeds B's outside basis by $360x.

B recognizes gain even though the distribution of money from the cancellation of the debt is treated under section 1.731–1(a)(1)(ii) of the regulations as occurring at the end of AB's taxable year. Because of the application of section 1.731–1(a)(1)(ii), however, A does not recognize gain in *Situation 2*. A's outside basis is increased by the allocation to A of $450x of the partnership's COD income, so the $90x distribution of money resulting from the decrease in A's share of the partnership liability does not exceed A's outside basis. After adjustment for the $90x distribution, A has an outside basis of $360x.

HOLDING

An allocation to a partner of a share of the partnership's cancellation of indebtedness income that differs from the partner's share of the cancelled debt under section 752(b) * * * has substantial economic effect under section 704(b) if (1) the deficit restoration obligations covering any negative capital account balances resulting from the COD income allocations can be invoked to satisfy other partners' positive capital account balances, (2) the requirements of the economic effect test are otherwise met, and (3) substantiality is independently established.

¶ 18,100

[¶ 18,102]

REVENUE RULING 97–38

1997–2 C.B. 69.

ISSUE

If a partner is treated as having a limited deficit restoration obligation under § 1.704–1(b)(2)(ii)(c) of the * * * Regulations by reason of the partner's liability to the partnership's creditors, how is the amount of that obligation calculated?

FACTS

In year 1, *GP* and *LP,* general partner and limited partner, each contribute $100x to form limited partnership *LPRS*. In general, *GP* and *LP* share *LPRS*'s income and loss 50 percent each. However, *LPRS* allocated to *GP* all depreciation deductions and gain from the sale of depreciable assets up to the amount of those deductions. *LPRS* maintains capital accounts according to the rules set forth in § 1.704–1(b)(2)(iv), and the partners agree to liquidate according to positive capital account balances under the rules of § 1.704–1(b)(2)(ii)(*b*)(*2*).

Under applicable state law, *GP* is liable to creditors for all partnership recourse liabilities, but *LP* has no personal liability. *GP* and *LP* do not agree to unconditional deficit restoration obligations as described in § 1.704–1(b)(2)(ii)(*b*)(*3*) (in general, a deficit restoration obligation requires a partner to restore any deficit capital account balance following the liquidation of the partner's interest in the partnership); *GP* is obligated to restore a deficit capital account only to the extent necessary to pay creditors. Thus, if *LPRS* were to liquidate after paying all creditors and *LP* had a positive capital account balance, *GP* would not be required to restore *GP*'s deficit capital account to permit a liquidating distribution to *LP*. In addition, *GP* and *LP* agree to a qualified income offset, thus satisfying the requirements of the alternate test for economic effect of § 1.704–1(b)(2)(ii)(*d*). *GP* and *LP* also agree that no allocation will be made that causes or increases a deficit balance in any partner's capital account in excess of the partner's obligation to restore the deficit.

LPRS purchases depreciable property for $1,000x from an unrelated seller, paying $200x in cash and borrowing the $800x balance from an unrelated bank that is not the seller of the property. The note is recourse to *LPRS*. The principal of the loan is due in 6 years; interest is payable semi-annually at the applicable federal rate. *GP* bears the entire economic risk of loss for *LPRS*'s recourse liability, and *GP*'s basis in *LPRS* (outside basis) is increased by $800x. *See* § 1.752—2.

In each of years 1 through 5, the property generates $200x of depreciation. All other partnership deductions and losses exactly equal

¶ 18,102

income, so that in each of years 1 through 5 *LPRS* has a net loss of $200*x*.

LAW AND ANALYSIS

Under § 704(b) * * * and the regulations thereunder, a partnership's allocations of income, gain, loss, deduction, or credit set forth in the partnership agreement are respected if they have substantial economic effect. If allocations under the partnership agreement would not have substantial economic effect, the partnership's allocations are determined according to the partners' interests in the partnership. The fundamental principles for establishing economic effect require an allocation to be consistent with the partners' underlying economic arrangement. A partner allocated a share of income should enjoy any corresponding economic benefit, and a partner allocated a share of losses or deductions should bear any corresponding economic burden. *See* § 1.704–1(b)(2)(ii)(*a*).

To come within the safe harbor for establishing economic effect in § 1.704–1(b)(2)(ii), partners must agree to maintain capital accounts under the rules of § 1.704–1(b)(2)(iv), liquidate according to positive capital account balances, and agree to an unconditional deficit restoration obligation for any partner with a deficit in that partner's capital account, as described in § 1.704–1(b)(2)(ii)(*b*)(*3*). Alternatively, the partnership may satisfy the requirements of the alternate test for economic effect provided in § 1.704–1(b)(2)(ii)(*d*). *LPRS*'s partnership agreement complies with the alternate test for economic effect.

The alternate test for economic effect requires the partners to agree to a qualified income offset in lieu of an unconditional deficit restoration obligation. If the partners so agree, allocations will have economic effect to the extent that they do not create a deficit capital account for any partner (in excess of any limited deficit restoration obligation of that partner) as of the end of the partnership taxable year to which the allocation relates. Section 1.704–(b)(2)(ii)(*d*)(*3*) (flush language).

A partner is treated as having a limited deficit restoration obligation to the extent of: (1) the outstanding principal balance of any promissory note contributed to the partnership by the partner, and (2) the amount of any unconditional obligation of the partner (whether imposed by the partnership agreement or by state or local law) to make subsequent contributions to the partnership. Section 1.704–1(b)(2)(ii)(*c*).

LP has no obligation under the partnership agreement or state or local law to make additional contributions to the partnership and, therefore, has no deficit restoration obligation. Under applicable state law, *GP* may have to make additional contributions to the partnership to pay creditors. However, *GP*'s obligation only arises to the extent that the amount of *LPRS*'s liabilities exceeds the value of *LPRS*'s assets available to satisfy the liabilities. Thus, the amount of *GP*'s limited deficit restoration obligation each year is equal to the difference between the amount of the partnership's recourse liabilities at the end of the year and the value of the partnership's assets available to satisfy the liabilities at the end of the year.

To ensure consistency with the other requirements of the regulations under § 704(b), where a partner's obligation to make additional contributions to the partnership is dependent on the value of the partnership's assets, the partner's deficit restoration obligation must be computed by reference to the rules for determining the value of partnership property contained in the regulations under § 704(b). Consequently, in computing *GP*'s limited deficit restoration obligation, the value of the partnership's assets is conclusively presumed to equal the book basis of those assets under the capital account maintenance rules of § 1.704–1(b)(2)(iv). *See* § 1.704–1(b)(2)(ii)(*d*) (value equals basis presumption applies for purposes of determining expected allocations and distributions under the alternate test for economic effect); § 1.704–1(b)(2)(iii) (value equals basis presumption applies for purposes of the substantiality test); § 1.704–1(b)(3)(iii) (value equals basis presumption applies for purposes of the partner's interest in the partnership test); § 1.704–(d) (value equals basis presumption applies in computing partnership minimum gain).

The *LPRS* agreement allocates all depreciation deductions and gain on the sale of depreciable property to the extent of those deductions to *GP*. Because *LPRS*'s partnership agreement satisfies the alternate test for economic effect, the allocations of depreciation deductions to *GP* will have economic effect to the extent that they do not create a deficit capital account for *GP* in excess of *GP*'s obligation to restore the deficit balance. At the end of year 1, the basis of the depreciable property has been reduced to $800x. If *LPRS* liquidated at the beginning of year 2, selling its depreciable property for its basis of $800x, the proceeds would be used to repay the $800x principal on *LPRS*'s recourse liability. All of *LPRS*'s creditors would be satisfied and *GP* would have no obligation to contribute to pay them. Thus, at the end of year 1, *GP* has no obligation to restore a deficit in its capital account.

Because *GP* has no obligation to restore a deficit balance in its capital account at the end of year 1, an allocation that reduces *GP*'s capital account below $0 is not permitted under the partnership agreement and would not satisfy the alternate test for economic effect. An allocation of $200x of depreciation deductions to *GP* would reduce *GP*'s capital account to negative $100x. Because the allocation would result in a deficit capital account balance in excess of *GP*'s obligation to restore, the allocation is not permitted under the partnership agreement, and would not satisfy the safe harbor under the alternate test for economic effect. Therefore, the deductions for year 1 must be allocated $100x each to *GP* and *LP* (which is in accordance with their interests in the partnership).

¶ 18,102

The allocation of depreciation of $200x to GP in year 2 has economic effect. Although the allocation reduces GP's capital account to negative $200x, while LP's capital account remains $0, the allocation to GP does not create a deficit capital account in excess of GP's limited deficit restoration obligation. If LPRS liquidated at the beginning of year 3, selling the depreciable property for its basis of $600x, the proceeds would be applied toward the $800x LPRS liability. Because GP is obligated to restore a deficit capital account to the extent necessary to pay creditors, GP would be required to contribute $200x to LPRS to satisfy the outstanding liability. Thus, at the end of year 2, GP has a deficit restoration obligation of $200x, and the allocation of depreciation to GP does not reduce GP's capital account below its obligation to restore a deficit capital account.

This analysis also applies to the allocation of $200x of depreciation to GP in years 3 through 5. At the beginning of year 6, when the property is fully depreciated, the $800x principal amount of the partnership liability is due. The partners' capital accounts at the beginning of year 6 will equal negative $800x and $0, respectively, for GP and LP. Because value is conclusively presumed to equal basis, the depreciable property would be worthless and could not be used to satisfy LPRS's $800x liability. As a result, GP is deemed to be required to contribute $800x to LPRS. A contribution by GP to satisfy this limited deficit restoration obligation would increase GP's capital account balance to $0.

Holding

When a partner is treated as having a limited deficit restoration obligation by reason of the partner's liability to the partnership's creditors, the amount of that obligation is the amount of money that the partner would be required to contribute to the partnership to satisfy partnership liabilities if all partnership property were sold for the amount of the partnership's book basis in the property.

* * *

[¶ 18,105]

b. *"Substantiality" of the Economic Effect*

The substantiality requirement of the regulations is intended to ensure that the allocation has an economic effect in substance and is not merely an attempt to minimize the tax liabilities of the partners. To be valid, there must be a reasonable possibility that the allocation "will affect substantially the dollar amounts to be received by the partners from the partnership, independent of tax consequences." Reg. § 1.704–1(b)(2)(iii)(*a*). For example, a partnership might invest $10,000 in taxable bonds and $12,000 in tax-exempt bonds, with both investments yielding about $1,000 of interest. An attempted allocation of the taxable interest to one partner and the tax-free interest to another would fail the substantiality requirement if it lacked any reasonable possibility of significance to the partners' respective economic interests. Reg. § 1.704–1(b)(5), Ex. 5. In what might prove to be more troublesome to some partnerships, this requirement is applied not only to specific allocations, such as the one illustrated, but also to the overall allocation for the year.

Transitory allocations are also vulnerable to challenge. Reg. § 1.704–1(b)(2)(iii)(*c*). Assume, for example, that a partnership agreement provides generally that income and loss will be divided equally but makes a special allocation to one partner of $20,000 in year 1 and a special allocation to another partner of $20,000 in year 2. The special allocations may be challenged on the ground that the substantiality test has not been met. If the challenge succeeds, each partner would be taxed on $10,000 for each year. See Reg. § 1.704–1(b)(5), Ex. 17.

[¶ 18,107]

REVENUE RULING 99–43

1999–2 C.B. 506.

ISSUE

Do partnership allocations lack substantiality under § 1.704–1(b)(2)(iii) of the * * * Regulations when the partners amend the partnership agreement to create offsetting special allocations of particular items after the events giving rise to the items have occurred?

FACTS

A and *B*, both individuals, formed a general partnership, *PRS*. *A* and *B* each contributed $1,000 and also agreed that each would be allocated a 50–percent share of all partnership items. The partnership agreement provides that, upon the contribution of additional capital by either partner, *PRS* must revalue the partnership's property and adjust the partners' capital accounts under § 1.704–1(b)(2)(iv)(*f*).

PRS borrowed $8,000 from a bank and used the borrowed and contributed funds to purchase nondepreciable property for $10,000. The loan was nonrecourse to *A* and *B* and was secured only by the property. No principal payments were due for 6 years, and interest was payable semi-annually at a market rate.

After one year, the fair market value of the property fell from $10,000 to $6,000, but the principal amount of the loan remained $8,000. As part of a workout arrangement among the bank, *PRS*, *A*, and *B*, the bank reduced the principal amount of the loan by $2,000, and *A* contributed an additional $500 to *PRS*. *A*'s capital account was credited with the $500, which *PRS* used to pay currently deductible expenses incurred in connection with the workout. All $500 of the currently deductible workout expenses were allocated to *A*. *B* made no additional contribution of capital. At the time of the workout, *B* was insolvent within the meaning of § 108(a) * * *. *A* and *B* agreed that, after the workout, *A* would have a 60–percent interest and *B* would have a 40–percent interest in the profits and losses of PRS.

As a result of the property's decline in value and the workout, *PRS* had two items to allocate between *A* and *B*. First, the agreement to cancel $2,000 of the loan resulted in $2,000 of cancellation of indebtedness income (COD income). Second, *A*'s contribution of $500 to *PRS* was an event that required *PRS*, under the partnership agreement, to revalue partnership property and adjust *A*'s and *B*'s capital accounts. Because of the decline in value of the property, the revaluation resulted in a $4,000 economic loss that must be allocated between *A*'s and *B*'s capital accounts.

Under the terms of the original partnership agreement, *PRS* would have allocated these items equally between *A* and *B*. *A* and *B*, however, amend the partnership agreement (in a timely manner) to make two special allocations. First, *PRS* specially allocates the entire $2,000 of COD income to *B*, an insolvent partner. Second, *PRS* specially allocates the book loss from the revaluation $1,000 to *A* and $3,000 to *B*.

While *A* receives a $1,000 allocation of book loss and *B* receives a $3,000 allocation of book loss, neither of these allocations results in a tax loss to either partner. Rather, the allocations result only in adjustments to *A*'s and *B*'s capital accounts. Thus, the cumulative effect of the special allocations is to reduce each partner's capital account to zero immediately following the allocations despite the fact that *B* is allocated $2,000 of income for tax purposes.

Law

Section 61(a)(12) provides that gross income includes income from the discharge of indebtedness.

Rev. Rul. 91–31, 1991–1 C.B. 19, holds that a taxpayer realizes COD income when a creditor (who was not the seller of the underlying property) reduces the principal amount of an under-secured nonrecourse debt.

Under § 704(b) and the regulations thereunder, allocations of a partnership's items of income, gain, loss, deduction, or credit provided for in the partnership agreement will be respected if the allocations have substantial economic effect. Allocations that fail to have substantial economic effect will be reallocated according to the partners' interests in the partnership (as defined in § 1.704–1(b)(3)).

Section 1.704–1(b)(2)(iv)(*f*) provides that a partnership may, upon the occurrence of certain events (including the contribution of money to the partnership by a new or existing partner), increase or decrease the partners' capital accounts to reflect a revaluation of the partnership property.

Section 1.704–1(b)(2)(iv)(*g*) provides that, to the extent a partnership's property is reflected on the books of the partnership at a book value that differs from the adjusted tax basis, the substantial economic effect requirements apply to the allocations of book items. Section 704(c) and § 1.704–1(b)(4)(i) govern the partners' distributive shares of tax items.

Section 1.704–1(b)(2)(i) provides that the determination of whether an allocation of income, gain, loss, or deduction (or item thereof) to a partner has substantial economic effect involves a two-part analysis that is made at the end of the partnership year to which the allocation relates. In order for an allocation to have substantial economic effect, the allocation must have both economic effect (within the meaning of § 1.704–1(b)(2)(ii)) and be substantial (within the meaning of § 1.704–1(b)(2)(iii)).

Section 1.704–1(b)(2)(iii)(*a*) provides that the economic effect of an allocation (or allocations) is substantial if there is a reasonable possibility that the allocation (or allocations) will substantially affect the dollar amounts to be received by the partners from the partnership independent of the tax consequences. However, the economic effect of an allocation is not substantial if, at the time the allocation becomes part of the partnership agreement, (1) the after-tax economic consequences of at least one partner may, in present value terms, be enhanced compared to the consequences if the allocation (or allocations) were not contained in the partnership agreement, and (2) there is a strong likelihood that the after-tax economic consequences of no partner will, in present value terms, be substantially diminished compared to the consequences if the allocation (or allocations) were not contained in the partnership agreement. In determining the after-tax economic benefit or detriment to a partner, tax consequences that result from the interaction of the allocation with the partner's tax attributes that are unrelated to the partnership will be taken into account.

Section 1.704–1(b)(2)(iii)(*b*) provides that the economic effect of an allocation (or allocations) in a partnership taxable year is not substantial if the allocations result in shifting tax consequences. Shifting tax consequences result when, at the time the allocation (or allocations) becomes part of the partnership agreement, there is a strong likelihood that (1) the net increases and decreases that will be recorded in the partners' respective capital accounts for the taxable year will not differ substantially from the net increases and decreases that would be recorded in the partners' respective capital accounts for the year if the allocations were not contained in the partnership agreement, and (2) the total tax liability of the partners (for their respective tax years in which the

¶ 18,107

allocations will be taken into account) will be less than if the allocations were not contained in the partnership agreement.

Section 1.704–1(b)(2)(iii)(c) provides that the economic effect of an allocation (or allocations) in a partnership taxable year is not substantial if the allocations are transitory. Allocations are considered transitory if a partnership agreement provides for the possibility that one or more allocations (the "original allocation(s)") will be largely offset by other allocations (the "offsetting allocation(s)"), and, at the time the allocations become part of the partnership agreement, there is a strong likelihood that (1) the net increases and decreases that will be recorded in the partners' capital accounts for the taxable years to which the allocations relate will not differ substantially from the net increases and decreases that would be recorded in such partners' respective capital accounts for such years if the original and offsetting allocation(s) were not contained in the partnership agreement, and (2) the total tax liability of the partners (for their respective tax years in which the allocations will be taken into account) will be less than if the allocations were not contained in the partnership agreement.

Section 761(c) provides that a partnership agreement includes any modifications made prior to, or at, the time prescribed for filing a partnership return (not including extensions) which are agreed to by all partners, or which are adopted in such other manner as may be provided by the partnership agreement.

ANALYSIS

PRS is free to allocate partnership items between *A* and *B* in accordance with the provisions of the partnership agreement if the allocations have substantial economic effect under § 1.704–1(b)(2). To the extent that the minimum gain chargeback rules do not apply,[1] COD income may be allocated in accordance with the rules under § 1.704–1(b)(2). This is true notwithstanding that the COD income arises in connection with the cancellation of a nonrecourse debt.

The economic effect of an allocation is not substantial if, at the time that the allocation becomes part of the partnership agreement, the allocation fails each of two tests. The allocation fails the first test if the after-tax consequences of at least one partner may, in present value terms, be enhanced compared to the consequences if the allocation (or allocations) were not contained in the partnership agreement. The

---

1. [As discussed below, at ¶ 18,125,] [u]nder certain circumstances, the COD income would be allocated between the partners in accordance with their shares of partnership minimum gain because the cancellation of the nonrecourse debt would result in a decrease in partnership minimum gain. *See* § 1.704–2(d). However, in this situation, there is no minimum gain be-cause the principal amount of the debt never exceeded the property's book value. Therefore, the minimum gain chargeback requirement does not govern the manner in which the COD income is allocated between *A* and *B*, and *PRS*'s special allocation of COD income must satisfy the substantial economic effect standard. *See* Rev. Rul. 92–97, 1992–2 C.B. 124.

¶ 18,107

allocation fails the second test if there is a strong likelihood that the after-tax economic consequences of no partner will, in present value terms, be substantially diminished compared to such consequences if the allocation (or allocations) were not contained in the partnership agreement.

A and *B* amended the *PRS* partnership agreement to provide for an allocation of the entire $2,000 of the COD income to *B*. *B*, an insolvent taxpayer, is eligible to exclude the income under § 108, so it is unlikely that the $2,000 of COD income would increase *B*'s immediate tax liability. Without the special allocation, *A*, who is not insolvent or otherwise entitled to exclude the COD income under § 108, would pay tax immediately on the $1,000 of COD income allocated under the general ratio for sharing income. *A* and *B* also amended the *PRS* partnership agreement to provide for the special allocation of the book loss resulting from the revaluation. Because the two special allocations offset each other, *B* will not realize any economic benefit from the $2,000 income allocation, even if the property subsequently appreciates in value.

The economics of *PRS* are unaffected by the paired special allocations. After the capital accounts of *A* and *B* are adjusted to reflect the special allocations, *A* and *B* each have a capital account of zero. Economically, the situation of both partners is identical to what it would have been had the special allocations not occurred. In addition, a strong likelihood exists that the total tax liability of *A* and *B* will be less than if *PRS* had allocated 50 percent of the $2,000 of COD income and 50 percent of the $4,000 book loss to each partner. Therefore, the special allocations of COD income and book loss are shifting allocations under § 1.704–1(b)(2)(iii)(*b*) and lack substantiality. (Alternatively, the allocations could be transitory allocations under § 1.704–1(b)(2)(iii)(*c*) if the allocations occur during different partnership taxable years).

This conclusion is not altered by the "value equals basis" rule that applies in determining the substantiality of an allocation. See § 1.704–1(b)(2)(iii)(*c*)(2). Under that rule, the adjusted tax basis (or, if different, the book value) of partnership property will be presumed to be the fair market value of the property. This presumption is appropriate in most cases because, under § 1.704–1(b)(2)(iv), property generally will be reflected on the books of the partnership at its fair market value when acquired. Thus, an allocation of gain or loss from the disposition of the property will reflect subsequent changes in the value of the property that generally cannot be predicted.

The substantiality of an allocation, however, is analyzed "at the time the allocation becomes part of the partnership agreement," not the time at which the allocation is first effective. See § 1.704–1(b)(2)(iii)(*a*). In the situation described above, the provisions of the *PRS* partnership agreement governing the allocation of gain or loss from the disposition of property are changed at a time that is after the property has been

¶ 18,107

revalued on the books of the partnership, but are effective for a period that begins prior to the revaluation. See § 1.704–1(b)(2)(iv)(*f*).

Under these facts, the presumption that value equals basis does not apply to validate the allocations. Instead, *PRS*'s allocations of gain or loss must be closely scrutinized in determining the appropriate tax consequences. *Cf.* § 1.704–1(b)(4)(vi). In this situation, the special allocations of the $2,000 of COD income and $4,000 of book loss will not be respected and, instead, must be allocated in accordance with the *A*'s and *B*'s interests in the partnership under § 1.704–1(b)(3).

Close scrutiny also would be required if the changes were made at a time when the events giving rise to the allocations had not yet occurred but were likely to occur or if, under the original allocation provisions of a partnership agreement, there was a strong likelihood that a disproportionate amount of COD income earned in the future would be allocated to any partner who is insolvent at the time of the allocation and would be offset by an increased allocation of loss or a reduced allocation of income to such partner or partners.

HOLDING

Partnership special allocations lack substantiality when the partners amend the partnership agreement to specially allocate COD income and book items from a related revaluation after the events creating such items have occurred if the overall economic effect of the special allocations on the partners' capital accounts does not differ substantially from the economic effect of the original allocations in the partnership agreement.

* * *

[¶ 18,110]

c. *Inability to Satisfy Substantial Economic Effect*

If the partnership allocation cannot be sustained under any variation of this safe harbor rule, the allocation for tax purposes is to be made in accordance with the "partner's interest in the partnership." Reg. § 1.704–1(b)(1)(i) and (3)(i). A partner's interest in the partnership is not, however, necessarily a single, fixed ratio determined by reference to some fundamental economic interest in the partnership. Rather, the partner's interest is determined for each item and is meant to reflect the manner in which the economic benefit or burden of that item is in fact borne by the partners. Not surprisingly, this residual formulation for allocation is based on the same principle as the safe harbor test: a valid tax allocation must reflect an underlying economic allocation. Indeed, if an allocation meets the safe harbor test, it will also comply with the partner's interest in the partnership test. This residual test, therefore, is used only if the partnership, through carelessness or design, fails to meet the complex technical requirements of the safe harbor rule.

[¶ 18,115]

Problems

1. Neeman and Marcus are the sole partners of a general partnership that owns and operates several department stores in various locations. Income and losses from operations are divided equally between the partners, except that 90 percent of the income or loss from the Cody, Wyoming, store is allocated to Neeman. The partnership maintains capital accounts that conform to the regulations and liquidating distributions are controlled by the positive balances in those accounts. However, no partner is obligated to restore a capital account deficit.

a. Assuming that all stores are profitable during the year, how must the income be allocated between the partners? See Reg. § 1.704–1(b)(2)(ii)(*i*) and (b)(3).

b. Assuming that the Cody store shows a loss for the year but that Neeman's share of the profits from the other stores exceeds that loss, how must the income be allocated?

c. Assume that the computation of the capital accounts of the partners does not conform to the regulatory requirements in several technical respects but nevertheless generally reflects the income and expense of the several stores. How would that deficiency affect the answer in Problem 1.a.?

d. Should the parties wish to incorporate their business, to what extent could they continue their existing financial arrangements?

2. Assume that the Neeman–Marcus partnership agreement provides that all depreciation on the Randolph, Vermont, store is allocated to Marcus and that, on the sale of that store, all gain will be allocated to Marcus. Assume further that the partners reasonably anticipate that the Randolph store will be sold for more than they paid to purchase it. How must the depreciation be allocated? See Reg. § 1.704–1(b)(2)(iii)(*c*) (last three sentences).

3. April and Mae each contribute $1,000 in cash to a partnership that was newly formed for the purpose of repairing Junecard washing machines. To finance their operations, the partnership borrows $8,000 on a recourse basis from a bank. Under the partnership agreement, 75 percent of all items of income and expense are allocated to April and 25 percent to Mae. The partnership meets the first two requirements of the substantial economic effect test, and, in addition, the partners are obligated to restore any capital account deficits upon the liquidation of the partnership. In its first year of operation, the partnership sustains a net loss of $4,000.

a. What will be the basis of the interests in the partnership following the bank borrowing? See Reg. § 1.752–2(f), Exs. 1 and 2.

b. How must the year 1 loss be allocated?

c. What will be the basis for the partnership interests and the capital account balances at the end of year 1?

d. If at the beginning of year 2 the partnership business is sold for $12,000, the bank loan repaid, and the partnership liquidated, what payments must be made among the parties?

e. How would your answer in Problem 3.d. change if the business is sold for $6,000?

4. General and Limited form a limited partnership to which each contributes $2,000. The partnership borrows $6,000 on a recourse basis and purchases depreciable property. The partnership meets the first two requirements of the substantial economic effect test, but neither partner is obligated by the partnership agreement to restore a capital account deficit. However, Limited is subject to a qualified income offset. All items of income and expense are shared equally except depreciation, which is allocated solely to Limited. Assume that the cash flow items of income and expense are equal and that the partnership thus incurs a loss attributable to depreciation of $1,000 per year. For which years will the partnership allocation formula be valid? See Reg. § 1.704–1(b)(2)(i), (ii)(a), (b), and (d). If in any year the allocation is invalid, to whom should the depreciation deduction be reallocated? See Reg. § 1.704–1(b)(3).

5. Assume that the partnership is a general partnership and the partnership agreement does not contain a qualified income offset. To whom are the depreciation deductions allocated and, if applicable, reallocated? See Reg. § 1.704–1(b)(3)(iii).

6. Returning to the General–Limited limited partnership in Problem 4, assume that at the beginning of year 4, a second limited partner is admitted to the partnership. At that time, the partnership property has a net value (in excess of the liability of $6,000) of $10,000, so the new partner contributes cash of $5,000 in exchange for a one-third interest in profits, losses, and capital—subject to the special allocation of depreciation to Limited. What effect would that event have on the allocation of depreciation for year 4? See Reg. § 1.704–1(b)(2)(iv)(f)(5)(i).

[¶ 18,120]

Note

The restatement of capital accounts to current value upon such events as the admission of a new partner is apparently permissible, rather than mandatory, under the capital account regulations. If the accounts are not restated, however, how would the assets of the partnership be distributed in a liquidation? In Problem 6, at ¶ 18,115, for

¶ 18,115

example, it would seem improper to distribute $1,000 of the liquidation proceeds to General and $5,000 to the new partner and to divide the balance equally among the three partners.

Regardless of whether the capital accounts are restated, the admission of a new partner creates a further issue: How must the pre-admission appreciation in the partnership properties be allocated? You may recognize that problem as the reverse of the transaction addressed by Section 704(c), discussed at ¶ 18,135. If capital accounts are not restated to current value, the regulations strongly encourage, but apparently do not require, the partners to allocate the pre-admission gain solely to the existing partners, here General and Limited. If capital accounts are restated to current value, the regulations do require that tax items attributable to revalued property be allocated using Section 704(c) principles (discussed at ¶¶ 18,135 and 18,145). These allocations are called "reverse Section 704(c) allocations." See Reg. § 1.704–1(b)(4)(i), (b)(2)(iv)(*f*), and (b)(5), Exs. 14 and 18; see also § 706(d)(2)(B)(iv), discussed at ¶ 18,205.

[¶ 18,125]

7. ALLOCATIONS ATTRIBUTABLE TO NONRECOURSE DEBT

Reg. § 1.704–2(b)(1) provides that taxpayers are precluded from sustaining an allocation of losses attributable to the expenditure of the proceeds of a nonrecourse borrowing under the substantial economic effect test. That safe harbor is denied for the stated reason that nonrecourse losses cannot have any economic effect since those losses, if incurred, will fall upon the nonrecourse lender, not the partnership.

The prohibition, however, creates only complexity, not a substantive restriction on allocations. The regulations continue to provide an even more tolerant safe harbor rule for the allocation of nonrecourse deductions, based on the Supreme Court decision in Commissioner v. Tufts, 461 U.S. 300 (1983). In *Tufts*, the Court held that, upon the disposition of property subject to an unpaid nonrecourse debt, the entire amount of the debt is included in the transferor's amount realized, even if the value of the property is lower. The minimum gain that must be recognized on such a disposition will, therefore, be the excess of the face amount of the debt over the adjusted basis of the property. Thus, depreciation deductions on property purchased with nonrecourse debt after the basis of the property falls below the amount of the debt will unavoidably be offset by the minimum gain realized on the subsequent disposition of the property. Under Reg. § 1.704–2, the allocation of deductions attributable to the nonrecourse debt generally will be valid, provided only that the partnership applies the *Tufts* principle on a partner-by-partner basis.

The allocation of nonrecourse deductions will be respected if the following requirements, set forth in Reg. § 1.704–2(e), are met:

1. The partnership meets the first two requirements of the substantial economic effect test concerning capital accounts (i.e., capital account balances are maintained in accordance with the Section 704(b) regulations and liquidating distributions are required to be made in accordance with the partners' positive capital account balances) and meets the third requirement of either Reg. § 1.704–1(b)(2)(ii)(*b*) or § 1.704–1(b)(2)(ii)(*d*) (i.e., partners with deficit capital account balances have an unconditional deficit restoration obligation or agree to a qualified income offset).

2. The allocation of nonrecourse deductions is consistent with some other allocation "of some other significant partnership item attributable to the property securing the [partnership's] nonrecourse liabilities" that meets the substantial economic effect test.

3. All other material partnership allocations and capital account adjustments are "recognized" under Reg. § 1.704–1(b).

4. The partnership agreement contains a "minimum gain chargeback." The definition of such a chargeback in Reg. § 1.704–2(f), covering a variety of factual possibilities, is extraordinarily complex, but the objective is clear. The *Tufts* gain—the "minimum gain"—recognized by the partnership on the disposition of property subject to nonrecourse debt must generally be allocated to the partners in the same proportion, and to the same extent, as those partners' previously claimed nonrecourse deductions (or distributions received of proceeds attributable to a nonrecourse debt); therefore, if that minimum gain (which justified the claiming of nonrecourse deductions earlier) drops in amount, the chargeback clause will promptly allocate other income to offset the capital account deficit that is no longer matched by a minimum gain.

In short, so long as the partners do not seek a greater benefit from a nonrecourse borrowing than the timing benefit to which they would be entitled on an investment not through a partnership, the allocation of a nonrecourse deduction will be respected under the Section 704(b) regulations.

The deductions subject to this rule, i.e., nonrecourse deductions, are those that create a minimum gain. Thus, the allocation of deductions attributable to property secured by a nonrecourse debt is subject to the more general rules described above until the basis of that property is reduced to an amount less than the face amount of the nonrecourse debt. Only to the extent of the annual increase in the excess of the face amount of the debt over the basis of the property are partnership losses treated as nonrecourse deductions subject to the rule described here.

One of the more confusing issues under prior law was whether a nonrecourse debt should be treated as a recourse debt if one or more of the partners guaranteed the repayment of all or a portion of the debt. The regulations under Section 704(b) do not take that approach but do severely limit the partnership's flexibility in allocating losses attributable to such "partner nonrecourse debt." All such losses must be allocated solely to the partners that bear the economic risk of loss on the debt in proportion to their shares of that risk. Reg. § 1.704–2(i)(1).

[¶ 18,130]

Problem

General and Limited form a limited partnership to which General contributes $100,000 and Limited contributes $100,000. The partnership agreement allocates 40 percent of profits and losses to General and 60 percent to Limited. The partnership agreement does not impose any explicit obligation to restore a capital account deficit but does contain both a qualified income offset provision and a minimum gain chargeback provision. The partnership purchases a building for $1,000,000 using nonrecourse debt of $800,000 (secured only by a mortgage on the building). Assume that partnership income equals deductions except for depreciation, which is $100,000 annually, and that the partnership pays all interest due on the debt but makes no repayments of principal.

    a.   Would the 60:40 special allocation of partnership losses be sustained for the first year of operations?

    b.   Would the allocation be permitted for the second year? What about the third year?

    c.   Assume that at the beginning of the fourth year the property is conveyed to the nonrecourse lender for no consideration other than the extinguishment of the $800,000 debt. What are the tax consequences to each partner?

8. ALLOCATIONS WITH RESPECT TO CONTRIBUTED PROPERTY

[¶ 18,135]

a. Section 704(c) Requirements for Allocation

Although Section 721 permits a partner's contribution of appreciated property without recognizing gain realized upon the exchange, the contributing partner is not allowed either to escape permanently taxation on the gain or to shift the tax consequences of the gain to other partners. Section 704(c)(1)(A), in a somewhat complicated formulation, denies both possibilities by requiring that gain or loss with respect to contributed property be allocated to take account of any difference between the tax basis and market value of the property at the time of the contribution. Recall that the contribution of such property would have been reflected in the capital accounts at market values. Section 704(c) in effect requires allocations for tax purposes that eliminate the disparity between the tax books and the capital accounts.

¶ 18,135

When nondepreciable contributed property is subsequently sold by the partnership at a gain or loss, the requirements of Section 704(c)(1)(A) are relatively straightforward. The extent of the gain or loss attributable to the difference between basis and value at the time of the contribution (referred to as the "built-in gain or loss") is allocated to the contributing partner. In the Al–Bea partnership (¶ 17,010), for example, if the property Al contributed were sold by the partnership for $100, the entire gain of $60 (i.e., amount realized of $100 minus the adjusted basis of $40) must be allocated to him. Gain or loss in excess of that amount is then allocated among the partners according to the partnership agreement and Section 704(b). The rules of Section 704(c) also apply to income generated by the collection of cash basis accounts receivable and deductions produced by the payment of cash basis accounts payable.

Regulations under Section 704(c) permit a partnership to make allocations "using a reasonable method that is consistent with the purpose of section 704(c)." Reg. § 1.704–3(a)(1). In particular, the regulations treat as "generally reasonable" three allocation methods: the "traditional method," the "traditional method with curative allocations," and the "remedial allocation method." Reg. § 1.704–3(b), (c), and (d). However, under an anti-abuse rule in the regulations, an allocation method will not be treated as reasonable if the contribution of property and the corresponding allocation of tax items are made "with a view to shifting the tax consequences of built-in gain or loss among the partners in a manner that substantially reduces the present value of the partners' aggregate tax liability." Reg. § 1.704–3(a)(10).

Section 704(c) applies on a property-by-property basis; accordingly, in determining whether a disparity exists between the tax basis and fair market value of contributed property, the regulations generally do not permit built-in gains and built-in losses on items of contributed property to be aggregated. Reg. § 1.704–3(a)(2). However, certain types of property—depreciable property, property with a zero basis, and inventory—may be aggregated if contributed by one partner. Reg. § 1.704–3(e)(2). (The regulations also contain a special aggregation rule for securities partnerships. See Reg. § 1.704–3(e)(3).) Only one allocation method may be used with respect to any one item of contributed property, but the regulations permit the use of different methods with respect to different items of contributed property (provided that the partnership and partners use a single reasonable method for each item of contributed property and that the overall method is reasonable under the facts and circumstances). Reg. § 1.704–3(a)(2). Is the flexibility of these regulations appropriate given the policy underlying the enactment of Section 704(c)?

The regulations contain a de minimis rule that relaxes the requirements of Section 704(c) in certain circumstances. This de minimis rule permits a partnership to disregard or defer the application of Section 704(c) if a partner contributes one or more items of property to a

¶ 18,135

partnership within a single taxable year of the partnership and the disparity between the book value and tax basis of the contributed property is a "small disparity." Reg. § 1.704–3(e)(1). A disparity is a "small disparity" for this purpose if the book value of all properties contributed by one partner during the partnership taxable year does not differ from the tax basis by more than 15 percent of the tax basis, and the total gross disparity is not more than $20,000. For example, suppose that Martha and Ken form a partnership, with Martha contributing property with an adjusted basis of $70,000 and a fair market value of $80,000 and Ken contributing $80,000 cash. Under the de minimis rule in the regulations, the partnership may disregard Section 704(c) with respect to the property contributed by Martha because the $10,000 disparity in the value and tax basis of the property does not exceed 15 percent of that tax basis (i.e., 15 percent of $70,000 equals $10,500) and the total disparity does not exceed $20,000.

Traditional method. Before the revision of Section 704(c) by the Tax Reform Act of 1984, partners were permitted, but not required, to make the allocations that are required by the current version of Section 704(c). The "traditional method" in the current regulations is based on the approach in the former Section 704(c) regulations developed when Section 704(c) allocations were elective. Under that method, when the partnership sells or exchanges contributed property, the partnership must allocate any built-in gain or loss to the contributing partner. Reg. § 1.704–3(b)(1). For example, returning to the Al–Bea partnership (¶ 17,-010), if the property Al contributed were sold by the partnership for $100, the entire taxable gain of $60 (i.e., amount realized of $100 minus the adjusted basis of $40) must be allocated to him under the traditional method.

The regulations, however, impose an important limitation on the magnitude of that permitted allocation under the traditional method. Reg. § 1.704–3(b)(1). Under the so-called ceiling rule, the partnership allocation of gain or loss is limited to the amount actually recognized by the partnership at the time of the disposition, even if that amount does not wholly eliminate the disparity between the tax books and capital accounts.[1] Returning to the Al–Bea partnership (¶ 17,010), if the property Al contributed were sold for only $90, thus resulting in taxable gain of $50, a theoretically correct result would be reached if the partnership could allocate to Al the precontribution gain of $60 plus one-half of the post-contribution loss of $10. The net allocation of a gain of $55 to Al would increase his basis to $95, and the allocation of a loss of $5 to Bea would reduce her basis to the same amount. Since their initial capital

---

1. New Section 704(c)(1)(C), enacted in 2004, explicitly provides that only the contributing partner can take into account a built-in loss and appears to override the ceiling rule in the regulations with respect to contributed property with a built-in loss. See L. Cunningham & N. Cunningham, The Logic of Subchapter K—A Conceptual Guide to the Taxation of Partnerships 90–93 (3d ed. 2006).

accounts of $100 would be reduced only by their share of the post-contribution loss, both of their tax bases for their partnership interests would be conformed to their capital accounts. Under the ceiling rule, however, the partnership is limited to allocating the actually recognized gain of $50 entirely to Al.

Traditional method with curative allocations. To correct distortions created by the ceiling rule, the traditional method with curative allocations permits a partnership to make "reasonable curative allocations" that reduce or eliminate disparities between book and tax items of noncontributing partners. Reg. § 1.704–3(c)(1). For this purpose, a curative allocation is an allocation of income, gain, loss, or deduction for tax purposes that differs from the partnership's allocation of the corresponding book item. Id. Thus, by definition, a curative allocation is one which is not reflected in the partners' capital accounts and has no economic effect. The regulations require the partnership to be consistent in its application of curative allocations with respect to each item of contributed property from year to year. Reg. § 1.704–3(c)(2).

To be considered reasonable, a curative allocation must not exceed the amount necessary to offset the effect of the ceiling rule. Reg. § 1.704–3(c)(3)(i). The regulations permit a partnership to make curative allocations to offset the effect of the ceiling rule for a prior taxable year if the allocations are made over a reasonable period of time and are provided for in the partnership agreement in effect for the year of contribution. Reg. § 1.704–3(c)(3)(ii). Further, a curative allocation generally is reasonable only if it is "expected to have substantially the same effect on each partner's tax liability as the tax item limited by the ceiling rule." Reg. § 1.704–3(c)(3)(iii)(A).

For example, returning to the Al–Bea partnership (¶ 17,010), suppose that the property Al contributed were sold by the partnership for $90 of long-term capital gain. As is true under the traditional method, the entire gain of $50 must be allocated to Al. Suppose further that the partnership invested the $100 cash contributed by Bea in other property that will produce long-term capital gain in the partnership's hands and now sells the purchased property for $120, realizing a book and tax gain of $20 that would be allocated $10 to each partner. Since the character of the gain on the sale of the property contributed by Al and the character of the property purchased with Bea's contribution are the same, the regulations permit the partnership to make a curative allocation, for tax purposes only, of $5 of Bea's tax gain on the sale of the purchased property to Al. Thus, even though for book purposes $10 of the gain would be allocated to each partner, for tax purposes $15 of the gain would be allocated to Al and only $5 to Bea. This curative allocation corrects the ceiling rule distortion.

Remedial allocation method. The regulations authorize yet a third method, the remedial allocation method, which allows a partnership to make remedial allocations to reduce ceiling rule disparities between tax items of noncontributing partners and corresponding book items. Reg. § 1.704–3(d)(1). These allocations are tax allocations of income, gain, loss, or deduction to the noncontributing partner that are offset by tax allocations in an identical amount to the contributing partner and have no effect on the partners' book capital accounts. Reg. § 1.704–3(d)(1) and (4)(ii). These remedial items have the same effect on a partner's tax liability and the partner's adjusted basis in the partnership interest as do other tax items, but they have no effect on the partnership's adjusted basis in its own property. Reg. § 1.704–3(d)(4)(i) and (ii).

Under this remedial allocation method, if the ceiling rule results in a book allocation to a noncontributing partner different from the partner's corresponding tax allocation, the partnership is permitted to make a remedial allocation of income, gain, loss, or deduction to the noncontributing partner equal to the full amount of the disparity caused by the ceiling rule, and a simultaneous, offsetting remedial allocation of deduction, loss, gain, or income to the contributing partner. Id. The regulations require that the remedial allocation have the same tax attributes as the tax item limited by the ceiling rule, including such attributes (when relevant) as source, character, or nature of the item limited by the ceiling rule. Reg. § 1.704–3(d)(3). For example, if the item limited by the ceiling rule is the partnership's loss from the sale of contributed property, to pass muster under this regulation the offsetting remedial allocation must be gain from the sale of that property. If the item limited by the ceiling rule is depreciation from contributed property, the offsetting remedial allocation must be income of the type generated by the property. Id.

To illustrate, returning to the Al–Bea partnership (¶ 17,010), suppose again that the property Al contributed were sold by the partnership for $90, with the partnership realizing $50 of long-term capital gain on the sale, all of which is allocated to Al. The remedial allocation method permits the partnership to create and allocate to Al $5 of long-term capital gain, and make an offsetting remedial allocation of $5 of long-term capital loss to Bea, thus eliminating the disparity between the book and tax allocations.

Remember that, although the remedial allocation method eliminates the distortions caused by the ceiling rule and thereby achieves the correct result under Section 704(c), it is not required to be used by a partnership. The regulations clearly permit a partnership to use the traditional method or the traditional method with curative allocations even though those methods result in disparities between the book and tax allocations. The regulations treat all three methods described above—traditional, traditional with curative allocations, and remedial—as "generally reasonable" provided that the anti-abuse rule in Reg. § 1.704–3(a)(10) is not violated.

¶ 18,135

Distributions of contributed property by the partnership. The original version of Section 704(c)(1) applied only to sales of contributed property by a partnership. Consequently, the contributing partner could avoid an allocation of the built-in gain or loss if the partnership distributed the contributed property to another partner or distributed property other than the contributed property to the contributing partner. To deter avoidance of the requirements of Section 704(c), Congress has enacted two provisions that accelerate the point at which the precontribution gain must be recognized.

Under Section 704(c)(1)(B), discussed at ¶ 22,090, if the contributed property is distributed to a partner other than the contributing partner within seven years of the contribution, the contributing partner must recognize the built-in gain or loss that would have been allocated to the partner had the property been sold for its fair market value. Section 737 has extended that concept to the distribution of property other than the contributed property to the contributing partner. As discussed at ¶ 22,-095, upon receipt of such a distribution, Section 737 requires the contributing partner to recognize the entire amount of the net gain that would be allocated to the partner under Section 704(c)(1)(B) if all the property contributed by the partner were distributed to other partners. However, the gain recognized under Section 737 is limited to the value of the property distributed minus the basis for the distributee's partnership interest.

Special anti-abuse rules for built-in loss property. As we have seen, Section 704(c)(1) is designed to prevent built-in gain or loss on contributed property from being shifted from the contributing partner to the noncontributing partners by requiring that the precontribution gain or loss be allocated to the contributing partner. However, under pre–2004 law, if the contributing partner transferred his or her partnership interest before the property was sold or distributed, Reg. § 1.704–3(a)(7) required that the built-in gain or loss be allocated to the transferee partner. If the contributing partner's interest was liquidated, rather than transferred to another person, there was no specific statutory or regulatory rule under pre–2004 law preventing the allocation of the built-in loss to the remaining partners. Thus, Congress became concerned that it was possible for built-in loss to be transferred to the remaining partners in situations where the contributing partner was no longer a partner at the time that the partnership sold or distributed the property. Congress was particularly concerned that this and other defects in the statute were being used in tax shelter transactions involving the transfer of losses among partners. See Staff of Joint Comm. on Tax'n, 109th Cong., 1st Sess., General Explanation of Tax Legislation Enacted in the 108th Congress, at 384–85 (2005).

To remedy this problem, Congress added Section 704(c)(1)(C) to the Code in 2004. Under this provision, if contributed property has a built-in loss, the built-in loss may be taken into account only in determining the

¶ 18,135

amount of items allocated to the contributing partner. In addition, except as may be provided in regulations to be issued by the Treasury and the IRS, in determining the amount of items to be allocated to the noncontributing partners, the partnership's basis in the property is treated as being equal to its fair market value at the time of contribution. Consequently, if the contributing partner's interest is transferred or liquidated, the partnership's adjusted basis in the contributed property is treated as being equal to its fair market value at the time of contribution and the built-in loss is eliminated. Neither a transferee partner nor any other partners may benefit from the built-in loss.[2]

Special rules for allocating depreciation recapture. Under Sections 1245 and 1250, a portion of a taxpayer's gain from the disposition of certain depreciable property may be recaptured, i.e., treated as ordinary income instead of capital gain or Section 1231 gain. The regulations contain special rules for allocating such depreciation recapture with respect to property contributed by a partner to the partnership. These rules generally require that any gain characterized as depreciation recapture be allocated to each partner in an amount equal to the lesser of (i) the partner's share of total gain from disposition of the property or (ii) the partner's share of the depreciation or amortization on the property. See Reg. §§ 1.1245–1(e)(2) and 1.1250–1(f). These rules attempt to insure that the recapture gain is allocated to the partners who received the benefit of the prior depreciation or amortization deductions on the property.

[¶ 18,140]

Problems

1. Marcia and Juan are equal partners. Several years ago Marcia contributed to the partnership unimproved land having a value of $1,000 and a basis of $400. Juan contributed cash of $1,000. The partnership has just sold the land for $1,400. How should the gain be allocated between the partners?

2. What is the effect on the capital accounts of the partners at the time of the contribution of the property? Of the sale for $1,400?

3. How would your answer in Problem 1 change if the land contributed by Marcia were sold by the partnership for $800 and the partnership uses the traditional method of allocation? See Reg. § 1.704–3(b). What is the effect on the capital accounts of the partners of this sale? See Reg. § 1.704–1(b)(2)(iv)(*g*)(*1*). Assume that the partnership has no other sale transactions during the year.

2. As will be discussed in Chapters 21 through 23, the 2004 legislation also amended Sections 734(b) and 743 to require mandatory downward basis adjustments to a partnership's inside basis in its property in certain cases where the partnership makes a distribution with respect to which there is a "substantial basis reduction" or a partner transfers a partnership interest with respect to which there is a "substantial built-in loss."

4. Suppose in Problem 3 that in the same taxable year in which the partnership sells the land contributed by Marcia, the partnership also sells corporate stock purchased by the partnership several years ago and held as an investment asset, recognizing a gain of $400. How should the gain on the sale of the land and on the sale of the corporate stock be allocated between the partners if the partnership elects to use the traditional method with curative allocations? See Reg. § 1.704–3(c).

5. How would your answer in Problem 3 change if the partnership had elected to use the remedial allocation method? See Reg. § 1.704–3(d).

6. What if the partnership in Problem 1 were to exchange the land for "like-kind property" (valued at $1,400) in a transaction governed by Section 1031? What if that like-kind property is eventually sold for $1,400? See Reg. § 1.704–3(a)(8)(i).

7. Assume in Problem 1 that the partnership sells other land that it had purchased and recognizes a gain of $700. Should $600 of that gain be allocated to Marcia to eliminate the disparity between her tax basis and her capital account?

[¶ 18,145]

b. Special Problems in Allocating Depreciation

If depreciable property is contributed to the partnership, the disparity between tax basis and capital accounts can also be eliminated through allocations of depreciation on the property. Section 704(c) appears to require such allocations, but the allocation arithmetic becomes considerably more complex.

Assume that Able and Baker form an equal partnership. Able contributes a building having a basis of $6,000 and a value of $10,000; Baker contributes cash of $10,000. The building is depreciated under the straight-line method over 10 years. The capital accounts will reflect equal contributions of $10,000. Since Baker has, however, effectively purchased half of the building for $5,000, he should be entitled to depreciation deductions of $500 annually. If the building is in fact worthless at the end of the decade, Baker will have lost half of his initial $10,000 investment.

For capital account calculations, depreciation in the first year will be 10 percent of $10,000, or $1,000, and $500 would be allocated to Baker. For tax purposes, however, the depreciation deduction for the partnership will be 10 percent of the basis of $6,000, or only $600. Under the traditional method, the depreciation deduction is first allocated to Baker (who was the noncontributing partner) in an amount equal to the depreciation allocated to him for capital account purposes. However, although not an issue in this Able–Baker partnership, under the ceiling rule, the amount allocated to Baker cannot exceed the actual deprecia-

¶ 18,140

tion deduction. The remainder of the deduction ($100) is allocated to Able.

If the property is used for 10 years, $5,000 of the book and tax depreciation will have been allocated to Baker, leaving him with a tax basis and capital account of $5,000. Able will have had depreciation deductions of $5,000 for capital account purposes and $1,000 for tax purposes. His basis and capital account will both be $5,000. Note that the net effect (not taking into account issues of timing) on Able is the same as if he had been taxed on the built-in gain of $4,000 and had been allowed tax deductions of $5,000.

As indicated above, under the traditional method, allocations of depreciation can be affected by the ceiling rule. In the case of depreciation, the ceiling rule will prevent the partnership from allocating the full book depreciation to the noncontributing partner for tax purposes, thus resulting in disparities between the tax basis and capital accounts. To correct this disparity, the partnership may elect to use either the traditional method with curative allocations or the remedial allocation method. Under the traditional method with curative allocations, the regulations permit the partnership to correct the disparity by making a curative allocation of tax depreciation from another item of depreciable partnership property or to allocate an additional amount of ordinary income from the sale of another partnership asset. Reg. § 1.704–3(c). Under the remedial allocation method, the partnership is permitted to correct the disparity by creating and making a tax allocation of additional depreciation from the property to the noncontributing partner in an amount equal to the full amount of the limitation caused by the ceiling rule and a simultaneous, offsetting allocation of ordinary income of the type produced by that property to the contributing partner. Reg. § 1.704–3(d)(1) and (3).

[¶ 18,150]

Problems

1.   Bill contributed depreciable property having a value of $1,000 and a basis of $600 to a partnership. Pete, an equal partner, contributed cash of $1,000. The property had a useful life of 10 years, and the partnership used a straight-line method of calculating depreciation deductions. The partnership used the traditional method of allocation. The partnership broke even every year, not counting the depreciation deductions. Determine the net effect of the partnership for each partner during those years.

After four years, at which time its adjusted basis was $240, the property was sold for $1,240. How should the gain be allocated? See Reg. § 1.704–3(b)(2), Ex. 1. How do the capital accounts compare to basis for tax purposes after your allocation?

2. Assume the same facts as in Problem 1, except that Bill's adjusted basis in the depreciable property contributed to the partnership is only $400. How would your answers in Problem 1 change?

3. How would your answers in Problem 2 change if the partnership had elected to use the traditional method with curative allocations? See Reg. § 1.704–3(c).

4. How would your answers in Problem 2 change if the partnership had elected to use the remedial allocation method? See Reg. § 1.704–3(d).

[¶ 18,155]

c. *Character of Gain or Loss*

As discussed earlier in this Chapter, under Section 702(b), the character of an item of income or loss resulting from the disposition of partnership property is generally determined at the partnership level. The combination of that rule with the broad grant of nonrecognition to contributions of property might invite a partner to try to alter the character of gain or loss by contributing property to the partnership prior to a sale. To discourage this potential abuse, Section 724 imposes a "taint" on the character of certain categories of property contributed to a partnership.

Income realized by a partnership on the collection or disposition of an unrealized receivable contributed by a partner will be ordinary income even if the partnership holds the receivable as an investment. § 724(a). Similarly, income or loss derived from the sale of property that was an inventory item in the hands of a contributing partner will also be ordinary income or loss to the partnership, even though the partnership is not a dealer in that type of property. § 724(b). However, the taint that attaches to contributions of inventory expires after five years. Id. Thereafter, the character of any income or loss from the sale of the inventory is determined by the activities of the partnership.

The possible conversion of a capital loss to an ordinary loss is also treated by Section 724(c). Any loss on the disposition of property that was a capital asset in the hands of a contributing partner must be treated as a capital loss to the partnership. However, this rule applies only to the extent of any built-in loss at the time of contribution and only during the five-year period following the contribution.

[¶ 18,160]

Problems

1. Developer contributed a block of residential lots that she had held for sale to customers in exchange for a 40–percent partnership interest. The partnership, however, was not a dealer in real estate. The lots had a basis to Developer of $70,000 but were worth $150,000 at the

time of the contribution. If the partnership sells the lots three years later for $170,000, to whom is the gain taxed? What is its character?

2. How would your answers in Problem 1 change if the lots are sold for $50,000?

3. How would your answers in Problem 1 change if the lots are sold for $170,000 seven years after the contribution?

4. Investor contributed a parcel of land in exchange for a 50–percent interest in the partnership. The partnership intended to develop and sell the land to customers. The land had been purchased by Investor for $100,000, but was worth only $70,000 at the time of the contribution. If the land is sold by the partnership for $50,000 three years after the contribution, to whom is the loss allocable? What is the character of the loss?

5. How would your answers in Problem 4 change if the land is sold for $90,000?

6. How would your answers in Problem 4 change if the land is sold for $50,000 seven years after the contribution?

9. ALLOCATION OF PARTNERSHIP LIABILITIES

[¶ 18,165]

a. *Introduction*

As discussed in Chapter 17, partnership level borrowing produces an increase in the basis of the partnership interests that corresponds to the increase in the basis of the partnership properties. That increase in the basis of the partnership interests will support the claiming of partnership losses by the partners and to that extent will allow the partners to avoid the limitations of Section 704(d), as will be discussed in Chapter 19. That increase in basis also will be used in determining the partner's gain or loss on disposition of the partnership interest and the partner's gain on the receipt of a cash distribution (or a distribution of marketable securities treated as a cash distribution), as will be discussed in Chapters 21 and 22.

Chapter 17 provided an introduction to the allocation of partnership liabilities under Section 752. As discussed in that Chapter, if the partnership liability is with recourse to the personal assets of one or more partners, the basis increase attributable to the liability is allocated among the partners in accordance with their relative obligations to contribute to the repayment of the loan following a constructive liquidation. See ¶ 17,040. However, reserved, until now, was a more detailed look at the regulations under Section 752, particularly the allocation of the basis increase attributable to a partnership's nonrecourse liabilities.

¶ 18,165

[¶ 18,170]

b. *Effect of Partnership Recourse Liabilities*

For purposes of the Section 752 regulations, a partnership liability is a recourse liability to the extent that any partner or a person related to a partner bears the economic risk of loss for that liability. Reg. § 1.752–1(a)(1). To the extent that no partner or a person related to a partner bears the economic risk of loss for a liability, it is a nonrecourse liability for Section 752 purposes. Reg. § 1.752–1(a)(2). Moreover, as discussed in Chapter 17, under Reg. § 1.752–2(a), a partner's share of a recourse liability is equal to the portion of the liability (if any) for which the partner or a person related to a partner bears the economic risk of loss. Thus, the economic risk of loss concept is a key to both determining whether a liability is a recourse or nonrecourse liability for purposes of these rules and to allocating a recourse liability among the partners. How does one determine whether and to what extent a partner bears the economic risk of loss for a partnership liability?

As a general matter, the regulations treat a partner as bearing the economic risk of loss for a partnership liability to the extent that, if the partnership "constructively liquidated," (i) the partner or a related person would be obligated to make a payment to any person (or a contribution to the partnership) because the liability becomes due and payable and (ii) the partner would not be entitled to reimbursement from another partner or person related to such partner. Reg. § 1.752–2(b)(1). To determine whether a partner has an obligation to make a payment on a partnership liability and thus, to that extent, bears the economic risk of loss for the liability, the regulations create the concept of a "constructive liquidation." See Reg. § 1.752–2(b)(1). This constructive liquidation process attempts to measure the maximum amount that a partner might have to contribute toward a partnership liability, and, thus, is an appropriate measure of the partner's share of the partnership liability and the corresponding basis increase attributable to the liability.

In that constructive liquidation, the following steps are deemed to occur simultaneously. First, all of the partnership's liabilities become payable in full. Second, except for certain property pledged by a partner to secure a partnership liability, all of the partnership's other assets, including money, are deemed to have a zero value. Third, the partnership disposes of all of its worthless property in a fully taxable transaction for no consideration (other than relief from nonrecourse liabilities to which any partnership asset is subject). Fourth, all items of partnership income, gain, loss, or deduction (including the gains and losses on the deemed dispositions) are allocated among the partners, and the partnership's books and capital accounts are adjusted to reflect these allocations. Finally, the partnership liquidates. Reg. § 1.752–2(b)(1).

The determination of whether a partner or related person has an obligation to make a payment is based on all the surrounding facts and circumstances and takes into account all statutory and contractual obligations (including guarantees, indemnification agreements, and reimbursement agreements) relating to the partnership liability. Reg. § 1.752–2(b)(3). The regulations treat a partner as bearing the economic risk of loss for a partnership liability to the extent of the fair market value of the partner's property that is pledged to secure a partnership liability or that is contributed to the partnership solely for the purpose of securing a partnership liability. Reg. § 1.752–2(h)(1) and (2).

Moreover, in determining the extent to which a partner has a payment obligation and the economic risk of loss, the regulations assume that all partners and all related persons who have obligations to make payments actually make the payments, irrespective of their actual net worth, unless the facts and circumstances indicate a plan to circumvent or avoid the obligation. Reg. § 1.752–2(b)(6). However, a partner's or related person's obligation to make a payment is reduced to the extent that the partner or related person is entitled to reimbursement from another partner or person related to another partner, whether by reason of state law, some provision of the partnership agreement, an indemnification agreement, or otherwise. Reg. § 1.752–2(b)(5).

As discussed in Chapter 17, for Section 752 purposes, an obligation is a liability "only if, when, and to the extent that incurring the obligation either (1) creates or increases the basis of any of the assets of the obligor (including cash); (2) gives rise to an immediate deduction by the obligor; or (3) gives rise to an expense that is not deductible by the obligor in computing taxable income and is not properly chargeable to the capital account. Reg. § 1.752–1(a)(4)(i). Thus, under this definition, accrued but unpaid expenses and accounts payable of a cash basis partnership are not "partnership liabilities." See also Rev. Rul. 88–77, 1988–2 C.B. 128. Further, a partnership liability is disregarded for Section 752 purposes if the liability is subject to contingencies that make it unlikely that it will ever be discharged. See, e.g., Reg. § 1.752–2(b)(4). Moreover, if the partnership's obligation to pay a liability would arise at a future time only after the occurrence of an event not determinable with reasonable certainty, the liability is ignored for Section 752 purposes until the event occurs. Id.[3]

In the case of tiered partnerships—i.e., one partnership (the upper-tier partnership) owns an interest in another partnership (the lower-tier partnership)—the Section 752 regulations logically enough treat the upper-tier partnership's share of the lower-tier partnership's liabilities

---

3. The regulations also contain detailed special rules regarding the partnership's assumption of certain liabilities from a partner, which are designed to prevent the acceleration or duplication of losses. See Reg. § 1.752–7. Any discussion of these regulations is beyond the scope of an introductory course in partnership taxation and, therefore, is beyond the scope of this book.

as a liability of the upper-tier partnership for purposes of applying Section 752 and its regulations to the partners of the upper-tier partnership. Reg. §§ 1.752–4(a) and 1.752–2(i). This rule, however, does not apply to any liability of the lower-tier partnership that is owed to the upper-tier partnership.

[¶ 18,175]

c. Effect of Partnership Nonrecourse Liabilities

Under Reg. § 1.752–3(a), the basis increase attributable to a nonrecourse liability of the partnership must be allocated among all of the partners under a three-tier system that is applied in sequential order. Under the first tier of that allocation system, the basis increase from a nonrecourse loan is first allocated to the partners to the extent of each partner's share of the partnership's minimum gain. Reg. § 1.752–3(a)(1). Recall in connection with the examination earlier in this Chapter of the regulations under Section 704(b), a so-called minimum gain is generated as the basis of property securing a nonrecourse debt is reduced below the face amount of that debt. The reduction in basis is produced by deductions attributable to the property subject to the debt, generally depreciation. A partner's share of the minimum gain will equal the partner's share of the nonrecourse deductions that produced the minimum gain. As a result, the higher the nonrecourse deductions allocated to a partner, the higher the allocation to that partner of the basis from the nonrecourse borrowing. Thus, the real allocation of the basis increase attributable to a nonrecourse borrowing is in proportion to the allocation of partnership losses.

Under the second tier of this allocation system, to the extent that the entire nonrecourse liability has not been allocated under the first tier above, a partner is allocated an amount of liability equal to the gain that would be allocated to the partner under Section 704(c) on contributed appreciated property if the partnership disposed of all partnership property subject to nonrecourse liabilities in satisfaction of those liabilities. Thus, basis allocated to a partner under this provision is limited to the extent of the gain represented by the excess of a nonrecourse debt over the basis of the property at the time of contribution. Reg. § 1.752–3(a)(2). The effect of Section 704(c) on the allocation of nonrecourse liabilities under Reg. § 1.752–3(a) is discussed and illustrated in Rev. Rul. 95–41, at ¶ 18,185.

For purposes of determining Section 704(c) minimum gain under this second tier, an amendment made to the regulations in 2000 provides that a partnership that holds multiple properties subject to a single nonrecourse liability may allocate the liability among the properties based on any reasonable method. The portion of the nonrecourse liability allocated to each property is then treated as a separate loan for purposes of this second tier. An allocation method is not reasonable if it allocates an amount of liability to a property in excess of the fair market value of the property. If any part of the liability is outstanding, a partnership generally may not change its allocation method. However, if one of the properties is no longer subject to the liability, the portion of the liability previously allocated to that property must be reallocated to the other properties that remain subject to the liability. Reg. § 1.752–3(b)(1).

Finally, under the third tier of this allocation system, any remaining unallocated basis attributable to a nonrecourse borrowing is to be allocated to the partners in proportion to their interests in partnership profits. In establishing this ratio, the partners are permitted to specify the controlling profit-sharing ratio so long as that ratio is "reasonably consistent" with other allocations (that have substantial economic effect) of "some other significant item of partnership income or gain." Reg. § 1.752–3(a)(3).

The regulations provide two alternative methods for allocating the liability under this third tier which the partnership may choose in lieu of an allocation based on the partners' share of profits. Under the first of those alternative methods, a partnership may allocate the excess nonrecourse liability among the partners in "the manner in which it is reasonably expected that the deductions attributable to [the] nonrecourse liabilities will be allocated." Under the second of those alternative methods, added to the regulations in 2000, a partnership may allocate the excess nonrecourse liability among the partners in accordance with their share of the excess Section 704(c) gain (i.e., the excess of the amount of Section 704(c) built-in gain over the amount of Section 704(c) minimum gain allocated in the second tier above) or excess reverse Section 704(c) gain (i.e., the excess of the amount of reverse Section 704(c) gain over the amount of Section 704(c) minimum gain allocated in the second tier above). Reg. § 1.752–3(a)(3). (The concept of "reverse Section 704(c) gain" is discussed at ¶ 18,120.)

If a loan is partly recourse and partly nonrecourse, the loan is treated as two different obligations and a portion of the basis adjustment is allocated under each set of rules. Reg. § 1.752–1(i). If a nonrecourse loan is obtained from a partner, or a person related to a partner, that partner is treated as bearing an economic risk of loss on the obligation. Thus, the entire basis increase attributable to such a loan is allocated to the lending partner. Reg. § 1.752–2(c)(1).

[¶ 18,180]

Note

How should the rules on allocation of partnership liabilities under Section 752 and its regulations apply to the liabilities of a limited liability company (LLC) that is classified as a partnership for federal tax purposes? In the usual situation, LLC debt, by definition, will not be recourse debt for Section 752 purposes because no member bears the economic risk of loss for the debt. Thus, the debt of an LLC generally will be treated as nonrecourse debt for purposes of these liability allocation rules. See Reg. § 1.751–1(a)(1) and (a)(2).

[¶ 18,185]

REVENUE RULING 95–41
1995–1 C.B. 132.

ISSUES

How does § 704(c) * * * affect the allocation of nonrecourse liabilities under § 1.752–3(a) of the * * * Regulations?

FACTS

A and B form a partnership, PRS, and agree that each will be allocated a 50 percent share of all partnership items. A contributes depreciable property subject to a nonrecourse liability of $6,000, with an adjusted tax basis of $4,000 and a fair market value of $10,000. B contributes $4,000 cash.

LAW

Section 1.752–3(a) provides that a partner's share of the nonrecourse liabilities of a partnership equals the sum of the amounts specified in § 1.752–3(a)(1)–(3).

Section 1.752–3(a)(1) provides that the partner's share of the nonrecourse liabilities of a partnership includes the partner's share of partnership minimum gain determined in accordance with the rules of § 704(b) and the regulations thereunder. See § 1.704–2.

Section 1.752–3(a)(2) provides that the partner's share of the nonrecourse liabilities of the partnership includes the amount of any taxable gain that would be allocated to the partner under § 704(c) (or in the same manner as § 704(c) in connection with a revaluation of partnership property) if the partnership disposed of (in a taxable transaction) all partnership property subject to one or more nonrecourse liabilities of the partnership in full satisfaction of the liabilities and for no other consideration.

Section 1.752–3(a)(3) provides that the partner's share of the nonrecourse liabilities of the partnership includes the partner's share of the excess nonrecourse liabilities (those not allocated under § 1.752–3(a)(1) and (a)(2)) of the partnership as determined in accordance with the partner's share of partnership profits. The partner's interest in partnership profits is determined by taking into account all facts and circumstances relating to the economic arrangement of the partners. The partnership agreement may specify the partners' interests in partnership profits for purposes of allocating excess nonrecourse liabilities, provided the interests so specified are reasonably consistent with allocations (that have substantial economic effect under the § 704(b) regulations) of some other significant item of partnership income or gain. Alternatively, excess nonrecourse liabilities may be allocated among the partners in accordance with the manner in which it is reasonably expected that the deductions attributable to those nonrecourse liabilities will be allocated. [Finally, under another method added to the regulations in 2000, a partnership may allocate an excess nonrecourse liability based on excess Section 704(c) gain or excess reverse Section 704(c) gain.]

Section 704(c)(1)(A) provides that income, gain, loss, and deduction with respect to property contributed to the partnership by a partner shall be shared among the partners so as to take account of the variation between the adjusted tax basis of the property to the partnership and its fair market value at the time of contribution.

Section 1.704–3(a)(3)(i) provides that the book value of contributed property is equal to its fair market value at the time of contribution and is subsequently adjusted for cost recovery and other events that affect the basis of the property.

Section 1.704–3(a)(3)(ii) provides that the built-in gain on § 704(c) property is the excess of the property's book value over the contributing partner's adjusted tax basis in the property upon contribution. The built-in gain is thereafter reduced by decreases in the difference between the property's book value and adjusted tax basis.

Analysis

Upon A's contribution of the depreciable property to PRS, there is $6,000 of § 704(c) built-in gain (the excess of the book value of the property ($10,000) over A's adjusted tax basis in the property at the time of contribution ($4,000)). As a result of the contribution, A's individual liabilities decreased by $6,000 (the amount of the nonrecourse liability which PRS is treated as having assumed). A's share of the partnership's nonrecourse liabilities is determined under § 1.752–3.

(1) First Tier Allocations:

Under § 1.752–3(a)(1), a partner's share of the nonrecourse liabilities of PRS includes the partner's share of partnership minimum gain determined in accordance with the rules of § 704(b) and the regulations thereunder. Section 1.704–2(d)(1) provides that partnership minimum gain is determined by computing, for each partnership nonrecourse liability, any gain the partnership would realize if it disposed of the property subject to that liability for no consideration other than full satisfaction of the liability, and then aggregating the separately computed gains. Pursuant to § 1.704–2(d)(3), partnership minimum gain is determined with reference to the contributed property's book value rather than its adjusted tax basis.

In contrast, § 704(c) requires that allocations take into account the difference between the contributed property's adjusted tax basis and its fair market value. Thus, because partnership minimum gain is computed using the contributed property's book value rather than its tax basis, allocations of nonrecourse liabilities under § 1.752–3(a)(1) are not affected by § 704(c). Moreover, because the book value of the property at the time of contribution ($10,000) exceeds the amount of the nonrecourse liability ($6,000), there is no partnership minimum gain immediately after the contribution, and neither A nor B receive an allocation of nonrecourse liabilities under § 1.752–3(a)(1) immediately after the contribution.

(2) Second Tier Allocations:

Under § 1.752–3(a)(2), a partner's share of the nonrecourse liabilities of the partnership includes the amount of taxable gain that would be allocated to the contributing partner under § 704(c) if the partnership, in a taxable transaction, disposed of the contributed property in full satisfaction of the nonrecourse liability and for no other consideration. If *PRS* sold the contributed property in full satisfaction of the liability and for no other consideration, *PRS* would recognize a taxable gain of $2,000 on the sale ($6,000 amount of the nonrecourse liability less $4,000 adjusted tax basis of the property). Under § 704(c) and § 1.704–3(b)(1), all of this taxable gain would be allocated to A. The hypothetical sale also would result in a book loss of $4,000 to *PRS* (excess of $10,000 book value of property over $6,000 amount of the nonrecourse liability). Under the terms of the partnership agreement, this book loss would be allocated equally between A and B. Because B would receive a $2,000 book loss but no corresponding tax loss, the hypothetical sale would result in a $2,000 disparity between B's book and tax allocations.

If *PRS* used the traditional method of making § 704(c) allocations described in § 1.704–3(d), A would be allocated a total of $2,000 of taxable gain from the hypothetical sale of the contributed property. Therefore, A would be allocated $2,000 of nonrecourse liabilities under § 1.752–3(a)(2) immediately after the contribution.

If *PRS* adopted the remedial allocation method described in § 1.704–3(d), *PRS* would be required to make a remedial allocation of $2,000 of tax loss to B in connection with the hypothetical sale to eliminate the $2,000 disparity between B's book and tax allocations. *PRS* also would be required to make an offsetting remedial allocation of tax gain to A of $2,000. Thus, A would be allocated a total of $4,000 of tax gain ($2,000 actual gain plus the $2,000 allocation of remedial gain) from the hypothetical sale of the contributed property. Therefore, if the partnership adopted the remedial allocation method, A would be allocated $4,000 of nonrecourse liabilities under § 1.752–3(a)(2) immediately after the contribution.

¶ 18,185

If *PRS* used the traditional method with curative allocations described in § 1.704–3(c), *PRS* would be permitted to make reasonable curative allocations to reduce or eliminate the difference between the book and tax allocations to *B* that resulted from the hypothetical sale. However, *PRS*'s ability to make curative allocations would depend on the existence of other partnership items and could not be determined solely from the hypothetical sale of the contributed property. Because any potential curative allocations could not be determined solely from the hypothetical sale of the contributed property, curative allocations are not taken into account in allocating nonrecourse liabilities under § 1.752–3(a)(2). Therefore, if *PRS* used the traditional method with curative allocations, *A* would be allocated $2,000 of nonrecourse liabilities under § 1.752–3(a)(2) immediately after the contribution.

(3) Third Tier Allocations:

Following the allocation under § 1.752–3(a)(2), *PRS* has excess nonrecourse liabilities that must be allocated between *A* and *B*. Section 1.752–3(a)(3) provides several alternatives for allocating excess nonrecourse liabilities.

(a) First, *PRS* may choose to allocate excess nonrecourse liabilities in accordance with the partners' shares of partnership profits. The partners' interests in partnership profits are determined by taking into account all the facts and circumstances relating to the economic arrangement of the partners. The partners' agreement to share the profits of the partnership equally is one fact to be considered in making this determination. Another fact to be considered is a partner's share of § 704(c) built-in gain to the extent that the gain was not taken into account in making an allocation of nonrecourse liabilities under § 1.752–3(a)(2). This built-in gain is one factor because, under the principles of § 704(c), this excess built-in gain, if recognized, will be allocated to *A*. *A*'s share of § 704(c) built-in gain that is not taken into account in making allocations under § 1.752–3(a)(2) is, therefore, one factor, but not the only factor, to be considered in determining *A*'s interest in partnership profits.

The amount of the § 704(c) built-in gain that is not considered in making allocations under § 1.752–3(a)(2) must be given an appropriate weight in light of all other items of partnership profit. For example, if it is reasonable to expect that *PRS* will have items of partnership profit over the life of the partnership that will be allocated to *B*, *PRS* may not allocate all of the excess nonrecourse liabilities to *A*. Rather, the remaining nonrecourse liabilities must be allocated between *A* and *B* in proportion to their interests in total partnership profits.

(b) Second, the *PRS* partnership agreement may specify the partners' interest in partnership profits for purposes of allocating excess nonrecourse liabilities, provided that the interests specified are reasonably consistent with allocations (that have substantial economic effect under the § 704(b) regulations) of some other significant item of partnership income or gain. The partnership agreement provides that each partner will be allocated a 50 percent share of all partnership items. Assuming that such allocations have substantial economic effect, *PRS* can choose to allocate the excess nonrecourse liabilities 50 percent to each partner. Section 704(c) allocations, however, do not have substantial economic effect under the § 704(b) regulations. See § 1.704–1(b)(2)(iv)(d). Accordingly, under this alternative, § 704(c) allocations cannot be used as a basis for allocating excess nonrecourse liabilities.

(c) [Third], *PRS* may choose to allocate the excess nonrecourse liabilities in accordance with the manner in which it is reasonably expected that the deductions attributable to the excess nonrecourse liabilities will be allocated. Because *A* and *B* have agreed to allocate all partnership items 50 percent to each partner, *A* and *B* each will be entitled to allocations of book depreciation of $5,000 over the life of the contributed property. The contributed property, however, has an adjusted tax basis of $4,000 and, regardless of the method used by the partnership under § 704(c), the entire $4,000 of tax depreciation over the life of the contributed property must be allocated to *B*. Therefore, *PRS* must allocate all of the excess nonrecourse liabilities to *B* if it chooses to allocate the excess nonrecourse liabilities in accordance with the manner that the deductions attributable to the excess nonrecourse liabilities will be allocated.

[Finally, an amendment to Reg. § 1.752–3(a)(3) in 2000 added an additional method that a partnership may choose to allocate an excess nonrecourse liability, one based on the excess Section 704(c) gain or excess reverse Section 704(c) gain. See the bracketed discussion below under "Holdings" concerning how those revised regulations affect the holdings in Rev. Rul. 95–41.]

HOLDINGS

(1) Allocations of nonrecourse liabilities under § 1.752–3(a)(1) are not affected by § 704(c).

(2) Allocations of nonrecourse liabilities under § 1.752–3(a)(2) take into account remedial allocations of gain that would be made to the contributing partner under § 1.704–3(d). Allocations of nonrecourse liabilities under § 1.752–3(a)(2) do not take into account curative allocations under § 1.704–3(c).

(3) Allocations of nonrecourse liabilities under § 1.752–3(a)(3) are affected by § 704(c) in the following manner:

(a) If the partnership determines the partners' interests in partnership profits based on all of the facts and circumstances relating to the economic arrangement of the partners, § 704(c) built-in gain that was not taken into account under § 1.752–3(a)(2) is one factor, but not the only factor, to be considered under § 1.752–3(a)(3).

(b) If the partnership chooses to allocate excess nonrecourse liabilities in a manner reasonably consistent with allocations (that have substantial economic effect under the § 704(b) regulations) of some other significant item of partnership income or gain, § 704(c) does not affect the allocation of nonrecourse liabilities under § 1.752–3(a)(3) because § 704(c) allocations do not have substantial economic effect.

(c) If the partnership chooses to allocate excess nonrecourse liabilities in accordance with the manner in which it is reasonably expected that the deductions attributable to the nonrecourse liabilities will be allocated, the partnership must take into account the allocations required by § 704(c) in determining the manner in which the deductions attributable to the nonrecourse liabilities will be allocated.

[Note that, as discussed above at ¶ 18,175, an amendment to Reg. § 1.752–3(a)(3) in 2000 changed the third tier to allow a partnership to allocate an excess nonrecourse liability under an additional method, one based on the excess Section 704(c) gain or excess reverse Section 704(c) gain. The preamble to the revised regulations makes clear that the holding in Rev. Rul. 95–41 that excess Section 704(c) gain is one factor, but not the only factor, to be used in determining the partners' interests in partnership profits for purposes of the third tier remains relevant if the partnership allocates the excess nonrecourse liability in the third tier based on the partners' interests in partnership profits rather than based on excess Section 704(c) gain. However, once a partnership has chosen to allocate the excess nonrecourse debt based on the excess Section 704(c) gain, that excess Section 704(c) gain cannot be double counted by again being taken into account in determining a partner's interest in partnership profits. See T.D. 8906, 2000–2 C.B. 470, 472.]

[¶ 18,190]

Problems

1.   Arlene and Judy each contribute $500 in cash to the capital of a new general partnership. The partnership purchases property from an unrelated seller for $1,000 in cash and a $9,000 recourse mortgage note. The partners have agreed to allocate profits and losses 40 percent to Arlene and 60 percent to Judy. Arlene and Judy are required to make up any deficit in their capital accounts.

What is each partner's share of the $9,000 partnership liability? See Reg. § 1.752–2(f), Ex. 2.

2.   Ethel and Fred form a limited partnership. Ethel, the general partner, contributes $2,000 and Fred, the limited partner, contributes $8,000 in cash to the partnership. The partners agree to allocate losses 20 percent to Ethel and 80 percent to Fred until Fred's capital account is reduced to zero; thereafter, all losses are allocated to Ethel. The partnership purchases depreciable property for $25,000 using its $10,000 cash

and a $15,000 recourse loan from a bank. Fred, the limited partner, guarantees payment of the $15,000 loan to the bank.

What is each partner's share of the $15,000 partnership liability? See Reg. § 1.752–2(f), Exs. 3 and 4.

3. How would your answer in Problem 2 change if the loan from the bank were nonrecourse in nature and secured only by a mortgage on the depreciable property? See Reg. § 1.752–2(f), Ex. 5.

4. General contributes $20 and Limited contributes $80 upon the formation of a limited partnership. The partners have agreed to allocate 20 percent of the partnership losses to General and 80 percent to Limited. However, 90 percent of the profits are allocated to General and 10 percent to Limited. The partnership borrows $100 on a recourse basis. The partnership uses the $100 of capital contributions and $100 of recourse loan proceeds to purchase depreciable property, worth $1,000, subject to a nonrecourse debt of $800 (i.e., the total consideration paid for the property is $1,000—cash contributions of $100, recourse loan proceeds of $100, and nonrecourse purchase money debt of $800). Assume that the partnership sustains a net loss from depreciation in each year of $100. Assume further that (i) capital accounts are properly maintained, (ii) positive balances in the capital accounts control liquidating distributions, (iii) no partner is obligated to restore a capital account deficit, and (iv) the agreement contains both a qualified income offset and a minimum gain chargeback.

Under the Section 752 and Section 704 regulations:

a. What is the initial basis of the partnership interest of General and Limited?

b. How must the partnership loss be allocated between the partners during the first four years of partnership operation?

c. What would the basis of the partnership interest be at the end of each of the first four years of partnership operation?

5. Badhardt & Sons is a limited partnership. Harry and Larry are the general partners. Bob is a limited partner who has already paid the maximum amount that he is obligated to contribute to the partnership. The three partners have agreed to allocate partnership profits and losses in the following way: 20 percent of profits and losses are allocated to each Harry and Larry; the 60 percent remainder is allocated to Bob. Analyze the effect on the basis of each partner's interest of a $12,000 borrowing by the partnership if:

a. The borrowing is a recourse loan.

b. The borrowing is a nonrecourse loan.

c. The borrowing is a nonrecourse loan, but three years later the partners agree to share profits equally.

d. The borrowing is a recourse loan, but the lender is Larry.

¶ 18,190

e. The borrowing is a nonrecourse loan, but the lender is Larry. See Reg. § 1.752–2(c)(1).

[¶ 18,195]

10. RETROACTIVE ALLOCATIONS

Under prior law, two rules of partnership taxation combined to create a significant tax avoidance opportunity. Under Section 706(a), partnership income and loss pass through to the partners on the last day of the partnership's taxable year. Under Section 761(c), the ratio in which those items are allocated among the partners can be amended at any time up to the date prescribed for filing the partnership tax return for the year. Those rules seemed to permit the retroactive allocation of losses sustained throughout the year to a partner admitted before the end of the partnership year. For example, assume that during year 1 the AB partnership has made quarterly payments of interest on a loan on the first day of March, June, September and December, and on December 31 postpaid rent for the entire year 1 on a building it occupies. On December 30 of year 1, however, C was admitted as a partner. To what extent may the partnership allocate to C deductions for interest and rent incurred and paid during year 1?

a. The Varying Interest Rule

[¶ 18,200]

REVENUE RULING 77–119

1977–1 C.B. 177.

Advice has been requested whether, under the circumstances described below, the modification of a partnership agreement will be recognized for Federal income tax purposes.

On December 31, 1975, D purchased an interest in ABC, a partnership, from the existing partners. The partnership agreement was modified on January 2, 1976, to provide that D would receive a 40 percent interest in the capital, a 45 percent interest in the profits, and 100 percent of the losses of the partnership for the partnership taxable year ending December 31, 1975. On its 1975 partnership return, the partnership reported an ordinary loss from its operations, all of which was allocated to D pursuant to the partnership agreement.

Section 704 * * * provides the general rule that a partner's distributive share of income, gain, loss, deduction, or credit shall be determined by the partnership agreement.

Prior to the Tax Reform Act of 1976, * * * section 704(b)(2) * * * provided, in part, that a partner's share of any item of income, gain, loss, deduction, or credit shall be determined in accordance with the partner's distributive share of the taxable income or loss of the partnership (exclusive of items requiring separate computation under section 702(a)) for the taxable year, if the principal purpose of any provision in the partnership agreement with respect to the partner's distributive share of such item is the avoidance or evasion of Federal income taxes.

Section 1.704–1(b)(2) of the * * * Regulations [formerly provided], in part, that if the principal purpose of any provision in the partnership agreement determining a partner's distributive share of a particular item is to avoid or evade the Federal income tax, the provisions shall be disregarded and the partners' distributive shares of that item shall be determined in accordance with the ratio in which the partners divide the general profits or losses of the partnership.

Section 761(c) * * * provides, in part, that a partnership agreement includes any modifications of the partnership agreement made prior to, or at, the time prescribed by law for the filing of the partnership return for the taxable year (not including extensions) that are agreed to by all the partners, or which are adopted in such other manner as may be provided by the partnership agreement.

In *Rodman v. Commissioner*, 542 F.2d 845 (2d Cir.1976), the court held that a taxpayer who purchased an interest in a partnership (joint venture) could not be allocated a distributive share of the profits and losses realized by the partnership before the taxpayer became a member. The court, citing *Helvering v. Horst*, 311 U.S. 112 * * * , stated that such a retroactive reallocation necessarily violates that well established prohibition against one taxpayer assigning taxable income to another. The court also stated that not only does the retroactive reallocation of income to a new partner violate the *Helvering v. Horst* general assignment of income prohibition, but that it necessarily follows from that conclusion that such an attempted assignment in the partnership agreement also falls within the caveat of section 704(b)(2) * * * that a term in a partnership agreement cannot be controlling for tax purposes where its principal purpose is the evasion of taxes.

Accordingly, in the instant case, the retroactive modification of the partnership agreement will not be recognized for Federal income tax purposes and *D*'s distributive share of the partnership's items of income, gain, loss, deduction, or credit may not include any part of such items realized or sustained prior to December 31, 1975.

[¶ 18,205]

b. Section 706(d)

Rev. Rul. 77–119 illustrates the abuses that widely occurred under prior law and the optimistic response of the IRS. Subsequently, Congress adopted a far more precise approach in Section 706(d). Section 706(d)(1) sets forth the general rule that when the interests of the partners change during the year the allocation of all partnership items for the year must take account of those varying interests. The effect of that general rule on the AB partnership would depend on how the expenses for the year were allocated between the periods that preceded and followed December 30. If the expense were allocated as if those periods were two separate tax years, none of the interest deduction could be allocated to C. If the expense were prorated over the days to which it related, no more than $\frac{2}{365}$ of the interest deduction could be allocated to C. While the partnership apparently may select either allocation method, in either event the ability to shift interest deductions to C is severely limited.

If the partnership selects the two separate tax years approach, however, the intent of Section 706(d)(1) would be undermined with respect to the rental payment. To prevent partnerships that use the cash basis method of tax accounting from manipulating the timing of making deductible payments, Section 706(d)(2) adds a further, and complex, rule. That provision requires cash basis partnerships to prorate specified "cash basis items" to each day in the taxable year to which the item is attributable if there is a change in any partner's interest during the year. Items attributable to a prior taxable year are assigned to the first day of the taxable year, and items attributable to a subsequent taxable year are assigned to the last day of the taxable year. Allocation among the partners is then made in proportion to their interests in the partnership on a daily basis. For the purposes of Section 706(d)(2), cash basis items include interest, taxes, rent, and compensation for services, although that list may be expanded by regulations to cover other items to which application of Section 706(d)(2) "is appropriate to avoid significant misstatements of the income of the partners." § 706(d)(2)(B). Thus, under this rule, no more than $\frac{2}{365}$ of either the interest or the rental payment incurred by the AB partnership may be allocated to C. The exact amount allocable to C will depend on the extent of C's interest in partnership losses during the last two days of year 1.

c. *Shifting Interests Not Accompanied by Contributions*

[¶ 18,210]

LIPKE v. COMMISSIONER

United States Tax Court, 1983.
81 T.C. 689, aff'd without published opinion, 751 F.2d 369 (2d Cir.1984).

FAY, JUDGE: * * *.

* * *

The facts have been fully stipulated and are so found.

Petitioners Clarence Rautenstrauch and Jennie Rautenstrauch resided in Florida when they filed their petition herein. All other petitioners resided in New York when they filed their petitions herein.

¶ 18,210

In 1972 petitioner Lawrence Reger (Reger), petitioner Clarence Rautenstrauch (Rautenstrauch), and Herbert M. Luksch (Luksch), formed March Equity Partners I, a limited partnership. The partnership was organized for the purpose of acquiring and operating apartment buildings in the suburbs of Buffalo, New York. Reger, Rautenstrauch, and Luksch were the general partners, and Luksch was also the initial limited partner. The general partners made a capital contribution in the total amount of $100. Shortly after formation of the partnership, limited partnership interests were sold to 14 investors for a total amount of $1,175,000, and Luksch's interest as a limited partner was liquidated. With one exception, the partnership agreement allocated all profits and losses to the limited partners.[5] At all relevant times, the partnership computed its taxable income on a calendar year basis using the accrual method of accounting.

In 1972 and 1973, the partnership acquired several apartment buildings. At all relevant times, these apartment buildings were subject to mortgages. In 1974 and 1975, the partnership experienced severe financial problems and defaulted on the mortgages. After the mortgagee foreclosed on one of the apartment buildings, the partnership obtained additional capital of $300,000 in order to avoid losing its remaining apartment buildings. Of the $300,000, $84,000 was contributed by 6 of the 14 original limited partners who together held interests in the partnership totaling 28 percent. The remaining $216,000 was contributed by petitioners James H. Williams (James), Francis M. Williams (Francis), Kenneth E. Lipke (Lipke), (herein sometimes collectively referred to as the new partners), and Reger (one of the general partners), in return for new limited partnership interests. All of these capital contributions were made on October 1, 1975. Also effective October 1, 1975, one of the original limited partners (herein the withdrawing partner) sold his entire limited partnership interest to several of the other original limited partners.

In connection with these additional capital contributions, effective October 1, 1975, the general and limited partners executed an amendment to the partnership agreement (herein the amendment). The amendment created two classes of limited partners. All of the original limited partners, except for the withdrawing partner, were designated as class A limited partners. Together with Reger and the new partners, the six original partners who made new capital contributions also became class B partners. Reger, Rautenstrauch, and Luksch continued as the general partners.

---

5. The partnership agreement allocated a residual interest in gains arising from "major capital events" to the general partners. In essence, a "major capital event" was defined as any transaction not in the ordinary course of business, such as the sale of real or personal property, condemnations, recovery of damages, etc.

¶ 18,210

The amendment also provided that the partnership was to be owned 49 percent by the class A limited partners, 49 percent by the class B limited partners, and 2 percent by the general partners. * * *

* * *

With the exception of the losses allocated to the withdrawing partner, the amendment reallocated 98 percent of all the partnership's 1975 losses to the class B limited partners. This reallocation was made expressly in consideration of the new capital contributions made to the partnership. The amendment also reallocated 2 percent of all the partnership's 1975 losses to the general partners.

On its 1975 return, the partnership reported losses of $933,825. * * * On their 1975 returns, petitioners (Lipke, J. Williams, F. Williams, Rautenstrauch, and Reger) reported their distributive shares of these losses. In his notices of deficiency, respondent disallowed that portion of the reported losses attributable to losses accrued by the partnership prior to October 1, 1975.[11]

The primary issue is whether the partnership properly allocated its 1975 losses among its partners. Respondent contends that section 706(c)(2)(B) prevents the partnership from reallocating losses accrued before October 1, 1975, to either the class B limited partners or to the general partners. Petitioners counter that prior to the Tax Reform Act of 1976, section 706(c)(2)(B) did not prevent the retroactive reallocation of losses to new partners. Petitioners further argue that even assuming former section 706(c)(2)(B) governs situations involving the admission of new partners, it does not prevent the retroactive reallocation of losses to those petitioners who were already partners when the reallocation was made. For the following reasons, we hold that the partnership's retroactive reallocation of losses to the class B limited partners was not permitted by section 706(c)(2)(B) because it was made as a result of additional capital contributions. It makes no difference that the additional capital was contributed by, and the resulting retroactive reallocation was made to, both new and existing partners. However, we also hold that the partnership's retroactive reallocation of losses to the general partners was permissible since it did not result from additional capital contributions and therefore constituted nothing more than a readjustment of partnership items among existing partners.

Section 702(a) requires a partner to report his distributive share of the partnership's income or loss. With certain exceptions, section 704(a) provides that a partner's distributive share is to be determined by the partnership agreement.[12] A partnership agreement includes any amend-

11. Respondent does not challenge the partnership's allocation of losses accrued from October 1, 1975, through December 31, 1975.

12. Respondent does not contend herein that the principal purpose of the partnership's allocation of its 1975 losses was the "avoidance or evasion of any tax" within

ments made before the time for filing the partnership return. Sec. 761(c). However, section 706(c)(2) provides for certain tax consequences to a partner whose partnership interest changes during the partnership's taxable year. Prior to the Tax Reform Act of 1976, that section provided in part as follows:

> The taxable year of a partnership shall not close (other than at the end of a partnership's taxable year as determined under subsection (b)(1)) with respect to a partner who sells or exchanges less than his entire interest in the partnership or with respect to a partner whose interest is reduced, *but such partner's distributive share of items described in section 702(a) shall be determined by taking into account his varying interests in the partnership during the taxable year*. [Emphasis added.]

In *Richardson v. Commissioner*, 76 T.C. 512 (1981), affd. 693 F.2d 1189 (5th Cir.1982), this Court ruled that even prior to the Tax Reform Act of 1976, section 706(c)(2)(B) was applicable to situations involving the admission of new partners.[13] Therein, we held that the reduction in the capital interests of the original partners resulting from the admission of the new partners constituted a reduction of interests within the meaning of section 706(c)(2)(B). The fact that the original partners' equity interests in the partnership remained the same was deemed to be irrelevant. Accordingly, under section 706(c)(2)(B) the original partners and the new partners were required to determine their distributive shares of partnership items by taking into account their varying interests in the partnership during the taxable year. Thus, a retroactive reallocation of partnership items to the new partners was not allowable. * * *

Although petitioners admit *Richardson* is directly on point with respect to the allocation of losses to the new partners in the instant case, they contend that the case was wrongly decided and now ask us to overrule it. However, buttressed by the affirmance of our decision by the Fifth Circuit Court of Appeals, we are fully satisfied with our decision in *Richardson* and are therefore unwilling to overrule it. * * * Accordingly, since petitioners James, Francis, and Lipke were newly admitted as partners on October 1, 1975, they are not entitled to report losses accrued by the partnership prior to that date.

We also hold that section 706(c)(2)(B) prevents the retroactive reallocation of losses to petitioner Reger as a limited partner even though he was already a partner when he made his additional capital contribution. Together with the new capital contributions made by the

---

the meaning of sec. 704(b)(2) as in effect during that year. * * *

13. After the phrase "with respect to a partner whose interest is reduced," the Tax Reform Act of 1976 inserted into sec. 706(c)(2)(B) the parenthetical "whether by entry of a new partner, partial liquidation of a partner's interest, gift, or otherwise." This Court determined in *Richardson v. Commissioner*, 76 T.C. 512 (1981), affd. 693 F.2d 1189 (5th Cir.1982), that this amendment merely codified prior law.

new partners and by six of the original limited partners, Reger's additional capital contribution reduced the capital interests of the noncontributing partners. For purposes of section 706(c)(2)(B), we find no difference between a reduction in partners' interests resulting from the admission of new partners, as in *Richardson*, and, as here, the reduction in partners' interests resulting from additional capital contributions made by existing partners. In both situations partners' interests were reduced and retroactive reallocations were made as a result of the additional capital contributions. We are unwilling to sustain, for example, the retroactive reallocations of losses made to petitioner Reger merely because he had previously contributed $34 to the partnership, and yet deny petitioners Lipke, James, and Francis that same benefit because they were new partners. That would create an illusory distinction which the language of section 706(c)(2)(B) simply does not require us to make.

With respect to the partnership's retroactive reallocation of losses to the general partners, however, we find that it did not result from additional capital contributions and therefore did not contravene the varying interest rules of section 706(c)(2)(B). Prior to October 1, 1975, the general partners held only a residual interest in gains arising from "major capital events." See note 5, *supra*. Pursuant to the October 1, 1975, amendment to the partnership agreement, however, the general partners were granted a 2–percent interest in the partnership's 1975 profits and losses including the losses accrued by the partnership during the preceding nine months. In contrast to the retroactive reallocation of losses to the class B limited partners, this reallocation to the general partners was not made in consideration for additional capital contributions. General partners Rautenstrauch and Luksch made no additional capital contributions and Reger's contribution was made in exchange for a limited partnership interest, not for an increase in his interest as a general partner. Accordingly, this reallocation of losses to the general partners was not directly accompanied by a reduction in any other partner's capital interest within the meaning of section 706(c)(2)(B). It constituted nothing more than a readjustment of partnership items among existing partners which, by itself, is permissible. * * *

Finally, we must determine how much of the partnership's 1975 losses can be allocated to the period after September 30, 1975. In his notice of deficiency, respondent allocated losses of $125,770 to that period. This determination was based on the partnership's interim closing of its books as of September 30, 1975, whereby it determined how much of its losses were allocable to the withdrawing partner.[14] Signifi-

---

14. The partnership allocated $78,021 of its 1975 losses to the withdrawing partner. Since the withdrawing partner owned a 10–percent interest in the partnership prior to his withdrawal on October 1, 1975, re-

spondent determined that the partnership must have accrued as of that date $780,210 of the $933,825 of losses the partnership reported on its 1975 return * * *, thus evidencing that the partnership accrued

cantly, petitioners do not dispute that respondent's determination in this respect accurately reflects the amount of losses incurred by the partnership during the relevant period. Rather, they simply argue that the partnership should be allowed to use the "year-end totals" method of accounting and thereby allocate losses of $212,431 to the period October 1, 1975, through December 31, 1975.[15]

We summarily reject petitioners argument. The amount of losses accrued by the partnership after September 30, 1975, is clearly shown by the partnership's interim closing of its books and allocation of losses to the withdrawing partner. See note 14, *supra*. There is simply no justification for now allowing the partnership to use the relatively less accurate "year-end totals" method of accounting for purposes of allocating losses to petitioners. Accordingly, we sustain respondent's determination in this respect. * * *

* * *

[¶ 18,215]

Problems

1. Hightower & Jones is a law partnership. During year 1, the five partners shared equally in profits and losses. Following their normal practice and in accordance with the terms of the partnership agreement, during January of year 3, the partners met to establish the profit-sharing ratio for the preceding year (year 2). They agreed that 40 percent of the profits for that year should be allocated to Rainmaker and the remaining 60 percent divided equally among the other four partners. Will the allocation be respected for federal income tax purposes?

2. At the beginning of year 1, the profits and losses of the ABC partnership were allocated 40 percent to Able and 30 percent each to Baker and Charlie. On July 1, the partnership admitted Don as a partner in exchange for a capital contribution of $20,000. At the same time, Charlie contributed an additional $5,000 to the partnership. None of the other partners made a contribution or received a distribution. At that time the partners agreed that the profits and losses of the entire year 1 should be allocated as follows: 10 percent to Able, 40 percent to Baker, 40 percent to Charlie, and 10 percent to Don. To what extent will that allocation be respected for federal income tax purposes? How must the profits for the year be allocated under their revised agreement?

---

losses of $153,804 in the last quarter of 1975. When this $153,804 is reduced by agreed depreciation adjustments of $28,034, the result is an accrued loss of $125,770 for that period.

15. The "year-end totals" method of accounting involves computing partnership income or loss at the end of the year and allocating that total ratably over the year. Thus, petitioners seek to allocate $212,431 of the partnership's total 1975 losses of $849,724 * * * to the last quarter of 1975.

3.   Ellen, Frances, and Gwen are equal partners in a cash method partnership. On October 1, Holly was admitted as an equal partner. On December 31, Ellen retired from the partnership. During September, the partnership received bills for six months' rental (beginning July 1) of $12,000 and for a $10,000 settlement that the partnership had agreed to pay on a tort claim against the firm. Both bills were paid in October. Of the deductions attributable to these items, what amount should be allocated to each of the partners? What allocations would be appropriate if the bills had not been paid until the following January?

4.   Realty Co. is a partnership that owns an apartment building. During the year the partnership sustained a loss of $24,000 from operations ratably over the year (i.e., $2,000 per month). In need of additional cash, the partnership on December 1 admitted Zeus in return for his contribution of $100,000. For the following year, Zeus will be entitled to 25 percent of profits and losses. What is the maximum amount of loss that can be allocated to Zeus for the year of his admission?

[¶ 18,220]

C.   FAMILY PARTNERSHIPS

Because partnership income is taxed directly to the partners, a considerable reduction in tax liabilities may be achieved if partnership interests are transferred from high-bracket taxpayers to family members in the lower income brackets. In principle, the tax law issues created by such a transfer are identical to the issues that arise from any attempt to assign income among family members although the interposition of the partnership entity can complicate the analysis.

[¶ 18,225]

1.   RECOGNITION OF TRANSFEREE PARTNER

For any family partnership, the first question that arises is whether the transferee family member should be recognized as a partner for income tax purposes. Section 704(e)(1) provides a partial answer to that question: if capital is a material income-producing factor in the business of the partnership, a transferee partner who is the bona fide owner of the partnership interest will be recognized. For making that determination, the regulations set forth a series of factors indicative of ownership that are derived from general assignment of income principles. Reg. § 1.704–1(e)(2). The general effect of this rule is to recognize for income tax purposes the transfer of an interest in a partnership that owns income-producing property to the same extent that the transfer of the underlying property would have been recognized.

¶ 18,225

Section 704(e)(1), of course, does not address partnerships in which capital is not a material income-producing factor. Thus, whether the transferee of an interest in a service partnership will be recognized is determined under case law rules and, in particular, under the decision of the Supreme Court in Commissioner v. Culbertson, 337 U.S. 733 (1949), as occurred in the following case.

[¶ 18,230]

CARRIAGE SQUARE, INC. v. COMMISSIONER

United States Tax Court, 1977.
69 T.C. 119.

[T (Condiotti) owned 79.5 percent of the stock of Carriage Square, Inc. On February 14, 1969, T's mother (using funds provided by T) created five trusts: one for T, one for T's wife, and a separate trust for each of T's three children. Each trust was funded with $1,000 in cash. On the same day, Carriage Square, as general partner, organized a limited partnership, Sonoma Development Company, with each trust as a limited partner "to carry on the business to acquire and develop residential property." Carriage Square contributed $556 to the capital of Sonoma and each trust contributed $1,000. Carriage Square was allotted a 10–percent share of the profits and each trust was allotted an 18–percent share. Under the terms of the limited partnership agreement, the limited partners were liable for debts only to the extent of their capital contribution plus their share of any retained profits. Carriage Square, as general partner, was required to devote only such time to the business of the partnership as might be required for the conduct thereof, it being expressly stated that the partnership venture was a sideline for the corporation. These transactions were consummated on the advice and at the direction of Barlow, T's accountant and tax adviser who prepared the various agreements, served as trustee of the trusts, and held 20.5 percent of the stock of Carriage Square. Actual development and construction undertaken by the partnership was financed by bank loans made to Sonoma, which were guaranteed by T and his wife. For the first three years, the income of the partnership was: $2,600 in 1969; $142,600 in 1970; and $177,742 in 1971. This income was allocated between Carriage Square (10 percent) and the trusts (90 percent) in accordance with the partnership agreement. Following an audit of the corporate returns of Carriage Square for the years 1969, 1970, and 1971, the IRS asserted a deficiency for each year based on an allocation of all the partnership income to the corporation.]

FORRESTER, JUDGE: * * *.

* * *

¶ 18,225

Respondent argues that he has properly allocated the income of Sonoma to petitioner, its sole general partner, for the years in question because such income was earned solely by the services performed and the financial risks assumed by petitioner.

Section 704(e)(1)[4] provides:

Sec. 704(e)(1). RECOGNITION OF INTEREST CREATED BY PURCHASE OR GIFT.—A person shall be recognized as a partner for purposes of this subtitle if he owns a capital interest in a partnership in which capital is a material income-producing factor, whether or not such interest was derived by purchase or gift from any other person.

Section 1.704–1(e)(1)(iv), Income Tax Regs., provides the following amplification of section 704(e)(1):

Sec. 704–1(e)(1)(iv). *Capital as a material income-producing factor.* For purposes of section 704(e)(1), the determination as to whether capital is a material income-producing factor must be made by reference to all the facts of each case. Capital is a material income-producing factor if a substantial portion of the gross income of the business is attributable to the employment of capital in the business conducted by the partnership. In general, capital is not a material income-producing factor where the income of the business consists principally of fees, commissions, or other compensation for personal services performed by members or employees of the partnership. On the other hand, capital is ordinarily a material income-producing factor if the operation of the business requires substantial inventories or a substantial investment in plant, machinery, or other equipment.

After carefully reviewing the record in the instant case, we hold that capital was not a material income-producing factor in Sonoma's business. We note at the outset that, with a total initial capital contribution of only $5,556, Sonoma earned $322,942 during its first three years.

Sonoma did employ large amounts of *borrowed* capital in constructing houses on the lots which it purchased from the Condiottis. While borrowed capital, under other circumstances, may be "capital" for section 704(e)(1) purposes, we hold that it is not in this instance. Petitioner, as Sonoma's only general partner, was the only partner in Sonoma whose liability for repayment of such borrowed capital was not substantially limited. Furthermore, Crocker would not have loaned such capital to Sonoma secured by partnership assets (or the general partner's assets) alone, but would loan such capital to Sonoma only after a continuing guarantee had been executed making the Condiottis liable for Sonoma's debts to Crocker in the event that Sonoma did not pay them.

---

4. Although such section is primarily directed toward "family partnership," its language is sufficiently broad to cover the instant case which does not involve a "family partnership" as defined in sec. 704(e)(3). * * *

Since Sonoma made a large profit with a very small total capital contribution from its partners and was able to borrow, and did borrow, substantially all of the capital which it employed in its business upon the condition that such loans were guaranteed by nonpartners, we think that section 1.704–1(e)(1)(i),[6] Income Tax Regs., prohibits the borrowed capital in the instant case from being considered as a "material income-producing factor." The regulation requires that such capital be "contributed by the partners." This view is supported by *Bateman v. United States*, 490 F.2d 549, 553 (9th Cir.1973):

> [H]ad the good will been personal to the Batemans, the transfers of interest to the trusts would not have received tax recognition. Under those circumstances, without the very substantial good will owned by BBC, the partnership would not have been one in which capital was a material income-producing factor. * * *

We hold, therefore, that Sonoma was not a partnership in which capital was a material income-producing factor and consequently section 704(e)(1) is inapplicable. However, the trusts must still be recognized as partners unless it appears that the parties did not in good faith and acting with a business purpose intend to join together as partners. *Commissioner v. Culbertson*, 337 U.S. 733 (1949) * * *.

We are unable to find that the parties acted with a business purpose because the trusts received a 90–percent share of Sonoma's profits even though they made no material contribution to the business. Their capital contribution was not material since Sonoma could borrow substantially all the money necessary to conduct its business as long as the Condiottis guaranteed its debts (which they did). The trusts provided no services and their liability was limited to the amount of their contributed capital plus their share of retained earnings. Furthermore, we cannot find that the parties in good faith intended to join together as partners where petitioner provided all the services necessary for the conduct of a partnership business, assumed substantially all risk of loss, and utilized its business contacts in obtaining the large loans required by the partnership business, but nevertheless was given only a share of the partnership profits which was exactly equal to its share of the capital contributions. Accordingly, we hold that the trusts were not bona fide partners of Sonoma so that respondent correctly allocated the income earned by Sonoma to petitioner.

* * *

Reviewed by the Court.

---

6. Sec. 1.704–1(e). Family partnerships—(1) In general—(i) Introduction. The production of income by a partnership is attributable to the capital or services, or both, *contributed by the partners*. The provisions of subchapter K, chapter 1 of the Code, are to be read in the light of their relationship to section 61, which requires, inter alia, that income be taxed to the person who earns it through his own labor and skill *and the utilization of his own capital*. [Emphasis supplied.]

GOFFE, J., concurring: I concur in the result that the trusts should not be recognized as limited partners but I cannot agree with the approach used by the majority. The majority holds that *borrowed* capital was not a material income-producing factor in the Sonoma limited partnership. There is an attempt to limit such holding to the facts of this case; nevertheless it places a qualification on the concept of "capital as a material income-producing factor" which concept is found in other areas of the tax law; i.e., e.g., definition of earned income from sources without the United States (sec. 911); * * * earned income for self-employment tax purposes (sec. 1.1402(a)–2(a), Income Tax Regs.); * * * and the qualification of retirement plans covering self-employed individuals * * *. The opinion of the majority is also out of touch with reality. Borrowed capital is almost invariably involved (usually to the maximum extent possible) in real estate developments. Moreover, the rationale adopted by the majority is gratuitous; it was not presented by respondent and, therefore, not argued by the parties in their briefs.

The majority emphasizes the unlimited liability of the general partner (petitioner) as distinguished from the limited liability of the limited partners (trusts). Such distinction is meaningless because the degree of liability between general partners and limited partners is not only customary it is definitional. Indeed, the regulations recognize this truism. Sec. 1.704–1(e)(3)(ii)(c), Income Tax Regs.

* * *

The facts of this case should be examined under the tests specified by the various portions of section 1.704–1(e), Income Tax Regs., entitled "Family Partnerships." The income of any partnership must be taxed to the person whose labor and skills earn the income and/or to the person whose own capital is utilized to produce the income. Sec. 1.704–1(e)(1), Income Tax Regs. Under section 752(a) * * *, the increases in petitioner's liabilities as a result of being a partner and the liabilities of the partnership assumed by petitioner are deemed to be contributions of money to the partnership yet the profits of the partnership were allocated among the partners in the ratio of their initial contributions which were nominal in comparison to the tremendous liabilities assumed by petitioner. Even under this broad principle, it is readily apparent that the income of the partnership was not taxed to the partner who provided the capital. In the usual limited partnership, the limited partners contribute substantial sums needed to earn the income and the general partner performs services.

In general, a person will be recognized as a partner for income tax purposes if he owns a capital interest in such partnership whether or not such interest is derived by purchase or gift from any other person. Sec. 1.704–1(e)(1)(ii), Income Tax Regs. However, in either the case of a purchase or a gift, the general rule is qualified as follows:

¶ 18,230

A donee or purchaser of a capital interest in a partnership is not recognized as a partner under the principles of section 704(e)(1) *unless such interest is acquired in a bona fide transaction, not a mere sham for tax avoidance or evasion* purposes, and the donee or purchaser is the real owner of such interest. To be recognized, a transfer must vest dominion and control of the partnership interest in the transferee. The existence of such dominion and control in the donee is to be determined from *all the facts and circumstances*. A transfer is not recognized if the transferor retains such incidents of ownership that the transferee has not acquired full and complete ownership of the partnership interest. *Transactions between members of a family will be closely scrutinized, and the circumstances, not only at the time of the purported transfer but also during the periods preceding and following it, will be taken into consideration in determining the bona fides or lack of bona fides of the purported gift or sale.* * * * [Sec. 1.704–1(e)(1)(iii), Income Tax Regs.; *Krause v. Commissioner*, 57 T.C. 890, 897 (1972). Emphasis added.]

* * *

The acquisition of each limited partnership interest was cast in terms of a purchase so such acquisitions should first be examined under the provisions of section 1.704–1(e)(4), Income Tax Regs. A purchase of a capital interest in a partnership will be recognized as bona fide if, considering all relevant factors, it has the usual characteristics of an arm's-length transaction. Sec. 1.704–1(e)(4)(ii)(*a*), Income Tax Regs. The purchase in the instant case had none of the characteristics of an arm's-length transaction. It was between related parties pursuant to an overall plan to avoid taxes. If the purchase is not arm's-length it can, nevertheless, be recognized if—

> [i]t can be shown, in the absence of characteristics of an arm's-length transaction, that the purchase was genuinely intended to promote the success of the business by securing participation of the purchaser in the business or by adding his credit to that of the other participants. [Sec. 1.704–1(e)(4)(ii)(*b*), Income Tax Regs.]

That test cannot be fulfilled because each of the trusts contributed only "seed money" of $1,000 each and were liable for no more. The trusts did nothing to promote the success of the business; they participated in nothing but profits.

The trusts, having failed to satisfy the tests for purchased interests in a family partnership, may be recognized only if they meet the requirements applicable to the acquisition of a partnership interest by gift. Sec. 1.704–1(e)(4)(i), Income Tax Regs. Indeed, the limited partnership interests were acquired by gifts of cash by Condiotti through his mother to Barlow as trustee for the benefit of himself, his wife and his three children. Sec. 1.704–1(e)(2)(i) provides:

¶ 18,230

> *Whether an alleged partner who is a donee of a capital interest in a partnership is the real owner of such capital interest, and whether the donee has dominion and control over such interest, must be ascertained from all the facts and circumstances of the particular case. Isolated facts are not determinative; the reality of the donee's ownership is to be determined in the light of the transaction as a whole.* The execution of legally sufficient and irrevocable deeds or other instruments of gift under state law is a factor to be taken into account but is not determinative of ownership by the donee for the purposes of section 704(e). *The reality of the transfer and of the donee's ownership of the property attributed to him are to be ascertained from the conduct of the parties with respect to the alleged gift and not by any mechanical or formal test.* Some of the more important factors to be considered in determining whether the donee has acquired ownership of the capital interest in a partnership are indicated in subdivisions (ii) to (x), inclusive, of this subparagraph. [Emphasis added.]

The reality of the transaction as a whole, as explained above, clearly shows that the general donee test of ownership cannot be satisfied. Moreover, the scheme fails to satisfy the specific test of section 1.704–1(e)(2)(iii):

> Controls inconsistent with ownership by the donee may be exercised indirectly as well as directly, for example, through a separate business organization, estate, trust, individual, or other partnership. Where such indirect controls exist, the reality of the donee's interest will be determined as if such controls were exercisable directly.

Here, the donor, Condiotti, and Barlow completely controlled petitioner, which was the sole general partner of Sonoma, which, under the partnership agreement, had the exclusive authority to make decisions of the partnership. In addition to the specific tests of retention of control by the donor, the final "catch-all" provision of section 1.704–1(e)(2)(vi), Income Tax Regs., applies:

> However, despite formal compliance with the above factors, other circumstances may indicate that the donor has retained substantial ownership of the interest purportedly transferred to the donee.

Not by the wildest stretch of the imagination can Barlow satisfy the tests imposed by the regulations on recognition of a trustee as a partner in a family partnership.

> *Trustees as partners.* A trustee may be recognized as a partner for income tax purposes under the principles relating to family partnerships generally as applied to the particular facts of the trust-partnership arrangement. A trustee who is unrelated to and independent of the grantor, and who participates as a partner and receives distribution of the income distributable to the trust, will ordinarily be recognized as the legal owner of the partnership

interest which he holds in trust unless the grantor has retained controls inconsistent with such ownership. However, if the grantor is the trustee, or if the trustee is amenable to the will of the grantor, the provisions of the trust instrument (particularly as to whether the trustee is subject to the responsibilities of a fiduciary), the provisions of the partnership agreement, and the conduct of the parties must all be taken into account in determining whether the trustee in a fiduciary capacity has become the real owner of the partnership interest. Where the grantor (or person amenable to his will) is the trustee, the trust may be recognized as a partner only if the grantor (or such other person) in his participation in the affairs of the partnership actively represents and protects the interests of the beneficiaries in accordance with the obligations of a fiduciary and does not subordinate such interests to the interests of the grantor. [Sec. 1.704–1(e)(2)(vii), Income Tax Regs. Emphasis added.]

Barlow is amenable to the will of Condiotti for numerous business reasons, the most apparent one being that Barlow is the only minority shareholder of petitioner and Condiotti is the only majority shareholder. * * *

* * *

* * * This brings us back to the conclusion stated earlier that the creation of the trusts and the limited partnerships was nothing more than a scheme to evade tax. Prior to their creation, Condiotti and his corporations, including petitioner, engaged in the identical business engaged in by the Sonoma limited partnership and Sonoma, in actuality, performed no useful function except the splitting up of income to five more taxpayers.

Although the parties here substantially carried out the formal steps in creating the trusts and the partnership, they represent shams. * * * The parties having flunked all of the tests, I would, therefore, hold that the trusts cannot be recognized as partners and sustain the Commissioner in his determination that all of the income of the Sonoma limited partnership is taxable to petitioner.

* * *

TANNENWALD, J., dissenting in part: I share the majority's concern over the attempt by Condiotti to spread the tax liability resulting from his business operation among petitioner and the numerous trusts established for the benefit of his family members. However, I cannot agree with the technique chosen by the majority to attack the effect of the partnership agreement and thereby allocate the entire income of the partnership to petitioner. Under my approach, part of the partnership income, albeit a small portion, would be allocated to the trusts, and it is for this reason that I record my dissent rather than concurrence.

Section 704(e)(1) provides that "[a] person shall be recognized as a partner" if two conditions are satisfied: first, the individual must own a capital interest in the partnership; second, capital must be a material income-producing factor in the partnership. The majority reasons that the interests of the trusts should not be recognized because the second requirement has not been satisfied. Its rationale is that capital was not a material income-producing factor in Sonoma's business because substantially all of the capital employed in the business was borrowed and the partnership was able to borrow such funds only because Condiotti, who was not a partner, guaranteed the loans. I cannot agree with this rationale.

Section 752(a) and the regulations thereunder make clear that liabilities resulting from funds borrowed by a partnership are treated as a contribution of capital by the partners and enter into the calculation of the partners' bases of their partnership interests. This is true of a limited partner in a situation where none of the partners has any personal liability, i.e., a nonrecourse borrowing by the partnership. It is also true, to a lesser extent, where there is personal liability on the part of another partner and the limited partner has not made the full capital contribution for which he is obligated. See sec. 1.752–1(e), Income Tax Regs. * * * This treatment is consistent with section 1.704–1(e)(1)(iv), Income Tax Regs., which deals with capital as a material income-producing factor. The regulation does not consider "borrowed" capital at all. Instead, it pinpoints "employment of capital in the business conducted by the partnership" and distinguishes businesses which require substantial inventories or a substantial investment in plant, machinery, or other equipment from businesses which derive their income primarily as compensation for services. What is determinative for such purposes is the function capital serves for the business, not the source from which it is obtained. * * *

What clearly emerges from the facts herein is that the partnership was in the business of purchasing land and constructing houses for sale on subdivided lots. Such transactions required the infusion of substantial sums of money. I perceive no valid reason why the fact that such funds were obtained from borrowings on the strength of Condiotti's credit should per se preclude a finding that capital was a material income-producing factor in the business of the partnership within the meaning of section 704(e)(1). Indeed, the majority's reasoning to the contrary, if carried to its logical conclusion, could cast doubt on the propriety of the allocation of income among partners in an ordinary limited real estate partnership with only one general partner, an approach which is fraught with substantial, if not insuperable, difficulties.

As I see it, capital was clearly a material income-producing factor in the business of Sonoma and the only issue herein is the impact, if any, of the borrowed funds upon the allocation of the partnership income among the petitioner and the trusts. Under section 704(e)(1), aside from the element of capital as a material income-producing factor, the question is whether the trusts' partnership status, and therefore the partnership, should be considered sham. While many aspects of the instant situation lend support for the basic thrust of respondent's argument that the partnership and the trusts' interests therein lacked economic reality and therefore should not be recognized, the fact of the matter is that the trusts did contribute capital, albeit in very small amounts. Perhaps these small capital contributions were not realistically required in the business of the partnership, but they were made and I am not prepared to say that, at least to the extent thereof, the trusts' partnership interest should not be recognized.[1] But there is still the further question as to the applicability of section 704(e)(2), which provides:

> In the case of any partnership interest created by gift, the distributive share of the donee under the partnership agreement shall be includible in his gross income, except to the extent that such share is determined without allowance of reasonable compensation for services rendered to the partnership by the donor, and *except to the extent that the portion of such share attributable to donated capital is proportionately greater than the share of the donor attributable to the donor's capital.* * * * [Emphasis added.]

Under this provision, each trust's share of income cannot exceed that amount justified by its share of the capital of the partnership.

Petitioner argues that this provision is inapplicable because the partnership interests were purchased with trust assets. This argument is answered by section 1.704–1(e)(4), Income Tax Regs., which provided that a purported purchase of a capital interest in a partnership will have to meet the same requirements as an interest created by gift, unless the purchase is recognized as bona fide under section 1.704–1(e)(4)(ii), Income Tax Regs.

I can think of few cases where the bona fides of the so-called purchases of the partnership interests by the trusts could be more open to question. The trusts herein were established and the partnership interests were acquired on the same day. The trusts were funded simply with a transfer of $1,000 to each trust and that entire amount was simultaneously invested in the partnership. While these elements standing alone might not be sufficient to justify ignoring the form of purchase, I think they are relevant when considered in the context of the allocation of partnership income in the instant case. The share of partnership income attributable to each trust, while proportionate to the initial capital investments by each partner, was grossly disproportionate when the role of Condiotti, and particularly the use of his credit standing, is

---

1. None of the cases relied upon by respondent to support his argument of lack of economic reality involved situations where the trusts made any payment. Respondent also argues that the trustee "was not in a position to act as an independent fiduciary." One of the tests in determining "sham" is whether a trustee-partner is "amenable to the will of the grantor." See sec. 1.704–1(e)(2)(vii), Income Tax Regs. Such amenability should not be inferred from the mere fact that the trustee involved herein was also Condiotti's accountant. * * *

taken into account. Nor is there any indication that investments by the trusts were intended to promote the success of the partnership's business either through the participation of the trusts or the use of their credit. In short, I think it more than appropriate to treat the trusts' partnership interests as having been acquired by gift within the meaning of section 704(e)(2).

There remains the question of how the partnership income should be allocated to reflect the exception of section 704(e)(2) in a situation where "the portion of such share attributable to donated capital is proportionately greater than the share of the donor attributable to the donor's capital." In this connection, the following provision of section 1.704–1(e)(3)(ii)(c) is pertinent:

> In the case of a limited partnership * * * consideration shall be given to the fact that a general partner, unlike a limited partner, risks his credit in the partnership business.

Given the limited participation by the trusts, the status of petitioner as the sole general partner with the concomitant full risk of loss thereby imposed upon it, and the pervasive role of petitioner's sole shareholder (Condiotti), including his assumption of the ultimate full risk of loss via his guaranty, it is clear to me that the capital represented by the borrowed funds should be considered as petitioner's capital.[3] Once that is done and the petitioner's capital thus determined, I would allocate the partnership income in accordance with the respective capital interests of the petitioner and the trusts.

* * *

[One other dissenting opinion has been omitted.]

[¶ 18,235]

Note

In applying the *Culbertson* rule, did the Tax Court examine the faith, good or bad, of the parties or their economic arrangement?

[¶ 18,240]

Problems

1. Greedee is one of three equal partners in an architectural firm. He proposes to transfer one-half of his interest to his 12–year-old

---

3. Petitioner appears to argue that, if respondent is not correct in his contention that the partnership should be considered a sham, then none of the income of Sonoma should be attributable to petitioner, because all of the activities of Sonoma were "earned" by Condiotti, who "ran the whole show." I would reject this argument to the extent that it can be construed as seeking to avoid the deficiency herein by claiming that the proper taxpayer is Condiotti (who is not before the Court) for two reasons: (1) Since I do not think the partnership should be ignored, petitioner's argument falls by the wayside, and (2) in any event, I would have serious doubts as to whether, under the circumstances herein, petitioner could ignore the form of the transaction adopted by the parties. * * *

daughter. Under what circumstances would the daughter be recognized as a partner?

2.   Following her graduation from law school, Cynthia was admitted to the law firm in which her father and two unrelated individuals were equal partners. Effective January 1, the partnership agreement was amended to provide that partnership income and loss would be allocated equally among the four partners. For that year, the partners billed the following hours:

    Father 2,000
    Cynthia 1,000
    Partner A 2,000
    Partner B 2,000

About one-half of the net income of the firm is attributable to the efforts of nonpartner employees. If the net income of the partnership for that year was $400,000, how must it be allocated among the partners? Cf. Reg. § 1.704–1(e)(3).

[¶ 18,245]

2.   APPORTIONMENT OF INCOME

If transferee family members are recognized as partners, Section 704(e)(2) seeks to prevent the improper assignment of income to the transferees. That provision may appear to do no more than codify otherwise applicable assignment of income principles. In fact, however, Section 704(e)(2) serves the important function of ensuring that those principles will be applied to family partnerships notwithstanding the more general grant of authority to allocate income among partners under Section 704(b). Moreover, under Section 704(e)(3), the assignment of income rules of Section 704(e)(2) are to be applied regardless of whether the transferee acquired the interest by gift or purchase. The rules of Section 704(e)(2) apparently are not exclusive. Where they are inapplicable, the IRS may invoke general assignment of income principles to reallocate income among members of a family.

The relationship between Section 704(e)(2) and the more recently revised Section 704(b) and 704(c) is far from clear. For example, assume that the donor partner had a 20–percent interest in profits and losses and in addition was entitled to a special allocation of depreciation with respect to one of the partnership properties. If the donor transfers one-half of the partnership interest to a child but retains the entire special allocation of depreciation, would Section 704(e)(2) require that one-half of the depreciation deduction also be allocated to the child or is that special allocation valid if it meets the requirements of the regulations under Section 704(b)? On the other hand, if the special allocation retained by the donor were of income, Section 704(e)(2) apparently would have no application. That rule bars only the allocation of a disproportionately large share of partnership income to donees. How would general assignment of income principles apply in this situation?

[¶ 18,250]

D. SIMPLIFIED FLOW–THROUGH REGIME FOR ELECTING LARGE PARTNERSHIPS

Under Sections 771 through 777, enacted as part of the Taxpayer Relief Act of 1997, a large partnership with at least 100 members may elect a simplified flow-through regime that reduces the number of items that must be separately computed and reported to each partner and makes certain other adjustments to the provisions of Subchapter K for these partnerships. Service partnerships and commodity trading partnerships, however, are generally not eligible to make this election. Congress enacted this simplified regime to ease the reporting burden for both the partnerships and their affected members and to facilitate IRS computer matching efforts. S. Rep. No. 33, 105th Cong., 1st Sess. 238–39 (1997).

Computation of electing large partnership's taxable income. An electing large partnership's taxable income is generally computed in the same manner as that of an individual, with certain modifications. § 773(a)(1). That partnership taxable income generally passes through as a net amount to the partners; however, as discussed below, certain items of partnership income, loss, deduction, or credit are separately stated and pass through to the partners as separate items. §§ 773(a)(1) and 772. The partnership is not allowed any deductions for personal exemptions under Section 151, net operating losses under Section 172, or the other itemized personal deductions such as medical expenses, alimony payments, or moving expenses. § 773(b)(1). The partnership is allowed a charitable deduction in computing its taxable income, and that deduction is subject to the percentage limitations in Section 170(b)(2). § 773(b)(2). The partnership's miscellaneous itemized deductions (as defined in Section 67(b))—the most important of which in this partnership setting are Section 212 deductions—are generally combined at the partnership level and subjected to a 70–percent floor at that level, instead of subjecting such expenses to the two-percent floor at the partner level. § 773(b)(3). Limitations in the Code are generally applied at the partnership level, although there are several exceptions to this rule. § 773(a)(2). Most elections relating to partnership income, deductions, and credits must be made at the partnership level, except that elections relating to foreign tax credits under Section 901 and cancellation of indebtedness income under Section 108 are made separately by each partner. § 773(a)(2).

Separately stated items of an electing large partnership. Each partner in an electing large partnership must take into account separate-

¶ 18,250

ly the partner's distributive share of certain items, as determined at the partnership level:

 (1) taxable income or loss from passive loss limitation activities;

 (2) taxable income or loss from other activities;

 (3) net capital gain or loss allocable to passive loss limitation activities;

 (4) net capital gain or loss allocable to other partnership activities;

 (5) tax-exempt interest;

 (6) applicable net alternative minimum tax adjustment separately computed for the passive loss limitation activities and for other partnership activities;

 (7) general credits;

 (8) Section 42 low income housing credit;

 (9) Section 47 rehabilitation credit;

 (10) foreign income taxes;

 (11) Section 29 alternative fuels credit; and

 (12) any other items to the extent that the IRS determines that separate treatment is appropriate.

§ 772(a).

Note that the following items have to be separately stated by most partnerships but do not have to be separately stated by electing large partnerships: long-term capital gains and losses; short-term capital gains and losses; Section 1231 gains and losses from the sale of property used in a trade or business; charitable contributions; miscellaneous itemized deductions that would be subject to Section 67 in the hands of an individual partner; and various separate alternative minimum tax preference items.

Note also that an electing large partnership generally nets capital gains and losses at the partnership level, but separates out its net capital gain or loss from passive activities and its net capital gain or loss from other partnership activities. Each partner separately takes into account its distributive share of the electing large partnership's net capital gain or loss from passive activities and from other activities and treats the net capital gain or loss as long-term capital gain or long-term capital loss. (However, special rules may be provided by regulation to deal with capital gains or losses that are subject to differing rates of tax. See Staff of Joint Comm. on Tax'n, 105th Cong., 1st Sess., General Explanation of Tax Legislation Enacted in 1997, at 355 (1997).) If an electing large partnership's net short-term capital gain exceeds its net long-term capital loss, that excess is combined with the partnership's other taxable income and is not separately stated. § 772(c)(4). Moreover, the partnership's Section 1231 gains and losses are netted at the partnership level;

if the net amount is a gain, it is treated as a long-term capital gain and netted with the partnership's other capital gains and losses, and if the net amount is a loss, it is treated as an ordinary loss and combined with the partnership's other taxable income.

Character of partnership items of an electing large partnership. The character of items of income, deduction, gain, and loss of an electing large partnership is generally determined at the partnership level under rules similar to Section 702(b). § 772(c)(1).

Other modifications. As a general matter, Section 771 provides that any provision of Subchapter K shall not apply to an electing large partnership to the extent that it is inconsistent with Sections 772 through 777. Section 774 makes certain other specific modifications to Subchapter K and other Code provisions for electing large partnerships. Section 776 contains special rules for electing large partnerships engaged in oil and gas activities. Finally, a special new unified audit system applies to electing large partnerships. See §§ 6240 through 6255.

Eligibility to elect large partnership treatment. A partnership is generally eligible to elect large partnership treatment if it had at least 100 partners during the prior taxable year. § 775(a)(1)(A). In applying this 100–partner threshold, any individual partner who is presently performing substantial services in connection with the partnership's activities, or who formerly performed such substantial services while a partner, is not counted. § 775(b)(1).

Service partnerships are generally not eligible to elect large partnership treatment. A partnership is an ineligible service partnership if substantially all of the partners are any of the following—

(i) individuals performing substantial services in connection with the partnership's business activities or are personal service corporations (as defined in Section 269A(b)) with owner-employees who perform such services;

(ii) retired partners who had performed such services; or

(iii) spouses of partners who are performing (or previously performed) such services.

§ 775(b)(2). In applying these provisions, the activities of a partnership include the activities of any other partnership in which the partnership owns directly an 80 percent or greater interest in partnership capital and profits. § 775(b)(3).

A partnership is not eligible to elect large partnership treatment if its principal activity is the buying and selling of commodities or options, futures, or forwards with respect to such commodities. § 775(c).

If a partnership treats itself as an electing large partnership on its partnership return, despite the fact that it has not filed an election or does not qualify to make the election, that treatment is binding on the partnership and its partners. Such erroneous treatment, however, is not binding on the IRS. § 775(d).

¶ 18,250

Chapter 19

PARTNER'S BASIS AND OTHER LIMITATIONS ON ALLOCATED LOSSES

[¶ 19,000]

A. INTRODUCTION

A critical element in implementing the single level of tax on partnerships is the computation of the basis of a partner's interest in the partnership. That computation results in a cumulative summary of the after-tax consequences of all transactions between the partner and the partnership: the partner's contribution of capital (including the deemed contribution resulting from a partnership borrowing), the subsequent allocations of income and loss to the partner, and any returns of capital from the partnership to the partner. Accordingly, at any point in time, the balance in the basis computation represents the partner's after-tax investment in the partnership and thus the amount that the partner may withdraw from the partnership free of tax. That amount also represents the maximum amount of loss attributable to the investment in the partnership that the partner is entitled to claim under Section 704(d). Compare § 165(b). There are, however, additional limitations on the claiming of partnership losses outside of Subchapter K that reflect policy considerations broader than the technical partnership taxation requirements. See, e.g., §§ 465 (the "at risk" rules) and 469 (the passive activity loss rules).

The computation of the basis of a partner's interest must be sharply distinguished from the computation of a partner's capital account. Like basis, the capital account records the history of the partner's transactions with the partnership. The capital account, however, reflects economic relationships; transactions are recorded in the account at their market value. Basis, of course, reflects only amounts for which tax liabilities have previously been settled and thus excludes the gains and losses that are included in market value but that have not yet been realized or recognized for tax purposes.

[¶ 19,005]

B. INITIAL BASIS

We have already seen that upon a contribution to the partnership, whether upon the formation of the partnership or thereafter, a partner obtains an initial basis (or increases an existing basis) for the partnership interest equal to the amount of cash plus the adjusted basis of any property contributed to the partnership. § 721. Moreover, under Section 752(a), that initial basis is increased by the partner's share of the liabilities of the partnership.

If the partner acquired the interest by a transfer from an existing partner, rather than by contribution, the new partner's initial basis is determined under the general rules of the Code. See § 742 and Chapter 21. That means that, if the interest was purchased, the initial basis for the interest will be the amount paid for the interest under Section 1012; if the interest is acquired by gift, the initial basis will carry over from the donor under Section 1015; if the interest is acquired from a decedent, the initial basis will be the fair market value of the interest at the date of the decedent's death under Section 1014, unless the interest represents income in respect of a decedent (see ¶¶ 25,010–25,015). Under the same principle, if the partnership interest is received as taxable compensation, the partner's initial basis, under the Section 1012 "tax cost" principle, will equal the taxable fair market value of the interest. In all events, that initial basis will be increased by the new partner's share of partnership liabilities under Section 752.

[¶ 19,010]

C. ADJUSTMENTS TO BASIS

To reflect the income tax history of partnership activities, the initial basis for the partnership interest must thereafter be continuously adjusted in the manner prescribed by Section 705. Naturally, basis must be increased by the items of income allocated to the partner. § 705(a)(1)(A). Since those items will be taxed to the partner even though they are not distributed, an upward basis adjustment is required to permit the later withdrawal of that amount without a second tax. For tax purposes, the partner's share of income not distributed by the partnership is viewed as an additional investment by the partner. By the same token, basis must be reduced by the amount of deductible losses allocated to the partner to prevent a second tax allowance for the same economic loss upon the disposition of the partnership interest. § 705(a)(2)(A).

¶ 19,010

Basis must also be increased by the partner's share of tax-exempt income. § 705(a)(1)(B). If that adjustment were not made, the distribution of the cash proceeds of the tax-exempt receipt might exceed the basis of the partnership interest and thus would be taxed to the partner.

Similarly, basis must be reduced by expenditures of the partnership that are not deductible. § 705(a)(2)(B). That provision, however, requires some elaboration. Subparagraph (B) requires that basis be reduced by expenditures of the partnership that are not deductible and are not chargeable to capital account. That final reference, however, is not to the capital accounts of the partners. Rather, it refers to expenditures that are not required to be capitalized under the capital expenditure rule. For capitalized expenditures of the partnership, such as the purchase of a building, partners reduce their basis as depreciation or other cost recovery allowances are claimed in the future and not when the initial expenditure is made. One clear application of subparagraph (B) is the reduction of basis required when the partnership incurs expenditures that are nondeductible, such as fines imposed by a government. Were basis not reduced, the partner would obtain a future loss deduction for that amount in violation of the legislative policies underlying the statutory prohibition against the deduction of fines. A less obvious application occurs when the partnership incurs the expenditures enumerated in Section 703(a)(2). Those items are not deductible by the partnership (and thus are not covered by Section 705(a)(2)(A)) but pass through to the partners and are deductible by them. Subparagraph (B) ensures that the basis of a partnership interest is reduced by the amount so deducted to prevent the partners from obtaining a double tax benefit for that amount. This principle is illustrated by Rev. Rul. 96–11, excerpted below.

Finally, in the converse of Section 722, the basis of the partnership interest must be reduced by distributions to the partner in the amount required by Section 733. That reduction will equal the amount of cash distributed and the basis that the distributed property acquires in the hands of the partner. While the computation of that basis is explored in detail in Chapter 22, in general, the basis of distributed property carries over from the partnership. Thus, the basis of a partnership interest is normally reduced by the partnership's basis in any property distributed to the partner.

The basis of a partnership interest may not be reduced below zero by either losses or distributions. § 705(a)(2). That limitation meshes with the prohibition against claiming losses in excess of basis and the tax imposed on distributions in excess of a partner's basis in the partnership interest.

It is sometimes observed that the aggregate of the outside bases for the partnership interests should equal the aggregate inside basis of the partnership properties and that the basis of a particular partnership interest should equal that partner's share of the inside partnership basis.

¶ 19,010

While those statements may be true in the simplest of partnerships, they do not represent reality for most partnerships. Too many kinds of transactions, such as transfers of partnership interests, may disturb those relationships.

[¶ 19,015]

REVENUE RULING 96–11

1996–1 C.B. 140.

ISSUE

If a partnership makes a charitable contribution of property, are the partners' bases in their partnership interests decreased to reflect the contribution?

FACTS

A and B each contribute an equal amount of cash to form PRS, a general partnership. Under the PRS agreement, each item of income, gain, loss, and deduction of the partnership is allocated 50 percent to A and 50 percent to B. PRS has unencumbered property, X, with a basis of $60x and a fair market value of $100x. PRS contributes X in a transaction that qualifies as a charitable contribution under § 170(c) * * *. The charitable contribution is not subject to the limitations of § 170(e)(1).

LAW AND ANALYSIS

Section 170(a) allows as a deduction any charitable contribution (as defined in § 170(c)) payment of which is made within the taxable year. The deduction provided by § 170(a) is subject to the limitations of § 170(b).

Section 1.170A-l(c)(1) of the * * * Regulations provides that, if a charitable contribution is made in property other than money, the amount of the contribution is the fair market value of the property at the time of the contribution reduced as provided by § 170(e)(1) and paragraph (a) of § 1.170A–4, or § 170(e)(3) and paragraph (c) of § 1.170A–4A.

Section 703(a)(2)(C) provides that the taxable income of a partnership is computed in the same manner as in the case of an individual except that the deduction for charitable contributions provided in § 170 is not allowed to the partnership. However, under § 702(a)(4) each partner takes into account separately the partner's distributive share of the partnership's charitable contributions (as defined in § 170(c)).

Section 1.170A-l(h)(7) provides that a partner's distributive share of charitable contributions actually paid by a partnership during its taxable year may be allowed as a deduction in the partner's separate return for the partner's taxable year with or within which the taxable year of the partnership ends, to the extent that the aggregate of the partner's share of the partnership contributions and the partner's own contributions does not exceed the limitations in § 170(b).

* * *

The adjustments to the basis of a partner's interest in a partnership under § 705 are necessary to prevent inappropriate or unintended benefits or detriments to the partners. Generally, the basis of a partner's interest in a partnership is adjusted to reflect the tax allocations of the partnership to that partner. This ensures that the income and loss of the partnership are taken into account by its partners only once. In addition, as provided in § 705(a)(1)(B) and (a)(2)(B), adjustments must also be made to reflect certain nontaxable events in the partnership. For example, a partner's share of nontaxable income (such as exempt income) is added to the basis of the partner's interest because, without a basis adjustment, the partner could recognize gain with respect to the tax-exempt income, for example, on a sale or redemption of the partner's interest, and the benefit of the tax-exempt income would be lost to the partner. Similarly, a partner's share of nondeductible expenditures must be deducted from the partner's basis in order to prevent that amount from giving rise to a loss to the partner on a sale or a redemption of the partner's interest in the partnership. *See* H.R. Rep. No. 1337, 83d Cong., 2d Sess. A225 (1954); S. Rep. No. 1622, 83d Cong., 2d Sess. 384 (1954).

In determining whether a transaction results in exempt income within the meaning of § 705(a)(1)(B), or a nondeductible, noncapital expenditure within the meaning of § 705(a)(2)(B), the proper inquiry is whether the transaction has a permanent effect on the partnership's basis in its assets, without a corresponding current or future effect on its taxable income. Pursuant to § 703(a)(2)(C), the contribution of X by *PRS* is not taken into account by *PRS* in computing its taxable income. Consequently, the contribution results in a permanent decrease in the aggregate basis of the assets of *PRS* that is not taken into account by *PRS*, in determining its taxable income and will not be taken into account for federal income tax purposes in any other manner. Therefore, for purposes of § 705(a)(2)(B), the contribution of X, and the resulting permanent decrease in partnership basis, is an expenditure of the partnership not deductible in computing its taxable income and not properly chargeable to capital account. * * *

Reducing the partners' bases in their partnership interests by their respective shares of the permanent decrease in the partnership's basis in its assets preserves the intended benefit of providing a deduction (in circumstances not under § 170(e)) for the fair market value of appreciated property without recognition of the appreciation. By contrast, reducing the partners' bases in their partnership interests by the fair market value of the contributed property would subsequently cause the partners to recognize gain (or a reduced loss), for example, upon a disposition of their partnership interests, attributable to the unrecognized appreciation in X at the time of this contribution.

Under the *PRS* agreement, partnership items are allocated equally between A and B. Accordingly, the basis of A's and B's interests in *PRS* is each decreased by $30x.

HOLDING

If a partnership makes a charitable contribution of property, the basis of each partner's interest in the partnership is decreased (but not below zero) by the partner's share of the partnership's basis in the property contributed.

[¶ 19,020]

D. TIMING AND PRIORITIES

So long as a partner retains a basis for the partnership interest, the precise order in which adjustments are made to that basis and the timing of those adjustments normally are of no significance. However, if the partnership makes distributions that might exceed the basis of a partner's interest, those refinements can assume considerable importance. Unfortunately, the rules governing these timing issues are not models of clarity.

In general, it appears that basis is not to be adjusted until the taxable year of the partnership closes as to the partner so that the net income or loss for the year can be computed. Reg. § 1.705–1(a)(1). However, under Section 731(a)(1), the amount of a cash distribution (or a distribution of marketable securities treated as cash under Section 731(c)) in excess of the basis for the partnership interest, as determined "immediately before" the distribution, is taxable. In combination, these two rules suggest that if a partner receives a distribution during the year that exceeds the basis for the partnership interest at the beginning of the year, the excess is taxed, notwithstanding that the partner's share of income for the year, on which the partner will also be taxed, exceeded the amount of the distribution. In an attempt to prevent this result, Reg. § 1.731–1(a)(1)(ii) provides that drawings or advances against the partner's distributive share of income are to be treated as year-end distributions. Does this solve the problem? Can all distributions be viewed as drawings against a distributive share? These issues are considered further in Chapter 22.

A similar question of ordering arises if the partnership both sustained a loss for the year and made distributions to partners. In that event, for the purpose of determining the amount of the loss allowable, the regulations require that the basis for the partnership interest first be increased under Section 705(a)(1) by the items of income for the year and then be decreased by the nontaxable amount of cash or the basis of property distributed. Reg. § 1.704–1(d)(2). As a result, the loss allowable for the year is limited to the basis for the partnership interest remaining after all distributions are taken into account. See Rev. Rul. 66–94, 1966–1 C.B. 166 (distributions are taken into account before losses in computing a partner's adjusted basis for her partnership interest under Section 705(a)). This ordering of losses and distributions is normally favorable to the partners: basis is first used to prevent immediate taxation of distributions while the claiming of partnership losses is merely deferred.

Similar timing issues are raised by the sale or gift of a partnership interest during the year. The timing of the basis adjustments attributable to income and loss for the year of transfer is considered in Chapter 21.

[¶ 19,025]

Problems

1. José and Katrina have an equal interest in the profits and losses of their partnership, which provides computer consulting services. José has a basis for his partnership interest of $5,000 and Katrina has a basis of $20,000. During the year, the partnership derived the following items of income and expense:

Receipts from customers	$20,000
Salary to employees	(30,000)
Capital loss	(10,000)
Tax-exempt interest income	6,000
Interest expense allocable to tax-exempt interest	(2,000)
Charitable contribution of cash	(4,000)

What will be the bases of their partnership interests at the end of the year?

2. How would your answer in Problem 1 change if the charitable contribution consisted of partnership property with an adjusted basis of $4,000 and a fair market value of $6,000? Assume that the contribution is not subject to the limitations of Section 170(e).

3. Assume in Problem 1 that the José-Katrina partnership made a year-end distribution of cash of $5,000 to each partner. What effect would that have on the partners?

E. LIMITATIONS ON THE DEDUCTION OF LOSSES

[¶ 19,030]

1. INADEQUATE BASIS

Losses allocated to a partner may not be deducted currently to the extent that they exceed the basis of the partnership interest. § 704(d).

That excess loss, however, is not forfeited. Rather, the loss is held in suspense and may be claimed by the partner in a future year in which the basis for the interest has been increased by allocations of partnership income or by contributions to the partnership. Reg. § 1.704–1(d)(1). For the purpose of determining the character of both the losses currently allowable and those carried forward, a proportionate fraction of each separately stated item of loss is subject to the Section 704(d) limitation. Reg. § 1.704–1(d)(2).

[¶ 19,035]

SENNETT v. COMMISSIONER

United States Court of Appeals, Ninth Circuit, 1985.
752 F.2d 428.

PER CURIAM:

Taxpayers William and Sandra Sennett claimed an ordinary loss deduction of $109,061 on their 1969 tax return. This loss represented William Sennett's share of the ordinary losses incurred in 1968 by Professional Properties Partnership ("PPP") when it repurchased his interest in the partnership. The Commissioner of Internal Revenue disallowed the deduction asserting *inter alia* that in 1969 Sennett had no basis in an interest in PPP since he had left the partnership in 1968 and is precluded by * * * § 704(d) and Treas. Reg. § 1.704–1(d) from claiming any loss. The Tax Court * * * ruled against petitioners. It held that a former partner may not claim a share of a loss that is incurred by the partnership after the withdrawal from the partnership of that partner. We agree and affirm.

FACTS

Sennett entered PPP as a limited partner in December 1967. PPP's total capital at that time was approximately $402,000. Sennett contributed $135,000 and received a 33.5% interest in the partnership. In 1967 PPP reported an ordinary loss of $405,329, and Sennett reported his allowable distributive share of $135,000.

Sennett sold his interest in PPP on November 26, 1968, with an effective date of December 1, 1968. The contract provided that PPP would pay Sennett $250,000, in annual installments with interest. Sennett agreed to pay PPP within one year the total loss allocated to Sennett's surrendered interest. PPP then sold twenty percent of Sennett's interest to a third party. PPP's return in 1968 reported a negative capital account of $109,061, corresponding to the eighty percent portion of the partnership interest PPP bought from Sennett and retained.

On May 15, 1969, Sennett and PPP executed an amended agreement which reduced PPP's obligation to $240,000, without interest if paid in full by December 31, 1969, or if paid one-half in 1969 and the rest in

¶ **19,035**

1970, at seven percent interest. PPP executed a promissory note to Sennett for $240,000, which Sennett signed as paid in full. Sennett meanwhile paid PPP $109,061, which was eighty percent of his share of PPP's losses. On his 1969 return Sennett reported $240,000 long-term capital gain and $109,061 as his distributive share of PPP's ordinary loss. The Commissioner disallowed the ordinary loss and maintained that, instead, there should be a long-term capital gain reported of $130,939 ($240,000 − $109,061). The Tax Court agreed and the Sennetts took this appeal.

ANALYSIS

The parties stipulated to the facts in the Tax Court proceedings. The task of the Tax Court was to apply the law to these facts. Review *de novo* is, therefore, appropriate. * * *

In deciding whether Sennett can deduct a $109,061 loss, we must look to * * * § 704(d). The statute provides:

> LIMITATION ON ALLOWANCE OF LOSSES.—A partner's distributive share of partnership loss (including capital loss) shall be allowed only to the extent of the adjusted basis of such partner's interest in the partnership at the end of the partnership year in which such loss occurred. *Any excess of such loss over such basis shall be allowed as a deduction at the end of the partnership year in which such excess is repaid to the partnership.* (Emphasis added.)

Treas. Reg. § 1.704–1(d)—in force in 1969 and having substantively the same effect now—interprets the statute as allowing only a partner to benefit from the carryover allowed by subsection 704(d). The Commissioner relies upon this regulation in disallowing the deduction, since Sennett was not a partner in the year he repaid the excess. Sennett does not deny this. Nor does he deny that his basis was zero when PPP purchased his interest and incurred the loss in 1968. Sennett argues instead that the regulation is merely an "interpretive regulation," and entitled to little or no weight. Sennett points to statutory language which allows the taxpayer to claim a deduction in the amount of the excess of basis in the partnership. He claims he repaid the loss in 1969 and is entitled to the deduction regardless of his lack of partner status.

This circuit has held that an interpretive regulation will be given effect if "it is a reasonable interpretation of the statute's plain language, its origin, and its purpose." *First Charter Financial Corp. v. United States*, 669 F.2d 1342, 1348 (9th Cir.1982). "A Treasury regulation 'is not invalid simply because the statutory language will support a contrary interpretation.' " *Id.* (quoting *United States v. Vogel Fertilizer Co.*, 455 U.S. 16, 26 * * * (1982)). As will be explained below, restricting carryover to partners is a reasonable interpretation in light of the wording of the statute and the legislative history.

Statutory language supports the Treasury Regulation. For example, the presence of the word "partner" at the beginning of subsection 704(d) strongly implies that a taxpayer must be a partner to take advantage of the carryover.

The Treasury Regulation's interpretation is also supported by a review of the legislative history of the statute. Section 704(d), as initially adopted by the House, allowed for deduction of the distributive share to the extent of adjusted basis. There was no provision for a carryover of the excess loss until the excess was repaid. H.R. Rep. No. 1337, 83d Cong., 2d Sess. 1 * * *. The bill the Senate passed, which was the version Congress enacted, provided for carryover. The accompanying Senate Report sums up both sentences of subsection 704(d) in a fashion that demonstrates the committee felt the subsection limited carryover to partners. It states:

> Your committee has revised subsection (d) of the House bill to provide that any loss in excess of the basis of a *partner's* partnership interest may be allowed as a deduction only at the end of the partnership year in which the loss is repaid, either directly, or out of future profits.

> Subsection (d), as amended, may be illustrated as follows. Assume that a partner has a basis of $50 for his interest, and his distributive share of partnership loss is $100. Under the subsection, the partner's distributive share of the loss would be limited to $50, thereby decreasing the basis of his interest to zero. The remaining $50 loss would not be recognized, unless the partner makes a further contribution of $50. If, however, the *partner* repays the $50 loss to the partnership *out of his share of partnership income for the following year*, then the additional $50 loss will be recognized at the end of the year in which such repayment is made.

S. Rep. No. 1622, 83d Cong., 2d Sess. 1 * * * (emphasis added).

Limiting carryover to those who are partners at the time of repayment, as Treas. Reg. § 1.704–1(d) does, effectuates congressional intent to allow deductions only to the extent of adjusted basis. When a partner repays the excess loss, it is, as the Senate Report notes, "a further contribution" to the partnership. The partner thereby increases his basis by an amount equal to the loss and reduces it to zero by taking the loss. Nor is the partnership element merely a formal distinction, since the partner repaying the excess loss increases his interest in the partnership and his exposure to loss. Sennett's position, in contrast, was that of a debtor with rights superior to those of partners.

Conclusion

Since Sennett was not a member of the partnership at the time he attempted to invoke the loss carryover provisions of section 704(d) by repaying his claimed share of the loss, he was not entitled to deduct a portion of PPP's 1967 and 1968 losses. The decision of the Tax Court rejecting the $109,061 deduction and setting taxpayer's long-term capital gain for the 1969 taxable year at $130,939 is affirmed.

[¶ 19,040]

Problems

1. Returning to the José-Katrina partnership in Problem 3 at ¶ 19,025, if in the following year the partnership derived no net income or loss but José made a cash contribution to the partnership of $10,000, what amount of loss would he be entitled to claim in that year and what would be the character of the loss?

2. Assume that José's original basis for his partnership interest was $5,000 because on the formation of the partnership he contributed property that had a basis of $5,000 and a value of $20,000. Would that alter the result reached in Problem 3 at ¶ 19,025?

3. Assume instead that José had contributed cash of only $5,000 to the partnership but had also delivered to the partnership his personal demand note for $15,000. Would that alter the result?

4. Assume instead that José had not delivered such a note but that the partnership had borrowed $30,000 from a bank following its formation. Would that alter the result? How does this situation differ economically from the facts of Problem 3?

[¶ 19,045]

2. SECTION 465 AT RISK LIMITATIONS

Section 465 was enacted to defend against certain tax shelters that created deductions on behalf of taxpayers beyond any economic resources which were at risk in the venture. The provisions of Section 465, which are complex and marked by a number of important restrictions, do not apply solely to investments through partnerships. However, the use of limited partnerships as vehicles for tax shelters was one of the primary targets of Section 465.

Partnerships have been used extensively as tax shelter devices, in large measure because the basis of a partner's interest in the partnership could be increased by an allocation of partnership liabilities for which the partner was not personally liable. This has permitted the flow-through of interest and depreciation deductions to a partner in excess of the partner's out-of-pocket investment and personal liability. These deductions have been applied to offset a partner's other income.

Section 465 attempts to remedy the tax shelter problem by requiring generally that the taxpayer's losses from an activity be allowed only to the extent of the aggregate amount which the taxpayer has "at risk" at the close of the taxable year. The amount at risk consists of the money

¶ 19,035

and other property contributed by the taxpayer to the activity plus amounts borrowed with respect to such activity for which the taxpayer is personally liable. § 465(b). Note that a partner's amount at risk in an activity conducted in the partnership form is *not* increased on account of a deficit capital account restoration provision in the partnership agreement where the deficit restoration obligation has not yet been triggered by a liquidation of the partner's interest. See Hubert Enterprises, Inc. v. Commissioner, 125 T.C. 72 (2005). As a result, Section 465 severely restricts the claiming of losses attributable to a nonrecourse borrowing. Losses disallowed by the at risk rules may be carried forward and claimed by a taxpayer in a future year in which the taxpayer has an amount at risk.

The rules of Section 465 apply only to individuals and to certain closely held C corporations. Thus, in the case of a partnership, the at risk rules are applied at the partner level, not the partnership level. Since the at risk rules are not applied at the partnership level, all of the partnership losses will pass through to the partners and may be used by those partners that are not subject to the Section 465 limitations. Before the 1986 Act, the most notable of several exclusions from the at risk requirements was "the holding of real property (other than mineral property)." The 1986 Act, however, applied the at risk rules to real estate investments placed in service after 1986, except for "qualified nonrecourse financing," which will be treated as an amount at risk. In general, a financing arrangement will be treated as qualified nonrecourse financing if the borrowing is with respect to holding real property and is obtained from a commercial lender or a governmental agency. § 465(b)(6). Loans from related persons may be treated as qualified nonrecourse financing under these provisions only "if the financing * * * is commercially reasonable and on substantially the same terms as loans involving unrelated persons." § 465(b)(6)(D)(ii).

Section 465 would seem to deny deductions even in circumstances where taxpayers have crossed the hurdles established by the regulations under Sections 704(b) and 752. Can you identify circumstances where this unhappy result (to the taxpayer) will occur?

[¶ 19,050]

3. PASSIVE ACTIVITY LOSS LIMITATIONS

Because the at risk rules of Section 465 had not adequately curtailed tax shelter activities, in 1986 Congress adopted the passive activity loss rules of Section 469. Like the at risk rules, the passive activity loss rules do not apply at the partnership level but rather bar the claiming of net losses from passive activities by individuals, trusts, or closely held C corporations, whether those losses are attributable to activities undertaken through a partnership or otherwise.

¶ 19,050

Section 469(c)(1) defines a "passive activity" as an activity involving the conduct of a trade or business in which the taxpayer does not "materially participate." Material participation is defined as involvement in the operations of the activity on a basis which is regular, continuous, and substantial. Accordingly, the characterization of a partnership's business and investment activities (and therefore the treatment of income and losses derived therefrom) for these purposes appears to depend on the involvement and responsibility of the partner in the conduct of those partnership activities.

The statute, however, provides several special rules concerning what constitutes a passive activity. For example, Section 469(c)(3)(A) provides that the term "passive activity" does "not include any working interest in any oil or gas property which the taxpayer holds directly or through an entity which does not limit the liability of the taxpayer with respect to such interest."

By contrast, Section 469(c)(2) provides that a rental activity is generally treated as a passive activity notwithstanding the taxpayer's material participation in the activity. However, this presumption does not apply to taxpayers in the real estate business who meet all of the requirements of Section 469(c)(7), including two principal requirements. First, more than half of the personal services performed by the taxpayer in trades or businesses for the taxable year must be performed in real property trades or businesses in which the taxpayer materially participates. Second, the taxpayer must perform more than 750 hours of services during the taxable year in real property trades or businesses in which the taxpayer materially participates. Moreover, there is a special rule in Section 469(i) allowing an individual to deduct up to $25,000 of passive activity loss per taxable year from rental real estate activities in which the individual actively participates. This $25,000 amount is subject to a phase-out provision, which reduces the $25,000 by 50 percent of the excess of the taxpayer's adjusted gross income over $100,000. § 469(i)(3).

The legislative history of these provisions clearly indicated, however, that the use of tax shelters in partnership form was a principal concern which led to the adoption of the new restrictions. Section 469(h)(2) provides that "no interest in a limited partnership as a limited partner shall be treated as an interest with respect to which a taxpayer materially participates." Similarly, Section 469(i)(6)(C) provides that "no interest as a limited partner in a limited partnership shall be treated as an interest with respect to which the taxpayer actively participates" for purposes of the special rule in Section 469(i). Accordingly, every loss attributable to limited partners will, unless a special exception is provided by statute or regulation, be treated as a passive loss subject to the Section 469 restrictions on deductibility.

¶ 19,050

Under Section 469, losses from passive activities may be deducted only against income from other passive activities. Thus, passive losses, which would include virtually all tax shelter losses, may not be used to offset income from active business activities, including salary income, or investment income. Losses disallowed may be carried forward and be deducted against passive income in future years or may be claimed upon the disposition of the taxpayer's interest in the passive activity. Section 469 has proven to be quite successful in eliminating the benefits of tax shelters designed to generate net tax losses.

[¶ 19,055]

4. JUDICIAL LIMITATIONS ON PARTNERSHIP LOSSES

The following case arose before Congress launched its serious statutory attacks on tax sheltering. However, the case remains significant for those taxpayers able to avoid the limitations of those provisions.

[¶ 19,060]

ESTATE OF FRANKLIN v. COMMISSIONER

United States Court of Appeals, Ninth Circuit, 1976.
544 F.2d 1045.

SNEED, CIRCUIT JUDGE:

This case involves another effort on the part of the Commissioner to curb the use of real estate tax shelters.[1] In this instance he seeks to disallow deductions for the taxpayers' distributive share of losses reported by a limited partnership with respect to its acquisition of a motel and related property. These "losses" have their origin in deductions for depreciation and interest claimed with respect to the motel and related property. These deductions were disallowed by the Commissioner on the ground either that the acquisition was a sham or that the entire acquisition transaction was in substance the purchase by the partnership of an option to acquire the motel and related property on January 15, 1979. The Tax Court held that the transaction constituted an option exercisable in 1979 and disallowed the taxpayers' deductions. * * * We

---

1. An early skirmish in this particular effort appears in *Manuel D. Mayerson*, 47 T.C. 340 (1966), which the Commissioner lost. The Commissioner attacked the substance of a nonrecourse sale, but based his attack on the nonrecourse and long-term nature of the purchase money note, without focusing on whether the sale was made at an unrealistically high price. In his acquiescence to *Mayerson*, * * * the Commissioner recognized that the fundamental issue in these cases generally will be whether the property has been "acquired" at an artificially high price, having little relation to its fair market value. "The Service emphasizes that its acquiescence in *Mayerson* is based on the particular facts in the case and will not be relied upon in the disposition of other cases except where it is clear that the property has been acquired at its fair market value in an arm's length transaction creating a bona fide purchase and a bona fide debt obligation." Rev. Rul. 69–77, 1969–1 Cum. Bull. 59.

affirm this disallowance although our approach differs somewhat from that of the Tax Court.

The interest and depreciation deductions were taken by Twenty-Fourth Property Associates (hereinafter referred to as Associates), a California limited partnership of which Charles T. Franklin and seven other doctors were the limited partners. The deductions flowed from the purported "purchase" by Associates of the Thunderbird Inn, an Arizona motel, from Wayne L. Romney and Joan E. Romney (hereinafter referred to as the Romneys) on November 15, 1968.

Under a document entitled "Sales Agreement," the Romneys agreed to "sell" the Thunderbird Inn to Associates for $1,224,000. The property would be paid for over a period of ten years, with interest on any unpaid balance of seven and one-half percent per annum. "Prepaid interest" in the amount of $75,000 was payable immediately; monthly principal and interest installments of $9,045.36 would be paid for approximately the first ten years, with Associates required to make a balloon payment at the end of the ten years of the difference between the remaining purchase price, forecast as $975,000, and any mortgages then outstanding against the property.

The purchase obligation of Associates to the Romneys was nonrecourse; the Romneys' only remedy in the event of default would be forfeiture of the partnership's interest. The sales agreement was recorded in the local county. A warranty deed was placed in an escrow account, along with a quitclaim deed from Associates to the Romneys, both documents to be delivered either to Associates upon full payment of the purchase price, or to the Romneys upon default.

The sale was combined with a leaseback of the property by Associates to the Romneys; Associates therefore never took physical possession. The lease payments were designed to approximate closely the principal and interest payments with the consequence that with the exception of the $75,000 prepaid interest payment no cash would cross between Associates and Romneys until the balloon payment. The lease was on a net basis; thus, the Romneys were responsible for all of the typical expenses of owning the motel property including all utility costs, taxes, assessments, rents, charges, and levies of "every name, nature and kind whatsoever." The Romneys also were to continue to be responsible for the first and second mortgages until the final purchase installment was made; the Romneys could, and indeed did, place additional mortgages on the property without the permission of Associates. Finally, the Romneys were allowed to propose new capital improvements which Associates would be required to either build themselves or allow the Romneys to construct with compensating modifications in rent or purchase price.

In holding that the transaction between Associates and the Romneys more nearly resembled an option than a sale, the Tax Court emphasized that Associates had the power at the end of ten years to walk away from

¶ 19,060

the transaction and merely lose its $75,000 "prepaid interest payment." It also pointed out that a *deed* was never recorded and that the "benefits and burdens of ownership" appeared to remain with the Romneys. Thus, the sale was combined with a leaseback in which no cash would pass; the Romneys remained responsible under the mortgages, which they could increase; and the Romneys could make capital improvements. The Tax Court further justified its "option" characterization by reference to the nonrecourse nature of the purchase money debt and the nice balance between the rental and purchase money payments.

Our emphasis is different from that of the Tax Court. We believe the characteristics set out above can exist in a situation in which the sale imposes upon the purchaser a genuine indebtedness within the meaning of section 167(a), * * * which will support both interest and depreciation deductions. They substantially so existed in *Hudspeth v. Commissioner*, 509 F.2d 1224 (9th Cir.1975) in which parents entered into sales-leaseback transactions with their children. The children paid for the property by executing nonnegotiable notes and mortgages equal to the fair market value of the property; state law proscribed deficiency judgments in case of default, limiting the parents' remedy to foreclosure of the property. The children had no funds with which to make mortgage payments; instead, the payments were offset in part by the rental payments, with the difference met by gifts from the parents to their children. Despite these characteristics this court held that there was a bona fide indebtedness on which the children, to the extent of the rental payments, could base interest deductions. *See also* * * * *Manuel D. Mayerson*, 47 T.C. 340 (1966).

In none of these cases, however, did the taxpayer fail to demonstrate that the purchase price was at least approximately equivalent to the fair market value of the property. Just such a failure occurred here. The Tax Court explicitly found that on the basis of the facts before it the value of the property could not be estimated. * * *[4] In our view this defect in the taxpayer's proof is fatal.

4. The Tax Court found that appellants had "not shown that the purported sales price of $1,224,000 (or any other price) had any relationship to the actual market value of the motel property...." * * *

Petitioners spent a substantial amount of time at trial attempting to establish that, whatever the actual market value of the property, Associates acted in the good faith *belief* that the market value of the property approximated the selling price. However, this evidence only goes to the issue of sham and does not supply substance to this transaction. "Save in those instances where the statute itself turns on intent, a matter so real as taxation must depend on objective realities, not on the varying subjective beliefs of individual taxpayers." *Lynch v. Commissioner*, 273 F. 2d 867, 872 (2d Cir. 1959). * * *

In oral argument it was suggested by the appellants that neither the Tax Court nor they recognized the importance of fair market value during the presentation of evidence and that this hampered the full and open development of this issue. However, upon an examination of the record, we are satisfied that the taxpayers recognized the importance of presenting objective evidence of the fair market value and were awarded ample opportunity to present their proof; appellants merely failed to present clear and admissible evidence that fair market value did indeed approximate the purchase

Reason supports our perception. An acquisition such as that of Associates if at a price approximately equal to the fair market value of the property under ordinary circumstances would rather quickly yield an equity in the property which the purchaser could not prudently abandon. This is the stuff of substance. It meshes with the form of the transaction and constitutes a sale.

No such meshing occurs when the purchase price exceeds a demonstrably reasonable estimate of the fair market value. Payments on the principal of the purchase price yield no equity so long as the unpaid balance of the purchase price exceeds the then existing fair market value. Under these circumstances the purchaser by abandoning the transaction can lose no more than a mere chance to acquire an equity in the future should the value of the acquired property increase. While this chance undoubtedly influenced the Tax Court's determination that the transaction before us constitutes an option, we need only point out that its existence fails to supply the substance necessary to justify treating the transaction as a sale *ab initio*. It is not necessary to the disposition of this case to decide the tax consequences of a transaction such as that before us if in a subsequent year the fair market value of the property increases to an extent that permits the purchaser to acquire an equity.[5]

Authority also supports our perception. It is fundamental that "depreciation is not predicated upon ownership of property *but rather upon an investment in property.* * * *." *Mayerson, supra* at 340. (italics added). No such investment exists when payments of the purchase price in accordance with the design of the parties yield no equity to the purchaser. * * * In the transaction before us and during the taxable years in question the purchase price payments by Associates have not been shown to constitute an investment in the property. Depreciation was properly disallowed. Only the Romneys had an investment in the property.

price. Such evidence of fair market value as was relied upon by the appellants, *viz.* two appraisals, one completed in 1968 and a second in 1971, even if fully admissible as evidence of the truth of the estimates of value appearing therein does not require us to set aside the Tax Court's finding. As the Tax Court found, the 1968 appraisal was "error-filled, sketchy" and "obviously suspect." * * * The 1971 appraisal had little relevancy as to 1968 values. On the other side, there existed cogent evidence indicating that the fair market value was substantially less than the purchase price. This evidence included (i) the Romney's purchase of the stock of two corporations, one of which wholly-owned the motel, for approximately $800,000 in the year preceding the "sale" to Associates ($660,000 of which was allocable to the sale property, according to Mr. Romney's estimate), and (ii) insurance policies on the property from 1967 through 1974 of only $583,200, $700,000, and $614,000. * * *

Given that it was the appellants' burden to present evidence showing that the purchase price did not exceed the fair market value and that he had a fair opportunity to do so, we see no reason to remand this case for further proceedings.

5. These consequences would include a determination of the proper basis of the acquired property at the date the increments to the purchaser's equity commenced.

Authority also supports disallowance of the interest deductions. This is said even though it has long been recognized that the absence of personal liability for the purchase money debt secured by a mortgage on the acquired property does not deprive the debt of its character as a bona fide debt obligation able to support an interest deduction. *Mayerson, supra* at 352. However, this is no longer true when it appears that the debt has economic significance only if the property substantially appreciates in value prior to the date at which a very large portion of the purchase price is to be discharged. Under these circumstances the purchaser has not secured "the use or forbearance of money." * * * Nor has the seller advanced money or forborne its use. * * * Prior to the date at which the balloon payment on the purchase price is required, and assuming no substantial increase in the fair market value of the property, the absence of personal liability on the debt reduces the transaction in economic terms to a mere chance that a genuine debt obligation may arise. This is not enough to justify an interest deduction. To justify the deduction the debt must exist; potential existence will not do. For debt to exist, the purchaser, in the absence of personal liability, must confront a situation in which it is presently reasonable from an economic point of view for him to make a capital investment in the amount of the unpaid purchase price. *See Mayerson, supra* at 352. Associates, during the taxable years in question, confronted no such situation. *Compare Crane v. Commissioner*, 331 U.S. 1, 11–12 * * * (1947).

Our focus on the relationship of the fair market value of the property to the unpaid purchase price should not be read as premised upon the belief that a sale is not a sale if the purchaser pays too much. Bad bargains from the buyer's point of view—as well as sensible bargains from buyer's, but exceptionally good from the seller's point of view—do not thereby cease to be sales. * * * We intend our holding and explanation thereof to be understood as limited to transactions substantially similar to that now before us.

AFFIRMED.

[¶ 19,065]

Notes

1. In *Estate of Franklin*, the Ninth Circuit, as a consequence of its finding that the nonrecourse debt was not genuine, disallowed completely the partners' depreciation deductions and interest deductions on the debt and did not allow any part of the nonrecourse debt to be included in the partnership's initial basis in the property for depreciation purposes. In Pleasant Summit Land Corp. v. Commissioner, 863 F.2d 263 (3d Cir.1988), cert. denied, 493 U.S. 901 (1989), the Third Circuit disagreed with the reasoning of *Estate of Franklin* and stated that while "a taxpayer holding property subject to a nonrecourse debt in excess of the market value of the property may have no incentive to pay off any

portion of the debt, * * * it is equally logical to recognize that the creditor holding the debt has no incentive to take back the property if the taxpayer offers to pay the debt up to the value of the property." 863 F.2d at 276. Thus, the court held that "it is appropriate to disregard only the portion of nonrecourse debt in excess of the fair market value of the property when it was acquired for purposes of calculations of the depreciation and interest deductions and to regard the nonrecourse debt as genuine indebtedness to the extent it is not disregarded." 863 F.2d at 276–77. Accordingly, if a nonrecourse debt of $1,000,000 is secured by depreciable property worth only $500,000, under the *Pleasant Summit* reasoning, only one half of the interest deductions and depreciation deductions would be disallowed.

Most courts, however, have rejected the *Pleasant Summit* reasoning and followed the *Estate of Franklin* decision. See, e.g., Lukens v. Commissioner, 945 F.2d 92 (5th Cir.1991); Lebowitz v. Commissioner, 917 F.2d 1314 (2d Cir.1990); Bergstrom v. United States, 37 Fed.Cl. 164 (1996). The *Estate of Franklin* view, thus, is the majority rule on this issue.

2.   As discussed above, until the passage of the 1986 Act, a prior version of Section 465(c)(3)(D) provided that the Section 465 at risk rules did not apply to the holding of real property. The application of the pre–1986 Act version of Section 465 would not, therefore, have eliminated the issue in *Franklin*. Does the current version of Section 465 wholly eliminate the *Estate of Franklin* problem? What about the restrictions on the deduction of passive activity losses in Section 469? Do they eliminate the *Estate of Franklin* problem?

Chapter 20

CHARACTERIZING TRANSAC-
TIONS BETWEEN PARTNERS
AND THE PARTNERSHIP

[¶ 20,000]

A. INTRODUCTION

One of the more difficult issues under Subchapter K is the proper characterization of transactions between a partner and the partnership. That difficulty is both conceptual and practical. On a conceptual level, the issue is whether a partner's transactions with the partnership are to be taxed under an aggregate or an entity approach. Stated differently, in taxing the transaction, will the partner be treated as acting in her capacity as partner or instead be treated as acting as a nonpartner third party? As is true elsewhere in Subchapter K, how that issue is resolved can have substantial income tax consequences to the parties and thus has important practical significance. Consider, for example, a partner who receives a payment as compensation for services rendered to the partnership. Under an entity approach, the payment would be treated as if it were made to a nonpartner third party service provider. Thus, the payment would be ordinary income to the partner and deductible by the partnership (and thus by the partners) even where the deduction produced an operating loss, subject of course to the normal capitalization rules of the Code. On the other hand, an aggregate approach generally would treat the payment as a portion of the partner's distributive share of partnership income, the character of which is determined by the nature of the partnership income, because the partner would be viewed as providing the services in her capacity as a partner and her distributive share in part is compensation for the partner services.

Before 1954, the case law was divided and somewhat muddled, with a majority of court decisions following the aggregate approach to characterizing transactions between a partnership and a partner and a minority following the entity approach. Initially, in the 1954 Code, Congress opted for flexibility and, in the original version of Section 707, gave partners wide latitude to select the characterization of their transactions. That very flexibility, however, created the administrative problem of attempting to characterize these payments and permitted the well-counseled to manipulate Section 707 for tax avoidance purposes. After 30 years of experience, Congress concluded that the flexibility of Section 707 had been abused and, in the Tax Reform Act of 1984, instructed the Treasury to draft regulations that would severely restrict the ability of the parties to select among possible tax consequences of their transactions.[1] Perhaps not surprisingly, those regulations have proven difficult to draft. The first installment of the regulations was not issued in final form until 1992. The second installment of the regulations was not issued even in proposed form until late 2004.

B. PAYMENTS FOR SERVICES AND THE USE OF PROPERTY

[¶ 20,005]

1. THE STATUTORY TRICHOTOMY

When a payment is made by the partnership to a partner as compensation for services or for the use of property, Section 707 creates three possible characterizations of the payment. The first issue that needs to be resolved in properly characterizing the payment under Section 707 is whether the partner-payee was acting in the capacity of partner or as a nonpartner third party in the transaction.

[¶ 20,010]

a. *The Entity Approach*

If the partner is deemed to have engaged in the transaction in a capacity other than as a partner, under Section 707(a)(1) the transaction will be taxed as a transaction with a nonpartner would be. When the payment is for services or for the use of property, that treatment requires that the payee partner be taxed on the salary or rent at ordinary income rates while the partnership will either deduct the payment or, if required by the generally applicable rules of the Code, capitalize that amount. The partnership deduction (or other tax benefit) must be allocated among the partners, including the payee partner, in accordance with their interests in this partnership outlay.

The timing of the reflection of the income and expense is determined by the cash or accrual accounting methods used by the partner and the

---

1. Sections 704(c)(1)(B) and 737, discussed in Chapter 22, represent further statutory retrenchment in this area. Moreover, the partnership anti-abuse rule in Reg. § 1.701–2, discussed at ¶ 16,085, further restricts the ability of taxpayers to manipulate Section 707 for tax avoidance purposes.

partnership, respectively. Formerly, by deferring a payment to a year subsequent to the year in which the payment was earned, an accrual method partnership might claim a deduction in a year earlier than the year in which a cash method partner was required to report the income. Today, however, that advantage of Section 707(a) payments has been eliminated. Under Section 267(e), the partnership is not allowed to accrue a deduction before the day on which the partner must include the payment in income. § 267(a)(2), (b), and (e).

The characterization of a Section 707(a) payment as if it were made to a nonpartner means that the payee partner may be treated as an employee of the partnership for certain other purposes of the Code (such as the various employee fringe benefit provisions). For example, in Armstrong v. Phinney, 394 F.2d 661 (5th Cir.1968), the court held that a partner could benefit from the Section 119 exclusion for meals and lodging provided to employees.

Section 707(a) may apply to payments from a partner to the partnership as well as to payments from the partnership. In addition, Section 707(a) may apply to loans of money to the partnership and to sales of property between the partner and the partnership, a matter considered below. Reg. § 1.707–1(a).

[¶ 20,015]

b. The Aggregate Approach

If Section 707(a) does not apply, then the payee partner generally will be treated as receiving a distributive share of partnership income and, upon payment, a partnership distribution taxed under Section 731. The character of the distributive share is determined by the nature of the partnership's income and thus may include capital gains or other tax-favored income. The amounts so allocated to the payee partner are simply excluded from the income of the other partners, and no mechanism exists that would require the capitalization of the payee partner's distributive share.

A partner is taxable on a distributive share of partnership income under the rules of Sections 702 and 706(a), which generally require the partner to include the share in income in the year for which the allocation is made and without regard to whether there is an actual distribution of that amount.

[¶ 20,020]

c. The Hybrid Approach

If a payment for services or the use of property falls outside of Section 707(a) but the amount owing is determined without regard to the income of the partnership (and thus is unlike a distributive share), the payment becomes a "guaranteed payment" under Section 707(c).

Guaranteed payments are treated as payments to nonpartners but only for the purposes of Sections 61 and 162. Thus, the payment will be taxed as ordinary income to the payee partner and will be either deducted or capitalized by the partnership, much like a Section 707(a) payment. However, for other purposes, a guaranteed payment is treated as a distributive share. Thus, the payment is not subject to withholding taxes and the payee is not treated as an employee for other purposes of the Code, such as payroll taxes and retirement or other employee benefits.

A guaranteed payment must be included in the income of the payee partner for the year in which the partnership deducted the payment. Reg. § 1.707–1(c). Thus, and by contrast to Section 707(a) payments, the partner must reflect the payment in accordance with the method of accounting used by the partnership. If the actual payment of a guaranteed payment is deferred by an accrual method partnership, even a cash method partner will be taxed on the payment before it is received, much like the taxation of a distributive share.

[¶ 20,025]

2. THE CONSEQUENCES OF CHARACTERIZATION

Under the simplest conditions, the income tax consequences of these three distinct characterizations may be identical. Consider the ABC partnership that earns net income for a year of $30,000, all of which is ordinary. The three partners have an equal interest in profits and losses except that a payment of $6,000 is made to A during the year in compensation for services. The consequences to the partners under each characterization would be as follows:

Section 707(a)

Partnership Income = $30,000 − 6,000 = $24,000

Partners' Income

	A	B	C
Distributive Share (before payment)....	$10,000	$10,000	$10,000
Deduction for Payment	(2,000)	(2,000)	(2,000)
Section 707(a) Payment	6,000		
Total	$14,000	$ 8,000	$ 8,000

Distributive Share

Partnership Income = $30,000

Partners' Income

	A	B	C
Distributive Share	$14,000	$ 8,000	$ 8,000

¶ 20,020

Guaranteed Payment

Partnership Income = $30,000 − 6,000 = $24,000

Partners' Income

	A	B	C
Distributive Share (before payment)....	$10,000	$10,000	$10,000
Deduction for Payment	(2,000)	(2,000)	(2,000)
Guaranteed Payment	6,000		
Total	$14,000	$ 8,000	$ 8,000

In practice, however, the consequences of the three possible characterizations will differ widely in a number of respects. The principal such differences, in addition to the timing differences described above, derive from the character of the payment to the payee and the application of the capitalization rules of the Code to the partnership. To illustrate, assume that one-half of the income of the partnership was a capital gain and that the payment to A was for services in connection with the sale of partnership interests and thus must be capitalized by the partnership.

Section 707(a)

Partnership Income

> Ordinary income = $15,000
> Capital gain = $15,000

Partners' Income

	A Ord. Inc.	A Cap. Gain	B Ord. Inc.	B Cap. Gain	C Ord. Inc.	C Cap. Gain
Distributive Share (before payment)						
Ordinary Income	$5,000		$5,000		$5,000	
Capital Gain		$5,000		$5,000		$5,000
Deduction for Payment	0		0		0	
Section 707(a) Payment	6,000					
Total	$11,000	$5,000	$5,000	$5,000	$5,000	$5,000

Distributive Share

Partnership Income

> Ordinary income = $15,000
> Capital gain = $15,000

¶ 20,025

Partners' Income

	A		B		C	
	Ord. Inc.	Cap. Gain	Ord. Inc.	Cap. Gain	Ord. Inc.	Cap. Gain
Distributive Share						
First $6,000	$3,000	$3,000				
$24,000 balance	4,000	4,000	4,000	4,000	4,000	4,000
Total	$7,000	$7,000	$4,000	$4,000	$4,000	$4,000

Guaranteed Payment

Partnership Income

Ordinary income = $15,000
Capital gain = $15,000

Partners' Income

	A		B		C	
	Ord. Inc.	Cap. Gain	Ord. Inc.	Cap. Gain	Ord. Inc.	Cap. Gain
Distributive Share (before payment)	$5,000	$5,000	$5,000	$5,000	$5,000	$5,000
Deduction for Payment	0		0		0	
Guaranteed Payment	6,000					
Total	$11,000	$5,000	$5,000	$5,000	$5,000	$5,000

A comparison of the results above should make it apparent why the IRS might resist characterizing the compensation of partners as a distributive share rather than as a Section 707(a) or 707(c) payment. To what extent would the objections of the IRS be well-founded?

3. DISTINGUISHING BETWEEN TYPES OF PAYMENTS

[¶ 20,030]

a. Section 707(a)

As mentioned above, under Section 707(a), the first step in determining the method of taxing transactions between partners and partnerships is to determine whether the partner was acting in the capacity of partner. The following case is one of the few that addresses this pivotal issue.

[¶ 20,035]

PRATT v. COMMISSIONER

United States Tax Court, 1975.
64 T.C. 203, aff'd in part, rev'd in part, 550 F.2d 1023 (5th Cir.1977).

SCOTT, JUDGE: * * *.

The issue for decision is whether management fees for services performed by petitioners for, and interest earned on, loans made by petitioners to two limited partnerships, of which petitioners were general partners, are deductible by the partnerships, and, if so, whether these amounts are includable in the income of petitioners who report income on the cash basis in the year accrued and deducted as business expenses by the partnerships which report on an accrual basis, even though petitioners did not receive payment of the amounts in the years of accrual by the partnerships. [The partners and partnerships all report income on the calendar year basis.]

* * *

Each of the limited partnership agreements contained the following provisions:

> Such General Partners shall contribute their time and managerial abilities to this partnership, and each such General Partner shall expend his best effort to the management of and for the purpose for which this partnership was formed. That for such managerial services and abilities contributed by the said General Partners, they shall receive a fee of five (5%) per cent of the Gross Base Lease Rentals of the said leases, and then the said General Partners shall receive ten (10%) per cent of all overrides and/or percentage rentals provided for in said leases as a fee for such managerial services.

* * *

> The General Partners shall give their personal services to the Partnership and shall devote thereto such time as they may deem necessary, without compensation other than the managerial fees as hereinbefore set out. Any of the Partners, General or Limited, may engage in other business ventures of every nature and description, independently or with others, * * *

The general partners had agreed that the management fees would be divided equally among the general partners who performed managerial services.

Petitioners contributed managerial services to the two partnerships and management fees were credited to accounts payable to them. These

¶ 20,035

fees were accrued and deducted annually by each of the partnerships
* * *.

* * *

[Petitioners also loaned funds at 6 percent interest to each of the limited partnerships.] In each of these years the partnership credited the interest * * * to the accounts payable to petitioners. Each of the partnerships accrued and deducted as interest expense in each of the years the amount of interest credited to petitioners to arrive at its net partnership income. The interest was not paid to petitioners and petitioners did not report their respective interest income on their respective income tax returns for the years 1967, 1968, and 1969.

* * *

Petitioners could have legally caused the two partnerships to pay the management fees and interest to them had they chosen to do so.

It was the intent of all the partners * * * that the management fees and interest were to be expenses to the partnerships.

* * *

Petitioners stated that without question each of the partnerships could accrue and deduct the amounts of management fees and interest credited to petitioners' accounts had the amount been due and credited to third parties rather than partners, * * * and that such third parties would not be required to include these amounts in their income if they reported their income on a cash basis until the amounts were actually or constructively received by them. Petitioners point out that the partnership statutes in subchapter K of the 1954 Code contain no provision analogous to section 267, * * * which disallows deduction to a corporation of accrued, but unpaid business expenses which are owed to certain related cash basis taxpayers unless payment is made within 2 1/2 months after the close of the corporation's taxable year. See sec. 267(a)(2). Petitioners further argue that even were the provisions of section 267 applicable to partnerships they would not qualify as related taxpayers under the provisions of section 267 since they did not own over a 50–percent interest in either partnership. Petitioners suggest that if we do not accept the position that the partnerships are entitled to deduct the accrued management fees and interest expense and petitioners are not for that reason required to include these amounts in their incomes for the years in which the partnerships take the deduction, then, rather than including the items in the incomes of each petitioner, the basis of each one's partnership interest should be decreased to the extent of the accrued fees and interest as provided in section 1.267(b)–1(b)(2), *example* (1), Income Tax Regs.[3]

---

3. Petitioners quote this example in their brief, underscoring the last sentence which states: "Furthermore, A's adjusted basis for his partnership interest must be

We agree with petitioners that section 267 is applicable only to corporations. [This is not true under current law. See §§ 267(a)(2), (b), and (e).] For that reason it has no application here, which disposes of petitioners' suggestion that we apply the provisions of section 1.267(b)–1(b)(2), Income Tax Regs., if we hold adversely to their primary contention in this case. However, the fact that section 267 does not apply to partnerships does not result in the conclusion that petitioners are entitled to treat the management fees and interest amounts as if they were not partners of the partnership accruing and deducting those items. The statutory scheme contained in subchapter K provides that in specified circumstances a partnership be treated as an entity separate from its members. See *Jackson E. Cagle, Jr.*, 63 T.C. 86, 94 (1974). However, a partnership is under subchapter K, as it was prior to the enactment of the 1954 Code, not a separate taxable entity subject to Federal income tax but the partners must include their distributive share of the partnership profits or losses in their income in computing their Federal income tax. Secs. 701 and 702. These provisions of subchapter K considered in the light of its legislative history show that whether the partnership is for a specific purpose considered as an aggregate of its partners or an entity is governed by the statutory provisions with the aggregate treatment prevailing as under prior law except where the statute provides otherwise. H.Rept. No. 1337, * * * 83d Cong., 2d Sess., pp. 65–68 (1954), and S.Rept. No. 1622, * * * 83d Cong., 2d Sess., pp. 89–94 (1954). Section 707(a) provides that, if a partner engages in a transaction with a partnership other than as a partner, the transaction shall, except as otherwise provided, be treated as occurring between the partnership and one who is not a partner, and section 707(c) provides that payments to a partner for services or the use of capital, if fixed without regard to the income of the partnership, are to be considered as made to one not a member of the partnership, but only for the purpose of including such amounts in the recipient's gross income and of allowing a business expense deduction to the partnership.

Petitioners contend that the management fees credited to them fall within the provisions of either [the prior law version of section] 707(a) or 707(c) and under either section are properly deductible by the partnership but not includable in their income for the years accrued by the partnership and credited to their accounts. Petitioners point to no provisions of the statute other than sections 707(a) and 707(c) under which management fees to partners for services to the partnership might be treated differently than such items were treated under the law prior to the enactment of the 1954 Code. Prior to the enactment of the provisions of section 707 of the 1954 Code, credits or payments to a partner for services, whether designated as fees or as salary, were not

decreased by the amount of his distributive share of such deductions. See section 705(a)(2)."

deductible by the partnership in computing the partnership income but were considered as part of the distributive share of partnership income of the partner to whom the credit or payment was made pursuant to the partnership agreement. *Frederick S. Klein*, 25 T.C. 1045 (1956). Therefore, if the management fees credited to petitioners do not qualify as transactions between a partner and a partnership, covered by section 707(a) or as guaranteed payments under section 707(c), they are part of the partners' distributive income from the partnership, includable in their distributive shares of profit or loss under section 706 for their taxable year in which the taxable year of the partnership ends and not proper deductions by the partnership in computing distributive partnership income.

In our view the management fees credited to petitioners were not "guaranteed payments" under section 707(c) even though, for reasons hereinafter discussed, we would not agree with petitioners' position that they were not required to include the amounts of the fees in their income for the years here in issue even if they were to be so considered.

Section 707(c) refers to payments "determined without regard to the income." The parties make some argument as to whether payments based on "gross rentals" as provided in the partnership agreements should be considered as payments based on "income." In our view there is no merit to such a distinction. The amounts of the management fees are based on a fixed percentage of the partnership's gross rentals which in turn constitute partnership income. To us it follows that the payments are not determined without regard to the income of the partnership as required by section 707(c) for a payment to a partner for services to be a "guaranteed payment."

Since we conclude that the management fees are not guaranteed payments under section 707(c), we must decide whether the provisions for such fees in the partnership agreement might be considered as a "transaction" engaged in by petitioners with the partnership in a capacity other than as a partner within the meaning of section 707(a). Initially, it might be noted that since section 707(c) deals specifically with continuing payments to a partner for services such as salary payments or the management fees here in issue, it is far from clear that such continuing payments were ever intended to come within the provisions of section 707(a). Section 707(a) refers to "transactions" between a partner and a partnership and is susceptible of being interpreted as covering only those services rendered by a partner to the partnership in a specific transaction as distinguished from continuing services of the partner which would either fall within section 707(c) or be, in effect, a partner's withdrawal of partnership profits. See *F. A. Falconer*, 40 T.C. 1011, 1015 (1963), where we stated as follows with respect to section 707(c):

Section 707(c) has no counterpart in the Internal Revenue Code of 1939. It initially appeared in the Internal Revenue Code of 1954. Since we have been unable to locate in our research any court decisions pertaining directly to the issue here presented, we approach the problem as one of first impression. * * * The legislative history of section 707(c) reveals that it was specifically intended to require ordinary income treatment to the partner receiving guaranteed salary payments and to give a deduction at the partnership level. [Footnote omitted.]

The touchstone for determining "guaranteed payments" is whether they are payable without regard to partnership income. And, in determining whether in a particular case an amount paid by a partnership to a partner is a "drawing" or a "guaranteed payment," the substance of the transaction, rather than its form, must govern. See sec. 1.707–1(a), Income Tax Regs. These are both factual matters to be judged from all the circumstances.

However, we need not decide whether a continuing payment to a partner for services was ever contemplated as being within the provisions of section 707(a).

Section 1.707–1(a) of the * * * Regulations with respect to a "partner not acting in capacity as partner" states that "In all cases, the substance of the transaction will govern rather than its form." Here, the record indicates that in managing the partnership petitioners were acting in their capacity as partners. They were performing basic duties of the partnership business pursuant to the partnership agreement. Although we have been unable to find cases arising under the 1954 Code concerning when a partner is acting within his capacity as such, a few cases arising under the provisions of the 1939 Code dealt with whether a payment to a partner should be considered as paid to him in a capacity other than as a partner. See *Leif J. Sverdrup,* 14 T.C. 859, 866 (1950); *Wegener v. Commissioner,* 119 F.2d 49 (5th Cir.1941), affg. 41 B.T.A. 857 (1940), cert. denied 314 U.S. 643 (1941). In *Wegener,* a joint venture was treated as a partnership for limited purposes, and the taxpayer-partner was found to be acting outside the scope of his partnership duties and in an individual capacity as an oil well drilling contractor, so that payments he received from the "partnership" for carrying out this separate and distinct activity were income to him individually as if he were an outsider. In the *Sverdrup* case, we recognized a payment to a taxpayer by a joint venture between a partnership of which the taxpayer was a member and a third party as compensation for work done on contracts being performed by the joint venture since "This sum was not a part of the income of the partnership of which he was a member, but was paid to him as an individual for services rendered to the joint venture."

Petitioners in this case were to receive the management fees for performing services within the normal scope of their duties as general

¶ 20,035

partners and pursuant to the partnership agreement. There is no indication that any one of the petitioners was engaged in a transaction with the partnership other than in his capacity as a partner. We therefore hold that the management fees were not deductible business expenses of the partnership under section 707(a). Instead, in our view the net partnership income is not reduced by these amounts and each petitioner's respective share of partnership profit is increased or loss is reduced by his credited portion of the management fees in each year here in issue. *Frederick S. Klein, supra.*

* * *

[¶ 20,040]

REVENUE RULING 81–301

1981–2 C.B. 144.

ISSUE

Is an allocation based on a percentage of gross income paid to an advisor general partner subject to section 707(a) * * *, under the circumstances described below?

FACTS

ABC is a partnership formed in accordance with the Uniform Limited Partnership Act of a state and is registered with the Securities and Exchange Commission as an open-end diversified management company pursuant to the Investment Company Act of 1940, as amended. Under the partnership agreement, *ABC*'s assets must consist only of municipal bonds, certain readily-marketable temporary investments, and cash. The agreement provides for two classes of general partners: (1) "director general partners" (directors) who are individuals and (2) one "adviser general partner" (adviser) that is a corporate investment adviser registered as such in accordance with the Investment Advisers Act of 1940 * * *.

Under the partnership agreement, the directors are compensated and have complete and exclusive control over the management, conduct, and operation of *ABC*'s activities. The directors are authorized to appoint agents and employees to perform duties on behalf of *ABC* and these agents may be, but need not be, general partners. Under the partnership agreement, the adviser has no rights, powers, or authority as a general partner, except that, subject to the supervision of the directors, the adviser is authorized to manage the investment and reinvestment of *ABC*'s assets. The adviser is responsible for payment of any expenses incurred in the performance of its investment advisory duties, including those for office space and facilities, equipment, and any of its personnel used to service and administer *ABC*'s investments. The adviser is not personally liable to the other partners for any losses incurred in the investment and reinvestment of *ABC*'s assets.

The nature of the adviser's services are substantially the same as those it renders as an independent contractor or agent for persons other than *ABC* and, under the agreement, the adviser is not precluded from engaging in such transactions with others.

Each general partner, including the adviser general partner, is required to contribute sufficient cash to *ABC* to acquire at least a one percent interest in the partnership. The agreement requires an allocation of 10 percent of *ABC*'s daily gross income to the adviser. After reduction by the compensation allocable to the directors and the adviser, *ABC*'s items of income, gain, loss, deduction, and credit are divided according to the percentage interests held by each partner.

The adviser's right to 10 percent of *ABC*'s daily gross income for managing *ABC*'s investment must be approved at least annually by a majority vote of the directors or a majority vote of all the partnership interests. Furthermore, the directors may remove the adviser as investment manager at any time on 60 days written notice to the adviser. The adviser can terminate its investment manager status by giving 60 days written notice to the directors. The agreement provides that the adviser will no longer be a general partner after removal or withdrawal as investment manager, but will continue to participate as a limited partner in the income, gains, losses, deductions, and credits attributable to the percentage interest that it holds.

Law and Analysis

Section 61(a)(1) * * * provides that, except as otherwise provided by law, gross income means all income from whatever source derived, including compensation for services, including fees, commissions, and similar items.

Section 702(a) * * * provides that in determining the income tax of a partner each partner must take into account separately such partner's distributive share of the partnership's items of income, gain, loss, deduction, or credit.

Section 707(a) * * * provides that if a partner engages in a transaction with a partnership other than as a member of such partnership, the transaction shall, except as otherwise provided in section 707, be considered as occurring between the partnership and one who is not a partner.

Section 1.707–1(a) of the * * * Regulations provides that a partner who engages in a transaction with a partnership other than in the capacity as a partner shall be treated as if not a member of the partnership with respect to such transaction. Such transactions include the rendering of services by the partner to the partnership. In all cases, the substance of the transaction will govern rather than its form.

Section 707(c) * * * provides that to the extent determined without regard to the income of the partnership, payments to a partner for services shall be considered as made to one who is not a member of the partnership, but only for purposes of section 61(a) and, subject to section 263, for purposes of section 162(a).

Although the adviser is identified in the agreement as an "adviser general partner," the adviser provides similar services to others as part of its regular trade or business, and its management of the investment and reinvestment of *ABC's* assets is supervised by the directors. Also it can be relieved of its duties and right to compensation at any time (with 60 days notice) by a majority vote of the directors. Further, the adviser pays its own expenses and is not personally liable to the other partners for any losses incurred in the investment and reinvestment of *ABC's* assets. The services performed by the adviser are, in substance, not performed in the capacity of a general partner, but are performed in the capacity of a person who is not a partner.

The 10 percent daily gross income allocation paid to the adviser is paid to the adviser in its capacity other than as a partner. Therefore, the gross income allocation is not a part of the adviser's distributive share of partnership income under section 702(a) * * * or a guaranteed payment under section 707(c).

HOLDING

The 10 percent daily gross income allocation paid to the adviser is subject to section 707(a) * * * and taxable to the adviser under section 61 as compensation for services rendered. The amount paid is deductible by the partnership under section 162, subject to the provisions of section 265.

Compare Rev. Rul. 81–300 [at ¶ 20,060], for an example of when section 707(c) * * * applies to services rendered by a partner for a partnership.

[¶ 20,045]

b.   *The 1984 Amendments*

Because of the language used by the courts in cases like *Pratt,* at ¶ 20,035, Congress became concerned that the line drawn by Section 707(c) and what is now Section 707(a)(1) between the aggregate and the entity approaches to payments to partners was inadequate. As discussed above, if a payment made to a partner would have to be capitalized by the partnership if it were made to a third party but the parties succeed in characterizing the payment as a distributive share, the remaining partners will be entitled to exclude that amount from their incomes and thus obtain tax benefits equivalent to a current deduction while the payee partner may be entitled to capital gains treatment for all or some portion of the payment. *Pratt* seemed to open just that possibility. Accordingly, in 1984, Congress amended Section 707 to add subparagraph (a)(2)(A). Under that provision, if a partner performs services for a partnership, the partnership allocates and distributes income to the partner, and "when viewed together" the services and the allocation and distribution "are properly characterized" as a transaction in which the partner is acting in a nonpartner capacity, then the payment will be treated as a Section 707(a) payment.

On its face, Section 707(a)(2)(A) appears to say very little. At most the provision reads like a codification of the step transaction doctrine that the courts could apply in the absence of the statutory provision. However, Section 707(a)(2) also authorizes the Treasury Department to issue regulations defining the scope of that provision, and, at the time of its enactment, there was every indication that the Treasury intended to issue extensive rules that would broadly recast payments to partners as Section 707(a) payments. While final regulations governing the transfer of property between a partner and the partnership were issued in 1992, regulations addressing the performance of services were not. Proposed regulations issued in late 2004, which govern the treatment of transactions between a partnership and its partners as disguised sales of partnership interests between the partners, also did not address the performance of services. Could one reason for the delay be that Section 707(a)(2)(A) is seriously misdirected? Is the capacity in which a partner is acting relevant to the tax avoidance that concerned Congress? That is, even if a partner is acting in the capacity of partner, should the partner's compensation be taxable at capital gains rates or should the capitalization rules of the Code be suspended? Would the amendment have made more sense as a modification of the definition of a guaranteed payment?

The committee reports to the 1984 legislation identified several factors that might be embodied in the regulations. See, e.g., Staff of Joint Comm. on Tax'n, 98th Cong., 2d Sess., General Explanation of the Revenue Provisions of the Deficit Reduction Act of 1984, at 227–28 (1984). Of these, the most important was said to be whether the partner bore an appreciable risk with respect to the amount of the payment. The more a partner bears the "entrepreneurial risk" of the fact and amount of payment, the more the payment resembles a share of profits rather than compensation to a nonventurer. Thus, short-term allocations of income that is virtually certain to be earned are more likely to be treated as Section 707(a) payments. Further insight into the Treasury's view of entrepreneurial risk may be gleaned from the regulations on property transfers, described below. The other factors identified in the legislative history were (a) whether partner status is transitory, (b) the temporal relationship of the services and the allocation and distribution, (c) whether partner status was obtained for tax reduction purposes and (d) whether the partner's continuing interest in profits is small relative to the allocation in question. Taking into account these factors, what results would be reached in *Pratt* (at ¶ 20,035) and in Rev. Rul. 81–301 (at ¶ 20,040)?

While the full scope of Section 707(a)(2)(A) remains unclear, it is reasonably clear that, in the taxation of the compensation of partners, Congress has attempted to materially shift the rules in favor of the entity approach.

[¶ 20,047]

Problems

1. LM Partnership recently constructed a large apartment complex, which can be reasonably expected to generate gross income of at least $1,000,000 per year indefinitely. Martha, an experienced construction engineer, performed services in connection with the construction of the partnership's apartment complex. She would normally charge a fee of $100,000 for her engineering services, but the partnership does not pay her any cash for the services. Instead, Martha contributes cash and her services in return for a ten-percent distributive share of partnership net income together with a special allocation of $25,000 of partnership gross income for the first four years after the apartment complex has been leased. Assume that the partnership reasonably anticipates that it will have sufficient cash flow to distribute $25,000 to Martha during each of those four years and that the partnership agreement contains a provision requiring it to do so. See Staff of Joint Comm. on Tax'n, 98th Cong., 2d Sess., General Explanation of the Revenue Provisions of the Deficit Reduction Act of 1984, at 229–30 (1984) (Example 1).

How should this arrangement be treated under the regulations to be issued by the Treasury and the IRS under Section 707(a)(2)(A)?

2. XY Partnership is organized to invest in securities. XY admits Sam, a stock broker, as one of its partners. Sam agrees to make stock trades for XY Partnership without charging his normal brokerage commissions. Sam contributes 51 percent of the partnership capital of XY and receives a 51–percent interest in XY's residual profits and losses. Sam also receives an allocation of gross income that is computed in a way that will approximate his foregone stock commissions. Assume that XY reasonably anticipates that it will have sufficient gross income to make this allocation. The partnership agreement has a provision giving Sam a priority distribution of cash from operations up to the amount of Sam's special gross income allocation. See Staff of Joint Comm. on Tax'n, 98th Cong., 2d Sess., General Explanation of the Revenue Provisions of the Deficit Reduction Act of 1984, at 230 (1984) (Example 2).

How should this arrangement be treated under the regulations to be issued by the Treasury and the IRS under Section 707(a)(2)(A)?

[¶ 20,050]

c. Section 707(c)

In *Pratt*, at ¶ 20,035, the court held that a payment could not be a "guaranteed payment" because it was determined with respect to partnership gross income, nor could it be a Section 707(a) payment because it was for services rendered as a partner. That seemed to leave the characterization of the payment as a distributive share even though it was not determined with respect to partnership taxable income. Under that analysis, a payment may be treated as a distributive share although it exceeds the net income of the partnership. Is that result reasonable?

[¶ 20,055]

GAINES v. COMMISSIONER

United States Tax Court, 1982.
T.C. Memo. 1982–731.

PARKER, JUDGE: * * *.

* * *

Issue No. 2: Guaranteed Payments

FINDINGS OF FACT

On their partnership returns for the year 1973, Lincoln Manor, Brookwood, Gaines Realty, and Riverbend each claimed as deductions certain guaranteed payments to partners. Gaines Properties was a general partner in each of these partnerships. The amounts claimed by the limited partnerships as deductions for guaranteed payments to partners and Gaines Properties' share of those guaranteed payments were as follows:

Partnership	Amount Claimed	Gaines Properties' Share
Lincoln Manner	$ 74,131.26	$ 23,750.00
Brookwood	109,666.00	88,666.00
Gaines Realty	125,881.00	91,106.00
Riverbend	216,087.00	104,168.50

Each of the four limited partnerships accrued and claimed deductions for these guaranteed payments. Lincoln Manor, Brookwood, Gaines Realty, and Riverbend all used the accrual method of accounting on their 1973 partnership returns. Gaines Properties reported its income using the cash receipts and disbursements method of accounting. Gaines Properties never received any of the guaranteed payments and did not report them in its income.

Respondent determined that Gaines Properties should have reported as income the guaranteed payments accrued and deducted by the four limited partnerships. Respondent, however, disallowed portions of the deductions that the four limited partnerships claimed for these guaranteed payments, on the ground that some portions were capital expenditures and not currently deductible.[14]

Issue No. 2: Guaranteed Payments

OPINION

Lincoln Manor, Brookwood, Riverbend, and Gaines Realty accrued and claimed deductions on their partnership returns for certain "guaranteed payments," including guaranteed payments to Gaines Properties, a general partner of each limited partnership. Gaines Properties never received these guaranteed payments. Respondent disallowed to the limited partnership portions of the claimed deductions for guaranteed payments, including some of the deductions attributable to the guaranteed payments to Gaines Properties. Notwithstanding this partial disallowance of deductions at the partnership level, respondent determined that the entire amount of the guaranteed payments to Gaines Properties, including the portion disallowed as deductions at the partnership level, should be included in Gaines Properties' income. Petitioners argue that the guaranteed payments that Gaines Properties did not receive, or at least such payments to the extent that the deductions therefor were disallowed at the partnership level, were not includable in Gaines Properties' income. Respondent argues that Gaines Properties' share of these guaranteed payments was includable in its income regardless of the fact that the deduction was partially disallowed at the partnership level and regardless of the fact that Gaines Properties, which used the cash method of accounting, never received the payments. We agree with respondent.

Section 707(c), as in effect in 1973, provided:

> To the extent determined without regard to the income of the partnership, payments to a partner for services or the use of capital shall be considered as made to one who is not a member of the partnership, but only for the purposes of section 61(a) (relating to gross income) and section 162(a) (relating to trade or business expenses).

This case does in fact involve "guaranteed payments" to a partner within the meaning of section 707(c) * * *. The fact that no actual payments were made does not affect the status of these transactions as section 707(c) guaranteed payments. "[D]espite the use of the word

---

14. It appears that respondent disallowed deductions of at least $40,000 of Gaines Properties' share of Brookwood's guaranteed payments, at least $24,000 of its share of Riverbend's guaranteed payments, and at least $22,641.56 of its share of Gaines Realty's guaranteed payments, a total disallowance of at least $86,641.56. In view of our holding on the guaranteed payments issue, we need not determine the exact amounts of Gaines Properties' share of guaranteed payments that respondent disallowed as deductions to the limited partnerships.

'payments' in both Section 707(c) and the Regulations thereunder, it is clear that no actual payment need be made; if the partnership deducts the amount under its method of accounting, the 'recipient' partner must include the amount in income in the appropriate year." W. McKee, W. Nelson and R. Whitmire, Federal Taxation of Partnerships and Partners (hereinafter McKee, Nelson and Whitmire), par. 13.03[2], pp. 13–16. See also *Pratt v. Commissioner*, 64 T.C. 203, 213 (1975), affd. on this point and revd. on other grounds 550 F. 2d 1023 (5th Cir.1977); sec. 1.707–1(c), Income Tax Regs. The parties stipulated that each of the four limited partnerships deducted "guaranteed payments." The partnership agreements of Brookwood and Gaines Realty expressly stated that certain payments to partners "shall constitute guaranteed payments within the meaning of section 707(c) of the Code." While the descriptions of such payments in the partnership agreements are not binding upon us * * *, the payments referred to in those two partnership agreements are clearly fixed sums determined without regard to partnership income. See sec. 707(c); sec. 1.707–1(c), Income Tax Regs. Furthermore, it is equally clear that the payments to the partners were for services in their capacities as partners.[15] Respondent in his notices of deficiency determined that these payments were in fact guaranteed payments under section 707(c), and petitioners did not dispute this determination. Accordingly, we hold that the payments here were guaranteed payments within the meaning of section 707(c).

The statutory language of section 707(c) addresses only the character of the guaranteed payments and not the timing. Respondent's regulation under section 707(c), sec. 1.707–1(c), Income Tax Regs., addresses the timing question, as follows:

> Payments made by a partnership to a partner for services or for the use of capital are considered as made to a person who is not a partner, to the extent such payments are determined without regard to the income of the partnership. However, a partner must include such payments as ordinary income for his taxable year within or with which ends the partnership taxable year in which the partnership deducted such payments as paid or accrued under its method of accounting. See § 706(a) and paragraph (a) of § 1.706–1.

As the regulation makes clear, the statutory authority for the timing of the inclusion of these guaranteed payments is section 706(a), which provides:

> In computing the taxable income of a partner for a taxable year, the inclusions required by section 702 and section 707(c) with respect to a partnership shall be based on the income, gain, loss, deduction, or

---

15. Transactions between a partner and his partnership when the partner is not acting in his capacity as a partner are governed by section 707(a), not section 707(c). W. McKee, W. Nelson, and R. Whitmire, Federal Taxation of Partnerships and Partners, par. 13.01[2]. See also *Pratt v. Commissioner*, 64 T.C. 203, 210–211 (1975), aff'd on this issue 550 F.2d 1023 (5th Cir. 1977).

credit of the partnership for any taxable year of the partnership ending within or with the taxable year of the partner.

The separate reference of section 707(c) guaranteed payments in the timing provisions of section 706(a) was explained by the Senate Report as simply—

> to make clear that payments made to a partner for services or for the use of capital are includible in his income at the same time as his distributive share of partnership income for the partnership year when the payments are made or accrued.... (S. Rept. No. 1622, * * * 83d Cong., 2d Sess. 385 (1954)).

In *Cagle v. Commissioner*, 63 T.C. 86 (1974), affd. 539 F. 2d 409 (5th Cir.1976), we held that includability and deductibility of guaranteed payments are two separate questions, and specifically that guaranteed payments are not automatically deductible simply by reason of their being included in the recipient's income. In *Cagle*, we stated 63 T.C. at 95:

> We think that all Congress meant was that guaranteed payments should be included in the recipient partner's income in the partnership taxable year ending with or within which the partner's taxable year ends and in which the tax accounting treatment of the transaction is determined at the partnership level. S. Rept. No. 1622, *supra* at pp. 94, 385, 387.

We believe our statement in *Cagle* is an accurate description of the Congressional intent. We have found nothing in the statutory language, regulations, or legislative history to indicate that includability in the recipient partner's income was intended to be dependent upon deductibility at the partnership level.

Petitioners seem to argue that there is a patent unfairness in taxing them on nonexistent income, namely income that they have neither received nor benefitted from (e.g. through a tax deduction at the partnership level). Their argument has a superficial appeal to it, but on closer analysis must fail. Except for certain very limited purposes, guaranteed payments are treated as part of the partner's distributive share of partnership income and loss. Sec. 1.707–1(c), Income Tax Regs. For timing purposes guaranteed payments are treated the same as distributive income and loss. Sec. 706(a); sec. 1.706–1(a) and sec. 1.707–1(c), Income Tax Regs. A partner's distributive share of partnership income is includable in his taxable income for any partnership year ending within or with the partner's taxable year. Sec. 706(a). As is the case with a partner's ordinary distributive share of partnership income and loss, any unfairness in taxing a partner on guaranteed payments that he neither receives nor benefits from results from the conduit theory of partnerships, and is a consequence of the taxpayer's choice to do the business in the partnership form.[16] We find no justification in the statute, regulations, or legislative history to permit these petitioners to recognize their income pro rata as deductions are allowed to the partnership. See also *Pratt v. Commissioner*, 64 T.C. 203, 213 (1975), affd. on this ground 550 F.2d 1023 (5th Cir.1977). We hold for respondent on the guaranteed payments issue.

* * *

[¶ 20,060]

REVENUE RULING 81–300

1981–2 C.B. 143.

Issue

Are the management fees paid to partners under the circumstances described below distributive shares of partnership income or guaranteed payments under section 707(c) * * *?

Facts

The taxpayers are the general partners in a limited partnership formed to purchase, develop and operate a shopping center. The partnership agreement specifies the taxpayers' shares of the profit and loss of the partnership. The general partners have a ten percent interest in each item of partnership income, gain, loss, deduction, or credit. In addition, the partnership agreement provides that the general partners must contribute their time, managerial abilities and best efforts to the partnership and that in return for their managerial services each will receive a fee of five percent of the gross rentals received by the partnership. These amounts will be paid to the general partners in all events.

Pursuant to the partnership agreement, the taxpayers carried out their duties as general partners and provided the management services required in the operation of the shopping centers. The management fee of five percent of gross rentals were reasonable in amount for the services rendered.

Law and Analysis

Section 707(a) * * * provides that if a partner engages in a transaction with a partnership other than in the capacity of a member of such partnership, the transaction shall, except as otherwise provided in this section, be considered as occurring between the partnership and one who is not a partner.

---

16. As part of a partner's distributive share of profit and loss, the guaranteed payments included in his income increase the partner's basis in his partnership interest. Sec. 705(a)(1) and (2).

¶ 20,060

Section 1.707–1(a) of the * * * Regulations provides that a partner who engages in a transaction with a partnership other than in the capacity of a partner shall be treated as if the partner were not a member of the partnership with respect to such transaction. The regulation's section further states that such transactions include the rendering of services by the partner to the partnership and that the substance of the transaction will govern rather than its form.

Section 707(c) * * * provides that to the extent determined without regard to the income of the partnership, payments to a partner for services, termed "guaranteed payments," shall be considered as made to one who is not a member of the partnership, but only for purposes of section 61(a) and, subject to section 263, for purposes of section 162(a).

In *Pratt v. Commissioner*, 64 T.C. 203 (1975), *aff'd in part, rev'd in part*, 550 F.2d 1023 (5th Cir.1977), under substantially similar facts to those in this case, both the United States Tax Court and the United States Court of Appeals for the Fifth Circuit held that management fees based on a percentage of gross rentals were not payments described in section 707(a) of the Code. The courts found that the terms of the partnership agreement and the actions of the parties indicated that the taxpayers were performing the management services in their capacities as general partners. *Compare* Rev. Rul. 81–301 [at ¶ 20,040].

When a determination is made that a partner is performing services in the capacity of a partner, a question arises whether the compensation for the services is a guaranteed payment under section 707(c) * * * or a distributive share of partnership income under section 704. In *Pratt*, the Tax Court held that the management fees were not guaranteed payments because they were computed as a percentage of gross rental income received by the partnership. The court reasoned that the gross rental income was "income" of the partnerships and, thus, the statutory test for a guaranteed payment, that it be "determined without regard to the income of the partnership," was not satisfied. On appeal, the taxpayer's argument was limited to the section 707(a) issue and the Fifth Circuit found it unnecessary to consider the application of section 707(c).

The legislative history of the Internal Revenue Code of 1954 indicates the intent of Congress to treat partnerships as entities in the case of certain transactions between partners and their partnerships. See S. Rep. No. 1622, 83d Cong., 2d Sess. 92 (1954). The Internal Revenue Code of 1939 and prior Revenue Acts contain no comparable provision and the courts had split on the question of whether a partner could deal with the partnership as an outsider. * * * This resulted both in uncertainty and in substantial computational problems when an aggregate theory was applied and the payment to a partner exceeded the partnership income. In such situations, the fixed salary was treated as a withdrawal of capital, taxable to the salaried partner to the extent that the withdrawal was made from the capital of other partners. * * * Terming such treatment as unrealistic and unnecessarily complicated, Congress enacted section 707(a) and (c) of the Code of 1954. Under section 707(a) the partnership is considered an unrelated entity for all purposes. Under section 707(c), the partnership is considered an unrelated entity for purposes of sections 61 and 162 to the extent that it makes a guaranteed payment for services or for the use of capital.

Although a fixed amount is the most obvious form of guaranteed payment, there are situations in which compensation for services is determined by reference to an item of gross income. For example, it is not unusual to compensate a manager of real property by reference to the gross rental income that the property produces. Such compensation arrangements do not give the provider of the service a share in the profits of the enterprise, but are designed to accurately measure the value of the services that are provided.

Thus, [in] view of the legislative history and the purpose underlying section 707 * * *, the term "guaranteed payment" should not be limited to fixed amounts. A payment for services determined by reference to an item of gross income will be a guaranteed payment if, on the basis of all of the facts and circumstances, the payment is compensation rather than a share of partnership profits. Relevant facts would include the reasonableness of the payment for the services provided and whether the method used to determine the amount of the payment would have been used to compensate an unrelated party for the services.

It is the position of the Internal Revenue Service that in *Pratt* the management fees were guaranteed payments under section 707(c) * * *. On the facts presented, the payments were not disguised distributions of partnership net income, but were compensation for services payable without regard to partnership income.

HOLDING

The management fees are guaranteed payments under section 707(c) * * *.

Compare Rev. Rul. 81–301 [at ¶ 20,040], for an example of when section 707(a) * * * applies to services rendered by a partner not acting in its capacity as a partner.

[¶ 20,065]

Notes

1. What would be the classification of these payments under the 1984 amendment to Section 707(a)?

2. The normal guaranteed payment is a fixed amount payable without regard to the income of the partnership. Classification becomes more difficult, however, if the payment is defined by reference both to

income and to a fixed amount. For example, assume that a partner is entitled to 30 percent of partnership net income but not less than $10,000. If the partnership derives net income of $60,000, the partner's distributive share is $18,000 and no part of that amount will be a guaranteed payment. However, if partnership net income is only $20,000, the partner will nevertheless receive $10,000. Of that, 30 percent of $20,000 or $6,000 will be a distributive share and $4,000 will be a guaranteed payment. Reg. § 1.707–1(c), Ex. 2. How will the tax consequences of these two potential characterizations differ for the partner and for the partnership?

3. In Rev. Rul. 91–26, 1991–1 C.B. 184, the IRS held that the value of a fringe benefit, such as accident and health insurance premiums, provided by a partnership to a partner for services rendered in her capacity as a partner, is a guaranteed payment if it is determined without regard to partnership income. Accordingly, the value of such fringe benefit is taxable as ordinary income to the recipient partner under Section 61(a), unless a Code section allowing exclusion of the fringe benefit "specifically provides that it applies to partners * * * because the benefit is treated as a distributive share of partnership income under [Reg. § 1.707–1(c)] for purposes of all Code sections other than sections 61(a) and 162, and a partner is treated as self-employed to the extent of his or her distributive share of income." Id. at 185. The partnership is entitled to deduct the cost of the fringe benefit provided to the partner as a guaranteed payment under Section 162 (subject to the capitalization requirements of Section 263). Rev. Rul. 91–26 alternatively allows the partnership to account for the accident and health insurance premiums as a reduction in distributions to the partner receiving the benefit. If this method of accounting for the accident and health premiums is followed by the partnership, the premiums are not deductible by the partnership and, hence, payment of the premiums does not affect the distributive shares of partnership income and deductions (and other payments). Regardless of which method of accounting for the premiums is used by the partnership, the recipient partner may partially deduct the cost of the premiums to the extent provided by Section 162(l).

4. Both Section 707(a) payments and Section 707(c) guaranteed payments are treated in a similar way for federal income tax purposes, except that Section 707(c) payments are treated as a distributive share of partnership income for purposes of determining when they are includible in the recipient partner's gross income (i.e., guaranteed payments are includible in the recipient partner's tax year in which, or with which, the partnership's tax year ends). Is this distinction justified from a tax policy point of view? In the light of the amendments to Section 707 made by the Tax Reform Act of 1984, should this distinction be eliminated? The Staff of the Joint Committee on Taxation recommended such a change in 1997. See Staff of Joint Comm. on Tax'n, 105th Cong., 1st Sess., Review

of Selected Entity Classification and Partnership Tax Issues, at 47 (1997).

[¶ 20,070]

Problems

In each of the following situations, how would the arrangement be characterized and how would the payee partner and the other partners be taxed?

1. Partner A, who is a CPA with a practice independent of the partnership, maintains the books and records of the partnership. The partnership pays Partner A $2,000 per year for this service without regard to partnership profits.

2. Assume in Problem 1 that instead of specifically paying Partner A for the record-keeping, the partnership agreed that her four-percent distributive share of partnership income would never be less than $2,000 (unless the total income of the partnership were less than $2,000).

3. In one year in Problem 1, Partner A also prepared the partnership information return. The partnership paid Partner A $1,000 for this service.

4. Partner B, a real estate agent, negotiated the acquisition of a building for the partnership. The partnership paid Partner B a standard commission of $10,000 for the services.

5. Assume in Problem 4 that the partnership did not pay a commission to Partner B but instead increased his distributive share of partnership income from four percent to six percent for a two-year period.

6. Partner C, who has no other business activity, is responsible for managing the portfolio investments of the partnership. For that service, five percent of partnership capital gains, less losses, on partnership trades, but not in excess of $300,000 annually, is allocated to Partner C.

7. Assume that the partnership in Problem 6 is an accrual method taxpayer while Partner C is on the cash method. If payment is not made to Partner C until the February following the year in which the services are performed, in which year must the transaction be reflected by the partnership and Partner C, assuming that the payment is governed by Section 707(a)? By Section 707(c)? Is a distributive share? How would Section 267(e) affect your analysis?

[¶ 20,075]

C. DISTINGUISHING BETWEEN SALES AND CURRENT DISTRIBUTIONS

The transfer of property from a partner to the partnership, or between two partners, can create characterization issues similar to those raised by the transfer of property from a shareholder to a corporation. Should the transfer be treated as a fully taxable sale, or is the transfer of the property entitled to nonrecognition under Section 721 and the payment to the partner a distribution, taxable (if at all) under Section 731? In the corporate area, this issue generally arises as taxpayers seek to avoid the carryover basis resulting from nonrecognition treatment under Section 351. In the partnership area, the positions of the parties are often reversed. The following cases illustrate the contexts in which the issue arises.

1. THE JUDICIAL BACKGROUND

[¶ 20,080]

OTEY v. COMMISSIONER

United States Tax Court, 1978.
70 T.C. 312, aff'd per curiam, 634 F.2d 1046 (6th Cir.1980).

HALL, JUDGE: * * * [T]he sole issue for decision is whether petitioners incurred net operating losses in 1972 which they are entitled to carry back to the years in issue. Resolution of this issue depends upon whether a payment by a partnership to petitioner (a partner) of $64,750 following petitioner's conveyance of real property to the partnership constitutes a sale of the property to the partnership or a contribution of the property to the partnership followed by a current distribution of $64,750, taxable, if at all, according to section 731.

* * *

Petitioner is in the real estate business. In 1963 petitioner inherited from his uncle real property at 2612–14 Heiman Street in Nashville ("Heiman Street property"). At the time petitioner acquired the property, its fair market value was $18,500. Petitioner took title to the property in joint tenancy with his wife.

The Heiman Street property was located in a blighted or red-line area of Nashville. There was in 1970 and 1971 a shortage of multi-family apartment complexes in Nashville. Sometime in 1971 petitioner and Marion Thurman ("Thurman"), a real estate developer, decided to develop the Heiman Street property into a moderate-income apartment complex, a type of complex for which there was then available FHA-insured financing. On October 19, 1971, petitioner and Thurman formed a partnership under the name of Court Villa Apartments for the purpose of building a 65–unit FHA-insured residential apartment on the Heiman Street property. Thurman, through his construction company, Marion Thurman Builders, was to build the rental units, and petitioner was to manage them.

On December 30, 1971, petitioner and his wife transferred title to the Heiman Street property to the partnership. At the time of the transfer, petitioner's basis in the property was $18,500 and the fair market value of the property was $65,000. This transfer was pursuant to the partnership agreement, which provided:

> John H. Otey, Jr. has contributed the land to the Joint Venture and the parties agree that the said Otey shall draw the first Sixty Five Thousand ($65,000) Dollars of loan proceeds from the Joint Venture as soon as the loan closes. Moreover the parties have together borrowed Fifteen Thousand ($15,000) Dollars from the Third National Bank and opened up a bank account in the name of COURT VILLA APARTMENTS. After the Sixty Five Thousand ($65,000) Dollars has been repaid to Otey, the parties agree that this loan shall be repaid to the Third National Bank.

The agreement further provided that profits and losses would be shared equally. Similarly, withdrawals and distributions of cash were to be made equally, except that as previously noted the first $65,000 of the loan proceeds was to be paid to petitioner.

On January 11, 1972, the partnership obtained a construction loan of $870,300 from the Third National Bank. Both petitioner and Thurman were jointly and severally liable for the loan. Pursuant to the partnership agreement, petitioner was paid $64,750 from the loan proceeds in four installments [during the year 1972].

Marion Thurman Builders built the apartment units for the partnership and was paid by the partnership from the construction loan. Thurman contributed no cash or other assets to the partnership. His contribution was his ability to get financing for the partnership through his good credit. During 1972, 1973 and 1974 the partnership reported losses on its Form 1065 (U.S. Partnership Return of Income).

The partners intended that petitioner's transfer of the Heiman Street property to the partnership was a contribution to the capital of the partnership and not a sale of the property to the partnership. On receipt of the $64,750 cash from the partnership in 1972, petitioner reduced his basis in his capital in the partnership. Since his basis, consisting of his $18,500 basis in the land contributed plus his liability for one-half of the borrowed construction money, exceeded the money distributed to him, he reported no income from this transaction on his 1972 return. Respondent, in his statutory notice, determined that petitioner realized gain from the "sale" of the Heiman Street property to the partnership in 1972 which should have been reported by petitioner on his 1972 return.

OPINION

Petitioner made a contribution of property worth $65,000 to a partnership of which he was a partner. Within a short period after such contribution, the partnership borrowed funds on which petitioner was jointly and severally liable, and pursuant to agreement distributed

$64,750 of such borrowed funds to petitioner, retaining petitioner's property. The distribution of $64,750 did not exceed petitioner's basis in the partnership. The question presented is whether petitioner in reality "sold" his property to the partnership. Respondent, relying on section 707, contends that he did.

Section 707 provides that "If a partner engages in a transaction with a partnership other than in his capacity as a member of such partnership, the transaction shall * * * be considered as occurring between the partnership and one who is not a partner," and section 1.707–1(a), Income Tax Regs., provides that "In all cases, the substance of the transaction will govern rather than its form."

Petitioner relies on section 721—"No gain or loss shall be recognized to a partnership or to any of its partners in the case of a contribution of property to the partnership in exchange for an interest in the partnership"—and section 731—"In the case of a distribution by a partnership to a partner * * * gain shall not be recognized to such partner, except to the extent any money distributed exceeds the adjusted basis of such partner's interest in the partnership immediately before the distribution."

We are cautioned, however, by section 1.731–1(c)(3), Income Tax Regs. as follows:

(3) If there is a contribution of property and within a short period:

(i) Before or after such contribution other property is distributed to the contributing partner and the contributed property is retained by the partnership, or

(ii) After such contribution the contributed property is distributed to another partner,

such distribution may not fall within the scope of section 731. Section 731 does not apply to a distribution of property, if, in fact, the distribution was made in order to effect an exchange of property between two or more of the partners or between the partnership and a partner. Such a transaction shall be treated as an exchange of property.

Thus we are faced with the question whether this transaction, which was in form a contribution of property to a partnership followed by a distribution of loan proceeds to the contributing partner, was in substance a sale of the property to the partnership by the partner.

Respondent relies on certain facts which he deems crucial. First, the property, which petitioner inherited from his uncle, was taken by petitioner in joint tenancy with his wife. To convey the property to the partnership, the wife had to join in the conveyance. Since she was not a partner, respondent concludes that at least as to half the real property there must have been a sale. However, since the wife apparently had only a legal title as joint tenant in the property, having contributed nothing to the acquisition, we find this argument unpersuasive. There is no indication in the record that petitioner intended to make a gift of half of the property to his wife and it appears the use of joint tenancy was merely intended as a convenient and customary means of reducing probate costs in the event of petitioner's death prior to his wife's death.

Second, respondent contends that because neither partner contributed any cash to the partnership, and all available cash had to come from borrowing, "it is unconvincing that a partner would withdraw funds for his personal use, when these funds were needed for the project." Respondent also points out that on the Department of Housing and Urban Development Mortgagor's Certificate of Actual Cost, the cost of the land was stated to be $64,750. Respondent then concludes that "considered as a whole, the facts portray a sale of property to the partnership." We disagree.

Subchapter K provides two possible methods of analyzing the transfer by petitioner of his Heiman Street property to the partnership, with sharply divergent tax consequences depending upon which analysis applies. Using the contribution approach, sections 721 and 731 treat a partner's contribution of property to his partnership as a non-recognizing transaction, producing neither gain nor loss, and withdrawals from the partnership are treated as reductions in basis rather than as taxable events. If these sections are applicable, we must sustain petitioner, because the immediate recourse borrowing by the partnership would (like most other borrowing) be a nontaxable event, increasing the basis of the parties in their partnership interest under sections 752(a) and 722. The distribution to a partner (petitioner) of part of the borrowed funds would not generate gain but would simply reduce pro tanto the distributee's basis under sections 731(a) and 733. This approach treats petitioner in a manner rather similar to a proprietor. Had petitioner simply decided to use his Heiman Street property as a proprietor for an FHA housing project and had he been able to obtain an FHA construction loan in an amount exceeding the cost of building the proposed structure, and diverted to his personal use $64,750 of the loan, no gain or loss would have been realized. This would be the case even had he been able to borrow the money only by agreeing to pay half his profits over to Thurman for acting as the co-signer on the loan. Sections 721 and 731 parallel this treatment.

But the Code also recognizes that in some cases partners do not deal with a partnership in their capacity as partners. Even though they are personally on both sides of a transaction with the partnership to the extent of their partnership interest, partners may on occasion deal with the partnership in a capacity other than as a partner and must treat such dealings with the partnership accordingly under section 707. This section, among other things, prevents use of the partnership provisions to render nontaxable what would in substance have been a taxable exchange if it had not been "run through" the partnership. For example, respondent has ruled that if two parties contribute to their partnership their equal interest in stock of two corporations and then liquidate the partnership with each taking all of the stock of one corporation, a taxable exchange has occurred. Rev. Rul. 57–200, 1957–1 C.B. 205. See sec. 1.731–1(c)(3)(ii), Income Tax Regs., *supra*. The partnership form may not be employed to evade the limitations in section 1031, and section 707 is the mechanism for guarding this gate.

Neither the Code and regulations nor the case law offers a great deal of guidance for distinguishing whether transactions such as those before us are to be characterized as a contribution (nontaxable) under section 721, as petitioner contends, or as a sale to the partnership other than in the capacity of a partner (taxable) under section 707, as respondent urges. It is at least clear from the above-quoted regulation under section 731 that application or not of section 707 is not always merely elective with a taxpayer. Occasions exist on which he must be thrust unwillingly within it in order for it to serve its above-described prophylactic function. And the regulations provide that "in all cases, the substance of the transaction will govern rather than its form." Sec. 1.707–1(a), Income Tax Regs.

The Code and regulations make more explicit the "ground rules" for the application of section 707 where performance of services by a partner for the partnership is involved as distinguished from a transfer of property. In the case of personal services, the characteristic which distinguishes ordinary distributions taxed under section 731 from "guaranteed payments" taxed under section 707 is the extent to which such payments are determined without regard to the income of the partnership. See sec. 707(c). Section 707 provides no explicit assistance analogous to section 707(c) where transfers of property are involved, but the guaranteed payments provision may provide useful indications of the drafters' intent. However, section 1.721–1(a), Income Tax Regs., does shed some light on the applicable rule. "Thus, if the transfer of property by the partner to the partnership results in the receipt by the partner of money or other consideration, including a promissory obligation fixed in amount and time for payment the transaction will be treated as a sale or exchange under section 707 rather than as a contribution under section 721."

A few cases have considered whether transfers of property by partners to partnerships were or were not taxable under section 707. In *Davis v. Commissioner*, * * * P–H Memo. T.C. par. 70,170 (1970), the taxpayer transferred land to a joint venture in which he was held to have been a partner. It was agreed that he would be paid for the property with the first available funds and in all events whether the project was a success or failure. In form the transaction was a sale. His 50–percent partner would have been required to put up half the purchase price if the venture could not pay. We there held the transaction was governed by section 707 and not by section 721. The taxpayer recognized long-term capital gain on the sale.

In *Oliver v. Commissioner,* * * * P–H Memo. T.C. par. 54,034 (1954), the taxpayer transferred 40 lots to a partnership in which he owned a 50 percent interest. In form, the transaction was a sale to the partnership, and the taxpayer claimed long-term capital gain treatment. However, the other partner contributed no capital, and the 40 lots constituted the sole capital of the partnership at its inception. We held that in substance the "sale" amounted to a capital contribution to the partnership. The taxpayer's capital account was credited with the taxpayer's cost of the lots and later with the excess of the FHA appraisal over that cost. There was no other partnership capital and had the taxpayer not contributed the lots there would have been no partnership business. While *Oliver* dealt with years preceding the 1954 Code, the issue decided therein of whether the transfer was in substance a sale or a capital contribution is essentially the same as whether section 707 or section 721 should apply under the law applicable to our case.

Willis argues that partners in effect may choose between coming within section 707 or section 721 by the choice they make between substantively identical methods of capitalizing their partnership. He does not construe the "substance of the transaction" language of regulation section 1.707–1(a) as authorizing respondent to recharacterize a transaction which is formally a sale, even if it is merely a method chosen for capitalizing the partnership, in the absence of an attempted end run around section 1031's limitations. 1 Willis, Partnership Taxation, §§ 14.08, 33.07 (2d ed., 1976).

Turning to the facts before us, a number of circumstances militate in favor of a conclusion that section 721 rather than section 707 should govern. In the first place, the form of the transaction was a contribution to capital rather than a sale, and there are no elements of artificiality in the form selected which should induce us to be particularly astute to look behind it. Without deciding here (because we need not decide) the extent to which Willis is correct in his view that partners may elect to capitalize their partnership under section 707 by employing the necessary formal steps, this partnership clearly did not so elect. Second, and most importantly, the capital in question (borrowed funds aside) was emplaced in the partnership at its inception and as a part of the very raison d'etre of the partnership. Without this transfer, the partnership would have had no assets and no business. It is therefore most difficult for us to agree with respondent that the transaction was between petitioner and the partnership *other than in petitioner's capacity as a partner*. See *Oliver v. Commissioner, supra.* Third, the capital in question was the *only* contributed capital of the partnership. To treat this as an outside transaction would require us to hold in effect that no non-borrowed capital was contributed at all. While such partnerships can of course exist, they are unusual and it would seem very strained to contend that this is such a case. The property had to be in the partnership to make the borrowing possible. Fourth, petitioner enjoyed here no guarantee by the partnership that he would be paid (and get to keep) the $65,000 in all events. Compare *Davis v. Commissioner, supra.* True, most of that sum was distributed to him almost at once out of borrowed funds, but he remained personally liable for the entire borrowing. Accordingly, we do not consider the transaction to be one described in section 1.721–1(a), Income Tax Regs., resulting "in the receipt by the partner of money or other consideration, including a promissory obligation fixed in amount and time for payment," and causing applicability of section 707. Provisions for preferential distributions out of borrowed funds to restore capital accounts to equality after non-pro rata partnership contributions do not necessarily demonstrate that the contributions were really sales. An important feature distinguishing transfers in the capacity of a partner from section 707 transactions is whether payment by the partnership to the partner is at the risk of the economic fortunes of the partnership. In the present case, whether partnership cash flow would ever suffice to repay the distributed $64,750 to the bank would depend on the partnership's subsequent economic fortunes. If they were adverse, petitioner could be called on to repay the loan himself. Fifth, the pattern here is a usual and customary partnership capitalization arrangement, under which the partner who put up a greater share of the capital than his share of the partnership profits is to receive preferential distributions to equalize capital accounts. The only unusual feature here is the immediate availability of the equalizing distribution out of excess borrowed funds. The normality of this general pattern would make it most unsettling were we to accept respondent's invitation to recharacterize the capitalization of the partnership on account thereof. Finally, although respondent relies briefly on the early cash distribution to petitioner of the excess borrowed funds, this payment does not constitute the kind of attempted end run around the limitations of section 1031 which the regulations properly seek to block. Were there no partnership at all, a taxpayer could borrow funds on the security of appreciated property and apply them to his personal use without triggering gain. Had the distributed funds come directly from the other partner, respondent's case would be stronger. While it may be argued that the funds have come indirectly from Thurman because his credit facilitated the loan, the fact is that the loan was a partnership loan on which the partnership was primarily liable, and both partners were jointly and severally liable for the full loan if the partnership defaulted. We do not view the factual pattern here as constituting a disguised sale of the land to Thurman or the partnership. For all the above reasons, we cannot sustain respondent in his attempted recharacterization of the transfer as a sale.

¶ 20,080

Respondent also places reliance upon the fact that the cost of the land transfer was stated to be $64,750 in cash in documents filed with the FHA. We do not view this as particularly significant since we do not believe that the implied "sale" label so affixed is determinative. To the extent labels are important, the label used in the partnership agreement itself is far more significant as an indication of the parties' true intent as between themselves.

We hold that the transfer constituted in substance what it was in form—the initial capitalization of the partnership. The early withdrawal of borrowed cash in an amount substantially equivalent to the agreed value of the contributed property reduced petitioner's basis in the partnership but did not create income to him. Secs. 731(a)(1) and 733.

* * *

[¶ 20,085]

JUPITER CORP. v. UNITED STATES

United States Court of Claims, 1983.
2 Cl.Ct. 58.

OPINION

LYDON, JUDGE:

In this case plaintiff seeks refunds of Federal income taxes it paid for calendar years ending December 31, 1965 and December 31, 1966, plus appropriate interest as provided by law. There are two issues to be resolved in this opinion: first, [issue omitted] and second, whether the IRS improperly classified amounts plaintiff received from a limited partnership in 1966 as the proceeds of a sale of a portion of plaintiff's partnership interest.

* * *

II.

The 1966 Partnership Distribution

The second issue litigated by the parties involved the characterization of a distribution of money plaintiff's wholly-owned subsidiary, Outer Drive East Corporation (hereinafter referred to as either ODE or plaintiff), received in 1966 from Randolph Outer Drive Venture (Venture), a limited partnership in which plaintiff was a general partner. Plaintiff received the distribution shortly after the Venture was reorganized to admit two new limited partners who contributed the money subsequently distributed to plaintiff. The IRS taxed this distribution as the proceeds of a sale of a portion of plaintiff's partnership interest under IRC section 741. Plaintiff, on the other hand, first stresses that section 721(a) provides, in essence, that upon the admission of new partners to a partnership, the existing partners will not recognize gain or loss for a contribution of property to the partnership in exchange for an interest in the partnership and then contends that the amount it received as a partner from the contribution to capital by the new limited partners to the partnership was a distribution of money by a partnership to a partner on which no gain is recognized under section 731(a), unless the amount distributed exceeds the partner's adjusted basis in his partnership interest. It is conceded that the amount distributed did not exceed the partner's adjusted basis in the partnership. The issues as framed by the briefs of the parties are whether there was a sale of a partnership interest and/or whether Treasury Regulation Section 1.731–1(c)[3] is applicable to the facts of this case.

As indicated previously, the decision of the Commissioner on this issue is endowed with a presumption of correctness which plaintiff has the burden to overcome. * * * After careful consideration of all the evidence, as discussed below, it is determined that plaintiff has successfully carried its burden of overcoming the Commissioner's presumption of correctness and has proved persuasively that the money it received from the Venture in 1966 was a bona fide distribution from the partnership which should not be taxed as the proceeds from a sale of a partnership interest. The Commissioner in reaching his determination did not have the benefit of a trial record on which to predicate his conclusion—a record which serves to rebut the presumption that would otherwise carry the day for him.

(1) Admission of New Limited Partners

The Venture was formed in 1962 to build a high-rise building containing 940 apartments, office and commercial spaces, a health club, 3 restaurants, a grocery store, and a parking garage (hereinafter referred to as the Project) on certain air rights which plaintiff had previously acquired over railroad yards on lakefront property in Chicago owned by the Illinois Central Railroad (IC). Plaintiff, through its wholly-owned subsidiary, ODE, owned a 77.5 percent general partnership interest in the Venture and was the Venture's only general partner. Empire Properties (Empire) owned the entire remaining 22.5 percent interest in the Venture as a limited partner. Empire was itself a limited partnership composed of members of a wealthy Chicago family which was active in real estate investments.

To finance the construction of the Project, the Venture obtained a $20,000,000 mortgage loan from a group of commercial banks. This loan was guaranteed by the Federal Housing Administration (FHA). Under the partnership agreement between plaintiff and Empire, plaintiff was obligated to supply all monies, in excess of the mortgage loan, needed to complete construction of the Project. Pursuant to this obligation, plaintiff loaned the Venture approximately $4,000,000, interest free, before construction of the Project was completed in 1964.

¶ 20,085

In 1965, the Venture began actively searching for investors interested in joining the Venture as limited partners. The Venture planned to use the amounts invested by new limited partners to repay the amounts it owed plaintiff. In the fall of 1965, plaintiff began negotiations with members of the Wilkow family, organizers of a Chicago based group of real estate investors, leading to the admittance of two limited partnerships formed by the Wilkow family into the Venture as limited partners. These two limited partnerships will be referred to collectively in this opinion as the Wilkow Group. The Wilkow Group was composed primarily of first and second generation elderly immigrants with relatively small individual amounts of money to invest. Most members of the Wilkow Group relied upon the income from their investments to supply them with daily needs. Therefore, these members required monthly or quarterly distributions of income from their investments. Since the principal invested often represented the entire savings of each member, the Wilkow Group only participated in investments which provided great security of principal and a secure, constant rate of return.

Plaintiff and the Wilkow Group approached the negotiations with the understanding that only a limited partnership interest would satisfy both the Wilkow Group's security needs and the plaintiff's objective to maintain management control of the Venture's operation. The Wilkow Group believed a general partnership interest involved too much risk. Plaintiff was seeking additional partners only as a means of raising capital; it did not want to give up any control of management to additional general partners.

Initial negotiations revealed that the Wilkow Group was willing to invest $4,650,000, if sufficiently secured, in exchange for a constant annual return rate of 8 percent. Subsequent negotiations established the characterization of this total investment. The Wilkow Group contributed $1,150,000 to the Venture's capital and loaned the Venture $3,500,000 at an interest rate of 4 percent. The loan amount calculated to replace plaintiff's loan to the Venture, which had been reduced to approximately $3,431,000 as of May 31, 1966, the date the Wilkow Group was admitted to the Venture.

The Venture was reorganized to admit the Wilkow Group as limited partners, with a total partnership interest of 20 percent, by the execution of an amended partnership agreement. This amended agreement provided the Wilkow Group with a secure rate of return equal to 8 percent on its total investment in the Venture. The amended agreement required the Venture to make the monthly payments of interest and principal on the Wilkow loan before making any distributions of partnership income to other partners. In a separate document, plaintiff and Empire pledged their respective partnership interests to the Wilkow Group as security for the loan. In addition, the amended agreement gave the Wilkow Group a cumulative right to monthly payments out of partnership income which was also given priority over distributions of

¶ 20,085

partnership income to other partners. The agreement provided that these cumulative monthly distributions would increase every 6 months so that the Wilkow Group's combined rate of return on the 4 percent loan and the contribution to capital would remain at 8 percent of the total amount originally invested as the repayment of loan principal decreased the amount of monthly interest the Wilkow Group received. These rights and preferences made the Wilkow Group's limited partnership interest unique from any partnership interest existing prior to the execution of the amended partnership agreement.

The original partnership agreement between plaintiff and Empire required the consent of both partners before any new partners could be admitted to the Venture. Plaintiff initially planned to proportionately reduce its interest and Empire's interest in the Venture by 20 percent to allow the admission of the Wilkow Group to the Venture as limited partners with a 20 percent partnership interest. However, Empire refused to consent to the admission of the Wilkow Group if the result was a reduction in Empire's proportioned partnership interest. The parties therefore structured the reorganization of the Venture so that plaintiff's partnership interest was decreased from 77.5 percent to 57.5 percent upon the admission of the Wilkow Group. Empire's partnership interest remained at 22.5 percent before and after the partnership reorganization.

Plaintiff was required to make other concessions to Empire to obtain its consent to the admission of the Wilkow Group to the Venture. The amended partnership agreement relieved Empire of any obligation to contribute the capital necessary to meet the monthly payments to the Wilkow Group in the event partnership income was insufficient. Plaintiff was required to loan Empire $500,000 which was to be repaid solely out of Empire's proceeds from the Venture.[19] This loan was, in effect, a prepayment of Empire's anticipated future distributions from the Venture. As a final inducement to Empire, plaintiff granted Empire the right to participate in any future development of air rights adjacent to the Project.

The Venture shortly distributed to plaintiff and Empire the total amount the Wilkow Group contributed and loaned to the partnership. Plaintiff received $3,431,000 as a repayment of its outstanding loan to the Venture. The remainder of the loan and the entire $1,150,000 contributed to capital were distributed to Empire and plaintiff in proportion to their pre-reorganization partnership interests. Empire paid to plaintiff the entire amount it received in this regard, approximately $258,000, as a partial repayment of the $500,000 loan which plaintiff made to induce Empire's consent. The Commissioner has not challenged the authenticity of the Wilkow Group's loan to the Venture or the

---

19. The validity of this loan was challenged by the Commissioner and upheld by the Tax Court in *Falkoff v. Commissioner*, 62 T.C. 200 (1974).

Venture's use of the money to repay plaintiff for plaintiff's outstanding loan to the Venture. In its deficiency notice, the Commissioner treated the admission of the Wilkow Group as a purchase and sale of 20 percent of plaintiff's partnership interest in exchange for cash in the amount of $1,150,000 (the Wilkow Group's contribution to capital) plus a reduction in plaintiff's liability in the amount of $3,847,124 (the Wilkow Group's assumption of 20 percent of the Venture's mortgage liability).

(2) Form and Substance of The Transaction

It has been noted that partnerships are "special animals" in the IRC. Code provisions "give partners great latitude in selecting the form the partnership takes and how economic benefits and burdens are allocated among the partners." * * * Indeed a principal objective of the partnership provision of the tax code "was to afford the parties 'flexibility' in allocating the tax burden of partnership transactions among themselves." McKee, Nelson & Whitmire, *Federal Taxation of Partnerships and Partners* ¶ 1.03 (1977), citing, H.R. Rep. No. 1337, 83d Cong., 2d Sess. 65 (1954). * * * The courts have generally recognized this legislative objective. For example, the Tax Court in *Foxman v. Commissioner*, 41 T.C. 535, 551 (1964) observed:

> One of the underlying philosophic objectives of the 1954 Code was to permit the partners themselves to determine their tax burdens *inter sese* to a certain extent, and this is what the committee reports meant when they referred to "flexibility."

The partnership provisions of the tax code achieve this flexibility by, *inter alia*, allowing a partner to choose either to sell his partnership interest to a third person or to reorganize the partnership to allow the admission of the third person as a new partner.

The major limitation on this flexibility has been expressed by the court in *Miller v. United States*, 181 Ct.Cl. 331, 344 n.3 (1967) as follows: "Of course, the true nature of the transaction and the intent of the parties must be ascertained. If a 'sale' is a sham it will be disregarded and a true sale is not made a liquidation by mere words." The parties must have intended to transfer the partnership interest in the form in which the transaction is cast. The legislative policy of flexibility does not permit a taxpayer to avoid the tax ramifications of a sale of a partnership interest simply by casting the intended sale in the form of a reorganization of the partnership. The form of the transaction must comport with the intentions of the parties. * * * In this case it is concluded that the form of the transaction was in keeping with its substance, and the intent of the parties.[20]

20. The Agreement for Admittance of Limited Partners to Limited Partnership contains the word "purchase" with reference to the acquired interest, but also contains the words, with reference to the cash payment by the Wilkow group to the partnership, "contribution to capital." These contractual formalisms and party emphasis thereon are not deemed relevant in this case. * * *

¶ **20,085**

The essential distinction between characterizing the transaction in the present case as either a sale of plaintiff's partnership interest or a contribution to the Venture followed by a distribution of capital to plaintiff is found in the intent of plaintiff, Empire, and the Wilkow Group. This determination of the parties' intent is a question of fact which is often difficult to resolve. * * *

In this case, the intent of the parties plays a crucial role in reaching a determination on the matter in issue. * * * The intent of plaintiff, Empire, and the Wilkow Group, as determined from an examination of the treatment of the transaction in the documents and the other surrounding circumstances was unquestionably to reorganize the Venture and admit the Wilkow Group as new limited partners, rather than to sell a portion of plaintiff's general partnership interest. The testimony, which is deemed credible, of all parties involved clearly supports this finding. This well established intent serves to carry the day for plaintiff. *See Otey v. Commissioner*, 70 T.C. 312 (1978), *affirmed*, 634 F.2d 1046, 1047–48 (6th Cir.1980) * * *. The parties did not choose the form of this transaction because it had better tax ramifications than an outright sale of plaintiff's partnership interest. The uncontradicted evidence in the record establishes that plaintiff would not have considered a sale, and the Wilkow Group would not have considered a purchase, of a portion of plaintiff's general partnership interest. The economic and legal prerequisites of plaintiff and the Wilkow Group mandated that the partnership be reorganized to admit the Wilkow Group as new limited partners.

The Wilkow Group's limited partnership interest did not exist prior to the reorganization of the Venture. This newly-created limited partnership interest gave the Wilkow Group cumulative rights to monthly distributions of income which had priority over all distributions to plaintiff and Empire. Neither plaintiff nor Empire owned such a cumulative priority right to the Venture's income prior to the reorganization. The Wilkow Group's limited partnership interest created by the reorganization carried no obligation to advance money needed by the Venture beyond the initial capital contribution and loan. Plaintiff's and Empire's partnership interests imposed such an obligation, to varying extents, both before and after the reorganization. Since the Wilkow Group's limited partnership interest was unique from the partnership interests owned by plaintiff and Empire, the Wilkow Group could not have purchased this interest directly from either partner.

Although plaintiff's general partnership interest was decreased from 77.5 percent to 57.5 percent after the reorganization, plaintiff remained in a more favorable position after the reorganization than it would have been if it had directly sold a 20 percent general partnership interest to the Wilkow Group. Both before and after the reorganization, plaintiff remained the sole general partner with 100 percent control of the management of the Venture. Plaintiff did not want to share its management responsibilities with any other partner. Furthermore, the Wilkow

Group was not interested in acquiring a share of the management responsibilities. The parties could not have accomplished these goals by a direct purchase and sale of a portion of plaintiff's general partnership interest.

A further indication that this transaction was intended, and could only have been accomplished, as a reorganization of the Venture is found in a change which the amended partnership agreement made in the rights and obligations of plaintiff and Empire vis-a-vis each other. Prior to the reorganization, plaintiff and Empire were both obligated to advance all amounts which the Venture required. After the reorganization, the amended partnership agreement expressly removed Empire's obligation to advance amounts which the Venture needed to make the monthly payments to the Wilkow Group. Of course, no change in the rights between plaintiff and Empire could have been accomplished solely by a direct sale of a portion of plaintiff's general partnership interest to the Wilkow Group.

The Wilkow Group's contribution to the Venture's capital was not treated as the proceeds of a sale of a portion of plaintiff's partnership interest. The amount was distributed to plaintiff and Empire according to their respective pre-reorganization partnership interests—77.5 percent to plaintiff and 22.5 percent to Empire. If plaintiff's intent was to sell a portion of its partnership interest to the Wilkow Group, it should have received 100 percent of the "purchase price" the Wilkow Group paid for the interest. The Commissioner's deficiency notice treats Empire's 22.5 percent portion of the Wilkow Group's capital contribution as having actually been received by plaintiff and subsequently paid over to Empire as an "expense of sale." The government's theory is that plaintiff was required to pay Empire 22.5 percent of the proceeds from the sale of the general partnership interest in exchange for Empire's consent to the transaction. There is no evidence in the record which even suggests that plaintiff received 100 percent of the Wilkow Group's contribution to capital and subsequently paid Empire a portion of these proceeds for its consent. Rather, the evidence establishes that the amounts contributed to capital was treated as partnership property and was distributed according to the provisions of the partnership agreement—77.5 percent to plaintiff and 22.5 percent to Empire.

The transaction involved in this case was not "a camouflaged sale of a partnership interest." *Cf. Crenshaw v. United States*, 450 F.2d 472, 476 (5th Cir.1971). The parties had legitimate business reasons for structuring the transaction as they did. In fact, the goals sought by the parties could not have been achieved by structuring the transaction as a sale of a portion of plaintiff's partnership interest. Plaintiff has carried its burden of proving that the transaction in issue was not a sale of its partnership interest. Plaintiff's proportionate share of the Wilkow Group's capital contribution was received as a distribution of partner-

¶ 20,085

ship property, rather than the proceeds of a sale as alleged by the Commissioner.

Section 731 provides the normal tax treatment of distributions from a partnership to a partner. Under this provision, the partner does not recognize gain when property (other than money) is distributed and does not recognize gain when money is distributed unless and only to the extent that the value of the money exceeds the partner's adjusted basis in his partnership interest. The statute contains two exceptions to the general rule of nonrecognition which arise when one of the following sections applies: section 736 (relating to payments to a retiring partner or deceased partner's successor in interest) or section 751 (relating to unrealized receivable and inventory items). The government does not contend that section 736 applies to the transaction in issue. Plaintiff admits that section 751 applies to require recognition of a small portion of the distribution, but plaintiff contends that section 731 operates to preclude any additional recognition of the gain it received from the distribution of the Wilkow Group's capital contribution.

(3) Treasury Regulation § 1.731–1(c)(3)

The government contends, as an alternative to its argument that the transaction in question was a camouflaged sale, that section 731 does not provide nonrecognition treatment to the distribution received by plaintiff because the parties wrongfully utilized the partnership entity to effect an exchange of property between them. In support of this claim, the government points to Treasury Regulation § 1.731–1(c)(3), which reads, in pertinent part, as follows:

> If there is a contribution of property to a partnership and within a short period:
>
> * * *
>
> (ii) After such contribution the contributed property is distributed to another partner,

such distribution may not fall within the scope of section 731. Section 731 does not apply to a distribution of property, if, in fact, the distribution was made in order to effect an exchange of property between two or more of the partners or between the partnership and a partner. Such a transaction shall be treated as an exchange of property.

This regulation provides an exception to section 731 only when the parties to a transaction, in fact, intended "to effect an exchange of property between two or more of the parties." Since it has already been determined that the plaintiff and the Wilkow Group neither intended a sale (or an exchange) of plaintiff's general partnership interest, nor, in fact, effected an exchange of such an interest, the government's reliance on this regulation to prevent the normal application of section 731 is misplaced.

¶ 20,085

This court reached the same conclusion in *Communications Satellite Corp. v. United States*, [223 Ct.Cl. 253 (1980)]. In that case, the court held that distributions to partners of amounts new partners paid for admission to the partnership were not proceeds from the sales of partnership interests. The court expressly rejected the government's contention that Treasury Regulation § 1.731–1(c)(3) removed the distributions from the normal nonrecognition treatment of section 731:

> This regulation does not automatically or necessarily require recognition of gain in every situation in which property contributed to a partnership is shortly thereafter distributed to one or more of the partners. The regulation states only that such distributions "may" not be within the scope of section 731. In applying the regulation, substance controls over form (see Treasury Regulation § 1.707–1(a) (1956)). To determine the substance of the transactions, we consider all of their aspects that shed any light upon their true character.

223 Ct.Cl. at 260 * * *. The court found sufficient evidence that the parties did not intend the substance of the transactions to be an exchange of partnership interests between established and incoming partners and therefore held that the regulation did not apply to prevent the normal section 731 nonrecognition treatment of the distributions to the established partners.

In the present case, as has previously been discussed, there is sufficient evidence that a sale or exchange of plaintiff's partnership interest for the Wilkow Group's cash was neither intended nor, in fact, effectuated. The regulation therefore does not apply. While the factual setting in *Communications Satellite Corp. v. United States, supra*, is different than that present in this case, a matter which defendant stresses, the thrust of the holding of that case is equally applicable here. In that case, as here, the facts supported a finding that the transactions in question did not constitute sales of a partnership interest and thus were outside the pale of Treasury Regulation § 1.731–1(c)(3).

The plaintiff's distribution of its proportionate share of the Wilkow Group's capital contribution should be taxed according to section 731 which provides nonrecognition treatment for the gain received which does not exceed plaintiff's basis in its partnership interest and which does not decrease plaintiff's interest in the Venture's "section 751 property." Such a holding gives due consideration to the intent of all parties to the transactions in question and to the flexibility underscoring the philosophic objectives of the partnership provisions of the IRC.

CONCLUSION OF LAW

In light of the findings and opinion, it is concluded that * * * plaintiff is entitled to recover a refund of taxes paid, together with interest thereon as provided by law, arising from the erroneous charac-

¶ **20,085**

terization by the IRS of the partnership distributions plaintiff received in 1966. * * *

[¶ 20,087]

Note

In Jacobson v. Commissioner, 96 T.C. 577 (1991), aff'd per curiam, 963 F.2d 218 (8th Cir.1992), a case arising before the effective date of the 1984 amendment of Section 707, a general partnership was formed by J and M. J transferred to the partnership appreciated property worth $15 million, but subject to liabilities of $7 million, in exchange for a 25–percent interest in the partnership while M transferred to the partnership cash of $6 million in exchange for a 75–percent interest. On the same day, the partnership transferred all $6 million of the cash to J, who reported the receipt as a distribution taxable under Section 731. The Tax Court recharacterized the transaction as a sale of a 75–percent interest in the property by J to M followed by a contribution by J and M of their interests in the property to the partnership in exchange for their partnership interests. Would it matter whether the property were viewed as sold to partner M or to the partnership?

[¶ 20,090]

2. THE 1992 REGULATIONS

In 1984, Congress responded to cases like *Otey* and *Jupiter* by enacting Section 707(a)(2)(B) to authorize regulations distinguishing between sales and contribution-distributions. Under that provision, if (1) there is a transfer of money or property both from a partner to the partnership and from the partnership to the contributing partner or to another partner and, (2) when viewed together, the transfers are properly characterized as a sale of the property, the transaction is to be treated as either a sale of the property between the partner and the partnership or between two partners and not as a contribution and distribution. In common with Section 707(a)(2)(A), that vague statutory language left much to be resolved by regulations.

In 1992, final regulations were issued that addressed the *Otey* problem of sales between partners and the partnership but generally did not address the *Jupiter* problem of indirect sales between partners. (Proposed regulations addressing indirect sales between partners were issued in late 2004 and are discussed at ¶ 20,095.) Under those final regulations, a contribution and a distribution are properly characterized as a sale if, when viewed together, the two events in substance amount to an exchange consisting of a transfer of property into the partnership in exchange for cash or other property transferred by the partnership, rather than a contribution to the partnership unrelated to the later distribution. Transfers to the partner will be treated as in exchange for the property if the transfer would not have been made but for the property transfer and the transfer to the partner is either made simultaneously with the property transfer or "is not dependent on the entrepreneurial risks of partnership operations." Reg. § 1.707–3(b)(1). In resolving both branches of that definition, the regulations apply a broad facts and circumstances test that alone would have produced a substantial amount of controversy. The regulations seek to minimize that controversy in two ways. First, the regulations list 10 factors, the presence of which "may tend to prove the existence of a sale." Reg. § 1.707–3(b)(2). For example, if the partner's right to receive a future transfer from the partnership is secured or guaranteed, that factor tends to indicate that the transfer from the partnership is not subject to an entrepreneurial risk and thus is the proceeds of a sale. Reg. § 1.707–3(b)(2)(iii).

Second, the regulations adopt a two-year presumption: If the partnership's transfer of property to a partner is made within two years of the partner's contribution of property to the partnership, the transactions are presumed to constitute a sale unless the facts and circumstances clearly show that the transfers do not constitute a sale, Reg. § 1.707–3(c)(1); if the transfers are separated by more than two years, they are presumed not to constitute a sale unless the facts and circumstances clearly show that the transfers constitute a sale, Reg. § 1.707–3(d). However, even partnership transfers to the partner that are thus presumed to constitute the proceeds of a sale will nevertheless be respected as distributions to the extent the transfers do not exceed the distribution to which the partner would have been entitled in the absence of the transfer of the property. Reg. § 1.707–3(f), Ex. 4.

The net effect of these rules seems to be that, if a partner receives a disproportionately large distribution from the partnership within two years of a transfer of property to the partnership and the partner had some assurance that the distribution would be made beyond mere anticipation of the success of the business, the IRS will probably treat the transaction as a sale and not as a contribution and distribution. If the amount treated as the proceeds of a sale is less than the value of the transferred property, the transaction is bifurcated, and, for the purpose of computing gain or loss, the partner must allocate the basis of the transferred property between the sale and contribution portions of the transaction. The sale portion of the transaction is treated as a sale for all purposes of the Code, including the installment sale and imputed interest rules. Reg. § 1.707–3(a)(2).

If the transfer to the partner is attributable to a borrowing by the partnership, the amount of the distribution that is treated as the proceeds of a sale is reduced by the partner's share of that liability. Reg. § 1.707–5(b)(1). To the extent of that continuing liability, the partner has not obtained a net consideration for the transfer. On the facts of *Otey*, for example, since Otey obtained a 50–percent interest in profits and losses, only one-half of the distribution of $64,750 to him (i.e., $32,375) would be treated as the proceeds of a sale (assuming that the

¶ 20,090

partnership borrowing was allocable to the distribution under the interest allocation rules of Temp. Reg. § 1.163–8T). Since one-half of Otey's basis in the transferred property was $9,250, Otey would have recognized a gain of $23,125 under the Section 707 regulations.

Payments to partners that constitute a mere return on invested capital are not payments in exchange for transferred property (or in exchange for the partner's interest in the partnership) even when those payments are insulated from entrepreneurial risk. To avoid treating such returns on capital as the proceeds of a sale, the regulations contain a series of safe harbor presumptions for identifying a return on partnership capital that override the more general definition of payments in exchange for transferred property. In general, a payment will be presumed to be a mere return on capital if the payment does not exceed a reasonable rate of return on the value of the partner's contribution to the partnership. Reg. § 1.707–4(a). Similarly, in general, a distribution to a partner that does not exceed the partner's share of the net cash flow from partnership operations is presumed not to be the proceeds of a sale of property. Reg. § 1.707–4(b).

Under general partnership tax principles, the assumption by the partnership of a partner's liability or the transfer of property subject to a liability is treated as a distribution of money to the partner to the extent that the liability transferred to the partnership exceeds the transferor-partner's share of the partnership liability. § 752(b) and (c). Accordingly, the transfer of encumbered property to a partnership or other assumption of a partner's liability in connection with a contribution of property might be viewed as a transfer of property to the partnership and a simultaneous transfer of money to the partner that would not have occurred but for the property transfer. Under such an approach, the transfer of encumbered property to a partnership automatically would be treated as a sale. The regulations, however, adopt a narrower approach. Reg. § 1.707–5(a).

Through a series of specific rules, the regulations seek to exclude from sale treatment transfers of property subject to liabilities incurred for business reasons and not in anticipation of the contribution of the property to the partnership. Thus, for example, if a liability encumbering the transferred property was incurred more than two years before the contribution, was incurred to acquire or improve the property, or was incurred in the ordinary course of a business transfer to the partnership, the assumption of the "qualified" liability is not treated as the proceeds of a sale. Reg. § 1.707–5(a)(6). If the liability is not excluded under one of these rules, the assumption of the liability (or the transfer of property subject to the liability) will be treated as the proceeds of a sale, unless the partner can "clearly establish" that the liability was not incurred in anticipation of the contribution. Reg. § 1.707–5(a)(7).[2]

2. Compare § 357(b), discussed at ¶¶ 2180 et seq.

¶ 20,090

If the assumption of the liability is treated as consideration received in a sale of the property, the amount of the liability that will be so treated is limited to the proportion of the liability from which the partner is relieved. Thus, the amount that will be treated as the proceeds of a sale is the full amount of the transferred liability less the contributing partner's share of that liability following the transfer. For example, if a partner transfers property worth $10,000 and having a basis of $1,000, but subject to a recourse liability incurred in anticipation of the contribution in the amount of $8,000, to a partnership in exchange for a 25–percent interest in profits and losses, only $6,000 of the liability will be treated as the taxable proceeds of a sale of the property. Thus, the partner would recognize a gain of $5,400 on the sale portion of the transaction, i.e., $6,000 minus $600 (the 10–percent portion of the basis in the property that is allocable to the sale portion).

The significance of these regulations to routine partnership transactions cannot be overemphasized. Partners may no longer safely assume that transfers of property to a partnership will constitute a nonrecognition transaction under Section 721 or that a distribution from a partnership in the years following a contribution will be free of tax under Section 731. All such transactions must now be reviewed by tax advisors for consistency with Section 707(a)(2)(B) and the regulations under that provision.[3]

[¶ 20,095]

3. THE 2004 PROPOSED REGULATIONS

In November 2004, proposed regulations were issued under Section 707(a)(2)(B) that, if and when finalized, will address the *Jupiter* problem of indirect sales between partners.[4] Under those proposed regulations, a contribution by one partner to a partnership (called the "purchasing partner" in the proposed regulations) and a distribution by the partnership to another partner (called the "selling partner" in these proposed regulations) would be treated as sale of the selling partner's partnership interest to the purchasing partner if, based on all the facts and circumstances, the partnership's distribution to the selling partner would not have been made but for the contribution to the partnership by the purchasing partner and, if the transfers are not made simultaneously, the later transfer "is not dependent on the entrepreneurial risks of partnership operations." Prop. Reg. § 1.707–7 (a)(1) and (b)(1). In resolving both branches of that definition, the proposed regulations would apply a broad facts and circumstances test. The proposed regulations list

3. Furthermore, as discussed in Chapter 22, Sections 704(c)(1)(B) and 737 also have a significant role to play in this area; and, as discussed in Chapter 16, the impact of the partnership anti-abuse rule in Reg. § 1.701–2 must be considered as well.

4. These proposed regulations have been widely criticized by practitioner-commentators and are likely to be substantially changed by the Treasury and the IRS before becoming final regulations.

10 factors, the presence of which "may tend to prove the existence of a sale." Prop. Reg. § 1.707–7(b)(2). For example, if the partner receiving the later transfer has a legally enforceable right to receive that later transfer or the right to receive the transfer is secured in any way, that factor tends to indicate that the transfer is not subject to an entrepreneurial risk and thus is the proceeds of a sale. Prop. Reg. § 1.707–7(b)(2)(ii).

The proposed regulations adopt a two-year presumption: If a purchasing partner makes a contribution to a partnership and the partnership distributes money or other property to a selling partner within a two-year period, regardless of the order of the transfers, the transfers are presumed to constitute a disguised sale of the selling partner's partnership interest to the purchasing partner unless the facts and circumstances clearly show that the transfers do not constitute a sale, Prop. Reg. § 1.707–7(c); if the transfers are separated by more than two years, they are presumed not to constitute a disguised sale unless the facts and circumstances clearly show that the transfers constitute a sale, Prop. Reg. § 1.707–7(d). However, even if the transfers are presumed to constitute a sale under this two-year rule, the proposed regulations provide that a distribution in liquidation of the selling partner's partnership interest will not be presumed to be a sale of the interest to the purchasing partner unless the facts clearly show that the liquidating distribution is part of a sale. Prop. Reg. § 1.707–7(e).

The proposed regulations have a safe harbor for transfers to and by service partnerships under which the rules in the proposed regulations would not apply to transfers of money (or marketable securities treated as money under Section 731(c)(1)) to and by a service partnership. Prop. Reg. § 1.707–7(g). This safe harbor recognizes "that partners frequently enter and exit service partnerships and, in most cases, those transactions are factually unrelated to each other and should not be treated as a disguised sale of a partnership interest." REG–149519–03, 2004–2 C.B. 1009, 1012.

These proposed regulations related to disguised sales of partnership interests would not apply to transfers incident to formation of a partnership. However, under certain circumstances, the rules in Reg. § 1.707–3(a), discussed above at ¶ 20,090, may apply to treat such transfers as disguised sales of property to the partnership. See Prop. Reg. § 1.707–7(a)(8).

The net effect of these proposed rules seems to be that, if one partner receives a disproportionately large distribution from the partnership within two years of a transfer of property to the partnership by another partner, regardless of which transaction takes place first, and the distributee partner had some assurance that the distribution would be made beyond mere anticipation of the success of the business, the IRS will probably treat the transaction as a sale, in whole or in part, of the

¶ 20,095

distributee partner's partnership interest to the contributing partner, and not as a contribution and distribution to which Sections 721 and 731 apply. Transfers that are treated as a sale of a partnership interest are treated as such a sale for all purposes of the Code, including the installment sale and imputed interest rules. Prop. Reg. § 1.707–7(a)(2)(i).

The proposed regulations provide that rules similar to those set forth in Reg. § 1.707–4, discussed above at ¶ 20,090, apply in determining the extent to which a transfer to a selling partner is treated as part of a sale of that partner's partnership interest to the purchasing partner. Prop. Reg. § 1.707–7(f). Thus, under those rules, payments to a partner that constitute a mere return on invested capital should not be treated as payments in exchange for the partner's interest in the partnership even when those payments are insulated from entrepreneurial risk. As discussed above, to avoid treating such returns on capital as the proceeds of a sale, Reg. § 1.707–4 contains a series of safe harbor presumptions for identifying a return on partnership capital that should override the more general definition of payments in exchange for the selling partner's partnership interest. In general, a payment to the selling partner is presumed to be a mere return on capital if the payment does not exceed a reasonable rate of return on the value of the selling partner's contribution to the partnership. Prop. Reg. § 1.707–7(f) and Reg. § 1.707–4(a). Similarly, in general, a distribution to a selling partner that does not exceed the partner's share of the net cash flow from partnership operations is presumed not to be the proceeds of a sale of that partner's partnership interest. Prop. Reg. § 1.707–7(f) and Reg. § 1.707–4(b).

The proposed regulations also contain rules for the treatment of liabilities. Under these rules, deemed contributions to and distributions from a partnership under Section 752 as a result of reallocations of partnership liabilities among partners are not treated as transfers of consideration. Prop. Reg. § 1.707–7(j)(1). If a partnership assumes a liability of a partner, the proposed regulations treat the partnership as transferring consideration to the partner to the extent that the amount of the liability exceeds the partner's share of the liability immediately after the partnership assumes it. Prop. Reg. § 1.707–7(j)(2). If a partner assumes a liability of the partnership, the proposed regulations treat the partner as transferring consideration to the partnership to the extent that the amount of the liability assumed exceeds the partner's share of the liability immediately before the partner assumed it. Prop. Reg. § 1.707–7(j)(3). The amount realized by a selling partner on the sale of that partner's partnership interest under these regulations includes any reduction in the selling partner's share of partnership liabilities treated as occurring on account of the sale. Prop. Reg. § 1.707–7(a)(4). However, unlike the regulations relating to disguised sales of property, discussed above at ¶ 20,090, these proposed regulations do not contain any special rules for so-called qualified liabilities.

¶ 20,095

Finally, the proposed regulations have rules regarding the timing of the sale of partnership interest. Under these rules, the sale of the partnership interest is treated as taking place on the date of the earliest of the transfers. See Prop. Reg. § 1.707–7(a)(2)(ii)(A). If the transfer by the partnership to the selling partner occurs before the transfer to the partnership by the purchasing partner, the proposed regulations treat the partners and the partnership as if, on the date of sale, the purchasing partner transferred to the partnership an obligation to deliver the purchasing partner's consideration in exchange for the consideration by the partnership to the selling partner, and then the purchasing partner transferred the selling partner's consideration to the selling partner in exchange for the selling partner's interest in the partnership. Prop. Reg. § 1.707–7(a)(2)(ii)(C). If the transfer by the partnership to the selling partner occurs after the transfer to the partnership by the purchasing partner, the proposed regulations treat the partners and the partnership as if, on the date of sale, the purchasing partner transferred to the partnership the purchasing partner's consideration in exchange for an obligation of the partnership to deliver the selling partner's consideration, and then the purchasing partner transferred that obligation to the selling partner in exchange for the selling partner's interest in the partnership. Prop. Reg. § 1.707–7(a)(2)(ii)(D).

[¶ 20,100]

Problems

1. Partner D transfers appreciated property worth $60,000 to the partnership in exchange for a 25–percent interest in partnership profits, losses, and capital. During the year, the partnership earns net income from operations of $40,000, which it distributes pro rata to the partners. What are the tax consequences of this transaction to Partner D?

2. Assume that in Problem 1, the partnership agreement had provided that, in the three years following Partner D's contribution, the first $20,000 of partnership distributions would be made to Partner D and all other distributions would be in proportion to the capital accounts of the partners. If there were no other agreement concerning the distribution to Partner D, would the transaction be treated as a sale? What of the distribution in the third year?

3. Rudi transfers Whiteacre, a highly appreciated piece of real estate, to a partnership that holds several other parcels of real property for investment in exchange for a 20–percent interest in the partnership. Fifteen months later, Whiteacre is distributed to a second partner in complete liquidation of that partner's interest. How would this transaction be treated under the 2004 proposed regulations? Should it matter if the liquidating distribution occurs more than seven years after Rudi's contribution?[5]

---

5. After you have studied Section 704(c)(1)(B), at ¶ 22,090, consider how that provision would apply here.

[¶ 20,105]

D. LIMITATIONS ON CERTAIN SALES

Consistent with the policy reflected in other Code provisions, two limitations are imposed upon the entity concept with respect to transactions between a partner and the partnership. The first limitation, in Section 707(b)(1), disallows certain losses upon the sale or exchange of property between a partner and the partnership. If a partner owns directly or indirectly a larger than 50 percent interest in capital or profits of the partnership, the loss will not be deductible. The same provision applies to disallow a loss in the case of a sale or exchange of property between two partnerships in which the same partners own more than 50 percent of the capital interests or profit interests. This limitation is consistent with Section 267(a)(1), which disallows losses upon sales of property between related taxpayers as defined therein, including transactions between a corporation and a shareholder who holds more than 50 percent of the corporation's outstanding stock.

The second limitation relates to the character of the gain from the sale of property which, in the hands of the transferee, is other than a capital asset. Section 707(b)(2) provides that if the sale is between a partnership and a partner owning a larger than 50 percent interest in the capital or profits of the partnership, the gain is taxed as ordinary income. The same rule applies to the gain upon a sale between two partnerships in which the same partners hold more than 50 percent of the capital interests or profit interests. Compare this provision with Section 1239, which treats as ordinary income gain from the sale of depreciable property between certain related parties, including an individual and a partnership in which the partner holds a greater than 50 percent interest. Section 707(b)(2) is much broader in scope, in that it is not limited to depreciable property but applies to any property which is not a capital asset as determined by its character in the hands of the purchaser.

In determining ownership under the foregoing provisions, Section 707(b)(3) provides that the rules of constructive ownership under Section 267(c) other than paragraph (3) shall be applicable.[6] This is particularly important in the case of a partnership involving family members. For example, in a mother-and-son partnership, losses and gains with respect to sales and exchanges between the partners and the partnership will invariably fall within the scope of the foregoing limitations. It should be added that, as to disallowed losses, the relief provisions of Section 267(d) are made applicable by Section 707(b)(1). Accordingly, the transferee

---

6. Note that Section 1239 also adopts the constructive ownership rules of Section 267(c) other than paragraph (3) thereof.

partner's or partnership's gain on a later sale of the property is not taxed to the extent of the transferor's disallowed loss.

[¶ 20,110]

Note

The IRS has ruled that if a loss on the sale of property between related partnerships is disallowed under Section 707(b)(1), the partners' bases in their partnership interests in the selling partnership are decreased under Section 705(a)(2) to reflect the disallowed loss. Rev. Rul. 96–10, 1996–1 C.B. 138. The IRS reasoned:

> Reducing the partners' bases in their partnership interests by their respective shares of the partnership's * * * [disallowed] loss preserves the intended detriment of not allowing losses from sales or exchanges between partnerships and related persons to be deducted. If the partners' bases in their partnership interests were not reduced by the amount of the partnership's disallowed loss, the partners could subsequently recognize this loss (or a reduced gain), for example, upon a disposition of their partnership interests.

1996–1 C.B. at 139.

In Rev. Rul. 96–10, the IRS also ruled that to the extent that gain from a subsequent sale of the property by the transferee partnership is not taxed by reason of Sections 707(b)(1) and 267(d), the partners' bases in their interests in the transferee partnership are increased under Section 705(a)(1) to reflect that nontaxable gain. The IRS explained the logic of that result, as follows:

> Increasing the partner[s'] bases in their partnership interests by their respective shares of the unrecognized gain on the sale of [the property] preserves the intended benefit of §§ 707(b)(1) and 267(d). If the partners' bases in their partnership interests were not increased by the amount of the partnership's unrecognized gain, the partners could subsequently recognize this gain (or a reduced loss), for example, upon a disposition of their partnership interests.

1996–1 C.B. at 139–40.

[¶ 20,115]

Problems

1. Susan owns a 55–percent interest in the L–M Partnership and a 60–percent interest in the X–Y Partnership. The other 45 percent of the L–M Partnership interests and 40 percent of the X–Y Partnership interests are owned by different parties that are unrelated to Susan or each other. Susan's adjusted basis in the L–M Partnership interest is $20,000 and her adjusted basis in the X–Y Partnership interest is $15,000. During the current year, the L–M Partnership sells a piece of unimproved land, in which the partnership has an adjusted basis of

$30,000, to the X–Y Partnership for $20,000 cash (the then fair market value of the property). Both partnerships break even from business operations during the year. What are the federal income tax consequences to Susan, the L–M Partnership, and the X–Y Partnership on account of this sale?

2.   Three years after the sale described in Problem 1, the X–Y Partnership sells the land to an unrelated purchaser for $35,000, its then fair market value. Susan's adjusted basis in her 60–percent X–Y Partnership interest at the time is $25,000. The X–Y Partnership breaks even from business operations during the year. What are the federal income tax consequences to Susan and the X–Y Partnership on account of this sale?

Chapter 21

SALE OF A PARTNERSHIP INTEREST

[¶ 21,000]

A. INTRODUCTION

The sale and purchase of a partnership interest most sharply illustrates the intertwining of the aggregate and the entity views of a partnership under Subchapter K. Under the familiar entity approach, the seller of an interest would be treated as selling a capital asset—the partnership interest—that was separate from the underlying assets of the partnership and would be taxed in the same manner as the seller of corporate stock. The sale would have no effect on the remaining partners; the tax basis of the partnership assets would not be adjusted to reflect the amount paid for the interest.

In general, this entity approach could be unduly favorable to sellers and unduly harsh to purchasers. Sellers would be able to convert their share of the potential ordinary income of the partnership into a capital gain on the sale of the interest. Even more inappropriately, sellers might exploit the liberal nonrecognition rules governing the transfer of property to partnerships by contributing ordinary income assets to the partnership in contemplation of a sale of the partnership interest at a profit that reflected the appreciation in the contributed assets. Purchasers, on the other hand, would be taxable on income recognized upon a subsequent sale of partnership properties although, in substance, the interest in those properties would have been purchased for fair market value when the interest in the partnership was acquired.

Under an aggregate approach, a partnership interest would be viewed as consisting of a fractional interest in each asset of the partnership. Thus, a seller of an interest in the partnership would be regarded as transferring an interest in each partnership asset. The purchase price would be allocated over all such assets and the character of the resulting gains and losses would be determined by the character of the individual

1052

assets. Following a study of this question, the American Law Institute proposed that Subchapter K be amended to adopt just such a "full fragmentation" approach. See Federal Income Tax Project: Subchapter K: Proposals on the Taxation of Partners 22–46 (A.L.I. 1984). By the same token, the purchaser would be treated as purchasing an interest in each of the partnership assets and would obtain a tax basis for that interest equal to the amount of the purchase price allocated to the asset concerned. As a result, the purchaser's share of the "inside" basis for the partnership assets would exactly equal the "outside" basis for the partnership interest but would differ from the inside basis in the partnership assets held by the other partners. The aggregate approach imposes a far more accurate tax burden on both the seller and the purchaser of a partnership interest than does the entity approach but only at a great cost in complexity. Before the dawning of the computer age, the complexity of computing partnership income under the aggregate view made that approach unthinkable in all but the simplest partnerships.

The existing Code does not rigorously adopt either an entity or an aggregate approach to sales of partnership interests. Rather, elements of both approaches are woven together by a series of provisions that are sometimes elective and sometimes mandatory and never quite produce exactly the right result under either approach. As you examine the following materials, think about how the treatment of sales of partnership interests might be changed to produce either a more precise tax result or a simpler result, or, if it is not asking too much, both.

[¶ 21,005]

B. TREATMENT OF THE SELLER—
IN GENERAL

Section 741 appears to adopt an entity approach to the taxation of the seller by providing that the gain or loss recognized on the sale of an interest in a partnership will be treated as attributable to the sale of a capital asset.[1] The cross-reference to Section 751(a), however, creates a

---

1. As mentioned at ¶ 17,008, if a partner has a divided holding period for the partnership interest sold, any capital gain or loss recognized under Section 741 is divided between long-term and short-term capital gain or loss in the same proportions as the holding period of the partnership interest is divided between the portion of the interest held for more than one year and the portion held for one year or less. Reg. § 1.1223–3(c)(1) and –3(f), Ex. 1. If a partner only sells or exchanges part of the partnership interest and has a divided holding period for the partnership interest, the holding period of the transferred interest is generally divided between long-term and short-term capital gain or loss in the same proportions as the long-term and short-term capital gain or loss that the transferor partner would realize if the entire partnership interest were transferred in a fully taxable transaction immediately before the actual sale or exchange. Reg. § 1.1223–3(c)(2)(ii) and –3(f), Ex. 5. However, a selling partner may elect to use the actual holding period of the portion of a partnership interest transferred in a publicly traded partnership

major exception to that general rule. Under Section 751(a), gain or loss on the sale will be recharacterized as ordinary income or loss to the extent that it reflects gain or loss in the ordinary income assets of the partnership. As a result, the taxation of the seller of a partnership interest becomes a compromise between the simplicity of the entity approach and the precision of the aggregate approach. As you study Section 751, however, you might conclude that it is not much of a compromise. How much more complicated would it be if the American Law Institute's full fragmentation approach were adopted and the proceeds of a sale were allocated over each item of partnership property?

[¶ 21,010]

1. EFFECT OF PARTNERSHIP LIABILITIES

When a partner sells an interest in a partnership, the partner's share of partnership liabilities will be reduced—normally to zero. That reduction, however, does not cause a constructive distribution to the partner under Section 752(b) because Section 752(d) handles the effect of the reduction more directly. Under the latter, the selling partner is treated exactly as if the partner had sold encumbered property in an individual capacity. That incorporates the rules of Crane v. Commissioner, 331 U.S. 1 (1947), and Commissioner v. Tufts, 461 U.S. 300 (1983). Thus, the amount realized by the selling partner will be increased by the partner's share of partnership liabilities immediately before the sale. Not too surprisingly, partners have sought a variety of methods for avoiding that result. The following ruling is the IRS's response to one such attempt.

[¶ 21,015]

REVENUE RULING 77–402
1977–2 C.B. 222.

Advice has been requested whether, under the circumstances described below, gain or loss on the sale or exchange of a partnership interest is recognized under section 741 * * *.

A, an individual, created *T*, an irrevocable trust. *A* and *B* (*A*'s spouse) are the trustees. All trust income is currently distributable for

---

(as defined in Section 7704(b)) if certain requirements are met. See Reg. § 1.1223–3(c)(2)(i) and –3(f), Ex. 6.

Note that the regulations authorize the IRS to issue guidance disregarding certain cash contributions (including de minimis cash contributions) for purposes of determining a selling partner's holding period in a partnership interest that is sold or exchanged. See Reg. § 1.1223–3(b)(5). In addition, the regulations contain a special rule that allows a partner to reduce cash contributions made within one year of a sale or exchange of a partnership interest by cash distributions received during that one-year period on a last-in, first-out basis, treating all cash contributions as if they were received immediately before the sale or exchange. See Reg. § 1.1223–3(b)(2), which is illustrated by an example at Reg. § 1.1223–3(f), Ex. 3.

life to *C*, *A* and *B*'s child. At *C*'s death, the corpus is distributable to *D*, *A* and *B*'s grandchild. *A* has expressly retained certain powers of the kind described in subpart E of part I of subchapter J of the Code. Therefore, for Federal income tax purposes, *T* is a "grantor trust" and *A* is considered the owner of the entire trust.

A, as the trustee, then used the funds that *A*, as grantor, initially contributed to *T*, to purchase on behalf of the trust an interest in *P*, a partnership. The principal activity of *P* is investing in real property, and *P* uses both recourse and nonrecourse financing. *P* properly elected to deduct accelerated depreciation, which generated large operating losses that *P*'s partners were entitled to deduct on their income tax returns. *A*, as owner of *T*, deducted the distributive share of partnership losses attributable to the partnership interest held by *T*.

When the adjusted basis of the partnership interest held by *T* had been reduced nearly to zero, and just before the so-called "cross-over point" (when *P* no longer generated losses but began generating income), *A*, as grantor, renounced the powers previously and expressly retained that initially resulted in *T* being classified as a grantor trust. Consequently, *T* ceased to be a grantor trust and *A* was no longer considered to be the owner of the trust. Thereafter, *C*, as life beneficiary, was subject to tax on the income generated by the trust.

Section 671 * * * provides, where it is specified in sections 673 through 679 that a grantor or another person shall be treated as the owner of any portion of a trust, that there shall be included in computing the taxable income and credits of the grantor or other person, the items of income, deductions, and credits of the trust attributable to the portion of the trust considered owned by such grantor or other person to the extent such items would be taken into account in computing the taxable income or credits of an individual.

Section 741 * * * provides that in the case of a sale or exchange of an interest in a partnership, gain or loss shall be recognized to the transferor partner.

Section 752(d) * * * provides that in the case of a sale or exchange of an interest in a partnership, liabilities shall be treated in the same manner as liabilities in connection with the sale or exchange of property not associated with partnerships.

In the instant case, since *A* was the owner of the entire trust, *A* was considered the owner of all the trust property for Federal income tax purposes, including the partnership interest. Since *A* was considered to be the owner of the partnership interest, *A*, not *T*, was considered to be the partner in *P* during the time *T* was a "grantor trust" under subpart E of part I of subchapter J * * *.

However, at the time *A* renounced the powers that gave rise to *T*'s classification as a grantor trust, *T* no longer qualified as a grantor trust, with the result that *A* was no longer considered to be the owner of the trust and trust property for Federal income tax purposes. Consequently, at that time, *A* is considered to have transferred ownership of the interest in *P* to *T*, now a separate taxable entity, independent of its grantor, *A*.

When a transfer of an interest in a partnership occurs and the transferor's share of partnership liabilities is reduced or eliminated, the transferor is treated as having sold the partnership interest for an amount equal to the share of liabilities reduced or eliminated. Under section 752(d) * * *, the amount realized by the transferor *A* includes the reduction in or elimination of such liabilities. * * * Any gain or loss realized on a sale or exchange of a partnership interest is recognized pursuant to section 741 * * *.

Accordingly, in the instant case, *A* realized an amount equal to the share of partnership liabilities that existed immediately before *T* converted from grantor to nongrantor status for Federal income tax purposes. The gain or loss realized by *A* is the difference between the amount realized from the reduction of the share of *P*'s liabilities and the adjusted basis in the partnership interest under section 705 * * * immediately prior to the change in *T*'s tax status. The gain or loss so realized must be recognized by *A* under section 741.

* * *

[¶ 21,020]

Note

When Section 752 was drafted, it was understood that, under footnote 37 in *Crane*, the amount realized on the transfer of property subject to a nonrecourse debt was limited to the value of the property and that rule was codified in Section 752(c). In *Tufts*, however, the Supreme Court reinterpreted *Crane* to hold that the amount realized would include the entire unpaid amount of a nonrecourse debt. That created a conflict with Section 752(c). Indeed, in *Tufts*, the taxpayers, who had sold their partnership interests, argued that under Section 752(d), as modified by Section 752(c), the amount realized attributable to the nonrecourse debt of the partnership could not exceed the value of the partnership properties. The Court reconciled its holding with Section 752(c) in the following language (461 U.S. at 314–17):

> Relying on the Code's § 752(c), * * * however, respondents argue that Congress has provided for precisely this type of asymmetrical treatment in the sale or disposition of partnership property. Section 752 prescribes the tax treatment of certain partnership transactions, and § 752(c) provides that "[f]or purposes of this section, a liability to which property is subject shall, to the extent of the fair market value of such property, be considered as a liability of

the owner of the property." Section 752(c) could be read to apply to a sale or disposition of partnership property, and thus to limit the amount realized to the fair market value of the property transferred. Inconsistent with this interpretation, however, is the language of § 752(d), which specifically mandates that partnership liabilities be treated "in the same manner as liabilities in connection with the sale or exchange of property not associated with partnerships." The apparent conflict of these subsections renders the facial meaning of the statute ambiguous, and therefore we must look to the statute's structure and legislative history.

Subsections (a) and (b) of § 752 prescribe rules for the treatment of liabilities in transactions between a partner and his partnership, and thus for determining the partner's adjusted basis in his partnership interest. Under § 704(d), a partner's distributive share of partnership losses is limited to the adjusted basis of his partnership interest. * * * When partnership liabilities are increased or when a partner takes on the liabilities of the partnership, § 752(a) treats the amount of the increase or the amount assumed as a contribution by the partner to the partnership. This treatment results in an increase in the adjusted basis of the partner's interest and a concomitant increase in the § 704(d) limit on his distributive share of any partnership loss. Conversely, under § 752(b), a decrease in partnership liabilities or the assumption of a partner's liabilities by the partnership has the effect of a distribution, thereby reducing the limit on the partner's distributive share of the partnership's losses. When property encumbered by liabilities is contributed to or distributed from the partnership, § 752(c) prescribes that the liability shall be considered to be assumed by the transferee only to the extent of the property's fair market value. * * *

The legislative history indicates that Congress contemplated this application of § 752(c). Mention of the fair market value limitation occurs only in the context of transactions under subsections (a) and (b). The sole reference to subsection (d) does not discuss the limitation. While the legislative history is certainly not conclusive, it indicates that the fair market value limitation of § 752(c) was directed to transactions between a partner and his partnership. * * *

By placing a fair market value limitation on liabilities connected with property contributions to and distributions from partnerships under subsections (a) and (b), Congress apparently intended § 752(c) to prevent a partner from inflating the basis of his partnership interest. Otherwise, a partner with no additional capital at risk in the partnership could raise the § 704(d) limit on his distributive share of partnership losses or could reduce his taxable gain upon disposition of his partnership interest. * * * There is no potential for similar abuse in the context of § 752(d) sales of partnership interests to unrelated third parties. In light of the above, we interpret subsection (c) to apply only to § 752(a) and (b) transactions, and not to limit the amount realized in a sale or exchange of a partnership interest under § 752(d).

[¶ 21,025]

2. EFFECT OF CURRENT YEAR'S INCOME

When an entire partnership interest is sold during the year, the partnership's taxable year closes as to the selling partner only. § 706(c)(2)(A). Under Section 706(a) the effect of this rule is to require that the selling partner's share of partnership income and loss for the year be included in the selling partner's taxable income on that day, while leaving the other partners to account for their shares of income at the end of the partnership's year. Under the regulations, however, the partnership is not required to compute the selling partner's share of income through an interim closing of the books. By agreement among the partners, the income attributable to the interest sold may be prorated between the buyer and seller based on the number of days in the year preceding and following the sale. Reg. § 1.706–1(c)(2)(ii).

If a partner sells less than the entire interest in the partnership, the taxable year of the partnership does not close and the transferor's share of partnership income is not includible in income until the last day of the partnership's year. However, partnership income must still be allocated between the transferor and the transferee by taking account of their varying interests during the year. § 706(d)(1).

In computing the tax consequences of the sale of a partnership interest, the income allocated to the seller is reflected first. Thus, the basis of the seller's partnership interest is adjusted under Section 705 by the seller's share of income and loss and that adjusted basis is subtracted from the proceeds of the sale (i.e., the "amount realized" on the sale of the partnership interest) to determine the gain or loss on the sale. See § 1001(a).

[¶ 21,030]

Problems

1. Mossback & Associates is a general partnership of five individuals. Its balance sheet on July 1 shows the following:

Assets	Basis	Value	Liabilities	
Cash	$ 4,000	$ 4,000	Loan from bank	$10,000
Building	12,000	30,000		
Land	14,000	26,000	Partner's Equity	

				Per Books	Value
Total	$30,000	$60,000		$20,000	$50,000

¶ 21,020

Each partner of Mossback has an equal interest in partnership profits and losses and each has a capital account (computed under tax accounting principles) of $4,000. On July 1, Alice sold her interest to Bart for cash of $10,000. Ignoring income or loss for the year (and Section 751), compute her gain on the sale.

2. Assume in Problem 1 that Mossback earned net income of $10,000 ratably over the year of the sale and that the partnership made no distributions to its partners during the year. Now what would be the consequences to Alice in the year of sale? Does the allocation of income of $1,000 to her alter the total amount on which she will be taxed or only its character?

3. What difference would it make to either Alice or Bart in Problem 2 if the partnership profit of $10,000 had been earned entirely in October?

4. In Problem 1, what will be Bart's initial basis for his partnership interest? What will be the amount of his capital account? See Reg. § 1.704–1(b)(2)(iv)(*l*).

[¶ 21,035]

C. SALES SUBJECT TO SECTION 751

Under Sections 741 and 751(a), the sale of any partnership interest is effectively divided into two parts: a sale of the partner's interest in the Section 751 property owned by the partnership and a sale of the remainder of the partnership interest. For each portion of the sale, gain or loss is computed and reported separately. See Reg. § 1.751–1(a)(2). Under the current regulations, the selling partner starts this determination by first determining the total amount of gain or loss on the sale of the partnership interest (i.e., by subtracting the partner's adjusted basis from the amount realized on the sale of the partnership interest). Then the selling partner determines the amount of her income or loss from the sale or exchange of her interest in the partnership's Section 751 property. That amount is the amount of income or loss that would have been allocated to the selling partner from Section 751 property (to the extent attributable to the partnership interest sold or exchanged) if the partnership had sold all of its property in a fully taxable transaction for cash in an amount equal to the fair market value of the property immediately before the partner's transfer of the partnership interest. The income or loss attributable to the sale or exchange of the Section 751 property is ordinary income or loss. Finally, the selling partner determines the amount of gain or loss on the sale of the partnership interest that will be treated as capital gain or loss under Section 741 by subtracting the amount of ordinary income or loss attributable to the Section 751 property from the partner's total amount of gain or loss on the sale of the partnership interest. Reg. § 1.751–1(a)(2).

To summarize, the computation required by Section 751(a) involves several steps: the selling partner's total amount of gain or loss on the sale of the partnership interest must be determined, the Section 751 property must be identified, the amount of income or loss that would have been allocated to the selling partner from a hypothetical sale of the partnership's Section 751 property must be determined and treated as ordinary income or loss, and that amount must be subtracted from the total amount of gain or loss on the sale of the partnership interest to determine the selling partner's capital gain or loss from the sale of the interest under Section 741.

[¶ 21,040]

1. SECTION 751 PROPERTY

Section 751 property includes both "unrealized receivables," defined in Section 751(c), and "inventory items," defined in Section 751(d). A casual reading of those subsections might suggest that only the most classic forms of business income are subject to Section 751(a) ordinary income or loss treatment. In fact, however, almost every asset that would produce ordinary income in whole or in part on a sale of that asset will be treated as Section 751 property.

a. *Unrealized Receivables*

[¶ 21,045]

LOGAN v. COMMISSIONER

United States Tax Court, 1968.
51 T.C. 482.

TANNENWALD, JUDGE: * * *.

FINDINGS OF FACT

* * *

Prior to March 1959, petitioner [Frank A. Logan] practiced law as a sole proprietor in Louisville. On March 1, 1959, he and Thomas S. Dawson (Dawson) formed a law partnership under the name of Logan & Dawson, agreeing to share profits and losses equally. Petitioner contributed assets to the partnership with an adjusted basis of $9,654.36. Dawson contributed no assets to the partnership. The partnership assumed a $7,500 personal note owed by petitioner but assumed no liability of Dawson's.

When the partnership was formed, petitioner had legal work in progress, some on a contingent fee basis, all of which had a zero basis. Petitioner contributed this work to the partnership, so that when the fees of some $60,000 were received therefor they became partnership income, rather than petitioner's personal income. In 1960, the petitioner decided to retire from active practice of law. Dawson agreed to buy his interest in the assets of the partnership and to assume all the liabilities of the partnership. On the date of the sale, the partnership had work in progress (unbilled fees), with a zero basis, which had not been completed and which, therefore, had not been billed. None of this work in progress was covered by express agreement with the client. The liabilities of the partnership were $6,179.51.

The agreement between petitioner and Dawson dated July 1, 1960, provided in part that:

> (2) Except as hereinafter provided in Paragraph 4, Logan agrees to and does hereby sell, assign and transfer to Dawson all of his right, title and interest in all the assets of every kind and nature of said partnership firm of Logan & Dawson, including but not limited to all unbilled fees and all physical assets of the partnership, such as books, files and records, office furniture, fixtures and equipment, lease and leasehold improvements at 606 Kentucky Home Life Building, Louisville, Kentucky, cash on hand, all accounts receivable, and the goodwill of the partnership. * * *

> (3) Dawson will assume and does hereby assume and agrees to pay all the liabilities of the firm of Logan & Dawson accrued or accruable at June 30, 1960, and in addition to other valuable considerations which Logan hereby acknowledges, Dawson will pay to Logan the sum of $10,000 for Logan's entire interest in the unbilled fees due to the partnership of Logan & Dawson, and in addition thereto Dawson will also pay to Logan the sum of $8,000 for Logan's entire interest in the net partnership assets of Logan & Dawson at June 30, 1960. Said sums shall be paid by Dawson to Logan in monthly installments of $1,000 each, the first such monthly installment to be due and payable on August 1, 1960, with each subsequent installment becoming due and payable on the first day of each month thereafter until the entire amount has been paid. It is agreed that the first ten monthly installments as herein provided shall be allocated to and shall be in payment of the $10,000 agreed to be paid for Logan's interest in unbilled partnership fees and that the last eight monthly installments shall be allocated to and be accepted in payment of the $8,000 herein agreed to be paid to Logan for his entire interest in the net partnership assets at June 30, 1960.

The term "unbilled fees," as used in the aforesaid agreement, was intended to cover the partnership's right to payment for services rendered prior to the date of sale for which payment had not been received.

Petitioner's initial basis in his partnership interest was $5,904.36. Petitioner's distributive share of the partnership profits was $50,467.52 over the life of the partnership; his total withdrawals were $44,453.02. Petitioner received $21,089.75 from the sale, consisting of $6,000 in cash

¶ 21,045

and \$3,089.75 in the form of an assumption by Dawson of petitioner's share of the partnership liabilities received in 1960 and \$12,000 received in 1961. Petitioner's basis in his partnership interest at the time of sale was \$11,258.61.

Under the dissolution agreement, \$4,000 of the amount received in 1961 was attributable to petitioner's interest in the "unbilled fees" of the partnership and \$8,000 to his remaining interest.

OPINION

On July 1, 1960, petitioner sold his interest in the assets of a two-man law partnership to his partner, Dawson. The parties agree that the transaction should be treated as a sale under section 741 rather than a liquidation of the partnership under section 736. * * * Secs. 1.736–1(a)(1)(i) and 1.741–1(b), Income Tax Regs. There is also no disagreement that the \$21,089.75 realized by petitioner from the sale (\$18,000 in cash and \$3,089.75 through the assumption by Dawson of petitioner's share of the partnership liabilities) should be allocated as provided in the agreement of sale. The dispute herein involves two issues: (1) Did the \$4,000 which petitioner received in 1961 for his interest in work in progress at the time of the sale (unbilled fees), which had a zero basis to the partnership, constitute a payment attributable to "unrealized receivables" and therefore taxable ordinary income under section 751? (2) What was petitioner's basis in his partnership interest for the purpose of determining his gain or loss upon receipt of the \$8,000 balance of the purchase price in that year?

Petitioner argues that, since there were no express agreements between the partnership and its clients with respect to the work in progress, the partnership had only rights *in quantum meruit* to collect fees therefor. * * * He therefore concludes that, at the time of sale, the partnership had no "right (contractual or otherwise) to payment for * * * services rendered or to be rendered" and thus no "unrealized receivables" within the meaning of section 751(c), with the result that the payment received for the "unbilled fees" is entitled to capital gains treatment. In so concluding, he points to respondent's regulations:

> The term "unrealized receivables" * * * means any rights (contractual or otherwise) * * * to payment for—

> (ii) Services rendered or to be rendered, to the extent that income arising from such rights to payment was not previously includible in income under the method of accounting employed by the partnership. *Such rights must have arisen under contracts or agreements in existence at the time of sale or distribution*, although the partnership may not be able to enforce payment until a later time. For example, the term includes trade accounts receivable of a cash method taxpayer, and rights to payment for work or goods

begun but incomplete at the time of the sale or distribution. [Sec. 1.751–1(c)(1)(ii), Income Tax Regs. Emphasis added.]

Section 751 was enacted "to prevent the conversion of potential ordinary income into capital gain by virtue of transfers of partnership interests." H. Rept. No. 1337, 83d Cong., 2d Sess., p. 70 (1954); S. Rept. No. 1622, 83d Cong., 2d Sess., p. 98 (1954). * * * If petitioner had remained in the partnership, he would eventually have shared in the payments for services performed by the partnership before July 1, 1960. His share would have been ordinary income to him. The $10,000 Dawson paid him for his interest in the work in progress on July 1, 1960, was thus a substitute for ordinary income. * * * The fruit petitioner left on the partnership tree may not have been ripe, but it was nonetheless fruit. * * *

The partnership clients were obligated to pay the firm reasonable compensation for work performed, whether the matters were pursued to completion or the services terminated prior thereto. Thus, under all circumstances, at the time of the sale the firm had a legal right to be paid for work done. At that time, its right was uncertain as to amount, but such uncertainty is not enough to avoid categorization as an "unrealized receivable." To be sure, such a right derives from an implied obligation, but it would be sheer semantic sophistry to construe "rights (contractual or otherwise)" to mean "rights arising under express contracts," as petitioner would have us do. Nor does the language of respondent's regulation require such a construction. The reference to "contracts or agreements in existence" clearly includes implied as well as express arrangements as shown by the example of "rights to payment for work * * * begun but incomplete at the time of the sale." See sec. 1.751–1(c)(1)(ii), *supra*.

We think that the right to an unbilled fee clearly falls within the ambit of section 751(c), which itself invites a liberal construction by stating that the phrase "unrealized receivables" *includes* certain specified rights, thereby implying that the statutory definition of the term is not necessarily self-limiting. Sec. 7701(b). Any other conclusion would frustrate the clearly expressed intention of Congress to give the phrase "unrealized receivables" broad application. See H. Rept. No. 1337, *supra* at 71, A235; S. Rept. No. 1622, *supra* at 99, 402. It would also be in derogation of the Supreme Court injunction that provisions according capital gains treatment should not be "so broadly applied as to defeat rather than further the purpose of Congress." See *Corn Products Co. v. Commissioner*, 350 U.S. 46, 52 (1955).

We hold that the $10,000 Dawson paid petitioner for his interest in the unbilled fees of the partnership was an amount attributable to unrealized receivables of the partnership. * * *

¶ 21,045

The second issue relates to the adjusted basis of [the] partnership interest. The root of the disagreement lies in the treatment of the liabilities of the partnership. We agree with respondent's treatment.

When the partnership was formed, petitioner contributed property with a basis of $9,654.36. The partnership assumed one of his personal liabilities in the amount of $7,500. Theoretically, this assumption by the partnership is treated as a distribution of money to petitioner, with a consequent decrease in the basis of his partnership interest. Sec. 705(a)(2) and 752(b). On the other hand, petitioner was simultaneously entitled to increase his basis by one-half of this amount. Sec. 1.722–1, ex. (1), Income Tax Regs. His basis in the partnership was therefore $5,904.36 ($9,654.36 less $7,500 plus $3,750). The parties agree that petitioner's basis was subsequently increased by $6,014.50, representing the excess of petitioner's share of the profits over the amounts withdrawn during the life of the partnership. Sec. 705(a). Petitioner's one-half share in the decrease of the liabilities of the partnership from $7,500 to $6,179.51 on the date of sale is treated as a distribution of money (sec. 752(b)) and decreases his basis by $660.25. Sec. 705(a)(2).

Petitioner seeks to increase his basis in two ways. First, he argues that some amount representing work in progress which he brought into the firm at its inception, and for which some $60,000 in fees was ultimately received, should be included. We disagree. Since petitioner's basis in those unbilled fees was zero, his contribution adds nothing to the basis of his partnership interest. Secs. 721 and 722. *Barnes v. United States*, 253 F. Supp. 116 (S.D.Ill.1966), cited by petitioner, is clearly distinguishable, since there the taxpayer bought into an existing partnership, paying cash for the interest, which included a share of the unrealized receivables of the partnership. The District Court allowed the taxpayer to attribute an allocable portion of his cost basis to the unrealized receivables upon the subsequent sale of his partnership interest.

Petitioner also seeks to increase his basis by one-half of the liabilities of the partnership at the time of sale. He contends that example (1) of section 1.751–1(g) of respondent's regulations supports his contention. There is a basic fallacy in petitioner's reasoning. Unquestionably one-half of the partnership liabilities at the date of sale should be included in his basis. The fact of the matter is, however, that the amount of his share of those liabilities was less than the amount of his share of the partnership liabilities at inception which were included in the original basis of his partnership interest. See above. Having been included once, they should not be included again. * * *

We conclude that petitioner had an adjusted basis of $11,258.61 in his partnership interest at the time of sale, the figure which respondent used.

* * *

¶ 21,045

[¶ 21,050]

Notes

1. In *Logan*, the Tax Court apparently treated fees attributable to work performed but unbilled as an unrealized receivable. What of the fees attributable to work to be performed in the future on existing engagements? Note carefully the language of Section 751(c)(2).

2. One recurring issue under Section 751(c) concerns the value of management contracts held by the partnership. For example, in Ledoux v. Commissioner, 77 T.C. 293 (1981), aff'd per curiam, 695 F.2d 1320 (11th Cir.1983), the partnership held a contractual right to operate a greyhound racing track for 20 years. The Tax Court treated that right as an unrealized receivable for the purposes of Section 751.

3. The definition of an unrealized receivable also includes the portion of the value of certain assets that would be taxed as ordinary income on a sale, such as the element of depreciation recapture in a Section 1231 asset. § 751(c).

[¶ 21,055]

b. Inventory Items

Most of the broad reach of Section 751(a) comes from the rather expansive definition of inventory found in Section 751(d). That definition includes not only traditional inventory items (Section 751(d)(1)) but also any property that on a sale would not be treated as a capital asset or Section 1231 asset. § 751(d)(2). Thus, for example, to the extent that a category of *Corn Products* assets exists after the Supreme Court's decision in Arkansas Best Corp. v. Commissioner, 485 U.S. 212 (1988), those assets would be included in the definition of inventory under Section 751(d)(2).

While the definition of inventory under Section 751(d) is clearly very broad, some elements of ordinary income may escape its grasp. For example, in some instances the Code provides for ordinary income taxation on the sale of an asset that is nevertheless a capital or Section 1231 asset and thus would seem outside the scope of Section 751(d)(2). One example would be corporate stock owned by the partnership the sale of which produce some ordinary income, see § 306(a)(1)(A), (discussed at ¶ 6110), but there are others.

Another capital asset the sale of which yields some ordinary income is a partnership interest in a partnership that holds Section 751 property. Under prior law a partnership might form a second-tier partnership to hold its Section 751 property. On a sale of an interest in the parent partnership, the selling partner might seek to avoid ordinary income treatment by claiming that the interest in the subsidiary partnership did not come within Section 751(d)(2) and thus that the parent partnership did not own any Section 751 property. That argument is now barred by

Section 751(f) which provides that the parent partnership will be treated as if it directly owned a proportionate share of any property owned by a lower-tier partnership.

A similar issue would be created by the potential application of the tax benefit rule at the partnership level. If a partnership holds a capital asset, the sale of which would produce ordinary income in part under the tax benefit rule (for example, a security with respect to which a loss due to worthlessness had been claimed), should that element of income be included in Section 751(d)(2)?

The final category of inventory within the meaning of Section 751(d) is property that, if held directly by the partner now selling a partnership interest, would be treated as inventory in the hands of that partner under the other two categories of Section 751(d). § 751(d)(3). How is that to be determined? The character of property is often determined by the purpose for which it is held, but how can that purpose be determined for one who had never actually held the property? Without question, Section 751(d)(3) would apply if the partner selling the interest was a dealer who recently contributed ordinary income property to a partnership that was not a dealer in that type of property. Should the application of the provision be limited to such step transaction-like cases? If so, what does Section 751(d)(3) add to Section 724?

In addition, as in the sale of almost any asset, a portion of the "gain" realized on the sale of a partnership interest may in fact be attributable to the claiming of deductions that reduced the basis for the interest but were not accompanied by an economic loss. Aside from the application of Section 751(a), should the tax benefit rule, applied at the partner rather than the partnership level, also override Section 741?

[¶ 21,060]

HOLBROOK v. COMMISSIONER

United States Tax Court, 1975.
T.C. Memo. 1975–294.

[The taxpayers held interests as limited partners in an oil and gas venture. Certain operating losses had been taken by the taxpayers as ordinary deductions over a period of four years, which reduced the basis of each partner's interest in the partnership. In 1968, the taxpayers sold their interests to the general partner at a price equal to their original investment. The amount realized by each was in excess of the adjusted basis of his or her partnership interest. Excerpted below is the portion of the Tax Court opinion that relates to the question of whether the gain realized on the sales constituted long-term capital gain or ordinary income.]

* * *

¶ 21,055

IRWIN, JUDGE: * * *.

* * *

[P]etitioners contend that they should be entitled to capital gain treatment. Respondent, on the other hand, argues that in substance petitioners were reimbursed for their investments. He submits that to the extent a sale occurred it was only to the extent of petitioners' bases in the partnership. The remainder of the amounts received, it is contended, constitute a recovery of partnership losses allocated to Holbrook and Childers and deducted on their tax returns, and should be treated as ordinary income under tax benefit principles.

We are not persuaded by respondent's arguments. * * * We can find no compelling authority to apply tax benefit principles to this situation.

We think the situation here contrasts to that in our recently court reviewed case of *Estate of David B. Munter*, 63 T.C. 663 (1975), wherein we held that the tax benefit rule applies where the identical item which had been previously expensed is later recovered. Here, there was no recovery of the operating losses as such. The recovery, if it be called that, is of the investment, a capital asset, not of the losses. Compare *Fribourg Navigation Co., Inc. v. Commissioner*, 383 U.S. 272 (1966). It is true that the operating losses reduced petitioners' bases but it does not follow that the payments for their interests in excess of the bases constitute ordinary income. Nothing in the Code suggests that to the extent losses reduce basis, that amount should be taxed as ordinary income if recovered on the sale of the interest. Compare *Arrowsmith v. Commissioner*, 344 U.S. 6 (1952). On the contrary, section 741 specifically provides that except as provided in section 751 gain from the sale of a partnership interest shall be considered as gain from the sale of a capital asset. Under section 751[(a)] only that portion of the partner's gain which is attributable to his share of the partnership's unrealized receivables and * * * inventory is treated as ordinary income. Section 751 does not produce ordinary income, however, to the extent that a partner has reduced his basis due to operating losses incurred by the partnership.

Although petitioners have the burden of proof, in our judgment they have overcome the presumption of correctness in respondent's determination and presented a prima facie case in support of a sale. This is not a situation involving a sham. As we interpret the evidence presented, it appears that Kissinger offered to buy back all of the limited partners' interests at their cost, which offers were accepted. Although the fair market value of the two interests herein was not established, in our judgment petitioners have presented a prima facie case of sale. The fact that the sale price may be greater than the fair market value does not prevent a finding that a sale in fact occurred. * * *

Accordingly, we find that Holbrook properly reported the difference between the face amount of his note and his adjusted basis as long-term

¶ 21,060

capital gain. With respect to Childers, he erred in failing to treat the payments received in each year as capital gain to the extent the amount received exceeded his partnership basis as allocated to each payment. Compare *Burnet v. Logan*, 283 U.S. 404 (1931).

* * *

[¶ 21,065]

Notes

1.   Is the reasoning of the court consistent with the later decision of the Supreme Court in Hillsboro Nat'l Bank v. Commissioner, 460 U.S. 370 (1983)? If not, can the decision nevertheless be justified by the very specific statutory framework created by Section 751?

2.   Before the Taxpayer Relief Act of 1997, inventory did not constitute a Section 751 asset unless the totality of the Section 751(d) items held by the partnership were substantially appreciated in value. To be substantially appreciated for this purpose, the aggregate value of all such inventory items had to exceed 120 percent of the aggregate adjusted basis to the partnership for those items. Former § 751(d)(1)(A). If this test was not met by the inventory items as a group, the partnership did not have any Section 751(d) assets even if certain inventory items were highly appreciated in value. Congress deleted the substantial appreciation requirement for inventory with respect to sales of partnership interests to reduce complexity and increase the effectiveness of Section 751(a) in properly treating income attributable to inventory as ordinary income. See S. Rep. No. 33, 105th Cong., 1st Sess. 192–93 (1997). As discussed at ¶ 22,110, however, Congress has retained in Section 751(b)(3) the substantial appreciation requirement for inventory with respect to disproportionate distributions of partnership property.

[¶ 21,070]

2.   DETERMINATION OF GAIN OR LOSS ON THE SECTION 751(a) AND THE SECTION 741 PORTIONS OF THE SALE

Once the total amount of the selling partner's gain or loss on the sale of the partnership interest has been determined and the Section 751 property has been identified, the selling partner's ordinary income or loss under Section 751(a) and capital gain or loss under Section 741 can be determined. As mentioned above, the current regulations at Reg. § 1.751–1(a)(2) adopt a hypothetical sale approach for determining the selling partner's ordinary income or loss under Section 751(a). That is, the selling partner has ordinary income or loss under Section 751(a) on the sale of the partnership interest in an amount equal to the amount of income or loss that would have been allocated to the selling partner from Section 751 property (to the extent attributable to the partnership interest sold or exchanged) if the partnership had sold all of its property

¶ 21,060

in a fully taxable transaction for cash in an amount equal to the fair market value of the property immediately before the partner's transfer of the partnership interest. This determination takes into account any remedial allocations under Reg. § 1.704–3(d) (see ¶ 18,135). Under Section 7701(g), the fair market value of the property on the partnership's hypothetical sale of the Section 751 property will include the full unpaid principal amount of any nonrecouse debt to which the Section 751 property is subject. The selling partner's gain or loss attributable to the sale or exchange of the Section 751 property is ordinary income or loss.

In order to avoid overstating the ordinary income attributable to an unrealized receivable, such as the unbilled fees involved in *Logan,* at ¶ 21,045, the partnership "basis" for purposes of determining the gain or loss on its hypothetical sale of the Section 751 property (including the unrealized receivable) must include the costs of earning the income that would not yet be deductible under the partnership's method of tax accounting. Reg. § 1.751–1(c)(2). Property that includes items of recapture that are defined as unrealized receivables by Section 751(c) is treated as two separate properties: the recapture property with a basis of zero and the balance of the property with a basis equal to the actual basis for the property.

Finally, the selling partner determines the amount of gain or loss on the sale of the partnership interest that will be treated as capital gain or loss under Section 741 by subtracting the amount of ordinary income or loss attributable to the Section 751 property from the partner's total amount of gain or loss on the sale of the partnership interest.[2] Thus, it is entirely possible that the seller will have ordinary income on the Section 751 portion of the sale and a capital loss on the balance of the transaction!

This process of calculating the Section 751(a) ordinary income or loss and the Section 741 capital gain or loss on a partner's sale of her partnership interest can be illustrated with the following example drawn in substantial part from Reg. § 1.751–1(g), Ex. 1:

> *Example.* A and B are equal partners in a personal service partnership, AB Partnership, which uses the cash method of tax accounting. Both A and B have held their partnership interests for

---

2. For purposes of determining a selling partner's holding period for a partnership interest that is sold or exchanged, Reg. § 1.1223–3(b)(4) disregards the contribution of a Section 751 asset to the partnership by the selling partner during the period within one year before the sale or exchange of the partnership interest if the selling partner recognizes ordinary income or loss on account of the Section 751 asset in a fully taxable transaction (either as a result of the sale of the partner's interest in the partnership or the sale of the Sec-

tion 751 asset by the partnership). The consequence of this rule is that if all of the partner's other contributions to the partnership occurred more than one year before sale of the partnership interest, the partner's holding period for the entire interest will be greater than one year (instead of partially long-term and partially short-term) and all of the partner's capital gain from sale of the partnership interest will be long-term capital gain. For an example illustrating the application of this rule, see Reg. § 1.1221–3(f), Ex. 2.

¶ 21,070

more than one year. B transfers its interest in the partnership to X for $60,000 when the AB Partnership's balance sheet is as follows:

Assets

	Basis	*Value*
Cash	$12,000	$12,000
Loans receivable	40,000	40,000
Capital Assets	28,000	20,000
Unrealized Receivables	0	56,000
Total	$80,000	$128,000

Liabilities and Capital Accounts

	Per Books	*Value*
Liabilities	$8,000	$8,000
Capital:		
A	36,000	60,000
B	36,000	60,000
Total	$80,000	$128,000

Assume that none of the AB Partnership's assets is Section 704(c) property and none of the capital assets is depreciable. B's undivided half interest in the AB Partnership property includes a half interest in the partnership's unrealized receivables, so Section 751(a) will apply to this sale of B's partnership interest.

First, B computes the total gain or loss on the sale of the partnership interest. B's total amount realized on the sale of the partnership interest is $64,000, consisting of the $60,000 cash received, plus, under Section 752, B's $4,000 share of the partnership liabilities assumed by X. B's basis for the partnership interest is $40,000 ($36,000, plus, under Section 752, B's $4,000 share of the partnership liabilities). Thus, B's total recognized gain on the sale of the partnership interest is $24,000.

Second, B determines the amount of ordinary income or loss on the Section 751(a) portion of the sale. If the AB Partnership had sold all of its Section 751 property immediately before B's sale of the partnership interest, B would have been allocated $28,000 of ordinary income with respect to the unrealized receivables (i.e., one-half of the $56,000 gain that the AB Partnership would have realized on a sale of those receivables). Thus, under Section 751(a), B has $28,000 of ordinary income on the sale of the partnership interest.

Finally, B determines the amount of capital gain or loss under Section 741 on the sale of the partnership interest by subtracting the $28,000 of ordinary income determined under Section 751(a) from B's total gain or loss on sale of the partnership interest of $24,000. Thus, B has a $4,000 capital loss under Section 741 on the sale of the partnership interest. Since B has held the partnership interest for more than one year, that loss will be a long-term capital loss.

[¶ 21,075]

Problems

1. Mice–By–Mail is a cash method general partnership of three individuals. The partnership has no liabilities and its year-end balance sheet shows the following:

| | Assets | |
	Basis	Value
Cash	$12,000	$ 12,000
Accounts receivable	0	18,000
Inventory	36,000	42,000
Section 1231 equipment	12,000	60,000
(cost: $36,000)		
Land	21,000	51,000
Goodwill	0	42,000
Total	$81,000	$225,000

| | Capital Accounts | |
	Per Books	Value
Ann	$27,000	$ 75,000
Bob	18,000	66,000
Carol	36,000	84,000
Total	$81,000	$225,000

Each partner has an equal interest in partnership profits and losses. The basis for each partner's interest in the partnership equals the amount of the capital account. As of the end of the year, Ann sold her interest to Don for cash of $75,000. Determine the amount of her ordinary income under Section 751(a) and her capital gain or loss under Section 741 on the sale of the partnership interest.

2. Assume that Ann had recently purchased her interest in the partnership for $72,000 and that the partnership has not made an election under Section 754. Ignoring Section 732(d), recompute her gain on a sale of her partnership interest. After studying Section 732(d), consider what benefit that subsection would be to Ann.

[¶ 21,080]

D. OTHER ENTITY VERSUS AGGREGATE ISSUES

The question of whether the aggregate or the entity approach to the sale of a partnership interest should prevail can arise in contexts not addressed by Section 751. When that occurs, how is the matter to be resolved?

¶ 21,080

1. INSTALLMENT SALE REPORTING OF GAIN FROM THE SALE OF A PARTNERSHIP INTEREST

[¶ 21,087]

REVENUE RULING 89–108

1989–2 C.B. 100.

ISSUE

If the property of a partnership includes inventory, to what extent may the installment method of reporting income under section 453 * * * be used to report income on the sale of an interest in that partnership?

FACTS

P was a partner in a partnership that held * * * inventory within the meaning of section 751(d) * * *. A portion of this property constituted inventory within the meaning of section 453(b)(2)(B). The partnership did not hold any unrealized receivables within the meaning of section 751(c). *P* sold *P*'s partnership interest in exchange for an installment note. The gain *P* recognized from the sale was, in part, attributable to the partnership inventory. Interests in the partnership were not traded on an established market, and therefore the provisions of section 453(k) did not make the sale ineligible for installment method reporting.

LAW AND ANALYSIS

Section 453(a) * * * states that, except as otherwise provided, income from an installment sale shall be taken into account under the installment method. Section 453(b)(1) defines an installment sale as a disposition of property where at least one payment is to be received after the close of the taxable year in which the disposition occurs. Section 453(c) defines the installment method as a method under which the income recognized for any taxable year from a disposition is that proportion of the payments received in that year which the gross profit (realized or to be realized when payment is completed) bears to the total contract price. Section 453(b)(2)(B) precludes installment method reporting in the case of a sale of personal property that is required to be included in inventory of the taxpayer if on hand at the close of the taxable year.

Section 741 * * * provides that, in the case of a sale or exchange of a partnership interest, gain or loss recognized to the transferor is considered gain or loss from the sale or exchange of a capital asset, except as otherwise provided in section 751.

Section 751(a) * * * provides that the amount received by a transferor partner in exchange for all or a part of a partnership interest shall be considered as an amount realized from the sale or exchange of property other than a capital asset, to the extent such an amount is attributable to unrealized receivables or inventory items * * *.

* * *

Under section 741 * * *, the sale of a partnership interest generally is treated as the sale of a single capital asset without regard to the nature of the underlying partnership property. *See* H.R. Rep. No. 1337, 83d Cong., 2d Sess. 70 (1954). In this respect, the tax treatment of the sale of a partnership interest differs from that accorded the sale of a sole proprietorship. *See, e.g., Williams v. McGowan,* 152 F.2d 570 (2d Cir. 1945), which held that the sale of an entire business as a going concern was the sale of the individual assets of the business. *See also* Rev. Rul. 68–13, 1968–1 C.B. 195, which holds that the installment sale of a sole proprietorship is generally considered to be a sale of individual assets of the proprietorship for purposes of applying section 453.

Section 751 * * * was enacted to prevent the conversion of certain potential ordinary income into capital gain upon the sale or exchange of a partnership interest. This section, in effect, severs certain income items from the partnership interest. H.R. Rep. No. 1337, *supra,* at 70, 71, and S. Rep. No. 1622, 83d Cong., 2d Sess. 99 (1954). Thus, to the extent a partnership interest represents * * * inventory or unrealized receivables described in section 751, the tax consequences to the transferor partner are "the same tax consequences which would be accorded an individual entrepreneur." H.R. Rep. No. 1337 at 71, and S. Rep. 1622, *supra,* at 99. In effect, the transferor partner is treated as disposing of the property described in section 751 "independently of the rest of his partnership interest." S. Rep. No. 1622 at 98, 99. *George Edward Quick Trust v. Commissioner,* 54 T.C. 1336 (1970), acq. * * *, *aff'd per curiam,* 444 F.2d 90 (8th Cir.1971); *Woodhall v. Commissioner,* T.C. Memo. 1969–279, *aff'd,* 454 F.2d 226 (9th Cir.1972).

Gain recognized under section 741 * * * on the sale of a partnership interest is reportable under the installment method. *See* Rev. Rul. 76–483, 1976–2 C.B. 131. However, because section 751 effectively treats a partner as if the partner had sold an interest in the section 751 property of the partnership, the portion of the gain that is attributable to section 751 property is reportable under the installment method only to the extent that income realized on a direct sale of the section 751 property would be reportable under such method. Because the installment method of reporting income would not be available on a sole proprietor's sale of the inventory, the installment method is not available for reporting income realized on the sale of a partnership interest to the extent attributable to the [partnership's] * * * inventory which constitutes inventory within the meaning of section 453(b)(2)(B).

Accordingly, *P*'s income from the sale of the partnership interest may not be reported under the installment method to the extent it

¶ 21,087

represents income attributable to the partnership's * * * inventory which would not be eligible for installment sale treatment if sold directly. The balance of the income realized by *P* from the sale of the partnership interest is reportable under the installment method.

HOLDING

Under section 453 * * *, the income from the sale of a partnership interest may not be reported under the installment method to the extent it represents income attributable to the partnership's * * * inventory (within the meaning of section 751(d) * * *) which would not be eligible for the installment sale treatment if sold directly. This holding is not to be construed as an interpretation of sections 453(k) and 453A(e).

[¶ 21,090]

Notes

1. Was the result in Rev. Rul. 89–108 compelled by Section 751? If not, was the IRS wise to rely so heavily on that Section? Is there a sounder basis for the result reached in the ruling?

2. Assume that the partnership had owned other assets, the sale of which by an individual could not be reported on the installment method but which were not "unrealized receivables" or "inventory items" within the meaning of Section 751. Could the portion of the gain from the sale of the partnership interest attributable to those assets be reported on the installment method?

[¶ 21,092]

2. CAPITAL GAIN LOOK–THROUGH RULES FOR SALES OR EXCHANGES OF PARTNERSHIP INTERESTS

As discussed at ¶ 18,030, the Taxpayer Relief Act of 1997 added substantial complexity to the tax treatment of capital gains and losses by creating several different categories of long-term capital gain, each having its own preferential rate. The 1997 Act and subsequent legislation lowered the capital gains tax rate in Section 1(h) for individual taxpayers whose ordinary income is taxed at marginal rates of 25 percent or higher to 20 percent for long-term capital gains from capital assets held for more than one year. This legislation lowered the capital gains tax rate for individual taxpayers whose ordinary income is taxed at marginal rates below 25 percent to 10 percent for long-term capital gains from capital assets held for more than one year. Legislation enacted in 2003, and extended in 2006, further reduced the preferential rates in Section 1(h) for long-term capital gains from capital assets held for more than one year to 15 percent for higher bracket taxpayers and to five percent (0 percent for taxable years starting after 2007) for lower bracket taxpayers.[3] However, these preferential capital gains tax rates do not apply to long-term capital gain from the sale of "collectibles," and long-term capital gain attributable to prior depreciation deductions taken with respect to depreciable real estate (so-called "unrecaptured Section 1250 gain"), which have their own higher preferential tax rates (i.e., a 28–percent rate for collectibles and a 25–percent rate for unrecaptured Section 1250 gain).

The statute specifically authorizes the Treasury to issue appropriate regulations to apply the provisions of Section 1(h) to sales and exchanges of interests in flow-through entities (including partnerships). § 1(h)(9). In 2000, three years before the capital gains rate reductions made in the 2003 legislation, the Treasury and the IRS issued those regulations. The regulations generally take an aggregate approach for determining into which categories the long-term capital gain from the sale of a partnership interest will fall (i.e., collectibles gain, unrecaptured Section 1250 gain, or gain qualifying for the most favorable preferential capital gains rates (i.e., under current law, 15 percent for higher bracket taxpayers and five percent/0 percent in 2008 and thereafter for lower bracket taxpayers)).

Under these rules, a taxpayer selling an interest in a partnership must first determine the portion of any gain or loss from the sale of the interest that is treated as ordinary income or loss under Section 751(a). The remainder of the gain or loss from the sale of the partnership interest will be treated as capital gain or loss under Section 741. If the selling partner's holding period for the entire partnership interest is one year or less, all of the remaining gain or loss will be short-term capital gain or loss; if the selling partner's holding period for the entire partnership interest is greater than one year, all of the remaining gain or loss will be long-term capital gain or loss. If the selling partner has a divided holding period for the partnership interest, the portions of the remaining gain or loss that are treated as long-term or short-term capital gain or loss will be determined in accordance with the rules in Reg. § 1.1223–3, discussed at ¶¶ 17,008 and 21,005 (footnote 1).

If the selling partner is an individual or noncorporate taxpayer qualifying for the preferential rates in Section 1(h), the partner must next determine the portion of any long-term capital gain from the sale of the partnership interest that will be treated as collectibles gain or unrecaptured Section 1250 gain. That portion is the amount of net gain that would be allocated to the partner if the partnership sold all of its collectibles and all of its depreciable real estate for cash equal to the fair market value of such assets in a fully taxable exchange (called "look-through capital gain" in the regulations). Reg. § 1.1(h)–1(b). The re-

---

3. These reductions in the preferential tax rates for capital gains will sunset (i.e., expire) for taxable years starting after 2010 and the pre–2003 preferential rates will again become the law, unless Congress further extends the effective date of or makes permanent the 2003 reductions in the capital gains rates.

mainder of the selling partner's long-term capital gain or loss from the sale of the partnership is called "residual long-term capital gain or loss" in the regulations and if a net gain, may qualify for the 15 percent (or 5 percent/0 percent) preferential rate under current law. See Reg. § 1.1(h)–1(c). In determining whether a partnership has any gain from collectibles or unrecaptured Section 1250 gain, the partnership is treated as owning its proportionate share of any collectibles or depreciable real estate of any partnership in which it owns an interest, either directly or indirectly through a chain of such partnerships. Reg. § 1.1(h)–1(d). For examples illustrating the application of these rules, see Reg. § 1.1(h)–1(f), Exs. 1–3 and 5.

[¶ 21,095]

E. TREATMENT OF THE PURCHASING PARTNER

The purchasing partner acquires a basis for the interest in the partnership that is determined under the general rules of Section 742. That means the partner's outside basis will be the sum of the amount paid for the interest plus an allocable share of partnership liabilities. §§ 1011, 1012, and 752.

Under the general rule of Section 743(a), however, which adopts the entity approach to the transfer of partnership interests, that new outside basis has no effect at all on the partnership's inside basis for its properties. In effect, the purchasing partner succeeds to the selling partner's share of the partnership's inside basis in its properties (except with respect to the built-in loss at time of contribution in properties contributed to the partnership by the selling partner).[4] While that rule is identical to the rule governing the purchase of corporate stock, including stock in S corporations, it can have unpleasant consequences. When the partnership sells property owned at the time that the partnership interest was purchased, the amount of gain recognized will be determined by the historic inside basis of the property. That gain will then be allocated to all partners, including the purchasing partner, although that partner will have purchased the partnership interest for an amount that reflected the fair market value of the partnership properties. As a result, the purchasing partner will be taxed on a gain that economically did not exist. Moreover, that element of gain will already have been taxed to the seller of the partnership interest.

---

4. Section 704(c)(1)(C) provides that only the contributing partner is entitled to take the built-in loss into account and no other partner may benefit from such loss, including the purchasing partner. In effect, the purchasing partner's share of the partnership's inside basis in the partnership properties is equal to the selling partner's share of such inside basis minus any amount of Section 704(c) built-in loss in the partnership properties contributed by the selling partner at the time of purchase. See L. Cunningham & N. Cunningham, The Logic of Subchapter K 147 (3d ed. 2006).

In principle, the overtaxation produced by Section 743(a) is only temporary. The gain allocated to the purchasing partner increases that partner's outside basis. Since by hypothesis that basis is already equal to the value of the partnership, the increase in basis will build a loss into the partnership interest that will equal the gain recognized on the sale of the partnership properties. That deferred loss, however, is not much comfort. The partner may not benefit from that basis for many years into the future.

[¶ 21,100]

1. SECTION 743(b) BASIS ADJUSTMENT

There is a way to avoid this acceleration of tax liabilities but only at a considerable cost in terms of complexity. If the partnership makes an election under Section 754,[5] the inside basis of the partnership properties is adjusted under Section 743(b) to reflect the outside basis of the purchasing partner—but with respect to the transferee partner only. Thus, if the Section 754 election is made, for purposes of calculating income, deduction, gain, and loss, the transferee partner will have a special basis in those partnership properties the bases of which are adjusted under Section 743(b). Reg. § 1.743–1(j)(1).

The special basis adjustment under Section 743(b) does not affect the common basis of the partnership property and has no effect on the partnership's computation of any item under Section 703.[6] Moreover, the Section 743(b) adjustment has no effect on the transferee partner's or any other partner's capital account. Reg. § 1.743–1(j)(1) and (2). Thus, the Section 743(b) adjustment has no effect on the other partners at all, as it properly should not.

The adjustment required by Section 743(b) is a two-or four-way street. If the purchasing partner's share of the partnership basis is an amount greater than the cost of the partnership interest, the special basis adjustment required if the Section 754 election is in effect will be an unfavorable downward adjustment. In addition, if the election is in effect, similar adjustments, discussed at ¶ 22,060, must be made following certain distributions to partners. § 734. Since the election can be harmful as well as helpful (and certainly is complex) and can be revoked only with the consent of the IRS, perhaps you can understand why many

---

5. As discussed at ¶ 21,108 below, as a result of a statutory change in 2004, Section 743 now *requires* a downward adjustment to the inside basis of the partnership properties, even though the purchasing partner does not make the Section 754 election, if the partnership has a "substantial built-in loss" immediately after the transfer of the partnership interest. § 743(a), (d).

6. An electing large partnership (as defined in Section 775) may elect to adjust the basis of partnership assets with respect to a transferee partner under Section 743(b). The computation of an electing large partnership's taxable income under Section 773 does not take into account any Section 743(b) basis adjustments. § 774(a)(1). The special rules that apply to electing large partnerships are discussed generally at ¶ 18,250.

partnerships accept the acceleration of tax liabilities rather than make the election. As the following case illustrates, that decision, however, may be regretted.

[¶ 21,105]

ESTATE OF DUPREE v. UNITED STATES

United States Court of Appeals, Fifth Circuit, 1968.
391 F.2d 753.

YOUNG, DISTRICT JUDGE:

The estate of Robert B. Dupree, deceased taxpayer, seeks a refund of income taxes paid by the deceased prior to his death for the year 1960.

In 1947, a limited partnership known as "Stroud's Motor Courts" was organized under the laws of Missouri for the purpose of operating the Park Plaza Motor Court, a motel in St. Louis, Missouri. The partnership had one general partner, Lemuel L. Stroud, and five limited partners. The major partnership asset, the motel, was held in the name of Lemuel L. Stroud and his wife, individually, but by written agreement, was held by them as property of the partnership.

The taxpayer and his wife, Katherine P. Dupree, owned as their community property, a 15% limited interest in the partnership. On September 25, 1957, Katherine P. Dupree died, leaving her one-half of the 15% partnership interest to her son, Robert P. Dupree. Thereafter, the taxpayer, Robert B. Dupree, and his son, Robert P. Dupree, each owned a 7½% interest in the partnership. The taxpayer, upon the death of his wife, obtained a new basis for his 7½% of the partnership interest pursuant to * * * Section 1014(b)(6). An audit completed in December, 1960, of Mrs. Dupree's estate tax return resulted in a determination by the Internal Revenue Service that the fair market value of the Dupree 15% interest in the partnership as of the date of her death was $142,500.00, so that the taxpayer's new basis in his 7½% partnership interest as of September 25, 1957, was $71,250.00.

On August 1, 1960, the motel was sold to Park Plaza Motor Motel, Inc., a corporation, in which Lemuel L. Stroud was a principal stockholder and president. The sale was reported in the final partnership return for its fiscal year ending March 31, 1961, as a capital gain and $52,441.31 was attributed to the taxpayer as his share of the gain.

The assets of the partnership were distributed to the various partners, and the taxpayer received $42,150.00 cash, and a 7½% interest in two promissory notes, the face value of one secured by a first lien in the face amount of $100,000.00, and a second secured by a second lien on the motel in the face amount of $600,000.00, so that the taxpayer's 7½% face value interest in the notes amounted to $52,500.00. The Internal Revenue Service stipulated that the fair market value of the second lien note was only 50% of its face value, or 300,000.00, so that the fair market value of the taxpayer's interest in that note was only $22,500.00, instead of $45,000.00.

The parties stipulated that if the motel was sold by the partnership, then after the sale, but before the distribution of the cash and the notes, the taxpayer's basis in his partnership interest was $127,706.95. The basis in the notes was reduced by the amount of cash money received by him ($42,150.00) to $85,556.95.

An audit of the final partnership return resulted in a determination by [the] Internal Revenue [Service] on March 19, 1962, that the partnership terminated in 1960, and not in 1961 as claimed on the return. A subsequent and related audit of taxpayer's individual return for the year 1960, resulted in a deficiency assessment of $17,388.77 additional tax based on a $52,441.31 capital gain by taxpayer from his share of the sale of the motel properties. The additional tax was paid and is the basis for this suit.

In charging the taxpayer with the capital gain of $52,441.31, no consideration was given to taxpayer's basis for his 7½% interest in the partnership (as distinguished from his 7½% interest in the assets of the partnership).

Subsequent to the audit of taxpayer's individual 1960 return, an amended partnership return was filed in September 1963, signed by M.L. Stroud, Jr., as "General Partner," with a Schedule A, which sought to exercise an election by the partnership under the provisions of Section 754 * * * to adjust the basis of partnership property under Sections 734(b) and 743(b) * * * for the taxable year ending December 31, 1960.

The taxpayer sought a summary judgment on two grounds: (1) that he had sustained an ordinary loss in 1960, for the difference between his basis in his 7½% interest in the notes received as proceeds from the motel sale and the actual face value of such interest; and (2) that a proper Section 743 election had been made. The district judge denied the motion.

In due course the case proceeded to a jury trial upon three issues raised by the plaintiff taxpayer:

> (1) That the taxpayer had an ordinary loss in 1960, as above noted;

> (2) That a proper election under Section 743 had been made by the amended return filed in 1963; and

> (3) That the partnership had in fact terminated prior to the sale of the motel properties.

At the conclusion of plaintiff's case-in-chief the Court granted the government's motion for directed verdict as to all three grounds. Taxpayer asserts here as error the denial of the summary judgment and the directed verdict.

I.

Under his first theory advanced as grounds for recovery, taxpayer contends he was not given credit for an ordinary loss of $33,056.95, allegedly realized by him in 1960, computed as follows:

Dupree's basis of his 7½% interest in partnership 8/1/60	$127,706.95
Less cash received	42,150.00
Dupree's basis of his 7½% interest in notes at face value	85,556.95
7½% of face value of notes	52,500.00
Claimed loss	$ 33,056.95

Taxpayer claims entitlement to take an ordinary loss deduction of the $33,056.95, under the provisions of Section 165(a) * * *. Taxpayer argues that it is obvious that the notes could never produce more than their face value ($52,500.00 for a 7½% interest) and that since his basis for his interest in them was $85,556.95, he sustained an ordinary loss immediately upon his receipt of such interest.

The taxpayer's position seeks to circumvent the mandate of Section 731 * * *. That section clearly defers for tax purposes recognition (as distinguished from realization) to a partner of a loss on notes received in a distribution from a partnership. The basis of the partner's interest in such notes, received in liquidation, is computed under Section 732(b) * * *.

While Section 165(a) is a broad relief measure, as pointed out by taxpayer, the specific language of Section 731 prevails over the general language of Section 165(a) as to a fact situation falling within the ambit of Section 731. In D. Ginsberg & Sons, Inc. v. Joseph Popkin, 285 U.S. 204 (1932), at page 208, * * * the Supreme Court held:

> "General language of a statutory provision, although broad enough to include it, will not be held to apply to a matter specifically dealt with in another part of the same enactment. * * * Specific terms prevail over the general in the same or another statute which otherwise might be controlling."

So, Section 731 prevailing, the loss—though unquestioned—would not be recognized in 1960.

In passing, we note that taxpayer's death deprived him of ever receiving income tax recognition of the loss sustained. Even if this were inequitable, there is no equity in tax law, Carlton v. United States of America, 385 F.2d 238 (5th Cir.1967), but it was not inequitable because the taxpayer was in no different position than any other citizen who held a capital asset which had dropped in value but who died before selling the asset and obtaining a recognizable tax loss on it.

II.

When the taxpayer received a stepped-up basis in the value of his partnership interest as a result of the death of his wife in 1957, the basis of his partnership interest became considerably larger than his proportionate share of the adjusted basis of the partnership property ($71,-250.00 vs. $14,973.27). Ordinarily, the fact that a taxpayer received a stepped-up basis in his partnership interest by virtue of a transfer on the death of a partner, does not affect the basis of the partnership property. However, Section 743(b) * * * permits an adjustment if the partnership makes an election under Section 754 * * *. The adjustment to the basis of the partnership's assets is for the benefit of the transferee partner only, and the special basis adjustment is measured by the difference between the transferee's basis for his partnership interest and his proportionate share of the partnership's basis for its assets at the time of the transfer.

In the case before us the transfer giving rise to a right of an election under Section 754, was that occasioned by the death of Mrs. Dupree in 1957. If a valid election had been effected, the taxpayer would have been entitled to a special basis adjustment by an increase of the basis of his proportionate share of partnership assets, in the amount of $56,276.73 (the difference between $71,250.00 and $14,973.27). Instead of a $52,441.31 capital gain he would have had a $3,834.42 loss on the sale of the motel properties. Although an election was attempted by the partnership, the validity of that election is in issue. The partnership in filing its original return on July 15, 1961, for the 1960 tax year, did not make the Section 754 election, but instead separately stated the taxpayer's distributive share of the gain realized from the sale of its assets without employing any special adjustment for his benefit. Subsequently, on September 24, 1963, as previously noted herein, the partnership filed an amendment to its 1960 return for the sole purpose of making the election under Section 754, for the 1960 tax year.

The government contends the election was too late to be effective. Assuming that an election could have been made for the first time for the 1960 taxable year (which position the government disputes), the government insists the election could not be by an amendment filed over two years after the original return for 1960 was due. We agree. Cases involving elections under other sections of the Internal Revenue Code have permitted an election to be validly exercised only in an original return or in a timely amendment, with "timely amendment" meaning if filed within the period provided by the statute for filing the original return. * * * We conclude that for a valid election to have been made for the taxable year 1960, it should have been timely made in the original return or by an amended return filed within the statutory time for filing the original return.

In view of our conclusion that the election was made too late to be valid, it is unnecessary to consider and decide the second defense of the government that an election could be made for the first time only in the year of the transfer—1957. We note that a recent district court case, Neel v. United States, 266 F.Supp. 7 (N.D.Ga., 1966), decided that issue adversely to the government but we express no opinion here as to that case or issue, declining instead to consider it because of it being unnecessary to do so in order to decide the case before us.

III.

As his third alternative theory for recovery, the taxpayer asserts that the individual partners—and not the partnership—sold the motel properties. He sought a jury verdict on that issue and cites as error the adverse directed verdict at the close of his case-in-chief.

Was there a complete absence of probative facts to support the taxpayer's position? * * * After a careful examination of the entire record, we agree with the conclusion of the district judge. There was no evidentiary basis for submitting this issue to the jury.

The record shows that prior to the 1960 motel properties sale, each limited partner executed statements recognizing the contemplated sale was that of property owned by the partnership and ratifying execution of contracts by Stroud as general partner; that the deed to the purchaser was from Stroud and his wife; that the check representing the cash portion of the purchase price was deposited in a new account opened in the name of the partnership; that the check was endorsed: "Lemuel L. Stroud, Jr., (partner)," the sales proceeds were distributed by the partnership to the partners by checks drawn on the partnership account; both the partnership's books and the March 1961 final partnership return treated the sale as one by the partnership; that the partnership paid a real estate sales commission on the sale; that after the sale for a period of several months the partnership dispensed substantial amounts in payment of creditors of the partnership; that in June 1961, the partners jointly executed a document canceling the certificate of limited partnership on file with the State of Missouri.

The only relevant evidence favorable to the position of the taxpayer was the testimony of Robert P. Dupree who testified that he "understood the partners were to dissolve the partnership and to sell the property and to receive the proceeds therefrom"; that it was his "preference that each partner should receive his separate note" from the sale; that he objected to the filing of the final partnership return prior to its filing; and that he and his father (the deceased taxpayer here) "were informed that the partnership was to terminate." Such evidence, accepted as true, merely states the desire of Robert P. Dupree and falls short of

¶ 21,105

any evidentiary basis for reasonable men to be able to conclude that the partnership did, in fact, terminate prior to the sale. That the partnership—and not the individual partners—sold the motel properties is the only conclusion that could, with reason, be reached on the evidence including all reasonable inferences to be deduced therefrom.

CONCLUSION

The claim of an ordinary loss in 1960 and the contention that a proper Section 743 election had been made were legal issues properly resolved by the district judge so that no error was committed in denying summary judgment or granting a directed verdict for the government as to them. The theory of a dissolution of the partnership prior to the sale failing to have any evidentiary support, there was no error in withdrawing that issue from the jury and directing a verdict as to it for the government. Accordingly, the judgment below is

Affirmed.

[¶ 21,107]

Note

In some cases, the combination of no basis adjustment under Section 743(b) because of the absence of a Section 754 election, a flow-through of income or loss under Section 702, a provision not recognizing such income or loss in the hands of the distributee partner, and a basis increase or decrease for such income nonetheless under Section 705 creates artificial losses or gains at the partner level. For example, suppose a corporation purchases a partnership interest at full fair market value but has no basis adjustment under Section 743(b) because the partnership has not made a Section 754 election. The partnership owns stock in the corporate partner that has a value substantially in excess of the partnership's adjusted basis in the corporate stock. If the partnership sells that stock at a gain, the corporate partner's distributive share of the gain will not be taxable under Section 1032 but will increase the corporate partner's basis in the partnership interest under Section 705. When the corporate partner sells that partnership interest, it will have a loss on the sale attributable to the flow-through of the nontaxable gain on the sale of its stock by the partnership, even though it has no economic loss on the sale of the partnership interest. If a Section 754 election had been in effect, however, the corporate partner would have had a Section 743(b) adjustment with respect to the stock that would offset its distributive share of the stock sale gain and thereby reduce the basis increase to its partnership interest under Section 705.

Accordingly, the IRS has issued regulations under Section 705 that apply when a corporation acquires an interest in a partnership that owns stock in the corporation, the partnership does not have a Section 754 election in effect, and the partnership later sells or exchanges the corporation's stock. In such a case, the regulations limit the corporate partner's basis increase or decrease under Section 705 on account of the sale or exchange of the stock to the amount of gain or loss that the corporate partner would have recognized (absent the application of Section 1032) if a Section 754 election had been in effect for the year in which the corporation acquired its partnership interest. See Reg. § 1.705–2(b)(1).

[¶ 21,108]

2. MANDATORY BASIS ADJUSTMENT FOR PARTNERSHIP WITH A SUBSTANTIAL BUILT–IN LOSS

More generally, the Section 754 election provides the purchasing partner with a tax avoidance technique. If the Section 743(b) adjustment would result in an increase to the inside basis of the partnership property because the partnership owns appreciated property with built-in gains, the purchasing partner will likely make the Section 754 election and avoid unfavorable distortions in the timing and character of partnership income. By contrast, if the Section 743(b) adjustment would result in a downward adjustment to inside basis because the partnership owns depreciated property with built-in losses, a well-advised purchasing partner likely would not make the Section 754 election in order to obtain the benefit of a deduction for those losses when the partnership sells the depreciated property. Although the pass-through of such losses as they are realized by the partnership will reduce the purchasing partner's outside basis in the partnership interest and thus result in more gain or less loss on a later sale of the partnership interest, the purchasing partner benefits by reason of the timing advantage of an earlier deduction and perhaps a change in character as well (e.g., a current ordinary deduction for his distributive share of the built-in loss on the sale by the partnership of an asset that is not a capital asset or Section 1231 asset and increased capital gain on the sale of the partnership interest under Section 741). In 2004, Congress decided that this election and other aspects of the partnership tax rules created opportunities for "the inappropriate transfer of losses among partners," which, among other things, "allowed partnerships to be created and used to aid tax-shelter transactions." H.R. Rep. No. 548, pt. 1, 108th Cong., 2d Sess. 283 (2004). Accordingly, Congress amended Section 743 (and Section 734, discussed in Chapter 22) to require a mandatory downward adjustment to the inside basis of the partnership property in certain cases.

Section 743(a) now generally requires a downward adjustment under Section 743(b) to the inside basis of the partnership properties on the transfer of a partnership interest if the partnership has a "substantial built-in loss" immediately after the transfer. Section 743(d)(1) treats a partnership as having a substantial built-in loss with respect to the transfer of a partnership interest if, immediately after the transfer, the partnership's aggregate adjusted basis in the partnership property exceeds the aggregate fair market value of such property by more than $250,000.[7] For example, assume that a selling partner sells her interest in a partnership to a purchaser for $1 million (its fair market value on the date of sale). Assume further that, immediately after the sale, the partnership's aggregate adjusted basis in the partnership properties is $5,270,000 and the aggregate fair market value of the partnership's properties is $5,000,000. Under Section 743(b), the partnership must make a downward adjustment to the inside basis of the partnership properties with respect to the purchasing partner and, as a result, the purchasing partner would not recognize any gain or loss if the partnership sold all of its properties for their aggregate fair market value immediately after the sale of the partnership interest. See H.R. Rep. No. 548, pt. 1, 108th Cong., 2d Sess. 284 (2004).

Section 743(e) provides an exception to the mandatory basis adjustment rule in the case of an "electing investment partnership," because Congress was concerned that such a partnership "would incur administrative difficulties" if the mandatory basis adjustment rule applied to it. H.R. Rep. No. 548, pt. 1, 108th Cong., 2d Sess. 283 (2004). Thus, such an electing investment partnership is not required to make the mandatory inside basis adjustment, but instead is subject to a partnership level loss limitation rule. Under this rule, in the case of a transfer of a partnership interest, the transferee partner's distributive share of losses (determined without regard to gains) from the sale or exchange of partnership property is not allowed, except to the extent that it is shown that such losses exceed the loss recognized by the transferor partner on the transfer of the partnership interest (and any loss recognized by any prior transferor to the extent not fully offset by a prior loss disallowance under this loss limitation rule). § 743(e)(1), (e)(2). To come with this loss limitation rule, instead of the mandatory basis adjustment rule in Section 743(a) and 743(b), the partnership must elect to have the rule apply and meet the detailed definitional requirements in Section 743(e)(6). Once made, the election is irrevocable, unless the IRS consents to a revocation. § 743(e)(6).[8]

---

7. Section 743(d)(2) gives the Treasury and the IRS broad regulatory authority to implement the purposes of this mandatory basis adjustment rule, including the issuance of regulations "aggregating related partnerships and disregarding property acquired by the partnership in an attempt to avoid" the purposes of the rule.

8. Section 743(f)(1) exempts a "securitization partnership" from both the mandatory basis adjustment rule and the loss limitation rule applicable to electing investment partnerships. Such a partnership is deemed by the statute to have no "substantial built-

in loss with respect to any transfer" and, consequently, no Section 743 basis adjustments need to be made by it unless it has made the Section 754 election. To come within this exception, a partnership has to meet two statutory requirements. First, it has to have as its "sole business activity" the issuance of securities that "provide for a fixed principal (or similar amount)" and that "are primarily serviced by the cash flows of a discrete pool (either fixed or revolving) of receivables or other financial assets that by their terms convert into cash in a finite period." Second, the sponsor of the pool must reasonably believe "that the

[¶ 21,110]

3. CALCULATING AND ALLOCATING THE SECTION 743(b) BASIS ADJUSTMENT

Unfortunately, the Section 743(b) basis adjustment is not as simple as increasing and decreasing the purchasing partner's share of partnership basis to the fair market value of the partnership properties. Instead, a single overall adjustment must be computed equal to the difference between the purchasing partner's outside basis for the partnership interest and that partner's share of the adjusted basis to the partnership of the partnership's property. Reg. § 1.743–1(b). A transferee's share of the adjusted basis to the partnership of partnership property is equal to the sum of the transferee partner's interest as a partner in the "partnership's previously taxed capital," plus the transferee partner's share of partnership liabilities. This concept of the partner's interest in the "partnership's previously taxed capital" is a new term added to the regulations when they were substantially revised in 1999 and is determined with reference to a hypothetical disposition by the partnership of all of its assets, immediately after the partnership interest transfer, in a fully taxable transaction for cash equal to the fair market value of those assets (called the "hypothetical transaction" in the regulations). Reg. § 1.743–1(d)(2). Reg. § 1.743–1(d)(1) defines "previously taxed capital" as an amount equal to—

(1) The amount of cash that the transferee would receive on a liquidation of the partnership following the hypothetical transaction, to the extent attributable to the acquired partnership interest; plus

(2) The amount of tax loss (taking into account any remedial allocations under Reg. § 1.704–3(d) (see ¶ 18,135)) that would be allocated to the transferee partner from the hypothetical transaction, to the extent attributable to the acquired partnership interest; and minus

(3) The amount of tax gain (taking into account any remedial allocations under Reg. § 1.704–3(d)) that would be allocated to the transferee partner from the hypothetical transaction (to the extent attributable to the acquired partnership interest).

Thus, the partner's share of the partnership's inside basis for its partnership properties must reflect not only the partner's varying interests in capital and profits but also any special allocations of income or loss under Section 704(b) and built-in gain or loss under Section 704(c). This is consistent with the basic policy of Section 743(b), which is to attempt to achieve conformity between the transferee partner's share of the inside basis of the partnership assets and the transferee partner's

receivables and other financial assets comprising the pool are not acquired so as to be   disposed of." § 743(f)(2).

outside basis in the partnership interest. The resulting adjustment should equal the amount of income (or loss) that would be allocated to the purchasing partner if all of the partnership properties were sold.

These computations are illustrated in the examples contained in Reg. § 1.743–1(d)(3). The following example is drawn from Example 2 in that regulation section:

Example. X, Y, and Z form a partnership in which the partners share profits and losses equally. X contributes unimproved land with an adjusted basis to X of $4,000 and a fair market value of $10,000, and Y and Z each contribute $10,000 cash, to the partnership. Each partner has $10,000 of capital credited to it on the partnership's books. During the partnership's first two taxable years, the land appreciates to $16,000. X sells its one-third interest in the partnership to A for $12,000, when a Section 754 election is in effect.

The amount of tax gain that would be allocated to A from a hypothetical sale of all of the partnership's assets immediately before the transfer of the partnership interest to A would be $8,000 ($6,000 of built-in gain under Section 704(c) (see ¶ 18,135), plus $2,000, one third of the partnership's additional gain of $6,000). Thus, A's interest in the partnership's previously taxed capital is $4,000 ($12,000, the amount of cash A would receive if the partnership liquidated immediately after the hypothetical transaction, decreased by $8,000, A's share of gain from the hypothetical transaction). The amount of A's basis adjustment under Section 743(b) is $8,000 (the excess of $12,000, A's cost basis for the acquired partnership interest under Sections 742 and 1012, over $4,000, A's share of the adjusted basis to the partnership of partnership property).

Once the total amount of the adjustment has been determined, the adjustment must be allocated over the partnership properties in accordance with the rules contained in the regulations under Section 755. Those regulations were substantially revised in 1999, 2000, and 2003, and contain three principal features. One principal feature of the revised regulations is that basis adjustments under Section 743(b) are allocated among partnership properties based on the amount of income, gain, or loss that the transferee partner would be allocated if, immediately after the transfer of the partnership interest, all of the partnership assets were disposed of in the "hypothetical transaction" discussed above. A second principal feature of the revised regulations is that so-called "two-way" adjustments to partnership property may occur. Thus, the portion of the basis adjustment allocated to one class of property may be an increase, while the portion allocated to the other class is a decrease; and, within a class of property, the portion of the basis adjustment allocated to one item of property may be an increase, while the portion allocated to another piece of property may be a decrease. Reg. § 1.755–1(b)(1)(i) and (ii). A third principal feature of these revised regulations is that this

¶ 21,110

allocation of basis adjustments between the classes of property must be made even if the total amount of the Section 743(b) basis adjustment is zero! Similarly, the allocation of the basis adjustment among items of property within a class must be made even though the total basis adjustment allocated to the class is zero. See Reg. § 1.755–1(b)(1)(i) and –1(b)(2)(ii), Ex. 2.

To make the required allocation, the regulations mandate a cumbersome two-step process. First, all partnership properties are divided into two classes: (1) capital assets and Section 1231 assets (denominated "capital gain property" in the regulations) and (2) all other property of the partnership (denominated "ordinary income property" in the regulations). Reg. § 1.755–1(a)(1). (Note that the definition of ordinary income property includes properties and potential gain treated as unrealized receivables under Section 751(c), including depreciation recapture, which for this purpose are treated as separate assets that are in the ordinary income property class. Reg. § 1.755–1(a)(1).) The adjustment must then be allocated between these two classes in the following way. The amount of the basis adjustment allocated to the class of ordinary income property is the total amount of income, gain, or loss that would be allocated to the transferee partner (to the extent attributable to the transferee's partnership interest) from the sale of all ordinary income property in the hypothetical sale transaction of all of the partnership assets described above. This determination must take into account any remedial allocations under Reg. § 1.704–3(d). The amount of the basis adjustment allocated to the class of capital gain property is the residual amount of the Section 743(b) adjustment—namely, the total amount of the Section 743(b) basis adjustment less the portion of the adjustment allocated to the class of ordinary income property. However, in no event may the amount of any decrease in basis allocated to capital gain property exceed the partnership's basis in capital gain property. If a decrease in basis allocated to capital gain property would, in the absence of this limit, exceed the partnership's basis in capital gain property, the excess instead must be applied to reduce the basis of ordinary income property. Reg. § 1.755–1(b)(2)(i).

Second, the allocation to each class must be further allocated to each item of property within the class under the complex and somewhat incomprehensible formulae set forth at Reg. § 1.755–1(b)(3)(i) and (ii). The amount of the basis adjustment allocated to each item within the ordinary income property class is:

> (1) The amount of income, gain, or loss that would be allocated to the transferee partner, to the extent attributable to the acquired partnership interest, from the sale of the ordinary income property item in the hypothetical transaction (taking into account any remedial allocations under Reg. § 1.704–3(d)); minus

¶ 21,110

(2) The product of (a) any decrease to the amount of the basis adjustment to ordinary income property made necessary because the partnership did not have sufficient basis in capital gain property to reduce, multiplied by (b) a fraction with a numerator that is the fair market value of the item of ordinary income property and a denominator that is the total fair market value of all of the partnership's items of ordinary income property. Reg. § 1.755–1(b)(3)(i).

The amount of the basis adjustment allocated to each item within the capital gain property class is:

(1) The amount of income, gain, or loss that would be allocated to the transferee partner, to the extent attributable to the acquired partnership interest, from the sale of the capital gain property item in the hypothetical transaction (taking into account any remedial allocations under Reg. § 1.704–3(d)); minus

(2) The product of (a) the total amount of gain or loss that would be allocated to the transferee partner from the hypothetical sale of all items of capital gain property (taking into account any remedial allocations under Reg. § 1.704–3(d)), minus the amount of the positive basis adjustment to all items of capital gain property or plus the amount of the negative basis adjustment to all items of capital gain property, multiplied by (b) a fraction with a numerator that is the fair market value of the item of capital gain property and a denominator that is the total fair market value of all of the partnership's items of capital gain property. Reg. § 1.755–1(b)(3)(ii).[9]

Stated much more simply, the allocation of the basis adjustment among the partnership properties within a class is made in accordance with the amount of gain or loss that would be allocated to the transferee partner on a hypothetical sale of the properties by the partnership. However, if the total basis adjustment allocated to a class does not equal the total amount of gain or loss that would be allocated to the transferee partner on a hypothetical sale of the partnership properties within that class, then the adjustment is reduced in proportion to the relative fair market values of the properties within the class. See Reg. § 1.755–

---

9. The regulations were revised in 2003 to provide two clarifying rules for making this allocation of the basis adjustment to items of capital gain property. First, if the transferee partner has no interest in the income, gain, losses, deductions with respect to an item of capital gain property, that item of property will not be taken into account in making the allocation. Reg. § 1.755–1(b)(3)(iii)(A). Second, in no event may the amount of any decrease in basis allocated to an item of capital gain property exceed the partnership's basis in capital gain property. If a decrease in basis allocated to an item of capital gain property would, in the absence of this limit, exceed the partnership's basis in that capital gain property, the excess instead must be applied to reduce the remaining basis, if any, of other items of capital gain property. This basis reduction is applied pro rata in proportion to the bases of such other items of capital gain property. Reg. § 1.755–1(b)(3)(iii)(B).

1(b)(3)(iv), Ex. 2; A. Gunn & J. Repetti, Partnership Income Taxation 144–45 (4th ed. 2005).

These allocation rules can be illustrated with the following Example drawn in part from Reg. § 1.755–1(b)(2)(ii), Ex. 1 and –1(b)(3)(iv), Ex. 1:

Example. X and Y form an equal partnership, the XY Partnership. X contributes $100,000 and Asset 1, capital gain property with an adjusted basis of $50,000 and a fair market value of $100,000. Y contributes $200,000. The XY Partnership uses cash to purchase Assets 2, 3, and 4. After two years, X sells her interest in the XY Partnership to O for $240,000. At the time of transfer, X's share of the partnership's basis in partnership assets is $150,000. Accordingly, O has a $90,000 basis adjustment under Section 743(b).

Immediately after X's transfer of her partnership interest, the adjusted basis and fair market value of the partnership's assets are, as follows:

Assets

	Adjusted Basis	Fair Market Value
Capital Gain Property:		
Asset 1	$50,000	$150,000
Asset 2	200,000	235,000
Ordinary Income Property:		
Asset 3	80,000	90,000
Asset 4	20,000	5,000
Total	$350,000	$480,000

If the XY Partnership sold all of its assets in a fully taxable transaction at fair market value immediately after X's transfer of her partnership interest to O, a $2,500 loss would be allocated to O from the ordinary income property (50 percent of the net depreciation in the ordinary income property). In addition, the total amount of capital gain that would be allocated to O is $92,500 ($50,000 Section 704(c) built-in gain from Asset 1, plus 50 percent of the $85,000 appreciation in the capital gain property, i.e., the remaining $50,000 of appreciation in Asset 1, after accounting for the Section 704(c) built-in gain, and the $35,000 of appreciation in Asset 2). Accordingly, of the $90,000 basis adjustment, ($2,500), a negative amount, is allocated to ordinary income property, and $92,500 is allocated to capital gain property.

The ($2,500) adjustment to ordinary income property is allocated between Asset 3 and Asset 4 as follows. In the hypothetical sale of partnership assets, O would be allocated $5,000 of gain from the sale of Asset 3. Therefore, O's adjustment with respect to Asset 3 is $5,000. O would be allocated $7,500 of loss with respect to Asset 4. Therefore, O's adjustment with respect to Asset 4 is ($7,500).

¶ 21,110

The $92,500 adjustment to capital gain property is allocated between Assets 1 and 2 as follows. In the hypothetical sale of partnership assets, O would be allocated $75,000 of capital gain from the sale of Asset 1. Therefore, O's adjustment with respect to Asset 1 is $75,000. O would be allocated $17,500 of capital gain from the sale of Asset 2. Therefore, O's adjustment with respect to Asset 2 is $17,500.

In identifying the properties of the partnership for the purpose of making these allocations, it is not sufficient to look only to the balance sheet of the partnership. Most partnerships own valuable intangibles, such as goodwill, that also must be taken into account. Since the failure to allocate any amount of the special basis adjustment to goodwill and other intangibles could result in an excessive increase in the basis of ordinary income property, a special rule governs the valuation of partnership assets for purposes of the allocations under Section 755 if the assets of the partnership constitute a trade or business. This rule requires that valuation be made using the residual method under Section 1060 for "applicable asset acquisitions," which involves a three-step process. First, the partnership must determine the fair market value of partnership properties other than Section 197 intangibles[10] "on the basis of all the facts and circumstances." Reg. § 1.755–1(a)(3). Second, the partnership determines the "partnership gross value," which generally is the amount that, if assigned to all partnership property, would result in a liquidating distribution to the partner equal to the transferee's basis in the transferred partnership interest. Reg. § 1.755–1(a)(4). Third, the partnership compares the partnership gross value to the aggregate fair market value of the partnership properties other than Section 197 intangibles. If the aggregate value of the partnership properties other than the Section 197 intangibles is equal to or greater than the partnership gross value, the regulations treat all Section 197 intangibles as having a value of zero for Section 755 purposes. In all other cases, the regulations treat the Section 197 intangibles as having a value equal to the excess of the partnership gross value over the value of the partnership properties other than Section 197 intangibles. That excess then must be allocated to (1) Section 197 intangibles other than goodwill and going concern value to the extent of such assets' actual fair market values and (2) then to goodwill and going concern value (i.e., the remaining amount of the excess, if any, is allocated to goodwill and going concern value). Reg. § 1.755–1(a)(5).

Once the purchasing partner's Section 743(b) special basis adjustment in specific assets has been identified, that basis will affect all partnership computations of income, gain, loss, and deduction with

---

10. For purposes of these Section 755 regulations, "Section 197 intangibles" include all Section 197 intangibles meeting the definition of that term in Section 197 as well as any goodwill or going concern value not meeting that definition. Reg. § 1.755–1(a)(2).

respect to the transferee partner. Thus, if an item of partnership property is sold, the transferee partner's share of the partnership gain or loss from the sale of the property must be reduced by the remaining amount of any positive basis adjustment to the property or increased by the remaining amount of any negative basis adjustment to the property. Reg. § 1.743–1(j)(3)(i). If the item of partnership property is depreciable, the transferee partner's distributive share of the partnership's depreciation is increased to reflect a recovery during the year of any positive basis adjustment (that recovery is made by treating the increased portion of the basis as if it were newly purchased recovery property placed in service when the partnership interest is transferred). Reg. § 1.743–1(j)(4)(i). If the Section 743(b) adjustment to depreciable property is a negative adjustment, that adjustment is recovered over the remaining recovery period for the property by reducing the partner's distributive share of the partnership's depreciation (first with respect to the particular item of property and, if in excess of that depreciation, then with respect to the partner's share of partnership depreciation with respect to other property; and, finally, if in excess of all such depreciation, the partner must recognize ordinary income in the amount of the excess). Reg. § 1.743–1(j)(4)(ii). The allocations of gain or loss from the sale of partnership property, or of depreciation, to the remaining partners are wholly unaffected by the special basis adjustment of the purchasing partner. Reg. § 1.743–1(j)(1).

One last important point bears mention here. As discussed in Chapter 18, under a change made in 2004, Section 704(c)(1)(C) now provides that (1) a built-in loss with respect to property contributed by a partner may be taken into account only by the contributing partner and (2) the basis of the contributed property is treated as being equal to its fair market value at the time of contribution for purposes of determining the amount of items allocated to the other partners. Thus, if the contributing partner transfers the partnership interest before the partnership sells the contributed property with the built-in loss, no other partner may be allocated any portion of the built-in loss. Neither the purchasing partner nor any other partner may benefit from this built-in loss. This rule will affect the determination and allocation of the Section 743(b) adjustment discussed above.

[¶ 21,115]

Problems

The Tree Farm is a partnership of John and Karla. Its books show the following properties, and it has no liabilities. Except as otherwise provided in Problem 3, assume that none of the partnership's assets listed below were contributed to the partnership by the partners. The partnership has made a Section 754 election.

¶ 21,110

	Basis	*Value*
Inventory X	$ 130	$ 70
Inventory Y	70	130
Equipment	200	700
Building...................................	600	1,000
Land......................................	400	1,200
Total	$1,400	$3,100

1.   Assume that the partners have an equal interest in profits, losses, and capital and that Karla sells her interest to Nancy for $1,550. Assume also that the partnership had purchased the equipment several years ago for $800 and has properly deducted $600 of depreciation with respect to the equipment. Compute the amount of Nancy's special basis adjustment and the allocation of that adjustment to specific partnership properties.

2.   Assume the same facts as in Problem 1, except that at the time of sale of the partnership interest, the land is worth only $100 and the partnership has goodwill with a fair market value of $1,100 and an adjusted basis of zero. Compute the amount of Nancy's special basis adjustment and the allocation of that adjustment to specific partnership properties.

3.   Assume the same facts as in Problem 1, except that the land was contributed by John when its value was $800 and its basis $400, but no other asset is subject to Section 704(c). Otherwise, the partners share in profits, losses, and capital equally. The basis for John's interest in the partnership is $500, and the basis for Karla's interest is $900.

a.   If Karla now sells her interest to Nancy for $1,550, what special basis adjustment will be available to Nancy and how must it be allocated over the partnership properties?

b.   If instead John sells his interest to Nancy for $1,550, how will the amount of the adjustments differ? See Reg. § 1.704–3(a)(7) and (a)(6)(ii).

[¶ 21,120]

F.   THE SALE OF AN INTEREST:
A COMPREHENSIVE
ILLUSTRATION

The effect of the several provisions just described may be easier to digest after examining the following illustration. The balance sheet for the ABC Partnership is as follows:

¶ 21,120

ABC Partnership

Assets	Book Value (Basis)	F.M. Value	Liabilities & Capital	Book Value	F.M. Value
Cash	$ 30,000	$ 30,000	Bank Loan	$ 20,000	$ 20,000
Accounts receivable	0	50,000			
Blueprints	20,000	30,000			
Fixed assets:			Capital:		
Furniture & equipment	10,000	20,000	A (20%)	18,000	36,000
Land	10,000	40,000	B (30%)	27,000	54,000
Building	40,000	30,000	C (50%)	45,000	90,000
	$110,000	$200,000		$110,000	$200,000

The ABC Partnership, which is engaged in providing architectural services, computes its income on the cash method. The furniture and equipment were purchased for $30,000 and depreciation to date has totaled $20,000. This property is subject to depreciation recapture under Section 1245. None of the partnership's assets have Section 704(c) built-in gain or loss. Although the ABC Partnership books do not reflect goodwill, assume that the partnership business is worth $230,000, which means that under the residual method of valuing goodwill, the partnership goodwill is worth $30,000 (and, of course, the partnership has a zero basis in that goodwill).

Assume that the entire interest of A, who held a 20–percent interest in both partnership capital and in profits and losses, is sold to D for cash of $42,000.

[¶ 21,125]

1. DETERMINATION OF GAIN (OR LOSS) ON THE SALE OF A PARTNER'S INTEREST

The sale would close the partnership year as to A. Thus, A's 20–percent share of partnership income and expense derived to date would be allocated to her as of the date of the sale. That allocation would increase or decrease the basis of her partnership interest for the purpose of computing gain or loss on the sale. For this illustration, however, it is assumed that no income or loss would be allocated to A.

A's amount realized on the sale would be $42,000 plus her $4,000 share of partnership liabilities, or $46,000. The basis for her partnership interest would be $18,000 plus her share of partnership liabilities, or $22,000. Thus, the overall gain on the sale would be $24,000. However, because the partnership has appreciated Section 751(a) property, some portion of that gain will be taxed as ordinary income. To determine that amount under the current Section 751 regulations, we must compute the amount of income or loss that would have been allocated to A from Section 751 property if the partnership had sold all of its property in a fully taxable transaction for cash in an amount equal to the fair market value of the property immediately before A's transfer of the partnership interest.

Because the partnership has no special allocations under Section 704(b) and no assets subject to the allocation rules of Section 704(c), that computation is not difficult in this case. If the ABC Partnership had sold all of its Section 751 property immediately before A's sale of the partnership interest, the partnership would have ordinary income of $70,000 from such sale. Because A has a 20–percent interest in both capital and profits, she would have been allocated $14,000 (i.e., 20 percent) of that ordinary income and that is the amount of her ordinary income on the sale of the partnership interest under Section 751(a). Notice that while the partnership might be entitled to an ordinary loss on the sale of the building under Section 1231, the building is not Section 751(a) property and the loss does not reduce the ordinary income on the sale. Thus, as to A, that loss is converted into a capital loss. A's Section 751(a) gain can be computed as follows:

Step One: Gain under Section 751(a)

Amount of Gain From Hypothetical Sale of the
Partnership's Section 751(a) Property:

Items of Partnership Property	Amount Realized	Partnership Basis	Ordinary Income
Accounts receivable	$50,000	$ 0	$50,000
Furniture and equipment—			
Depreciation recapture	10,000	0	10,000
Inventory (blueprints)	30,000	20,000	10,000
Total	$90,000	$20,000	$70,000

A's 20% share of this ordinary income is $14,000.

Finally, after the Section 751(a) calculation is complete, Section 741 applies to the balance of the sale. To the extent that the ABC Partnership has property which is not Section 751(a) property, A is selling her interest in the partnership, viewed as an entity without regard to the underlying assets. A determines the amount of gain or loss on the sale of the partnership interest that will be treated as capital gain or loss under Section 741 by subtracting the amount of ordinary income or loss attributable to the Section 751 property from the partner's total amount of gain or loss on the sale of the partnership interest.

Step Two: Gain under Section 741

A's Total Gain on Sale of Partnership Interest	$24,000
A's Ordinary Income under Section 751(a) (as Determined in Step One)	– 14,000
A's Section 741 Gain	$10,000

¶ **21,125**

A therefore is required to report a capital gain of $10,000 under Section 741 as well as ordinary income of $14,000 under Section 751 on the sale of her partnership interest.

[¶ 21,130]

2. DETERMINATION OF BASIS TO THE PURCHASER

The basis of the purchased partnership interest to D will be the sum of the $42,000 cash paid for the interest plus his $4,000 share of the liabilities of the partnership, or $46,000. If the partnership has not filed the Section 754 election, the sale will not affect the inside basis for the partnership properties. (The mandatory basis adjustment in Section 743(a) does not apply here because the partnership has no "substantial built-in loss," as defined in Section 743(d)(1).) Thus, for example, if the partnership were to sell the blueprints for $30,000 and retain the cash proceeds, D's share of the gain would be $2,000. He would be taxed on that gain and would increase the basis of his interest to $48,000, although the value of that interest would remain unchanged at $46,000.

If the partnership has made the Section 754 election, D's special basis adjustment must be computed and allocated to specific properties. Under the current regulations, the amount of the adjustment is the difference between D's $46,000 basis for the partnership interest and D's share of the adjusted basis to the partnership of the partnership's property. D's share of the adjusted basis of the partnership property is equal to the sum of D's interest in the "partnership's previously taxed capital," plus D's share of partnership liabilities. D's interest in the partnership's previously taxed capital is $18,000–equal to the amount of cash D would receive on a liquidation of the partnership following the hypothetical cash sale of all of its assets for their fair market values (including the goodwill valued at $30,000), $42,000 (20 percent of $210,000, i.e., the $230,000 proceeds from the hypothetical sale minus $20,000 used to pay off the partnership liabilities before the hypothetical liquidation); plus $2,000, the amount of tax loss that would be allocated to D from this hypothetical cash sale (20 percent of the partnership's $10,000 loss from the sale of the building); minus $26,000, the amount of tax gain that would be allocated to D from this hypothetical cash sale (20 percent of the partnership's $130,000 of gain from the sale of the inventory (blueprint), accounts receivable, furniture and equipment, land, and goodwill). Thus, D's share of the adjusted basis of the partnership property is D's $18,000 share of the partnership's previously taxed capital plus B's $4,000 share of partnership liabilities, or $22,000. The $24,000 difference between D's $46,000 basis in the purchased partnership interest and D's $22,000 share of the partnership's adjusted basis in its property is the amount of the total Section 743(b) adjustment. That

$24,000 adjustment must then be allocated among the partnership properties under Section 755.

The first step in the Section 755 allocation is to divide the partnership's properties into two categories: (1) capital assets and Section 1231 assets ("capital gain property") and (2) all other property of the partnership ("ordinary income property"). Note that the definition of ordinary income property largely parallels the definition of Section 751(a) property and includes properties and potential gain treated as unrealized receivables under Section 751(c). Thus, the depreciation recapture in the furniture and equipment is treated as a separate asset with a fair market value of $10,000 and an adjusted basis to the partnership of zero. The amount of the basis adjustment allocated to the class of ordinary income property is the total amount of income, gain, or loss that would be allocated to D, the transferee partner, from the sale of all ordinary income property in the hypothetical sale transaction of all of the partnership assets. As shown above in the connection with the determination of D's Section 751(a) gain on the sale of the partnership interest, the ABC Partnership would have $70,000 total gain on a hypothetical sale of all its ordinary income property and D's share of that gain would be $14,000 (i.e., 20 percent of $70,000).

The amount of the basis adjustment allocated to the class of capital gain property is the residual amount of the Section 743(b) adjustment–namely, the total amount of the Section 743(b) basis adjustment of $24,000 less the $14,000 portion of the adjustment allocated to the class of ordinary income property, or $10,000.

The next step required under Section 755 is to further allocate that adjustment within each class. The amount of the $14,000 basis adjustment allocated to each item within the ordinary income property class is the amount of income, gain, or loss that would be allocated to D from the sale of the ordinary income property item in the hypothetical sale transaction:

Items of Ordinary Income Property	Market Value	Partnership Basis	Ordinary Income	D's Share of Ordinary Income
(1) Accounts receivable	$50,000	$ 0	$50,000	$10,000
Furniture and equipment—				
(2) Depreciation recapture	10,000	0	10,000	2,000
(3) Inventory (blueprints)	30,000	20,000	10,000	2,000
Total				$14,000

Thus, the amount of the adjustment allocated to the accounts receivable is $10,000, to the depreciation recapture is $2,000, and to the inventory (blueprints) also is $2,000.

The amount of the $10,000 basis adjustment allocated to each item within the capital gain property class is (1) the amount of income, gain, or loss that would be allocated to D from the sale of the capital gain property item in the hypothetical transaction; minus (2) the product of (a) the total amount of gain or loss that would be allocated to D from the hypothetical sale of all items of capital gain property, minus the amount of the positive basis adjustment to all items of capital gain property, multiplied by (b) a fraction with a numerator that is the fair market value of the item of capital gain property to the partnership and a denominator that is the total fair market value of all of the partnership's items of capital gain property. In this example, as in many simple cases, element (2) of this calculation does not come into play because it equals zero (i.e., the total amount of gain that would be allocated to D from a hypothetical sale of all of the partnership's capital gain property equals here the amount of the positive basis adjustment to all items of capital gain property). Thus, it works out that the amount of the $10,000 basis adjustment allocated to each item within the capital gain property class is the amount of gain or loss that would be allocated from the sale of each item of capital gain property in the hypothetical sale transaction. (As mentioned above, note that the portion of the furniture and equipment apart from the depreciation recapture is treated as an item of capital gain property with an adjusted basis and fair market value of $10,000.)

Items of Capital Gain Property	Market Value	Basis	Capital Gain or (Loss)	D's Share of Capital Gain
Furniture and equipment	$10,000	$10,000	$ 0	$ 0
Land.	40,000	10,000	30,000	6,000
Building	30,000	40,000	(10,000)	(2,000)
Goodwill	30,000	0	30,000	6,000
Total				$10,000

Thus, D must allocate $6,000 of the basis adjustment to the land, ($2,000), a negative amount, of the adjustment to the building, and $6,000 of the adjustment to the goodwill. Note that under the current regulations even though the overall adjustment within the capital gain property class is positive, the portion of the adjustment allocated to some properties can be positive and the portion allocated to other properties can be negative.

If the partnership sold all of its assets, D would not have any net gain or loss; his total inside basis equals the value of his interest in the partnership properties. Moreover, if the partnership sold the land, for example, none of the gain would be taxable to D, because D's $6,000 share of the gain from the sale of the land would be offset by his $6,000 special basis adjustment under Section 743(b) with respect to the land. Similarly, if the partnership sold the building for a loss of $10,000, D would not have a deductible loss for his $2,000 share of the loss because it would be offset by his ($2,000) special basis adjustment with respect to the building.

¶ 21,130

Chapter 22

CURRENT DISTRIBUTIONS
TO PARTNERS

[¶ 22,000]

A. INTRODUCTION

In introducing the tax rules governing the formation of partnerships, it was noted that Subchapter K embodies a strong policy against the taxation of property transfers between partners and their partnership. This Chapter examines the second aspect of that policy: the taxation of distributions of cash or other property to partners.

In sharp contrast to the rules governing corporate distributions under Subchapter C, the historic approach under Subchapter K has been to exempt distributions from tax at both the partner and the partnership levels to the maximum extent possible. That exemption is not permanent; the tax that otherwise would be imposed at the time of distribution is deferred through an adjustment to the basis of the distributed property.

Nevertheless, the tax benefit from the principle of deferral can be very substantial—sometimes more substantial than Congress or the Treasury Department is willing to tolerate. In Chapter 16, we discussed Reg. § 1.701–2, which authorizes the IRS to disregard the form of a partnership transaction if the partnership is being used in a transaction (or a series of related transactions) with a principal purpose of reducing the partners' federal tax liability in a manner inconsistent with the intent of Subchapter K. Moreover, we have already seen in Chapter 20 that by an amendment to Section 707, Congress has trimmed back the deferral of tax on some partnership distributions by authorizing regulations that would characterize certain distributions as fully taxable sales and the Treasury Department has issued regulations under revised Section 707 that do just that. In this Chapter, we will examine five additional Code provisions that trim back the deferral of tax on partnership distributions:

(1) If a partner contributes appreciated or depreciated property to a partnership and the partnership distributes such property to another partner within seven years of the contribution, Section 704(c)(1)(B) generally requires the contributing partner to recognize gain or loss as if the property had been sold at its fair market value at the time of distribution (see ¶ 22,090);

(2) If a partner contributes appreciated property to a partnership and the partnership distributes other property to the contributing partner within seven years of the contribution, Section 737 generally requires the partner to recognize the precontribution gain on the contributed property to the extent that the partnership distributes other property to the partner with a value that exceeds the partner's basis in the partnership interest (see ¶ 22,095);

(3) Section 731(c) treats certain "marketable securities" as cash for purposes of the partnership distribution rules and, thus, the distributee partner generally will be taxed on a distribution of such securities if their fair market value exceeds the partner's basis in the partnership interest (see ¶ 22,100);

(4) In certain situations, under Section 732(f)(4), a corporate partner will have to recognize long-term capital gain on a partnership distribution of stock in another corporation controlled by the corporate partner (see ¶ 22,022); and

(5) Section 751(b) treats a partnership distribution as a taxable sale or exchange (rather than a nontaxable distribution) if the distributee partner receives an interest in certain ordinary income assets of the partnership (i.e., substantially appreciated inventory or unrealized receivables) in exchange for the partner's interest in certain other partnership property (or receives an interest in certain other partnership property in exchange for the partner's interest in substantially appreciated inventory or unrealized receivables) (see ¶ 22,110).

B. PARTNER LEVEL CONSEQUENCES

[¶ 22,005]

1. CASH DISTRIBUTIONS

Distributions of cash to a partner generally are not subject to tax except to the extent that the distribution exceeds the basis of the partner's interest in the partnership. § 731(a)(1). Since partners are taxed directly on their share of partnership income whether it is distributed or not, the mere transfer of the fruits of that income to a partner should not be subject to an additional tax. To the extent that the distribution is not taxed, the partner's basis in the partnership interest must be reduced. §§ 733(1) and 705(a)(2). Since a partner's outside basis represents the sum of the capital contributions to the partnership plus the income previously taxed to the partner (or minus the losses previously flowing through to the partner), a cash distribution in excess of that basis would constitute a gain that had not been previously taxed and thus must be taxed at the time of distribution. If there is a taxable gain, the gain is taxed in the same manner as gain from the sale of a partnership interest. § 731(a) (flush language). Because current distributions are not closed transactions, no loss can be recognized until the partner retires. § 731(a)(2).

These rules apply only to transfers to a partner that are treated as distributions for tax purposes. If, for example, a partnership loans money to a partner, the transaction is governed by Sections 707 and 752. In addition, some transfers to partners may be treated as the proceeds of a sale or as compensation by Section 707(a)(2) and thus be excluded from the application of the distribution rules. See ¶ 20,090.

We noted earlier (at ¶ 19,020) that partnership distributions made during a year might become taxable because a partner's basis for the partnership interest apparently is not adjusted for the partnership's income of the year until the end of the year. Partnerships commonly avoid that difficulty by advancing funds to partners during the year against their share of partnership earnings for the year. If the advance is respected as a loan, it will not be treated as a distribution until year-end and will benefit from the basis adjustment for that year. Reg. § 1.731–1(a)(1)(ii) and (c)(2). What steps might be taken to ensure that a transfer will be treated as a loan rather than a distribution?

Because the contribution of cash by a partner results in an increase in the partner's basis in the partnership interest, the pro rata distribution of cash by a partnership is rarely taxable. The following case, however, proves that rarely does not mean never.

[¶ 22,010]

HELMER v. COMMISSIONER

United States Tax Court, 1975.
T.C. Memo. 1975–160.

[Two brothers, T.L. and George Helmer, operated a cattle-raising business as a 50–50 partnership and entered into an option agreement with a third party to sell certain lands owned by the partnership. Under the terms of the agreement, the consideration for the option which totaled $300,000 was to be applied to the purchase price in the event the option were exercised. There was no provision for repayment of the amounts paid under the agreement in the event the option was not exercised. During the taxable years in issue, consideration for the option was paid directly to the partners. These distributions exceeded the bases of the interests of the respective partners in the partnership. The optionee, however, had not exercised the option. After determining that there was a partnership and that the land was owned by the partnership, the Tax Court discussed the tax consequences of the distribution of the option proceeds.]

WILES, JUDGE: * * *.

* * *

Section 731 generally provides that to the extent a distribution of money by a partnership to a partner exceeds the adjusted basis of his interest in the partnership immediately prior to such distribution, gain will be recognized by such partner. * * *

* * *

* * * [P]etitioners alternatively contend that no gain arose upon distribution of cash to T.L. and George Helmer because receipt of the option consideration created a partnership liability. Section 752 generally provides that any increase in a partner's share of liability of a partnership should be treated as a contribution of money by such partner. This results in an increase in the basis of the partner's partnership interest by the amount of such liability. Section 1.752–1(a)(1), Income Tax Regs. Petitioners contend that receipt of the option payments by the partnership created a liability of the partnership and increased their adjusted bases in the partnership by such amounts. Therefore distribution of the money received was not in excess of their adjusted bases. Respondent contends that no such liability arose and therefore no adjustments can be made in their bases.

We are faced with a unique situation.[4] Helmer Brothers received payments pursuant to the option agreement when there was no forfeiture of any of the option payments, the option had not been terminated, nor had any portion of the option been exercised by the optionee. Respondent, in his brief, conceded that the income from the option payments was deferrable by the partnership until characterized as ordinary income (because of a default by the optionee) or capital gains (because of an exercise of the option by the optionee). Respondent does contend, however, that the amounts distributed to T.L. and George Helmer were in excess of their bases because no liability arose upon receipt of such money.

---

4. We believe that the problem created in this case is analogous to the receipt of tax-exempt income under section 705(a)(1)(B) which permits a partner's basis to be increased by the amount of such income so that upon distribution there will be no recognition of gain in excess of basis. We also note that the situation may run counter to the general concept of subchapter K that the partnership is a conduit as to income and loss items. Neither party, however, raised the issue whether, under other provisions of subchapter K, there would not be recognition of income to the petitioners in this case. We therefore express no opinion with regard to issues other than those raised by the parties * * *.

We agree with respondent that no liability arose upon receipt of the option payments by Helmer Brothers. There were no provisions in the option agreement for repayment of the amounts paid under the agreement should the agreement terminate. The moneys received under the option agreement were received without any restrictions except that upon exercise of the option such amounts would be applied against the purchase price. Thus, the restriction only affected the character of the gain in the partnership's hands. It is this lack of ability to determine character of income (not any liability to repay or to perform) that causes the deferral of the recognition of the income by the partnership until the option is either exercised or lapsed. * * * *Virginia Iron Coal & Coke Company*, 37 B.T.A. 195 (1938), affd. 99 F.2d 919 (C.A.4, 1938), cert. denied 307 U.S. 630 (1939). The option agreement, however, created no liability on the part of the partnership to repay the funds paid nor to perform any services in the future. Therefore we hold that no liability arose under section 752 and the partners' bases cannot be increased by such amounts. [The partners were, thus, taxed to the extent that the distribution of the option proceeds exceeded the bases in their partnership interests.]

* * *

[¶ 22,012]

Note

As mentioned at ¶ 17,008, if a partner has taxable capital gain on account of a distribution from the partnership, the capital gain or loss recognized is divided between long-term and short-term capital gain or loss in the same proportion as the long-term or short-term capital gain or loss that the distributee partner would realize if her entire partnership interest were transferred in a fully taxable transaction immediately before the distribution. Reg. § 1.1223–3(d)(2) and –3(f), Ex. 8.

Partnership distributions to a partner generally do not affect the determination of a partner's holding period in a partnership interest. Reg. § 1.1223–3(d)(1) and –3(f), Ex. 7. However, the regulations contain a special rule that allows a partner to reduce cash contributions made within one year of a distribution by the partnership that results in taxable gain or loss to the partner under Section 731 by cash distributions received during that one-year period on a last-in, first-out basis, treating all cash contributions as if they were received at the time of the taxable distribution. See Reg. § 1.1223–3(b)(2), which is illustrated by an example at Reg. § 1.1223–3(f), Ex. 8. Moreover, certain deemed contributions of cash under Section 752(a) and deemed distributions of cash under Section 752(b) are disregarded for purposes of determining the holding period for a partner's interest in the partnership. See Reg. §§ 1.1223–3(b)(3) and 1.704–1(b)(2)(iv)(*c*).

¶ 22,012

[¶ 22,015]

Problems

1.   Aside from the point raised in footnote 4 of the Tax Court's *Helmer* decision, at ¶ 22,010, what steps might the parties have taken to avoid tax on this distribution?

2.   Videos Unlimited is a calendar year partnership that earns a steady income of $10,000 per month. At the end of March it transferred $15,000 to Bridget, a 20–percent partner, who had a zero basis for her partnership interest at the beginning of the year. If no further transfers are made to her this year, what will be the tax consequences of her receipt of the $15,000 distribution?

3.   What would be the result in Problem 2 if the $15,000 were referred to by the parties as an "advance"? Should so labeling the distribution defer its tax effect if the partner in fact had no obligation to repay the distribution without regard to the actual income of the partnership for the year? See Reg. § 1.731–1(a)(1)(ii) and (c)(2).

[¶ 22,020]

2.   PROPERTY DISTRIBUTIONS

Under Section 731, as a general rule, distributions to a partner of noncash property are not subject to tax.[1] Rather, a property distribution is a nonrecognition transaction in which gain or loss is deferred through basis adjustments in a manner very similar to the operation of other nonrecognition provisions of the Code. The basis of distributed property in the hands of the partnership carries over to the property in the hands of the partner. § 732(a)(1); Reg. § 1.732–1(a). However, to prevent a tax-free step-up in the partner's basis, the basis of the property cannot exceed the basis of the distributee partner's interest in the partnership (reduced by any cash distributed to the partner in the same transaction). § 732(a)(2); Reg. § 1.732–1(a). If the distributee partner is entitled to a special basis adjustment in the distributed property under Section 743(b) because the partnership had a Section 754 election in effect when the partner's interest was acquired, the carryover basis of the property must be increased or decreased by that adjustment. Reg. § 1.732–2.[2]

At the same time, the basis for the distributee's partnership interest must be reduced by the basis for the distributed property. § 733(2); Reg. § 1.733–1. In effect, the partner's pre-distribution basis for the partner-

---

1.   As noted at ¶ 22,000, this general rule of nontaxability of partnership distributions of noncash property is subject to a growing number of exceptions that are discussed later in this Chapter: Sections 731(c) (see ¶ 22,100), 704(c)(1)(B) (see ¶ 22,090), 737 (see ¶ 22,095), 732(f)(4) (see ¶ 22,022), and 751(b) (see ¶ 22,110).

2.   Note that if the distributee partner receives a distribution of property with respect to which *another partner* has a Section 743(b) basis adjustment, the distributee partner does not take that other partner's basis adjustment into account under Section 732. See Reg. § 1.743–1(g)(2)(i).

ship interest must be allocated among all distributions and the remaining partnership interest, with that basis allocated first to cash, second to other property to the extent of the partnership's basis in that property, and finally to the partnership interest. When the dust settles, the gain in the distributed property is preserved (or possibly increased) by the carryover basis, and the gain in the partnership interest is preserved in the bases for the several properties now owned by the partner.

An example may help illustrate these rules. Assume that a partner has a basis of $10,000 for a partnership interest, although the value of the interest is far greater, and that the partnership distributes to the partner $3,000 in cash and Property A which has a basis of $3,000 to the partnership and a value of $8,000. The partner will not recognize any gain. After the distribution, the $10,000 pre-distribution basis for the partnership interest will be allocated over the assets held by the partner as follows:

Cash	$3,000
Property A	3,000
Partnership interest	4,000

See Reg. § 1.732–1(a), Exs. 1 and 2. Notice that in this simple illustration involving only one distributed property the value of Property A is irrelevant to the computations of the partner's possible gain on the cash distribution and basis in the various assets. However, for the purpose of computing the partners' capital accounts, the value of Property A would indeed be relevant. The distributee partner's capital account would be reduced by the cash and the value of the property distributed.

If the partnership distributes more than one property to a partner and the partnership basis cannot simply carry over to the properties in the hands of the partner because the aggregate bases of the properties distributed exceed the basis of the partnership interest, the pre-distribution basis for the partnership interest must be allocated over the properties under the somewhat complicated special rule contained in Section 732(c). Under the two-tier rule of that provision, basis must first be allocated to any unrealized receivables or inventory items to the extent of the partnership's basis in those assets. § 732(c)(1)(A)(i); Reg. § 1.732–1(c)(1)(i). That rule will avoid any increase in the amount of ordinary income on which the distributee partner will be taxed on a later sale of the property. If the distributee partner's basis in the partnership interest is less than the full amount of the partnership's basis in the distributed unrealized receivables and inventory, that shortfall in basis must be allocated among the unrealized receivables and inventory. § 732(c)(1)(A)(ii); Reg. § 1.732–1(c)(1)(i). That basis shortfall, called a basis "decrease" by Section 732(c), is first allocated to (and, thus, reduces the distributee partner's basis in) the inventory items with unrealized depreciation in proportion to their amounts of unrealized depreciation. § 732(c)(1)(A)(ii) and (c)(3)(A); Reg. § 1.732–1(c)(2)(i). Any remaining basis shortfall not allocated under this rule is allocated to the unrealized receivables and inventory items in proportion to the partnership's adjusted basis in the properties (as reduced by the allocations made under the rule described in the prior sentence). § 732(c)(1)(A)(ii) and (c)(3)(B); Reg. § 1.732–1(c)(2)(i).

The distributee partner's basis in the partnership interest remaining after the allocations to unrealized receivables and inventory is allocated to the other partnership properties distributed to the extent of the partnership's basis in those properties immediately before the distribution. § 732(c)(1)(B)(i); Reg. § 1.732–1(c)(1)(ii). If the partner's remaining basis in the partnership interest is less than the partnership's basis in the other distributed properties, that basis shortfall ("decrease") is first allocated to the distributed properties with unrealized depreciation in proportion to their respective amounts of unrealized depreciation. § 732(c)(1)(B)(ii) and (c)(3)(A); Reg. § 1.732–1(c)(2)(i). Any remaining shortfall in basis is allocated to the other distributed properties in proportion to the partnership's basis in those properties (as reduced by the allocations made under the rule described in the prior sentence). § 732(c)(1)(B)(ii) and (c)(3)(B); Reg. § 1.732–1(c)(2)(i).

Assume that in the previous example, the partner had received inventory having a basis of $9,000 to the partnership and a value of $15,000, instead of cash. Following the distribution, the partner's $10,000 basis in the partnership interest would be allocated as follows:

Inventory	$9,000
Property A	1,000
Partnership interest	0

Now, to illustrate the complicated mechanics of these allocation rules when there is a basis shortfall, assume in the previous example, that the partner (who has a basis of $10,000 in the partnership interest) had received the following partnership properties in the distribution: inventory having a basis of $8,000 to the partnership and a value of $15,000, Property A having a basis of $3,000 to the partnership and a value of $5,000, and Property B having a basis of $4,000 to the partnership and a value of $2,000. The partner will not recognize any gain or loss on the distribution under Section 731 and the basis of the distributed properties will be determined under Section 732(c).

First, under Section 732(c)(1)(A)(i), the distributee partner will first allocate the basis in the partnership interest to the distributed inventory item in an amount equal to the partnership's $8,000 basis in the inventory; thus, the partner carries over the partnership's $8,000 basis in the inventory. Second, under Section 732(c)(1)(B)(i), the partner's remaining $2,000 basis in the partnership interest is first allocated to the extent of the partnership's basis in each other distributed property:

Property A, $3,000, and Property B, $4,000, for a total of $7,000. However, under Section 732(c)(1)(B)(ii) and 732(c)(3), because the partner's remaining basis in the partnership interest is only $2,000, a downward adjustment ("basis decrease") of $5,000 ($7,000 minus $2,000) is required. The basis decrease is first allocated to the property having unrealized depreciation, Property B, to the extent of the $2,000 unrealized depreciation in that property, thus reducing the basis in Property B from $4,000 to $2,000. The remaining $3,000 of basis decrease is allocated between Property A and Property B in proportion to their adjusted bases (after taking into account the adjustment to the basis in Property B already made); accordingly, three-fifths of the decrease, or $1,800, is allocated to Property A, reducing the basis in that property from $3,000 to $1,200, and two-fifths of the decrease, or $1,200, is allocated to Property B, further reducing the basis in that property from $2,000 to $800. To summarize, following the distribution, the partner's $10,000 basis in the partnership interest would be allocated as follows:

Inventory	$8,000
Property A	1,200
Property B	800
Partnership interest	0

Before the Taxpayer Relief Act of 1997, the distributee partners allocated their basis in the partnership interest among the distributed properties in proportion to the partnership's adjusted basis in the distributed properties (without regard to the fair market value of the properties distributed). Congress modified the basis allocation rules to take into account the relative amounts of unrealized appreciation or depreciation in the properties distributed because it was concerned that the prior law rules placed a premium on tax planning and permitted "basis shifting transactions in which basis is allocated so as to increase basis artificially, giving rise to inflated depreciation deductions or artificially large losses." S. Rep. No. 33, 105th Cong., 1st Sess. 190 (1997).

Despite this legislative change to the allocation rules, these partnership distribution rules still create ample other opportunities for tax planning or abuse—depending on one's perspective and the aggressiveness of the plan. For example, a partnership planning a cash distribution that would exceed the bases of the partners' interests might consider purchasing property instead and distributing that property to the partners. What would that accomplish? Could that tax advantage be challenged successfully? Would Section 707(a)(2) be relevant? What about the partnership anti-abuse rule in Reg. § 1.701–2?

Historically, as discussed at ¶ 22,110, the major exception to the general rule of nontaxability of partnership distributions of noncash property was Section 751(b), which focuses on one area of potential abuse: disproportionate distributions that amount to sales or exchanges of the distributee partner's interest in the partnership's ordinary income assets for other partnership property or vice versa. In recent years, Congress has focused on another area of potential abuse involving partnership distributions: use of partnership distributions of noncash property to avoid or defer the recognition of precontribution gain or loss by the contributing partner under Section 704(c). As discussed at ¶¶ 22,090 and 22,095, Sections 704(c)(1)(B) and 737 significantly restrict the scope of nonrecognition under Section 731 for partners who obtained their partnership interests in return for appreciated property. In addition, as discussed at ¶ 22,100, Congress has focused on yet another area of perceived abuse—distributions of marketable securities that are equivalent to cash. Section 731(c) now generally treats such distributions as cash distributions that may result in taxable gain to the distributee partner. Finally, in 1999, Congress enacted Section 732(f) (discussed in the next section at ¶ 22,022) to deal with another area of potential tax avoidance involving partnership distributions.

[¶ 22,022]

3. DISTRIBUTIONS OF STOCK OF A CONTROLLED CORPORATION TO A CORPORATE PARTNER

In 1999, Congress enacted Section 732(f) to deal with potential tax avoidance involving the distribution by a partnership to a corporate partner of stock in another corporation controlled by the corporate partner (the "distributed corporation") immediately after the distribution or at any time thereafter. (A corporate partner controls a distributed corporation for this purpose if it owns at least 80 percent of the total voting power and total value of the distributed corporation's stock. § 732(f)(5).) Congress explained its concerns, as follows:

> If corporate stock is distributed by a partnership to a corporate partner with a low basis in its partnership interest, the basis of the stock is reduced in the hands of the partner so that the stock basis equals the distributee partner's adjusted basis in its partnership interest. No comparable reduction is made in the basis of the corporation's assets, however. The effect of reducing the stock basis can be negated by a subsequent liquidation of the corporation under section 332.

REASONS FOR CHANGE

> The Committee is concerned that the downward adjustment to the basis of property distributed by a partnership may be nullified if the distributed property is corporate stock. The distributed corporation can be liquidated by the corporate partner, so that the stock basis adjustment has no effect. Similarly, if the corporations file a consolidated return, their taxable income may be computed without

reference to the downward adjustment to the basis of the stock. These results can occur either if the partnership has contributed property to the distributed corporation, or if the property was held by the corporation before the distribution. Therefore, the provision requires a basis reduction to the property of the distributed corporation.

S. Rep. No. 201, 106th Cong., 1st Sess. 49–50 (1999) (footnote omitted).

Under the general rule in Section 732(f)(1), the distributed corporation must reduce its adjusted bases in its assets by the amount of the excess of (1) the partnership's adjusted basis in the stock of the distributed corporation immediately before the distribution, over (2) the corporate partner's adjusted basis in that distributed stock immediately after the distribution under Section 732(a) and (c). This basis adjustment is allocated among the distributed corporation's properties in accordance with the rules in Section 732(c) discussed above. However, this basis reduction provision will not apply if the corporate partner (i) does not have control of the distributed corporation immediately after the distribution but later acquires control of the distributed corporation and (ii) establishes to the IRS's satisfaction that the partnership's distribution of the stock was not part of a plan to acquire control of the distributed corporation. § 732(f)(2).

The statute provides two limits on this basis reduction. First, Section 732(f)(3)(A) provides that this basis reduction will not exceed the amount by which (1) the sum of total adjusted bases of the property owned by the distributed corporation and the cash held by the distributed corporation exceeds (2) the corporate partner's adjusted basis in the stock of the distributed corporation. For example, if the distributed corporation has cash of $40,000 and other property with total adjusted bases of $60,000 and the corporate partner's adjusted basis in the stock of the distributed corporation is $20,000, then the basis reduction under Section 732(f) could not exceed $80,000 (($40,000 + $60,000) − $20,000). Second, Section 732(f)(3)(B) provides that the adjusted bases of property (other than money) of the distributed corporation cannot be reduced below zero under this provision.

Section 732(f)(4)(A) requires the corporate partner to recognize long-term capital gain to the extent that the amount of the basis reduction (after applying the limit in Section 732(f)(3)(A)) exceeds the basis of property (other than cash) of the distributed corporation. To prevent potential double taxation of the same amount, the corporate partner thereafter increases its adjusted basis in the stock of the distributed corporation by the amount of gain recognized under Section 732(f)(4)(B). For example, if the basis adjustment were $80,000, and the distributed corporation has cash of $40,000 and other property with total adjusted bases of $60,000, then the distributed corporation would have to reduce the adjusted bases of its noncash property to zero and the corporate partner would have to recognize capital gain of $20,000 (the amount by which the $80,000 basis adjustment exceeds the distributed corporation's total adjusted bases in its noncash property). In this example, the corporate partner would also increase its basis in the stock of the distributed corporation by the gain recognized of $20,000.

Section 732(f)(8) authorizes the Treasury and the IRS to issue regulations to avoid double counting and to prevent abuse of the provision. The legislative history indicates that Congress intended these yet to be issued regulations to prevent taxpayers from avoiding the purposes of the provision through the use of tiered partnerships. See S. Rep. No. 201, 106th Cong., 1st Sess. 52 (1999).

[¶ 22,025]

4. ELECTIVE BASIS ADJUSTMENT TO DISTRIBUTEE

While the basis rules of Section 732 are generous in their deferral of gain on distributions, the carryover basis can have harsh consequences when highly appreciated property is distributed to a new partner. Although the partner's interest in the partnership assets, including the asset distributed, will have been purchased at fair market value, on a distribution the partner will assume the low partnership basis for the asset. Upon a later sale of the asset, the partner will recognize a taxable gain, although there may not have been any economic gain at all. The partner will have only shifted a correspondingly small proportion of the basis for the partnership interest to the distributed property. Thus, the partner will have an offsetting loss inherent in the partnership interest, but that loss will not be recognized until retirement from the partnership.

As we have seen, if the partnership had the Section 754 election in effect when the distributee partner purchased the interest, these results would be avoided. The partner would have been entitled to a special basis adjustment that would follow the property upon its distribution to the new partner.

Under Section 732(d), similar relief is available to distributee partners of partnerships that have not made that election. Upon a distribution of property within two years of the purchase of a partnership interest, the partner may elect to obtain the same basis for the distributed property as the property would have had under Section 743(b) if the Section 754 election were in effect. Reg. § 1.732–1(d)(1)(iii). As a result, a greater proportion of the basis for the partnership interest is shifted to the distributed property, thus eliminating both the potential artificial gain in the property and the potential artificial loss in the partnership interest.

In certain cases, the adjustment under Section 732(d) may be forced on the taxpayer by the IRS. Under regulations authorized by the statute, a partner who acquired her partnership interest in a transfer to which the Section 754 election was not in effect is required to apply the special basis rule in Section 732(d) to a distribution to her if (1) at the time of the acquisition of her interest, the fair market value of all noncash property of the partnership exceeded 110 percent of its adjusted basis to the partnership, (2) an allocation of basis under Section 732(c) upon a liquidation of her interest immediately after the transfer of the interest would have resulted in a shift of basis from nondepreciable property to depreciable property, and (3) a basis adjustment under Section 743(b) would change the basis to her of the property actually distributed. This rule applies whether or not the distribution is made within two years after the transfer of the partnership interest to the distributee partner. Reg. § 1.732–1(d)(4). Note that although the changes to the allocation rules in Section 732(c) made by the 1997 Act make the basis shifting distortions at which this rule is aimed less likely to occur, they did not eliminate the possibility of such distortions. See T.D. 8847, 1999–2 C.B. 701, 702.

[¶ 22,030]

5. DISPOSITION OF DISTRIBUTED PROPERTY

Generally, the consequences of a sale by a partner of property distributed from the partnership are governed by the general rules of the Code and not by Subchapter K. That general rule, however, would permit the conversion of ordinary income to capital gain through the distribution of inventory to a partner who is not a dealer in that property. Accordingly, Section 735(a) attaches a character taint to certain distributions that is similar (but not identical) to the taint attached by Section 724 to contributed property. Under Section 735(a), any gain or loss on the disposition of Section 751–type assets distributed by a partnership, that is, unrealized receivables or inventory (but determined without regard to appreciation), will be ordinary income or loss. However, for inventory items, the Section 735(a) taint applies only to sales or exchanges occurring within five years following the distribution. § 735(a)(2). If tainted property is exchanged for other property in a nonrecognition transaction, the taint carries over to the replacement property. § 735(c)(2)(A).

The recapture items that are treated as unrealized receivables under Section 751 are not subject to the tainting rule of Section 735. § 751(c) (flush language). However, because distributions are carryover basis transactions, the ordinary recapture income contained in distributed property is normally preserved in the hands of the distributee partner. See, e.g., § 1245(a)(2)(A).

Under Section 735(b), the holding period for all types of distributed property in the hands of the distributee partner includes the holding period of the partnership. Thus, the long-term character of a capital asset or Section 1231 asset is not lost by a distribution of the property to a partner. That tacking rule does not apply in measuring the five-year taint attached to inventory by Section 735(a).

[¶ 22,035]

Problems

1. Al–Phred–Bet is a partnership of three equal partners. The partnership was formed six years ago and all partnership contributions were made at that time. It has no liabilities and its assets consist of the following:

	Basis	Value
Cash	$30,000	$30,000
Inventory Item I	12,000	12,000
Capital Asset X	2,000	30,000
Capital Asset Y	1,000	9,000
Capital Asset Z	15,000	15,000
Goodwill	0	84,000
	$60,000	$180,000

Fred has a basis for his interest in the partnership of $20,000. The partnership will make a distribution to him of $30,000 which will reduce his interest from one-third to one-fifth. Ignoring any income or loss for the year, compute the gain recognized by Fred, the basis of the distributed property, and the remaining basis for his partnership interest if the distribution consists of one of the following:

a. Cash of $30,000.

b. Capital Asset X.

c. Cash of $21,000 and Capital Asset Y. See Reg. § 1.731–1 (a)(1)(i) and § 1.732–1(a), Ex. 2.

d. Cash of $3,000, Inventory Item I, and Capital Asset Z.

e. Cash of $12,000, Capital Asset Y, and three-fifths of Capital Asset Z.

2. If Fred sells Inventory Item I after it has been distributed to him under the following circumstances, what will be the federal income tax consequences to him?

a. It is sold for $20,000 after four years.

b. It is exchanged for property of a like kind after four years without the recognition of any gain, and the replacement property is sold for $20,000 two years later.

c. It is sold for $10,000 after three years.

3. Assume that Betty recently purchased her one-third interest in the Al–Phred–Bet partnership for $60,000 and that the partnership had not made the Section 754 election. Six months later the partnership

distributed to her Capital Asset X, which became an inventory item in her hands.

a. Compare the effect on Betty of electing and not electing a basis adjustment under Section 732(d).

b. If Betty contemplates selling her partnership interest but retaining Capital Asset X, should she make the election?

[¶ 22,040]

6. EFFECT OF PARTNERSHIP LIABILITIES

The liabilities of the partnership may enter into the computations of the effect of a distribution in several ways. Initially, as discussed in Chapters 17 and 18, the basis of any partnership interest may have been increased under Section 752 by the liabilities of the partnership. That component of basis will also protect a partner from tax on the distribution of cash. Indeed, one planning technique for avoiding tax on cash distributions is to cause the partnership to incur liabilities that will increase the basis of partnership interests.

Second, if there is a shift in the proportionate interests of the partners in profits or losses, the allocation of basis attributable to partnership liabilities may change. That change in proportionate interest may be produced by a distribution of property, by the admission of a partner, or just by a change in the allocation of profits and losses. Regardless of why the change in proportionate interest occurs, under Section 752(a) and (b) the resulting reduction and increase in liabilities produces constructive contributions of money by some partners and constructive distributions of money to other partners which change the allocation of basis. The distribution rules of Sections 731 through 733 also apply to the constructive distributions of money created by Section 752(b). Such a distribution will reduce the basis of the partnership interest and can result in taxable gain.

Note that the IRS has indicated in two revenue rulings that it will not treat actual and deemed distributions differently for purposes of Reg. § 1.731–1(a)(1)(ii). Thus, in Rev. Rul. 92–97, at ¶ 18,100, the IRS treated a deemed distribution of money to a partner under Section 752(b) resulting from a cancellation of partnership debt as an advance or drawing of money under Reg. § 1.731–1(a)(1)(ii) against that partner's share of cancellation of indebtedness income. Further, in Rev. Rul. 94–4, 1994–1 C.B. 195, the IRS treated a deemed distribution of money under Section 752(b) resulting from a decrease in a partner's share of partnership liabilities as an advance or drawing of money under Reg. § 1.731–1(a)(1)(ii) to the extent of that partner's distributive share of income for the partnership taxable year.

Third, the property distributed to a partner may be subject to a liability. Under Section 752(a) that increase in the individual liabilities of the partner is treated as a contribution of money that increases the basis of the partnership interest. In addition, however, the distribution of encumbered property will also result in a reduction of partnership liabilities and thus a constructive distribution, which may affect the distributee partner as well as the remaining partners.

The net effect of all of these rules is to create a series of distributions and contributions. The order in which these events are deemed to occur could have a significant effect on the tax liability of the partner.

[¶ 22,045]

REVENUE RULING 79-205

1979-2 C.B. 255.

ISSUES

When a partnership makes a nonliquidating distribution of property, (1) is a partner permitted to offset the increase in the partner's liabilities against the decrease in the partner's liabilities in determining the extent of recognition of gain or loss, and (2) is partnership basis adjusted before or after the property distribution?

FACTS

A and B are general partners in M, a general partnership, which was formed for the purposes of owning and operating shopping centers.

On December 31, 1977, M made nonliquidating distributions in a single transaction of a portion of its property to A and B. A and B are equal partners in M. M, A and B are calendar year taxpayers. No assets of the type described in section 751(a) * * * were distributed by M to either A or B.

Immediately prior to the distribution A had an adjusted basis for A's interest in M of 1,000x dollars, and B had an adjusted basis for B's interest in M of 1,500x dollars. The property distributed to A had an adjusted basis to M of 2,000x dollars, and was subject to liabilities of 1,600x dollars. The property distributed to B had an adjusted basis to M of 3,200x dollars and was subject to liabilities of 2,800x dollars. A's individual liabilities increased by 1,600x dollars by reason of the distribution to A. B's individual liabilities increased by 2,800x dollars by reason of the distribution to B. A's share and B's share of the liabilities of M each decreased by 2,200x dollars (½ of 1,600x + ½ of 2,800x dollars) by reason of the distributions. The basis and fair market value of the properties distributed were greater than the liabilities to which they were subject.

* * *

¶ 22,040

ANALYSIS & HOLDING

In general, partnership distributions are taxable under section 731(a)(1) * * * only to the extent that the amount of money distributed exceeds the distributee partner's basis for the partner's partnership interest. This rule reflects the Congressional intent to limit narrowly the area in which gain or loss is recognized upon a distribution so as to remove deterrents to property being moved in and out of partnerships as business reasons dictate. See *S. Rep. No. 1622*, 83rd Cong., 2nd Sess., page 96 (1954). Here, since partner liabilities are both increasing and decreasing in the same transaction offsetting the increases and decreases tends to limit recognition of gain, thereby giving effect to the Congressional intent. Consequently, in a distribution of encumbered property, the resulting liability adjustments will be treated as occurring simultaneously, rather than occurring in a particular order. Therefore, on a distribution of encumbered property, the amount of money considered distributed to a partner for purposes of section 731(a)(1) is the amount (if any) by which the decrease in the partner's share of the liabilities of the partnership under section 752(b) exceeds the increase in the partner's individual liabilities under section 752(a). The amount of money considered contributed by a partner for purposes of section 722 is the amount (if any) by which the increase in the partner's individual liabilities under section 752(a) exceeds the decrease in the partner's share of the liabilities of the partnership under section 752(b). The increase in the partner's individual liabilities occurs by reason of the assumption by the partner of partnership liabilities, or by reason of a distribution of property subject to a liability, to the extent of the fair market value of such property.

Because the distribution was part of a single transaction, the two properties are treated as having been distributed simultaneously to A and B. Therefore, all resulting liability adjustments relating to the distribution of the two properties will be treated as occurring simultaneously, rather than occurring in a particular order.

TREATMENT OF PARTNER A

A will be deemed to have received a net distribution of $600x$ dollars in money, that is, the amount by which the amount of money considered distributed to A ($2,200x$ dollars) exceeds the amount of money considered contributed by A ($1,600x$ dollars). Since $600x$ dollars does not exceed A's basis for A's interest in M immediately before the distribution ($1,000x$ dollars), no gain is recognized to A.

Under section 732(a) * * *, the basis to A of the property distributed to A is the lesser of (i) the adjusted basis of the property to the partnership ($2,000x$ dollars), or (ii) the adjusted basis of A's partnership interest ($1,000x$ dollars) reduced by the amount of money deemed distributed to A ($600x$ dollars). Therefore, the basis of the property in A's hands is 400x dollars. Under section 733, the adjusted basis of A's partnership interest (1,000x dollars) is reduced by the amount of money deemed distributed to A (600x dollars) and by the basis to A of the distributed property (400x dollars). The adjusted basis of A's partnership interest is therefore reduced to zero.

TREATMENT OF PARTNER B

B will be deemed to have made a net contribution of 600x dollars, that is, the amount by which the amount of money considered contributed by B (2,800x dollars) exceeds the amount of money considered distributed to B (2,200x dollars). In applying sections 732(a) and 733 * * * to B, the adjustment to B's basis in B's partnership interest attributable to the liability adjustments resulting from the distributions will be treated as occurring first, and the distribution of property to B as occurring second. By so doing, B's basis for the distributed property is increased and B's basis in B's partnership interest is decreased. This allocation gives greater effect to the general rule of section 732(a)(1), which provides for the partner to have the same basis in distributed property as the partnership had for that property.

Therefore, the first step is that B's basis for B's partnership interest (1,500x dollars) is increased under sections 722 and 705(a) by the amount of the net contribution deemed made by B (600x dollars), and is equal to 2,100x dollars. Next, under section 732(a) * * *, the basis to B of the property distributed to B is the lesser of (i) the adjusted basis of the property to the partnership (3,200x dollars), or (ii) the adjusted basis of B's partnership interest (2,100x dollars) reduced by the amount of money deemed distributed to B (zero). Therefore, the basis of the property in B's hands is 2,100x dollars. Under section 733, the adjusted basis of B's partnership interest (2,100x dollars) is reduced by the amount of money deemed distributed to B (zero) and by the basis to B of the distributed property (2,100x dollars). The adjusted basis of B's partnership interest is therefore zero.

[¶ 22,050]

Problem

SuLu is a partnership of two individuals, each of whom has a 50–percent interest in partnership capital, profits, and losses. The partnership was formed eight years ago and all partnership contributions were made at that time. Sue and Lou each have a basis of $50,000 for their partnership interests (including their share of the partnership's liabilities). The gross value of the partnership assets is $180,000 and the partnership has recourse liabilities totaling $60,000. The partnership will make a distribution having a net value of $30,000 to Sue, which will reduce her interest to one-third. What will be the result to Sue and Lou if the partnership distributes:

¶ 22,045

a.   Unencumbered property having a value of $30,000 and a basis of $15,000.

b.   Property having a gross value of $90,000 and a basis of $75,000, but subject to a liability of $60,000, which Sue assumes.

[¶ 22,055]

C.   PARTNERSHIP LEVEL CONSEQUENCES

Under Section 731(b), the partnership will not recognize any gain or loss on a distribution to a partner unless Section 751 applies. However, the distribution will result in a loss to the partnership of the basis for the distributed property, and in some cases that can result in an increase of gain recognized by the partnership and taxed to the remaining partners in future years. Consider the ABC partnership, which has the following assets:

	Basis	*Value*
Cash	$40,000	$ 40,000
Capital Asset N	40,000	40,000
Capital Asset L	10,000	40,000
	$90,000	$120,000

The partnership interest of each of the three partners has a basis of $30,000 and a value of $40,000. If the partnership sold all of its assets and dissolved, each of the partners thus would have a net gain of $10,000.

Assume that the partnership distributes the $40,000 in cash to A. Under Section 731, A will have a gain of $10,000. The partnership, however, will be left with property having a value of $80,000 but a basis of $50,000. If the partnership now sold its remaining assets, B and C would each have a gain of $15,000. Plainly B and C would be overtaxed. What has occurred is that, by distributing a high-basis asset (cash) to A, A has obtained a disproportionately large fraction of the total partnership basis for its assets. That left B and C with a disproportionately small basis and an increase in their potential gain.

If we follow the example through, we will see that the effect on B and C is only temporary. The hypothetical sale of all of the assets of the partnership would produce a gain to each partner of $15,000, which would increase the basis for each of their partnership interests to $45,000. Since the value of each partnership interest would be only $40,000, each partnership interest would have a built-in loss of $5,000. Ultimately that loss will offset the excess gain taxed to each of B and C, but that loss will not be recognized until a partner retires—and perhaps not then if property is distributed. In any event, that deferred loss is small comfort in comparison to the accelerated gain.

This overtaxation of the remaining partners did not occur simply because cash was distributed to A. It will occur anytime that the average basis of the assets distributed is higher than the average basis of the assets held by the partnership immediately before the distribution. On those facts, a disproportionately large proportion of the partnership inside basis will have been distributed.

On the other hand, if an asset with a disproportionately small basis is distributed, the distributee partner may be overtaxed and the partnership may obtain an accelerated loss (or reduction of gain). Assume that the partnership distributes Capital Asset L to A in liquidation of A's partnership interest. Under Section 732(b), A would be entitled to step up the basis in Asset L to the $30,000 basis in the partnership interest, which would defer the gain of $10,000. However, following the distribution, the partnership would have property with an aggregate basis and value of $80,000 and thus on a hypothetical sale of all assets would not have any gain or loss at all. Since the sale would not produce a change in the basis of B's or C's partnership interest, each would have a gain of $10,000 on the liquidation of the partnership, but the distribution of Capital Asset L has permitted the deferral of that gain.

Recall that the Treasury Department has issued an anti-abuse regulation, which authorizes the IRS to disregard the form of a partnership transaction if the partnership is being used in a transaction (or series of related transactions) with a principal purpose of reducing the partners' federal tax liability in a manner inconsistent with the intent of Subchapter K. See Reg. § 1.701–2, discussed at ¶ 16,085. Under what circumstances will the IRS use this regulatory authority to recast partnership transactions designed to exploit the basis distortions resulting from the Section 732 basis rules? See, e.g., Reg. § 1.701–2(d), Exs. 9, 10, and 11.

[¶ 22,060]

1. THE SECTION 754 ELECTION

These results, both favorable and unfavorable, will be avoided if the partnership has made the Section 754 election. Under Section 734(b), the basis of the property retained by a partnership following a distribution will be adjusted in the following four situations:

1. The basis will be increased by (a) the gain recognized on a distribution of cash or (b) the amount by which the basis of distributed property is reduced because the partnership basis for the property exceeded the basis of the partnership interest of the distributee partner.

2. The partnership basis will be reduced by (a) the loss recognized to the distributee partner or (b) the amount by which the basis of the distributed property is increased on a liquidating distri-

bution because the basis of the partnership interest exceeded the basis of the property in the hands of the partnership.[3]

Notice that these adjustments under Section 734 are not triggered by every distribution of a disproportionate amount of basis but only when the disproportion is sufficient to result in gain (or loss) or lost (or gained) basis.[4]

Moreover, under a statutory change made in 2004, a mandatory downward adjustment to the property retained by the partnership must be made if the distribution results in a "substantial basis reduction" even if no Section 754 election is in effect. § 734(b).[5] A substantial basis reduction exists with respect to a distribution if the downward adjustment to the partnership's properties that would have made if a Section 754 election were in effect exceeds $250,000. § 734(d)(1).[6]

In the example above at ¶ 22,055, under these rules, what basis adjustment will the partnership obtain if cash is distributed to A? If Capital Asset L is distributed? Are those results correct?

[¶ 22,065]

2. ALLOCATING THE SECTION 734(b) BASIS ADJUSTMENT

If a basis adjustment must be made under Section 734, the adjustment must be allocated over the assets of the partnership in accordance with the rules contained in the regulations under Section 755. Under the current regulations, the rules governing the allocation in the case of the distribution are somewhat different than the rules that govern the allocation of the special basis adjustment obtained by the purchaser of a partnership interest, discussed in Chapter 21 (see ¶ 21,110).

The properties of the partnership are first divided into two classes: capital and Section 1231 assets (denominated "capital gain property" in the regulations) and all other properties (denominated "ordinary income property" in the regulations). Adjustments required under Section 734(b)(1)(B) and (b)(2)(B) by reason of a difference between the distribu-

3. Note that an electing large partnership (as defined in Section 775) may continue to elect to adjust the basis of partnership property under Section 734(b) if property is distributed to a partner. The special rules that apply to electing large partnerships are discussed generally at ¶ 18,250.

4. Note also that in the case of a distribution of marketable securities treated as cash under Section 731(c) (see ¶ 22,100), no Section 734 adjustment is made to the basis of partnership property by reason of any gain recognized by a partner, or any step-up in the basis in the distributed marketable securities, under Section 731(c). See § 731(c)(5); Reg. § 1.731–2(f)(2).

5. Sections 734(d)(2) and 743(d)(2) give the Treasury and the IRS broad regulatory authority to implement the purposes of this mandatory basis adjustment rule, including the issuance of regulations "aggregating related partnerships and disregarding property acquired by the partnership in an attempt to avoid" the purposes of the rule.

6. This mandatory basis adjustment rule does not apply to a "securitization partnership" (as defined in Section 743(f)). § 734(e). For a discussion of securitization partnerships, see ¶ 21,108.

tee partner's adjusted basis in the distributed property under Section 732 and the adjusted basis of the property to the partnership immediately before the distribution then must be made to property of the same class as that of the distributed property. Thus, when the partnership's adjusted basis of distributed capital gain property immediately before the distribution exceeds the basis of the property to the distributee partner under Section 732, the basis of the partnership's remaining undistributed capital gain property is increased by such excess. On the other hand, when the distributee partner's basis in the distributed capital gain property under Section 732 exceeds the partnership's adjusted basis of such property immediately before the distribution, the basis of the partnership's remaining undistributed capital gain property is reduced by such excess. Similarly, if ordinary income property is distributed to a partner and the distributee partner's basis in the property under Section 732 is not the same as the partnership's adjusted basis in the property immediately before the distribution, the Section 734 adjustment is made only to undistributed ordinary income property remaining in the partnership. Reg. § 1.755–1(c)(1)(i). However, when the adjustment is required because a gain or loss was recognized to the distributee partner under Section 731(a), the adjustment can be made only to capital gain property. Reg. § 1.755–1(c)(1)(ii).

Once the amount of the adjustment has been determined and the class to which the adjustment must be made has been identified, the allocation to specific properties must be made. Unlike the rule that is applicable to allocations following sales (discussed in Chapter 21), positive adjustments under Section 734 are allocated first to appreciated assets in proportion to the relative appreciation in those assets (but only to the extent of each property's unrealized appreciation); any remaining positive adjustment must be allocated among the properties within the class in proportion to their fair market values. Similarly, negative adjustments under Section 734 are allocated first to assets within the class that have depreciated in value in proportion to the relative depreciation in those assets (but only to the extent of each property's unrealized depreciation); any remaining negative adjustment must be allocated among the properties in the class in proportion to their adjusted bases (as reduced under the allocation rule in the first part of this sentence). Reg. § 1.755–1(c)(2) and (c)(6), Ex.

Consistent with the general prohibition throughout the federal tax law against the concept of a negative basis, the regulations under Section 755 provide that the basis of partnership properties may not be decreased under Section 734(b)(2) below zero. Reg. § 1.755–1(c)(3). When an adjustment cannot be allocated to undistributed partnership properties because of this limitation or because the partnership owns no property of the character required to be adjusted, the adjustment is carried forward and made when the partnership acquires property of a like character to which an adjustment can be made. Reg. § 1.755–1(c)(4).

¶ 22,065

One final point should be noted here. Section 755(c), as added to the Code in 2004, provides that in making any downward adjustment to the inside basis of the partnership's properties under Section 734(b), no allocation of such adjustment may be made to stock in a corporation that is a partner of the partnership. Nor may any allocation of the adjustment be made to stock in any person related to a corporate partner of the partnership (within the meaning of Sections 267(b) and 707(b)(1)). § 755(c)(1). Any amount not allocated to corporate stock owned by the partnership by reason of this rule must be allocated to other partnership property. § 755(c)(2). If the amount required to be allocated to the other partnership property exceeds the partnership's adjusted basis in such other property immediately before the allocation, the partnership must recognize gain in the amount of such excess. § 755(c). Congress enacted this provision because of its concern that certain tax avoidance transactions were being undertaken that exploited the interaction of the partnership basis adjustment rules and the rules preventing gain recognition to a corporation from its issuance of stock to increase the tax basis of depreciable assets and to decrease by a corresponding amount the basis of the stock of a corporate partner. The result was a creation of duplicate tax deductions at no economic cost. See H.R. Rep. No. 548, pt. 1, 108th Cong., 2d Sess. 287 (2004).

[¶ 22,067]

3. EFFECT OF OPERATING DISTRIBUTIONS ON PARTNERS' CAPITAL ACCOUNTS

Recall from Chapter 18 that in order for a special allocation of partnership income, gain, loss, or deduction to be respected for federal income tax purposes under Section 704(b), the regulations contain several requirements, including a requirement that throughout the full term of the partnership, the partnership maintain capital accounts in accordance with the rules in the regulations. See Reg. § 1.704–1(b)(2)(ii)(*b*) and–1(b)(2)(iv). One of the events that triggers capital account adjustments is a nonliquidating distribution. Reg. § 1.704–1(b)(2)(iv)(*b*). Since a distribution represents a decrease in the distributee partner's interest in the partnership, the regulations logically enough require that the distributee partner's capital account be reduced by any cash or the fair market value of any property distributed to the partner. Reg. § 1.704–1(b)(2)(iv)(*b*). However, to prevent distortion of the partners' capital account by reason that Section 731(b) generally prevents the partnership from recognizing gain on the distribution, the regulations require the partners' capital accounts to be adjusted to reflect the manner in which unrealized gain or loss inherent in the distributed property would have been allocated among the partners if the partnership had made a taxable disposition of the property. Reg. § 1.704–1(b)(2)(iv)(*e*)(*1*).

For example, assume that a partnership with four equal partners (John, Paul, George, and Ringo) distributes a capital asset to John having a fair market value of $100,000 and an adjusted basis and book value to the partnership of $20,000. Under Section 731(b), the partnership will not recognize any tax gain on the distribution to John. However, for capital account purposes, the partnership is treated as having made a taxable disposition of the capital asset for $100,000 (its fair market value) and recognized gain of $80,000. The partnership allocates $20,000 of the gain to each of the four partners, increasing each partner's capital account by that amount. John then reduces his capital account by the $100,000 fair market value of the property distributed, leaving him with a net downward adjustment of $80,000 to his capital account by reason of the distribution.

This adjustment to the capital accounts for unrealized gain or loss inherent in the property distributed should not be made to the extent that the unrealized gain or loss is already reflected on the partners' capital accounts. See Reg. § 1.704–1(b)(2)(iv)(f). For example, if the capital gain property distributed to John in the example above had been contributed by John at a time when its adjusted basis was $20,000 and its fair market value was $40,000, it would have been reflected in the capital accounts at the $40,000 fair market value and only the post-contribution unrealized gain of $60,000 would be triggered on distribution and allocated to the four partners in the amount of $15,000 each in order to increase each partner's capital account by that amount.

Finally, the regulations allow, but do not require, the partnership to revalue all of the remaining properties on its books and adjust the partners' capital accounts accordingly in the case of a distribution of cash or other property (other than a de minimis amount), but only if such adjustment is made principally for a substantial nontax business purpose. See Reg. § 1.704–1(b)(2)(iv)(f)(5)(ii).

[¶ 22,070]

Problem

Thunderbirds is a partnership of three individuals. Each partner has an equal interest in profits and losses but has a capital account computed under tax accounting principles. The partnership was formed six years ago and all partnership contributions were made at that time. The partnership has no liabilities and the following assets (none of which were contributed to the partnership by the partners):

	Basis	Value
Inventory M	$ 500	$ 500
Inventory N	900	1,000
Capital Asset X	400	1,100
Capital Asset Y	2,000	2,200
Total	$3,800	$4,800

¶ 22,067

Chuck, who has a basis of $600 for his partnership interest, has received a distribution consisting of Inventory M and Capital Asset X.

a. What is Chuck's tax basis for the distributed assets?

b. If the partnership has made the Section 754 election, what adjustments to the basis of the remaining partnership assets must be made?

[¶ 22,075]

4. TIERED PARTNERSHIP DISTRIBUTIONS

The following ruling involves two situations in which property distributions are made to a partner from a partnership (the upper-tier partnership) that owns an interest in another partnership (the lower-tier partnership) and both partnerships have Section 754 elections in effect. The ruling considers what basis adjustments to partnership property must be made under Section 734(b) by the upper-tier partnership and the lower-tier partnership.

[¶ 22,080]

REVENUE RULING 92–15

1992–1 C.B. 215.

Issues

(1) An upper-tier partnership (*UTP*), has an interest in a lower-tier partnership (*LTP*), and both partnerships have elections in effect under section 754 * * *. If *UTP* distributes property to a partner and, as a consequence of the distribution, adjusts the basis of its interest in *LTP* under section 734(b), does *LTP* also adjust the basis of its property under section 734(b)?

(2) An upper-tier partnership (*UTP*) distributes its interest in a lower-tier partnership (*LTP*) to a partner of *UTP*, while both partnerships have elections in effect under section 754 * * *. If section 732(a)(2) applies to limit the distributee partner's basis in the distributed partnership interest, does *UTP* increase the basis of its undistributed property to the extent provided in section 734(b)(1)(B)?

Facts

A and *B* are partners in partnership *UTP*, each with a 50 percent interest in the capital, profits and losses of the partnership. *A*'s partnership interest in *UTP* has an adjusted basis of zero and a fair market value of 160x dollars. *UTP* has no liabilities and only two properties, capital asset *X* and a 10 percent interest in the capital, profits and losses of partnership *LTP*. Asset *X* has an adjusted basis to *UTP* of 140x dollars and a fair market value of 240x dollars. *UTP*'s interest in *LTP* has an adjusted basis to *UTP* of 30x dollars and a fair market value of 80x dollars.

LTP has no liabilities and only two properties, capital asset *Y* and noncapital asset *Z*. Asset *Y* has an adjusted basis of 200x dollars and a fair market value of 700x dollars. Asset *Z* has an adjusted basis of zero and a fair market value of 100x dollars. *UTP*'s share of the adjusted basis of *LTP*'s properties is 20x dollars.

For the taxable year in which the events described in Situations 1 and 2 occur, *UTP* and *LTP* make valid elections under section 754 * * *. Capital assets *X* and *Y*, and noncapital asset *Z*, are not assets described in section 751. Section 732(d) does not apply to *A*.

Situation 1

UTP distributes one-half of capital asset *X* to partner *A*, in order to reduce *A*'s 50 percent interest in *UTP* to 20 percent, and increase *B*'s interest to 80 percent. The distribution reduces the value of *A*'s partnership interest in *UTP* to 40x dollars.

Situation 2

UTP distributes its partnership interest in *LTP* to partner *A* in order to reduce *A*'s 50 percent interest in *UTP* to 33 percent. The distribution reduces the value of *A*'s partnership interest in *UTP* to 80x dollars.

LAW AND ANALYSIS

Section 734(a) * * * provides that the basis of partnership property is not adjusted as the result of a distribution of property to a partner unless the partnership has an election in effect under section 754 * * *.

Section 743(a) * * * provides that the basis of partnership property is not adjusted as the result of a transfer of an interest in a partnership unless the partnership has an election in effect under section 754 * * *.

Section 754 * * * provides that if a partnership files an election in accordance with regulations prescribed by the Secretary, the basis of partnership property is adjusted, in the case of a distribution of property, in the manner provided in section 734(b), and, in the case of a transfer of a partnership interest, in the manner provided in section 743(b).

Section 734(b) * * * provides that, in the case of a distribution of property to a partner, a partnership that has a section 754 election in effect increases or decreases the adjusted basis of partnership property under specified circumstances. Under section 734(b)(1)(A), the amount of increase is the amount of any gain recognized to the distributee partner with respect to the distribution. Under section 734(b)(1)(B), in the case of distributed property to which section 732(a)(2) applies, the amount of increase also includes the excess of the adjusted basis of the distributed property immediately before the distribution over the basis of the distributed property to the distributee. The partnership does not make the adjustment described in the preceding sentence if the distributed property is an interest in another partnership that does not have an election in effect under section 754 * * *.

Section 732(a)(1) * * * provides that the basis of property (other than money) distributed by a partnership to a partner other than in liquidation of the partner's interest is generally equal to the property's adjusted basis to the partnership immediately before the distribution. Section 732(a)(2), however, limits the basis of the property to the distributee partner to the adjusted basis of the partner's interest in the partnership reduced by any money distributed in the same transaction.

Section 734(c) * * * requires the allocation of any basis adjustment among partnership properties in accordance with section 755 * * *.

Section 743(b) * * * provides that, in the case of a transfer of an interest in a partnership by sale or exchange or upon the death of a partner, a partnership that has a section 754 election in effect increases or decreases the adjusted basis of partnership property under specified circumstances.

Section 743(c) * * * requires the allocation of any basis adjustment among partnership properties in accordance with section 755 * * *.

Section 755(a)(1) * * * provides that the basis adjustment is allocated among partnership properties in a manner that reduces the difference between the fair market value and the adjusted bases of those properties. Section 755(b) provides that in applying the allocation rules of section 755(a), increases or decreases in the adjusted basis of partnership property arising from a distribution of, or a transfer of an interest attributable to, (1) capital assets and property described in section 1231(b) ("capital assets"), or (2) any other property of the partnership, are allocated to partnership property of like character.

Section 1.755–1[(c)](1) of the * * * Regulations provides that where there is an adjustment to the basis of undistributed partnership property under section 734(b)(1)(B) * * *, the adjustment is allocated to remaining partnership property of a character similar to that of the distributed property.

* * *

Section 741 * * * provides that, except as provided in section 751, the gain or loss from the sale or exchange of an interest in a partnership is considered to be a gain or loss from the sale or exchange of a capital asset.

Section 708(b)(1)(B) * * * provides that a partnership is considered terminated if, within a 12 month period, there is a sale or exchange of 50 percent or more of the total interest in partnership capital and profits. Section 1.708–l(b)[(2)] of the regulations provides that the liquidation of a partnership interest is not a sale or exchange for purposes of section 708(b)(1). Section 761(e) provides that, for purposes of sections 708 and 743, any distribution of an interest in a partnership (not otherwise treated as an exchange) is treated as an exchange.

Situation 1

UTP distributes one-half of capital asset X to partner A, reducing the value of A's partnership interest to 40x dollars. Under section 732(a)(1) * * *, A's basis in the distributed half of asset X would be equal to the basis of the distributed half of asset X to UTP immediately before the distribution, or 70x dollars. Section 732(a)(2), however, limits A's basis in the distributed half of asset X to A's basis in its UTP partnership interest, or zero. Because UTP has a section 754 election in effect, under section 734(b)(1)(B), UTP increases the adjusted basis of its remaining property by 70x dollars, the excess of the adjusted basis of the distributed property to UTP immediately before the distribution (70x dollars) over the basis of the distributed property to A (zero).

Section 755(b) * * * and section 1.755–1[(c)](1) of the regulations provide that the basis adjustment to undistributed partnership property under section 734(b)(1)(B) is allocated to remaining partnership property of a character similar to that of the distributed property. UTP's remaining property is the undistributed half of asset X and its interest in LTP, both of which, like asset X, are capital assets. Section 755(a) generally requires a reduction of the difference between the fair market value and the adjusted basis of undistributed property. In this case, the undistributed half of asset X and UTP's partnership interest in LTP each have a difference of 50x dollars between fair market value and adjusted basis. Section 1.755–1[(c)(2)(i)] requires that a section 734(b) basis increase be allocated among partnership assets in proportion to the difference between the value and the basis of each. Accordingly, the 70x dollar basis adjustment is allocated equally among UTP's two assets, so that UTP increases its basis in the undistributed half of asset X from 70x dollars to 105x dollars, and increases its basis in LTP from 30x dollars to 65x dollars.

Because both UTP and LTP have made elections under section 754 * * *, it is appropriate to treat UTP's distribution of one-half of asset X to A and the subsequent 35x dollar increase to UTP's basis in LTP as an event that triggers a section 734(b) basis increase of 35x dollars to UTP's share of LTP's assets. Under section 755(b) * * * and section 1.755–1[(c)](1) of the regulations, the basis adjustment to undistributed partnership property under section 734(b)(1)(B) is allocated to remaining partnership property of a character similar to that of the distributed property. Accordingly, LTP increases its basis in UTP's share of asset Y from 20x dollars to 55x dollars. This adjustment to basis is for UTP only and does not affect the basis in *LTP* property of other partners of *LTP*. No adjustment is made to *UTP*'s share of *LTP*'s basis in noncapital asset *Z*.

Although *A*'s interest in *UTP* is reduced from 50 percent to 20 percent, the reduction of *A*'s interest in *UTP* is effected by a distribution, which is not considered a sale or exchange of a *UTP* interest for purposes of section 708 * * *. *Cf.* section 1.708–1(b)[(2)] of the regulations.

Under the facts addressed by this ruling, *UTP* and *LTP* were allowed to increase the basis of undistributed property. Under other circumstances, upper- and lower-tier partnerships might be required to decrease the basis of undistributed property in accordance with the principles described above. For example, if a partner in an upper-tier partnership (with a section 754 election in effect) is distributed property in liquidation of the partner's interest, and the partner has a higher basis in its partnership interest than in the distributed partnership property, the upper-tier partnership must decrease its adjusted basis in its remaining partnership property under section 734(b)(2) * * *. If this adjustment results in a reduction in the upper-tier partnership's basis in its partnership interest in a lower-tier partnership (which also has a section 754 election in effect), the lower-tier partnership must decrease its adjusted basis in the upper-tier partnership's proportionate share of the lower-tier partnership's assets under section 734(b)(2) as well.

Situation 2

UTP distributes its partnership interest in *LTP* to partner *A*, reducing *A*'s 50 percent interest in *UTP* to 33 percent. Under section 732(a)(2) * * *, *A*'s basis in the distributed *LTP* interest is equal to *A*'s basis in its *UTP* partnership interest, or zero. Because both *UTP* and *LTP* have section 754 elections in effect, under section 734(b)(1)(B), *UTP* increases the adjusted basis of its remaining property (asset *X*) by $30x$ dollars, the excess of the adjusted basis of the distributed property to *UTP* immediately before the distribution ($30x$ dollars) over the basis of the distributed property to *A* (zero).

UTP makes the above basis adjustment only because both *UTP* and *LTP* have elections in effect under section 754 * * *. See the last sentence of section 734(b), which limits the applicability of section 734(b)(1)(B).

Under section 761(e) * * *, *UTP*'s distribution of its interest in *LTP* is treated as an exchange of the interest in *LTP* for purposes of section 743. Because *LTP* has a section 754 election in effect, under section 743(b)(2) *LTP* would decrease the adjusted basis of its property by $20x$ dollars, the excess of *A*'s proportionate share of the adjusted basis of *LTP*'s property ($20x$ dollars) over the basis of *A*'s interest in *LTP* (zero). * * *

¶ 22,080

Under section 761(e) * * *, *UTP*'s distribution of its interest in *LTP* is treated as an exchange of a 10 percent interest in *LTP* for purposes of the partnership termination provisions in section 708. *See* Rev. Rul. 87–50, 1987–1 C.B. 157. The reduction of *A*'s interest in *UTP* is not considered a sale or exchange for purposes of section 708. *Cf.* section 1.708–1(b)(1)(ii) of the regulations.

HOLDINGS

(1) If partnership *UTP* and partnership *LTP* have elections in effect under section 754 * * *, if *UTP* distributes property to a partner and one of *UTP*'s undistributed properties is an interest in partnership *LTP*, and if *UTP* adjusts the basis of its interest in *LTP* under section 734(b), then this adjustment is an event that is deemed to require *LTP* to adjust the basis of its property under section 734(b) by the same amount. This adjustment to basis is for *UTP* only and does not affect the basis in *LTP* property of other partners of *LTP*.

(2) If partnership *UTP* distributes its interest in partnership *LTP* to a partner of *UTP* while both partnerships have elections in effect under section 754 * * *, and if section 732(a)(2) applies to the distributed partnership interest, *UTP* increases the basis of its undistributed property to the extent provided in section 734(b)(1)(B).

[¶ 22,085]

Note

What the IRS seems to have done in *Situation 1* of this ruling is treat the partnership-level basis adjustment, which in fact resulted from a Section 734(b) adjustment following a distribution by the upper-tier partnership, as if it were produced by a transfer of the interest in the lower-tier partnership. As a result, the ruling allows a special basis adjustment in the lower-tier partnership's assets only to the one partner, the upper-tier partnership—the adjustment that would have been mandated by Section 743(b) if a transfer had in fact occurred.

The substantive result reached in *Situation 1* may be correct. Nevertheless, it is not at all clear that the Code supports that result. In general, a Section 754 election promotes conformity between inside and outside basis, and the ruling furthers that conformity. However, the adjustments required by a Section 754 election are finite and closely described; Section 754 falls far short of mandating conformity of inside and outside partnership basis under all circumstances. At the very least, Rev. Rul. 92–15 stakes out an aggressive ruling position that might not be followed by a court.

D. TREATMENT OF PRECONTRIBUTION GAIN OR LOSS ON CERTAIN IN–KIND PARTNERSHIP DISTRIBUTIONS: SO–CALLED "MIXING BOWL" TRANSACTIONS

[¶ 22,090]

1. DISTRIBUTIONS OF CONTRIBUTED PROPERTY TO ANOTHER PARTNER (SECTION 704(c)(1)(B))

Under Section 704(c)(1)(A), discussed at ¶ 18,135, a partner that contributes property to a partnership with precontribution appreciation or depreciation is generally allocated the precontribution gain or loss when the partnership later sells the property. The original version of Section 704(c)(1) applied only to a later sale of the contributed property by the partnership. Consequently, if the partnership distributed the property to another partner instead of selling it, the contributing partner could avoid an allocation of the precontribution gain or loss. Under Section 731(b), the partnership would not recognize a gain or loss on the distribution; thus, there would be no gain or loss to allocate to the contributing partner. The precontribution appreciation or depreciation in the contributed property would be shifted to the distributee partner by operation of the basis rule in Section 732.

To prevent this end-run around Section 704(c)(1), Congress, in 1989, added Section 704(c)(1)(B) to the Code. Under Section 704(c)(1)(B)(i), if a partner contributes property to a partnership and the partnership distributes the property to another partner within seven years[7] of the contribution, the contributing partner will recognize gain or loss equal to the gain or loss that would have been allocated to the partner under Section 704(c)(1)(A) if the property had been sold at its fair market value at the time of distribution. Reg. § 1.704–4(a). The character of the contributing partner's gain or loss is the same as the character would have been to the partnership if the property had been sold by the partnership to the distributee partner at the time of the distribution. § 704(c)(1)(B)(ii); Reg. § 1.704–4(b).

Section 704(c)(1)(B) requires that appropriate adjustments be made to the basis of the contributing partner's partnership interest and to the basis of the partnership in the distributed property to reflect the gain or loss recognized by the contributing partner. § 704(c)(1)(B)(iii). Thus, the contributing partner's basis in the partnership interest is increased or decreased by the amount of gain or loss recognized under § 704(c)(1)(B). Reg. § 1.704–4(e)(1). Similarly, the partnership's basis in the distributed

---

7. Before a change made by the Taxpayer Relief Act of 1997, this period was five years. The regulations continue to reflect the prior law.

property is increased or decreased (prior to the distribution) by the amount of the gain or loss recognized by the contributing partner. Thus, this adjustment is taken into account in determining the distributee partner's adjusted basis in the distributed property under Section 732. Reg. § 1.704–4(e)(2).

The regulations make clear that these basis adjustments to partnership property as a result of gain or loss recognized to the contributing partner under Section 704(c)(1)(B) are not elective in nature and must be made regardless of whether the partnership has a Section 754 election in effect. Moreover, any adjustments to the bases of partnership property (including the distributed property) under Section 734(b) pursuant to the Section 754 election must be made after and take into account the adjustments to basis made as a result of the gain or loss recognized to the contributing partner under Section 704(c)(1)(B). Reg. § 1.704–4(e)(3).

The statute contains two exceptions to the general rule in Section 704(c)(1)(B). First, Section 704(c)(1)(B) does not apply if the contributed property is distributed back to the contributing partner. See also Reg. § 1.704–4(c)(6). In such a case, the contributing partner will receive, on distribution, a substituted basis in the contributed property under Section 732 and, thus, will be subject to tax on the precontribution gain or loss on a later sale of the property. Since the abuse that Section 704(c)(1)(B) was designed to prevent (i.e., avoidance of the precontribution gain or loss by the contributing partner) is not present, there is no need to require the contributing partner to recognize gain or loss at the time of distribution.

Second, Section 704(c)(1)(B) contains a special rule that applies if the contributing partner receives a distribution of property of a like kind (as defined in Section 1031) to the contributed property within the earlier of (1) 180 days after the contributed property is distributed to another partner or (2) the due date for the contributing partner's return for the taxable year in which the distribution of the contributed property to another partner occurs. Under this special rule, the contributing partner is treated as if the contributed property had been received in the distribution up to the value of the like-kind property received. § 704(c)(2) (flush language); Reg. § 1.704–4(d)(3). Thus, to the extent of the value of the like-kind property received, the contributing partner is not subject to gain or loss recognition under Section 704(c)(1)(B) on the distribution of the contributed property to another partner.

The regulations provide that Section 704(c)(1)(B) does not apply to a transfer by a partnership of all of its assets and liabilities to another partnership, followed by a distribution of the interest in the transferee partnership in liquidation of the transferor partnership as part of the same plan. Reg. § 1.704–4(c)(4). In addition, the regulations provide that Section 704(c)(1)(B) does not apply to an incorporation of a partnership

¶ 22,090

if the partnership is liquidated as part of the incorporation transaction. The latter exception applies to incorporation of the partnership by any method other than by an actual distribution of partnership assets to the partners followed by a contribution of those assets to a corporation. Reg. § 1.704–4(c)(5). Both exceptions recognize that in these transactions, the partners are converting their interest in a partnership into an interest in another partnership or a corporation and, under the rules of either Section 732 or Section 358, the built-in gain or loss in the liquidated partnership interest is preserved in the transferee partnership interest or stock received by the contributing partner. See PS–76–92; PS–51–93, 1995–1 C.B. 1001, 1005.

In addition, as discussed at ¶ 24,040, the regulations provide that precontribution gain or loss otherwise required to be recognized under Section 704(c)(1)(B) is not triggered by a constructive partnership termination under Section 708(b)(1)(B). Reg. § 1.704–4(c)(3).

Section 704(c)(3) provides that Section 704(c)(1)(B) (and its exceptions) may apply to a successor of the contributing partner (e.g., a purchaser or donee of the contributing partner's partnership interest). See also Reg. §§ 1.704–4(d)(2) and–3(a)(7). Thus, for example, if the partner who originally contributed appreciated property to the partnership sells his or her partnership interest to a successor, the successor will recognize gain under Section 704(c)(1)(B) if the contributed property is distributed to another partner within seven years of the original contributing partner's contribution. In the case of a built-in loss on contributed property, however, Section 704(c)(1)(C), added to the Code in 2004, would prevent a successor partner from recognizing such built-in loss because the statute now provides that the basis of the contributed property is treated as equal to its fair market value at the time it was contributed to the partnership for purposes of making allocations to any partner other than the contributing partner, including a successor in interest of the contributing partner.

Finally, the regulations contain an anti-abuse rule that, in the case of a transaction a principal purpose of which is to achieve a tax result that is inconsistent with the purpose of Section 704(c)(1)(B), authorizes the IRS to recast the transaction for federal tax purposes as appropriate to achieve tax results that are consistent with the purpose of Section 704(c)(1)(B). Reg. § 1.704–4(f)(1). Determining whether a tax result is inconsistent with the purpose of Section 704(c)(1)(B) is made on the basis of all the facts and circumstances. Two examples illustrate the application of this anti-abuse rule. See Reg. § 1.704–4(f)(2), Exs. 1 and 2.

[¶ 22,095]

2. DISTRIBUTIONS OF OTHER PROPERTY TO THE CONTRIBUTING PARTNER (SECTION 737)

Suppose that a partner contributes appreciated property to a partnership but is redeemed out of the partnership for other property before the contributed property is distributed to another partner. In that case, Section 704(c)(1)(B) would not apply to the distribution. Moreover, as discussed at ¶ 20,090, Section 707(a)(2)(B) would also probably not apply if the distribution occurred more than two years after the contribution. Thus, the contributing partner would be able to avoid or defer recognition of the precontribution appreciation in the contributed property in violation of the policy underlying Sections 704(c)(1) and 707(a)(2)(B) even though she could be viewed as having effectively sold the contributed property in return for the distributed property. To prevent this perceived abuse, Congress, in 1992, enacted Section 737 to buttress Sections 704(c)(1) and 707(a)(2)(B).

Section 737 requires a contributing partner to recognize the precontribution gain that otherwise would be recognized under Section 704(c) if she contributes appreciated property to a partnership and within seven years[8] of the contribution receives property other than money (or marketable securities treated as money under Section 731(c)) as a distribution from the partnership. Under Section 737(a), the amount of the recognized gain is the lesser of

> (i) the fair market value of the distributed property (other than money or marketable securities treated as money) less the distributee partner's basis in the partnership interest immediately before the distribution reduced by the money (or the fair market value of marketable securities treated as money) received in the distribution—called an "excess distribution" in the regulations, or

> (ii) the distributee partner's "net precontribution gain."

Reg. § 1.737–1(a) and (b). Section 737(b) defines "net precontribution gain" as the net gain that the distributee partner would have recognized under Section 704(c)(1)(B) if all property that had been contributed by that partner to the partnership within seven years before the distribution and that is held by the partnership immediately before the distribution had been distributed by the partnership to another partner. See also Reg. § 1.737–1(c). The character of the gain recognized by the distributee partner is determined by reference to the proportionate character of the net precontribution gain. § 737(a) (flush sentence); Reg. § 1.737–1(d).

Section 737 requires basis adjustments for both the distributee partner and the distributing partnership to reflect the gain recognized under Section 737(a). Under Section 737(c)(1), the distributee partner increases the adjusted basis of the partnership interest by the amount of gain recognized under Section 737(a). Reg. § 1.737–3(a). For purposes of determining the basis of the distributed property (other than money), this basis increase is treated as occurring immediately before the distribution. Reg. § 1.737–3(b). Under Section 737(c)(2), the partnership

---

8. Before a change made by the Taxpayer Relief Act of 1997, this period was five years. The regulations continue to reflect the prior law.

increases its adjusted basis in the contributed property to reflect the gain recognized by the distributee partner. Reg. § 1.737–3(c)(1).

The regulations make clear that these basis adjustments to partnership property as a result of gain recognized by the distributee partner under Section 737 are not elective in nature and must be made regardless of whether the partnership has a Section 754 election in effect. Moreover, any adjustments to the bases of partnership property under Section 734(b) pursuant to the Section 754 election must be made after and take into account the adjustments to basis made as a result of the gain recognized to the distributee partner under Section 737. Reg. § 1.737–3(c)(4).

Section 737(d) contains two exceptions to the general rule in Section 737(a). Under the first exception in Section 737(d)(1), if any portion of the distributed property consists of property that had been contributed by the distributee partner to the partnership, that property is not taken into account in determining the amount of recognized gain under Section 737(a)(1) or the amount of the net precontribution gain under Section 737(b). However, if the property distributed is an interest in an entity, this exception does not apply to the extent that the value of the interest is attributable to property contributed to the entity after the interest had been contributed to the partnership. § 737(d)(1) (second sentence); Reg. § 1.737–2(d)(2). Under the second exception in Section 737(d)(2), Section 737 does not apply to the extent that Section 751(b) applies to the distribution.

The regulations provide that Section 737 does not apply to a transfer by a partnership of all of its assets and liabilities to another partnership, followed by a distribution of the interest in the transferee partnership in liquidation of the transferor partnership as part of the same plan. Reg. § 1.737–2(b)(1). In addition, the regulations provide that Section 737 does not apply to an incorporation of a partnership if the partnership is liquidated as part of the incorporation transaction. This exception applies to incorporation of the partnership by any method other than by an actual distribution of partnership assets to the partners followed by a contribution of those assets to a corporation. Reg. § 1.737–2(c). These exceptions are similar to the exceptions contained in the Section 704(c)(1)(B) regulations and are based on the same policy rationale (discussed at ¶ 22,090).

The Section 737 regulations have an additional exception for certain divisive partnership transactions in which the partnership transfers all its Section 704(c) property contributed by a partner to another partnership and distributes its partnership interest in the transferee partnership in complete liquidation of the interest of the partner that originally contributed the Section 704(c) property to the partnership. Reg. § 1.737–2(b)(2). This exception recognizes that the contributing partner remains subject to Section 737 with respect to the built-in gain preserved in the interest in the transferee partnership.

In addition, as discussed at ¶ 24,040, the regulations provide that taxation of the precontribution gain otherwise required to be recognized under Section 737 is not triggered by a constructive partnership termination under Section 708(b)(1)(B). Reg. § 1.737–2(a).

Finally, the regulations contain an anti-abuse rule that, in the case of a transaction a principal purpose of which is to achieve a tax result that is inconsistent with the purpose of Section 737, authorizes the IRS to recast the transaction for federal tax purposes as appropriate to achieve tax results that are consistent with the purpose of Section 737. Reg. § 1.737–4(a). Determining whether a tax result is inconsistent with the purpose of Section 737 is made on the basis of all the facts and circumstances. The regulations contain two examples which illustrate the application of this anti-abuse rule. See Reg. § 1.737–4(b), Exs. 1 and 2.

[¶ 22,100]

E. DISTRIBUTIONS OF MARKETABLE SECURITIES (SECTION 731(c))

In 1994, Congress focused on another area of potential abuse involving partnership distributions—a partner's tax-free exchange of her share of appreciated partnership assets for an increased share of the partnership's marketable securities. Congress viewed such an exchange as "the virtual economic equivalent of a sale of a partner's share of the partnership assets" and the prior law distinction in treatment between a distribution of cash and a distribution of marketable securities ("which are nearly as easily valued and as liquid as cash") as "elevat[ing] form over substance, caus[ing] taxpayers to choose the form of transactions for tax reasons rather than economic reasons, and * * * not promot[ing] accurate income measurement." H.R. Rep. No. 826, pt. 1, 103d Cong., 2d Sess. 187–188 (1994). To limit the deferral or avoidance of federal income tax upon the receipt of marketable securities by a partner with unrealized appreciation in her partnership interest, Congress added Section 731(c) to the Code.

Section 731(c) provides that for purposes of determining the amount of gain that a partner recognizes under Section 731(a)(1) or Section 737 upon a partnership's distribution of marketable securities, the fair market value of the securities as of the date of distribution is treated as money. This means that the distributee partner will generally recognize gain to the extent that the sum of the money received and the fair market value of the marketable securities received exceeds the partner's basis in the partnership interest.

¶ 22,095

For purposes of Section 731(c), "marketable securities" is defined to mean financial instruments and foreign currencies that are, as of the date of distribution, actively traded. § 731(c)(2)(A). Financial instruments include financial products such as stock and other equity interests, evidences of indebtedness, options, forward or future contracts, notional principal contracts, and derivatives. § 731(c)(2)(C). In addition, "marketable securities" include certain other specified types of assets, such as an interest in an open-ended mutual fund, any financial instrument that is readily convertible into, or exchangeable for, money or marketable securities, any financial instrument the value of which is determined substantially by reference to marketable securities, and an interest in certain actively traded precious metals. § 731(c)(2)(B)(i) through (iv). Moreover, an interest in an entity is a marketable security if substantially all of the entity's assets consist of marketable securities, cash, or both. § 731(c)(2)(B)(v).[9]

There are five exceptions to the general rule under Section 731(c)(1) that upon a distribution of marketable securities, the distributee partner recognizes gain to the extent that the sum of the money and the fair market value of the marketable securities distributed exceeds the partner's basis in her partnership interest. Under the first exception in Section 731(c)(3)(B), more accurately thought of as a gain limitation rule, the distributee partner is allowed to receive a distribution of marketable securities without recognizing the gain that is attributable to the partner's share of the partnership's net appreciation with respect to securities of the same class and issuer as the distributed securities. The theory is that to that extent the distributee partner is not exchanging her share of the appreciation in other partnership assets for an increased share of the partnership's marketable securities, and, hence, the perceived abuse that Section 731(c) was designed to prevent is not occurring. Specifically, Section 731(c)(3)(B) and Reg. § 1.731–2(b)(2) provide that the amount of marketable securities treated as money is reduced by the excess of (i) the distributee partner's distributive share of any net gain that she would take into account if all securities of the type distributed that are held by the partnership immediately before the transaction were sold for their fair market value, over (ii) the distributee partner's distributive share of any net gain that she would take into account if all securities of that type that are held by the partnership immediately after the transaction are sold. For purposes of this gain limitation rule, the regulations treat all marketable securities held by

---

9. The regulations define "substantially all" to mean that at least 90 percent of the assets of the entity (by value) at the time of distribution of an interest in the entity consist of marketable securities, cash, or both. Reg. § 1.731–2(c)(3)(i). If less than 90 percent but at least 20 percent of the assets of an entity consist of marketable securities, cash, or both, the regulations treat an interest in the entity as a marketable security, but only to the extent that the value of the interest is attributable to marketable securities, cash, or both. § 731(c)(2)(B)(vi); Reg. § 1.731–2(c)(3)(ii).

¶ 22,100

the partnership as being of the same class and issuer as the distributed securities. Reg. § 1.731–2(b)(1).

To illustrate this gain limitation rule, consider the following example based on an example in the legislative history. See H.R. Rep. No. 826, pt. 1, 103d Cong., 2d Sess. 192–93 (1994). Suppose that a partnership holds 300 shares of the common stock of ABC Corporation, a marketable security, as well as other assets. The distributee partner holds a one-third interest in the partnership's capital and profits. Each share of ABC Corporation stock held by the partnership has a basis of $10 and a fair market value of $100. The distributee partner's adjusted basis in her partnership interest is $5,000. The partnership distributes all the shares of ABC Corporation to the distributee partner. How much gain is she required to recognize under Section 731(c)?

Under the general rule in Section 731(c)(1), the $30,000 fair market value of the ABC Corporation stock would be treated as money for purposes of Sections 731(a)(1) and 737. However, under the gain limitation rule in Section 731(c)(3)(B), the $30,000 amount is reduced by $9,000 (i.e., one-third of $27,000, the amount of gain that the distributee partner would have taken into account if the partnership had sold all 300 shares of the ABC Corporation stock, in which it had a total basis of $3,000, for their $30,000 fair market value). Thus, under Section 731(a)(1) and 731(c), the distributee partner recognizes a gain of $16,000 (i.e., $30,000 value of the distributed securities treated as money under Section 731(c)(1), reduced by $9,000 under the gain limitation rule in Section 731(c)(3)(B), and further reduced by the distributee partner's $5,000 basis in her partnership interest).

Under the second exception, Section 731(c) generally does not apply to the distribution of a marketable security if the distributed security was contributed by the distributee partner. § 731(c)(3)(A)(i); Reg. § 1.731–2(d)(1)(i). However, under an anti-stuffing rule in the regulations, this exception does not apply to the extent that the value of the distributed security is attributable to marketable securities or cash contributed (directly or indirectly) to the entity to which the distributed security relates. Reg. § 1.731–2(d)(2).

The third exception provides that, if certain conditions in the regulations are met, Section 731(c) will not apply to a distribution of a marketable security that was not a marketable security when it was acquired by the partnership. § 731(c)(3)(A)(ii); Reg. § 1.731–2(d)(1)(iii). This exception is also subject to the anti-stuffing rule described above.

The fourth exception provides that Section 731(c) does not apply to the distribution of a marketable security if the security was acquired by the partnership in a nonrecognition transaction and if certain other conditions in the regulations are met. Reg. § 1.731–2(d)(1)(ii). This exception is also subject to the anti-stuffing rule.

¶ 22,100

Finally, the fifth exception provides that Section 731(c) generally does not apply to a distribution of marketable securities by an investment partnership to an eligible partner. § 731(c)(3)(A)(iii); Reg. § 1.731–2(e).

If Section 731(c) applies to a distribution of marketable securities, the distributee partner's adjusted basis in the distributed marketable securities is equal to their basis as determined under Section 732, increased by the amount of gain recognized by reason of Section 731(c). § 731(c)(4)(A); Reg. § 1.731–2(f)(1)(i). This basis increase is allocated among the distributed marketable securities in proportion to the amounts of unrealized appreciation in the respective securities (determined before the increase in basis under this provision). § 731(c)(4)(B); Reg. § 1.731–2(f)(1)(i).

The distributee partner's adjusted basis in her partnership interest and the partnership's adjusted basis in its remaining assets after the distribution are to be determined without regard to this provision. § 731(c)(5). Thus, the rules in Section 733 for determining the distributee partner's basis in her partnership interest are applied as if no gain were recognized by the distributee partner under Section 731(c) and no adjustment were made to the basis of property under Section 731(c)(4). Accordingly, in a nonliquidating distribution, the distributee partner's basis in her partnership interest is reduced under Section 733 by the basis of the distributed marketable securities (as determined under Section 732) and without regard to Section 731(c). Reg. § 1.731–2(f)(1)(ii). Moreover, no adjustment is made to the basis of partnership property under Section 734 as a result of gain recognized to the partner under Section 731(c). § 731(c)(5); Reg. § 1.731–2(f)(2).

To illustrate these basis rules, consider the following example based on an example in the legislative history. See H.R. Rep. No. 826, pt. 1, 103d Cong., 2d Sess. 193 (1994). Suppose that a partnership distributes to a partner (in a nonliquidating distribution), two marketable securities: Marketable Security X (with a basis of $60 and a fair market value of $100) and Marketable Security Y (with a basis of $40 and a fair market value of $100). The distributee partner has a basis of $120 in her partnership interest. After taking into account, under Section 731(c)(3)(B), the distributee partner's share of partnership appreciation in securities of the same type (class and issuer) as Marketable Securities X and Y, assume that the partner will recognize $40 of gain by reason of Section 731(c). What is the distributee partner's basis in the distributed securities? What is her basis in the partnership interest after the distribution?

Under Section 731(c)(4)(B), $16, 40 percent of the gain, is allocated to Marketable Security X, and $24, 60 percent of the gain, is allocated to Marketable Security Y. Thus, the distributee partner's basis in the Marketable Security X is $76 (the $60 basis determined under Section

732, increased by $16 under Section 731(c)(4)), and in Marketable Security Y is $64 (the $40 basis determined under Section 732, increased by $24 under Section 731(c)(4)). The distributee partner's basis in her partnership interest after the distribution is $20, i.e., her basis in the interest before the distribution of $120, reduced under Section 733 by the sum of the partnership's bases in Marketable Security X ($60) and Marketable Security Y ($40), or a total reduction of $100.

Section 731(c)(6) provides that any gain recognized under Section 731(c) is ordinary income to the extent that the basis of any marketable security that is an unrealized receivable or an inventory item (within the meaning of Section 751, discussed at ¶¶ 21,035 et seq. and 22,110) is increased by reason of this provision. Moreover, the committee reports make clear that Section 751(b) should apply before Section 731(c). See H.R. Rep. No. 826, pt. 1, 103d Cong., 2d Sess. 195 n.17 (1994) (citing § 731(d)). Any gain recognized by reason of Section 731(c) that does not fall within this special characterization rule should be treated under Section 731(a)(1) as gain from the sale or exchange of the distributee partner's partnership interest.

The regulations contain rules for coordinating the tax treatment of distributions of marketable securities under Section 731(c) with the rules in Sections 704(c)(1)(B) and 737. Under these coordination rules, the tax consequences of a distribution are determined by applying Section 704(c)(1)(B) first, Section 731(c) second, and Section 737 last. Reg. § 1.731–2(g)(1)(i). Accordingly, the basis increase or decrease in a partner's interest in the partnership as a result of gain or loss recognized by the partner under Section 704(c)(1)(B) is taken into account in determining the distributee partner's gain on the distribution of the marketable securities under Section 731(c) and in determining the distributee partner's basis in the distributed securities. Reg. § 1.731–2(g)(1)(ii). As stated by the IRS, this coordination rule "reflects the fact that the general effect of [S]ection 704(c)(1)(B) is to treat the contributing partner as having contributed property with a full fair market value basis at the time of contribution." PS–2–95, 1996–1 C.B. 853, 855.

By contrast, the basis increase in the partner's partnership interest by reason of any gain recognized under Section 737 is not taken into account for Section 731(c) purposes. Reg. § 1.731–2(g)(1)(iii)(B). As stated by the IRS, this coordination rule is "consistent with Section 737, which generally treats a distribution of money as occurring before, and independently of, a distribution of other property." PS–2–95, 1996–1 C.B. 853, 855.

Finally, the regulations contain an anti-abuse rule, issued under the authority of Section 731(c)(7). Under that rule, if a principal purpose of a transaction is to achieve a purpose inconsistent with Section 731(c) and the regulations, the IRS can recast the transaction to achieve results that are consistent with Section 731(c). Reg. § 1.731–2(h). The determi-

¶ 22,100

nation of whether such a purpose exists is determined on the basis of all the facts and circumstances. The regulations indicate that the IRS may use this anti-abuse rule to prevent avoidance of Section 731(c) through such devices as changes in partnership allocations and distribution rights, multiple distributions, or related entities. As an example, under these regulations, the IRS may seek to prevent avoidance of Section 731(c) in the situation where a partnership distributes substantially all of its assets (other than marketable securities and cash) to some partners, with the substantive effect of a distribution of the marketable securities to the remaining partners.

[¶ 22,105]

Problems

KVTA is a partnership of four equal partners: Katherine, Valerie, Tiffany, and Alexandra. The partnership was formed on January 1 of year 1. On that date, the four partners contributed the following properties to the partnership:

		Basis	*Value*
Katherine	Capital Asset W	$1,000	$2,000
Valerie	Capital Asset X	500	2,000
Tiffany	Capital Asset Y	2,000	2,000
Alexandra	C Corporation Stock	100	500
	Capital Asset Z	2,000	1,500

At the time of Alexandra's contribution of the C Corporation stock to the partnership, C Corporation had assets worth $500. (The stock contributed to the partnership by Alexandra was all of the outstanding stock of the corporation.) The partnership uses the "traditional method" of making Section 704(c) allocations under Reg. § 1.704–3(b). Assume that the partners' bases in their partnership interests at the time of the transactions described below are the same as their original bases for the partnership interests. Except as otherwise provided in Problem 12, below, assume that none of the partnership's assets are marketable securities (within the meaning of Section 731(c)(2)).

Ignoring any income or loss for the year of distribution, determine the federal income tax consequences to the partners from the following alternative transactions:

1. On July 1 of year 7, the partnership sells Capital Asset X for $2,000 (its then fair market value).

2. On July 1 of year 7, the partnership distributes Capital Asset X (which has a value of $2,000) to Tiffany.

3. On July 1 of year 7, the partnership distributes Capital Asset Y (which has a value of $2,000) to Katherine.

4. On July 1 of year 7, the partnership distributes Capital Asset Z (which has a value of $1,500) to Valerie.

¶ 22,105

5. How would your answer in Problem 2 change if the distribution to Tiffany took place on July 1 of year 2 (when Capital Asset X had a value of $2,000)? See § 707(a)(2)(B) and Reg. § 1.704–4(a)(2).

6. How would your answer in Problem 2 change if Capital Asset X had a value of $4,000 on July 1 of year 7? (Assume that the total value of all partnership assets at the time of distribution is $16,000.)

7. How would your answers in Problems 2 through 5 change if the distributions were made on July 1 of year 8?

8. How would your answer in Problem 2 change if, at the time of distribution of Capital Asset X to Tiffany, Valerie were no longer a partner because Jeanie had purchased Valerie's partnership interest on January 1 of year 2 for $2,000 (its then value)?

9. On July 1 of year 7, the partnership distributes Capital Asset W (which has a value of $2,000) to Tiffany. On September 1 of year 7, the partnership distributes Capital Asset Y (which also has a value of $2,000) to Katherine. Assume that Capital Asset W and Capital Asset Y are like-kind properties (within the meaning of Section 1031).

10. On July 1 of year 7, the partnership distributes Capital Asset X (which has a value of $2,000) back to Valerie.

11. On July 1 of year 6, the partnership contributes Capital Asset X to C Corporation as a contribution to capital. On July 1 of year 7, the partnership distributes the C Corporation stock (which has a value of $2,500) back to Alexandra. (Assume the total value of all partnership assets at the time of distribution is $10,000.)

12. On July 1 of year 7, the partnership distributes Capital Asset X (which for purposes of this Problem 12 is a marketable security, within the meaning of Section 731(c)(2), and the only marketable security owned by the partnership) to Katherine. At the time of distribution, Capital Asset X has a fair market value of $4,000 and the total value of all partnership assets is $16,000.

F. DISTRIBUTIONS THAT ALTER A PART-NER'S INTEREST IN ORDINARY IN-COME PROPERTY

[¶ 22,110]

1. CURRENT LAW

Any distribution to a partner has the effect of an exchange of the partner's interest in some partnership property for an interest in other property unless the distribution is entirely pro rata. The distributee's interest in the distributed property increases while the interest in the partnership and its remaining properties decreases. If distributions of property were fully taxable events, this exchange of properties could not be used to manipulate tax liabilities because the gain in distributed property would be recognized at the time of distribution and taxed to all partners. However, because distributions generally are carryover basis transactions, Congress feared that partners could use the distribution rules to reduce their tax liabilities improperly. For example, a partnership might distribute its ordinary income properties to a low bracket partner, or a partner having operating loss carryovers, while leaving the higher bracket partners taxable only at capital gains rates.

In an effort to minimize, if not eliminate, that ability to shift the liability for the tax on ordinary income, Congress enacted Section 751(b). Under that provision to the extent that a distribution increases or decreases the distributee partner's interest in the partnership's unrealized receivables or inventory items that have substantially appreciated in value, the distribution is treated as a fully taxable sale. In concept, Section 751(b) is more astonishing than it is complex. In practice, however, it is both.

In Chapter 21, the definitions of "unrealized receivables" in Section 751(c) and "inventory items" in Section 751(d) were discussed in connection with the application of Section 751(a) on the sale of a partnership interest. See ¶¶ 21,045–21,050 (definition of unrealized receivables) and 21,055–21,065 (definition of inventory items). Those same definitions apply for purposes of Section 751(b) as well with one major modification.

Under the disproportionate distribution rules in Section 751(b), an inventory item does not constitute a Section 751(b) asset unless the totality of the Section 751(d) inventory items held by the partnership are substantially appreciated in value. § 751(b)(1)(A)(ii). For making that determination, the Code contains a very precise formula. The aggregate value of all such inventory items must exceed 120 percent of the aggregate adjusted basis to the partnership for those items.[10] § 751(b)(3)(A). If this test is not met by the inventory items as a group, the partnership will not have any substantially appreciated inventory items for Section 751(b) purposes even if certain inventory items are highly appreciated in value. However, an item of inventory property is excluded in applying this test if a principal purpose for acquiring such property was avoidance of Section 751(b). § 751(b)(3)(B). Moreover, even

---

10. Before a change made by Congress in 1993, former Section 751(d)(1) contained a two-pronged formula for determining whether the partnership's inventory items had substantially appreciated in value. The aggregate value of all such inventory items had to exceed 120 percent of the aggregate adjusted basis to the partnership for those items, and that aggregate value had to exceed 10 percent of the value of all partnership property, excluding cash. In 1993, Congress deleted the 10 percent of value test to prevent taxpayers from avoiding Section 751 by manipulating the partnership's gross assets. See, e.g., H.R. Rep. No. 111, 103d Cong., 1st Sess. 642 (1993). The 1993 Act also added the provision disregarding inventory that is acquired principally to avoid Section 751(b) "to prevent circumvention of the [appreciated inventory] rule." Id.

if a partnership does not have any substantially appreciated inventory items, it may still have Section 751(b) assets if it has unrealized receivables under Section 751(c).

The regulations provide that among the ordinary income assets included in Section 751(d)(2) are accounts receivable, notwithstanding that the receivables are unrealized receivables and thus are also treated as Section 751(c) assets. Reg. § 1.751–1(d)(2)(ii).[11] The regulations do not contemplate a double counting of the ordinary income items of the partnership; the definition solely affects the computation of appreciation in the inventory items for purposes of Section 751(b)(3). Is that definition necessary to prevent manipulation of the definition of substantial appreciation? Should that regulation be read to include the accounts receivable of an accrual basis partnership? The receivable would be realized and thus would not be included within Section 751(c). What is the effect of including realized receivables within the scope of Section 751(d) for purposes of the substantial appreciation test in Section 751(b)(3)?

The operation of Section 751(b) is better illustrated than merely explained. Assume that a partnership of three equal partners has just the following assets and no liabilities:

	Basis	*Value*
Inventory Item I	$3,000	$9,000
Cash	3,000	3,000
Capital Asset X	3,000	15,000
	$9,000	$27,000

Each partner has a capital account and basis for her partnership interest equal to $3,000. The partnership makes a distribution to partner A of Inventory Item I. Notice that in the absence of Section 751(b), no gain would be recognized on this distribution to any partner, and partner A would hold the inventory with a carryover basis of $3,000. Thus, the partnership would have shifted all of the ordinary gain in partnership properties to partner A.

Under Section 751(b), the first step is to determine the extent to which distributee partner A's interest in unrealized receivables and

---

11. This regulation was issued under an earlier version of the statute when the substantial appreciation requirement for inventory items was set forth in Section 751(d)(1) and applied to both sales of partnership interests governed by Section 751(a) and disproportionate partnership distributions governed by Section 751(b). As discussed in Chapter 21, the Taxpayer Relief Act of 1997 broadened the scope of Section 751(a) by deleting the substantial appreciation requirement for inventory items in the context of sales of partnership interests but retained the substantial appreciation requirement for inventory items in the context of partnership distributions. The 1997 Act did not change the wording of the requirement but moved it from Section 751(d)(1) to Section 751(b)(3). In the light of this legislative change, Reg. § 1.751–1(d)(2)(ii) should be read as now applying to the determination of whether a partnership's inventory items satisfy the substantial appreciation requirement in Section 751(b)(3).

substantially appreciated inventory items has increased or decreased. In a sacrifice of accuracy (but perhaps a gain in simplicity), that determination is made by reference to the gross value of the partnership assets and not by reference to relative appreciation. When the partners' interests in capital differ from their interests in profits and losses, those differing ratios must be taken into account in determining the change in the distributee partner's interest in the value of the partnership properties. Here, however, prior to the distribution, partner A held a one-third interest in the value of all partnership properties. Thus, the value of partner A's interest in the Section 751(b) assets of the partnership prior to the distribution was $3,000. After the distribution, the value of partner A's interest in Section 751(b) assets had increased to $9,000. Thus, partner A's interest in Section 751(b) assets has increased by $6,000. Correspondingly, the value of partner A's interest in non-Section 751(b) assets has declined from $6,000 (one third of $18,000) to zero. It can be seen, therefore, that partner A effectively has exchanged an interest in $6,000 of non-Section 751(b) assets for $6,000 of Section 751(b) assets.

The general effect of Section 751(b) is to treat that exchange as a taxable event to both partner A and the remaining partners. Since it would be the remaining partners who otherwise would be avoiding a tax on ordinary income, under Section 751 the partnership is treated as exchanging $6,000 of Inventory Item I with partner A for $6,000 of non-Section 751(b) assets in a taxable transaction.

In order for that exchange to occur, however, partner A must first have the non-Section 751(b) assets that she is treated as exchanging—and that is where Section 751(b) becomes rather fanciful: First, partner A is treated exactly as if she received an actual distribution of $6,000 of non-Section 751(b) assets (which in reality is not what she is getting but rather is what she is giving up). Partner A's basis in the non-Section 751(b) assets that she constructively receives is determined under the normal carryover basis rules of Section 732 and will reduce the basis of her partnership interest.

Next, partner A is treated as if she exchanged those non-Section 751(b) assets for $6,000 of the inventory that she did in fact receive. That exchange is taxable to both parties. The effect of all this on the partnership is not hard to figure out. The partnership is treated as selling $6,000 of Inventory Item I, which has a basis of $2,000, and thus recognizes ordinary income of $4,000. The effect on partner A can become a bit trickier. Since the amount of her gain depends on the basis of the non-Section 751(b) property constructively distributed to her (and transferred back to the partnership), we have to determine what property that was. While that determination can become quite complex, here it is not: partner A has given up her interest in cash of $1,000 and $5,000 of Capital Asset X with a basis of $1,000, and she is treated as receiving a distribution of those assets. On the constructive transfer of those properties back to the partnership, partner A would have a capital gain of $4,000 on the constructive exchange of $5,000 of Capital Asset X. Moreover, the partnership will be treated as if it had purchased $5,000 of Capital Asset X.

All of these constructive steps are given the tax consequences that actual steps would have. Thus, partner A will have $6,000 of Inventory Item I with a basis of $6,000. Similarly, the partnership will have $5,000 of Capital Asset X with a cost basis of $5,000. Adding that to the $2,000 basis in the portion of Capital Asset X that was not treated as distributed to A gives the partnership a basis for Capital Asset X of $7,000. Note that the partnership obtains this step-up in basis under Section 751 even if the Section 754 election has not been made. The effect of the constructive distributions on the basis of partner A's interest in the partnership would be:

Initial Basis	$3,000
Less Distributions	
Cash	(1,000)
Capital Asset X	(1,000)
Remaining Basis	$1,000

Following all of these constructive steps, partner A is now treated as receiving a distribution of the balance of the actual distribution. Since $6,000 of Inventory Item I has been accounted for, she is now treated as receiving a distribution of $3,000 of Inventory Item I with a basis of $1,000. Since that basis is the same as the remaining basis for her partnership interest, that amount becomes her basis in the distributed inventory. Added to the $6,000 basis she obtained in the constructive exchange, her total basis in Inventory Item I becomes $7,000. Of partner A's overall gain of $6,000 in the partnership, $4,000 will have been taxed and $2,000 deferred. Whew!

[¶ 22,115]

Problems

1.   A cash method partnership, which has no liabilities, owns the following properties:

	Basis	*Value*
Accounts receivable	$ 0	$ 50
Inventory	1,100	1,400
Section 1231 equipment (cost $3,000)	1,400	2,000
Land	2,000	5,000
Total	$4,500	$8,450

What are the partnership's "unrealized receivables" and "inventory items which have appreciated substantially in value" for Section 751(b) purposes?

¶ 22,110

2. Assume in Problem 1 that the partnership sells on credit one item of inventory that had a basis of $100 and a value of $300. Now what would be the partnership's "inventory items which have appreciated substantially in value" for Section 751(b) purposes?

3. A partnership has the following assets:

	Basis	*Value*
Cash	$ 90	$ 90
Inventory Item X................	10	70
Inventory Item Y................	140	140
Total	$240	$300

If the partnership distributes cash of $30 and Inventory Item X in retirement of the interest of a partner who owned a one-third interest in the partnership, will Section 751(b) apply? Has ordinary income been shifted to the retiring partner?

4. Top Banana Imports is a two-person partnership having no liabilities and the following assets:

	Basis	*Value*
Cash	$ 6,000	$ 6,000
Inventory.....................	6,000	24,000
Building......................	18,000	18,000
Trademark	0	24,000
Total	$30,000	$72,000

Paul owns a 50–percent interest in partnership profits, losses, and capital. The tax basis for his partnership interest is $12,000. The partnership was formed eight years ago, and all partnership contributions were made at that time.

If the partnership distributes the Building to Paul, reducing his interest to one-third, what will be the tax consequences to him and to the partnership? What will be the final basis of the Building to Paul?

5. In Problem 4, assuming that Top Banana had made a Section 754 election, what further basis adjustments must be made? Note that the portion of the Building that Paul is treated as receiving in the constructive Section 751 exchange is not treated as received in a distribution governed by Sections 731 through 733.

6. Olde Tyme Nurseries is a partnership of three individuals, each of whom has an equal interest in partnership profits, losses, and capital. The partnership was formed eight years ago, and all partnership contributions were made at that time. The partnership has no liabilities and the following assets:

¶ 22,115

	Basis	*Value*
Cash	$45,000	$45,000
Lots (Inventory)	15,000	45,000
Land, parcel #1	0	45,000
Land, parcel #2	45,000	45,000
Total	$105,000	$180,000

The partnership will make a distribution to Jayne of $15,000 in cash and $15,000 in Lots, which will reduce her interest in the partnership from one-third to one-fifth. Assuming that Jayne's adjusted basis in her partnership interest is $35,000, trace the tax consequences of the distribution to her and to the remaining partners.

7. In Problem 6, Jayne might be regarded as receiving Lots in exchange for her interest in either parcel #1 or parcel #2. Under those circumstances, the regulations provide that the parties may specify which properties are included in the exchange. Reg. § 1.751–1(g), Exs. 3(c) and 4(c). What difference does it make to Jayne which parcel is specified? What difference does it make to the partnership which parcel is specified?

[¶ 22,120]

2. ALTERNATIVE APPROACHES FOR REFORM OF SECTION 751(b)

The daunting complexity of Section 751(b) and the regulations thereunder creates administrative difficulties for partnerships trying to comply with the requirements of the Section 751(b) regulations and likely leads to noncompliance with those requirements, not to mention the difficulties it creates for the IRS in trying to enforce these rules. Moreover, many of the tax abuses involving the use of partnership distributions that are the target of Section 751(b) may be prevented in large part under current law by other provisions in Subchapter K that have been added to the Code since Section 751(b) was enacted, such as Sections 704(c), 731(c), and 737, and the mandatory basis adjustment rule in Section 734 added in 2004. This has led some leading commentators to recommend repeal of Section 751(b). See, e.g., Federal Income Tax Project: Subchapter K: Proposals on the Taxation of Partners 47–55 (A.L.I. 1984).

Another reform alternative to outright repeal of Section 751(b) would be substantial revision of the complicated regulations under the provision. The IRS discusses several possible approaches for amending the Section 751(b) regulations in the following Notice.

[¶ 22,125]

IRS NOTICE 2006–14

2006–1 C.B. 498.

Section 1.   Purpose

This notice invites public comments on certain distributions treated as sales or exchanges under § 751(b) * * *.

Section 2.   Background

Section 751 was enacted to prevent the conversion of ordinary income into capital gain and the shifting of ordinary income among partners. See H.R. Rep. No. 1337, at 70 (1954) * * *. Section 751(a) provides for recharacterization of capital gain or loss when an interest in a partnership is sold or exchanged to the extent of the selling partner's share of unrealized receivables and inventory items of the partnership. Section 751(b) overrides the nonrecognition scheme of § 731 for certain current and liquidating partnership distributions that alter a partner's share of unrealized receivables and substantially appreciated inventory items (disproportionate distributions). Section 751(b)(1) provides:

(1) GENERAL RULE.-To the extent a partner receives in a distribution—

(A) partnership property which is–(i) unrealized receivables, or (ii) inventory items which have appreciated substantially in value, in exchange for all or a part of his interest in other partnership property (including money), or

(B) partnership property (including money) other than property described in subparagraph (A)(i) or (ii) in exchange for all or part of his interest in partnership property described in subparagraph (A)(i) or (ii), such transactions shall, under regulations prescribed by the Secretary, be considered as a sale or exchange of such property between the distributee and the partnership (as constituted after the distribution).

The legislative history of § 751 demonstrates that Congress was primarily concerned with unrealized appreciation in unrealized receivables and inventory items of a partnership.

The provisions relating to unrealized receivables and appreciated inventory items are necessary to prevent the use of the partnership as a device for obtaining capital-gain treatment on fees or other rights to income and on appreciated inventory. Amounts attributable to such rights would be treated as ordinary income if realized in normal course by the partnership. The sale of a partnership interest or distributions to partners should not be permitted to change the character of this income. *The statutory treatment proposed, in gener-*

al, regards the income rights as severable from the partnership interest and as subject to the same tax consequences which would be accorded an individual entrepreneur.

S. Rep. No. 1622, at 99 (1954) * * * (emphasis added).

The current regulations under § 751(b) require the identification of two classes of assets: (1) hot assets (unrealized receivables as defined in § 751(c) and substantially appreciated inventory as defined in § 751(b)(3) and (d)); and (2) cold assets (assets other than unrealized receivables and substantially appreciated inventory). In computing the distributee partner's income under § 751(b), the current regulations provide that the distributee partner's share of the partnership's hot assets and cold assets before and after the distribution must be compared. For purposes of this comparison, each partner's share of the partnership's hot and cold assets is determined by reference to the gross value of the assets. If the distribution results in an exchange of all or a portion of the distributee partner's share of one class of assets (relinquished assets) for assets in the other class (acquired assets), it is necessary to construct a deemed exchange by identifying which relinquished assets are treated as exchanged for which acquired assets.

For example, if a partner receives more than the partner's share of the partnership's hot assets in a distribution, that partner is treated as exchanging a portion of the partner's interest in certain cold assets of the partnership for the other partners' shares of the acquired hot assets. In order to accomplish the exchange, the distributee partner is treated as (1) receiving the relinquished assets (the cold assets) in a nonliquidating distribution and (2) engaging in a taxable exchange (with the partnership) of those assets for the acquired assets (the hot assets). Both the distributee partner and the other partners may recognize income or loss on the exchange. The distributee partner and the partnership then hold the exchanged assets (or portions thereof) with a cost basis under § 1012. The rest of the actual distribution (the part that is not subject to § 751(b)) is characterized under the general rules for partnership distributions prescribed in §§ 731 through 736.

The current regulations under § 751(b) were published in 1956 and have not been amended to reflect significant changes in subchapter K and in the operations of contemporary partnerships. Moreover, the current § 751(b) regulations have been widely criticized as being extraordinarily complex and burdensome and as not achieving the objectives of the statute. As a result, a distribution may reduce a partner's *pro rata* share of the unrealized appreciation in the partnership's hot assets without triggering § 751(b), and a distribution can trigger § 751(b) even if the partner's *pro rata* share of the unrealized appreciation is not reduced.

¶ 22,125

The Treasury Department and the Service are considering several possible methods, discussed below, for addressing the issues associated with the current § 751(b) regulations.

Section 3.   Discussion

(a) Determining the partners' shares of partnership property

The current regulations under § 751(b) provide little guidance on how each partner's share of partnership property is determined. Two economic rights are inherent in most partnership interests: a right to partnership capital, and a right to partnership profits and losses. A partner may have a different interest in each of these rights, and those interests may vary over time. Moreover, a partner's share of unrealized partnership items may be affected by both the economic arrangement of the partners and certain requirements of subchapter K, such as § 704(c).

The legislative history of § 751(b) emphasizes "income rights" of the partners and suggests that these rights may be treated as severable and subject to the same tax consequences as those of an individual entrepreneur. S. Rep. No. 1622, at 99. Consistent with this legislative history, in order to determine whether a distribution may be subject to § 751(b), commentators have suggested that new regulations could require partnerships and their partners to compare the amounts of ordinary income that would be recognized by the partners if the partnership's hot assets (including distributed assets) were sold or exchanged for fair market value in a taxable transaction both before and after the distribution (hypothetical sale approach). If the amount of ordinary income that would be allocated to any partner (including the distributee) as a result of such a sale or exchange is reduced as a result of a distribution from the partnership, an analysis under § 751(b) would be required. The hypothetical sale approach, combined with the application of § 704(c) principles, could provide rules that achieve the objective of the statute in a less burdensome manner.

Under § 704(c), if partnership property is sold or exchanged, the built-in gain or loss in contributed or revalued partnership property must be allocated to the contributing or appropriate historic partner (§ 704(c) principles). *See* § 704(c)(1)(A) and §§ 1.704–1(b)(4)(i), 1.704–3(a)(2), and 1.704–3(a)(6). As a result of the application of § 704(c) principles, there can be layers of appreciation in partnership assets (due to successive revaluations), each of which may be allocable separately. Moreover, distributed § 704(c) property and § 704(c) property with a substantial built-in loss must be analyzed separately to determine each partner's appropriate share of the unrealized gain or loss. See, e.g., § 704(c)(1)(B) and (C). As a result, § 704(c) generally operates to preserve each partner's share of the built-in appreciation and depreciation in partnership assets. If the regulations under § 751(b) were amended to specify that § 704(c) principles are taken into account for purposes of determining whether a partner's share of partnership hot assets has been altered by a distribution, significantly fewer distributions would trigger § 751(b).

Example 1. Assume that A, B, and C each contribute $120 to partnership *ABC*. *ABC* purchases land for $210, which appreciates in value to $300. At a time when the partnership also has $90 of zero-basis unrealized receivables and cash of $50, *ABC* distributes $90 to C, reducing C's interest in *ABC* from 1/3 to 1/5. If, immediately before the distribution, the partnership's assets are revalued and the partners' capital accounts are increased to reflect each partner's share of the unrealized appreciation in the partnership's assets, C's entire pre-distribution share of the partnership's unrealized income in the accounts receivable (1/3 of $90, or $30) is preserved in C's capital account after the distribution. *ABC* will have the following post-distribution balance sheet (before the application of section 751(b)):

Assets	Basis	Value	Capital	Basis	Value
Cash	$60	$60	A	$120	$180
Unrealized Receivables	$0	$90	B	$120	$180
Land	$210	$300	C	$30	$90
Total	$270	$450		$270	$450

If § 704(c) principles were applicable for purposes of § 751(b), the distribution to C would not trigger § 751(b), as C's pre-distribution share of the unrealized income in the receivables ($30) is fully preserved in its capital account after the distribution. Section 704(c) principles would require the partnership to allocate that share of appreciation to C when it is recognized.

Special rules may be necessary to address distributions of hot assets to a partner where the adjusted basis of the distributed assets (and the unrealized appreciation in those assets) is different in the hands of the distributee partner than it was in the hands of the partnership. Under §§ 732(a)(2) and (b), the adjusted basis of distributed hot assets is reduced (and the unrealized appreciation in those hot assets is increased) if the distributee partner's basis in its partnership interest is insufficient to absorb the partnership's adjusted basis in the distributed hot asset. If the partnership has a § 754 election in effect at the time of the distribution, § 734(b)(1)(B) permits the partnership to increase the adjusted basis of the partnership's retained hot assets to the extent of the reduction in the basis of the distributed hot assets under § 732(a)(2) or (b). Under these circumstances, the hot asset appreciation remaining in the partnership is reduced. As such, one of the issues raised by use of a hypothetical sale to measure changes in a partner's interest in hot asset appreciation is the extent to which basis adjustments under §§ 732 and 734(b) should be taken into account.

Moreover, a hypothetical sale at any one point in time does not take into account future allocations that are planned or expected. For example, a partner's allocations with respect to a particular asset may vary over time. Measuring income or loss on a hypothetical sale of that asset at a particular time may not accurately reflect that partner's income rights with respect to that asset over the life of the partnership.

Once it is determined that a partner's share of the income rights in the partnership's hot assets has been reduced by a distribution, the tax consequences of the distribution under § 751(b) must be determined.

(b) Determining the tax consequences of disproportionate distributions

The current § 751(b) regulations impose a complex deemed distribution/exchange approach for determining the tax consequences of a disproportionate distribution. One possible way to simplify this determination would be to treat a disproportionate distribution as triggering a taxable sale of the partners' shares of relinquished hot assets to the partnership immediately before the distribution (hot asset sale approach). The hot asset sale approach would apply § 751(b) in a fully aggregate manner that is arguably consistent with its legislative history (under which each partner's tax treatment should be that of an individual entrepreneur).

This approach could be combined with the hypothetical sale approach. Thus, new regulations could provide that § 751(b) applies if any partner's share of the net unrealized appreciation in hot assets of the partnership is reduced as a result of a distribution from the partnership. Under the hot asset sale approach, for any partner whose share of hot assets is reduced (selling partner), whether or not the selling partner is the distributee, the selling partner would be treated as receiving the relinquished hot assets in a deemed distribution and selling to the partnership the relinquished share of the hot assets immediately before the actual distribution. The selling partner would recognize ordinary income from the deemed sale, and the partner's basis in the partnership interest and the partner's capital account would be adjusted to reflect the consideration treated as contributed to the partnership. The assets deemed sold to the partnership would have a cost basis under § 1012. Under the hot asset sale approach there would be no deemed exchange for cold assets, thereby eliminating the need to identify cold assets to be exchanged and to construct a deemed distribution of those assets.

The hot asset sale approach can be straightforward if the distributee partner's share of hot asset appreciation is reduced by the distribution. In this situation, the partnership would be treated as distributing the relinquished share of hot assets to the distributee who sells the hot assets back to the partnership, recognizing ordinary income, with appropriate adjustments to the distributee partner's basis in the partnership interest and capital account. The asset deemed sold would take a cost basis, and the distribution would be governed by §§ 731 through 736.

Example 2. Assume *A*, *B* and *C* are each 1/3 partners in a partnership that holds one hot asset and one cold asset, each with a basis of $0 and a fair market value of $150. *A*, *B*, and *C* each have an adjusted basis in the partnership interest of $0, and a $50 share of hot asset appreciation. *A* is fully redeemed by a distribution of 2/3 of the cold asset ($100). Immediately before the distribution, the partnership's assets are revalued and the partners' capital accounts are increased to $100 to reflect each partner's share of the unrealized appreciation in the partnership's assets. Because the entire $150 of hot asset appreciation remains in the partnership after the distribution, *A*'s share of that appreciation has been reduced by $50. Under the hot asset sale approach, PRS would be treated as distributing the relinquished share of the hot asset ($50) to *A* and then purchasing that share for $50. *A* would recognize income of $50 and would be treated as contributing the $50 to PRS. *A*'s basis in the partnership interest would increase to $50 and *A*'s capital account would be restored to $100. The portion of the hot asset deemed sold would take a cost basis, increasing the partnership's basis in the hot asset to $50.

In this example, because *A*'s basis in its partnership interest is $50, the basis of the distributed cold asset would be increased under § 732(b) to $50 in *A*'s hands. The cold asset remaining in the partnership has a $0 basis and would not be subject to a basis reduction under § 734(b) even if the partnership had a § 754 election in effect. In these circumstances, $50 of capital gain is potentially eliminated from the system, however.

The hot asset sale approach also raises certain complications where the distributee partner has insufficient basis in its partnership interest to absorb the partnership's adjusted basis in the distributed hot assets. This can lead to results inconsistent with the intent of § 751(b).

Example 3. Assume the same facts as Example 2, except that instead of distributing 2/3 of the cold asset to *A*, the partnership fully redeems *A* by a distribution of 2/3 of the hot asset ($100). Because only $50 of hot asset appreciation remains in the partnership after the distribution, *B*'s and *C*'s shares of that appreciation have been reduced by $25 each. Under the hot asset sale approach, *PRS* would be deemed to distribute the relinquished share of the hot asset ($50) equally to *B* and *C* and each would be treating as selling $25 worth of the hot asset to the partnership. *B* and *C* would each recognize $25 of ordinary income and would be treated as contributing $25 to the partnership. The portion of the hot asset deemed sold would take a cost basis, increasing the partnership's basis in the distributed portion of the distributed hot asset to $50. Because *A*'s basis in its partnership interest is $0, however, the basis of the distributed hot asset would be reduced under § 732(b) to $0 in *A*'s hands. If the partnership had a § 754 election in effect, the partnership would increase the basis of the retained hot asset under § 734(b) by $50. After the distribution, *A*'s share of unrealized income in hot assets would

¶ 22,125

still be $100, and B and C, who each recognized $25 of ordinary income, would recognize no additional ordinary income.

Commentators have suggested that, in these situations, it may be appropriate to permit or require the distributee partner to recognize capital gain to the extent the adjusted basis of the distributed hot assets exceeds that partner's basis in the partnership interest. In Example 3, A could elect, or be required, to recognize capital gain equal to the amount by which the adjusted basis of the distributed hot assets exceeds that partner's basis in the partnership interest ($50), thereby increasing A's basis to $50. The distributed hot asset would take a $50 basis in A's hands under § 732(b), and no § 734(b) adjustment would be made to the retained hot asset. If A recognizes capital gain on the distribution, future regulations could permit an equivalent increase to the basis of the partnership's retained cold assets.

SECTION 4. REQUEST FOR COMMENTS

The Treasury Department and the Service are conducting a study of the current § 751(b) regulations and are considering alternative approaches to achieving the purpose of the statute that would provide greater simplicity. For example, it may be possible to provide safe harbor methods for calculating the share of ordinary income or capital gain that should be recognized as a result of a disproportionate distribution that may reduce some administrative burden but still serve the purpose of the statute. In this regard, the Treasury Department and the Service request comments on the approaches discussed in this Notice (as well as other possible approaches) to determining a partner's share of hot assets and to prescribing the tax consequences of a disproportionate distribution. Comments are requested concerning the following issues:

A. For purposes of determining each partner's share of partnership assets before and after a distribution that may be subject to § 751(b),

    1. Whether the hypothetical sale approach (combined with the application of § 704(c) principles) for determining each partner's share of partnership assets provides an accurate and appropriate measure for purposes of § 751(b). In particular,

        a. Whether special rules would be necessary to address situations in which the distributee partner's interest in unrealized appreciation in hot assets prior to the distribution exceeds the partner's interest in partnership capital after the distribution;

        b. Whether the hypothetical sale approach should be modified to take into account changes in allocations that are planned or may occur in the future or changes in the partner's interest in anticipated future appreciation and depreciation in partnership assets;

c.   The extent to which regulations adopting the hypothetical sale approach should take into account the distributee partner's basis in the partnership interest and basis adjustments under §§ 734(b) and 743(b), including basis adjustments resulting from the distribution;

d.   Whether the partners' shares of partnership liabilities should be considered in determining the partners' shares of partnership assets, and how the rules of § 752 should be coordinated with those of § 751(b).

2.   Whether § 751(b) should be limited to transactions that change the partners' shares of unrealized appreciation in hot assets or should also apply to transactions that change the partners' shares of unrealized depreciation in hot assets.

3.   Whether other approaches to determining a partner's share of partnership hot and cold assets should be considered.

B.   For purposes of simplifying the tax consequences of a distribution that is subject to § 751(b), whether the hot asset sale approach is an appropriate method of applying § 751(b) or whether other approaches should be considered. Comments are specifically requested on the following:

1.   Whether the regulations should provide a simple safe harbor that approximates the appropriate taxation of a disproportionate distribution and, if so, the appropriate parameters and availability of such a safe harbor.

2.   Whether the current § 751(b) regulations should be generally retained or retained in combination with a safe harbor, or whether the current § 751(b) regulations should be completely revised to adopt a new paradigm such as the hot asset sale approach.

3.   Whether mandatory or elective capital gain recognition should be included in the hot asset sale approach.

* * *

[¶ 22,130]

Note

Now that you have studied Section 751(b) of current law, what do you think of the alternative approaches for revising the regulations under Section 751(b)? Do the Treasury and the IRS have the necessary regulatory authority under the current statute to make the changes that are suggested in this Notice? Would amendment of the Section 751(b) regulations solve the administrative problems created by these regulations or is outright repeal of the statutory provision warranted?

Chapter 23

LIQUIDATING DISTRIBUTIONS

[¶ 23,000]

A. INTRODUCTION

There is no inherent reason why the taxation of distributions in complete liquidation of a partner's interest in a partnership should be any more complex than the taxation of current distributions. However, it is. The fundamental reason for the added complexity has less to do with taxation than with determining just when a partner should be treated as having retired from the partnership for income tax purposes. Consider, for example, an arrangement under which a retiring partner receives a lump-sum payment geared to the book value of the partnership on the day of retirement in year 1 plus annual payments over the next five years equal to 20 percent, 10 percent, 10 percent, 5 percent, and 5 percent of the firm's net profits for the year concerned. The partner may have retired for state law purposes in year 1, but should that be controlling for tax purposes? The percentage payments in years 2 through 6 look a great deal like a declining distributive share of partnership income.

Rather than arbitrarily specify when a partner is to be treated as retired for income tax purposes, the Code has adopted a more flexible, but more complex, solution in Section 736. A portion of the payments to a retiring partner (or the estate of a deceased partner) is treated like a liquidating distribution that is taxed very much like a current distribution. However, the other portion of the payments is treated like a payment to a continuing partner. Moreover, although recent legislative changes have significantly reduced the flexibility in this area, in some limited circumstances, the partners themselves have considerable latitude in determining how a payment is to be treated for tax purposes.

[¶ 23,005]

B. THE STRUCTURE OF SECTION 736

All liquidating distributions to a retiring partner or with respect to the retirement of a deceased partner's interest are governed by Section 736. That provision, however, does not itself prescribe the income tax consequences of the distributions. Rather, Section 736 is a definitional provision that directs taxpayers to the appropriate provisions of Subchapter K for the taxation of the transaction.

Section 736 divides liquidating distributions to retiring or deceased partners into two categories: so-called Section 736(a) payments and Section 736(b) payments. Surprisingly, perhaps, that division is not based on the nature of the payments but rather on the nature of the partnership properties. Section 736(b) governs payments in exchange for the retiring partner's interest in partnership property (other than, in the case of a retiring general partner in a services partnership, unrealized receivables and goodwill if the partnership agreement does not provide a payment for goodwill). Section 736(a) governs all other payments in exchange for the retiring partner's interest. However, as a practical matter, Section 736(a) has a narrow scope and will include only (i) payments for the retiring partner's interest in unrealized receivables and in goodwill not included in the Section 736(b) payments (i.e., payments to a retiring general partner in a services partnership for the partner's share of unrealized receivables and goodwill if the partnership agreement does not provide a payment for goodwill) and (ii) payments to the retiring partner in any type of partnership in excess of the value of the partner's interest in partnership property (i.e., payments in the nature of deferred compensation or mutual insurance).

The statutory dichotomy is not free of complexity. Payments for a retiring partner's interest in realized receivables and, apparently, in the partnership's basis in goodwill must be treated as Section 736(b) payments, even in the case of a retiring general partner in a services partnership. Reg. § 1.736–1(b)(2) and (3). The treatment of distributions in kind is not fully clear. At least to the extent of the partner's interest in the distributed property, the distribution should be governed by Section 736(b). Moreover, the distribution of unrealized receivables in kind is probably governed by Section 736(b) since the distribution is not a payment for the partner's interest in the receivable. However, no reason appears why the Section 736(a) payment for an unrealized receivable cannot be in the form of any other type of property.

For most partnerships, the mandatory allocation of payments between subsections (a) and (b) will control the entire amount of the liquidating distribution. However, in some partnerships, retiring partners are entitled to liquidating distributions in an amount that exceeds the value of their interest in the tangible value of the partnership. To the extent that those payments are to a retiring general partner in a services partnership for partnership goodwill, their classification is subject to the control of the parties. If the partnership agreement specifically provides for payments for goodwill, the payments will be governed by Section 736(b). If the partnership agreement does not provide for payments for goodwill, the payments will be treated as Section 736(a) payments. Since the partnership agreement may be amended to provide or not provide for payments for goodwill at the time a partner retires, Section 736 effectively permits the parties in a services partnership to elect the desired treatment for this category of payments. However, the computation of the total amount of the payments treated as attributable to goodwill may be subject to the allocation rules of Section 1060.

[¶ 23,010]

C. SECTION 736(b) PAYMENTS

Section 736(b) payments are treated as distributions and thus are taxed under the rules of Sections 731 and 732 in a manner almost identical to the taxation of current distributions. In common with current distributions, gain will not be recognized (unless Section 751(b) applies) to the retiring partner except to the extent that any cash distributed (or the fair market value of certain marketable securities distributed) exceeds the basis for the partnership interest. However, in contrast to current distributions, a loss can be recognized on a liquidating distribution. Because the basis of Section 751 property (or of cash) cannot be greater in the hands of the partner than in the hands of the partnership, a loss on the liquidation of a partner's interest cannot be deferred if the distribution consists solely of cash, unrealized receivables, or inventory (without regard to appreciation). When the distribution consists solely of one or more of those categories of assets and the basis for the partnership interest is greater than the sum of the cash and the tax basis of the distributed receivables and inventory, a loss is allowed for the excess under Section 731(a)(2). See Reg. §§ 1.731–1(a)(2) and 1.732–1(c)(3). As in the event of a gain, the loss is treated as a loss from the sale or exchange of the partnership interest.

Since the partnership interest will disappear following a liquidating distribution, the allocation of basis to any property distributed to the retiring partner must differ from the allocation in a current distribution. Under Section 732(b) the entire basis for the partnership interest, after reduction for any cash distributed, must be allocated among the properties distributed. That allocation, however, is made under the complex rules of Section 732(c), which was first discussed in Chapter 22 in connection with the allocation of basis following a current distribution. Thus, the basis for the liquidated partnership interest is first allocated to any distributed unrealized receivables and inventory in an amount equal to the partnership basis in those properties (but not in excess of that partnership basis). § 732(c)(1)(A)(i); Reg. § 1.732–1(c)(1)(i). If the liquidating partner's basis in the partnership interest is less than the full amount of the partnership's basis in the distributed unrealized receivables and inventory, that shortfall in basis must be allocated among the unrealized receivables and inventory. § 732(c)(1)(A)(ii); Reg. § 1.732–1(c)(1)(i). That basis shortfall, called a basis "decrease" by Section 732(c), is first allocated to (and, thus, reduces the liquidating partner's basis in) the inventory items with unrealized depreciation in proportion to their amounts of unrealized depreciation. § 732(c)(1)(A)(ii) and (c)(3)(A); Reg. § 1.732–1(c)(2)(i). Any remaining basis shortfall not allocated under this rule is allocated to the unrealized receivables and inventory items in proportion to the partnership's adjusted basis in those properties (as reduced by the allocations made under the rule described in the prior sentence). § 732(c)(1)(A)(ii) and (c)(3)(B); Reg. § 1.732–1(c)(2)(i).

The liquidating partner's basis in the partnership interest remaining after the allocations to unrealized receivables and inventory is allocated to the other partnership properties distributed to the extent of the partnership's basis in those properties. § 732(c)(1)(B)(i); Reg. § 1.732–1(c)(1)(ii). If the partner's remaining basis in the partnership interest exceeds the partnership's basis in the other distributed properties, that basis excess must be allocated among those properties. That basis excess, called a basis "increase" by Section 732(c), is first allocated to (and, thus, increases the liquidating partner's basis in) the other distributed properties with unrealized appreciation in proportion to their amounts of unrealized appreciation. § 732(c)(1)(B)(ii) and (c)(2)(A); Reg. § 1.732–1(c)(2)(ii). Any remaining basis is allocated to the distributed properties in proportion to their respective fair market values. § 732(c)(1)(B)(ii) and (c)(2)(B); Reg. § 1.732–1(c)(2)(ii) and (c)(4), Ex. 1. As discussed above, if the liquidating partner's basis in the partnership interest before the liquidating distribution exceeds the cash and the adjusted bases to the partnership of the unrealized receivables and inventory items distributed to the partner and there is no other property distributed to the partner to which the excess can be allocated under the allocation rules described above, the liquidating partner is treated as sustaining a capital loss under Section 731(a)(2) to the extent of the unallocated basis of the partnership interest. Reg. § 1.732–1(c)(3) and–1(c)(4), Ex. 4.

Alternatively, if the partner's remaining basis in the liquidated partnership interest is less than the partnership's basis in the other distributed properties, that basis shortfall ("decrease") is first allocated to the distributed properties with unrealized depreciation in proportion to their respective amounts of unrealized depreciation. § 732(c)(1)(B)(ii) and (c)(3)(A); Reg. § 1.732–1(c)(2)(i) and –1(c)(4), Ex. 2. Any remaining shortfall in basis is allocated to the other distributed properties in proportion to the partnership's basis in those properties (as reduced by the allocations made under the rule described in the prior sentence). § 732(c)(1)(B)(ii) and (c)(3)(B); Reg. § 1.732–1(c)(2)(i).

To illustrate these allocation rules, assume that a partner has a basis of $24,000 in the partnership interest and the partnership interest has a fair market value of $30,000. The partnership distributes three assets to the partner in liquidation of the partnership interest: inventory having a basis to the partnership of $3,000 and a value of $18,000, Property A having a basis to the partnership of $7,000 and a value of $4,000, and Property B having a basis to the partnership of $4,000 and a value of $8,000. Under Section 732(c)(1)(A)(i), the liquidating partner must first allocate the basis in the partnership interest to the distributed inventory item in an amount equal to the partnership's $3,000 basis in the inventory; thus, the liquidating partner carries over the partnership's $3,000 basis in the inventory. Second, under Section 732(c)(1)(B)(i), the partner's remaining $21,000 basis in the partnership interest is first allocated to the extent of the partnership's basis in each other distributed property: Property A, $7,000, and Property B, $4,000, for a total of $11,000. However, under Section 732(c)(1)(B)(ii) and 732(c)(2), because the partner's basis in the partnership interest ($24,-000) exceeds the partnership's total basis in the distributed assets ($14,000), an upward adjustment ("basis increase") of $10,000 is required. That basis increase is first allocated to the distributed property having unrealized appreciation, Property B, in the amount of the $4,000 unrealized appreciation in that property, thus increasing the basis in Property B from $4,000 to $8,000. The remaining basis increase of $6,000 is allocated in accordance with the respective fair market values of Properties A and B—accordingly, one-third of that basis increase, or $2,000, is allocated to Property A, increasing the basis in that property from $7,000 to $9,000, and two-thirds of the basis increase, or $4,000, is allocated to Property B, increasing the basis in that property from $8,000 to $12,000.

Before legislative changes to the Code made in 1997, a distributee partner allocated the basis in the liquidated partnership interest in proportion to the partnership's adjusted basis in the distributed properties (without regard to the fair market value of the properties distributed). As discussed in Chapter 22, Congress modified the basis allocation rules because it was concerned that the prior law rules placed a premium on tax planning (particularly in the context of in-kind liquidating distributions) and permitted "basis shifting transactions" which generated inflated depreciation deductions or loss deductions with respect to the distributed property. S. Rep. No. 33, 105th Cong., 1st Sess. 190 (1997).

In the case of a liquidating distribution of marketable securities to which Section 731(c) applies, the adjusted basis of the marketable

¶ 23,010

securities as determined under Section 732 is increased by the gain recognized by the retiring partner under Section 731(c). If more than one marketable security is distributed, the Section 731(c) recognized gain is allocated among the distributed securities in proportion to the amounts of unrealized appreciation in those securities. § 731(c)(4); Reg. § 1.731–2(f)(1)(i).

If the liquidating partnership does not have a Section 754 election in effect, any partnership bases in distributed assets that are not carried over to the liquidating partner under the allocation rules of Section 732(c) are lost. This principle is illustrated with the following example that is drawn in part from Reg. § 1.732–1(c)(4), Ex. 3:

> *Example.* A partnership has three equal partners, including Molly, and has no Section 754 election in effect. Molly has an adjusted basis in her partnership interest of $18,000. The partnership distributes the following assets to her in liquidation of her entire partnership interest: $12,000 cash, inventory items having an adjusted basis to the partnership of $14,000, and real property having an adjusted basis to the partnership of $9,000. The cash distributed reduces Molly's basis in the partnership interest to $6,000. That basis must be allocated entirely to the inventory items under Section 732(c), giving Molly a $6,000 basis in those items. Therefore, her basis in the real property is zero and $8,000 of the partnership's basis in the inventory items and the partnership's entire $9,000 basis in the real property is lost. None of the remaining assets in the partnership will be adjusted following the liquidating distribution to Molly because no Section 754 election was in effect.

By contrast, if a Section 754 election is in effect, the basis of the remaining partnership properties must be adjusted under Section 734 following Section 736(b) liquidating distributions in the same manner as adjustments are made following current distributions.

As discussed in Chapter 22, under a statutory change made in 2004, even if a Section 754 election is not in effect, a partnership is required to decrease its basis in the remaining partnership properties if a liquidating distribution results in a "substantial basis reduction." § 734(b)(2).[1] A substantial basis reduction exists with respect to a liquidating distribution if the basis decrease that would have been made to the partnership's remaining properties had a Section 754 election been in effect exceeds $250,000. § 734(d).[2]

---

1. Sections 734(d)(2) and 743(d)(2) give the Treasury and the IRS broad regulatory authority to implement the purposes of this mandatory basis adjustment rule, including the issuance of regulations "aggregating related partnerships and disregarding property acquired by the partnership in an attempt to avoid" the purposes of the rule.

2. The statute contains an exception to this basis decrease requirement under Section 734(b) in the case of a "securitization partnership." See §§ 734(e) and 743(f) (discussed at ¶¶ 21,108 and 22,060).

Suppose that the partner whose interest is liquidated had contributed property to the partnership with a built-in loss and that such property is not distributed in the liquidating distribution. Under Section 704(c)(1)(C), which was added to the Code in 2004, the built-in loss can only be allocated to the contributing partner and the property is treated as having a basis equal to its fair market value at the time of contribution for purposes of allocating partnership items to the other partners. Consequently, the built-in loss is eliminated when the contributing partner's partnership interest is liquidated.

Moreover, Section 751(b) also applies to liquidating distributions but with an important difference from its application to current distributions. Section 751(b) applies only to Section 736(b) payments, not to Section 736(a) payments. Since payments to a retiring general partner in a services partnership for unrealized receivables are never subject to Section 736(b) and payments for goodwill may not be, those properties are disregarded in determining the extent to which the retiring partner has exchanged Section 751(b) property for other assets of the partnership. Ordinary income treatment for payments to a retiring general partner in a services partnership that are attributable to unrealized receivables is secured directly under Section 736(a), rather than indirectly under Section 751(b).

One last issue bears mention here. Recall from Chapter 18 that partnership liquidations are an important element of the capital account analysis that underlies the substantial economic effect test in the partnership allocation regulations under Section 704(b). To comply with the requirements of those regulations, liquidating distributions must be made in accordance with the positive capital account balances of the partners. See Reg. § 1.704–1(b)(2)(ii)(*b*)(*2*). The regulations also require that the partners' capital accounts be adjusted to reflect the book gain or loss inherent in the property distributed in liquidation of a partner's partnership interest just as is done in the case of a partnership operating distribution (discussed at ¶ 22,067). See Reg. § 1.704–1(b)(2)(iv)(*e*)(*1*). At the time of the liquidation of a partner's interest in the partnership, a partnership also may, but is not required to, revalue its remaining properties and make adjustments to the remaining partners' capital accounts to reflect such revaluation, provided that such adjustment is made principally for a substantial nontax business purpose. See Reg. § 1.704–1(b)(2)(iv)(*f*)(*5*)(*ii*).

¶ **23,010**

[¶ 23,015]

D. SECTION 736(a) PAYMENTS

The amount of a liquidating distribution that does not constitute a Section 736(b) payment is governed by Section 736(a). Section 736(a), however, adds to the flexibility, and complexity, of liquidating distributions by creating two categories of Section 736(a) payments. To the extent that the Section 736(a) payments are determined without regard to partnership net income and thus would meet the definition of a guaranteed payment, the tax consequences of the payments are governed by Section 707(c). § 736(a)(2). Thus, the amount of those payments will be taxed as ordinary income to the retiring partner and will be deductible by the partnership. Reg. § 1.736–1(a)(4). Should the regulations to Section 707(a)(2) modify that blanket rule?

On the other hand, if the payments are determined by reference to the income of the partnership, the payments are simply treated as a continuing distributive share of partnership income. § 736(a)(1). The character of the income to the retiring partner will be determined at the partnership level and the income allocated to the retiring partner will be excluded from the income of the remaining partners. This treatment of Section 736(a) payments survives even the termination of the partnership as Rev. Rul. 75–154, at ¶ 23,020, indicates.

Under current law, Section 736(a) has a narrow scope. It applies only to payments to a retiring general partner in a partnership in which capital is not a material income-producing factor for the partner's share of unrealized receivables and goodwill (if the partnership agreement does not provide a payment for goodwill) and apparently to payments to a retiring general partner in any type of partnership (whether or not capital is a material income-producing factor) in excess of the value of a retiring partner's share of partnership property (including goodwill). All other payments to a retiring partner are governed by Section 736(b). For purposes of Section 736, capital is not a material income-producing factor in a partnership "where substantially all the gross income of the business consists of fees, commissions, or other compensation for personal services performed by an individual." H.R. Rep. No. 111, 103d Cong., 1st Sess. 783 (1993).

Before the effective date of changes made by Congress in 1993, Section 736(a) had a broader scope and included all payments for a retiring partner's share of the partnership's unrealized receivables as well as payments for a retiring partner's share of the partnership's goodwill if the partnership agreement did not provide a payment for goodwill. The 1993 legislation substantially narrowed the scope of Section 736(a) by amending Section 736(b) to provide that payments for unrealized receivables and goodwill must now be treated as Section

736(b) payments, except in the case of payments to a retiring general partner of a services partnership for the partner's share of unrealized receivables and goodwill if the partnership agreement does not provide a payment for goodwill.[3] The reasons for this narrowing of the scope of Section 736(a) are explained in the following excerpt from the legislative history of the 1993 legislation:[4]

> By treating a payment for unstated goodwill and unrealized receivables as a guaranteed payment or distributive share, present law in effect permits a deduction for an amount that would otherwise constitute a capital expenditure. This treatment does not measure partnership income properly. It also threatens to erode the rule requiring capitalization of such payments generally. Under present law, a prospective buyer of a business may structure the transaction so as to currently deduct such an amount by first entering into a partnership with the seller and then liquidating the seller's partnership interest.

> Section 736 was intended to simplify the taxation of payments in liquidation. Instead, it has created confusion as to whether a particular payment is a payment in liquidation or is made pursuant to a sale of the partnership interest to the continuing partners. The proposal reduces this confusion by eliminating a primary difference between sales and liquidations.

> The special treatment of goodwill was apparently predicated on the assumption that the adverse positions of the taxpayers will result in a stated price equal to the true value of the goodwill. That assumption is false. If the value of the preferential rate (if any) and the income deflection are not equal, the stated goodwill and total retirement payments will likely be set so as to maximize the combined tax savings for both retiring and continuing partners.

> It is recognized, however, that general partners in service partnerships do not ordinarily value goodwill in liquidating partners. Accordingly, such partners may continue to receive the special rule of present law.

* * *

The bill generally repeals the special treatment of liquidation payments made for goodwill and unrealized receivables. Thus, such

---

3. The 1993 legislation also narrowed the scope of Section 736(a) in one other respect. Through an amendment to Section 751(c), recapture-type income items are no longer treated as unrealized receivables for Section 736 purposes. Thus, payments with respect to those items must now be treated as Section 736(b) payments for partnership property. Of course, Section 751(b) may apply to those payments.

4. The 1993 amendment to Section 736 basically follows a similar proposal made by the American Law Institute in 1984. For a more comprehensive discussion of the reasons for this change to Section 736, see Federal Income Tax Project: Subchapter K: Proposals on the Taxation of Partners 56–66 (A.L.I. 1984).

¶ **23,015**

payments would be treated as made in exchange for the partner's interest in partnership property, and not as a distributive share or guaranteed payment that could give rise to a deduction or its equivalent. The bill does not change present law with respect to payments made to a general partner in a partnership in which capital is not a material income-producing factor. The determination of whether capital is a material income-producing factor would be made under principles of present and prior law. For purposes of this provision, capital is not a material income-producing factor where substantially all the gross income of the business consists of fees, commissions, or other compensation for personal services performed by an individual. The practice of his or her profession by a doctor, dentist, lawyer, architect, or accountant will not, as such, be treated as a trade or business in which capital is a material income-producing factor even though the practitioner may have a substantial capital investment in professional equipment or in the physical plant constituting the office from which such individual conducts his or her practice so long as such capital investment is merely incidental to such professional practice. In addition, the bill does not affect the deductibility of compensation paid to a retiring partner for past services.

Unrealized receivables

The bill also repeals the special treatment of payments made for unrealized receivables (other than unbilled amounts and accounts receivable) for all partners. Such amounts would be treated as made in exchange for the partner's interest in partnership property. Thus, for example, a payment for depreciation recapture would be treated as made in exchange for an interest in partnership property, and not as a distributive share or guaranteed payment that could give rise to a deduction or its equivalent.

H.R. Rep. No. 111, 103d Cong., 1st Sess. 782–83 (1993).

[¶ 23,020]

REVENUE RULING 75–154

1975–1 C.B. 186.

Advice has been requested regarding the treatment for Federal income tax purposes of payments made to a retired partner under the circumstances described below.

ABC partnership was formed in 1968 to conduct a management consulting business. Under the terms of the partnership agreement, upon retirement, the retiring partner was entitled to receive, in addition to amounts paid for his interest in partnership property, a specified amount payable in monthly installments over a three-year period following his retirement. There was no provision in the partnership agreement with respect to the payment to a retiring partner for goodwill. Partner *C* retired on January 2, 1972, and received 12 monthly payments from the partnership during 1972. On January 2, 1973, all of the business and financial activities of the partnership ended and *A* and *B* withdrew from the business. The former partners, *A* and *B*, assumed their share of the remaining liability to *C* and made the required payments for the years 1973 and 1974.

Under section 708 * * * an existing partnership shall be considered as terminated only if no part of any business, financial operation, or venture of the partnership continues to be carried on by any of its partners in a partnership, or within a 12–month period there is a sale or exchange of 50 percent or more of the total interest in partnership capital and profits.

Section 736(a) * * * provides, in general, that payments made in liquidation of the interest of a retiring partner or a deceased partner shall, except as provided in section 736(b), be considered (1) as a distributive share to the recipient of partnership income if the amount thereof is determined with regard to the income of the partnership, or (2) as a guaranteed payment described in section 707(c) if the amount thereof is determined without regard to the income of the partnership. Under section 707(c), to the extent determined without regard to the income of the partnership, payments to a partner for services or for the use of capital shall be considered as made to one who is not a member of the partnership, but only for the purposes of section 61(a) (relating to gross income) and section 162(a) (relating to trade or business expenses).

Section 736(b)(1) * * * provides, in part, that payments made in liquidation of the interest of a retiring partner or a deceased partner shall, to the extent such payments are determined to be made in exchange for the interest of such partner in partnership property, be considered as a distribution by the partnership and not as a distributive share of partnership income or guaranteed payment under section 736(a).

Section 736(b)(2) * * * provides, in part, that for purposes of section 736(b), payments in exchange for an interest in partnership property shall not include amounts paid for unrealized receivables of the partnership (as defined in section 751(c)), or goodwill of the partnership, except to the extent that the partnership agreement provides for a payment with respect to goodwill.

Section 751(c) * * * provides, in part, that the term "unrealized receivables" includes, to the extent not previously includible in income under the method of accounting used by the partnership, any rights (contractual or otherwise) to payment for goods delivered, or to be delivered, to the extent the proceeds therefrom would be treated as amounts received from the sale or exchange of property other than a capital asset, or services rendered, or to be rendered.

Thus, since the amounts paid to *C*, other than the amounts paid for his interest in partnership property under section 736(b) * * *, were determined without regard to the income of the partnership, they qualify as guaranteed payments described in section 707(c). In the instant case, the guaranteed payments were deductible by the partnership under section 162(a) and includible in the gross income of the retired partner under section 61(a).

Section 1.736–1(a)(6) of the * * * Regulations provides, in part, that a retiring partner or a deceased partner's successor in interest receiving payments under section 736 * * * is regarded as a partner until the entire interest of the retiring or deceased partner is liquidated. Therefore, if one of the members of a 2-[member] partnership retires under a plan whereby he is to receive payments under section 736, the partnership will not be considered terminated, nor will the partnership year close with respect to either partner, until the retiring partner's entire interest is liquidated, since the retiring partner continues to hold a partnership interest in the partnership until that time.

Section 1.736–1(a)(6) of the regulations prevents the termination of a partnership under section 708 * * *, only in those situations in which the partnership would otherwise be terminated because of the withdrawal of a retiring or a deceased partner who is entitled to receive payments under section 736(a)(2). However, in the instant case, section 1.736–1(a)(6) of the regulations does not prevent the termination of the partnership under section 708, even though *C* was receiving liquidating payments under section 736(a)(2). It was the withdrawal of *A* and *B* that caused the partnership to terminate, not *C*'s prior retirement.

Accordingly, the partnership did not continue to exist under section 736 * * *, but terminated under section 708 when partners *A* and *B* discontinued the financial operation of the partnership and withdrew from the business.

It has been previously held that payments that would have been deductible by a partnership had it continued in existence were deductible by the former partners after termination of the partnership. * * *

Thus, in the instant case, after the partnership terminated, payments made by former partners *A* and *B*, in satisfaction of the liability to retired partner *C*, are deductible by them as trade or business expenses under section 162(a) * * * in the year paid, since the payments would have been deductible by the partnership if it had not terminated. Furthermore, the payments to *C* are includible in *C*'s gross income under section 61(a) in the year received.

¶ 23,020

[¶ 23,025]

E. PLANNING FOR LIQUIDATIONS: SECTION 736(a) v. SECTION 736(b)

When payments to a retiring partner will exceed the value of the partner's interest in the property shown on the books of the partnership, the parties, in some limited circumstances, have the opportunity to select the desired tax treatment of the excess payments. To the extent that those payments are to a retiring general partner in a services partnership and are attributable to partnership goodwill, they may be treated as either Section 736(a) payments or as Section 736(b) payments. But which treatment should the partners select? Section 736(b) payments for goodwill may be entitled to capital gain treatment under Section 1221 or Section 1231, except to the extent that Section 1245 requires the recapture as ordinary income of any prior amortization deductions taken under Section 197. As a result, many partners assume that the partnership agreement should provide for payments for goodwill. However, the partnership does not obtain any tax benefit for Section 736(b) payments attributable to goodwill unless the Section 754 election is in effect. Even then, the partnership benefit may be limited to a basis adjustment unless amortization under Section 197 applies. Thus, Section 736(b) payments may result in a capital gains tax to the retiring partner but provide to the remaining partners only the (possible) benefit of increased amortization deductions.

On the other hand, while Section 736(a) payments are generally taxed as ordinary income to the retiring partner, they are deductible or excludable from the income of the remaining partners. As a result, if all of the partners face the same marginal rates of tax, Section 736(a) payments do not result in any increase in the income tax liabilities of the partners as a group. In most instances, therefore, Section 736(a) payments will produce a lower overall income tax burden than will Section 736(b) payments.

Whether the parties select Section 736(a) or Section 736(b), even the most careful tax planning can be upset by inadequate drafting of the partnership agreement. For example, in Commissioner v. Jackson Investment Co., 346 F.2d 187, 190 (9th Cir.1965), the partnership agreement was amended upon the retirement of a partner to provide for a payment of $40,350 in three annual installments as "a guaranteed payment, or a payment for good will." Not surprisingly, the court had a difficult time in determining whether the parties intended the payments to be taxed under Section 736(a) or Section 736(b). Reversing the Tax Court, the Ninth Circuit held that the amendment sufficiently provided for a payment for goodwill to invoke Section 736(b).

¶ 23,025

Finally, as discussed earlier in this Chapter, the 1993 legislative amendments by substantially reducing the scope of Section 736(a) have narrowed the tax differences between sales and liquidations of partnership interests. Accordingly, the planning opportunities in this area have been significantly reduced (but not eliminated).

[¶ 23,030]

F. RELATIONSHIP BETWEEN SECTIONS 752 AND 736

The amount distributed to a retiring partner includes not only the sum of the cash and property actually distributed but also the constructive distribution required by Section 752(b) to the extent that the partner is relieved from liability on partnership debt. It is not fully clear, however, when that constructive distribution occurs under the Section 752 regulations. For tax purposes, a retired partner who is receiving Section 736(a) payments is treated as a continuing partner regardless of his or her status under state law. Reg. § 1.736–1(a)(6). As a result, the retired partner's share of partnership liabilities presumably continues to be determined under Section 752. Under the Section 752 regulations, a partner's share of recourse liabilities is a function of the partner's relative economic risk of loss as measured by a constructive liquidation analysis. Reg. § 1.752–2. That risk of loss, however, would be determined by the liabilities of a retired partner for partnership debts under state law and the partnership agreement. If, as will usually be the case, the retired partner would not have any obligation to make a payment to the partnership or a creditor in a constructive liquidation, the partner would not seem to bear any risk of loss and thus should be treated as receiving a constructive distribution equal to the partner's entire share of partnership recourse liabilities on the date of retirement. On the other hand, if (under state law or the partnership agreement) the retired partner continues to bear the economic risk of loss for the partnership's recourse liabilities, the retired partner should not be treated as receiving a constructive distribution of the partner's share of the recourse liabilities until the partnership makes payments on those liabilities or until the partner receives the final liquidation payment and is no longer treated as a partner of the partnership for federal income tax purposes.

A partner's share of nonrecourse liabilities is determined primarily by the partner's share of partnership minimum gain, rather than liabilities to the partnership or others. Reg. § 1.752–3(a)(1). Since a mere retirement would not appear to alter a partner's share of minimum gain, the partner should not be treated as receiving a distribution attributable to an amount of the nonrecourse debt equal to the minimum gain until the payments for the partner's interest are complete and the partner is no longer treated as a continuing partner for income tax purposes.

[¶ 23,035]

G. TAXING DEFERRED SECTION 736 PAYMENTS

Payments to retiring partners typically are made over a period of years. When that occurs, it is necessary to divide each payment into its Section 736(a) and Section 736(b) components. Fortunately, the regulations permit all of the partners to agree to an allocation of the annual payments between these two components so long as the total amount of the Section 736(b) payments is not altered. Reg. § 1.736–1(b)(5)(iii). In the absence of such an agreement, the method of allocation varies depending on whether the total payment to be made is fixed. Reg. § 1.736–1(b)(5). To the extent that the amount of the payments is fixed, the fraction of each fixed payment treated as a Section 736(b) payment must equal the ratio of the total fixed Section 736(b) payments to the total fixed Section 736(a) and Section 736(b) payments. The balance of each fixed payment is treated as a Section 736(a) payment. Payments that are not fixed in amount are first treated as Section 736(b) payments until the total amount of the Section 736(b) payments has been received.

Since Section 736(a) payments are treated as a distributive share or guaranteed payment, the retiring partner must include those payments in income for the taxable year with or within which ends the partnership taxable year for which the payment is a distributive share, just as if the retiring partner were an actual partner. Reg. § 1.736–1(a)(5). However, since Section 736(b) payments are treated as distributions, those payments are taxable only as they are made. Thus, distributions (including constructive distributions under Section 752) are first applied against the basis for the partnership interest and become taxable only in the year in which cash distributions exceed that basis. However, if Section 751(b) applies to the distribution and creates a constructive sale between the retiring partner and the partnership, that sale occurs in the year of retirement and the gain must be reported in accordance with the rules governing the taxation of sales generally. If no payments are received in the year of retirement, should that mean that the sale is an installment sale reportable under Section 453?

Another question that arises is whether Section 736(b) payments made to a retiring partner over a period of years should be subject to the imputed interest rules of Sections 483 and 1272. Would it matter whether the partnership issued its note to the retiring partner reflecting its obligation to make the Section 736(b) payments? Under present law, the partnership's obligation to make those Section 736(b) payments is not treated as a liability for Section 752 purposes and probably is not subject to the imputed interest rules. By contrast, the installment sale of a partnership interest, which would similarly defer tax on the selling partner's gain, is subject to the imputed interest rules.

Suppose that a partnership with a Section 754 election in effect agrees to make deferred payments to a retiring partner in complete liquidation of that partner's partnership interest that are treated as distributions under Section 736(b)(1). When is the basis of partnership property adjusted under Section 734(b)? In Rev. Rul. 93–13, 1993–1 C.B. 126, the IRS held that the Section 734(b) basis adjustments to partnership property must correspond in timing and amount with the recognition of gain or loss by the retiring partner with respect to those payments.

[¶ 23,040]

H. THE COMPREHENSIVE ILLUSTRATION REVISITED

As we told you, the taxation of liquidating distributions is complex. Much of that complexity results because even a simple Section 736 problem requires the application of about one half of all the rules of partnership taxation! The following illustration may thus serve as a convenient review of all of the rules governing partnership distributions—and more. At ¶¶ 21,120 et seq., we examined in some detail the consequences of a sale of a partnership interest from A to D. Now assume that, instead, A received a distribution from the partnership in complete retirement of her interest. Notice that the partnership is engaged in a business in which capital is not a material income-producing factor for Section 736 purposes. A's basis for the partnership interest was $22,000, including a $4,000 share of liabilities. On the date of retirement, A is relieved of any liability to the bank. The $42,000 cash payment to A from the partnership is to be made in three equal annual installments of $14,000. A's 20–percent share of the value and inside basis of the partnership properties is as follows:

Retiring Partner's Interest

Item	Value	Basis
Cash	$ 6,000	$ 6,000
Accounts receivable	10,000	0
Inventory (blueprints)	6,000	4,000
Furniture and equipment	4,000	2,000
Land	8,000	2,000
Building	6,000	8,000
Goodwill	6,000	0
Total	$46,000	$22,000

Step One: Characterization

The first step in computing A's tax liability is to divide the total payment into its Section 736(a) and (b) components. Since the partnership is a service partnership and A, the retiring partner, is a general partner, the $10,000 unrealized gain in the accounts receivable is a Section 736(a) asset. In addition, assuming that the partnership agreement does not provide for payments for goodwill, all payments in excess of the value of A's interest in tangible partnership property will be treated as Section 736(a) payments. Notice that although the appreciation in the furniture and equipment would be subject to depreciation recapture under Section 1245, such recapture-type income items are not treated as unrealized receivables for Section 736 purposes. Thus, the total Section 736(b) payments will equal $30,000 while the total Section 736(a) payments will equal $16,000.

Step Two: Section 751(b)

Since the $30,000 Section 736(b) payment is treated as a distribution, Section 751(b) will apply if the partnership has unrealized receivables within the meaning of Section 751(c) but not treated as unrealized receivables for Section 736 purposes (the depreciation recapture on the furniture and equipment) and substantially appreciated inventory under Section 751(b)(3), and A's interest in those assets is reduced. Here, we know that the depreciation recapture is a Section 751(c) unrealized receivable and that the inventory is substantially appreciated, and we also know that A has exchanged her entire interest in those assets for cash. Thus, Section 751(b) applies, and A is treated as receiving a constructive distribution of her share of the depreciation recapture item and the inventory and selling those assets back to the partnership for cash. Under Section 732(c)(1), A's basis for the constructively distributed Section 751(b) assets will be a carryover basis of zero for the depreciation recapture and $4,000 for the inventory. The results of this series of constructive transactions are:

(a) The basis for A's partnership interest is reduced by $4,000 to $18,000 under Section 733;

(b) A will recognize ordinary income of $4,000 under Section 735;

(c) The partnership will not recognize any gain or loss; and

(d) The partnership's basis for the depreciation recapture in the furniture and equipment will increase by $2,000 and in the inventory by $2,000.

Step Three: Section 736(b)

In the year of retirement, A receives a distribution of $14,000 plus her $4,000 share of liabilities, or $18,000. In the absence of any agreement to the contrary, 30/46 of that distribution is to be treated as a Section 736(b) payment. Of that approximately $11,740, $8,000 was treated as received in the constructive sale under Section 751(b). Thus, A is treated as receiving a distribution of $3,740 taxable under Section 731. Since A's basis for her partnership interest exceeds that amount, the

¶ 23,040

distribution is not taxed but reduces A's basis to $14,260. The second year Section 736(b) payment of 30/46 of $14,000, or about $9,130, will similarly not be taxable and will reduce A's basis to $5,130. However, the final Section 736(b) payment of $9,130 will exceed A's remaining basis by $4,000. That amount will thus be subject to tax as a capital gain.

Step Four: Section 736(a)

Because the $16,000 Section 736(a) payment is not determined with respect to partnership income, it is treated as a guaranteed payment. In the first year, the Section 736(a) payment will equal 16/46 of $18,000, or about $6,260. In the second and third years, the Section 736(a) payment will equal 16/46 of $14,000, or $4,870, and thus will total $16,000 over the three payments. Those amounts will be taxable to A as ordinary income and will be deductible by the other partners in accordance with their interest in partnership losses.

Step Five: The Section 754 Election

If the partnership has made the Section 754 election, in the year of the final payment, it must adjust the basis of its assets to reflect the $4,000 gain recognized by A on the payments treated as distributions under Section 736(b) (the partnership has already obtained a tax benefit for the Section 736(a) payments). The adjustment is to be made to the appreciated capital assets and Section 1231 assets in proportion to the relative appreciation in those assets.

[¶ 23,045]

Problems

1. In the comprehensive illustration, what would have been the effect on A and on the partnership if the partnership agreement provided for a payment of $6,000 to A attributable to goodwill? Would such a provision be desirable?

2. In the comprehensive illustration, what would have been the effect on A and the partnership if capital were a material income-producing factor for the partnership?

3. To test fully your understanding of the taxation of dispositions of partnership interests, compare the results reached in the two versions of the comprehensive illustration to the several parties. Initially, at least, assume that, in the liquidating distribution, all payments for goodwill were treated as Section 736(b) payments. To make the illustrations consistent, assume that following the liquidating distribution, a new partner contributed cash of $42,000 to the partnership in exchange for a 20–percent interest in profits and losses. Note, but do not pursue, the possibility that such a distribution-contribution might be recharacterized under Section 707(a)(2)(B).

a. Which approach would be most favorable to the retiring partner?

¶ 23,040

b. Which approach would be most favorable to the continuing partners?

c. Which approach would be most favorable to the new partner?

d. Which approach produces the most favorable overall result to the parties?

e. How does the treatment of goodwill affect your conclusion?

4. What other differences between sales and liquidating distributions can you identify?

5. A cash method partnership has the following properties and no liabilities:

	Value	Basis
Cash	$15,000	$15,000
Accounts Receivable	9,000	0
Capital Asset X	12,000	6,000
Capital Asset Y	9,000	9,000
Total	$45,000	$30,000

Keith, who owns a one-third interest in partnership profits, losses, and capital, has a basis for his partnership interest of $10,000. Assuming that the partnership is a services partnership in which capital is not a material income-producing factor, none of the partnership's assets consist of "marketable securities" (within the meaning of Section 731(c)(2)), and the partnership has not made a Section 754 election, what will be the consequences to Keith and to the partnership if his interest is retired through a distribution consisting of:

a. Cash of $15,000?

b. Cash of $20,000?

c. Accounts Receivable of $3,000 and Capital Asset X?

d. Cash of $6,000 and Capital Asset Y?

e. Cash of $6,000 and Accounts Receivable of $9,000?

f. If the partnership did have a Section 754 election in effect, what would be the consequences to the partnership in Problems 5.a. through 5.e.?

g. Cash of $5,000 in each of the next three years?

h. How would your answer in Problem 5.g. change if, shortly before Keith's retirement, the partnership borrowed $15,000 (on a recourse basis)?

6. How would your answers in Problem 5 change if capital were a material income-producing factor in the partnership?

¶ 23,045

[¶ 23,050]

I. LIQUIDATIONS DISTINGUISHED FROM SALES

When a partner leaves a partnership, instead of receiving a liquidating distribution from the partnership, the partner may sell the partnership interest to the remaining partners. If the interest is sold to each of the continuing partners in the proportion of their interests in the partnership, the economic consequences of such a sale will closely resemble the consequences of a liquidating distribution. The tax consequences of a sale, however, are different from the consequences of a distribution and are very different from the consequences of a Section 736(a) payment. It might be supposed that at least it would be apparent when the transaction constitutes a sale taxable under Section 741 and when it constitutes a distribution taxable under Section 736. That, however, has not proven to be the case.

[¶ 23,055]

COONEY v. COMMISSIONER

United States Tax Court, 1975.
65 T.C. 101.

FEATHERSTON, JUDGE: * * *.

* * *

The issue presented for decision requires a determination of the tax consequences to the continuing members of petitioners' law firm of the payments to the withdrawing partners. Those payments took the form of cash and the discharge of the withdrawing partners' shares of certain partnership liabilities. Four of the continuing partners, petitioners in the instant proceeding, contend that, under section 736(a), those payments were made in liquidation of the withdrawing partners' interests in the partnership and that, consequently, such payments are deductible in computing the partnership's taxable income for 1967.

One of the withdrawing partners, who is not a party to these proceedings but was a witness at the trial, has taken the position that, within the meaning of section 741, the withdrawal transaction was a sale of his partnership interest and that the payments he received are taxable to him as capital gain. If he is correct, the payments made to the withdrawing partners would not reduce the surviving partnership's taxable income for 1967.

To protect the revenue, respondent has taken inconsistent positions—denying the deductions claimed by petitioners but determining that the amounts received by the withdrawing partners are taxable to them as ordinary income. In the instant proceedings, respondent takes the position that the withdrawal transaction was a sale under section 741 and not, as petitioners contend, a liquidation under section 736.

Section 741 deals with the sale or exchange of a partnership interest. It provides that, except as to section 751 assets, gain or loss from the sale or exchange of a partnership interest shall be considered as the sale or exchange of a capital asset. As to the exception, section 751(a) provides that to the extent the amount of money received by a transferor in exchange for his interest in the partnership is attributable to "unrealized receivables," among other items, such amount shall be considered as money realized from the sale of property other than a capital asset. Accordingly, the amount paid to a withdrawing partner from the "sale" of his partnership interest, even though attributable to unrealized receivables, is not deductible by the partnership but is treated as a capital investment.

Section 736 deals with the liquidation of a partnership. Insofar as it pertains to the instant case, that section divides payments to a withdrawing partner into two categories: (1) Payments representing a withdrawing partner's interest in partnership property (other than unrealized receivables), including goodwill, to the extent the partnership agreement provides for a payment for goodwill, sec. 736(b); sec. 1.736–1(b), Income Tax Regs., and (2) payments representing the value of the withdrawing partner's share of unrealized receivables and goodwill where the partnership agreement does not provide for a payment with respect to goodwill. Sec. 736(a) and 736(b)(2); sec. 1.736–1(a)(3), Income Tax Regs. [Under current Section 736, as amended in 1993, payments for a withdrawing partner's share of unrealized receivables and goodwill are treated as Section 736(a) payments only if (1) capital is not a material income-producing factor for the partnership, (2) the retiring partner is a general partner, and (3) in the case of goodwill, the partnership agreement does not provide for a payment for goodwill.] Payments in category (1) are treated as a "distribution by the partnership" (see secs. 731 and 751(b)) and are not deductible by the partnership in computing its taxable income. Payments in category (2) are treated by the partnership "as a distributive share to the recipient of partnership income," if the amount thereof is determined *with* regard to partnership income (sec. 736(a)(1)), or as a "guaranteed payment," if the amount thereof is determined *without* regard to partnership income (sec. 736(a)(2)). The payments here in issue are unrelated to partnership income and, consequently, if section 736 applies, they are "guaranteed payment[s]." See S. Rept. No. 1622, * * * 83d Cong., 2d Sess. 395 (1954).

The critical distinction between a sale of a partnership interest under section 741 and a liquidation of such an interest under section 736 is that a sale is a transaction between a third party or the continuing partners individually and the withdrawing partner, whereas a liquidation is a transaction between the partnership as such and the withdrawing partner. Sec. 1.736–1(a), Income Tax Regs. * * *. This means that the partners themselves, through arm's-length negotiations, to a large extent can "determine whether to take the 'sale' route or the 'liquidation' route, thereby allocating the tax burden among themselves." *David A. Foxman*, 41 T.C. 535, 551 (1964), affd. 352 F.2d 466 (3d Cir.1965); * * * see generally H. Rept. No. 1337, * * * 83d Cong., 2d Sess. 65 (1954); S. Rept. No. 1622, * * * 83d Cong., 2d Sess. 89 (1954).

As we view the record in the instant case, it leaves little doubt that the instant transaction was a liquidation of the withdrawing partners' interests in the partnership. The partnership agreement and the withdrawal agreement are not cast in the terms of a purchase and sale. Rather they prescribe a formula for the liquidation of a withdrawing partner's interest. The partnership agreement provides that each withdrawing partner will receive (1) the balance in his capital account; (2) the balance in his income account, including his share of current earnings to the date of withdrawal; (3) his share of unrealized receivables; and (4) his share of the value of the leased library, furniture, and fixtures. As to clients who elect to continue to be served by one of the withdrawing partners, the partnership would bill all such clients for work which had been done unless "the withdrawing partner consents to the deduction of the amount of the bill from payments otherwise required to be made to him *in liquidation of his partnership interest.*" (Emphasis added.) Thus, the agreement negotiated by the parties is not only consistent in principle with a liquidation, but its language expressly so describes a partner's withdrawal.

Moreover, the whole thrust of the partnership agreement and the withdrawal agreement was that the partnership would continue and that the amounts to which the withdrawing partners were entitled would be paid by the partnership rather than the continuing partners individually. Indeed, the partnership agreement provides that the withdrawal of any partner "shall have no effect upon the continuance of the partnership business" and that the interests of the remaining partners shall be adjusted so as to absorb, on a proportionate basis, the former interest of the withdrawing partner. Consistently, the promissory notes given to liquidate the withdrawing partners' interests were paid by partnership checks drawn on the partnership bank account. We think it is clear, therefore, that the transaction was one between the withdrawing partners and the partnership as such.

It is true, as emphasized by respondent, that the withdrawal agreement provides that, in consideration of the amounts payable under that formula, "the withdrawing partners do hereby each set-over, convey, confirm and transfer to the surviving partners all their right, title and interest" in the partnership assets. But, these words in themselves do not show the transaction was a sale. To the contrary, this language was

¶ 23,055

appropriate in order to make it clear that the withdrawing partners were relinquishing their interests in the partnership assets.

It is also true, as respondent emphasizes, that the withdrawal agreement was signed by "Glenn B. Hester, Individually, for and on behalf of the surviving partners" and that the notes given to the withdrawing partners were signed by all the continuing partners. However, the reference to "surviving partners" in the withdrawal agreement indicates that Hester signed on behalf of the surviving partnership rather than as agent for the other partners as individuals. Because the partners are jointly and severally liable for partnership obligations, the legal consequences are the same as if the papers had been signed in the name of the partnership.

As to the promissory notes, the partnership agreement provides that no partner may, without the consent of the other partners, "make * * * any commercial paper * * * on behalf of the partnership." Thus, either an amendment to that agreement or the signatures of all the partners on the notes were required. Obviously, the simplest procedure was to have each continuing partner sign the notes. Under the law of Georgia, moreover, an obligation undertaken by all the members of a partnership, within the scope of its business, binds the partnership, which, of course, places liability on the individual partners. * * * Therefore, appearance of the individual partners' signatures on the promissory notes does not show that the individual partners rather than the partnership were the obligors.

We think it is clear that the transaction was a liquidation rather than a sale and that petitioners' distributive shares from their law partnership during 1967 must be reduced by the payments to or on behalf of the withdrawing partners. Respondent argues that the actual value of the partnership's unrealized receivables as of December 31, 1966, did not exceed $75,000, even though they were assigned a value of $271,214.88 pursuant to the formula prescribed by the partnership agreement, and maintains that the difference between the two amounts was a payment for goodwill. We are not certain from a study of respondent's briefs whether this argument was intended to be advanced only as part of his contention that the transaction was a sale under section 741 or was also addressed to the tax consequences of a liquidation under section 736. If the argument was intended to refer to the determination of petitioners' tax liability under section 736, it is sufficient to point out that the partnership agreement expressly declares that, on the withdrawal of any partner, "no allowance shall be made to him * * * with respect to the value of the good will of the firm." In such circumstances, under section 736(b)(2)(B), payments in excess of the value of the unrealized receivables, including payments in lieu of goodwill, are income payments taxable to the withdrawing partners and deductible by the continuing partnership. * * *

¶ 23,055

In reaching this conclusion, we do not intend to hold that partners are free to disregard the objective facts in structuring their liquidation agreements. In the instant case, our conclusion is predicated on the finding that petitioners' law partnership had no substantial assets other than its unrealized receivables and goodwill, and the partnership agreement expressly provided that no value would be attributed to goodwill. In such circumstances, section 736(b)(2)(B) leaves us no latitude. No part of the payment can be treated as a payment for goodwill. The entire amounts paid to the withdrawing partners are guaranteed payments under section 736(a)(2).

* * *

[¶ 23,060]

Note

In the introduction to these chapters on partnership taxation we noted that the hallmark of the 1954 legislation was flexibility. As the preceding chapters have demonstrated, however, over the years Congress progressively has replaced that flexibility with mandatory rules. That altered philosophy is reflected in the amendments made by Congress in 1993, which substantially reduced the scope of Section 736(a) and thereby reduced (but certainly did not eliminate) the tax differences between sales and liquidations of partnership interests. Did Congress go far enough in these amendments or too far? What justification exists today for allowing the partners to elect between the sale and the liquidation patterns of taxation upon the retirement of a partner? Indeed, what justification exists for allowing the partners to elect between the Section 736(a) and the Section 736(b) patterns of taxation for payments attributable to goodwill in the case of a retiring general partner in a partnership in which capital is not a material income-producing factor? One possible explanation for cases like *Cooney* is that the parties were attempting to "whipsaw" the IRS by taking inconsistent positions. Is that relevant to the continuation of the more limited elective treatment of retirements under current law?

[¶ 23,065]

J. ABANDONING PARTNERSHIP INTERESTS

When a partner realizes a loss upon withdrawing from a partnership, the loss generally will be a capital loss. As the following case discusses, even if no assets are distributed to the withdrawing partner, the relief from partnership liabilities will create a constructive distribution under Section 752(b) that is treated as a sale or exchange by Section 731, thus producing a capital loss. There may be, however, a small window through which a partner can obtain an ordinary loss.

¶ 23,055

[¶ 23,070]

CITRON v. COMMISSIONER

United States Tax Court, 1991.
97 T.C. 200.

GERBER, JUDGE: * * * The primary issue for our consideration is whether petitioners are entitled to a loss either due to a theft or embezzlement or, in the alternative, due to abandonment. If petitioners are entitled to a loss, secondary issues involve the amount of the loss and whether it should be characterized as capital or ordinary.

FINDING OF FACT

* * *

Petitioner became a limited partner in Vandom, a California limited partnership, on September 26, 1980, by the cash investment of $60,000. * * * Petitioner obtained the $60,000 by means of a loan from Crocker National Bank. * * * No promissory notes or obligations were assumed by or for Vandom by the limited partners. No funds necessary for Vandom's operation were borrowed. Instead, Vandom's operation was funded by the capital contributions of the four partners.

The general partner of Vandom was Vandom, Inc. Robert Burge (Burge) was president of Vandom, Inc. * * *

The purpose of Vandom was to produce a motion picture to be named "Girls of Company C," also known as "The Girls of Charley Company." Burge wrote and developed the script for the motion picture in February 1980. The filming was completed in September 1980 and was the only movie made or activity conducted by Vandom. The completed movie film is referred to in the industry as the "negative." Upon the completion of Vandom's activity concerning the negative, it was in the possession of Pacific Film Lab, a company in which neither Vandom nor Vandom, Inc., had an interest. In May 1981 Burge asked Pacific Film Lab for the negative for purposes of cutting and editing.

Joe Bardo (Bardo), doing business through a corporation known as "Millionaire Productions" (Millionaire), was an executive producer of the movie. * * * Bardo was also the subdistributor and videotape distributor of the movie. After the negative was delivered to Bardo, Burge made several requests for its return, which Bardo did not heed. Burge also had prior dealings with Bardo involving two other movies, and Burge believed that Bardo had improperly sold foreign rights to those movies and had not remitted money owed to Burge or his related entities.

At the time of Bardo's refusal to return the negative, Vandom retained a work print of the movie (a copy of the negative), which cannot be used to generally and commercially reproduce and release the type of

¶ 23,070

movie Vandom was attempting to make. Burge advised the Vandom limited partners of Bardo's refusal and told them that the movie could not be made without the negative. Subsequently, Burge met three times with the limited partners between July and the end of December 1981. At the third meeting Burge explained that his attorneys' efforts to obtain the negative had been unsuccessful and that Bardo would not answer Burge's telephone calls. The limited partners were advised that an expensive and lengthy lawsuit would have to be brought against Bardo to recover the negative. Burge also advised the limited partners that with additional investment an X-rated version of the movie could be made from the work print which might allow the recovery of a portion of the investment in Vandom.

Petitioner had no expertise in the movie industry and relied upon Burge's statements. The limited partners had no contractual requirement to advance additional money beyond their $60,000 investments. Petitioner and the other three limited partners decided that they did not want to advance additional money or participate in the conversion of the work print to an X-rated film. Petitioner believed that it could damage his professional reputation and jeopardize his position with Glendale Adventist Medical Center, where he was the only "non-Adventist" on the staff of an Adventist Church affiliated hospital. At that same third meeting during December 1981, petitioner advised Burge that he did not wish to advance more money or participate in any of the proposed future activities of Vandom. At that meeting the limited partners voted to dissolve Vandom. There was no written agreement reflecting the dissolution or evidence indicating that documentation of the dissolution had been filed with the California Secretary of State. Thereafter, Burge instructed the certified public accountant to prepare a final tax return for Vandom because there would be no further activity for the partnership and that there should be a complete writeoff of the investment. The accountant inquired whether there would be future income and Burge advised that there would be no income from the film. The accountant prepared the partnership return reporting a $270,000 loss.

* * *

No assets, liabilities, or capital were reflected as of December 31, 1981, on Vandom's 1981 Schedule L attached to its partnership return. Per Vandom's certified public accountant, Vandom had no liabilities at the end of the 1981 year. Vandom's 1981 return reflected only $3,560 of accounts payable as of the beginning of the taxable year, with an offsetting asset in the form of a deferred expense. No liabilities were reflected in connection with the limited partners' relationship with Vandom.

* * *

¶ 23,070

At the end of 1981 petitioner did not expect to receive anything back from the Vandom limited partnership interest. The Vandom partnership agreement, Article XIV(b), provides that the partnership shall pay the value of a limited partner's interest within three months after termination of his interest. Petitioner did not receive any amount under Article XIV(b).

The accountant prepared a Schedule K–1 for each of the limited partners' 1981 taxable year. Petitioner's Schedule K–1 reflected a loss of $60,000 and he claimed a $60,014 loss on Schedule E of his 1981 income tax return. Per the accountant, no financial transaction occurred for Vandom after December 31, 1981. * * * Respondent disallowed the entire $60,014 loss claimed by petitioners.

OPINION

Petitioners claimed a $60,000 ordinary loss, in connection with the investment as a limited partner. Although the loss was first shown as a loss reflected on a Schedule K–1, for purposes of this case it is claimed alternatively as a theft or embezzlement loss, or as a loss due to abandonment. We first consider whether petitioners incurred a "theft or embezzlement" loss.

Theft or Embezzlement Loss

* * *

[The court held that the petitioners were not entitled to a theft or embezzlement loss.]

Abandonment Loss

Having decided that petitioners did not show that there had been a theft or embezzlement under California law, we next consider whether petitioner abandoned his partnership interest during the 1981 taxable year and, if he did, the amount of his loss and whether it is ordinary or capital.

To be entitled to deduct an abandonment loss under section 165, a taxpayer must show: (1) An intention on the part of the owner to abandon the asset, and (2) an affirmative act of abandonment. * * *

In determining a taxpayer's intent to abandon, the "subjective judgment of the taxpayer * * * as to whether the business assets will in the future have value is entitled to great weight and a court is not justified in substituting its business judgment for a reasonable, well-founded judgment of the taxpayer." * * * Here, respondent does not dispute the fact that petitioners may have formed an intent to abandon the partnership interest. Respondent places emphasis on the argument that petitioners have failed to show an affirmative act of abandonment during 1981. Petitioners counter that the record does reflect affirmative acts of abandonment. Specifically, petitioner points out that he told

¶ 23,070

Burge at the December 1981 meeting that he would not provide additional money to the partnership and that he would not become involved in the making of an X-rated film. Petitioner also stated to Burge that he would not have anything further to do with the partnership and the movie. Petitioner also refers us to the fact that the limited partners voted to dissolve the partnership at the December 1981 meeting. Thereafter, Burge told the accountant to file the final partnership return for the period ending December 31, 1981.

Little has been written concerning the abandonment of a partnership interest. Tangible property is capable of physical abandonment, but abandonment of a partnership interest (an intangible property interest) should be accompanied by some express manifestation. Considering the passive nature of a limited partnership interest, the need to manifestly express the intent to abandon is especially important. * * * California has adopted the Uniform Limited Partnership Act, and Cal. Corp. Code sec. 15518 (West 1977) defines a limited partnership interest as "personal property." We could find no reason to treat this personal property differently from other types of personal property. In *Echols v. Commissioner*, 935 F.2d 703 (5th Cir.1991), revg. 93 T.C. 553 (1989), the Circuit Court held that a partner could and did abandon his partnership interest for Federal tax purposes. In so holding, it was pointed out that neither Texas State law nor the Internal Revenue Code or underlying regulations specified physical methods or legal procedures for abandoning an interest in a partnership. Accordingly, we proceed to decide whether petitioner abandoned his limited partnership interest during 1981.

* * *

Respondent also relied upon *Echols v. Commissioner*, 93 T.C. 553, but that case was reversed by the Court of Appeals for the Fifth Circuit on July 15, 1991, after completion of the briefing in this case. In that case the taxpayer was a 37.5–percent partner in a partnership which had (as its sole asset) undeveloped real property purchased in anticipation of an adjacent highway project. After the highway project stalled due to local opposition and the real estate market went into a slump, another 37.5–percent partner transferred his interest to the taxpayer in exchange for the taxpayer's assumption of the recourse debt outstanding on the realty. The remainder of the debt was nonrecourse. The taxpayer and the remaining 25–percent partner attempted to and finally sold a 50–percent interest in the realty to a third party who defaulted on his payment after a little more than one year. Thereafter, the taxpayer met with the 25–percent partner and informed him that he would no longer make payment of his 75–percent portion of the mortgage and taxes. The taxpayer also offered to convey his interest to anyone who would assume his portion of the partnership debt. At that time, the value of the realty had declined to less than the mortgage balance. The taxpayer did nothing more during that year and claimed a capital loss. The next year the mortgagees foreclosed on the realty. Under those facts, we held that there was a failure to manifest abandonment through some act apparent to those outside the partnership, as distinguished from the case of *Middleton v. Commissioner*, 77 T.C. 310, 322 (1981), affd. per curiam 693 F.2d 124 (11th Cir.1982). See *Echols v. Commissioner*, 93 T.C. at 555–558. The Court of Appeals for the Fifth Circuit, however, held that abandonment should not be viewed solely from a partnership perspective and that the taxpayer's actions were sufficient to constitute an abandonment of his partnership interest during 1976. *Echols v. Commissioner*, 935 F.2d 703 * * *. There is no requirement that a taxpayer relinquish title in order to establish a loss if such "loss is reasonably certain in fact and ascertainable in amount." *Middleton v. Commissioner*, 77 T.C. at 322.

In this case, the partners borrowed the money necessary to produce the movie, and they were personally obligated to pay the debt even if no movie or asset was ever in existence. In other words, there were no interested parties, such as mortgagees, to whom to manifest the abandonment. The limited partners here voted to dissolve and abandon the interest or rights that they may have had in the negative. They were not interested in participating in the conversion of the working print into an X-rated movie, and petitioner communicated to the general partner that he no longer had any interest in the partnership or the movie. Based upon those events and that communication, Burge proceeded (without the financial assistance or involvement of petitioner) to make an X-rated movie and to pursue through legal action the negative held by Bardo and his company. We find the facts of this case to be distinguishable from those in the cases cited by respondent. Here, petitioner manifested his intent to abandon by an overt act of abandonment to the parties in interest (the general partner and all limited partners). Burge proceeded to close down the partnership (directing that a final partnership return be filed) and to treat the movie and the rights to it as no longer belonging to the limited partners, including petitioner.

Having found that petitioner abandoned his interest in the partnership as of the end of 1981, we must now decide whether the loss is capital or ordinary. If petitioner's loss is from the sale or exchange of a capital asset, the amount of capital loss allowable for the taxable year is the lower of $3,000 or the excess of capital losses over capital gains. Secs. 165(f), 1211, and 1212(b). If, on the other hand, the loss is ordinary, the limitation of section 1212(b) would not be applicable.

Although partnership interests are property and should be subject to the abandonment principles in the same manner as any other property, some distinctions have been made and commentary expressed concerning whether the abandonment of a partnership interest should or could result in an ordinary loss. Because subchapter K generally provides for sales, exchanges, and other dispositions of partnerships and partnership interests, it has been suggested that some potential for overlap may exist between subchapter K and section 165.

This Court, in the context of the Internal Revenue Code of 1939, has decided that abandonment (forfeiture) of a partnership interest was not a sale or exchange and could be accorded ordinary (rather than capital) 1056 treatment. * * * No changes were made in the loss provisions of the Internal Revenue Code of 1954 which would dictate a change in the case precedent under the 1939 Code. There is limited precedent, in other courts, under the Internal Revenue Code of 1954 that the worthlessness of a partnership interest (a capital asset) may result in an ordinary loss. *Zeeman v. United States*, 275 F.Supp. 235, 253 (S.D.N.Y.1967), affd. and remanded on other issues 395 F.2d 861 (2d Cir.1968).

We have addressed several post-Internal Revenue Code of 1954 cases where taxpayers were found to have capital losses because they were relieved of liabilities by means of their abandonment resulting in a sale or exchange. See, for example, *Freeland v. Commissioner*, 74 T.C. 970, 982–983 (1980), and *Middleton v. Commissioner*, 77 T.C. 310, 319–324 (1981), affd. per curiam 693 F.2d 124 (11th Cir.1982). More specifically, in a partnership setting we held that a decrease in a taxpayer's individual liabilities by reason of the assumption of debt by the partnership can constitute a deemed distribution under section 752(b). *O'Brien v. Commissioner*, 77 T.C. 113, 118–120 (1981). In that case it was reasoned that distributions deemed as such were sales or exchanges of a partnership interest within the meaning of section 731(a), resulting in capital gain or loss pursuant to section 741.

Respondent argues in this case that if we find that petitioner abandoned his partnership interest during 1981, such abandonment resulted in a sale or exchange within the meaning of section 741 because the partnership had a $3,560 liability at the end of its taxable year.

Petitioner counters that respondent is in error concerning the $3,560 liability. Petitioner points out that the $3,560 liability only appears as an opening balance on the balance sheet on Vandom's final return (Form 1065 for the 1981 year) and that no liabilities are reflected for the partnership as of the close of the 1981 year. The certified public accountant for Vandom testified and confirmed that there were no liabilities in reference to the limited partners. Because respondent has incorrectly interpreted the facts, his argument on this point must fail because there was no debt to be assumed by the partnership. * * *

* * *

* * * Accordingly, we must decide whether abandonment of a partnership interest (where there are no liabilities owed by the partnership) would result in ordinary loss under post–1939 versions of the Internal Revenue Code.[11]

---

11. Although we decide that abandonment of a partnership interest may result in ordinary, rather than capital, losses, the requirement that there be no partnership

We have not, under the 1954 or later versions of the Internal Revenue Code, decided whether abandonment of assets (including partnership interests), where no partnership liabilities exist, results in ordinary, rather than capital, loss. See *Stilwell v. Commissioner*, 46 T.C. 247, 252 n. 3 (1966). It is noted that *Stilwell* involved a liquidation of a two-man partnership where we found no terminology had been used to indicate that a sale or exchange had occurred.

The effect of liabilities was touched upon in *La Rue v. Commissioner*, 90 T.C. 465, 482–483 (1988), where we stated:

> Losses allowed by section 165 may be either ordinary or capital in character. Section 1222 defines a capital loss as a loss from the sale or exchange of a capital asset. A partnership interest is a capital asset under section 741. We must determine whether an actual or constructive sale or exchange occurred here.
>
> The touchstone for sale or exchange treatment is consideration. If, in return for assets, any consideration is received, even if nominal in amount, the transaction will be classified as a sale or exchange. * * *

Respondent's argument here follows the above-quoted principle, but then goes further by reference to Rev. Rul. 76–189, 1976–1 C.B. 181. That ruling expresses the view that even where a partnership has no assets or liabilities at termination, any loss of a partner is subject to section 731 and results in capital loss. There are no cases which support this view and we treat respondent's rulings merely as the position of a party. * * * Section 731 is specifically concerned with "Recognition of Gain or Loss on *Distribution*." (Emphasis supplied.) Because section 731 concerns distributions and literally requires a distribution to be operative, respondent, in the ruling, treats the transaction as though an actual distribution had taken place.

No rationale or support[14] is provided in the ruling for the supposition deeming the existence of a distribution for purposes of section 731. In order to decide this case under the theory used by respondent in the

---

liabilities is likely to limit the pervasiveness of this holding. Additionally, it would not be a usual occurrence for a business or investor to abandon a valuable asset which has no debt associated with it. Moreover, satisfaction of the debt prior to abandonment may be too high a "price" to "pay" for the tax savings attributable to avoiding the current $3,000 capital loss limitation.

14. It may be that respondent is attempting to take partnership interests out of the realm of sec. 165 and to have them exclusively and consistently treated under subchapter K. Although some may agree

that would be a good or appropriate policy consideration * * *, it is not our role to make the proper or appropriate policy considerations in the promulgation or enforcement of the laws. It also seems paradoxical that two taxpayers with substantially similar situations would be treated differently because of $1 or more of unpaid liabilities existing upon abandonment. On the other hand, one may also argue that it is good policy to treat taxpayers who abandon assets the same, irrespective of the type of asset, so long as sec. 165 requirements are met.

ruling, we would be compelled to impute a sale or exchange, even though none had occurred. This we decline to do. Section 165 losses are not limited to certain types of assets, and sections 701 through 761 are not literally exclusive for purposes of abandonment. Section 752(b), for example, may come into play in situations where abandonment results in a decrease in a partner's liabilities. That section deems such an event to constitute a "distribution of money to the partner." In that event, the case precedent, sections 731 and 741, and other considerations may result in capital gain or loss due to abandonment of a partnership interest.

Accordingly, petitioners are entitled to ordinary loss treatment with respect to the abandonment of the Vandom partnership interest during 1981.

* * *

Reviewed by the Court.

[The dissenting opinion has been omitted.]

[¶ 23,075]

REVENUE RULING 93–80
1993–2 C.B. 239.

ISSUE

Is a loss incurred on the abandonment or worthlessness of a partnership interest a capital or an ordinary loss?

FACTS

Situation 1. PRS is a general partnership in which *A*, *B*, and *C* were equal partners. During 1993, *PRS* became insolvent, and *C* abandoned *C*'s partnership interest. *C* took all steps necessary to effect a proper abandonment, including written notification to *PRS*. *PRS*'s partnership agreement was amended to indicate that *C* was no longer a partner. At the time *C* abandoned the partnership interest, *PRS*'s only liabilities were nonrecourse liabilities of 120*x* dollars, shared equally by *A*, *B*, and *C*. *C* had a remaining adjusted basis in the partnership interest of 180*x* dollars. *C* did not receive any money or property on leaving the partnership.

Situation 2. LP is a limited partnership in which *D* and *E* were general partners and *F* was one of the limited partners. During 1993, *LP* became insolvent, and *F* abandoned *F*'s limited partnership interest. *F* took all steps necessary to effect a proper abandonment, including written notification to *LP*. *LP*'s partnership agreement was amended to indicate that *F* was no longer a partner. At the time *F* abandoned the partnership interest, *F* had a remaining adjusted basis of 200*x* dollars in the partnership interest. *F* did not bear the economic risk of loss for any of the partnership liabilities and was not entitled to include a share of the partnership liabilities in the basis of *F*'s partnership interest. *F* did not receive any money or property on leaving the partnership.

LAW

Section 165(a) * * * allows a deduction for any loss sustained during the taxable year and not compensated for by insurance or otherwise. Section 165(b) provides that the basis for determining the amount of a deduction for any loss is the adjusted basis provided in section 1011 for determining the loss from the sale or other disposition of property. Section 1.165–1(b) of the * * * Regulations provides that a loss must be evidenced by closed and completed transactions, fixed by identifiable events, and actually sustained during the taxable year.

Section 165(f) * * * provides that losses from sales or exchanges of capital assets are allowed only to the extent allowed in [section] 1211 or 1212. Under section 1.165–2 of the regulations, however, absent a sale or exchange a loss that results from the abandonment or worthlessness of nondepreciable property is an ordinary loss even if the abandoned or worthless asset is a capital asset (such as a partnership interest).

To establish the abandonment of an asset, a taxpayer must show an intent to abandon the asset, and must overtly act to abandon the asset. * * *

* * *

In Rev. Rul. 70–355, 1970–2 C.B. 51, a taxpayer paid cash for an interest as a limited partner in a partnership, and the taxpayer's capital account was credited with an amount less than the cash paid. The partnership agreement provided that losses would first be allocated against each partner's capital account and any balance would be shared only by the general partners. In a subsequent taxable year, the partnership sustained a loss in its business operations, entered into bankruptcy, and dissolved. The taxpayer's distributive share of the partnership loss for the taxable year reduced the taxpayer's capital account to zero. In addition, the taxpayer's adjusted basis in the partnership interest, which was greater than the taxpayer's capital account, was reduced by the taxpayer's distributive share of the loss. However, the taxpayer's adjusted basis in the partnership interest was not reduced to zero. The taxpayer did not receive any cash or other consideration in liquidation of the taxpayer's partnership interest.

Rev. Rul. 70–355 concludes that the taxpayer's loss is deductible as an ordinary loss under section 165(a) * * *. The taxpayer's loss was composed of the taxpayer's distributive share of the partnership loss equal to the taxpayer's capital account and the balance of the taxpayer's adjusted basis in the partnership interest.

¶ **23,075**

In Rev. Rul. 76–189, 1976–1 C.B. 181, *D* purchased a one-third interest in the *ABC* partnership from taxpayer *A*. *ABC* sustained a net loss from its business operations for the taxable year and terminated at the end of that taxable year. At termination, *ABC* had no remaining assets or liabilities. *D*'s distributive share of the partnership loss did not reduce *D*'s basis in *D*'s partnership interest to zero.

Rev. Rul. 76–189 concludes that *D* has an ordinary loss deduction for *D*'s distributive share of the partnership loss under section 702(a) * * * and a capital loss deduction for any remaining adjusted basis in *D*'s partnership interest under section 731(a) on the date the partnership terminated. This was so even though there was no actual or deemed distribution from the partnership.

ANALYSIS

The abandonment or worthlessness of a partnership interest may give rise to a loss deductible under section 165(a) * * *. Whether a loss from the abandonment or worthlessness of a partnership interest is capital or ordinary depends on whether or not the loss results from the sale or exchange of a capital asset.

Sections 731 and 741 * * * apply to any transaction in which the partner receives an actual distribution of money or property from the partnership. These provisions likewise apply to any transaction in which a partner is deemed to receive a distribution from the partnership (*e.g.*, section 752(b)). Thus, whether there is an actual distribution or a deemed distribution, the transaction is treated as a sale or exchange of the partnership interest, and any loss resulting from the transaction is capital (except as provided in section 751(b)). Such a transaction is not treated for tax purposes as involving a loss from the abandonment or worthlessness of a partnership interest regardless of the amount of the consideration actually received or deemed received in the exchange.

Any decrease in a partner's share of partnership liabilities is deemed to be a distribution of money to the partner under section 752(b). The section 752(b) deemed distribution triggers the distribution on liquidation rule of section 731(a) for recognition of loss. For purposes of determining whether or not section 752(b) applies to create a deemed distribution upon abandonment or worthlessness, liability shifts that take place in anticipation of such event are treated as occurring at the time of the abandonment or worthlessness under general tax principles. *See also* section 1.731–1(a)(2) of the regulations providing that the liquidation of a partner's interest in a partnership may take place by means of a series of distributions.

A loss from the abandonment or worthlessness of a partnership interest will be ordinary if there is neither an actual nor a deemed distribution to the partner under the principles described above. Even a *de minimis* actual or deemed distribution makes the entire loss a capital

¶ 23,075

loss. *Citron v. Commissioner*, 97 T.C. 200, 216 n.14 (1991). In addition, the loss will be ordinary only if the transaction is not otherwise in substance a sale or exchange. For example, a partner's receipt of consideration from another partner (or a party related thereto) may, depending upon the facts and circumstances, establish that a purported abandonment or worthlessness of a partnership interest is in substance a sale or exchange.

Partner *D* in Rev. Rul. 76–189 satisfied all of the requirements for ordinary loss treatment. Partner *D* did not receive any actual distributions, and *D* was not deemed to receive any distributions under section 752(b) * * * as a result of liability shifts. Nevertheless, Rev. Rul. 76–189 denied *D* ordinary loss treatment because the Service concluded that for partnership terminations section 731 applied as if an actual distribution had taken place. The Service will no longer follow Rev. Rul. 76–189.

The taxpayer in Rev. Rul. 70–355 also satisfied all of the requirements for ordinary loss treatment. Unlike Rev. Rul. 76–189, however, Rev. Rul. 70–355 concludes that the taxpayer's loss is ordinary without discussing the relevance of partnership liabilities in determining whether a partner has an ordinary loss under section 165(a) * * * upon the abandonment or worthlessness of a partnership interest. Further, some taxpayers have interpreted the partnership's bankruptcy as an essential fact in Rev. Rul. 70–355. Thus, although the conclusion in Rev. Rul. 70–355 is consistent with the conclusion in this revenue ruling, to avoid further confusion, Rev. Rul. 70–355 is clarified and superseded.

In *Situation 1*, when *C* abandons the interest in *PRS*, which has liabilities in which *C* shares, a deemed distribution of $40x$ dollars is made to *C* under section 752(b) * * *. The deemed distribution reduces the basis of *C*'s interest to $140x$ dollars ($180x - 40x = 140x$). Because there is a deemed distribution to *C*, section 731(a) applies and any loss allowed is capital. Thus, *C*'s entire $140x$ dollars loss from abandoning the *PRS* interest is a capital loss even though the deemed distribution under section 752(b) is only $40x$ dollars. The results would be the same if *C*'s interest in *PRS* were found to be worthless. Because *C* shares in the liabilities of *PRS*, a deemed distribution is made to *C* on a finding of worthlessness, section 731 applies, and any loss allowed is capital.

In *Situation 2*, *F* permanently abandons *F*'s interest in *LP*. Section 731 * * * does not apply because *F* did not receive any actual or deemed distribution from the partnership. *F* received nothing in exchange for *F*'s interest in *LP*. Accordingly, *F* realizes an ordinary loss of $200x$ dollars for the adjusted basis of *F*'s partnership interest, which may be deducted under section 165(a) as an ordinary loss subject to all other applicable rules of the Code. The results would be the same if *F*'s partnership interest in *LP* had become worthless.

¶ 23,075

HOLDING

A loss incurred on the abandonment or worthlessness of a partnership interest is an ordinary loss if sale or exchange treatment does not apply. If there is an actual or deemed distribution to the partner, or if the transaction is otherwise in substance a sale or exchange, the partner's loss is capital (except as provided in section 751(b)).

EFFECTS ON OTHER REVENUE RULINGS

Rev. Rul. 70–355 is clarified and superseded. Rev. Rul. 76–189 is revoked.

* * *

[¶ 23,080]

Problem

TVA is a limited partnership in which Tiffany, Valerie, and Alexandra are equal general partners and Katherine is one of the limited partners. During the current year, TVA became insolvent, and Tiffany abandoned her general partnership interest and Katherine abandoned her limited partnership interest. Both Tiffany and Katherine took all steps necessary to effect a proper abandonment, and TVA's partnership agreement was amended to provide that Tiffany and Katherine were no longer partners of TVA. At the time Tiffany abandoned her partnership interest, TVA's only liabilities were nonrecourse liabilities of $90, shared equally by Tiffany, Valerie, and Alexandra. Assume that none of TVA's liabilities were allocable to Katherine under the Section 752 regulations and she was not entitled to include any share of TVA's liabilities in the basis of her partnership interest. At the time of abandonment of the partnership interests, Tiffany had an adjusted basis of $60 in her general partnership interest, and Katherine had an adjusted basis of $100 in her limited partnership interest. Neither Tiffany nor Katherine received any money or property on leaving the partnership.

What are the federal income tax consequences to Tiffany and Katherine on the abandonment of their partnership interests?

Chapter 24

PARTNERSHIP TERMINATIONS

[¶ 24,000]

A. VOLUNTARY TERMINATIONS OF THE BUSINESS

When the partners decide to terminate partnership operations, they may proceed in any of several ways. The partnership may sell all of its assets, discharge its liabilities, and distribute any remaining proceeds. Or the partners may individually sell their partnership interests, either to a single purchaser or to several purchasers. Both of these procedures will be taxed under the rules discussed in the prior chapters. In general, under either approach, the entire gain or loss in the partnership properties will be recognized and taxed to the partners although, upon a partnership level sale, the element of ordinary income will be identified on an asset-by-asset basis while, upon a sale of the interests in the partnership, Section 751(a) will apply.

Alternatively, the partnership may distribute the partnership properties to the partners who may retain or sell those properties. Again, the consequences of such a liquidating distribution are governed by the rules discussed above, with one exception. Since the partnership is not continuing, Section 736 cannot apply. Rather, all distributions will be taxed under Section 731 and, if the distribution is not pro rata, under Section 751(b).[1] Under this regime, gain or loss generally will not be recognized, and the partners will have an aggregate basis for the property distributed to them equal to the basis they had for their partnership interests. §§ 731 and 732. In addition, Section 735 may apply to determine the character of the distributee partner's gain or loss on a later disposition of the distributed property.

---

1. Somewhat inconsistently, Section 736 does apply to the retirement of the first partner from a two-person partnership be- cause the partnership does not terminate until the final liquidating distribution is made. Reg. § 1.736–1(a)(6).

The following ruling considers the application of Section 751(b) to a non-pro rata distribution in connection with the complete liquidation of a partnership.

[¶ 24,005]

REVENUE RULING 77–412

1977–2 C.B. 223.

Advice has been requested concerning the Federal income tax consequences upon the complete liquidation of a two person partnership involving the non-pro rata distribution of "section 751 property" to the partners.

* * *

Section 751(b)(1) * * * provides that where a partner receives, in a distribution, partnership section 751 property [i.e., for Section 751(b) purposes, unrealized receivables and substantially appreciated inventory items] in exchange for all or a part of such partner's interest in other partnership property (including money), or receives other partnership property (including money) in exchange for all or a part of an interest in partnership section 751 property, such transaction shall be considered as a sale or exchange of such property between the distributee and the partnership (as constituted after the distribution). Consequently, section 751(b) * * * applies to that part of the distribution to a partner that consists of the non-pro rata distribution of the partnership section 751 property in exchange for other property, or the non-pro rata distribution of other partnership property in exchange for section 751 property.

In *Yourman v. United States*, 277 F. Supp. 818 (S.D.Calif.1967), the court held that section 751 * * * applied to a non-pro rata distribution of section 751 property of a partnership even though the partnership did not continue in existence after the distribution.

Accordingly in the case of a two person partnership, to the extent that a partner either receives section 751 property in exchange for relinquishing any part of such partner's interest in other property, or receives other property in exchange for relinquishing any part of the interest in section 751 property, the distribution is treated as a sale or exchange of such properties between the distributee partner and the partnership (as constituted after the distribution), even though after the distribution the partnership consists of a single individual.

For example, the non-pro rata distribution by a two person partnership of section 751 property to its partners, A and B, as part of a distribution resulting in a complete liquidation of the partnership, can be viewed in two ways, both of which result in the same tax consequences to each party to the transaction. In the non-pro rata distribution, partner A receives more partnership section 751 property than A's underlying interest in such property, while partner *B* receives more partnership other property than *B*'s interest in such property. Partner *A* may be treated as the distributee partner who has exchanged part of an interest in partnership property other than section 751 property with the partnership as constituted after the distribution (partner *B*) for section 751 property. Partner *A* would be treated as realizing gain or loss on a sale or exchange of the property other than section 751 property, and the partnership as constituted after the distribution would realize ordinary income or loss on the exchange of the section 751 property.

Partner *B* may be treated as the distributee partner who has exchanged part of an interest in the partnership section 751 property with the partnership as constituted after the distribution (partner *A*) for other property. Partner *B* would be treated as realizing ordinary income or loss on the exchange of the section 751 property, and the partnership as constituted after the distribution would realize gain or loss on a sale or exchange of the other property. However, regardless of which partner is considered to be the distributee and which is considered to be the remaining partner, the Federal income tax consequences are the same to each partner.

[¶ 24,010]

Note

Because property, rather than cash, may be received in a liquidating distribution, the economic consequences of liquidations may be sufficiently different from the economic consequences of sales to justify the difference in income tax consequences. However, when the business of the partnership is to be continued by a corporation owned by the former partners, those economic distinctions will disappear. Should the income tax distinctions then likewise disappear? Consider that question as you read the following ruling.

[¶ 24,015]

REVENUE RULING 84–111

1984–2 C.B. 88.

* * *

FACTS

The three situations described [below] involve partnerships *X*, *Y*, and *Z*, respectively. Each partnership used the accrual method of accounting and had assets and liabilities consisting of cash, equipment, and accounts payable. The liabilities of each partnership did not exceed the adjusted basis of its assets. The three situations are as follows:

¶ 24,015

Situation 1

X transferred all of its assets to newly-formed corporation R in exchange for all the outstanding stock of R and the assumption by R of X's liabilities. X then terminated by distributing all the stock of R to X's partners in proportion to their partnership interests.

Situation 2

Y distributed all of its assets and liabilities to its partners in proportion to their partnership interests in a transaction that constituted a termination of Y under section 708(b)(1)(A) * * *. The partners then transferred all the assets received from Y to newly-formed corporation S in exchange for all the outstanding stock of S and the assumption by S of Y's liabilities that had been assumed by the partners.

Situation 3

The partners of Z transferred their partnership interests in Z to newly-formed corporation T in exchange for all of the outstanding stock of T. This exchange terminated Z and all of its assets and liabilities became assets and liabilities of T.

In each situation, the steps taken by X, Y, and Z, and the partners of X, Y, and Z, were parts of a plan to transfer the partnership operations to a corporation organized for valid business reasons in exchange for its stock and were not devices to avoid or evade recognition of gain. * * *

LAW AND ANALYSIS

Section 351(a) * * * provides that no gain or loss will be recognized if property is transferred to a corporation by one or more persons solely in exchange for stock * * * in such corporation and immediately after the exchange such person or persons are in control (as defined in section 368(c)) of the corporation.

Section 1.351–1(a)(1) of the * * * Regulations provides that, as used in section 351 * * *, the phrase "one or more persons" includes individuals, trusts, estates, partnerships, associations, companies, or corporations. To be in control of the transferee corporation, such person or persons must own immediately after the transfer stock possessing at least 80 percent of the total combined voting power of all classes of stock entitled to vote and at least 80 percent of the total number of shares of all other classes of stock of such corporation.

Section 358(a) * * * provides that in the case of an exchange to which section 351 applies, the basis of the property permitted to be received under such section without the recognition of gain or loss will be the same as that of the property exchanged, decreased by the amount of any money received by the taxpayer.

¶ 24,015

Section 358(d) * * * provides that where, as part of the consideration to the taxpayer, another party to the exchange assumed a liability of the taxpayer or acquired from the taxpayer property subject to a liability, such assumption or acquisition (in the amount of the liability) will, for purposes of section 358, be treated as money received by the taxpayer on the exchange.

Section 362(a) * * * provides that a corporation's basis in property acquired in a transaction to which section 351 applies will be the same as it would be in the hands of the transferor.

Under section 708(b)(1)(A) * * *, a partnership is terminated if no part of any business, financial operation, or venture of the partnership continues to be carried on by any of its partners in a partnership. Under section 708(b)(1)(B), a partnership terminates if within a 12–month period there is a sale or exchange of 50 percent or more of the total interest in partnership capital and profits.

Section 732(b) * * * provides that the basis of property other than money distributed by a partnership in a liquidation of a partner's interest shall be an amount equal to the adjusted basis of the partner's interest in the partnership reduced by any money distributed. Section 732(c) * * * provides rules for the allocation of a partner's basis in a partnership interest among the assets received in a liquidating distribution.

Section 735(b) * * * provides that a partner's holding period for property received in a distribution from a partnership (other than with respect to certain inventory items defined in section 751(d)(2)) includes the partnership's holding period, as determined under section 1223, with respect to such property.

Section 1223(1) * * * provides that where property received in an exchange acquires the same basis, in whole or in part, as the property surrendered in the exchange, the holding period of the property received includes the holding period of the property surrendered to the extent such surrendered property was a capital asset or property described in section 1231. Under section 1223(2), the holding period of a taxpayer's property, however acquired, includes the period during which the property was held by any other person if that property has the same basis, in whole or in part, in the taxpayer's hands as it would have in the hands of such other person.

Section 741 * * * provides that in the case of a sale or exchange of an interest in a partnership, gain or loss shall be recognized to the transferor partner. Such gain or loss shall be considered as a gain or loss from the sale or exchange of a capital asset, except as otherwise provided in section 751.

Section 751(a) * * * provides that the amount of money or the fair value of property received by a transferor partner in exchange for all or part of such partner's interest in the partnership attributable to unrealized receivables of the partnership, or to inventory items of the partnership that have appreciated substantially in value, shall be considered as an amount realized from the sale or exchange of property other than a capital asset.

Section 752(a) * * * provides that any increase in a partner's share of the liabilities of a partnership, or any increase in a partner's individual liabilities by reason of the assumption by the partner of partnership liabilities, will be considered as a contribution of money by such partner to the partnership.

Section 752(b) * * * provides that any decrease in a partner's share of the liabilities of a partnership, or any decrease in a partner's individual liabilities by reason of the assumption by the partnership of such individual liabilities, will be considered as a distribution of money to the partner by the partnership. Under section 733(1) * * *, the basis of a partner's interest in the partnership is reduced by the amount of money received in a distribution that is not in liquidation of the partnership.

Section 752(d) * * * provides that in the case of a sale or exchange of an interest in a partnership, liabilities shall be treated in the same manner as liabilities in connection with the sale or exchange of property not associated with partnerships.

* * * As described below, depending on the format chosen for the transfer to a controlled corporation, the basis and holding periods of the various assets received by the corporation and the basis and holding periods of the stock received by the former partners can vary.

* * * Recognition of the three possible methods to incorporate a partnership will enable taxpayers to avoid * * * potential pitfalls and will facilitate flexibility with respect to the basis and holding periods of the assets received in the exchange.

HOLDING

* * *

Situation 1

Under section 351 * * *, gain or loss is not recognized by X on the transfer by X of all of its assets to R in exchange for R's stock and the assumption by R of X's liabilities.

Under section 362(a) * * *, R's basis in the assets received from X equals their basis to X immediately before their transfer to R. Under section 358(a), the basis to X of the stock received from R is the same as the basis to X of the assets transferred to R, reduced by the liabilities assumed by R, which assumption is treated as a payment of money to X under section 358(d). In addition, the assumption by R of X's liabilities decreased each partner's share of the partnership liabilities, thus, decreasing the basis of each partner's partnership interest pursuant to sections 752 and 733.

On distribution of the stock to X's partners, X terminated under section 708(b)(1)(A) * * *. Pursuant to section 732(b), the basis of the stock distributed to the partners in liquidation of their partnership interests is, with respect to each partner, equal to the adjusted basis of the partner's interest in the partnership.

Under section 1223(1) * * *, X's holding period for the stock received in the exchange includes its holding period in the capital assets and section 1231 assets transferred (to the extent that the stock was received in exchange for such assets). To the extent the stock was received in exchange for neither capital nor section 1231 assets, X's holding period for such stock begins on the day following the date of the exchange. * * * Under section 1223(2), R's holding period in the assets transferred to it includes X's holding period. When X distributed the R stock to its partners, under sections 735(b) and 1223, the partners' holding periods included X's holding period of the stock. Furthermore, such distribution will not violate the control requirement of section 368(c) * * *.

Situation 2

On the transfer of all of Y's assets to its partners, Y terminated under section 708(b)(1)(A) * * *, and, pursuant to section 732(b), the basis of the assets (other than money) distributed to the partners in liquidation of their partnership interests in Y was, with respect to each partner, equal to the adjusted basis of the partner's interest in Y, reduced by the money distributed. Under section 752, the decrease in Y's liabilities resulting from the transfer to Y's partners was offset by the partners' corresponding assumption of such liabilities so that the net effect on the basis of each partner's interest in Y, with respect to the liabilities transferred, was zero.

Under section 351 * * *, gain or loss is not recognized by Y's former partners on the transfer to S in exchange for its stock and the assumption of Y's liabilities, of the assets of Y received by Y's partners in liquidation of Y.

Under section 358(a) * * *, the basis to the former partners of Y in the stock received from S is the same as the section 732(b) basis to the former partners of Y in the assets received in liquidation of Y and transferred to S, reduced by the liabilities assumed by S, which assumption is treated as a payment of money to the partners under section 358(d).

Under section 362(a) * * *, S's basis in the assets received from Y's former partners equals their basis to the former partners as determined under section 732(c) immediately before the transfer to S.

¶ **24,015**

Under section 735(b) * * *, the partners' holding periods for the assets distributed to them by Y includes Y's holding period. Under section 1223(1), the partners' holding periods for the stock received in the exchange includes the partners' holding periods in the capital assets and section 1231 assets transferred to S (to the extent that the stock was received in exchange for such assets). However, to the extent that the stock received was in exchange for neither capital nor section 1231 assets, the holding period of the stock began on the day following the date of the exchange. Under section 1223(2), S's holding period of the Y assets received in the exchange includes the partner's holding periods.

Situation 3

Under section 351 * * *, gain or loss is not recognized by Z's partners on the transfer of the partnership interests to T in exchange for T's stock.

On the transfer of the partnership interests to the corporation, Z terminated under section 708(b)(1)(A) * * *.

Under section 358(a) * * *, the basis to the partners of Z of the stock received from T in exchange for their partnership interests equals the basis of their partnership interests transferred to T, reduced by Z's liabilities assumed by T, the release from which is treated as a payment of money to Z's partners under sections 752(d) and 358(d).

T's basis for the assets received in the exchange equals the basis of the partners in their partnership interests allocated in accordance with section 732(c). T's holding period includes Z's holding period in the assets.

Under section 1223(1) * * *, the holding period of the T stock received by the former partners of Z includes each respective partner's holding period for the partnership interest transferred, except that the holding period of the T stock that was received by the partners of Z in exchange for their interests in section 751 assets of Z that are neither capital assets nor section 1231 assets begins on the day following the date of the exchange.

* * *

[¶ 24,020]

Notes

1. If a partnership or an LLC classified as a partnership for federal tax purposes elects to change its classification to that of a corporation, the regulations treat the partnership as if it had contributed all of its assets and liabilities to the corporation in exchange for stock in the corporation. Then, the regulations treat the partnership as liquidating itself by distributing the stock in the corporation to its partners. Reg. § 301.7701–3(g)(1)(i). These regulations, however, do not affect the

validity of the holdings in Rev. Rul. 84–111, in which the IRS indicates that it will generally respect the form undertaken by the taxpayers in effecting a partnership-to-corporation conversion. See REG–105162–97, 1997–2 C.B. 649, 650.

2. The regulations provide that the amount of any gain recognized to the partnership on the Section 351 exchange is determined without regard to a Section 743 basis adjustment in the property transferred to the corporation. Instead, the partner with the special basis adjustment is allowed to use that adjustment to reduce its allocable share of any gain recognized by the partnership on the Section 351 exchange. Reg. § 1.743–1(h)(2)(ii). This approach taken in the regulations of determining any recognized gain at the partnership level and allowing the partner to use the Section 743 adjustment as an offset against its allocable share of the gain is similar to the treatment of a sale of partnership property with a special basis adjustment (discussed in Chapter 21). See REG–105162–97, 1997–2 C.B. 649, 651.

The regulations also provide that a corporate transferee's basis under Section 362 in the property transferred by a partnership in a Section 351 exchange includes any special basis adjustment under Section 743 (other than a basis adjustment that reduced a partner's gain, as described in the paragraph above). Reg. § 1.743–1(h)(2)(i). The partnership's adjusted basis in the stock received in the Section 351 exchange is not affected by any Section 743 adjustment in property transferred to the corporation. However, a partner with a Section 743 basis adjustment in property transferred to the corporation has a basis adjustment in the stock received by the partnership in the Section 351 exchange equal to the partner's basis adjustment in the property transferred, reduced by any basis adjustment that reduced the partner's gain under the rule described above. Reg. § 1.743–1(h)(2)(iii).

3. Suppose that an unincorporated state law entity that is classified as a partnership for federal tax purposes converts into a state law corporation under a state law formless conversion statute. In Rev. Rul. 2004–59, 2004–1 C.B. 1050, the IRS ruled that Rev. Rul. 84–111 does not apply and that the following is deemed to occur: the partnership contributes all its assets and liabilities to the corporation in exchange for stock in the corporation, and, immediately thereafter, the partnership liquidates and distributes the stock to its partners.

B. STATUTORY TERMINATIONS

[¶ 24,025]

1. GENERALLY

A partnership does not terminate for income tax purposes merely because it is technically dissolved under state law. Rather, and regardless of the intention of the partners, a partnership will terminate for income tax purposes only if either of the two events specified in Section 708(b)(1)(A) or 708(b)(1)(B) occurs. If a partnership is terminated under Section 708, its taxable year closes and the income and loss of the partnership are allocated among all of the partners on the date of the termination. § 706(c)(1) and Reg. § 1.708–1(b)(3).

[¶ 24,030]

a. *Complete Cessation of Business in the Partnership Form—Section 708(b)(1)(A)*

Not surprisingly, a termination will occur if "no part" of any business operation is carried on by the partnership. § 708(b)(1)(A). Apparently, even minimal activity, such as the management of accounts receivable derived from the sale of an active business, will prevent a termination under this provision. Why might the parties desire to delay a termination of the partnership for income tax purposes?

A termination also will occur under Section 708(b)(1)(A) if one of the partners in a two-member partnership sells her partnership interest to the other partner, causing the partnership to be reclassified as an entity disregarded from its owner and thereby terminating business operations in the partnership form. This principle is illustrated by the following ruling involving a two-member LLC that becomes a disregarded entity when one of the members sells his interest to the other member or both members sell their interests to a third party.

[¶ 24,035]

REVENUE RULING 99–6
1999–1 C.B. 432.

Issue

What are the federal income tax consequences if one person purchases all of the ownership interests in a domestic limited liability company (LLC) that is classified as a partnership under § 301.7701–3 of the * * * Regulations, causing the LLC's status as a partnership to terminate under § 708(b)(1)(A) * * *?

Facts

In each of the following situations, an LLC is formed and operates in a state which permits an LLC to have a single owner. Each LLC is classified as a partnership under § 301.7701–3. Neither of the LLCs holds any unrealized receivables or substantially appreciated inventory for purposes of § 751(b). For the sake of simplicity, it is assumed that neither LLC is liable for any indebtedness, nor are the assets of the LLCs subject to any indebtedness.

   Situation 1. A and *B* are equal partners in *AB*, an LLC. *A* sells *A*'s entire interest in *AB* to *B* for $10,000. After the sale, the business is continued by the LLC, which is owned solely by *B*.

   Situation 2. C and *D* are equal partners in *CD*, an LLC. *C* and *D* sell their entire interests in *CD* to *E*, an unrelated person, in exchange for $10,000 each. After the sale, the business is continued by the LLC, which is owned solely by *E*.

   After the sale, in both situations, no entity classification election is made under § 301.7701–3(c) to treat the LLC as an association for federal tax purposes.

Law

   Section 708(b)(1)(A) and § 1.708–1(b)(1) of the * * * Regulations provide that a partnership shall terminate when the operations of the partnership are discontinued and no part of any business, financial operation, or venture of the partnership continues to be carried on by any of its partners in a partnership.

   Section 731(a)(1) provides that, in the case of a distribution by a partnership to a partner, gain is not recognized to the partner except to the extent that any money distributed exceeds the adjusted basis of the partner's interest in the partnership immediately before the distribution.

   Section 731(a)(2) provides that, in the case of a distribution by a partnership in liquidation of a partner's interest in a partnership where no property other than money, unrealized receivables (as defined in § 751(c)), and inventory (as defined in § 751(d)(2)) is distributed to the partner, loss is recognized to the extent of the excess of the adjusted basis of the partner's interest in the partnership over the sum of (A) any money distributed, and (B) the basis to the distributee, as determined under section 732, of any unrealized receivables and inventory.

   Section 732(b) provides that the basis of property (other than money) distributed by a partnership to a partner in liquidation of the partner's interest shall be an amount equal to the adjusted basis of the partner's interest in the partnership, reduced by any money distributed in the same transaction.

   Section 735(b) provides that, in determining the period for which a partner has held property received in a distribution from a partnership (other than for purposes of § 735(a)(2)), there shall be included the holding period of the partnership, as determined under § 1223, with respect to the property.

   Section 741 provides that gain or loss resulting from the sale or exchange of an interest in a partnership shall be recognized by the transferor partner, and that the gain or loss shall be considered as gain or loss from a capital asset, except as provided in § 751 (relating to unrealized receivables and inventory items).

¶ 24,035

Section 1.741–1(b) provides that § 741 applies to the transferor partner in a two-person partnership when one partner sells a partnership interest to the other partner, and to all the members of a partnership when they sell their interests to one or more persons outside the partnership.

Section 301.7701–2(c)(1) provides that, for federal tax purposes, the term "partnership" means a business entity (as the term is defined in § 301.7701–2(a)) that is not a corporation and that has at least two members.

In *Edwin E. McCauslen v. Commissioner*, 45 T.C. 588 (1966), one partner in an equal, two-person partnership died, and his partnership interest was purchased from his estate by the remaining partner. The purchase caused a termination of the partnership under § 708(b)(1)(A). The Tax Court held that the surviving partner did not purchase the deceased partner's interest in the partnership, but that the surviving partner purchased the partnership assets attributable to the interest. As a result, the surviving partner was not permitted to succeed to the partnership's holding period with respect to these assets.

Rev. Rul. 67–65, 1967–1 C.B. 168, also considered the purchase of a deceased partner's interest by the other partner in a two-person partnership. The Service ruled that, for the purpose of determining the purchaser's holding period in the assets attributable to the deceased partner's interest, the purchaser should treat the transaction as a purchase of the assets attributable to the interest. Accordingly, the purchaser was not permitted to succeed to the partnership's holding period with respect to these assets. *See also* Rev. Rul. 55–68, 1955–1 C.B. 372.

ANALYSIS AND HOLDINGS

Situation 1. The *AB* partnership terminates under § 708(b)(1)(A) when *B* purchases *A*'s entire interest in *AB*. Accordingly, *A* must treat the transaction as the sale of a partnership interest. Reg. § 1.741–1(b). *A* must report gain or loss, if any, resulting from the sale of *A*'s partnership interest in accordance with § 741.

Under the analysis of *McCauslen* and Rev. Rul. 67–65, for purposes of determining the tax treatment of *B*, the *AB* partnership is deemed to make a liquidating distribution of all of its assets to *A* and *B*, and following this distribution, *B* is treated as acquiring the assets deemed to have been distributed to *A* in liquidation of *A*'s partnership interest.

B's basis in the assets attributable to *A*'s one-half interest in the partnership is $10,000, the purchase price for *A*'s partnership interest. Section 1012. Section 735(b) does not apply with respect to the assets *B* is deemed to have purchased from *A*. Therefore, *B*'s holding period for these assets begins on the day immediately following the date of the sale. See Rev. Rul. 66–7, 1966–1 C.B. 188, which provides that the holding

¶ 24,035

period of an asset is computed by excluding the date on which the asset is acquired.

Upon the termination of *AB*, *B* is considered to receive a distribution of those assets attributable to *B*'s former interest in *AB*. *B* must recognize gain or loss, if any, on the deemed distribution of the assets to the extent required by § 731(a). *B*'s basis in the assets received in the deemed liquidation of *B*'s partnership interest is determined under § 732(b). Under § 735(b), *B*'s holding period for the assets attributable to *B*'s one-half interest in *AB* includes the partnership's holding period for such assets (except for purposes of § 735(a)(2)).

Situation 2. The *CD* partnership terminates under § 708(b)(1)(A) when *E* purchases the entire interests of *C* and *D* in *CD*. *C* and *D* must report gain or loss, if any, resulting from the sale of their partnership interests in accordance with § 741.

For purposes of classifying the acquisition by *E*, the *CD* partnership is deemed to make a liquidating distribution of its assets to *C* and *D*. Immediately following this distribution, *E* is deemed to acquire, by purchase, all of the former partnership's assets. Compare Rev. Rul. 84–111, 1984–2 C.B. 88 (Situation 3), which determines the tax consequences to a corporate transferee of all interests in a partnership in a manner consistent with *McCauslen*, and holds that the transferee's basis in the assets received equals the basis of the partnership interests, allocated among the assets in accordance with § 732(c).

E's basis in the assets is $20,000 under § 1012. *E*'s holding period for the assets begins on the day immediately following the date of sale.

* * *

[¶ 24,037]

Note

The proposed regulations under Section 707(a)(2)(B), which treat certain contribution-distribution transactions as disguised sales of partnership interests between the partners, may apply to transfers to and from a partnership, even if, after the application of the rules in those regulations, a partnership termination under Section 708(b)(1)(A) results. See Prop. Reg. § 1.707–7(a)(7). These proposed regulations are discussed at ¶ 20,095.

[¶ 24,040]

b. Constructive Terminations—Section 708(b)(1)(B)

More surprisingly, a termination will occur if sales or exchanges of 50 percent or more of the partnership interests occur within a 12–month period—even if the dispositions are unrelated. § 708(b)(1)(B). This type of termination is often called a "constructive" or "technical" termination. The potential severity of this constructive termination rule is mitigated by a generous definition of what constitutes sale or exchange of an interest—transfers by testamentary or inter vivos gift, the admission of new partners, and the liquidation of a partnership interest do not count, although sales to existing partners do. Reg. § 1.708–1(b)(2). Nevertheless, a partnership may suffer an inadvertent termination in a number of surprising ways. For example, the liquidation of an upper-tier partnership would result in the exchange of its interest in a lower-tier partnership. § 761(e). Similarly, the acquisition of a corporate partner in a tax-free merger or "C" reorganization would constitute an exchange of the partnership interest.

If a partnership is terminated under Section 708(b)(1)(B), the following is treated as occurring under Reg. § 1.708–1(b)(4). The partnership is deemed to contribute all of its assets and liabilities to a new partnership in exchange for an interest in the new partnership. Immediately thereafter, the terminated partnership is deemed to liquidate by distributing interests in the new partnership to the purchasing partner and the other remaining partners in proportion to their interests in the terminated partnership.

There are numerous tax consequences to this constructive contribution-liquidation transaction. For example, all of the elections made by the terminated partnership, including the Section 754 election, are invalidated and must be renewed. Thus, a termination gives the partnership an opportunity to escape from elections that have proven unwise.

Any special basis adjustment a partner has in assets of the terminated partnership under Section 743(b) as a result of the Section 754 election carries over to the new partnership, regardless of whether the new partnership makes a Section 754 election. Reg. § 1.743–1(h)(1). Moreover, a Section 754 election that is in effect for the taxable year of the terminated partnership in which the sale occurs applies to the incoming purchasing partner. Accordingly, the bases of the partnership assets with respect to that partner are adjusted under Sections 743 and 755 before their deemed contribution to the new partnership. See Reg. § 1.708–1(b)(5) (incorporating the principles of the now obsolete Rev. Rul. 86–73, 1986–1 C.B. 282). In effect, the purchasing partner is treated as a partner of the terminated partnership for the instant before the contribution of the partnership assets by the terminated partnership to the new partnership occurs.

The deemed contribution of assets to a new partnership and the distribution of the new partnership interests to the partners of the terminated partnership are ignored for purposes of maintaining capital accounts under Section 704(b). As a result, the constructive termination does not change the capital accounts of the purchasing partner or the remaining partners (which carry over to the new partnership) or the books of the partnership. Reg. §§ 1.704–1(b)(2)(iv)(*l*), 1.704–1(b)(5), Ex. 13(v), and 1.708–1(b)(4), Ex. (ii).

Recall that Section 704(c)(1)(B), discussed at ¶ 22,090, provides that if property contributed by one partner to the partnership is distributed to another partner within seven years of the contribution, the contributing partner must recognize Section 704(c) gain or loss as if the partner had sold the property for its fair market value at the time of distribution. Recall also that under Section 737, discussed at ¶ 22,095, a partner who contributes appreciated property to a partnership must recognize gain if within seven years of the contribution that partner receives property other than money as a distribution from the partnership. Does a constructive partnership termination under Section 708(b)(1)(B) trigger the recognition of gain or loss under those provisions?

The regulations under Sections 704(c)(1)(B) and 737 make clear that these provisions do not apply to the deemed distribution of new partnership interests as a result of the constructive partnership termination; thus, recognition of precontribution gain or loss is not triggered by a constructive partnership termination under Section 708(b)(1)(B). A later distribution of property by the new partnership to a partner of the new partnership is subject to Sections 704(c)(1)(B) and 737 to the same extent that a distribution from the terminated partnership would have been subject to those provisions. Reg. §§ 1.704–4(c)(3) and 1.737–2(a).

Moreover, the deemed contribution of the assets to a new partnership does not create any additional Section 704(c) property; instead, property contributed to the new partnership is treated as Section 704(c) property in the hands of the new partnership only to the extent that the property was Section 704(c) property in the hands of the terminated partnership immediately before the termination of the partnership. Reg. § 1.704–3(a)(3)(i). However, the new partnership does not have to use the same method as the terminated partnership with respect to the Section 704(c) property deemed contributed to it by the terminated partnership. Reg. § 1.704–3(a)(2). For purposes of Sections 704(c) and 737, a constructive termination of the partnership does not begin a new seven-year period with respect to the built-in gain and built-in loss property that the terminated partnership is deemed to contribute to the new partnership. See Reg. § 1.704–4(a)(4)(ii).

Finally, recall that under Section 731(c), discussed at ¶ 22,100, a partnership's distribution of "marketable securities" is generally treated as a cash distribution which triggers the recognition of gain to the distributee partner. The regulations provide, however, that the deemed distribution of partnership interests under Reg. § 1.708–1(b)(4) does not trigger the application of Section 731(c). Reg. § 1.731–2(g)(2).

¶ 24,040

[¶ 24,045]

Notes

1. An electing large partnership (as defined in Section 775) is not terminated by reason of a change in ownership of 50 percent or more of its interests during a 12–month period. The constructive termination rules of Section 708(b)(1)(B) do not apply to such a partnership. § 774(c). This rule recognizes the practical reality that electing large partnerships need to have readily transferable interests. The special simplified regime applicable to electing large partnerships is discussed generally at ¶ 18,250.

2. The proposed regulations under Section 707(a)(2)(B), which treat certain contribution-distribution transactions as disguised sales of partnership interests between the partners, do not apply to the deemed transfers resulting from a partnership termination under Section 708(b)(1)(B). See Prop. Reg. § 1.707–7(a)(8). These proposed regulations are discussed at ¶ 20,095.

[¶ 24,050]

2. TIERED PARTNERSHIPS

A sale or exchange of an interest in an upper-tier partnership that holds an interest in a lower-tier partnership may have federal tax consequences for the lower-tier partnership if the sale of the interest in the upper-tier partnership results in a termination of the upper-tier partnership under Section 708(b)(1)(B). In such a case, the upper-tier partnership is treated as exchanging its entire interest in the lower-tier partnership. Thus, the termination of the upper-tier partnership will in turn cause a termination of the lower-tier partnership if the upper-tier partnership's interest together with any other interests sold or exchanged in the lower-tier partnership during a 12–month period meets the 50–percent threshold for constructive partnership terminations under Section 708(b)(1)(B). Reg. § 1.708–1(b)(2) (which has incorporated the principles of the now obsolete Rev. Rul. 87–50, 1987–1 C.B. 157).

Suppose that the sale of the interest in the upper-tier partnership does not terminate the upper-tier partnership? What effect will that sale have on the lower-tier partnership, i.e., will it be treated as a sale of the upper-tier partnership's interest in the lower-tier partnership for purposes of determining whether sales of interests in the lower-tier partnership meet the 50–percent threshold in Section 708(b)(1)(B). The following ruling, which was issued under a prior version of the regulations and is now obsolete, answers these questions. The principles of the ruling are still valid, however, and have been incorporated into Reg. § 1.708–1(b)(2).

[¶ 24,055]

REVENUE RULING 87–51

1987–1 C.B. 158, declared obsolete by T.D. 8717, 1997–1 C.B. 125.

ISSUE

In a multi-tiered partnership arrangement, if a partner of an upper-tier partnership sells a partnership interest of less than 50 percent of the capital and profits of the upper-tier partnership, then, for purposes of section 708(b)(1)(B) * * *, is that sale also considered a sale of the partner's proportionate share of the upper-tier partnership's interest in a lower-tier partnership?

FACTS

AB is a partnership that holds a 50 percent interest in the capital and profits of *XYZ*, another partnership. *A*, a partner in *AB*, sold *A*'s 40 percent interest in the capital and profits of *AB*, and, within twelve months of the sale by *A*, *X*, a partner in *XYZ*, sold all of *X*'s 30 percent interest in the capital and profits of *XYZ*. There were no other sales of interests in either *AB* or *XYZ* during the same twelve month period.

LAW AND ANALYSIS

Section 708(b)(1)(B) * * * provides that a partnership will be considered terminated if within a 12–month period there is a sale or exchange of 50 percent or more of the total interest in partnership capital and profits.

Section 741 * * * provides that, in the case of a sale or exchange of an interest in a partnership, gain or loss shall be recognized to the transferor partner. Such gain or loss shall be considered as gain or loss from the sale or exchange of a capital asset, except as otherwise provided in section 751 (relating to unrealized receivables and inventory items which have appreciated substantially in value).

In the present situation, *A* sold a 40 percent partnership interest in *AB*, which held a 50 percent partnership interest in the partnership *XYZ*. In addition, within twelve months of the sale by *A*, *X* sold a 30 percent interest in *XYZ*. If *A*'s sale of a 40 percent partnership interest in *AB* is also considered a sale of a 20 percent (40 percent of 50 percent) interest in *XYZ*, then *A*'s sale of the 20 percent interest combined with *X*'s sale of a 30 percent interest in *XYZ* within twelve months would result in the termination of *XYZ* under section 708(b)(1)(B) * * *.

Under the provisions of subchapter K of the Code, a partnership is considered for various purposes to be either an aggregate of its partners or an entity, transactionally independent of its partners. Generally, subchapter K adopts an entity approach with respect to transactions involving partnership interests. *See* Rev. Rul. 75–62, 1975–1 C.B. 188.

¶ 24,055

Whether an aggregate or entity theory of partnerships should be applied to a particular Code section depends upon which theory is more appropriate to such section. *See* S. Rep. No. 1622, 83d Cong., 2d Sess. 89 (1954), and H.R. Rep. No. 2543, 83d Cong., 2d Sess. 59 (1954); *Casel v. Commissioner*, 79 T.C. 424 (1982). The termination of a partnership under section 708(b)(1)(B) depends on whether there was a sale or exchange of a partnership interest and on whether there was transfer of at least 50 percent of the total interest in partnership capital and profits. Because section 708(b)(1)(B) is an entity-oriented provision, an entity approach is more appropriate for that section.

Thus, in a multi-tiered partnership arrangement, the sale of a partner's interest in the capital and profits of an upper-tier partnership that is itself a partner in a lower-tier partnership is not a sale of the partner's proportionate share of the underlying assets of the upper-tier partnership for purposes of section 708(b)(1)(B). Rather, under section 741, the sale of *A*'s interest in *AB* is considered the sale of a single capital asset, the interest in *AB*. Accordingly, only *X*'s sale of a 30 percent partnership interest in *XYZ* qualifies for the determination of whether there has been a sale or exchange of 50 percent or more of the total interest in the partnership capital and profits of *XYZ*.

HOLDING

In a multi-tiered partnership arrangement, the sale of a partner's interest in an upper-tier partnership that does not trigger a termination of the upper-tier partnership is not considered a sale of that partner's proportionate share of the upper-tier partnership's interest in a lower-tier partnership for purposes of the termination provisions of section 708(b)(1)(B) * * *.

* * *

[¶ 24,060]

Note

Reg. § 1.708–1(b)(2) and Rev. Rul. 87–51 use an entity view of partnership taxation in applying Section 708(b)(1)(B) to the transfer of interests in multi-tier partnerships. Thus, *XYZ*, the lower-tier partnership, did not terminate under Section 708(b)(1)(B) even though there was a 50–percent change in the ultimate owners of interests in *XYZ* during a 12–month period (consisting of a direct sale of a 30–percent interest by *X* and an indirect sale of a 20–percent interest by *A*, an indirect 20–percent partner in *XYZ* through ownership of a 40–percent interest in *AB*, the upper-tier partnership that owns a 50–percent interest in *XYZ*). Does the entity view of partnership taxation achieve consistent and sensible results under Section 708(b)(1)(B) when applied to these multi-tier partnerships?

¶ 24,055

[¶ 24,065]

Problems

1. X and Y formed the XY Partnership several years ago with cash contributions. X and Y each has an equal interest in partnership capital and profits. The partnership has no liabilities. X and Y each has an adjusted basis of $20,000 for her partnership interest as of July 1 of the current year. On that date, X sells her interest in the partnership for $45,000 cash to Z. The partnership had the following assets on that date:

Assets	*Partnership's A.B.*	*F.M.V.*
Cash	$10,000	$10,000
Accounts receivable	5,000	5,000
Inventory	10,000	30,000
Building used in the business	15,000	45,000
Total	$40,000	$90,000

Assuming that the partnership has never filed an election under Section 754 and that Z does not elect under Section 732(d), determine the federal income tax consequences to the XY Partnership and to X, Y, and Z as a result of the sale of X's partnership interest to Z.

2. How would your answer change in Problem 1 if the partnership had an election in effect under Section 754?

3. How would your answer change in Problem 1 if the partnership did not have an election in effect under Section 754 but Z made an election under Section 732(d)?

C. PARTNERSHIP MERGERS AND DIVISIONS

[¶ 24,070]

1. MERGERS

General rule. If two or more partnerships merge or consolidate into one partnership, Section 708(b)(2)(A) generally treats the resulting partnership as a continuation of the partnership the members of which own an interest of more than 50 percent in the capital and profits of the resulting partnership. In 2001, the Treasury and the IRS issued final regulations on the federal income tax consequences of partnership mergers. Those regulations provide that, if, under the more than 50 percent interest test, the resulting partnership can considered to be a continuation of more than one of the merging or consolidating partnerships, it is treated as the continuation solely of the partnership that is credited with the contribution of the greatest net fair market value of assets to the resulting partnership (unless the IRS otherwise permits). For purposes of this rule, the regulations determine the fair market value of the contributed assets net of liabilities. All other merging or consolidated partnerships are treated as terminated. If the members of none of the merging partnerships have an interest of more than 50 percent in the capital and profits of the resulting partnership, then the regulations treat all of the merging partnerships as terminated and a new partnership as resulting. Reg. § 1.708–1(c)(1). Any elections in effect for the terminated partnerships end on the date of termination.

> *Example.* X owns 70 percent of the XY Partnership and owns 51 percent of the XZ Partnership. The two partnerships merge and form the XYZ Partnership. The XY Partnership contributes assets with a net fair market value of $500,000 and the XZ Partnership contributes assets with a net fair market value of $750,000. Because X owns more than 50 percent of the profits and capital of both the XY and XZ Partnerships, the XYZ Partnership could be treated as a continuation of either partnership. However, because the XZ Partnership is credited with a greater net fair market value of contributed assets to the resulting partnership, the regulations treat XYZ as a continuation of the XZ Partnership and treat the XY Partnership as terminated. See id.

Recognized forms of partnership merger or consolidation under the regulations. The regulations recognize two forms of partnership merger or consolidation for federal income tax purposes: the assets-over form and the assets-up form. Under the assets-over form of merger or consolidation, the merged or consolidated partnership that is treated as terminated under these regulations contributes all of its assets and liabilities to the resulting partnership in exchange for an interest in the resulting partnership. Then the terminating partnership immediately distributes interests in the resulting partnership to its partners in liquidation of the terminating partnership. Reg. § 1.708–1(c)(3)(i).

Under the assets-up form of merger or consolidation, the merged or consolidated partnership that is treated as terminated under these regulations liquidates by distributing its assets and liabilities to its partners. Then those partners immediately contribute the distributed assets to the resulting partnership in exchange for the resulting partnership's partnership interests. The IRS will respect the assets-up form of partnership merger or consolidation despite the partners' transitory ownership of the terminating partnership's assets, provided that the distribution occurs in a manner that, under the laws of the applicable jurisdiction, those partners are treated as the owners of the terminating partnership's assets. Reg. § 1.708–1(c)(3)(ii).

Under a default rule in the regulations, a merger or consolidation that does not follow any particular form for the merger or that uses a form that does not clearly conform to the assets-up form of merger described in the regulations is treated as an assets-over form of merger for federal income tax purposes even if it does not follow that form. See Reg. § 1.708–1(c)(3)(i) and (c)(5), Ex. 4.

¶ 24,070

For a transaction to be respected as following the assets-up form of partnership merger, instead of being treated as an assets-over merger under the default rule, the regulations require the terminating partnership to actually undertake all the steps necessary under the laws of the applicable jurisdiction to convey ownership of the assets distributed to the partners. This requirement is not met by the partners of the terminating partnership assigning their right to receive title to assets to the resulting partnership or directing the terminating partnership to transfer title to the assets to the resulting partnership. T.D. 8925, 2001–1 C.B. 496, 497. However, T.D. 8925 indicates that this does not mean that an actual transfer and recording of a deed or certificate of title is required for most types of assets. Moreover, the regulations make clear that a partnership can use the assets-up form of partnership merger even where the terminating partnership owns certain assets, such as undivided interests in goodwill, that would be difficult, if not impossible, for the partners to hold outside of the partnership. Id. Note that the regulations do not require that the partners actually assume the liabilities of the terminating partnership, although each partner will be deemed under Section 752 to have assumed a share of the resulting partnership's liabilities. See Reg. § 1.708–1(c)(5), Ex. 3; T.D. 8925, 2001–1 C.B. 496, 497.

The regulations require consistency in the characterization of a merger or consolidation in which all of the assets and liabilities of a terminating partnership are transferred to a single resulting partnership. Thus, the regulations do not respect bifurcated mergers or consolidations for federal income tax purposes in which the partnership undertakes the assets-over form with respect to some assets and the assets-up form with respect to other assets. In such a case, under the default rule, the partnership merger is treated as an assets-over form of merger. However, when more than two partnerships are combined, each combination is viewed as a separate merger that may be structured to conform to either the assets-over form or assets-up form of merger. See T.D. 8925, 2001–1 C.B. 496, 498.

The regulations also do not respect the interests-over form of partnership merger or consolidation in which the partners in the terminating partnership transfer their partnership interests to the resulting partnership in exchange for interests in the resulting partnership. Under the default rule in the regulations, because such a merger does not follow the assets-up form, it is treated as an assets-over merger for federal income tax purposes. Thus, the terminating partnership is treated as contributing its assets and liabilities to the resulting partnership in exchange for interests in that partnership and the terminating partnership is treated as distributing the interests in the resulting partnership to its partners in liquidation of their interests in the terminating partnership. See Reg. § 1.708–1(c)(5), Ex. 4; REG–111119–99, 2000–1 C.B. 455, 456. Is the position of the Treasury and the IRS on this issue

¶ 24,070

consistent with the IRS's recognition of the interests-over form of incorporating an existing partnership described in *Situation 3* of Rev. Rul. 84–111, at ¶ 24,015?

Anti-abuse rule. The regulations authorize the IRS to recharacterize transactions that are structured to follow the assets-up or assets-over forms but that are in substance part of a larger series of transactions that are inconsistent with those forms. In such cases, the IRS can disregard the form of the merger and recast the transactions in line with their substance. Reg. § 1.708–1(c)(6)(i). For example, if, pursuant to a prearranged transaction, assets that are contributed by partners to the resulting partnership in an assets-up form of partnership merger are contributed to a new partnership and the interests in the new partnership are distributed in liquidation of their interests in the resulting partnership, the IRS will disregard the form of the transactions and recast them as in substance a taxable exchange of interests in the original partnership for interests in the resulting partnership. Reg. § 1.708–1(c)(6)(ii).

Tax consequences of assets-over and assets-up forms of partnership merger. The basic tax consequences of the assets-over form of partnership merger are as follows. The partnership's contribution of its assets and liabilities in exchange for interests in the new partnership is a nonrecognition transfer under Section 721. Section 752(b) treats liabilities of the terminating partnership assumed by the resulting partnership as cash distributions to the partners relieved of the debt to the extent that they exceed any liabilities assumed by the partners as a result of becoming partners in the resulting partnership. Reg. § 1.752–1(f) and (g), Ex. 2. Each partner must apply the amount of this deemed distribution to reduce the basis of the interest in the terminating partnership and, if the deemed distribution exceeds such basis, must recognize taxable capital gain from the sale of the partnership interest under Sections 731(a)(1) and 741. Finally, under Section 732(b), the partners' bases in their new partnership interests are equal to their bases in the interests in the terminating partnership, reduced by any net decrease in the partners' shares of the liabilities or increased by any net increase in the partners' shares of the liabilities as a result of the merger. Note that because no actual property distributions occur as part of the assets-over form of merger, there is no gain recognition triggered under Section 704(c).

The basic tax consequences of an assets-up merger are as follows. When the terminating partnership distributes all of its assets and liabilities, the distributee partner's tax consequences on the distribution are determined under Sections 731, 704(c)(1)(B), and 737. The partners' bases in the assets are the same as their bases in the partnership interests under Section 732(b). When the partners contribute the assets and liabilities to the resulting partnership, no gain or loss is recognized on the transfer under Section 721, and the resulting partnership's bases in those assets are a carryover of the partners' bases in the assets under Section 723. Under Section 1223(1), each partner's holding period for the assets is the same as the partner's holding period for the partnership interest in the terminating partnership, and, under Section 1223(2), that holding period becomes the holding period of the resulting partnership in the assets when the assets and liabilities are contributed to the resulting partnership. If, as part of the assets-up merger, the partnership distributes property with built-in gain within seven years of its contribution to any partner other than the contributing partner, the contributing partner will have to recognize the built-in gain under Section 704(c)(1)(B). See REG–111119–99, 2000–1 C.B. 455, 456.

Special buy-out rule in the regulations for exiting partners. Suppose that one or more partners of a terminating partnership do not want to become members of the resulting partnership in an assets-over form of partnership merger. The regulations contain a special buy-out rule that allows a resulting partnership to purchase the interests of one or more partners in a terminating partnership without triggering the disguised sale rules under Section 707(a)(2)(B) and having the transfer of money or other property to one or more partners treated as a disguised sale of the partnership assets. To come within this buy-out rule, the merger agreement must state that the resulting partnership is purchasing interests from a particular partner or partners, must state the amount being paid for each interest purchased, and must state that the selling partner consents to treat the transaction as a sale of the partnership interest. The selling partner does not have to be a party to the merger agreement, but must consent to having the transaction treated as a sale of the partnership interest for the buy-out rule to apply. Reg. § 1.708–1(c)(4); T.D. 8925, 2001–1 C.B. 496, 498.

If this buy-out rule applies, the resulting partnership is treated as purchasing the partnership interest of the exiting partner. Consequently, the resulting partnership inherits the exiting partner's capital account in the terminating partnership and any Section 704(c) built-in gain or reverse Section 704(c) allocations as well. (Section 704(c)(1)(C), enacted in 2004, presumably would prevent the resulting partnership from inheriting any Section 704(c) built-in losses of the exiting partner.) Any built-in gain or reverse Section 704(c) allocations attributable to the purchased partnership interest are apportioned among the partners who were partners in the terminating partnership immediately before the merger. The resulting partnership's basis in the purchased partnership interest is equal to the amount paid to the exiting partner under Section 742. Immediately thereafter the resulting partnership is treated as receiving a distribution of property in liquidation of the partnership interest upon the transfer by the terminating partnership of its assets as part of the assets-over merger. The resulting partnership obtains a substituted basis in the assets equal to its basis in the liquidated partnership interest under Section 732(b) and obtains no special basis adjustment under Section 743(b). See Reg. § 1.708–1(c)(5), Ex. 5; REG–111119–99, 2000–1 C.B. 455, 457; T.D. 8925, 2001–1 C.B. 496, 498–99.

Suppose that the exiting partners of the terminating partnership sell 50 percent or more of the total interests in the terminating partnership under this buy-out rule. In that case, because the regulations treat the buy-out as occurring immediately before the merger, a partnership termination under Section 708(b)(1)(B) will be treated as occurring immediately before the merger. See T.D. 8925, 2001–1 C.B. 496, 499.

[¶ 24,075]

2. DIVISIONS

General rule. Under Section 708(b)(2)(B), when a partnership divides into two or more partnerships, any resulting partnership or partnerships are treated as a continuation of the prior partnership if the members of the resulting partnership had an interest of more than 50 percent in the capital and profits of the prior partnership. In 2001, the Treasury and the IRS issued final regulations on the federal income tax consequences of partnership divisions. Under those regulations, any other resulting partnership not meeting the foregoing test is not treated as a continuation of the prior partnership and is instead treated as a new partnership. If the members of none of the resulting partnerships owned a more than 50 percent interest in the prior partnership, none of the resulting partnerships is treated as a continuation of the prior partnership. In such a case, each resulting partnership is treated as a new partnership, and the prior partnership is treated as terminated. The partnership interest of any member of the prior partnership who does not become a member of any of the resulting partnerships is treated as having been liquidated as of the date of the division. Reg. § 1.708–1(d)(1).

Example. Partnership LMNO is in the manufacturing and real estate businesses. L owns a 40–percent interest and M, N, and O each own a 20–percent interest in partnership capital and profits. On September 1 of the current year, the partners decide to separate the manufacturing and real estate businesses into two separate partnerships. Partnership LM obtains the manufacturing business and partnership NO obtains the real estate business. Because the partners of the resulting partnership LM owned more than 50 percent of the capital and profits of partnership LMNO (i.e., L owned a 40–percent interest and M owned a 20–percent interest), partnership LM is treated as a continuation of partnership LMNO. Because the partners of partnership NO did not own more than 50 percent of the capital and profits of partnership LMNO, partnership NO is not treated as a continuation of partnership LMNO. Instead, NO is treated as a new partnership formed at the start of the day on September 2 of the current year. See Reg. § 1.708–1(d)(5), Ex. 1.

¶ 24,070

Definition of "divided partnership"; effect of division on partnership elections. For purposes of these regulation provisions, the divided partnership is the continuing partnership that is treated for federal income tax purposes as transferring the assets and liabilities to the recipient partnerships, either directly under the assets-over form or indirectly under the assets-up form. If the resulting partnership that in form transferred its assets and liabilities with the division is a continuation of the prior partnership, then the regulations treat that resulting partnership as the divided partnership. If a partnership divides into two or more partnerships and only one of these partnerships is a continuation of the prior partnership because only that partnership has partners who owned more than a 50 percent interest in the capital and profits of the prior partnership, then that partnership is treated as the divided partnership. If more than one resulting partnership would be treated as a continuation of the prior partnership, the regulations treat the continuing resulting partnership with the assets having the greatest fair market value (net of liabilities) as the divided partnership. Reg. § 1.708–1(d)(4)(i).

All resulting partnerships that are treated under these regulations as continuing are bound by the prior partnership's preexisting elections. However, any elections made by a resulting partnership after the division do not bind the other resulting partnerships. Reg. § 1.708–1(d)(2)(ii).

Recognized forms of partnership division under the regulations. The regulations recognize two forms of partnership division for federal income tax purposes: the assets-over form and the assets-up form. In the assets-over form of partnership division, the divided partnership transfers certain assets and liabilities to a recipient partnership in exchange for interests in the recipient partnership. Then immediately thereafter the divided partnership distributes the interests in the recipient partnership to some or all of its partners in liquidation of their partnership interests in the divided partnership. Reg. § 1.708–1(d)(3)(i)(A). If none of the resulting partnerships is treated as a continuation of the prior partnership, the regulations treat the prior partnership as transferring all of its assets and liabilities to new resulting partnerships in exchange for interests in the resulting partnerships. Then immediately thereafter the divided partnership liquidates by distributing the interests in the new resulting partnerships to the prior partnership's partners. Reg. § 1.708–1(d)(3)(i)(B).

In the assets-up form of partnership division, the divided partnership distributes certain of its assets and liabilities to some or all of its partners in liquidation of their interests in the divided partnership. Then immediately thereafter the partners contribute the assets and liabilities to a recipient partnership in exchange for interests in that recipient partnership. For this form of partnership division to be respected for federal income tax purposes, the partners receiving the distribution must be treated as the owners of the assets under the laws of the applicable jurisdiction, however transitory that ownership. For a particular transfer to a particular recipient partnership to be respected for tax purposes, the regulations require that all of the assets that are transferred from the divided partnership to the recipient partnership be distributed to, and then contributed by, the partners of the recipient partnership. Reg. § 1.708–1(d)(3)(ii)(A) and (d)(5), Ex. 2.

Under a default rule in the regulations, a division that does not follow a form for the division or that uses a form that does not clearly conform to the assets-up form of division described in the regulations is treated as an assets-over form of division for federal income tax purposes. See Reg. § 1.708–1(d)(3)(i) and (d)(5), Exs. 3 and 6.

Note that to constitute a partnership division under these regulations, at least two partners of the prior partnership must be members of each resulting partnership. Thus, the regulations would not treat as a partnership division a transaction in which a three-member partnership with two businesses distributes one of those businesses to a partner in liquidation of that partner's interest and the liquidated partner transfers the business to a new partnership with another party. See T.D. 8925, 2001–1 C.B. 496, 499.

Anti-abuse rule. The regulations authorize the IRS to recharacterize transactions that are structured to follow the assets-up or assets-over forms of partnership division but that are in substance part of a larger series of transactions that are inconsistent with those forms. In such cases, the IRS can disregard the form of the division and recast the transactions in line with their substance. Reg. § 1.708–1(d)(6).

[¶ 24,077]

3. APPLICATION OF MIXING BOWL RULES TO PARTNERSHIP MERGERS

As mentioned above, one issue that arises in partnership mergers and divisions is how the mixing bowl rules in Sections 704(c)(1)(B) and 737 should apply following such merger or division transactions. The following ruling, Rev. Rul. 2004–43, provides the IRS view on this issue in the context of a partnership merger effected in the assets-over form of merger transaction. Although the IRS revoked this ruling in Rev. Rul. 2005–10, it indicated that the Treasury and the IRS would issue regulations "implementing the principles" enunciated in Rev. Rul. 2004–43. See Rev. Rul. 2005–10, 2005–1 C.B. 492; IRS Notice 2005–15, 2005–1 C.B. 527.

[¶ 24,078]

REVENUE RULING 2004–43

2004–1 C.B. 842, revoked by Rev. Rul. 2005–10, 2005–1 C.B. 492.

ISSUES

1) Does § 704(c)(1)(B)* * * apply to § 704(c) gain or loss that is created in an assets-over partnership merger?

2) For purposes of § 737(b), does net precontribution gain include § 704(c) gain or loss that is created in an assets-over partnership merger?

FACTS

Situation 1. On January 1, 2004, *A* contributes Asset 1, with a basis of $200x and a fair market value of $300x to partnership *AB* in exchange for a 50 percent interest. On the same date, *B* contributes $300x of cash to *AB* in exchange for a 50 percent interest. Also on January 1, 2004, *C* contributes Asset 2, with a basis of $100x and a fair market value of $200x to partnership *CD* in exchange for a 50 percent interest. *D* contributes $200x of cash to *CD* in exchange for a 50 percent interest.

On January 1, 2006, *AB* and *CD* undertake an assets-over partnership merger in which *AB* is the continuing partnership and *CD* is the terminating partnership. At the time of the merger, *AB*'s only assets are Asset 1, with a fair market value of $900x, and $300x in cash, and *CD*'s only assets are Asset 2, with a fair market value of $600x and $200x in cash. After the merger, the partners have capital and profits interests in *AB* as follows: *A*, 30 percent; *B*, 30 percent; *C*, 20 percent; and *D*, 20 percent.

The partnership agreements for *AB* and *CD* provide that the partners' capital accounts will be determined and maintained in accordance with § 1.704–1(b)(2)(iv) of the * * * Regulations, distributions in liquidation of the partnership (or any partner's interest) will be made in accordance with the partners' positive capital account balances, and any partner with a deficit balance in the partner's capital account following the liquidation of the partner's interest must restore that deficit to the partnership (as set forth in § 1.704–1(b)(2)(ii)(b)(2) and (3)). *AB* and *CD* both have provisions in their partnership agreements requiring the revaluation of partnership property upon the entry of a new partner. *AB* would not be treated as an investment company (within the meaning of § 351) if it were incorporated. Neither partnership holds any unrealized receivables or inventory for purposes of § 751. *AB* and *CD* do not have a § 754 election in place. Asset 1 and Asset 2 are nondepreciable capital assets.

On January 1, 2012, *AB* has the same assets that it had after the merger. Each asset has the same value that it had at the time of the merger. On this date, *AB* distributes Asset 2 to *A* in liquidation of *A*'s interest in *AB*.

Situation 2. The facts are the same as in Situation 1, except that on January 1, 2012, Asset 1 has a value of $275x$, and *AB* distributes Asset 1 to *C* in liquidation of *C*'s interest in *AB*.

Law

Under § 704(b) and the regulations thereunder, allocations of a partnership's items of income, gain, loss, deduction, or credit provided for in the partnership agreement will be respected if the allocations have substantial economic effect. Allocations that fail to have substantial economic effect will be reallocated according to the partners' interests in the partnership.

Section 1.704–1(b)(2)(iv)(*f*) provides that a partnership may, upon the occurrence of certain events (including the contribution of money to the partnership by a new or existing partner), increase or decrease the partners' capital accounts to reflect a revaluation of the partnership property.

Section 1.704–1(b)(2)(iv)(*g*) provides that, to the extent a partnership's property is reflected on the books of the partnership at a book value that differs from the adjusted tax basis, the substantial economic effect requirements apply to the allocations of book items. Section 704(c) and § 1.704–1(b)(4)(i) govern the partners' distributive shares of tax items.

Section 1.704–1(b)(4)(i) provides that if partnership property is, under § 1.704–1(b)(2)(iv)(*f*), properly reflected in the capital accounts of the partners and on the books of the partnership at a book value that differs from the adjusted tax basis of the property, then depreciation, depletion, amortization, and gain or loss, as computed for book purposes, with respect to the property will be greater or less than the depreciation, depletion, amortization, and gain or loss, as computed for federal tax purposes, with respect to the property. In these cases the capital accounts of the partners are required to be adjusted solely for allocations of the book items to the partners (see § 1.704–1(b)(2)(iv)(*g*)), and the partners' shares of the corresponding tax items are not independently reflected by further adjustments to the partners' capital accounts. Thus, separate allocations of these tax items cannot have economic effect under § 1.704–1(b)(2)(ii)(*b*)(*1*), and the partners' distributive shares of tax items must (unless governed by § 704(c)) be determined in accordance with the partners' interests in the partnership. These tax items must be shared among the partners in a manner that takes account of the variation between the adjusted tax basis of the property and its book value in the same manner as variations between the adjusted tax basis and fair market value of property contributed to the partnership are taken into account in determining the partners' shares of tax items under § 704(c).

Section 704(c)(1)(A) provides that income, gain, loss, and deduction with respect to property contributed to the partnership by a partner shall be shared among the partners so as to take account of the variation between the basis of the property to the partnership and its fair market value at the time of contribution.

Section 1.704–3(a)(2) provides that, except as provided in § 1.704–3(e)(2) and (3), § 704(c) and § 1.704–3 apply on a property-by-property basis.

Section 1.704–3(a)(3)(i) provides that property contributed to a partnership is § 704(c) property if at the time of contribution its book value differs from the contributing partner's adjusted tax basis. For purposes of § 1.704–3, book value is determined as contemplated by § 1.704–1(b). Therefore, book value is equal to fair market value at the time of contribution and is subsequently adjusted for cost recovery and other events that affect the basis of the property.

Section 1.704–3(a)(3)(ii) provides that the built-in gain on § 704(c) property is the excess of the property's book value over the contributing partner's adjusted tax basis upon contribution. The built-in gain is thereafter reduced by decreases in the difference between the property's book value and adjusted tax basis.

Section 1.704–3(a)(6) provides that the principles of § 1.704–3 also apply to "reverse § 704(c) allocations" which result from revaluations of partnership property pursuant to § 1.704–1(b)(2)(iv)(*f*).

Section 1.704–3(a)(7) provides that, if a contributing partner transfers a partnership interest, built-in gain or loss must be allocated to the transferee partner as it would have been allocated to the transferor partner. If the contributing partner transfers a portion of the partnership interest, the share of built-in gain or loss proportionate to the interest transferred must be allocated to the transferee partner. [However, under Section 704(c)(1)(C), added to the Code in late 2004 after this revenue ruling was issued, built-in loss may be allocated only to the contributing partner and not to any other partner, including a transferee of the contributing partner's partnership interest.]

Section 704(c)(1)(B) provides that if any property contributed to the partnership by a partner is distributed (directly or indirectly) by the partnership (other than to the contributing partner) within seven years of being contributed: (i) the contributing partner shall be treated as recognizing gain or loss (as the case may be) from the sale of the property in an amount equal to the gain or loss which would have been allocated to the partner under § 704(c)(1)(A) by reason of the variation described in § 704(c)(1)(A) if the property had been sold at its fair market value at the time of the distribution; (ii) the character of the gain or loss shall be determined by reference to the character of the gain or loss which would have resulted if the property had been sold by the partnership to the distributee; and (iii) appropriate adjustments shall be made to the adjusted basis of the contributing partner's interest in the partnership and to the adjusted basis of the property distributed to reflect any gain or loss recognized under § 704(c)(1)(B).

Section 1.704–4(c)(4) provides that § 704(c)(1)(B) and § 1.704–4 do not apply to a transfer by a partnership (transferor partnership) of all of its assets and liabilities to a second partnership (transferee partnership) in an exchange described in § 721, followed by a distribution of the interest in the transferee partnership in liquidation of the transferor partnership as part of the same plan or arrangement. Section 1.704–4(c)(4) also provides that a subsequent distribution of § 704(c) property by the transferee partnership to a partner of the transferee partnership is subject to § 704(c)(1)(B) to the same extent that a distribution by the transferor partnership would have been subject to § 704(c)(1)(B).

Section 1.704–4(d)(2) provides that the transferee of all or a portion of the partnership interest of a contributing partner is treated as the contributing partner for purposes of § 704(c)(1)(B) and § 1.704–4 to the extent of the share of built-in gain or loss allocated to the transferee partner.

Section 708(a) provides that, for purposes of subchapter K, an existing partnership shall be considered as continuing if it is not terminated.

Section 708(b)(2)(A) provides that in the case of the merger or consolidation of two or more partnerships, the resulting partnership shall, for purposes of § 708, be considered the continuation of any merging or consolidating partnership whose members own an interest of more than 50 percent in the capital and profits of the resulting partnership.

Section 1.708–1(c)(3)(i) provides that when two or more partnerships merge or consolidate into one partnership under the applicable jurisdictional law without undertaking a form for the merger or consolidation, or undertake a form for the merger or consolidation that is not described in § 1.708–1(c)(3)(ii), any merged or consolidated partnership that is considered terminated under § 1.708–1(c)(1) is treated as undertaking the assets-over form for federal income tax purposes. Under the assets-over form, the merged or consolidated partnership that is considered terminated under § 1.708–1(c)(1) contributes all of its assets and liabilities to the resulting partnership in exchange for an interest in the resulting partnership, and immediately thereafter, the terminated partnership distributes interests in the resulting partnership to its partners in liquidation of the terminated partnership.

Section 737(a) provides that, in the case of any distribution by a partnership to a partner, the partner shall be treated as recognizing gain in an amount equal to the lesser of (1) the excess (if any) of (A) the fair market value of property (other than money) received in the distribution over (B) the adjusted basis of the partner's interest in the partnership immediately before the distribution reduced (but not below zero) by the amount of money received in the distribution, or (2) the net precontribution gain of the partner. Gain recognized under the preceding sentence shall be in addition to any gain recognized under § 731. The character of the gain shall be determined by reference to the proportionate character of the net precontribution gain.

Section 737(b) provides that for purposes of § 737, the term "net precontribution gain" means the net gain (if any) which would have been recognized by the distributee partner under § 704(c)(1)(B) if all property which (1) had been contributed to the partnership by the distributee partner within seven years of the distribution, and (2) is held by the partnership immediately before the distribution, had been distributed by the partnership to another partner.

Section 1.737–1(c)(1) provides that the distributee partner's net precontribution gain is the net gain (if any) that would have been recognized by the distributee partner under § 704(c)(1)(B) and § 1.704–4 if all property that had been contributed to the partnership by the distributee partner within seven years of the distribution and is held by the partnership immediately before the distribution had been distributed by the partnership to another partner other than a partner who owns, directly or indirectly, more than 50 percent of the capital or profits interest in the partnership.

Section 1.737–1(c)(2)(iii) provides that the transferee of all or a portion of a contributing partner's partnership interest succeeds to the transferor's net precontribution gain, if any, in an amount proportionate to the interest transferred.

Section 1.737–2(b)(1) provides that § 737 and § 1.737–2 do not apply to a transfer by a partnership (transferor partnership) of all of its assets and liabilities to a second partnership (transferee partnership) in an exchange described in § 721, followed by a distribution of the interest in the transferee partnership in liquidation of the transferor partnership as part of the same plan or arrangement.

Section 1.737–2(b)(3) provides that a subsequent distribution of property by the transferee partnership to a partner of the transferee partnership that was formerly a partner of the transferor partnership is subject to § 737 to the same extent that a distribution from the transferor partnership would have been subject to § 737.

ANALYSIS

Section 1.704–4(c)(4) describes the effect of an assets-over partnership merger on pre-existing § 704(c) gain or loss for purposes of § 704(c)(1)(B). Under § 1.704–4(c)(4), if the transferor partnership in an assets-over merger holds contributed property with § 704(c) gain or loss, the seven year period in § 704(c)(1)(B) does not restart with respect to that gain or loss as a result of the merger. Section 1.704–4(c)(4) does not prevent the creation of new § 704(c) gain or loss when assets are contributed by one partnership to another partnership in an assets-over merger. Section 704(c)(1)(B) applies to this newly created § 704(c) gain or loss if the assets contributed in the merger are distributed to a partner other than the contributing partner (or its successor) within seven years of the merger.

Section 1.737–2(b)(1) and (3) describes the effect of an assets-over partnership merger on net precontribution gain that includes pre-existing § 704(c) gain or loss. Under § 1.737–2(b)(3), if the transferor partnership in an assets-over merger holds contributed property with § 704(c) gain or loss, the seven year period in § 737(b) does not restart with respect to that gain or loss as a result of the merger. Section 1.737–2(b)(3) does not prevent the creation of new § 704(c) gain or loss when assets are contributed by one partnership to another partnership in an assets-over merger. This gain or loss must be considered in determining the amount of net precontribution gain for purposes of § 737 if the continuing partnership distributes other property to the contributing partner (or its successor) within seven years of the merger.

Section 1.704–3(a)(6)(i) provides that the principles of § 1.704–3 apply to reverse § 704(c) allocations. In contrast, the regulations under § 704(c)(1)(B) and § 737 contain no similar rule requiring that the principles of § 704(c)(1)(B) and § 737 apply to reverse § 704(c) allocations. Under those regulations, § 704(c)(1)(B) and § 737 do not apply to reverse § 704(c) allocations.

In both of the situations described above, on the date of the partnership merger, CD contributes cash and Asset 2 to AB in exchange for an interest in AB. Immediately thereafter, CD distributes, in liquidation, interests in AB to C and D. Asset 2 has a basis of $100x$ and a fair market value of $600x$ upon contribution. Of the $500x$ of built in gain in Asset 2, $100x$ is pre-existing § 704(c) gain attributable to C's contribution of Asset 2 to CD, and $400x$ is additional § 704(c) gain created as a result of the merger. As the transferees of CD's partnership interest in AB, C and D each succeed to one-half of CD's $400x$ of § 704(c) gain in Asset 2 (each $200x$). Section 1.704–3(a)(7). Thus, C's share of § 704(c) gain is $300x$, and D's share of § 704(c) gain is $200x$.

The entry of CD as a new partner of AB causes partnership AB to revalue its property. When CD enters as a new partner of AB, Asset 1 has a basis of $200x$ and a fair market value of $900x$. Of the $700x$ of built-in gain in Asset 1, $100x$ is pre-existing § 704(c) gain attributable to the contribution of Asset 1 by A. The revaluation results in the creation of $600x$ of reverse § 704(c) gain in Asset 1. This layer of reverse § 704(c) gain is shared equally by A and B ($300x$ each). Thus,

¶ 24,078

A's share of § 704(c) gain is $400*x*, and *B*'s share of § 704(c) gain is $300*x*. The calculation of § 704(c) gain in each asset is summarized in the following table.

	Adjusted Tax Basis	Value on Date of Contribution	§ 704(c) Gain on Date of Contribution	Value on Date of Merger	§ 704(c) Gain Created by Merger	Total § 704(c) Gain After Merger
Asset 1	$200*x*	$300*x*	$100*x*	$900*x*	$600*x*	$700*x*
Asset 2	$100*x*	$200*x*	$100*x*	$600*x*	$400*x*	$500*x*
Cash	$500*x*	$500*x*	$0*x*	$500*x*	$0*x*	$0*x*
Total	$800*x*	$1,000*x*	$200*x*	$2,000*x*	$1,000*x*	$1,200*x*

The partners' share of § 704(c) gain in each of *AB*'s assets after the merger is summarized in the following table.

	A's Share of § 704(c) Gain	B's Share of § 704(c) Gain	C's Share of § 704(c) Gain	D's Share of § 704(c) Gain	Total § 704(c) Gain
Asset 1	$400*x*	$300*x*	$0*x*	$0*x*	$700*x*
Asset 2	$0*x*	$0*x*	$300*x*	$200*x*	$500*x*
Cash	$0*x*	$0*x*	$0*x*	$0*x*	$0*x*
Total	$400*x*	$300*x*	$300*x*	$200*x*	$1,200*x*

In *Situation 1*, the distribution of Asset 2 to *A* occurs more than seven years after the contribution of Asset 2 to *CD*. Therefore, § 704(c)(1)(B) does not apply to the $100*x* of pre-existing § 704(c) gain attributable to that contribution. However, the distribution of Asset 2 to *A* occurs within seven years of the contribution of Asset 2 by *CD* to *AB*. The contribution of Asset 2 by *CD* to *AB* creates § 704(c) gain of $400*x*. As the transferees of *CD*'s partnership interest in *AB*, *C* and *D* each succeed to one-half of the $400*x* of § 704(c) gain created by the merger. Section 1.704–3(a)(7). Section 704(c)(1)(B) applies to that § 704(c) gain, causing *C* and *D* each to recognize $200*x* of gain.

The distribution of Asset 2 to *A* occurs more than seven years after the contribution of Asset 1 to *AB*, and A made no subsequent contributions to *AB*. Therefore, *A*'s net precontribution gain for purposes of § 737(b) at the time of the distribution is zero. *AB*'s $600*x* of reverse § 704(c) gain in Asset 1, resulting from a revaluation of *AB*'s partnership property at the time of the merger, is not net precontribution gain. Accordingly, *A* will not recognize gain under § 737 as a result of the distribution of Asset 2.

In *Situation 2*, § 704(c)(1)(B) does not apply to the distribution by the continuing partnership of Asset 1 to *C* on January 1, 2012. The distribution of Asset 1 to *C* occurs more than seven years after the contribution of Asset 1 to *AB*, and § 704(c)(1)(B) does not apply to the reverse § 704(c) gain in Asset 1 resulting from a revaluation of *AB*'s partnership property at the time of the merger. Accordingly, neither *A* nor B will recognize gain under § 704(c)(1)(B) as a result of the distribution of Asset 1 to C.

The distribution of Asset 1 to C occurs more than seven years after the contribution of Asset 2 to CD. Therefore, C's net precontribution gain at the time of the distribution does not include C's \$100x of preexisting § 704(c) gain attributable to that contribution. However, the distribution of Asset 1 to C occurs within seven years of the contribution of Asset 2 by CD to AB. The contribution of Asset 2 by CD to AB creates net precontribution gain of \$400x. As the transferees of CD's partnership interest in AB, C and D each succeed to one-half of CD's \$400x of net precontribution gain in Asset 2. Section 1.737–1(c)(2)(iii). Thus, C's portion of CD's net precontribution gain created by the merger is \$200x. The excess of Asset 1's fair market value, \$275x, over the adjusted tax basis of C's interest in AB immediately before the distribution, \$100x, is \$175x, which is less than C's \$200x of net precontribution gain. Therefore, C will recognize \$175x of capital gain under § 737 as a result of the distribution. Because no property is distributed to D and none of the property treated as contributed by D is distributed to another partner, D recognizes no gain under § 737 or § 704(c)(1)(B).

HOLDINGS

1) Section 704(c)(1)(B) applies to newly created § 704(c) gain or loss in property contributed by the transferor partnership to the continuing partnership in an assets-over partnership merger, but does not apply to newly created reverse § 704(c) gain or loss resulting from a revaluation of property in the continuing partnership.

2) For purposes of § 737(b), net precontribution gain includes newly created § 704(c) gain or loss in property contributed by the transferor partnership to the continuing partnership in an assets-over partnership merger, but does not include newly created reverse § 704(c) gain or loss resulting from a revaluation of property in the continuing partnership.

* * *

[¶ 24,080]

D. CONVERSIONS OF PARTNERSHIP INTERESTS

In the following rulings, the IRS analyzes the federal income tax consequences of converting a general partnership into a limited partnership and of converting an interest in a domestic partnership into an interest in a domestic LLC or vice versa.

[¶ 24,085]

REVENUE RULING 84–52

1984–1 C.B. 157.

ISSUE

What are the federal income tax consequences of the conversion of a general partnership interest into a limited partnership interest in the same partnership?

FACTS

In 1975, X was formed as a general partnership under the Uniform Partnership Act of state M. X is engaged in the business of farming. The partners of X are A, B, C, and D. The partners have equal interest[s] in the partnership.

The partners propose to amend the partnership agreement to convert the general partnership into a limited partnership under the Uniform Limited Partnership Act of State M, a statute that corresponds in all material respects to the Uniform Limited Partnership Act. Under the certificate of limited partnership, A and B will be limited partners, and both C and D will be general partners and limited partners. Each partner's total percent[age] interest in the partnership's profits, losses, and capital will remain the same when the general partnership is converted into a limited partnership. The business of the general partnership will continue to be carried on after the conversion.

LAW AND ANALYSIS

Section 741 * * * provides that in the case of a sale or exchange of an interest in a partnership, gain or loss shall be recognized by the transferor partner.

Under section 1001 * * *, if there is a sale or other disposition of property, the entire amount of the gain or loss realized thereunder will be recognized, unless another section of subtitle A provides for nonrecognition.

Under section 721 * * *, no gain or loss is recognized by a partnership or any of its partners upon the contribution of property to the partnership in exchange for an interest therein.

Section 708 * * * provides that a partnership is considered to be continuing if it is not terminated. A partnership is terminated if (1) no part of any business, financial operation, or venture of the partnership continues to be carried on by any of its partners in a partnership, or (2) within a 12–month period there is a sale or exchange of 50 percent or more of the total interest in partnership capital and profits.

¶ 24,085

Section 1.708–1(b)(1)(ii) of the * * * Regulations provides that a contribution of property to a partnership does not constitute a sale or exchange for purposes of section 708 * * *.

Section 722 * * * generally provides that the basis of an interest in a partnership acquired by a contribution of property equals the transferor partner's adjusted basis in the contributed property.

Section 1223(1) * * * provides that the holding period of property received in exchange for other property includes the holding period of the property exchanged, if the property received has the same basis (in whole or in part) as the property exchanged.

Under section 731 * * *, if a partnership distributes money to a partner, then that partner will generally recognize gain only to the extent that the amount of money distributed (or deemed distributed) exceeds the adjusted basis of the partner's interest in the partnership immediately before the distribution.

Under section 733 * * *, if there is a distribution by a partnership to a partner and if there is no liquidation of that partner's interest, then the adjusted basis of that partner's interest in the partnership must be reduced (but not below zero) by the amount of money distributed to the partner.

Section 752(a) * * * states, in part, that any increase in a partner's share of the partnership's liabilities is considered to be a contribution of money by the partner to the partnership.

Section 752(b) * * * states in part, that any decrease in a partner's share of a partnership's liabilities is considered to be a distribution of money by the partnership to the partner.

Section 1.752–1(e) of the regulations provides rules for determining a partner's share of partnership liabilities with respect to both limited partnerships and general partnerships.

Under the facts of this revenue ruling, A, B, C, and D, will remain partners in X after X is converted to a limited partnership. Although the partners have exchanged their interests in the general partnership X for interests in the limited partnership X, under section 721 * * *, gain or loss will not be recognized by any of the partners of X except as provided in section 731 * * *.

HOLDINGS

(1) Except as provided below, pursuant to section 721 * * *, no gain or loss will be recognized by A, B, C, or D under section 741 or section 1001 * * * as a result of the conversion of a general partnership interest in X into a limited partnership in X.

(2) Because the business of X will continue after the conversion and because, under section 1.708–1(b)(1)(ii) of the regulations, a transaction

¶ 24,085

governed by section 721 * * * is not treated as a sale or exchange for purposes of section 708 * * *, X will not be terminated under section 708 * * *.

(3) If, as a result of the conversion, there is no change in the partners' shares of X's liabilities under section 1.752-1(e) of the regulations, there will be no change to the adjusted basis of any partner's interest in X, and C and D will each have a single adjusted basis with respect to each partner's interest in X (both as limited partner and general partner) equal to the adjusted basis of each partner's respective general partner interest in X prior to the conversion. *See* Rev. Rul. 84–53, [1984–1 C.B. 159].

(4) If, as a result of the conversion, there is a change in the partners' shares of X's liabilities under section 1.752-1(e) of the regulations, and such change causes a deemed contribution of money to X by a partner under section 752(a) * * *, then the adjusted basis of that partner's interest shall, under section 722 * * *, be increased by the amount of such deemed contribution. If the change in the partners' shares of X's liabilities causes a deemed distribution of money by X to a partner under section 752(b) * * *, then the basis of that partner's interest shall, under section 733 * * *, be reduced (but not below zero) by the amount of such deemed distribution, and gain will be recognized by that partner under section 731 * * * to the extent the deemed distribution exceeds the adjusted basis of that partner's interest in X.

(5) Pursuant to section 1223(1) * * *, there will be no change to the holding period of any partner's total interest in X.

The holdings contained herein would apply with equal force if the conversion had been of a limited partnership to a general partnership.

[¶ 24,090]

REVENUE RULING 95–37

1995–1 C.B. 130.

ISSUES

(1) Do the federal income tax consequences described in Rev. Rul. 84–52, 1984–1 C.B. 157, apply to the conversion of an interest in a domestic partnership into an interest in a domestic limited liability company (LLC) that is classified as a partnership for federal tax purposes?

(2) Does the taxable year of the converting domestic partnership close with respect to all the partners or with respect to any partner?

(3) Does the resulting domestic LLC need to obtain a new taxpayer identification number?

Law and Analysis

In Rev. Rul. 84–52, a general partnership formed under the Uniform Partnership Act of State *M* proposed to convert to a limited partnership under the Uniform Limited Partnership Act of State *M*. Rev. Rul. 84–52 generally holds that (1) under § 721 * * *, the conversion will not cause the partners to recognize gain or loss under §§ 741 or 1001, (2) unless its business will not continue after the conversion, the partnership will not terminate under § 708 because the conversion is not treated as a sale or exchange for purposes of § 708, (3) if the partners' shares of partnership liabilities do not change, there will be no change in the adjusted basis of any partner's interest in the partnership, (4) if the partners' shares of partnership liabilities change and cause a deemed contribution of money to the partnership by a partner under § 752(a), then the adjusted basis of such a partner's interest will be increased under § 722 by the amount of the deemed contribution, (5) if the partners' shares of partnership liabilities change and cause a deemed distribution of money by the partnership to a partner under § 752(b), then the basis of such a partner's interest will be reduced under § 733 (but not below zero) by the amount of the deemed distribution, and gain will be recognized by the partner under § 731 to the extent the deemed distribution exceeds the adjusted basis of the partner's interest in the partnership, and (6) under § 1223(1), there will be no change in the holding period of any partner's total interest in the partnership.

The conversion of an interest in a domestic partnership into an interest in a domestic LLC that is classified as a partnership for federal tax purposes is treated as a partnership-to-partnership conversion that is subject to the principles of Rev. Rul. 84–52.

Section 706(c)(1) provides that, except in the case of a termination of a partnership and except as provided in § 706(c)(2), the taxable year of a partnership does not close as the result of * * * the entry of a new partner, the liquidation of a partner's interest in the partnership, or the sale or exchange of a partner's interest in the partnership.

Section 706(c)(2)(A)(i) provides that the taxable year of a partnership closes with respect to a partner who sells or exchanges the partner's entire interest in a partnership. Section 706(c)(2)(A)(ii) provides that the taxable year of a partnership closes with respect to a partner whose interest is liquidated * * *.

In the present case, the conversion of an interest in a domestic partnership into an interest in a domestic LLC that is classified as a partnership for federal tax purposes does not cause a termination under § 708. *See* Rev. Rul. 84–52. Moreover, because each partner in a converting domestic partnership continues to hold an interest in the resulting domestic LLC, the conversion is not a sale, exchange, or liquidation of the converting partner's entire partnership interest for purposes of § 706(c)(2)(A). *See* Rev. Rul. 86–101, 1986–2 C.B. 94 (the taxable year of

¶ 24,090

a partnership does not close with respect to a general partner when the partnership agreement provides that the general partner's interest converts to a limited partnership interest on the general partner's death because the decedent's successor continues to hold an interest in the partnership). Consequently, the conversion does not cause the taxable year of the domestic partnership to close with respect to all the partners or with respect to any partner.

Because the conversion of an interest in a domestic partnership into an interest in a domestic LLC that is classified as a partnership for federal tax purposes does not cause a termination under § 708, the resulting domestic LLC does not need to obtain a new taxpayer identification number.

HOLDINGS

(1) The federal income tax consequences described in Rev. Rul. 84–52 apply to the conversion of an interest in a domestic partnership into an interest in a domestic LLC that is classified as a partnership for federal tax purposes. The federal tax consequences are the same whether the resulting LLC is formed in the same state or in a different state than the converting domestic partnership.

(2) The taxable year of the converting domestic partnership does not close with respect to all the partners or with respect to any partner.

(3) The resulting domestic LLC does not need to obtain a new taxpayer identification number.

The holdings contained herein would apply in a similar manner if the conversion had been of an interest in a domestic LLC that is classified as a partnership for federal tax purposes into an interest in a domestic partnership. The holdings contained herein apply regardless of the manner in which the conversion is achieved under state law.

This revenue ruling does not address the federal tax consequences of a conversion of an organization that is classified as a corporation into an organization that is classified as a partnership for federal tax purposes. *See, e.g.*, §§ 336 and 337.

* * *

[¶ 24,095]

Notes

1. By its terms, Rev. Rul. 95–37 does not apply to the conversion of an organization that is classified as a corporation into an organization that is classified as a partnership for federal tax purposes. Such a conversion would result in the liquidation of the corporation for tax purposes and would trigger application of the tax rules discussed in Chapter 8. Reg. § 301.7701–3(g)(1)(ii). The potential tax liability at the

¶ 24,095

entity level on the liquidation of the corporation serves as a significant tax deterrent to conversions of existing corporations into partnerships or LLCs.

2. In Rev. Rul. 95–55, 1995–2 C.B. 313, the IRS held that the registration of a New York general partnership as a registered limited liability partnership is treated as a partnership-to-partnership conversion that is subject to the principles of Rev. Rul. 84–52. Accordingly, such registration is not treated as a termination of the general partnership under Section 708.

Chapter 25

DEATH OF A PARTNER

[¶ 25,000]

A. INTRODUCTION

On the death of a partner, one of three things will occur. The estate or another successor to the deceased partner's interest may replace the decedent as a partner. In that event, the successor will be recognized as a new partner for income tax purposes. Alternatively, the interest of the deceased partner may be liquidated in one or more distributions, the taxation of which will be governed by Section 736. Finally, if the agreement among the partners so provides, the interest of the deceased partner may be sold as of the date of death to either new or existing partners. Not surprisingly, the income tax consequences of these three possibilities differ. Adding to those possibilities, the successor to the deceased partner's interest may sell or liquidate that interest.

[¶ 25,005]

B. EFFECT ON CURRENT YEAR'S INCOME

While the death of a partner will normally cause a technical dissolution of the partnership under state law, death alone does not cause a termination of the partnership for income tax purposes. See § 708. Nevertheless, under current law, the taxable year of a partnership closes with respect to a partner whose entire interest in a partnership terminates, whether that termination occurs "by reason of death, liquidation, or otherwise."[1] § 706(c)(2)(A). Thus, the partnership's income for the

---

1. Before the Taxpayer Relief Act of 1997, a partnership's taxable year generally did not close upon a partner's death. See Estate of Hesse v. Commissioner, 74 T.C. 1307 (1980). Thus, under prior law, the entire partnership income for the year of the partner's death was generally taxable to the estate or other successor in interest, even though the deceased partner may have made withdrawals against that income and used the proceeds for the benefit of others.

year of death must be apportioned between the decedent and the successor in interest under the varying interest rule of Section 706(d)(1), and the decedent's share of the partnership's income or loss for the year of death must be reported on the decedent's final tax return.

C. BASIS ADJUSTMENTS

[¶ 25,010]

1. FAIR MARKET VALUE BASIS

Under Section 1014, the tax basis of property acquired from a decedent, including a partnership interest, becomes its value at the date of the decedent's death, unless the property represents income in respect of a decedent.[2] The successor to the interest of the deceased partner will benefit from that basis adjustment regardless of whether the partnership interest is sold, liquidated, or retained by the successor. However, unless a Section 754 election is in effect, the successor in interest will not benefit from the outside basis adjustment extended by Section 1014 until the interest is sold or liquidated.

If the partnership does have a Section 754 election in effect and the interest is purchased by the other partners (or by a new investor) or the successor in interest to the deceased partner continues as a partner, the inside basis of the partnership properties also will be adjusted to reflect the adjustment of the outside basis under Sections 742 and 1014. § 743(b). Under a statutory change made in 2004, the partnership also will be required to make a downward adjustment to the inside basis of its assets if it has a "substantial built-in loss" (within the meaning of Section 743(d)) immediately after the transfer, even though it has no Section 754 election in effect. The partnership has a substantial built-in loss for this purpose if the adjusted bases of its assets exceed the fair market value of those assets by more than $250,000.

On the other hand, if the interest of the deceased partner is liquidated under Section 736 through cash distributions, Section 734 rather than Section 743 controls the inside basis adjustment. Unfortunately, Section 734 does not operate correctly when the outside basis has become unrelated to the inside basis, as occurs following a Section 1014 basis adjustment. As explained at ¶ 22,065, under Section 734(b)(1)(A), if the partnership has a Section 754 election in effect, the basis of partnership property is increased following a distribution of cash only by the amount of gain recognized to a distributee under Section 731(a)(1).

---

2. As a result of tax legislation enacted in 2001, the fair market value at date of death basis rules in Section 1014 will be repealed (see Section 1014(f)) and replaced with the modified carryover basis rules in Section 1022. As enacted, however, this change will not take effect until 2010, and is scheduled to sunset in 2011 (meaning that in 2011, the Section 1014 rules will again become the law), unless Congress extends or makes permanent the repeal of Section 1014.

¶ 25,005

When the distribution follows death, no gain will be recognized because the outside basis of the distributee will have been increased under Section 1014 and thus no adjustment to the partnership basis will occur.

If property, rather than cash, is distributed in the liquidation of the deceased partner's interest, this flaw in the structure of Section 734(b) can even result in a reduction of the inside basis of the partnership properties. Because of the high outside basis, the basis of the distributed property to the distributee normally will be increased under Section 732(b). When that occurs, under Section 734(b)(2)(B) the basis of the remaining partnership properties must be correspondingly decreased. This result occurs if the partnership has a Section 754 election in effect or, under a change made in 2004, if there is a substantial basis reduction. A substantial basis reduction for this purpose is a downward adjustment in excess of $250,000 that would be made to the inside basis of the partnership's assets if a Section 754 election were in effect. § 743(d)(1).

[¶ 25,015]

2. CARRYOVER BASIS: INCOME IN RESPECT OF A DECEDENT

Wholly aside from the taxation of partnerships, the basis adjustment under Section 1014 does not apply to items of income attributable to the decedent but not taxable before death—so-called items of income in respect of a decedent. §§ 1014(c) and 691. The exemption from tax extended by Section 1014 to the beneficiaries of the decedent does not extend to income earned by the decedent, or attributable to sales made by the decedent, but not subject to tax before the date of death because of the method of accounting employed by the decedent. Rather, the properties that embody those elements of income, such as accounts receivable and installment notes, do not obtain a fair market value basis and thus remain fully taxable to the estate or other successor in interest that receives the income. In principle, Section 691 should apply equally to income earned through a partnership. Unfortunately, the relationship between Section 691 and Subchapter K is not always that clear or logical.

If the death of a partner produces a liquidation of the partner's interest taxable under Section 736, a portion of the payments received by the successor to the deceased partner's interest will be treated as income in respect of a decedent. Under Section 753, the entire amount of the Section 736(a) payments must be so treated. Thus, even though goodwill would otherwise constitute property to which the Section 1014 basis adjustment would apply, payments for goodwill in a service partnership that are treated by the partners as Section 736(a) payments are treated as income in respect of a decedent. The entire amount of the Section 736(a) payments thus will be taxable to the recipient of the payments in the same manner as if the payments had been received by the decedent. By virtue of Section 753, the basis adjustment produced by Section 1014 is limited to the value at the date of the deceased partner's death of the partnership properties with respect to which Section 736(b) payments are made.

If the interest of the deceased partner is not liquidated, no provision of the Code directly addresses the application of Section 691. That matter, however, has been the subject of some litigation.

[¶ 25,020]

QUICK TRUST v. COMMISSIONER

United States Tax Court, 1970.
54 T.C. 1336 (acq.), aff'd per curiam, 444 F.2d 90 (8th Cir.1971).

TANNENWALD, JUDGE: * * *.

* * *

When Quick died he was an equal partner in a partnership which had been in the business of providing architectural and engineering services. In 1957, the partnership had ceased all business activity except the collection of outstanding accounts receivable. These receivables, and some cash, were the only assets of the partnership. Since partnership income was reported on the cash basis, the receivables had a zero basis.

Upon Quick's death in 1960, the estate became a partner with Maguolo and remained a partner until 1965 when it was succeeded as a partner by petitioner herein. The outstanding accounts receivable were substantial in amount at that time. In its 1960 return, the partnership elected under section 754 to make the adjustment in the basis of the partnership property provided for in section 743(b) and to allocate that adjustment in accordance with section 755. On the facts of this case, the net result of this adjustment was to increase the basis of the accounts receivable to the partnership from zero to an amount slightly less than one-half of their face value. If such treatment was correct, it substantially reduced the amount of the taxable income to the partnership from the collection of the accounts receivable under section 743(b) and the estate and the petitioner herein were entitled to the benefit of that reduction.

The issue before us is whether the foregoing adjustment to basis was correctly made. Its resolution depends upon the determination of the basis to the estate of its interest in the partnership, since section 743(b)(1) allows only an "increase [in] the adjusted basis of the partnership property by the excess of *the basis to the transferee partner of his interest in the partnership* over his proportionate share of the adjusted basis of the partnership property." (Emphasis added.) This in turn depends upon whether, to the extent that "the basis to the transferee partner" reflects an interest in underlying accounts receivable arising out of personal services of the deceased partner, such interest constitutes income in respect of a decedent under section 691(a)(1) and (3). In such event, section 1014(c) comes into play and prohibits equating the basis of Quick's partnership interest with the fair market value of that interest at the time of his death under section 1014(a).

Petitioner argues that the partnership provisions of the Internal Revenue Code of 1954 adopted the entity theory of a partnership, that the plain meaning of those provisions, insofar as they relate to the question of basis, requires the conclusion that the inherited partnership interest is separate and distinct from the underlying assets of the partnership, and that, therefore, section 691, and consequently section 1014(c), has no application herein.

Respondent counters with the assertion that the basis of a partnership interest is determined under section 742 by reference to other sections of the Code. He claims that, by virtue of section 1014(c), section 1014(a) does not apply to property which is classified as a right to receive income in respect of a decedent under section 691 and that the interest of the estate and of petitioner in the proceeds of the accounts receivable of the partnership falls within this classification. He emphasizes that, since the accounts receivable represent money earned by the performance of personal services, the collections thereon would have been taxable to the decedent, if the partnership had been on the accrual basis, or to the estate and to petitioner if the decedent had been a cash basis sole proprietor. Similarly, he points out that if the business had been conducted by a corporation, the collections on the accounts receivable would have been fully taxable, regardless of Quick's death. Respondent concludes that no different result should occur simply because a cash basis partnership is interposed.

The share of a general partner's successor in interest upon his death in the collections by a partnership on accounts receivable arising out of the rendition of personal services constituted income in respect of a decedent under the 1939 Code. *United States v. Ellis*, 264 F.2d 325 (C.A.2, 1959); *Riegelman's Estate v. Commissioner*, 253 F. 2d 315 (C.A.2, 1958), affirming 27 T.C. 833 (1957). Petitioner ignores these decisions, apparently on the ground that the enactment of comprehensive provisions dealing with the taxation of partnerships in the 1954 Code and what it asserts is "the plain meaning" of those provisions render such decisions inapplicable in the instant case. We disagree.

The partnership provisions of the 1954 Code are comprehensive in the sense that they are detailed. But this does not mean that they are exclusive, especially where those provisions themselves recognize the interplay with other provisions of the Code. Section 742 specifies: "The basis of an interest in a partnership acquired other than by contribution shall be determined under part II of subchapter O (sec. 1011 and following)." With the exception of section 722, which deals with the basis

¶ 25,020

of a contributing partner's interest and which has no applicability herein, this is the only section directed toward the question of the initial determination of the basis of a partnership interest. From the specification of section 742, one is thus led directly to section 1014 and by subsection (c) thereof directly to section 691. Since, insofar as this case is concerned, section 691 incorporates the provisions and legal underpinning of its predecessor (sec. 126 of the 1939 Code),[10] we are directed back to a recognition, under the 1954 Code, of the decisional effect of *United States v. Ellis, supra,* and *Riegelman's Estate v. Commissioner, supra.*

Thus, to the extent that a "plain meaning" can be distilled from the partnership provisions of the 1954 Code, we think that it is contrary to petitioner's position. In point of fact, however, we hesitate to rest our decision in an area such as is involved herein exclusively on such linguistic clarity and purity. See *David A. Foxman,* 41 T.C. 535, 551, n.9 (1964), affd. 352 F. 2d 466 (C.A.3, 1965). However, an examination of the legislative purpose reinforces our reading of the statute. Section 751, dealing with unrealized receivables and inventory items, is included in Subpart D of Subchapter K, and is labeled "Provisions Common to Other Subparts." Both the House and Senate committee reports specifically state that income rights relating to unrealized receivables or fees are regarded "as severable from the partnership interest and as subject to the same tax consequences which would be accorded an individual entrepreneur." See H. Rept. No. 1337, 83d Cong., 2d Sess., p. 71 (1954); S. Rept. No. 1622, 83d Cong., 2d Sess., p. 99 (1954). And the Senate committee report adds the following significant language.

> *The House bill provides that a decedent partner's share of unrealized receivables are* [sic] *to be treated as income in respect of a decedent.* Such rights to income are to be taxed to the estate or heirs when collected, with an appropriate adjustment for estate taxes. * * * *Your committee's bill agrees substantially with the House in the treatment described above* but also provides that other income apart from unrealized receivables is to be treated as income in respect of a decedent. [See S. Rept. No. 1622, *supra,* p. 99; emphasis added.]

In light of the foregoing, the deletion of a provision in section 743 of the House bill which specifically provided that the optional adjustment to basis of partnership property should not be made with respect to unrealized receivables is of little, if any, significance. H.R. 8300, 83d Cong., 2d Sess., sec. 743(e) (1954) (introduced print). The fact that such deletion was made without comment either in the Senate or Conference Committee reports indicates that the problem was covered by other sections and that such a provision was therefore unnecessary.[12] Similar-

---

10. According to the House committee report at the time the 1954 Code was enacted, section 1014(c) "makes explicit the rule of existing law." See H. Rept. No. 1337, 83d Cong., 2d Sess., p. A267 (1954).

12. Nor do we consider it significant that efforts have been made to clarify the

ly, the specific reference in section 753 to income in respect of a decedent cannot be given an exclusive characterization.[13] That section merely states that certain distributions in liquidation under section 736(a) shall be treated as income in respect of a decedent. It does not state that no other amounts can be so treated.

Many of the assertions of the parties have dealt with the superstructure of the partnership provisions—assertions based upon a technical and involuted analysis of those provisions dealing with various adjustments and the treatment to be accorded to distributions after the basis of the partnership has been determined. But, as we have previously indicated * * *, the question herein involves the foundation, not the superstructure, i.e., what is the basis of petitioner's partnership interest?

Petitioner asserts that a partnership interest is an "asset separate and apart from the individual assets of the partnership" and that the character of the accounts receivable disappears into the character of the partnership interest, with the result that such interest cannot, in whole or in part, represent a right to receive income in respect of a decedent. In making such an argument, petitioner has erroneously transmuted the so-called partnership "entity" approach into a rule of law which allegedly precludes fragmentation of a partnership interest. But it is clear that even the "entity" approach should not be inexorably applied under all circumstances. See H. Rept. No. 2543, 83d Cong., 2d Sess., p. 59 (1954). Similarly, the fact that a rule of nonfragmentation of a partnership interest (except to the extent that the statute otherwise expressly provides) may govern sales of such an interest to third parties * * * does not compel its application in all situations where such an interest is transferred. In short, a partnership interest is not, as petitioner suggests, a unitary res, incapable of further analysis.

A partnership interest is a property interest, and an intangible one at that. A property interest can often be appropriately viewed as a bundle of rights. Indeed, petitioner suggests this viewpoint by pointing out that the partnership interest herein is "merely a right to share in the profits and surplus of the Partnership." That partnership interest had value only insofar as it represented a right to receive the cash or other property of the partnership. Viewed as a bundle of rights, a major constituent element of that interest was the right to share in the proceeds of the accounts receivable as they were collected. This right was admittedly not the same as the right to collect the accounts receivable; only the partnership had the latter right. But it does not follow from this

situation involved herein. See reports of House Committee on Ways and Means and Senate Finance Committee to accompany H.R. 9662 (Trust and Partnership Income Tax Revision Act of 1960) (H. Rept. No. 1231, 86th Cong., 2d Sess., pp. 36, 99 (1960); S. Rept. No. 1616, 86th Cong., 2d Sess., p. 124 (1960)). Both reports specifi-

cally state that no inferences are to be drawn from the proposed action as to the proper treatment under existing law. H. Rept. No. 1231, *supra*, pp. 37 and 100; S. Rept. No. 1616, *supra*, pp. 124 and 126.

13. The cross-reference to sec. 753 in sec. 691(e) has no legal effect. Sec. 7806(a).

¶ 25,020

dichotomy that the right of the estate to share in the collections merged into the partnership interest. Nothing in the statute compels such a merger. Indeed, an analysis of the applicable statutory provisions points to the opposite conclusion.

Accordingly, we hold that section 691(a)(1) and (3) applies and that the right to share in the collections from the accounts receivable must be considered a right to receive income in respect of a decedent. Consequently, section 1014(c) also applies and the basis of the partnership interest must be reduced from the fair market value thereof at Quick's death. The measure of that reduction under section 1014 is the extent to which that value includes the fair market value of a one-half interest in the proceeds of the zero basis partnership accounts receivable. See sec. 1.742–1, Income Tax Regs. It follows that the optional adjustment to basis made by the partnership under section 743(b) must be modified accordingly and that respondent's determination as to the amount of additional income subject to the tax should be sustained. See Rev. Rul. 66–325, 1966–2 C.B. 249.

Petitioner would have us equate the absence of statutory language specifically dealing with the problem herein and purported inferences from tangential provisions with an intention on the part of Congress entirely to relieve from taxation an item that had previously been held subject to tax. We would normally be reluctant to find that Congress indirectly legislated so eccentrically. * * * In any event, as we have previously indicated, we think the enacted provisions prevent us from so doing herein.

* * *

[¶ 25,025]

WOODHALL v. COMMISSIONER

United States Court of Appeals, Ninth Circuit, 1972.
454 F.2d 226.

CHOY, CIRCUIT JUDGE:

W. Lyle Woodhall died on January 20, 1964, leaving Mrs. Woodhall as his sole heir and executrix. For 1964, Mrs. Woodhall filed a joint income tax return as surviving spouse. She also filed a fiduciary income tax return for the estate for part of 1964. For 1965, she filed an individual tax return and a fiduciary return.

The Commissioner of Internal Revenue determined deficiencies against Mrs. Woodhall for the years 1964 and 1965. The ground was that she had not declared as income certain amounts which came to her from the sale of her husband's interest in a partnership. Mrs. Woodhall petitioned the Tax Court for a declaration that she did not owe the deficiencies. The Tax Court upheld the Commissioner's determination and Mrs. Woodhall appeals. We affirm.

From January 1958 until his death, Woodhall was equal partner with his brother, Eldon Woodhall, in a lath and plaster contracting business known as Woodhall Brothers.

In December 1961, the brothers executed a written buy-sell agreement, which provided that "upon the death of either partner the partnership shall terminate and the survivor shall purchase the decedent's interest in the partnership." The price was to be determined according to a formula set out in the agreement. The formula defined accounts payable and included certain valuations for fixed assets, inventory, accounts receivable and other assets. It is the accounts receivable item that generates this controversy over Mrs. Woodhall's income for 1964 and 1965.

Because the partnership reported income on a cash basis, Woodhall had not paid taxes on his share of the accounts receivable which were outstanding at the time of his death. Mrs. Woodhall, in filing her tax returns as an individual and as executrix of her husband's estate, did not report as income the amounts allocated to the accounts receivable. Instead Mrs. Woodhall's tax returns stated that no gain had been realized by the sale of her husband's partnership interest because the tax basis of the interest was the fair market value at the time of death and this was the same as the sale price.

The issue presented is whether portions of payments received by Mrs. Woodhall, as executrix of the estate and as surviving spouse, constitute income in respect of a decedent under § 691(a)(1) * * * and are therefore subject to income taxes to the extent that such portions are allocable to unrealized receivables.

Generally, the sale of a partnership interest is an occasion for determining the character of gain or loss "to the transferor partner" as provided by § 741. In the case at bar, however, there was technically no "transferor partner" to accomplish the sale. The Woodhall Brothers partnership terminated automatically upon the death of Woodhall by operation of the buy-sell agreement, as well as under common law. Mrs. Woodhall, as executrix of the estate and as holder of a community property interest, was the transferor.

A tax regulation recognizes that § 741 applies when the sale of the partnership interest results in a termination of the partnership [Reg. § 1.741-1(b)]. The question arises whether a termination of the partnership by operation of a written agreement of the parties upon the death of one partner has the same effect.

The legislative history of § 741 explicitly deals with this question. The House report reads as follows:

"Transfer of an interest in a partnership (§§ 741–743, 751)

¶ **25,025**

(1) General rules.—Under present decisions the sale of a partnership interest is generally considered to be a sale of a capital asset, and any gain or loss realized is treated as capital gain or loss. It is not clear whether the sale of an interest whose value is attributable to uncollected rights to income gives rise to capital gain or ordinary income

* * *

(2) Unrealized receivables or fees * * * In order to prevent the conversion of potential ordinary income into capital gain by virtue of transfers of partnership interests, certain rules have been adopted * * * which will apply to *all* dispositions of partnership interests

* * *

A decedent partner's share of unrealized receivables and fees will be treated as income in respect of a decedent. Such rights to income will be taxed to the estate or heirs when collected * * *

* * *

The term 'unrealized receivables or fees' is used to apply to any rights to income which have not been included in gross income under the method of accounting employed by the partnership. The provision is applicable mainly to cash basis partnerships which have acquired a contractual or other legal right to income for goods or services." House Report No. 1337, to accompany H.R. 8300 (Pub. L. 591), 83rd Cong., 2d Sess., pp. 70–71 (1954) (emphasis added) * * *.

The Senate report is similar, with only technical amendments which do not alter the basic statement of purpose in the House report. Senate Report No. 1622, to accompany H.R. 8300 (Pub. L. 591), 83rd Cong., 2d Sess., p. 396 (1954).

Mrs. Woodhall's approach to the issue was much different. On the sale of her husband's partnership interest, she attempted to elect to establish the tax basis as the fair market value on the date of her husband's death. By this means, the sale price would be the same as the fair market value; there would be no gain and so no income to be taxed.

Mrs. Woodhall contends that the payments she received for the accounts receivable do not come within § 691(a), pertaining to income in respect of a decedent. § 691(f) [now § 691(e)], she points out, makes cross-reference to § 753, for application of § 691 to income in respect of a deceased partner. § 753, in turn, refers to § 736 which provides that payments by a partnership for a deceased partner's interest in unrealized receivables shall be considered income in respect of a decedent under § 691. Mrs. Woodhall argues that a payment by a surviving partner is distinct from a payment by a partnership. Thus, she would have us interpret § 753, in conjunction with § 736, exclusively. In effect, this means that no payment other than one by a partnership which

¶ 25,025

continues after one partner's death could constitute income in respect of a deceased partner. We reject this reading of the statutes.

The approach suggested by Mrs. Woodhall is not an appropriate characterization of the transfer of funds to her. Reading § 691 in the light of § 741, it is clear that Congress intended that the money Mrs. Woodhall received as an allocation from the unrealized accounts receivable be treated as income in respect of a decedent.

The Court of Appeals for the Eighth Circuit has just recently ruled that accounts receivable of a partnership shared in by a successor in interest of a deceased partner constituted income in respect of a decedent. *Quick's Trust v. Commissioner of Internal Revenue*, 444 F.2d 90 (8th Cir.1971.) The instant case is substantially the same.

We hold that the Commissioner rightly determined deficiencies against Mrs. Woodhall in the tax years 1964 and 1965.

In addition to this primary issue, Mrs. Woodhall contends that, if the receivables were taxable to her, then she should be allowed an offsetting deduction for her husband's share of the unpaid payables outstanding at the date of his death.

Mrs. Woodhall is not entitled to any deduction in respect of a decedent based on the accounts payable. Section 691(b)(1) permits deductions only "when paid." Eldon Woodhall, as the surviving partner, assumed all the partnership liabilities and, in fact, paid them. Since Mrs. Woodhall did not pay the liabilities, she cannot deduct them.

Affirmed.

[¶ 25,030]

Notes

1. The scope of Section 691 will differ depending on whether Sections 736 and 753 or the rule of *Quick Trust*, at ¶ 25,020, applies. For example, if a general partnership interest in a partnership in which capital is not a material income-producing factor is liquidated and the partnership agreement does not provide a payment for goodwill, the Section 736(a) payments for goodwill will be treated as income in respect of a decedent and thus will be fully taxable (but fully deductible by the partnership). However, if the partnership interest is sold or is retained by the successor in interest, the basis of the partnership interest will be increased under Section 1014 by the value of the deceased partner's interest in goodwill. That basis increase would eliminate any tax attributable to the goodwill on the receipt of the proceeds of a sale of the partnership interest. Is that difference in treatment desirable? What other differences might occur? In planning for the death of a partner, does this difference suggest that the interest should be sold or liquidated? Which approach would be most favorable to the estate? Which

approach would result in the lowest overall tax burden to all of the parties?

2. As the Tax Court held in *Quick Trust*, in the case where a partnership interest is transferred as a result of a partner's death, because the transferee's basis under Section 1014 does not include the fair market value of assets that represent income in respect of a decedent, the basis adjustment under Section 743(b) likewise does not reflect the value of those assets. Thus, Reg. § 1.755–1(b)(4)(i) provides that no part of the Section 743(b) adjustment is allocated to assets that represent income in respect of a decedent. Instead, the entire basis adjustment is allocated to the other assets owned by the partnership. See Reg. § 1.755–1(b)(4)(ii), Ex.

[¶ 25,035]

3. PROPERTY CONTRIBUTED BY THE DECEASED PARTNER WITH A BUILT–IN LOSS

Suppose that the decedent partner had contributed property to the partnership with a basis exceeding its fair market value at the time of contribution (i.e., property having a so-called built-in loss). Under a change made in 2004, Section 704(c)(1)(C) now provides that (1) the built-in loss may be taken into account only by the contributing partner and (2) the basis of the contributed property is treated as being equal to its fair market value at the time of contribution for purposes of determining the amount of items allocated to the other partners. Thus, when the decedent dies and the partnership interest passes to a successor, the built-in loss is eliminated and will be of no benefit to the successor or any of the other partners.

Index

References are to Paragraph Numbers

ACCUMULATED EARNINGS TAX
Business needs, 7070
Purpose to avoid tax, 7040
Unreasonable accumulations, 7055

ACQUISITIONS, TAXABLE
Asset acquisitions, 8085
    Allocation of purchase price, 8095
    Seller's consequences, 8085
In general, 8075–8080
Stock acquisitions, 8100
    Section 338 election, 8120–8123

AFFILIATED GROUP
See Consolidated Returns

ALLOCATION OF INCOME
Arms' length standard, 1130, 14,015
Common control, 14,045
Comparable uncontrolled price method, 14,020
Illegal income, 14,030
Intangible property, 14,025

ALTERNATIVE MINIMUM TAX
Alternative minimum taxable income
    Determination, 1030
Credit for prior year minimum tax liability, 1035
Description, 1025
Exemption for small corporations, 1045
Liability, 1025
    Credits against, 1040
Tentative minimum tax, 1025

AVOIDANCE OF TAX
Assignment of income, 2260–2265, 18,045–18,055, 18,220–18,245
Assumption of liabilities, 2170–2195, 2205–2245
Business purpose, 1071, 9055–9060, 16,085
Economic substance, 1073, 9065–9075, 16,085
Partnership anti-abuse rules, 16,085
Step transaction doctrine, 1071, 9065–9075, 16,085

BOOT TRANSACTIONS
Allocation, 2115–2120
Corporate organization, 2000, 2105–2110
General effect of boot, 2105–2110

BOOT TRANSACTIONS—Cont'd
Nonqualified preferred stock, 2025, 2040, 10,040, 10,205, 10,240, 11,025
Recognition
    Reorganizations, 10,240–10,320
    Timing, 2130

C CORPORATIONS
See Corporations

CAPITAL GAINS AND LOSSES
Generally, 1020, 18,030
Holding period
    Partnership interest, 17,008, 21,005
    S corporation interest,
Losses on debts and investments, 3100–3135
Original issue discount, 3085
Partnership, disposition of property contributed to partnership, characterization of, 18,155–18,160
Partnership, disposition of property distributed to partner, characterization of, 22,030–22,035
Partnership income and expense, characterization of, 18,020–18,025
    Electing large partnership, 18,250
Partnership interest, sale of, characterization, 21,005, 21,035–21,075, 21,092, 21,125
S corporation income and expense, characterization of, 15,225, 15,245
S corporation interest, sale of, characterization, 15,385–15,390

CARRYOVER AND CARRYBACK OF TAX ATTRIBUTES
Attribution rules, 13,045
Built-in gains and losses, 13,080
Consolidated return regulations, 13,115
    Sections 382 and 383 and consolidated groups, 13,120
    Separate return limitation (SRLY) rules, 13,125
    SRLY limitation on built-in losses, 13,130
Earnings and profits, 13,010
Net operating loss carryovers, 13,020
Limitations after worthless stock deduction, 13,105

CARRYOVER AND CARRYBACK OF TAX ATTRIBUTES—Cont'd
NOL Carrybacks
General rules, 13,135
Limitation following CERT, 13,140
Ongoing significance of Section 269, 13,110
Overview, 13,000
Section 381, 13,005
Section 382
Consolidated groups, 13,115
Effect of ownership change, 13,060
Rules to prevent avoidance of, 13,095
Stock, 13,050
Testing period, 13,055
Triggering event, 13,040
Section 383 restrictions, 13,085
Section 384 restrictions, 13,090
Value of stock of old loss corporation, 13,065

CHOICE OF ENTITY CONSIDERATIONS, 1055, 15,010–15,015, 16,060–16,065, 16,090

CLASSIFICATION OF ENTITIES, 1075–1090, 16,060–16,080
Check-the-box regulations, 1082–1087, 16,070–16,077

CONSOLIDATED RETURNS
Affiliated groups, defined, 1050, 14,055
Consolidated income and loss, 14,060
Excess loss accounts, 14,080
Generally, 1050, 14,050
Intercompany transactions, 14,065
Investment adjustments, 14,070
S corporations as members of affiliated group, 15,170

CORPORATE DIVISIONS
Active business, 12,010–12,025
Carryover of corporate attributes, 12,185–12,195
Combined with taxable acquisition, 12,090
Combined with tax free acquisition, 12,100–12,170
Case law and administrative developments before 1997, 12,100
Determination of control involving asset transfers, 12,160
Gain recognition triggered under Section 355(e), 12,115
Regulations under Section 355(e), 12,120–12,150
Consequences of failure to qualify under Section 355, 12,175
Consequences to distributee shareholders, 12,070–12,080
Consequences to distributing corporation, 12,085
Consolidated return changes, 12,170
Corporate business purpose and continuity of interest requirements, 12,045–12,055
Device requirement, 12,030–12,040

CORPORATE DIVISIONS—Cont'd
Disqualified investment corporations, 12,172
Distribution of rights, 12,180
Effects on distributees and distributing corporations, 12,070–12,085
Failure to qualify, 12,175
Incident to "D" reorganizations, 12,065
Introduction, 12,000
Requirements to prevent bail-out of corporate earnings, 12,005–12,055

CORPORATE INCOME TAX
Allocation of income
See Allocation of income
Computation, 1005
Dividend-received deduction, 4100
Domestic production deduction, 1007
History, 1000
Rates of tax, 1015

CORPORATE TAX INTEGRATION, 1060–1067

CORPORATIONS
Accounting methods, 1005
Agent or nominee, 1115–1125
Assignment of income, 1130, 2260–2265
See also Allocation of Income
Assumption of liabilities, 2170–2195, 2205–2245, 10,305–10,315, 15,030–15,035
Basis adjustments in a Section 351 incorporation, 2140–2155
Capital contributions
Nonrecognition events, 2285–2295
Sales or loans distinguished, 3010–3040
Shareholder guarantees, 3060–3070, 15,300–15,310
Capital structure, 3005, 15,040
Cash basis business
Cash method taxpayers, 2255
Liabilities in excess of basis, 2190–2200
Classes of stock, 3005
Computation of taxable income, 1005
Control
Accommodation transfers, 2075–2095
Defined, 2040
Meeting control requirement, 2045–2095
Transaction denied nonrecognition, 2100
Controlled groups
Limitation on multiple allowances, 14,010
Defined, 1075, 16,060–16,075
Dividends
See Dividend Distributions; Stock Dividends
80–percent stock test, 2040
Exchange for stock, 2015, 3050
Liquidations
See Liquidation of Corporation
Organization
Contributions to capital, 2285–2295, 3000–3005

CORPORATIONS—Cont'd
Organization—Cont'd
Existing business incorporation, 2255–2280
Expenditures, 2305
Nonrecognition treatment on incorporation transfers, 2000, 15,025–15,035
Personal service corporations, 1015, 1130
Policy considerations, 1060–1067, 3140, 10,325, 15,017, 15,090, 15,095
Recognition of the corporate entity, 1095–1125
Sham corporations, 1110
Small business companies, 3080
Stock versus debt, 3010–3040
Transfer of property, 2010

DEFINITIONS
Affiliated group, 1050, 14,055
Control of corporation, 2040
Corporations, 1075, 16,060–16,080
Disqualified investment corporations, 12,172
Earnings and profits, 4025
Limited liability companies, 1055, 16,065
Nonqualified preferred stock, 2025, 9030, 10,240
Partnerships, 16,025–16,080
Passive investment income, 15,450
Reorganizations, 9005–9020
Section 306 stock, 6145
Section 351 incorporations, 2010–2095
Triangular reorganizations, 9010, 10,150–10,180

DIVIDEND DISTRIBUTIONS
Constructive dividends, 4080–4095
Corporate shareholders
Anti-abuse provisions, 4105
Dividends distinguished from sales, 4115
Dividends-received deduction, 4100
Earnings and profits
Allocation of, 4035
Current and accumulated, 4030
Defined, 4025
General Utilities doctrine, 4055
Qualified dividends, 4042
Property distributions
Corporate level consequences, 4055
Distribution of corporate obligations, 4065
Effect on earnings and profits, 4060
Loss property, 4055, 4090
Shareholder taxation
See Shareholders
Stock dividends
See Stock dividends

DOMESTIC PRODUCTION DEDUCTION, 1007

ECONOMIC SUBSTANCE DOCTRINE, 1071–1073

ENTITY CLASSIFICATION
See Classification of Entities

LIMITED LIABILITY COMPANIES (LLCs), 1055, 16,065

LIQUIDATION OF CORPORATIONS
Controlled subsidiaries
Nonrecognition of gain or loss, 8040
Installment sales of stock, 8020
General Utilities doctrine, 8075
Nonsubsidiary
Corporate level consequences, 8025
Loss property, 8025
Shareholder level consequences, 8010
Plan of liquidation, 8005

PARTIAL LIQUIDATIONS
See Redemption of Stock

PARTNERSHIPS
Anti-abuse rules, 16,085
At risk limitations (Sec. 465), 19,045
Basic rules of Subchapter K, 16,010–16,015
Basis of partnership interest
Adjustments, 19,010–19,015, 21,100–21,115
Death of a partner, 25,010–25,035
Debt, effect on, 17,025–17,055, 18,165–18,190
Initial, 19,005, 21,095
Limitations on deduction of losses, 19,030–19,040
Purchasing partner, 21,095–21,110
Sale of partnership interest, 21,010–21,030
Timing and priorities, 19,020
Capital accounts
Allocations of partnership income and deductions, relationship to, 18,070–18,107, 18,115, 18,125–18,130
Compensatory partnership interest, 17,065
Defined, 17,010
Initial based on contributions, 17,010
Liquidating distributions, effect of, 23,010
Operating distributions, effect of, 22,067
Capital contributions
Capital contribution versus sale, 17,020
Tax versus financial accounting, 17,010
Taxation of transfer to the partnership, 17,005
Choice of entity considerations, 1115, 15,010–15,015, 16,060–16,065, 16,090
See also Classification of Entities
Conversions of partnership interests
General partnership interest into limited partnership interest, 24,080–24,085
Partnership interest into LLC interest, 24,090–24,095
Current distributions to partners
Capital accounts, effect on, 22,067

PARTNERSHIPS—Cont'd
Current distributions to partners—Cont'd
  Cash, 22,005–22,015
  Disposition of distributed property, 22,030, 22,035
  Distribution of controlled corporate stock to corporate partner, 22,022
  Distributions altering partner's interest in ordinary income property, 22,110–22,130
  Elective basis adjustment, 22,025, 22,035
  Liabilities, effect, 22,040–22,050
  Mandatory basis adjustment, 22,060, 25,010
  Marketable securities, 22,100, 22,105
  "Mixing bowl" rules, 22,090–22,095, 22,105
  Partnership level consequences, 22,055–22,070
  Precontribution gain or loss treatment, 22,090–22,095, 22,105
  Property, 22,020–22,035
  Sales compared, 20,075–20,100
  Section 751(b), 22,110–22,130
  Section 754 election, 22,060–22,065, 22,070
  Tiered partnership distributions, 22,075–22,080
Death of a partner
  Basis adjustments, 25,010–25,035
  Effect on current year's income, 25,005
  Income in respect of a decedent, 25,015–25,030
  Mandatory basis adjustment, 25,010
Debt, effect on basis, 17,025–17,055, 18,165–18,190
Defined, 16,025–16,080
Distributions
  See Partnerships, Current distributions to partners; Partnerships, Liquidating distributions
Divisions of partnerships, 24,075
Electing large partnerships, special rules, 18,250
Electing out of Subchapter K, 16,055
Family partnerships, 18,220–18,245
Formation, 17,000–17,100
Guaranteed payments, taxation of, 20,020, 20,050–20,070
Holding period for partnership interest, 17,008, 21,005, 22,012
Income or loss
  Allocation, 18,065–18,215
  Basis in partnership interest, effect on, 19,010, 19,020–19,025
  Computation and classification, 18,005–18,040
  Elections of partnership, 18,020, 18,035–18,040
  Reporting and taxing, 18,000
  Sale of partnership interest, effect of current year's income, 21,025

PARTNERSHIPS—Cont'd
Judicial limitations on deduction of losses, 19,055–19,065
Limited liability company compared, 1055, 16,065
Limited partnership compared, 1055, 16,060
Liquidating distributions
  Abandonment of partnership interest, 23,065–23,080
  Deferred payments, 23,035
  Elective basis adjustment, 23,010
  Mandatory basis adjustment, 23,010
  Planning, 23,025
  Relationship between Sections 752 and 736, 23,030
  Sale of partnership interest compared, 23,050–23,060
  Section 736(a) payments, 23,015, 23,045
  Section 736(b) payments, 23,010, 23,045
  Structure of Section 736, 23,005
  Taxation, illustration of, 23,040
  Types of payments, 23,010–23,020
Mergers of partnerships, 24,070, 24,077–24,078
Organization expenses, 17,105
Passive activity loss limitations, 19,050
Payments for services and use of property
  Consequences of characterization, 20,025
  Guaranteed payments, 20,050–20,070
  Statutory trichotomy, 20,005–20,020
  Types of payments, distinguishing between, 20,030–20,070
Publicly traded partnership, 16,080
S corporation compared, 1055, 15,010
Sale of partnership interest
  Application of entity versus aggregate approach, 21,000
  Basis to purchaser, determination, 21,095, 21,130
  Capital gain look-through rules, 21,092
  Current year's income, effect of, 21,025
  Elective basis adjustment, 21,100–21,107, 21,110–21,115
  Gain or loss of selling partner, determination of, 21,125
  Holding period for partnership interest, 17,008, 21,005, 21,070, 22,012
  Installment sale reporting of seller's gain, 21,087–21,090
  Liabilities, effect of, 21,010–21,020
  Mandatory basis adjustment, 21,108
  Purchasing partner, treatment of, 21,095–21,115, 21,130
  Section 751, sales subject to, 21,035–21,075
  Seller, treatment of, 21,005–21,030, 21,092, 21,125
  Taxation, illustration of, 21,120–21,130
Services, contribution of
  Capital account, effect on, 17,065
  Contribution of property compared, 17,060

PARTNERSHIPS—Cont'd

Services—Cont'd

Liquidation value safe harbor, 17,084–17,085

Receipt of capital interest, 17,065, 17,090

Receipt of profits interest, 17,070–17,083, 17,090

Section 83 consequences, 17,065, 17,075, 17,084–17,085

Taxation of partnership, 17,065

Taxation of service provider, 17,005, 17,060

Statutory framework, 16,005

Syndication expenses, 17,105

Taxable year of partnership, 18,015

Terminations

Statutory, 24,025–24,065

Voluntary, 24,000–24,020

PERSONAL HOLDING COMPANIES

Defined, 7010

Professional corporation as, 7020

PERSONAL SERVICE CORPORATIONS, 1015, 1130

POLICY ISSUES

Corporate tax integration, 1160–1067

Distinctions between debt and equity, 3140

Judicial doctrines, role of, 1070–1074

Proposals for reform of taxation of acquisitions, 10,325

Reorganizations, 10,325

Section 751(b), application to partnership distributions,

Statutory interpretation–textualism versus purposivism, 1071, 15,287–15,288

Subchapter S regime, 15,017, 15,090–15,095

REDEMPTION OF STOCK

Acquisitive technique

Buyer's tax considerations, 5195–5215

Seller's tax considerations, 5170–5190

Attribution rules, 5015

"Bad blood" exception, 5105

Entity waiver, 5060

Basis shifting, 5022

Complete terminations of interest, 5025–5045, 5175

Death taxes, 5115

Distributing company, effect on, 5125

Equivalent to dividend, 5080

Partial liquidations, 5225

Safe harbor, 5225

Substantial contraction, 5230

Related corporations, 5130

Brother-sister sales, 5135

Corporate shareholders, 5155

Parent-subsidiary sales, 5140

Relationship to Section 351, 5145

S corporations, 15,375–15,380

Substantially disproportionate, 5010

REINCORPORATION

See Reorganizations

REORGANIZATIONS

"A" reorganization

Continuity of business enterprise requirement, 10,060–10,075

Continuity of shareholder interest requirement, 9080–9100, 10,040–10,055

Definition, 9010, 10,015–10,025

Disregarded entity mergers, 10,030

Problems, 10,035

Acquisition framework, 10,010

Acquisitions partly tax-free, 10,200–10,235

"B" reorganization

Creeping reorganizations, 10,140

Definition, 9010

Problems, 10,145

Solely for voting stock requirement, 10,125–10,135

Basis in reorganizations, 9035

"C" reorganization

Boot relaxation rule, 10,115

Concept of "substantially all" property, 10,080–10,110

Definition, 9010

Disposition of unwanted assets, 10,095–10,110

Problems, 10,120

Solely for voting stock requirement, 10,115

Corporate divisions

See Corporate Divisions

"D" reorganization

Definition, 9010, 11,085

Nondivisive "D" reorganization, 11,085–11,095

Definition, 9005

"E" reorganization

Bailout potential, 11,010–11,020

Definition, 9015, 11,005

Introduction, 11,005

No continuity of shareholder interest or business enterprise required, 11,030–11,040

Nonqualified preferred stock as boot, 11,025

Problems, 11,050

Section 306 stock, 11,045

"F" reorganization

Definition, 9015

Introduction, 11,055

Linked to another transaction, 11,065–11,075

No continuity of shareholder interest or continuity of business enterprise requirement, 11,080

Only one participating corporation may participate, 11,060

"G" reorganization, 9005

Holding period of nonrecognition property, 9040

Judicial requirements, 9050–9105

REORGANIZATIONS—Cont'd

Judicial requirements—Cont'd

Business purpose requirement, 9055–9060

Continuity of business enterprise requirement, 9105, 10,060–10,075

Continuity of shareholder interest requirement, 9080–9100, 10,040–10,055

Step transaction doctrine, 9065–9075

Substance over form, 9065–9075

Liquidation of affiliate

80 percent control, 10,280

Liquidation-reincorporation transactions

Application of "D" reorganization rules, 11,105–11,115

Application of "F" reorganization rules, 11,120

Not meeting statutory reorganization requirements, 11,125–11,135

Potential tax benefits, 11,100

Multi-step acquisitions, 10,185–10,195

Nonrecognition of gain or loss, 9030

Overview of acquisitive reorganizations, 10,000

Preferred stock recapitalization preceding stock purchase, 10,205

Proposals for reform of taxation of acquisitions, 10,325

Purchase of target's shares followed by tender offer, 10,200

Requirements of acquisitive reorganizations, 10,005–10,180

Tax accounting aspects, 9045

Treatment of boot, 10,240–10,315

Assumption of liabilities, 10,305

Definition, 10,315

Treatment of assumed liabilities as other than boot, 10,310

Concept of stock or securities, 10,265–10,290

Contingent or escrowed stock, 10,280

Debt obligations as securities, 10,265

Determination of basis, 10,300

Horizontal double dummy transaction, 10,235

Nonrecognition by corporate parties, 10,295

Recognition by shareholders and creditors, 10,240

Recognized gain having effect of distribution of dividends, 10,245

Warrants to buy stock, 10,290

Triangular reorganizations

Background, 10,150

Definition, 9010

Forward triangular merger, 9010, 10,155

Reverse triangular merger, 9010, 10,165–10,180

Triangular "B" and "C" reorganizations, 10,155

Types, 9010

REORGANIZATIONS—Cont'd

Use of Section 351, 10,210

S CORPORATIONS

Accounting methods, 15,230

Accumulated adjustments account, 15,350

Basis of corporation in property contributed by shareholders, 15,035

Basis of shareholders

Computation, 15,030, 15,280–15,288, 15,315

Debt, 15,290–15,300

Effect of operations, 15,280–15,288

Guarantees, 15,300–15,310

Restoration of basis, 15,315

Built-in gains, 15,410–15,425

Cancellation of indebtedness income, 15,287–15,288

Computation of income, 15,220–15,230

Debt of entity, 1055, 15,010, 15,290–15,310

Dispositions at death, 15,395

Distributions, 15,020, 15,330–15,380

Distributions of property in kind, 15,240–15,245

Earnings and profits, 15,335–15,340

Electing small business trust, 15,105, 15,145–15,150

Election of S status

Corporate requirements, 15,165–15,200

Desirability, 1055, 15,010–15,015

Eligibility generally, 15,090

Filing procedure, 15,045–15,085

Termination, 15,205–15,210, 15,445, 15,455–15,470

Elections by corporation, 15,230

Family-owned corporations, 15,265–15,275

Fringe benefits, 15,235

Ineligible corporations, 15,165, 15,455

LIFO inventory, 15,405

Losses, limitation on the deduction of, 15,280–15,285, 15,290–15,325

Midstream elections, 15,400–15,453

Multi-tier structures and partnerships, 15,195–15,200

No carryback or carryforward of losses from C corporation year to S corporation year, 15,453

One class of stock limitation on eligibility, 15,180–15,190

Partnerships compared, 15,010

Pass-through of income and losses, 15,020, 15,220–15,230, 15,250–15,260, 15,280–15,315

Passive investment income, 15,435–15,450

Definition, 15,450

Post-termination transition period, 15,470

Pre–1983 S corporations, 15,335, 15,365

Qualified subchapter S subsidiary, 15,175

Qualified subchapter S trusts, 15,125–15,130, 15,140

Safe harbor debt, 15,190

Second-tier elective distributions, 15,360

Shareholders

S CORPORATIONS—Cont'd
Shareholders—Cont'd
  Allocation of portions of corporate income and expense, 15,250–15,260, 15,385–15,395, 15,460–15,465
  Basis, 15,030, 15,280–15,315
  Eligibility, 15,095–15,160
  Taxation, 15,020, 15,215, 15,330–15,390
Stock
  One class limitation, 15,180–15,190
  Redemptions, 15,375–15,380
  Sales and other dispositions, 15,385–15,395
  Worthlessness, 15,320
Subsidiaries, 15,170–15,175
Tax shelter limitations, 15,325
Termination of election
  Impact on reporting of income, 15,460–15,465
  Ineligible shareholder, 15,205–15,210
  Methods, 15,455, 15,465
  Passive investment income, 15,445, 15,455
  Post-termination transition period, 15,470
Three-tier distribution scheme, 15,345–15,360, 15,370

SHAREHOLDERS
Fifteen percent tax rate on qualified dividend income, 4000
Guarantees, 3060–3075, 3120

SHAREHOLDERS—Cont'd
Losses, 3100–3130
Section 1244 stock, 3125
Taxation, 1020, 3080–3095

SECURITIES
Classification, stock versus debt, 3010
Conversion, 3090
Losses, 3100
Taxation, 3080
Types, 3005

STATUTORY INTERPRETATION, 1071, 15,287–15,288

STOCK DIVIDENDS
Disproportionate distributions, 6040
  Redemptions as, 6040
Distributions on preferred stock, 6055
Election to receive stock or property, 6025
History of taxation, 6005
Impact on distributing company, 6080
Nontaxable, 6010
Section 306 stock, 6100–6175
  Defined, 6145, 6172
  Exceptions to, 6120–6135
  Redemptions of, 6115
Reorganizations, issued in, 6170
  Sales of, 6110
Recapitalizations, in, 6070
Taxable, 6020

STOCK REDEMPTION
See Redemption of Stock

†